WEST'S LAW SCHOOL ADVISORY BOARD

PRINCIPLES OF INTERNATIONAL BUSINESS TRANSACTIONS

Third Edition

By

Ralph H. Folsom
Professor of Law
University of San Diego

Michael Wallace Gordon
John H. and Mary Lou Dasburg Professor of Law Emeritus
University of Florida

John A. Spanogle, Jr.
William Wallace Kirkpatrick Professor of Law
The George Washington University

Michael P. Van Alstine
Professor of Law
University of Maryland Francis King Carey School of Law

CONCISE HORNBOOK SERIES®

WEST®

Mat #41381282

610 Opperman Drive
St. Paul, MN 55123
1-800-313-9378

Printed in the United States of America

ISBN: 978–0–314–28659–8

Preface

The authors have collaborated on *International Business Transactions: A Problem–Oriented Coursebook*, and its spin-off editions, *IBT: Contracting Across Borders, IBT: Trade and Economic Relations* and *IBT: Foreign Investment*. Many students studying with these popular coursebooks, and others interested in an introduction to the field, have enjoyed our easy-to-read *International Business Transactions* Nutshell and its companion, the *International Trade and Economic Relations* Nutshell.

Principles of International Business Transactions is part of the West Academic Publishing's Concise Hornbook series. Our coverage moves sequentially from international sales and letters of credit to regulation of international trade to transfers of technology to foreign investment to dispute settlement. *Principles* is intended to provide extensive depth, analysis and citations. It can be used in connection with any international business, sales, trade, investment or economic law course, or independently as a treatise. We welcome feedback.

RALPH H. FOLSOM
rfolsom@sandiego.edu

MICHAEL W. GORDON
gordon@law.ufl.edu

JOHN A. SPANOGLE
aspanogle@law.gwu.edu

MICHAEL P. VAN ALSTINE
mvanalst@law.umaryland.edu

May 2013

Summary of Contents

Table of Contents

PRINCIPLES OF INTERNATIONAL BUSINESS TRANSACATIONS

Third Edition

Chapter 1

INTERNATIONAL SALES LAW

Table of Sections

It is a common misconception, often formed in first-year Contracts courses, that Article 2 of the Uniform Commercial Code (UCC) governs all contracts for the sale of goods, both domestic and international. The UCC may indeed apply to international sales of goods, provided that the transaction in dispute bears an "appropriate relation" to a UCC state. *See* UCC Rev. § 1–301(b) (former § 1–105(1)). Other countries have their own choice-of-law rules to determine which body of domestic law applies to a particular transaction. One prominent example is the European Union's Regulation on the Law Applicable to Contractual Obligations (2009), which applies in all EU member states. For sale of goods transactions, this so-called "Rome I" Regulation chooses "the law of the country where the seller has his habitual residence." *See* Article 4(1).

What is substantially less well known is that the United States and dozens of other countries also have adopted an international treaty, the United Nations Convention on Contracts for the International Sale of Goods (CISG), which provides rules for the international sale of goods. By virtue of the Supremacy Clause of the U.S. Constitution, this treaty operates as supreme federal law—and thus preempts state laws like the UCC—for transactions within its scope. As a result, this treaty must be the starting point for any analysis of sales transactions with international connections.

§ 1.1 Introduction to the CISG

The United Nations Convention on Contracts for the International Sale of Goods (1980)[1]—which is commonly known, even internationally, by the acronym CISG—governs the sale of goods between parties in the United States and those in nearly eighty other countries. The Convention grew out of the failure of two earlier conventions—the so-called "ULIS" and "ULF"[2]—to address the diversity of cultures and legal traditions involved in international contracting. Following extensive negotiations, the CISG was adopted and opened for signature and ratification by a U.N.-sponsored diplomatic conference held in Vienna in 1980. The Convention then entered into force on January 1, 1988, thirteen months after the ratifica-

---

[1] United Nations Convention on Contracts for the International Sale of Goods, Apr. 11, 1980, U.N. Doc. A/CONF. 97/18 (1980), *reprinted in* 19 I.L.M. 671 (1980).

[2] The ULIS (Convention Relating to a Uniform Law on the International Sale of Goods (1964)) addressed substantive rights and obligations; the ULF (Convention Relating to a Uniform Law on the Formation of Contracts for the International Sale of Goods (1964)) addressed formation issues.

tions of the United States, China, and Italy exceeded the prescribed acceptance threshold of ten member states (which the CISG somewhat confusingly refers to as "Contracting States").

As of March, 2013, seventy-nine countries are Contracting States to the CISG, representing well over three-quarters of the world's trade in goods. The list of Contracting States includes countries from all parts of the world and from all legal traditions, as well as nearly every major trading partner of the United States, from Canada and Mexico, to Japan and China, to Germany and France, and to South Korea and Singapore. (Notable exceptions include the United Kingdom and India.) In addition to the United States, the Contracting States of the CISG are: Albania, Argentina, Armenia, Australia, Austria, Belarus, Belgium, Benin, Bosnia and Herzegovina, Brazil (effective in 2014), Bulgaria, Burundi, Canada, Chile, China, Colombia, Croatia, Cuba, Cyprus, Czech Republic, Denmark, Dominican Republic, Ecuador, Egypt, El Salvador, Estonia, Finland, France, Gabon, Georgia, Germany, Greece, Guinea, Honduras, Hungary, Iceland, Iraq, Israel, Italy, Japan, Kyrgyzstan, Latvia, Lebanon, Lesotho, Liberia, Lithuania, Luxembourg, Macedonia, Mauritania, Mexico, Moldova, Mongolia, Montenegro, the Netherlands, New Zealand, Norway, Paraguay, Peru, Poland, Republic of Korea, Romania, the Russian Federation, Saint Vincent and Grenadines, San Marino, Serbia, Singapore, Slovakia, Slovenia, Spain, Sweden, Switzerland, Syria, Turkey, Uganda, Ukraine, Uruguay, Uzbekistan, and Zambia. As a result of this broad acceptance, courts and arbitral tribunals have already generated thousands of opinions interpreting the CISG.

Each year, the roll of Contracting States of the CISG continues to grow, and more states are expected to ratify or otherwise accept the CISG in the near future. This will increase the impact and effectiveness of the CISG in unifying international sales law. A current and complete list of Contracting States to this Convention is available at UNCITRAL's website, www.uncitral.org.

The CISG resulted from the work of a specialized body of the United Nations, the United Nations Commission on International Trade Law (UNCITRAL), whose mandate is the unification and harmonization of international trade law. The purpose of such unification is to reduce legal obstacles to international trade, decrease transaction costs, enhance predictability and certainty, and promote the orderly development of new legal concepts as international commerce evolves in the future.

Substantial English language resource materials are available for understanding and applying the CISG. These include prominent treatises,[3] hundreds of journal articles, comprehensive online compilation of materials[4] and court opinions,[5] and an authoritative collection of the drafting records for the Convention.[6] UNICTRAL also maintains a searchable database of abstracts of CISG cases from around the world[7] as well as a Digest with analytical summaries arranged by individual Articles of the Convention.[8] As explained below,[9] these materials are of particular importance because decisions by foreign courts should serve as persuasive precedent on the Convention.

In addition to the CISG, UNCITRAL is responsible for a series of further treaties in the field of international commercial law. The most significant of these for present purposes is the 1974 Convention on the Limitation Period in the International Sale of Goods (as amended by Protocol in 1980). This Convention, which the United States and two dozen other countries have ratified as of 2013, provides special rules for what American lawyers would call the "statute of limitations" for international sale of goods transactions. (For more detail on this treaty, see *The Limitation Convention*, § 1.40 below.) Other such UNCITRAL treaties—thus far, substantially less successful—include the Convention on the Use of Electronic Communications in International Contracts (2005); the Convention on the Assignment of Receivables in International Trade (2001); the Convention on Independent Guarantees and Standby Letters of Credit (1995); and the Convention on International Bills of Exchange and International Promissory Notes (1988).

Separately, UNCITRAL has prepared "model laws" for consideration by individual countries as domestic legislation. Prominent

---

3 *See* COMMENTARY ON THE UN CONVENTION ON THE INTERNATIONAL SALE OF GOODS (CISG) (P. Schlechtriem & I. Schwenzer, eds., 3rd ed., 2010); UN CONVENTION ON CONTRACTS FOR THE INTERNATIONAL SALE OF GOODS (CISG) (S. Kröll, L. Mistelis & M. Perales Viscasillas, eds., 2011); DRAFTING CONTRACTS UNDER THE CISG (H. Flechtner, R. Brand, and M. Walter, eds., 2008).

4 *See* the CISG Database of Pace University, www.cisg.law.pace.edu.

5 *See* http://www.unilex.info/dynasite.cfm?dssid=2376&dsmid=14315; http://www.cisg.law.pace.edu/cisg/text/caseschedule.html.

6 *See* John O. Honnold, DOCUMENTARY HISTORY FOR THE UNIFORM LAW ON INTERNATIONAL SALES (1989). These records are also available at http://www.cisg.law.pace.edu/cisg/conference.html.

7 *See* CASE LAW ON UNCITRAL TEXTS (CLOUT), available at http://www.uncitral.org/uncitral/en/case_law/abstracts.html.

8 UNCITRAL DIGEST OF CASE LAW ON THE CISG (2012 ed.), http://www.uncitral.org/uncitral/en/case_law/digests/cisg.html (hereinafter CISG DIGEST 2012).

9 *See* the analysis of CISG Article 7 in § 1.9 *infra*.

among these are the Model Law on International Commercial Arbitration (1985, as amended in 2006), which has served as a model for legislation in over sixty countries and seven states of the United States; the Model Law on Cross-Border Insolvency (1997), which the United States adopted through a new Chapter 15 of the Bankruptcy Code; the Model Law on Electronic Commerce (1996), which has influenced more than forty national laws, uniform acts in nearly every state of the U.S. and nearly every province of Canada, and various European Union directives; and a new Model Law on Public Procurement (2011). UNCITRAL is continuing its work on promoting international uniformity in other areas of commercial law, with present projects on international security interests and on online dispute resolution.

UNCITRAL is not the only international organization involved in proposing legal instruments for the unification and harmonization of international commercial law. Another prominent body, the International Institute for the Unification of Private Law (UNIDROIT), has prepared a variety of formal treaties in the field, including a Convention on International Factoring (1988), a Convention on International Financial Leasing (1988), and a promising (and, with 52 ratifications as of 2013, already quite successful) Convention on International Interests in Mobile Equipment (2001). The last instrument is designed to serve as a framework treaty to be supplemented by later "protocols" that focus on specific types of collateral.[10] The Organization of American States (OAS) also has been active in this field on a hemisphere-wide basis.

In addition, UNIDROIT has prepared and issued the Principles of International Commercial Contracts (1994, as revised in 2004 and again in 2010). The Principles provide rules for all types of international commercial contracts, not just sales of goods, and their provisions are substantially more comprehensive. If the CISG is the international analog to UCC Article 2 in U.S. law, then the Principles are the international analog to the Restatement of Contracts in U.S. law. The Principles are not intended to be adopted as a convention or enacted as formal domestic law. Rather, they are designed for use principally by international commercial arbitrators, and even by judges where local law is ambiguous (and so permits). Some of the specific concepts are discussed later in this chapter. The substantive rules of the Principles are often different from those of the CISG, because the Principles were drafted by independent experts

[10] As of 2013, UNIDROIT has completed three such protocols: On "Matters Specific to Space Assets" (Berlin, 2012); on "Matters Specific to Railway Rolling Stock" (Luxembourg, 2007); and on "Matters Specific to Aircraft Equipment" (Cape Town, 2001).

(not official delegations of governments), and the drafters could thus adopt what they considered to be the "best practices" in international commercial contracts.

§ 1.2 The Legal Status of the CISG

In the United States, the CISG has the constitutional status of preemptive federal law. This is so because the Convention operates as a so-called "self-executing treaty," which means that it functions as directly applicable federal law without the need for implementing legislation by Congress.[11] The CISG thus obtained domestic legal force by virtue of the Senate consent procedure defined in the treaty clause of Article II, Section 2, of the Constitution. And because ratified treaties function as supreme federal law under Article VI of the Constitution, the CISG preempts all state law within its scope, including Article 2 of the UCC.[12]

The CISG also creates a federal cause of action in favor of aggrieved buyers and sellers in ordinary commercial litigation in the courts of the United States.[13] Thus, for example, a sale of goods contract between a private party in the United States and one in Canada would be governed by the CISG, not by the UCC, and U.S. federal courts would have jurisdiction to hear disputes arising out of such a contract.[14] Moreover, the rules for interpreting the CISG and for filling gaps in its provisions impose, as explored in more detail below,[15] severe restrictions on the ability of courts to resort to domestic law (such as the UCC) to resolve contested issues.

§ 1.3 The CISG's Structure and Sphere of Application

The goal of the CISG is to promote legal certainty in international sales transactions by creating a uniform set of legal rules to

---

[11] *See* Medellín v. Texas, 552 U.S. 491, 505 (2008)(observing that a self-executing treaty "operates of itself" as domestic law "without the aid of any legislative provision"). President Reagan expressly declared that the CISG is self-executing upon submission to the Senate in 1983. *See Letter of Transmittal from the President of the United States to the Senate With Legal Analysis of the United Nations Convention on Contracts for the International Sale of Goods*, Sept. 21, 1983, Sen. Treaty Doc. No. 98–9, *reprinted in* 22 I.L.M. 1368, 1369 (1983).

[12] *See, e.g.,* Beth Schiffer Fine Photographic Arts, Inc. v. Colex Imaging, Inc., 2012 WL 924380, at *7 (D.N.J. 2012); Usinor Industeel v. Leeco Steel Prods., Inc., 209 F. Supp. 2d 880, 884 (N.D. Ill. 2002).

[13] *See* BP Oil Int'l, Ltd. v. Empresa Estatal Petroleos de Ecuador, 332 F.3d 333, 336 (5th Cir. 2003).

[14] This is so because 28 U.S.C. § 1331(a) confers on the district courts "original jurisdiction of all civil actions arising under . . . treaties of the United States."

[15] *See* the discussion of CISG Article 7 in § 1.9 *infra*.

operate in the place of the diverse domestic legal systems of the ratifying countries. The Convention does not even permit Contracting States to declare reservations to limit the effect of any of its substantive provisions[16] (but for a short list of expressly stated exceptions). On the other hand, the CISG applies only to international transactions as defined therein. It does not affect purely domestic sales transactions, and permits the parties (as explored below) to "opt out" of its application by a sufficiently clear contractual agreement.

In addition to rules governing its scope, the CISG contains provisions on contract formation; the respective rights and performance obligations of sellers and buyers; the rights and remedies upon breach; the passing of the risk of loss from the seller to the buyer; as well as most other significant subjects in international sales transactions. The Convention is structured in four principal parts:

Part I Scope and general principles;

Part II Contract formation;

Part III The substantive rights and obligations of the buyer and the seller; and

Part IV The non-substantive "diplomatic" provisions relating to ratification, reservations, withdrawal, etc.

As noted, in the United States the CISG operates as a "self-executing treaty," with the result that as of 1988 it has functioned as directly applicable, preemptive federal law without the need for separate implementing legislation.

To achieve its goal of certainty and predictability, it is important that the CISG's scope of application be clear, both as to the circumstances where it applies, and those where it does not. The first six articles of the CISG define its sphere of application, but the principal rules are found in Article 1. That Article provides that the CISG will apply if a transaction (1) involves a contract for the sale of goods; (2) is "international"; and (3) bears a stated relation to at least one country that has ratified or otherwise accepted the CISG (again, so-called "Contracting States").

(1) On the first requirement, the CISG unfortunately does not define "contract," "sale," or "goods." Nonetheless, pursuant to the

---

16 CISG, art. 98.

basic rule for interpreting the CISG (see below[17]), these notions must be defined "autonomously," that is, by reference to the principles reflected in the Convention itself and not through a resort to domestic law. Thus, on the basis of the rules in Articles 30 and 53—which respectively require the seller to deliver "property in" the goods and the buyer to pay a "price"—it is broadly accepted that the subject matter of the transaction must involve the passing of title for a price (and thus not a bailment, gift, or lease). One court accordingly has observed that the essential nature of a contract governed by the CISG is that it involves the delivery of goods in exchange for money.[18]

An "autonomous" interpretation likewise permits a definition of the term "goods." A variety of CISG provisions make clear that the term refers to items that have a physical existence and are moveable at the time of agreed delivery.[19] Examples include provisions that refer to the "weight" of items, to the seller's "delivery" at a defined "place," and to the buyer taking "possession of" and the "preserv[ing]" the goods.[20] Courts have accordingly held that "goods" must be "moveable and tangible" (although not necessary in solid form).[21]

(2) The CISG clearly defines the requirement for an "international" sale of goods. This is determined not by the location or delivery of the goods (such as whether they cross a national border), but rather by the "places of business" of the persons involved in the transaction. Specifically, under Article 1(1) a contract for the sale of goods is international if, at the time of contract formation, the parties have their respective "places of business" in different states (with "states" being sovereign countries, not the states of the United States).

What is "a place of business"? The CISG does not define the term, but according to scholarly commentary and court opinions a "place of business" requires some level of both permanence and in-

[17] *See* the analysis of CISG Article 7 in *The General Provisions of the CISG infra.*

[18] CLOUT Case No. 328, *Kantonsgericht* [Provincial Court] of Zug, Switzerland (21 October 1999).

[19] For an analysis of whether software may qualify as a "good" see § 1.5 *infra.*

[20] *See, e.g.,* art. 30 (referring to the seller's obligation to "deliver" goods); art. 31 (defining the "place" at which seller is obligated to deliver); art. 53 (stating buyer's obligation to "take delivery"); art. 56 (stating a rule for when the price is fixed according to the "weight of the goods"); and art. 86 (referring to the buyer's obligation to preserve the goods after taking possession of them).

[21] *See CISG* DIGEST 2012, *supra* footnote 8, art. 1, para. 28. *See also* Schwenzer/Hachem, art. 1, paras. 16–17, in Schlechtriem & Schwenzer, *supra* note 3.

dependence. Reference to the equally authoritative[22] French (*establissement*) and Spanish (*establecimiento*) language versions support this view. Judicial interpretations are in accord,[23] with one court observing that a place of business "requires a certain duration and stability as well as a certain amount of autonomy."[24]

On this basis, courts have found that none of the following constitutes a "place of business" under the CISG: a mere warehouse where the contract goods are located; a booth at an exhibition; the place where a party's representative happened to negotiate the contract; and a seller's "liaison office" that did not have autonomy in business decisions.[25] A branch office, on the other hand, may well suffice as long as it has some level of permanence and independent decision-making authority.

For emphasis, Article 1(3) also declares that neither the nationality of the parties (*e.g.*, where a business is incorporated) nor their "civil or commercial character" (*e.g.*, whether or not domestic law would consider a party a "merchant") is to be taken into consideration in determining whether the CISG applies. One Austrian appellate court thus expressly declared that the nationality of the parties is irrelevant to the application of the CISG in a transaction between an Austrian corporation and an Austrian-German joint venture because the relevant places of the business of the two sides were in different CISG member states.[26] However, under Article 1(2) the CISG will not apply even if the parties are from different states if this fact "does not appear" from information available to them upon the conclusion of the contract. Thus, if one party is represented by a local agent who does not disclose (before contract formation) the foreign place of business of its principal, the Convention should not govern the transaction. One should note, however, that the question of whether an intermediary is an agent or instead acts on its own account is a matter for domestic law, not the CISG.[27]

A special problem arises if a party has more than one location that qualifies as a "place of business" (which is quite common for

---

[22] Like other UNCITRAL texts, the CISG has six official language texts: English, French, Spanish, Chinese, Russian, and Arabic.

[23] *See* CISG DIGEST 2012, *supra* footnote 8, art. 1, para. 5.

[24] *Oberlandesgericht* [Appellate Court] of Stuttgart, Germany, 28 February 2000, http://cisgw3.law.pace.edu/cases/000228g1.html.

[25] *See* CISG DIGEST 2012, *supra* footnote 8, art. 1, para. 5.

[26] CLOUT Case 746, *Oberlandesgericht* [Appellate Court] of Graz, Austria (29 July 2004).

[27] *See* CISG DIGEST 2012, *supra* footnote 8, art. 1, para. 7; Caterpillar, Inc. v. Usinor Industeel, 393 F. Supp. 2d 659, 669–673 (N.D. Ill. 2005) (applying Illinois law of agency to a transaction otherwise governed by the CISG).

large multi-national enterprises). If, for example, a seller has its place of business in the United States and the buyer has places of business in both Germany and the United States, the CISG may or may not apply depending on which place of business of the buyer is the relevant one. In such a case, CISG Article 10 provides that the relevant place of business is the one with the "closest relationship to the contract and its performance." Thus, the determinative "place of business" under the CISG is not a party's "main" or "principal" business location or even its "seat" under domestic law. Instead, the analysis will turn on which of a party's different business locations has the closest the relationship to the transaction.

Nonetheless, the duel considerations of "the contract" and "its performance" may cause difficulties in application to specific facts where, for example, one office is more closely associated with the formation of the contract and a second office is more closely associated with a party's performance of its contractual obligations. When such circumstances arise, courts will need to weigh the relative significance of the two considerations to determine which predominates. Article 10(a)—in parallel to Article 1(2), see above—provides some assistance in this regard, for it limits the usable facts to those circumstances "known to or contemplated by *the parties*" (emphasis supplied) at or before the conclusion of the contract. This should avoid a surprise application of the CISG where a domestic party deals principally with a local office and knows little about a possible foreign place of business. On the other hand, well-advised parties may ensure that the CISG, and not foreign domestic law, will apply by stating in the contract which office of each party they believe to have "the closest relationship" to the transaction. In short, because the Convention here focuses on the knowledge of "the parties," each party should ensure that the other is aware of its status.

A small number of courts have directly addressed the significance of Article 10(a) for the application of the CISG. Thus, for example, a U.S. District Court found that the CISG did not govern a transaction in which a U.S. company designed software for use in Germany by a German company, because the buyer's relevant place of business was its U.S. subsidiary to which the software was first sent and from which payment was made.[28] On the other hand, where a Canadian seller had a U.S. distributor, but the transaction was in part negotiated in Canada and the goods were manufactured there—all of which was known to the U.S.-based buyer—a court

[28] American Mint v. GO Software, Inc., 2006 WL 42090 (M.D. Pa. 2006). *See also* McDowell Valley Vineyards, Inc. v. Sabate USA Inc., 2005 WL 2893848 (N.D. Cal. 2005)(holding that the CISG did not apply because the relevant place of business of a French seller was its U.S.-based subsidiary).

found that the transaction was between places of business in different states, and thus that the CISG applied.[29]

(3) Finally, the CISG governs only those contracts for the international sale of goods that have a sufficient relation to one or more Contracting States—that is, countries that have ratified, acceded to, or otherwise accepted the Convention before the relevant transaction (or, if contract formation is at issue, before the proposal to conclude a contract, *see* Article 100). The CISG defines two different ways to satisfy this requirement. First, under Article 1(1)(a) the Convention will apply if the parties have their places of business in different states and *both* of these states are CISG Contracting States. Under this option, therefore, the CISG will govern a contract of sale (unless the parties expressly "opt out" under Article 6, see § 1.4 below), where one party has its place of business in the United States and the other has its place of business in France, China, Mexico, or any other CISG Contracting State. This option thus does not depend upon the vagaries of conflicts of law doctrines, and provides certainty both to the parties in designing the transaction and to the courts in analyzing and deciding the issues that arise therein.

Under Article 1(1)(b), the CISG also could apply if the applicable domestic conflict of law rules (known by the civil law term "the rules of private international law") lead to the application of the law of a Contracting State. Thus, the CISG could govern a transaction between a seller in Germany (a Contracting State) and a buyer in the United Kingdom (not a Contracting State) if the forum's domestic choice of law rules lead to the application of German law (which includes the CISG).[30] This option is sometimes referred to as the "indirect application" of the CISG.

This possibility does not apply, however, for courts in the United States. When it ratified the CISG, the United States declared an allowed reservation under Article 95 that it would not be bound by Article 1(1)(b). The effect of this reservation is that courts in the United States will apply the CISG only when the parties' respective places of business are in different states and *both* of those states are CISG Contracting States. Thus, for example, the CISG will not apply to a sales contract between parties with respective places of business in the United States and the United Kingdom (again, a non-Contracting State), even if applicable choice-of-law rules would

---

29 Asante Technologies v. PMC-Sierra, Inc., 164 F. Supp. 2d 1142, 1147–1149 (N.D. Cal. 2001).

30 This would be the case for courts in EU countries because, as noted in the Introduction to this Chapter, the "Rome I" regulation applies the law of the seller's home country for sale of goods contracts.

require that a U.S. court apply U.S. law. What law should the court apply in such a case? Instead of the CISG, United States law for domestic sales transactions would govern, which means the UCC as applicable in forty-nine states (all but Louisiana).

The United States declared the Article 95 reservation upon ratification in 1986 based on a belief that the UCC is a superior approach to sales law as compared to the CISG.[31] At the time, the assumption was that the principal benefit of the uniform rules in the CISG was to avoid the uncertainty of the various choice-of-law regimes around the world and that resort to the alternative of Article 1(1)(b) would reintroduce that uncertainty. Certain U.S. interests also believed that if a court first had to resolve choice-of-law issues and then determined that domestic United States law applied, it might as well apply the "best" United States law—the UCC.

Beyond the U.S., only six of seventy-nine states have declared a reservation to the application of Article 1(1)(b). Moreover, to ensure consistency of application, the drafting history and scholarly commentary on the reservation indicate that even a foreign court should not consider the reserving states as CISG "Contracting States" for purposes of Article 1(1)(b).[32] (Germany in fact expressly declared this upon its ratification of the CISG.) Thus, in our U.S.-U.K. example above, even if the litigation somehow were brought in France (a CISG Contracting State that has not made an Article 95 reservation), the French court should apply the UCC (not the CISG), if French choice-of-law rules point to United States law. Nonetheless, with the growing world-wide acceptance of the Convention (and thus the increasing application of Article 1(1)(a)), the Article 95 reservation of the United States is rapidly decreasing in significance.

§ 1.4 Party Autonomy and Choice of Law Clauses

One of the most important provisions for understanding the basic philosophy and scope of the CISG is Article 6. That provision states the core principle of "party autonomy," that is, the power of the parties to "exclude application of th[e] Convention" and to "derogate from or vary the effect of any of its provisions." The agreements of the parties, in other words, take precedence over the provisions of the CISG. In its most fundamental sense, this includes the

[31] *See* U.S. State Department, *Legal Analysis of the United Nations Convention on Contract for the Internal Sale of Goods* (1980), Appendix B, *reprinted in* 22 I.L.M. 1368, 1380 (1983).

[32] *See* CISG DIGEST 2012, *supra* footnote 8, art. 1, para. 19.

power of the parties to declare that the CISG will not govern their transaction at all (the power to "opt out" of the Convention).

Thus, even if the CISG otherwise is applicable under Article 1, the parties may choose to exclude it in favor of the application of the law of a specific domestic legal system. Special care is required, however, to exercise this power in an effective way. First, and most important, CISG Article 6 grants the power to the parties (in the plural). As a result, an international trader cannot be assured that a unilateral choice of law clause in its standard business terms will be effective. The recent case of *Hanwha Corp. v. Cedar Petrochemicals, Inc.* illustrates this point.[33] There, a South Korea-based buyer and a New York-based seller exchanged standard business forms that had conflicting choice-of-law clauses. Even though both parties tried to choose domestic law to govern the transaction, the absence of an agreement between them on one choice (in derogation of the CISG) meant that the court applied the CISG, and especially its contract formation rules.

Moreover, several courts have recognized that an effective exclusion of the CISG requires a clear, unequivocal, and affirmative agreement of the parties. To be sure, the documentary records of the CISG show that the drafters rejected a proposal to require an "express" exclusion, and on this basis, some courts and arbitral tribunals have noted the possibility of an implied agreement to opt-out of the Convention. Nonetheless, the delegates at the 1980 Vienna Conference also rejected a proposal to include in Article 6 a textual recognition of "implicit" exclusions out of a fear that courts would reach such a result on insufficient evidence.[34] The result is that most courts have recognized high standards for an exclusion of the CISG, including an emphasis on the need for a real and unequivocal agreement between the parties.[35]

Finally, the parties must also affirmatively opt-out of the CISG by specific reference. A mere contractual designation of a particular country's laws will not suffice, especially if that country is a Contracting State to the CISG. Thus, a simple statement that, for example, a contract "shall be governed by New York law" will not effectively exclude the CISG. Indeed, courts addressing such clauses have commonly held that a choice of the law of a CISG Contracting State means, for international sale of goods transactions, merely a

---

[33] 760 F. Supp. 2d 426 (S.D.N.Y. 2011).

[34] *See* Deliberations of the First Committee at the 1980 Vienna conference (A/CONF.97/C.I.SR.4), *reprinted in* Honnold, Documentary History, *supra* note 6, at 469–475.

[35] *See* CISG DIGEST 2012, *supra* footnote 8, art. 6, para. 2.

choice of the CISG, with the result that the CISG nonetheless applies. As a U.S. federal Court of Appeals declared in a case where the parties' contract designated Ecuadorian law, "[g]iven that the CISG *is* Ecuadorian law, a choice of law provision designating Ecuadorian law merely confirms that the treaty governs the transaction."[36] The same rule applies, under preemption doctrines, if the parties choose the law of a state of the United States, and U.S. courts have consistently so held.[37]

As a result, if the parties wish to exercise their Article 6 "opt out" power in favor of pure domestic law, they must do so through express language that both (a) affirmatively excludes the Convention by name, and (b) expressly identifies the agreed domestic law. (*E.g.*: "The law of the State of New York, including as applicable the New York Uniform Commercial Code, shall govern all disputes relating to this transaction. The parties hereby exclude application of the United Nations Convention on Contracts for the International Sale of Goods (CISG)").[38] Even if the parties do not wish to exclude the CISG (or cannot reach a corresponding agreement), they are well advised to designate a default domestic law. This is so because the CISG, similar to other instruments, does not represent a complete legal regime for all issues that may arise between the parties.

Article 6 also permits partial derogation from the CISG, for it expressly empowers the parties to "derogate from or vary the effect of" any of its provisions.[39] This more general implication of the principle of "party autonomy" means that the parties' agreement takes precedence even over the express rules in the CISG. Thus, for example, one court held that a contractual requirement of notice of breach "within five working days from the delivery" took precedence over Article 39(1)'s allowance of a "reasonable time."[40] In the same vein, courts and arbitral tribunals have held, for example, that the

---

[36] BP Oil Int'l, Ltd. v. Empresa Estatal Petroleos, 332 F.3d 333, 337 (5th Cir. 2003)(emphasis in original). One U.S. court misleadingly indicated in dicta that a mere choice of domestic law may suffice to exclude the CISG, but the court's opinion only addressed the effectiveness of a forum selection. *See* American Biophysics v. Dubois Marine Specialties, 411 F. Supp. 2d 61 (D.R.I. 2006).

[37] *See, e.g.,* Travelers Property Cas. Co. of America v. Saint-Gobain Technical Fabrics Canada Ltd., 474 F. Supp. 2d 1075, 1081–1082 (D. Minn. 2007); American Mint LLC v. GOSoftware, Inc., 2005 WL 2021248 (M.D. Pa. 2005).

[38] Parties that have agreed so to exclude the CISG are also well advised to exclude application of the companion treaty on the Limitation Period in the International Sale of Goods. *See* Limitation Convention, § 1.40 *infra*.

[39] The parties do not have this power with respect to any requirement that a contract be concluded in writing if a Contracting State has declared a corresponding reservation under Article 96. *See* discussion of CISG article 12 in § 1.8, *infra*.

[40] *Rechtbank* [Local Court] of Arnhem, the Netherlands (11 February 2009), available at http://cisgw3.law.pace.edu/cases/090211n1.html.

parties may, by agreement, derogate from CISG rules on the concept of "delivery," on the required place of delivery, and on liability upon breach.[41]

If the parties may "opt out" of the CISG, may they also "opt in"? Because the principle of party autonomy is widely accepted in domestic sale of goods law as well,[42] the answer here should be "yes." As a more specific matter, if the parties have their places of business in different states, CISG Article 1(1)(b) should permit them, by way of a choice of law clause, to use such rules of "private international law" to "opt in" to the Convention.[43] The choice of law clause used to accomplish this result can be relatively simple ("this contract shall be governed by the laws of France") because, as explained above, a choice of the laws of France (a CISG Contracting State) should yield an application of the CISG.[44] To avoid misunderstanding, however, parties are well advised to state their intent in this regard explicitly, *e.g.*: "This contract shall be governed by the laws of France, including the United Nations Convention on Contracts for the International Sale of Goods."

Unfortunately, many U.S. attorneys unthinkingly seek to "opt out" of the CISG for all contracts under all circumstances, simply because they do not understand it as well as they understand the UCC. Such an impulse, however, may work a disservice to their clients' interests. If an attorney represents the seller in an international transaction, for example, the UCC and its "perfect tender" and "implied warranty" rules may be less favorable than the corresponding rules under the CISG.[45] In such cases, automatic rejection of the CISG may prejudice the client's interests, unless the attorney can be assured that comparable seller-friendly rules will make it into the express terms of the contract. One respected author has observed in this vein that routinely opting out of the CISG, or even simply negotiating an international sales contract, without understanding how the treaty affects the client's interests, may constitute malpractice.[46]

---

[41] *See CISG* DIGEST 2012, *supra* footnote 8, art. 6, para. 6 (with citations).

[42] *See, e.g.*, UCC Rev. § 1–301(a) (former § 1–105(1)); EU Rome I Regulation on the Law Applicable to Contractual Obligations, art. 3(1).

[43] *See supra* § 1.3, text accompanying note 30.

[44] *See supra* § 1.3, text accompanying note 36.

[45] *See* §§ 1.19 and 1.32 *infra*.

[46] *See* Ronald Brand, *Professional Responsibility in a Transnational Practice*, 17 J. Law & Com. 301, 335–336 (1998). Unfortunately, knowledge of the CISG and its status as directly applicable and preemptive federal law is alarmingly limited. A recent survey across the spectrum of states (Florida, New York, California, Hawai'i, and Montana) revealed that only 30% of practitioners were "thoroughly" or "moder-

§ 1.5 Transactions Excluded from the CISG

CISG Article 2 expressly excludes from the scope of the Convention a number of specific types of transactions. The most prominent of these exclusions is a sale of goods to consumers. The drafters of the CISG excluded such transactions in order to avoid conflicts with special national legislation (usually "mandatory law") designed to protect consumers. CISG Article 2(a) thus states that the Convention does not apply to goods "bought for personal, family or household use," a term which should be familiar to U.S. attorneys, since it is parallels language in the UCC[47] and the federal Truth in Lending Act.[48]

The switch in focus in Article 2(a) from a "sale" of goods to goods "bought" and the use of the preposition "for" have important implications for the application of the exclusion. According to the widely prevailing view, the determinative fact is the buyer's intention regarding the use of the goods at the time of contract conclusion.[49] Standard examples includes automobiles, leisure boats, motorcycles, and recreational trailers.[50] An Austrian appellate court thus ruled in one case that the CISG did not apply to a purchase of Lamborghini automobile because the buyer's intent at the time of purchase was for personal use, even though he actually put it into use for other purposes.[51] On the other hand, a purchase of goods by an individual for commercial or professional purposes remains subject to the Convention. Moreover, the intended purchase must be *exclusively* for consumer use. As the drafters accordingly observed at the 1980 Vienna convention, the exclusion should not apply—and thus the CISG should apply—to the purchase of dual use items such as a camera partly used by a professional photographer, toiletries used by a business, and an automobile bought by a dealer for resale.[52]

As may be clear from this discussion, the relevant time for assessing the consumer goods exclusion is at the conclusion of the contract. Moreover, as protection for a surprise application of domestic

---

ately" familiar with the CISG. The results for judges were even starker, with 82% reporting that they were "not at all familiar" with the CISG. See Peter Fitzgerald, *The International Contracting Practices Survey Project*, 27 J.L. & Com. 1 (2008).

[47] UCC § 9–102(a)(23).

[48] 15 USC § 1602(i).

[49] *See CISG* DIGEST 2012, *supra* footnote 8, art. 2, para. 3.

[50] *Id.*

[51] *See* CLOUT Case No. 190, *Oberster Gerichtshof* [Supreme Court] of Austria (11 February 1997).

[52] *See CISG* DIGEST 2012, *supra* footnote 8, art. 2, para. 4.

law, CISG Article 2(a) states that the exclusion does not apply if, at that time, the seller "neither knew nor ought to have known" of the buyer's intended use for personal purposes. Although the seller has the burden of proof on this score, this exception to the exclusion injects objective considerations into the analysis, such as the nature and quantity of the goods purchased, the extent to which the buyer's name indicates a business entity, and the delivery address. Thus, a German appellate court held that the CISG applied to the sale of a car from a salesman in Germany to a buyer in Finland, regardless of the buyer's subjective intent, because the seller reasonably assumed that the buyer also was an entrepreneur.[53] The allocation of the burden of proof may nonetheless explain the results in some cases. In the Lamborghini sale noted above, for example, the Austrian court observed that the seller had not presented sufficient evidence that it neither knew nor ought to have known of the buyer's personal use.[54]

Article 2(b) excludes sales by auction, whether public (*i.e.*, under authority of law) or private.[55] The rationale for this exclusion is that such transactions are held at a specific location and often under the assumption that the local law of that location governs. The necessary attributes of an auction—a pre-announced public sale in which the contract is awarded immediately to the highest bidder—place important limitations on the scope of this exclusion. Thus, the CISG should apply notwithstanding Article 2(b) to sales *to* an auction house, sales at commodity exchanges, and even public procurement transactions. For the same reason, online "auctions" (such as on eBay), where sales are drawn out over time and are open to international bidders, should not fall within the "auction" exclusion of Article 2(b)(subject of course to the separate consumer sale exception in Article 2(a)).[56]

Execution sales and sales orders by governmental authority are also excluded from the CISG.[57] Such sales commonly are subject to mandatory special legislation or judicial rules. The word "otherwise" in Article 2(c) makes clear that the exclusion extends to sales by third parties as required or allowed under the authority of law. Thus, sales by creditors (such as in execution of a judgment), by ju-

---

[53] *See Oberlandesgericht* [Appellate Court] of Hamm, Germany, 2 April 2009, available at http://cisgw3.law.pace.edu/cases/090402g1.html.

[54] *See* CLOUT Case No. 190, *Oberster Gerichtshof* [Supreme Court] of Austria (11 February 1997).

[55] Contrast UCC § 2–328.

[56] *See* Schwenzer/Hachem, art. 2, para. 21, in Schlechtriem & Schwenzer, *supra* note 3.

[57] CISG, art. 2(c).

dicial bodies, or in a bankruptcy proceeding all are excluded from the scope of the CISG.

Sales of some intangible rights or claims—investment securities (stocks, shares), negotiable instruments, and money—are expressly excluded from the CISG, even though they may have a tangible "token."[58] Again, these exclusions were designed to avoid conflicts with mandatory rules of domestic law. Thus, a Swiss court held that a contract for the purchase of corporate shares is not covered by the CISG.[59] The "negotiable instruments" exclusion is, however, more limited than might appear at first glance. First, it only applies to documents that are formally negotiable (*i.e.*, those under which the transfer of the paper itself transfers a right to a monetary claim). Moreover, the exclusion does not extend to negotiable documents of title for goods (bills of lading, warehouse receipts), because the purchase of such a document (such as in documentary sale transactions) in legal substance involves a transfer of rights in the underlying goods. Finally, although Article 2(d) excludes sales of "money," one arbitral tribunal held that the CISG applied to a sale of souvenir coins.[60]

CISG Article 2(e) also states that the Convention does not apply to sales of "ships, vessels, hovercraft, or aircraft."[61] Under the two predecessor conventions to the CISG—the ULIS and ULF[62]—such sales were excluded only to the extent that such ships, etc., were subject to such official registration (in the nature of real estate). This requirement does not appear in the text of the CISG, however. Moreover, sales of sailboats and other leisure watercraft should be excluded irrespective of the lack of knowledge exception for consumer sales discussed immediately above. Nonetheless, because such exclusions generally are interpreted narrowly, the prevailing view is that the CISG nonetheless applies to a sale of parts for such water- or aircraft, even if the parts may be subject to registration.[63] One must note, in any event, that this exclusion is idiosyncratic, for Article 2(e) does not apply to other transportation vehicles such as locomotives, trains, and automobiles.

---

[58] CISG, art. 2(d) and 2(f).

[59] *See* CLOUT Case No. 260, *Cour de Justice* [District Court] of Genève, Switzerland (9 October, 1998).

[60] *See* CLOUT Case No. 988, China International Economic and Trade Arbitration Commission (2000).

[61] CISG, art. 2(e).

[62] *See supra* note 2.

[63] *See CISG* DIGEST 2012, *supra* footnote 8, art. 2, para. 10. *See also*, *e.g.*, United Tech. Int'l v. Malev Hungarian Airlines (Metropolitan Court of Hungary (10 January 1992), available at http://cisgw3.law.pace.edu/cases/920110h1.html.

Finally, Article 2(f) excludes sales of electricity. Courts should interpret this exclusion, like the others in Article 2, narrowly. Thus, the exception does not apply—and thus the CISG should apply—to sales of other sources of energy such as gas, coal, or oil.

§ 1.6 "Hybrid" and Other Sales Transactions Excluded from the CISG

Section 1.3 above noted that, by general consensus, the term "goods" means items with a physical existence that are moveable at the time of agreed delivery.[64] This straightforward definition nonetheless may mask a variety of subtle and important issues concerning the scope of the CISG.

Software Contracts. For modern commerce, the most prominent example of these difficult scope issues involves contracts for the transfer of intangible rights (such as intellectual property) contained or reflected in a tangible medium (*e.g.*, a computer disc). According to the general view, transactions that in their essence involve only the transfer of intangible rights are not within the scope of the Convention. Thus, a pure sale of know-how, information, or an ownership interest in a business enterprise is not subject to the CISG.[65] One court accordingly held that the CISG did not apply to a contract to conduct a marketing study, even though the contract required delivery in the form of a formal written report.[66] The court there emphasized that the concept of "goods" requires that the tangible thing delivered be the principal object of the contract. Similarly, contracts that solely involve a transfer of intellectual property rights (patents, copyrights, or trademarks) are licenses, and not a sale of goods (even if, again, the rights are delivered in a tangible medium). On the other hand, the mere fact that a sale of goods includes or is subject to intellectual property rights does not take the transaction out of the scope of the CISG.[67]

The applicability of the CISG to a sale of computer software, in contrast, has generated substantial controversy. One matter, however, is clear from the outset: The question of whether software transactions are within the scope of the CISG must be determined "autonomously," that is, on the basis of the CISG and without resort

[64] *See supra* notes 20-21 and accompanying text.

[65] *See* Schwenzer/Hachem, art. 1. paras. 19–22, in Schlechtriem & Schwenzer, *supra* note 3.

[66] *See* CLOUT Case No. 122, *Oberlandesgericht* [Appellate Court] of Köln, Germany (26 August 1994).

[67] Indeed, certain provisions of the CISG expressly cover the role of intellectual property rights in sales within its scope. *See, e.g.*, CISG, arts.41 and 42.

to rules or concepts of domestic law.[68] By general consensus, the CISG may indeed apply to a sale of software. A sale of physical electronic goods (*e.g.*, computers, electronic hardware, computer components,) is certainly within the scope of the CISG.[69] And the mere fact that most modern products include embedded software also should not affect the nature of a transaction as a sale of goods.

The challenge comes with transactions whose essential nature is purely a sale of software. There seems to be general consensus that a sale of standard computer software through a tangible medium (such as a CD ROM) is within the scope of the CISG.[70] Some commentators go much further, however, and argue that the CISG should apply to any sale of software, irrespective of the mode of delivery (and even purely over the internet).[71]

Courts and arbitral tribunals have delivered a mixed message. Some have seemed to follow the more liberal view that the CISG applies to all software sales;[72] at least one court has held, in contrast, that software developed and sold for an internet website did not involve goods.[73] Others have drawn a distinction between "standard" and specially designed software. Thus, two early German courts suggested that the CISG should apply only to sales of "standard software"—presumably, software generally available on a mass-market basis—as opposed to a program specially designed for the buyer and installed through the services of the seller.[74]

An analogy from the non-electronic world may be helpful in analyzing software sales. A contract calling for the submission of a manuscript for a book is not a contract for the sale of goods, even

---

[68] *See* the analysis of CISG Article 7 in *The General Provisions of the CISG infra.*

[69] *See, e.g.,* CLOUT Case No. 281, *Oberlandesgericht* [Appellate Court] of Koblenz, Germany (17 September 1993); *Handelsgericht* [Commercial Court] of Zürich, Switzerland, February 17, 2000, available at http://cisgw3.law.pace.edu/cases/000217s1.html.

[70] *See* CLOUT Case No. 749, *Oberster Gerichtshof* [Supreme Court] of Austria (21 June 2005); CLOUT Case No. 281, *Oberlandesgericht* [Appellate Court] of Koblenz, Germany (17 September 1993).

[71] *See S*chwenzer/Hachem, art. 1. para. 18, in Schlechtriem & Schwenzer, *supra* note 3.

[72] Decision of District Court of Arnhem (Netherlands), 28 June 2006, available at http://cisgw3.law.pace.edu/cases/060628n1.html; CLOUT Case No. 281, *Oberlandesgericht* [Appellate Court] of Koblenz, Germany (17 September 1993).

[73] *See Østre Landsret* [Appellate Court] of Denmark, March 7, 2002, available at http://cisgw3.law.pace.edu/cases/020307d1.html (with commentary by Joseph Lookofsky).

[74] *See* CLOUT Case No. 122, *Oberlandesgericht* [Appellate Court] of Köln, Germany (26 August 1994): CLOUT Case No. 131, *Landgericht* [State Court] of München, Germany (8 February 1995).

though the manuscript will be on paper or a disc. The essence of such a transaction is for the author's services. However, a contract for the sale of a commercial lot of printed books (or only one book) is for the sale of tangible items—the books, and not the printer's services. No such bright line may exist in software sales, because these may involve some adaptation to the user's precise situation. Nevertheless, a criterion based on the difference between "off the shelf" software and individually designed software may be helpful even when the software sold exhibits some characteristics of each, because one characteristic or the other may predominate.

In any event, most mass-market sales of software directly over the internet likely will be consumer sales (for "personal, family or household use") and thus will be excluded from the CISG under Article 2(a).

Hybrid Sales and Services Contracts. "Services" contracts are expressly excluded from the CISG.[75] Many contracts, however, involve obligations both to sell goods and to provide related services. CISG Article 3(2) provides a rule to address such situations. Under that rule, the CISG does not apply to a transaction in which the "preponderant part of the obligations of the party who furnishes the goods consists in the supply of labour or other services." The authorities seem to be in agreement that the "preponderant part" test focuses on "the economic value of the obligations relating to the supply of labour and services and the economic value of the obligations regarding the goods."[76] One court thus held that the CISG applied to a transaction in which fifty percent or more of the purchase price was attributed to the sale of a water tank, even though the contract also required installation services for the tank.[77] This conclusion certainly obtains if the seller merely provides ancillary services such as onsite assembly, training of personnel, or continuing maintenance services. If the CISG applies to a mixed sales and services contract, then it governs both aspects of the transaction (unless of course the parties actually conclude two separate contracts).[78]

---

75 CISG, art. 3(2).

76 CISG DIGEST 2012, *supra* footnote 8, art. 3, para. 4 (citing cases).

77 CLOUT Case No. 196, *Handelsgericht* [Commercial Court] of Zürich, Switzerland (26 April 1995).

78 *See* Schwenzer/Hachem, art. 3, paras. 12, 16–17, in Schlechtriem & Schwenzer, *supra* note 3.

Distribution Agreements. Distribution (or "framework") agreements in their usual form are not covered by the CISG.[79] The rationale is that such contracts address the "organization of the distribution" instead of the delivery of specified goods.[80] Thus, distribution agreements, like franchising and marketing contracts, are regarded as service contracts and not contracts for sale of goods. The CISG will govern, however, the separate contracts under those distribution agreements that involve actual orders for goods.[81] As one U.S. court stated, a distribution contract would be within the CISG only if it contains definite terms for the delivery of specific goods.[82] That case involved a distribution contract that identified certain goods; the dispute between the parties involved, however, not those goods, but rather separate goods ordered under a later transaction. The same analysis applies to joint venture agreements.[83]

Hybrid Supply Contracts for Future Goods. CISG Article 3(1) also has a separate, though conceptually related, rule governing contracts "for the supply of goods to be manufactured or produced" in the future. This rule addresses what are known in the United States as "maquiladora" transactions, in which a domestic business ships component parts to a business in Mexico (or other low-wage country) for assembly and return shipment to the United States. (Mexico is a CISG Contracting State.) Article 3(1) states as a basic rule that such transactions "are to be considered sales." It then makes an exception, however, for those transactions in which the purported buyer ("the party who orders the goods") provides "a substantial part of the materials necessary for [the] manufacture or production" of the goods.

Note here the deliberate use of "a substantial part" in CISG Article 3(1), in contrast to "the preponderant part" rule in Article 3(2). This would seem to indicate that the purported buyer need not provide more than fifty percent of the necessary materials in order for this exclusion to apply. Substantial disagreement exists, however,

---

[79] *See, e.g.*, Multi–Juice, S.A. v. Snapple Beverage Corp., 2006 WL 1519981 (S.D.N.Y. 2006); Viva Vino Import Corp. v. Farnese Vini S.R.L., 2000 WL 1224903 (E.D. Pa. 2000). *See also* CISG DIGEST 2012, *supra* note 8, art. 1, para. 24 (citing numerous cases).

[80] CLOUT Case No. 192, *Obergericht* [Appellate Court] of Luzern, Switzerland (8 January 1997).

[81] *See, e.g.,* Foreign Trade Court of Arbitration Award No. T–8/08, Serbian Chamber of Commerce (28 January 2009); CLOUT Case No. 273, *Oberlandesgericht* [Appellate Court] of München, Germany (9 July 1997).

[82] Helen Kaminski PTY Ltd. v. Marketing Australia Products Inc. 1997 WL 414137 (S.D.N.Y. 1997).

[83] Amco Ukrservice v. American Meter Co., 2004 WL 816923 (E.D. Pa. 2004).

over the precise contours of the term "a substantial part."[84] A reasonable resolution of this disagreement would rely principally on the relative value and volume of the buyer- and seller-supplied goods and, secondarily, on the importance of the buyer-supplied materials for the functionality or marketability of the final product.[85]

Hybrid Sales and Real Estate Transactions. The subject of contracts for the sale of goods attached to real estate has been a difficult one under domestic legal systems.[86] The CISG has no specific provision on the subject. Nonetheless, the consensus understanding on the definition of "goods" should resolve most of the difficult issues in practical application. Under that definition, goods must be moveable at the time of agreed delivery.[87] For sales of to-be-extracted minerals as well as of growing crops and timber, the CISG should apply if such goods are, or should be, moveable at the time of delivery according to the terms of the parties' contract.

Barter Transactions. Barter transactions (sometimes referred to internationally as "countertrade") represent a difficult conceptual issue for the application of the CISG. Is such a transaction, in which goods are exchanged for other goods, a "sale"? A couple of Russian arbitral tribunals and some commentators have answered in the affirmative.[88] This view, however, runs contrary to the description in CISG Article 53 of the essential obligation of the buyer to "pay the price," words usually related to tender of money and not to a tender of goods. As a result, the "prevailing opinion" is that the CISG does not apply to purely barter transactions.[89]

Countertrade transactions sometime specify a price when structured to use three interrelated contracts—one for the sale of the primary goods, a second for the exchange sale of the countertrade goods, and a protocol to define the relationship between other two. In such a case, the two sales contracts could be governed by the CISG. However, many such sales contracts, especially structural

---

84 This dispute arises in part from a difference between the English ("a substantial part") and French language versions ("an essential part").

85 *See* Schwenzer/Hachem, art. 3, para. 6, in Schlechtriem & Schwenzer, *supra* note 3. Contrary to the misguided view of one French court, purely knowledge-based specifications or instructions supplied by the buyer should not count as "materials" for purposes of Article 3(1).

86 *See* UCC §§ 2–105(1), 2–107.

87 *See* footnotes 20-21 and accompanying text *supra*.

88 *See, e.g.,* Tribunal of International Commercial Arbitration of the Russian Federation Chamber of Commerce and Industry (9 March 2004), available at http://cisgw3.law.pace.edu/cases/040309r1.html; Schwenzer/Hachem, art 1, para. 11, in Schlechtriem & Schwenzer, *supra* note 3.

89 *See* Schwenzer/Hachem, art. 1, para. 11, in Schlechtriem & Schwenzer, *supra* note 3.

arrangements on the exchange of the goods, are not sufficiently specific in identifying the quantities and types of goods to be purchased under the countertrade agreement. Thus, although the purported contract would be governed by the CISG, the Convention might well determine that no valid contract was formed.[90]

Other Mixed Transactions. By general consensus, the CISG does not apply to franchise agreements (the essence of which is the temporary transfer of intellectual property rights); "turn-key" contracts (the essence of which is that a contractor must complete a work, typically a building, for immediate operation); or financial leasing arrangements (which involve a transfer of only temporary rights).[91] Nonetheless, by express terms the CISG applies to installment contracts as well as modification contracts for transactions already within its scope.[92]

§ 1.7 Issues Expressly Excluded from the Convention

The Convention expressly *includes* from its coverage two sets of issues that arise under a sale contract, and expressly *excludes* three sets of issues. As to the latter, one must return to the substantive law of the domestic legal regime that applies under choice of law doctrines (in CISG terminology, "the rules of private international law"). The issues expressly covered by the Convention—indeed, its sum and substance—are (a) the formation of the contract, and (b) the rights and obligations of the parties to the contract.[93] The expressly excluded issues are the (a) "validity" of the contract or its provisions,[94] (b) property (or title) to the goods,[95] and (c) liability for death or personal injury.[96]

In the structure of the CISG, Article 4's basic inclusion of "formation" issues refers to Part II of the Convention[97] and its inclusion of the "rights and obligations" of the parties refers to Part III of the

---

[90] For further discussion of this issue, *see* § 1.13 *infra*.

[91] *See CISG* DIGEST 2012, *supra* note 8, art. 1, paras. 25–26; Schwenzer/-Hachem, art. 3, paras. 21–22, in Schlechtriem & Schwenzer, *supra* note 3.

[92] *See* CISG, art. 73 and art. 29.

[93] CISG, art. 4.

[94] CISG, art. 4(a).

[95] CISG, art. 4(b).

[96] CISG, art. 5.

[97] CISG, arts. 14–24.

Convention.[98] Included within the concept of "obligations" is remedies for beach.[99]

CISG Article 4's reference to the rights and obligations "of the seller and the buyer" nonetheless leaves open an important issue over whether the CISG would also govern the rights and obligations of persons who were not immediate parties to the sales contract. Such persons would include both "remote sellers" (such as manufacturers of the product or its parts that had sold to an intermediate seller in the chain of distribution) and "remote buyers" (sub-buyers of the goods that purchased from an intermediate buyer). This issue has raised substantial challenges for courts and scholars, especially because the modern trend (under the UCC in the United States at least) has been to abolish such a "privity" bar for many "implied warranty" claims.[100]

The archetypical form of this issue involves a manufacturer that sells a product along with a standard form "warranty in a box" and a retailer that resells the goods "as is" to a remote purchaser. The language of CISG Article 4 strongly suggests that the CISG provides no basis for a claim by the remote purchaser against the manufacturer, as the latter is not a *seller* in the "downstream" contract. And indeed, the strong trend of courts is to conclude that the CISG does not apply to such claims. As a U.S. federal court recently observed, "district courts have consistently found that, unless the buyer or the seller is acting through an agent who is selling the goods directly to a third party, a remote purchaser does not have a cause of action to sue an upstream seller under the CISG. Instead, the rights and obligations of remote purchasers are governed by the otherwise applicable state law."[101]

Note, however, that this conclusion may create substantial complexity in application to actual disputes. If all three parties—foreign manufacturer, U.S. reseller, and U.S. downstream purchas-

---

[98] CISG, arts. 25–88.

[99] The Convention includes within the general chapter on the "Obligations of the Seller" a section on the "Remedies for Breach of Contract by the Seller." *See* Part III, Ch. II, § III. It likewise includes within the general chapter on the "Obligations of the Buyer" a section on the "Remedies for Breach of Contract by the Buyer." *See* Part III, Ch. III, § III.

[100] This development is subject to important limitations. *See* Lee v. Mylan Inc., 806 F. Supp. 2d 1320, 1325–1326 (M.D. Ga. 2011)(observing that "[m]any states have eliminated the requirement of vertical privity" for certain implied warranty claims, but noting limitations); Pulte Home Corp. v. Parex, Inc., 579 S.E.2d 188, 192–193 (Va. 2003)(limiting remedies for such claims).

[101] Beth Schiffer Fine Photographic Arts, Inc. v. Colex Imaging, Inc., 2012 WL 924380 (D.N.J. 2012).*See also* Caterpillar Inc. v. Usinor Industeel, 393 F. Supp. 2d 659, 676 (N.D. Ill. 2005)(same).

er—are brought into the same lawsuit, different bodies of law may apply to the different sides of the potential triangle: (a) As between the foreign manufacturer and the U.S. reseller, the CISG would govern (if the manufacturer is from a CISG member state); (b) as between the U.S. reseller and the U.S. purchaser, in contrast, the UCC likely would apply; but (c) although the CISG would not apply as between the foreign manufacturer and the U.S. remote purchaser because of the absence of a contractual relationship, the courts seem prepared to recognize a claim under the UCC (depending on the approach of the applicable state law to "privity" issues).

CISG Article 4 has also been used to exclude many non-sale issues, especially agency issues, from analysis under the CISG. Such issues include the liability of a purported "agent" who represented a non-existing principal; whether a person paid by a buyer was an agent of the seller or not; and whether a right to payment could be assigned.[102] This issue—that is, who is an actual party to a potential contract—plays an important role in whether the CISG applies in the first place.[103] Separately, some courts have held that the CISG does not displace "promissory estoppel" claims under domestic law,[104] but there are strong reasons to question this result. In its essence, promissory estoppel is a contract claim; if, therefore, a party cannot satisfy the requirements for contractual liability under the CISG, it should not be permitted—under federal preemption—to circumvent that result by resort to an alternative version of contractual liability under state law. The CISG clearly should not apply, in contrast, to non-contractual unjust enrichment claims (except with respect to remedies for breach of a contract governed by the CISG[105]) nor to related business tort claims.

CISG Article 4(a) also excludes issues of "validity" from the coverage of the Convention. Unfortunately, the CISG does not define "validity." Nonetheless, the exclusion of validity issues clearly arose because the CISG was not designed to police sales contracts for fairness or otherwise address core defenses to contract enforce-

---

[102] *See, e.g.,* CLOUT Case No. 378, *Tribunale di Vigevano*, Italy (12 July 2000); CLOUT Case No. 189, *Oberster Gerichtshof* [Supreme Court] of Austria (20 March 1997). *See also generally* CISG DIGEST 2012, *supra* note 8, art. 1, para. 7 (citing cases).

[103] *See supra* § 1.3. As one recent federal court noted, however, the mere allegation that a party is an agent does not preclude an analysis of whether that party is a co-seller under the CISG. *See* 2P Commercial Agency S.R.O. v. Familant, 2012 WL 6615889 (M.D. Fla. 2012).

[104] Caterpillar, Inc. v. Usinor Industeel, 393 F. Supp. 2d 659, 675–676 (N.D. Ill. 2005); Geneva Pharmaceuticals Technology Corp. v. Barr Laboratories, Inc., 201 F. Supp. 2d 236 (S.D.N.Y. 2002), *rev. on other grounds*, 386 F.3d 485 (2004).

[105] CISG articles 81 through 84 provide specific rules for restitutionary remedies in the event of an avoidance of a contract.

ment. Thus, it is generally accepted that the concept of validity "refers to any issue by which the domestic law would render the contract void, voidable, or unenforceable."[106] As a result, domestic law will continue to apply even in CISG transactions for contract defenses based on fraud, negligent misrepresentation, duress, illegality, incapacity, and similar notions. Other domestic regulatory statutes, such as unfair competition laws, also are preserved under CISG Article 4(a).

The impact of the general contract doctrine of mistake, however, requires more careful analysis. Where the concept of mistake is based on facts existing at the time of contract formation and functions as a defense to enforcement, domestic law should apply.[107] But Article 4 permits such a resort to domestic law "except as otherwise expressly provided in this Convention," and the CISG has a number of provisions that might conflict with, and thus displace, some domestic law "mistake" doctrines. Thus, for example, if the "mistake" relates to a party's expression of intent, CISG Article 8(1) provides the governing rule.[108] Similarly, the CISG displaces domestic law claims based on post-formation events—which some legal systems categorize as a "subsequent mistake"—because CISG Article 79 exhaustively covers issues of impracticability, hardship, and the like.[109]

CISG Article 4(a) excludes from the Convention's scope not only issues of validity of a contract as a whole but also "of any of its provisions or of any usage." Thus, there has been a fair amount of litigation concerning the validity of individual clauses in standard business terms and concerning domestic statutes regulating the subject. There is now general agreement that such issues of validity are a matter of domestic law[110] (although not the basic question of whether such terms become part of the contract in the first place[111]). Thus, recent cases have held that the validity of clauses on

---

[106] *See CISG* DIGEST 2012, *supra* note 8, art. 4, para. 9 (quoting cases).

[107] *See, e.g.*, CLOUT Case No. 426, *Oberster Gerichtshof* [Supreme Court] of Austria (13 April 2000); *Bundesgerichtshof* [Supreme Civil Court] of Germany (27 November 2007), available at http://cisgw3.law.pace.edu/cases/071127g1.html.

[108] For more on CISG Article 8, see § 1.10 *infra*.

[109] For more on CISG Article 79, see § 1.25 *infra*. Other examples of CISG rules that displace domestic law claims founded on a party's "mistake" include Article 27 (for errors in transmission); Articles 35–44 (for mistakes about the conformity or quality of the goods); and Article 71 (for mistakes about the solvency of the other party).

[110] *See CISG* DIGEST 2012, *supra* footnote 8, art. 4, para. 9; Schwenzer/Hachem, art. 4, para. 38, in Schlechtriem & Schwenzer, *supra* note 3.

[111] Part II of the Convention exhaustively covers the issue of contract formation. *See* §§ 1.12–1.16 *infra*.

damage limitation,[112] liquidated damages, non-competition, forum selection, and assignments of rights are a matter for domestic law.[113] Similarly, the validity of contracts or clauses on the settlement of disputes, assignment of receivables, set-offs, assumption or acknowledgement of debts, and the rights of third parties are not governed by the CISG.[114] The subject of the statute of limitations (the "limitation period") on claims in international sales transactions is covered by a companion treaty to the CISG.[115]

The validity exclusion in CISG Article 4 has triggered special issues with specific reference to United States law. The first is whether the restrictions in the UCC on disclaimers of warranty fall in this category. For example, UCC § 2–316 imposes special linguistic and form rules for a valid disclaimer of the warranty of merchantability, including the use of the term "merchantability" and a requirement that it be conspicuous.[116] Is this an issue of "validity" as contemplated by the CISG? A second issue concerns the UCC restrictions on clauses that exclude or limit the buyer's remedies to repair or replacement, and thereby exclude the remedies of avoidance of the contract (refusal to accept delivery of the goods) or an action for damages, especially consequential damages.[117] A third issue concerns clauses that provide for a significantly larger payment to the aggrieved party than any actual or reasonably expected damages. The relevant UCC provision makes such clauses "void as a penalty."[118]

On the first issue, one U.S. federal court has expressly concluded that the CISG does not displace the UCC's requirement for a valid warranty disclaimer.[119] This is in accord with the view originally expressed by Professor Hartnell that, because the UCC warranty disclaimer provisions are designed to protect fairness, they qualify as rules of "validity" excluded from the scope of the CISG by Article 4(a).[120] Other scholars have disagreed with this view.[121] As a gen-

---

[112] MSS, Inc. v. Maser Corp., 2011 WL 2938424 (M.D. Tenn. July 18, 2011).

[113] *See CISG* DIGEST 2012, *supra* footnote 8, art. 4, paras. 9 and 14 (citing cases).

[114] *See id.*, art. 4, para. 14 (citing cases).

[115] *See* § 1.40 *infra.*

[116] UCC § 2–316(2).

[117] UCC § 2–719(2).

[118] UCC § 2–718(1), last sentence.

[119] Norfolk Southern Ry. Co. v. Power Source Supply, Inc., 2008 WL 2884102, at *5 (W.D. Pa. 2008).

[120] *See* Helen Hartnell, *Rousing the Sleeping Dog: The Validity Exception to the Convention on Contracts for the International Sale of Goods*, 18 YALE INT'L L.1 (1993).

[121] *See* John Honnold, UNIFORM LAW FOR INTERNATIONAL SALES UNDER THE 1980 UNITED NATIONS CONVENTION § 230 (H. Flechtner, ed., 4th ed. 2009)(declaring

eral proposition, the CISG cases from other jurisdictions, especially those concerning pre-formulated standard business terms, have held that even agreements on warranty limitations are subject to a review for validity under domestic law.[122] But one might reasonably draw a distinction between (a) whether local public policy prohibits conduct completely and (b) whether it defines specific linguistic requirements for limiting the seller's obligations. Under this approach, the courts would view general contract defenses (such as unconscionability) as issues of validity outside of the CISG; but, given that CISG Article 35 expressly permits the parties to "agree otherwise" regarding conformity of the goods, the courts could find that the specific linguistic formulations defined by the UCC for warranty disclaimers are displaced by the specific provisions of the CISG.[123]

On the second issue, there seems to be general agreement that the validity of clauses limiting the liability of the seller or the remedies of the buyer is a matter for domestic law.[124] Thus, a recent federal court has expressly concluded that the validity of a consequential damages limitation was governed by the UCC, not the CISG.[125] However, such clauses may not in any event leave a buyer with no remedy at all nor, as the Austrian Supreme Court has held, otherwise conflict with the core remedial values of the Convention (such as the right to declare a contract avoided).[126]

General agreement also exists on the third issue, the status of liquidated damages and penalty clauses: The validity of such clauses likewise is an issue of validity under CISG Article 4(a) and thus is a matter for domestic law.[127] Common law courts hold such clauses to be invalid, even in contracts otherwise subject to the CISG. The wide acceptance of this conclusion may be due to the fact that the UCC makes such clauses substantively "void," rather than

---

that "the particular verbal formulations or warranty requirements specified in the U.C.C. for disclaiming" implied warranties do not apply to CISG contracts); Bruno Zeller, CISG AND THE UNIFICATION OF INTERNATIONAL TRADE LAW 71 (2007)(same).

[122] *See Oberster Gerichtshof* [Supreme Court] *of* Austria (7 September 2000), available at http://cisgw3.law.pace.edu/cases/000907a3.html.

[123] *See* CISG, art. 35 and the discussion in §§ 1.19 *infra.*

[124] *See* Schwenzer/Hachem, art. 4, para. 43, in Schlechtriem & Schwenzer, *supra* note 3.

[125] *See* 2P Commercial Agency S.R.O. v. Familant, 2012 WL 6615889 (M.D. Fla. 2012).

[126] *See Oberster Gerichtshof* [Supreme Court] of Austria (7 September 2000), available at http://cisgw3.law.pace.edu/cases/000907a3.html. *See also* Schwenzer/Hachem, art. 4, para. 43, in Schlechtriem & Schwenzer, *supra* note 3.

[127] *See* Schwenzer/Hachem, art. 4, para. 44, in Schlechtriem & Schwenzer, *supra* note 3, and, *e.g.*, decision of Appellate Court (*Oberlandesgericht*), Hamburg, Germany, 25 January 2008, available at http://cisgw3.law.pace.edu/cases/080125g1.html.

merely subject to special linguistic requirements. It may also be due to the foundations of the common law rule against "penalty" clauses in basic public policies against non-compensatory remedies and potential *in terrorem* use of such contract rights.[128]

Another set of issues excluded from CISG coverage concerns property rights to the goods, including title to the goods and the security rights and obligations of third parties to the contract.[129] It is clear that disputes over ownership of the goods are not covered by the CISG and must be determined under local law.[130] The primary issue raised in litigation over this provision has been the effect of "retention of title" clauses, by which the seller attempts to retain title in the goods after delivery and until the buyer pays for them. The legal status of such clauses is a property issue and is therefore outside the scope of the CISG.[131] Thus, any determination of the effect of such clauses depends upon applicable domestic law (in the U.S., UCC Article 9), even though the CISG applies to the analysis of the remainder of the contract.

§ 1.8 The General Provisions of the CISG

CISG Articles 7 through 13 contain its "general principles." These provisions deal with interpretation of the Convention and filling gaps in its provisions (Article 7), interpretation of party intent and usages of trade (Article 8 and 9), a few definitions (Articles 10 and 13), and a general removal of form requirements such as the Statute of Frauds (Articles 11 and 12). Article 7 is designed to assist in interpretation of the Convention itself, while Articles 8 and 9 provide rules on the interpretation of party intent, both preformation and as reflected in their contract terms. In specific, Article 8 concentrates on statements and conduct by the parties themselves as indications of their contractual agreement, while Article 9 concentrates on sources external to the parties, such as trade usages. (Section 1.3 above has already analyzed the provisions of Article 10 concerning multiple business offices and the application of the CISG in the first place.)

---

[128] For an historical perspective see Lloyd, *Penalties and Forfeitures*, 29 HARV. L. REV. 117 (1915).

[129] CISG, art. 4(b).

[130] *See, e.g.*, Usinor Industeel v. Leeco Steel Prods., 209 F. Supp. 2d 880 (N.D. Ill. 2002).

[131] *See CISG* DIGEST 2012, *supra* footnote 8, art. 4, para. 13 (citing cases).

§ 1.9 Interpretation of the CISG

At first glance, CISG Article 7(1) appears to be a set of "pious platitudes," without any particular analytical content. This provision, however, plays an essential role in defining the nature of the Convention and its relationship with domestic law. At its most fundamental, Article 7(1) is designed to inhibit local courts from applying local norms and rules, rather than the Convention, to international sales disputes governed by the CISG. It first directs that interpretation of the Convention must heed its "international character." The purpose of this provision is to ensure that local courts respect the fact that the Convention reflects a broad international compromise among domestic legal systems. Courts must thus interpret the CISG on its own ("autonomously"), without resort to domestic interpretive norms or substantive rules. Thus, for example, in interpreting the concepts stated in the Convention, such as "reasonable time," the required regard for the "international character" of the Convention imposes on the courts an obligation to follow international practice developed within the CISG, rather than domestic practice or precedent.

The requirement of an international perspective is stressed further by a second directive in Article 7(1)—that interpretation of the CISG must "promote uniformity of its application." This directive serves both to highlight the persuasive authority of foreign decisions interpreting the CISG and to emphasize (again) that local decisions on domestic sales law should not be relevant. Even the doctrine of "good faith" under the CISG is muted. Although UCC Rev. § 1–304 (former § 1–203) imposes an obligation of good faith on the parties to sales (and other) transactions, CISG Article 7(1) only refers to good faith in the interpretation of the Convention, not of the parties' contract (although some courts have shown recent flexibility on this score via Article 7(2), see immediately below).

Unfortunately, some courts in the United States have missed the essential message of Article 7(1) when they have turned to the domestic UCC to assist in interpreting the CISG. The Second Circuit started U.S. courts on this false path in 1995 when it stated that, where the language of a CISG provision tracks that of an analogous UCC provision, UCC case law may help to inform interpretation of the CISG.[132] Many subsequent courts have followed this statement without further analysis. The Seventh Circuit, for example, has observed that the CISG is the "international analog" to Article 2 of the UCC, and that where provisions are "the same or simi-

---

[132] Delchi Carrier S.p.A. v. Rotorex, 71 F.3d 1024, 1028 (2nd Cir. 1995).

lar" the UCC can be informative to the court.[133] These statements in principal part seem to serve as a means of easing the burden of the courts based on the equally misleading premise, often repeated, that there is "virtually no case law under the Convention."[134] Similarly, U.S. courts routinely fail to consider foreign interpretive decisions under the Convention.[135]

These observations fundamentally miss the core directives of Article 7(1) that interpretation of the Convention must heed its "international character" and "promote uniformity of its application." Thus, unless the drafting history of the Convention reveals that a particular provision is based on a UCC rule, a coincidental linguistic parallel between the UCC and the CISG may be merely a "false friend" (just as a parallel with French or Chinese norms does not mean that the CISG follows those domestic law approaches). As a matter of domestic law, a particular federal appellate decision may have a *stare decisis* effect on inferior courts. But within the scheme of an international treaty such as the CISG, decisions of foreign courts should have an equal persuasive value as domestic ones. Moreover, foreign interpretive decisions for the CISG are both abundant and easily accessible.[136] Indeed, one internet site alone lists 2,500 full text cases and 10,000 annotations.[137]

Article 7(2) continues this approach with respect to apparent gaps in the express provisions of the Convention. Reflective of a civil code interpretive approach, this provision states as a primary rule that gaps in the CISG "are to be settled in conformity with the general principles on which it is based." This approach (unlike that of the domestic UCC) thus again mandates that courts first attempt to fill regulatory gaps on an "autonomous" basis—that is, with reference to the broader principles reflected in the *Convention itself.* On this basis, courts and scholars have distilled from common themes in the CISG's provisions certain fundamental principles (which might be viewed as "inductive general principles"), including reasonableness, a duty to communicate relevant information, full compensation in the event of breach, a form of traditional estoppel, and

---

[133] Chicago Prime Packers, Inc. v. Northam Food Trading Co., 408 F.3d 894 (7th Cir. 2005).

[134] *See, e.g.,* Hilaturas Miel, S.L. v. Republic of Iraq, 573 F. Supp. 2d 781, 799 (S.D.N.Y. 2008)(*quoting* Delchi Carrier S.p.A. v. Rotorex, 71 F.3d 1024, 1028 (2nd Cir. 1995)).

[135] For a positive counterexample see Forestal Guarani S.A. v. Daros Intern., Inc., 613 F.3d 395, 399–400 (3rd Cir. 2010)(examining the competing views of foreign courts on a disputed CISG issue).

[136] For a comprehensive analysis of the CISG's interpretive scheme see Michael P. Van Alstine, *Dynamic Treaty Interpretation*, 146 U. PA. L. REV. 687 (1998).

[137] http://www.cisg.law.pace.edu/cisg/text/digest-cases-toc.html.

even a requirement of good faith in the exercise of discretionary powers.[138] In the same way, courts have found a general principle that a party relying on a CISG right or power has the burden to prove the factual prerequisites and a party claiming an exception to a CISG rule has the burden of proving the factual prerequisites of that exception, at least where the structure of the CISG implies such a result.[139]

It is only if a thorough search for CISG general principles fails that Article 7(2) permits resort to domestic law principles determined under applicable choice-of-law rules. The danger to uniform application is that local courts will discover many "gaps" and no usable "general principles" derivable from the Convention, and then easily fall back on their own familiar supplementary principles of law. The fundamental philosophy of the CISG is that local courts must assiduously resist this impulse.

§ 1.10 Interpretation of the Party Intent and Usages

Article 8 establishes rules for interpreting party expressions and conduct as well as any final contract between them. It establishes a three-tier hierarchy: (1) Where the parties have a common understanding concerning their intent or the meaning of a provision, that common understanding will prevail. (2) Where the parties do not have a common understanding or intent, but one party "knew or could not have been unaware" of the other party's (subjective) intent, under Article 8(1) the latter party's interpretation prevails. The idea here is that a party's *actual* intent should prevail where the other party knows of that *actual* intent. And (3) in all other cases, and especially where the meaning of a disputed term is ambiguous, under Article 8(2) the parties' statements and conduct are determined by the traditional "reasonable person" standard. In evaluating party conduct and statements, Article 8(3) instructs courts to look to "all relevant circumstances," including the negotiating history of the contract (contrary to the American parol evidence rule) and the parties' prior practices and subsequent conduct.

Fortunately, U.S. courts seem to have taken this hierarchy to heart. In *MCC-Marble Ceramic Center, Inc. v. Ceramica Nuova d'Agostino, S.p.A.*, for example, a federal Court of Appeals inter-

---

[138] *See CISG* DIGEST 2012, *supra* footnote 8, art. 7, paras. 10–32 (citing numerous cases). *See also* Van Alstine, *Dynamic Treaty Interpretation*, *supra* note 136, at 749–753.

[139] *See CISG* DIGEST 2012, *supra* footnote 8, art. 4, para. 4. *See also* Honnold/Flechtner, *supra* note 121, Article4, § 70.1.

preted Article 8(1) to require consideration of a party's subjective intent in interpreting the statements and conduct of the parties in the formation of a contract.[140] Article 8(3) also can direct a court to a very different approach to contract interpretation than is usual in other U.S. contract cases. Its requirement that a court give consideration to all relevant circumstances is a clear direction to consider parol evidence, even in interpreting a subsequent and final written agreement. As a more recent federal court has observed, "CISG allows all evidence of the parties' intent to be admitted to interpret the terms of the agreement" in direct rejection of domestic rules that favor final writings.[141] Some courts and scholars likewise have relied on the interpretive rules in Article 8 to promote the actual intent of the parties in "battle of the forms" situations and thus to avoid mechanical application of the traditional "last shot" doctrine.[142]

CISG Article 9 addresses express and implied acceptance of usages of trade. Article 9(1) first provides that the parties are bound by "any usage" to which they have "agreed." Such agreements need not be in writing and, although the drafting history suggests a higher standard, the Austrian Supreme Court has held that even implicit agreements on usages are binding.[143] Further, "any" usage may be so incorporated, including local ones, not just international usage. If so incorporated, a usage is considered to be part of the express contract items.[144] However, because Article 6 allows the express terms of the contract to vary the provisions of the Convention, agreed usages will prevail over CISG provisions. The one exception to the last statement is Article 12, which is applicable only if one of the parties has its place of business in a Contracting State that has declared a reservation under Article 96. Under that reservation (see "form requirements" immediately below), contracts must be evidenced by a writing if so required by the local law of the Contracting State.

Article 9(1) also binds the parties to "any practices which they have established between themselves." Where the parties have established such practices, they prevail over common industry usages. As the Eleventh Circuit observed in *Treibacher Industrie, A.G. v.*

---

140 144. F.2d 1384 (11th Cir. 1998).

141 ECEM European Chemical Marketing B.V. v. Purolite Co., 2010 WL 419444, at *13 (E.D. Pa. 2010).

142 *See* § 1.16 *infra*.

143 *See* CLOUT Case No. 425, *Oberster Gerichtshof* [Supreme Court] of Austria (21 March 2000).

144 For numerous examples of such agreed usages see CISG DIGEST 2012, *supra* footnote 8, art. 9, para. 6.

Allegheny Technologies, Inc., "the parties' usage of a term in their course of dealings controls that term's meaning in the face of a conflicting customary usage of the term."[145]

Article 9(2) concerns the incorporation of usages by implication. In the drafting of the CISG, both less developed countries (LDCs) and nonmarket economies (NMEs) demanded a limit on the application of trade usages by implication. The result was a rule that, if the parties do not expressly agree to incorporate a usage, it may apply in the parties' contractual relationship only if (a) "the parties knew or ought to have known" of it; (b) it is international (not merely local) in nature; and (c) it is both "widely known to" and "regularly observed by" others in that particular international trade. This seems to set a very high standard for a party seeking to rely on an implied trade usage, and in particular with regard to the identification of the specific "international trade" involved.

§ 1.11 Form Requirements

Article 11 provides that a contract for the international sale of goods need not be evidenced by any writing and may be proven by any means. Thus, there is no equivalent in the Convention of the Statute of Frauds. This provision likewise makes clear that CISG contracts may be concluded or evidenced by electronic communications.[146]

Nonetheless, Articles 12 and 96 allow a Contracting State to declare a reservation that the local law of that Contracting State will govern the form requirements for a sales contract "where any party has his place of business in that State." Such a reservation, however, is applicable only to the extent that the domestic law of the State making the reservation "requires contracts of sale to be concluded in or evidence by writing."[147] The United States has not made this declaration, so its Statute of Frauds provisions in UCC § 2–201 are not applicable to contracts under the Convention. In fact, only eight Contracting States have declared an Article 96 reservation; but prominently included among these are Russia, China, Chile, and Argentina, with the result that their domestic law on writing requirements would continue to apply for CISG contracts.

The existence of an Article 96 reservation by one of these states may not, however, be the final word on transactions involving their

---

[145] 464 F.3d 1235, 1239 (11th Cir. 2006).

[146] *See also* CISG Advisory Council Opinion No.1, *Electronic Communications under CISG* (2003).

[147] CISG, art. 96.

residents. According to what appears to be the minority view, if one party has its relevant place of business in such a state, that state's writing requirements apply.[148] The apparent majority view, in contrast, first requires application of the forum state's conflict of law rules. It is only if those rules lead to the application of a reserving state's law that its writing requirements will apply. The Third Circuit recently endorsed this majority approach.[149]

If a state's Article 96 reservation applies to a transaction, however, the parties may not under CISG Article 6 agree otherwise.[150] This gives the local law the effect of "mandatory law" under the Convention. Nonetheless, Article 13 provides that a telex or a telegram may satisfy the "writing" requirement, and thus regardless of the formal requirements of the local law: Articles 12 and 96 only make unenforceable those contracts which are "other than in writing" (a Convention term), and Article 13 then defines "writing," as used in the CISG, to include a telex or telegram. Nonetheless, the telex and telegram of course long ago yielded to electronic communication, so the effect of Article 13 will be limited.

§ 1.12 Contract Formation—In General

The CISG has a separate "Part" (Part II) for its contract formation provisions.[151] Under Article 92, a Contracting State may declare a reservation at the time of ratification that it will not be bound by Part II, even though it is bound by the rest of the CISG. Only the Scandinavian countries, however, have declared such a reservation (and even they recently have been retreating from this stance).

Every first-year American law student studies about "offer, acceptance and consideration," but all of these three elements of contract formation are not present in other legal systems. Civil law emphasizes the agreement process, and does not include a "consideration" requirement. Nonetheless, an examination of the consideration cases will show that few such disputes arise in true commercial transactions. Rather, they tend to involve family members arguing over failed promises (uncles attempting to induce nephews not to smoke and the like). Thus, it should not be surprising to learn that the CISG has no requirement of "consideration" in its contract formation provisions.

---

[148] *See CISG* DIGEST 2012, *supra* footnote 8, art. 12, para. 4 (citing cases).

[149] Forestal Guarani S.A. v. Daros Intern., Inc., 613 F.3d 395, 399–400 (3rd Cir. 2010).

[150] CISG, art. 12.

[151] CISG, arts. 14–24.

As was discussed in the previous section, the writing requirements of the Statute of Frauds also are not applicable, unless one of the parties has a place of business in a Contracting State that has declared a reservation under Article 96. However, the parties to an informal contract may agree to require any formalities they desire, including requiring that a contract may be validly concluded only with a written, signed final agreement. Such a term, if agreed by both parties, is an enforceable derogation from CISG Article 11.

Part II of the CISG focuses on "offer"[152] and "acceptance."[153] In Convention terminology, a contract "is concluded at the moment when an acceptance of an offer becomes effective."[154] Again, there is no need for consideration, and no similar required formalities.

Nonetheless, it is also clear that the parties can conclude a contract without a clearly identifiable offer and acceptance, and that such contracting arrangements fall within the scope of CISG rules.[155] Thus, the conduct of the parties can reflect an agreement on the existence of a contract between them, and the CISG would recognize such an agreement as a binding contract without a formal offer or acceptance. This results from the fundamental principle of "party autonomy" contained in CISG Article 6.[156] Whether this would allow recognition of a contract in the case of a "merchant's letter of confirmation," which in some countries will lead to contract formation in the absence of a timely objection, remains the subject of substantial dispute.[157]

§ 1.13 Contract Formation—The Offer

Article 14 defines three requirements for an "offer." First, it must be "a proposal for concluding a contract," which is a standard notion. Second, it must indicate "an intention to be bound in case of acceptance," which will distinguish an offer from a general sales catalogue, an advertisement, or a purchase inquiry. Article 14(2) elaborates on this concept by making proposals addressed to the general public presumptively not offers "unless the contrary is clearly indicated." Third, an offer must be "sufficiently definite." Article 14 expressly identifies in this regard only three essential elements: goods, quantity, and price; by implication, other terms

---

152 CISG, arts. 14–17.

153 CISG, arts. 18–22.

154 CISG, art. 23.

155 *See CISG* DIGEST 2012, *supra* footnote 8, *Formation of the Contract*, para. 5.

156 *See* § 1.4 *supra*.

157 *See CISG* DIGEST 2012, *supra* footnote 8, *Formation of the Contract*, para. 13 (citing cases).

can be left open, but not these three.[158] A proposal satisfies this definiteness requirement if it merely "indicates" the goods, which does not seem to require that they be described with any particularity. Similarly, an offer is sufficiently definite if it "expressly or impliedly fixes or makes provision for determining the quantity and the price."

Examples of sufficiently definite quantity terms include "an order of up to 250,000 pounds" of soy lecithin, "three truckloads" of eggs where the parties understood that this mean full truckloads, and "10,000 tons +/-5 per cent" of a particular good.[159]

Thus, flexible quantity provisions do not seem to prevent proposals from being regarded as offers. One court accordingly held that a proposal to sell a chemical "in commercial amounts" was "sufficiently definite."[160] In particular, open quantity contracts, such as those for requirements, output, or exclusive dealings, in most cases should cause little difficulty for the courts. In each such contract, a "provision for determining the quantity" likely will arise through party performance, even if the precise number cannot be fixed in advance. Thus, an order for an approximate quantity of natural gas met the requirements of Article 14, because it complied with usage regularly applied in the natural gas trade.[161] On the other hand, a mere distribution agreement without specific quantities was held not to make adequate provision for determining the quantity.[162] Thus, in view of the requirements of CISG Article 14 it is usually preferable to include either estimated quantity amounts or minimum quantity amounts, to assure that there is a fixed or determinable quantity provision.

Assortment arrangements, under which one party has discretion over the choice of goods from among an assortment, are a final problem concerning "definiteness."[163] A clause that permits either the buyer or the seller to specify the assortment of goods during the performance of the contract would seem to make a provision for determining both quantity and type of goods. The major hurdle in such cases is the requirement that the offer "indicate[] the goods."

---

[158] *See CISG* DIGEST 2012, *supra* footnote 8, art. 14, para. 7.

[159] *See CISG* DIGEST 2012, *supra* footnote 8, art. 14, para. 93 (citing cases).

[160] Geneva Pharmaceuticals Tech Corp. v. Barr Labs, Inc., 201 F. Supp. 2d 236, 281–282 (S.D.N.Y. 2002), *aff'd*, 386 F.3d 485 (2nd Cir. 2004).

[161] CLOUT Case No. 176, *Oberster Gerichtshof* [Supreme Court] of Austria (6 February 1996), also available at http://cisgw3.law.pace.edu/cases/960206a3.html.

[162] Helen Kaminski PTY Ltd. v. Marketing Australia Products Inc. 1997 WL 414137 (S.D.N.Y. 1997).

[163] Compare UCC § 2–311.

But Article 14(1) does not require that the offer "specify" the goods, and so clauses that allow later selection of assortment are presumably authorized, if the parties take care in describing the type of goods from which the assortment will be selected. Nonetheless, the alternatives must also satisfy the requirement of a definite price.[164]

The CISG requirement for a definite price seems more restrictive than the comparable UCC provision on open, or flexible, price contracts,[165] and it was so intended. This is so because many civil law states do not recognize such open-price contracts. Some have argued that a true "open price" contract is possible under the CISG, provided that the parties have expressed a knowing intent to be bound.[166] This could be accomplished, however, only with a sufficiently clear party intent on a means to determine the price, and not, unlike the UCC, by a mere judicial resort to the market price.

CISG Article 55—which permits reference to the price "generally charged . . . under comparable circumstances"—may be helpful here. Although this provision only applies where a contract has already been "validly concluded" (which assumes a valid offer[167]), the cases have not been so doctrinaire. Most often these more flexible cases have found that, by conduct or dealings, parties have "implicitly" agreed on a price under the interpretive rules of CISG Article 8.[168] Thus, where the offer indicated a range of prices for goods with a range of quality, the court held that the offer was sufficiently definite, since it was possible to price each item according to its quality.[169] Likewise, in two cases where the seller and buyer agreed to a sale with no price term, but the seller then shipped and the buyer accepted the goods, the courts found that a binding contract existed.[170] Nonetheless, the cases are clear that CISG Article 55 is "not a means for judicial price-setting."[171] Thus, where the parties agreed to a sale without stating a price, but essentially "agreed to agree"

---

164 *See* CLOUT Case No. 53, *Legfelsóbb Biróság* [Supreme Court] of Hungary (25 September 1992)(holding that proposals to an aircraft buyer did not satisfy the CISG's definiteness requirement because they did not provide the price for some elements of the various alternatives), also available at http://cisgw3.law.pace.edu/cases/920925h1.html.

165 *See* UCC § 2–305.

166 *See* Mohs, art. 55, para. 5, in Schlechtriem & Schwenzer, *supra* note 3.

167 *See CISG* DIGEST 2012, *supra* footnote 8, art. 14, para. 15.

168 *See* § 1.10 *supra*.

169 CLOUT Case No. 106, *Oberster Gerichtshof* [Supreme Court] of Austria (10 November 1994).

170 CLOUT Case No. 215, *Bezirksgericht* [District Court] of St. Gallen, Switzerland (3 July 1997); *Landgericht* [State Court] of Neubrandenburg, Germany (3 August 2005), also available at http://cisgw3.law.pace.edu/cases/050803g1.html.

171 *See CISG* DIGEST 2012, *supra* footnote 8, art. 55, para. 3.

later on the price for each shipment, the purported offer neither contained a price term nor made a provision for determining the price as required for a valid contract by Article 14(1).[172]

More generally, the Convention's language is flexible enough to authorize most forms of flexible pricing. A contract will sufficiently "make provision for determining the price" where the price is to follow a specified index, or is subject to an escalator clause, or is to be set by a third party. Arguably, the latter would include "lowest price to others" clauses. The only serious problem not resolved under this analysis may be an order for a replacement part in which no price is stated. It is here that Article 55 is certainly useful. The offeror may have "implicitly" agreed to pay the seller's current price for such goods, and Article 55 fixes the price as that generally charged at the time the contract was "concluded."

§ 1.14 Contract Formation—Firm Offers and Other Offer Issues

CISG Article 14 provides the prerequisites of an offer, but the three following articles concern the withdrawal, revocation and termination of an offer.[173] Many of these provisions resemble the civil law in substance, scope and style, more than comparable common law models. "Withdrawal" of an offer—with the effect that it does not become "effective" in the first place[174]—is permissible only before the offer reaches the offeree.[175] After this, the only recourse of the offeror is to attempt to "revoke" the offer.

Under the CISG, in general a revocation of an offer must reach the offeree before the offeree has dispatched an acceptance.[176] The offeror does not have this power, however, for all offers.

One of the consequences of the abandonment of the "consideration" requirement is that there is no foundation for the strict common law approach to the revocability of an unaccepted offer. Traditional common law doctrine makes an offer freely revocable until accepted, unless the parties had an agreement supported by consideration to keep it open (*i.e.*, had concluded a related "option contract"). In German law, in contrast, an offer is binding and irrevo-

---

[172] CLOUT Case No. 139, Tribunal of International Commercial Arbitration of Russia (2 March 1995).

[173] CISG, arts. 15–17.

[174] CISG, art. 15(1)

[175] CISG, art. 15(2).

[176] CISG, art. 16(1).

cable unless the offeror states that it is revocable.[177] These two approaches are in conflict, and the compromise adopted by the CISG uses neither.

Under the second paragraph of Article 16, an offer governed by the Convention[178] in principle is revocable, but subject to two important exceptions. First, an offer is not revocable if it "indicates" that it is irrevocable.[179] Second, the offeror loses the power of revocation in the case of reasonable reliance by the offeree.[180] The first of these approaches incorporates civil law norms, while the second applies common law norms. In adopting this position, the Convention rejects both the common rule that an offer is always revocable and the German civil law rule that an offer is not revocable unless it is expressly states otherwise. This approach is similar in concept to a merchant's "firm offer" under the UCC,[181] but no "signed writing" is required.

An offeror can indicate that an offer is irrevocable "by stating a fixed time for acceptance or otherwise."[182] The first reference seems relatively clear, and would include a statement that an offer will be held open for a specified period and no longer. But, what is included in "or otherwise"? For example, does it include a statement that an offer will *lapse* after a specified period? That does not necessarily waive the offeror's right to revoke the offer earlier, but the delegates at the Diplomatic Conference could not agree on how their language applied in that hypothetical case.[183] In any event, the "or otherwise" language should embrace any other aspects of the offer (as interpreted under Article 8), including those that permit reference to the circumstances surrounding the negotiation of the contract or the nature of the parties' relationship.

The possibility of irrevocability through reasonable and actual offeree reliance is similar in concept to (but should not be influenced

---

177 *See* German Civil Code art. 145.

178 Under CISG article 100, the Convention applies to a proposal made on or after the time when it has entered into force under CISG article 1. On this latter point see § 1.3 *supra*.

179 CISG, art. 16(2)(a).

180 CISG, art. 16(2)(b).

181 UCC § 2–205.

182 CISG, art. 16(2)(a).

183 *See* Gyula Eorsi, *Article 16*, in COMMENTARY ON THE INTERNATIONAL SALES LAW: THE 1980 VIENNA CONVENTION (C.M. Bianca & M. Bonell, eds., 1987)(observing that "[t]he common law delegations maintained that even if the offer states a fixed time for acceptance, this, in itself, does not necessarily mean that the offer is irrevocable. . . . Thus, the common law delegations were inclined to read the civil law language in the common law way.").

by) the notion of an "option contract" created through reasonable reliance by an offeree under Section 87(2) of the Second Restatement of Contracts. For emphasis, however, the § 87(2) requirements are idiosyncratic to U.S. domestic law and courts should not consult them for guidance in developing the autonomous law required by the CISG (for no gap exists as contemplated by CISG Article 7(2)).[184] Finally, in either of the two means for irrevocability under Article 16, the offer must also meet the Article 14 requirements, including an indication of the goods and a fixed or determinable price and quantity.

Despite the seeming ambiguity of these concepts and the Convention language, no reported cases have actually applied Article 16(2). Courts presented with these issues may consult the principles of CISG Article 8 on the interpretation of party expressions. Under 8(1), the issue for the irrevocability of an offer would be whether the offeree knew or could not have been unaware that the offeror intended the offer to be revocable.[185] If both offeror and offeree are from common law states, there may be such an intention, although it is not conclusive since both parties' understandings arise from a common law background in which offers are revocable in the absence of consideration or a signed writing. If both parties are from civil law backgrounds the opposite construction of intention may be possible. One might argue that Article 8 is irrelevant to this determination, because CISG Article 16(2)(a) focuses on what the offer indicates, not on what the person making the offer intended to indicate. However, it is unlikely that the drafters of the CISG intended to set aside the general interpretive rules of Article 8 in the application of the Convention's substantive provisions, including the rules in Article 16. In any event, what is "reasonable" reliance for purposes of CISG Article 16(2)(b) must be determined on an international level and not based on domestic law practices or precedents.

§ 1.15 Contract Formation—Acceptance

The CISG's definition of an "acceptance" of an offer generally follows traditional notions. CISG Article 18(1) defines an acceptance as a statement or "other conduct" by an offeree "indicating assent to an offer." The same basic notion applies to proposals to modify or terminate a contract.[186] Also, a party who negotiates over or indi-

---

[184] *See* Geneva Pharmaceuticals Technology Corp. v. Barr Laboratories, Inc., 201 F. Supp. 2d 236, 286–287 (S.D.N.Y. 2002)(observing in dicta that domestic promissory estoppel claims for reliance on an offer governed by the CISG would be preempted).

[185] *See* § 1.10 *supra*.

[186] *See CISG* DIGEST 2012, *supra* footnote 8, art. 18, para. 2.

cates acceptance of an offer in a foreign language bears the risk of the detailed meaning of that foreign language.[187]

CISG Article 18(1) also declares that "silence or inactivity" does not "in itself" amount to acceptance. Nonetheless, the rules for interpreting party intent[188] make clear that negotiations and other prior conduct of the parties may establish an implicit understanding that lengthy silence followed by an absence of an affirmative objection indicates an acceptance. Thus, a U.S. District Court held in *Filanto, S.p.A. v. Chilewich Int'l Corp.* that a course of prior dealings, including exchanges of draft contracts, required an offeree to object promptly to an offer and that a lengthy failure to object to a proposed final draft, followed by the beginning of performance by the offeror, amounted to an acceptance.[189]

The *Filantro* decision creates some analytical challenges regarding the interaction between federal law on arbitration agreements and the contract formation rules of the CISG.[190] In part, the decision seems to indicate that there can be a contract to arbitrate formed separately from the sales contract. There is in principle no necessary conflict between federal arbitration law and the CISG, for the CISG elevates the agreement of the parties ("party autonomy") over even its express provisions.[191] But courts must take care to ensure that the parties' dealings in fact reflect a separate intent to arbitrate. In any event, the true value of the *Filanto* decision lies in its recognition, on the foundation of the interpretive rules of the Convention, that a court "may consider previous relations between the parties in assessing whether a party's conduct constituted acceptance."[192] As discussed immediately below, the *Filanto* decisions—now reflected in later court decisions as well—also repre-

---

[187] *See id.*, art. 18, para. 2.

[188] *See* CISG, art. 8(3) and CISG, art. 9(1)(stating that the parties are bound by "any practices which they have established between themselves"). On both points see § 1.10 *supra*.

[189] 789 F. Supp. 1229 (S.D.N.Y. 1992). Interestingly, this opinion is principally an analysis of the "federal law of contracts" that has grown up around the 1958 New York Convention on the Recognition and Enforcement of Arbitral Awards and the federal legislation implementing that treaty. 9 U.S.C. §§ 201–209. The court found that the implicit acceptance by the offeree created an express "agreement in writing" for purposes of the Federal Arbitration Act.

[190] *See, e.g.*, Peter Winship, *The U.N. Convention and the Emerging Caselaw*, in EMPTIO–VENDITIO INTERNATIONES 227–237 (1997); Michael P. Van Alstine, *Consensus, Dissensus and Contractual Obligation Through the Prism of Uniform International Sales Law*, 37 VA. INT'L L. 1 (1996); Gary Nakata, *Filanto S.p.A. v. Chilewich Int'l Corp.: Sounds of Silence Bellow Forth Under the CISG's International Battle of the Forms*, 7 TRANSNAT'L LAW.141 (1994).

[191] *See* § 1.4 *supra*.

[192] 789 F. Supp. at 1240.

sents judicial hostility to a retreat to the dated "last shot" doctrine in a "battle of the forms" under the CISG.

Article 18(2) determines when an "indication of acceptance" is effective for "concluding" the contract. Thus, along with Articles 16(1) and 22, it forms the Convention's approach to "the mailbox rule"—except that the CISG rules are different. At common law, "the mailbox rule" passes the risk of loss or delay in the transmission of an acceptance to the offeror when the offeree dispatches the acceptance.[193] It also chooses that point in time to terminate the offeror's power to revoke an offer and to terminate the offeree's power to withdraw the acceptance. Under the CISG, in contrast, an acceptance is not effective until it "reaches" (is delivered to) the offeror.[194] Thus, risk of loss or delay in transmission of an acceptance is on the offeree, who must now inquire should it not receive acknowledgement of receipt. Moreover, the acceptance must "reach" the offeror within the time fixed in the offer (or, failing that, within a reasonable time).

Nonetheless, this rule is balanced by CISG Article 16(1), which provides that the offeror's power to revoke is terminated upon dispatch of the acceptance—which is the common law rule. However, the offeree's power to withdraw the acceptance terminates only when the acceptance reaches the offeror. Thus, an acceptance sent by a slow transmission method allows the offeree to speculate for a brief time while the offeror is bound. An email message, for example, will release the offeree from the not-yet-received acceptance.

Even though Article 18(1) states that acceptance by conduct alone is possible, the remaining paragraphs of Article 18 seem to imply that in the usual case the offeree must notify the offeror that acceptance by conduct is forthcoming. Article 18(3) indicates that acceptance by conduct without notice is possible only when that procedure is allowed by the offer, by usage, or by the parties' prior course of dealing. If so allowed, the acceptance by conduct without notice—such as shipment of the goods—is effective upon the performance of the act, rather than upon the delivery of the goods to the offeror (when knowledge of the acceptance would otherwise reach the offeror). Notification of the acceptance may reach the offeror indirectly through third parties, such as banks or carriers.

Finally, the CISG provides that a contract may be modified by the parties through a "mere agreement,"[195] a point emphasized by a

---

[193] *See* Adams v. Lindsell, 1 Barn. & Ald. 681, 106 Eng. Rep. 250 (K.B. 1818).

[194] CISG, art. 18(2).

[195] CISG, art. 29.

U.S. Court of Appeals in a dispute over a settlement agreement.[196] If a contract writing permits modification only in writing, however, the contract cannot be otherwise modified, unless a party by its conduct induces the other party to act in reliance on an unwritten modification.[197]

§ 1.16 Contract Formation—The Battle of the Forms

One of the most vexing of modern contract formation issues is the "battle of the forms." This "battle" arises when the respective lawyers of the buyer and the seller prepare carefully crafted forms, but the parties themselves pay little attention to the forms when they actually negotiate their contract. The parties focus instead on the business terms (price, specification and quantity of goods, performance time); it is only if and when a dispute arises that the parties pull out the forms and review them carefully. The CISG's approach to this vexing issue of the "battle of the forms" differs markedly from that of the UCC (the infamous § 2–207).

To begin the battle, the CISG, although in a circuitous fashion, generally follows the traditional "mirror-image" analysis. Under CISG Article 19(1), if the buyer's purchase order form and the seller's reply order acknowledgment form—the typical arrangement—differ in any respect, the reply functions not as an acceptance, but instead as a rejection and counteroffer. Article 19(2) seems to inject some flexibility, for it states that a reply may "constitute[] an acceptance"—and thus form a contract—even with additional or different terms if both (a) such terms do not "materially alter" the terms of the offer and (b) the offeror does not object "without undue delay." In such a case, the terms of the contract are those in the offer "with the modifications contained in the acceptance."[198]

What Article 19(2) gives, however, Article 19(3) takes away almost entirely. The latter defines as "material" nearly every term of noteworthy interest to the parties, including "among other things," those relating to "price, payment, quality and quantity of the goods, place and time of delivery, extent of one party's liability to the other or the settlement of disputes." In the great run of "battle of the forms" cases under the CISG, therefore, the reply document (again, usually the seller's order acknowledgement form prepared in detail by the seller's lawyers) will not function as a legal acceptance of the

---

[196] Valero Marketing & Supply Co. v. Greeni Oy, 242 Fed. Appx.840, 844–845 (3rd Cir. 2007).

[197] CISG, art. 29(2). The same rules apply to a termination of a contract. *Id.*

[198] CISG, art. 19(2).

buyer's offer. Instead, will operate as a rejection of the offer and as a counteroffer. Pursuant to CISG Article 17, the rejection also terminates the original offer. Thus, the parties do not "conclude" a contract by exchanging forms, and if one party reneges on its promises, before performance, no contract exists.

Nonetheless, in the vast majority of transactions involving exchanges of such forms, the parties fail to notice, or disregard, the technical conflicts between the forms and simply proceed to performance of the contemplated transaction. Once the seller ships the goods and the buyer accepts and pays for them, there is little doubt that the parties have formed a contract governing their transaction—but what are its terms? To put the same question in a different way, is the seller's shipment of the goods "conduct" by the seller under CISG Article 18(1) that accepts the terms in the buyer's purchase order? Or, is the buyer's acceptance of and payment for the goods "conduct" that accepts the terms in the seller's order acknowledgement form? The common law analysis would give effect to the terms of the last form sent by either party, with the reasoning that this last form (usually the seller's) would be a rejection and counteroffer and terminate all prior unaccepted offers. The only offer left to accept through conduct, therefore, is this last counteroffer. This is the "last shot" principle, and, on the surface, CISG Articles 17, 18(3), and 19 seem to follow it. The drafting history of the CISG, however, is at best ambiguous; it shows instead that the drafters simply were unable to come to an agreement and consciously left the matter unresolved.[199] By near universal consensus of courts and scholars, this does not, however, represent a gap in the CISG that would permit resort to domestic law.[200]

It is worth noting that both the United States and civil law jurisdictions have developed more sophisticated methods of dealing with the "battle of the forms" than the "mirror-image" rule followed by the "last shot" principle—interestingly, in the United States by statute (UCC § 2–207) and in some civil code countries by judicial innovation. These approaches rely on different mechanisms, but commonly seek to rely on a deeper assessment of actual party intent in the place of the traditional inflexible rules.[201] Despite the superfi-

---

199 *See* Van Alstine, *Dynamic Treaty Interpretation*, *supra* note 136, at 771, note 348 (citing the relevant drafting history of the Convention).

200 *See* Schroeter, art. 19, para. 33, in Schlechtriem & Schwenzer, *supra* note 3.

201 Under UCC § 2–207 differences (even material ones) between the parties' forms do not preclude contract formation, unless the reply is "expressly" made conditional on the applicability of its terms. Without such a clause, the material additional terms in the reply (often the seller's acknowledgment form) drop out under UCC § 2–207(2). This is a "first shot" rule, which rewards the initiator of the transaction (the first offeror) by giving it the terms of its offer. In the case of actual conflicts, however,

cial clarity of CISG Articles 18 and 19, it thus is not surprising that courts and scholars have shown great resistance to going back to 19th century contract principles.

Nonetheless, the reflexive initial response under the CISG supported the traditional "last shot" approach. In this view, again, the ultimate performance by the parties was viewed as an expression of mutual assent to the *entirety* of whichever form happened to be sent last.[202] The more recent and growing trend of opinion among courts and scholars, however, has relied instead on the flexible interpretive rules of the Convention (*see* § 1.10 above) and the core principle of party autonomy (*see* § 1.4 above) to resolve this issue.[203]

The fundamental principle of party autonomy in CISG Article 6 makes clear that the parties may form a contract without regard to the formal offer-acceptance scheme. The more modern view on the battle of the forms under the CISG takes account of the fact that the parties rarely focus on, or even read, the standard business terms they commonly exchange as a matter of habit. Thus, the parties' performance of their transaction most often merely reflects an agreement on the existence of a contract—and decidedly not on the application of the form that happened to be last exchanged. In the words of CISG Article 8(1), each party "could not have been unaware" of the actual intent of the other to rely on its own standard terms. But if both nonetheless perform the essential aspects of their transaction, they obviously have agreed at least on the existence of a contract between them. As a result, their contract consists only of the terms on which their forms are in agreement (and of course any other agreed terms), together with the background rules of the Con-

---

the majority view holds that both offeror and offeree terms are "knocked out" of the contract. Where, in contrast, the reply is "expressly" conditional on the applicability of its terms, subsequent performance by the parties will mean a contract only on the terms on which offer and acceptance agree (an "overlap" rule). *See* § 2–207(3).

The German Civil Code, as a formal matter, adopts a "mirror image" approach. *See* Art. 150(2). German courts nonetheless have focused on a fundamental norm of "good faith" ("*Treu und Glauben,*" *see* Art. 242) to craft a more flexible solution. Under this view, the non-negotiated standard forms of the parties do not become part of the contract, especially if one or both has an express term that insists on the application of all of its own terms. For a review of this approach of German courts see Van Alstine, *Consensus, supra* note 190, at 97–100.

[202] *See, e.g.*, Allan E. Farnsworth, *Article 19*, at 179, in COMMENTARY ON THE INTERNATIONAL SALES LAW: THE 1980 VIENNA SALES CONVENTION (C. Bianca & M. Bonell, eds., 1987); Clark Kelso, *The United Nations Convention on Contracts for the International Sale of Goods: Contract Formation and the Battle of the Forms*, 21 COLUM. J. TRANSNAT'L L. 529, 554 (1983).

[203] To be sure, some residue of the traditional view remains in court decisions. *See* Larry A. Dimatteo, *et al.*, *The Interpretive Turn in International Sales Law: An Analysis of Fifteen Years of CISG Jurisprudence*, 24 NW. J. INT'L LAW & BUS. 299 (2004)(reviewing court decisions on the issue).

vention. All other proposed terms do not become part of the contract—a so-called "knock-out" rule (or better, "overlap" rule)—in absence of a clear agreement on those terms.[204] The German Supreme Civil Court in fact has described this modern approach as "most likely the prevailing view."[205]

United States courts, following on the *Filanto* case described in § 1.15 above, have agreed with this essential focus on the parties' actual intent. In one prominent case, the Ninth Circuit Court of Appeals held that where the parties formed an oral contract their mere performance of the transaction did not indicate assent to the terms of a document sent by one of them.[206] And again, all that is required for a contract under the CISG is an agreement on the price, quantity and description.[207] In such cases, all of the additional terms in the parties' respective forms are proposals for modifications. Since a modification requires an agreement between the parties, none of the proposed additional terms become part of the contract.[208] All the missing terms are filled in with CISG terms, which is, in effect, the "overlap" rule. The courts have held that a form sent out after such an oral agreement, followed by conduct of the other party, does not show agreement to the form's terms, thus rejecting a possible application of the "last shot" rule. In *Filanto*, discussed above, the court likewise used prior conduct of the parties to find the existence of a contract where exchange of forms was followed by one party's silence.

The approach of foreign courts tends to be in accord. In the German Supreme Civil Court decision mentioned above, a seller of dairy products received an oral order from a buyer. The seller responded with a written acceptance along with standard business terms that limited the buyer's warranty rights. The court found, however, that in battle of the forms cases under the CISG the parties respective standard business terms "become part of the contract only to the extent that they do not conflict."[209] Thus, although the buyer performed the transaction after receipt of the seller's reply,

---

[204] For a comprehensive explanation of this approach see Van Alstine, *Consensus, supra* note 190, at 81–102.

[205] *See* Decision of the German *Bundesgerichtshof* [Supreme Civil Court] (9 January 2002), available at http://cisgw3.law.pace.edu/cases/020109g1.html.

[206] Chateau des Charmes Wines Ltd. v. Sabate USA Inc., 328 F.3d 528, 531 (9th Cir. 2003); Solae, LLC v. Hershey Can. Inc., 557 F. Supp. 2d 452, 457–458 (D. Del. 2008)(same).

[207] *See* §§ 1.13, 1.15.

[208] *See also* CISG, art. 29(1)(requiring an "agreement" to modify a contract).

[209] *See* Decision of *Bundesgerichtshof* [Supreme Civil Court] of Germany (January 9, 2002), available at http://cisgw3.law.pace.edu/cases/020109g1.html.

the seller's limitation on warranty claims did not become part of the contract.

All of these authorities seem to agree that the mirror-image and last-shot doctrines should not be resurrected, and that there are more sophisticated analytical tools to resolve the battle of the forms under the CISG.

Business enterprises nonetheless often believe they can "win" the battle of the forms by inserting a clause in their standard business terms to the effect that "our terms and conditions prevail over all others and we reject any terms proposed by [buyer/seller]." But if the other side does the same, and the parties nonetheless perform the transaction, they obviously have not insisted on their respective terms as a condition to contract formation. As the German Supreme Civil Court case demonstrates—where, incidentally, the seller's form included just such a clause—actual, express agreement is the only way to ensure application of one's desired contract terms.

In summary, and in comparison to the UCC, the CISG generally follows the traditional offer-acceptance scheme. But it may reduce the flexibility of the parties regarding some open price transactions, and it expands the "firm offer" concept to more offers. On the battle of the forms, the courts have generally avoided the traditional "last shot" principle. Instead, based on a growing consensus among courts and scholars, the more modern approach has looked beyond the superficial wording of CISG Article 19 and focused on deeper principles in the Convention, especially the importance of the actual intent of the parties, to follow a "knock-out rule" that favors the standard terms of neither buyer nor seller.

§ 1.17 Seller's Performance Obligations—In General

Part III of the CISG sets forth the basic performance obligations of the seller and the buyer. After some initial general provisions (such as on the core notion of "fundamental breach" in Article 25), Part III contains separate chapters for the obligations of the seller (Articles 30–52) and of the buyer (Articles 53–65).

CISG Article 30 defines the fundamental obligations of the seller. Under that provision, the seller is obligated to deliver the goods and any related documents as provided in the parties' contract and to transfer to the buyer "the property in the goods." The following articles provide further detail.[210] In addition, the seller is

---

[210] CISG, arts. 31–34.

obligated to deliver goods that conform to the contract as to quantity, quality, description, and freedom from third-party claims.[211]

Domestic law may influence the content of some of these obligations, because under Article 4(b) the Convention "is not concerned with" the effect of the contract on "the property in the goods sold."[212] Domestic law, therefore, determines whether "the property" passes from the seller to the buyer at the "conclusion" (formation) of the contract, upon delivery, or at some other time;[213] whether a certificate of title is required;[214] and whether the seller may retain title as security for the purchase price or other debts.[215]

§ 1.18 Seller's Obligations—Delivery

"Delivery" under the CISG is a limited concept, and relates only to transfer of possession of or control over the goods. The CISG's drafters did not attempt to consolidate all incidents of sale—physical delivery, passing of risk of loss, passing of title, liability for the price, and ability to obtain specific performance, etc.—into a single concept or make them turn on a single event, as has been done in some sales statutes.[216] Instead, they generally followed the format of the UCC—although not the specific rules—in providing separate provisions for each of these incidents.

Place of Delivery. As to the place of delivery, the CISG recognizes four distinct types of delivery terms: (1) delivery contracts, under which the seller must deliver the goods at a specified distant place; (2) shipment contracts, which "involve carriage of the goods," but do not require delivery at any particular distant place; (3) sales contracts where the goods are at a known location and are not expected to be transported; and (4) sales contracts without a specified place of delivery and where goods are not expected to be transported. Each of these options is examined below.

(1) In a delivery contract, the seller may be obligated to deliver the goods at the buyer's place, or at a sub-buyer's place, or at any other specified distant location. But the CISG addresses this option only in the nature of a default in the event the parties have not agreed on one of the other three arrangements. In specific, CISG

---

[211] CISG, arts. 35–44.

[212] *See* § 1.7 *supra*.

[213] For domestic law in the United States, see UCC §§ 2–401 to 2–403.

[214] For domestic law in the United States, see UCC §§ 2–319 to 2–323.

[215] For domestic law in the United States, see UCC §§ 2–507, 2–703 and 1–201(b)(35).

[216] *See* U.K. Sale of Goods Act 1979, §§ 17–20.

Article 31 provides express rules only for those contracts under which the seller "is not bound to deliver the goods at any other particular place." Thus, the CISG has no specific rules describing the seller's duties in delivery contracts, and as a result, the identification of the seller's specific delivery obligations is left to interpretation of the contract terms only. A common practice in international sales transactions is to define such obligations through commercial terms such as "DAP," "DAT," or specific forms of "FOB."[217] In any event, the goods must be conforming when delivered,[218] not merely when shipped.

(2) In a shipment contract, the seller has no obligation to deliver the goods at any particular place, but it is clear that transportation of the goods by an independent third party carrier is involved. Subject (as always) to the parties' contractual agreements, a shipment contract may require the seller to take more than one action to accomplish its obligation of "delivery." First, Article 31 requires that the seller transfer ("hand over") the goods to a carrier—the first independent carrier.[219] This means that the seller must actually deliver possession to the carrier.[220] (Because the seller must "hand over" the goods to the carrier and not to the buyer, transactions requiring that the buyer assume responsibility for carriage seem excluded from this provision.) There is no duty under the CISG for seller to arrange for the carriage of the goods, such as the one imposed by the UCC.[221] Commercial terms may impose such a duty,[222] but the Convention does not. Second, Article 32 provides that if the goods are not "clearly identified to the contract" by the shipping documents or by their own markings, the seller must "give notice to the buyer of the consignment specifying the goods."[223] Third, if the seller is bound to arrange for carriage of the goods, it must make such carriage contracts as are "appropriate in the circumstances" and according to the "usual terms" for such transportation.[224] Finally, depending upon the contract's terms, the seller must either "effect insurance" coverage of the goods during transit

---

217 For more detail on these commercial terms, see Chapter 2 *infra*.

218 *Cf.* CISG, arts. 36 (stating that the goods must be conforming when the risk of loss passes) and 69 (stating that the risk of loss passes when the buyer takes over the goods or wrongfully fails to do so). For more on risk of loss, see § 1.24 *infra*.

219 CISG, art. 31(a).

220 *See CISG* DIGEST 2012, *supra* footnote 8, art. 31, para. 7.

221 *See* UCC § 2–504(a).

222 For more detail see Chapter 2 *infra*.

223 CISG, art. 32(1).

224 CISG, art. 32(2).

or, at the buyer's request, give the buyer the information necessary to effect insurance.[225]

(3) and (4) The CISG has different rules for transactions where carriage of the goods is not "involved." Absent a contrary agreement, if the parties knew at the time of the conclusion of the contract where the goods were or were to be produced, the buyer is expected to pick them up at that location.[226] In all other cases where transportation is not involved, delivery is required only at the seller's place of business.[227] In either such transaction, the seller's obligation under the CISG is merely to put the goods "at the buyer's disposal" at the appropriate place.[228] This means that "the seller has done that which is necessary for the buyer to be able to take possession."[229] The Convention is not clear on whether this requires notification to the buyer, but it would require notification to any third party bailees to allow the buyer to take possession.

Where the delivery of the goods is to be accomplished by tender or delivery of documents, Article 34 requires only that the seller adhere to the terms of the contract. The second and third sentences of Article 34 also establish the principle that a seller who delivers defective documents early may cure the defects until the date due under the contract, if possible, and the buyer must take the cured documents, even though the original tender and cure has caused damage to the buyer. Of course, in the latter case the buyer nonetheless will retain any right to recover damages from the seller.

Time of Delivery. CISG Article 33 defines the time requirements for the seller's performance. That Article focuses again on the contract terms: the seller must deliver the goods or any documents (a) on or before a fixed or determinable date as set in the contract, (b) within a fixed or determinable time period as set in the contract (unless the buyer has a power to choose a date), or (c) if no date or time period is set, within a "reasonable time."[230] "Reasonable time" is not defined, and will depend on the surrounding circumstances and trade usage, but at least it should preclude a demand for immediate delivery.

---

[225] CISG, art. 32(3).

[226] CISG, art. 31(b).

[227] CISG, art. 31(c).

[228] CISG, arts. 31(b), (c).

[229] *See CISG* DIGEST 2012, *supra* footnote 8, art. 31, para. 9 (quoting the UNCITRAL Secretariat's commentary on the CISG).

[230] CISG, art. 33(a)-(c).

The Convention has no express provisions concerning the seller's duties regarding export and import licenses and taxes, and thus leaves the determination of these incidents of delivery to the contract terms, or usage. Where these issues are not covered by the contract terms or usage, the nature of the seller's delivery obligation often will provide the needed guidance. Thus, if the seller is not obligated to arrange transportation, these responsibilities should fall to the buyer; if, in contrast, the seller is obligated to deliver at a particular destination inside the buyer's country, the seller generally will have the responsibility to obtain export and import licenses. The issue becomes complicated where delivery is to be made only at a port in the buyer's country; in such a case, the *buyer's* separate obligation to perform all reasonable acts to "enable the seller to make delivery" generally will include the import (but not export) license.[231] In any event, it is quite common in international transactions for the parties to agree on an incorporation of international "commercial terms" ("FOB," "CIF," etc.), and in particular the so-called "Incoterms," which expressly address export and import licenses and related issues.[232]

§ 1.19 Seller's Obligations—Quality of the Goods

Under the CISG, the seller's obligation is to deliver goods of the quantity, quality, description and packaging required by the contract.[233] In determining whether the quality of the goods conforms to the contract, the Convention eschews such separate and independent doctrines as "warranty" and "strict product liability" from the common law approaches, as well as "fault" or "negligence" from the civil law. Instead, the CISG focuses on the simpler concept that the seller is obligated to deliver the goods as "required by" the contract.[234] It then defines certain default obligations of the seller and creates certain related presumptions.[235] This approach produces results that are comparable to the "warranty" structure of the UCC, but without the divisions between express and implied warranties.[236] This facial similarity should not, however, lead courts to ap-

---

[231] *See* CISG, art. 60 (requiring buyer to "do[] all the acts which could reasonably be expected of him in order to enable the seller to make delivery"). *See also* CISG DIGEST 2012, *supra* footnote 8, art. 60, para. 2 (relating to import licenses).

[232] For more detail on these commercial terms, see Chapter 2 *infra*.

[233] CISG, art. 35.

[234] CISG, art. 35(1).

[235] CISG, art. 35(2).

[236] The UCC creates a series of "warranties" from seller to buyer. Some warranties are "express" (*see* UCC § 2–313), others are "implied" (*see* UCC §§ 2–314 and 2–315). The primary reason for the differentiation under UCC concepts is that "implied" warranties can be "disclaimed" under UCC § 2–316(2), while "express" warranties generally cannot.

ply idiosyncratic UCC notions, precedents, and practices to transactions governed by the CISG.[237]

The basic obligation of the seller is that the goods must conform to the contract requirements regarding "quantity, quality and description" as well as in their packaging.[238] An early Federal Court of Appeals decision applying the CISG thus held that failure of the goods to comply with affirmative contractual performance standards (contractual specifications regarding cooling capacity and power consumption) constituted a breach.[239] Any trade usage recognized by the CISG would also be applicable to the contractual description.[240]

To this, the CISG adds certain presumptions that will apply unless the seller secures a contractual limitation. First, the goods must be fit for "the purposes for which goods of the same description would ordinarily be used"[241] and be "contained or packaged in a manner usual for such goods."[242] The CISG imposes no conditions on this obligation of the seller relating to fitness for ordinary use. And because the CISG generally applies only to commercial contracts, there is no need for the UCC limitation to "merchant" sellers.[243]

Nonetheless, this leaves one important unresolved issue—whether the "ordinary use" is defined by the seller's location or the buyer's location, if the "ordinary use" in the two is different. Although some scholars support a contrary position, an early decision of the German Supreme Civil Court declared the now prevailing view that the seller generally is not obligated to deliver goods that conform to public laws and regulations enforced at the buyer's place of business, subject to three important exceptions: (1) if the public laws and regulations of the buyer's state are identical to those enforced in the seller's state; (2) if the buyer informed the seller about those regulations; *or* (3) if, due to "special circumstances," the seller knew or should have known about the regulations in the buyer's state.[244] The concept of "special circumstances" includes the seller

---

[237] *See* the discussion of the interpretive rules of the CISG, especially in Article 7(1), in § 1.9 *supra*.

[238] CISG, art. 35(1). Compare UCC § 2–313.

[239] Delchi Carrier S.p.A. v. Rotorex Corp., 71 F.3d 1024 (2d Cir.1995).

[240] CISG, art. 9(2).*See also* § 1.10 *supra*.

[241] CISG, art. 35(2)(a). Compare UCC § 2–314(2)(c).

[242] CISG, art. 35(2)(d). Compare UCC § 2–314(2)(e).

[243] Compare UCC § 2–314(1).

[244] *See* CLOUT Case No. 123, *Bundesgerichtshof* [Supreme Civil Court] of Germany (8 March 1995).

having a branch office in the buyer's state. A U.S. federal court subsequently endorsed this approach,[245] as have courts of other jurisdictions.[246] One might also add that the seller likewise should be liable where a use is "ordinary" in the international trade of the goods involved. To secure a broader obligation, the buyer must conclude an express contractual agreement under Article 35(1) or satisfy the criteria for fitness for a "particular purpose" (see immediately below).

Second, the goods must be fit for any particular use made known to the seller.[247] From its structure, this provision prescribes an interesting arrangement for the burden of proof. First, it will arise only if the buyer can prove that its "particular purpose" was "expressly or impliedly" made known to the seller at or before "the time of the conclusion of the contract." But if the buyer satisfies the factual predicates, the obligation nonetheless does not exist if the seller can prove[248] either that the buyer in fact did not rely or that it was unreasonable for the buyer to rely on the seller's skill and judgment (which switches the burden of proof on this element as compared to the UCC[249]). The CISG states no express requirement that the buyer inform the seller of the buyer's reliance; the seller need only know of the buyer's particular purpose. More important, there is no requirement that the buyer inform the seller of any of the difficulties involved in designating or designing goods to accomplish the particular use. Courts may address abuse of this issue through a careful application of the "reasonable reliance" criterion.

Finally, the goods must conform to any goods the seller "has held out to the buyer as a sample or model."[250] This is in addition to any express contractual descriptions of the goods.[251]

Each of these obligations, however, arises out of the contract, with the result that the parties may "agree otherwise" and limit the seller's obligations concerning quality (a more flexible concept than

---

[245] Medical Marketing Int'l, Inc. v. Internazionale Medico Scientifica, S.R.L., 1999 WL 311945 (E.D. La. 1999).

[246] *See CISG* DIGEST 2012, *supra* footnote 8, art. 35, para. 9 (citing cases).

[247] CISG, art. 35(2)(b). Compare UCC § 2–315.

[248] Although courts have not agreed on the details, this allocation of the burden of proof arises from the structure of the rule in Article 35(2)(b): The obligation applies if the buyer proves the factual predicates, "except" if one of the latter two facts exists. If the seller wishes to rely on these latter exceptions, it must prove that they exist. *See CISG* DIGEST 2012, *supra* footnote 8, art. 35, para. 17 (citing cases).

[249] *See* UCC § 2–315.

[250] CISG, art. 35(2)(c) UCC § 2–313(1)(c)(which categorizes this obligation as an "express warranty").

[251] *See* Schwenzer, art. 35, para. 26, in Schlechtriem & Schwenzer, *supra* note 3.

"disclaimer of warranties" under the UCC[252]). And as a federal Court of Appeals correctly held in *Chicago Prime Packers, Inc. v. Northam Food Trading Co.*,[253] the buyer has the burden to prove any such a nonconformity. In any event, the buyer need not prove the exact nature of the defect, only that the goods did not conform to contractual requirements.[254]

The obligations of the seller under Article 35(2) relating to nonconformities of quality do not apply where the buyer knew or "could not have been unaware" of the nonconformity at the time the contract was "concluded."[255] Thus, knowledge gained at the time of delivery or inspection of the goods will not affect the seller's obligation. Courts have held, however, that the seller may not rely on this exemption where, although the buyer has general knowledge of a defect or state of quality in the goods, the seller knows of specific facts not disclosed to the buyer.[256]

The relevant time for assessment of a nonconformity of the goods is "when the risk [of loss] passes to the buyer"[257]—a concept explored in more detail below.[258] How long do these obligations continue? Although the less developed countries sought a statutory provision requiring "a reasonable time" for the duration of such obligations, the drafters did not include such a provision. Instead, the CISG defers to the contract, and speaks of long term obligations of quality that arise from a "guarantee . . . for a period of time."[259] However, it is clear that any nonconformity concerning the quality of the goods which exists at the time the risk of loss passes is actionable, even if discovered later. The buyer must prove, however, that the defect actually was present at that point (typically, at delivery) and was not caused by third parties or the buyer's own use or lack of oversight of the goods. Nonetheless, the seller will be liable if defects arose later (such as in transit) due to inadequate packaging in violation of the seller's obligations under Article 35.[260] Pursuant to CISG Article 37, however, the seller may remedy any deficiencies in quantity, quality, and the like up to the agreed delivery

[252] Compare UCC § 2–316(2).

[253] 408 F.3d 894 (7th Cir. 2005).*See also* CISG DIGEST 2012, *supra* footnote 8, art. 4, para. 7; Schwenzer, art. 35, para. 54, in Schlechtriem & Schwenzer, *supra* note 3.

[254] Schmitz-Werke GmbH & Co. v. Rockland Indus., Inc., 37 Fed. Appx.687 (4th Cir. 2002).

[255] CISG, art. 35(3).

[256] *See CISG* DIGEST 2012, *supra* footnote 8, art. 35, para. 16. *See also* Schwenzer, art. 35, para. 34, in Schlechtriem & Schwenzer, *supra* note 3.

[257] CISG, art. 36.

[258] *See* § 1.24 *infra.*

[259] CISG, art. 36(2).

[260] *See CISG* DIGEST 2012, *supra* footnote 8, art. 36, para. 6 (citing cases).

date, provided this would not cause the buyer unreasonable inconvenience or expense.

The CISG also imposes certain obligations on the buyer—explored in more detail below[261]—in order to preserve its rights relating to nonconforming goods. The buyer may lose its right to rely on a nonconformity if it does not inspect the goods "within as short a time as is practicable" under the circumstances[262] or does not give notice to the seller "specifying the nature of the lack of conformity" within a reasonable time after the buyer discovered or "ought to have discovered it."[263]

If the seller knows of a nonconformity, however, the CISG may impose an obligation of disclosure. CISG Article 40 imposes on the seller an obligation to notify the buyer of any "facts" relating to a nonconformity of which the seller knew or "could not have been unaware." If the seller does so notify the buyer in such a case, then the seller may not rely on the buyer's failure to inspect the goods promptly or to notify the seller of any discovered defects.[264] Thus, even though the buyer may lose its right to rely on a nonconformity due its own failure to inspect or notify, the right revives if the seller, in turn, knew of the nonconformity and did not notify the buyer of it.[265]

May the seller exclude these obligations concerning the quality of the goods by terms in the contract—and, if so, how? As a basic rule, CISG Article 6 states that the parties may, by agreement, derogate from *any* provision of the Convention. And Article 35 expressly affirms this point with the specific reference to the seller's obligations concerning the conformity of the goods with the statement that such obligations apply only "except where the parties have agreed otherwise."[266] Nonetheless, it is also clear that the standard formulation under the UCC—"disclaimer of implied warranties"[267]—will be inapposite, because the CISG describes the seller's

---

[261] *See* § 1.22 *infra.*

[262] CISG, art. 38.

[263] CISG, art. 39.

[264] *See* CISG, arts. 38 and 39. For more on these obligations of the buyer see § 1.22 *infra.*

[265] CISG, art. 40.

[266] CISG, art. 35(2).

[267] *See* UCC § 2–316. A "standard manufacturer's warranty" commonly reads as follows:

> Seller warrants this product to be free from defects in material and workmanship for [amount of time]. Seller makes no other EXPRESS WARRANTY and NO IMPLIED WARRANTIES. Buyer's exclusive remedy for breach of any of Seller's ob-

obligations neither as "warranties" nor as "implied." Careful international sellers will need to employ different verbal formulations, ones that deal directly with the description of the goods and their expected use as defined in the CISG (not the UCC).

If a contract is framed in the usual language for contracts subject to the UCC, but it is actually governed by the CISG, a court would have two possible analytical approaches. One would arise from the concept that the term "warranties" has little meaning in the CISG context, and the drafters deliberately avoided using it, because the term has many different meanings in different legal regimes. Thus, use of such language by a seller should not be allowed to destroy the obligations imposed by the express terms of the CISG. The other approach would allow a court to inquire into the intent of the parties (under CISG rules) to determine what they meant with their contractual terms of "warranty," "express" and "implied"—*i.e.*, whether they were familiar with the United States domestic legal approach in this area. If so, CISG Article 8(1) would allow the court to interpret the language according to the parties' intentions.[268]

One continuing issue of controversy in this regard is the extent to which local law regulating disclaimers might apply for international contracts governed by the CISG. Such local law covers a spectrum, from prohibitions on "unconscionable" disclaimers (especially in printed standard terms) to the special linguistic and similar requirements set out in the UCC.[269] Today, however, there seems to be agreement that the former raises a question of "validity", which CISG Article 4(a) excludes from the scope of the Convention, and leaves to applicable domestic law.[270] As argued above,[271] the latter, in contrast, should not raise questions of "validity" as contemplated by CISG Article 4(a). As a result, the UCC's specific statutory requirements for an exclusion of warranties should not apply for CISG contracts. The distinction should depend upon whether the local public policy prohibits conduct completely, as opposed to allowing the parties to limit the seller's obligations within certain specified conditions. Accordingly, the courts should draw a distinction

---

ligations (including breach of warranty) is limited to a repair or replacement of defective parts without charge to Buyer.

[268] This would include, importantly, "all relevant circumstances" of the case, including the parties' prior dealings and negotiations. *See* § 1.10 *supra* and in particular MCC-Marble Ceramic Center, Inc. v. Ceramica Nuova d'Agostino, S.p.A., 144 F.2d 1384 (11th Cir. 1998).

[269] *See* UCC § 2–316.

[270] *See* § 1.7 *supra.*

[271] *See* text accompanying notes 121-123 in § 1.7 *supra.*

between general contract defenses (such as unconscionability and fraud) and the specific UCC provisions that set requirements for exclusion of the express or implied warranties created by the UCC itself (*e.g.*, that the disclaimer be "conspicuous" or use particular words such "merchantability").

§ 1.20 Obligations—Property Issues

Even though CISG Article 4(b) states that the Convention is not concerned with "property in" (title to) the goods sold, it imposes obligations on the seller that the goods be free of any claims concerning title and claims founded in infringement of intellectual property rights.[272] In specific, the seller generally is obligated to deliver goods "free from any right or claim of a third party."[273] As discussed in § 1.7 above,[274] the issue of who actually has valid title to particular goods is outside the scope of the Convention, and thus is governed by otherwise-applicable domestic law. But the scope of the seller's obligation to deliver what it has promised, including on clear title to the goods, is within the scope of the Convention.

A subtler issue is whether the seller is required to convey only a valid title to the goods, or also title that will not be subject to third-party claims at all. The UCC in the United States generally requires that the seller provide a warranty of "quiet possession."[275] The legal issue is whether the Convention language should be interpreted to require that the seller convey title that is free from all claims, or only title that is free from valid claims. The language in the English version is not clear, and the debates and drafting history suggest conflicting interpretations. Nonetheless, the language in the French and Spanish versions suggests that the goods are to be free from all claims. Some scholars have argued that the seller's obligation is not breached by third-party claims that are frivolous on their face, and in that respect seem to follow the general approach under the UCC.[276] The prevailing view, however, holds that the seller is obligated to protect the buyer even from spurious claims and if such arise, the seller must reimburse the buyer the costs of defense.[277] The parties may derogate from the terms of the-

---

[272] CISG, arts.41, 42.

[273] CISG, art. 41. Compare UCC § 2–312

[274] *See* text accompanying notes 129-131*supra*.

[275] *See* UCC § 2–312, and especially Comment 1.

[276] *See, e.g.*, Pacific Sunwear of California, Inc. v. Olaes Enterprises, Inc., 84 Cal. Rptr. 3d 182 (2008)(holding that the seller's obligation in UCC § 2–312(3) does not extend to a "frivolous claim," one that is "totally and completely without merit").

[277] *See* Honnold/Flechtner, *supra* note 121, Article 41, § 266; Schwenzer, art. 41, para. 11, in Schlechtriem & Schwenzer, *supra* note 3.

se provisions of the CISG by agreement, but the buyer's knowledge that the goods are subject to a bailee's lien does not necessarily imply such an agreement. Instead, buyer may expect the seller to discharge the lien before tender of delivery. This rule does not apply, however, if the buyer agreed to take the goods subject to the right or claim.[278]

In addition to good title, seller is obligated to deliver the goods free from patent, trademark and copyright claims assertable under the law of the buyer's "place of business" or the place where both parties expect the goods to be used or resold.[279] This obligation is, however, subject to multiple qualifications. First, the seller's obligations arise only with respect to claims of which the seller "knew or could not have been unaware."[280] Second, the seller has no obligation with respect to intellectual property rights or claims of which the buyer "knew or could not have been unaware" when the contract was formed.[281] Third, the seller is not liable for claims that arise out of its use of technical drawings, designs or other specifications furnished by the buyer, if the seller's action is in "compliance with" the buyer's specifications.[282] It is clear that this provision applies when the seller is following specifications required by the contract, but its application is not clear when the seller is merely following "suggestions" of the buyer as to how best to meet more general contract provisions. Fourth, the seller is excused from these obligations if the buyer does not give notice of breach[283]—unless the seller actually "knew" of the claim and "the nature of it" in the first place.[284]

With all these qualifications on the seller's obligation regarding intellectual property rights, does the mere assertion of an intellectual property infringement claim create a violation of the seller's title obligations? In order to have a violation, the buyer must show that "seller knew or could not have been unaware" of the third party claims. Moreover, there seems to be general agreement that the buyer bears the burden of proof that the seller had this level of knowledge.[285] And one survey of the legislative history concludes that it does not require the seller to research the trademark and copyright registries of the buyer's country, but only requires the

---

[278] CISG, art. 41.

[279] CISG, art. 42.

[280] CISG, art. 42(1).

[281] CISG, art. 42(2)(a).

[282] CISG, art. 42(2)(b).

[283] CISG, art. 43(1).

[284] CISG, art. 43(2). Compare UCC § 2–312(3).

[285] *See CISG* DIGEST 2012, *supra* footnote 8, art. 4, para. 7 (citing cases).

seller to use due care.[286] That interpretation would preclude a warranty of quiet enjoyment, because the buyer has no absolute claim, only a knowledge or negligence-based claim.

A seller might also argue that mistake of law will provide an excuse, or at least that it has performed its obligations concerning intellectual property rights, if it has relied on trustworthy information from a lawyer. If it entered the transaction on the basis of such trustworthy information that the use or resale of the goods would not infringe on third-party intellectual property rights, the seller may be able to argue that it could not have "known" of the possible infringement claims.

The UCC approach to these problems is to allow the buyer, when sued by a third party claimant, to "vouch in" the seller, so as to allow the seller to defend itself directly.[287] Given the differences in local procedural rules, the CISG understandably contains no such "vouching in" provision. Thus, buyers who are confronted with third party claims are left to local procedural devices for protection.

§ 1.21 Buyer's Performance Obligations—Payment and Acceptance of Delivery

The CISG imposes two primary obligations on the buyer for a sales contract governed by the Convention: to pay the price, and to take delivery of the goods.[288] The former duty is the more important of the two.[289] In addition, the buyer may have several derivative preliminary duties, which one might refer to as "enabling steps."[290] These include taking such actions as are required to enable payment[291] or enable delivery,[292] and providing specifications on "the form, measurement or other features of the goods."[293]

---

[286] *See* Allen Shinn, *Liabilities Under Article 42 of the U.N. Convention on the International Sale of Goods*, 2 MINN. J. GLOBAL TRADE 115 (1993).

[287] *See* UCC § 2–607(5).

[288] CISG, art. 53.

[289] If the parties have validly concluded a contract by "fix[ing] or mak[ing] provision for determining . . . the price" (*see* § 1.13 *supra*), CISG Article 55 permits reference to "the price generally charged . . . for such goods under comparable circumstances in the trade concerned." This provision would have particular relevance when the parties actually perform a transaction without a prior price arrangement and for replacement parts. Separately, CISG Article 56 provides that an price fixed by weight of the goods "in cases of doubt" means the net weight.

[290] *See* Honnold/Flechtner, *supra* note 121, Article 54, § 323.

[291] CISG, art. 54.

[292] CISG art. 60(a).

[293] CISG art. 65. If the buyer fails to make such specifications, the seller may do so upon advance notice to the buyer. CISG art. 65(1), (2).

Time of Payment. Unless the sale contract expressly grants credit to the buyer, the sale is a cash sale, and the seller may make payment a condition of delivery of the goods or the handing over of related documents.[294] Further, payment is due when the seller places the goods, or their documents of title, "at buyer's disposal" in accordance with the contract and the Convention.[295] If the sales contract involves carriage of the goods, the seller has the right to ship them under negotiable documents of title and then to demand payment against those documents, even if the parties have not agreed on any particular method of payment.[296]

Nonetheless, the buyer in general has a right to withhold payment until it has had an "opportunity to examine the goods."[297] If, however, the parties have agreed on a "payment against documents" transaction (such as through the use of the commercial terms "CFR" or "CIF"[298]), the buyer has thereby agreed to pay upon tender of the documents, regardless of whether the goods have yet arrived, and without inspection of the goods.[299]

Place of Payment. If the buyer is to pay against "handing over" of the documents, or handing over the goods, the place of "handing over" is the place of payment. Otherwise, the seller's place of business is the place of payment, unless the contract provides otherwise.[300] Such a rule requires the buyer to "export" the funds to the seller, which is a critical issue when the buyer is from a country with a "soft" currency, or with other restrictions on the transfer of funds. The buyer's duty of payment also includes a cooperation obligation to the effect that it must take all necessary steps to enable payment to be made, including whatever formalities may be imposed by the buyer's country to obtain administrative authorization to make a payment abroad.[301] Like any other contractual obligation under the CISG, failure to take such steps may reflect a breach by the buyer even before payment is due.

Acceptance of Delivery. The buyer's second obligation, to take delivery, also carries duties of cooperation. The CISG refers to this as the obligation of the buyer to "tak[e] over the goods" (or, as appli-

[294] CISG, art. 58(1).

[295] *Id.*

[296] CISG, art. 58(2).

[297] CISG, art. 58(3).

[298] *See* Chapter 2, §§ 2.10 and 2.11 *infra.*

[299] CISG, art. 58(3).

[300] CISG, art. 57(1). If the seller changes its place of business after contract formation, it must bear any resultant costs. CISG, art. 57(2).

[301] CISG, art. 54.

cable, the documents governing the goods).[302] This obligation also may have significance for the passing of the risk of loss when the contract contemplates shipment of the goods. In such a case, the risk of loss of or damage to the goods passes to the buyer when it fails to "take over" the goods in due time and the buyer thereby commits a breach by failing to take delivery.[303]

Taking delivery does not, however, imply acceptance of any defects; the buyer retains the right to inspect the goods, give notice of any lack of conformity, or resort to any remedies for late or improper delivery.[304] The buyer may also reject the goods if the seller delivers early or to the extent the seller delivers excess goods it is also generally accepted that the buyer may reject in the event of a "fundamental breach" (*see* § 1.28 below).[305]

Nonetheless, the buyer must do "all the acts" that "could reasonably be expected" in order to enable the seller to make delivery.[306] This includes a duty to make the expected preparations to permit the seller to make delivery and may include such acts as providing for containers, arrangement of carriage (where this is not the seller's obligation), local transportation, unloading, and import licenses.[307]

§ 1.22 Buyer's Inspection and Notice of Defects

The buyer has a right to inspect the goods before taking delivery;[308] but it also loses the right to rely on any nonconformities if it does not timely notify the seller of such nonconformities.[309] Timeliness of inspection is important, for the buyer must examine the goods "within as short a period as is practicable" under the circumstances.[310] Timeliness will of course depend decisively upon the nature of the goods and similar circumstances. Thus, courts have held that a buyer fulfilled its duty by inspecting within a month, but

---

302 CISG, art. 60(a).

303 CISG, art. 69(1).For more on the passing of the risk of loss see § 1.24 *infra*.

304 *See CISG* DIGEST 2012, *supra* footnote 8, art. 60, para. 8. *See also* § 1.22 *infra* (regarding these rights of the buyer).

305 *See id.*, para. 9.

306 CISG, art. 60(b).

307 *See CISG* DIGEST 2012, *supra* footnote 8, art. 60, para. 2.

308 CISG, art. 38(1). Compare UCC § 2–513, which gives the buyer a right to inspect the goods before it must either accept or pay for them. Even when shipment of the goods is involved, the buyer may inspect the goods after arrival and before acceptance or payment, unless otherwise agreed. UCC § 2–513(1). However, the buyer is not permitted to inspect before payment where the contract provides for payment against documents. UCC § 2–513(3).

309 CISG, art. 39(1).

310 CISG, art. 38(1).

other courts have reached the opposite conclusion where the buyer inspected two months, one month, one week, and even a few days after delivery.[311] A U.S. court has found that a buyer lost its rights to rely on a nonconformity in frozen ribs when it failed to inspect them for over a month.[312]

Where the contract involves the carriage of goods, the buyer may defer the inspection until the goods have arrived at their destination.[313] Likewise, if the seller knew or ought to have known at the conclusion of the contract that the buyer would redirect the goods in transit or redispatch them after arrival, the buyer's inspection obligation may be deferred until the ultimate arrival.[314]

The buyer may also have a natural incentive to inspect at the place of delivery (*e.g.*, shipment) because under the most commonly used commercial terms (FOB, FAS, CIF, CFR), the risk of loss in transit will pass to the buyer at the place or port of shipment.[315] Numerous specialized inspection companies will, for a fee, inspect goods for a distant buyer.

The buyer's duty to notify the seller of nonconformities involves both timeliness and content. The buyer must so notify the seller "within a reasonable time" after it "discovered or ought to have discovered" a nonconformity.[316] The "ought to have discovered" option of course has direct relevance to the buyer's obligation to timely inspect the goods upon delivery. In contrast to the ambiguity on this point under the UCC,[317] the CISG also expressly requires that the notice "specify[] the nature of the lack of conformity."[318]

If the buyer fails to duly notify the seller, the buyer may not rely on the lack of conformity as a foundation for breach.[319] As a spe-

---

[311] *See CISG* DIGEST 2012, *supra* footnote 8, art. 38, paras. 16 and 17 (citing numerous cases).

[312] Chicago Prime Packers, Inc. v. Northam Food Trading Co., 320 F. Supp. 2d 702, 711–14 (N.D. Ill. 2004).

[313] CISG, art. 38(2).

[314] CISG, art. 38(3).

[315] *See generally* Chapter 2 *infra*.

[316] As with all other notices respecting performance obligations, if a buyer chooses an appropriate means for sending a notice of a nonconformity to the seller, a delay or error in transmission does not deprive the buyer of the right to rely on the notice. *See* CISG, art. 27.

[317] Compare § 2–607(3)(a)(stating only that the buyer must "notify" the seller of any discovered breach).

[318] CISG, art. 39(1). For a comprehensive review of the cases examining the required content of such a notice see CISG DIGEST 2012, *supra* footnote 8, art. 39, paras. 16–17 (citing numerous cases).

[319] *Id.*

cial protection for remote or unsophisticated parties, however, the buyer retains a right to reduce the contract price or to claim damages (but not lost profits),[320] if it has "a reasonable excuse" for the failure to give the required notice.[321] This latter provision was included in the CISG as a result of pressure from developing countries, which argued that it often is difficult for their businesses to inspect and notify promptly. In any event, the CISG contains an interesting rule requiring the buyer to give notice of a nonconformity "at the latest within a period of two years from the date on which the goods were actually handed over to the buyer."[322]

There has been more litigation over the effectiveness of notices of nonconformity than over almost any other single issue, but the results are usually not surprising.[323] Several courts have attempted to set "presumptive periods" for notices of nonconformity, but the measuring points have differed: Some have set a presumptive period—from as short as eight days to as long as six weeks—measured as of the time of delivery (thus encompassing both the inspection period and the notice period). Others have set a presumptive period—from as little as a few days to as much as a month—measured only with reference to the duty of timely notice. On the latter, many courts have argued for the "noble month" as a presumptive period of notice under normal circumstances.[324]

As with inspections, most often the issue of timeliness will turn on the specific facts of each case, but especially on the nature of the goods and the difficulty of discovering defects.[325] One U.S. court thus indicated that, for a complicated piece of machinery, notice "within a matter of weeks" was not practicable.[326] In any event, courts in the United States have commonly held that issues of the timeliness of notice under CISG Article 39 are so intensely factual as to preclude resolution by summary judgment.[327]

---

[320] On these two remedies see §§ 1.33 and 1.35 *infra*.

[321] CISG, art. 44.

[322] CISG, art. 39(2).

[323] *See CISG* DIGEST 2012, *supra* footnote 8, art. 38, paras. 16 and 17 (citing numerous cases).

[324] On all of these points see CISG DIGEST 2012, *supra* footnote 8, art. 39, para. 24 (citing numerous cases).

[325] For a comprehensive review of the relevant factors identified by the courts see CISG DIGEST 2012, *supra* footnote 8, art. 39, paras. 25–27 (citing numerous cases).

[326] *See* Miami Valley Paper, LLC v. Lebbing Engineering & Consulting GmbH, 2009 WL 818618, *7 (S.D. Ohio 2009).

[327] *See, e.g.*, Electrocraft Arkansas, Inc. v. Super Elec. Motors, Ltd, 2010 WL 3307461 (E.D. Ark. 2010); Miami Valley Paper, LLC v. Lebbing Engineering & Consulting GmbH, 2009 WL 818618, *7 (S.D. Ohio 2009).

As noted above,[328] however, the seller may not rely on the failure of the buyer to give a timely notice if the relevant lack of conformity relates to facts already known to the seller or of which it "could not have been unaware" and did not disclose to the buyer.[329] Moreover, a seller may be deemed to have waived (as a "general principle" of the Convention[330]) its right to timely notice. The German Supreme Civil Court thus held in one case that the seller made such a waiver when it agreed to give credit to the buyer after the buyer raised potential concerns.[331]

§ 1.23 Seller's Rights to Cure

If the seller delivers nonconforming goods, it will often wish to cure the defects even after delivery. It is for that reason that the Convention requires early notice by the buyer to the seller of any defects in the goods or their tender of delivery. The primary issues arise from defects in quantity or quality of the goods and the timeliness of the delivery. The Convention has different rules for cure which depend upon whether the defects were discovered before or after the contract date for delivery.

Pre-Delivery Date Cure. Where a non-conforming tender is made before the contract date for delivery, the seller has the right to remedy any lack of conformity, "provided that the exercise of this right does not cause the buyer unreasonable inconvenience or unreasonable expense."[332] If the seller cures the non-conformity, it is still liable to the buyer for any damages caused by the defects.[333] The same rules apply with respect to nonconformities in any documents covering the goods (such as a bill of lading).[334]

CISG Article 37 expressly identifies the cure options available to the seller: delivery of any missing part for or quantity of the goods; delivery of replacement goods; and "remedying any lack of conformity" in the goods delivered. Whether the seller has a "right" to rely on other forms of cure, such as offering a money allowance to

---

328 *See* text accompanying notes 264-265 in § 1.19 *supra.*

329 CISG, art. 40.

330 *See* CISG, art. 7(2) and § 1.9 *supra.*

331 CLOUT case No. 235, *Bundesgerichtshof* [Supreme Civil Court] of Germany (25 June 1997).

332 CISG, art. 37. Compare UCC § 2–508(1), which allows a seller who tenders delivery before the contract delivery date to cure any nonconformity, provided it gives timely notice of an intent to do so and accomplishes the cure before the contract delivery date. For more on a comparison of the CISG and the UCC in this regard see § 1.32 *infra.*

333 CISG, art. 37.

334 CISG, art. 34.

the buyer,[335] is not clear. Given the objectives of Article 37, the list of specific forms of remedy should not be read as exclusive and the buyer should be obligated to accept a tendered cure as long as it does not cause unreasonable inconvenience or unreasonable expense.

CISG Article 37 makes clear that the seller "may" cure the nonconformity of a tender before the date for delivery. Thus, if the buyer refuses to permit the seller to effect a cure, the buyer, at a minimum, will lose its right to rely on the nonconformity involved. Moreover, one could argue that such a refusal by the buyer may amount to a breach,[336] thus making the buyer liable for any damages suffered by the seller.[337]

Post-Delivery Date Cure. Even after the date for delivery has passed, the seller may remedy the non-conformity, but its right to do so is subject to more exacting conditions. Similar to the pre-delivery date option, the seller may resort to such a cure if it can do so "without unreasonable delay and without causing the buyer unreasonable inconvenience or uncertainty of reimbursement of expenses."[338] But the seller must also must cure "without unreasonable delay."[339] Unlike the specific references in CISG Article 37 to various ways a seller might remedy a nonconforming tender, CISG Article 48 states only that the seller "may remedy . . . any failure." Thus, the right to cure after delivery extends to every kind of breach of contract by the seller. And given that the basic objectives of Article 48 are the same as that of Article 37, the seller should not be limited in the form of cure as long as the conditions are satisfied. Even if the seller cures the non-conformity, it will again be liable to the buyer for any damages caused by the defects.[340]

The seller's right to post-delivery date cure is expressly subject to the buyer's right to declare an "avoidance" of the contract, espe-

---

335 This would be the analog of the buyer's right to reduce the price corresponding to any nonconformity. *See* CISG, art. 50.

336 CISG, art. 61(1).

337 CISG, art. 74. For a general review of damages under the CISG see §§ 1.35 and 1.39 *infra*.

338 CISG, art. 49(1).

339 *Id.* Compare UCC § 2–508(2) which gives to the seller a more limited right to cure after the contract delivery date. It is available only if the seller had "reasonable grounds to believe" that, although defective, the nonconforming tender "would be acceptable" to the buyer. If so, the seller must notify the buyer of the intention to cure, and then may "substitute a conforming tender" within a reasonable time of the contract delivery date.

340 *Id.*

cially for a "fundamental" breach.[341] (On both notions, see § 1.28 below.) Nonetheless, the authorities are not in agreement on the details of this limitation, especially with respect to the influence of an offered cure on the existence of a fundamental breach in the first place (a point explored in more detail in § 1.32 below).[342] In any event, if a buyer wishes to take such an action, it must comply with all of the requirements of CISG Article 49. For the standard case of a "fundamental breach," this would mean that the seller's breach "substantially deprives" the buyer of its contractual rights. But in most cases it should be difficult for the buyer to meet this standard if the seller has made a timely offer of cure and can demonstrate an ability to effect that cure within a reasonable time.[343] Moreover, the entire thrust of the CISG provisions on the seller's right to cure (and more generally, the buyer's remedies) is to require cooperation between the parties in resolving disputes over timeliness of delivery and conformity of the goods.

If the conditions for post-delivery date cure (*i.e.*, no unreasonable delay, expense, or inconvenience) are satisfied, the buyer otherwise has no right to refuse a cure by the seller.[344] But given the factual uncertainty of the conditions, the CISG also has a special provision that permits the seller to force the buyer to take a position on any post-delivery cure: The seller may state a reasonable time within which it will effect the cure and then request that the buyer "make known" whether it will accept that performance. If the buyer agrees or does not respond at all, the seller has a right to perform within the stated period. And in the interim the buyer may not resort to any inconsistent remedy (including avoidance of the contract).[345]

§ 1.24 Risk of Loss

The identification of the moment at which the risk of loss of or damage to the goods passes from the seller to the buyer is especially important for transactions governed by the CISG. This is because—although not required for the CISG to apply[346]—significant geographical distances often separate the parties, and as a result most

---

[341] CISG, art. 48(1)(stating that the right to cure is "[s]ubject to article 49," which addresses the buyer's right to declare the contract avoided).

[342] *See* Müller-Chen, art. 48, paras. 14–17, in Schlechtriem & Schwenzer, *supra* note 3.

[343] For more on avoidance for a fundamental breach see § 1.28 *infra.*

[344] CISG, art. 48(1).

[345] CISG, art. 48(2).

[346] *See* discussion of CISG article 1 in § 1.3 *supra.*

contracts governed by the CISG will involve transportation of the goods.

The basic rule under the CISG is that the buyer bears the risk of loss to the goods during their transportation by a carrier, unless the contract provides otherwise.[347] Such a contractual agreement to allocate the risk of loss typically comes through the inclusion of a "commercial term" (such as FOB or CIF), and such agreements supersede the CISG provisions under CISG Articles 6 and 9.[348] More generally, the CISG makes clear that loss or damage to the goods after the risk of loss has passed to the buyer leaves it liable to pay the price (unless the loss or damage was due to an act or omission of the seller).[349]

In absence of a contrary contractual agreement, CISG Articles 67 through 70 set forth specific risk of loss rules which depend on the nature of the seller's delivery obligation. A first set of rules (see (a) and (b) below) relates to transactions that "involve[] carriage of the goods":

(a) If the contract does not obligate the seller to hand over the goods "at a particular place" (a "shipment contract"), the risk of loss will pass to the buyer when the goods are delivered "to the first carrier" for shipment to the buyer.[350] If instead the contract obligates the seller to hand over the goods to the <u>carrier</u> "at a particular place," then the risk of loss passes when the seller hands over goods to the carrier at that place.[351] In either situation, the goods need not be on board the means of transportation—any receipt by a carrier will do. Further, the seller need not "hand over" the goods to an ocean-going or international carrier—possession by the local trucker who will haul them to the port is sufficient. However, if the seller uses its own vehicle to transport the goods, the seller bears the risk until the goods are handed over to an independent carrier, or to the buyer.

(b) If, however, the contract requires the seller to deliver the goods to the <u>buyer</u> at the buyer's location or "at" some other distant

[347] CISG, art. 67(1). Compare UCC § 2–509(1).

[348] For a full discussion of risk of loss under commercial terms, see Chapter 2 *infra*. As noted there, the most widely accepted of these commercial terms are the Incoterms. Many courts have held that the Incoterms qualify under CISG Article 9(2) as a "usage . . . which in international trade is widely known to, and regularly observed by, parties to" international sales contracts. As a result, the risk of loss rules of the Incoterms would supplant the default rules of the CISG.

[349] CISG, art. 66.

[350] CISG, art. 67(1), first sentence.

[351] *Id.*, second sentence.

location (a "destination contract"), the seller bears the risk of loss until it puts the goods at the buyer's disposal at that location at the delivery time and the buyer becomes aware of that fact.[352]

Thus, in a contract between a Buffalo, N.Y., seller and Beijing, China, buyer: (1) in a shipment contract under the CISG, the risk would pass to the buyer when the goods were delivered to the first carrier in Buffalo; (2) in a destination contract (where the seller is obligated to deliver at Beijing), the seller would bear the risk during transit, and the risk would not pass to the buyer until the goods were put at the buyer's disposal in Beijing. (Again, as discussed in Chapter 2 below, specific commercial terms—such as FOB, FAS, and CIF—have more detailed rules on risk of loss.)

A second set of risk of loss rules applies to transactions that do not involve carriage of the goods from the seller to the buyer:

(c) If the goods are not to be transported by a carrier (*e.g.*, when the buyer or an agent are close to the seller and will pick up the goods), the risk passes to the buyer when it "takes over" the goods or, if it is late in doing so, when the goods are "placed" at its "disposal" and it commits a breach by not taking delivery.[353] The goods cannot, however, be at the buyer's "disposal" until they have first been identified to the contract.[354]

(d) If the goods are already in transit when sold, the risk passes when the contract is "concluded."[355] If, however, "the circumstances so indicate"—especially if the buyer has concluded insurance cover during transit—the risk of loss will pass when the goods are delivered to the carrier that has issued documents governing the transit.[356] On the other hand, if at the conclusion of the contract the seller knew or ought to have known of a loss or damage in transit and did not disclose this to the buyer, the risk of loss to that extent remains with the seller.[357]

The challenge for the buyer under this latter rule is that it may be practically impossible to determine whether damage to goods in a ship's cargo hold occurred before or after the parties concluded the sales contract.

---

[352] CISG, art. 69(2).

[353] CISG, art. 6(1).

[354] CISG, art. 67(2).

[355] CISG, art. 68, first sentence.

[356] CISG, art. 68, second sentence. *See also* Hager/Schmidt-Kessel, art. 68, paras. 5–6, in Schlechtriem & Schwenzer, *supra* note 3.

[357] CISG, art. 68, third sentence.

In most situations, title and risk are treated separately. Thus, manipulation of title through the use of documents of title, such as negotiable bills of lading, is irrelevant and has no effect on the point of transfer of risk of loss.[358] Just as title and risk are treated separately, so also breach and risk generally are treated separately. The one exception to this approach (discussed immediately above) is where the buyer is obligated to pick up the goods and commits a breach by failing to do so in a timely manner.[359] In all other cases, including any breach by the seller, the basic risk of loss rules are not changed by claims of breach.[360] Thus, a breach by the seller, even if a "fundamental breach," is irrelevant to determining the point at which the risk of loss passes to the buyer. In specific, if the seller has in fact already committed a fundamental breach, the risk of loss rules in Articles 67, 68, and 69 will not impair the remedies available to the buyer on account of that breach (and especially the right to avoid the contract).[361] And an unrelated non-fundamental breach in a shipment contract will not create a right for the buyer to avoid the contract simply because the goods are lost or damaged in transit (because the risk of loss will already have passed to the buyer upon delivery to the carrier).

§ 1.25 Excuses for Non-Performance

Unexpected Impediments. The CISG, like the domestic UCC,[362] has a general provision that recognizes an excuse for non-performance. But the CISG provision, Article 79, is different in fundamental respects, and comprehensively regulates the cognate subjects of impossibility, impracticability, frustration, and changed circumstances. Because of this, courts should not consult the rules and precedents developed under the UCC for guidance in applying CISG Article 79. Thus, for instance, Article 79, unlike its UCC counterpart, may excuse a non-performance by either the seller or the buyer, and extends to "any" obligations (not just the seller's delivery obligation). More important, as explained below, the CISG intentionally uses terms and concepts that do not correspond to domestic law approaches such as that in the UCC.

A party asserting an excuse under CISG Article 79 must prove three elements:

---

358 CISG, art. 67(1), third sentence.

359 CISG art. 69(1).

360 This is different from the approach of the UCC. Compare UCC § 2–510.

361 CISG, art. 70.

362 *See* UCC § 2–615.

(a) First, the party must prove that its failure to perform was "due to an impediment beyond [its] control."[363] The choice of the nontraditional notion of "impediment" here was a calculated one in order to avoid possible associations with any particular domestic legal regime.[364] The drafters of the CISG provisions thus deliberately rejected a proposal to use the word "circumstances," rather than "impediment."[365] "Impediment" was thought to reflect a requirement of a specific external force that prevents a party's performance, rather than a change in the general economic climate (even if unexpected). Thus, recessions or increases in inflation rates should not qualify as impediments. Nonetheless, and notwithstanding the reference to "impediment," the standard for exemption is not strict impossibility. Rather, the prevailing view is that an extreme hardship will suffice, that is, such extreme difficulty in performance as constitutes impossibility as a practical matter under the circumstances.[366] A recent Court of Cassation (roughly, the Supreme Court) of Belgium expressly so held.[367] Nonetheless, even this standard is an exacting one: Even a one hundred percent cost increase should not suffice, and "a party may have to accept even a tripled market price."[368]

Although Article 79 does not expressly address the point, in principle the excuse it describes should apply as well to a defective performance—such as delivery of nonconforming goods or a breach relating to third party property claims. This follows from the reference to an allowed excuse for a failure to perform "any" of a party's obligations. Nonetheless, as reflected in the drafting deliberations and in the concerns of some scholars, the circumstances in which such an excuse might be possible should be extremely narrow.[369]

(b) Second, the affected party must show that it "could not reasonably be expected" to have taken the impediment into account at the time of the conclusion of the contract. This "unforeseeability"

---

[363] CISG, art. 79(1). Inherent in the phrase "due to" this is a causation requirement, that is, that the impediment is the sole cause of the party's inability to perform.

[364] *See* Honnold/Flechtner, *supra* note 121, Article 79, §§ 425–427.

[365] *See id.*, § 427.

[366] *See* Schwenzer, art. 79, para. 30, in Schlechtriem & Schwenzer, *supra* note 3; Honnold/Flechtner, *supra* note 121, Article 79, §432.2.

[367] *Hof van Cassatie* [Court of Final Resort] of Belgium (19 June 2009), available at http://cisgw3.law.pace.edu/cases/090619b1.html.

[368] *See* Schwenzer, art. 79, para. 30, in Schlechtriem & Schwenzer, *supra* note 3.

[369] On the concerns about extending Article 79 to defective performances see Honnold/Flechtner, *supra* note 121, Article 79, § 427; Nicholas, *Impracticability and Impossibility in the U.N. Convention on Contracts for the International Sale of Goods*, in INTERNATIONAL SALES: THE UNITED NATIONS CONVENTION ON CONTRACTS FOR THE INTERNATIONAL SALE OF GOODS § 5–1 (N. Galston & H. Smit eds., 1984).

test requires proof that a reasonable person in the claimant's position at the time of contract formation would not have anticipated that the impediment to performance would occur. This is the element on which claims for excuse most often founder, for international buyers and sellers are expected to "take into account" the great variety of risks that attend international contracting.

(c) Finally, the affected party must demonstrate that it could not reasonably have avoided or overcome the impediment or its consequences. The party must thus be expected to bear increased costs for overcoming even an unexpected impediment—such as from alternative modes or routes of transport, reallocation of supply, or the hiring of extra staff.[370]

While the CISG provisions may seem open-ended and subject to widely varying interpretations, the cases applying CISG Article 79 have been remarkably consistent: With rare and narrow exceptions, the decisions have all ruled against the party seeking excuse. Thus, courts have found that unexpected import regulations on radioactivity in food and increased costs for tomatoes from adverse weather conditions were not valid excuses for sellers, and that significantly decreased market prices for purchased goods and a failure of a third party to transmit the buyer's payment to the seller were not valid excuses for buyers.[371]

Many of the cases involve a default by the seller's suppliers. On the surface, CISG Article 79 seems to provide some protection for the seller in such cases. The Article's second paragraph states that a party is excused if its failure is "due to the failure by a third person whom [it] has engaged to perform the whole or part of the contract." But there is less here than appears at first read. For one thing, the standards for such an excuse are very stringent: The non-performing party (most often, the seller) is excused by a default of a third party (the supplier) only if it can show that *both* it and its supplier satisfy the requirements of CISG Article 79.[372] Thus, the seller also must prove that some unforeseeable and uncontrollable "impediment" prevented the supplier from performing. Financial difficulties of the supplier do not meet that standard, and the seller thus assumes the risk of the supplier's ability to continue to perform.

But as a more fundamental matter, Article 79(2) only applies when a party has "engaged" a third person "to perform . . the con-

[370] *See CISG* DIGEST 2012, *supra* footnote 8, art. 79, para. 19 (citing cases).

[371] *See CISG* DIGEST 2012, *supra* footnote 8, art. 79, para. 13 (citing cases).

[372] CISG, art. 79(2)(a) and (b).

tract." Based on this language, the strongly prevailing view among courts and scholars is that the excuse does not extend to mere upstream suppliers with which the seller has a separate contract, because the seller does not "engage" them to "perform" its formal contractual obligations to the buyer.[373]

The excuse under CISG Article 79 is available only for as long as the impediment continues;[374] and the party seeking excuse must notify the other party to the contract both of the "impediment" and of its effect on performance.[375] Moreover, even if the party claiming an excuse proves all of the elements, it is protected only from damage claims. It is not protected from other remedial actions by the other party, such as avoidance of the contract or restitution of benefits received from the other party or derived from goods received.[376]

As a final note, some U.S. courts unfortunately have established a troubling pattern in the application of CISG Article 79. These courts, though small in number, have not looked to either the literature or the voluminous foreign case law under the CISG when applying Article 79. Instead, they have looked for guidance to case law under the UCC merely because "no American court has specifically . . . interpreted Article 79."[377] Some arbitrators may be following the same misguided path.[378] These decisions fail to recognize that CISG Article 79 reflects a deliberately different approach and one that comprehensively regulates the subject to the exclusion of domestic law regimes.[379]

Reliance on One's Own Acts or Omissions. CISG Article 80 separately declares that a party may not rely on a failure to perform "to the extent that such a failure was caused by" its own acts or omissions. Thus, where a party's own actions are the cause of a breach by the other party, the breach does not provide a ground to assert rights under the Convention. This is similar in concept to the notion

---

[373] *See CISG* DIGEST 2012, *supra* footnote 8, art. 79, para. 21; Schwenzer, art. 99, para. 37, in Schlechtriem & Schwenzer, *supra* note 3.

[374] CISG, art. 79(3).

[375] CISG, art. 79(4).

[376] CISG, art. 79(5)(providing that the excuse does not prevent either party "from exercising any right other than a claim to damages").

[377] Raw Materials, Inc. v. Manfred Forberich GmbH & Co., 2004 WL 1535839 (N.D. Ill. 2004). *See also* Hilaturas Miel, S.L. v. Republic of Iraq, 573 F. Supp. 2d 781, 798–800 (S.D.N.Y. 2008).

[378] Macromex SRL v. Globex Int'l, Inc., 2008 WL 1752530 (S.D.N.Y. 2008)(affirming an arbitral award).

[379] *See, e.g.*, Carla Spivack, *Of Shrinking Sweatsuits and Poison Vine Wax: A Comparison of Basis for Excuse under UCC § 2–615 and CISG Article 79*, 27 U. PA. J. INT'L ECON. LAW 757 (2006).

of "good faith" under the UCC and the common law;[380] but like all other such facial similarities, the precedents and practices developed under U.S. law are not determinative for the CISG. Nonetheless, in words that will be familiar to U.S. lawyers, the Supreme Court of Poland has declared that CISG Article 80 "imposes on the parties the duty of loyalty and abstention from any acts that would hinder the performance of the contract."[381] Courts have thus applied Article 80 to prevent a party from relying on a variety of remedies otherwise permitted for nonperformance, including a right to damages, to avoid the contract, and to use the non-performance as a contractual defense.[382]

§ 1.26 Breach and Remedies—In General

The CISG provides no formal definition for the traditional concept of breach of contract. Rather, it states simply that if the seller fails to perform "any" of its obligations, the buyer has a general right to damages as well as a right to certain more specific remedies.[383] Likewise, it states that if the buyer fails to perform "any" of its obligations, the seller has a general right to damages as well as a right to certain other more specific remedies.[384]

The CISG sets forth the rules for the buyer's and the seller's respective remedies upon breach in separate, though parallel, chapters. The buyer's remedies are in Part III, Chapter II (Articles 45 through 52). The seller's remedies are in Part III, Chapter III (Articles 61 through 65). The rules for determining damages for both parties, however, are combined in still another chapter, Part III, Chapter V (Articles 74 through 77).

In general, the drafters of the remedy provisions of the CISG faced special challenges because of the divergent approaches of civil and common law legal systems. These challenges are illustrated by two facts: First, specific performance is the primary remedy at civil law, while an action for damages is preferred at common law. Second, at civil law, a finding of "fault" is usually required for imposition of any recovery of damages, while under the common law an aggrieved party need show only breach of any nature. The CISG drafters attempted to bridge both gaps.

---

[380] *See* UCC § 1–304; Restatement (Second) of Contracts, § 205.

[381] Decision of Supreme Court of Poland (11 May 2007), available at http://cisgw3.law.pace.edu/cases/070511p1.html.

[382] *See CISG* DIGEST 2012, *supra* footnote 8, art. 80, para. 7 (citing cases).

[383] CISG, art. 45(1)(a), (b).

[384] CISG, art. 61(1)(a), (b).

As described in more detail below, the buyer has four potential types of remedies under the CISG: "avoidance" of the contract;[385] a self-help right of price adjustment;[386] specific performance;[387] and an action for damages.[388] The first two of these remedies in many circumstances may be undertaken without judicial intervention, but the latter two will require proceedings in a court or before an arbitral tribunal. Separately, even in the event of a breach by the seller the buyer may have certain obligations to protect the goods after delivery.[389] The CISG also specifically provides that the buyer does not lose its right to damages by resorting to one of the other allowed remedies.[390]

If the buyer breaches, the seller has three potential types of remedies: "avoidance" of the contract (which may include a right to reclaim the goods);[391] an action for the price (which functions much in the nature of specific performance);[392] and an action for damages.[393] The first of these remedies may be undertaken without judicial intervention, but the last two involve proceedings in a court or before an arbitral tribunal. The seller likewise may have certain obligations to protect the goods upon non-payment by the buyer.[394] Like the buyer, the seller does not lose a right to damages by resorting to another allowed remedy.[395]

The buyer and the seller also each may have a right to suspend performance in the event of well-grounded doubts about performance by the other party.[396] Merchants commonly prefer such practical, informal rights because of their low cost; and merchants who have traded with each other in the past, and hope to do so in the future, are much more likely to use these rights than to go to court. Similarly, when it is clear that the other party absolutely will not

---

385 *See* § 1.30 *infra* and CISG, art. 49.

386 *See* § 1.31 *infra* and CISG, art. 50.

387 *See* § 1.32 *infra* and CISG, art. 46, which in the United States is also subject to art. 28.

388 *See* § 1.35 *infra* and CISG, art. 45(1)(b), referring to arts. 74–77.

389 See § 1.35 *infra* and CISG, arts. 86–88.

390 CISG, art. 45(2). A separate provision makes clear that no court may grant an additional grace period if the buyer resorts to one of its allowed remedies. CISG, art. 45(3).

391 *See* § 1.37 *infra* and CISG, art. 64.

392 *See* § 1.38 *infra* and CISG, art. 62, which in the United States may or may not be subject to art. 28.

393 *See* § 1.39 *infra* and CISG, art. 61(1)(b), referring to arts. 74–77.

394 *See* § 1.39 *infra* and CISG, arts. 85, 87–88.

395 CISG, art. 61(2). As with the buyer, no court may grant an additional grace period if the seller resorts to one of its allowed remedies. CISG, art. 61(3).

396 CISG, art. 71.

perform, merchants prefer to declare the entire transaction avoided without filing a lawsuit, and the CISG provides a mechanism for doing so.[397] Comparable rights exist with respect to installment contracts.[398] We will thus analyze these informal, practical, and non-judicial rights before turning to the more specific and formal remedies set forth in the CISG.[399]

§ 1.27 Breach—Right to Suspend Performance

Under CISG Article 71, a party who has yet to perform may suspend its performance if it "becomes apparent" that the other party "will not perform a substantial part" of the required counter-performance.[400] A party who suspends performance must notify the other party of that suspension.[401] Although the CISG does not expressly identify the consequence of failing to do so, courts have uniformly held that in absence of timely notice the claimant may not rely on the right to suspend.[402] Thus, even if substantive grounds exist, a suspension of performance without the requisite timely notice may trigger the other party's rights to a remedy for breach under the other provisions of the CISG, including a right to damages.[403]

CISG Article 71 is neutral between buyers and sellers. Thus, a buyer who has agreed to prepay for the goods may suspend that performance if it is apparent that the seller will not perform as a result of either (a) a "serious deficiency" in the seller's "ability to perform,"[404] or (b) the seller's conduct in preparing to perform or in actually performing.[405] Such obligations of the seller regarding preparation for performance may include making appropriate transportation arrangements,[406] assisting the buyer in concluding insurance cover,[407] or obtaining and timely presenting proper documents covering the goods.[408]

---

[397] CISG, art. 72.

[398] CISG, art. 73.

[399] *See* §§ 1.27–1.29 *infra.*

[400] CISG, art. 71(1).

[401] CISG, art. 71(3).

[402] *See CISG* DIGEST 2012, *supra* footnote 8, art. 71, para. 11 (citing cases).

[403] For the buyer's rights, see CISG, art. 45(1); for the seller's, see CISG, art. 61(1).

[404] CISG, art. 71(1)(a).

[405] CISG, art. 71(1)(b).

[406] CISG, art. 32(2).

[407] CISG, art. 32(3).

[408] CISG, art. 34.

In the same way, a seller who has not yet shipped the goods may suspend that performance if it learns that there is a "serious deficiency" in the creditworthiness of the buyer.[409] The seller may also suspend its performance if the buyer fails to perform necessary, agreed-upon preliminary steps, such setting up a required bank guarantee or a letter of credit[410] or providing specifications for the goods.[411]

Despite the facial neutrality of the provision between sellers and buyers, the right to suspend performance has the greatest significance for sellers. This is so because the sellers often must ship goods before payment, and thus assume the risk of later nonpayment by the buyer. Unfortunately, the decisions under the CISG thus far have left some uncertainty for sellers wishing to rely on their right to suspend performance in such cases. The Austrian Supreme Court has held that a seller may not suspend performance merely because the buyer has failed to pay for prior installments of goods shipped under a contract.[412] It stated that the seller was entitled to suspend its performance only if it could establish that the buyer was unable to pay (financial difficulty or insolvency), and that proof of the buyer's unwillingness to pay was insufficient.

Two other decisions seem to send a less strict message. In one, a Belgian court held that a seven month delay in the buyer's payment for an initial installment of goods allowed a seller to suspend performance in delivering the second installment.[413] The court reasoned that the seller could have a reasonable suspicion that the buyer would not pay for the second installment, but there is no indication that the buyer was in any financial difficulties or had any inability to pay. Thus, the unwillingness of the buyer to pay for prior deliveries was sufficient.

A more recent case from the United States is in accord. In *Doolim Corp. v. R Doll, LLC*,[414] a U.S. District Court held that a buyer's three months' delay in paying for two initial installments justified the seller in suspending future shipments. Along with a later failure to open a letter of credit, the court stated that the initial nonpay-

---

[409] CISG, art. 71(1)(a).

[410] CISG, art. 71(1)(b). *See CISG* DIGEST 2012, *supra* footnote 8, art. 71, para. 6 (citing cases).

[411] *See* CISG, art. 65.

[412] Clout Case No. 238, *Oberster Gerichtshof* [Supreme Court] of Austria (12 February 1998).

[413] *Rechtbank van Koophandel* [Commercial Court] of Hasselt, Belgium (1 March 1995), also available at UNILEX, Case D. 1995–7.0.

[414] 2009 WL 1514913 (S.D.N.Y. 2009).

ment made it apparent that the buyer "would be, at the very least, seriously deficient in its performance of its remaining contractual obligations."[415]

These seemingly inconsistent cases arise from a focus on different language in CISG Article 71: The Austrian court focused on Article 71(1)(a), which refers to a serious deficiency in an actual "ability" to pay; the other decisions focused on the basic rule in Article 71(1), which requires only that it become "apparent" that the other party will not perform. Certainly, the grounds stated in subparagraphs (a) and (b) to Article 71(1) reflect an exclusive list. But, as the court in *Doolim Corp.* correctly reasoned, the existence of objective, "well-grounded fears" of non-payment by the buyer should suffice to make it "apparent" that the buyer will not perform a substantial part of its overall payment obligation. This applies to both options, that is, as a result of (a) a "serious deficiency" in the buyer's ability to pay, or (b) the buyer's "conduct" in preparing or performing its already existing payment obligations.

Separately, the CISG permits a seller to suspend performance after shipment but before delivery of the goods—a so-called right of stoppage in transit.[416] The CISG provision, however, only deals with rights and duties between the parties to the contract. Thus, it may give the seller the right, but not a practical ability, to prevent delivery by a carrier. The CISG does not require the carrier to comply with a seller's request; instead, it expressly leaves the carrier's obligations to other law.[417] If the seller has possession of a negotiable bill of lading to its order, then the carrier is obligated under the contract of carriage to deliver the goods to the seller. The CISG provision does not state any criteria for determining whether the stoppage is authorized, so the buyer has no ground under the sales contract to object to the seller's stoppage or to challenge it.

However, if the buyer is already the holder of the negotiable bill of lading, then the carrier is obligated to follow the buyer's instructions.[418] If the carrier does so, then the CISG provides no relief for the seller. If the carrier has not delivered the goods to the buyer, the seller may seek to obtain the bill of lading from the buyer and to

---

415 *Id.*, at *6.

416 CISG, art. 71. A related right to stop goods in transit may arise from an "avoidance" of the contract by the seller. *See infra* §§ 1.28 (on avoidance in general) and 1.37 (on the seller's specific rights upon avoidance).

417 CISG, art. 71(2), last sentence. Thus, for example, the Federal Bills of Lading Act in the United States declares that where goods are covered by a negotiable bill of lading the rights of a good faith purchaser of the bill for value are superior to any right to stop goods in transit. 49 U.S.C. § 80105(b). *See also* UCC § 7–502(b)(same).

418 For more on this point, see Chapter 3 *infra*.

enjoin the buyer from presenting the bill to the carrier. These remedies are not expressly provided for by the CISG; but the first sentence of CISG Article 71(2) expressly states that the seller is entitled to stop delivery even though the buyer "holds a document which entitles [it] to obtain [the goods]." The remedies discussed merely give effect to this right. This reasoning also applies to a transaction in which the buyer is the consignee of a non-negotiable bill of lading.

After the carrier has delivered the goods to the buyer, then it is no longer possible to stop delivery under the CISG. All that the seller would have is an *in personam* claim against for the purchase price.[419] Although CISG Article 71 states the substantive grounds, the CISG is otherwise silent on whether the seller has an *in rem* right to recover the goods, and thus this is a matter for domestic law.[420]

Under CISG Article 71(3), the right to stop goods in transit—like the right to suspend in general—ceases if the other party "provides adequate assurance" that it will perform.[421] Although not expressly stated, the assurance must come within a reasonable time, as this is a "general principle" of the Convention.[422] In such a case, the original party must continue with its performance. As of 2013, no cases have applied this provision.

§ 1.28 Breach—Contract Avoidance and Fundamental Breach

Either a buyer or a seller may declare a contract "avoided" in the event of a nonperformance or defective performance by the other party.[423] The CISG addresses the buyer's and the seller's respective rights to take such an action in separate sections of the Convention. The specific situations of buyers and sellers thus will be analyzed in separate sections below.[424]

Nonetheless, the concept of "avoidance of the contract" is central to the general breach and remedial scheme of the CISG and appears in a variety of provisions applicable to both buyer and sell-

---

[419] CISG, arts. 61(1)(a), 62. *See also* § 1.37 *infra*.

[420] CISG, art. 4(b).

[421] CISG, art. 71(3).

[422] *See* CISG, art. 7(2), and the discussion of the CISG's gap-filling "general principles" in § 1.9 *supra*.

[423] CISG, arts.49(1), 64(1).

[424] See §§ 1.32 and 1.38.

er.[425] In CISG terminology, "avoidance of the contract" is the equivalent of "cancellation of the contract" under the UCC.[426] But, importantly, this concept under the CISG is fundamentally different from the notion of "avoidance" under the UCC.[427]

In its essence, a justified declaration of avoidance brings a contract to an end and releases both parties from their obligations under it, but preserves the right to damages by the aggrieved party.[428] To be effective, a declaration of avoidance must be made by notice to the other party.[429] For an aggrieved buyer, the legal result is a right to refuse to accept delivery of goods or to return defective goods, and in either case to refuse to pay for the goods. For an aggrieved seller, a justified avoidance means a right to stop goods in transit or to refuse to deliver them in the first place.

Again, the specific situations of the buyer and the seller regarding avoidance will be addressed below. But the principal ground for declaring a contract avoided under the CISG is in the event of a "fundamental breach."[430] What constitutes a "fundamental breach"? The Convention definition requires "such detriment to the other party as to substantially deprive him of what he is entitled to expect under the contract."[431] The drafting history of this provision seems to support a stricter standard than the "substantial impairment" test of the UCC;[432] and in any event courts should avoid any resort to UCC principles or practices in analyzing a "fundamental breach" under the CISG.[433]

A fundamental breach requires more than a failure of a party to perform a contractual obligation (whether from the terms of the contract itself or from the default rules of the CISG). The "fundamental" nature of such a breach also will arise not simply from the amount of damages it will cause but also, and especially, from "the

---

[425] *See, e.g.*, §§ 1–29 and 1.30 *infra*. The concept of fundamental breach also may be relevant to the passage of risk. *See* CISG, art. 70 and § 1.24 *supra*.

[426] Compare UCC § 2–106(4). *See also* Dingxi Longhai Dairy, Ltd. v. Becwood Technology Group L.L.C., 635 F.3d 1106, 1108 n.2 (8th Cir. 2011) (recognizing this similarity). Under the UCC, where a party cancels a contract for breach, it nonetheless retains "any remedy for breach of the whole contract or any unperformed balance." *Id.*

[427] *See* UCC § 2–613 (stating that a contract is "avoided" if a "casualty to identified goods" causes a total loss).

[428] CISG, art. 81.

[429] CISG, art. 26.

[430] *See* CISG, arts. 49(1)(a), 64(1)(a).

[431] CISG, art. 25.

[432] UCC §§ 2–608, 2–612.

[433] *See* Schroeter, art. 25, para. 12, in Schlechtriem & Schwenzer, *supra* note 3.

importance of the interest which the contract and its individual obligations have created for the promisee."[434] The reference to expectation is defined with reference to the CISG's rules for interpreting contracts, and thus most often will involve an objective test that compares the claimed failure of performance to the reasonable expectation of the aggrieved party.[435] It follows, therefore, that the parties may define expressly in their contract the standards for a fundamental breach.[436] The motivations or reasons for a party's breach, such as an economic desire to escape from a losing contract, are not relevant, however, to the analysis of a "fundamental breach."

A fundamental breach includes of course a complete failure to perform an essential contract duty (*e.g.*, final nondelivery or final nonpayment). Other possibilities of their nature will depend decisively on the facts of each case, but may include a failure to perform beyond a reasonable time where time is of the essence, defects in the goods such that they are unusable and cannot be resold, and an unjustified denial of contract rights. A cumulation of several violations also may suffice if as a result the aggrieved party loses the principal benefit of, or interest in, the expected contract performance.[437]

United States court decisions seem not to have required an overwhelmingly high standard for a "fundamental breach." Nor have they required "perfect tender" or allowed non-functional defects to be considered a fundamental breach. In one case, compressors for air conditioning units did not have either the cooling capacity or the power consumption contained in the contract specifications. The court held that cooling capacity was an important factor in determining the value of air conditioner compressors, so that the buyer did not in fact receive the goods it was entitled to expect.[438] In the other case, mammography units were seized for non-compliance with U.S. administrative regulations. When the court decided that the seller was obligated to furnish goods that conformed to the buyer's laws,[439] it held that a breach of that obligation was a fundamental breach.[440] A third U.S. court stated that a buyer's refusal to

---

434 *See id.*, para. 21.

435 *See* the discussion of CISG, art. 8 in § 1.10 *supra*.

436 *See* Björklund, art. 25, paras. 16–17, in Kröll, et al, *supra* note 3; Schroeter, art. 25, paras.21–22, in Schlechtriem & Schwenzer, *supra* note 3.

437 *See CISG* DIGEST 2012, *supra* footnote 8, art. 25, paras.6–12 (citing cases).

438 Delchi Carrier S.p.A. v. Rotorex Corp., 71 F.3d 1024 (2d Cir.1995).

439 *See* analysis accompanying footnotes 244-245 in § 1.19 *supra*.

440 Medical Marketing Int'l, Inc. v. Internazionale Medico Scientifica, S.R.L., 1999 WL 311945 (E.D. La. 1999).

make "large" progress payments on schedule likely would be a fundamental breach.[441] In still another case, a court found that a buyer's refusal to accept substantially conforming substitute goods amounted to a fundamental breach.[442]

Foreign cases seem to have followed a similarly flexible approach. The German Supreme Civil Court thus found a fundamental breach where a buyer was unable to use, or otherwise reprocess, substandard steel wire delivered by the seller.[443] Similarly, a French court found a fundamental breach where a buyer of sugared wine was not able to use or resell it.[444] On the other hand, when a seller contracted to deliver in "July, August, September" and thus the buyer expected monthly installment deliveries, it was not a fundamental breach to deliver the goods on September 26.[445] The court held that such tender of delivery was within the agreed delivery period, so any delay was not a fundamental defect.

A number of cases have related to resale of the goods. In one case, a court rejected a claim of a fundamental breach in an exclusive dealership arrangement merely because an agent of the seller sold to another retailer in the buyer's exclusive territory.[446] The court so held based on the reasoning that the seller had no knowledge of the agent's conduct and such knowledge also could not be imputed to the seller. On the other hand, where a seller stated at contract formation that the resale location of the goods was critically important, and the buyer thus stated that it intended to resell in South America, a resale elsewhere was held to be a fundamental breach.[447] The court thus explicitly concluded that such a resale "substantially deprived" the seller of what it was entitled to expect under the contract.[448]

---

[441] Shuttle Pkg. Syst. v. Tsonakis, 2001 WL 34046276 (W.D. Mich. 2001).

[442] Valero Marketing & Supply Company v. Greeni Oy, 2006 WL 891196 (D.N.J. 2006). On the other hand, one court held that a mere delay in delivery, absent special circumstances, would not amount to a fundamental breach. Macromex SRL v. Globex Int'l, Inc., 2008 WL 1752530 (S.D.N.Y. 2008).

[443] CLOUT case No. 235, *Bundesgerichtshof* [Supreme Civil Court] of Germany (25 June 1997).

[444] CLOUT Case No. 150, *Cour de Cassation* [Court of Final Resort] of France (23 January 1996).

[445] CLOUT Case No. 7, *Amtsgericht* [Local Court] of Oldenburg, Germany (24 April 1990).

[446] CLOUT Case No. 6, *Landgericht* [State Court] of Frankfurt a.M., Germany (16 September 1991).

[447] CLOUT Case No. 154, *Cour d'appel* [Court of Appeal] of Grenoble, France (22 February 1995).

[448] CISG, art. 25, first clause.

This last case also illustrates the final requirement for a fundamental breach: CISG Article 25 declares that a breach is not fundamental if "the party in breach did not foresee and a reasonable person of the same kind and in the same circumstances would not have foreseen such a result."[449] The relevant time for assessing this question of foreseeability is the conclusion of the contract.[450] Thus, in the last cited case, the court emphasized that the buyer knew, or could reasonably have foreseen, at the conclusion of the contract that an agreement precluding resale where other distributors of the seller sold the contract goods could cause a substantial detriment for the seller.[451]

§ 1.29 Breach—Anticipatory Breach

Unlike the UCC,[452] the CISG describes no general right of an insecure party to request assurance when doubt exists about the other party's ability or willingness to perform. As described in § 1.27 above, CISG Article 71 sets forth certain grounds for a party to suspend its own performance, which the other party may cut off with an "adequate assurance" of performance. But the CISG otherwise does not expressly empower an insecure party to initiate such a dialogue.

Instead, CISG Article 72 declares a general right to declare a contract entirely avoided in the event of a "fundamental breach" by one party. Where it is clear that one party will commit such a breach when its future performance comes due (anticipatory breach), CISG Article 72(1) gives the other party the power to declare the contract avoided even before the time for that performance.

The preconditions for such a declaration are few, but stringent. First, a declaring party must give reasonable notice to the other party, but only "if time allows." Second, and more important, the conduct of the other party must amount to a "fundamental breach" (as discussed in § 1.28 above). Third, the mere possibility of a breach in the future does not suffice; it must be "clear" under the circumstances that the other party will commit the required fundamental breach. Thus, for example, an Australian court held that

---

[449] CISG, art. 25, second clause.

[450] CLOUT Case No. 275, *Oberlandesgericht* [Appellate Court] of Düsseldorf, Germany (24 April 1997); CLOUT Case No. 681, China International Economic and Trade Arbitration Commission (18 August 1997).

[451] CLOUT Case No. 154, *Cour d'appel* [Court of Appeal] of Grenoble, France (22 February 1995).

[452] *See* UCC § 2–609(4).

the buyer's failure to open a letter of credit justified a declaration of avoidance by the seller.[453] Other examples include a buyer's failure to pay for prior deliveries; a seller's unfounded stoppage of the goods in transit; and where a party made its own performance contingent on conditions not defined by the contract.[454]

The combined requirement of a "clear" indication of a fundamental breach, however, often will leave the other party in substantial doubt. This highlights a final requirement: that, after receipt of the notice, the other party does not give an "adequate assurance" that it in fact will perform. One U.S. court in fact emphasized the absence of such an assurance in its determination that the seller had a right to declare the sales contract avoided due to an anticipatory fundamental breach by the buyer.[455]

Where the other party actually declares that it will not perform its obligations when due, the requirements for avoidance under Article 72 seemingly are less stringent. In such a case, CISG Article 72(3) provides that a party need not give notice of an intent to declare an avoidance. In addition, the other party does not have a right to cut off such an avoidance through a subsequent assurance of performance. Nonetheless, the twin requirements of a "clear" indication of a future "fundamental breach" remain. This often will leave an aggrieved party in substantial doubt about whether it has a right to declare an avoidance for anticipatory breach. It is in such circumstances that the right of a party to suspend its own performance, pending an adequate assurance from the other party, will be most valuable.[456]

§ 1.30 Breach—Installment Contracts

The CISG has special rules for breach of an "instalment contract"—that is, where the contract involves at least two successive deliveries of the goods. For such a contract, the goods need not be of the same type; but the deliveries must be under the same contract as a unit (as opposed to under separate unrelated contracts). With respect to a breach of such contracts, CISG Article 73 defines different rules for an individual installment as opposed to a breach that affects the whole contract.

---

[453] CLOUT Case No. 631, Supreme Court of Queensland, Australia (17 November 2000).

[454] *See CISG* DIGEST 2012, *supra* footnote 8, art. 72, paras.6–7 (citing cases).

[455] Doolim Corp. v. R Doll, LLC, 2009 WL 1514913, at *6–7 (S.D.N.Y. 2009).

[456] *See* CISG, art. 71 and § 1.27 *supra*.

For an individual installment, if a party fails to perform in such as way as to constitute "a fundamental breach of contract with respect to that instalment," the other party may declare the contract avoided "with respect to that instalment."[457] If, however, such a breach also gives the aggrieved party "good grounds to conclude" that a fundamental breach will occur in the future installments, it may declare the contract avoided for the future as well (provided it does so within a reasonable time).[458] Thus, in one case a French court found that a buyer's breach of a resale limitation amounted to a fundamental breach with respect to the seller's delivery of a first installment of goods.[459] But the buyer also had stated unequivocally that "its resale actions are of no concern to" the seller. That statement gave the seller good grounds to conclude that the buyer would continue to breach the contract with regard to future installments as it had with respect to the first installment. As a result, the court concluded that the seller was justified in declaring an avoidance of the entire contract.

Separately, the CISG grants a special right to an aggrieved buyer to declare an avoidance of the whole contract (or affected portions) if a breach on one delivery has a broader effect on the contract performances.[460] If the buyer can show that, "by reason of their interdependence," past or future deliveries "could not be used for the purpose contemplated by the parties at the time of the conclusion of the contract," it may declare an avoidance with respect to those past or future deliveries as well.[461] One court has held, however, that both parties must be aware of this interdependence in order to justify a buyer's resort to this special power of avoidance.[462]

§ 1.31 Buyer's Remedies for Breach by Seller

CISG Articles 45 through 52 define the remedies available to the buyer upon a breach by the seller. As described in detail below, if the seller breaches any of its obligations, the buyer has four basic types of remedies: (a) "avoidance" of the contract; (b) a special remedy that allows a "self-help" reduction in the price due; (c) specific performance; and in any event (d) an action for damages.

---

457 CISG, art. 73(1).

458 CISG, art. 73(2).

459 CLOUT Case No. 154, *Cour d'appel* [Court of Appeal] of Grenoble, France (22 February 1995).

460 CISG, art. 73(3).

461 This structure thus differs in important respects from the UCC provisions on installment contracts in § 2–612.

462 CLOUT Case No. 880, Tribunal Cantonal of Vaud, Switzerland (11 April 2002).

Before turning to those remedies, it is appropriate to recall that the CISG imposes certain conditions on the buyer's right to assert claims against the seller. As noted in § 1.22 above, to preserve any remedy for a delivery of nonconforming goods by the seller, the buyer must: inspect the goods in "as short a period as is practicable"; notify the seller of the nonconformity "within a reasonable time" of discovery; and permit the seller to attempt to cure any nonconformity, if the cure does not cause "unreasonable delay" or "inconvenience." Similarly, the buyer loses the right to assert claims based on the existence of third-party property rights in the goods if it does not give notice to the seller of the claim "within a reasonable time" of discovery.[463]

§ 1.32 Buyer's Remedies—Avoidance of the Contract

The CISG provides two separate grounds for the buyer to declare an "avoidance of the contract" upon a breach by the seller. First, CISG Article 49(1)(a) permits the buyer to use this remedy in the event of a "fundamental breach," regardless of the type of breach or when it occurs. Second, in the specific case of a non-delivery, CISG Article 49(1)(b) allows the buyer to declare an avoidance if the seller does not perform within an additional deadline set by the buyer. We will examine these two alternatives in turn.

As an essential background for both, recall first that an "avoidance of the contract" by the buyer is a method of refusing to accept or to keep defective goods, with a corresponding right not to pay for the goods.[464] In this respect, "avoidance" under the CISG is comparable to the rights of a buyer under the UCC to "reject" the goods actually delivered before "acceptance,"[465] or to "revoke the acceptance" of goods previously accepted.[466] However, the CISG does not adopt the UCC's distinctions between "rejection" of the goods, "acceptance" of the goods, and "revocation of acceptance."[467] Further, CISG does not attach special legal significance to the concept of "acceptance" of the goods; as a result, the buyer's taking delivery of the goods is not a crucial factual or legal step in the analysis of the buyer's position under the CISG.

Avoidance for Fundamental Breach. Instead, the fundamental concept under the CISG is to limit use of this remedy to situations

---

[463] For more detail on all of these points see § 1.22 *supra*.

[464] *See* the discussion in § 1.28 *supra*.

[465] UCC §§ 2–601, 2–612.

[466] UCC §§ 2–606, 2–608.

[467] UCC §§ 2–601, 2–602, 2–608, 2–612.

which involve "fundamental breach" by the seller, regardless of when the breach occurs.[468] This is the first of the two alternatives noted above for a buyer's right to declare an avoidance of the contract. Section 1.28 above analyzed in detail the CISG's definition of a "fundamental breach." In summary, a buyer has a right to declare an avoidance on this basis if a seller's failure to perform "any" of its obligations "substantially deprive[s]" the buyer of what it is "entitled to expect under the contract."[469] Such a declaration of avoidance must be made by notice to the seller.[470] But the right to declare an avoidance for a fundamental breach is lost if the buyer does not make the declaration (a) in respect of late delivery, within a reasonable time after the buyer has become aware of delivery, or (b) in respect of all other breaches, within a reasonable time after the buyer knew or ought to have known of the breach.[471] The purpose of this notice is to give the seller an opportunity to cure the defects.[472]

Even if the buyer seeks to avoid the contract after a "fundamental breach" by the seller, the latter has a right to "cure" any defect in its performance. As discussed in more detail in § 1.23 above, if the seller's nonconforming tender is early, the seller may cure by making a conforming tender up to the delivery date in the contract, whether the nonconformity would create a fundamental breach or not.[473] The seller's right to cure on this basis also survives the buyer's declaration of "avoidance of the contract," because it will be very difficult to sustain a finding of fundamental breach where the seller has made a timely offer of cure before the delivery date has even arrived. If the seller's tender of a cure is made *after* the delivery date in the contract, it still has a right to cure through late performance, but only if it can do so "without unreasonable delay," and without causing the buyer unreasonable inconvenience or uncertainty of reimbursement of expenses.[474]

One controversy in this regard is whether the seller retains a post-delivery right to cure after a fundamental breach has already occurred. As noted above, the authorities seem to take conflicting views on the point.[475] One view holds that the buyer's right to declare a complete avoidance of the contract on such a basis takes pri-

---

468 CISG, art. 49(1)(a).

469 CISG, art. 25.

470 CISG, art. 26.

471 CISG, art. 49(2)(b)(i).

472 *See* discussion of "cure" in § 1.23 *supra*.

473 *See also* CISG, art. 37.

474 CISG, art. 48(1). Again, for more detail on this point see § 1.23 *supra*.

475 *See* § 1.23 and Müller-Chen, art. 48, paras. 14–17, in Schlechtriem & Schwenzer, *supra* note 3.

ority over the seller's right to cure after the delivery date.[476] Nonetheless, one must be careful not to make too much of this argument, for the possibility of a timely cure will influence the existence of a fundamental breach in the first place. Thus, some courts have expressly held that the availability of timely repairs by the seller (or, presumably, third parties) precludes a finding of a fundamental breach. As UNCITRAL's Digest of Case Law on the CISG states, "[c]ourts are reluctant to consider a breach fundamental when the seller offers and effects speedy repair without any inconvenience to the buyer."[477] More generally, other courts have indicated that the assessment of a fundamental breach is strongly influenced by the buyer's ability to procure suitable substitutes in a timely manner.[478]

In any event, the entire thrust of the CISG provisions on the buyer's remedies is to require cooperation between the parties in resolving disputes over timeliness of delivery and conformity of the goods. Moreover, as noted below, CISG Article 77 imposes an obligation on an aggrieved party to take reasonable steps to mitigate its damages.[479]

The CISG's rules on avoidance and cure may leave the seller of goods in a significantly better position as compared to the UCC, if the buyer claims a relatively minor fault in the goods. First, under the UCC the buyer may reject the goods merely because a tender is not "perfect,"[480] but this is definitely not allowed under the CISG. In addition, although the seller has a right to cure defects under both regimes, the right under the UCC has either time limitations or knowledge requirements[481] that do not exist under the CISG. Finally, under either the UCC or the CISG the buyer will have a right to damages; but under the CISG, the buyer may return the goods only in the event of a "fundamental breach." Thus, the seller is less likely to find the goods rejected for an asserted minor nonconformity, and stranded an ocean or continent away.

Must performance offered as cure after delivery of defective goods meet a strict "nonconformity" test, or is it still subject to the "fundamental breach" test? The CISG has no express provision on this issue. Nonetheless, it would be paradoxical that if a seller effects a cure (*e.g.*, repair or replacement) that substantially gives the

---

476 *See* § 1.23 *supra*.

477 *See CISG* DIGEST 2012, *supra* footnote 8, art. 25, para. 9 (citing cases).

478 *See id.*, art. 25, para. 8 (citing cases) and art. 49, para. 16 (citing cases).

479 *See* § 1.35 *infra*.

480 *See* UCC § 2–601.

481 *See* UCC § 2–508.

buyer what it entitled to expect under the contract,[482] the buyer nonetheless may declare an avoidance for fundamental breach. On the other hand, if the seller does not achieve this result on a first attempt at a cure, the likelihood of a subsequent cure "without unreasonable delay" and "without causing the buyer unreasonable inconvenience" decreases significantly.[483] Perhaps the seller, having breached once, should be considered to be on probation and must "get it right" during that probationary period (at least to clear up any existing fundamental breach).

In any event, even if the seller is able to effect a complete cure—whether before or after the delivery date—the buyer retains a right to damages caused by the defective goods.[484]

Recall also, finally, that CISG Article 73(3) grants an aggrieved buyer with respect to a single installment a right to avoid the whole contract (or affected portions) if the interdependence of deliveries means that future deliveries cannot be used for the purpose contemplated at time of contracting.[485] Similarly, CISG Article 51 states that, even for a single delivery contract, the buyer may declare an avoidance of the entire contract if a seller's failure to make a complete delivery or a completely conforming delivery amounts to a fundamental breach of the entire contract.

Avoidance and "Nachfrist." Given the uncertainties of the "fundamental breach" test, it often will be difficult for the buyer, or its attorney, to know how to react to any particular breach—and whether "avoidance" of the contract is permissible or not. Incorrect analysis could put the buyer in the position of making a fundamental breach through its response. CISG Articles 47 and 49(1)(b) attempt to cure these uncertainties by offering the buyer an alternative method of formulating a supposedly strict standard for performance. Based on the German law notion of *Nachfrist* ("additional deadline"), if the seller fails to deliver the goods on the agreed delivery date, the buyer may notify the seller that performance is due by a stated new date.[486] If the seller fails to perform—or declares that it will not perform—by the new deadline, the buyer has a right to declare an avoidance of the contract even if no fundamental breach has yet occurred.[487] Such a declaration of avoidance must again be

---

[482] *See* CISG, art. 25 (defining the opposite of the statement in the text as a fundamental breach).

[483] *See* CISG, art. 48(1).

[484] CISG, arts.37, 48(1).

[485] *See* § 1.30 *supra.*

[486] CISG, art. 47(1).

[487] CISG, art. 49(1)(b).

made by notice to the seller.[488] And if the seller has already delivered the goods, the buyer loses the right to declare an avoidance on this basis unless it does so within a reasonable time after the expiration of the "*Nachfrist*."[489]

However, by its express terms, the CISG allows this alternative ground for avoidance by the buyer only for "non-delivery" by the seller. Thus, it is not clear whether the seller's delivery of nonconforming goods during the additional period permits avoidance or not. In other words, must the quality of a late delivery by the seller meet a strict standard of "nonconformity," or only the standard of the "fundamental breach" test? In any event, if the buyer sets such an additional deadline for performance, it may not resort in the interim to any remedy for breach of contract, unless the seller declares that it will not perform in any event.[490]

How long of an additional period must the buyer give the seller? Article 47 requires that it be "of reasonable length," but unless there is a custom on this issue the buyer will have no certainty that the period given in the *Nachfrist* notice is long enough, especially if long distances are involved. In one German decision, the court held that three to four weeks was a reasonable time for a car sale contract.[491] In another, however, the court indicated that an additional period of two weeks was too short, but nonetheless upheld the buyer's declaration of avoidance seven weeks later because the seller had offered only a partial delivery of conforming goods in the interim.[492] This latter holding conforms with a general practice of courts to substitute a reasonable period in the event the buyer fixes an unreasonably short period.[493]

The cases sometimes involve buyers who quickly complain about the goods, hoping that the seller will cure the defect, and then officially declare avoidance much later (often months). They usually are not permitted to avoid the contract—the courts holding that their original complaints about the goods do not amount either to the setting of a clear deadline as required for a "Nachfrist" or to a formal declaration of avoidance, and that their later declarations

---

488 CISG, art. 26.

489 CISG, art. 49(2)(b)(ii). The same rule applies if the seller declared an intent to cure under CISG Article 48 and then (a) did not do so, or (b) the buyer rightfully refused to permit such a cure. CISG, art. 49(2)(b)(iii).

490 CISG, art. 47(2).

491 CLOUT Case No. 332, *Oberlandesgericht* [Appellate Court] of Naumburg, Germany (27 April 1999).

492 CLOUT Case No. 136, *Oberlandesgericht* [Appellate Court] of Celle, Germany (24 May 1995).

493 *See CISG* DIGEST 2012, *supra* footnote 8, art. 47, para. 5.

come too late.[494] The message of these cases is that buyers must make a clear choice either to set a deadline for final performance by the seller or make a timely declaration of avoidance for fundamental breach. As one U.S. Appellate Court observed, however, the CISG's light requirements for a valid modification of a contract ("mere agreement") may mean that the parties' interactions after a defective or late delivery amount to a formal agreement to amend their contract.[495]

Restitution and Obligation to Preserve Goods. As noted in § 1.28 above, avoidance of the contract releases both parties from their contractual obligations, but also preserves the right to damages for the aggrieved party.[496] A party that has already performed in such a case has a corresponding right of restitution against the other.[497] Thus, if the buyer properly avoids the contract, it is entitled to a return of any money already paid to the seller, but also must return to the seller any goods already delivered.

The CISG imposes certain important conditions and obligations on a buyer that wishes to declare a contract avoided. First, the buyer loses the right to make such a declaration—or require delivery of substitute goods—if it cannot return the goods to the seller "substantially in the condition in which he received them."[498] This rule does not apply, however, if (a) the buyer was not at fault for the inability so to return the goods, (b) the harm to the goods was a result of a proper inspection upon delivery, or (c) the buyer sold or otherwise consumed the goods in the ordinary course of its business.[499] Even if one of these exceptions does not apply, the buyer retains all of the other remedies it has for seller's breach.[500]

In addition, CISG Articles 85 through 88 impose certain obligations on the buyer to preserve the goods pending their return to the seller. A buyer who declares an avoidance after delivery of the goods must take "reasonable" steps to preserve them.[501] This may include depositing the goods in a warehouse at the seller's expense.[502] If the seller has no agent in the buyer's location, but the goods have been

---

[494] *See CISG* DIGEST 2012, *supra* footnote 8, art. 12, para. 4 (citing cases).

[495] Valero Marketing & Supply Co. v. Greeni Oy, 242 Fed. Appx. 840, 844–845 (3rd Cir. 2007).

[496] CISG, art. 81(1).

[497] CISG, art. 81((2).

[498] CISG, art. 82(1).

[499] CISG, art. 82(2).

[500] CISG, art. 83.

[501] CISG, art. 86(1).

[502] CISG, art. 87.

"placed at [the buyer's] disposal at their destination," the buyer must take possession of them "on behalf of the seller" if this can be done without payment of the price (*i.e.*, without paying for a negotiable bill of lading) and without "unreasonable inconvenience or unreasonable expense."[503] After such a taking of possession on behalf of the seller, the buyer must again take "reasonable" steps to preserve them. If the goods are perishable, an aggrieved buyer in possession may be required to attempt to sell them and remit any proceeds to the seller, less the costs of preservation and sale.[504] The CISG does not, however, contain any provisions that would require an aggrieved buyer in possession to follow the seller's instructions, such as to resell on the seller's behalf, whether seemingly reasonable or not.[505]

Finally, the buyer must account to the seller for any benefits derived from temporary possession of the goods before return.[506]

§ 1.33 Buyer's Remedies—Non-Judicial Reduction in Price

In addition to refusing to accept goods that do not conform to the contract through "avoidance" as discussed immediately above, an aggrieved buyer has a separate informal remedy that appears to give it a power of self-help. Under the CISG, a buyer who receives nonconforming goods "may reduce the price" it pays to the seller.[507] This remedy is available whether the buyer has already paid or not, but if the buyer has paid, the remedy is likely to require an action in court. The buyer may not resort to this remedy, however, if the seller has cured any defects in the goods[508] or the buyer wrongfully refuses to grant the seller an opportunity to make such a cure.[509]

The Convention spells out a formula for calculating the permissible amount of the price reduction: The buyer is entitled to reduce the price "in the same proportion as the value that the goods actually delivered bears to the value that conforming goods would have had at that time."[510] Thus, the buyer may reduce the price according to the difference between the actual value of the nonconforming goods and the contractually required value of those goods. If the

503 CISG, art. 86(2).

504 CISG, art. 88(2).

505 Compare UCC § 2–603.

506 CISG, art. 84(2).

507 CISG, art. 50.

508 *See* CISG, arts. 37 and 48 and § 1.23 *supra*.

509 CISG, art. 50.

510 *Id.*

market price has not changed between the time of contracting and the delivery date, this formula should give the same result as under the UCC.[511] In any event, one U.S. District Court has indicated that, if the buyer resells the defective goods, the resale price is evidence of their value at the time of delivery and that the seller is entitled to discover that resale price.[512]

This type of self-help provision is familiar at civil law, as a method of compensating an aggrieved buyer when there is no civil law cause of action for damages (such as when the seller is not "at fault").[513] The UCC also allows an aggrieved buyer to exercise self help in reducing the price of non-conforming goods, but this remedy appears to be not widely used.[514] Unlike the UCC provisions, there is no requirement of prior notice to the seller by the buyer before exercising this option (although of course the buyer must give notice of the defect itself[515]). Proposals at the CISG Diplomatic Conference to require a "declaration of price reduction" by the buyer were not accepted.[516]

There is little guidance in the provision on how to determine the value of the actual goods delivered at the time of delivery, or as to what evidence of value should be sent to the seller. The provision, therefore, seems better suited to deliveries that are defective as to quantity, rather than as to quality. Nonetheless, the buyer's right to reduce the price clearly applies to defects in quality as well.[517] The general view among authorities is that the remedy is not available for defects in title or a breach founded on the existence of third-party property claims.[518]

---

[511] *See* UCC § 2–714 (measuring damages for breach of warranty by the difference between the value of accepted goods and "the value they would have had if they had been as warranted"). The price reduction measure under the CISG may cause a different result as compared to the UCC if the market price of the goods has changed between formation and delivery. *See* Harry Flechtner, *More U.S. Decisions on the U.N. Sales Convention: Scope, Parol Evidence, "Validity," and Reduction of Price Under Article 50*, 14 J. LAW & COM. 153 (1995).

[512] Interag Co. Ltd. v. Stafford Phase Corp., 1990 WL 71478, at *4 (S.D.N.Y. 1990).

[513] On the civil law foundation of Article 50, see Eric Bergsten & Anthony Miller, *The Remedy of Reduction of Price*, 27 AM. J. COMP. L. 255 (1979).

[514] UCC § 2–717.

[515] *See* CISG, art. 39 and § 1.22 *supra*.

[516] *See* Bergsten & Miller, *supra* note 513.

[517] On the seller's obligations regarding the quality of goods see § 1.19 *supra*.

[518] *See* Müller-Chen, art. 50, para. 2, in Schlechtriem & Schwenzer, *supra* note 3.

As noted, a buyer intending to use this self-help remedy must allow the seller to attempt to cure, if the seller so requests.[519] On the other hand, a seller who is excused from performance by an Article 79 "impediment"[520] will still be vulnerable to a price reduction under Article 50. A buyer that has claimed a price reduction may not, however, simultaneously demand that a defect be remedied by repair or delivery of substitute goods,[521] although it may combine a price reduction with a claim for damages to obtain full compensation).[522]

§ 1.34 Buyer's Remedies—Specific Performance

The more formal remedies available to an aggrieved buyer through court or arbitral tribunal proceedings are an action for specific performance and an action for damages. (The seller has parallel judicial remedies in the form of an action for the price and an action for damages.[523])

The CISG gives to the buyer who has not received the agreed performance from the seller a specifically enforceable right to "require performance" by the seller.[524] This reflects the basic civil law theory that legal compulsion of performance is the best relief to an aggrieved buyer, and that the seller's actual performance is preferable to substitutional relief (such as a monetary award).[525] The reference to the seller's "obligations" is not limited, and so can include court compulsion to provide goods of the agreed description quantity, quality and title (including intellectual property rights), as well as adhering to the agreed time, place and manner of delivery.

The buyer's right to specific performance is subject to two important qualifications: First, the buyer must not have already resorted to an "inconsistent" remedy; and, second, a court (such as in a common law jurisdiction) need not grant such a remedy "unless the court would do so under its own law" for comparable contracts.[526] Thus, the CISG gives the buyer the right to seek specific performance, rather than damages, but does not compel it to do so;

---

[519] CISG, art. 50.

[520] *See* § 1.25 *supra*.

[521] *See* CISG, art. 46 (although this remedy may not be available in the United States, see § 1.34 *infra*).

[522] *See* Müller-Chen, art. 50, para. 18, in Schlechtriem & Schwenzer, *supra* note 3.

[523] *See* §§ 1.38 and 1.39 *infra*.

[524] CISG, art. 46.

[525] For a background and comparison see Shael Herman, *Specific Performance: A Comparative Analysis*, 7 EDINBURGH L. REV. 5 [Part I] and 194 [Part II] (2003).

[526] CISG, art. 28.

and it permits a court to grant such a remedy, but does not compel it to do so. Even in civil law jurisdictions, buyers will often prefer damages and purchase of substitute goods, because of the expense and delays inherent in seeking formal court orders requiring performance.

The provision permits the buyer to seek specific performance, but *does not require* it to do so. The buyer may still elect between seeking a performance remedy or a substitutional (*i.e.*, damages) remedy. Thus, any preference for this remedy must arise from the buyer's perspective, not from the court's. Even in civil law jurisdictions, buyers will often prefer to recover damages and purchase substitute goods, because of the expense and delays inherent in litigation.[527] Nonetheless, the first limitation noted above reflects the notion that a buyer cannot require *specific* performance of a contractual duty if it has already sought a *substitutional* remedy. The CISG in this respect imposes an election of remedies rule: A buyer may not seek this specific remedy if it has already resorted to an "inconsistent remedy." The buyer is not entitled to specific performance, therefore, if it has already declared an avoidance of the contract (whether for fundamental breach or failure of the seller to meet a *Nachfrist*);[528] has effected a reduction in price;[529] or sought damages tied directly to the seller's failure to deliver the goods (as opposed to consequential damages).[530]

The second limitation on the remedy of specific performance is much more significant in the United States. Under CISG Article 28, a court "is not bound" to order specific performance "unless the court would do so under its own law" in respect of similar contracts of sale. This rule will have a negligible effect on civil law courts because they are authorized to order the seller's performance in many more cases.[531] Thus, if specific performance is sought in a civil law court, it will usually apply CISG Article 46 and order the seller to perform its obligations, and a buyer desiring this remedy should, if possible, bring its claim in such a court.

---

527 There is significant evidence that substitutional relief is often sought in civil law commercial disputes. *See, e.g.*, Henrik Lando and Caspar Rose, *On the Enforcement of Specific Performance in Civil Law Countries*, 24 INT'L REV. L. & ECON. 473, 478 (2004)(stating that damages are "by far the dominant form of relief" in civil law countries as well); Jacob Ziegel, *The Remedial Provisions of the Vienna Sales Convention: Common Law Perspectives*, Ch. 9, in INTERNATIONAL SALES (N. Galston and H. Smit, eds. 1984).

528 *See* § 1. 32 *supra* and CISG, arts. 26, 49(1)(a), (b).

529 *See* § 1.33 *supra* and CISG, art. 50.

530 *See* § 1.35 *infra* and CISG, arts. 45(1)(b), 74–77.

531 *See* Tallon, *Remedies, The French Report*, in CONTRACT LAW TODAY 263–288 (D. Harris and D. Tallon, eds. 1989).

This would not, however, be the analytical approach of a common law court. Although the UCC is designed to empower courts to order specific performance, the case law does not demonstrate widespread interest in compelling performance.[532] If the goods are "unique" and they exist, then it is more likely the court will order specific performance. If, however, substitute goods are readily available in the market, it is less likely that the court would order specific performance. A U.S. court would be likely to issue a specific performance order for requirements or output contracts involving "particular or peculiarly available" goods.[533] With those exceptions, a U.S. court generally would not be required by CISG Article 46 to issue an order compelling the delivery of goods by the seller. And, in a noteworthy exception to the general principle of "party autonomy" in CISG Article 6, the parties may not derogate from this limitation through contractual agreement.[534] Thus, a buyer desirous of a specific performance remedy should not bring its claim in a common law court.[535]

If the remedy of specific performance is available, the buyer may require performance by the seller of any of its breached obligations.[536] Where the goods have not been delivered, this would mean a requirement that the seller deliver the goods. If the seller has delivered, but the goods do not conform to the contract, the buyer may require delivery of conforming substitute goods if the nonconformity amounts to a "fundamental breach," and the buyer has given the seller proper notice (either as part of the initial notice of nonconformity or separately within a reasonable time).[537] Likewise, the buyer may require the seller to repair nonconforming goods, unless this is "unreasonable having regard to all the circumstances."[538] The principal difference between replacement and repair is that a buyer need not show that the non-conformities constitute a fundamental breach when requesting repair.

---

532 UCC § 2–716(1).

533 UCC § 2–716, comment 2.

534 *See* CLOUT Case No. 651, *Tribunale di Padova*, Italy (11 January 2005).

535 Because the reference point in CISG Article 28 is "the court" in which an action is proceeding, the applicable law for granting specific performance is that of the forum, without regard to choice of law rules. *See* Müller-Chen, art. 28, para. 9, in Schlechtriem & Schwenzer, *supra* note 3.

536 CISG, art. 46(1).

537 CISG, art. 46(2).

538 CISG, art. 46(3).

§ 1.35 Buyer's Remedies—Action for Damages

In accordance with traditional notions, the CISG also provides an aggrieved buyer (as well as an aggrieved seller, *see* below[539]) with an action for damages.[540] Like other remedies, the buyer's right to damages exists if the seller fails to perform any of its obligations under the contract.[541] The right to damages exists even when the buyer has avoided the contract and when the seller has successfully cured defects in its performance.[542] There is no requirement that the buyer prove that the seller was "at fault" as a prerequisite to a recovery of damages. Both direct and consequential damages are recoverable; and expectancy, reliance and restitutionary interests are all protected depending on the specific context.

CISG Articles 74 through 78 define the basic rules for the calculation of a claim for damages for both seller and buyer. Article 74 defines the basic principle that an aggrieved party is entitled to "a sum equal to the loss, including loss of profit, suffered as a consequence of the breach." As the Second Circuit correctly observed in *Delchi Carrier S.p.A. v. Rotorex Corp.*, this rule is "designed to place the aggrieved party in as good a position as if the other party had properly performed the contract."[543] In a claim based on a seller's delivery of nonconforming goods, this court also concluded that the buyer may recover profits from any lost downstream sales, measured by the price less variable costs only (*i.e.*, not including fixed overhead costs).[544]

Recovery of damages under the CISG is subject to certain, in part familiar, limitations. First, CISG Article 74 expressly states that damages (especially consequential damages) may not exceed the loss that the party in breach "foresaw or ought to have foreseen at the time of the conclusion of the contract." Some U.S. courts have observed that this rule is "identical to the well-known rule of *Hadley v. Baxendale*."[545] This, however, is an example of *faux amis* ("false friends"), in which courts wrongly assume that similar

---

539 *See* § 1.39 *infra*.

540 CISG, art. 45(1)(b).

541 *Id.*

542 CISG, art. 45(2).

543 71 F.3d 1024, 1029 (2d Cir. 1995)(quoting John Honnold, *Uniform Law for International Sales Under the 1980 United Nations Convention* 503 (2d ed. 1991).

544 *Id.* at 1029–1030. *See also* Al Hewar Environmental & Public Health Establishment v. Southeast Ranch, LLC, 2011 WL 7191744, at *2 (S.D. Fla. 2011)(awarding an aggrieved buyer damages from lost profits on downstream sales).

545 Tee Vee Toons, Inc. v. Gerhard Schubert GmbH, 2006 WL 2463537, at *9 (S.D.N.Y. 2006)(citing Hadley v. Baxendale, 9 Ex. 341, 156 Eng. Rep. 145 (1854)). *See also* Delchi Carrier S.p.A. v. Rotorex Corp., 71 F.3d 1024, 1030 (2d Cir. 1995)(same).

means "identical." First, unlike the common law foreseeability rule, CISG Article 74 states that recovery is available if the loss suffered is a "possible" (not "probable") consequence of the breach.[546] Second, the CISG rule has a more ambiguous reference to matters of which the party in breach "ought to have known" at the time of contract formation. Finally, the CISG rule refers explicitly to the two layers of foreseeability, that of the loss itself and, separately, that of the "facts and matters" of which the party in breach knew or ought to have known as a possible consequence of the breach.

CISG Article 77 sets forth the second limitation on the recovery of contract damages: that an aggrieved buyer must take "reasonable measures" to mitigate its damages. If such a party fails to do so, the party in breach may claim a reduction in damages "in the amount by which the loss should have been mitigated."[547] With reference to a breach by the seller, this limitation commonly will require an aggrieved buyer to enter into a substitute purchase in order to prevent or mitigate its damages.[548]

Finally, it is generally understood that an aggrieved party must prove its damages to a reasonable degree of certainty.[549] This follows from the general principles of reasonableness and that a proponent has the burden of proof on a claim and of a claimant.[550]

Where a buyer has declared an avoidance of the contract, the CISG provides alternative specific measures of recovery. Article 75 first allows the recovery, in addition to the general damages under Article 74, of the difference between the contract price and the "price in [a] substitute transaction," which in the case of an aggrieved buyer means the purchase of replacement goods.[551] This measure is only allowed, however, if the replacement purchase occurs in a reasonable manner and within a reasonable time after avoidance.

---

[546] *Compare* CISG, art. 74, last sentence, *with* RESTATEMENT (SECOND) OF CONTRACTS, § 351(1). For a thorough discussion of the differences between the Common Law and CISG, see Arthur Murphey, *Consequential Damages in CISG and the Legacy of Hadley*, 23 GEO. WASH. J. INT'L L. & ECON.415 (1989).

[547] CISG, art. 77.

[548] *See* Schwenzer, art. 77, para. 10, in Schlechtriem & Schwenzer, *supra* note 3.

[549] CISG Advisory Council Opinion No. 6, *Calculation of Damages under CISG Article 74*, § 2 (2006), available at http://www.cisgac.com/default.php?ipkCat=128&ifkCat=148&sid=148.*See also* Tee Vee Toons, Inc. v. Gerhard Schubert GmbH, 2006 WL 2463537, at *10 (S.D.N.Y. 2006)(referring to proof with "sufficient certainty")(citing Delchi Carrier S.p.A. v. Rotorex Corp., 71 F.3d 1024, 1029 (2d Cir. 1995)).

[550] For a discussion of these "general principles" of the Convention see § 1.9 *supra*.

[551] Compare UCC § 2–712(providing for damages in the event of a "cover" purchase by the buyer).

As an alternative, Article 76 permits recovery based on the difference between the contract price and the "current price" (*i.e.*, the market price) for the goods. Where this current price differential is used, the price in the market is to be measured at the time of "avoidance,"[552] unless the buyer had already "taken over" the goods at the time of avoidance. In the latter case, the market price is measured at the time of "taking over."[553] The relevant market for determining the current price is the place where delivery of the goods should have been made or, if no such price exists there, "at such other place as serves as a reasonable substitute."[554] The Article 76 measure may not be used at all, however, if no "current price" is available at any such place.

Although the Convention provides for recovery under either Article 75 or Article 76, if the buyer actually makes a replacement purchase, it may not use the latter.[555] The Convention gives no guidance, however, on how to determine whether any particular purchase by the buyer is a replacement purchase, or is instead an ordinary buildup of inventory.

The CISG measures of the buyer's damages are remarkably similar to those in the UCC. The U.S. leading case applying the CISG's damages rules remains *Delchi Carrier S.p.A. v. Rotorex Corp.* There, the court correctly ruled that UCC case law could not be used to interpret CISG provisions unless the language of the UCC provision tracks that of the CISG provision.[556] But the court observed that the broad, general language of CISG Article 74 reflects a traditional and fundamental principle of full compensation.[557]

The case involved a buyer which had lost sales due to the seller's delivery of nonconforming goods, and which sought loss of profits for the sales lost until substitute, conforming goods had been found. The court found that the standard contract price vs. market price differential would not fully compensate the buyer for the "loss, including lost profits, suffered by" the buyer as declared in CISG Article 74.[558] The lost profit damages were, however, recoverable

---

552 CISG, art. 76, first sentence.

553 CISG, art. 76, second sentence.

554 CISG, art. 76(2).

555 CISG art. 76 (stating that the measure is available "if [the buyer] has not made a purchase . . . under article 75").

556 71 F.3d 1024, 1028 (2d Cir. 1995).

557 *Id.*, at 1029–1030 (emphasizing the language in CISG Article that "[d]amages . . . consist of a sum equal to the loss . . . suffered by the other party as a consequence of the breach").

558 *Id.*

only to the extent that they were reasonably foreseeable by the parties. In measuring the buyer's lost profits, the court found that the CISG had no specific provision on the treatment of fixed and variable costs in determining the buyer's lost profits. It therefore followed the traditional principle that only the variable costs saved by the buyer are to be deducted from the lost sales revenues.

The courts also allowed the buyer to recover, as additional consequential and incidental damages:

(1) the costs of the buyer's attempts to cure, including reinspection and testing;

(2) the costs of expedited delivery of substitute conforming goods from another seller;

(3) the costs of storing the non-conforming goods;

(4) the shipping and customs costs for the non-conforming goods;

(5) the costs of materials and tools usable only with the non-conforming goods; and

(6) the labor costs related to the production line shutdown.[559]

In most of the world, the losing party pays also the winner's attorney's fees, typically according to a statutory formula. This is regarded as part of the damages necessary to make the aggrieved party whole. One U.S. appellate court has held, however, that such an award would be merely procedural and, therefore, not part of the substantive law of the Convention.[560] The problem with this decision is that it engaged carefully neither with the interpretive rules in CISG Article 7 nor with the thoughtful analyses of foreign courts on the subject (which is also required by Article 7(1)).[561] Essentially every court and arbitral tribunal outside of the United States has found, however, that the basic principle of full compensation reflect-

---

559 *Id.*, at 1029–031.

560 Zapata Hermanos Sucesores, S.A. v. Hearthside Baking Company, Inc., 313 F.3d 385, 389–390 (7th Cir. 2002). *See also* San Lucio, S.R.L. v. Import & Storage Services, LLC, 2009 WL 1010981 (D.N.J. 2009)(also denying attorney's fees, but with no analysis of the CISG whatsoever). *But see* Granjas Aquanova S.A. de C.V. v. House Mfg. Co. Inc., 2010 WL 4809342, at *2 (E.D. Ark. 2010)(noting the criticism of *Zapata* and suggesting the matter remains in doubt).

561 *See, e.g.*, CISG AC Opinion No. 6, *supra* note 549, Comment 5.2 (criticizing the procedural/substantive distinction in as reflected in Zapata as "outdated and unproductive"); Peter Schlechtriem, *Legal Costs as Damages in the Application of UN Sales Law*, 25 J.L. & COM. 71 (2007–08).

ed in CISG Article 74 requires an award of reasonable attorney's fees as well.[562]

Incidental damages relating to interest are allowed separately in Article 78 (although substantial dispute exists over how to calculate the interest rate).[563] But CISG Article 79 declares that damages are not recoverable in the event an unforeseeable impediment has prevented the other party's performance.[564]

§ 1.36 Seller's Remedies for Breach by Buyer

The CISG provisions on the seller's remedies for a breach by the buyer parallel the structure for the buyer's remedies upon breach discussed above. Under CISG Articles 61 through 65, if the buyer fails to perform "any" of its obligations,[565] the seller has three basic types of remedies: (a) a non-judicial "avoidance" of the contract; (b) an action for the price (a form of specific performance); and in any event (c) an action for damages.

§ 1.37 Seller's Remedies—Avoidance of the Contract

Again in parallel with the buyer's rights upon breach, the CISG provides two separate grounds for the seller to declare an "avoidance of the contract" upon a breach by the buyer. First, Article 64(1)(a) permits the seller to make such a declaration in the case of a "fundamental breach" by the buyer, regardless of the type of breach or when it occurs. Second, if the buyer does not pay the price or accept delivery of the goods, Articles 63 and 64(1)(b) give the seller a right to declare an avoidance if the buyer does not perform within an additional deadline set by the seller. We will again examine these two alternatives in turn.

Under either option, the effect of an "avoidance of the contract" by the seller is a right not to perform its contractual obligations, and especially to refuse to deliver the goods to the buyer.[566] Further, because the CISG does not attach special legal significance to the concept of "acceptance" of the goods, the seller's delivery of the goods to the buyer is not a crucial factual or legal step in the analy-

---

562 See CISG DIGEST 2012, *supra* footnote 8, art. 74, para. 27 (citing cases).

563 For a review of this controversy see Michael P. Van Alstine, *The UNCITRAL Digest, the Right to Interest, and the Interest Rate Controversy*, in DRAFTING CONTRACTS UNDER THE CISG (R. Brand, ed., 2008).

564 For more on this excuse for nonperformance see § 1.25 *supra*.

565 CISG, art. 61(1).

566 *See* the discussion in § 1.28 *supra*.

sis of the seller's position under the CISG. Thus, as compared to the UCC, the CISG may put an aggrieved seller in a substantially better position regarding stopping the goods in transit or reclaiming them from the buyer. (*See* immediately below.)

To assert either option for avoidance, the seller must make a corresponding declaration by notice to the buyer.[567] In either case, the seller also retains its right to any damages caused by the buyer's breach.[568]

Avoidance for Fundamental Breach. The seller's principal right to declare an avoidance of the contract arises upon a "fundamental breach" by the buyer.[569] Section 1.28 above analyzed in detail the CISG's definition of a "fundamental breach." In summary, the seller has a right to declare an avoidance on this basis if the buyer's failure to perform "any" of its obligations[570] "substantially deprive[s]" the seller of what it is "entitled to expect under the contract."[571] The standard examples from the case law of such fundamental breaches by the buyer are a definitive failure to pay the price (or a significant portion thereof) and a final failure to take delivery of the goods (which is especially important in long-distance transactions).[572] But if the buyer has already paid the purchase price, the right to declare an avoidance for a fundamental breach is lost if the seller does not make the declaration (a) in respect of late performance, before the seller "has become aware that the performance has been rendered," or (b) in respect of any other breach, within a reasonable time after the seller knew or ought to have known of the breach.[573]

Avoidance and "Nachfrist." The uncertainties over the precise application of the "fundamental breach" test in practice also affect a seller, for it too will have difficulty in knowing whether a particular breach by the buyer will justify an "avoidance" of the contract. Here as well, incorrect analysis could put the seller in the position of making a fundamental breach through its response. CISG Articles 63 and 64(1)(b) thus also give the seller an alternative method for ensuring that the buyer will perform its obligations—or at least making clear that the buyer will not do so. Thus, in the event the buyer fails to perform, the seller may set a *Nachfrist* ("additional deadline"), that is, "an additional period of time . . . for performance

---

[567] CISG, art. 26.

[568] CISG, art. 61(2).

[569] CISG, art. 64(1)(a).

[570] CISG, arts. 61(1), 64(1)(a).

[571] CISG, art. 25.

[572] *See CISG* DIGEST 2012, *supra* footnote 8, art. 64, paras. 3–6 (citing cases).

[573] CISG, art. 64(2)(b)(i).

by the buyer."[574] Then, if the buyer fails to perform—or declares that it will not perform—by the new deadline, the seller has a right to declare an avoidance of the contract even if no fundamental breach has yet occurred.[575] This option only exists with respect to the buyer's obligations to pay the price and take delivery of the goods. Finally, the additional deadline for performance must be "of reasonable length"[576] in order to permit the buyer to perform at least to a level that will retain the integrity of the contract (especially, a right to delivery of the goods).

If the seller sets such an additional deadline for performance, it may not resort in the interim to any remedy for breach of contract, unless the buyer declares that it will not perform within the deadline. But even if the buyer so performs, the seller will retain its rights to any remaining damages from the delay in the buyer's performance.[577]

Again, such a declaration of avoidance must be made by notice to the buyer.[578] If the buyer has already paid the price, the seller loses the right to declare an avoidance on this basis unless it does so within a reasonable time after the expiration of the "*Nachfrist*" (or after the buyer has declared that it will not perform).[579]

The Seller's Right of Reclamation. A seller's justified declaration of avoidance may also trigger a right to reclaim the goods from the buyer after delivery. That is, if an unpaid seller is unable (for any reason) to obtain the price, it may through a declaration of avoidance seek to obtain the return of its goods from the defaulting buyer. The UCC places substantial limitations on such a right.[580] But the CISG's description of the rights upon avoidance may allow such a reclamation. First, the CISG's grant to the seller of a power of avoidance upon breach by the buyer does not distinguish between pre-and post-delivery situations.[581] In addition, if one party has already performed, an avoidance of the contract creates a right of "restitution from the other party of whatever the first party has supplied" under the contract.[582] In the case of the seller, this should

---

574 CISG, art. 63(1).

575 CISG, art. 64(1)(b).

576 CISG, art. 63(1). For a discussion of court decisions on what is a "reasonable" length of time in particular cases see § 1.32 *supra*.

577 CISG, art. 63(2).

578 CISG, art. 26.

579 CISG, art. 64(2)(b)(ii).

580 *See, e.g.*, UCC §§ 2–507 and 2–702, and their comments.

581 CISG, art. 64.

582 CISG, art. 81(2).

mean a right of restitution of goods already delivered. This analysis is available only so long as third parties (*e.g.*, buyer's creditors and trustees in bankruptcy) are not involved, for the CISG excludes from its scope issues of title to the goods and third party rights.[583] Notwithstanding this rule, the CISG would seem to grant to the seller, as between it and the buyer, a right to *possession* of the goods upon a justified avoidance of the contract. This should create the legal ground for a right of replevin under domestic law (and notwithstanding that the CISG generally does not require a court to order "specific performance" of a contract[584]).

Restitution and Obligation to Preserve Goods. Like the buyer's situation upon breach by the seller, avoidance of the contract releases both parties from their contractual obligations.[585] And as noted immediately above, if either party has already performed, it has a corresponding right of restitution against the other.[586]

If the buyer fails to take delivery of the goods or to pay the price when concurrent performance is required, the CISG imposes certain obligations on the seller regarding preservation of the goods. First, if the seller is in possession of or otherwise controls the goods, it must take reasonable steps to preserve them pending ultimate delivery to the buyer.[587] It may do so by depositing the goods in a public warehouse at the expense of the buyer.[588] The seller may then make payment of any such expenses a condition to delivery of the goods.[589] If, however, there is an "unreasonable delay" in the buyer taking delivery or paying the price, the seller may sell the goods to a third party "by any appropriate means"[590] and must do so if the goods are subject to rapid deterioration.[591] It may then take out of the proceeds any related expenses, but must account to the buyer for any excess.[592]

---

583 CISG, art. 4(b). *See also* § 1.7 *supra*.

584 *See* CISG, art. 28 and §§ 1.34 *supra* and 1.38 *infra*.

585 CISG, art. 81(1).

586 CISG, art. 81((2).

587 CISG, art. 86(1).

588 CISG art. 87.

589 CISG, art. 85.

590 CISG, art. 88(1).

591 CISG, art. 88(2). The same rule applies if the costs of preservation are excessive as compared to the value of the goods. *Id.*

592 CISG, art. 88(3).

§ 1.38 Seller's Remedies—Specific Performance—Action for the Price

The preferred remedy for an aggrieved seller, if the buyer should breach, is a cause of action for the price, which is the seller's functional equivalent of an action for specific performance. A cause of action for damages, but not the price, is distinctly secondary.

CISG Article 62 gives the seller an unqualified right to require the buyer to pay the price (although formally no CISG Article expressly states that the seller has a cause of action for payment of the price). There are, however, important conditions on the exercise of such a right: First, the seller of course must itself have performed as required by the contract.[593] Second, the payment of the price must actually be due.[594] Third, the seller must not have already resorted to an "inconsistent" remedy.[595] Prominent examples of this would be a declaration of an avoidance of the contract (for the seller may not "keep its contract and have it too") and a resale of the goods with an eye to recovering corresponding damages.

Finally, and perhaps most important, such an action for the price may reflect a claim "for specific performance." As noted above, CISG Article 28 declares that a court need only grant such a remedy if it would do so "in respect of similar contracts of sale not governed by the Convention."[596] For a time, some doubt existed on whether this rule was relevant to the seller's action for the price. The problem lied in the fact that the Convention and the UCC have different concepts of "specific performance." From the UCC perspective the only provision which specifically mentions an action for "specific performance" is UCC § 2–716, which is expressly limited to a cause of action by the buyer. The seller is given no comparable general cause of action to compel performance of the buyer's obligations, except for a limited right to seek payment of the price—a monetary award.[597] Thus, from the UCC perspective the action for the price under UCC § 2–709 is merely another action for a monetary judgment, not one to compel conduct. From the CISG perspective there is no separate action for the price as a monetary judgment, only CISG Article 62, which allows a court to compel three different types of conduct—payment of the price, taking delivery, or

---

[593] *See* §§ 1.17–1.20 *supra*.

[594] CISG, art. 58.

[595] CISG, art. 62.

[596] *See* the discussion in § 1.34 *supra* (relating to a claim of specific performance by the buyer).

[597] UCC § 2–709.

performance of other obligations. Payment of the price is within a list of specific performances which a court is authorized to compel.

Today, however, there is near universal agreement that an action for the price reflects a claim to specific performance.[598] As a result, an aggrieved seller seeking the full contract price must meet the requirements of UCC § 2–709, as well as those of CISG Article 62, before a U.S. court could order this remedy as opposed to calculating a general right to damages. This thus is one of the extremely rare circumstances in which a U.S. court may resort directly to the UCC even for a contract governed by the CISG.

Some of the buyer's obligations are not monetary, such as preparing to take delivery of the goods or opening a letter of credit. The CISG also authorizes a court to compel such conduct by the buyer,[599] if again the court would do so in a non-Convention case. In all such cases, therefore, a seller desirous of recovering the price should file its claim in a jurisdiction (such as a civil law court) that does not impose the more rigorous conditions of the UCC.

§ 1.39 Seller's Remedies—Action for Damages

The CISG also grants to the seller a right to damages if the buyer fails to perform "any" of its obligations.[600] This right exists even when the seller has avoided the contract.[601] Like the rights of the buyer, there is no requirement that the seller prove that the buyer was "at fault" as a prerequisite to a recovery of damages. And, again, both direct and consequential damages are recoverable and as appropriate expectancy, reliance and restitutionary interests are all protected.

The general rules for the calculation of the seller's right to damages are the same as in the discussion of the buyer's remedies for a breach by the seller.[602] Again, CISG Article 74 defines the basic principle that an aggrieved party is entitled to "a sum equal to the loss, including loss of profit, suffered as a consequence of the breach." And as the Second Circuit has correctly observed, this rule is "designed to place the aggrieved party in as good a position as if

---

[598] *See CISG* DIGEST 2012, *supra* footnote 8, art. 62, para. 6; Mohs, art. 62, para. 14, in Schlechtriem & Schwenzer, *supra* note 3; Bell, art. 62, paras. 11, in Kröll, et al, *supra* note 3.

[599] CISG, art. 62 (referring to requiring the buyer to "take delivery or perform [its] other obligations").

[600] CISG, art. 61(1)(b).

[601] CISG, art. 61(2).

[602] CISG, arts. 74–77. *See also* § 1.35 *supra*.

the other party had properly performed the contract."[603] In parallel with the rules for recovery by the buyer,[604] however, certain familiar limitations apply: First, recoverable damages may not exceed the loss that the buyer "foresaw or ought to have foreseen at the time of the conclusion of the contract;"[605] second, the seller may not recover damages that it could have avoided through "reasonable measures";[606] and the seller must prove its damages to a reasonable degree of certainty.[607]

The same two general alternatives also exist for the measurement of the seller's damages: (a) under Article 75, the difference between the contract price and the price in a "substitute transaction," which in the case of an aggrieved seller is a resale of the goods;[608] and (b) under Article 76, the difference between the contract price and the "current price" (*i.e.*, the market price) for the goods at the time of avoidance of the contract.[609] The Convention provides for recovery according to either of these measures, but if the seller actually resells the goods, only the first is available.[610]

Again, the Article 76 recovery is based on the difference between the contract price and the "current price" for the goods. Where this current price differential is used, the price in the market is to be measured at the time of "avoidance,"[611] unless the goods had already been "taken over" at the time of avoidance. In the latter case, the current price is measured at the time of the "taking over."[612] The relevant place for determining the current price is where delivery of the goods should have been made or, if no such price exists there, "at such other place as serves as a reasonable substitute."[613] The Article 76 measure may not be used at all, however, if no "current price" is available at any such place.

---

[603] Delchi Carrier S.p.A. v. Rotorex Corp., 71 F.3d 1024, 1029 (2d Cir. 1995)(quoting John Honnold, UNIFORM LAW FOR INTERNATIONAL SALES UNDER THE 1980 UNITED NATIONS CONVENTION 503 (2d ed. 1991)).

[604] *See* the discussion in § 1.35 *supra*.

[605] CISG, art. 74.

[606] CISG, art. 77.

[607] CISG Advisory Council Opinion No. 6, *supra* note 549, § 2. *See also* Tee Vee Toons, Inc. v. Gerhard Schubert GmbH, 2006 WL 2463537, at *10 (S.D.N.Y. 2006)(referring to proof with "sufficient certainty")(citing Delchi Carrier S.p.A. v. Rotorex Corp., 71 F.3d 1024, 1029 (2d Cir. 1995)).

[608] CISG, art. 75. Compare UCC § 2–706.

[609] CISG, art. 76. Compare UCC § 2–708(1).

[610] CISG, art. 76(1)(stating that this measure is available only if the seller "has not made a . . . resale").

[611] CISG, art. 76, first sentence.

[612] CISG, art. 76, second sentence.

[613] CISG, art. 76(2).

The major practical issue concerning aggrieved sellers is that the "lost volume" seller is not adequately protected by these alternative measures of damages.[614] Nonetheless, CISG Article 74 states as a general principle that an aggrieved party is entitled to all damages "including loss of profit" suffered "as a consequence of the breach." On this basis, courts have granted full protection to aggrieved sellers by awarding "lost profits" damages, and by subtracting from those losses only the variable costs saved by the termination of the first sales contract.[615] Thus, for example, the Supreme Court of Austria held in one case that a seller could recover its lost volume profit, provided that it could have completed another sale at the market price.[616] As this case indicates, such a recovery requires, however, that the seller actually had the intent and capacity to conclude the second sale in addition to the breached first sales contract.

The seller likewise is entitled to incidental damages relating to interest on unpaid claims (although, again, substantial dispute exists over how to calculate the interest rate).[617]

§ 1.40 The Limitation Convention

Following its acceptance of the CISG, the United States in 1994 also ratified a parallel treaty that addresses the limitation period for international sales contracts (which U.S. lawyers would know as the "statute of limitations"): The Convention on the Limitation Period in the International Sale of Goods.[618] Over two dozen other countries have ratified this Limitation Convention (as amended by a 1980 Protocol).

The provisions on the scope of the Limitation Convention in many respects parallel those of the CISG. The Limitation Convention applies to "claims . . . arising from a contract of international sale of goods or relating to its breach, termination, or invalidity."[619] Similar to the CISG, the Limitation Convention applies if, at the time of the conclusion of a contract, the parties have their "places of business" in different states and both such states are member states

---

614 Compare UCC § 2–708(2).

615 *See* CISG DIGEST 2012, *supra* footnote 8, art. 74, para. 32 (citing cases).

616 CLOUT case No. 427, *Oberster Gerichtshof* [Supreme Court] of Austria (28 April 2000).

617 CISG, art. 78. For a review of this controversy see Van Alstine, *The UNCITRAL Digest, supra* note 563.

618 Like the CISG, information about this Convention and the status of ratification is available on the website of UNCITRAL, http://www.uncitral.org/uncitral/en/uncitral_texts/sale_goods.html.

619 Limitation Convention art. 1(1).

of the Convention.[620] But it also applies if the relevant conflict of law rules make the law of a member state applicable to the contract of sale.[621] Unlike the CISG, the United States has not declared a reservation to this latter option, with the result that the Limitation Convention may well apply to a transaction even if the CISG does not. If a party has more than one place of business, the relevant place is the one with the "closest relationship" to the contract and its performance.[622]

In parallel with CISG Article 6, Article 3(2) of the Limitation Convention permits the parties to exclude its application to their transaction.[623] The Limitation Convention also does not apply to sales to consumers, as well as a variety of other specific transaction types also excluded by the CISG.[624] The Convention likewise excludes a variety of specific types of claims, most notably those based on personal injuries, judgments, or negotiable instruments.[625] Finally, and again in parallel with the CISG, the Limitation Convention does not apply where the "preponderant part" of the seller's obligations consists of services or where the buyer supplies a "substantial part" of the component parts or materials the seller uses to sell the resultant goods to the buyer.[626]

The basic period of limitation under the Convention is four years,[627] a period that begins to run on the date on which the claim "accrues."[628] The Convention makes clear that the commencement of this period is not postponed by any notice requirement or by a provision in an arbitration agreement to the effect that no rights arise until the arbitration award is rendered.[629] Once the limitation period has expired, the Convention declares that the affected claim shall not "be recognized or enforced in any legal proceeding."[630] If, on the other hand, the obligated party (known as the "debtor"[631])

---

[620] Limitation Convention, arts. 2(a)(defining an "international" contract) and 3(1)(a)(stating the basic rule).

[621] Limitation Convention art. 2.

[622] Limitation Convention, art. 2(c). Compare CISG, art. 10.

[623] *Id.*, art. 3(2).

[624] *Id.*, art. 4. *See also* CISG art. 2 and § 1.5 *supra.*

[625] Limitation Convention, art. 5.

[626] *Id.*, art. 6. Compare CISG art. 3.

[627] Limitation Convention, art. 8.

[628] *Id.*, art. 9(1).

[629] *Id.*, art. 9(2).

[630] *Id.*, art. 25(1).

[631] *Id.*, art. 1(3)(c).

nonetheless performs his obligation thereafter, it does not have a claim to restitution.[632]

Article 10 of the Limitation Convention sets forth the important rules on when specific causes of action "accrue": (a) A cause of action for a standard breach of contract accrues "on the date on which such breach occurs";[633] (b) a claim arising from "a defect or other lack of conformity" in the goods accrues on the date on which "the goods are actually handed over" to the buyer or the buyer refuses such delivery;[634] and a claim based on fraud accrues on the date on which the fraud "was or reasonably could have been discovered."[635]

The Convention also contains an analog to the UCC's "warranty of future performance" exception to when a cause of action for breach of warranty generally accrues.[636] Under Article 11, if the seller has given an "express undertaking" relating to the goods "which is stated to have effect for a certain period of time," the limitation period for a breach of such undertaking will commence not on tender of delivery, but rather on the date on which the buyer "notifies the seller of the fact on which the claim is based."[637] Recall in this regard that under CISG Article 39 the buyer loses a right to rely on a nonconformity if it does not give sufficient notice to the seller within a reasonable time.[638] Putting the two rules together, if the buyer satisfies its notice obligation, a cause of action for breach of an express undertaking that extends to the future will accrue within a reasonable time after the buyer "discovered or ought to have discovered" the breach.[639] A conceptually similar provision states that if a party may declare a contract terminated before the date of performance by the other party, the limitation period commences on the date such a declaration is made to the other party, and if such a declaration is not made, on the date of performance.[640]

The Limitation Convention also has detailed rules on the cessation and extension of the limitation period. First, the period ceas-

---

[632] *Id.*, art. 26.

[633] *Id.*, art. 10(1).

[634] *Id.*, art. 10(2).

[635] *Id.*, art. 10(3).

[636] Compare UCC § 2–725(2).

[637] The same provision makes clear an issue left unresolved by UCC § 2–725(2), specifically that in such a case the limitation period will commence at the latest "on the date of the expiration of the period of the undertaking." Limitation Convention, art. 11.

[638] *See* § 1.22 *supra*.

[639] CISG art. 39.

[640] Limitation Convention, art. 12.

es when the aggrieved party undertakes an act that, under the law of the forum, "is recognized as commencing judicial proceedings" or as otherwise raising a claim in an existing proceeding.[641] For arbitration proceedings, the period ceases when a claim is commenced according to the agreement or applicable law or, in absence of this, when the arbitration request is made.[642] Counterclaims are deemed raised at that same time as the claim against which they are directed.[643] In the event a court dismisses a proceeding without prejudice, the applicable period of limitation "shall be deemed to have continued to run," but if less than one year remains at that time, a party will have one year to assert its claim.[644] If a breaching party acknowledges its obligation either expressly in writing or implicitly by making a payment, a new four-year period of limitation applies. Finally, the Limitation Convention has a form of "impracticability" exception in the event of an uncontrollable and unavoidable circumstance that prevents a party from asserting a claim in a timely manner. In such a case, the limitation period is extended until one year after the circumstance ceases to exist.[645]

The Limitation Convention also has certain rules that differ from U.S. concepts in important particulars. First, Article 22 precludes the parties from modifying the Convention's limitation period in advance, even by an express contractual agreement. The party in breach may extend the period, but only after it has begun to run.[646] Second, the Convention also sets an absolute ten year limitation period from when any particular period has "commenced to run."[647] Finally, and unusually, the Limitation Convention includes a form of a procedural rule that precludes a party from relying on the expiration of a limitations period unless it has timely raised a corresponding defense in a relevant legal proceeding.[648]

---

641 *Id.*, art. 13.

642 Limitation Convention, art. 14. *See also id.*, art. 15 (stating special rules for death or incapacity of the breaching party, bankruptcy, and dissolution or liquidation of a corporate entity).

643 *Id.*, art. 16.

644 *Id.*, art. 17. For claims against jointly and severally liable parties see *id.*, art. 18.

645 *Id.*, art. 21.

646 *Id.*, art. 22(b).

647 *Id.*, art. 23.

648 *Id.*, art. 24.

Chapter 2

COMMERCIAL TERMS

Table of Sections

§ 2.1 Introduction

Chapter 1 illustrated how different rules may apply for domestic and international sales of goods—for the United States, the Uniform Commercial Code (UCC), and the Convention on Contracts for the International Sales of Goods (CISG), respectively.[1] There are also differences between domestic and international "commercial terms," which provide rules for the rights and obligations of the buyer and seller regarding the delivery of the goods under a sales contract.

Given the complexity and detail of this subject, parties to international sales transactions will often wish to adopt an agreed "commercial term" to define the allocation of responsibilities between the seller and the buyer regarding delivery of the goods. Such

[1] United Nations Convention on Contracts for the International Sale of Goods, Apr. 11, 1980, U.N. Doc. A/CONF. 97/18 (1980), *reprinted in* 19 I.L.M. 671 (1980) (hereinafter CISG).

terms include, for example, FOB (Free on Board), FAS (Free Alongside Ship), and CIF (Cost, Insurance and Freight). The UCC has its own definitions of such terms.[2] The CISG, on the other hand, does not have such definitions, and the CISG rules on delivery terms are quite sparse.[3] Instead of incorporating detailed rules on the subject, the drafters of the CISG were able to rely upon a written formulation of industry norms on the meaning of individual commercial delivery terms for international transactions. That written formulation is contained in "Incoterms," published by the International Chamber of Commerce (I.C.C.).[4] Indeed, as described in Section 2.3 below, the Incoterms are widely recognized as an international "usage" for international contracts under the CISG, and therefore are available to fill in gaps in the CISG's provisions.

Incoterms is an acronym for "International Commercial Terms," a set of rules first published by the I.C.C. in 1936. The Incoterms have been updated periodically since that time. The current version of Incoterms was published in 2010, and is known as "Incoterms 2010." These revisions of Incoterms have made the Incoterms definitions of commercial terms substantially different from the UCC definitions of similar terms.

§ 2.2 The Purpose of Commercial Terms

Where the goods are to be carried from one location to another as part of the sale transaction, the parties will often adopt a commercial term to state the delivery obligation of the seller. As noted in the Introduction, these terms are defined in the UCC, but the UCC definitions are seldom used intentionally in international trade. In fact, the UCC definitions are becoming obsolete in domestic trade, because they are premised primarily on water-borne traffic and do not address new business practices associated with air freight, containerization, or multi-modal transportation practices.[5]

In international commerce, the Incoterms represent by far the dominant source of definitions for commercial terms. The Incoterms provide specific rules for determining the obligations of both the seller and the buyer depending on the specific commercial term they choose (FOB, CIF, etc.). The Incoterms Rules state what acts the seller must do to deliver, what acts the buyer must do to accommo-

---

[2] UCC §§ 2–319 to 2–324.

[3] CISG, arts. 31–34. *See also* the more detailed discussion in Chapter 1, § 1.18.

[4] INCOTERMS 2010 (ICC Publ. No. 715, 2010)(hereinafter, INCOTERMS 2010).

[5] An effort at a comprehensive revision of UCC Article 2 would have deleted the commercial terms definitions entirely, but that effort failed because no state has adopted the Revised Article 2.

date delivery, what costs each party must bear, and at what point in the delivery process the risk of loss passes from the seller to the buyer. Each of these obligations may be different for different commercial terms. Thus, the obligations, costs, and risks of the seller and the buyer are different under FOB than they are under CIF.

§ 2.3 The Incoterms Rules as Trade Usages

Because the I.C.C. is a non-governmental entity, Incoterms is neither national legislation nor an international treaty. Thus, they cannot be "the governing law" of any contract. Instead, they are a written form of custom and usage in the trade, which the parties can, and often do, expressly incorporate in their international contracts for the sale of goods. Alternatively, if the Incoterms are not expressly incorporated in the contract, they nonetheless may have effect as an implicit term of the contract in the form of an international trade usage. Courts in the United States have expressly so held,[6] as have courts in France, Germany, and elsewhere.[7] This description has allowed Incoterms to qualify under the CISG as a "usage . . . which in international trade is widely known to, and regularly observed by, parties to" international sales contracts.[8]

Although, as noted, the UCC has definitions for some commercial terms (*e.g.*, F.O.B., F.A.S., C.I.F.), these definitions are expressly subject to "agreement otherwise."[9] Thus, an express reference to Incoterms will supercede the UCC provisions, and United States courts have so held.[10] Such incorporation by express reference is often made in American international sales contracts, especially in Atlantic Ocean trade. Even if a contract does not include an express reference, and the UCC is the governing law rather than CISG, Incoterms can still be applicable as a "usage of trade" under the UCC (as under the CISG).[11] The UCC criteria for such a usage is "a practice or method of dealing having such regularity of observance . . . as to justify an expectation that it will be observed with respect to

---

6 *See* BP Oil Int'l Ltd. v. Empresa Estatal Petroleos de Ecuador, 332 F.3d 333 (5th Cir. 2003); China North Chem. Indus. Corp. v. Beston Chem. Corp., 2006 WL 295395 (S.D. Tex. 2006); St. Paul Guardian Ins. Co. v. Neuromed Medical Systems & Support, GmbH, 2002 WL 465312 (S.D.N.Y. 2002); Texful Textile Ltd. v. Cotton Express Textile, Inc., 891 F. Supp. 1381 (C.D. Cal. 1995).

7 UNCITRAL DIGEST OF CASE LAW ON THE CISG (2012 ed.), art. 9, ¶19, available at http://www.uncitral.org/uncitral/en/case_law/digests/cisg.html.

8 CISG, art. 9(2).

9 UCC §§ 2–319(1)(2), 2–320(2).

10 *See, e.g.,* Phillips Puerto Rico Core, Inc. v. Tradax Petroleum Ltd., 782 F.2d 314 (2nd Cir. 1985); Animal Science Products, Inc. v. China Nat. Metals & Minerals Import & Export Corp., 702 F.Supp.2d 320, 371 n. 53 (D.N.J. 2010), *rev'd on other grounds*, 654 F.3d 462 (3rd Cir. 2011).

11 UCC § 1–303(c).

the transaction in question."[12] A usage need not be "universal" nor "ancient," just "currently observed by the great majority of decent dealers."[13] Thus, one federal court has held that a CFR term in a shipment from Ecuador to the United States implicitly incorporated the Incoterms as a usage.[14] Moreover, as noted in Section 2.5 below, the Incoterms 2010 now expressly recognize that they may be used in "both domestic and international trade."

§ 2.4 The 2010 Revision of Incoterms

Incoterms—a copyrighted work of the ICC—are periodically revised, typically about once every ten years. As noted, the last revision was in 2010 and is set forth in ICC Publication No. 715.

The 2010 revisions of the Incoterms, which formally entered into effect on January 1, 2011, were designed principally to respond to general developments in international trade and transport practices and otherwise to simplify and clarify uncertain aspects of Incoterms 2000. The revisions had two principal purposes. First, they distilled and organized the eleven defined commercial terms into two general categories: those limited to sea and inland waterway transport, and those permitted for any mode of transport. The former category includes the most frequently used terms in large international transactions, CIF and FOB, as well as more specific versions CFR (Cost and Freight) and FAS (Free Alongside Ship). The latter category includes the seven other terms that are also occasionally used in water transport, but are more common for air, land, and rail transportation.

The second principal purpose of Incoterms 2010 was to address specific legal and factual developments relating to the transportation of goods. The most significant of these was electronic communication. Thus, the new rules endorse the substitution of paper communications with an "equivalent electronic record or procedure." Moreover, they broadly embrace such electronic communications where either the parties so agree or such is "customary" in the trade.[15] This reference to trade custom is significant because it will increasingly authorize buyers and sellers to fulfill communication and documentation requirements with electronic equivalents. More-

---

[12] *Id.*

[13] *See* UCC § 1–303, comment 4.

[14] BP Oil Int'l Ltd. v. Empresa Estatal Petroleos de Ecuador (Petro Ecuador), 332 F.3d 333 (5th Cir. 2003).

[15] In each of the eleven Incoterms Rules, A1 (for the seller) and B1. (for the buyer) state that a paper document may be replaced by "an equivalent electronic record or procedure" provided only that this is "agreed between the parties or customary."

over, the new Incoterms intentionally adopted an open-ended definition of "electronic records" to permit the rules to adapt to new technologies as they arise in the future.[16]

Incoterms 2010 also expressly recognize that they may be used in "both domestic and international trade."[17] The goal of this language was to facilitate the use of Incoterms in customs-free trade zones such as the European Union (where international borders are less significant) as well as in large domestic legal systems (such as in the place of the UCC in the United States).[18]

§ 2.5 The Categories of Commercial Terms

Incoterms 2010 give the parties a menu of eleven (formerly, thirteen) different commercial terms ("Incoterms Rules") to describe the delivery obligations of the seller and the reciprocal obligations of the buyer to accommodate delivery. One can align these eleven Rules along a spectrum according to the respective responsibilities of the seller and the buyer. At one end of the spectrum would be EXW (Ex Works), under which the seller must merely make the goods available at its own place of business (or other named place);[19] at the other end would be DDP (Delivered Duty Paid), which obligates the seller to place the goods at the buyer's disposal at the destination location and to assume the responsibility and cost of both export and import customs clearance.[20] The others fall along the spectrum and thus permit the parties to choose the term that best fits their specific commercial transaction. The eleven Incoterms rules—listed alphabetically—are as follows:

1. CFR (Cost and Freight)

2. CIF (Cost, Insurance and Freight)

3. CIP (Carriage and Insurance Paid)

4. CPT (Carriage Paid To)

5. DAP (Delivered at Place)

6. DAT (Delivered at Terminal)

---

16 For more on electronic bills of lading see Chapter 3, § 3.19.

17 *See* INCOTERMS 2010, *supra* note 4, at 8.

18 *Id.*

19 *See id.*, at 15 (stating that "EXW represents the minimum obligation for the seller").

20 *See id.*, at 69 (stating that "DDP represents the maximum obligation for the seller").

7. DDP (Delivered Duty Paid)

8. EXW (Ex Works)

9. FAS (Free Alongside Ship)

10. FCA (Free Carrier)

11. FOB (Free On Board).

One may organize these eleven different terms in a variety of ways. One is a division between the one term that does not assume that a carrier will be involved (EXW), and the ten other terms. Another, noted above, is along a spectrum of responsibilities (from EXW to DDP). A third, also suggested above, is between those four terms that may only be used for water-borne transportation (FAS, FOB, CFR, CIF) and the seven other terms, which are applicable to any mode of transportation, including multi-modal transportation (CIP, CPT, DAP, DAT, DDP, EXW, and FCA). The UCC has none of the latter seven terms, even though the types of transactions they are designed for arise routinely. The parties may nonetheless be able to achieve the same results with careful adjustments to the UCC designations "F.O.B. place of shipment," "F.O.B. place of destination," "C. & F.", and "C.I.F."

The ten terms requiring transportation can also be divided into "shipment contract" terms (FCA, FAS, FOB, CFR, CIF, CPT, and CIP)—although the precise agreements of the parties may affect this—and "destination contract" terms (DAP, DAT, and DDP). The UCC and the CISG each distinguish in some form between "shipment" and "destination" contracts, although not with the same specific rules.[21] The underlying notion is that in shipment contracts the seller need merely put the goods in the hands of a carrier and arrange for their transportation, but transportation is at the buyer's risk and expense.[22] In destination contracts, in contrast, the seller is responsible for putting the goods in the hands of the carrier, arranging their transportation, and bearing the cost and risk of transportation to the named location.[23] Unfortunately, many aspects of transportation usages have changed since the UCC was drafted in 1952, and the UCC concepts do not always fit the practices that the newly updated Incoterms are able to address.

---

21 Compare UCC §§ 2–503, 2–504, and CISG, art. 31.

22 Compare UCC § 2–504.

23 Compare UCC § 2–503(1), (3).

§ 2.6 The Format of Incoterms

The Incoterms obligations are arranged in a mirror-image format that sets forth ten specific obligations in adjacent columns, with "the seller's obligations" in the left column and "the buyer's obligations" in the right. Each column has numbered paragraphs, and each numbered paragraph refers to the comparable obligation of each party. Thus, for example, for each Incoterm Rule, "A4" covers the seller's obligations regarding "delivery" and "B4" the buyer's obligations on the same subject. The other obligations covered include licenses and other formalities, contracts of carriage and insurance, risk of loss, division of costs, notices, transportation documents or equivalent electronic messages, and inspections:

A1/B1. The first set of parallel paragraphs contains a statement of the basic obligations of the seller and the buyer: The seller must deliver the goods and a commercial invoice (or its electronic equivalent), and the buyer must pay the contract price.

A2/B2. The second set of paragraphs allocates the responsibilities of the parties regarding export and import licenses, customs formalities, and (in a new reference) "security clearances."

A3/B3. The third set of paragraphs allocates the responsibilities of the parties to arrange and pay for carriage and insurance during transportation of the goods.

A4/B4. The fourth set of paragraphs specifies the extent of both the seller's delivery obligation and the buyer's obligation to take delivery.

A5/B5. The fifth set of paragraphs specifies when the risk of loss is transferred from the seller to the buyer.

A6/B6. The sixth set of paragraphs allocates the costs of transportation between the parties, including not only the freight and insurance costs already allocated in A3/B3, but also loading costs and the administrative costs of customs clearance, even when no import duties are charged.

A7/B7. The seventh set of paragraphs defines what notices each party must give to the other, when such notices must be given, and what each notice should say.

A8/B8. The eighth set of paragraphs specifies the type of transport document or other proof of delivery that the seller must provide to the buyer and the buyer's obligation to accept such a document.

A9/B9. The ninth set of paragraphs allocates who must pay the costs of packaging the goods, marking the packages, "checking operations" (quality, measuring, weighing, counting), and any preshipment inspection. It does not, however, state whether the buyer has a right to post-shipment inspection before paying for the goods.

A10/B10. Finally, the tenth set of paragraphs sets forth miscellaneous obligations, such as duties of assistance and cooperation. New in Incoterms 2010 is a requirement of cooperation by both parties regarding any "security-related information" that either may need to fulfill obligations to customs or other governmental authorities.

§ 2.7 The Incoterms Rules for Sea and Inland Waterway Transport

The following sections will address each of the Incoterms Rules. They are addressed in the two principal groupings identified by the ICC: the rules for sea and inland waterway transport, and the rules for any mode or modes of transport. Because FOB and CIF are by far the most commonly used terms in international trade, Sections 2.8 and 2.10, respectively, will provide more detail on the obligations of the parties under such terms. But note at the outset here that, although similar in some respects, the FOB and CIF terms contemplate fundamentally different transportation transactions.

§ 2.8 ____The Free on Board (FOB) Term

Under the Incoterms Free on Board (FOB) commercial term, the essential agreement between the parties is that the seller merely must deliver the goods on board a ship arranged for and identified by the buyer at a named port of (outbound) shipment. Thus, this term is appropriate only for water-borne transportation.

Like the other Incoterm Rules, the basic obligation of the seller under an FOB term is to deliver the goods and a corresponding commercial invoice "in conformity with the contract of sale," as well as any other proof of conformity the parties specified in the sales contract.[24] For its part, the buyer is obligated to pay the price of the goods as specified in the sales contract.[25] And like the other Rules, any document (such as the commercial invoice) required under the

---

[24] INCOTERMS 2010, FOB A1.

[25] INCOTERMS 2010, FOB B1.

FOB term may be in the form of an "equivalent electronic record or procedure if agreed between the parties" or such is "customary" in the trade.[26]

With respect to customs issues, the FOB term obligates the seller to obtain, "at its own risk and expense," any necessary *export* licenses and other official authorizations and to "carry out all customs formalities necessary for the export of goods."[27] The buyer thus must procure "at its own risk and expense," any *import* licenses or similar authorizations, and also take care of any customs formalities "for the import of goods and their transport through any country."[28] The seller is responsible for the costs of packaging the goods, marking the packages, "checking operations" (quality, measuring, weighing, counting), and any pre-shipment inspection mandated by export authorities.[29] Each side must also provide assistance to the other regarding any documents or information, especially "security-related information," needed to fulfill their respective obligations to customs or other governmental authorities.[30]

The seller under an FOB term must bear the costs and risks of inland transportation to the named port of shipment (that is, the outbound port, typically in the seller's home country). But it has no obligation to arrange transportation or insurance for the goods in transit after delivery at that shipment port.[31] The FOB term instead expressly places the obligation to arrange the contract for the carriage of goods on the buyer.[32] The seller "may" arrange carriage "on usual terms at the buyer's risk and expense," if requested by the buyer, or if it is "commercial practice" for the seller to do so and the buyer does not timely object.[33] But even under such circumstances, the seller may refuse to make such arrangements if it promptly so notifies the buyer.[34] Although the seller is not obligated to arrange for insurance, it must provide the buyer with any information nec-

---

26 *Id.*, second paragraph.

27 INCOTERMS 2010, FOB A2.

28 INCOTERMS 2010, FOB B2.

29 INCOTERMS 2010, FOB A9, B9.

30 INCOTERMS 2010, FOB A10, B10.

31 INCOTERMS 2010, FOB A3.

32 INCOTERMS 2010, FOB B3(a)(stating that the buyer "must contract, at its own expense[,] for the carriage of goods from the named port of shipment," unless the seller has made the carriage contract on its behalf).

33 INCOTERMS 2010, FOB A3(a).

34 *Id.*

essary to obtain insurance.[35] But, curiously, the FOB term does not obligate the buyer to make any contract of insurance.[36]

FOB A4 provides more detail on the seller's delivery obligation: The seller must deliver the goods "on board" the vessel nominated by the buyer within the time agreed and in the manner customary at the shipment port. Alternatively, the seller may "procure" rights to goods already loaded on a ship.[37] This option acknowledges the common practice of reselling goods, especially commodities, in "string sales," under which the seller obtains rights over the goods—such as by obtaining the corresponding negotiable bill of lading—when they are already in transit. In either case, the seller must notify the buyer of the delivery.[38] For its part, the FOB term obligates the buyer to notify the seller of the ship on which the goods are to be loaded[39] and accept the delivery when made.[40]

The costs and risks for the buyer and seller under an FOB term track the seller's basic obligation regarding delivery of the goods. The risk of loss or damage to the goods will pass from the seller to the buyer once the goods are "on board the vessel" (or when the seller has otherwise "procured" the goods in transit).[41] But if the buyer fails to nominate the vessel in time or the vessel is delayed in arriving, the buyer will bear the risk of loss or damage from the contractually agreed delivery time for the goods.[42]

The cost point under an FOB term is the same (decidedly unlike the CIF term discussed below[43]): The seller bears the cost of transporting the goods only "until they have been delivered in accordance with A4" (*i.e.*, until they are "on board" the vessel), and the buyer is responsible for the freight and other costs from that point on.[44] The seller is also responsible for the "checking operations" (such as quality, measuring, weighing, and counting) that are necessary for delivering the goods "on board the vessel," as well as the costs of packaging the goods "in a manner appropriate for their

---

[35] INCOTERMS 2010, FOB A3(b).

[36] INCOTERMS 2010, FOB B3(b).

[37] INCOTERMS 2010, FOB A4.

[38] INCOTERMS 2010, FOB A7. The seller must also notify the buyer if the nominated vessel is not timely available for loading. *Id.*

[39] INCOTERMS 2010, FOB B7.

[40] INCOTERMS 2010, FOB B4.

[41] INCOTERMS 2010, FOB A5, B5.

[42] INCOTERMS 2010, FOB B5.

[43] *See* § 2.10 *infra.*

[44] INCOTERMS 2010, FOB A6, B6. The seller is also responsible for any export licenses or formalities and the buyer for any import licenses or formalities. *Id.*, FOB A6(b), B6(c).

transport."[45] However, the buyer must pay the cost of any pre-shipment inspection not required by the country of export.[46] Moreover, the buyer is responsible for any additional costs that arise from its failure to nominate the vessel in time or from any delayed arrival of that ship.[47]

Because the seller has no obligations regarding the outbound carriage of the goods, its responsibility regarding the transport document are quite limited. It need merely provide to the buyer "usual proof that the goods have been delivered in accordance with A4."[48] Thus, the seller is not obligated to obtain a negotiable bill of lading covering the goods. As a result, the Incoterms FOB term is not appropriate for a "payment against documents" transaction (unless of course the parties otherwise expressly agree).

The Incoterms FOB definition has no provisions on the time and place of payment, on post-shipment inspection of the goods, or on transfer of title. These matters, therefore, must be resolved under otherwise-applicable law. In the United States, the UCC generally provides that payment is due at the time of delivery, but that the buyer has a right to inspect the goods themselves before such payment.[49] UCC Article 2 generally disdains title concepts regarding sale of goods transactions, but does provide that title generally passes when the seller completes its obligations regarding "physical delivery" of the goods.[50]

The UCC also has a definition for "F.O.B.," but that definition is divided into "F.O.B. place of shipment," "F.O.B. place of destination," and "F.O.B. vessel" varieties.[51] Only the latter—which also may be appended to either of the first two varieties—relates directly to water-borne transportation. It is most closely aligned with the Incoterms FOB term in that it also obligates the seller to deliver the goods on board the ship and does not require it to arrange transportation to a final destination.[52] Under the UCC, however, the term "F.O.B. vessel" requires the buyer to pay against a tender of docu-

---

[45] INCOTERMS 2010, FOB A9. The seller must also assist the buyer with regard to obtaining any necessary documents or information required for security clearances or for the importation of the goods. *Id.*, FOB A10.

[46] INCOTERMS 2010, FOB B9.

[47] INCOTERMS 2010, FOB B6.

[48] INCOTERMS 2010, FOB A8.

[49] UCC §§ 2–511(1), 2–513(1). For transactions governed by the CISG, see Chapter 1, §§ 1.17 through 1.22.

[50] UCC § 2–401(2). This rule applies even if the seller has reserved title in the goods or has shipped them under a document of title. *Id.*

[51] UCC § 2–319(1)(c).

[52] UCC § 2–319(1)(c).

ments, such as a negotiable bill of lading, before the goods arrive at their destination and before the buyer has any post-shipment opportunity to inspect the goods.[53] This obligation does not align at all well with the Incoterms FOB Rule.

§ 2.9 ____The Free Alongside Ship (FAS) Term

The Incoterms Free Alongside Ship (FAS) commercial term is similar to the FOB term except—as its title implies—with respect to the precise point of delivery. Under an FAS term, the seller is obligated to deliver the goods alongside a ship arranged for and named by the buyer at a named port of shipment (or, again, to "procure" rights to goods already in transit).[54] The seller must bear the costs of inland transportation to the named port of shipment.[55] The risk of loss also will transfer to the buyer at the time the goods are delivered alongside the ship.[56] The seller has no obligation to arrange transportation or insurance for the outbound (or water-borne) part of the carriage,[57] but does have a duty to notify the buyer that the goods have been delivered alongside the ship.[58] The seller must provide a commercial invoice[59] and the "usual proof" that the goods have been so delivered[60] (or an equivalent electronic record for either[61]). The seller is obligated to obtain any licenses or other approvals for export clearance, and the buyer has the same obligation regarding import clearance.[62]

Again, the Incoterms FAS definition has no provisions on payment, post-shipment inspection, or title; as noted for the FOB term above, otherwise-applicable domestic law or the CISG must provide answers to these issues.[63] Under the UCC "F.A.S. vessel" term,[64] the buyer must pay against a tender of documents, such as a negotiable bill of lading, before the goods arrive at their destination and before the buyer has any post-shipment opportunity to inspect the goods.[65] Otherwise, the UCC "F.A.S." term is similar to the Incoterms "FAS"

---

53 UCC § 2–319(4).

54 INCOTERMS 2010, FAS A4, B4.

55 INCOTERMS 2010, FAS A5, B5.

56 INCOTERMS 2010, FAS A6, B6.

57 INCOTERMS 2010, FAS A3, B3.

58 INCOTERMS 2010, FAS A7.

59 INCOTERMS 2010, FAS A1.

60 INCOTERMS 2010, FAS A8.

61 INCOTERMS 2010, FAS A1.

62 INCOTERMS 2010, FAS A2, B2.

63 *See* § 2.8 above.

64 UCC § 2–319(2).

65 UCC § 2–319(4).

term, including obligating the seller only to deliver the goods alongside a named vessel and not obligating the seller to arrange transportation to a final destination. The Incoterms FAS term does not require that the seller obtain a negotiable bill of lading or that buyer pay against documents, but also does not restrict the buyer's right of inspection before payment.

§ 2.10 The Cost, Insurance and Freight (CIF) Term

Under the Incoterms Cost, Insurance and Freight (CIF) commercial term, the seller is obligated to arrange for both transportation and insurance to a named destination port and to deliver the goods on board the ship arranged by the seller. Thus, the term also is appropriate only for water-borne transportation.

Many of the standard obligations of the seller and the buyer under a CIF term are similar to those for the FOB term. Under a CIF term, the seller also is obligated to pay the cost of the goods and provide a commercial invoice "in conformity with the contract of sale,"[66] and the buyer is obligated to pay the price as provided in the contract.[67] Again, the parties may, by agreement or by custom, use an equivalent electronic record or procedure for any required document.[68] The seller also is responsible for any license or other official authorization required for exporting the goods, and the buyer is responsible for the same issues regarding importing the goods.[69] The seller again is responsible for the costs of packaging the goods, marking the packages, "checking operations" (quality, measuring, weighing, counting), and any pre-shipment inspection mandated by export authorities.[70] And each side must provide assistance to the other regarding any documents or information, especially "security-related information," needed to fulfill their respective obligations to customs or other governmental authorities.[71]

Also similar to the FOB term, the seller under the CIF term must deliver the goods by "placing them on board the vessel" or by "procuring" goods already loaded on a ship.[72] In either case, the seller must perform its delivery obligation within the agreed time[73]

---

66 INCOTERMS 2010, CIF A1.

67 INCOTERMS 2010, CIF B1.

68 INCOTERMS 2010, CIF A1, B1.

69 INCOTERMS 2010, CIF A2, B2.

70 INCOTERMS 2010, CIF A9, B9.

71 INCOTERMS 2010, CIF A10, B10.

72 INCOTERMS 2010, CIF A4.

73 *Id.*

and provide whatever notice is required "to enable the buyer to take the goods."[74]

The risk of loss point under a CIF term also is the same as that for an FOB term. Under CIF as well, the risk of loss or damage to the goods will pass from the seller to the buyer once the seller has completed its delivery obligation, *i.e.*, when it has placed the goods "on board the vessel" at the shipment port or "procured" the goods in transit.[75] But if the buyer fails to give any required notification to the seller, the buyer will bear the risk of loss or damage from the agreed date of shipment.[76]

The striking contrast with the FOB term lies, however, in the seller's obligations regarding transport and insurance, and regarding the costs related to those obligations. Under the CIF term, the seller is obligated to conclude a contract "for the carriage of the goods from . . . the place of delivery to the named port of destination."[77] (As noted immediately above, the place of delivery most often is the shipment port.) The carriage contract must be on the "usual terms" and provide for carriage "by the usual route in a vessel of the type normally used" for the goods involved.[78] The seller also must bear the *costs* of such carriage to the destination port, including the transportation costs to and the loading costs at the shipment port.[79]

In addition, the seller is obligated to procure cargo insurance covering the goods from the point of delivery to the destination port.[80] The insurance must be from a company of "good repute," cover 110% of the contract price for the goods, and entitle the buyer to claim directly from the insurer.[81] Indeed, the 2010 Incoterms CIF Rule explicitly identifies the minimum allowed coverage with reference to the "Institute Cargo Clauses" prepared by maritime insurance carriers.[82] And, again, the seller is obligated to assume the *costs* of this insurance coverage to the destination port.[83]

---

[74] INCOTERMS 2010, CIF A7.

[75] INCOTERMS 2010, CIF A5, B5.

[76] INCOTERMS 2010, CIF B5.

[77] INCOTERMS 2010, CIF A3(a).

[78] *Id.*

[79] INCOTERMS 2010, CIF A6(a), (b).

[80] INCOTERMS 2010, CIF A3(b).

[81] *Id.*

[82] CIF A3(b) states that the minimum allowed coverage is that "provided by Clauses (C) of the Institute Cargo Clauses (LMA/IUA) or any similar clauses." *Id.* The Institute Cargo Clauses (last updated in 2009) are the product of insurance industry working groups (including the International Underwriting Association and

Thus, the CIF term establishes a system that separates the cost point from the delivery and risk of loss point. The seller must arrange and pay for the transportation to the *port of destination*, but has completed its delivery obligations when the goods are placed "on board the vessel" at the *port of shipment*. For its part, the buyer must "take delivery" of the goods at the *port of shipment*.[84] Similarly, the seller must arrange and pay for insurance during transportation to the *port of destination*, but the risk of loss transfers to the buyer at the time the goods are on board the vessel at the *port of shipment*. Thus, the buyer bears the risk of damages that occur to the goods during transit, but in the event of a loss may resort to the insurance coverage arranged and paid for by the seller. And because the seller must pay for freight and insurance to the destination port, it must take those costs into account when it quotes a price to the buyer upon the formation of the sales contract.

A second fundamental way in which the CIF term differs from the FOB term relates to the transport document the seller must obtain upon shipment of the goods. Indeed, this required transport document defines the essence of the CIF transaction as a "payment against documents" transaction. CIF A8 first states the basic obligation of the seller to provide the buyer "with the usual transport document for the agreed port of destination."[85] But the most important obligation of the seller lies in the description of the details for this transport document. In specific, the second paragraph of CIF A8 declares that the document must (a) "cover the contract goods," (b) "enable the buyer to claim the goods from the carrier at the port of destination," and (c) unless the parties agree otherwise, "enable the buyer to sell the goods in transit by the transfer of the document to a subsequent buyer or by notification to the carrier."[86]

The last requirement on this list the most important. As a practical matter, the only secure way for the seller to "enable the buyer to sell the goods in transit" as described there is to obtain a *negotiable* bill of lading from the carrier and to tender that negotiable document to the buyer through a series of banks. The banks will allow the buyer to obtain possession of the document (and thus con-

---

the Lloyds Market Association) and define levels of insurance coverage that include "(C)-Minimum cover," through "(B)-Intermediate cover," and "(A)-All Risks."

[83] INCOTERMS 2010, CIF A6(c). In addition, the seller must provide, at the buyer's "request, risk and expense," any information that the buyer needs to obtain additional insurance. CIF A3(b).

[84] INCOTERMS 2010, CIF B4. The buyer is also obligated to "receive" the goods "from the carrier at the named port of destination." *Id.*

[85] INCOTERMS 2010, CIF A8, first paragraph.

[86] *Id.*, second paragraph.

trol over the goods) only after it pays for the goods. Thus, the buyer "pays against documents," most often while the goods are still on the ship at sea. The buyer, therefore, will have to pay without an opportunity to inspect the goods themselves, although it will have a right to inspect the bill of lading to ensure that it is in conformity with the sales contract.[87] And after such payment, only a negotiable bill of lading—as Chapter 3 below describes in greater detail[88]—will "represent the goods" in a way that will permit the buyer to sell them "by the transfer of the document to a subsequent buyer."[89] In contrast, as the ICC Guide to Incoterms 2010 declares, a nonnegotiable bill—aka an ocean waybill or sea waybill, among other names—"cannot be used . . . for transferring rights to the goods by the transfer of the document."[90]

The Incoterms CIF Rule again does not address issues of the formal title to the goods themselves, as federal courts have expressly recognized.[91] Nonetheless, upon issuance of a negotiable bill of lading covering the goods, the person properly in possession of the bill (the "holder," again see Chapter 3[92]) will obtain title to the goods as well.[93] The Incoterms CIF definition also has no *express* provisions on either payment or post-shipment inspection of the goods. But again, because the nature of the CIF term contemplates a "payment against documents" transaction, the buyer as a practical matter will have to pay upon presentation of the negotiable bill of lading and without an opportunity to inspect the goods.

The UCC also has a definition of "C.I.F.," which requires the buyer to "make payment against tender of the required documents."[94] The UCC "C.I.F." term is otherwise similar to Incoterms CIF, in that it requires the seller to deliver the goods to the carrier at the port of shipment and bear the risk of loss only to that port,

---

[87] INCOTERMS 2010, CIF B8 (stating that the buyer is obligated to accept the transport document as long as it is "in conformity with the contract").

[88] *See* in particular § 3.3.

[89] INCOTERMS 2010, CIF A8, second paragraph. A less secure alternative that would "enable the buyer to sell the goods in transit . . . by notification to the carrier" is to obtain a nonnegotiable document with an *irrevocable* designation of the buyer or its bank as consignee.

[90] *See* Jan Ramberg, ICC GUIDE TO INCOTERMS 2010, at 72–73 (ICC Publ. No. 720E, 2010). Regarding this nature of a nonnegotiable bill of lading see Chapter 3, § 3.2.

[91] *See, e.g.,* Italverde Trading, Inc. v. Four Bills of Lading, 485 F. Supp. 2d 187, 200 (E.D.N.Y. 2007)("CIF within the meaning of the Incoterms does not govern change in title."): St. Paul Guardian Ins. Co. v. Neuromed Medical Systems & Support, GmbH, 2002 WL 465312, at *4 (S.D.N.Y. 2002)(same).

[92] *See* Chapter 3, § 3.3.

[93] *See* Federal Bill of Lading Act, 49 U.S.C. § 80105(a), and UCC § 7–502(a)(2).

[94] UCC § 2–320(4).

but it also requires the seller to pay the freight and insurance costs to the port of destination.[95]

§ 2.11 The Cost and Freight (CFR) Term

The Incoterms Cost and Freight (CFR) commercial term is similar to the CIF term, except that the seller has no obligations with respect to either arranging or paying for insurance coverage of the goods during transportation. Under the CFR term, the seller is obligated to arrange for transportation to a named destination point and then to deliver the goods on board the ship arranged for by the seller (or to "procure" rights to the goods already in transit).[96] Thus, the term is appropriate only for water-borne transportation.

The seller must arrange the transportation and pay the freight costs to the *destination port*,[97] but has completed its delivery obligations when the goods are placed "on board the vessel" at the *port of shipment*.[98] The seller has no express obligation to arrange or pay for insurance on the goods during transportation,[99] and the risk of loss transfers to the buyer at the time the goods are on board the vessel at the *port of shipment*.[100] The seller must give the buyer any notice needed to enable the buyer to take the goods and the buyer must notify the seller of any specific required location at the destination port.[101] The seller also is responsible for any license or other official authorization required for the exportation of the goods, and the buyer is responsible for the same issues regarding the importation of the goods.[102] The seller must provide a commercial invoice and "the usual transport document" for the destination port (or an equivalent electronic record for either).[103] Finally, like the CIF term, the seller under a CFR term must procure a transport document that will "enable the buyer to sell the goods in transit by the transfer of the document to a subsequent buyer or by notification to the carrier."[104]

As with CIF, the Incoterms CFR definition has no provisions on either payment or post-shipment inspection. However, like CIF, the

---

95 UCC § 2–320(1), (2).

96 INCOTERMS 2010, CFR A1, A4.

97 INCOTERMS 2010, CFR A3(a), A6.

98 INCOTERMS 2010, CFR A4.

99 INCOTERMS 2010, CFR A3(b).

100 INCOTERMS 2010, CFR A5, B5.

101 INCOTERMS 2010, CFR A7, B7.

102 INCOTERMS 2010, CFR A2, B2.

103 INCOTERMS 2010, CFR A1.

104 INCOTERMS 2010, CFR A8.

practical requirement of a negotiable bill of lading will mean that a CFR term will involve a payment against documents transaction. Both the UCC[105] and prior versions of Incoterms regarded this term as requiring payment against documents while the goods were still at sea, thus restricting port-shipment inspection of the goods before payment. The same norm should continue to apply under the 2010 version of Incoterms CFR.

§ 2.12 The Incoterms Rules for Any Mode or Modes of Transport

As noted in Sections 2.8 through 2.11 above, the Incoterms FOB, FAS, CIF, and CFR Rules are appropriate only for "sea and inland waterway transport." But the Incoterms also include Rules that are available for any mode of transport, including multi-modal transportation. The following Sections will describe the seven Rules that fall in this category (CIP, CPT, DAP, DAT, DDP, EXW, and FCA).

§ 2.13 ____The Ex Works (EXW) Term

Under the Incoterms Ex Works (EXW) commercial term, the seller must only tender the goods by placing them "at the disposal of the buyer" at an agreed point. But if there is no agreed point, the seller "may select the point that best suits its purpose," and this most often will be its own premises. Thus, the seller has no obligation to deliver the goods to a carrier or to load the goods on any vehicle. Indeed, the seller is not even obligated to arrange for any licenses or authorizations necessary for export.[106] In short, the EXW term "represents the minimum obligation of the seller" and thus "should be used with care."[107] It is best suited for those sellers who are new to international export transactions where the buyer has substantial experience and expertise.

The seller has no obligation to arrange for transportation or insurance,[108] but must give the buyer any notice necessary for it to take delivery of the goods.[109] The seller must provide a commercial invoice, or an equivalent electronic record, but has no obligation to obtain a document of title (or any other transport document).[110] The

---

[105] *See* UCC § 2–320(3)(referring to a "C&F" term that in most respects is functionally equivalent to the Incoterms CFR Rule).

[106] INCOTERMS 2010, EXW, A2, B2.

[107] INCOTERMS 2010, EXW, at 15.

[108] INCOTERMS 2010, EXW, A3.

[109] INCOTERMS 2010, EXW, A7.

[110] INCOTERMS 2010, EXW, A1, A8.

Incoterms definition has no effect upon either payment or inspection rights under the contract (although of course the buyer must assume any costs of pre-shipment inspection). The risk of loss transfers to the buyer at the time the goods are placed at the buyer's disposal.[111] This rule is contrary to the default rules of both the UCC and the CISG, which delay passing the risk in a non-delivery transaction until the buyer's actual receipt of the goods,[112] because the seller is more likely to have insurance and because the seller has a greater ability to protect the goods.

§ 2.14 The Free Carrier (FCA) Term

Under the Incoterms Free Carrier (FCA) commercial term, the seller is obligated to deliver the goods, cleared for export, into the custody of a carrier nominated by the buyer, usually the first carrier in a multi-modal transportation scheme.[113] The seller has no obligation to pay for transportation costs or insurance.[114] However, the seller "may" arrange transportation at the buyer's expense if requested by the buyer, or if it is "commercial practice" for the seller to do so and the buyer does not timely object.[115] But even under these circumstances, the seller may refuse to make such arrangements as long as it so notifies the buyer. Even if the seller does arrange transportation, it has no obligation to arrange for insurance coverage during transportation.[116]

The seller completes its delivery obligation when the goods have been loaded at its premises on the transport arranged by the buyer or otherwise put into the custody of the carrier or other person nominated by the buyer.[117] The seller then need only notify the buyer when the goods have been so delivered.[118] The risk of loss transfers to the buyer upon such delivery, although the buyer may not receive notice until after that time.[119] The seller must provide a commercial invoice or an equivalent electronic record, any necessary export license, and "the usual proof that the goods have been delivered."[120] The Incoterms definition has no provisions on either payment or post-shipment inspection.

---

[111] INCOTERMS 2010, EXW, A5, B5.

[112] *See* UCC § 2–509(3) and CISG, *supra* note 1, art. 69.

[113] INCOTERMS 2010, FCA, A2, A4.

[114] INCOTERMS 2010, FCA, A6.

[115] INCOTERMS 2010, FCA, A3(a).

[116] INCOTERMS 2010, FCA, A3(b).

[117] INCOTERMS 2010, FCA, A4.

[118] INCOTERMS 2010, FCA, A7.

[119] INCOTERMS 2010, FCA, A5, B5.

[120] INCOTERMS 2010, FCA, A1, A2, A8.

This FCA term is the Incoterms commercial term that is most comparable to the UCC's "F.O.B. place of shipment" term under § 2–319(1)(a). However, there are two levels of confusion. One is that Incoterms has its own "FOB" term, which is different; this creates a risk of a false comparison between the UCC "F.O.B." term and the Incoterms "FOB" term. The other is that the obligations under FCA and the UCC "F.O.B. place of shipment" term are, in fact, different. Under the UCC's "F.O.B. place of shipment" term, the seller must arrange transportation[121] while the seller need do so under Incoterms FCA only by special agreement. Further, under the UCC, the seller under an F.O.B. place of shipment term must also "obtain and promptly deliver . . . any document necessary to enable the buyer to obtain possession of the goods."[122] Under Incoterms FCA, the seller need merely provide, at the buyer's request, "assistance" in obtaining a transport document.[123]

§ 2.15 ___The Carriage and Insurance Paid To (CIP) Term

The Incoterms Carriage and Insurance To Paid (CIP) and Carriage Paid To (CPT) commercial terms are similar to its CIF and CFR terms, except that they may be used for any type of transportation, including multimodal transportation (and thus not just for waterborne transportation). The CIP term is the analog to the CIF term. Under the CIP term, the seller is obligated to arrange[124] and pay for[125] both transportation and insurance to a named *destination* place. However, the seller completes its delivery obligations by handing the goods over to the carrier at the place of *shipment* within the agreed time.[126] The risk of loss likewise passes to the buyer upon delivery to the first carrier at the place of *shipment*.[127] Thus, unlike CIF, the CIP term is appropriate for multimodal transportation and for container transport.

Under CIP, the seller must notify the buyer that the goods have been delivered to the first carrier, and also give any other notice required to enable the buyer "to take the goods."[128] The seller must provide a commercial invoice, or an equivalent electronic record, any necessary export license, and "the usual transport docu-

---

[121] UCC §§ 3–319(1), 2–504.

[122] UCC § 2–504(b).

[123] INCOTERMS 2010, FCA, A8.

[124] INCOTERMS 2010, CIP, A3.

[125] INCOTERMS 2010, CIP, A6.

[126] INCOTERMS 2010, CIP, A4.

[127] INCOTERMS 2010, CIP, A5, B5.

[128] INCOTERMS 2010, CIP, A7.

ment."[129] But—unlike CIF—the seller is obligated to obtain a document that would "enable the buyer to sell the goods in transit" (such as a negotiable bill of lading) *only if* this is "agreed or customary."[130] Thus, unless the parties expressly agree to a "payment against documents" term or a special trade usage exists, the CIP commercial term does not require payment against documents or restrict inspection rights before payment. These Incoterms definitions contain no other payment or post-shipment inspection provisions. As with all of the other seven Incoterms rules that apply for any mode of transport, the UCC does not recognize a CIP or CPT term.

§ 2.16 ___The Carriage Paid (CPT) Term

The Incoterms Carriage To Paid (CPT) is the analog to the CFR term, except that, again, it may be used for any type of transportation, including multimodal transportation. Under the CPT term, the seller is obligated to arrange[131] and pay for[132] transportation to a named *destination* place. However, the seller completes its delivery obligations by handing the goods over to the carrier at the place of *shipment* within the agreed time.[133] The risk of loss likewise passes to the buyer upon delivery to the first carrier at the place of *shipment*.[134] Thus, the CPT term, like the CIP term, is appropriate for multimodal transportation and for container transport. The seller completes its delivery obligations,[135] and the risk of loss passes to the buyer, upon delivery to the first carrier at the place of *shipment*.[136]

But unlike the CIP term, under a CPT term the seller has no obligation to arrange or pay for insurance on the goods during transportation.[137] In other words, CPT has the same relationship to CIP that CFR has to CIF. The difference is that, because the seller under a CIP/CPT term completes its delivery obligation by "handing [the goods] over to the carrier" (and not by loading them on a waterborne vessel), these two terms—unlike CIF/CFR—are appropriate for multimodal transportation and for container transport.

---

129 INCOTERMS 2010, CIP, A1, A2, A8.

130 INCOTERMS 2010, CIP, A8.

131 INCOTERMS 2010, CPT, A3(a).

132 INCOTERMS 2010, CPT, A6.

133 INCOTERMS 2010, CPT, A4.

134 INCOTERMS 2010, CPT, A5, B5.

135 INCOTERMS 2010, CPT, A4.

136 INCOTERMS 2010, CPT, A5, B5.

137 INCOTERMS 2010, CPT A3(b).

The remaining rules for the CPT term are the same as those for CIP. Thus, the seller must provide a commercial invoice, or an equivalent electronic record, any necessary export license, and "the usual transport document," and then notify the buyer that the goods have been delivered.[138] Also, unlike CFR, the seller under a CPT term is obligated to obtain a document that would "enable the buyer to sell the goods in transit" *only if* such is "agreed or customary."[139] Thus, unless the parties expressly agree to a "payment against documents" term or a special trade usage exists, the CPT commercial term does not require payment against documents or restrict inspection rights before payment.

§ 2.17 ___The Delivered at Place (DAP) Term

The Incoterms 2010 have two new terms, DAP (Delivered at Place) and DAT (Delivered at Terminal), which replace four former terms (DES, DEQ, DAF, and DDU). Both can again be used for any type of transportation, including multimodal transport. In both, the seller is required to arrange transportation, pay the freight costs, and bear the risk of loss to a named destination point. Although these definitions have no provisions on insurance during transportation, because the seller bears the risk of loss during transport, it is well-advised to arrange and pay for insurance or it otherwise will act as a self-insurer. There are also no provisions on payment or post-shipment inspection; but the DAP term also does not require that the seller procure a negotiable bill of lading. Thus, there is no reason to imply a "payment against documents" requirement if none is expressly stated. On the other hand, the parties (as always) are free to agree expressly on both a destination commercial term and a payment against documents term.

Under the Incoterms DAP term, the seller bears the responsibility, costs, and risks of delivering the goods at the destination specified in the contract.[140] The seller completes its delivery obligations under DAP when the goods reach the named place and are placed "at the disposal of the buyer on the arriving means of transport ready for unloading" by the buyer.[141] Thus, the seller is obligated to arrange and pay for transportation to the named destination port and (although not obligated) is well advised to arrange and pay for insurance on the goods during transportation.[142] The risk of loss also will transfer to the buyer when the seller completes

---

[138] INCOTERMS 2010, CPT, A1, A2, A7, A8.

[139] INCOTERMS 2010, CPT, A8.

[140] INCOTERMS 2010, DAP, A3, A4, A5, A6.

[141] INCOTERMS 2010, DAP, A4.

[142] INCOTERMS 2010, DAP, A3, A6.

its delivery obligation at the named destination.[143] The seller must clear the goods for export and for transport "through any country prior to delivery," but is not responsible for import duties or other import formalities.[144] The seller, finally, must provide to the buyer any document necessary to enable the buyer to take the goods.[145]

§ 2.18 The Delivered at Terminal (DAT) Term

The Incoterms DAT rule is similar to DAP, for the seller again bears the responsibility, costs, and risks of delivering the goods to the terminal at the location specified in the contract.[146] Unlike DAP, however, the seller also is responsible for unloading the goods from the arriving means of transport.[147] The seller completes its delivery obligations when the goods are unloaded from the arriving means of transport and are placed at the disposal of the buyer "at the named terminal" at the place of destination.[148] Terminal includes all forms of terminals (whether quay, container or rail yard, or road, rail, or air terminal). The risk of loss also passes to the buyer at that point.[149] Like DAP, the seller is responsible for export clearance and for clearance through any country along the way to the delivery terminal, but is not responsible for import duties or other import formalities.[150] Finally, the seller must again provide to the buyer any document necessary to enable the buyer to take the goods.[151]

The DAT term is especially valuable for sellers who wish to control their supply chain in order to signal reliability to customers, control costs, and maintain quality of the goods. Sellers of this type also may wish to rely on established relationships with freight forwarders or carriers or to ship their goods to multiple customers under a single bill of lading or in a single container.

§ 2.19 The Delivered Duty Paid (DDP) Term

The final Incoterm rule, DDP (Delivered Duty Paid), places the highest level of responsibility on the seller (and thus the lowest responsibility on the buyer).[152] Under the DDP commercial term, de-

---

143 INCOTERMS 2010, DAP, A5.

144 INCOTERMS 2010, DAP, A2.

145 INCOTERMS 2010, DAP, A8.

146 INCOTERMS 2010, DAT, A3, A4, A5, A6.

147 INCOTERMS 2010, DAT, A4.

148 *Id.*

149 INCOTERMS 2010, DAT, A5.

150 INCOTERMS 2010, DAT, A2.

151 INCOTERMS 2010, DAT, A8.

152 *See* INCOTERMS 2010, *supra* note 4, at 69 (stating that "DDP represents the maximum obligation for the seller").

livery occurs and the risk of loss passes when the goods are placed at the buyer's disposal, "ready for unloading," at the named place in the country of destination.[153] The buyer's only noteworthy responsibility is to arrange and pay for the unloading of the goods from the arriving means of transport.[154]

But unlike all other Incoterms Rules, the seller under a DDP term not only is responsible for export clearance, but also must deliver the goods to the buyer cleared for importation into the destination country.[155] Thus, the seller must obtain the import license, pay all import duties and terminal charges, and complete all customs formalities at its risk and expense.[156] The seller must again provide to the buyer any document necessary to enable the buyer to take the goods at the named destination.[157] The closest UCC commercial term is "F.O.B. destination,"[158] but it lacks substantial detail as compared to the Incoterms DDP term.

---

[153] INCOTERMS 2010, DDP, A4, A5.

[154] INCOTERMS 2010, DDP, B6.

[155] INCOTERMS 2010, DDP, A2.

[156] INCOTERMS 2010, DDP, A2, A3, A6.

[157] INCOTERMS 2010, DDP, A8.

[158] UCC § 2–319(1)(b).

Chapter 3

BILLS OF LADING

Table of Sections

§ 3.1 Introduction to Bills of Lading

Bills of lading play a significant, indeed essential, role in international sales transactions. A bill of lading is a document issued by a carrier upon receipt of goods from a shipper (commonly, the seller in a sales transaction). Such a document serves three independent, but related functions:

(1) It first serves as the shipper's contract of carriage with the carrier. This contract sets forth the terms under which the carrier undertakes to transport the goods and either expressly includes the carrier's tariffs or incorporates them by reference;

(2) A contract of bailment, which serves as a receipt given by the carrier to the shipper describing the goods received from the shipper; and

(3) A document of title covering the goods.[1]

Bills of lading make it possible to have a cash international sales transaction without a letter of credit issued by a bank. This is typically accomplished through the use of a "negotiable" bill of lading and a series of collecting banks. The banks will act on behalf of the shipper and require that the buyer pay the price in full as a condition to delivery of physical possession of the negotiable bill of lading. Because it serves as a special form of a document of title covering the goods, presentation of such a bill is a requirement for the carrier's delivery of the goods to the buyer.

The common law and both state and federal law recognize two different types of bills of lading: a nonnegotiable (or "straight") bill of lading, and a negotiable (or "order") bill of lading. These are also known in the trade as "white" and "yellow" for the different colors of paper on which they are often printed. They are specifically described below in Sections 3.2 and 3.3. The following Sections then examine the essential role of negotiable bills of lading in "payment against documents" transactions and the special risks for buyers and sellers that highlight that essential role.[2]

State, federal, and international law all have rules governing bills of lading. Uniform Commercial Code Article 7 (as revised in 2003) broadly regulates "Documents of Title," including bills of lading. But the regulation of bills of lading, and in particular the relationship of the carrier to its customers, also is the subject of four international conventions and three U.S. federal statutes. Until recently, only three conventions—the so-called Hague Rules, Hague/Visby Rules, and Hamburg Rules—were in existence, each of which was progressively more customer-oriented. The multiplicity of treaties governing the terms and usage of bills of lading created actual conflicts in the legal concepts that may apply to a single transaction. Concerns about these conflicts thus led to the negotiation and conclusion of an entirely new treaty, the so-called "Rotterdam Rules," and as of 2013 there are positive signs that the United States will adopt this treaty. These international conventions are the subject of the analysis in Section 3.10 below.

---

1 *See* Kawasaki Kisen Kaisha Ltd. v. Regal-Beloit Corp., ___ U.S. ___, 130 S. Ct. 2433, 2439 (2010)(stating that a bill of lading "records that a carrier has received goods from the party that wishes to ship them, states the terms of carriage, and serves as evidence of the contract for carriage")(*quoting* Norfolk Southern R. Co. v. James N. Kirby, 543 U.S. 14, 18–19 (2004)).

2 *See* §§ 3.6–3.9 *infra*.

As of 2013, however, the United States has accepted only the Hague Rules, which it has enacted into domestic law as the Carriage of Goods by Sea Act (COGSA).[3] The United States also has in force more limited pre-COGSA legislation, the Harter Act, which governs certain narrow aspects of the domestic transport of goods.[4] The most important federal law regulating bills of lading, however, is the Federal Bills of Lading Act (FBLA, also known by its earlier name, the Pomerene Act).[5] Sections 3.11 through 3.14 below will examine in detail these various U.S. laws governing bills of lading.

The fundamental function of a negotiable bill of lading lies in its status as a legal embodiment of the rights to the goods described therein. This status ensures that the carrier delivers ("turns out") the goods only according to the nature and terms of the bill of lading covering those goods. But the status also provides the material for the three most common disputes over bills of lading: (a) misdelivery of the goods by the carrier; (b) misdescription of the goods in the bill of lading; and (c) forgery of necessary signatures on the bill of lading. Sections 3.15 through 3.18 below will examine these disputes in detail.

Shippers and carriers also use a variety of specialized terms to describe specific aspects of bills of lading. Thus, for example, they often refer to an "on board" bill of lading. An "on board" or "loaded" bill of lading is issued once the goods have been loaded on board the vessel bound for the required destination. A "clean" bill of lading is one that has no clause or notation on its face indicating visible or possible defects in the packaging or condition of the goods. Simple comments regarding amount, weight, or other descriptions provided by the shipper will not, however, "foul" the bill of lading, provided that they do not incorporate other documents indicating defects in the cargo.

In addition, the parties can negotiate either a "through" bill of lading, or a "multimodal" or "combined transport" bill of lading. Such forms involve an agreement by the carrier to transport and deliver the goods to their final destination using any required connecting carriers (such as railroads, trucks, and air carriers). In such

---

3 COGSA is now in a statutory note to 46 U.S.C. § 30701.

4 46 U.S.C. § 30701 et seq.

5 49 U.S.C. § 80101 et seq.

a case, a single bill of lading may govern all of the links in the transportation chain.[6]

Finally, this area of law, like many others, is entering into the electronic age. Electronic substitutes for nonnegotiable bills of lading have been in use for about two decades and have proved to be successful. However, electronic substitutes for negotiable bills of lading have been less successful and are still in the developmental stage. Section 3.19 below will examine the progress toward the use of such electronic bills of lading.

§ 3.2 Nonnegotiable ("Straight") Bills of Lading

A nonnegotiable, or "straight," bill of lading is a receipt for the goods, and serves as a contract with the carrier stating the terms and conditions of carriage. A straight bill of lading is issued to a named person, the consignee.[7] Under the FBLA, a straight bill of lading is one stating that "the goods are to be delivered to a consignee."[8] The FBLA also obligates a carrier issuing such a bill to state "nonnegotiable" or "not negotiable" on the bill of lading itself.[9]

Straight bills of lading are not negotiable documents. As a result, an indorsement on a straight bill of lading does not make the bill negotiable or give any rights to the transferee.[10]

Possession of the actual straight bill of lading also does not confer rights over the goods or against the carrier to a person in possession of the paper. Instead, the carrier is obligated to deliver only to the consignee named on the nonnegotiable bill;[11] in fact, the consignee does not need to be in possession of the bill of lading or produce the document in order to obtain the goods from the carrier.[12]

---

[6] *See* Kawasaki Kisen Kaisha Ltd. v. Regal-Beloit Corp., ___ U.S. ___, 130 S. Ct. 2433, 2439 (2010)(observing that "[a] through bill of lading covers both the ocean and inland portions of the transport in a single document"). *See also* UCC § 7–302(a).

[7] 49 U.S.C. § 80101(1)(defining a consignee as "the person named in a bill of lading as the person to whom the goods are to be delivered").

[8] 49 U.S.C. § 80103(b)(1). *See also* UCC § 7–104(b).

[9] 49 U.S.C. § 80103(b)(2).

[10] 49 U.S.C. § 80103(b)(1)(A), (B).

[11] 49 U.S.C. § 80110(a)(stating that "the carrier must deliver goods covered by a bill of lading on demand of the consignee named in a nonnegotiable bill"); *id.*, § 80110(b)(2)(stating that the carrier "may deliver the goods covered by a bill of lading to . . . the consignee named in a nonnegotiable bill").

[12] *See, e.g.,* Quanzhou Joerga Fashion Co., Inc. v. Brooks Fitch Quanzhou Joerga Fashion Co., Inc. v. Brooks Fitch Apparel Group, LLC, 2012 WL 4767180 (S.D.N.Y. 2012)(stating that for a nonnegotiable bill of lading "production of the original bill is not actually a precondition to the delivery of the goods"). For a discussion of earlier such cases see Felix W.H. Chan, *A Plea for Certainty: Legal and Practical*

But because the carrier fulfills its duty under the straight bill of lading only by delivering and transferring title to the goods to the consignee, the carrier is liable if it delivers to any other person.[13] The shipper of the goods (often, the seller) can even change its mind at any time prior to the delivery of the goods and stop delivery or reroute delivery to another party by so instructing the carrier. Nonetheless, some courts have noted that the carrier also may deliver according to the specific instructions of the consignee, even if not to the consignee itself.[14]

Straight bills of lading are commonly used between related parties or merchants with established business relationships as it is the simplest method of conducting business. Similarly, such bills of lading are often used in container transport, on short sea routes, and for air transport where the goods are likely to arrive as soon as the bill of lading. Straight bills of lading are also called "air waybills," "sea waybills" and "freight receipts," depending upon the intended method of main transportation for the goods. In fact, the sea waybill is the European equivalent to the U.S. straight bill of lading. Such nonnegotiable receipts also may be used under specific Incoterms (most notably, FOB and FAS) where no requirement of a transferrable document exists.[15]

§ 3.3 Negotiable ("Order") Bills of Lading

A negotiable, or "order," bill of lading also serves as (1) a contract with the carrier, (2) a receipt for the goods, and, especially, (3) a document of title for the goods. For such a bill of lading, physical possession is essential to determining the rights to the goods and the delivery obligations of the carrier.

Under the FBLA, a bill of lading is negotiable if it states that the goods are to be delivered "to the order of a consignee,"[16] unless

---

Problems in the Presentation of Nonnegotiable Bills of Lading, 29 HONG KONG L.J. 44, 52 (1999).

[13] 49 U.S.C. § 80111(a)(1).

[14] *See, e.g.*, PolyGram Group Distrib., Inc. v. Transus, Inc., 990 F. Supp. 1454, 1459 (N.D. Ga. 1997)(holding that delivery to a street address specified as consignee's place of business on a straight bill of lading along with the signature of a general contractor working at that address satisfied delivery requirements imposed by the bill of lading).

[15] *See* INCOTERMS 2010, at 10 (ICC Publ. No. 715, 2010)(stating that "with EXW, FCA, FAS and FOB the delivery document may simply be a receipt").

[16] 49 U.S.C. § 80103(a)(1)(a). *See also* UCC § 7–104(a). UCC Article 7 expressly recognizes a negotiable bill of lading in "bearer" form (*see* § 7–104(a)), but the FBLA does not refer to such a possibility. A bearer bill of lading is one made out simply to "bearer" and may be transferred by delivery alone. Thus, anyone in possession may demand delivery of the goods from the carrier. Because of the inherent risks of such a

the bill states "on its face" that it is not negotiable.[17] With the words "to the order of," a bill of lading creates a power of transfer ("negotiation")—that is, a power to give an "order" to the carrier—in favor of the named consignee. As a result, the consignee has the power to transfer rights over the goods by transferring the bill of lading and thereby to "order" the carrier to deliver to the transferee.[18]

The consignee exercises its power of negotiation by delivering possession of the bill along with its "indorsement."[19] An indorsement may be made in two ways: (1) "in blank," that is, with the bare signature ("*Michael Van Alstine*"); or (2) by a "special indorsement," which identifies the next intended holder by name ("Deliver the goods to Ralph Folsom, or order. *Michael Van Alstine*").[20] In either case, a proper negotiation will make the transferee a "holder," that is, a person entitled to demand delivery from the carrier.[21] With a blank indorsement, any person in possession becomes a "holder." With a special indorsement, in contrast, only the named indorsee (if in possession) becomes the holder, and only that person can demand delivery from the carrier (or indorse the bill of lading to still another party so as to make it the holder).[22] And only the original consignee (or a subsequent holder) can make its own indorsement—a forgery (however well made) of the holder's signature is not effective as an indorsement.[23] Thus, the special indorsement protects the interests of the parties from thieves and forgers much better than a blank indorsement.

By obtaining possession of the actual negotiable bill of lading, properly indorsed over to it, a person becomes the holder and acquires rights over the goods and against the carrier.[24] In turn, the carrier is liable to the holder of a negotiable bill of lading for misdelivery if it delivers the goods to anyone but the holder.[25] Thus, possession of the negotiable bill of lading becomes crucial. The carrier

---

practice, negotiable bills of lading issued to "bearer" are substantially less common in international transactions.

[17] 49 U.S.C. § 80103(a)(1)(a).

[18] *See* 49 U.S.C. § 80101(5)(defining an "order" as "an order by indorsement on a bill of lading").

[19] 49 U.S.C. § 80104(a)(1).

[20] *Id.*

[21] 49 U.S.C. § 80101(4)(defining a "holder" as "a person having possession of, and a property right in, a bill of lading").

[22] 49 U.S.C. § 80110(b).

[23] *See* Adel Precision Products Corp. v. Grand Trunk Western R. Co., 332 Mich. 519, 51 N.W.2d 922 (1952). For a more detailed analysis of a forgery on a bill of lading see §§ 3.16 and 3.18 *infra*.

[24] 49 U.S.C. § 80110(a).

[25] 49 U.S.C. § 80113(a).

must see the actual bill of lading to confirm that the person demanding the goods has possession of the bill and that the bill has the proper chain of indorsements over to that person. It is in this sense that the negotiable bill of lading is an especially secure "document of title," because possession of it, properly indorsed to the possessor, controls title to the document, title to the goods, and the direct obligation of the carrier to deliver the goods only to the holder.[26]

A negotiable bill of lading retains its status as a transferrable document of title regardless of the number of transferees. Thus, a transferee by negotiation ("holder") from the original consignee has the power to "negotiate" the bill of lading to a further transferee. With transfer of possession and a further proper indorsement, the downstream transferee will then become the "holder" of the bill. Once again, this act of negotiation vests in the new holder the rights over the goods and against the carrier with regard to the delivery of those goods.

The holder of a negotiable bill of lading does not obtain absolute title to the goods in all cases, but nearly so. The FBLA provides that upon a proper negotiation the transferee acquires the title to the goods that the transferor "had the ability to convey to a purchaser in good faith for value."[27] Thus, if the consignee was not the owner of the goods in the first place—for example if a thief originally stole the goods from the "true owner" at gunpoint—then no holder of the bill of lading will have title to the goods because the shipper's claim of title was "void" from the beginning. However, if the owner voluntarily parted with the goods but was defrauded by the shipper, then the shipper obtains "voidable" title and can pass good title to a holder of the document who purchases it in good faith for value without notice.[28] The rights of such a good faith holder for value are also superior to any seller's lien or right to stop delivery of the goods in transit.[29]

Some commercial nations recognize only straight bills of lading and not negotiable bills of lading, but most commentators believe the U.S. system of recognizing both types of bills of lading is prefer-

---

[26] 49 U.S.C. §§ 80105(a), 80110(b). For a more detailed examination of the delivery obligations of the carrier, and thus its liability for "misdelivery," see § 3.16 *infra*.

[27] 49 U.S.C. § 80105(a).

[28] The FBLA does not define the "purchaser in good faith for value." The UCC, in contrast, provides more detailed guidance on the notion of a good faith purchaser of a bill of lading. *See* UCC § 7–503(a) (with reference to § 2–403).

[29] 49 U.S.C. § 80105(b).

able. And as described below, a negotiable bill of lading is an essential component of the "payment against documents" transaction[30] as well as the commercial letter of credit transaction,[31] and is required for Incoterms CIF and CFR contracts (among others).[32]

§ 3.4 The Payment against Documents Transaction

How does the "payment against documents" transaction work? When the buyer and the seller are forming their contract for the sale of the goods, the seller will insist that the buyer "pay against the documents," rather than after delivery and inspection of the goods themselves. Such a payment term must be bargained for and expressed in the sales contract. As discussed in Chapter 2, an agreement also may arise from the nature of specific commercial terms (such as CIF and CFR). But it otherwise will not normally be implied. Such an arrangement often is especially important to a seller in an international transaction. If the buyer rejects the goods after international shipment, the seller is left with goods at a foreign location and with no payment from the buyer. Its options are then limited to assuming the expense and hassle of a return shipment or a distress sale at the foreign port.

If the parties' contract includes a "payment against documents" arrangement, the seller will pack the goods and prepare a commercial invoice. If the commercial term requires it (*e.g.*, under a CIF term[33]), the seller will also procure an insurance certificate (another form of contract) covering the goods in transit. The seller then delivers the goods to the carrier, which issues a bill of lading and designates to whom the goods should be delivered. In the case of a negotiable bill of lading, it will require the carrier to deliver the goods only "to the order of the shipper" (seller)—*i.e.*, only to the seller or a person the seller may designate by an appropriate indorsement.

As stated immediately above, the bill of lading serves as both a carrier contract and as a receipt for the cargo given to the carrier. Under the terms of the bill of lading contract, the carrier promises, in return for payment of the freight charge, to deliver the goods to either (1) the named "consignee" in a straight or nonnegotiable bill of lading, or (2) the person in possession or the "holder" of a properly indorsed order or negotiable bill of lading. The issuance by the car-

---

30 *See* §§ 3.4 and 3.5 *infra*.

31 *See* § 6.1 in Chapter 6 *infra*.

32 *See* the analysis of these commercial terms in Chapter 2, *supra*.

33 *See* the discussion of the CIF term in Chapter 2, *supra*.

rier of a bill of lading serves to assure the parties that (1) the goods have been delivered to the carrier, and (2) that they are destined for the buyer either as consignee under a straight bill of lading or as the holder of a negotiable bill of lading.

§ 3.5 ___The Necessity of a Negotiable Bill of Lading

Unless otherwise agreed, a "payment against documents" transaction will require use of a negotiable bill of lading. Because the negotiable bill of lading acts as a document of title that can transfer rights by transfer of the bill, the buyer is able to obtain delivery of the goods *only if* the buyer has physical possession of a properly indorsed bill of lading. The buyer can acquire physical possession of a properly indorsed bill of lading only by paying in full the balance owed on the goods for the shipment.

Since a negotiable bill of lading controls the right to obtain the goods from the carrier, the collecting banks can control the carrier's delivery of the goods to the buyer by simply retaining possession of the order bill of lading. In other words, when a bank undertakes to collect funds from the buyer for the seller, it receives the bill of lading from the seller that has been issued by the carrier. The bank's control over the negotiable bill of lading as a document of title confers control over the goods. The buyer cannot obtain possession of the goods from a carrier without physical possession of the negotiable bill of lading. Therefore, after the banks have received that piece of paper from the seller, they—acting on behalf of the seller—will demand payment (or an adequate assurance that the buyer will pay) before they give the buyer physical possession of the negotiable bill of lading and therefore the ability to obtain the goods from the carrier.

If a nonnegotiable ("straight") bill of lading were to be used in the payment against documents transaction, an almost insoluble problem would arise regarding the identification of the consignee. As noted in Section 3.2 above, with a nonnegotiable bill of lading the carrier is obligated to deliver only to the named consignee. If the seller were named as consignee, the buyer would be obligated to pay against a document that did not give it rights over the goods. But if the buyer were named as consignee, it would be able to obtain delivery of the goods from the carrier even without payment, and thus the seller would lose the valuable protection inherent in a "payment against documents" transaction.

§ 3.6 ____Payment

Once the seller has obtained a negotiable bill of lading made out to its "order," how does this payment arrangement actually work? First, the seller prepares and forwards along with the bill of lading a "draft," together with an invoice and any other documents required by the sales contract. This draft also is a negotiable instrument.[34] Like a check drawn on a bank, the draft functions as a legal vehicle for "withdrawing" from the buyer the amount owed to the seller under the sales contract. The seller uses the banking system as a collection agent for the draft. The draft (sometimes also called a "bill of exchange") will usually be a "sight draft," which is payable on demand ("on sight") when presented to the buyer. The draft is drawn for the amount due under the sales contract, and it is payable to the seller's order.

The seller then indorses both the negotiable draft and the negotiable bill of lading and delivers them along with any other required documents to its local bank (which for ease of reference we will refer to as the "Seller's Bank"). If no letter of credit is involved in the transaction, Seller's Bank will usually take these documents only "for collection," although it is also possible for the bank to "discount," or buy, the documents outright and become the owner. If Seller's Bank acts for collection only, the seller will also provide a collection form that describes the condition for release of the bill of lading to the buyer (typically, full payment).

Seller's Bank is then required to send the draft, the bill of lading, and the other accompanying documents for presentment to the buyer.[35] Seller's Bank deals with "for collection" items individually, without assuming that they will be honored, and therefore without giving the seller a provisional credit in the seller's account until the buyer pays the draft. It and other involved banks likewise have no obligation relating to the goods themselves other than to follow the seller's reasonable instructions.[36]

If no intermediary banks are involved, Seller's Bank will deliver the draft, with the bill of lading and the other attached documents, through "customary banking channels" to the "presenting bank" (which typically will be the buyer's local bank, referred to

---

[34] *See* UCC § 3–104(a), (e). In the United States, the UCC provides special rules for the obligations of banks dealing with such "documentary drafts." *See* UCC Article 4, Part 5. *See also* § 4–104(6)(defining "documentary draft").

[35] *See* UCC § 4–501.

[36] *See* UCC § 4–403 (stating that the bank presenting the draft "is under no obligation with respect to the goods represented by [a bill of lading] except to follow any reasonable instructions seasonably received").

here as "Buyer's Bank"). Buyer's Bank will then notify the buyer of the arrival of the documents and demand that the buyer "honor" the draft. This means that the buyer must pay the amount of a demand (or "sight") draft or "accept"—bindingly promise to pay later—a draft payable at a later time (a "time draft"). The buyer may require the bank to "exhibit" the draft and other documents (especially, the bill of lading) to allow the buyer to determine whether they conform to the contract. The buyer typically has three banking days after presentment to decide whether to honor the draft, if mere notice is sent. However, if the draft and documents are exhibited directly to the buyer, the buyer must decide whether or not to honor the draft by the close of business on that same day, unless there are extenuating circumstances.

An international sale of goods transaction involving payment against documents is illustrated by the following diagram:

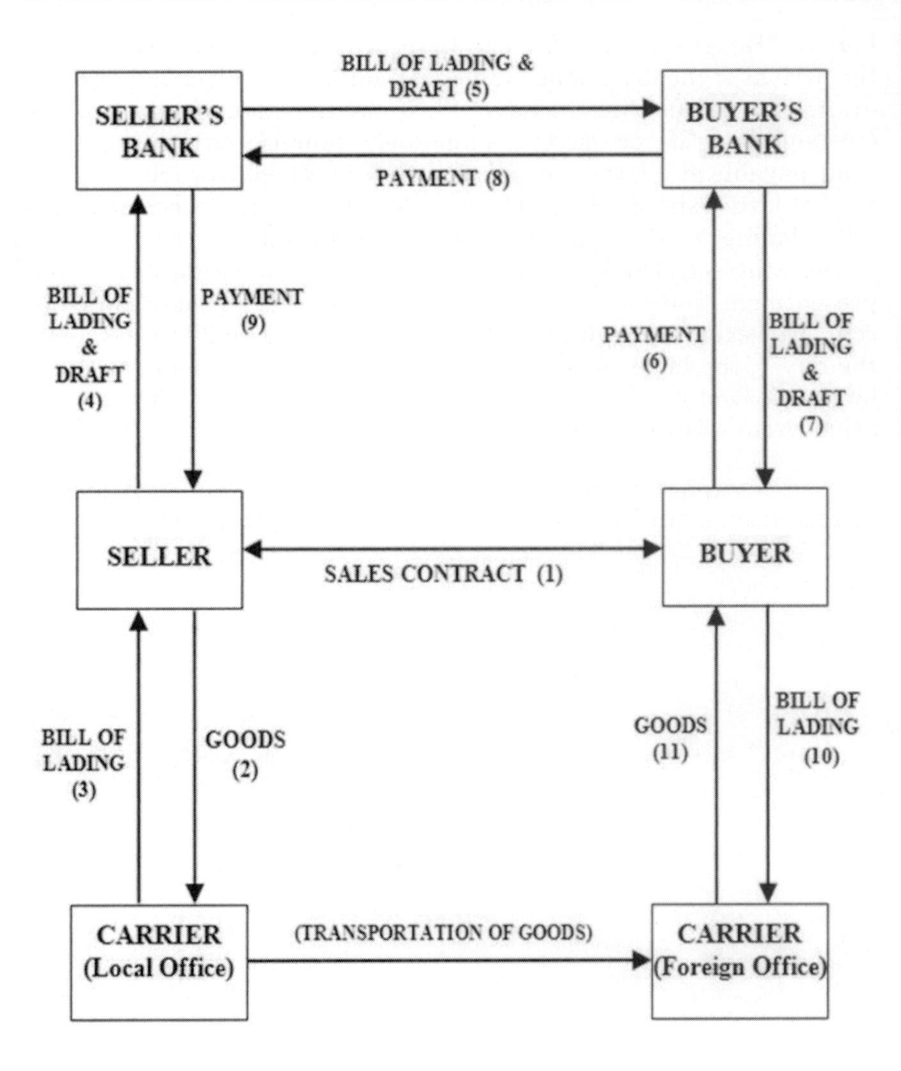

Upon presentation by Buyer's Bank (again, acting on behalf of the seller), the buyer must "pay against the documents" and not the goods themselves. This is why it is preferable to specify the terms of the documents in the original contract for the sale of goods. Once the buyer has paid, or arranged to pay, Buyer's Bank will give possession of the bill of lading to the buyer. Only then will the buyer be able to obtain the goods from the carrier. The buyer never sees the goods, only the documents—so it inspects the documents rigorously to determine that they comply exactly with the requirements of the sales contract. Substantial performance by the seller in the tender of documents is not acceptable.

§ 3.7 ____Risks for the Parties—In General

Both parties face certain risks in this type of transaction, some of which have nothing to do with the formal payment arrangement. For example, the goods could be lost or stolen. With respect to this risk, the parties must consider the value of the goods, the amount of time required to secure additional or replacement goods, and the demand for the goods in the marketplace.

Some of these problems are recognized and dealt with in the standard handling of the "payment against documents" transaction. For example, as noted above, a "payment against documents" transaction often arises through the use of a CIF commercial term. With such a term, the seller is obligated to arrange and pay for insurance coverage for the time after delivery of the goods to the carrier. But this payment arrangement also may leave the buyer exposed, especially because it will have an obligation to pay before inspecting the goods themselves. To address this problem, buyers have sought to require an "inspection certificate," a protective device that is in common use in modern transactions.

These and similar risks are the subject of the discussion in the Sections immediately below. Other risks that relate directly to the use of bills of lading are discussed in §§ 3.15 through 3.18 below.

§ 3.8 ____The Risks for the Seller

What can go wrong from the seller's point of view? The seller will be paid before the documents or the goods are released to the buyer. If the buyer pays the buyer's bank, the proceeds are remitted immediately and automatically to the seller's bank account in the seller's nation. Therefore, the seller will not lose control of the goods without being paid for them.

However, the seller has shipped the goods to a foreign buyer prior to receiving any payment, and with no guarantee of payment from anyone other than the buyer. The buyer may refuse to pay the sight draft with documents attached when it arrives. This would give the seller a cause of action, but often the seller can only assert its right in the buyer's home jurisdiction. Such a suit abroad will bring extra expense, delay, and uncertainty. In particular, the seller could feel that it will be the target of discrimination in the courts of another country.

The seller would still have control of the goods, because after dishonor of the draft, the collecting banks will return the bill of lading to the seller. However, the goods would now be at a foreign destination—one at which the seller likely has no agents, and no particular prospects for resale. In addition, if the seller wishes to bring the goods back to its base of operations (and normal sales territory), it would have to arrange and pay a second transportation charge, and this may be substantial in relation to the value of the goods. The seller will be somewhat better situated under a documentary transaction, because the buyer may review only the documents (especially, the bill of lading) in deciding whether it will pay. But a dishonor of the draft by the buyer also can create economic circumstances in which the seller's only rational option is a distress sale at a foreign location. This risk to the seller is inherent in the "payment against documents" transaction, unless the seller requires that the buyer also arrange for the issuance of a letter of credit. (See Chapter 6 for a complete description and discussion of the letter of credit transaction.)

§ 3.9 ____The Risks for the Buyer

What can go wrong from the buyer's point of view? In exchange for its payment of the purchase price of the goods, the buyer has a document from the carrier entitling it to delivery of the goods, likely an insurance certificate protecting the buyer against casualty loss in transit, and—if it had the foresight to secure such a right in advance (see immediately below)—perhaps an inspection certificate confirming that the goods conform to the sales contract. Therefore, the buyer should receive what it bargained for—delivery of conforming goods or insurance proceeds sufficient to cover any loss.

However, without the ability to inspect the actual goods before payment, the buyer cannot be absolutely assured that they conform to the contract. The buyer will be forced to rely on information provided in the bill of lading, such as a description of the goods, quantity of boxes or weight of the cargo prior to payment for the goods. There could be misstatements on the bill of lading, such that the description conforms to the requirements of the sales contract, but upon delivery, the buyer could find that the goods actually do not conform. Such a nonconformity could range from the seller shipping scrap paper to it shipping the correct goods but in the wrong size, color, or type. Similarly, the buyer could find that the labeling on the packaging is incorrect (which can cause problems with customs agents in both countries).

The buyer also may face other risks relating to the conduct of the carrier. These include that the carrier stored or handled the goods inappropriately such that they are damaged in transit. Separately, the seller or a third party may have obtained the bill of lading by fraud or forgery in the first place, or a thief could have stolen and forged the bill later. Some of these risks are inherent in any transaction using a bill of lading, and will be considered in Sections 3.15 through 3.18 below. But they assume special significance for the buyer in a "payment against documents" transaction under which it must pay before getting access to the goods themselves.

§ 3.10 International Conventions

The regulation of the terms of a bill of lading, as well as the more general relationship between a carrier and its customers, is the subject of four international conventions and three U.S. federal statutes. As noted in the Introduction to this Chapter, until recently, only three conventions were in existence: The so-called Hague Rules;[37] the Hague/Visby Rules (which build on the Hague Rules, but amend them in noteworthy ways);[38] and Hamburg Rules.[39] Each of these treaties governs contracts of carriage and bills of lading, but they follow differing approaches.[40]

The Hague Rules were adopted in 1924, and set forth rules governing shipowner liability to shippers for cargo loss and damage. The Hague Rules define the basic "due diligence" obligations of the carrier,[41] provide seventeen defenses against carrier and shipowner

---

[37] Convention for the Unification of Certain Rules of Law Relating to Bills of Lading, Aug. 25, 1924, 51 Stat. 233, T.S. No. 931, 120 L.N.T.S. 155 (hereinafter the Hague Rules). As noted, the United States has enacted this treaty as the Carriage of Goods by Sea Act (COGSA), which now appears as a statutory note to 46 U.S.C. § 30701.

[38] Protocol to Amend the International Convention for the Unification of Certain Rules of Law Relating to Bills of Lading, Brussels, Feb. 23, 1968, 1412 U.N.T.S. 127 (entered into force June 23, 1977)(Hague-Visby Rules), available at http://www.admiraltylaw.com/statutes/hague.html. Numerous countries have adopted the Hague-Visby Rules, including Belgium, China, Denmark, Ecuador, Finland, France, Italy, the Netherlands, Norway, Poland, Singapore, Sweden, and the United Kingdom. For the full list see the 2010 CMI YEARBOOK OF THE COMITE MARITIME INTERNATIONAL, http://www.comitemaritime.org/Uploads/Yearbooks/Yearbook%20 2010.pdf.

[39] United Nations Convention on the Carriage of Goods by Sea, Hamburg, Mar. 31, 1978, U.N. Doc A/Conf.89/13, U.N. Doc. A/RES/48/34 (entered into force Nov. 1, 1992) (hereinafter the Hamburg Rules), also available at 17 I.L.M. 608 (1978). As of March, 2013, thirty-four countries are Contracting States to the Hamburg Rules. *See* http://www.uncitral.org/uncitral/en/uncitral_texts/transport_goods.html.

[40] For discussions on the development of and change to these international conventions, see Hakan Karan, THE CARRIER'S LIABILITY UNDER THE INTERNATIONAL MARITIME CONVENTIONS: THE HAGUE, HAGUE-VISBY, AND HAMBURG RULES (2004); Samuel Mandelbaum, *Creating Uniform Worldwide Liability Standards for Sea Carriage of Goods Under the Hague, COGSA, Visby and Hamburg Conventions*, 23 TRANSP. L.J. 471, 477 (1996); and Benjamin Yancey, *Comparative Aspects of Current Importance: The Carriage of Goods: Hague, COGSA, Visby and Hamburg* 57 TUL. L. REV. 1238 (1983).

[41] Hague Rules, art. 3.

liability,[42] preclude contractual exculpatory clauses in bills of lading,[43] and limit liability to a minimum of $500 per package or customary freight unit.[44] (Because the United States has enacted the Hague Rules into domestic law, Section 3.13 examines the content of these rules in more detail below.)

The Hague-Visby Rules of 1968 were based on, but made noteworthy amendments to, the Hague Rules. This "Visby Amendment" addressed certain issues that had arisen under the Hague Rules, such as the scope of carrier defenses and the inadequacy of the $500 per package provision in light of multimodal transportation and containerized packaging. The Hague-Visby Rules retain most of the long list of defenses for carriers[45] and define the term "package" to include containerized cargo.[46] These Rules also increase the per package liability to $666 (or $2 per kilogram, whichever is higher),[47] but expressly remove that limitation for damage caused by the carrier's own intentional or reckless actions.[48]

The Hamburg Rules of 1978 were a major departure from the Hague and Hague-Visby Rules, for they substantially decreased carrier and shipowner defenses and increased their potential liability. The Hamburg Rules thus limit the available defenses to carriers, and in fact leave only three of the seventeen defenses provided in the previous conventions;[49] they increase the liability per package to approximately $1,169 per package or customary shipping unit, but also provide the shipper an opportunity to recover based on the weight of the cargo instead;[50] and they include liability for on deck cargo and shipments without a bill of lading for the first time (such liability having been specifically excluded by the prior conventions).[51] A substantial majority of the thirty-four countries that have adopted the Hamburg Rules are developing or landlocked states, whose businesses are most likely to benefit from expansive

---

42 *Id.*, art. 4(2).

43 *Id.*, art. 3(8).

44 *Id.*, art. 4(5)(as adjusted under COGSA § 4(5)).

45 Hague-Visby Rules, *supra* note 38, art. IV(e).

46 *Id.*, art. IV(5)(c).

47 *Id.*, art. IV(5)(a).

48 *Id.*, art. IV(5)(e)

49 Hamburg Rules, art. 5.

50 *Id.*, art. 6.

51 *Id.*, art. 9. For an in-depth review of the Hamburg Rules, see Robert Force, *A Comparison of the Hague, Hague-Visby, and Hamburg Rules: Much Ado About (?)*, 70 TUL. L. REV. 2051 (1996).

liability rules for carriers.[52] The Hague Rules and the Hague-Visby Rules, in contrast, are more favorable to carriers and thus have been adopted mostly by the world's maritime states.[53]

Some nations have chosen one set of rules to apply as mandatory law; others, such as those that have adopted the Hague-Visby Rules, apply different rules depending on whether the shipment is inbound or outbound (because those rules are not applicable of their own force for inbound shipments).[54]

As noted in the Introduction, concerns about the conflicts between these three "international" treaty efforts led to comprehensive negotiations under the auspices of the United Nations Commission on International Trade Law (UNCITRAL) to bring about true international uniformity. The result of this new effort was a fourth treaty on the subject of the obligations of carriers in international trade, the United Nations Convention on Contracts for the International Carriage of Goods Wholly or Partly by Sea (2009).[55] These so-called Rotterdam Rules are the product of two decades of negotiation and drafting by interested parties from a broad range of perspectives and thus may be acceptable to a noteworthy majority of states, whether principally supportive of buyers, sellers, or carriers. As of 2013, however, only two states (Spain and Togo) have ratified the Rotterdam Rules, and it has not yet entered into force.[56] The United States has signed the treaty, and there are some positive indications that it may ratify in the near future.

If they were to enter into force, the Rotterdam Rules would comprehensively cover the relationship between the carrier and its customers, including with respect to the basic obligations of the carrier;[57] the carrier's liability for loss, damage, or delay,[58] as well as the limitations on that liability;[59] the rules for deck cargo and related issues;[60] the delivery of the goods;[61] the obligations of the shipper

---

[52] *See* Status of Convention, available at the website of UNCITRAL, http://www.uncitral.org/uncitral/en/uncitral_texts/transport_goods/Hamburg_status.html

[53] *See* 1 William Tetley, MARINE CARGO CLAIMS 11 (4th ed., 2008).

[54] Hague-Visby Rules, *supra* note 38, art. X.

[55] G.A. Res. 63/122, Annex, U.N. Doc. A/RES/63/122 (Feb. 2, 2009). The text of the Rotterdam Rules is available at http://www.uncitral.org/uncitral/en/uncitral_texts/transport_goods/2008rotterdam_rules.html.

[56] The status of ratification of the Rotterdam Rules is available at http://www.uncitral.org/uncitral/en/uncitral_texts/transport_goods/rotterdam_status.html.

[57] Rotterdam Rules, *supra* note 55, arts. 11–16.

[58] *Id.*, arts. 17–23.

[59] *Id.*, arts. 59–61.

[60] *Id.*, arts. 24–26.

to the carrier;[62] the rules for "transport documents" (especially bills of lading);[63] the transfer of negotiable transport documents and the resultant rights of the party with control over the goods;[64] and time limitations, jurisdiction, and arbitration.[65] These Rules also expressly contemplate, and create the legal framework for, the issuance and transfer of electronic bills of lading.[66]

As discussed below, as of 2013, the United States remains committed to the Hague Rules, which it has enacted into its domestic law as the Carriage of Goods by Sea Act (COGSA).

§ 3.11 Overview of United States Law

Article 7 of the UCC would appear to regulate the rights and obligations arising out of bills of lading, for—in addition to warehouse receipts—it comprehensively addresses the subject. In fact, however, in large measure the UCC is preempted by federal law.[67] The Federal Bills of Lading Act (formerly called the Pomerene Act)[68] governs the issue, transfer, and transferability of all bills of lading issued by any common carrier for the transportation of goods in either interstate commerce or international commerce from the United States to another country.[69] The rules of UCC Article 7 governing the issuance and transfer of bills of lading thus continue to apply only to purely intrastate transactions, inbound international shipments, and international shipments that do not reach the United States (provided U.S. law applies at all and the court obtains jurisdiction).[70]

As discussed below, certain aspects of the form and content of bills of lading are also governed by two other federal statutes, the

---

[61] *Id.*, arts. 43–49.

[62] *Id.*, arts. 27–34.

[63] *Id.*, arts. 35–42.

[64] *Id.*, arts. 56–56. For a comprehensive analysis of these Rotterdam Rules see Michael Sturley, Tomotaka Fujita & G.J. Van der Ziel, THE ROTTERDAM RULES: THE UN CONVENTION ON CONTRACTS FOR THE INTERNATIONAL CARRIAGE OF GOODS WHOLLY OR PARTLY BY SEA (2010).

[65] Rotterdam Rules, *supra* note 55, arts. 62–78.

[66] *Id.*, arts. 8–10, 35, 45–47, 57.

[67] *See* National Union Fire Ins. Co. v. Allite, Inc., 430 Mass. 828, 724 N.E.2d 677, 679 (2000)(holding that the FBLA preempts Article 7 of the UCC for interstate and outbound international transportation of goods).

[68] 49 U.S.C. §§ 80101 *et seq.*

[69] 49 U.S.C. § 80102.

[70] *See* Thypin Steel Co. v. Certain Bills of Lading, in Rem, 1996 WL 223896 (S.D.N.Y. 1996); T.C. Ziraat Bankasi v. Standard Chartered Bank, 644 N.E.2d 272 (N.Y. 1994).

Harter Act,[71] and COGSA.[72] With this multiplicity of statutes governing the terms and use of a bill of lading, conflicting concepts from overlapping statutes can be expected. Thus, for example, as one federal court has observed, the Supreme Court has not "spoken directly to the question of whether COGSA completely preempts state law" and "the courts that have reached the question have come to differing conclusions."[73] In many situations, therefore, lawyers will need to consider the possible application of both state and federal law to bill of lading transactions.[74]

§ 3.12 The Harter Act

The Harter Act, codified under the shipping title of the United States Code,[75] governs liability for cargo between the vessel owner or carrier and the shipper in domestic trade. The Harter Act was a restatement of the common law as of 1893 that applied to the duties and liabilities of a vessel to its cargo.[76]

The Harter Act prohibits and nullifies language in a bill of lading that limits a carrier's liability for "negligence or fault in loading, stowage, custody, care, or proper delivery."[77] Basically, the Harter Act defines the carrier's basic obligation of "due diligence"[78] and limits the carrier's ability to contract away this liability in preparing the vessel for the carriage of the goods and in handling the goods while in its possession.[79]

In significant measure, COGSA (see immediately below) displaced the Harter Act for international shipments. The one area in which the Harter Act remains potentially relevant for international transactions is with respect to carrier liability for events that occur after the goods have been offloaded in a domestic port. This conclusion obtains, as the Supreme Court has recently observed, because COGSA governs bills of lading for the carriage of goods only "from

[71] 46 U.S.C. § 30701 *et seq.*

[72] COGSA appears as a statutory note to 46 U.S.C. § 30701.

[73] Continental Ins. Co. v. Kawasaki Kisen Kasha, Ltd., 542 F. Supp. 2d. 1031, 1034 (N.D. Cal. 2008). *See also* UTI, U.S., Inc. v. Bernuth Agencies, Inc., 2012 WL 4511304 (S.D. Fla. 2012)(also examining the scope of COGSA preemption of state law).

[74] For a more comprehensive discussion of the possible conflicts between state and federal law see Michael Crowley, *The Limited Scope of the Cargo Liability Regime Covering Carriage of Goods by Sea: The Multimodal Problem*, 79 TUL. L. REV. 1461, 1474–78 (2005).

[75] 46 U.S.C. § 30701 *et seq.*

[76] *See* The Delaware, 161 U.S. 459, 471–72 (1896).

[77] 46 U.S.C § 30704.

[78] *Id.*, § 30706.

[79] *Id.*, § 30705.

the time when the goods are loaded on to the time when they are discharged from the ship."[80]

§ 3.13 ___The Carriage of Goods by Sea Act (COGSA)

The Carriage of Goods by Sea Act (COGSA) is the principal U.S. statute governing the international transport of goods. Together with the FBLA discussed in Section 3.14 below, COGSA defines the rights and obligations of a carrier in its relations with its customers (principally, the shipper and its transferees), including the rights and obligations derived from bills of lading issued for international transport.

COGSA is derived from the ratification by the United States of the Hague Rules.[81] Indeed, as one federal appellate court has observed, COGSA is "virtually identical" to the Hague Rules.[82] At the time COGSA was enacted in 1936, there was no international uniformity regarding cargo liability derived from bills of lading. For example, in the United States, carriers could not limit their liability and were treated as insurers of the cargo, while in the United Kingdom, they were permitted (under the principle of freedom of contract) to disclaim all liability. Because of this, a principal goal of the Hague Rules, and thus COGSA, was to establish uniform rules for ocean bills of lading, and especially for the liability of the vessel owner or carrier to the shipper in international trade.[83]

COGSA applies to every bill of lading or document of title that evidences a contract for the carriage of goods by sea "to or from ports of the United States in foreign trade,"[84] and thus does not automatically apply to bills of lading issued in the United States. COGSA sets forth the responsibilities and liabilities of the carrier and the ship, including seaworthiness of the vessel (which includes the proper manning, maintenance, equipment, supplies, and prepa-

---

[80] Norfolk S. Ry. Co. v. Kirby, 543 U.S. 14, 29 (2004)(*quoting* COGSA § 1(e)).

[81] 46 U.S.C. § 30701 (statutory note). Upon a restructuring of the maritime laws in 46 U.S.C. in 2006, Congress moved COGSA to a "statutory note" in order not to interfere with the negotiations over the Rotterdam Rules. This change had no effect on the continued validity of COGSA.

[82] Federal Ins. Co. v. Union Pacific R. Co., 651 F.3d 1175, 1179 (9th Cir. 2011).

[83] *See* Robert C. Herd & Co., Inc. v. Krawill Mach. Corp., 359 U.S. 297, 301 (1959). The international counterpart in the United Kingdom in the early 1900s was the Carriage of Goods by Sea Act of 1924. More modern versions include the U.K.'s Carriage of Goods By Sea Act of 1971 (which implemented the Hague-Visby Rules) and the Carriage of Goods By Sea Act of 1992 (which provided more details for bills of lading).

[84] COGSA, § 13.

ration of the vessel so that it is fit for the cargo),[85] and proper care and loading of cargo.[86]

Unlike the Harter Act, COGSA does not require due diligence as a condition precedent to the use of a statutory defense,[87] except for liability under the seaworthiness requirement.[88] In addition, COGSA states that a carrier will be held liable for damaged cargo resulting from an unreasonable deviation from the terms of the contract of carriage, for example, discharging the cargo and reloading it on another vessel, stowage in contravention to specific terms of contract of carriage, or a change in route to take on cargo resulting in delay of delivery.[89] Furthermore, COGSA provides a carrier with seventeen defenses for uncontrollable causes of loss, including defective navigation or management of the ship; fires; dangers of the sea; acts of God or war or public enemies; seizure by foreign authorities; certain labor problems; inherent defects in the goods; insufficiency of packing or marks; and more generally any other cause "without the actual fault and privity of the carrier."[90]

One of the most well-known provisions of COGSA is the $500 per package limitation of liability for loss or damage to cargo.[91] This limitation was the regulatory trade-off for the prohibition against limitation of liability clauses in the carriage contract itself.[92] The shipper may obtain an increase in the $500 per package limit; indeed, some courts have found that the carrier must give the shipper a "fair opportunity" to do so.[93] But as one federal court has observed, "in the modern commercial context, it is rare for a shipper to declare the value of the goods [because] carriers typically demand a much higher freight when a shipper declares the value of the cargo as compensation for shouldering increased potential liability."[94] Moreover, neither the carrier nor the ship is liable for any increased liability if the shipper has "knowingly and fraudulently misstated

[85] *Id.*, § 3(1).

[86] *Id.*, § 3(2).

[87] *Id.*, § 4(2).

[88] *Id.*, § 4(1).

[89] *Id.*, § 4(4).

[90] *Id.*, § 4(2).

[91] *Id.*, § 4(5).

[92] *Id.*, § 3(8).

[93] *See e.g.*, Kukje Hwajae Ins. Co. v. M/V Hyundai Liberty, 408 F.3d 1250, 1255 (9th Cir. 2005). *But see* Ferrostaal, Inc. v. M/V Sea Phoenix, 447 F.3d 212, 228–229 (3rd Cir. 2006)(rejecting this doctrine as inconsistent with the express language of COGSA).

[94] Delphi-Delco Electronics Systems v. M/V NEDLLOYD EUROPA, 324 F. Supp. 2d 403, 413 (S.D.N.Y. 2004).

the value of the goods on the bill of lading."[95] Regardless of the valuation or maximum amount of liability, a carrier or ship is not liable for more than the damage actually sustained.[96] An additional protection under COGSA is that claims must be filed within a year following delivery of the subject goods.[97]

COGSA contains some provisions that overlap with the Harter Act. COGSA will prevail over the Harter Act regarding liability arising from an act, negligence or default in navigation or management of a vessel used for carriage of goods by sea.[98] As noted above, however, when damage to goods occurs on land (*i.e.*, after discharge from the ship), the Harter Act will prevail and prohibit any disclaimers against liability.[99] The Harter Act by its terms still governs prior to loading and after discharge of cargo until delivery under the bill of lading is made.[100] Nonetheless, federal courts have held that a bill of lading covering an international shipment may extend COGSA's liability regime even to the time after discharge of the goods.[101]

COGSA also has important provisions relating to bills of lading. First, it expressly obligates the carrier, on the request of the shipper, to issue a bill of lading that describes "among other things" (a) the marks identifying the goods as provided by the shipper, (b) the number or weight of the goods (as applicable), and (c) "the apparent order and condition of the goods."[102] On all such issues, however, the carrier is not obligated to provide a description as to a fact it "had no reasonable means of checking."[103] Once the carrier has provided such a description, COGSA declares that the bill of lading is "prima facie evidence of the receipt by the carrier of the goods as therein described."[104] As discussed in Section 3.17 below, this essen-

---

95 *Id.*, § 4(5).

96 COGSA, § 4(5).

97 *Id.*, § 6.

98 *Id.*, § 1(e)(defining "carriage of goods" to mean "the period from the time when the goods are loaded on to the time when they are discharged from the ship").

99 *See* § 3.12 above. *Compare* also COGSA § 4(2)(a) *with* Harter Act, 46 USC § 30704.

100 COGSA, *supra* note 81, § 11 (stating that COGSA does not supercede the Harter Act or other federal statutes insofar as they relate to duties, responsibilities and liabilities of the ship or carrier prior to the time when the goods are loaded or after the time the goods are discharged from the ship.).

101 *See, e.g.,* Greenpack of Puerto Rico, Inc. v. American President Lines, 684 F.3d 20, 26–28 (1st Cir. 2012); Federal Ins. Co. v. Union Pacific R. Co., 651 F.3d 1175, 1179 (9th Cir. 2011).

102 COGSA, § 3(3).

103 *Id.*

104 *Id.*, § 3(4).

tial rule establishes the foundation for carrier liability for a "misdescription" of the goods in a bill of lading.

§ 3.14 The Federal Bills of Lading Act (FBLA)

The Federal Bills of Lading Act (FBLA), codified under the transportation title of the United States Code (Title 49), governs the creation, transferability, and transfer of bills of lading in defined international and interstate shipments. Congress originally enacted the FBLA (then known as the Pomerene Act) in 1916, and recodified it with slight clarifications as the FBLA in 1994. The recodification did not change the substance of the Act, but it did reword and consolidate the prior provisions and change all the section numbers.

The FBLA governs all interstate and outbound international shipments that use a bill of lading issued by a common carrier.[105] In specific, the statute governs a bill of lading if the goods are shipped between a place in one state and through to another state or from a place in the United States "to a place in a foreign country."[106] To that extent, the FBLA entirely preempts the UCC. But the UCC continues to cover *purely* intrastate shipments. Some courts have reasoned that the UCC also may apply by default to inbound international shipments[107] and international shipments that do not touch the United States, but are litigated in the United States.[108]

Unlike COGSA, the FBLA regulates only the rights and obligations arising out of bills of lading. It thus addresses the issuance of bills of lading;[109] the form and requirements for negotiation and the rights obtained upon transfer;[110] the rights of carriers upon nonpayment;[111] and the obligations of the carrier regarding descriptions and delivery of the goods.[112]

As Sections 3.2 and 3.3 above described in detail, the most fundamental distinction in the FBLA is between negotiable (or "order") bills of lading and nonnegotiable (or "straight") bills of lading.[113]

---

105 49 U.S.C. § 80102.

106 *Id.*

107 Hual AS v. Expert Concrete, Inc., 45 UCC Rep. Serv. 2d 882 (N.Y. Sup. 2001).

108 T.C. Ziraat Bankasi v. Standard Chartered Bank, 644 N.E.2d 272 (N.Y. 1994).

109 49 U.S.C. § 80103. *See also* 49 U.S.C. § 80114 (addressing lost, stolen, or destroyed bills of lading).

110 49 U.S.C. §§ 80104–80108.

111 49 U.S.C. § 80109.

112 49 U.S.C. §§ 80110–80113.

113 *See* especially 49 U.S.C. § 80103.

Those sections also described how the FBLA's important rules governing the transfer of rights under bills of lading affect the carrier's obligations regarding delivery of the goods. It is in this respect in particular that the distinction between nonnegotiable and negotiable bills of lading becomes significant: For a nonnegotiable bill of lading, the carrier must deliver the goods only to the consignee named on the bill;[114] for a negotiable bill of lading, in contrast, the carrier must deliver the goods only to the person in possession of the bill and only if the bill has been properly indorsed over to that person (the "holder").[115]

The FBLA does not define "carrier," so it is not clear whether documents issued by freight forwarders are covered. Further, the term "bill of lading" is not defined, so it is not clear whether air waybills or inland waterway documents are included. Nonetheless, depending on the specific circumstances and especially the functional roles of each, strong arguments support application of the FBLA to both subjects.

§ 3.15 Liabilities and Inherent Risks Regarding Bills of Lading

The FBLA also has several important liability rules that address certain risks uniquely related to transactions that use a bill of lading. The most prominent of these risks are the following: (1) where the carrier delivers the goods to the wrong person ("misdelivery"); (2) where the carrier delivers goods that do not conform to the description on the bill of lading ("misdescription"); and (3) where a bill of lading contains a forgery and thus creates potential warranty liability for transferors.

Sections 3.15 through 3.18 below will examine each of these subjects in detail. But to set the context here, the FBLA establishes important obligations for a carrier regarding delivery of the goods and in this way it sets the foundation both for (a) analyzing whether a carrier is liable for "misdelivery" (or conversion) and (b) the available defenses to such a claim.[116] For example, the carrier (as noted above[117]) must deliver the goods to the consignee under a nonnegotiable bill of lading or to the holder of a negotiable bill of lading.[118] Likewise, for a negotiable bill of lading it must obtain and cancel

---

[114] For more detail, see § 3.2 above.

[115] For more detail, see § 3.3 above.

[116] *See* 49 U.S.C. §§ 80110 and 80111, and § 3.16 *infra*.

[117] *See* §§ 3.2 and 3.3 *supra*.

[118] 49 U.S.C. § 80111(a).

the bill at the time of delivery.[119] These essential obligations will define whether the carrier has delivered the goods to the wrong person and thus is liable for "misdelivery."

The FBLA's liability rules also set the foundation for an analysis of a "misdescription" claim. On the basis of COGSA's obligation that a bill of lading contain a description of the goods,[120] a carrier is liable under the FBLA for nonreceipt or misdescription if the bill of lading either indicates receipt of cargo where no cargo was received or describes the goods in a manner that does not correspond to the goods actually delivered.[121] The FBLA provides, however, certain defenses for a carrier regarding nonreceipt and misdescription claims. The most prominent of these arises when all of the following are true: the goods are loaded by the shipper, the bill of lading indicates that the shipper provided the description for the goods, and the carrier is not aware of information contrary to that included on the bill.[122]

Finally, the FBLA provides for automatic representations and warranties by a person that negotiates or otherwise transfers a bill of lading for value. The statutory warranties set the foundation for analyzing claims of forgery on a bill of lading.[123] These warranties include that the bill is genuine; that the transferor has title to the goods and the right to transfer the bill; and that the transferor is not aware of any fact affecting the validity of the bill.[124] Again, however, as analyzed in more detail below, the FBLA recognizes a form of defense to such liability.[125]

§ 3.16 Misdelivery

A claim against the carrier for delivering the goods to the wrong person depends decisively on whether the goods were covered by a nonnegotiable or a negotiable bill of lading. Under a nonnegotiable bill of lading, the carrier (as described in detail in § 3.2 above) obligates itself to deliver the goods at the stated destination point only to the consignee named in the bill of lading.[126] As a result, the carrier is liable to the consignee of a straight bill of lading for mis-

---

[119] 49 U.S.C. § 80111(c). For more detail, see § 3.16 *infra.*

[120] *See* COGSA, § 3(3), and § 3.13 *supra.*

[121] *See* 49 U.S.C. § 80113(a) and § 3.17 *infra.*

[122] 49 U.S.C. § 80113(b) and (c). For more detail, see § 3.17 *infra.*

[123] *See* 49 U.S.C. § 80107(a) and § 3.18 *infra.*

[124] 49 U.S.C. § 80107(a)(1)-(4). For more detail, see § 3.18 *infra.*

[125] *See* 49 U.S.C. § 80107(a).

[126] 49 U.S.C. § 80110(b)(2). The carrier will have a defense, however, if it delivers to the person with the actual legal right to possession. 49 U.S.C. § 80110(b)(1).

delivery if it delivers the goods to anyone but the consignee (or a person whom the consignee delegates to receive them).[127] Thus, straight bills of lading are not appropriate for a "payment against documents" transaction,[128] and the case reports are full of litigation where an attorney tried a short-cut using a straight bill of lading, and sacrificed the client's interests in the process.

Under a negotiable bill of lading, in contrast, the FBLA obligates the carrier to deliver the goods at the destination point only to the "holder" of the bill of lading.[129] Thus, possession of the physical bill of lading becomes crucial. The carrier must see the bill of lading both to determine who has possession and to determine to whom the indorsements run.

As a result, for goods covered by a negotiable bill of lading the carrier is liable for misdelivery if it delivers the goods to anyone but the holder.[130] As discussed above,[131] a negotiable bill of lading is a special form of a document of title. A person in possession of a negotiable bill of lading, if properly indorsed over to the person, is the "holder" and has title to the document, title to the goods, and the direct right against the carrier to delivery of the covered goods. For this reason, the negotiable bill of lading is appropriate for a "payment against documents" transaction.[132] As the analysis in Sections 3.4 through 3.9 above illustrates, with "payment against documents" transactions, the collecting banks—acting on behalf of the seller—can use their possession of the required negotiable bill of lading to control title to and possession of the goods until the banks have collected the purchase price from the buyer.

If, therefore, the carrier delivers goods covered by a negotiable bill of lading to someone other than the holder, the carrier is liable in damages to the person with ultimate rights over the goods (almost always the holder). As the court observed in *Ace Bag & Burlap Co., Inc. v. Sea-Land Service, Inc.*, "where the carrier delivers goods to a person not entitled to their possession and without production of the bill of lading . . ., the carrier [is] liable for damages to anyone having title to or a right to possession of the goods."[133] However, some courts have observed, based on estoppel principles, that the

---

[127] 49 U.S.C. § 80111(a)(1). For certain limited exceptions see 49 U.S.C. § 80111(d).

[128] *See also* § 3.5 *supra*.

[129] 49 U.S.C. § 80110(b)(3).

[130] 49 U.S.C. § 80111(a)(1).

[131] *See* § 3.3 *supra* (analyzing negotiable bills of lading in more detail).

[132] *See* § 3.5 *supra*.

[133] 40 F. Supp. 2d 233, 239 (D.N.J. 1999).

carrier may deliver the goods to another person if it does so on the explicit instructions of the holder.[134]

The difference between the carrier's delivery obligations for a nonnegotiable as compared to a negotiable bill of lading is illustrated by a recent federal court case that involved three separate bills of lading, all of which named a Russian buyer as consignee.[135] Two of the bills were nonnegotiable and one was negotiable, but the seller kept possession of all three pending payment by the buyer. The court held that the carrier properly delivered the goods to the consignee-buyer under the two nonnegotiable bills of lading; but it found that the carrier had misdelivered under the negotiable bill of lading because it did not require presentation of the physical bill as a condition to delivery of the goods to the buyer.[136]

The FBLA nonetheless recognizes a form of an excuse in the event of a technical misdelivery. If the carrier happens to deliver to the person with the actual legal right to possession of the goods, it will not be held liable to the holder of the bill of lading.[137] A federal court thus recently held that a carrier was not liable when goods were stolen while in the possession of Honduran customs authorities. Even though the bill of lading was not available upon delivery, the court found that under the applicable local law and circumstances the customs authorities were "persons entitled to possession" of the goods as contemplated by the FBLA.[138]

Nonetheless, a variety of other provisions in the FBLA highlight the significance of possession for a negotiable bill of lading. Thus, the FBLA sets forth a formal obligation of the carrier to take possession of the bill of lading and cancel it upon delivery of the goods. If the carrier does not do so, it will be liable in damages "to a person purchasing the bill for value in good faith whether the pur-

---

[134] *See, e.g.,* Chilewich Partners v. M.V. Alligator Fortune, 853 F. Supp. 744, 752–753 (S.D.N.Y. 1994)(holding that a carrier was not liable where it delivered goods to a third-party at the specific direction of the holder of a negotiable bill of lading).

[135] Edelweiss (USA), Inc. v. Vengroff Williams & Assoc., Inc., 59 A.D.3d 588, 873 N.Y.S.2d 714 (2009). The case involved a malpractice claim against a lawyer for not timely filing the claim against the carrier, but the ultimate issue revolved around the delivery obligations of the carrier in the first place. *Id.*, at 715.

[136] *Id.*, at 717.

[137] 49 U.S.C. § 80110(b)(1). *See also* 49 U.S.C. § 8011(a)(1)(stating that basic liability rule for misdelivery applies if the carrier delivers the goods "to a person not entitled to their possession").

[138] Ace Bag & Burlap Co., Inc. v. Sea–Land Serv., Inc., 40 F. Supp. 2d 233, 239–40 (D.N.J.1999). *See also* New Edge Intern., LLC v. Trans-Net, Inc., 2009 WL 5214414 (W.D. Wash. 2009)(same regarding delivery to Russian customs authorities).

chase was before or after delivery."[139] And this liability attaches even if the carrier had delivered the goods to "a person entitled to the goods" (such as an original holder),[140] unless the delivery was made by judicial process, to satisfy a lien for unpaid fees, or because the goods were unclaimed or perishable.[141] Even where a claimant obtains a court order for delivery because of a lost, stolen or destroyed bill of lading, the carrier will be liable to a good faith purchaser of a negotiable bill of lading without notice.[142] For this reason, the FBLA permits a court in such circumstances to require that the recipient of the delivery post a bond.[143]

Under the FBLA, as under the UCC, any forgery of a necessary indorsement is not effective to create or transfer rights, regardless of the expertise of the forger. This is so because by definition a forgery is an unauthorized signature, and without the actual or authorized signature of a holder upon transfer ("indorsement") the transferee cannot become the holder. Even a signature by a purported agent is treated as a forgery if the signature was made without actual, implied, or apparent authority. The protection is illustrated by a situation in which a thief steals a negotiable bill of lading from the holder in possession under a special indorsement (that is, one made by naming that specific party only[144]). As such, the holder's indorsement is necessary to transfer rights to the document and the goods to any other party. Without that indorsement, the thief is not a holder and has no rights (even if in possession).[145] If the thief transfers the document to another party, that party—even if it acted in good faith—also is not a holder and cannot obtain rights under the document without the true holder's signature. And the carrier is still obligated to deliver the goods only to the holder.[146] Thus, if a collecting bank or another party takes the document under a special indorsement, it is protected against theft of the paper and forgery, because the carrier does not discharge its obligation by delivering to the forger.

---

139 49 U.S.C. § 80111(c).

140 *Id.*

141 49 U.S.C. § 80111(d).

142 49 U.S.C. § 80114(b).

143 49 U.S.C. § 80114(a).

144 *See* 49 U.S.C. § 80104(a)(1)(stating that a negotiable bill of lading may be negotiated by an indorsement "to a specified person").

145 *See* 49 U.S.C. § 80104(a)(1)(declaring that "[i]f the goods are deliverable to the order of a specified person, then the bill must be indorsed by that person"). The situation is different if the prior holder indorsed "in blank." *See* 49 U.S.C. § 80104(a). In such a case, the bill becomes a "bearer" bill, and the carrier may deliver to anyone in possession. 49 U.S.C. § 80110(b)(3)(B).

146 49 U.S.C. § 80110(b)(3).

If, in short, the carrier delivers to a forger, or to someone who received the document from the forger, without the holder's indorsement, the carrier is liable for misdelivery.[147] The forger of course is also liable (in the unlikely event that he can be found).

The FBLA also creates certain statutory warranties by transferors of bills of lading. "Unless a contrary intention appears," every person who negotiates or otherwise transfers a bill of lading warrants that it had "a right to transfer the bill and title to the goods."[148] A forged necessary indorsement will constitute a breach of this warranty. The concept is that each person who takes the bill of lading should "know its transferor." If the goods are misdelivered, the party most easily found is the one who received the goods, and that party is liable for the transfer that resulted in the (mis)delivery of the goods. That party—which is the person most likely to be able to find its own transferor—then has a warranty action against that transferor. Each such transferor, in turn, has a warranty action against its transferor—and so on back up the chain of transfers. This is not very efficient, but the purpose is to push liability back up the chain of transfers to the person who took from the forger (and, if he can be found, to the forger himself). In the meantime, the person with legal rights to the goods will collect from the misdelivering carrier, which (perhaps) will collect from its insurer.[149]

This warranty liability also can extend to collecting banks that transfer the document for value. If the buyer pays, and the collecting banks transmit those funds to the forger, then an argument exists that the banks have received value. However, such banks have several potential escape valves. One is to disclaim the warranty liability when indorsing or transferring the bill of lading. As noted, the FBLA provides that its transfer warranties do not arise if "a contrary intention appears."[150] Thus, an indorsement, "XYZ Bank—no warranties, prior indorsements not guaranteed," would clearly disclaim liability for such a warranty. Banks may similarly argue that banking custom relieves them from any duty to examine documents, with the result that an implicit blanket statutory "contrary intention" exists as a matter of custom. A second avenue is to claim that the bank is only holding the document "as security for a debt," be-

---

[147] 49 U.S.C. § 80111(a)(1). *See also* Adel Precision Products Corp. v. Grand Trunk Western R. Co., 332 Mich. 519, 51 N.W.2d 922 (1952).

[148] 49 U.S.C. § 80107(a)(2). For more on these statutory warranties see § 3.18 below.

[149] An indorsement does not, however, by itself make the indorser a guarantor of the obligations of the carrier or previous indorsers. 49 U.S.C. § 80107(d).

[150] 49 U.S.C. § 80107(a).

cause the statute exempts such holders from warranty liability.[151] The difficulty with this avenue is that a collecting bank does not pay the seller until after it receives payment, so it never becomes a creditor, secured or otherwise. Finally, if a bank incorporates by reference the International Chamber of Commerce's (ICC) *Uniform Rules for Collections* (1995) when it forwards the documents, it may effectively avoid liability for problems not apparent on the face of the documents.

Each of these approaches has analytical difficulties, but they may indicate a blanket intention to disclaim the statutory warranties by implication. In any event, any bank found to have warranty liability can pass this liability back to its transferor, as long as it can identify and find that transferor.

One party that clearly will be subject to liability in the case of a misdelivery, however, will be the carrier. In such a case, the FBLA provides that the carrier is liable to "a person having title to, or right to possession of," the goods.[152] For a negotiable bill of lading, this of course will be the holder (if still in possession). But this will not be the case with a forged indorsement, because the carrier will have received possession of the bill from the forger and should have cancelled it as part of its standard practices, with the consequence that no formal holder of the bill of lading will exist.[153] The proper claimant then will be the person who otherwise has preeminent rights to the goods themselves, which likely will be the original holder of the bill.[154]

For defects in transfer not based on forgeries, however, the FBLA is less forgiving for the original holder. If the owner of the bill is deprived of possession by "fraud, accident, mistake, duress, loss, theft, or conversion," the validity of the owner's negotiation of the bill is not affected as against a transferee who has given value for the bill in good faith and without notice of the problem.[155] Such a

---

[151] 49 U.S.C. 80107(b)("A person holding a bill of lading as security for a debt and in good faith demanding or receiving payment of the debt from another person does not warrant by the demand or receipt (1) the genuineness of the bill; or (2) the quantity or quality of the goods described in the bill.")

[152] 49 U.S.C. § 80113.

[153] 49 U.S.C. § 80101(4)(defining a "holder" as "a person having possession of, and a property right in, a bill of lading").

[154] *See* 49 U.S.C. § 80105(a)(1)(stating that a person who takes by a negotiation—here, the original holder—"acquires title to the goods" as held by its transferor). For otherwise-applicable domestic law see UCC §§ 2–401 (relating to title), 2–702 (relating to a seller's right to reclaim the goods, 1–201(b)(35)(providing that a seller's reservation of title has the effect of a security interest), and 9–609 (providing that a secured party has a right of possession).

[155] 49 U.S.C. § 80104(b).

transferee will become the holder as a result of a valid negotiation of the bill (assuming, again, that no forgery occurred).[156]

Finally, the UCC has clearer rules on statutory warranties and ones that are more favorable to the banks. If the UCC governs a transaction, such as under an "inbound" international shipment, statutory transfer warranties apply that are quite similar to those under the FBLA.[157] But the UCC has a special rule that generally releases collecting banks from these warranties. A collecting bank or "other intermediary known to be entrusted with documents of title on behalf of another" warrants "only its good faith and authority."[158] This protection of "mere intermediaries" applies even if they actually purchased the right to receive delivery of the goods (such as by purchasing the bill).[159]

§ 3.17 ___Misdescription

A carrier responsible for transporting goods under a contract with a shipper is not a party to the sales contract between (*i.e.*, is not in "privity" with) the seller and the buyer. Therefore, the carrier has no obligation to deliver goods that conform to the sales contract. However, when a shipper (most often the seller in the sales transaction) delivers goods to a carrier for transport in international trade, COGSA obligates the carrier on request to issue a bill of lading covering the goods.[160] COGSA then also obligates the carrier to provide in the bill of lading information on "[e]ither the number of packages or pieces, or the quantity, or weight, as the case may be, as furnished in writing by the shipper" as well as on "the apparent order and condition of the goods."[161] The carrier is not obligated to provide a description, however, with respect to facts it "had no reasonable means of checking."[162]

Nonetheless, once the carrier has provided such a description of the goods, COGSA (as noted above) declares that the bill of lading is "prima facie evidence of the receipt by the carrier of the goods as

---

156 *Id.* The result under the UCC is similar. Under § 7–502(a)(2), if a bill of lading is "duly negotiated" to a holder, that person thereby obtains title to the underlying goods. Under §7–501(a)(5), due negotiation requires that the transferee take in good faith, for value, and without notice of any defenses.

157 UCC § 7–507.

158 UCC § 7–508. *See also* T.C. Ziraat Bankasi v. Standard Chartered Bank, 644 N.E.2d 272 (N.Y. 1994).

159 *Id.*

160 COGSA, § 3(3).

161 *Id.*

162 *Id.*

therein described."[163] And under the FBLA, a carrier is liable for any failure to deliver goods that correspond to the description in the bill of lading.[164] This obligation is owed to the owner of the goods under a nonnegotiable bill of lading and to the holder of a negotiable bill of lading, provided that the owner or holder "gave value in good faith relying on the description of the goods in the bill."[165]

The problem with this obligation is that the carrier usually does not know what it is carrying, because (among other reasons) the goods often are in containers. Thus, the carrier knows that it received a container labeled "1000 Apple iPads." But it will not, and is not expected to, open the container to check whether it in fact contains iPads, or to count how many items actually are there. Even if it opened the container, the carrier would not be expected to check whether each iPad is in working order. And even if it did so check, it is not likely to have the expertise to determine whether each iPad can perform as expected or is otherwise fit for the ordinary uses of such a device. Thus, the carrier is not expected to warrant the description and capability of packaged goods given to it to transport.

To solve this problem, the FBLA allows carriers to disclaim their obligations to deliver goods that conform to the description in the bill of lading. This is accomplished through what are generally known as "Shipper's weight, load, and count" or "SLC" clauses.[166] The FBLA sets forth the specific language to make such a disclaimer, including:

"contents or condition of contents of pack-ages unknown";

"said to contain"; and

"shipper's weight, load, and count."

But the Act also makes clear that these exact linguistic formulas are not required; "words of the same meaning" will suffice.[167]

The FBLA defines two further requirements for the effectiveness of such a clause. First, the goods must actually have been load-

---

[163] *Id.*, § 3(4). *See also* § 3.13 above.

[164] 49 U.S.C. § 80113(a).

[165] *Id.*

[166] *See, e.g.,* Distribuidora Internacional Alimentos v. Amcar Forwarding, Inc., 2011 WL 902093 (S.D. Fla. 2011)(stating that "'a bill of lading containing the recital 'shipper's load and count' places the burden of proof and correct loading on the shipper' who then accepts responsibility for the description and count of the goods")(*quoting* Dublin Co. v. Ryder Truck Lines, Inc., 417 F.2d 777 (5th Cir. 1969)).

[167] 49 U.S.C. § 80113(b).

ed on the vessel by the shipper. If the carrier loads the goods, an SLC clause is not effective to disclaim liability for a description of the goods on the bill of lading.[168] When goods are loaded by a carrier, the carrier has a direct ability to count the number of packages and at least note the condition of the packages and thus is obligated to "determine the kind and quantity" (although not the quality) of the goods.[169] Moreover, for bulk freight, even where it is loaded by the shipper, the carrier must still determine the kind and quantity of the freight if the shipper so requests and provides adequate facilities for the carrier to weigh the freight. In situations where the carrier must count packages or weigh the goods, disclaimers such as "shipper's weight, load, and count" will not be effective.[170]

The requirement that the shipper actually load the goods seems appropriate for disclaimers of the "shipper's weight, load, and count" variety; but it seems inapposite for disclaimers of the "said to contain" or "contents or condition of contents of packages unknown" variety. Nonetheless, the carrier will be liable for a misdescription even with an otherwise clear "SLC" disclaimer if it issues a bill of lading and the shipper in fact never loaded anything at all on board the carrier's vessels.

Second, a disclaimer is effective only to the extent that the carrier "does not know whether any part of the goods were received or conform to the description."[171] If the carrier has actual knowledge of a problem, it may not passively allow the shipper to provide a misdescription in the bill of lading. The protection of an SLC disclaimer, in other words, is available only to the uninformed carrier.

As noted, COGSA also permits the carrier to refuse to add to a bill of lading information that it has "no reasonable means of checking."[172] Nonetheless, the carrier must make at least a "reasonable inspection" of the goods under the circumstances.[173] If such an inspection reveals information that contradicts that provided by the shipper, the carrier must so note it on the bill of lading. In such a case of readily apparent information about number, quantity, or

---

[168] *Id.*, § 80113(b)(1).

[169] 49 U.S.C. § 80113(d)(2). *See also* Distribuidora Internacional Alimentos v. Amcar Forwarding, Inc., 2011 WL 902093 (S.D. Fla. 2011)("When the goods are loaded by a common carrier, . . . the carrier is responsible for verifying that the quantity of the goods described on the bill of lading matches what is actually loaded for transit."); Elgie & Co. v. S.S. "S. A. Nederburg", 599 F.2d 1177, 1180–81 (2nd Cir. 1979)(same), *cert. denied*, 444 U.S. 1072 (1980).

[170] 49 U.S.C. § 80113(d)(1).

[171] *Id.*, § 80113(b)(3).

[172] COGSA, § 3(3)(c).

[173] *See* 1 William Tetley, MARINE CARGO CLAIMS 654 (4th ed., 2008).

weight, the carrier is not permitted to hide behind an SLC clause. However, the carrier is not required to check most quality terms, such as what goods are in a container and whether or not they are in operating condition.[174]

The intersection of these rules arises when the carrier accepts a sealed container supposed to contain 2,000 tin ingots weighing 35 tons, and issues a bill of lading for a container "said to contain 2,000 tin ingots." If the container is empty or weighs less than a ton, and this information is readily apparent to the carrier, the carrier's disclaimer is not likely to provide protection.[175]

Indeed, some courts have connected a loss of SLC clause protection with a loss of the $500 per package limitation of liability set forth in COGSA.[176] Thus, a number of courts have found a carrier liable for the full value of misdescribed goods where a bill of lading contains false information that either is "readily apparent" to the carrier or relates to the carrier's own conduct in handling the goods.[177]

If, however, a carrier satisfies the three elements for a valid SLC clause, the bill of lading will no longer represent "*prima facie* evidence" (as stated in COGSA) of what the carrier received from

---

[174] By its terms, the FBLA only applies to outbound shipments from the United States (*see* 49 U.S.C. § 80102), with the result that the status of SLC clauses for inbound shipments remains unclear. Nonetheless, recent opinions have upheld SLC clauses for inbound shipments as well. *See, e.g.*, American Nat. Fire Ins. Co. v. M/V Seaboard Victory, 2009 WL 6465299 (S.D. Fla. 2009)(*citing* Plastique Tags, Inc. v. Asia Trans Line, Inc., 83 F.3d 1367, 1369 (11th Cir. 1996)).

[175] *See, e.g.*, Berisford Metals Corp. v. S/S Salvador, 779 F.2d 841 (2nd Cir. 1985); Delphi-Delco Elecs. Sys. v. M/V Nedlloyd Europa, 324 F.Supp.2d 403, 10 (S.D.N.Y. 2004)(holding a carrier liable where a bill of lading "erroneously states that goods have been received on board when they have not been so loaded").

[176] *See* text accompanying notes 91-97 *supra*.

[177] *See, e.g.*, Y-Tex Corp. v. Schenker, Inc., 2011 WL 2292352 (W.D. Wash. 2011)(removing COGSA's $500 liability limit because the carrier blindly accepted false information on two misidentified containers and did not "check[] the seal which was visible from the outside of the containers to verify the weight"); Mitsui Marine Fire & Ins. Co. v. Direct Container Line, Inc., 119 F. Supp. 2d 412, 416 (S.D.N.Y.)(observing that "for a carrier to lose the package limitation, it is enough that a bill of lading be erroneous" with regard to the carrier's own conduct, "regardless of whether that carrier acted fraudulently"), *aff'd*, 21 Fed. Appx. 58 (2nd Cir. 2001). The progenitor of this line of cases is Berisford Metals Corp. v. S/S Salvador, 779 F.2d 841 (2nd Cir. 1985). *But see* St. Paul Travelers Ins. Co. v. M/V Madame Butterfly, 700 F. Supp. 2d 496, 506 (S.D.N.Y. 2010)("Courts have limited the false bill of lading exception to the COGSA package limitation 'to misrepresentations concerning the physical condition or location of the goods at the time the bill of lading was issued.'")(*quoting* Delphi-Delco Electronics Systems v. M/V NEDLLOYD EUROPA, 324 F. Supp. 2d 403, 411 (S.D.N.Y. 2004)), *aff'd*, 2011 WL 1901738 (2nd Cir. 2011).

the shipper.[178] In other words, the burden of proof will switch to the shipper or other entitled party to prove that the carrier actually was the cause for the loss of or damage to the goods. As a federal court recently observed, in the case of a valid SLC clause, "a shipper must prove that the goods were damaged or lost while in the carrier's custody."[179] In the typical case, the shipper will not have access to sufficient information to meet that burden.

Thus, what is established is a system in which the carrier is responsible for checking readily observable facts—quantity, the number of cartons, obvious information about the weight of a shipment, and the like. It is likely to check such matters in any event, at least to be certain that cartons are not inadvertently left behind and to determine the appropriate freight charge. For any information thus found that contradicts information provided by the shipper, the carrier must provide an appropriate notation on the bill of lading (although of course this likely will "foul" the bill from the shipper's perspective and thus trigger further discussions). However, the carrier is not required to check goods sealed in a container or otherwise investigate their quality or functionality. Thus, it can truthfully say that it has received 1,000 cartons "said to contain" Apple iPads, without opening the cartons or testing whether the tablet computers work. For such information, a valid SLC clause will protect the carrier from misdescriptions on the bill of lading. But it must note at least readily apparent information such as the number of cartons of claimed iPads or whether the cartons or containers are damaged.[180]

§ 3.18 ____Forged Bills of Lading

If the carrier issues a bill of lading for which there are no goods, the carrier is likely to be liable for misdescription as described above. However, suppose the carrier never issued a bill of

---

[178] COGSA expressly yields to the rules in the FBLA, including with reference to the effectiveness of SLC clauses. *See* COGSA, § 3(4)(stating with respect to the "prima facie evidence" rule for a bill of lading that "nothing in this chapter shall be construed as repealing or limiting the application of any part of" the FBLA).

[179] American Nat'l Fire Ins. v. M/V Seaboard Victory, 2009 WL 6465299 at *7 (S.D. Fla. 2009)(*citing* Plastique Tags, Inc. v. Asia Trans Line, Inc., 83 F.3d 1367, 1369–1370 (11th Cir. 1996)).

[180] *See, e.g.,* Jain Irrigation System, Ltd. v. Chemcolit, Inc., 2000 WL 1802069 (S.D. Tex. 2000)(holding that the carrier was not liable for goods misdescribed on a bill of lading because the bill contained a valid "said to contain" clause, the shipper loaded the goods, and the carrier knew of no contrary information); Dei Dogi Calzature S.P.A. v. Summa Trading Corp., 733 F. Supp. 773, 775–76 (S.D.N.Y. 1990)(stating that a carrier is not liable to a shipper for losses resulting from receipt of a container filled with water instead of leather items, where the bill of lading contained a "said to contain" clause and the shipper in fact loaded the freight).

lading in the first place. Instead, a person unrelated to the carrier created the bill of lading and then forged the carrier's signature or signature stamp (*i.e.*, without the authority of the carrier). A buyer who pays upon receipt of such a forged bill of lading (such as in a "payment against documents" transaction) will have paid out the funds—probably through a series of banks—but will find that the carrier has no goods to deliver. In such a case, the buyer will have no misdelivery or misdescription claim against the carrier, for no one ever delivered goods to the carrier that it could misdescribe or misdeliver. If the carrier did not issue the bill of lading and its "signature" is a forgery or is otherwise unauthorized, that signature is not "effective," and carrier will not be liable on the bill, absent collusion or (perhaps) some sort of actionable negligence.

The forger is liable for the fraud, if he can be found. But unlike the forged indorsement situation, there is no one who has received any goods, for there never were any goods to deliver. Nonetheless, like the forged indorsement situation, each party that transferred the bill of lading for value makes warranties to later parties, and the first warranty is that "the bill is genuine."[181] If the bill of lading itself is forged, that warranty is breached. Thus, later transferees can assert breach of warranty actions against all parties who transferred the bill in return for payment. The concept is that the last person to purchase the bill will "know its transferor," and be able to recover against that transferor. That transferor can, in turn, recover against its transferor, and so on up the chain of transfers, until the loss falls either on the forger or on the person that took the bill from the forger.

Again, collecting banks that have transferred the document for value can be subject to this warranty liability.[182] But again, such banks will have the same three potential escape valves discussed in Section 3.17 above regarding forged indorsements: (1) an express disclaimer of warranty that indicates "a contrary intention"; (2) a claim that the bank is holding the document only "as security for a debt"; and (3) the limitation in the ICC Collection Rules that banks need examine only the appearance of the documents. Again, each of these approaches has analytical difficulties, but they may reflect a blanket, implicit indication to disclaim the statutory warranties. In any event, any bank found to have warranty liability can pass this liability back to its transferor, as long as it can identify and find that transferor.

---

[181] 49 U.S.C. § 80107(a)(1).

[182] *See* § 3.17 *supra*.

Finally, if UCC Article 7 applies, such as for an inbound shipment, it will generally exempt banks that are "mere intermediaries" (*e.g.*, collecting banks) from the transfer warranties regarding the genuineness of bills of lading.[183]

§ 3.19 Electronic Bills of Lading

The FBLA does not define "bill of lading," but it also does not expressly require that a bill of lading be written on a piece of paper or signed in physical form. Thus, use of electronic bills of lading would seem to be a technical possibility. Nonetheless, all of the primary rules of the FBLA are founded on an implicit assumption that the bill of lading—at least a negotiable one—is a paper document. The references to indorsement (whether in blank or to a specified person), to transfer by "delivery," to "possession" of the bill, and to a "holder" all leave the impression that a paper document is required.

However, telecommunications technology can provide electronic messages that perform the main functions of the bill of lading: as a receipt, a transport contract, and a document of title. Thus, several types of bill of lading equivalents are currently in use; but most of them are used only as receipts for the goods generated by the carrier. This is especially true for nonnegotiable bills of lading (a.k.a. waybills), which do not need to be presented to a carrier to obtain possession of the goods. Thus, as a federal court recently observed, "[s]ince the physical document is no longer necessary to the transaction, [a] waybill may be transmitted electronically or telexed between the parties."[184]

With this foundation, several efforts have been made to facilitate and create electronic carrier-issued international receipts for goods. For example, the Interstate Commerce Commission (I.C.C.) now authorizes the use of uniform electronic bills of lading, both negotiable and nonnegotiable, for motor carrier and rail carrier use.[185] More generally, as noted some federal courts have recognized the effectiveness of electronic bills of lading, at least in certain respects.[186] These developments, however, relate to the role of bills of lading merely in evidencing a carriage contract and in communicating information about the goods, the shipper, and the consignee.

---

[183] UCC §§ 7–507, 7–508.

[184] Quanzhou Joerga Fashion Co., Inc. v. Brooks Fitch Quanzhou Joerga Fashion Co., Inc. v. Brooks Fitch Apparel Group, LLC, 2012 WL 4767180 (S.D.N.Y. 2012).

[185] *See* 49 C.F.R. Part 1035.

[186] *See, e.g.*, Quanzhou Joerga Fashion Co., Inc. v. Brooks Fitch Quanzhou Joerga Fashion Co., Inc. v. Brooks Fitch Apparel Group, LLC, 2012 WL 4767180 (S.D.N.Y. 2012); Delphi-Delco Electronics Systems v. M/V NEDLLOYD EUROPA, 324 F. Supp. 2d 403, 413 (S.D.N.Y. 2004).

The recognition by the I.C.C. and the court cases does not address issues relating to the formal legal rights and obligations of the parties to the electronic bill. Thus, the bills do not allow for further sale or rerouting of the goods in transit, or for using the bills of lading to finance the transaction. Under the I.C.C. regulations, for example, negotiable uniform electronic bills of lading must "provide for indorsement on the back portion,"[187] but there is no explanation of how an electronic message has a "back portion," or how "indorsement" is to be effected.

Carriers also have attempted to create programs that utilize electronic carrier-issued international receipts for goods. Most of these efforts relate to nonnegotiable electronic waybills under which shippers provide relevant information through the carrier's website and the shipper or consignee then prints out a waybill document at either the origin or destination. Atlantic Container Lines, for example, has used dedicated lines between terminals at its offices in different ports to send messages between those offices. It generates a Data Freight Receipt which is given to the consignee or notify party. Such a receipt is not negotiable, however, and gives buyers and banks little protection from further sale or rerouting of the goods by the shipper in transit. This program is an advance over the initial efforts because it includes a "no disposal" term in the shipper-carrier contract. Thus, this electronic message protects the buyer from further sale or rerouting by the seller in transit. But it still cannot be used to finance the transfer, because the electronic receipt, even if it named a bank as consignee, is not formally a negotiable document of title. The receipt is believed to give the bank only the right to prevent delivery to the buyer, not a positive right to take control of the goods for itself.

Chase Manhattan Bank also attempted to create the Seaborne Trade Documentation System (SEADOCS), which involved a Registry for negotiable electronic bills of lading for oil shipments. The Registry acted as custodian for an actual paper negotiable bill of lading issued by a carrier, and maintained a registry of transfers of that bill from the original shipper to the ultimate "holder." The transfers were made by a series of electronic messages, each of which could be authenticated by "test keys", or identification numbers, generated by SEADOCS. SEADOCS would then, as agent, indorse the paper bill of lading in its custody. At the end, SEADOCS would electronically deliver a paper copy of the negotiable bill of lading to the last indorsee to enable it to obtain the goods from the carrier. While SEADOCS was a legal success, showing that such a

---

[187] 49 CFR § 1035.1.

program was technically feasible, it was not a commercial success, and survived for less than a year.[188]

The Comité Maritime International has adopted Rules for Electronic Bills of Lading (the "CMI Rules").[189] Under these rules, any carrier can issue an electronic bill of lading as long as it will act as a clearinghouse for subsequent transfers. Upon receiving goods, the carrier sends an electronic message to the shipper describing the goods, the contract terms and a "private key."[190] The shipper then has the "right of control and transfer" over the goods, and is called a "holder."[191] Under CMI Rules 4 and 7, an electronic message from the shipper that includes the private key can be used to transfer the shipper's rights to a third party, who then becomes a new holder. The carrier then cancels the shipper's "private key" and issues a different private key to the new holder.[192] Upon arrival, the carrier delivers the goods to then-current holder or a consignee designated by the holder.

To take advantage of the CMI Rules, the original parties to the transaction must agree that the CMI Rules will govern the "communications" aspects of the transaction—the rules are voluntary and do not automatically have the force of law.[193] But such an agreement may come merely through a reference in the carriage contract. The CMI Rules are not intended to govern the substantive laws of bills of lading provisions, only the electronic transfers of the electronic bill of lading. The Rules thus reflected an attempt to create an "electronic" writing that functions as a negotiable document of title by contract and estoppel. However, this attempt by private parties to create a negotiable document cannot serve the essential function of binding third parties, a power usually reserved to legislatures. In addition, there is some concern that the CMI Rules do not address certain important issues, such as what happens when the system fails.

The Commission of the European Committees has sponsored the BOLERO electronic bill of lading initiative, which is based on the CMI Rules, and is now a separate enterprise. However, under

---

188 *See* Susan Beecher, *Can the Electronic Bill of Lading Go Paperless*, 40 INT. LAW. 627, 635–638 (2006).

189 Comité Maritime International Rules for Electronic Bills of Lading, available at http://comitemaritime.org/Rules-for-Electronic-Bills-of-Lading/0,2728,12832,00.html.

190 *Id.*, art. 4.

191 *Id.*, art. 7.

192 *Id.*

193 *Id.*, art. 1.

the BOLERO system neither a bank nor a carrier is the repository of the sensitive information regarding who has bought and sold the cargo covered by the electronic bills of lading. Instead, BOLERO establishes as the operator of the central registry a "cloud-based" third entity that is independent of the shipper, the carrier, the ultimate buyer, and all intermediate parties. More recently, the BOLERO system operators have teamed with the Society for Worldwide Interbank Financial Telecommunication (SWIFT) to create a "Core Messaging Platform" for the presentation of formal electronic documents such as bills of lading ("eBL"). (Indeed, in 2013 BOLERO received a patent for this technology.) The system involves all counterparties agreeing to a "Rulebook," which provides for the dispatch and receipt of legally binding electronic bills of lading and, most important, a formal "fingerprinting" to ensure recognition of only one "original" bill. Thus far, however, this system also has not been able to establish a secure foundation for broad use of electronic bills of lading.

The largest challenge in all of these efforts, however, has been in making an electronic bill of lading negotiable so that it remains authentic, unique, confidential, and transferrable in a way to bind third parties. Most bankers have been skeptical of the device created by the CMI Rules, including as clarified in the BOLERO system. The registries maintained by each carrier do not have the same level of security associated with normal SWIFT procedures. (*See* "Electronic Letters of Credit" in Chapter 3.) In addition to fraudulent transactions, there is a risk of misdirected messages. Thus, a bank could find itself relying on non-existent rights from a fraudulent actor impersonating the carrier. Although the new BOLERO system seeks to minimize these risks, the banks are concerned as to whether carriers will accept liability for losses due to such fraudulent practices. The banks are also concerned that the full terms and conditions of the CMI and BOLERO Rules are not available to or perhaps binding on subsequent "holders." Thus, the CMI and BOLERO Rules have not yet seemed to find wide acceptance, at least in the United States, and bills of lading are still primarily paper-based in both the "payment against documents" and letter of credit transactions.

Other systems also have been tried. The "Global Trade System" employed a nonnegotiable waybill with a clause that tried to give it aspects of a negotiable bill of lading.[194] The Trade Card System was an Internet-based, paper-less system, which allowed electronic set-

---

[194] For further discussion of these systems, see Marek Dubovic, *The Problems and Possibilities for using Electronic Bills of Lading as Collateral*, 23 ARIZ. J. INT'L & COMP. L. 437 (2006).

tlement of payments for purchases of goods and related services.[195] These systems were confined to registered users, but both offered financing for commercial transactions." Both systems, however, had difficulties in providing bills of lading that could be used as collateral. The 2007 UNCITRAL Legislative Guide on Secured Transactions in fact is founded on the notion of paper documents of title.[196]

Two recent legal developments nonetheless may facilitate and promote the future development of secure and commercially viable electronic bills of lading. First, recent revisions to the UCC expressly contemplate "electronic documents of title," including electronic bills of lading. Revised UCC Article 1 defines an electronic document of title as one "evidenced by a record consisting of information stored in an electronic medium"[197] and then broadly defines a "record" to include information that is "stored in an electronic medium and is retrievable in perceivable form."[198] The 2003 revisions to UCC Article 7 then address issues concerning the security of electronic bills of lading through the concept of "control."[199] At the core of this concept is a requirement that "a single authoritative copy of the document exists which is unique, identifiable, and [with certain defined exceptions] unalterable." Article 7 then has specifically tailored rules for the "negotiation" of an electronic document of title.[200]

Second, the recently concluded "Rotterdam Rules" create an explicit legal framework for the creation, transfer, and enforcement of "negotiable electronic transport records."[201] Deliberately medium and technology neutral, these rules should both accommodate and foster future technological innovations.[202] Thus, the only requirements for the use of a "negotiable electronic transport record" are functional: it must arise subject to procedures that provide for (a) a method for the issuance and the transfer of the record to an intended holder, (b) an assurance that the record "retains its integrity," (c)

---

[195] *Id.*

[196] Footnote 25 of the UNCITRAL Legislative Guide on Secured Transactions expressly notes that—although not designed to discourage use of electronic documents of title—it was "prepared against the background of negotiable instruments and negotiable documents in paper form." *See* http://www.uncitral.org/uncitral/uncitral_texts/security.html.

[197] UCC § 1–201(b)(16).

[198] UCC § 1–201(b)(31).

[199] UCC § 7–106(b).

[200] UCC § 7–501(b).

[201] Rotterdam Rules, *supra* note 55, arts. 1(10)(b), 1(19), 8–10.

[202] *Id.*, art. 1(21)(defining the "issuance" of a negotiable "electronic transport record" merely as requiring procedures "that ensure that the record is subject to exclusive control from its creation until it ceases to have any effect or validity"); and *id.*, arts. 9, 51(4), and 57 (providing more detail).

the manner by which the holder can "demonstrate that it is the holder," and (d) the manner of confirming the delivery to the holder or of terminating the record.[203] Although only two countries have ratified the Rotterdam Rules as of 2013, as noted above there are positive indications that many countries will do so (including the United States).

Separately, Customs and Border Protection (CPB) has established a system for paperless customs clearance through the use of an electronic interface on a dedicated agency website. Since September 2008, new Foreign Trade Regulations have mandated the electronic filing of export information via Electronic Export Information ("EEI") forms for any export over $2500 (other than to Canada). This new online Automated Export System ("AES") has replaced the filing of hard copy Shipper's Export Declaration (SED) forms. The purpose of the system was to assist U.S. Customs in enforcement goals and to spot potential terrorist threats.

---

[203] *Id.*, art. 9.

Chapter 4

SALES AGENT AND DISTRIBUTORSHIP AGREEMENTS

Table of Sections

§ 4.1 Need for a Written Agreement

Most products sold to purchasers in foreign lands involve the use of some person or entity in the foreign nation as the sales agent or distributor.[1] A small company may retain an agent who handles many different, but usually compatible, products. A large company often has its own foreign agent or distributor, who may be the exclusive agent.[2]

It should be obvious that the commercial relationship between a U.S. producer and its foreign agent or distributor *should* be reduced to a written agreement. Because two different nations' laws may be involved, and probably two different cultures, the agree-

---

[1] See generally, D. Campbell (ed.), International Agency and Distribution Law (three volumes—2008). Certainly a company in one nation may accept orders placed from abroad. Such sales require no foreign, local representation. The retention of a foreign agent or distributor often follows periodic but increasing sales placed directly to the home office from abroad. Increasingly, the internet is used.

[2] While the direct sale from an order placed from abroad may be the prelude to the first use of an agent or distributor, the successful use of an agent or distributor may in turn subsequently lead to manufacturing the products in the foreign nation. Later chapters deal with both licensing such production as well as direct foreign investment.

ment should be sufficiently detailed to deal with the legal consequences reflecting such differences.[3]

There are times when an agreement is not in writing. That is often thought to make termination easier by the agent or distributor, but that may be a false expectation. Foreign laws are designed to protect local agents and distributors; oral agreements may simply muddy the waters, but nevertheless result in a foreign judgment against the U.S. business. Another thought that may be equally dangerous is to use the standard agreement developed and used in the United States. Agency and distributor agreements should be tailored to fit each separate nation, with careful attention to local law.

Contract law is obviously the central focus of a cross-border agreement that creates an agency or distributorship. That includes an important method of distributing products (*e.g.*, fast food), or services (*e.g.*, hotel accommodations)—the franchise. While the entity from which the goods or services originate will often have the bargaining edge by mere size and legal resources, and demand provisions that provide for exclusive resolution of any dispute in its nation and under its law, courts within the nation where the goods are sold or services provided are very likely to find some way to reject the U.S. choice of law and forum and apply their own law in their own courts. That may be based on express laws governing sales agents, distributorships or franchises (including provisions within a trade area such as the EU or NAFTA), or simply on a prevalent civil law notion that contractual obligations should be governed by the law of the country where such obligations are incurred, an application of *lex loci domicili*.

§ 4.2 Problems Most Prevalent upon Termination

A U.S. producer/seller may have its own complete distribution network in each foreign country in which it does business. Much more likely is that the U.S. company will use some local person or entity for the distribution of its goods. Local distributors are used by U.S. companies just beginning to sell goods abroad, as well as by large multinationals with long experience abroad, but which do not have their own distribution networks. As in the case of any commercial contract, there are many possible areas for disagreement. But the most difficult issues involving distribution agree-

---

[3] Eberhard H. Rohm & Robert Koch, Choice of Law in International Distribution Contracts: Obstacle or Opportunity, 11 N.Y. Int'l L. Rev. 1 (1998).

ments arise upon termination, especially when the foreign agent or distributor is terminated against its will.

Termination issues are sufficiently difficult when both parties are in the United States. They are exacerbated when the seller is in one nation, such as the United States, and the distributor is in another nation, particularly a developing nation.[4] The foreign distributor, often an individual or comparatively small corporation, may believe that it has been treated unfairly by the quite likely much larger foreign seller. This is especially true when the local distributor has worked for a long time to develop clients and goodwill for the foreign company. The consequence of complaints by local agents and distributors that they have been mistreated, especially terminated unfairly, by large foreign corporations, has been the enactment of host-nation regulation of many forms of distribution agreements.[5] These laws may be very favorable to the local agent or distributor, and one may look in vain for provisions in these foreign laws which offer the foreign producer or supplier compensation when the local distributor has performed unsatisfactorily.

The form of damages against the U.S. company may be lost profits that are the probable result of the termination. Damages may also include overhead and goodwill, an even in some nations a form of severance compensation.

An effecting contract should cover pricing, specific quantity of goods to be ordered or sold, geographic territory, exclusive or nonexclusive arrangement, agreement duration, and liability insurance.

---

[4] It is not only developing nations which attempt to regulate the distribution of goods. Agency law in general affects such distribution and may be quite different and quite complex in other countries. See for example the law of Mexico, as discussed by Ignacio Gomez Palacio in Symposium, Establishing an Agency or Distributorship in Mexico, 4 U.S.–Mexico L. J. 72 (1996); in Italy, as discussed in D. Dobson & R. Gaudenzi, Agency and Distributorship Laws in Italy: Guidelines for the Foreign Principal, 20 Int'l L. 997 (1986) and in G. LaVilla & M. Caetella, The Italian Law of Agency and Distributorship Agreements (1977); in Germany, as discussed in F. Staubach, The German Law of Agency and Distributorship (1977); in France, as discussed in J. Guyenot, The French Law of Agency and Distributorship Agreements (1976), or in Belgium, as discussed in A. Hansebout, Mind Your Belgian Distributor! ALTIUS (2009).

[5] For example, the "Statement of Motives" of the Puerto Rican law applicable to distribution agreements states:

> The Commonwealth of Puerto Rico cannot remain indifferent to the growing number of cases in which domestic and foreign enterprises, without just cause, eliminate their dealers, concessionaries [sic], or agents, as soon as these have created a favorable market and without taking into account their legitimate interests.

Quoted in Fornaris v. Ridge Tool Co., 423 F.2d 563, 565 (1st Cir.1970), *reversed* 400 U.S. 41, 91 S.Ct. 156, 27 L.Ed.2d 174 (1970).

§ 4.3 Effect of Changing Export Laws in the United States

A company dealing abroad through a foreign agent or distributor must be aware also of U.S. laws that may affect the distribution of goods abroad. The United States has exerted with some frequency extraterritorial authority by way of laws that affect U.S. businesses doing business abroad. These rules usually have been motivated by political goals (*e.g.*, the removal of a dictator from office), and have no direct relation to either the U.S. seller or the foreign buyer. The political goals may be strongly objected to by the foreign agent's or distributor's government. These rules may have significant impact. The U.S. party may be prohibited from exporting to the foreign nation, which leaves the foreign agent or distributor without products to sell, and therefor in jeopardy of serious financial losses. The U.S. exporter may be in breach of a distribution agreement if it is unable to fulfill orders. The agreement should have an *excuse for nonperformance* clause which covers such an event. Which U.S. laws may have such an effect are not easily identified. Foreign policy has caused various U.S. presidents to use export controls as a response to foreign political actions, such as in 1982 when the United States limited the transfer of goods to Europe that were destined for use in the construction of a gas pipeline from the then USSR.

§ 4.4 Choice of Form

The two forms most frequently used to distribute products abroad are (1) an independent foreign agent, or (2) an independent foreign distributor. Usually the choice is made by the U.S. exporter. But in doing business abroad, especially in developing nations, the choice of the form of distribution may not be the prerogative of the U.S. company. The choice may be mandated by local law. Furthermore, there may be quite different choices under foreign laws, but the goal is likely to be the same: protection of local agents or distributors.

§ 4.5 Independent Foreign Agent

An independent foreign agent, who may be called a "sales representative" or "commission agent", is a person in the foreign nation who does not take title to the goods and who usually is paid in some combination of stipend and commissions. This person does not bear the risk that the buyer might not pay. That risk remains with the U.S. supplier. The foreign agent usually does not have the power to bind the U.S. supplier,[6] but may be considered to have implied power to do so, and certainly may be given express authority to do so.[7]

The independent agent obtains orders for sales abroad and sends those orders to the U.S. seller. Thus, usually there is no need for the agent to store goods in its nation, the agent is a go-between for the U.S. distributor and foreign customer. The agreement reached by the agent and foreign buyer is usually subject to approval by the U.S. company; the agent does not usually have the authority to bind the U.S. principal.

Agency law may differ substantially in a foreign nation, especially nations with civil law tradition systems.[8] Furthermore, the laws of some nations blur the distinction between the two forms of distribution, and thus use of one form may not achieve the protection sought.

The law of the agent's nation may regulate the nature of the agency relationship substantially more than is the practice in the United States. Civil law commercial codes may provide extensive detail regarding the agency relationship. Additionally, these rules may be mandatory and not subject to alteration by contract. Foreign law may outline different forms of agency with quite carefully delineated powers. The powers may or may not be in conflict with what the U.S. party might wish to arrange by contract.

§ 4.6 Independent Foreign Distributor

An independent foreign distributor, in contrast to the usual kind of agent, buys the company's products and resells them through the foreign distributor's network.[9] The foreign distributor, in taking title to the goods, consequently assumes such risk as not being able to resell them. The distributor is the one whom the purchaser must pay, and therefore the distributor is at risk for nonpayment. Because the distributor essentially is buying the goods for

---

[6] The word "agent" in foreign sales use may mean more than or less than the legal meaning of the word in U.S. law. U.S. agency law usually involves a consensual relationship where the agent has certain power to bind the principal. But that power may be limited or removed altogether. It is important to realize that the general meaning of "agent" may differ from country-to-country, which emphasizes the need for contractual clarity in defining the relationship.

[7] Agents are frequently used for sales to foreign governments, where contracts are often for very substantial amounts.

[8] The civil law tends not to recognize the responsibility of a principal for acts of an undisclosed agent.

[9] The distributor, in contrast to an agent, thus has to make a financial commitment, and consequently is usually a larger and more formal entity than a foreign direct agent.

resale, it must find storage for the goods prior to final sale and distribution. Usually, it must also undertake actively promoting and market the products.

Unlike the uncertainty existing in the case of the independent agent, the independent distributor does not have power to bind the supplier. That is because the distributor buys the goods for resale, rather than entering into contracts on behalf of the principal as in the case of an agent. Of course, the distributor might additionally have power to act as an agent for goods it does not obtain as a distributor. In such case, the issue of the power to bind the principal may arise.

If an independent foreign distributor is chosen, the language in the distribution agreement should be as clear as possible in noting a principal-principal as opposed to a principal-agent relationship. Language used when establishing an independent contractor relationship may be useful in establishing an independent distributor relationship.

§ 4.7 Laws Protecting Agents and Distributors

Countries often have special laws that govern the distribution agreement between their nationals and foreign businesses.[10] This is in addition to the domestic agency laws that apply to any agency relationship.[11] There are far fewer countries that have laws governing agreements between foreign business and local independent *distributors*.[12] The distinction between the two is sometimes blurred, but nevertheless remains an important distinction. For example, antitrust laws in some nations are enforced against distributorships but not against agencies. This may affect assigning a distributor exclusive selling rights.[13] Of course, when the agency form is that of an *employee* agent rather than an *independent* agent, the agency clearly may be exclusive. Some developing nations do not even recognize the distinction between their nationals as agents and their nationals as distributors, and govern both in

---

[10] Some nations mandate the use of local agents for the distribution of foreign goods. This tends to be the rule in developing nations, and includes much of the Middle-East.

[11] Appointment of an agent, particularly with power to bind the principal, may constitute doing business and subject the foreign business to jurisdiction and taxation.

[12] An example is Belgium, one of the few nations in the European Union to have legislation regulating distributorship agreements.

[13] Chile allows an exclusive agency but not an exclusive distributorship.

one law.[14] But to be fair, what the U.S. supplier calls its foreign distributor is less important than being able to determine and formalize the characteristics of the relationship. If the characteristics suggest an agency, the host nation is likely to consider the person as an agent. The same is true for distributors.[15]

Where foreign laws exist to govern distribution agreements they are likely to be designed to (1) benefit local agents/distributors, especially in the area of termination; (2) restrict (or prohibit) the use of agents/distributors, essentially to protect the public from unfair agents/distributors; or (3) apply domestic *labor* law to the distribution agreement, especially in the area of a severance payment.

Civil law tradition nations tend to be more likely to restrict freedom to contract than common law tradition nations. Laws regulating agency and distributorship agreements in civil law countries may be separate and specific, or may be found in the civil or commercial codes.[16] Developing nations are most likely to have special laws affecting the agency/distributorship relationships.

Even where host nation law mandates the use of local agents or distributors, it may be possible to use a local business entity as the agent even though the agency is majority owned by the U.S. company. But some host nations that mandate the use of local distributors additionally require at least majority host nation ownership of artificial entities (i.e., local corporations).[17]

---

[14] This is true of many Latin American nations, but not of Brazil. Developing nations in other areas of the world, i.e., Africa and Asia, are more inclined to follow the general rule of regulating agents but not distributors.

[15] Carolita L. Oliveros, International Distribution Issues: Contract Materials, ALI–ABA 19th Annual Advanced Course, March 18–20, 2004, SJ075 ALI–ABA 777 (an extensive coverage of some 44 nations); Michael Dean, International Distribution Overview of Relevant Distribution Laws: Europe, SJ075 ALA–ABA 245 (2004); E. Charles Routh, Agency, Representation and Distribution Agreements in Asia, SJ078 ALI–ABA 397 (2004); Dennis Campbell & Louis Lafili, Distributorships, Agency and Franchising in an International Arena: Europe, The United States, Japan and Latin America (1990).

[16] Distribution of products within the European Union involves national laws and EU law. Common or civil law tradition based national laws, depending on the EU member state involved, are likely to govern the nature of the relationship, such as the powers of persons designated as agents. European Union law is likely to govern such aspects of distribution as territorial restrictions and price maintenance. See especially the EU "Vertical Restraints Regulation", discussed in Section 22.12 *infra*.

[17] Many nonmarket economies mandated local sales through a government state trading organization (STO) or foreign trade organization (FTO), a requirement which substantially has been abandoned, along with many other trade restrictions. But remnants of state involvement persist in some nations in transition from non-

§ 4.8 Aspects of Control

The sale of goods abroad to an independent distributor usually means the seller relinquishes control over such aspects as where the product may be resold and the price.[18] Loss of control over establishing the price may be enough to cause the seller to adopt an independent *agency* form of distribution, which may but does not assure ability to set the resale price.[19] Because title remains in the U.S. seller until the goods are sold in the foreign country by the agent, the seller should be able to set the price.[20] The agent only has authority to find a buyer, but not set the terms of the sale. That remains the function of the seller.

A further element of control is the ability to appoint sub-agents or sub-distributors without the approval of the principal. An agent normally has no such authority, but an independent distributor will be able to hire and fire at will, unless there is some agreement regarding whom the distributor uses to deal with the foreign company's products.

If the agent is actually *employed* by the U.S. company, there is no question about the issue of control.[21] But when an agent is an employee, the employer becomes subject to labor laws of the host nation. That may create such problem as being unable to terminate the employee at will, at least without making a substantial severance payment.[22] It is not only developing nations' laws which grant greater rights to employees. The industrialized nations of Europe treat labor in a very different way than does the United States.[23]

---

market to market economies, and there remain a number of nations still firmly committed to nonmarket policies.

[18] The U.S. export-control laws govern re-export and may place a burden on the U.S. exporter to assure that the goods are not re-exported to certain destinations. See infra Chapter 16.

[19] In many developing nations the government establishes price controls.

[20] That may be a wholesale price and the U.S. seller may not be able to further control the retail price.

[21] An employee-agent may be on commissions alone or a salary plus commissions. The independent agent is more likely to be solely on commissions.

[22] Many developing nations have special agency/distributor laws because their labor laws do not apply to these relationships. Agents and distributors are thought to be able to bargain better than employees, but when that has proven not to be the case, it has been "remedied" by either enacting a special agent/distributor law, or by applying the labor laws to the agency/distributorship relationships.

[23] See Clyde W. Summers, Worker Participation in the U.S. and West Germany: A Comparative Study from an American Perspective, 28 Am.J.Comp.L. 367 (1980).

The U.S. company therefore may prefer to use an independent agent who is carefully kept independent of the company, and linked to the company as an agent by contract rather than by employment. Control will be contractually designated, but host-nation laws are likely to affect the contract. Some foreign nations do not distinguish carefully between an agent who is an employee and an agent who is not.[24] Where the distinction is made, and statutory protection is not given to the independent agent, the choice of an agent who is not an employee will usually be the preference of the U.S. company.

The fact that some laws may not acknowledge the distinction between an employee-agent and an independent agent does not mean that all laws will overlook that distinction. For example, the tax laws generally will accept the distinction, and thus income from sales by an employee-agent is income to the corporation, but not necessarily so in the case of an independent agent. Furthermore, a foreign nation may exert extraterritorial jurisdiction over the U.S. company which *employs* an agent in the foreign nation, but decline to do so when the U.S. company uses an *independent* agent in the foreign nation.

Choice of an independent distributor rather than an employee-agent may create antitrust problems. The distributorship agreement becomes an agreement between two different and independent entities, and provisions such as an exclusive distributorship arrangement may conflict with local laws. The European Union imposes rules on exclusive distributorships which differ from those in the United States. Prohibitions on selling outside an exclusive territory, such as one of the EU nations, will not be recognized, although one may be able to mandate that the distributor *solicit* business exclusively in the applicable territory. European Union rules also address and prohibit resale price maintenance and minimum prices.

Antitrust concerns similar to those involving exclusive distributorship arrangements may exist where the foreign independent distributor is prohibited from selling competing goods. This may create a problem with U.S. law in that it may foreclose other U.S. companies from entering the foreign market. It may conflict with host nation antitrust principles as well.

---

[24] Italy grants to self-employed agents nearly all the rights granted to employee agents. See A.H. Puelinck & H.A. Tielemans, The Termination of Agency and Distributorship Agreements: A Comparative Survey, 3 Nw.J.Int'l L. & Bus. 452, 456 (1981).

Use of an employee-agent may avoid these issues, because there is only a single entity involved and the control over the employee is obviously greater than over an independent agent. When there is any question regarding restraints on competition, the antitrust laws of both the United States and the foreign host nation must be consulted. The most developed antitrust law outside the United States is in the European Union. While many of the EU antitrust concepts parallel those in the United States, there are many significant differences, mandating an understanding of both.

The ability to control the agent by means of the distribution agreement may depend upon whether the agent is in a country with a common law tradition or a country with a civil law tradition. Common law tradition nations tend to allow greater freedom to contractually create the full terms of the agreement, including termination provisions. Civil law tradition nations, contrastingly, more often include statutory restraints on freedom to contract, especially with regard to the right to terminate and rights created upon termination. Whether the nation has a common law or civil law tradition system, laws are dynamic and the attitude toward distribution agreements may change. Laws governing the transfer of technology and intellectual property have very substantially changed in the past two decades in developing nations, several of which realized that restrictive laws diminished the amount and quality of technology offered. Knowing foreign law usually means associating with local counsel. No one distributing products in many countries can be an expert in all the host-nation laws—the use of local counsel is critical.

§ 4.9 Areas to Consider

There are many areas of control which should be considered, not only those mentioned above dealing with setting prices and hiring sub-agents. Where control exists, the agent/distributor may be limited in many actions. That may include the ability to incur expenses on behalf of the principal, or to carry competing lines of products. Such actions as making corrupt payments to foreign officials may be closely monitored where control exists. There is an obvious benefit to having control. But with control may come responsibility for actions of the agent that appear to a third party to be within the agent's authority. Such responsibility may be avoided by using a distributor who is fully independent of the company. But where the host foreign nation does not recognize this independence, the worst of both worlds may exist. The company may have no control over the agent/distributor, but may be held responsible for much of the conduct of the agent/distributor.

A U.S. entity should not expect that developed countries will have the least protective agency and distributorship laws and developing countries the most protective. Mexico does not have specific indemnification rights on termination, even where the termination is not done for just cause.

A final area that has arisen more frequently, but has not been resolved, is the application of U.S. federal labor and employment rules and such matters as meeting the requirements of the American Disabilities Act (ADA) in a foreign country. Assume a U.S. entity trains foreign workers on U.S. made work policies that comply with U.S. federal laws. May the foreign distributor impose those rules, even when it is willing to do so?[25] May a distinction be made between subsidiaries abroad owned by the U.S. entity, and agents or distributors abroad but extensively controlled by the U.S. entity?

---

[25] See, e.g., Spector v. Norwegian Cruise Line, Ltd., 545 U.S. 119 (2005).

Chapter 5

COUNTERTRADE AGREEMENTS

Table of Sections

§ 5.1 Countertrade in the Post World War II Years

Countertrade is barter in modern clothes. It developed rapidly as a form of doing business with the USSR and Eastern European nations in the 1970s and 1980s, before major economic and political reforms tended to diminish its emphasis as a means of doing business.[1] Although some nations announced that as part of their reforms from nonmarket to market economies they would discontinue the use of countertrade, some of the same reasons that previously existed which encouraged the use of countertrade, i.e., shortage of hard currency, have persisted and have caused these nations to continue its use. Increased countertrade has been part of the dynamic growth in world trade since World War II, and part of the changing conditions in trading patterns.[2] By the 1990s countertrade was part of the fabric of international trade, especially for developing nations with inconvertible currencies and little access to hard currencies.

1 The Council for Mutual Economic Aid (CMEA or COMECON), the socialist bloc's modest attempt at economic integration, had requirements that member-nation sellers had to obtain contracts to sell their goods before they could import Western goods.

2 It has been estimated as accounting for 8–10 percent of world trade. Group of Thirty (G30) Report (Mar. 1986). A United States International Trade Commission report in 1985 suggested that 5.6 percent of U.S. exports involved countertrade. ITC country specific studies sometimes discuss the impact of countertrade. See, *e.g.*, Survey of Views on the Impact of Granting Most Favored Nation Status to the Soviet Union, USITC Publication 2251 (1990) at 2-28.

Thus, Thailand trades fruit for buses from China. While countertrade is often disparaged by the U.S. government, it continues. Pepsico has traded its famous product for Russia's—Stolichnaya vodka.

The use of countertrade has not depended on the size of the transaction. It has been used for some very large natural resource ventures in the former Soviet Union, and for many relatively small transactions in Eastern European nations. The success that countertrade achieved in nonmarket economy nations caused it to spread; it has been used increasingly in transactions with developing nations.[3] Countertrade is not limited to nonmarket or developing nation trade, however. One form of countertrade, *offsets* (discussed below), is being used for many military equipment and large civilian aircraft sales to developed nations. It is thus no longer considered the "dark" side of international trade, but a legitimate form of doing business.

The above comments illustrate classifying the use of countertrade by the characteristics of a nation's economy, such as nonmarket economy nations, developing nations, and developed or industrialized nations. The classification might also be based upon a product or service, such as aircraft. Countertrade has often been the only form of sales available where the goods or services were not of sufficiently high priority to gain import permission and consequent access to scarce hard currency. The exporter of sophisticated computer hardware usually has had little trouble in demanding traditional forms of documentary sales, cash in the form of some hard currency in return for the needed goods. But where the goods or services are of less priority for a nation's perceived development needs,[4] or where the goods or services are available from many sources, countertrade may be the only way to successfully market them.[5]

§ 5.2 Why Engage in Countertrade?

Before one characterizes countertrade as any form of rightful heir to free trade, it must be acknowledged as a form of trade which is often an involuntary transaction. It consumes more time than a

---

[3] It was largely the product of the debt crisis in the early 1980s, certainly as much as the success of countertrade by nonmarket economies.

[4] This is especially true where there is a development plan which outlines what the nation's needs are for the next 5–10 years. If the products planned for export to such a country are not on the "list", they will be unlikely to be approved as a transaction involving scarce hard currency.

[5] Scott J. Lochner, "Guide to Countertrade and International Barter," 19 Int'l L. 725 (1985). A useful resource is the weekly report on barter at www.barternews.com.

cash transaction. It gives the U.S. exporter products it may not want and cannot easily sell, sometimes because of poor quality. In view of such unattractive characteristics of countertrade, why do U.S. and other industrialized nations' companies engage in countertrade? In a great many cases not because they want to, but because it is the only way to trade or invest in the particular product or service. Additionally, it may be the way to gain a foothold in a market, to be positioned favorably for the time when countertrade is not mandatory and exchangeable currency is available.

The U.S. company would almost always prefer to be paid in dollars or another hard currency. Those currencies are freely convertible. The reason for countertrade is often that the foreign party (or that party's nation) is short of convertible currency. It is easier to understand the complexities of countertrade when it is accepted that it is usually not the preferred method of trade, but does have some justifications that lead parties to agree to one form of countertrade or another.

One might use countertrade to avoid or evade taxation, but that is not a common characteristic of a professional, commercial transaction. It is rather more common between individuals who know each other, such as a person who has a hobby making concrete garden statuary and trades a fountain to a local restaurant for a dozen "free" dinners. Or the plumber who does some work on a lawyer's house in exchange for a will.[6] Tax avoidance was probably not an issue, but a consequence of not even thinking it might be necessary to include the value of each item received as income. These simple transactions constitute countertrade, but in its most simple form—barter.

Countertrade as a form of international trade may be used to penetrate new markets which have been closed due to traditional trading relationships or patterns.[7] Some persons have viewed countertrade as a necessary way of prying open formerly closed markets.[8] Purchasers often build good relations with suppliers and tend to avoid even listening about other available substitutes. It is commonplace in Japan especially, and often misunderstood in the United States as creating intentional trade barriers. Coerced or volun-

---

6 This is obviously more likely in a small town where people frequently "exchange" their work products, than in a large city. One may reasonably doubt that a large New York City law firm engages in such barter of its services.

7 Erwin Amann and Dalia Marin, "Risk–Sharing in International Trade: An Analysis of Countertrade," XLII J. Indus. Econ. 63 (1994).

8 Stanislaw J. Soltysinski, "Statement: In Defense of Countertrade," 5 J. Com. Bus. & Capital Market L. 341 (1983).

tary countertrade may be an effective way to create new markets for new products.[9]

Countertrade is not only intended to keep scarce hard currency within the nation that demands countertrade, but to create jobs as well. It thus is not only practiced by third world and nonmarket economies, but by many industrialized nations.[10] Selling military equipment, or large aircraft, is very likely to involve some countertrade as part of the sales agreement. This is a voluntary form of countertrade, part of the negotiating process to obtain a sale, and viewed as a legitimate part of fair trade, or trading on an "even playing field." Selling commercial aircraft from the United States to Japan is likely to involve manufacturing some of the aircraft parts in Japan. Japan announced in 2013 that it would soon sell new regional jets; it had gained experience in countertrade with Boeing because it had been involved in design developments. If a U.S. aircraft industry company does not agree to countertrade, Airbus in Europe is likely to win the contract by agreeing to such form of countertrade.

The motivation and even government mandate or private interest decision to engage in countertrade will vary from country-to-country. Some Eastern European nations made countertrade mandatory, before 1988, but the trend is away from such restrictive use. Some nations use countertrade to attempt to maintain a general balance of trade in all industries, and others try to maintain a balance in each industrial sector (e.g., vehicles) or even each separate industry (e.g., trucks). Because countertrade tends to increase when a nation has a serious shortage of hard currency, the rules of the countertrade game are constantly changing. Participants enter and exit usually not according to any philosophical commitment to or rejection of countertrade, but because sales are best or only achieved by playing the countertrade game.

Because various forms of countertrade are often given different names, some definitions should be useful. They are not always carefully separated in use, but they help to illustrate how many varia-

---

[9] It is estimated that countertrade grew from about two percent of world trade in 1976 to something between five percent and 25 percent by the mid–1980s. Philip Rowberg, Jr., Countertrade as a Quid Pro Quo for Host Government Approval of a Joint Venture, in David N. Goldsweig (ed.), Joint Venturing Abroad: A Case Study (ABA 1985). The movement towards market economies in Eastern Europe and former USSR countries has reduced countertrade because some of those nations consider countertrade a characteristic identified with the socialist, nonmarket form of economy they have rejected.

[10] Australia, Belgium and Canada, for example. See Cedric Guyot, Countertrade Contracts in International Business, 20 Int'l Lawyer 921, 943 (1986).

tions of centuries-old "barter" modern commerce has been able to create.

§ 5.3 Barter

"Countertrade" has many faces. It is often nothing more than simple "*barter*," two parties exchanging goods, usually of similar value. Any difference in the values is normally paid in cash, but barter is often thought of as a transaction without cash, partly because the parties lack any currencies. It is actually the one form of countertrade that is usually accomplished without any cash involvement. As young people we probably all at one time engaged in barter, trading "things" with friends, perhaps stamps, or baseball cards, or dolls, or marbles, or Pokemon cards. We never thought of involving any money in the exchange. The reason for the exchange may well have been that we did not have any money, and thus added to our collections by disposing of items less desired or duplicated. That sounds remarkably like a modern countertrade transaction by a nation short of hard currency or lacking credit.

Barter may be on a much larger scale than exchanging marbles or one rifle for fifteen buffalo hides. Many commercial transactions, particularly with Eastern European countries in the 1970s and 1980s, were basically barter transactions. But countertrade has never been exclusively a characteristic of nonmarket nations. New Zealand has exchanged lamb for Iranian oil. A U.S. liquor company exported bourbon in exchange for bananas. The list of such examples is very long.

Barter agreements are not always simple, cash-less, single-document arrangements. They sometimes involve two separate documentary sales, often with letters of credit, and a linking or protocol agreement which includes provisions that make the transaction an exchange or barter transaction. But this tends to be more descriptive of a more complex form of barter, most likely *counterpurchase*.

§ 5.4 Counterpurchase

Counterpurchase occurs usually after one party, for example a company in the United States, finds a market for its goods in another, for example Poland. The U.S. company agrees to purchase Polish products of the same value as the U.S. company's proposed exports. The Polish goods are usually unrelated to the U.S. goods. It sounds like barter described above. But barter usually has two parties interested in each other's goods. In much counterpurchase, where it may be fairly called an involuntary transaction, one party would prefer to sell its goods for cash, but is forced into a countertrade agreement because of the currency shortage of the other nation. A company, whether Boeing or Airbus, selling commercial aircraft to Poland, would prefer to be paid in dollars or pounds or euros. The company really does not want glassware, or canned hams, or coal. But if it wishes to sell the aircraft, it may have to accept the Polish products and arrange for their sale in the United States or some third nation.[11]

The counterpurchase agreement will provide for the date by which the seller must purchase the agreed amount of countertrade goods. Some nations require all agreements to be 100 percent counterpurchase, that is the seller must purchase as much as it sells. Such an arrangement effectively means there will be no net exchange of currency. But the nation demanding countertrade may even attempt to negotiate 150 percent countertrade, requiring that the foreign party essentially sell, on behalf of the nation demanding countertrade, some of its products and return hard currency for the 50 percent excess. For example, a U.S. company sells a lathe valued at $10,000 to a Chilean company, and must take $15,000 in value in Chilean goods. But the U.S. company does not keep the $15,000 received for selling those goods, it must turn over to the Chilean company $5,000. The U.S. company has become little more than a sales agent for Chilean goods, at least with respect to the $5,000 worth of goods.

There is always concern that if the U.S. exporter purchases the foreign countertrade goods *before* selling its own goods, the foreign nation will use the hard currency obtained from such sale for some purpose other than to obtain the U.S. exporter's products. In such case, it is wise for the U.S. company to demand the establishment of an escrow account in a third nation and have all the hard currency resulting from the U.S. purchase deposited in that account, to be used by the foreign nation only to buy specified products from the U.S. exporter.

Counterpurchase accounts for a considerable percentage of countertrade, perhaps as much as 50–60 percent. There are many potential problems, both with regard to locating products for countertrade in the foreign nation, establishing their value, drafting the agreement, and selling the products in the United States or a third nation. The countertrade or protocol agreement must be carefully drafted, although it is likely that some control of its terms will be

---

[11] Because it involves imports of the Polish products into the United States or a third nation, tariffs and non-tariff barriers may have to be confronted.

maintained by the foreign nation, which may have laws or regulations governing such issues as the required percentage of counterpurchase, time limits for meeting such purchase commitment, and penalties for failure to meet the time limit.

One issue frequently involved in either common barter or the more sophisticated counterpurchase is setting a value for the goods. Returning to trading items as a child, if you were trying to trade an 1898 postage stamp, you might have said it was "worth" three 1904 stamps. But your friend may have disagreed, saying the 1904 stamps were rarer and at best the trade should be one for one. The same problem may occur in modern countertrade. In establishing the price you wish to receive for your lathe sold to the Chilean party, you may inflate the price above what would be the cash price so as to cover the "extra" costs attributable to countertrade. One of these costs is the uncertainty of the value of the products received from Chile. You may be asked to and accept Chilean wine as the countertrade products. But at what price will the wine sell in the United States—$6 or $12 a bottle? The Chilean company may argue the latter, but unless there is an established market for such wine in the United States, the price agreed per bottle is somewhat of a "rolling of the dice". One can understand why companies forced into countertrade may increase substantially the price of their goods in order to cover some very unknown costs of countertrade.[12]

§ 5.5 Compensation or Buyback

Compensation or buyback involves a relationship linking the seller's product and the countertrade goods.[13] The seller's "product" is sometimes equipment, or technology, or even an entire manufacturing plant. In return the seller receives products produced by the foreign purchaser with the equipment or technology, or in the manufacturing plant constructed by the seller. Obviously, it may take a long period of time to pay for the value of a plant by way of accepting products produced in that plant, and the agreement will be for a considerable duration. One of the most notable examples of buyback involved the Occidental Petroleum Company's sale to the USSR of an ammonia plant, paid for by taking part of the ammonia production once the plant was operating.

---

[12] Waide Warner, Jr., William Megevick, Emily Altman, Credit Agreements and Collateral Arrangements in International Infrastructure Projects, PLI 2000 Project Financing, PLI No. A0–003F, Mar. (2000)

[13] See Leo G.B. Welt, Unconventional Forms of Financing: Buyback/Compensation/Barter, 22 N.Y.U. J. Int'l L. & Pol. 461 (1990); Jerzy Rajski, Some Legal Aspects of International Compensation Trade, 35 Int'l & Comp.L.Q. 128 (1986).

There is usually less concern about the disposition of *compensation* goods in contrast to *counterpurchase* goods. Counterpurchase may involve very different goods than what the U.S. company sold, i.e., airplanes for canned hams, or liquor for bananas. In compensation agreements, the goods are often products with which the seller is familiar, and possibly even sells in the regular course of its business. Thus, a U.S. automobile manufacturer might establish a plant in China, and take in exchange a percentage or fixed number of the production, which it in turn markets along with the production of its own U.S. plants.[14] An obvious concern in such case is to assure that the Chinese products meet quality standards of the U.S. company's other plants. Returning countertrade products is costly and has proven all too frequent in many countertrade arrangements with nonmarket and developing nations. At least in a compensation agreement, the seller may have some say over quality in the production of the goods. In a counterpurchase agreement, contrastingly, it will be necessary to carefully examine any prospective products to assure that they will be marketable in the United States or a third nation.

Compensation agreements are often for very large dollar amounts. A chemical plant may be constructed in return for many years of a percentage of the production. An automobile manufacturing plant may also require many automobiles over many years to pay for the cost of the plant. Counterpurchase agreements may be for large amounts, such as the sale of airplanes, but they are usually much smaller-value contracts than compensation agreements.

§ 5.6 Offsets

Sometimes used interchangeably to describe either counterpurchase or compensation forms of countertrade, an *offset* arrangement is technically quite different. It is frequently used in the aerospace industry, especially in the defense industry where there may be military alliances such as NATO. But it is also important for civilian aircraft sales. Offsets constitute an agreement by the foreign seller (e.g., Boeing or Airbus) to include as part of the sale in the foreign nation (e.g., China) the use of parts or services from local suppliers. It is really a local content requirement and is becoming increasingly more common.[15] The local supplier could be owned by the U.S. party (a foreign subsidiary), and might be established for that very purpose. Often a joint venture is established to provide the local pro-

---

[14] The experience of producing the "Jeep" in the People's Republic of China is related in Jim Mann, Beijing Jeep (1989).

[15] It might also involve regular counterpurchase, buying unrelated products and selling them in the home nation or a third nation.

duction. The net result is that some of the production takes place in the foreign nation which is purchasing the item, expectantly at less cost to the nation's possibly limited supply of hard currency, and with an increase in local jobs.

The U.S. government has been sufficiently concerned that offset agreements have a damaging impact on the U.S. economy that Congress in 1984 amended the Defense Production Act to require annual reporting by the President on the impact of offsets on "defense preparedness, industrial competitiveness, employment, and trade."[16] The general view of the U.S. government is not favorable toward countertrade, yet it realizes that countertrade is often required for U.S. firms to be competitive. Curiously, it (actually the Department of Defense) has promoted the use of offsets for many defense-related items.

Offsets have been used and encouraged by such nations as Belgium and Canada for 20 years. Most firms in Western Europe, as well as Canada, Australia, and New Zealand, use offsets for large military contracts. For example, Boeing in the United States agreed with the United Kingdom to use a 130 percent offset in sales of military aircraft.[17]

The Feingold Amendment to the Foreign Relations Authorization Act in 1995 amended the Arms Export Control Act to require the President to certify to Congress whether an offset agreement involving certain high-value weapon sales abroad constitutes a government-to-government or a direct commercial sale.[18] U.S contractors may not give incentive payments to U.S. persons to persuade them to buy goods or services from a foreign country which has an offset agreement with the contractor. The amendment arose from concern that Northrop offered more than $1 million to a customer of Harnischfeger Industries to encourage the customer to buy machinery from a Finnish company to help meet Northrup's offset obligations in a $3 billion sale of jet fighters to Finland. A Memorandum

---

16 50 U.S.C.A. app. § 2099 (1986). Subsequent amendments have extended the reporting requirements. The reporting process and results of the report prepared in 1985 are discussed in Judith K. Cole, Evaluating Offset Agreements: Achieving a Balance of Advantages, 19 Law & Pol'y Int'l Bus. 765, 781 (1987).

17 Economist 89 (Dec. 20, 1986).

18 Current reporting requirements are in the Defense Production Act Amendments of 1992. Contractor reporting is required for offset agreements exceeding $5 million for the sale of weapons systems or defense related items to foreign purchasers. 15 C.F.R. Part 701—"Reporting of Offsets Agreements in Sales of Weapons Systems or Defense Related Items to Foreign Countries or Foreign Firms." See 59 FR 61796 (2 Dec. 1994).

of Understanding (MOU) between Finland and the United States only discouraged offsets, it did not prohibit them.

Offsets are prohibited in the NAFTA agreement, but there is a major exception for defense procurement.[19]

§ 5.7 Switch Trading

Switch trading is less a form of countertrade than a procedure for clearing accounts among a number of transactions, or even among a number of nations. If a U.S. seller of airplanes to Brazil is unable to find sufficient Brazilian products to meet the counterpurchase percentage requirement in the contract, it may learn that Brazil is selling certain goods to Canada and has a surplus of Canadian dollars which the Brazilian government is willing to apply to the U.S. agreement. These Canadian dollars are called "clearing dollars." But Brazil may wish to retain all the Canadian-transaction hard currency for other uses, because it lacks scarce hard currencies of any denomination.

If the clearing transaction is with a nation with soft currency, it may be easier to work the switch. For example, if the Brazilian goods are sold in Argentina rather than Canada, Brazil may welcome the U.S. seller taking Argentine currency, since it is not acceptable in many international transactions (and may be available to the seller at a discounted price). The U.S. seller may be willing to take the Argentine currency if it is buying products from Argentina, or commencing an investment there and needs some local currency.[20]

Companies usually turn to professional help for switch trading. There are a number of multinational companies which act as countertrade facilitators using computer technology. Usually based in developed nations, e.g., London or Vienna, these facilitators bear the risk, buying the product from the seller, paying for it with vouchers (which are exchangeable for products or services from the firm's clients), or sometimes cash plus vouchers. The services obtained might even be travel (accommodations) and advertising.[21] The persons who arrange these clearing transactions are called "switch traders". They obviously add an additional cost to the

---

[19] See Richard J. Russin, Offsets in International Military Procurement, 24 Pub. Cont. L.J. 65 (1994).

[20] The Argentine adoption of the dollar as a dual currency temporarily increased the acceptability of the Argentine peso in international transactions, including switch trading.

[21] See G. Cassidy, Financing Strategies—Barter's Rebirth, East–West Commersant, Dec. 1, 1995.

transaction. Indeed, countertrade has several "hidden" costs which may arise to take away or diminish an expected profit. One of those costs is the higher cost of negotiating a countertrade agreement than a simple single documentary sale. Such costs will be added to the selling price.

§ 5.8 Bilateral Clearing Accounts

Occasionally two nations will agree to purchase goods from each other in a determined amount. They are "clearing units" or an artificial use of a set currency, usually the dollar. The trade is designed to remain in balance. If it becomes out of balance the clearing units may be sold, often at a discount and often using a switch trader.

§ 5.9 Investment Commitment

In this form the seller agrees to invest a certain amount of money in the foreign country. The amount to be invested may be a percentage of the sales of the seller's products, or a fixed amount to be taken out of the proceeds of such sales in a fixed amount/percentage over a period of time. In some cases, companies invest the proceeds of their sales not because of any investment commitment, but because there is a shortage of hard currency in the foreign nation and the seller is essentially locked into leaving the proceeds of the sale of the goods in the country. An investment is often the most appropriate use of such funds.

§ 5.10 Future of Countertrade

Countertrade began to intensify in use a decade or two after World War II, mainly as the hard currency-short Eastern European nations increased trade with Western nations that were reluctant to buy the former nations' products. But countertrade quite rapidly spread to many other parts of the world, especially developing nations that were also short of hard currency. Latin American countertrade increased substantially in the early 1980s. Once free of Soviet domination, most of the Eastern European nations stated that they would reduce countertrade as part of their market economy oriented reforms, but that has proven to depend on these nations' ability to successfully market their products abroad.

Some countertrade may distort free or nearly free markets, partly because it is bilateral rather than multilateral trade.[22] Im-

[22] William D. Zeller, Countertrade, The GATT, and the Theory of the Second Best, 11 Hastings Int'l & Comp. L. Rev. 247 (1988).

ports under a countertrade agreement may disadvantageously affect the market, and may cause unemployment and depressed prices. Because it is often difficult to identify a true price for the countertrade goods, it is hard to identify and measure dumping. Whatever distortions in free trade are attributed to countertrade, it is a method of international trading that sophisticated trading enterprises must learn and add to more common forms. However negative the United States may be towards the use of countertrade, there are no laws that prohibit its use. Indeed, the Department of Commerce issues a report occasionally on offsets in defense trade that illustrate its extensive use. The expertise in countertrade transactions has lagged behind the number of transactions. Experience and a long-term approach to countertrade are necessary ingredients to success. Some companies have suggested that it takes at least three years to show results from an in-house countertrade entity, and a General Electric spokesperson noted that GE had "nurtured" its trading capability over a 20 year period.[23] Countertrade is thus usually considered to be a service center in the same way as market research or finance, rather than a separate profit center.[24] However it is considered, company willingness to use countertrade may result in rewards for the additional effort.

Countertrade is here to stay. The United Nations Commission on International Trade Law believed that countertrade was a sufficiently important part of world trade to have published in 1993 a 183 page Legal Guide on International Countertrade Transactions.

To be successful in countertrade arrangements, a company must learn how to accomplish some very complex negotiating, which cannot but help it in other trading as new, esoteric forms arise. Additionally, a company that has been willing to accept countertrade to gain entry to a market may be in a very advantageous position when the nation becomes better off in accumulating hard currency required for direct cash purchases.

---

[23] Int'l Trade Rpt. 489 (Oct. 17, 1984). But in 1986 GE Trading announced that it was halting its countertrade program. Losses on large transactions caused several major countertraders to make similar announcements. But others, including Mitsui and Mitsubishi, were making announcements to increase countertrade.

[24] The company may bill product divisions for the countertrade services when a sale is made.

Chapter 6

DOCUMENTARY LETTERS OF CREDIT

Table of Sections

§ 6.1 Introduction—The Transactional Problem

Unlike most domestic sales transactions, in a sale of goods across national borders the exporter-seller and importer-buyer may not have previously dealt with one another; or each may know nothing about the other; or each may be unfamiliar with the other's national legal system. The seller does not know, among other things: (1) whether the buyer is creditworthy or trustworthy; (2) whether information received on these subjects from the buyer's associates is reliable; (3) whether exchange controls will hinder payment by the buyer (especially if the buyer's country has a "soft" currency, but payment is in a "hard" currency); (4) how great the exchange risk is if payment is to be in the buyer's currency; and (5) what delays may be involved in receiving unencumbered funds from the buyer.

For its part, the buyer does not know, among other things: (1) whether the seller can be trusted to ship the goods if the buyer prepays; (2) whether the goods shipped will be of the quantity and quality contracted for; (3) whether the goods will be shipped by a reliable carrier and properly insured; (4) whether the goods might be damaged in transit; (5) whether the seller will furnish to the buyer sufficient ownership documentation covering the goods to allow the buyer to claim them from the carrier; (6) whether the seller will provide the documentation necessary to satisfy customs and valuation regulations (*e.g.*, country of origin certificates, health and other inspection certificates, *etc.*); and (7) what delays may be involved in receiving unencumbered possession and use of the goods at the buyer's location.

Where the parties are strangers, these risks are significant, possibly overwhelming. Most important, because they operate at a distance from each other, the seller and the buyer cannot concurrently exchange the goods for the payment of funds *without the help of third parties.* An international letter of credit can work to bridge this and similar problems. In specific, a documentary sale with a confirmed letter of credit can distribute the potentially large risks reviewed above to third parties that have specialized knowledge and can more efficiently and effectively evaluate each risk assumed. This distribution of individual risks can reduce the overall transaction risk to near insignificance.

§ 6.2 The Documentary Sale Transaction with a Confirmed Letter of Credit

The third party intermediaries enlisted are banks (at least one in the buyer's home country and usually a second one in the seller's home country) and at least one carrier. Thus, the parties involved are: (1) the buyer; (2) the bank at which the buyer does its banking (hereafter, "Buyer's Bank"); (3) the seller; (4) a bank with an office in the seller's country (hereafter "Seller's Bank"); and (5) at least one carrier. These parties are able to take a large risk not subject to firm evaluation by any one of them, and divide it into several small, calculable risks, and then allocate these smaller risks to the parties best able to evaluate them. Thus, the documentary sale with a letter of credit demonstrates that not all risk allocation is a "zero sum game," but may in fact create a "win-win" situation.

The transaction involves a series of contracts—but not all of the parties to the transaction will be parties to each contract. The contracts include: (a) the sale of goods contract between the buyer and the seller; (b) the bill of lading, a contract with and a receipt issued by the carrier; and (c) the letter of credit, which represents a promise by Buyer's Bank (and, if confirmed, also by Seller's Bank) to pay the seller under certain conditions concerning proof that the seller has shipped the goods.

(a) The contract underlying the entire series of transactions is the contract for the sale of goods. The buyer and the seller are parties to this contract, but not the banks or the carrier. This contract obligates the seller to deliver the agreed quantity and quality of goods, and the buyer to take the goods and pay the agreed price. As described in Chapter 2, the law governing international sale of goods contracts in modern commerce is commonly, and increasingly so, the United Nations Convention on Contracts for the International Sale of Goods (CISG). (For a detailed examination of the scope and content of this international treaty, *see* Chapter 2.)

(b) In international documentary sales, the buyer and the seller usually are in geographically distant locations from each other, and most often this also involves transportation of the goods. Thus, an international carrier of the goods is usually required, and either the seller or the buyer will make a contract with the carrier to transport the goods. (For our illustration, the seller will make that contract.) The seller—or, in the language of a contract of carriage, the "shipper"—makes a contract with the carrier that obligates the carrier to transport the goods to the buyer's location or some other distant place.

This second contract in our transaction will be expressed in a "bill of lading," which is "issued" by the carrier. Under the terms of the bill of lading contract, the carrier promises, in return for payment of the freight charge, to deliver the goods to either (1) the named "consignee" in a nonnegotiable (or "straight") bill of lading, or (2) the person properly in possession ("holder") of a negotiable (or "order") bill of lading.[1] Of its nature, the documentary sale transaction (especially one involving a letter of credit) will involve a negotiable bill of lading, so that the buyer is able to obtain delivery of the goods *only if* it has physical possession of the bill of lading properly indorsed over to it.[2] As a special form of a "document of title" covering the goods, such a bill of lading controls access to and delivery of the goods.

---

1 For more on these two different types of bills of lading see Chapter 3, §§ 3.2 and 3.3.

2 For more detail on the necessity of a negotiable bill of lading for such transactions see Chapter 3, § 3.5.

(c) Before it delivers the goods to the carrier, the seller ("shipper") wants assurance that the payment for the goods will be forthcoming. A simple promise from the foreign buyer may not be sufficient. Even a promise from a bank in the buyer's country may not be sufficient, because the seller likely does not fully trust foreign banks either. Instead, the seller wants a firm, legally binding promise from a bank known to it, preferably one in the seller's jurisdiction and locality.

What the seller wants is the third contract in our transaction—a confirmed, irrevocable letter of credit. A letter of credit is a specialized contract involving a promise by a bank (Buyer's Bank) that it will pay to the seller the amount of the contract price subject to defined conditions. In the distinctive language of letter of credit law, the promise will be that the bank "will honor drafts drawn on the bank by the seller." But again, the seller also will want a payment promise from a bank in its own country and region. Thus, if required by the sales contract, the buyer also must arrange for a "confirmed" letter of credit. This occurs through Buyer's Bank requesting a bank in the seller's location *also* to obligate itself, through a separate "confirmation" letter sent to the seller, to honor the drafts presented by the seller. Often, the seller will learn of both actions in the one confirmation letter from its local bank.

The banks' promises will be conditioned upon the seller presenting documentary evidence that the goods have been shipped via a carrier to arrive at the buyer's location, along with any other documents required by the contract for the sale of goods. What would furnish such evidence? The key document is the bill of lading issued by the carrier (the second contract in our transaction), which furnishes evidence that the seller has shipped the goods as described therein.

Further, a negotiable (or "order") bill of lading will be required, one that also controls the right to obtain the goods from the carrier. Thus, and as described in more detail in Chapter 3 above, a negotiable bill of lading issued by the carrier and delivered by the seller to Seller's Bank will serve three distinct functions: (1) it will provide evidence that the goods have been delivered to the carrier; (2) it will show that the goods are destined for the buyer and not some third party; and (3) it will assure the banks that they can control the carrier's ultimate delivery of the goods to the buyer by simply retaining possession of the order bill of lading.[3] In other words, when a bank pays the seller under the letter of credit, it receives from the seller a

---

3 For more detail, see Chapter 3, § 3.3.

"document of title" issued by the carrier that gives the bank control over the carrier's delivery of the goods. The buyer cannot obtain possession of the goods from the carrier without physical possession of the bill of lading. Thus, after paying the seller under the letter of credit and receiving the bill from the seller, the bank can preclude the buyer from obtaining the goods from the carrier until the buyer has reimbursed the bank (or made a binding commitment to do so).

How does the international documentary transaction involving a letter of credit work? Consult the following diagram:

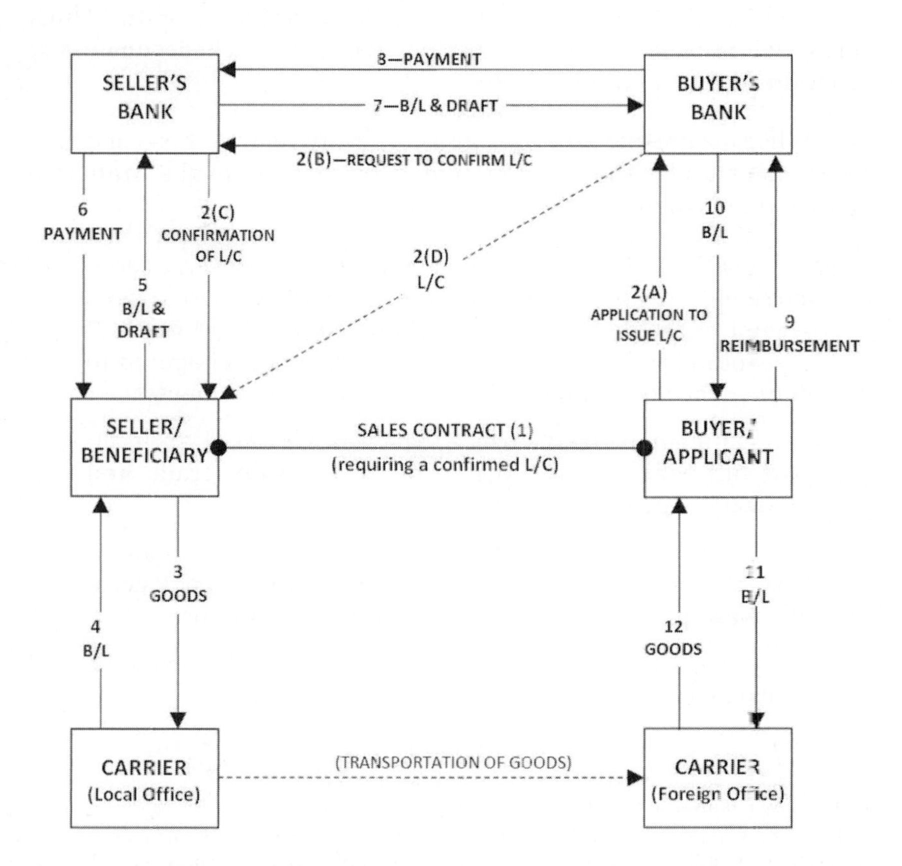

The process begins with the sale of goods contract. When the parties form their contract, the seller will insist that it include both a "price term" (*i.e.*, the amount) and a "payment term" (*i.e.*, the method of payment). To avoid the risk of nonpayment by the buyer, the seller must bargain for and include in the sales contract a term that requires payment by a letter of credit issued by a bank. Such an agreement will not normally be implied.

For maximum protection, the seller will seek payment by "Confirmed, Irrevocable Letter of Credit," and should also specify in detail what documents it will need to present to obtain payment. The reason for specifying this payment term in the sales contract is that, under standard default rules, the buyer generally will have a right to inspect the *goods* before payment. This is not the case with a "payment against documents" transaction;[4] but even here, the buyer will have a right to inspect the *documents* before payment, and this inspection will come after the seller has shipped the goods with the carrier. The same is true with respect to the documents that will be required by the banks for payment under a letter of credit. Thus, the seller is well advised to specify precisely which documents it must present to obtain payment.

What documents will the banks typically require as a condition to payment under the letter of credit? In addition to the draft (see below), they usually require the following:

(1) A transport document, and for large ocean-borne carriage a *negotiable* bill of lading, showing the carrier's receipt of the described goods. As noted, the legal effect of a negotiable bill of lading is that the carrier is obligated to deliver the goods only to the "holder" of the document;[5]

(2) a commercial invoice, which is a form of an itemized bill that sets out the terms of the sale, grade and quantity of goods, amount owed, *etc.*;[6]

(3) a packing list, which is a separate confirmation from the seller's shipping department of what goods actually were packed in any sealed cartons or containers;

(4) a policy of marine insurance (if the goods are to be transported by sea);[7]

---

4 *See* Chapter 3, §§ 3.4–3.6.

5 *See* Chapter 3, § 3.3. The transportation document may also be a non-negotiable waybill or similar document. For more on these documents see § 6.15 *infra*. Such documents are not appropriate for a "payment against documents" transaction, however, because (as described in more detail in Chapter 3, see § 3.5) non-negotiable bills of lading will not "represent the goods" in a legal sense, and thus the buyer would pay without thereby obtaining legal control over the goods.

6 As noted in § 6.5 *infra*, the principal source for the rules governing international letters of credit is the *Uniform Customs and Practices for Documentary Credits*, a copyrighted publication of the International Chamber of Commerce. *See* ICC UNIFORM CUSTOMS AND PRACTICE FOR DOCUMENTARY CREDITS—UCP 600 (ICC Publ. No. 600, 2007))(hereinafter UCP). With regard to the need for a commercial invoice see UCP, art. 18.

7 *See* UCP, art. 28.

(5) a certificate of inspection, which is issued by a commercial inspecting firm and independently confirms that the required number and type of goods were shipped (although the buyer must separately contract for such an inspection, and then ensure that presentation of the certificate is included as a condition in the letter of credit); and

(6) a certificate of origin, which documents the source of the goods sold and—depending on the trade agreements between the exporting and importing country—may be used by customs personnel in the importing country to determine tariff assessments.

The parties' contract may require the presentation of other documents, depending on the nature of the goods.[8] But as described below, the letter of credit may not require that the beneficiary satisfy any non-documentary conditions.[9]

If the parties' contract includes a letter of credit payment term, the buyer—in the language of letter of credit law, the "applicant"[10]—will contract Buyer's Bank to serve as the "issuing bank"[11] for the letter of credit. The letter will then name the seller as the "beneficiary."[12] The letter of credit is a direct promise by the issuing bank that it will pay the contract price to the seller/beneficiary, if the seller presents to it the documents specified in the letter of credit. Buyer's Bank will be aware of the buyer's creditworthiness, and will make appropriate arrangements to ensure reimbursement from the buyer (through either immediate payment or future repayment of a loan secured by appropriate collateral). These arrangements will be made before the letter of credit is issued, for with an irrevocable letter of credit, Buyer's Bank is independently bound after issuance to pay according to the credit's terms.

If the sales contract requires a "confirmed" letter of credit, the buyer must also arrange for a payment promise by a local bank in the seller's area (again, we will refer to this bank here as "Seller's Bank"). Buyer's Bank then will forward its letter of credit to the seller through Seller's Bank, and request that Seller's Bank add its "confirmation," thereby becoming a "confirming bank."[13] By merely indicating, "We confirm this credit," Seller's Bank makes a direct

---

8 Examples might include, where required by local law or custom, an export license, food safety certificate, or a health inspection certificate.

9 *See* UCP, art. 7. *See also* UCC § 5–108(g).

10 *See* UCP, art. 2; UCC § 5–102(a)(2).

11 *See* UCP, art. 2. *See also* UCC § 5–102(a)(9)(defining an "issuer").

12 For each of these terms see UCP, art. 2, and UCC § 5–102(a).

13 *See* UCP, art. 2. *See also* UCC § 5–102(a)(4)(defining a "confirmer").

and independent promise to the seller that it will pay the stated amount (typically, the sales contract price), if the seller presents the required documents. In this respect, the confirming bank assumes the same basic obligations to the beneficiary as did the issuing bank. (Why do the banks provide these services? For an appropriate fee, of course.)

If the sales contract does not require a confirmation of the credit, Buyer's Bank nonetheless may choose to forward the letter of credit through an "advising bank" located near the seller.[14] Such a bank will not be obligated to the seller; it merely acts as the agent of the issuing bank and has only a duty to communicate the terms of the credit accurately. An advising bank may—but is not obligated to—later take the presented documents from the seller and forward them to Buyer's Bank for collection purposes only.[15]

Another role a bank in a letter of credit transaction may play is as a "nominated bank." This term broadly covers any bank "with which the credit is available,"[16] and thus would include a confirming bank as well. In its broadest sense, a nominated bank is one the issuer authorizes to accept documents presented under a credit and pay the beneficiary.[17] A confirming bank is a nominated bank that also undertakes *in advance* to accept a presentation for payment under the credit; but a nominated bank that is *not also* a confirming bank is authorized, but not obligated, to do so.[18]

Once the letter of credit is issued and confirmed, the seller will pack the goods, prepare a commercial invoice, and, where required, procure an insurance certificate (another form of contract) covering the goods in transit to the buyer. If an inspection certificate is required by the sales contract, the goods will be made available to the designated inspection firm (which is engaged according to another contract); this firm will issue a certificate stating that the goods conform to the description in the sales contract. If so required by the sales contract, the seller also will prepare the necessary documents for the customs officials in its home country (*e.g.*, an export license) and those in the buyer's country (*e.g.*, a certificate of origin). (The details on the respective obligations of the seller and the buyer re-

[14] UCP, art. 2. The UCC refers to such a bank as an "adviser." *See* § 5–102(a)(1).

[15] Under non-letter of credit law, such a bank is known as a "collecting bank." *See* UCC § 4–105(5).

[16] *See* UCP, art. 2; UCC §§ 5–102(a)(11), 5–107(b).

[17] The UCC terms such a bank a "nominated person." *See* UCC § 5-107(b).

[18] *See* UCP, art. 12(a) ("Unless a nominated bank is the confirming bank, an authorization to honour or negotiate does not impose any obligation on that nominated bank to honour or negotiate[.]")

garding transportation and delivery are typically defined by a "commercial term," such as FOB or CIF.[19])

The seller will then send the goods to the carrier, which issues the negotiable bill of lading as a combination receipt and contract. As described above, the letter of credit almost always will require a negotiable bill of lading (at least for large transactions), and commonly will require the carrier to deliver the goods only "to the seller or order"—*i.e.*, only to the seller or a person the seller designates by an appropriate indorsement.[20]

The seller now has the complete set of the required documents, and takes these documents to Seller's Bank, which, as a confirming bank, is obligated to pay the seller upon presentation of conforming documents. Because the letter of credit is merely a promise to pay, the seller must use a legal vehicle to "draw on" the credit. To do this, the seller prepares a "draft"[21] and then presents it to the bank along with the other required documents. The draft (sometimes known by an earlier term, "bill of exchange") also is a negotiable document, *i.e.*, one that can be transferred from one "holder" to another. The draft functions like a check written by the seller and drawn on Buyer's Bank (the original issuer) for the amount stated in the letter of credit.

A draft can be payable on demand or at a defined later time. If a demand draft (or "sight draft") is agreed, the bank—in our case, Seller's Bank (the confirming bank)—will pay the amount immediately, usually by crediting the seller's account or by sending the funds to an account at another bank designated by the seller.

If, in contrast, the parties' contract (and thus the letter of credit) specifies a "time draft" (*e.g.*, "30 days after sight"), the payment to the seller/beneficiary will be delayed. In such a case, the confirming bank or issuing bank need not pay upon presentment, but it must "accept" the time draft (*i.e.*, stamp its name on it) when the documents are presented.[22] This "acceptance" creates a binding obligation on the part of the bank that it will pay at the later time stated in the draft.[23] The obligation of such an "acceptor" is directly enforceable by the original presenter of the draft or by any other "holder"[24] to whom that person sells ("negotiates") the draft after

19 For more detail on commercial terms see Chapter 2.

20 Again, for more on these issues see Chapter 3.

21 *See* UCC §§ 3–104(e), 4–104(6).

22 *See* UCC § 3–409.

23 *See* UCC § 3–413.

24 *See* UCC §§ 1–201(b)(21), 3–301.

acceptance.[25] Thus, if the confirming bank accepts a time draft and the buyer later becomes insolvent, the bank that has accepted the draft must still pay when the stated time expires. With the bank obligated on the time draft, the seller can immediately raise funds by selling the paper—or pledging it as collateral—on the strength of the bank's binding obligation to pay on maturity.

In return for the payment or acceptance, the seller will indorse both the draft and the negotiable bill of lading over to Seller's Bank—thereby making it the "holder"—and transfer the other required documents to it. Seller's Bank will, in turn, indorse the draft and the bill of lading and present both with the other required documents to Buyer's Bank.[26] As the issuer of the letter of credit, Buyer's Bank is obligated to "honor" the draft and thus to reimburse Seller's Bank if the draft and the other documents from the seller conform to the requirements in the letter of credit. Because the two banks likely already will have a correspondent relationship, Seller's Bank typically will simply debit the account of Buyer's Bank held at Seller's Bank and notify Buyer's Bank of this action.

Buyer's Bank then advises the buyer that the documents have arrived and that payment is due. Since the buyer and Buyer's Bank usually have an established relationship, the typical agreement will be that Buyer's Bank may simply charge the amount of the draft to buyer's account, and forward the documents to the buyer. If the buyer has arranged for credit from Buyer's Bank, the credit will be advanced when the draft and documents arrive. If no preexisting relationship exists between the buyer and Buyer's Bank, then the buyer will be required to pay (or to arrange sufficient credit for) the draft before the bill of lading is released to it. As the documents are forwarded from the seller to Seller's Bank and then to Buyer's Bank, each will indorse the bill of lading to the next party. Ultimately, upon obtaining reimbursement from the buyer, Buyer's Bank will indorse the negotiable bill of lading over to the buyer, thereby, again, making it the "holder."

The buyer, like the banks, must pay "against the documents" and not the goods themselves. This is why it is necessary to specify the terms of the documents in the original contract for the sale of goods, and then repeat those specifications precisely in the letter of credit. Once the buyer has paid (or arranged to pay) Buyer's Bank, the buyer will obtain possession of the negotiable bill of lading. Because such a bill of lading is a "document of title" that legally repre-

[25] *See* UCC §§ 3–201, 3–301, 3–413.

[26] For more on such a "presentation" by the confirming bank to the issuing bank see text accompanying footnotes 152-153 *infra* and UCP arts. 2, 7(c).

sents the goods, only then will the buyer have the power to obtain the goods from the carrier.

Note that the buyer has effectively paid for the goods while they are at sea, long before their arrival. In fact, the buyer was in effect bound to pay for the goods as soon as the draft and required documents were presented to Seller's Bank. If the goods fail to arrive or are damaged in transit, the buyer must look to its Insurance Certificate for protection and reimbursement.[27] When the goods arrive, the carrier may not release them to the buyer unless the buyer is in possession of the negotiable bill of lading, properly indorsed to the buyer.[28] Further, from its nature, a transaction involving a negotiable bill of lading will prohibit the buyer from even inspecting the goods—until it has obtained physical possession of the bill of lading and presented it to the carrier. Thus, until the banks are satisfied that they will be paid by the buyer, they can control the goods by controlling the bill of lading.

§ 6.3 ___Risk Allocation in the Letter of Credit Transaction

The defining attribute of the irrevocable, confirmed letter of credit transaction is the allocation of risks to and among the various players. If the seller ships conforming goods, it has independent promises of payment from both the buyer and two banks. The banks' promises are enforceable despite assertions of non-conformity of the *goods*, so long as the *documents* conform to the requirements of the letter of credit. For their part, the banks never see the goods, only the documents. Because of this, they inspect the documents rigorously to determine that they comply exactly with the description in the letter of credit—for the documents are their only protection. As Sections 6.6 through 6.8 below will describe in detail, substantial performance by the beneficiary is not acceptable with respect to the documents required by the letter of credit.

Thus, as a practical matter, the seller is at risk only if Seller's Bank fails, Buyer's Bank fails, and the buyer is either unable or unwilling to pay. But this is a constellation of events so unlikely that seller should have no noteworthy concern. And most important, if Seller's Bank unjustifiably refuses to perform its payment obliga-

---

[27] This of course assumes that such insurance exists. But in the typical case, a letter of credit transaction will also involve a "CIF" commercial term. Such a term obligates the seller to arrange and pay for insurance covering the goods in transit. *See* Chapter 2, § 2.10.

[28] *See* Chapter 3, § 3.3 (describing in more detail these obligations of the carrier under a negotiable bill of lading).

tion, the seller has a cause of action in a local court—which will use a familiar language and involve a familiar legal system—against a "deep pocket defendant."

The position of Seller's Bank also is generally secure, even though it is obligated to pay against presentation of the documents. Because it is entitled to reimbursement, it is practically at risk only if both Buyer's Bank and buyer fail or refuse to perform their obligations. And Seller's Bank also should be in the best position to assess its principal risk, *i.e.*, nonpayment by Buyer's Bank: (a) It has the credit risk concerning the solvency of Buyer's Bank, but it is better situated to evaluate this risk than either the buyer or the seller; and (b) it has the risk that Buyer's Bank will wrongfully refuse to perform its obligations as issuer on the letter of credit, but because it has multiple direct and institutional relationships with Buyer's Bank, it is in a better position to induce compliance than the other parties.

Buyer's Bank, in turn, is at risk only if the buyer fails or refuses to perform. Buyer's Bank has an independent obligation to pay if the documents conform to the requirements in the letter of credit, with the result that it bears the risk that the buyer cannot pay (becomes insolvent) or will not pay (refuses to reimburse). But these again are risks that Buyer's Bank is best able to evaluate: It is in a particularly good position to investigate and evaluate the risk of the buyer's insolvency, for it either has an established relationship with the buyer or can familiarize itself with the buyer's reputation and financial circumstances in the local market. It also is able either to obtain funds from the buyer when issuing the letter of credit or sue the buyer for breach of contract (again, under the local legal system) if the buyer wrongfully refuses to pay. And Buyer's Bank has an opportunity to evaluate all of these risks before issuing the letter of credit, and thus can adjust its price (the fee or interest rate it charges) to compensate for any increased risk. Moreover, Buyer's Bank (and Seller's Bank before it) has the security of the negotiable bill of lading, which will enable it to control the goods until it obtains reimbursement. In the worst case, the banks can resell the goods into the market to limit their losses.

On the other hand, for its payment of the price to Buyer's Bank, the buyer has a document from the carrier entitling it to delivery of the goods, an insurance certificate protecting the buyer against casualty loss in transit, and perhaps an inspection certificate warranting that the goods conform to the sales contract. In other words, the buyer should receive what it bargained for—

delivery of conforming goods or insurance proceeds sufficient to cover any loss.

In short, with an irrevocable, confirmed letter of credit, one large risk in a sales transaction has been divided into several smaller ones, with each smaller risk allocated to the party best able to evaluate it. The lack of substantial remaining risk in the vast bulk of these transactions is evidenced by the fact that the usual bank charge for the issuance of a letter of credit is merely one to two percent of the amount of the credit.

§ 6.4 The Law Governing Letters of Credit

The law relating to letters of credit developed before World War I principally in the courts of England, and thereafter in state and federal courts in the United States.[29] With the advent of the Uniform Commercial Code in the middle of the last century, however, letter of credit law became statutory law in the United States through the adoption of this uniform law by the individual states. In specific, Article 5 of the UCC carefully regulates most rights and obligations of the parties arising out of letters of credit. It broadly defines its scope to cover any "definite undertaking . . . by an issuer to a beneficiary at the request or for the account of an applicant . . . to honor a documentary presentation by payment."[30] A letter of credit may be in any form that is authenticated (typically by signature) of the issuer or by agreement or practice.[31]

UCC Article 5 now exists in a revised version. In 1995, the Uniform Law Commissioners and the American Law Institute updated and clarified the Article, and since then all fifty states and the District of Columbia have enacted the revised version into law. Even the State of New York has come along, although after a long delay.

Nonetheless, as is true with the rest of the UCC, most of Article 5 is not mandatory law; rather, nearly all of its provisions defer to the agreement of the parties as expressed in the terms of their contract.[32]

Moreover, for international letters of credit, the practically more significant rules are found in the Uniform Customs and Practices for Documentary Credits (UCP). The UCP (like the Inco-

---

[29] *See* John F. Dolan, THE LAW OF LETTERS OF CREDIT §§ 3.01–3.04 (Rev. ed., 1999).

[30] UCC § 5–102(10).

[31] *Id.*, § 5–104.

[32] *See* UCC § 5–103(c).

terms[33]) are a set of copyrighted contract terms prepared and published by the International Chamber of Commerce (ICC). The ICC published the original version of the UCP in 1933, and since then has updated it with new versions approximately every ten years. The most recent version of the UCP is the 2007 Revision (No. 600).[34]

The UCP applies, by its own terms, to any documentary credit (which it refers to merely as a "credit") "when the text of the credit expressly indicates that it is subject to these rules."[35] The overwhelming majority of international letters of credit in fact contain such an express reference to the UCP. And as the next Section describes in detail, UCC Article 5 explicitly validates an incorporation of the UCP rules into a letter of credit.

Finally, UNCITRAL—the U.N. institution responsible for the CISG—also has drafted a potentially relevant treaty, the United Nations Convention on Independent Guarantees and Stand-by Letters of Credit (1995).[36] This treaty governs a commercial letter of credit if it "expressly states" that it is subject to the treaty.[37] As of March 2013, however, only eight countries have ratified the treaty (and not the United States nor any other major trading country).

§ 6.5 ____The Uniform Customs and Practices for Documentary Credits (UCP)

The UCP constitutes a rather detailed set of rules that define the rights and obligations of the banks involved in a letter of credit transaction. But its legal status is as a statement of contract terms and banking trade usage, and not as generally applicable positive law. Thus, in an important sense there is no need for a "choice of law" analysis as between the UCC and the UCP. The former is legislation, and the latter merely reflects—through an incorporation by reference—agreed contractual terms. Nonetheless, because most of the provisions in UCC Article 5 are not mandatory law,[38] the UCP provisions would seem to prevail over the "gap-filler" provisions of UCC Article 5 without further analysis.

The unusual aspect of the UCP, however, is that it takes effect by a *unilateral* declaration of a bank in the letter of credit, and not

---

[33] For a detailed discussion of the Incoterms, see Chapter 2.

[34] *See* UCP 600, *supra* footnote 6.

[35] UCP, art. 1.

[36] Dec. 11, 1995, 2169 U.N.T.S. 190, available at UNCITRAL's website, http://www.uncitral.org/pdf/english/texts/payments/guarantees/guarantees.pdf.

[37] *Id.*, art. 1(2).

[38] *See* note 32, *supra*.

by a contractual agreement with the beneficiary.[39] This would seem to require a more specialized authorization by law, and the UCC expressly grants such an authorization. Section 5–116 declares that the liability of banks "is governed by any rules of custom or practice, such as the Uniform Customs and Practices for Documentary Credits, to which the letter of credit, confirmation, or other undertaking is expressly made subject."[40] This rule applies even in the case of a direct conflict between the UCC and the UCP, except with respect to the UCC's rare "nonvariable" provisions.[41] Thus, as one New York court recently observed, "[t]he UCP does not have the force of law, but is binding if the terms of a letter of credit explicitly incorporate its provisions."[42]

The rules set forth in the UCC and the UCP nonetheless generally are quite similar in scope and substance, and indeed one key purpose of the 1995 revision of Article 5 was to align the UCC more closely with the UCP. However, some differences remain.[43] Moreover, the UCP does not purport to define a comprehensive regulatory system for letters of credit. UCC § 5–116(c) also makes clear that, even if incorporated in a specific letter of credit, the UCP controls only to the extent of a conflict with the UCC.

The most prominent example of this is that the UCP has no rules that address fraud or forgery or the enjoining of payment by a bank when such issues arise.[44] As a result, UCC Article 5, and not the UCP, will provide the legal rules to resolve issues related to allegations of fraud or forgery in letter of credit transactions. But the UCP provisions will govern the great variety of other letter of credit issues that do not involve fraud. Based on this relationship between the UCP and the UCC, this Chapter will focus on the UCP rules for all non-fraud issues; Chapter 7 (on standby letters of credit) will then review the law governing fraud issues.[45] This division also aligns with the fact that litigation over allegations of fraud is comparatively rare for documentary credit transactions, but occurs with some frequency with standby letters of credit. For the latter cases, the UCC's fraud rules come into play with regularity.

---

[39] *Compare* UCC Rev. § 1–301(a)(permitting "the parties" to agree that the law of another jurisdiction will govern their transaction).

[40] UCC § 5–116(c).

[41] UCC § 5–103(c)(listing the few provisions of Article 5 that the parties may not vary even by express agreement).

[42] Fortis Bank (Nederland) N.V. v. Abu Dhabi Islamic Bank, 2010 WL 7326395, at *1 (N.Y. Sup. 2010).

[43] For an example of such a difference see footnote 146 *infra*.

[44] *See* UCC § 5–109(a), (b).

[45] *See* Chapter 7, §§ 7.11–7.13.

Finally, one provision noticeably absent from the UCP is a term that addresses the background law applicable to the transaction in absence of a party choice of one jurisdiction or another. For such choice of law issues, therefore, one must turn to otherwise applicable law. In the United States, the UCC allows the parties, or a bank through the letter of credit alone, to select the law of any jurisdiction as the applicable law.[46] Separately, it provides a default rule if such a choice is not made.[47] In specific, in absence of a choice of law, the liability of a bank is governed by the law of the jurisdiction where it is "located."[48] In the case of multiple banks with different roles (issuing bank, confirming bank, *etc.*), this rule creates the very real possibility that no one body of law will govern an entire letter of credit transaction; instead a series of different laws, each dependent on the location of the involved bank, may apply for each of the different parties' liabilities. Nonetheless, the UCC rule addresses only the liabilities of the issuing bank, a nominated person (including a confirming bank), and an adviser, and does not include the applicant. Apparently, the choice of law for the applicant is left to the contract between the applicant and the issuer, or to general conflict doctrines.

The UCP recognizes four different types of banks in the letter of credit transaction: an issuing bank; an advising bank; a confirming bank, and a nominated bank.[49] Under the UCC, each could be located in a different jurisdiction: (a) An *issuing bank* is usually located in the buyer's jurisdiction and promises to honor drafts on itself upon a presentation of conforming documents as stated in the letter of credit.[50] (b) An *advising bank* is usually located in the seller's jurisdiction and "advises" the seller (the beneficiary) of the documentary credit "at the request of the issuing bank;" but it makes no promise to pay the beneficiary against the documents.[51] An advising bank merely must exercise "reasonable care" to check the authenticity of the credit and convey its terms to the beneficiary. (c)

---

46 UCC § 5–116(a). The general choice of law provisions in UCC Article 1 allow choice of the law of any state or nation if the "transaction bears a reasonable relation to" that state or nation. UCC Rev. § 1–301(a) (former §1–105(1)).

47 UCC § 5–116(b). The general choice of law provisions in UCC Article 1 provide that the court in a state which has enacted the UCC shall use its own law (its own state's version of the UCC) if the transaction bears an "appropriate relation" to the forum state. UCC Rev. § 1–301(b)(former § 1–105(1), last sentence).

48 UCC § 5–116(b). If a bank has more than one, all branches are deemed to be "separate juridical entities." *Id.*

49 *See* UCP, art. 2.

50 UCP, arts. 2 (tenth definition), 7. The UCC equivalent is the "issuer." *See* UCC §§ 5–102(a)(9), 5–108(a).

51 UCP, arts. 2 (first definition), 9. The UCC equivalent is the "adviser." *See* UCC §§ 5–102(a)(1), 5–107(c).

A *confirming bank* also is usually located in the seller's jurisdiction. Such a bank "adds its confirmation to a credit upon the issuing bank's authorization or request."[52] In this way, it makes its own, independent promise to the beneficiary to pay upon the presentation of conforming documents.[53] (d) A *nominated bank* is often located in the seller's jurisdiction, but may be in a third jurisdiction. The term "nominated bank" broadly covers any bank "with which the credit is available."[54] Thus, a nominated bank may or may not also be a confirming bank.[55]

Outside the United States, foreign courts will use their own choice of law doctrines. (U.S. courts also generally will uphold a choice of law clause in a letter of credit contract.[56]) But a choice of law clause stated in the underlying sales contract is not necessarily applicable to the letter of credit contract. In absence of a choice of law clause, the traditional doctrine is that the applicable law is the law of the place of performance of the contract, or, in the letter of credit context, the place of payment of the credit against presentation of the documents. Thus, where only an issuer is involved, the law of the issuer's location is applicable. For a confirmed letter of credit, the law of the confirming bank applies, because that is the jurisdiction in which the beneficiary presents the documents and demands payment.

The traditional doctrine generally applies the same law to all segments of the credit transaction. Article 5 changes this approach, however, and permits the application of different rules to the obligations of the issuer and of the confirmer.[57] This, in turn, could lead, for example, to the use of different standards for determining strict compliance with the requirements of a letter of credit.[58] And the law governing the liability of a nominated bank most often cannot be determined until after the beneficiary has chosen to present the documents to such a bank for honor.

---

[52] UCP art. 2 (sixth definition). The UCC equivalent is the "confirmer." *See* UCC §§ 5–102(a)(4), 5–107(a).

[53] *See* UCP art. 8.

[54] *See* UCP, art. 2 (twelfth definition). The UCC equivalent is the "nominated person." *See* UCC §§ 5–102(a)(11), 5–107(b).

[55] For more detail on the basic obligations of these banks under letters of credit see § 6.9 *infra*.

[56] *See, e.g.,* Lipcon v. Underwriters at Lloyd's, London, 148 F.3d 1285 (11th Cir. 1998), *cert. denied*, 525 U.S. 1093 (1999); Bonny v. Society of Lloyd's, 3 F.3d 156 (7th Cir. 1993), *cert. denied*, 510 U.S. 1113 (1994).

[57] *See* UCC § 5–116(b) and noted 46-48, *supra*.

[58] *See* the discussion of the "strict compliance" standard in § 6.6 below.

§ 6.6 The Fundamental Legal Principles of Letter of Credit Law

Two fundamental principles underlie the regulatory scheme defined by the UCP's letter of credit rules. The first is that the banks' obligations under the letter of credit are independent of the buyer's and the seller's obligations under the contract for the sale of goods—the Independence Principle.[59] The second is that the banks deal only with documents, and not with the goods or any issues concerning performance of the sales contract.[60] But because they are obligated to pay the beneficiary on this basis alone (and thus never see the goods), banks insist on strict compliance with all documentary conditions—the Strict Compliance Principle.[61] Sections 6.7 and 6.8 below will examine these two fundamental principles in more detail. The following Sections will then describe the basic obligations of banks that issue, confirm, or otherwise are nominated to accept a presentation under a letter of credit.

§ 6.7 ____The Independence Principle

The most fundamental principle of letter of credit law is that the banks' obligations to pay upon the presentation of conforming *documents* is independent of the performance of the underlying transaction for the sale of the *goods*. As a U.S. District Court recently observed, the independence principle "means that a letter of credit 'takes on a life of its own,' endowing the transaction with the simplicity and certainty that are its hallmarks" and indeed the principle "is universally viewed as essential to the proper functioning of letters of credit."[62]

UCP Article 4 accordingly declares that a credit "by its nature is a separate transaction from the sale or other contract on which it may be based." Letters of credit often refer to the underlying contract between the buyer and the seller. But even with such a refer-

---

[59] UCP art. 4. *See also* In re Central Illinois Energy, L.L.C., 482 B.R. 772, 782 (C.D. Ill. 2012); Jaffe v. Bank of America, N.A. 395 Fed. Appx. 583 (11th Cir. 2010).

[60] UCP, art. 5 and § 6.7 *infra*.

[61] *See* UCP art. 14(a), (d) and § 6.8 *infra*.

[62] In re Central Illinois Energy, L.L.C., 482 B.R. 772, 782 (C.D. Ill. 2012). *See also* ACE American Ins. Co. v. Bank of the Ozarks, 2012 WL 3240239, at *5 (S.D.N.Y. 2012)("The central purpose of the letter-of-credit mechanism would be defeated if courts felt free to examine the merits of underlying contract disputes in order to determine whether letters of credit should be paid.")(*quoting* Alaska Textile Co., Inc. v. Chase Manhattan Bank, N.A., 982 F.2d 813, 815–816 (2nd Cir. 1992)).

ence the UCP emphasizes that "[b]anks are in no way concerned with or bound by such contract."[63]

This basic principle carries with it two important corollaries. First, the obligations of an issuing bank or a confirming bank are not subject to claims or defenses by the applicant (the buyer) that the beneficiary (the seller) has not performed its obligations under the sales contract.[64] The banks have made their own, separate undertakings to the beneficiary that they will pay if the beneficiary performs its obligations under *the letter of credit contract*, regardless of whether it performs its obligations under *the sales contract*. Indeed, this independence principle broadly relates to all events outside of the letter of credit transaction. A U.S. District Court recently summarized the breadth of this principle as follows:

> Because of the "independence principle," an issuing or confirming bank must honor a proper demand even though the beneficiary has breached the underlying contract; even though the insolvency of the account party renders reimbursement impossible; and notwithstanding supervening illegality, impossibility, war or insurrection.[65]

The second corollary is one that runs in the opposite direction: In asserting its claim against a bank, the beneficiary may not rely on rights outside of the letter of credit transaction. UCP Article 4 thus states that the beneficiary "can in no case avail itself of the contractual relationships existing between banks or between the applicant and the issuing bank."

The one exception to the independence principle relates to allegations of fraud or forgery. Although the banks' obligations under the letter of credit generally are independent of the sales contract, they may still be subject to claims by the applicant (the buyer) that payment under a letter of credit will facilitate a material fraud by the beneficiary (the seller). As noted above,[66] the UCP has no provisions concerning fraud or forgery, and as a result UCC Article 5 (where U.S. law is applicable) will provide the governing rules.[67]

---

63 UCP, art. 4(a).

64 *Id.*

65 ACE American Ins. Co. v. Bank of the Ozarks, 2012 WL 3240239, at *5 (S.D.N.Y. 2012)(*quoting* Alaska Textile Co., Inc. v. Chase Manhattan Bank, N.A., 982 F.2d 813, 815–816 (2nd Cir. 1992))(citations omitted).

66 *See* § 6.5 *supra*.

67 *See* UCC § 5–109.

Chapter 7 will examine this law governing fraud and forgery in more detail.[68]

§ 6.8 ___The Strict Compliance Principle

The second fundamental principle of letter of credit law is that in fulfilling their obligations the banks deal only with the documents required by the letter of credit.[69] UCP Article 5 thus declares, "Banks deal with documents and not with goods, services or performance to which the documents may relate." But because the documents are the only basis on which the banks may determine their payment obligations, they insist on a standard of "strict compliance" with all documentary conditions. Under this longstanding approach of the UCP, "[e]ven slight discrepancies in compliance with the terms of a letter of credit justify refusal to pay."[70]

The modern versions of the UCP have introduced a slightly different linguistic formulation for the standard of conformity. As a general matter, the UCP provides that a presentation of documents must be "in accordance with the terms and conditions of the credit."[71] UCP Article 14(a) then provides more detail. That article first states that the banks must examine a presentation to determine "on the basis of the documents alone" whether or not they appear, "on their face," to constitute a complying presentation. This provision thus makes clear that the banks must assess conformity with the letter of credit by looking *only* at the "four corners" of the documents presented by the beneficiary.

Unfortunately, the UCP does not provide an explicit definition of a "complying presentation." Article 14(d) states only that data in a presented document "need not be identical to, but must not conflict with," the terms of other required documents and the letter of credit. The same provision defines the measurement standard as "the context of the credit" and "international standard banking practice."[72] This latter language has generated some judicial and

---

[68] *See* Chapter 7, §§ 7.11–7.13.

[69] For an examination of the documents typically required by a letter of credit see § 6.9 *infra*.

[70] *See, e.g.*, Creaciones Con Idea, S.A. de C.V. v. MashreqBank PSC, 51 F. Supp. 2d 423, 427 (S.D.N.Y. 1999)(*quoting* Hellenic Republic v. Standard Chartered Bank, 631 N.Y.S.2d 320, 321 (App. Div. 1995)).

[71] UCP, art. 2.

[72] UCP, art. 14(d).

scholarly debate, but, as described below, the prevailing view is that a "strict compliance" standard remains.[73]

The primary document for describing the goods in a documentary sale transaction is the commercial invoice. The UCP states that the description in the commercial invoice "must correspond with that appearing in the credit."[74] Descriptions of the goods in all other documents "may be in general terms not conflicting with" the description in the credit.[75] And if a letter of credit requires, but does not provide specifics on, a document other than the commercial invoice, a transport document (usually, the bill of lading), or an insurance document, the UCP provides that the document need merely fulfill the general "function" of such a document.[76]

The archetypical case of the strict compliance doctrine is an English court's determination that "machine shelled groundnut kernels" was not the same description as "Coromandel groundnuts," even though merchants in the trade for such goods understood that the either label was accurate.[77] The court there emphasized that the banks are not expected to know, or to find out, what specific terms mean outside of the banking world.

In recent years, the revisions to the linguistic formulation of the compliance standard in the UCP have generated debate about the status of the "strict compliance" test. The specific flash point for controversy has been the language that describes the touchstone of compliance as "international standard banking practice."[78] For guidance, the ICC periodically publishes a booklet entitled the "International Standard Banking Practice (ISBP)";[79] but this manual provides only guidelines and is not authoritative.

In any event, modern opinions (as well as revised Article 5[80]) have rejected a nascent line in some American cases that seemed to

---

73 To provide at least some guidance, the ICC publishes and periodically updates an "International Standard Banking Practice" (ISBP) manual. *See* ICC Publ. No. 681E (2007).

74 UCP, art. 18(c).

75 UCP, art. 14(e).

76 UCP, art. 14(f).

77 J.H. Rayner & Co. Ltd. v. Hambros Bank Ltd. [1943] 1 K.B. 37 (Court of Appeal).

78 UCP arts. 2(a), 14(d).

79 *See* ICC Publ. 681E (2007).

80 *See* § 5–108 and Comment 1.

permit payment upon substantial performance by the beneficiary.[81] Instead, the prevailing view among courts and scholars is that the "strict compliance" standard, properly calibrated, continues to apply under the UCP as well.[82]

Nonetheless, a clear typographical error seems to represent the edge of the strict compliance standard. The 2007 version of the ICC's "International Standard Banking Practice" manual states as an example of such an obvious "misspelling or typographical error" a description of the goods as "fountan pen" instead of "fountain pen."[83] This seems to apply, however, only to a case of an obvious typographic or linguistic error. Thus, one court held that an issuer was justified in dishonoring where the letter of credit mistakenly identified the beneficiary as "Sung Jin Electronics," while the documents were correctly addressed to "Sung Jun Electronics."[84] The court found that it was not obvious in the context of the transaction that this reflected a mere linguistic error.

What is left, as the court in *Voest-Alpine Trading USA Corp. v. Bank of China* sensibly explained, is "a common sense, case-by-case approach [that] permit[s] minor deviations of a typographical nature because such a letter-for-letter correspondence between the letter of credit and the presentation documents is virtually impossible."[85] That case involved seven different discrepancies in the presented documents as compared to the requirements of the letter of credit. The discrepancies included failures to denote documents as originals, minor misstatements of the names of the parties, adding digits to the letter of credit number, and presenting a survey dated after the bill of lading was issued. Otherwise, however, the documents conformed, such that "the whole of the documents relate[d] to the transaction."[86] The court thus held that the discrepancies were not sufficient, even under the strict compliance standard, to permit the issuing bank to reject the documents and dishonor.

---

[81] *See* Flagship Cruises, Ltd. v. New England Merchants Nat. Bank, 569 F.2d 699 (1st Cir. 1978); Banco Español de Credito v. State Street Bank and Trust, 385 F.2d 230 (1st Cir. 1967), *cert. denied*, 390 U.S. 1013 (1968).

[82] *See, e.g.,* Continental Cas. Co. v. SouthTrust Bank, N.A., 933 So.2d 337, 340 (Ala. 2006); Shin-Etsu Chemical Co., Ltd. v. 3033 ICICI Bank Ltd., 777 N.Y.S.2d 69, 74 (App. Div. 2004). *See also* J. White & R. Summers, Uniform Commercial Code 1096 (6th ed., 2010)(observing that "although [UCP] Articles 2a and 14d refer to compliance with international banking standards, [this] arguably constitutes strict compliance in today's world").

[83] *See* ISBP Manual, *supra* footnote 73, at 22.

[84] Hanil Bank v. Pt. Bank Negara Indonesia, 148 F.3d 127 (2nd Cir. 1998).

[85] 167 F. Supp. 2d 940, 947 (S.D. Tex. 2000).

[86] *Id.*, 947–949. For an analysis of this opinion see Lisa Pietrzak, *Sloping in the Right Direction: A First Look at UCP 600 and the New Standards as Applied to Voest-Alpine*, 7 ASPER REV. INT'L BUS. & TRADE L. 179 (2007).

Many of the strict compliance cases seem to revolve around discrepancies in transportation documents or terms.[87] Express conditions in the credit that loading, presentment, or other acts must be performed by a certain time will be strictly enforced.[88] The same is true for a discrepancy in the location for shipment or delivery,[89] or with respect to the required form of transport document. Thus, one court held that a credit calling for "Full Set Clean on board ocean bills of lading" was not satisfied by "truckers bills of lading," even though the latter were customary in the country involved.[90] Nor is a requirement for a "Full Set Clean on Board Bills of Lading" satisfied by air waybills, even if air delivery is preferable under the circumstances.[91] Indeed, the UCP emphasizes the importance of a "clean" transport document with a rule that banks may only accept such a document if it bears "no clause or notation expressly declaring a defective condition of the goods or their packaging."[92]

§ 6.9 The Basic Obligations of Banks

The Issuing Bank. The issuing bank, as the originator of a letter of credit, has the primary obligation to pay the stated amount upon presentation of complying documents. UCP Article 7 thus states that if the presented documents "constitute a complying presentation," the issuing bank "must honour" and thus pay according to the terms of the letter of credit.[93] An issuing bank is "irrevocably" bound to do so "as of the time it issues the credit."[94] The obligation to honor arises either when the conforming documents are presented directly to the issuing bank or when a nominated bank (especially a confirming bank) refuses to take or pay for the documents.[95]

---

[87] *See, e.g.*, Uniloy Milacron, Inc. v. PNC Bank, N.A., 2008 WL 3884316 (W.D. Ky. 2008); Beyene v. Irving Trust Co., 762 F.2d 4 (2nd Cir. 1985).

[88] *See, e.g.*, Beyene v. Irving Trust Co., 762 F.2d 4 (2nd Cir. 1985); Voest-Alpine Int'l Corp. v. Chase Manhattan Bank, NA, 545 F. Supp. 301 (S.D.N.Y. 1982), *aff'd in part, rev'd in part* 707 F.2d 680 (2nd Cir. 1983).

[89] *See, e.g.*, Bank of Nova Scotia v. Angelica-Whitewear Ltd., 36 Dom. L.R. 4th 161 (Can. 1987); Bucci Imports, Ltd. v. Chase Bank Int'l, 518 N.Y.S.2d 15 (App. Div. 1987).

[90] Marine Midland Grace Trust Co. of N.Y. v. Banco Del Pais, S.A., 261 F. Supp. 884 (S.D.N.Y. 1966).

[91] Board of Trade v. Swiss Credit Bank, 597 F.2d 146 (9th Cir.1979).

[92] UCP, art. 27.

[93] The obligation to honor involves either immediate payment or, in the case of an agreed payment at a later date, an "acceptance" of the related draft or other documents. For the concept of acceptance, see the text accompanying footnotes 21-25 *supra*.

[94] UCP, art. 7(b).

[95] UCP, art. 7(a)(i)-(v).

Where another bank is authorized to accept documents and pay under a letter of credit (*i.e.*, in the case of a "nominated bank"), the issuing bank also has an obligation to such a bank. In specific, UCP Article 7(c) provides that the issuing bank "undertakes to reimburse a nominated bank that has honoured or negotiated a complying presentation and forwarded the documents to the issuing bank."[96] The standard example of this is where a confirming bank has first honored a presentation by paying the beneficiary. (The concept of a "negotiation" covers the case where a confirming bank does not simply honor a presentation, but rather "purchases" the related drafts for its own account—*i.e.*, to make a profit beyond its small fee.[97]) The UCP also explicitly states that the issuing bank's obligation to reimburse a nominated bank "is independent of the issuing bank's undertaking to the beneficiary."[98]

Confirming Bank. Recall that a confirming bank is one that that "adds its confirmation" to a credit at the authorization or request of the issuing bank.[99] A "confirmation" represents an independent obligation, "in addition to that of the issuing bank," to honor a complying presentation under the letter of credit.[100] The confirming bank becomes "irrevocably" bound as soon as it adds its confirmation.[101]

As against the beneficiary, the obligations of a confirming bank parallel those of the issuing bank. Under UCP Article 8, a confirming bank also "must honour" a presentation, provided as always that the documents comply with the requirements of the letter of credit.[102] Like the issuing bank, the confirming bank's obligation to honor arises either when the conforming documents are presented directly to it or when some other nominated bank refuses to take or pay for the documents.[103]

Nominated Bank. Under the UCP, a "nominated bank" is one that the issuer expressly or impliedly authorizes to accept documents presented under a credit. Indeed, the term includes any bank at all if the issuer makes the credit "available with any bank" (aka,

---

96 UCP, art. 7(c).

97 UCP, art. 2 (eleventh definition)

98 UCP, art. 7(c).

99 UCP, art. 2 (seventh definition).

100 UCP, art. 2 (sixth definition).

101 UCP, art. 8(b).

102 UCP, art. 8(a).

103 UCP, art. 8(a)(i)-(v). A confirming bank also owes an obligation to reimburse another nominated bank that has honored a complying presentation. This obligation is independent of that owed to the beneficiary. UCP, art. 8(c).

a "freely negotiable credit").[104] Thus, a nominated bank may or may not also be a confirming bank. The distinguishing point is that a confirming bank also *obligates itself* in advance to accept a presentation, whereas other nominated banks are authorized, but not obligated, to do so.[105]

The legal position of the nominated bank flows directly from this description. Absent a confirmation or express agreement, the authorization to accept a presentation "does not impose any obligation on th[e] nominated bank to honour or negotiate."[106] Indeed, even the receipt and forwarding of documents by a nominated bank does not constitute an honor or negotiation of the documents.[107]

If, on the other hand, a nominated bank in fact chooses to honor or negotiate complying documents under a letter of credit, it is entitled to reimbursement from the issuing bank or a confirming bank.[108]

§ 6.10 The Banks' Obligations upon Presentation of Documents

As noted above, under the UCP banks deal only in documents.[109] Indeed, the UCP's very definition of a "credit" is one that requires a "presentation," a term that relates only to "documents."[110] The UCP also provides a variety of more detailed requirements for letters of credit. These include that the credit must state: (1) either the specific bank(s) with which it is available (*i.e.*, to which bank(s) a presentation may be made) or that it is available with "any bank"; (2) when payment must be made upon presentation (*e.g.*, "on sight" or "30 days after presentation"); (3) an expiry date; and (4) the location of the bank(s) for presentation.[111]

When documents are "presented" to an issuing bank or to a confirming bank (or another nominated bank that has decided to act upon its nomination), it has two principal duties: One is to examine the documents to determine whether they conform to the terms of

[104] *See* UCP, art. 2 (twelfth definition). The UCC equivalent is the "nominated person." *See* UCC §§ 5–102(a)(11), 5–107(b).

[105] *See* UCP, art. 12(a).

[106] UCP, art. 12(a).

[107] UCP, art. 12(c).

[108] UCP, art. 7(c), 8(c).

[109] *See* § 6.8 and UCP, art. 5.

[110] UCP, art. 2 (thirteenth definition) (defining a "presentation" as "either the delivery of documents under a credit to the issuing bank or nominated bank or the documents so delivered").

[111] UCP, art. 6(a)-(d).

the letter of credit (see § 6.11 below); the second is to act upon any discrepancies found (see § 6.12 below).

§ 6.11 ____Obligation to Examine the Documents for Discrepancies

Unfortunately, discrepancies in documents presented under letters of credits are an everyday occurrence. Indeed, some estimates are that over two-thirds of all presentations contain at least one discrepancy,[112] and that one-half of presentations are rejected on this basis. That rate of error should not be surprising if one understands that the presentation may consist of many pages of documents. Moreover, as described above, the prevailing view on the standard for identifying a discrepancy remains "strict compliance" with the terms of the letter of credit.[113]

The existence of a discrepancy in a presentation has direct consequences for the rights of the presenter, the obligations of the bank, and the right of the bank to seek reimbursement from another bank and the applicant (the buyer):

(a) If the bank determines that a presentation complies with the letter of credit, it "must honour" and pay the beneficiary (or "accept" a time draft).[114] In such a case, the bank is entitled to reimbursement. But if it refuses to pay in such a case, it will be liable to the presenter ("wrongful dishonor");[115]

(b) If, in contrast, the documents do not comply, the bank "may refuse to honor."[116] In such a case, the presenter has no claim to payment under the letter of credit;[117]

(c) Finally, if the documents do not comply, but the bank nonetheless honors (or waives its right to dishonor), it generally is not entitled to reimbursement ("wrongful honor").[118]

---

[112] *See* Ronald J. Mann, *The Role of Letters of Credit in Payment Transactions*, 98 MICH. L. REV. 2494, 2497 (2000) (finding that only twenty-seven percent of presentations conformed to the requirements of the letter of credit).

[113] *See* § 6.8 *supra*.

[114] UCP, art. 15(a), 15(b). Such a bank may also "negotiate," *i.e.*, purchase the draft from the presenter. *Id.* For the concept of "acceptance" see the text accompanying footnotes 22-25 *supra*.

[115] *See* § 6.13 *infra*.

[116] UCP, art. 16(a).

[117] For other obligations of the banks upon a dishonor (especially notice) see § 6.12 *infra*.

[118] For more on this issue see § 6.14 *infra*.

Given the central importance of the assessment of a nonconformity, the UCP provides a variety of more detailed rules on the rights and performance obligations of the banks. The following paragraphs explore these rules.

Examination of Documents Alone. It is worth emphasizing that the first protection of banks is that they must determine the existence of a discrepancy "on the basis of the documents alone." The UCP stresses this point by stating that examination extends only to the "face" of the documents presented.[119] Thus, if the banks find that a document does not comply, they are under no obligation to investigate other circumstances that may or may not clarify the discrepancy.[120]

Irrelevance of Usages or Customs. The banks also are not responsible for knowing, and are not expected to investigate, the customs or usages that may apply in a particular trade outside of the banking trade. The famous case (noted above) of *J.H. Rayner & Co. Ltd. v. Hambro's Bank, Ltd.* thus made clear that the bank there was not bound to know the general merchant's understanding of "Coromandel groundnuts."[121] The UCP has no explicit rule on this point, unlike the UCC.[122] It is nonetheless generally understood that for the UCP as well, as a U.S. District Court has declared, "[t]he bank is not expected or required to be familiar with or to consider the customs of, or the special meaning or effect given to particular terms in, the trade."[123]

Nondocumentary Conditions. As a corollary to the principle that the examination for conformity with the letter of credit involves "the documents alone," the banks may consider only those conditions that may be satisfied by documentary evidence. UCP Article 14 states this rule explicitly: "If a credit contains a condition without stipulating the document to indicate compliance with the condition," the banks must "deem such condition as not stated and

---

[119] UCP, art. 14(h).

[120] UCP Article 14 also has some highly specific rules on information in a document. *See* UCP, art. 14(i) (stating that a required document may be dated before the issuance of the letter of credit, but not after the presentation); 14(j) (stating that the addresses of the beneficiary and the applicant need not be the same as stated in the credit, but must be within the stated country).

[121] *See supra* footnote 77.

[122] *See* UCC § 5–108(f)(3).

[123] Thiagarajar Mills, Ltd. v. Thornton, 47 F. Supp. 2d 918, 924 (W.D. Tenn. 1999)(*quoting* Marino Indus. Corp. v. Chase Manhattan Bank, N.A., 686 F.2d 112, 115 (2nd Cir. 1982)).

. . . disregard it."[124] As a result, letters of credit must state precisely the documents, and the terms of the documents, against which payment is to be made. And if the issuing bank or the applicant (the buyer) wants to condition payment on a certain fact, they must ensure that the fact can be evidenced by a document. Upon a presentation, the banks are obligated to disregard any other form of a condition.

Anomalous documents. Another unfortunately common occurrence is that a beneficiary presents a document *not* required by the letter of credit. One might term these "anomalous documents." Derivative of the rule on nondocumentary conditions, the UCP requires that the banks ignore such documents: "A document presented but not required by the credit will be disregarded and may be returned to the presenter."[125]

Original Documents. The UCP 600 has a new provision designed specifically to address controversies over the subject of "original" documents engendered by ambiguities in earlier versions. The new version continues to require the presentation of "at least" one original of each document stipulated in the credit.[126] And the UCP has special detail on this requirement for the crucial commercial invoice: This document must (1) "appear to have been issued by the beneficiary," (2) "be made out in the name of the applicant," and (3) "be made out in the same currency as the credit."[127] But other provisions temper the seeming strictness of the "original document" requirement. First, one provision removes a requirement of a formal "signature" on the commercial invoice.[128] Two other provisions then require that a bank accept a presented document as an original, in absence of a contrary indication, if (a) it bears "an apparently original signature, mark, stamp, or label of the issuer," or (b) "states that it is original."[129]

Right to Seek a Waiver. In many situations, the discrepancies discovered by the banks may be trivial, and the applicant/buyer may want the payment made, and the goods delivered, despite the discrepancy. (Businesses most often are interested in "getting the deal done," not creating lawsuits.) To accommodate this, the UCP

---

[124] UCP, art. 14(h). *See also* In re Central Illinois Energy, L.L.C., 482 B.R. 772, 782 (C.D. Ill. 2012)("If a letter of credit contains nondocumentary conditions, the issuer is authorized to disregard them and treat them as if they were not stated.").

[125] UCP, art. 14(g).

[126] UCP, art. 17(a).

[127] UCP, art. 18(a).

[128] UCP, art. 18(a)(iv).

[129] UCP, art. 17(b), 17(c).

allows, but does not require, a bank, "in its sole judgement," to consult the applicant (its customer) for a waiver of discrepancies.[130] In the overwhelming majority of cases, applicants in fact waive the discrepancies discovered by the bank. Thus, the system has continued to work despite frequency of discrepancies, because the non-bank parties (the buyer and the seller) typically want the transaction to be completed despite the technical protections offered by letter of credit law.

Errors in Transmission. The UCP also has a general provision that protects banks against errors in the transmission of documents or similar technological problems.[131] In specific, Article 35 states that a bank "assumes no liability or responsibility for the consequences arising out of delay, loss in transit, mutilation or other errors arising in the transmission of" a letter of credit or associated communications. The same is true for errors in "translation or interpretation of technical terms."[132] Where the errors occur in the relationship with the beneficiary, these rules seem to provide complete protection to the banks. But as to transmissions *between* banks, the UCP has no specific rule.[133] And the UCC states only that the banks must observe "standard practice of financial institutions that regularly issue letters of credit" and are "not responsible for . . . an act or omission of others."[134]

§ 6.12 ___Obligation of Timely Notification of Discrepancies

The second principal obligation of a bank upon a presentation of documents is that it give timely notice of any discrepancies found. In this respect, the new UCP 600 provides a variety of important clarifications.

Duty of Notice. First, if a bank decides to dishonor a presentation (*i.e.*, not pay under the letter of credit), the UCP requires that it send a "notice to that effect" to the presenter.[135] This notice must

[130] UCP, art. 16(b). Some past courts have held that an issuer may not consult in bad faith with the applicant for the sole purpose of discovering discrepancies. *See* E & H Partners v. Broadway Nat. Bank, 39 F. Supp. 2d 275, 284–285 (S.D.N.Y. 1998); Banker's Trust Co. v. State Bank of India, 1 Lloyd's Rept. 578 (1991), *aff'd*, 2 Lloyd's Rept. 443 (Ct. App. 1991).

[131] As noted in § 6.16 below, most communications between banks occur via the SWIFT system.

[132] UCP, art 35.

[133] The one exception is that a confirming or issuing bank must honor a presentation by a nominated bank even if the documents are lost in transit. *See* UCP, art. 35, second para.

[134] *See* UCC § 5–108(e), (f)(2).

[135] UPC, art. 16(c).

state the following information: (a) that the bank is refusing to honor or negotiate (*i.e.*, purchase) the documents; (b) "each discrepancy in respect of which the bank refuses to honour or negotiate"; and (c) that the bank is either returning the documents to the presenter or holding them pending further instructions from the presenter or the applicant.[136] On this latter issue, the UCP 600 has a new provision that allows the bank instead to follow prior instructions given by the *beneficiary* (the seller) or other presenter.[137] (This is separate from the right of the bank to consult the applicant for a waiver of discrepancies.[138]) This is an important provision, for it may allow the seller to speculate on a possible rise in the price of the goods between the date of shipment and the date of arrival.[139]

To ensure that the required notice of dishonor arrives in a timely fashion, the UCP also specifies the means for communication. The notice must be sent "by telecommunication," and if this is not possible, "by other expeditious means."[140] As one court thus held, the use of a courier is not sufficiently expeditious to fulfill this obligation.[141]

Single Notice Requirement. UCP 600 also states that the bank has only one opportunity to give a notice of any discrepancy. In specific, Article 16(c) allows the bank to give only "a single notice," which, as noted above, must set forth all discrepancies on which the bank is relying for a dishonor decision. And, as noted below, the bank will be precluded from relying on any discrepancy not included in this "single notice."[142]

Timing of Notice. The UCP 600 states a clear rule for the time within which a bank must make a decision on dishonoring a presentation. If a bank determines that a presentation does not comply, it must give a notice to that effect "no later than the close of the fifth banking day following the day of presentation."[143] This new rule—which replaced a flexible "reasonable time" standard—extends to the issuing bank, any confirming bank, and any nominated bank

---

136 *Id.*, art. 16(c)(i)-(iii).

137 UCP, art. 16(c)(iii)(d).

138 *See* the discussion of this right in § 6.11 above.

139 *See* Roberto Bergami, *What Can UCP 600 Do for You?*, 11 VINDONOBA J. INT'L L. & ARBITRATION 1, 9 (2007).

140 UCP art. 16(d).

141 Hamilton Bank, N.A. v. Kookmin Bank, 245 F.3d 82, 89–90 (2nd Cir. 2001).

142 *See* "Strict Preclusion Rule" immediately below.

143 UCP, art. 16(d). *See also id.*, 14(b)(stating that the banks shall have "a maximum of a five banking days . . . to determine if a presentation is complying").

that acts on its nomination.[144] A "banking day" means any day "on which a bank is regularly open" at the location of the presentation.[145] This strict five-day rule for letters of credit covered by the UCP differs from the traditional rule stated in UCC Article 5 ("a reasonable time . . . but not beyond the seventh business day" after presentation).[146]

As noted above, the UCP allows, but does not require, the bank to consult with the applicant (the buyer) for a waiver of discrepancies. But the UCP makes clear that this does not extend the five-day notice period.[147] Thus, the "five banking days" deadline includes not only time to examine the documents, but also any time required to consult the buyer about waiving the discrepancies and to prepare and dispatch the notice of dishonor. The latter limitations had created difficulties with the earlier "reasonable time" standard (which, as noted, continues in the UCC).

Strict Preclusion Rule. The new UCP 600 also includes a strict rule on the failure of a bank to adhere to the timely notice requirement. If an issuing bank or a confirming bank fails to fulfill that obligation, "it shall be precluded from claiming that the documents do not constitute a complying presentation."[148] This preclusion thus covers both (a) a failure to give notice within the strict five-day period *and* (b) any discrepancies not stated in the allowed "single notice" of dishonor. Any such failure triggers an automatic preclusion for discrepancies not timely stated, and without requiring proof of a waiver or estoppel. Thus, banks that reject documents have only one chance to identify all the discrepancies on which they can ever rely. The rationale for this rule is that the presenter should have notice of all discrepancies at once, so that it can determine whether they are curable and whether the cure is cost-effective. But the rule can also lead the banks to delay notification as long as permitted to ensure that they discover all possible defects.

The strict rule of preclusion has two exceptions. First because the formal language of the rule refers to "discrepancies," some courts have held that the preclusion does not apply if the letter of credit had already expired or been cancelled before the presenta-

---

[144] UCP, art. 16(c), (d). This time period applies even if the letter of credit thereafter expires by its own terms. *See id.*, art. 14(b).

[145] UCP, art. 2 (third definition).

[146] UCC § 5–108(b).

[147] UCP, art. 16(b).

[148] UCP, art. 16(f).

tion.[149] However, the simple fact that the beneficiary sent documents that were clearly discrepant, or even that the beneficiary knew that they were discrepant, will not excuse the issuing bank from observing the notice requirements.[150]

Second, the notice requirement does not apply to fraud or forgery. As noted above, the UCP does not address such issues, with the result that otherwise applicable law will govern. Where UCC Article 5 applies, a failure to give a notice of dishonor "does not preclude the issuer from asserting as a basis for dishonor fraud or forgery."[151]

Rights of Confirming Banks. The requirement of timely notice of all grounds for dishonor should apply as well to a presentation made by a confirming bank (or other nominated bank) to the issuing bank. The UCP does not explicitly address this point. But it states that the notice obligation applies in favor of a "presenter," and defines that term as a "beneficiary, *bank* or other party" that delivers documents to a bank seeking payment under a letter of credit.[152] Moreover, courts that have addressed presentations by a confirming bank to an issuing bank have expressly proceeded on the foundation that the notice obligations in UCP Article 16 apply there as well.[153] Thus, when, after paying the beneficiary, a confirming bank in turn presents the documents to the issuer, the latter has five banking days to give a "single notice" of all discrepancies on which it relies in refusing to reimburse the confirming bank.

§ 6.13 Wrongful Dishonor of a Credit

If the issuing bank or the confirming bank refuses to pay upon presentation of the documents, such a "dishonor" may be rightful or wrongful. If discrepancies in fact exist between the presented documents and the specifications in the credit, the banks are entitled to

---

[149] *See, e.g.*, CVD Equipment Corp. v. Taiwan Glass Indus. Corp., 2011 WL 1210199, at *5 (S.D.N.Y. 2011); Todi Exports v. Amrav Sportswear, 1997 WL 61063, at *4 (S.D.N.Y. 1997).

[150] *See, e.g.*, Hamilton Bank, N.A. v. Kookmin Bank, 245 F.3d 82, 89–90 ((2nd Cir. 2001); Bombay Industries, Inc. v. Bank of New York, 1997 WL 860671, at *3–4 (N.Y. Sup. 1997).

[151] UCC § 5–108(d).

[152] UCP, art. 2 (thirteenth definition)(emphasis supplied). *See also id.* (fourteenth definition)(defining a "presentation").

[153] *See* CVD Equipment Corp. vs. Taiwan Glass Indus. Corp., 2011 WL 1210199 (S.D.N.Y. 2011)(holding in the case of a presentation by a confirming bank under the UCP that "[t]he rule could not be more clear" that the issuing bank must give notice within five banking days); Fortis Bank SA NV v Stemcor UK Ltd [2011] EWHC 538 (Comm)(2011)(applying the preclusion rule in UCP 16(f) to an issuing bank responding to a presentation by a confirming bank).

dishonor, although to do so they must follow the notice procedures specified in the UCP.[154] If discrepancies in fact exist and it follows the procedures, the bank has no liability on the credit, and no successful litigation on the credit[155] should ensue. Most of the cases involving rightful dishonor involve litigation over the timeliness and effectiveness of the notice of dishonor required by the UCP rules.

If, in contrast, the bank refuses to pay when the presented documents in fact strictly comply with the letter of credit, it has committed a wrongful dishonor and thus is in breach of one or more contracts. First, it is in breach of the letter of credit contract, for which the beneficiary will have a cause of action. Second, it may be a breach of the credit application agreement between the applicant and the issuer, for which the applicant may have a cause of action. Both issues are now governed by statute, but the latter is also informed by general contract law.

The UCP has no provisions on the formal issue of causes of action. But UCC Article 5 expressly gives the beneficiary of a letter of credit whose presentation was wrongfully dishonored a cause of action against the issuer.[156] It defines the amount of damages the aggrieved beneficiary may claim as "the amount of money that is the subject of the dishonor."[157] This amount does not necessarily equate to the actual damages suffered by the beneficiary. The beneficiary has no obligation to mitigate damages, but if it in fact avoids part of the loss, the recovery is reduced by the amount of the loss avoided. In addition, the aggrieved beneficiary can recover incidental damages and interest, but not consequential damages.[158]

If the issuer wrongfully dishonors a presentation, the applicant (the buyer) may also be damaged. The most common harm is damage to the applicant's reputation in the trade, and an unwillingness of suppliers to accept subsequent letters of credit from the buyer. Prior to the revision of UCC Article 5 in 1995, the consensus view was that, because it was not a formal party to the letter of credit, the applicant could not bring an action on the letter of credit itself for wrongful dishonor.[159] Instead, the applicant's right to sue the

---

[154] *See* generally UCP art. 16. For further discussion see §§ 6.9–6.12, *supra*.

[155] The buyer and the seller may nonetheless pursue their dispute under the sales contact For this dispute, the CISG or (as applicable) the UCC will govern. *See* Chapter 1.

[156] UCC § 5–111(a).

[157] *Id.*

[158] *Id.*

[159] *See, e.g.*, Interchemicals Co. v. Bank of Credit, 635 N.Y.S.2d 194 (App. Div. 1995).

issuer for wrongful dishonor would arise out of (and follow the terms of) the credit application agreement, and would be analyzed under ordinary contract law. In fact, issuing banks commonly require the applicant to enter into "reimbursement agreements" that broadly cover their relationship.

The 1995 version of UCC Article 5 reverses this reasoning. UCC § 5–111(b) states that if the issuer wrongfully dishonors a presentation, the applicant also "may recover damages." The most important aspect of this rule is that the applicant may recover only incidental damages, and not consequential damages, even if foreseeable.[160] Thus, the applicant's recovery for the most common form of harm—damage to reputation—would seem to be foreclosed in the statutory action. However, the contract cause of action under the credit application agreement may survive the enactment of the statutory cause of action, because the Official Comments state that "this section does not bar recovery of consequential or even punitive damages for breach of statutory or common law duties outside of this article."[161] But because most rules of UCC Article 5 defer the agreement of the parties,[162] the contract between the issuer and the applicant may place noteworthy restrictions on the right of the applicant to seek damages for wrongful dishonor.

§ 6.14 Wrongful Honor of the Credit

If the issuing or confirming bank honors a presentation under a letter of credit and pays the beneficiary (or accepts a time draft), its actions may be rightful or wrongful. If no discrepancies exist between the specifications in the credit and the documents presented, the banks are obligated to honor the presentation. They are then entitled to reimbursement from the applicant. In such a case, the beneficiary also has received payment or the acceptance of its time draft, so its claims should be satisfied and no litigation on the credit should ensue.

The bank will then seek reimbursement from the applicant under the credit application agreement or applicable law. If the documents are conforming, so that the banks rightfully honored the beneficiary's presentation, the applicant has no defense to the reimbursement claim. The issuer has performed its contractual obligation to the applicant and is entitled to the counter-performance (reimbursement). The UCC expressly recognizes this right.[163] Practical

---

[160] *Id.*

[161] *Id.*, Official Comment 4.

[162] § 5–103(c).

[163] *See* UCC § 5–108(i).

challenges nonetheless may exist for the issuer in asserting this right. If, for example, the issuer granted credit to the applicant, the issuer has consciously taken the risk that the applicant might be unable to pay. To avoid this risk, the issuer should insist on a pledge of collateral, obtain a third party's guarantee, or demand pre-payment.

On the other hand, if the documents have discrepancies and the issuer honors the beneficiary's presentation anyway, that is a wrongful honor. The issuer may still seek reimbursement from the applicant and may have the practical ability to debit the applicant's account with the bank. This would force the applicant to litigate in order to obtain a recrediting of its account.[164]

Curiously, the UCP has no provisions that directly address the subject. It merely states that a "complying presentation" is one that does not "conflict with" the terms of the letter of credit under "international standard banking practice."[165] If this is the case, the UCP expressly recognizes that a confirming bank or other nominated bank that has honored a presentation is entitled to reimbursement from the issuing bank.[166] But it has no express rule on the right of the issuing bank to seek reimbursement from the applicant.

UCC Article 5 also leaves at least some room for dispute on the issue. Its structure reflects a principle that the issuer is entitled to reimbursement only if it honored a complying presentation. Thus, it states that the issuer "shall dishonor a presentation that does not appear . . . to comply."[167] It then provides that the issuer is entitled to reimbursement only if it has honored a presentation "as permitted or required" in Article 5.[168] From this foundation, § 5–111(b) also grants to the applicant a cause of action for damages in the event of a "wrongful honor." But this rule states that the right to damages is founded on a "breach of [the issuer's] obligation to the applicant."[169]

The uncertainty comes from the fact that the UCC's statutory rights and obligations are subject to the parties' agreement. As a result, the terms of the credit application agreement (or "reim-

---

164 For an example, see Oei v. Citibank N.A., 957 F. Supp. 492 (S.D.N.Y 1997).

165 UCP, art. 14(d).

166 UCP, art. 7(c).

167 UCC § 5–108(a).

168 UCC § 5–108(i).

169 UCC § 5–111(b). For examples, see Imptex Intern. Corp. v. HSBC Bank USA, N.A., 859 N.Y.S.2d 147 (App. Div. 2008); Oei v. Citibank, N.A., 957 F. Supp. 492 (S.D.N.Y.1997).

bursement agreement") may be more important than the provisions of either the UCC or the UCP. In specific, such agreements may include a disclaimer of, or limitation on, the liability of the issuer for wrongful honor, and thus may create a contractual right to reimbursement where no such statutory right exists.

If the issuer has wrongfully honored the beneficiary's presentation, and cannot obtain reimbursement from the applicant, it may seek to recover from the beneficiary. Such a right in favor of the issuer may exist directly against the beneficiary on a breach of warranty, or indirectly as an assignee or subrogee of the applicant's rights. The UCC provides that the beneficiary gives a warranty to the issuer that there is no fraud or forgery of the documents; but that warranty is not so broad as to cover all discrepancies in the documents, or even simple breach of contract.[170] The beneficiary also gives a warranty to the applicant, but the warranty is different in substance. The beneficiary warrants to the applicant only that the documents do not violate the sales contract or other agreement.[171] The difference between these warranties arises from a goal of promoting finality to the letter of credit transaction, so that litigation between parties to the letter of credit transaction is not infected with disputes over the sales transaction.[172]

§ 6.15 The Special Role of the Transportation Document in the Letter of Credit Transaction

Although, for the description of the goods, the commercial invoice is the document that must "strictly conform" to the letter of credit, the most important document required by a letter of credit commonly is the transportation document. Prior versions of the UCP were premised on ocean bills of lading, evidencing an assumption that the goods would be carried by sea. New developments in the transport industry, however, have created new technological applications. Thus, the recent revisions of the UCP provide separate, detailed articles for multi-modal transport documents;[173] negotiable ocean bills of lading;[174] non-negotiable sea waybills;[175] charter party bills of lading;[176] air transport documents;[177] road, rail or in-

---

[170] UCC § 5–110(a)(1).

[171] UCC § 5–110(a)(2).

[172] UCC § 5–110, Official Comment 2.

[173] UCP, art. 19.

[174] UCP art. 20.

[175] UCP art. 21.

[176] UCP, art. 22.

[177] UCP, art. 23.

land waterway transport documents;[178] and courier receipts, post receipts, and certificates of posting.[179]

Nonetheless, the most common form of required transport document in large international transactions remains the negotiable ocean bill of lading. Under the UCP, an ocean bill of lading must name the port of loading, the port of discharge, and the carrier, and be signed by the carrier or its agent.[180] Banks have no duty, however, to check the signature or initials accompanying an "on board" notation, absent a special arrangement.[181] The bill of lading also may merely identify an "intended vessel." In such a case, any "on board" notation must specify the vessel on which the goods have been loaded.[182] The medieval custom of issuing "a set" of bills of lading, and hoping one of them would arrive and be honored, is now disapproved: The UCP requires as a norm only one original bill of lading.[183] If the original documents are lost or destroyed, a bank may accept copies of the documents as originals, if the copies have been signed. Allowable signatures includes handwriting, facsimiles, perforated signatures, stamps, symbols, and other mechanical and electronic methods.[184]

In addition to nonnegotiable "waybills,"[185] two modern transportation practices are worthy of mention. A "charter party" bill of lading does not identify the carrier, and thus involves special risks. The UCP nonetheless now recognizes this as a permissible transport document for use with a letter of credit. But it also relieves the banks from any duty to examine the terms of the charter party contract,[186] under the assumption that only sophisticated parties with considerable knowledge of the trade will use them.

A second form of increasingly common transport document is a "multimodal" bill of lading. In multimodal transportation arrangements, the bill of lading—as its name implies—will cover the goods through "at least two different modes of transport."[187] An example would be where the goods are first loaded on a truck and then transferred to a railroad, before being loaded on a ship for ocean

---

[178] UCP, art. 24.

[179] UCP, art. 25.

[180] UCP, art. 20(a)(i). For more on negotiable bills of lading see Chapter 3, § 3.3

[181] UCP art. 20(a)(ii).

[182] *Id.*

[183] UCP, art. 20(a)(iv).

[184] For more detail on electronic "authentications" of documents, see Chapter 8.

[185] *See* UCP, art. 21.

[186] UCP, art. 22(b).

[187] UCP, art. 19.

transport. Such a bill of lading is likely to be issued by a freight forwarder and not by a single carrier (because many carriers may be involved). Thus, it does not name a carrier and does not represent a receipt directly from the carrier, which is the norm for documents of title such as negotiable bills of lading. However, the UCP allows its use if the letter of credit authorizes a signature by a named agent of the carrier and the freight forwarder issues it in that capacity as a multi-modal transport document.[188]

§ 6.16 Electronic Letter of Credit Transactions

Electronic communications have taken over some aspects of letter of credit practice, but not others. They dominate the issuance process in bank-to-bank communications, and are sometimes used by applicants to initiate the issuance process. However, for a variety of reasons banks and other interested parties have not yet been able to create an entirely paperless transaction. First, the beneficiary still commonly wants a piece of paper committing the banks to pay upon specified conditions. Second, even with an electronic letter of credit, most industries have not accepted electronic forms in the place of the significant documents typically required by a letter of credit. The principal example is an electronic negotiable bill of lading, which, for the reasons discussed in Chapter 3,[189] has not yet found broad or stable acceptance. Thus, in the presentation phase for letters of credit, the parties commonly still use physical documents, while funds settlement (payment) likely will be electronic.

Over three quarters of letter of credit communication between banks—including the issuance, advice, and confirmation of letters of credit—is paperless; and nearly all informal communication is electronic. While bank-to-bank communication is electronic, bank-to-beneficiary (seller) communication is still paper-based. Letter of credit issuers can now communicate directly with beneficiaries' computers, however, and use of this practice both is widespread and should be expected to increase. The UCP rules also now expressly contemplate "teletransmission," which will continue to facilitate the use of electronic practices.[190]

Most bank-to-bank communications concerning letters of credit are routed through the dedicated lines of SWIFT (the Society for Worldwide Interbank Financial Telecommunication). SWIFT is a Belgian not-for-profit organization owned by banks as a cooperative venture for the transmission of financial transaction messages. It

[188] UCP, art. 19(a).

[189] *See* Chapter 3, § 3.19.

[190] UCP, art. 11.

requires all such messages to be structured in a uniform format, and uses standardized elements for allocating message space and for message text. Thus, messages can be communicated on a computer-to-computer basis without being re-keyed.

A bank issuing a letter of credit communicates that message to the nearest SWIFT access point. The message is then routed on a dedicated data transmission line to a regional processor, where it is validated (see below). From the regional processor, it is routed over a dedicated line to one of three main data centers, one each in the United States, the Netherlands, and Switzerland. From there it is routed through a regional processor to a SWIFT access point and to the receiving bank. The message switching, and sometimes necessary storage, can be performed by computers, if the standardization of the format of the financial messages is sufficiently developed and comprehensive. SWIFT seems to have achieved this level of uniformity.

The bank that receives a SWIFT electronic letter of credit message need not send a reply stating that it accepts the request to confirm (or merely advise) or the authorization to negotiate or pay the letter of credit. It needs only to perform by advising, confirming, negotiating, or paying, and it is entitled to reimbursement by the issuing bank. However, the SWIFT messages only transmit the letter of credit and their authorizations and requests. SWIFT messages do not effect the settlements of letters of credit or other transfers of funds between issuing banks and other banks. SWIFT is not a clearing house for bank settlements like, for example, CHIPS (Clearing House for Interbank Payment Systems). Under the SWIFT letter of credit system, participating banks must use other arrangements (such as CHIPS) to settle their accounts and accomplish a transfer of funds.

SWIFT relies upon both encryption of messages and authentication to provide security to its users. The authentication of SWIFT messages is accomplished by the use of algorithms, which are mathematical formulas that calculate the contents of a message from header to trailer. If a SWIFT message requires authentication, and all letter of credit messages do, the issuing bank computes the contents and compiles a result based on the number of characters and data fields. At the regional processor, SWIFT checks the authentication trailer for the number of characters in the authentication. However, a more rigorous authentication will be performed by the receiving bank, using an algorithm contained in an authentication key provided by the issuing bank. The computations involving these authentication procedures will indicate a mismatch if the message is fraudulent or has been altered. There are also "log in" procedures, application-selection procedures, message numbering and error-checking capabilities, and control of access to the system hardware. SWIFT also retains records of each transaction. In all, the security devices are numerous and complex.

Most SWIFT messages are delivered within minutes of their issuance by a bank, although delays of up to two hours are possible. Thus, delays in the system are slight, but present. When is the issuer of an electronic letter of credit bound? The UCP provides no set rules on the issue, but UCC Article 5 establishes that such messages are effective and enforceable upon transmission by the issuer, not delivery to the receiving bank,[191] and SWIFT rules require no reply. This UCC rule conforms to the understanding of bankers involved in the trade.

Under SWIFT rules, Belgian law governs all relations between SWIFT and its users. SWIFT is liable for negligence or fraud of its own employees and agents and for those parts of the communication system that it controls, such as regional processors, main switches and the dedicated lines that connect them. But SWIFT disclaims liability for those parts of the communication system that it does not control, such as the bank computers that issue and receive messages and the dedicated lines from bank to a regional processor. Even where SWIFT is liable, its liability is limited to "direct" damages (loss of interest); the contracts with SWIFT thus expressly disclaim liability for indirect, special, or consequential damages.

It is now possible for an applicant (buyer, in the documentary credit transaction) to draft a proposed electronic letter of credit. The electronic proposed credit can then be transmitted to the issuing bank for issuance through the SWIFT system. This procedure is usually used where the applicant seeks multiple credits and there is a master agreement between the issuing bank and the applicant. The issuing bank will first check to see whether the proposed credit is authorized and contains the required security codes. Then, it will determine whether it is within the previously authorized credit limits and is stated in the standardized elements and uniform format for electronic messages. Both SWIFT and UCP requirements must be analyzed, and changes in the proposed message may be necessary. Thus, the procedures are not yet fully automatic.

On the other end of the electronic communications, the beneficiary (the seller, in the documentary sale)—which must be induced

---

[191] UCC § 5–106(a).

to part with value (*i.e.*, ship the goods) on the basis of the bank's promises—wants a "hard copy," a written letter of credit in the traditional form. The receiving bank (such as a confirming bank) will, therefore, convert the SWIFT electronic message into such a written, paper credit. However, the SWIFT message has been designed for bank-to-bank use, and not necessarily for use by beneficiaries, which creates some problems. First, it does not bear a signature in the traditional sense, even though it has been thoroughly authenticated within the computer-based transmission mechanisms. Thus, the beneficiary is entitled to doubt whether the sending bank is bound to the beneficiary to perform by the written credit derived from the SWIFT electronic message.

The issue is usually framed as this: "Is the SWIFT message to be considered to be *the* operative credit instrument as far as the beneficiary is concerned?" The issue is of importance to beneficiaries not only in the original issuance of the credit, but also in the myriad of amendments to the credit that may follow. Under SWIFT rules, SWIFT users treat the electronic message as a binding obligation, and treat the authentication as the functional equivalent of a signature. However, the beneficiary is not a SWIFT user, and banking practice has been that a beneficiary can rely on an electronic message only after it has been issued in a paper-based format, properly signed or otherwise authenticated. The UCC makes clear that a letter of credit "may be issued in any form," including an electronic format;[192] but that provision does not necessarily answer the question as to whether the unsigned, paper-based transcription of a SWIFT message, generated by the recipient of that message, is the operative credit instrument and binds the issuing bank.

Under the UCP, whether an electronic message is the operative credit instrument or not depends upon the terminology in the message itself. UCP Article 11(a) states a basic rule that an authenticated electronic message "will be deemed to be the operative credit," and that "any subsequent mail confirmation shall be disregarded."[193] It also states, however, that if the electronic message states "full details to follow (or words of similar effect)," then the electronic message will not be the operative credit, and the issuing bank "must then issue the operative credit . . . without delay in terms not inconsistent" with the electronic message.[194]

---

192 UCC § 5–104.

193 UCP, art. 11(a).

194 *Id.*.

However, there is some doubt as to whether SWIFT-generated transcriptions are subject to the UCP. SWIFT internal rules provide that credits issued through its system are subject to the UCP, but the transcription into a hard copy may bear no reference to the UCP. UCP Article 1 states that the UCP provisions govern "where the text of the credit expressly indicates that it is subject to these rules."

Chapter 3 discussed the attempts to create an electronic bill of lading.[195] If successful, an electronic bill of lading could help facilitate the electronic letter of credit transaction. However, to date, while an electronic bill of lading can replace a nonnegotiable (or straight) bill of lading, market participants have remained skeptical about its ability to replace a negotiable bill of lading. A number of institutions and business have tried, thus far without great success, to replicate the security of paper-based negotiable bills of lading. But some change may be on the horizon. As described in Chapter 3, the new provisions of UCC Articles 1 and 7 on "electronic documents of title" as well as the new "Rotterdam Rules" of 2009 may provide a stable legal foundation for a broader acceptance of electronic bills of lading in the future.[196] Moreover, in early 2012 the ICC and SWIFT agreed to collaborate toward creation of a new "Bank Payment Obligation (BPO)" system designed to create a stable foundation for electronic letters of credit. This collaboration between the two leading international institutions in the field of letter of credit law is likely to bring about important advancements in electronic letters of credit.

---

195 *See* Chapter 3, § 3.19.

196 *See id.*

Chapter 7

STANDBY LETTERS OF CREDIT

Table of Sections

§ 7.1 Introduction

Just like traditional letters of credit, standby letters of credit are mechanisms for allocating risks among parties in commercial transactions. By arranging for placement in the hands of a neutral third party the responsibility for making a payment, if and when specified conditions are met, one party to a transaction is able to avoid the risk of nonpayment or nonperformance.

Foreign governments, or other developers with sufficient bargaining power, often require a financial assurance (by way of a financial guarantee) by multinational enterprises (MNEs) that they will supply goods, perform services, or construct a project competently and in accordance with the terms of the governing contract. Performance bonds can serve as an adequate assurance, but under prior U.S. federal law, banks were not allowed to issue guarantees, performance bonds, or insurance policies.[1] In response, however, they developed an alternative—*the "standby" letter of credit*. This form of a letter of credit is issued by the seller's (or other perform-

[1] *See* 12 U.S.C. § 24 (Seventh).

er's) bank and runs in favor of the purchaser—truly a backwards arrangement as compared to the commercial letters of credit described in Chapter 6 above.

A standby credit is payable against a writing that certifies that the seller or other performer has not performed its obligations. Such a credit is not for the purpose of ensuring that *the buyer* performs its payment obligation to the seller upon shipment of goods; instead, it is used as a form of guarantee or insurance that *the seller* will perform its obligations to a buyer or developer. Thus, although not allowed to issue guarantees, performance bonds, or insurance policies, banks can achieve essentially the same end through standby letters of credit. The result is the creation of a new commercial device, which is now commercially accepted for its own value and has supplanted the performance bond in many fields of endeavor. The standby letter of credit has become an indispensable tool for financing international commercial transactions.

§ 7.2 The Transaction Pattern of a Standby Letter of Credit

As noted in the Introduction, the financial assurance in a standby letter of credit runs in the opposite direction of a standard commercial letter of credit: Instead of assuring performance by the buyer (*i.e.*, payment), it backstops ("stands by") the performance by the seller. Consult the following diagram as an illustration of the stages of the issuance of and resort to a standby letter of credit:

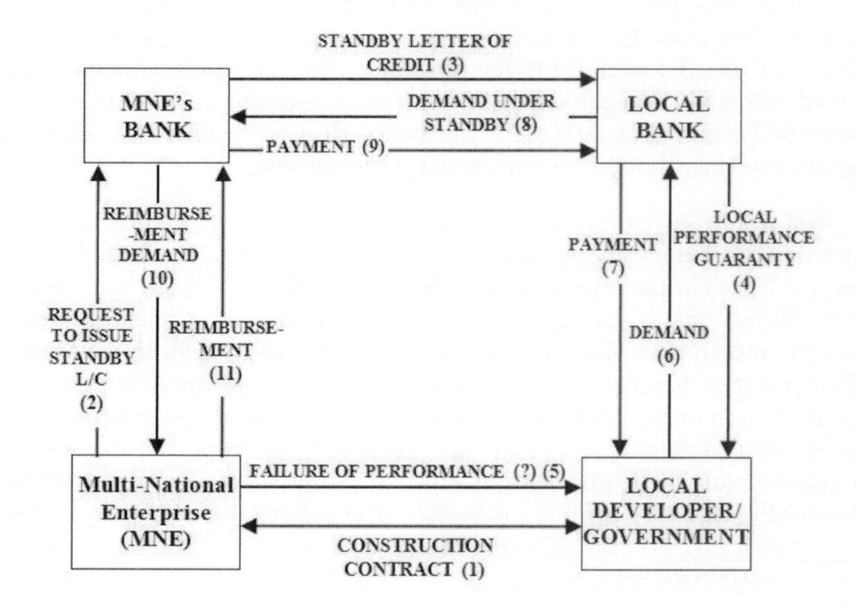

The following is an example of a standby letter of credit issued by a seller's bank in favor of the country of India.

". . . TO: THE PRESIDENT OF INDIA

INDIA

BY ORDER OF: ELECTRONICS SYSTEMS

DIVISION OF DYNAMICS CORPORATION OF AMERICA

For account

of same

GENTLEMEN:

WE HEREBY ESTABLISH OUR IRREVOCABLE CREDIT IN YOUR FAVOR, FOR THE ACCOUNT INDICATED ABOVE, FOR A SUM OR SUMS NOT EXCEEDING IN ALL FOUR HUNDRED TEN THOUSAND FOUR HUNDRED SEVENTY TWO AND 60/100 US DOLLARS (US$410,472.60)—AVAILABLE BY YOUR DRAFT(S) AT sight,

DRAWN ON: us

Which must be accompanied by:

1. Your signed certification as follows: "The President of India being one of the parties to the Agreement dated March 14, 1971 signed and exchanged between the President of India and the Dynamics Corporation of America for the license to manufacture, purchase and supply of radio equipment as per Schedule I thereof for the total contract value of $1,368,242.00, does hereby certify in the exercise of reasonable discretion and in good faith that the Dynamics Corporation of America has failed to carry out certain obligations of theirs under the said Order/Agreement. . . ."[2]

In this credit, the seller (applicant or "account party") has contracted to have the seller's bank (issuing bank) issue an irrevocable letter of credit in favor of the foreign government (beneficiary) that payment will be made upon presentation of a simple documentary

[2] This standby letter of credit is from Dynamics Corp. of America v. Citizens & Southern Nat. Bank, 356 F. Supp. 991 (N.D. Ga. 1973).

statement by the beneficiary. The required statement is merely a unilateral declaration by the beneficiary, "in the exercise of reasonable discretion and in good faith," that the account party has failed to carry out its obligations under a contract. Some standbys require no documentary statement of default, but provide for payment merely upon the beneficiary's demand (a so-called "suicide credit").

This transaction is almost a reverse mirror image of the letter of credit in the documentary sale. In the standby credit, the account party (applicant) is the seller or contractor, the beneficiary is the purchaser (not the seller), and the documents do not control the goods and have no independent value of their own. As noted, often the required documentation is a mere certification by the beneficiary that the contractor has failed to perform under the contract or, perhaps, has failed to return an advance payment.

§ 7.3 Differences with a Commercial Letter of Credit

The function of a standby letter of credit differs substantially from that of the traditional ("commercial") letter of credit, even though the same basic rules of law apply to both. The fundamental difference is that the payment obligation of the issuing bank under a commercial letter of credit arises upon the presentation of documents that show the *beneficiary has performed* (typically, shipped the goods). Thus, the parties expect that the beneficiary will draw on a commercial letter of credit as an essential aspect of deal (*i.e.*, even if everything is fine in the underlying transaction). In contrast, the payment obligation of the issuing bank under a standby letter of credit arises upon the presentation of documents that show the *principal has failed to perform*. Thus, the parties expect that a standby letter of credit will become relevant only if something goes wrong in the underlying transaction.

The standby letter of credit is primarily a risk-shifting device that protects the beneficiary in the event of default by its contractor. It thus provides the beneficiary with swift and easy access to funds upon default, much as if the contractor had left a cash deposit with the beneficiary. The standby letter of credit is often preferable to a cash deposit, however, because it does not require the contractor to part with any funds until after payment is demanded on the credit.

Under the standby letter of credit the beneficiary generally may draw only after the contractor defaults on the underlying contract. A commercial letter of credit usually requires a third party (*e.g.*, a carrier) to generate some of the documents that the beneficiary must present to the issuer (*e.g.*, a bill of lading); under the standby letter of credit, in contrast, the beneficiary itself usually generates all of the necessary documents (often a simple statement that the contractor is in default).

Due to their contingent nature, standby letters of credit are riskier for a bank than ordinary letters of credit. Similar to a commercial letter of credit, the bank does not and cannot "look behind" the documentary claim that its customer (the applicant) has failed to perform, nor may the bank delay payment in order to investigate the validity of the claim. The bank also cannot assert any defenses that the contractor may have against the beneficiary(except fraud or forgery, see below[3]). But with a standby letter of credit, the bank commonly will have only the bare claim of the beneficiary (and few if any other documents) to examine in making its payment decision. Standby letters of credit also typically are unfounded (that is, they are not supported by funds on deposit with the bank), because banks do not anticipate having to pay out on them; the customer simply promises to reimburse the bank if it is forced to pay out on the letter of credit.

Under "suicide" credits, *i.e.*, those payable upon a simple demand by the beneficiary, the exposure of the applicant may be enormous. This is so because the legal protections against arbitrary or unfounded demands are limited to cases of provable and material fraud or forgery.[4] Thus, standby credits tend, by their nature, to rely more heavily on the good faith of the parties than do commercial credit transactions. This necessary reliance on good faith—which carries with it an increased risk of fraud—exists because the payment decision by the issuing bank will be based solely on the unilateral decision of the beneficiary to demand payment. This also is unlike a commercial credit, under which the beneficiary must present documents generally prepared by third parties, such as carriers or inspection firms, to justify the demand for payment.

§ 7.4 The Law Governing Standby Letters of Credit

As with commercial letters of credit, the principal sources of the legal rules applicable to standby letters of credit are Article 5 of the Uniform Commercial Code (UCC) and the Uniform Customs

---

3 *See* §§ 7.11–7.13 *infra*.

4 Again, see §§ 7.11–7.13 *infra*.

and Practices for Documentary Credits (UCP).[5] As the following sections describe, both of these legal instruments make clear that they may apply to standby letters of credit as well.

Both UCC Article 5 and the UCP exist in revised versions. The Uniform Commissioners and the American Law Institute revised Article 5 in 1995, and all fifty-one U.S. jurisdictions have since enacted the revised version into law. The most recent version of the UCP is the 2007 Revision (UCP 600). The rules set forth in the two generally are the same in substance, but some differences exist. The most prominent example of this is that the UCP has no rules that address allegations of fraud or forgery, or the enjoining of payment by a bank in the event of such allegations. As a result, UCC Article 5, and not the UCP, will provide the legal rules to resolve issues related to such allegations in letter of credit transactions, including standby letters of credit.

§ 7.5 ____Uniform Commercial Code Article 5

Article 5 of the UCC has had a considerable influence on the development of the law governing letters of credit. Until the formulation of the United Nations Convention on Independent Guarantees and Standby Letters of Credit in 1995,[6] it was the only comprehensive statutory effort to regulate the subject. Although, like the rest of the UCC, Article 5 is merely an attempt at uniform law on a state level, every U.S. state (and the District of Columbia) adopted the original and has now adopted the revised version. The result is near complete statutory uniformity throughout the United States. Article 5's broad definition of a "letter of credit" also makes clear that it may apply to standby credits.[7]

Article 5 has provided a structure for the development of letter of credit law on an international basis as well. This is particularly true on issues of fraud: While the original version of UCC Article 5, released in 1952, reflected existing general principles of letter of credit law, it captured the fraud exception in a manner that has been highly influential. Reflective of the increasing relationship between state, national, and international law, the 1995 revision of

---

[5] *See* ICC UNIFORM CUSTOMS AND PRACTICE FOR DOCUMENTARY CREDITS—UCP 600(ICC Publ. No. 600, 2007)(hereinafter UCP).

[6] United Nations Convention on Independent Guarantees and Standby Letters of Credit, December 11, 1995, 2169 U.N.T.S. 190, available at http://www.uncitral.org/pdf/english/texts/payments/guarantees/guarantees.pdf. (hereinafter Convention on Standby Credits).

[7] UCC § 5–102(10)(defining a letter of credit as any "definite undertaking . . . by an issuer to a beneficiary at the request or for the account of an applicant . . . to honor a documentary presentation by payment").

Article 5 unfolded along with, and was influenced by, the formulation of the U.N. Convention and the revision of the UCP. The revised Article 5 also embraces new practices in letter of credit law, including by recognizing electronic technology[8] and deferred payment arrangements.[9]

As is true with the rest of the UCC, most of Article 5 is not mandatory law; rather, nearly all of its provisions defer to the agreement of the parties as expressed in the terms of their contract.[10] In specific recognition of this, § 5–116 expressly allows a bank, by unilateral declaration in the letter of credit, to incorporate the rules of the UCP. In such a case, the UCC will defer to the UCP in the event of any conflict between the two,[11] except with respect to the UCC's rare "nonvariable" provisions.[12]

Since 1933, the ICC has published and periodically updated the UCP to provide a uniform set of rules regarding the obligations of banks in letter of credit transactions. The legal status of the UCP is merely as a statement of contract terms and banking trade usage, and not as generally applicable positive law. But as noted, the UCP has broad international influence by virtue of an express incorporation of its terms in most letters of credit, and the express validation of such incorporations by UCC Article 5.

§ 7.6 ___The Uniform Customs and Practices for Documentary Credits (UCP)

A standby letter of credit, like its commercial credit counterpart,[13] may incorporate the UCP. By its terms, the UCP applies to any documentary credit "when the text of the credit expressly indicates that it is subject to these rules."[14] And if a bank includes such an express reference, the UCP rules "are binding on all parties" to the credit except as otherwise expressly modified or excluded.[15] Since 1983, the UCP has also expressly included standby letters of credit within its scope. The present version (UCP 600) thus states that, if (again) a standby includes an express incorporation, the

---

8 UCC §§ 102(a)(14) and 5–104.

9 UCC § 102(a)(8)(iii).

10 *See* UCC § 5–103(c).

11 *See* UCC § 5–116(c).

12 UCC § 5–103(c)(listing the few provisions of Article 5 that the parties may not vary even by express agreement).

13 *See* Chapter 6, § 6.5.

14 UCP, art. 1.

15 *Id.*

UCP rules apply "to the extent to which they may be applicable."[16] Standby letters of credit also may have confirming banks; but it is quite common for a standby to serve instead as support for a local performance guaranty by foreign banks.

Nonetheless, it is clear that the UCP was designed principally to cover the documentary letter of credit transaction and not the standby transaction. It thus includes numerous provisions that have little relevance to standbys, such as references to transportation documents. As a more fundamental matter, the UCP is structured on the basis of extensive documentary presentations. Under a standby credit, the beneficiary is the party entitled to receive performance, not to perform. But the UCP contemplates that the beneficiary will create or procure a variety of documents in the course of its performance. The result is that most of the provisions of the UCP simply are not relevant to standby credits.

§ 7.7 The Fundamental Legal Principles of Standby Letters of Credit

The two fundamental principles of commercial letters of credit also apply to standby credits.[17] The first is that the banks' obligations under the letter of credit are independent of the buyer's and seller's obligations under the sale of goods or other underlying contract—the *independence principle.*[18] Even if the letter of credit refers to the underlying contract, the UCP emphasizes that "[b]anks are in no way concerned with or bound by such contract."[19] The banks' payment obligation thus is not subject to defenses arising out of the underlying transaction, with the result that, with exceptions noted below,[20] the disputes between the buyer and the seller in the underlying contract are irrelevant to the banks' payment decision. Historically, the independence principle arose in order to ensure predictability of payment for sellers that otherwise were often reluctant to send goods abroad without such an assurance.

The second fundamental principle of letter of credit law is that the banks deal only with documents required by and presented under the letter of credit.[21] Because of this limitation, the consensus view is that the UCP requires that the presented documents strictly comply with the requirements of the letter of credit—the *strict com-*

---

16 *Id.*

17 *See* Chapter 6, §§ 6.6–6.8.

18 *See* UCP, art. 4 and Chapter 6, § 6.7.

19 UCP, art. 4(a).

20 *See* §§ 7.11–7.13 *infra* (addressing the subject of fraud and forgery).

21 *See* UCP, art. 5 and Chapter 6, § 6.8.

pliance principle. Thus, if the documents presented conform precisely to the terms of the letter of credit, the issuing bank and confirming bank (if any) are obligated to honor the presentation and either pay the beneficiary immediately or "accept" its "time draft" for later payment.[22] But if the documents do not "strictly comply," the banks may not pay out under the letter of credit.

Some legal commentators question whether these traditional rules covering letters of credit should be applied to standby credits. The reasoning is that standby credits serve a different function: They do not provide a *primary* vehicle to assure payment to a seller/exporter, but rather a *secondary* assurance of performance for a foreign government or developer if a seller/contractor fails to deliver on its contract (to supply goods, services, or raw materials, or to construct a project). However, as noted, the text of both the UCP and UCC Article 5 make it clear that their respective drafters intended to cover standby letters of credit, and to apply the independence and the strict compliance principles to this form of bank credits as well.

§ 7.8 New International Rules for Standby Letters of Credit

Even though both the UCP and UCC Article 5 include standby letters of credit within their coverage, it is clear, as noted above, that they were designed to cover the documentary letter of credit transaction and not the standby transaction. Thus, they impose many unnecessary document-related conditions on the use of standbys. In response to these difficulties, the United Nations Commission on International Trade Law (UNCITRAL) developed the U.N. Convention on Independent Guarantees and Stand-by Letters of Credit (1995).[23]

For the same reason, the ICC has developed a separate set of rules for standby credits, the International Standby Practices (ISP 98), which became effective in 1999.[24] The ISP 98 was designed to replace the UCP and be its equivalent in international practice regarding standby letters of credit. (A further set of ICC rules, The Uniform Rules for Demand Guarantees (URDG 758),[25] addresses

---

[22] Regarding the concept of "acceptance" of a draft, see the text accompanying footnotes 21–25 in Chapter 6.

[23] *See* Convention on Standby Credits, *supra* footnote 6.

[24] INTERNATIONAL STANDBY PRACTICES 1998 (ISP 98) (ICC Publ. No. 590, 1998).

[25] ICC UNIFORM RULES FOR DEMAND GUARANTEES (URDG 758) (ICC Publ. No. 758, 2010).

the subject of demand guarantees, a civil law instrument more commonly used in foreign countries.)

§ 7.9 ___TheUnited Nations Convention on Independent Guaranteesand Stand-by Letters of Credit (1995)

The United Nations Convention on Independent Guarantees and Stand-by Letters of Credit, like the CISG, is a formal international treaty drafted under the auspices of UNCITRAL. The U.N. Convention was adopted and opened for signature by the U.N. General Assembly by resolution 50/48 of December 11, 1995. The Convention entered into force by its own terms on January 1, 2000.[26] As of March, 2013, however, the Convention has only eight Contracting States (Belarus, Ecuador, El Salvador, Gabon, Kuwait, Liberia, Panama and Tunisia), and no state has adopted the Convention in over seven years.

Nonetheless, now that the Convention has entered into force, letters of credit can be issued subject to its provisions. Indeed, even in countries that have not adopted the Convention, standby letters of credit may be issued subject to it if so permitted by the choice of law rules of the issuer's state. Because most such rules emphasize party autonomy, the law of many different countries may permit an issuer to choose the Convention as the law governing a standby letter of credit.

The Convention is designed to facilitate the use of independent guarantees and standby letters of credit. It applies to an "international undertaking,"[27] a term that covers both instruments. Under Article 4, a letter of credit is "international" if the place of business of any two of the following typical actors are in different countries: the issuer, the beneficiary, the applicant, an "instructing party" (an entity that applies for the letter of credit on behalf of the applicant), and a confirmer.[28] The Convention nonetheless gives full freedom to the parties to exclude its application,[29] with the result that otherwise-applicable domestic law will apply. The Convention expressly applies only to independent guarantees and standby letters of credit; but it allows issuers of other forms of international credits—such

---

[26] The status of the Convention is available on UNCITRAL'S website http://www.uncitral.org/uncitral/en/uncitral_texts/payments/1995Convention_guarantees_status.html.

[27] Convention on Standby Credits, art. 1(1).

[28] *Id.*, art. 4(1).

[29] *Id.*

as standard commercial credits—to "opt into" the Convention by express reference.[30]

The Convention provides choice of law rules, and allows the parties to choose the applicable law. If the parties do not agree on a choice of law, the Convention provides a default rule that the law of the issuer's place of business shall govern the transaction.[31] More generally, the Convention's rules are not mandatory, and thus are subject to any contrary agreement of the parties. In this way, it allows the parties to choose rules more closely tailored to their specific transaction, such as the UCP, ISP, or URDG.

The Convention also has express rules on the "independence" of an undertaking.[32] Under the basic rule, an undertaking is independent if the bank's obligation to the beneficiary is not dependent upon "the existence or validity of the underlying transaction, or upon any other undertaking."[33] Likewise, the undertaking must not be "subject to any term or condition not appearing in the undertaking."[34] Finally, the undertaking may not be subject to any "future, uncertain act or event" except for the presentation of documents.[35] In other words, this Convention also adopts a standard that any conditions on payment must have a "documentary" character. The effect of this rule is that an undertaking that is subject to "non-documentary" conditions is outside the scope of the Convention.

Like the CISG, the Convention contains a general rule that interpretation of its provisions must heed its "international character" and the need to promote uniformity in its application.[36] Likewise, interpretation of the Convention must have regard for the observance of good faith in the international practice associated with independent guarantees and standby credits.[37]

The Convention provides general rules on issuance, form, and expiry of undertakings[38] as well as on the amendment, transfer, or assignment of proceeds of undertakings.[39] But the focus of the Convention is on the relationship between the issuer and the benefi-

---

30 *Id.*, art. 1(2).

31 *Id.*, arts. 21, 22.

32 *Id.*, art. 3.

33 *Id.*, art. 3(a).

34 *Id.*, art. 3(b).

35 *Id.*

36 *Id.*, art. 5. Compare CISG, art. 7(1).

37 *Id.*

38 *Id.*, arts. 7, 11, 12.

39 *Id.*, arts. 8–10.

ciary. The relationship between the issuer and the account party largely falls outside its scope. Not surprisingly, the Convention states that the terms and conditions of the undertaking generally define the rights and obligations of the issuer and the beneficiary.[40] Beyond this, Article 14 of the Convention states the basic principle that an issuer must "act in good faith and exercise reasonable care" and must adhere to "generally accepted standards of international practice" for standby letters of credit.

The core provision of the Convention, however, is found in Article 16 on "examination of [the] demand and accompanying documents." Under that provision, the issuer must examine any demand for payment in accordance with the Article 14 standard, and determine "whether documents are in facial conformity with the terms and conditions of the undertaking, and are consistent with one another." The bank also has a "reasonable time, but not more than seven business days" following the demand to examine the documents and, if it decides not to honor, to give the beneficiary notice to that effect.[41] This notice must be by "expeditious means" and must "indicate the reason for the decision not to pay."[42]

The Convention also provides rules for allegations of fraud and the grounds for injunctive relief.[43] Sections 7.11 through 7.13 below will analyze these provisions in more detail.

§ 7.10 The International Standby Practices (ISP 98)

The ICC's International Standby Practices (ISP 98) document defines uniform rules with specific reference to standby letters of credit. Its goal is to create a set of widely accepted norms that will streamline and standardize the customs and practices for standby credits. With this specialized focus, it is able to address, and thus provide greater clarity on, the issues unique to standby credits. Similar to the UCP, the ISP 98 clarifies the terminology and restates basic principles, but with specific reference to standby credits.[44]

Because in many respects standby and commercial credit practices are the same, the ISP has a number of rules that are similar to those in the UCP. Like the UCP, the ISP 98 permits the parties to

---

40 *Id.*, art. 13(1).

41 *Id.*, art. 16(2).

42 *Id.*

43 *Id.*, arts. 19, 20.

44 ISP 98, Rules 1.06, 1.07, 1.10.

incorporate all of its rules by simple reference in the standby credit.[45] The ISP 98 nonetheless differs from the UCP in style and approach. The ISP 98 contains 89 rules, in contrast to the UCP's 39, and covers many issues on which the UCP is silent. The most significant differences between the UCP and the ISP 98 exist in the issuer's and the beneficiary's respective rights and obligations.

ISP 98 applies to any international or (notwithstanding its title) domestic standby credit that expressly indicates that it is subject to the ISP 98 rules.[46] Thus, like the UCP, the ISP 98 will apply to any independent undertaking issued subject to it. The choice of which set of rules to select is, therefore, left to the parties. The ISP 98 is designed to be compatible with the U.N. Convention on Standby Credits and also with local law, whether statutory or judicial.

Neither the UCP nor the ISP 98 contains rules concerning when the issuer may or should refuse a complying presentation on the ground that the beneficiary's draw is (allegedly) fraudulent. The UCP has no reference to the subject at all. For its part, the ISP 98 states expressly that it does not address "defenses to honor based on fraud, abuse or similar matters."[47] For such issues, therefore, the parties must look to otherwise applicable law such as the UCC (or, where applicable, the U.N. Convention on Standby Credits).

The ISP 98 contains an express rule permitting electronic presentation of documents under a standby credit.[48] It thus enables members of the SWIFT banking communication system to make electronic presentation in situations where the only required document is a demand, whether or not the credit expressly permits it.[49] In addition, ISP 98 proposes basic definitions to cover cases in which the standby credit permits or requires presentation of documents by electronic means. While electronic presentation is relatively easy for standbys, it is much more difficult for commercial letters of credit that require presentation of documents of title.

The ISP 98 applies to the obligation of the applicant to reimburse the issuer of a standby letter of credit, and even creates indemnification obligations on the part of the applicant against certain costs of the issuer.[50] It also permits the issuer to waive unilat-

---

45 ISP 98, Rules 1.06, 1.07, 1.10.

46 ISP 98, Rule 1.01(b).

47 ISP 98, Rule 1.01(b).

48 ISP 98, Rule 3.06.

49 For more on the SWIFT system see Chapter 6, § 6.16.

50 ISP 98, Rule 8.03.

erally certain provisions of a standby letter of credit, without affecting the applicant's reimbursement obligations to the issuer.[51] But like the UCC and the UCP, it otherwise contains few provisions concerning the contractual rights as between the issuer and the account party (applicant). These concern the issuer's rights to demand reimbursement for charges and expenses as well as to limit its liability to the applicant for wrongful honor or dishonor.[52]

On the issue of the time frame for the issuer to respond to a demand for payment, the ISP 98 follows the traditional rule of a "reasonable time" not to exceed seven banking days (now limited to five under the UCP[53]).[54] But to balance the uncertainty of the reasonable time standard, the ISP 98 also establishes a three-day safe harbor for examination of documents, within which notice of dishonor is deemed to be timely.[55] The statement of discrepancies in a notice of dishonor need not be detailed.[56]

The ISP also sets out standards for documentary compliance.[57] Rule 4.01 states the general principle that a demand for payment must comply on its face with the terms and conditions of the standby credit. The rest of Rule 4 then contains specific rules for applying this principle.

§ 7.11 The "Fraud Defense"

One important tension that arises from a strict application of the "independence principle" in letter of credit law is the effect of fraud. The independence principle promotes the utility of the letter of credit transactions by offering certainty of payment to the beneficiary if it complies with the credit's requirements. But where a required document is forged or fraudulent, or the beneficiary has engaged in material fraud beyond a "mere" breach of the underlying sales contract, a counter-principle comes into play. As one court long ago observed, "[t]here is as much public interest in discouraging fraud as in encouraging the use of letters of credit."[58] The famous case in this regard is *Sztejn v. J. Henry Schroder Banking*

---

[51] ISP 98, Rule 3.11.

[52] For more on the UCC and UCP approaches to these issues see Chapter 6, §§ 6.13 and 6.14.

[53] *See* Chapter 6, § 6.12.

[54] ISP Rule 5.01.

[55] *Id.*

[56] ISP 98, Rule 5.02 and Official Comments thereto.

[57] ISP 98, Rule 4.09.

[58] Dynamics Corp. of America v. Citizens & Southern Nat. Bank, 356 F. Supp. 991 (N.D. Ga. 1973).

Corp.,[59] in which the court observed that the principle of "the independence of the bank's obligation under the letter of credit" should not be extended to protect an unscrupulous beneficiary where its fraudulent actions become apparent before the bank decides to honor a presentation.

Thus, the law is subject to two competing principles, and the courts have attempted to accommodate both when allegations arise that a payment will facilitate a material fraud or otherwise is tainted by forged or fraudulent documents. Vexing problems arise when an applicant makes a claim of fraud and, more particularly, of a fraud in the underlying transaction—where the conflict with the independence principle is most severe. Nonetheless, the UCC and, in varying degrees, other legal systems recognize the "fraud exception" to the independence principle. The policy underlying this exception is that the courts will not allow their process to be used by a dishonest person to carry out a fraud. However, an enduring debate exists about how broad this "fraud exception" should be.

§ 7.12 ___The Fraud Defense under the UCC

As noted above, neither the UCP nor the ISP 98 has provisions that address the subject of fraud. As a result, otherwise applicable law will step in to "fill the gap." Indeed, the UCC expressly provides that, even where a credit incorporates rules of custom or practice such as the UCP or ISP, the UCC will continue to apply in absence of a conflict.[60] With the UCP and ISP 98 silent, no such conflict exists on the issue of fraud.

The courts generally have been skeptical of fraud claims in documentary letter of credit transactions. Even here, however, some cases exist. An example is *Mid–America Tire, Inc. v. PTZ Trading Ltd.*[61] There, the Supreme Court of Ohio first observed that, given the UCP's silence on the subject, the UCC fraud rules apply even to a documentary credit that incorporates the UCP. Citing UCC § 5–109, the court then held that it had the authority to issue an injunction in the event of fraud in either the letter of credit transaction or the underlying sales transaction. It further held that the relevant standard of "material fraud"[62] requires actions that "vitiate the transaction," and thereby deprive the applicant of the benefits of

---

59 31 N.Y.S.2d 631 (N.Y. Sup. 1941).

60 UCC § 5–116(c). *See also, e.g.*, Northrop Grumman Overseas Serv. Corp. v. Banco Wiese Sudameris, 2004 WL 2199547, at *3 n.6 (S.D.N.Y. 2004); Amwest Sur. Ins. Co. v. Concord Bank, 248 F. Supp. 2d 867, 877 (E.D. Mo. 2003).

61 768 N.E.2d 619 (Ohio 2002).

62 *See* UCC § 5–109(b).

the underlying contract. It also observed that the courts must consider the fraudulent acts of agents of the beneficiary in deciding whether to enjoin payment under a letter of credit.

In another case, a U.S. insurer sought to enjoin a draw by a Bermuda reinsurer on a letter of credit allegedly tainted by fraud.[63] The court granted injunctive relief, holding that the possibility of a later monetary award against a defendant already in receivership would be an inadequate legal remedy, and that a choice of forum clause in the underlying contract did not control the proper forum for actions involving the letter of credit. In a related case, a different court denied injunctive relief. That court held that a choice of forum clause in the underlying contract could affect the rights of parties to the letter of credit, thus turning the independence principle completely on its head.[64]

Such cases involving documentary credits, however, are comparatively rare. In contrast, injunctions against payment due to fraud are not at all uncommon in standby letter of credit transactions. A principal reason for the difference is that some of the limiting concepts for documentary credits, such as the extensive documentary requirements and the "strict compliance" standard, become largely meaningless when the "document" involves a mere allegation by one party that the other party failed to perform properly in the underlying contract. When the limitations that give structure to a transaction become meaningless, the transaction can become a breeding ground for fraud.

UCC § 5–109 imposes, however, a series of important limitations on the availability of the fraud exception.

Protection of Good Faith Intermediary Banks. The first is an absolute requirement that an issuer honor a presentation by certain intermediary banks that have already paid in good faith. Thus, § 5–109(a)(1) provides that "the issuer shall honor" a conforming presentation made by either (i) "a nominated person who has given value in good faith without notice of forgery or material fraud," or (ii) "a confirmer who has honored its confirmation in good faith."[65] Thus, a confirming bank that has paid against conforming docu-

---

[63] Hendricks v. Bank of America, N.A., 408 F.3d 1127 (9th Cir. 2005).

[64] American Patriot Ins. Agency, Inc. v. Mutual Risk Mgmt., Ltd., 364 F.3d 884 (7th Cir. 2004).

[65] This protection also applies to certain other intermediaries in quite rare circumstances. *See* UCC § 5–109(a)(1)(requiring honor for a holder in due course of a draft taken after the issuer or a nominated bank has already accepted it); *id.* (requiring honor for certain good faith assignees of a deferred obligation already assumed by an issuer or nominated bank).

ments in good faith is entitled to reimbursement even if strong evidence of fraud or forgery later surfaces. The same applies for other nominated banks (*i.e.*, those authorized but not obligated to honor a presentation) if they have paid in good faith and without notice. Under the UCC, therefore, if such a good faith intermediary bank has already paid the beneficiary, and the documents appear on their face to comply with the credit, the issuing bank *must* provide reimbursement, even if the documents are forged or fraudulent or the beneficiary has perpetrated a material fraud.

Authorization to Pay Even Over Allegations of Fraud. A second protection for the banks applies to presentations by all other persons (*e.g.*, the beneficiary or any other intermediary bank). In such cases, the issuing bank *may* still pay—even if the applicant has already claimed that the documents are forged or fraudulent, or that there is fraud in the underlying transaction.[66] The only requirement is that the issuer act "in good faith," and Article 5 defines this term with the very limited notion of "honesty in fact."[67] Thus, an issuing bank or confirming bank may honor a presentation even in the face of allegations of fraud as long as it is not itself involved in deceitful activity.

Such a bank may accede to the applicant's desires and refuse to pay, but for a variety of reasons it is not very likely to do so. First, the banks have a limited ability to evaluate the available evidence of fraud, especially on their own, and have little desire to become involved in the buyer-seller dispute in any event. Second, the banks agree to take their small fee (typically, one to two percent of the credit amount) on the premise that they are mere administrative actors in the transaction, not the ultimate judge and jury of all disputes. Third, the banks likely will be reluctant to develop a reputation as an unreliable source of funds in letter of credit transactions. Fourth, a decision to dishonor almost certainly will cause a lawsuit by the beneficiary for wrongful dishonor, with all of the attendant litigation and attorneys' fees for the bank. Finally, if the issuing bank honors a conforming presentation in good faith, even with no investigation whatsoever, Article 5 makes clear that it has an absolute right of reimbursement from the applicant.[68] Thus, all of the incentives point in the direction of the issuer honoring and allowing the applicant and the beneficiary to fight it out among themselves.

---

66 UCC § 5–109(b).

67 UCC § 5–102(a)(7).

68 UCC § 5–108(i).

Direct Resort to Judicial Injunctions. The applicant (the buyer) may, however, seek to block payment on its own by requesting an injunction from a court. The UCC grants an applicant the right to seek such a court order based on fraud or forgery.[69] Indeed, it permits an injunction against payment if *either* (a) the beneficiary itself is involved in a "material fraud" in the underlying transaction, or (b) even without the knowledge or involvement of the beneficiary, a document required by the letter of credit is "forged or materially fraudulent."[70] In either case, if the applicant obtains an injunction from a court having proper jurisdiction, the issuing bank will be compelled to refuse to pay. But UCC Article 5 leaves only a very narrow avenue for this option, and for good reason. To beneficiaries, the possibility of an injunction creates great uncertainty about prompt payment, because they may know nothing about a foreign judicial system and may fear the worst. This undermines the basic utility of letters of credit as secure payment vehicles in international sales transactions.

UCC § 5–109(b) thus limits the right to an injunction based on the fraud exception in several important ways:

First, as indicated above, a court may not issue an injunction against payment to an intermediary bank that has already honored a conforming presentation in good faith.[71]

Second, the fraud must be "material," and this is a severe standard. The meaning of "material" of course will be decided on a case-by-case basis. Nonetheless, courts generally have imposed a very high burden, and have required proof of fraud that has "so vitiated the entire transaction that the legitimate purposes of the independence of the issuer's obligation would no longer be served."[72]

Third, the applicant must present actual and sufficient evidence of fraud or forgery, not merely allegations of it.[73]

Fourth, the applicant must satisfy all of the traditional equitable requirements for injunctive and similar relief. Thus, it must

---

[69] UCC § 5–109(b).

[70] *Id.*

[71] UCC § 5–109(b)(1).

[72] *See, e.g.*, Ground Air Transfer, Inc. v. Westates Airlines, Inc., 899 F.2d 1269 (1st Cir. 1990).*See also*Hook Point, LLC v. Branch Banking and Trust Co., 725 S.E.2d 681, 684 (S.C. 2012); Smart & Associates LLC v. Independent Liquor (NZ) Ltd., 2012 WL 5463028, at *5–6 (W.D. Ky. 2012). *See also* § 5–109, Comment 1 (endorsing this standard).

[73] UCC § 5–109(b)(4)(permitting an injunction "only . . . on the basis of information submitted to the court").

demonstrate that it would suffer irreparable harm without an injunction and that a later money judgment would not be an adequate remedy (that there is "no adequate remedy at law"). In most jurisdictions, the applicant must also show that the balance of harm does not weigh too heavily against the beneficiary and that an injunction would not be contrary to the public interest.[74]

Fifth, a court must require as a condition of an injunction that the beneficiary, the issuer, and any affected confirming or nominated banks are "adequately protected."[75] This typically means that the applicant must post a bond against any losses by affected third parties. The Comments to § 5–109 expand this concept to include even protection against incidental damages, such as legal fees.

Finally, UCC § 5–109(b) adds a significant limitation with regard to fraud in the underlying transaction. A forgery or a fraud in a document required by the letter of credit may permit an injunction if perpetrated by anyone. But as to conduct in the underlying transaction, an injunction is permissible only if payment would facilitate a material fraud "by the beneficiary," and not by some third party, such as a carrier.

The importance of this distinction is illustrated by the approach of other common law courts. English and Canadian courts, for example, also have recognized the "fraud exception" based upon fundamental contract principles and the persuasive precedent of the American cases. These courts require, however, proof that the *beneficiary itself* was involved in the fraudulent activities; a fraud or forgery by any other party, including in the letter of credit transaction, will not suffice. Thus, the House of Lords in the famous case of *The American Accord*, while recognizing the basic fraud exception, refused to extend it to protect the buyer when the fraud was committed by a third party (a loading broker) without the beneficiary's knowledge.[76]

This different approach is illustrated by comparing three different scenarios in which a credit requires an "on board" bill of lading dated May 15: (1) if the applicant can prove that the beneficiary fraudulently delivered worthless trash to the carrier (instead of the required goods) to meet the May 15 deadline, a court may issue an injunction against honor; (2) if the applicant can prove that the beneficiary fraudulently altered a May 16 bill of lading to state May

[74] UCC § 5–019(b)(3).

[75] UCC § 5–109(b)(2).

[76] United City Merchants (Investments) Ltd. v. Royal Bank of Canada (The American Accord), [1983] 1.A.C.168.

15, a court may issue an injunction against honor; but (3) if the carrier or another third party fraudulently puts a May 15 date on a bill of lading actually issued on May 16, a court may *not* issue an injunction against honor. Indeed, the English Court of Appeals has refused to allow any flexibility in the requirement of beneficiary involvement, even if a document presented under the letter of credit is so fraudulent as to be a "nullity."[77] Under § 5–109 of the UCC, in contrast, a court may issue an injunction in all three cases, including if a document required by the letter of credit is forged or materially fraudulent, but the beneficiary is not involved in any way. In such a case, the identity of the perpetrator is irrelevant.

The traditional difference between fraud doctrines and breach of contract concepts was that the former considers the state of mind of a party, while the latter focuses only on whether a particular performance conformed to the contractually agreed standard. Fraud concepts have expanded enormously since the middle of the last century, however, and conduct that would not have been actionable then now may well amount to "fraud." The modern fraud doctrines often do not require any evil intent; rather, the law now requires merely that a party state a fact with indifference about its truthfulness or make an innocent statement of fact under circumstances that leave the impression of complete knowledge, when that is not true. In spite of all of this, in letter of credit law the courts have continued to place a high burden on applicants to demonstrate "material fraud" by the beneficiary.

Because of this, courts commonly decline to enjoin payment because of insufficient evidence of fraud. Applicants thus have sought other means for protection. One option is a "notice injunction." Under this vehicle, an applicant with only limited evidence of fraud may nonetheless be able to convince a court to require that an issuer give notice to the applicant (usually a matter of days) before honoring a presentation by the beneficiary. This would permit the applicant to accelerate its efforts to obtain sufficient evidence to justify a preliminary or permanent injunction against payment by the issuer under the letter of credit.

As suggested above, injunctions against honor are rare in traditional commercial letters of credit, but are more common in standby letters of credit. The principal reason for this is the extremely limited documentary presentations typically required with standbys. Often, the beneficiary need merely make a documentary

---

[77] *See* Montrod Ltd. v. Grundkötter Fleischvertriebs GmbH, [2002] 1 W.L.R. 1975.

demand that states an entitlement to payment, and this may create a special enticement to demand payment as soon as any problems arise. Substantial political and economic upheavals thus often trigger "aggressive" demands under standby letters of credit. One prominent example is the political changes brought about by the revolution in Iran in the 1970s. After an initial period of strict adherence to the independence principle, U.S. courts became increasingly skeptical of demands made by Iranian governmental institutions and began issuing injunctions against honor under standby letters of credit that supported pre-revolution projects.[78] One court found similarly convincing evidence of fraud in the chaos surrounding the recent events in Iraq such as to justify an injunction against honoring a demand under a standby letter of credit.[79]

§ 7.13 ___Claims of Fraud under the U.N. Convention on Independent Guaranteesand Stand-by Letters of Credit

One principal purpose of the U.N. Convention on Independent Guarantees and Stand-by Letters of Credit is to establish greater international uniformity regarding the proper response of issuers and courts to allegations of fraud or abuse under standby letters of credit. The Convention thus includes two important provisions (Articles 19 and 20) that address this subject: Article 19 covers the right of a bank to refuse payment, and Article 20 the authority of a court to grant a "provisional measure" against payment upon the request of an applicant.

Under Article 19, a bank, "acting in good faith," may refuse to pay if it is "manifest and clear" that: (1) a document is not genuine or has been falsified; (2) no payment is due on the basis asserted by the presenter; or (3) "the demand has no conceivable basis."[80] The same Article then describes five expansions on the third option. These include that (a) a covered risk "has undoubtedly not materialized"; (b) a court or arbitral tribunal has already declared the underlying obligation as "invalid"; (c) the underlying obligation "has undoubtedly been fulfilled to the satisfaction of the beneficiary"; (d) fulfillment of that obligation "has clearly been prevented by wilful

---

[78] *See, e.g.*, Harris Corp. v. Nat'l Iranian Radio and Television, 691 F.2d 1344 (2nd Cir. 1982).

[79] *See* Archer Daniels Midland Co. v. JP Morgan Chase Bank, N.A., 2011 WL 855936 (S.D.N.Y. 2011).

[80] Convention on Standby Credits, *supra* note 6, art. 19(1).

misconduct of the beneficiary"; or (e) a confirming or similar bank seeking reimbursement has made payment "in bad faith."[81]

As is apparent from these requirements, the Convention imposes a rigorous standard for dishonor based on allegations of fraud. Nonetheless, it seeks to strike a balance between the different interests and considerations involved in letter of credit transactions. By setting a high standard but granting discretion to the issuer, acting in good faith, the Convention permits dishonor in egregious cases of fraud, but also takes into account the concern of issuers over preserving the commercial reliability of undertakings as promises that are independent from underlying transactions.

At the same time, Article 20 provides that, if the issuer is nonetheless intent on honoring the presentation, the applicant may itself seek provisional court measures to prevent that action.[82] These may include blocking payment or freezing the proceeds of an undertaking.[83] But this right exists *only* for the grounds recognized in Article 19.[84] Moreover, the Convention imposes other important limitations on the right to such "provisional relief" by a court. First, such relief must be based on "immediately available strong evidence."[85] Second, the evidence must show a "high probability" that one of the grounds recognized in Article 19 is present. Third, in deciding whether to block payment of the proceeds, the court must take into account whether failing to do so "likely" will cause the applicant "serious harm."[86] Finally, as a condition to issuing such an order, the court "may require the [applicant] to furnish such form of security as the court deems appropriate."[87] Like the UCC, therefore, the court may require that the applicant post a bond against any losses by affected third parties.

---

[81] *Id.*, art. 19(2).

[82] *Id.*, arts. 19(3), 20.

[83] *Id.*, art. 20(1)(a), (b).

[84] *Id.*, art. 20(3). Provisional court orders blocking payment or freezing proceeds are also authorized in the case of use of an undertaking for a criminal purpose. *Id.*

[85] *Id.*, art. 20(1).

[86] *Id.*, art. 20(1)(b).

[87] *Id.*, art. 20(2).

Chapter 8

INTERNATIONAL ELECTRONIC COMMERCE

Table of Sections

§ 8.1 Introduction

The modern confluence of computerization, the Internet, dedicated intranets, "cloud computing," and a variety of other communications technologies is having a profound effect on established business models and traditional contracting practices. This "E-Commerce" involves transactions in an intangible, digital world, one marked by an immediacy and rapidity of communication quite literally unthinkable only a few decades ago. This affects a whole variety of previously settled assumptions about transactional relationships, as well as the management, communication, and security of information.[1]

[1] The phenomenon, of course, is not new. Concerns about the impact of new technologies is a constant feature of commerce. Consider the following statement from the middle of the 1800s:

> The businessman of the present day must be continually on the jump, the slow express train will not answer his purpose, and the poor merchant has no other way in which to work to secure a living for his family. He *must* use the telegraph."

Initially, the rapid growth of E-Commerce in the modern economy caught the legal regimes of the world unprepared. None was ready for the legal problems caused by the new means for concluding business deals, for effecting payment, and for exchanging communications and information. Although the courts at first did their best to bend or adapt traditional legal rules to accommodate the new transaction patterns, substantial uncertainties remained. Moreover, the rapidity of change has meant that modern communications and business technologies in significant respects represent a "moving target" for lawmakers and the courts. Even as lawmakers began to step in, the statutory rules were limited and uncoordinated. Thus, although some fundamental legal rules are the same across jurisdictions, even today noteworthy inconsistencies exist in the rules applicable to E-Commerce transactions that cross national borders.

A lack of consistency across legal regimes of course is not new; but in one significant respect the problems that arise from such inconsistencies are especially challenging for E-Commerce transactions: Often, the parties often do not know when an E-Commerce transaction involves dealings across national boundaries. A website with a ".com" address may be located anywhere in the world. Thus, the website addresses of the parties, which may be the only information each has about the other, may not reveal the transborder nature of their transaction.

As a more general matter, E-Commerce also raises a number of important challenges for the traditional rules of contract law. These include writing and signature requirements; the authentication of the parties' expressions of contractual assent; the security and integrity of communications; and express and implied terms for both commercial and consumer contracts. E-Commerce also raises jurisdictional issues, which range from choice of law to sufficient contacts for the exercise of personal jurisdiction and to "presence" in a jurisdiction for purposes of regulation by public authorities. Public authorities may see a special need for such regulation in E-Commerce transactions not only to prevent fraud, but also to address privacy concerns, intellectual property rights, and taxation issues, among others. In all of these areas, the traditional legal rules premised on paper transactions—whether statutory or common law—are inadequate to address the multiplicity of challenges that arise from electronic communications and contracting.

Statement in 1868 by W.E. Dodge, *quoted in* Tom Standage, THE VICTORIAN INTERNET 166 (1999)(emphasis in the original).

Thus, there was and is a growing need not only for statutory rules to facilitate E-Commerce, but also for uniform solutions across jurisdictional borders. The most fundamental concern is over whether parties may form a contract by electronic means in the first place. This basic issue has led in recent years to a burst of legislative activity at the state, federal, and international levels:

International Efforts. At the international level, lawmakers could promote the adoption of similar rules across jurisdictions by either an international treaty or proposed model legislation. The initial efforts in this direction came in the latter form. In 1996, UNCITRAL (the organization responsible for the CISG) first proposed a Model Law on Electronic Commerce.[2] This Model Law reflects a minimalist approach to legislation, and merely seeks to facilitate E-Commerce transactions, not regulate them. UNCITRAL followed this effort in 2001 with a Model Law on Electronic Signatures, the goal of which is merely to ensure that legal regimes do not deny legal effect to signatures made in an electronic form.[3] Both model laws are now available to domestic legal systems to provide a foundation for electronic contracting.

More recently, UNCITRAL has proposed a formal treaty, the United Nations Convention on the Use of Electronic Communications in International Contracts (2005).[4] This treaty also is designed to ensure that a communication or contract is not "denied validity or enforceability on the sole ground that it is in the form of an electronic communication."[5] But unlike the Model Law, the goal of this treaty is to function as formal, positive law for ratifying countries.

Sections 8.5 and 8.7 below will examine these international efforts to facilitate electronic contracting in more detail.

Domestic Legislation. In the United States, a federal statute from 2000, the Electronic Signatures in Global and National Commerce Act (E-SIGN),[6] has served as a significant impetus to the legal enforceability of E-Commerce transactions. E-SIGN was not adopted to displace the substantive rules of contract law, but rather

---

2 U.N. Doc. A/RES/51/162, 16 December, 1996, available at http://www.uncitral.org/uncitral/en/uncitral_texts/electronic_commerce/1996Model.html.

3 U.N. Doc. A/CN.9/WG.IV/WP.88, 30 January 2001, available at http://www.uncitral.org/pdf/english/texts/electcom/ml-elecsig-e.pdf.

4 UN Doc. A/60/515, 22 November 2005, available at http://www.uncitral.org/pdf/english/texts/electcom/06-57452_Ebook.pdf

5 *Id.*, art. 8(1).

6 Electronic Signatures in Global and National Commerce Act of 2000, 15 U.S.C. §§ 7000 et seq. (hereinafter E-SIGN).

to facilitate the use of electronic records and signatures in interstate and foreign commerce. At its core is the familiar principle that electronic signatures, records, and contracts may not be denied validity or effect solely because they are in an electronic form. E-SIGN permits the states to adopt their own conforming legislation in its place, but it has achieved its principal purpose because every State has done so.[7]

Indeed, even before E-SIGN, the National Conference of Commissioners on Uniform State Laws (NCCUSL)—one of two institutions responsible for drafting the UCC—prepared two separate uniform acts to facilitate electronic commerce transactions. The first is the Uniform Electronic Transactions Act (UETA),[8] which is similar in scope and substance to the UNCITRAL Model Law. Forty-seven of the fifty states have adopted UETA (and in this way exercised their power to displace E-SIGN). The second legal effort is the Uniform Computer Information Transactions Act (UCITA),[9] which applies specifically to transactions involving the transfer of computer information, such as software licensing transactions over the internet. Unlike UETA, however, UCITA has not been widely accepted, with only two state adoptions (Maryland and Virginia).

Sections 8.8 and 8.9 below will examine in more detail these various domestic legislative efforts to facilitate E-Commerce transactions.

The European Union. The European Union also has been active in addressing electronic legal transactions on a regional level. In specific, it has adopted two "directives" on the subject: The Directive on Electronic Commerce[10] and the Directive on Electronic Signatures.[11] Separately, the European Union has recognized that the increased physical distance and increasingly impersonal interactions between sellers and buyers raise special legal challenges for consumer transactions, including an enhanced risk of deceptive

---

7 *See* §§ 8.8 and 8.9 *infra*.

8 The Uniform Electronic Transactions Act (1999), available at http://www.uniformlaws.org/shared/docs/electronic%20transactions/ueta_final_99.pdf (hereinafter UETA).

9 The Uniform Computer Information Transactions Act (2002), available at http://www.uniformlaws.org/shared/docs/computer_information_transactions/ucita_final_02.pdf. (hereinafter, UCITA)

10 Directive 2000/31/EC of the European Parliament and of the Council of 8 June 2000 on Electronic Commerce, available at http://eur-lex.europa.eu/LexUriServ/LexUriServ.do?uri=CELEX:32000L0031:EN:HTML.

11 Directive 1999/93/EC of the European Parliament and of the Council of 13 December 1999 on a Community Framework for Electronic Signatures, available at http://eur-lex.europa.eu/LexUriServ/LexUriServ.do?uri=CELEX:31999L0093:EN:HTML.

practices and concerns about privacy and data protection. The European Union has adopted a variety of directives on these subjects as well.

Sections 8.10 through 8.13 below will examine these European Union initiatives in more detail.

Before turning to these more formal legal regimes, the next section will briefly address private efforts to take advantage of electronic means of communication and contracting. Against the backdrop of limited world-wide legal uniformity, private parties have attempted to regulate their dealings through traditional contractual arrangements. But as the more modern legislative efforts to facilitate electronic commercial transactions at an international level take hold, the value of these private contractual arrangements will only increase.

§ 8.2 Private Contractual Measures Enabling E-Commerce—Trading Partner Agreements

Trading Partner Agreements were among the first tools private parties developed to address the issues raised by E-Commerce, but they continue to serve a valuable role in a number of different types of business relationships today. These agreements function under a variety of different names and forms (including "EDI" or "electronic data interchange" agreements). They nonetheless share the central idea that a prearranged (or prescribed) contractual agreement regulates the transactions and communications between the parties through some form of electronic platform. The agreement may be between only two parties, such as where a supplier creates a platform for regular orders by a customer on a dedicated website on the supplier's server. But such an agreement also may regulate a whole network of interrelated business transactions, whether under a master contract covering all parties or under a series of standardized individual contracts based on an agreed model.

Modern "cloud" computing, under which electronic communications, documents, and information are saved on a single third-party server, is increasingly making such multi-party arrangements both feasible and practical. Whether provided by a telecommunications company, an internet service provider, or a more specialized business organization, "cloud" computing arrangements permit parties to create a platform for regularized interaction based on a master contract. An example is the effort by the organizers of the "BOLERO" system to create the legal infrastructure for electronic bills of lading.[12] The BOLERO system requires all involved parties—shippers, carriers, banks, and consignees—to consent to a framework set of contractual rules (the "BOLERO Rule Book").[13] The legal interactions between the parties are then conducted on a dedicated and secure "cloud" computing site under the control of the BOLERO system. Such trading partner arrangements function best—or perhaps only—in a "closed system," where every party is a member of the network pursuant to a single framework contractual arrangement.

§ 8.3 Legislative Measures Enabling E-Commerce—in General

Given the speed with which electronic technology is changing business practices, many legislators and commentators believe that a gradual adaptation of existing legal rules through case law is simply inadequate. And as merchants push for more certainty in the legal rules governing transactions in electronic form, legislatures on the national, regional, and international levels want to demonstrate their receptiveness to these new ways of doing business. This has led to a rapid increase in statutes, codes, and model laws on E-Commerce around the world.

The new statutory schemes nonetheless have different purposes. Some are "enabling" measures designed simply to clarify or confirm the ability to form contractual agreements electronically. This is the most basic function for any statutory E-Commerce measure. As legal systems become more comfortable with electronic communication and contracting, more modern statutory measures are turning to the special substantive issues that arise in "cyberspace" transactions.

Thus, for example, some new statutory schemes address the special challenges relating to "standard" contracts in electronic transactions. This is a phenomenon as old as the printing press, but the ease of reproduction of contract terms in electronic form has raised with new urgency the traditional concerns about procedural and substantive fairness: Are the standard electronic terms unconscionable? Are they sufficiently clear and conspicuous so as to bind the user? Do such transactions raise special public policy issues, such as concerning rights to privacy? Do the customary legal remedies work with E-Commerce transactions? And are there particular problems with choice of law and choice of forum in the global mar-

---

12 For more on the BOLERO system see Chapter 3, § 3.19.

13 *See* www.bolero.net.

ketplaces that exist only in cyberspace? These are questions that a variety of affected bodies of law will continue to confront for some years to come.

§ 8.4 The UNCITRAL Model Law on Electronic Commerce

The first significant international effort to address electronic commerce and contracting came in the form of a "model law" proposed by the United Nations Commission on International Trade Law (UNCITRAL), the organization that developed the CISG.[14] A model law is not designed to function as law by itself, but rather to serve as a coherent set of principles for domestic adoption by individual legal systems. In this respect, the Model Law on Electronic Commerce has been quite successful: As of 2013, it has already influenced more than forty national laws,[15] various European Union Directives, and uniform acts in nearly every state and province in the United States and Canada.[16] Further enactments are expected.

The Model Law follows a minimalist approach to legislation, for it seeks to merely validate and facilitate E-Commerce transactions, not to regulate them comprehensively. Its fundamental principle is equality of treatment for paper documents and electronic "data messages."[17] With this foundation, Articles 5 to 10 of the Model Law address the legal recognition of data messages;[18] the admissibility and evidentiary weight of data messages;[19] the concepts of "writing,""signature," and "original document" in electronic commerce;[20] and the retention of data messages.[21] Articles 11 to 15 then furnish a set of rules that address the formation of electronic contracts and the communication of data messages.[22]

---

14 For a detailed examination of the CISG see Chapter 1.

15 Prominent examples of the countries that have adopted legislation based on the UNCITRAL Model Law on Electronic Commerce are Australia, China, Colombia, France, India, Iran, Ireland, Mexico, New Zealand, Pakistan, Panama the Philippines, the Republic of Korea, Singapore, and South Africa. *See* http://www.uncitral.org/uncitral/en/uncitral_texts/electronic_commerce/1996Model_status.html.

16 *See id.*

17 *Id.*, art. 1(a)(defining a "data message" as "information generated, sent, received or stored by electronic, optical or similar means").

18 Model Law on Electronic Commerce , *supra* note 2, art. 5.

19 *Id.*, art. 9.

20 *Id.*, arts 6, 7, 8.

21 *Id.*, art. 10.

22 *Id.*, arts. 11–15.

§ 8.5 ___Equality of Treatment

As noted above, the fundamental goal of the UNCITRAL Model Law on Electronic Commerce is to ensure that electronic messages enjoy the same legal status as paper documents. The Model Law thus provides that a "data message" is not to be denied legal effect, validity, or enforceability solely because it is in electronic form.[23] Similarly, if a rule of law requires that a party present or retain a document in its "original form," an electronic data message will suffice if: (a) "there exists a reliable assurance as to the integrity of the information from the time when it was first generated in its final form;" and (b) any such information "is capable of being displayed to the person to whom it is to be presented."[24] But like paper-based records, information contained in a data message of course is not necessarily valid simply because it is in an electronic form.[25]

The Model Law also addresses the admissibility and evidentiary weight of a data message in legal proceedings. Article 9 provides that information in a data message cannot be denied admissibility as evidence "on the sole ground that it is a data message" or, if the message is the best evidence that a party can obtain, "on the grounds that it is not in its original form."[26] Thus, the fact that evidence exists in electronic form is not a ground to deny the *admissibility* of a data message. But the evidentiary *weight* of the data message will depend on the extent to which it was generated, stored, and communicated in a reliable manner.[27]

Similarly, a data message may satisfy any applicable "writing" or record retention requirement under domestic law. But to achieve a level of formality that parallels paper documents, the Model Law provides that the information in a data message satisfy three requirements: First, it must be "accessible so as to be usable for subsequent reference"; second, it must be "retained in the format in which it was generated, sent or received" or in a format that "can be demonstrated" to be accurate; and finally, it must be retained such that it permits "identification of the origin and destination of a data message and the date and time when it was sent or received."[28] The retention requirement thus implies that the information in an elec-

---

[23] *Id.*, art. 5.

[24] *Id.*, art. 8(1).

[25] *See* UNICTRAL Model Law on Electronic Commerce, Guide to Enactment, ¶ 46.

[26] *Id.*, art. 9(1).

[27] *Id.*, art. 9(2).

[28] *Id.*, art. 10(1).

tronic data message must be accessible, retrievable, identifiable with the original, and accurate.

The legal requirements for a valid electronic "signature" are similar. The Model Law provides that a data message will satisfy the requirements for a signature under domestic law if a method exists that is "reasonable for the circumstances" to identify both the identity of the person sending the message and that person's approval of the message.[29] Thus, three requirements exist for an effective electronic signature: The method by which the electronic signature is made must be (1) reliable under the circumstances, (2) sufficient to identify the person, (3) sufficient to identify the person's approval of the data massage.

Because of the significance of signatures for a variety of legal rules (writing requirements, evidence of assent, etc.), UNCITRAL also has prepared a Model Law on Electronic Signatures (2001) of similar content[30] that legal systems may adopt separately from the Model Law on Electronic Commerce. Intentionally medium-neutral,[31] this Model Law likewise declares that an electronic signature is sufficient with respect to a "date message" if the signature "is as reliable as was appropriate for the purpose for which the data message was generated or communicated, in the light of all the circumstances."[32] As of 2013, over twenty countries have adopted legislation based on the Model Law on Electronic Signatures.[33]

§ 8.6 Contract Formation

The UNCITRAL Model Law on Electronic Commerce also contains targeted provisions on the subjects of contract formation and the communication of data messages. In specific, the Model Law has rules on formation, the attribution of messages, and the acknowledgment and receipt of data messages. The law provides, however, that these more specialized rules may be varied by agreement of the parties.[34]

---

29 *Id.*, art. 7(1)(b).

30 *See* Model Law on Electronic Signatures, *supra* note 3.

31 *Id.*, art. 3.

32 *Id.*, art. 6(1).

33 For a list of the countries that have adopted such domestic legislation see http://www.uncitral.org/uncitral/en/uncitral_texts/electronic_commerce/2001Model_status.html.

34 Model Law on Electronic Commerce , *supra* note 2, art. 11 (providing that the parties also may agree that they will be bound only by paper-based communications, such as a formally-signed written document).

The Model Law addresses the recognition of a contract formed through an exchange of data messages in its Article 11. Like the Model Law's general principle on data messages, that provision declares that a contract may not be "denied validity or enforceability on the sole ground" that it was formed by exchange of data messages.[35] This rule extends to cases in which both the offer and the acceptance are communicated by electronic means as well as those in which only the offer or only the acceptance is communicated electronically.[36]

The Model Law also contains a set of rules on the "attribution" of data messages.[37] These rules address both sides of two-way electronic communications, that is, under what circumstances a data message is binding as a message of the originator, and under what circumstances the originator is bound by the addressee's response or action. First, a party is bound as an originator of a data message if it actually sent that message.[38] Second, a party is bound by a data message if the sender had the authority to act on the party's behalf in respect of that data message.[39] On similar reasoning, a party is bound as an originator if the data message was sent automatically by an information system programmed by or on behalf of the party.[40] Third, the addressee is "entitled to regard" a data message as being that of the originator if either (a) the addressee properly applied an authentication procedure previously agreed to by the originator for that purpose,[41] or (b) the data message resulted from the action of a person whose relationship with the originator was such that it enabled that person to gain access to the method used by the originator to identify a message as its own.[42]

If a data message is deemed that of the originator or the addressee is otherwise is entitled to rely it, then the addressee also is "entitled to act on th[e] assumption" that the data message was authorized.[43] This is not true, however, if the addressee "knew or ought to have known" that the data message in fact was not from or not authorized by the originator.[44]

---

35 *Id.*, art. 11(1).

36 *Id.*

37 *Id.*, art. 13.

38 *Id.*, art. 13(1).

39 *Id.*, art. 13(2)(a).

40 *Id.*, art. 13(2)(b).

41 *Id.*, art. 13(3)(a).

42 *Id.*, art. 13(3)(b).

43 *Id.*, art. 13(5).

44 *Id.*, art. 13(5), last sentence.

A major problem with electronic data messages is that they get lost—or are caught in spam or similar computer filters—much more often than messages sent in paper form. Thus, acknowledgment of receipt of electronic messages is much more important to the parties than is acknowledgment of paper-based messages, and they thus often agree that data messages must be acknowledged to be effective. If the parties so agree, the UNCITRAL Model Law provides that the required acknowledgment may be accomplished either by an agreed-upon method or, in absence of such a method, by any sufficiently clear communication or conduct.[45] Even where the parties have not agreed to require acknowledgment, the originator of a data message may unilaterally require it by stating in the body of the message that it is conditional on acknowledgment.[46] In such a case, the data message "is treated as though it has never been sent, until the acknowledgement is received."[47] Receipt of a message generally requires that the message enter an information system outside the control of the originator or its agents.[48] The UNCITRAL Model Law also contains detailed rules that address when a data message is deemed sent and received.[49]

Other provisions in the UNCITRAL Model Law are specific to the contracts for the carriage of goods and to transportation documents.[50] These provisions generally permit electronic data messages to replace bills of lading and waybills, even where local statutes require a paper document.[51] They also provide that legal requirements for the use of paper documents in carriage contracts are satisfied by such data messages.[52]

§ 8.7 The UNCITRAL Convention on the Use of Electronic Communications in International Contracts

UNCITRAL also has prepared a formal treaty on the subject of electronic communications and contracting, the United Nations Convention on the Use of Electronic Communications in International Contracts (2005).[53] Like the Model Law on Electronic Commerce, the fundamental purpose of this treaty is to validate com-

45 *Id.*, art. 14(2).

46 *Id.*, art. 14(3).

47 *Id.*

48 *Id.*, art. 15(1).

49 *Id.*, art. 15(2), (4).

50 *Id.*, arts. 16–17.

51 *Id.*, art. 16(1)-(5).

52 *Id.*, art. 16(6).

53 *See* Convention on Electronic Communications, *supra* note 4.

munications or contracts in electronic form. But unlike the Model Law, UNICTRAL has proposed this legal product as a treaty, which, like the CISG, would take effect as formal, positive law in the ratifying countries.

By its terms, the Convention applies to electronic communications between parties whose "places of business" are in different states, provided at least one party has its place of business in a Contracting State.[54] The parties may "opt into" the Convention, but may also "opt out" or otherwise vary the effect of the Convention.[55] The Convention does not apply, however, to communications concerning transactions with consumers nor those involving negotiable instruments, documents of title, wills or trusts, or certain types of financial matters.[56]

The core principles of the Convention parallel those of the Model Law on Electronic Commerce. First, the Convention declares that a communication or a contract may not be "denied validity or enforceability on the sole ground that it is in the form of an electronic communication."[57] Second, it emphasizes that nothing in its rules "requires that a communication or a contract be made or evidenced in any particular form."[58] Third, it expressly validates contracts concluded on an entirely automated basis,[59] but defines specific remedies for input errors by natural persons relating to automated message systems.[60] Finally, to further its general goal of ensuring functional equivalence between paper documents and electronic communications and contracts, it states that the electronic forms must be "accessible so as to be usable for subsequent reference"[61] and that electronic signatures must identify the person and indicate assent by sufficiently reliable methods.[62]

Although this Convention formally entered into force on March 1, 2013, thus far only three countries have ratified it.[63] As a result, the extent of its future influence remains quite unclear. A principal

---

54 *Id.*, art. 1(1).

55 *Id.*, art. 3.

56 *Id.*, art. 2(1), (2).

57 *Id.*, art. 8(1).

58 *Id.*, art. 9(1).

59 *Id.*, art. 12.

60 *Id.*, art. 14.

61 *Id.*, art. 9(2).

62 *Id.*, art. 9(3).

63 The three countries are the Dominican Republic, Honduras and Singapore. *See* http://www.uncitral.org/uncitral/en/uncitral_texts/electronic_commerce/2005Convention_status.html.

reason for this is that many advanced countries, including the United States and the member states of the European Union, already have in place comprehensive legislative schemes that regulate the same subject as UNCITRAL's proposed treaty. The following sections will examine those domestic legislative schemes in more detail.

§ 8.8 The United States—The Federal E-SIGN Act

As noted in the Introduction to this Chapter, the principal impetus for the recognition and validation of electronic commerce in the United States was the federal Electronic Signatures in Global and National Commerce Act (E-SIGN).[64] The provisions of E-SIGN broadly cover electronic signatures, electronic contracts, and electronic records, and apply to "any transaction in or affecting interstate or foreign commerce."[65] A "transaction" is similarly broadly defined in the Act as any "action or set of actions relating to the conduct of business, consumer, or commercial affairs between two or more persons."[66]

E-SIGN declares two fundamental principles, "notwithstanding any statute, regulation, or other rule of law": (1) "a signature, contract, or other record . . . may not be denied legal effect, validity, or enforceability solely because it is in electronic form"; and (2) "a contract . . . may not be denied legal effect, validity, or enforceability solely because an electronic signature or electronic record was used in its formation."[67] The Act also has more specific rules relating to the accuracy and ability to retain contracts and other records,[68] notarization of documents,[69] and electronic agents.[70]

E-SIGN has special provisions for consumer contracts. It assumes that many consumers will want a paper (hardcopy) record of the transaction, while others prefer not to be bothered with paper. The Act thus provides that if a law requires that information be provided to a consumer in writing, the use of an electronic record satisfies the requirement if: (1) "the consumer has affirmatively

---

[64] *See* E-SIGN, *supra* note 6. For a case questioning, but not deciding, the constitutionality of E-SIGN, see People v. McFarlan, 744 N.Y.S. 2d 287, 293 (Sup. Ct. 2002).

[65] 15 U.S.C. § 7001(a).

[66] *Id.*, § 7006(13).

[67] *Id.*, § 7001(a)(1), (2).

[68] *Id.*, § 7001(d), (e).

[69] *Id.*, § 7001(g).

[70] *Id.*, § 7001(h).

consented to such use and had not withdrawn such consent," and (2) before such consent, the consumer is provided with a "clear and conspicuous statement" informing him or her of any right or option to have the record made available on paper and of the right to withdraw the consent.[71] The consumer must also have some ability to access the electronic records to which the consent applies.[72] However, this requirement may be met if the consumer confirms electronically that he or she can access the electronic records in the specified formats, or acknowledges or responds affirmatively to an electronic query that asks whether the consumer can access the electronic record. If any changes occur to hardware or software requirements for such access, the consumer must be informed of this and that it may withdraw its consent to the use of electronic records.[73] Any consent by a consumer applies only to the particular transaction that gave rise to the obligation to provide the record.

The most important aspect of E-SIGN for present purposes, however, is the fact that it may be superseded by a state statute. Indeed, the Act explicitly declares that a state may "modify, limit, or supersede" its provisions if the state either (a) enacts the Uniform Electronic Transactions Act (UETA) as adopted by the NCCUSL (see Section 8.9 below), or (b) otherwise specifies rules and procedures that are consistent with E-SIGN.[74] Effectively all States have taken advantage of authorization; indeed as of 2013 forty-seven have enacted UETA.[75] Thus, the most important practical statute for validating and facilitating electronic communications and contracting is UETA.[76]

Moreover, even under E-SIGN, a party may give notice that it will not be bound by electronic messages, and thus negate E-SIGN's rules.[77] In addition, E-SIGN does not apply at all for transactions governed by the UCC (but this exclusion does not extend to UCC

---

71 *Id.*, § 7001(c)(1)(A)-(B).

72 *Id.*, § 7001(c)(1)(C).

73 *Id.*, § 7001(c)(1)(D).

74 *Id.*, § 7002(a).

75 *See* http://uniformlaws.org/Act.aspx?title=Electronic Transactions Act. The three states that have not adopted UETA are New York, Illinois, and Washington. But each has adopted legislation that in nearly all significant respects parallels the rules in UETA.

76 New York has not adopted UETA, and one court has questioned whether the e-commerce statute adopted by New York conforms to E-SIGN in all respects. *See* People v. McFarlan, 744 N.Y.S. 2d 287, 294 (Sup. Ct. 2002). More recent courts have observed, however, that the New York legislation "appear[s] to have chosen to incorporate the substantive terms of E–SIGN into New York state law." Martin v. Portexit Corp. 948 N.Y.S.2d 21 (Ct. App. 2012)(*quoting* Naldi v. Grunberg, 80 A.D.3d 1,12, 908 N.Y.S.2d 639 (2010)).

77 *Id.*, § 7001(b)(2).

Article 2 (on sales of goods) or Article 2A (on leases of goods)).[78] More generally, E-SIGN makes clear that it does not alter the obligations of persons under any requirements imposed by another statute, regulation, or other rule of law except with respect to the validity and enforceability of electronic signatures, contracts or records.[79]

§ 8.9 ___State Laws, Especially UETA

UETA. As described in the preceding Section, the most important source for legal validation of electronic communications and contracts in the United States is uniform law adopted at the state level. In specific, NCCUSL (also now known as the Uniform Law Commission) has produced two different uniform acts to facilitate electronic commerce. By far the most significant of the two is the Uniform Electronic Transactions Act (UETA).[80] As noted above, forty-seven states have enacted UETA into their domestic law to displace E-SIGN based on the express authorization in E-SIGN itself.[81]

Nonetheless, like E-SIGN, UETA is designed to validate and facilitate the use of electronic records at a very basic level. UETA also is similar in scope and substance to E-SIGN[82] as well as to the UNCITRAL Model Law on Electronic Commerce.[83] In fact, in nearly all significant respects, each of the principles discussed below regarding UETA conforms to the provisions in E-SIGN.

UETA applies to all types of electronic messages and contracts. It thus broadly defines its scope to cover any "action or set of actions occurring between two or more persons relating to the conduct of business, commercial, or governmental affairs."[84] Like E-SIGN, UETA does not apply to wills or to transactions governed by the UCC, with the exception of Articles 2 and Article 2A (to which UETA does apply).[85]

The core principles of UETA are found in Section 7. At its most basic, that section mandates equal recognition of electronic con-

---

78 *Id.*, § 7003.

79 *Id.*, § 7001(b)(1).

80 *See* UETA, *supra* note 8.

81 *See supra* note 75.

82 *See* § 8.8 *supra*.

83 *See* § 8.4 *supra*.

84 UETA, *supra* note 80, §§ 2(16)(so defining the term "transaction"), and 3(a) (stating that the Act applies to electronic records and signatures "relating to a transaction").

85 *Id.*, § 3(b)(1), (2).

tracts and communications with paper documents. In specific, it declares in four subparagraphs that:

(a) a record or signature "may not be denied legal effect or enforceability solely because it is in electronic form";

(b) a contract "may not be denied legal effect or enforceability solely because it is in electronic form";

(c) if a law requires a record to be in writing, "an electronic record satisfies the law"; and

(d) if a law requires a signature, "an electronic signature satisfies the law."[86]

Central to an understanding of these basic principles of UETA is its definition of "electronic records" and "electronic signatures." In both respects, UETA is technology-neutral, for it does not require that businesses and consumers use or accept any specific type or method of electronic interaction in order to conduct a transaction. The Act thus defines an "electronic record" very broadly as any record "created, generated, sent, communicated, received or stored by electronic means."[87]

The definition of an "electronic signature" is similarly capacious. It includes any "electronic sound, symbol or process attached to or logically associated with a contract or other record and executed or adopted by a person with the intent to sign the record."[88] This definition is broad enough to include telephone keypad agreements (*e.g.*, "press 9 to agree") and internet "click wrap" agreements (*e.g.*, "click here if you agree"). The last phrase of the definition of an electronic signature is significant, however. Although under UETA a recording may satisfy any writing requirement, a surreptitious recording cannot satisfy the signature requirement because the speaker did not intend the recording to be a signature.[89] Thus, the person or entity accepting an electronic "sound, symbol or process" as a signature must exercise care to ensure that the person supposedly bound in fact intended to connect itself with the electronic contract or record.

---

86 UETA, *supra* note 80, § 7(a)-(d).

87 *Id.*, § 2(7). UETA also has detailed rules on when and where electronic records are deemed sent and received. *See id.*, § 15.

88 *Id.*, § 2(8).

89 *See* Sawyer v. Mills, 295 S.W.3d 79 (Ky. 2009).

UETA (like E-SIGN) does not alter the existing contract law as to the validity and enforceability of contracts. Rather, it provides substitute methods to satisfy certain basic formalities of contract law. Thus, where a "Statute of Frauds" provision requires a contract to be in writing, UETA states that an electronic record will suffice. But to ensure a level of reliability comparable to paper documents, UETA requires that an electronic record be in a form that "accurately reflects the information" in the record and "remains accessible for later reference."[90]

UETA generally follows an "opt-in" approach; that is, it only applies to transactions "between parties each of which has agreed to conduct transactions by electronic means."[91] Nonetheless, such an agreement may be explicit or implicit and thus may arise even from the parties' conduct.[92] On the other hand, the Act makes clear that all of its provisions "may be varied by agreement."[93]

UETA also has detailed "attribution" rules. Section 9 of the Act provides that an electronic signature or record is attributable to a person only if it is in fact produced by an act of that person.[94] This may poses challenges in some cases, but UETA is quite flexible on the point. The same provision also states the act of a person "may be shown in any manner," including by security procedures designed to identify a person.[95]

Finally, UETA expressly contemplates, and validates, transactions concluded on an entirely automated basis (*i.e.*, by "electronic agents").[96] The Act likewise provides that a contract may be formed "by the interaction of an electronic agent and an individual."[97] Conceptually, this is essentially the extension of basic agency principles to the computer, with the computer acting on the instructions programmed by its "principal."

UCITA. The second uniform law produced by the Uniform Law Commission to address electronic commerce is the Uniform Computer Information Transactions Act (UCITA).[98] Unlike UETA, UCITA applies with specific reference to one category of transac-

---

90 *Id.*, § 12.

91 *Id.*, § 5(b).

92 *Id.*

93 *Id.*, § 5(d).

94 *Id.*, § 9(a).

95 *Id.*

96 *Id.*, § 14(1).

97 *Id.*, § 14(2).

98 *See* UCITA, *supra* note 9.

tions, *i.e.*, to those involving the sale or other distribution of, or access to, "computer information."[99] The term "computer information" is broadly defined as "information in electronic form which is obtained from or through the use of a computer."[100] Distilled to their essence, these rules mean that UCITA principally applies to software licensing transactions concluded or conducted via computer, and thus especially to transactions over the internet. UCITA then sets forth detailed provisions specifically tailored to such transactions. Thus, for example, UCITA has provisions on express and implied warranties that are customized for software transactions.[101]

The format of UCITA is similar to UCC Article 2 on sales of goods. Indeed, at an early stage in the process the drafters intended it to become UCC Article 2B; but this effort was rejected by the American Law Institute—NCCUSL's partner in UCC projects—as not sufficiently balanced. NCCUSL then took over the project on its own, and UCITA was the result. As of 2013, however, only two states have adopted UCITA (Maryland and Virginia).[102] Moreover, at least four states have enacted "bomb shelter" statutes to ensure that UCITA is not applied against their residents.[103] And in 2003, NCCUSL stated that it would not push for further enactments of UCITA, although it did not withdraw its original endorsement.

UCITA generally has provisions that parallel E-SIGN and UETA with regard to the validation of electronic records, contracts, and signatures.[104] But its rules on electronic signatures (which it refers to as "authentications"[105]) are even broader. Beyond executing or adopting "an electronic symbol, sound, message, or process," a party may be deemed to have authenticated (signed) a record under UCITA if it merely "made use of" or had "access" to computer information.[106] UCITA also has detailed substantive rules regarding offers and acceptances for electronic contracts,[107] including by "electronic agents."[108]

---

99 UCITA, *supra* note 98, § 103.

100 *Id.*, § 102(10).

101 *Id.*, §§ 401–410. *See also* Baney Corp. v. Agilysis NV, L.L.C, 773 F. Supp. 2d 593 (D. Md. 2011)(holding a supplier liable for a breach of warranty under UCITA § 402(a) with regard to defects in a software program).

102 *See* http://uniformlaws.org/Act.aspx?title=Computer Information Transactions Act.

103 The four states are Iowa, North Carolina, Vermont and West Virginia.

104 UCITA, *supra* note 98, § 107.

105 *Id.*, § 102(6).

106 *Id.*, § 108.

107 *Id.*, §§ 201–207.

108 *Id.*, § 206.

The other controversial provisions of UCITA relate, first, to choice of law and choice of jurisdiction clauses. As to the former, it broadly validates choice of law clauses (including, of course, a choice of UCITA), and then states that in absence of such a choice the licensor's home jurisdiction applies, "in all respects for purposes of contract law."[109] If a licensor has its place of business in a UCITA state (Maryland or Virginia), therefore, UCITA applies by default.[110]

As to choice of jurisdiction clauses, UCITA permits the parties to choose an exclusive forum for dispute resolution, unless the choice is "unreasonable and unjust."[111] Together with the broad rules choosing the governing law (and for proving "assent," see immediately below), the validation of choice of jurisdiction clauses gives substantial power to licensors (at least those in Maryland or Virginia) to ensure that UCITA governs their transactions.

Perhaps the most controversial aspects of UCITA relate to manifestations of assent. On this, UCITA first states the basic principle that both parties must indicate their assent to an electronic record (such as contractual terms prepared by a licensor) and that both must have had an opportunity to review the record or terms before manifesting assent.[112] The controversy comes with a rule that a person assents to contractual terms if, after an "opportunity to review,"[113] it engages in any conduct or makes any statement "with reason to know that the other party or its electronic agent may infer" such assent.[114] Moreover, under UCITA a licensor has the practical power to change a contract's terms unilaterally. This is so because it can demonstrate that a licensee has assented to a change merely by subsequently "obtain[ing] or us[ing]" the licensed product.[115] Thus, a licensee could become bound to contract modifications merely by using the product it has already purchased.[116]

---

109 *Id.*, § 109(a), (b). A choice of law clause will not, however, displace mandatory consumer protection laws. *Id.*, § 109(a).

110 *Id.*, § 109(d).

111 *Id.*, § 110.

112 *Id.*, § 112(a).

113 A person has such an "opportunity to review" a record if, *inter alia*, "it is made available in a manner that ought to call it to the attention of a reasonable person and permit review." *Id.*, § 112(e)(1). For a case holding that a person did not have such an opportunity to review with respect to terms not prominently displayed on an internet website see Cvent, Inc. v. Eventbrite, Inc., 739 F. Supp. 2d 927, 937 (E.D. Va. 2010).

114 *Id.*, § 112(a)(2).

115 *Id.*, § 112(d).

116 Such a licensee may then have a "right to return" the related software, but that right is limited in noteworthy respects. *See id.*, § 112(e)(3).

§ 8.10 The European Union—Background to the eEurope Initiative

Like the United States, the European Union has made substantial efforts to develop regulatory solutions to the issues raised by electronic commerce. Beginning with an "eEurope Initiative" in the late 1990s,[117] as supplemented by "action plans" (eEurope 2002 and eEurope 2005[118]), these efforts were an attempt to address in a comprehensive way the impact of technology on European society.

From a legal perspective, the eEurope Initiative resulted in legislative products that in some ways are quite similar to the federal and state statutes in the United States noted above, but in other ways are quite different (especially regarding consumer protection). The principal measures designed as "enabling legislation" for E-Commerce are the 1999 Electronic Signatures Directive,[119] and the 2000 Electronic Commerce Directive.[120] Section 8.11 below will briefly review these Directives.

Separately, the European Union has adopted legislation designed to protect the legal and economic interests of consumers in the impersonal and distant transactions that electronic communications and commerce make possible. Section 8.12 will review these Directives in more detail.

Finally, the European Union's distinctive approach to data privacy is worthy of brief review. In 1995, the European Union adopted the Data Protection Directive[121] which required the member states limit in substantial respects the collection and sharing of information relating to natural persons. This of course is an issue of ever increasing significance as, for example, Facebook and similar social media sites collect ever more detailed information on the lives of their users. Although beyond the scope of "enabling legislation" as such, the significance of this issue justifies a review of the Data Protection Directive (see Section 8.13 below).

---

117 *See eEurope—An Information Society for All*, COM(99) 687 final, 8 December 1999, available at http://aei.pitt.edu/3532/.

118 *See eEurope 2005 Action Plan: An Information Society for Everyone*, http://europa.eu/legislation_summaries/information_society/strategies/l24226_en.htm

119 *See* Electronic Signatures Directive, *supra* note 11.

120 *See* Electronic Commerce Directive, *supra* note 10.

121 Directive 95/46/EC of 24 October 1995 on the Protection of Individuals with Regard to the Processing of Personal Data and on the Free Movement of Such Data, http://eur-lex.europa.eu/LexUriServ/LexUriServ.do?uri=CELEX:31995L0046:EN:HTML.

§ 8.11 E.U. Directives Enabling E-Commerce

The European Union's two principal legislative vehicles that recognize and facilitate electronic commerce are the Electronic Signatures Directive and the Electronic Commerce Directive[122] Under the European Union's legal infrastructure, a "Directive" does not function as directly applicable law on its own, but rather requires that the twenty-seven member states adopt or adapt their own domestic legislation to conform to principles described therein.

Electronic Signatures Directive. The Electronic Signatures Directive, as the name implies, establishes the basic principle that the European Union member states must "ensure that an electronic signature is not denied legal effectiveness and admissibility solely on the grounds" that it is in electronic form.[123] More generally, the Directive requires that the member states ensure that electronic signatures are permitted "to circulate freely" within the European Union.[124] The definition of "electronic signature" is intentionally flexible and means merely "data in electronic form which are attached to or logically associated with other electronic data and which serve as a method of authentication."[125] In this respect, the Electronic Signatures Directive is technology-neutral, in that it seeks merely to associate an electronic record with a particular party. The Directive also contemplates a more secure, high-tech system in the form of "advanced electronic signatures." The idea here was that third party "Certification Services Providers" (CSPs) would issue unique and highly secure "qualified certificates" for specific transactions.[126] However, subsequent technological advances—as well as risks of liability for CSPs in the event of errors[127]—have meant that this option has almost entirely disappeared in favor of the more flexible general electronic signature.

Electronic Commerce Directive. The second major piece of European Union legislation designed to facilitate electronic commerce

---

[122] *See* Electronic Signatures Directive, *supra* note 11 and Electronic Commerce Directive, *supra* note 10.

[123] Electronic Signatures Directive, *supra* note 11, art. 5(2).

[124] *Id.*, art. 4(2).

[125] *Id.*, art. 2(1).

[126] *See id.*, arts. 2(2)(defining an "advanced electronic signature"); 2(9) (defining a "certificate" to mean "an electronic attestation which links signature verification data to a person and confirms the identity of that person"); and 2(10)(defining a "certification service provider" as an entity that, inter alia, "issues certificates"). *See also id.*, art. 5(1)(conferring special legal significance on "advanced electronic signatures" subject to certain other requirements).

[127] *Id.*, art. 6.

is, appropriately, the Electronic Commerce Directive.[128] Issued in 2000, the broad goal of this Directive is to facilitate the provision of "information society services," including, among other things, the establishment of service providers and the use of electronic communications and contracts.[129] On the first point, the Directive thus precludes member states from requiring prior approval for online providers of commercial services ("information society service providers—ISSPs") or from imposing "any other requirement having equivalent effect."[130]

But a more specific goal of the Directive is a familiar one: to remove the legal obstacles to the enforceability of electronic contracts. Article 9 of the Directive thus states that European Union member states "shall ensure that their legal system allows contracts to be concluded by electronic means."[131] The same provision also obligates member states to ensure that the legal requirements for contract formation "neither create obstacles for the use of electronic contracts nor result in such contracts being deprived of legal effectiveness and validity on account of their having been made by electronic means."[132]

The Directive provides, however, that any contract terms and general conditions for the transaction "must be made available in a way that allows [the recipient] to store and reproduce them."[133] It also requires that electronic communications from ISSPs "clearly identify" the sender as well as their specific nature. Thus, "commercial communications," "promotional offers," and "promotional competitions or games," respectively, must be "clearly identifiable as such."[134]

The Directive establishes greater disclosure requirements for ISSPs in transactions with consumers. In specific, in such transactions ISSPs must provide the following information "clearly, comprehensibly and unambiguously and prior to the order being placed by the recipient of the service": (a) the required technical actions to conclude the contract; (b) whether the contract will be filed and be accessible; (c) the technical means to correct "input errors" by the consumer prior to concluding the contract; and (d) the language(s)

---

[128] Electronic Commerce Directive, *supra* note 10.

[129] *Id.*, Preamble, ¶¶ 1, 2.

[130] *Id.*, art. 4(1). The Directive also has specific rules on required disclosures by ISSPs, see *id.*, art. 5, and well as on their liability. *See id.*, arts. 12–15.

[131] *Id.*, art. 9(1).

[132] *Id.*

[133] *Id.*, art. 10(3).

[134] *Id.*, art. 6(a)-(d).

offered for contracting. Where a consumer places an order by electronic means, ISSPs must also acknowledge receipt "without undue delay and by electronic means."[135]

§ 8.12 ___TheDistance Selling Directive and Other E.U. Consumer Protection Directives

For transactions with consumers, the European Union generally follows a much more protective policy than does the United States. The significance of this issue has only increased as electronic commerce has enabled transactions at much greater distances and on a much more impersonal basis. This has prompted the European Union to adopted a variety of directives aimed at protecting consumers from unfair and deceptive practices.

The most significant of these in practical terms is the 1997 Directive on the Protection of Consumers in respect of Distance Contracts (the Distance Selling Directive).[136] The Distance Selling Directive is intended to promote European consumer confidence in E-Commerce by guaranteeing that local consumer protection laws—including those laid down in the Directive itself—apply to contracts concluded at a distance and may not be circumvented by choice of law clauses.[137] To advance this goal, the Directive imposes disclosure requirements on suppliers and grants a general right of withdrawal to consumers. In this way, it seeks to limit the effect of the aggressive marketing techniques and deceptive practices that may be particularly prevalent in online transactions.

The Directive nonetheless applies to contracts concluded by any means where the supplier is not in the physical presence of the consumer. Thus, it applies to contracts created by mail, telephone, videophone, fax, and email, for example, as well as those concluded online.[138] In order to achieve its goal of an "approximate" level of consumer protection in such distance selling transactions throughout the European Union, the Directive required each member state to implement its provisions in their national law by the end of 2000.[139]

---

[135] *Id.*, art. 11.

[136] Directive 1997/7/EC of the European Parliament and of the Council of 20 May 1997 on *the* Protection of Consumers in respect of Distance Contracts, http://eur-lex.europa.eu/LexUriServ/LexUriServ.do?uri=CELEX:31997L0007:EN:HTML.

[137] *Id.*, art. 12.

[138] *Id.*, at 2 and Annex 1.

[139] *Id.*, art. 15.

The Directive imposes a number of obligations on suppliers and grants certain important rights to consumers in distance selling contracts. The most important of these is the right of consumers to "withdraw" from the contract. Within seven days from the receipt of the goods or the provision of the services, the consumer has a right to withdraw from the contract "without penalty and without giving any reason."[140] The only cost that may be imposed on the consumer is the cost of returning the goods.[141] Thereafter, the supplier must process the consumer's reimbursement as soon as possible and in any event within thirty days.[142] The supplier must also inform the consumer of this right upon contract formation and again in writing in the course of contract performance,[143] and, if the supplier fails to do so, the time period for the consumer to exercise the right of withdrawal expands to three months.[144]

The Directive requires specific disclosures to consumers, in a "clear and comprehensible form," prior to concluding a distance selling contract. These include information on a variety of basic details about the supplier; the cost, terms, and conditions of the transaction; and, significantly, the consumer's right to withdraw or cancel the transaction.[145] The supplier must also provide a confirmation of most of this information either in writing or in some other "durable" media accessible to the consumer prior to delivery or completion of performance of the contract.[146] Orders placed through distance selling must ordinarily be filled within thirty days.[147] The Distance Selling Directive also completely bans unsolicited marketing by certain types of technologies, including automated calling machines or faxes (and presumably, by extension, email spam), and allows others only if there is no clear objection by the consumer.[148]

The European Union also has adopted consumer protection directives of general application that are relevant to transactions conducted by electronic means. The first is the Directive on Unfair

---

140 *Id.*, art. 6(1).

141 *Id.* For limitations on the right of withdrawal see *id.*, art. 6(3).

142 *Id.*, art. 6(2).

143 *Id.*, arts. 4(1)(f), 5(1).

144 *Id.*, art. 6(1).

145 *Id.*, art. 4.

146 *Id.*, art. 5. This confirmation obligation does not apply to services provided on a one-time basis. *Id.*, art. 5(2).

147 *Id.*, art. 7.

148 *Id.*, art. 10. A more specialized E.U. Directive addresses distance marketing of financial services. *See* Directive 2002/65/EC of the European Parliament and of the Council of 23 September 2002 Concerning the Distance Marketing of Consumer Financial Services, available at http://eur-lex.europa.eu/LexUriServ/LexUriServ.do?uri=CELEX:32002L0065:EN:HTML.

Contract Terms of 1993.[149] This rule-based Directive governs non-negotiated contracts with consumers and reflects a much more paternalistic approach than the general unconscionability doctrine of U.S. law. It contains a list of terms that are never effective in contracts with consumers and subjects all others to a substantive review for fairness.[150]

A second consumer protection directive of note is the Consumer Goods Directive of 1999.[151] This Directive might be seen as a complement to the Directive on Unfair Contract Terms, but with reference to contractual promises made regarding the quality of goods sold to consumers. In general, the seller must ensure that the goods conform to the contract, comply with any description given by the seller, are fit for any specific purpose made known to the seller, and are of a comparable quality to similar goods.[152] If the seller fails to meet these obligations, it is liable to the consumer for any resultant damages.[153]

A final consumer protection directive relevant to electronic commerce is the Unfair Commercial Practices Directive of 2005.[154] This Directive broadly prohibits commercial practices that distort the economic decision-making of consumers. Included among such practices are advertising with misleading information,[155] misleading omissions,[156] and other aggressive commercial tactics.[157]

§ 8.13 ___The E.U. Personal Data Protection Directive

The European Union has adopted a personal data protection directive that applies as well to international electronic commerce.

---

[149] Council Directive 93/13/EEC of 5 April 1993 on Unfair Terms in Consumer Contracts, available at http://eur-lex.europa.eu/LexUriServ/LexUriServ.do?uri=CELEX:31993L0013:EN:HTML.

[150] *Id.*, art. 3 and Annex.

[151] Directive 1999/44/EC of the European Parliament and of the Council of 25 May 1999 on Certain Aspects of the Sale of Consumer Goods and Associated Guarantees, available at http://eur-lex.europa.eu/LexUriServ/LexUriServ.do?uri=CELEX:31999L0044:EN:HTML.

[152] *Id.*, art. 2.

[153] *Id.*, art. 4.

[154] Directive 2005/29/EC of the European Parliament and of the Council of 11 May 2005 Concerning Unfair Business-to-Consumer Commercial Practices, available at http://eur-lex.europa.eu/LexUriServ/LexUriServ.do?uri=CELEX:32005L0029:EN:HTML.

[155] *Id.*, art. 6 (also defining a practice as misleading if it contains false information or otherwise deceives the consumer).

[156] *Id.*, art. 7.

[157] *Id.*, art. 8.

The Data Protection Directive requires each European Union member state to regulate the processing of personal data in accordance with certain described principles.[158]

The purpose of the Data Protection Directive is to protect "the fundamental rights and freedoms of natural persons, and in particular their right to privacy with respect to the processing of personal data."[159] It accomplishes this goal by declaring that the processing of any information relating to natural persons must be fair, current, legitimate, accurate, and proportional to the related purpose. "Personal data" is broadly defined as "any information relating to an identified or identifiable natural person."[160] The Directive then places severe restrictions on the "processing" of such personal data. This term also is exceptionally broad and covers "any operation or set of operations which is performed upon personal data, whether or not by automatic means."[161]

The Data Protection Directive applies to any processing of personal data by entities ("controllers"[162]) that are established in, or use any equipment in, a member state of the European Union.[163] In most cases, it permits the processing of personal data only with the "unambiguous" consent of the individual involved or when the processing is "necessary" for contract performance (*e.g.*, billing), to serve "important public interests," or to protect the individual's "vital interests."[164] The processing of data revealing racial or ethnic origin, political opinions, religious beliefs, philosophical or ethical persuasion, or health or sexual life is rarely permitted without the individual's "explicit" consent.[165]

The Directive also requires that controllers provide information to the affected individuals on a variety of subjects, including the purposes for both the collection and the processing of personal data.[166] Such disclosure obligations apply to virtually all websites that

---

[158] The Data Protection Directive, *supra* note 121. Switzerland also has adopted a "Federal Act on Data Protection" (1992, as amended 2008), available at http://www.admin.ch/ch/e/rs/2/235.1.en.pdf.

[159] *Id.*, art. 1(1).

[160] *Id.*, art. 2(a).

[161] *Id.*, art. 2(b). The term "processing" expressly includes the "collection, recording, organization, storage, adaptation or alteration, retrieval, consultation, use, disclosure by transmission, dissemination or otherwise making available, alignment or combination, blocking, erasure or destruction." *Id.*

[162] *Id.*, art. 2(d).

[163] *Id.*, art. 4.

[164] *Id.*, art. 7.

[165] *Id.*, art. 8.

[166] *Id.*, arts. 10, 11.

invite registration or otherwise collect data on users. Affected individuals have a right to obtain access, "without constraint at reasonable intervals and without excessive delay or expense," to the personal data collected by controllers.[167] The individuals then may object either to any processing of personal data for marketing purposes or, "on compelling legitimate grounds," to processing of any kind.[168] All processing also must also be confidential and secure.[169] The Directive requires that member states provide for private civil liability and public administrative remedies for violations of its requirements.[170]

Data processors are required to make extensive disclosures to governments authorities as well. Each member state is obligated to designate or establish a "supervisory authority" to implement and oversee compliance with the Directive's requirements.[171] Data controllers must then provide extensive disclosures to these supervisory authorities regarding the processing of personal data.[172] The national authorities are empowered where appropriate to access, demand erasure, or block the processing of information held by data processors.[173]

For international commercial transactions, the most important provision in the Data Protection Directive is Article 25. That provision mandates that member states prohibit the transfer of personal data to persons in non-member states (such as the United States) unless those states offer an "adequate level of protection." This prohibition applies unless the Directive otherwise permits the processing of personal data, such as with the "unambiguous" consent of the affected individual or (within the narrow confines noted above) when "necessary" and for a "legitimate purpose."[174]

Practically speaking, the Data Protection Directive governs most global businesses, for the simple reason that is very difficult to segregate European Union data from data collected elsewhere. Both online and offline data processors fall within its scope. The Directive's impact has been felt, for example, in restrictive orders denying U.S. direct mail companies access to European mailing lists.

---

167 *Id.*, art. 12.

168 *Id.*, art. 14.

169 *Id.*, arts. 16, 17.

170 *Id.*, arts. 22–24.

171 *Id.*, art. 28(1).

172 *Id.*, arts. 18, 19.

173 *Id.*, art. 28.

174 *Id.*, art. 7.

The European Commission and the U.S. Department of Commerce have sought to defuse the sensitive issue of the "adequacy" of U.S. law on personal data privacy. Early in 2000, the United States and the European Union reached a "safe harbor" agreement for U.S. firms based on seven privacy principles designed to satisfy the European Union "adequacy" requirement.[175] The twist in this safe harbor arrangement is that compliance takes place in the United States in accordance with U.S. law and is carried out primarily by the private sector. To qualify for the safe harbor, a data processing organization must either (1) join a self-regulatory privacy program that adheres to the safe harbor's requirements, or (2) develop its own privacy policy that conforms to the safe harbor requirements. Such an organization can self-certify annually to the Department of Commerce in writing that it agrees to adhere to the safe harbor's requirements, including those on notice, choice, access, and enforcement. The organization must also state in its published privacy policy that it adheres to the safe harbor. The Department of Commerce maintains a list of all organizations that file self-certification letters and makes both the list and the self-certification letters publicly available.

Such organizations must have in place procedures for verifying compliance with the safe harbor requirements as well as a dispute resolution system that investigates and resolves individual complaints. They then must timely remedy any problems arising out of a failure to comply with the principles. Under the Federal Trade Commission Act, a company's failure to abide by commitments to implement the safe harbor principles might be considered deceptive and actionable by the FTC.

A few hundred (mostly small) U.S. companies have signed up with self-regulatory privacy groups (such as BBBOnline[176]) to obtain shelter from the EU's Data Protection Directive. But many thousands have created their own self-certification programs and have declared their compliance with the Data Protection Directive by registration with the Department of Commerce.[177] Many companies employ online pop-up screens that state the purpose for the collection of data and the intended future uses, and then—on the basis of a "click here if you agree" box—rely upon the customer's click as creating a record of "unambiguous" consent. Many organizations in the European Union have developed an array of similarly directed contract systems. As noted, many U.S. companies assert

175 *See* http://export.gov/safeharbor/eu/eg_main_018475.asp.

176 *See* http://www.auto.bbb.org/BBB-EU-Safe-Harbor-Participants/.

177 *See* https://safeharbor.export.gov/list.aspx.

that they are in compliance with the safe harbor requirements. Others have selectively curtailed their use of "cookies" to track online users. Many, perhaps most, seem blissfully unaware of the scope and intensity of the Data Protection Directive.

In 2012, the European Commission also announced a draft European General Data Protection Regulation to supersede the Data Protection Directive.[178] Unlike a directive, a regulation functions as directly applicable and binding law without implementation by the individual member states. The goal is that work on this project will be completed by 2014 and that the new General Data Protection Regulation will go into effect in 2016.

[178] Draft General Data Protection Regulation, available at http://ec.europa.eu/justice/data-protection/document/review2012/com_2012_11_en.pdf.

Chapter 9

AN INTRODUCTION TO THE WTO, IMF AND U.S. TRADE AUTHORITIES

Table of Sections

The need to balance the protection of local industries from harm by foreign competitors and the encouragement of trade across national borders is a recurrent theme in the law of international business transactions. There has been a shift in recent years toward freer international trade because of diminished restrictions on imported goods. However, trade problems associated with the movement of goods across national borders still arise because of restrictive trade devices which impede or distort trade. Common devices include tariff barriers (e.g., import duties and export duties) as well as certain nontariff trade barriers (NTBs) such as import quotas, import licensing procedures, safety, environmental and other minimum manufacturing standards, import testing requirements, complex customs procedures (including valuation), government procurement policies, and government subsidies or countervailing measures. For example, during a part of 1982, France required that all video recorders entering France had to do so through a small customs post at Poitiers and carry documentation written in French. Product distribution practices have been an effective NTB in Japan. The Japanese have also banned from importation a food preservative which is essential to preserve the edibility of certain agricultural products from abroad.

Efforts by countries to limit disruptive trade practices are commonly found in bilateral treaties of friendship, commerce and navigation (FCN), which open the territory of each signatory nation to imports arriving from the other signatory nation. Such bilateral FCN treaty clauses are usually linked to other preferential trade agreements. In a bilateral arrangement, such linkage will most often be through a reciprocal "most favored nation" (MFN) clause. In a MFN clause, both parties agree not to extend to any other nation trade arrangements which are more favorable than available under the bilateral treaty, unless the more favorable trade arrangements are immediately *also* available to the signatory of the bilateral treaty. In various parts of the world, two or more countries have joined in customs unions or free trade areas in order to facilitate trade between those countries and to acquire increased bargaining power in trade negotiations. The European Union and NAFTA are prime examples.

The General Agreement on Tariffs and Trade (GATT, 1947), now replaced by the World Trade Organization (WTO), was an international arrangement with over one hundred countries as Contracting States which regularly held multilateral trade negotiations (MTN) seeking ways of making international trade more open. These periodic negotiations cumulatively reduced tariff barriers by an average of up to eighty percent below those existing three decades before. After the most recent multilateral negotiations, the Uruguay Round, average tariff rates of developed countries on dutiable manufactured imports were cut from 6.3 percent to 3.9 percent. Tariff reductions are one of the success stories of GATT. But not all nations participated in the GATT or are members of its replacement, the WTO. For example, Iran is still seeking membership in the WTO. China did not join until 2001, Vietnam in 2007, Russia in 2012. Nontariff trade barriers (NTBs) are also addressed in the WTO Covered Agreements, which include agreements designed to lessen or to eliminate NTBs such as complex customs valuation procedures, import licensing systems, product standards, subsidies and countervailing duties, and dumping practices.

U.S. international trade law is primarily found in the frequently amended Tariff Act of 1930 and the Trade Act of 1974. Much of the content of these statutes is derived from World Trade Organization principles. Additional statutes of note include the NAFTA Implementation Act of 1993, the Uruguay Round Agreements Act of 1994, the Export Administration Act of 1979, the Foreign Corrupt Practices Act of 1977, and the Caribbean Basin Economic Recovery Act of 1983.

The international trade of the United States is regulated by a number of different governmental bodies. The International Trade Administration is part of the Commerce Department, which in turn is part of the Executive Branch of the federal government. The Commerce Department also contains the Office of Export Licensing and the Office of Anti-boycott Compliance. The International Trade Commission is an independent federal government agency, and the Court of International Trade is part of the Judicial Branch of the United States government. Lastly, the Office of the United States Trade Representative works directly under the President.

§ 9.1 The General Agreement on Tariffs and Trade (1947)

Participants in the Bretton Woods meetings in 1944 recognized a post–War need to reduce trade obstacles in order to foster freer trade. They envisioned the creation of an International Trade Organization (ITO) to achieve the desired result. Fifty-three countries met in Havana in 1948 to complete drafting the Charter of an ITO that would be the international organizational umbrella underneath which negotiations could occur periodically to deal with tariff reductions. A framework for such negotiations had already been staked out in Geneva in 1947, in a document entitled the General Agreement on Tariffs and Trade (GATT). Twenty-three nations participated in that first GATT session, India, Chile, Cuba and Brazil representing the developing world. China participated; Japan and West Germany did not. Stringent trading rules were adopted only where there were no special interests of major participants to alter them. The developing nations objected to many of the strict rules, arguing for special treatment justified on development needs, but they achieved few successes in drafting GATT.

The ITO Charter was never ratified. The United States Congress in the late 1940s was unwilling to join more new international organizations, thus U.S. ratification of the ITO Charter could not be secured. Nonetheless, and moving by way of the President's power to make executive agreements, the United States did join twenty-one other countries, as Contracting Parties, in signing a Protocol of Provisional Application of the General Agreement on Tariffs and

Trade (61 Stat.Pts. 5, 6) (popularly called the "GATT Agreement"). One notable feature of this protocol was the exemption of existing trade restraints of the Contracting States. The GATT 1947 Agreement evolved from its "provisional" status into the premier international trade body, GATT the organization based in Geneva. It was through this organization that tariffs were steadily reduced over decades by means of increased membership and GATT negotiating Rounds. Today, the GATT 1947 Agreement has been superceded by the substantially similar GATT 1994 Agreement, part of the World Trade Organization "package" of trade agreements that took effect in 1995.

Trade in Goods: Core GATT Principles

One of the central features of GATT 1947 and 1994 is Article I, which makes a general commitment to the long standing practice of "most favored nation treatment" (MFN) by requiring each Contracting Party to accord unconditional MFN status to goods from all other Contracting Parties. Thus, any privilege or tariff granted by a Contracting Party to products imported from any other country (not necessarily a WTO member) must also be "immediately and unconditionally" granted to any "like product" imported from any Contracting Parties. There are two major exceptions to the MFN obligation of Article I: Free trade areas and customs unions (see Chapter 21) and differential and more favorable treatment of goods from developing countries (see Chapter 10).

GATT Article III incorporates the practice of according "national treatment" to imported goods by providing, with enumerated exceptions, that they shall receive the same tax and regulatory treatment as domestic goods. In this context, national treatment requires that the products of the exporting GATT Contracting State be treated no less favorably than domestic products of the importing State under its laws and regulations concerning sale, internal resale, purchase, transportation and use. Two major exceptions apply to Article III: Government procurement policies (see Section 9.10) and some subsidization of domestic industries (see Chapter 13).

In addition to requiring MFN and national treatment, GATT prohibits use of certain kinds of quantitative restrictions. Subject to exceptions such as balance of payment crises, Article XI prohibits "prohibitions or restrictions" on imports and it specifically prohibits the use of "quotas, import or export licenses or other measures" to restrict imports from a Contracting Party. If utilized, Article XIII requires non-discrimination in quantitative trade restrictions, by barring an importing Contracting State from applying any prohibition or restriction to the products of another Contracting State, "unless the importation of the like product of all third countries . . . is similarly prohibited or restricted." (emphasis added).

The WTO has significantly reduced the number of trade quotas. The Agreement on Textiles eliminated quotas long maintained under the Multi–Fibre Arrangement. Voluntary export restraints (quotas) are severely limited by the Safeguards Agreement In addition, the WTO removes trade quotas by advancing "tariffication," replacing quotas with tariffs—sometimes even at extraordinarily high tariff rates. Tariffication is the approach adopted in the WTO Agricultural Agreement. Import licensing schemes are also being phased out under WTO agreements.

There are four important exceptions to all GATT 1994 rules. These concern national security (Article XXI), balance of payments (Articles XII and XVII:B), "safeguards" against import surges (see Chapter 15), and public health, morals or policy (such as product standards or conservation of exhaustible natural resources) (Article XX).

GATT Procedures

While GATT does permit nondiscriminatory "duties, taxes and other charges," the powers of a Contracting Party are limited even as to these devices. First, GATT Article X requires that notice be given of any new or changed national regulations which affect international trade, by requiring the prompt publication of those "laws, regulations, judicial decisions and administrative rulings of general application." Second, the Contracting Parties commit themselves "from time to time" to a continuing series of multilateral tariff negotiations (MTN) to seek further reductions in tariff levels and other barriers to international trade. Such negotiations are to be "on a reciprocal and mutually advantageous basis." GATT negotiated tariff rates (called "concessions" or "bindings"), which are listed in the "tariff Schedules", are deposited with GATT by each participating country. These concessions must be granted to imports from any Contracting Party, both because of the GATT requires MFN treatment, and also because Article II specifically requires use of the negotiated rates.

The 1947 GATT Agreement and its subsequent multinational negotiating rounds were quite successful in reducing tariff duty levels on trade in goods. See Section 9.2 below. This was its original purpose, and the mechanism was well-adapted to accomplishing that purpose. However, its effectiveness was also limited to trade in goods, and primarily to reduction of tariffs in such trade. It was not designed to affect trade in services, trade-related intellectual property rights or trade-related investment measures. As tariff duty rates declined, the trade-distorting effects of these other issues became relatively more important.

Even within "trade in goods," the 1947 GATT had limitations. It included a Protocol of Provisional Application which allowed numerous grandfathered exceptions to Members' obligations under the GATT Agreement. The Protocol exempted from GATT disciplines the national laws of Member States which were already enacted and in force at the time of adoption of the Protocol. Further, the 1947 GATT did not have an institutional charter, and was not intended to become an international organization on trade. It did later develop institutional structures and acquired quasi-organizational status, but there was always a lack of a recognized structure. This lack was most often perceived in the inability of GATT to resolve disputes which were brought to it. Dispute settlement procedures were dependent upon the acquiescence of all Member States, including the losing state, which understandably almost never acquiesced.

Framers of GATT 1947 were well aware that a commitment to freer trade could cause serious, adverse economic consequences from time to time within part or all of a country's domestic economy, particularly its labor sector. The GATT contains at least seven safety valves (in nine clauses of the Agreement) to permit a country, in appropriate circumstances, to respond to domestic pressures while remaining a participant in GATT. Two safety valves deal with antidumping duties and countervailing subsidies. See Chapters 12 and 13. Another concerns "safeguard procedures." See Chapter 15.

§ 9.2 The GATT Multinational Trade Negotiations (Rounds)

Under the auspices of GATT Article XXVIII, the Contracting Parties committed themselves to hold periodic multinational trade negotiations (MTN or "Rounds"). They have completed eight such Rounds to date, and the WTO Doha Round is marginally ongoing.

While the first five Rounds concentrated on item by item tariff reductions, the "Kennedy Round" (1964–1967) was noted for its achievement of across-the-board tariff reductions. In 1961, GATT began to consider how to approach the increasing trade disparity with the developing world. In 1964, GATT adopted Part IV, which introduced a principle of "diminished expectations of reciprocity".

Reciprocity remained a goal, but developed nations would not expect concessions from developing nations which were inconsistent with developmental needs. For the developing nations, nonreciprocity meant freedom to protect domestic markets from import competition. Import substitution was a major focus of developmental theory in the 1960s, and developing nations saw keeping their markets closed as a way to save these domestic industries. Although they also sought preferential treatment of their exports, that was a demand which would remain unsatisfied for another decade and longer.

The "Tokyo Round" (1973–1979) engendered agreements about several areas of nontariff barrier (NTB) trade restraints. Nearly a dozen major agreements on nontariff barrier issues were produced in the Tokyo Round. In the early 1970s, national and regional generalized preference schemes (GSP) developed to favor the exports of developing nations. The foreign debt payment problems of the developing nations suggest that they need to generate revenue to pay these debts, and that developmental theory must shift from import substitution to export promotion.

In 1986, the "Uruguay Round" of multilateral trade negotiations began at a Special Session of the GATT Contracting States. This Uruguay Round included separate negotiations on trade in goods and on trade in services, with separate groups of negotiators dealing with each topic. Subtopics for negotiation by subgroups included nontariff barriers, agriculture, subsidies and countervailing duties, intellectual property rights and counterfeit goods, safeguards, tropical products, textiles, investment policies, and dispute resolution. The negotiating sessions were extraordinarily complex, but were able to achieve a successful conclusion at the end of 1993, giving birth to the World Trade organization in 1995.

In 1999 an attempt at launching a "Seattle Round" led by President Clinton failed with violence in the streets. Two years later, the "Doha Round" was successfully launched in Qatar covering all existing WTO fields as well as E-commerce, trade and the environment, debt and finance, and special and differential treatment and assistance for developing countries. Developed WTO countries have been pushing foreign investment, competition policy, transparency in procurement, and trade facilitation topics. At Cancun in 2003, the WTO developing nations rejected these topics, focusing on agricultural trade barriers to their exports. Scheduled for completion in 2005, in July 2008 the Doha Round of WTO negotiations collapsed after marathon sessions. India and China, in particular, insisted upon Special Safeguard Mechanisms against surges in agricultural imports, provisions the U.S. and EU did not accept. Apart from cotton, the members were in agreement on all other areas of the Doha Round negotiations. At this writing, the Doha Round remains on life support.

§ 9.3 The World Trade Organization (WTO) and GATT 1994

The WTO is the product of the Uruguay Round of GATT negotiations, which was successfully completed in 1994. The Uruguay Round produced a package of agreements, the Agreement Establishing the World Trade Organization and its Annexes, which include the General Agreement on Tariffs and Trade 1994 (GATT 1994) and a series of Multilateral Trade Agreements (the Covered Agreements), and a series of Plurilateral Trade Agreements.[1]

GATT 1947 and GATT 1994 are two distinct agreements. GATT 1994 incorporates the provisions of GATT 1947, except for the Protocol of Provisional Application, which is expressly excluded. Thus, the problems created by exempting the existing national laws at the time of the adoption of the Protocol will now be avoided by this exclusion in the Covered Agreements. Otherwise, in cases involving a conflict between GATT 1947 and GATT 1994, GATT 1947 controls. The WTO will be guided by the decisions, procedures and customary practices under GATT.

Annexed to the WTO Agreement are several Multilateral Trade Agreements. As to trade in goods, they include Agreements on Agriculture, Textiles, Antidumping, Subsidies and Countervailing Measures, Safeguards, Technical Barriers to Trade, Sanitary and Phytosanitary Measures, Pre-shipment Inspection, Rules of Origin, and Import License Procedures. In addition to trade in goods, they include a General Agreement on Trade in Services and Agreements on Trade–Related Aspects of Intellectual Property Rights and Trade–Related Investment Measures. Affecting all of these agreements is the Understanding on Rules and Procedures Governing the Settlement of Disputes. All of the Multilateral Trade Agreements are binding on all Members of the World Trade Organization.

In addition to the Multilateral Trade Agreements, there are also Plurilateral Trade Agreements which are annexed to the WTO Agreement. These agreements, however, are not binding on all WTO Members, and Members can choose to adhere to them or not. They include Agreements on Government Procurement, Trade in

---

1 *See* 33 Int. Legal Mat. 1130 (1994).

Civil Aircraft, International Dairy and an Arrangement Regarding Bovine Meat. States which do not join the plurilateral trade agreements do not receive reciprocal benefits under them.

WORLD TRADE ORGANIZATION AGREEMENTS

AGREEMENT ESTABLISHING THE WORLD TRADE ORGANIZATION

ANNEX 1A: AGREEMENTS ON TRADE IN GOODS

1 General Agreement on Tariffs and Trade 1994

- (a) Understanding on the Interpretation of Article II:1(b)
- (b) Understanding on the Interpretation of Article XVII
- (c) Understanding on Balance-of-Payments Provisions
- (d) Understanding on the Interpretation of Article XXIV
- (e) Understanding on the Interpretation of Article XXV
- (f) Understanding on the Interpretation of Article XXVIII
- (g) Understanding on the Interpretation of Article XXXV

2 Uruguay Round Protocol GATT 1994

3 Agreement on Agriculture

4 Agreement on Sanitary and Phytosanitary Measures

5 Agreement on Textiles and Clothing

6 Agreement on Technical Barriers to Trade

7 Agreement on Trade–Related Investment Measures

8 Agreement on Implementation of Article VI

9 Agreement on Implementation of Article VII

10 Agreement on Preshipment Inspection

11 Agreement on Rules of Origin

12 Agreement on Import Licensing Procedures

13 Agreement on Subsidies and Countervailing Measures

14 Agreement on Safeguards

ANNEX 1B: General Agreement on Trade in Services and Annexes

ANNEX 1C: Agreement on Trade–Related Aspects of Intellectual Property Rights, Including Trade in Counterfeit Goods

ANNEX 2: Understanding on Rules and Procedures Governing the Settlement of Disputes

ANNEX 3: Trade Policy Review Mechanism

ANNEX 4: Plurilateral Trade Agreements

ANNEX 4(a) Agreement on Trade in Civil Aircraft

ANNEX 4(b) Agreement on Government Procurement

ANNEX 4(c) International Dairy Arrangement

ANNEX 4(d) Arrangement Regarding Bovine Meat

The duties of the World Trade Organization are to facilitate the implementation, administer the operations and further the objectives of all these agreements. Its duties also include the resolution of disputes under the agreements, reviews of trade policy and cooperation with the International Monetary Fund (IMF) and the World Bank. To achieve these goals, the WTO Agreement provides a charter for the new organization, but for only minimalist institutional and procedural capabilities, and no substantive competence. Thus, there is a unified administration of pre-existing and new obligations under all agreements concerning trade in goods, including the Uruguay Round Agreements. In addition, the administration of the new obligations on trade in services and intellectual property were brought under the same roof.

The WTO as an institution has no power to bring actions on its own initiative. Under the provisions of the WTO Agreement, only the Members of WTO can initiate actions under the Dispute Settlement Understanding. Enforcement of WTO obligations is primarily through permitting Members to retaliate or cross retaliate against other members, rather than by execution of WTO institutional orders. See Section 9.6 below.

§ 9.4 WTO Decision–Making, Admission

The World Trade Organization is structured in three tiers. One tier is the Ministerial Conference, which meets biennially and is composed of representatives of all WTO Members. Each Member has an equal voting weight, which is unlike the representation in the IMF and World Bank where there is weighted voting, and financially powerful states have more power over the decision-making process. The Ministerial Conference is responsible for all WTO functions, and is able to make any decisions necessary. It has the power to authorize new multilateral negotiations and to adopt the results of such negotiations. The Ministerial Conference, by a three-fourths vote, is authorized to grant waivers of obligations to Members in exceptional circumstances. It also has the power to adopt interpretations of Covered Agreements. When the Ministerial Conference is in recess, its functions are performed by the General Council.

The second tier is the General Council which has executive authority over the day to day operations and functions of the WTO. It is composed of representatives of all WTO Members, and each member has an equal voting weight. It meets whenever it is appropriate. The General Council also has the power to adopt interpretations of Covered Agreements.

The third tier comprises the councils, bodies and committees which are accountable to the Ministerial Conference or General Council. Ministerial Conference committees include Committees on Trade and Development, Balance of Payment Restrictions, Budget, Finance and Administration. General Council bodies include the Dispute Settlement Body, the Trade Policy Review Body, and Councils for Trade in Goods, Trade in Services and Trade–Related Intellectual Property Rights. The Councils are all created by the WTO Agreement and are open to representatives of all Member States. The Councils also have the authority to create subordinate organizations. Other committees, such as the Committee on Subsidies and Countervailing Measures are created by specific individual agreements.

Of the General Council bodies, the two which are likely to be most important are the Dispute Settlement Body (DSB) and the Trade Policy Review Body (TPRB). The DSB is a special meeting of the General Council, and therefore includes all WTO Members. It has responsibility for resolution of disputes under all the Covered Agreements, and will be discussed in more detail below under Dispute Resolution.

The purpose of the Trade Policy Review–Mechanism (TPRM) is to improve adherence to the WTO agreements and obligations, and to obtain greater transparency. Individual Members of WTO each prepare a "Country Report" on their trade policies and perceived adherence to the WTO Covered Agreements. The WTO Secretariat also prepares a report on each Member, but from the perspective of the Secretariat. The Trade Policy Review Body (TPRB) then reviews the trade policies of each Member based on these two reports. At the end of the review, the TPRB issues its own report concerning the adherence of the Member's trade policy to the WTO Covered Agreements. The TPRB has no enforcement capability, but the report is sent to the next meeting of the WTO Ministerial Conference. It is then up to the Ministerial Conference to evaluate the trade practices and policies of the Member.

Consensus Rules

The process of decision-making in the WTO Ministerial Conference and General Council relies upon "consensus" as the norm, just as it did for decision-making under GATT 1947. "Consensus", in this context means that no Member formally objects to a proposed decision. Thus, consensus is not obtained if any one Member formally objects, and has often been very difficult to obtain, which proved to be a weakness in the operation of GATT. However, there are many exceptions to the consensus formula under WTO, and some new concepts (such as "inverted consensus", discussed below) which are designed to ease the process of decision-making under WTO.

Article IX(1) of the WTO Agreement first provides that "the practice of decision-making by consensus" followed under GATT shall be continued. The next sentence of that provision, however, states that "where a decision cannot be arrived at by consensus, the matter at issue shall be decided by voting", except where otherwise provided. The ultimate resolution of the conflict between these two sentences is not completely clear.

There are a number of exceptions to the requirement for consensus that are expressly created under the WTO Agreement. One such exception is decisions by the Dispute Settlement Body, which has its own rules (see below). Another set of exceptions concerns decisions on waivers, interpretations and amendments of the Covered Agreements. Waivers of obligations may be granted and amendments adopted to Covered Agreements only by the Ministerial Conference. Amendments of Multilateral Trade Agreements usually require a consensus, but where a decision on a proposed amendment cannot obtain consensus, the decision on that amendment is to be made in certain circumstances by a two-thirds majority vote. In "exceptional circumstances", the Ministerial Conference is authorized to grant waivers of obligations under a Covered Agreement by a three-fourths vote. Another exception to the consensus requirement allows procedural rules in both the Ministerial Conference and the General Council to be decided by a majority vote of the Members, unless otherwise provided.

Admission to the WTO

Admission to the World Trade Organization is by "consensus." In theory, this gives each member a veto over applicant countries. In reality, no nation wishing to join has ever formally been vetoed, though many have been long delayed. Iran's desire to join has basically been frustrated by U.S. refusal to negotiate on WTO entry. It took, for example, well over a decade to negotiate acceptable terms of entry for the People's Republic of China and Russia. Such negotiations are handled individually by member states, not by the WTO as an organization. United States negotiations with China were particularly lengthy and difficult, one principal issue being whether China should be admitted as a developing or developed nation. (The issue was fudged, with China treated differently within the WTO package of agreements.)

Essentially, applicant counties make an offer of trade liberalization commitments to join the WTO. This offer is renegotiated with interested member nations, some 40 nations regarding China including the European Union which negotiates as a unit (NAFTA does not). Regarding China, the last member to reach agreement on WTO admission was Mexico, which extracted stiff promises against the dumping of Chinese goods. The various commitments made by the applicant in these negotiations are consolidated into a final accession protocol which is then approved by "consensus."

§ 9.5 WTO Agreements and U.S. Law

The WTO Covered Agreements concern not only trade in goods, but also trade in services (GATS), and trade-related aspects of intellectual property (TRIPS). The basic concepts that GATT applied to trade in goods (described above) are now applied to these areas through GATS and TRIPS. In the WTO Covered Agreements, the basic concepts of GATT 1947 and its associated agreements are elaborated and clarified. In addition, there is an attempt to transform all protectionist measures relating to agriculture (such as import bans and quotas, etc.) into only tariff barriers, which can then be lowered in subsequent MTN Rounds (a process known as "tariffication"). WTO also contains some superficial provisions on trade-related investment measures (TRIMS). Some of the WTO provisions, particularly those concerning trade in goods, will be discussed in more detail below in relation to United States trade law.

As of 2013, there were over 155 Member States of the World Trade Organization. The United States enacted legislation to implement WTO and the Covered Agreements on December 3, 1994. The implementing legislation was submitted to Congress under the "fast track" procedures of 19 U.S.C.A. § 2112, which required that the agreement and its implementing legislation be considered as a whole by Congress, and which also prohibits Congressional amendments to the implementing legislation. The Congressional authority for "fast track" procedures also required that the President give ninety days notice of his intention to enter into such an agreement. Similar fast track procedures were in place for the Doha Round of WTO negotiations under the Trade Promotion Authority Act of 2002, but expired in July of 2007.

Neither GATT 1947 nor the WTO Agreement, GATT 1994 and the other Covered Agreements have been ratified as treaties, and therefore comprise international obligations of the United States only to the extent that they are incorporated in United States' implementing legislation. GATT 1947 was not considered controlling by the courts of the United States, and these courts have always held themselves bound to the U.S. legislation actually enacted.[2] The WTO Covered Agreements will be considered to have a non-self-executed status, and therefore are likely to be regarded in the same manner as GATT 1947.

§ 9.6 WTO Dispute Settlement/U.S. Disputes/ China Disputes

The WTO provides a unified system for settling international trade disputes through the Dispute Settlement Understanding (DSU) and using the Dispute Settlement Body (DSB). The DSB is a special assembly of the WTO General Council, and includes all WTO Members. There are five stages in the resolution of disputes under WTO: 1) Consultation; 2) Panel establishment, investigation and report; 3) Appellate review of the panel report; 4) Adoption of the panel and appellate decision; and 5) Implementation of the decision adopted. There is also a parallel process for binding arbitration, if both parties agree to submit this dispute to arbitration, rather than to a DSB panel. In addition, during the implementation phase (5), the party subject to an adverse decision may seek arbitration as a matter of right on issues of compliance and authorized retaliation.

Although the DSU offers a unified dispute resolution system that is applicable across all sectors and all WTO Covered Agreements, there are many specialized rules for disputes which arise under them. Such specialized rules appear in the Agreements on Textiles, Antidumping, Subsidies and Countervailing Measures, Technical Barriers to Trade, Sanitary and Phytosanitary Measures, Customs Valuation, General Agreement on Trade in Services, Financial Services and Air Transport Services. The special provisions in these individual Covered Agreements govern, where applicable, and prevail in any conflict with the general provisions of the DSU.

Under WTO, unlike under GATT 1947, the DSU practically assures that panels will be established upon request by a Member. Further, under WTO, unlike under GATT 1947, the DSU virtually ensures the adoption of unmodified panel and appellate body decisions. It accomplishes this by requiring the DSB to adopt panel reports and appellate body decisions automatically and without amendment unless they are rejected by a consensus of all Members. This "inverted consensus" requires that all Members of the DSB,

---

[2] *See, e.g.*, Suramerica de Aleaciones Laminadas, C.A. v. United States, 966 F.2d 660 (Fed.Cir.1992).

including the Member who prevailed in the dispute, decide to reject the dispute resolution decision; and that no Member formally favor that decision. Such an outcome seems unlikely. This inverted consensus requirement is imposed on both the adoption of panel reports or appellate body decisions and also on the decision to establish a panel.

The potential resolutions of a dispute under DSU range from a "mutually satisfactory solution" agreed to by the parties under the first, or consultation phase, to authorized retaliation under the last, or implementation, phase. The preferred solution is always any resolution that is mutually satisfactory to the parties. After a panel decision, there are three types of remedies available to the prevailing party, if a mutually satisfactory solution cannot be obtained. One is for the respondent to bring the measure found to violate a Covered Agreement into conformity with the Agreement. A second is for the prevailing Member to receive compensation from the respondent which both parties agree is sufficient to compensate for any injury caused by the measure found to violate a Covered Agreement.

Finally, if no such agreement can be reached, a prevailing party can be authorized to suspend some of its concessions under the Covered Agreements to the respondent. These suspended concessions, called "retaliation," can be authorized within the same trade sector and agreement; or, if that will not create sufficient compensation, can be authorized across trade sectors and agreements.

Consultation

Any WTO Member who believes that the Measures of another Member are not in conformity with the Covered Agreements may call for consultations on those measures. The respondent has ten days to reply to the call for consultations and must agree to enter into consultation within 30 days. If the respondent does not enter into consultations within the 30 day period, the party seeking consultations can immediately request the establishment of a panel under DSU, which puts the dispute into Phase 2.

Once consultations begin, the parties have 60 days to achieve a settlement. The goal is to seek a positive solution to the dispute, and the preferred resolution is to reach whatever solution is mutually satisfactory to the parties. If such a settlement cannot be obtained after 60 days of consultations, the party seeking consultations may request the establishment of a panel under DSU, which moves the dispute into Phase 2.

Third parties with an interest in the subject-matter of the consultations may seek to be included in them. If such inclusion is rejected, they may seek their own consultations with the other Member. Alternatives to consultations may be provided through the use of conciliation, mediation or good offices, where all parties agree to use the alternative process. Any party can terminate the use of conciliation, mediation or good offices and then seek the establishment of a panel under DSU, which will move the dispute into Phase 2.

Panel establishment, investigation and report

If consultations between the parties fail, the party seeking the consultations (the complainant) may request the DSB to establish a panel to investigate, report and resolve the dispute. The DSB must establish such a panel upon request, unless the DSB expressly decides by consensus not to establish the panel. Since an "inverted consensus" is required to reject the establishment of the panel and the complainant Member must be part of that consensus, it is very likely that a panel will be established. Roughly 100 panels were established in the first five years of operation of the DSU.

The WTO Secretariat is to maintain a list of well-qualified persons who are available to serve as panelists. The panels are usually composed of three individuals from that list who are not citizens of either party. If the parties agree, a panel can be composed of five such individuals. The parties can also agree to appoint citizens of a party to a panel. Panelists may be either nongovernmental individuals or governmental officials, but they are to be selected so as to ensure their independence. Thus, there is a bias towards independent individuals who are not citizens of any party. If a citizen of a party is appointed, his government may not instruct that citizen how to vote, for the panelist must be independent. By the same reasoning, a governmental official of a non-party Member who is subject to instructions from his government would not seem to fit the profile of an independent panelist.

The WTO Secretariat proposes nominations of the panelists. Parties may not normally oppose the nominations, except for "compelling reasons." The parties are given twenty days to agree on the panelists and the composition of the panel. If such agreement is not forthcoming, the WTO Director–General is authorized to appoint the panelists, in consultation with other persons in the Secretariat.

Complaints brought to DSB panels can involve either violations of Covered Agreements or nonviolation nullification and impairment of benefits under the Covered Agreements. A prima facie case of nullification impairment arises when one Member infringes upon the "obligations assumed under a Covered Agreement." Such infringement creates a presumption against the infringing Member, but the presumption can be rebutted by a showing that the complaining Member has suffered no adverse effect from the infringement.

The panels receive pleadings and rebuttals and hear oral arguments. Panels can also engage in fact development from sources outside those presented by the parties. Thus, the procedure has aspects familiar to civil law courts. A panel can, on its own initiative, request information from any body, including experts selected by the panel. It can also obtain confidential information in some circumstances from an administrative body which is part of the government of a Member, without any prior consent from that Member. A panel can establish its own group of experts to provide reports to it on factual or scientific issues. In a series of rulings commencing with the *Shrimp–Turtles* decision in 1998, the WTO Appellate Body has affirmed the right of panels and itself to elect to receive unsolicited informational and argumentative briefs or letters from non-governmental organizations (NGOs), business groups and law firms.

A panel is obligated to produce two written reports—an interim and a final report. A panel is supposed to submit a final written report to the DSB within six months of its establishment. The report will contain its findings of fact, findings of law, decision and the rationale for its decision. Before the final report is issued, the panel is supposed to provide an interim report to the parties. The purpose of this interim report is to apprize the parties of the panel's current analysis of the issues and to permit the parties to comment on that analysis. The final report of the panel need not change any of the findings or conclusions in its interim report unless it is persuaded to do so by a party's comments. However, if it is not so persuaded, it is obligated to explain in its final report why it is not so persuaded.

The decisions in panel reports are final as to issues of fact. The decisions in panel reports are not necessarily final as to issues of law. Panel decisions on issues of law are subject to review by the Appellate Body, which is Phase 3, and explained below. Any party can appeal a panel report, and as is explained below it is expected that appeals will usually be taken.

Appellate review of the panel report

Appellate review of panel reports is available at the request of any party, unless the DSB rejects that request by an "inverted consensus." There is no threshold requirement for an appellant to present a substantial substantive legal issue. Thus, most panel decisions are appealed as a matter of course. However, the Appellate Body can only review the panel reports on questions of law or legal interpretation.

The Appellate Body is a new institution in the international trade organization and its process. GATT 1947 had nothing comparable to it. The Appellate Body is composed of seven members (or judges) who are appointed by the DSB to four year terms. Each judge may be reappointed, but only once, to a second four year term. Each judge is to be a recognized authority on international trade law and the Covered Agreements. To date, Appellate Body members have been drawn mostly from the academe and retired justices. They have come from Germany, Japan, Egypt, India, New Zealand, the Philippines, Argentina, the United States and other WTO member nations. The review of any panel decision is performed by three judges out of the seven. The parties do not, however, have any influence on which judges are selected to review a particular panel report. There is a schedule, created by the Appellate Body itself, for the rotation for sitting of each of the judges. Thus, a party might try to appear before a favored judge by timing the start of the dispute settlement process to arrive at the Appellate Body at the right moment on the rotation schedule, but even this limited approach has difficulties.

The Appellate Body receives written submissions from the parties and has 60, or in some cases 90, days in which to render its decision. The Appellate Body review is limited to issues of law and legal interpretation. The panel decision may be upheld, modified, or reversed by the Appellate Body decision. Appellate Body decisions will be anonymous, and ex parte communications are not permitted, which will make judge-shopping by parties more than usually difficult.

Adoption of the panel or Appellate Body decision

Appellate Body determinations are submitted to the DSB. Panel decisions which are not appealed are also submitted to the DSB. Once either type of decision is submitted to the DSB, the DSB must automatically adopt them without modification or amendment at its next meeting unless the decision is rejected by all Members of the DSB through the form of "inverted consensus" discussed previously.

An alternative to Phases 2 through 4 is arbitration, if both parties agree. The arbitration must be binding on the parties, and there is no appeal from the arbitral tribunal's decision to the DSB Appellate Body.

Implementation of the decision adopted

Once a panel or Appellate Body decision is adopted by the DSB, implementation is a three-step process. In the first step, the Member found to have a measure which violates its WTO obligations has "a reasonable time" (usually 15 months) to bring those measures into conformity with the WTO obligations. That remedy is the preferred one, and this form of implementation is the principal goal of the WTO implementation system. To date, most disputes have resulted in compliance in this manner. If the adequacy of compliance is disputed, such disputes typically return to the WTO panel that rendered decision on the merits which also determines, acting as an arbitrator, the amount (if any) of authorized retaliation. The retaliation process is discussed below.

Compensation

If the violating measures are not brought into conformity within a reasonable time, the parties proceed to the second step. In that second step, the parties negotiate to reach an agreement upon a form of compensation which will be granted by the party in violation to the injured party. Such compensation will usually comprise trade concessions by the violating party to the injured party, which are over and above those already available under the WTO and Covered Agreements. The nature, scope, amount and duration of these additional concessions is at the negotiating parties' discretion, but each side must agree that the final compensation package is fair and is properly related to the injury caused by the violating measures. Presumably, any such concessions need not be extended under MFN principles to all WTO members. Few such compensation agreements have ever been achieved.

Authorized Retaliation

If the parties cannot agree on an appropriate amount of compensation within twenty days, the complainant may proceed to the third step. In the third step, the party injured by the violating measures seeks authority from the DSB to retaliate against the party whose measures violated its WTO obligations. Thus complainant seeks authority to suspend some of its WTO obligations in regard to the respondent. The retaliation must ordinarily be within the same sector and agreement as the violating measure. "Sector" is sometimes broadly defined, as all trade in goods, and sometimes narrowly defined, as in individual services in the Services Sectoral Classification List. "Agreement" is also broadly defined. All the agreements listed in Annex IA to the WTO Agreement are considered a single agreement. If retaliation within the sector and agreement of the violating measure is considered insufficient compensation, the complainant may seek suspension of its obligations across sectors and agreements.

The DSB must grant the complainant's request to retaliate within 30 days unless all WTO members reject it through an "inverted consensus." (Article 22.6, D.S.U.) However, the respondent may object to the level or scope of the retaliation. The issues raised by the objection will be examined by either the Appellate Body or by an arbitrator. The respondent has a right, even if arbitration was not used in Phases 2 through 4, to have an arbitrator review in Phase 5 the appropriateness of the complainant's proposed level and scope of retaliation. The arbitrator will also examine whether the proper procedures and criteria to establish retaliation have been followed. The Phase 5 arbitration is final and binding and the arbitrator's decision is not subject to DSB review.

In addition to objecting to the level of authorized retaliation, the responding WTO member may simultaneously challenge the assertion of noncompliance (Article 21.5, D.S.U.). This challenge will ordinarily be heard by the original panel and must be resolved within 90 days. Thus the request for authorized retaliation and objections thereto could conceivably be accomplished before noncompliance is formally determined. In practice, WTO dispute settlement has melded these conflicting procedures such that compliance and retaliation issues are decided together, typically by the original panel.

Retaliation in Action

Retaliation has rarely been authorized and even less rarely imposed. The amount of a U.S. retaliation permitted against the EU after the WTO *Bananas* and *Beef Hormones* decisions were not implemented by the EU was contested. The arbitration tribunals for this issue were the original WTO panels, which did not allow the entire amount of the almost $700 million in retaliatory tariffs proposed by the United States. The U.S. was authorized and levied retaliatory tariffs amounting to about $300 million against European goods because of the EU failure to implement those WTO decisions. Since 2000, Congress has authorized rotating these tariffs in "carousel" fashion upon different European goods. The threat of carousel retaliation contributed to settlements of these disputes. The $300 million in authorized U.S. retaliation was dwarfed by a WTO decision allowing the EU to impose up to $4 billion in retaliatory tariffs on U.S. exports after twice finding U.S. extraterritorial export tax benefits (FSCs) to be illegal subsidies. The EU commenced imposing this retaliation gradually in 2004, which caused Congress to repeal the offending IRC provisions shortly thereafter.

In a landmark ruling, a WTO panel acting as an arbitrator has authorized Ecuador to remove protection of intellectual property rights regarding geographical indicators, copyrights and industrial designs on European Union goods for sale in Ecuador. This authorization is part of Ecuador's $200 million compensation in the Bananas dispute. The WTO panel acknowledged that Ecuador imports mostly capital goods and raw materials from the European Union and that imposing retaliatory tariffs on them would adversely harm its manufacturing industries. This risk supported "cross-retaliation" under Article 22.3 of the DSU outside the sector of the EU trade violation. Cross-sector retaliation was also authorized against the U.S. after losing a GATS dispute to Antigua on Internet gambling restraints. The United States settled this dispute with nearly all other WTO members via compensation.

Both "compensation" in the second step and "retaliation" in the third step of implementation provide only for indirect enforcement of DSB decisions. There is no mechanism for direct enforcement by the WTO of its decisions through WTO orders to suspend trade obligations. Some commentators believe that retaliation will be an effective implementation device; others believe that it will prove ineffective. The division represented by these conflicting views represents two different approaches to the nature of both international law and international trade law.

One approach seeks a rule-oriented use of the "rule of law"; the other seeks a power-oriented use of diplomacy. The United States and less developed countries have traditionally sought to develop a rule-oriented approach to international trade disputes. The European Union and Japan have traditionally sought to use the GATT/WTO primarily as a forum for diplomatic negotiations, although the EU now ranks second in number of WTO proceedings. These different views created part of the conflict at the December 1999 Seattle WTO meeting (which failed to launch the Millennium Round). If the DSB is a court, its proceedings should be open and "transparent." However, if it is just another form of government-to-government diplomacy, that has always been held in secret.

U.S. Involvement in WTO Dispute Resolution

The WTO dispute resolution process has been invoked more frequently than many expected. The United States has been a complainant or a respondent in dozens of disputes. It lost a dispute initiated by Venezuela and Brazil (WT/DS 2 and 4) concerning U.S. standards for reformulated and conventional gasoline. The offending U.S. law was amended to conform to the WTO ruling. It won on a complaint initiated jointly with Canada and the European Union (WT/DS 8, 10 and 11) regarding Japanese taxes on alcoholic beverages. Japan subsequently changed its law. When Costa Rica complained about U.S. restraints on imports of underwear (WT/DS 24), the U.S. let the restraints expire prior to any formal DSB ruling at the WTO. Similar results were reached when India complained of U.S. restraints on wool shirts and blouses (WT/DS 23). The United States won a major dispute with Canada concerning trade and subsidies for periodicals (WT/DS 31). This celebrated *Sports Illustrated* dispute proved that WTO remedies can be used to avoid Canada's cultural industries exclusion under NAFTA.

In the longstanding *Bananas* dispute (WT/DS 27) noted above, the United States joined Ecuador, Guatemala, Honduras and Mexico in successfully challenging EU import restraints against so-called "dollar bananas." The EU failed to comply with the Appellate Body's ruling, and retaliatory measures were authorized and imposed. In April 2001, the *Bananas* dispute was settled on terms that converted EU quotas to tariffs by 2006. A patent law complaint by the U.S. against India (WT/DS 50) prevailed in the DSB and ultimately brought changes in Indian law regarding pharmaceuticals and agricultural chemicals.

In *Beef Hormones* (WT/DS 26 and 48), also noted above, the European Union lost twice before the Appellate Body for want of proof of a "scientific basis" for its ban on hormone beef. It refused to alter its import restraints and absorbed $200 million in retaliatory tariffs on selected exports to Canada and the United States. In 2009, an arguably pro-European settlement was reached. The U.S. effectively got a higher quota to export hormone-free beef to the EU, in return for phasing out over four years its retaliatory tariffs on EU goods. The U.S. threat of carousel sanctions, i.e. rotating goods subject to retaliation, was instrumental to this settlement. Meanwhile, because the U.S. beef industry failed to timely ask for a continuation of the retaliatory tariffs, the Federal Circuit ruled in 2010 that they expired in 2007. Refunds were given to importers of EU products who paid those tariffs.

The United States prevailed against Argentina regarding tariffs and taxes on footwear, textiles and apparel (WT/DS 56). It lost a challenge (strongly supported by Kodak) to Japan's distribution rules regarding photo film and paper (WT/DS 44). In this dispute the U.S. elected *not* to appeal the adverse WTO panel ruling to the Appellate Body. In contrast, the European Union took an appeal which reversed an adverse panel ruling on its customs classification of computer equipment (WT/DS 62, 67 and 68). The U.S. had commenced this proceeding. Opponents in many disputes, Japan, the United States and the European Union united to complain in WT/DS 54, 55, 59 and 64 that Indonesia's National Car Programme was discriminatory and in breach of several WTO agreements. They prevailed and Indonesia altered its program.

India, Malaysia, Pakistan and Thailand teamed up to challenge U.S. shrimp import restraints enacted to protect endangered sea turtles (WT/DS 58). The WTO Appellate Body generally upheld their complaint and the U.S. has moved to comply. The adequacy of U.S. compliance is being challenged by Malaysia. The European Union and the United States jointly opposed Korea's discriminatory taxes on alcoholic beverages (WT/DS 75 and 84). This challenge was successful and Korea now imposes flat non-discriminatory taxes. The United States also complained of Japan's quarantine, testing and other agricultural import rules (WT/DS 76/1). The U.S. won at the WTO and Japan has changed its procedures.

In a semiconductor dumping dispute, Korea successfully argued that the U.S. was not in compliance with the WTO Antidumping Agreement (WT/DS 99/1). The United States amended its law, but Korea has instituted further proceedings alleging that these amendments are inadequate. The United States did likewise after Australia lost a subsidies dispute relating to auto leather exports (WT/DS 126/1). The reconvened WTO panel ruled that Australia had indeed failed to conform to the original adverse DSB decision. A U.S. challenge concerning India's quotas on imports of agricultural, textile and industrial products was upheld (WT/DS 90/1). India and the United States subsequently reached agreement on a timeline for removal of these restraints.

Closer to home, New Zealand and the United States complained of Canada's import/export rules regarding milk (WT/DS 103/1). Losing at the WTO, Canada agreed to a phased removal of the offending measures. The United States also won against Mexico in an antidumping dispute involving corn syrup (WT/DS 132/1), but lost a "big one" when the DSB determined that export tax preferences granted to "Foreign Sales Corporations" of U.S. companies were illegal (WT/DS 108/1). Another "big one" went in favor of the United States. The European Union challenged the validity under the DSU of unilateral retaliation under Section 301 of the Trade Act of 1974 (WT/DS 152/1). Section 301 has been something of a bete noire in U.S. trade law, but the WTO panel affirmed its legality in light of Presidential undertakings to administer it in accordance with U.S. obligations to adhere to multilateral WTO dispute settlement.

U.S. involvement in WTO dispute settlement continues to be extensive. The Appellate Body ruled that U.S. countervailing duties against British steel based upon pre-privitization subsidies were unlawful (WT/DS 138/1). The European Union prevailed before a WTO panel in its challenge of the U.S. Antidumping Act of 1916 (WT/DS 136), since repealed. U.S. complaints against Korean beef import restraints and procurement practices were upheld (WT/DS 161/1, 163/1). Canada's patent protection term was also invalidated by the WTO under a U.S. complaint (WT/DS 170/1). European Union complaints concerning U.S. wheat gluten quotas (WT/DS 166/1) and the royalty free small business provisions of the Fairness in Music Licensing Act of 1998 (WT/DS 160/1) have been sustained. The *Wheat Gluten* dispute questions the legality of U.S. "causation" rules in escape clause proceedings under Section 201 of the Trade Act of 1974.

A WTO Panel ruled in 2002 that the Byrd Amendment violates the WTO antidumping and subsidy codes. The Byrd Amendment (Continued Dumping and Subsidy Act of 2000) authorizes the Customs Service to forward AD and CVD duties to affected domestic producers for qualified expenses. Eleven WTO members including the EU, Canada and Mexico challenged the Amendment. This ruling was affirmed by the WTO Appellate Body and retaliation was authorized. Late in 2005, the U.S. repealed the Byrd Amendment, subject to a contested two-year phase out. The Appellate Body also ruled against Section 211 of the Omnibus Appropriations Act of 1998 denying trademark protection in connection with confiscated assets (the "HAVANA CLUB" dispute). U.S. compliance with these rulings has been slow in forthcoming. The United States and other complainants prevailed in a 2002 WTO proceeding against Indian local content and trade balancing requirements for foreign auto manufacturers. These requirements violated the TRIMs agreement.

In March of 2004, the European Union commenced raising tariffs against U.S. goods under the WTO retaliation authorized out of the FSC/export tax subsidy dispute. Monthly increments were planned until either the U.S. complied or the EU reached the maximum of roughly $4 billion annually it was authorized to retaliate. In the Fall of 2004, the United States repealed the extraterritorial income exclusion and the EU subsequently removed its retaliatory tariffs. In 2004, also, Antigua–Barbuda won a WTO panel ruling under the GATS against certain U.S. Internet gambling restraints. Retaliation was authorized, and the U.S. settled by offering compensation to all WTO members. The U.S. won a panel decision against Mexico's exorbitant telecom interconnection rates, but lost a 2004 cotton subsidy challenge by Brazil. Retaliation by Brazil was authorized.

The United States also lost a second dispute with the EU about pre-privatization countervailable subsidies, in particular the legality of the U.S. "same person" methodology. (WT/DS212/AB/R). The U.S. won an SPS dispute against Japanese quarantine of U.S. apples (WT/DS245/AB/R), while losing an important softwood lumber "zeroing" methodology complaint brought by Canada. (WT/DS257/AB/R). In 2006, the Mexico–United States "sugar war" came to a head before the Appellate Body. Mexico's 20% soft drink tax on beverages not using cane sugar, its 20% distribution tax on those beverages, and related bookkeeping requirements were found to violate GATT Article III and not exempt under Article XX(d). Subsequently, the two countries settled their dispute by agreeing, effective in 2008, to free trade in sugar and high fructose corn syrup. Further in 2006, the U.S. failed to persuade the Appellate Body to require the European Union under GATT Article X (3) to undertake a major overhaul of its customs law system targeting inconsistencies therein among the 27 member states.

In 2010, the United States agreed to pay $147 million annually to provide technical assistance to Brazilian cotton farmers. In return, Brazil has suspended retaliatory tariffs and cross-sector IP sanctions authorized by the WTO because of U.S. cotton subsidy violations. In 2009, a WTO panel ruled that Airbus had received $20 billion in illegal EU "launch" subsidies. By 2010, that same panel found Boeing the recipient of $5 billion in federal research contract subsidies that violated the WTO Subsidies Code.

The United States has also settled a number of disputes prior to WTO panel decisions, and remains in consultation on other disputes that may be decided by a WTO panel. For the latest summary of all WTO disputes, including many not involving the United States, see www.wto.org.

China and WTO Disputes

Canada, the European Union and the United States complained against Chinese duties on imported auto parts (10 percent) that rose to those on complete autos (25 percent) if the imported parts exceeded a fixed percentage of the final vehicle content or price, or if specific combinations of imported auto parts were used in the final vehicle. In addition, extensive record keeping, reporting and verification requirements were imposed when Chinese auto companies used imported parts. In July of 2008, a WTO panel ruled that these "internal charges" violated Articles III (2) and III (4) of the GATT, reproduced in the Documents Supplement to this coursebook. The core Panel ruling found China's auto parts measures discriminatory in favor of domestic producers, a violation of the national treatment standard for taxes and regulations. This ruling marked the first time since China's admission to the WTO in 2001 that China has been held in breach of its WTO commitments and obligations. See WT/DS 339, 340, 342/R (July 18, 2008) (Affirmed by the Appellate Body Oct. 16, 2008).

Less than one month after losing this dispute, China enacted a clever "green tax" on gas-guzzling autos, most of which just happen to be imported. The sales tax on cars with engine capacities over 4.1 litres has been doubled to 40%. Autos with engines between 3 and 4.1 litres are taxed at 25%, up from 15%. Most Chinese-made cars have engines with 2.5 litres or less. Autos with engines between 1 and 3 litres remain taxed at 8% and 10%. The smallest cars with engines below 1 litre have their sales tax reduced from 3 to 1 percent. This green tax could achieve protective results similar to China's Auto Parts tariff structure and could be challenged under GATT Article III.

Other disputes challenging China's compliance with WTO law are pending. They concern China's value-added tax on integrated circuits, discriminatory tax refunds, reductions and exemptions, protection and enforcement of intellectual property rights (2009 WTO panel ruled against China), trade and distribution of publications and audiovisual entertainment products (2009 WTO panel ruled against China), commodity export tariffs and restrictions (2011 WTO Panel ruled against China) and treatment of foreign financial information suppliers. The United States is a complaining party to all of these disputes. China, in turn, has challenged U.S. safeguard measures applied to Chinese steel exports (2010 WTO

Panel rejected challenge) and tires (2011 WTO Panel rejected challenge), and U.S. antidumping and countervailing duties on paper products from China (2011 WTO Panel ruled against U.S. dual assessment of AD and CVD duties). It has also applied AD duties to U.S. exports, e.g. chicken.

§ 9.7 Import Quotas and Licenses under the WTO

Quantity restrictions, such as numerical quotas on the importation of an item or upon a type of item, continue to exist, despite GATT Article XI which calls for their elimination. Import quotas may be "global" limitations (applying to items originating from anywhere in the world), "bilateral" limitations (applying to items originating from a particular country) and "discretionary" limitations. Quantitative limitations may have arisen from a Treaty of Friendship, Commerce and Navigation or from a narrow international agreement, such as agreements on trade in textiles and textile products. Discretionary limitations, when coupled with a requirement that importation of items must be licensed in advance by local authorities, provide an effective vehicle for gathering statistical data and for raising local revenues. "Tariff-rate quotas" admit a specified quantity of goods at a preferential rate of duty. Once imports reach that quantity, tariffs are normally increased.

The WTO has significantly reduced the number of trade quotas. The Agreement on Textiles eliminates in 2005 the quotas long maintained under the Multi–Fibre Arrangement. The demise of MFA textile quotas in 2005, as widely expected, accelerated Chinese and other Asian textile exports to the United States. Responding to domestic pressures, President Bush set temporary quotas in the Fall of 2004 against surges of Chinese bras, bathrobes and knit fabrics. More such restraints are permitted until 2008. Voluntary export restraints (quotas) are severely limited by the Safeguards Agreement. In addition, the WTO removes trade quotas by pressuring for "tariffication," or replacing them with tariffs—sometimes even at extraordinarily high tariff rates. Tariffication is the approach adopted in the Agriculture Agreement. It is expected that such high tariff rates will be reduced in subsequent negotiating Rounds. Import licensing schemes are also being phased out under WTO agreements.

§ 9.8 GATT/WTO Nontariff Trade Barrier Codes

There are numerous nontariff trade barriers applicable to imports. Many of these barriers arise out of safety and health regulations. Others concern the environment, consumer protection, product standards and government procurement. Many of the relevant rules were created for legitimate consumer and public protection reasons. They were often created without extensive consideration of their international impact as potential nontariff trade barriers. Nevertheless, the practical impact of legislation of this type is to ban the importation of nonconforming products. Thus, unlike tariffs which can always be paid, and unlike quotas which permit a certain amount of goods to enter the market, nontariff trade barriers have the potential to totally exclude foreign exports.

Multilateral GATT negotiations since the end of World War II have led to a significant decline in world tariff levels, particularly on trade with developed nations. As steadily as tariff barriers have disappeared, nontariff trade barriers (NTBs) have emerged. Health and safety regulations, environmental laws, rules regulating products standards, procurement legislation and customs procedures are often said to present NTB problems. Negotiations over nontariff trade barriers dominated the Tokyo Round of the GATT negotiations during the late 1970s. A number of optional NTB "codes" (sometimes called "side agreements") emerged from the Tokyo Round. These concerned subsidies, dumping, government procurement, technical barriers (products standards), customs valuation and import licensing. In addition, specific agreements regarding trade in bovine meats, dairy products and civil aircraft were also reached. The United States accepted all of these NTB codes and agreements except the one on dairy products. Most of the necessary implementation of these agreements was accomplished in the Trade Agreements Act of 1979.

Additional GATT codes were agreed upon under the Uruguay Round ending in late 1993. They revisit all of the NTB areas covered by the Tokyo Round Codes and create new codes for sanitary and phyto-sanitary measures (SPS), trade-related investment measures (TRIMs), preshipment inspection, rules of origin, escape clause safeguards and trade-related intellectual property rights (TRIPs). However, the WTO nontariff barrier codes (save a few plurilateral codes) are **mandatory** for all members. The United States Congress approved and implemented these Codes in December of 1994 under the Uruguay Round Agreements Act.

One problem with nontariff trade barriers is that they are so numerous. Intergovernmental negotiation intended to reduce their trade restricting impact is both tedious and difficult. There are continuing attempts through the World Trade Organization to come to grips with additional specific NTB problems. Furthermore, various trade agreements of the United States have been undertaken in this field. For example, the Canadian–United States Free Trade Area Agreement and the NAFTA built upon the existing GATT agreements to further reduce NTB problems between the United States, Canada and Mexico.

Some of the difficulties of NTBs are illustrated in the *EU Beef Hormones* case. The EU, adhering to "precautionary principles," banned imports of growth-enhancing hormone-treated beef from the U.S. and Canada as a health hazard. The Appellate Body ruled that, since the ban was more strict than international standards, the EU needed scientific evidence to back it up. However, the EU had failed to undertake a scientific risk assessment, and the EU's scientific reports did not provide any rational basis to uphold the ban. In fact, the primary EU study had found no evidence of harm to humans from the growth-enhancing-hormones. The Appellate Body ruled that the ban violated the EU's SPS obligations and required the EU to produce scientific evidence to justify the ban within a reasonable time, or to revoke the ban. Arbitrators later determined that 15 months was a reasonable time, but the EU failed to produce such evidence and the U.S. retaliated. Late in 2004, the EU commenced new WTO proceedings asserting that more recent scientific studies and precaution justified its ban and require removal of U.S. retaliation. This WTO proceeding also went against the EU, again for want of adequate proof of scientific basis.

§ 9.9 The WTO Agreement on Agriculture

Agricultural issues played a central role in the Uruguay Round negotiations and are critical to the Doha Round as well. More than any other issue, they delayed completion of the Uruguay Round from 1990 to 1993. The agreement reached in December of 1993 is a trade liberalizing, market-oriented effort. Each country has made a number of commitments on market access, reduced domestic agricultural support levels and export subsidies. The United States Congress approved of these commitments in December of 1994 by adopting the Uruguay Round Agreements Act.

Broadly speaking nontariff barriers (NTBs) to international agricultural trade are replaced by tariffs that provide substantially the same level of protection. This is known as "tariffication." It applies to virtually all NTBs, including variable levies, import bans, voluntary export restraints and import quotas. Tariffication applies specifically to U.S. agricultural quotas adopted under Section 22 of the Agricultural Adjustment Act. All agricultural tariffs, including those converted from NTBs, are to be reduced by 36 and 24 percent by developed and developing countries, respectively, over 6 and 10 year periods. Certain minimum access tariff quotas apply when imports amount to less than 3 to 5 percent of domestic consumption. An escape clause exists for tariffed imports at low prices or upon a surge of importation depending upon the existing degree of import penetration.

Regarding domestic support for agriculture, some programs with minimal impact on trade are exempt from change. These programs are known as "green box policies." They include governmental support for agricultural research, disease control, infrastructure and food security. Green box policies were also exempt from GATT/WTO challenge or countervailing duties for 9 years. Direct payments to producers that are not linked to production are also generally exempt. This will include income support, adjustment assistance, and environmental and regional assistance payments. Furthermore, direct payments to support crop reductions and *de minimis* payments are exempted in most cases.

After removing all of the exempted domestic agricultural support programs, the agreement on agriculture arrives at a calculation known as the Total Aggregate Measurement of Support (Total AMS). This measure is the basis for agricultural support reductions under the agreement. Developed nations reduced their Total AMS by 20 percent over 6 years, developing nations by 13.3 percent over 10 years. United States reductions undertaken in 1985 and 1990 meant that little or no U.S. action was required to meet this obligation. Agricultural export subsidies of developed nations were reduced by 36 percent below 1986–1990 levels over 6 years and the quantity of subsidized agricultural exports by 21 percent. Developing nations had corresponding 24 and 14 percent reductions over 10 years.

All conforming tariffications, reductions in domestic support for agriculture and export subsidy alterations were essentially exempt from challenge for 9 years within the GATT/WTO on grounds such as serious prejudice in export markets or nullification and impairment of agreement benefits. However, countervailing duties could be levied against all unlawfully subsidized exports of agricultural goods except for subsidies derived from so-called national "green box policies" (discussed above).

§ 9.10 The Optional WTO Public Procurement Code

Where public procurement is involved, and the taxpayer's money is at issue, virtually every nation has some form of legislation or tradition that favors buying from domestic suppliers. The Tokyo Round GATT Procurement Code was not particularly successful at opening up government purchasing. Only Austria, Canada, the twelve European Union states, Finland, Hong Kong, Israel, Japan, Norway, Singapore, Sweden, Switzerland and the United States adhered to that Procurement Code. This was also partly the result of the 1979 Code's many exceptions. For example, the Code did not apply to contracts below its threshold amount of $150,000 SDR (about $171,000 since 1988), service contracts, and procurement by entities on each country's reserve list (including most national defense items). Because procurement in the European Union and Japan is often decentralized, many contracts fell below the SDR threshold and were therefore GATT exempt. By dividing up procurement into smaller contracts national preferences were retained. United States government procurement tends to be more centralized and thus more likely to be covered by the GATT Code. This pattern may help explain why Congress restrictively amended the Buy American Act in 1988.

Chapter 13 of the North American Free Trade Area Agreement opened government procurement to U.S., Canadian and Mexican suppliers on contracts as small as $25,000. However, the goods supplied must have at least 50 percent North American content. These special procurement rules effectively created an exception to the GATT Procurement Code which otherwise applied. The thresholds are $50,000 for goods and services provided to federal agencies and $250,000 for government-owned enterprises (notably PEMEX and CFE). These regulations are particularly important because Mexico, unlike Canada, has not traditionally joined in GATT/WTO procurement codes. In December 2011 Canada-U.S. procurement provisions were incorporated in a long awaited agreement to expand the WTO Procurement Code. This expansion selectively brings more types of procurement contracts, notable service contracts, and more sub-central government entities within the Code's coverage. Contract value thresholds are also selectively lowered.

The Uruguay Round Procurement Code took effect in 1996 and replaced the 1979 Tokyo Round GATT Procurement Code. The Uruguay Round (WTO) Code expanded the coverage of the prior GATT Code to include procurement of services, construction, government-owned utilities, and some state and local (subcentral) contracts. The

U.S. and the European Union applied the new Code's provisions on government-owned utilities and subcentral contracts as early as April 15, 1994. Most developing nations have opted out of the WTO Procurement Code.

Various improvements to the procedural rules surrounding procurement practices and dispute settlement under the WTO Code attempt to reduce tensions in this difficult area. For example, an elaborate system for bid protests is established. Bidders who believe the 1979 Code's procedural rules have been abused will be able to lodge, litigate and appeal their protests. The WTO Procurement Code became part of U.S. law in December of 1994 under the Uruguay Round Agreements Act. The United States has made, with few exceptions, all procurement by executive agencies subject to the Federal Acquisition Regulations under the Code's coverage (i.e., to suspend application of the normal Buy American preferences to such procurement). Thirteen U.S. states have not ratified the WTO Procurement Code. The economic stimulus and auto bail-out legislation of the Obama administration have raised questions of U.S. compliance with the Code.

§ 9.11 The General Agreement on Trade in Services (GATS)

Because protectionist barriers to international trade in services were stifling, the United States and several other countries insisted that there should be a General Agreement on Trade in Services (GATS). In the United States, services account for over two-thirds of the Nation's GNP and provide jobs for nearly two-thirds of the work force. Services account for almost one-third of U.S. exports.

Market access for services is a major focus of the General Agreement on Trade in Services (GATS), a product of the Uruguay Round of Negotiations. The GATS defines the supply of services broadly to include providing services across borders or inside member states with or without a commercial presence therein. The core commitment is to afford most-favored-nation treatment to service providers, subject to country-specific exemptions, such as audio-visual services in the EU.

The U.S. Congress approved and implemented the GATS agreement in December of 1994 under the Uruguay Round Agreements Act. Subsequently, early in 1995, the United States refused to extend most-favored-nation treatment to financial services. The European Union, Japan and other GATS nations then entered into an interim 2–year agreement which operated on MFN principles.

Financial services was revisited in 1996–97 with further negotiations aimed at bringing the United States into the fold. These negotiations bore fruit late in 1997 with 70 nations (including the United States) joining in an agreement that covers 95 percent of trade in banking, insurance, securities and financial information. This agreement took effect March 1, 1999.

National laws that restrict the number of firms in a market, that are dependent upon local "needs tests" or that mandate local incorporation are regulated by the GATS. Various "transparency" rules require disclosure of all relevant laws and regulations, and these must be administered reasonably, objectively and impartially. Specific service market access and national treatment commitments are made by various governments in schedules attached to the agreement. These commitments may be modified or withdrawn after 3 years, subject to a right of compensation that can be arbitrated. Certain mutual recognition of education and training for service-sector licensing will occur. State monopolies or exclusive service providers may continue, but must not abuse their positions. Detailed rules are created in annexes to the GATS on financial, telecommunications and air transport services.

The GATS has reduced unilateral U.S. action under Section 301 to gain access to foreign markets for U.S. service providers. This reduction flows from U.S. adherence to the Dispute Settlement Understanding (DSU) that accompanies the Uruguay Round accords. The DSU obligates its signatories to follow streamlined dispute settlement procedures under which unilateral retaliation is restrained until the offending nation has failed to conform to a World Trade Organization ruling.

GATS, and the 1996 Protocol on Telecommunications and 1997 Protocol on Financial Services, have generated only a handful of WTO disputes:

1. EC—Regime for the Importation, Sale and Distribution of Bananas, WT/DS 27/AB/R (1997) (traders of goods may also be traders of services, such as wholesaling or retailing, GATS Articles II and XVII apply to de jure and de facto discrimination).

2. Canada—Certain Measures Concerning Periodicals, WT/DS 31/AB/R (1997) (GATT and GATS co-exist, no override).

3. Canada—Certain Measures Affecting The Automotive Industry, WT/DS 139, 142/ R (2000) (coverage under GATS must be determined before assessment of consistency with GATS obligations).

4. Mexico—Measures Affecting Telecommunication Services WT/DS 204/R (2004) (Mexican cross-border interconnection rates not cost-oriented and unreasonable in breach of Telecoms Annex, failure to allow access to private leased-circuits also violated commitments) (settled with rate reductions and increased access).

5. United States—Measures Affecting The Cross–Border Supply of Gambling and Betting Services, WT/DS 285/AB/R (2005) (gambling included in U.S. recreational services' commitments, U.S. import ban amounted to "zero quota" in breach of GATS Article XVI, necessary to protect public morals under Article XIV defense but discriminatory enforcement regarding Interstate Horseracing Act fails to meet "chapeau" requirements) (U.S. pays compensation to all GATS signatories except Antigua and Barbuda, the complaining party. . . . $21 million retaliation authorized in 2008).

§ 9.12 The WTO and Rules of Origin

The Uruguay Round accord on rules of origin is, in reality, an agreement to agree. A negotiations schedule was established along with a WTO Committee to work with the Customs Cooperation Council on harmonized rules of origin. Certain broad guiding principles for the negotiations are given and considered binding until agreement is reached. These principles are:

- rules of origin applied to foreign trade must not be more stringent than applied to domestic goods.
- rules of origin must be administered consistently, uniformly, impartially and reasonably.
- origin assessments must be issued within 150 days of a request and remain valid for three years.
- new or modified rules or origin may not be applied retroactively.
- strict confidentiality rules apply to information submitted confidentially for rule of origin determinations.

§ 9.13 The WTO TRIPs Agreement

The Uruguay Round accords of late 1993 include an agreement on trade-related intellectual property rights (TRIPs). This agreement is binding upon the over 155 nations that are members of the World Trade Organization. In the United States, the TRIPs agreement must be ratified and implemented by Congress. There is a general requirement of national and most-favored-nation treatment among the parties.

The TRIPs Code covers the gamut of intellectual property. On copyrights, there is protection for computer programs and databases, rental authorization controls for owners of computer software and sound recordings, a 50–year motion picture and sound recording copyright term, and a general obligation to comply with the Berne Convention (except for its provisions on moral rights). On patents, the Paris Convention prevails, product and process patents are to be available for pharmaceuticals and agricultural chemicals, limits are placed on compulsory licensing, and a general 20–year patent term is created. For trademarks, service marks become registrable, internationally prominent marks receive enhanced protection, the linking of local marks with foreign trademarks is prohibited, and compulsory licensing is banned. In addition, trade secret protection is assisted by TRIPs rules enabling owners to prevent unauthorized use or disclosure. Integrated circuits are covered by rules intended to improve upon the Washington Treaty. Lastly, industrial designs and geographic indicators of alcoholic beverages (e.g., Canadian Whiskey) are also part of the TRIPs regime.

Infringement and anticounterfeiting remedies are included in the TRIPs, for both domestic and international trade protection. There are specific provisions governing injunctions, damages, customs seizures, and discovery of evidence.

Late in 2001, the Doha Round of WTO negotiations were launched. These negotiations have reconsidered the TRIPs agreement, particularly as it applies to developing nations. In addition, a Declaration on the TRIPs Agreement and Public Health was issued at the Qatar Ministerial Conference. This Declaration includes the following statement:

> We agree that the TRIPs Agreement does not prevent Members from taking measures to protect public health. Accordingly, while reiterating our commitment to the TRIPs Agreement, we affirm that the Agreement can and should be interpreted and implemented in a manner sup-

portive of WTO Members' right to protect public health and, in particular, to promote access to medicines for all.

By mid–2003, a "Medicines Agreement" was finally reached on how to implement this Declaration. Compulsory licensing and/or importation of generic copies of patented medicines needed to address developing nation public health problems are authorized. Such activities may not pursue industrial or commercial policy objectives, and different packaging and labeling must be used in an effort at minimizing the risk of diversion of the generics to developed country markets. Under pressure from the United States, a number of more advanced developing nations (such as Mexico, Singapore and Qatar) agreed not to employ compulsory licensing except in situations of national emergency or extreme urgency. Canada, on the other hand has licensed production of drugs of Rwanda and other nations incapable of pharmaceutical production.

Dozens of TRIPs complaints have been initiated under WTO dispute settlement procedures. Most have been settled, but a few have resulted in WTO Panel and Appellate Body Reports:

1. India—Patent Protection for Pharmaceutical and Agricultural Chemical Products, WT/DS 50/AB/R (1998) ("mailbox rule" patent applications for subjects not patentable in India until 2005 inadequate, denial of exclusive marketing rights in breach of TRIPs Article 70.9).

2. Canada—Term of Patent Protection, WT/DS 170/AB/R (2000) (pre–TRIPs Canadian patents must receive 20 year term).

3. U.S.—Section 110 (5) Copyright Act, WT/DS 160/ R (2000) (copyright exemption for "homestyle" dramatic musical works consistent with Berne Convention, "business use" exemption inconsistent with Berne and therefore in breach of TRIPs) (settled by payment).

4. Canada—Pharmaceutical Patents, WT/DS 114/ R (2000) (Canadian generic pharmaceutical regulatory review and stockpiling patent rights' exceptions not sufficiently "limited").

5. U.S.—Section 211 Appropriations Act, WT/DS 176/AB/R (2002) (prohibition against registering marks confiscated by Cuban government, e.g. HAVANA CLUB rum, without original owner's consent violates Paris Convention and TRIPs, trade names covered by TRIPs).

6. EC—Trademarks and Geographical Indications WT/DS 174, 290/R (2005) (EC regulation violates national treatment and most-favored treatment obligations to non-EC nationals, procedural violations also found).

7. China—Measures Affecting The Protection and Enforcement of Intellectual Property Rights, WT/DS 362R (Jan.26, 2009) (China's implementation of TRIPs upheld as to criminal law thresholds and disposal of confiscated, infringing goods by customs authorities, rejected as to denial of copyright protection for works not authorized for release in China).

8. China—Measures Affecting Trading Rights and Distribution Services for Certain Publications and Audiovisuals Entertainment Products, WT/DS 363/AB/R (Dec. 31, 2009) (China's ADV restrictions limited to state-owned or approved channels violate WTO Accession Protocol, GATT 1994 and GATS; Restraints not necessary to protect public morals).

9. European Communities—Information Technology Tariffs, WT/DS 375–377 (Aug.16, 2010) (EU tariffs on cable converter boxes with Net capacity, flat panel computer screens and printers that also scan, fax or copy violated 1996 Information Technology Agreement zero tariff rules).

§ 9.14 U.S. International Trade Administration (ITA)

The international trade of the United States is regulated by a number of different governmental bodies. The International Trade Administration is part of the Commerce Department, which in turn is part of the Executive Branch of the federal government. The Commerce Department also contains the Office of Export Licensing and the Office of Anti-boycott Compliance. The International Trade Commission is an independent federal government agency, and the Court of International Trade is part of the Judicial Branch of the United States government. Lastly, the Office of the United States Trade Representative works directly under the President.

The International Trade Administration (ITA) is an administrative agency. In broadest terms, the ITA is to foster, promote and develop world trade, and to bring U.S. companies into the business of selling overseas. At a practical level, the ITA is designed to be helpful to the individual business by providing it with information concerning the "what, where, how and when" of imports and exports, such as information sources, requirements for a particular trade license, forms for an international license agreement or procedures to start a business in a foreign country. The ITA provides business data and educational programs to United States businesses. In addition to these duties, the ITA also decides whether there are subsidies in countervailing duty (CVD)[3] cases or sales at less than fair value in antidumping duty (AD) cases.[4] Prior to 1980, such decisions were made by the Treasury Department. The ITA is not, however, involved in decision-making in escape clause (Section 201), market disruption (Section 406) and unfair import practices (Section 337) proceedings.

§ 9.15 U.S. International Trade Commission (ITC)

The United States International Trade Commission (ITC) is an independent bipartisan agency created in 1916 by an act of Congress. The ITC is the successor to the United States Tariff Commission. In 1974, the name was changed and the ITC was given additional authority, powers and responsibilities. The Commission's present powers and duties include preparing reports pertaining to international economics and foreign trade for the Executive Branch, the Congress, other government agencies and the public. To carry out this responsibility, the ITC conducts investigations which entail extensive research, specialized studies and a high degree of expertise in all matters relating to the commercial and international trade policies of the United States. Statutory investigations conducted by the ITC include unfair import trade practice determinations (Section 337 proceedings),[5] domestic industry injury determinations in antidumping and countervailing duty cases,[6] and escape clause and market disruption import relief recommendations.[7] The ITC also advises the President about probable economic effects on domestic industries and consumers of modifications on duties and other trade barriers incident to proposed trade agreements with foreign countries.

The ITC is intended to be a quasi-judicial, bipartisan, independent agency providing trade expertise to both Congress and the Executive. Congress went to great lengths to create a bipartisan body to conduct international trade studies and provide reliable expert information. The six Commissioners of the ITC are appointed

---

3 See Chapter 13.

4 See Chapter 12.

5 See Chapter 24.

6 See Chapters 12 and 13.

7 See Chapter 15.

by the President and confirmed by the United States Senate for nine year terms, unless appointed to fill an unexpired term. The presence of entrenched points of view is inhibited because a Commissioner who has served for more than five years is not eligible for reappointment. Not more than three Commissioners may be members of the same political party. The Chairman and Vice–Chairman are designated by the President for two year terms. No Chairman may be of the same political party as the preceding Chairman, nor may the President designate two Commissioners of the same political party as Chairman and Vice–Chairman. Congress further guaranteed the independence of the ITC from the Executive Branch by having its budget submitted directly to the Congress. This means that its budget is not subject to review by the Office of Management and Budget.

§ 9.16 U.S. Court of International Trade (CIT)

The United States Court of International Trade (CIT) is an Article III court under the United States Constitution for judicial review of civil actions arising out of import transactions and certain federal statutes affecting international trade. It grew out of the Board of General Appraisers (a quasi-judicial administrative unit within the Treasury Department which reviewed decisions by United States Customs officials concerning the amount of duties to be paid on imports in actions arising under the tariff acts) and the United States Customs Court which had essentially the same jurisdiction and powers. The President, with the advice and consent of the Senate, appoints the nine judges who constitute the Court of International Trade. Not more than five of the nine judges may belong to any one political party.

The geographical jurisdiction of the Court of International Trade extends throughout the United States, and it is also authorized to hold hearings in foreign countries. The court has exclusive subject-matter jurisdiction to decide any civil action commenced against the United States, its agencies or its officers arising from any law pertaining to revenue from imports, tariffs, duties or embargoes or enforcement of these and other customs regulations. This includes disputes regarding trade embargoes, quotas, customs classification and valuation, country of origin determinations and denials of protests by the U.S. Customs Service.

The court's exclusive jurisdiction also includes any civil action commenced by the United States that arises out of an import transaction, and authority to review final agency decisions concerning antidumping and countervailing duty matters, the eligibility of workers, firms and communities who are economically harmed by foreign imports for trade adjustment assistance, disputes concerning the release of confidential business information, and decisions to deny, revoke or suspend the licenses of customs brokers. However, the CIT does *not* have jurisdiction over disputes involving restrictions on imported merchandise where public safety or health issues are raised. This limitation on CIT jurisdiction arises because such issues involving domestic goods would be determined by other regulatory bodies, and only referral to United States District Courts can ensure uniform treatment of both imports and domestically produced goods.

The standard for the judicial review exercised by the CIT varies from case to case. In some instances, such as confidentiality orders, a *de novo* trial is undertaken. In others, notably antidumping and countervailing duty cases, the standard is one of substantial evidence or arbitrary, capricious or unlawful action or an abuse of discretion. In trade adjustment assistance litigation, the administrative determinations are considered conclusive absent substantial evidentiary support in the record with the CIT empowered to order the taking of further evidence. Unless otherwise specified by statute, the Administrative Procedure Act governs the judicial review by the CIT of U.S. international trade law. The CIT possesses all the remedial powers, legal and equitable, of a United States District Court, including authority to enter money judgments for or against the United States, but with three limitations. First, in an action challenging a trade adjustment ruling, the court may not issue an injunction or writ of mandamus. Second, the CIT may order disclosure of confidential information only as specified in Section 777(c)(2) of the Tariff Act of 1930. Third, the CIT may order only declaratory relief for suits brought under the provision allowing the court accelerated review because of a showing of irreparable harm.

The CIT must give due deference to Customs Service regulations under *Chevron* rules[8] even when undertaking *de novo* review.[9] CIT decisions are first appealed to the Court of Appeals for the Federal Circuit (formerly to the Court of Customs and Patent Appeals), and ultimately to the United States Supreme Court.

---

[8] Chevron, U.S.A., Inc. v. Natural Resources Defense Council, Inc., 467 U.S. 837, 104 S.Ct. 2778, 81 L.Ed.2d 694 (1984).

[9] United States v. Haggar Apparel Co., 526 U.S. 380, 119 S.Ct. 1392, 143 L.Ed.2d 480 (1999).

§ 9.17 The USTR, Fast Track and U.S. Trade Agreements

Removing trade barriers is usually done on a reciprocal basis, and requires lengthy bargaining and negotiations between the sovereigns. Congress is not adapted to carry on such negotiations, so it routinely delegates limited authority to the President to negotiate agreements reducing trade restrictions. Recent efforts to reduce trade restrictions have been multilateral, bilateral and trilateral. Congress has intermittently given quite broad authority to the President, or his representative, to reduce or eliminate United States tariffs on a reciprocal "fast track" basis. Fast track originated as a compromise after Congress refused to ratify two major components of the Kennedy Round of GATT negotiations. NAFTA and the Uruguay Round WTO agreements were negotiated and implemented under fast track procedures, discussed below.

In response to Section 1104 of the Trade Agreements Act of 1979,[10] the President reviewed the structure of the international trade functions of the Executive Branch. Although this did not lead to the establishment of a new Department of International Trade and Investment, it did lead to enhancement of the Office of the Special Representative for Trade Negotiations,[11] which has since been renamed the United States Trade Representative (USTR). The powers of the USTR were expanded and its authority given a legislative foundation. The USTR is appointed by the President, with the advice and consent of the Senate.[12] The Office of the USTR has been the principal vehicle through which trade negotiations have been conducted on behalf of the United States. Among other things, the USTR has had continuing responsibility in connection with implementation of the WTO Agreements and U.S. free trade agreements. The USTR is the contact point for persons who desire an investigation of instances of noncompliance with any trade agreement.

In 1988, the duties of the USTR were significantly expanded in conjunction with an overhaul of Section 301 of the Trade Act of 1974.[13] Section 301 creates a controversial unilateral trade remedy which principally has been used to obtain foreign market access for U.S. exports. Prior to 1988, the President directly administered Section 301. Thereafter, as amended by the Omnibus Trade and Competitiveness Act, the USTR assumed this role along with new duties

---

10 P.L. 96–39.

11 The office had been established by an Executive Order in 1963.

12 19 U.S.C.A. § 2171.

13 See Chapter 19.

governing the Super 301 and Special 301 procedures created in 1988. Moreover, since the 1988 Act expanded the coverage of Section 301 and introduced mandatory (not discretionary) remedies, the USTR has been in the spotlight of many domestic industry complaints about foreign governments. Such complaints can reach breaches of international agreements as well as unjustifiable, unreasonable or discriminatory foreign country practices.

The Trade Act of 2002 (P.L. 107–210) authorized President Bush to negotiate international trade agreements on a fast track basis, a procedure that requires Congress to vote within 90 legislative days up or down, without amendments, on U.S. trade agreements. In return, Congress receives substantial notice and opportunity to influence U.S. trade negotiations conducted by the USTR. See 19 U.S.C. § 3801 et seq. The President and the USTR quickly completed and Congress approved free trade agreements with Chile and Singapore, and thereafter with Morocco, Australia, Central America/Dominican Republic, Peru, Jordan, Oman, and Bahrain. The President's fast track authority expired in July of 2007 with agreements for Colombia, Panama and Korea completed but not approved by Congress. Several years later these agreements were ratified under the Obama administration. For U.S. free trade partners, fast track suggests that once they reach a deal Congress cannot alter it, though in recent years Congress has effectively tacked on additional requirements, notably regarding labor and the environment.

Recognizing that China is a rapidly developing economic superstar, the United States under the Obama administration is pursuing what resembles a "containment" strategy by promoting a "Trans-Pacific Partnership." This strategy seeks to bring the U. S., Australia, New Zealand, Malaysia, Chile, Peru, Brunei, Singapore, and notably Vietnam into a broad trade, technology and investment alliance. Mexico, Canada and Japan have expressed interest in joining this alliance. In 2013, the United States and the European Union commenced difficult negotiations on a Transatlantic Trade and Investment Partenership agreement.

Hundreds of bilateral free trade agreements lattice the world, including for example the European Union and South Africa, Canada and Costa Rica, China and Chile, Japan and Singapore. Mexico has dozens of bilateral free trade agreements. The EU is working on bilateral FTAs with India and Canada. Japan and India are negotiating bilaterally with Canada. At this point the only nation without a bilateral free trade deal is Mongolia. A variety of factors help explain why bilaterals have become the leading edge of international trade law and policy. Difficulties encountered in the Uruguay, "Seattle" and Doha Rounds of multilateral trade negotiations are certainly crucial. GATT/WTO regulatory failures regarding bilaterals have also fueled this reality. Yet these "negatives" do not fully explain the feeding frenzy of bilaterals.

A range of attractions are also at work. For example, bilaterals often extend to subject matters beyond WTO competence. Foreign investment law is a prime example, and many bilaterals serve as investment magnets. Government procurement, optional at the WTO level, is often included in bilaterals. Competition policy and labor and environmental matters absent from the WTO are sometimes covered in bilaterals. In addition, bilaterals can reach beyond the scope of existing WTO agreements. Services is one "WTO-plus" area where this is clearly true. Intellectual property rights are also being "WTO-plussed" in bilateral free trade agreements. Whether this amounts to competitive trade liberalization or competitive trade imperialism is a provocative question.

§ 9.18 An Introduction to the IMF

Most nations have a national currency and pursue an internal monetary policy to meet their own political and economic goals. Twelve EU nations have joined in a common currency, the Euro, managed by the European Central Bank. No central authority controls a world monetary system; monetary policy is decentralized. Since 1944, nations have coordinated national monetary policies principally through the International Monetary Fund (IMF). Both the IMF and the International Bank for Reconstruction and Development (the "World Bank") arose out of the Bretton Woods Conference in 1944. The World Bank was to facilitate loans by capital surplus countries (e.g., then the United States) to countries needing foreign investment for economic redevelopment after World War II. The IMF was to stabilize currency exchange rates, assist countries in their balance of payments, and repair other war damage to the international monetary system. Twenty-nine countries including the United States became party to the IMF Articles of Agreement in 1945. Today, over 150 countries are members of the IMF.

IMF Operations

The IMF goals are to facilitate the expansion and balanced growth of international trade, to assist in the elimination of foreign exchange restrictions which hamper the growth of international trade, and to shorten the duration and lessen the disequilibrium in the international balances of payments of members. The mitigation of wide currency fluctuations is achieved through a complex lending system which permits a country to borrow money from other Fund members or from the Fund (by way of "Special Drawing Rights" or "SDRs") for the purpose of stabilizing the relationship of its currency to other world currencies. These monetary drawing arrangements permit a member country to support its national currency's relative value when compared with national currencies of other countries, especially the "hard" ("reserve") currencies such as the Swiss franc, the Euro, Japanese yen, and United States dollar.

In recent years, IMF loans have normally been "conditioned" upon adoption of specific economic reforms by debtor states, especially in Asia and Latin America. This has led to the perception that the IMF is the world's "sheriff", setting the terms for refinancing national debts and protecting the interests of commercial bank creditors. The IMF does function as the first line of negotiation in an international "debt crisis," and commercial and national banks often conform their loans to IMF conditions. These IMF conditions can have dramatic political and social repercussions in debtor nations.

From 2006 onwards, nations paid off their IMF debt in record numbers. Argentina did so with an assist from Venezuela. Brazil, Russia, Bolivia, Uruguay, Indonesia, the Philippines and others joined in the flight from IMF loan conditions. The IMF's loan portfolio stood at $100 billion in 2003. By 2008, that portfolio was approaching zero, the IMF was running a budget deficit, cutting staff and proposing sales of gold reserves. Many commentators wondered aloud what was the role of the IMF without loans?

The global financial and economic crisis that commenced late in 2008 muted this commentary. The IMF "pre-approved" unconditional, short-term loans to nations it deems sound but facing liquidity problems, such as Mexico, Brazil and South Korea. Conditional IMF loans were made to Iceland, Pakistan, Ukraine and Hungary. The IMF is heavily involved with crisis-driven EURO bailouts, notably those involving Greece, Portugal, Ireland and Cyprus. Injections of new capital have made it clear that the IMF is back in the loan business for years to come.

The IMF, like any bureaucracy in search of a mission, also drafted a Code of Best Practices for "Sovereign Wealth Funds" (SWFs). Such Funds are said to hold over $3 trillion, and are expanding rapidly. Abu Dhabi, Saudi Arabia, Kuwait, Singapore, Russia, China and Norway (for example) all have large SWFs, many of which played an important role in bailing out U.S. banks and securities firms with heavy sub-prime loan exposure. In 2008, developing nations (particularly their central banks) bought over 50 percent of the net foreign purchases of U.S. government securities. In a role reversal, the United States has become heavily dependent on SWF and developing world capital inflows to finance its large national debt and enormous international trade deficit. The primary concern is that SWFs and developing nations might use their power for political purposes. Their emergence further diminishes the need for IMF loans. As yet the SWFs have not "conditioned" their lending or investment decisions.

Special Drawing Rights (SDRs)

The International Monetary Fund has established a form of international money which is not a national currency and is called a Special Drawing Right (SDR). Certificates of deposit are denominated in SDRs; short-term SDR loans may be obtained commercially; and some OPEC nations have begun to value their national currencies in SDRs. Mechanically, an SDR is an international medium of exchange having a 1991 composite value based 39 percent on the U.S. dollar, 32 percent on the Euro, 18 percent on the Japanese yen, and 11 percent on the British pound. Each exchange rate fluctuation in any one of these "basket currencies" produces commensurately only a smaller, fractional fluctuation in the value of an SDR. In the wake of the global financial crisis that commenced in 2008, China has been promoting the SDR as an alternative to the U.S. dollar's dominance.

Although the SDR has been talked about as if it is a supranational currency, the SD "Right" is more technically a "unit of account" created by an IMF process. When an IMF member country, having a negative balance of payments position, runs short of its currency "reserves" (which may be its stocks of "hard" "reserve" currencies or gold), the member country may exercise its "Right" to make a "Special Drawing" from the IMF Special Drawing Account (e.g., the country may exercise its Special Drawing Right to ask the IMF to arrange for that country to receive $40 million (U.S.) worth of currency other than gold). Upon receipt of the Drawing "request", the IMF approaches another member country having a fuller stock of "reserves" (which "back up" its national currency), and requests that country to provide currency to the requesting country (e.g. to provide $40 million worth of currency other than gold).

In return for having supplied the currency, the supplying country acquires additional Special Drawing Rights (e.g. worth $40 million) which it may revoke if ever its currency "reserves" get too low. Each IMF Member Country participating in the SDR scheme has a finite allocation of SDRs available for its possible use. A net result of the SDR scheme is that countries "swap" currencies to help other countries from time to time in maintaining existing, relative values between their national currency and other currencies of the world.

Chapter 10

UNITED STATES TARIFFS AND DUTY FREE IMPORTS

Table of Sections

---

§ 10.1 U.S. Tariffs, Duty Free Entry

This chapter focuses on United States tariffs under the Harmonized Tariff Schedule (HTS). Column 1 tariffs, known as most-favored-nation (MFN) tariffs, are the lower and most likely to be applicable. Column 2 tariffs, originating in the Smoot–Hawley Tariff Act of 1930, are the higher and least likely to be applicable. United States tariffs generally take one of three forms. The most common is an ad valorem rate. Such tariffs are assessed in proportion to the value of the article. Tariffs may also be assessed at specific rates or compound rates. Specific rates may be measured by the pound or other weight. A compound rate is a mixture of an ad valorem and specific rate tariff. Tariff rate quotas involve limitations on imports at a specific tariff up to a certain amount. Imports in excess of that amount are not prohibited, but are subject to a higher rate of tariff. Thus tariff rate quotas tend to restrict imports that are in excess of the specified quota for the lower tariff level.

Some goods may enter the United States at less than most-favored-nation tariff levels or duty free. This occurs because of special tariff preferences incorporated into United States law (outlined below). It is important to realize that these preferences create valuable trading opportunities for U.S. importers and exporters located in qualified nations. These people are the clients for whom lawyers work to secure duty free entry into the United States market. Duty free entry is, of course, the ultimate goal of all exporters and importers involved in United States trade. Various free trade and customs union agreements (including NAFTA and other FTAs of the United States) achieving duty free outcomes are discussed in Chapter 21. The European Union is reviewed in Chapter 26.

Perhaps the widest of the duty free programs is known as the Generalized System of Preferences (GSP) adopted through the GATT. The GSP is a complex system of duty free tariff preferences benefiting selected goods originating in developing nations and intended to foster their economic improvement. A second program is the Caribbean Basin Economic Recovery Act of 1983 (also known as the Caribbean Basin Initiative), which permits certain goods to enter the United States market duty free. To a significant degree, the CBI duty free program was duplicated in the Andean Trade Preference Act of 1991 initially benefiting Colombian, Ecuadorian, Bolivian and Peruvian goods. Another important "duty free" category allows fabricated U.S.-made components shipped abroad for assembly to return to the U.S. without tariffs on the value of the components. Authorization for this importation is found in Section 9802.00.80 of the Harmonized Tariff Schedule. Goods of this type are subject to a United States Customs duty limited in amount to the value added by foreign assembly operations. This provision is perhaps best known in connection with Mexican maquiladoras.

- The least restrictive rules of origin for duty free entry of goods into the United States apply to its insular possessions. These include American Samoa, Guam, Johnson Island, Kingman Reef, Midway Islands, Puerto Rico, the U.S. Virgin Islands and Wake Island. Generally speaking, goods from such possessions may contain up to 70 percent foreign value and still be admitted duty free.

- Some of these duty free programs overlap and effectively compete with each other. It might be helpful to think of them in terms of concentric geographic circles. The widest circle is Section

9802.00.80 which applies to the entire globe. The next circle represents the GSP system and most developing nations. Inside that circle is the Caribbean Basin Initiative, the Andean Initiative, and U.S. insular possessions followed by the North American, and other U.S. Free Trade Agreements. A manufacturer based in the Caribbean may seek duty free entry into the United States market under Section 9802.00.80, the GSP program or the CBI, but not U.S. free trade agreements, save the Dominican Republic. To most developing nations, these are selectively discriminatory duty free programs that undermine their GSP benefits.

- Unusual trade opportunities can arise by linking U.S. duty free entry programs with those of the European Union (EU). For example, the Union has its own complicated and different GSP program, its equivalent of Section 9802.00.80, and two selective duty free programs for developing nations. The latter are known as its Mediterranean Policy and Lomé/Cotonou Conventions.[1] A producer in Israel can quite possibly gain duty free access to the EU (under its Mediterranean Policy) and to the United States (under the Israeli-U.S. FTA). A producer in Jamaica might achieve similar results under the Lomé/Cotonou Conventions, the CBI and/or the GSP programs of the EU and the United States.

§ 10.2 The Origins of United States Tariffs

Article I, Section 8, of the United States Constitution authorizes Congress to levy uniform tariffs on imports. Tariff legislation must originate in the House of Representatives. Although tariffs were primarily viewed as revenue-raising measures at the founding of the nation, it was not long before tariffs became used for openly protectionist purposes. The Tariff Act of 1816 initiated this change in outlook. During much of the Nineteenth Century, the United States legislated heavy protective tariffs. These were justified as necessary to protect the country's infant industries and to force the South to engage in more trade with the North (not with Europe). Exceptions were made to the high level of tariffs for selected United States imports under conditional most-favored-nation reciprocity treaties. The first of these treaties involved Canada (1854) and Hawaii (1875).

As the United States moved into the 20th Century, additional tariffs in excess of the already high level of protection were authorized. "Countervailing duty" tariffs were created in 1890 to combat export subsidies of European nations, particularly Germany. After

1 See, generally, R. Folsom, Principles of European Union Law (West Group), Chapter 6.

1916, additional duties could also be assessed if "dumping practices" were involved. Early American dumping legislation was largely a reaction to marketplace competition from foreign cartels. Throughout all of these years the constitutionality of protective tariffs was never clearly resolved. In 1928, however, the United States Supreme Court firmly ruled that the enactment of protective tariffs was constitutional.[2] This decision, followed by the crash of the stock market in 1929, led to the enactment of the Smoot–Hawley Tariff Act of 1930. This Act set some of the highest rates of tariff duties in the history of the United States. It represents the last piece of tariff legislation that Congress passed without international negotiations. These tariffs remain part of United States law and are generally referred to as "Column 2 tariffs" under the Harmonized Tariff Schedule (HTS).

Since 1930, changes in the levels of tariffs applicable to goods entering the United States have chiefly been achieved through international trade agreements negotiated by the President and affirmed by Congress. During the 1930s and 40s, the Smoot–Hawley tariffs generally applied unless altered through bilateral trade agreements. The Reciprocal Trade Agreements Act of 1934[3] gives the President the authority to enter into such agreements, and under various extensions this authority remains in effect today. An early agreement of this type was the Canadian Reciprocal Trade Agreement of 1935.

§ 10.3 Column 1 Tariffs and the GATT/WTO

The Trade Agreements Extension Act of 1945 authorized the President to conduct multilateral negotiations in the trade field. It was out of this authority that the General Agreement on Tariffs and Trade (GATT) was negotiated. The GATT became effective on January 1, 1948 and was implemented in the United States by executive order. Indeed, despite its wide-ranging impact on United States tariff levels since 1948, the GATT was never ratified by the United States Congress. Nevertheless, it is the source of the principal tariffs assessed today on imports into the United States. These duties, known as most-favored-nation (MFN) tariffs or "Column 1 tariffs," have been dramatically reduced over the years through successive rounds of trade negotiations. They are unconditional MFN tariffs, meaning that reciprocity is not required in order for them to apply. Multilateral tariff agreements have predominated over bilateral negotiations since 1948.

---

[2] J.W. Hampton, Jr. & Co. v. United States, 276 U.S. 394, 48 S.Ct. 348, 72 L.Ed. 624 (1928).

[3] 48 Stat. 943 (1934).

The term "most-favored-nation" is misleading in its suggestion of special tariff arrangements. It is more appropriate and since 1998 officially correct to think of MFN tariffs as the "normal" level of U.S. tariffs, to which there are exceptions resulting in the application of higher or lower tariffs. After the Tokyo Round of GATT negotiations in 1978, the average MFN tariff applied to manufactured imports into the United States was approximately 5.6 percent. Reductions in this level to approximately 3.5 percent have been accomplished under the Uruguay Round of 1994.

Tariff cuts on a wide range of information technology products were agreed to late in 1996. By the year 2000, the United States, the European Union and most of East Asia had abolished tariffs on computers, electrical capacitors, calculators, ATM's, fax and answering machines, digital copiers and video cameras, computer diskettes, CD–ROM drives, computer software, fiber optical cables and hundreds of other items. This agreement covers more than 90 percent of all information technology trade.

In early 1997, agreement on liberalizing trade and reducing tariffs on basic telecommunications equipment was reached by 69 nations. This agreement took effect Feb. 5, 1998. Later that year, a WTO declaration imposed standstill obligations on all members to continue to refrain from applying customs duties to electronic commerce while negotiations are underway for more permanent rules in this area.

§ 10.4 Column 2 Tariffs

Between 1948 and 1951 the United States granted Column 1 most-favored-nation tariff treatment to goods originating from virtually every part of the world. Commencing in 1951, goods originating in nations controlled by communists were withdrawn from such tariff treatment. This had, and to some degree continues to have, the effect of treating the importation of goods from communist nations under Column 2 United States tariff headings. As a practical matter, very few such imports can overcome the high Smoot–Hawley tariffs embodied in Column 2.

The designation of which nations are "communist" for these purposes has varied over time. Yugoslavia was generally not treated as a communist country and its goods therefore entered under Column 1 MFN tariffs. Goods from the Balkans presently do so as well. Central and Eastern European nations were sometimes treated as communist countries, particularly during the 1950s and 1960s. This is no longer the case, and at this point nearly every European and

Baltic nation has been granted MFN status under United States tariff law. Belarus, Kazakhstan, Turkmenistan, Georgia, Azerbaijan, Tajikstan, Moldava, Kyrgyszstan, Armenia, Uzbekistan, the Russian Federation and Ukraine are also MFN beneficiaries. It is perhaps more useful, therefore, to indicate those nations that do not presently benefit from most-favored-nation tariff treatment. These include Cuba and North Korea. Goods from some of these nations are totally embargoed as a matter of national security; the law in this area is covered in Chapter 18. The most current listing of those nations whose products are subject to Column 2 tariffs can be found in General Headnote 3(b) to the HTS.

§ 10.5 The Jackson–Vanik Amendment

Section 402 of the 1974 Trade Act presently governs American grants of most-favored-nation tariff status.[4] This is commonly known as the "Jackson–Vanik Amendment." Under its terms, no products from a nonmarket economy nation may receive MFN treatment, nor may that country participate in U.S. financial credit or guaranty programs, whenever the President determines that it denies its citizens the right or opportunity to emigrate, imposes more than nominal taxes on visas or other emigration documents, or imposes more than nominal charges on its citizens as a result of their desire to leave. These statutory conditions are widely thought to have been the product of United States desires to have the Soviet Union permit greater exodus of its Jewish population during the early 1970s. However, the passage of the Jackson–Vanik Amendment was an important factor in the Soviet decision to withdraw from a broad trade agreement with the United States at that time, and led to sharply curtailed Jewish emigration from the Soviet Union.

The application of Jackson–Vanik by the President is subject to a waiver by executive order whenever the President determines that such a waiver will substantially promote the objectives of freedom of emigration and the President has received assurances that the emigration practices of a particular nonmarket economy nation will lead substantially to the achievement of those objectives. If the President decides to exercise this waiver authority, the waiver must be renewed annually and reported to Congress. These reports and the exercise of presidential waivers have over the years been contentious. At one point Congress had the power to veto presidential waivers under the Jackson–Vanik Amendment. However, a 1983 decision of the United States Supreme Court strongly suggested

---

[4] 19 U.S.C.A. § 2432.

that these veto powers were unconstitutional.[5] The Customs and Trade Act of 1990 amended the Trade Act of 1974 so as to permit Congress to jointly resolve against presidential Jackson–Vanik waivers. These resolutions can be vetoed by the President, and the President's veto can in turn by overridden by Congress. It is thought that these amendments resolved the constitutional problems associated with Congressional vetoes of presidential action.

Congress and the President have disagreed significantly over the renewal of most-favored-nation treatment for Chinese goods. Questions surrounding China's emigration policies, and its general human rights record, were downplayed by U.S. authorities for many years prior to Tiananmen Square. As internal discord within China increased, especially in Tibet and more generally in connection with the Democracy Movement, the Jackson–Vanik amendment came to the forefront of Sino–American trade relations. President Bush's renewal of China's most favored nation status in 1990, 1991 and 1992 was heavily criticized.

Jackson–Vanik became the political fulcrum of Sino–American trade relations. Congress threatened but did not achieve a veto of the President's renewal of MFN tariffs for Chinese goods. Early in 1992, Congress adopted the United States–China Act of 1991. This law would have prohibited the President from recommending further extensions of MFN status to China unless he reports that the PRC has accounted for citizens detained or accused in connection with Tiananmen Square and has made significant progress in achieving specified objectives on human rights, trade and weapons proliferation. President Bush vetoed the Act and the Congress was unable to override that veto.

In 1993, President Clinton renewed China's MFN status subject to some general human-rights conditions, including "significant progress" in releasing political prisoners, allowing international groups access to prisons and respect for human rights in Tibet. This seemed to pacify Congress for the moment. But it engendered hostility and resistance in China. Less publicly, the United States business community opposed the linkage of human rights to MFN tariffs as its PRC trade and investment commitments and opportunities were endangered. China, meanwhile, had developed the world's fastest growing economy and it decided to force the issue. If anything, abuse of human rights in the PRC actually increased early in 1994, notably prior to a well-publicized visit of the U.S. Secre-

---

5 See Immigration and Naturalization Service v. Chadha, 462 U.S. 919, 103 S.Ct. 2764, 77 L.Ed.2d 317 (1983).

tary of State. With Congress increasingly split on the issue, President Clinton made what will probably prove to be an historic reversal in policy. In June of 1994, he renewed China's MFN tariff status without human rights conditions, limiting its coverage only as regards Chinese-made ammunition and guns.

President Clinton renewed China's MFN tariff status each year after 1994. Congress did not seek to override these decisions. In 1998, for the first time, President Clinton waived the Jackson–Vanik requirements for Vietnam. President George W. Bush did likewise. This waiver survived Congressional scrutiny. It opened the door to EXIMBANK and OPIC programs, as well as Column 1 MFN tariffs on Vietnamese goods entering the United States.

WTO members like China since 2001, Vietnam since 2007 and Russia since 2012 receive MFN tariff status automatically and unconditionally. Hence the Jackson-Vanik amendment no longer has significant application.

§ 10.6 U.S. Generalized System of Tariff Preferences—Statutory Authorization

The Generalized System of Preferences (GSP) originated in United Nations dialogues between the developed and the developing world. The third world successfully argued that it needed special access to industrial markets in order to improve and advance their economies. One problem with this approach is that it is contrary to the unconditional most-favored-nation principle contained in the GATT. Nevertheless, in 1971 the GATT authorized its parties to establish generalized systems of tariff preferences for developing nations. The European Union, Japan and nearly all other developed nations adopted GSP systems before the United States. Although similar in purpose, each of these systems is governed by a unique body of law of the "donor" country.

It was not until the Trade Act of 1974 that a GSP system was incorporated into United States tariff law. The Trade Act authorized GSP tariff preferences for ten years. The program was renewed in the Trade Act of 1984 for an additional nine years ending in July 1993. Incremental extensions have since been made pending a program review. The Trade Promotion Authority–Trade Adjustment Assistance Act of 2002 (TPA–TAA) renewed the GSP program through 2006 retroactive to its expiration on Sept. 30, 2001. Annual GSP renewals have followed. At this point, tens of billions of dollars worth of goods enter the U.S. market duty free under the GSP program, but it is estimated that more imports could achieve this status if traders better understood the GSP.

Title V of the Trade Act of 1974 contains the provisions authorizing the United States GSP program.[6] The United States GSP system, as presently operated, designates certain nations as "beneficiary developing countries." Unless a country is so designated, none of its imports can enter duty free under the GSP program. In addition, only selected goods are designated "eligible articles" for purposes of the GSP program. Thus, for duty free entry under the GSP program to occur, the goods must originate from a beneficiary nation and qualify as eligible articles.

§ 10.7 U.S. Generalized System of Tariff Preferences—USTR Petition Procedures

Any United States producer of an article that competes with GSP imports can file a petition with the United States Trade Representative (USTR) to have a country or particular products withdrawn from the program. This petitioning procedure can also be used in the reverse by importers and exporters to obtain product or beneficiary country status under the United States GSP program. The President is given broad authority to withdraw, suspend or limit the application of duty free entry under the GSP system.[7] Specific products from specific countries may be excluded from GSP benefits. In one case, for example, the President's decision to withdraw GSP benefits for "buffalo leather and goat and kid leather (not fancy)" from India was affirmed.[8] In another decision, the President's discretionary authority to deny GSP benefits to cut flowers from Colombia was similarly upheld.[9]

The President is required to take into consideration the impact of duty free entry on U.S. producers of like or directly competitive products. There is a set of regulations, codified at 15 C.F.R. Part 2007, which details the petitioning procedures used in connection with the certification of GSP eligible products or countries. These regulations require the domestic competitor to cite injury caused by duty free GSP imports. Within 6 months after the petition is filed, and a review by the United States Trade Representative (USTR) acting with the advice of the International Trade Commission (ITC)

---

6 19 U.S.C.A. §§ 501–506.

7 See 19 U.S.C.A. § 2464(a).

8 Florsheim Shoe Co. v. United States, 744 F.2d 787 (Fed.Cir.1984)

9 Sunburst Farms, Inc. v. United States, 797 F.2d 973 (Fed.Cir.1986).

has been undertaken, a decision on the petition will be rendered by the USTR.

§ 10.8 U.S. Generalized System of Tariff Preferences—Competitive Need Limitations

There are two statutory limitations on the applicability of duty free GSP entry. These are known as the "competitive need" limitations. They are found in Section 504 of the Trade Act of 1974, codified at 19 U.S.C.A. § 2464(c). The first statutory limitation focuses upon dollar volumes. Duty free entry is not permitted to any eligible product from a beneficiary country if during the preceding year that country exported to the United States more than a designated dollar volume of the article in question. There is a statutory formula for establishing this dollar volume limitation. In recent years, the maximum dollar volume limitation has ranged between 75 and 80 million dollars. The second statutory limitation on duty free GSP entry is framed in terms of percentages. Duty free entry is denied to products if during the preceding year the beneficiary country exported to the United States 50 percent or more of the total U.S. imports of that particular product.[10]

A complex system of waivers applies to the competitive need formulae. These are administered by the USTR and the President acting on advice of the International Trade Commission.[11] Basically, there are five possibilities for waivers of the competitive need limitations. The first can occur if the President decides that there is no like or directly competitive article produced in the United States and the imported product is exempt from the percentage but not the dollar value competitive need limitation. The second can occur under circumstances where the President determines that the imports in question are de minimis. The third possibility involves imports from the least developed developing nations, after notice to Congress. A list of these countries can be found in HTS General Note 3(c)(ii)(B). A fourth opportunity for a competitive need waiver exists when there has been an historical preferential trade relationship between the United States and the source country, and there is a trade agreement between that country and the United States, and the source country does not discriminate against or otherwise impose unjustifiable or unreasonable barriers to United States commerce.

---

[10] See West Bend Co. v. United States, 10 C.I.T. 146 (1986) (competitive impact still must be proven).

[11] See 19 U.S.C.A. § 2464(c).

Lastly, the President is authorized to waive the competitive need requirements of the GSP program if the International Trade Commission decides that the imports in question are not likely to have an adverse effect on the United States industry with which they compete, and the President determines that such a waiver is in the national economic interest.[12] In making waiver determinations, the President must consider generally the extent to which the beneficiary country has assured the United States that it will provide equitable and reasonable access to its markets and basic commodity resources. The President must also consider the extent to which the country provides adequate and effective means for foreigners to secure and exercise intellectual property rights. Once a waiver of the competitive need limitations is granted, it remains in effect until circumstances change and the President decides that it is no longer justified. Attorneys can play a useful role in monitoring Department of Commerce trade statistics to determine how close imports are coming under the competitive need formulae to restriction. By shifting to purchases of similar goods from another country, importers can preserve duty free entry and avoid the affects of these statutory restraints.

§ 10.9 U.S. Generalized System of Tariff Preferences—Country Eligibility

At present, thousands of products from over one hundred countries benefit from duty free GSP entry into the United States.[13] A list of GSP qualified nations and territories is presented in HTS General Note 3(c)(ii). Goods from insular possessions of the United States (e.g., American Samoa and the U.S. Virgin Islands) ordinarily receive duty free GSP entry "no less favorable" than allowed GSP beneficiary nations.[14] The President's power over the list of eligible countries and eligible products is wide and politically sensitive. For example, the President is required to evaluate, in determining whether a country is eligible under the U.S. GSP program, if it is upholding "internationally recognized workers' rights." Such rights include the right of association, the right to organize and bargain collectively, a prohibition against forced or compulsory labor, a minimum age for employment of children, and acceptable working conditions (minimum wages, hours of work, and occupational safety and health.)[15] In 2002, the definition of "core worker rights" for GSP

---

[12] See 19 U.S.C.A. § 2464(c)(3)(A).

[13] See Executive Order 11888 (Nov. 24, 1975, 40 F.R. 55276, extensively amended, for a detailed listing of eligible products and countries).

[14] 19 U.S.C.A. § 2462(d).

[15] 19 U.S.C.A. 2462(a).

country eligibility purposes was updated to include the ILO prohibition on the worst forms of child labor. The President must report annually to the Congress on the status of internationally recognized workers' rights in every GSP beneficiary country, but the issue is not open to private challenge.[16]

The President must also consider whether the foreign country is adequately protecting United States owners of intellectual property, (compliance with TRIPs is not necessarily sufficient), and whether its investment laws adversely affect U.S. exports. In addition, when designating GSP beneficiary nations, the Trade Act requires the President to take into account various factors which amount to a U.S. agenda on international economic relations:

(1) the desires of the country;

(2) its level of economic development;

(3) whether the EU, Japan or others extend GSP treatment to it;

(4) the extent to which the country provides equitable and reasonable access to its markets and its basic commodity resources, and the extent to which it will refrain from unreasonable export practices;

(5) the extent to which it provides adequate and effective intellectual property rights; and

(6) the extent to which it has taken action to reduce trade distorting investment practices (including export performance requirements) and reduced barriers to trade in services.[17]

No communist nations and no oil restraining OPEC nations (Indonesia, Ecuador and Venezuela are excepted) may benefit from the GSP program. Furthermore, the President must not designate countries that grant trade preferences to other *developed* nations. The President must also consider, in making GSP decisions, whether beneficiary countries are cooperative on drug enforcement, whether they are expropriators of U.S. property interests, whether they offer assistance to terrorists, and whether they are willing to recognize international arbitration awards. The President may

---

[16] See International Labor Rights Education & Research Fund v. Bush, 752 F.Supp. 495 (D.D.C.1990), *affirmed* 954 F.2d 745 (D.C.Cir.1992).

[17] 19 U.S.C.A. § 2462(c).

waive the expropriation requirement if it is determined that the country in question has paid prompt, adequate and effective compensation or entered into good faith negotiations or arbitration with the intent to do so.

The statutory bar against communist, oil restricting OPEC and preferentially trading countries as GSP beneficiaries is absolute. The bar against expropriating, drug dealing, arbitration award unenforcement, terrorist aiding and workers rights nonrecognition beneficiaries is discretionary with the President. The goods of such nations may still qualify if the President determines that GSP duty free entry would be in the national economic interest of the United States.[18] In applying these country eligibility criteria, past Presidents have disqualified a variety of nations from the U.S. GSP program. For example, Romania, Nicaragua, Paraguay, Chile, Burma, the Central African Republic and Liberia have all been disqualified in the past for failure to meet the workers' rights standards. Argentina and Honduras have lost GSP benefits for perceived failures to adequately protect U.S. pharmaceutical patents. Panama under General Noriega was rendered ineligible in 1988 because of the failure to cooperate on narcotics. Intellectual property piracy led to the suspension of Ukraine's country eligibility in the GSP program.

The President's review of a country's eligibility under the GSP program is ongoing. This has led to the reinstatement of GSP beneficiary nations. Russia was made a GSP beneficiary by President Clinton in the Fall of 1993. Any country designated as a beneficiary nation under the GSP program that is subsequently disqualified by exercise of Presidential discretion, or graduated, must receive 60 days notice from the President with an explanation of this decision.[19] This, in effect, presents the opportunity to reply and negotiate.

Since the GSP program originated within the GATT/WTO nearly all the beneficiary countries are members of that organization. It is not, however, mandatory for a developing nation to be a member of the WTO in order to receive GSP trade benefits from the United States. China is a WTO member, but for other reasons its goods do not qualify for GSP duty free entry. Other nations whose goods are not eligible are specifically listed in the Trade Act: Australia, Austria, Canada, European Union States, Finland, Iceland,

---

18 19 U.S.C.A. § 2462(b).

19 19 U.S.C.A. § 2462(a).

Japan, Monaco, New Zealand, Norway, Republic of South Africa, Sweden, and Switzerland.[20]

§ 10.10 U.S. Generalized System of Tariff Preferences—Product Eligibility

For each designated GSP beneficiary country, the President also issues a list of products from that country that qualify for duty free entry into the United States. The statutory authorization for the United States GSP program generally excludes leather products, textiles and apparel,[21] watches,[22] selected electronics and, certain steel, footwear and categories of glass from being designated as eligible articles.[23] All these goods are thought to involve particular "import sensitivity."

The UNCTAD Certificate of Origin Form A is ordinarily required of the foreign exporter when GSP eligible merchandise is involved. A complex body of "rules of origin" determine where goods are from for purposes of the United States GSP program. Basically, for goods to originate in a beneficiary country, at least 35 percent of the appraised value of those goods must be added in that nation.[24] The statutory rules of origin for GSP eligible goods are found in 19 U.S.C.A. § 2463(b).[25] A federal Circuit Court of Appeals has ruled

---

[20] 19 U.S.C.A. § 2462(b).

[21] See Luggage and Leather Goods Mfrs. of America, Inc. v. United States, 588 F.Supp. 1413 (C.I.T.1984) (man-made fiber flat goods are textile and apparel articles).

[22] See North American Foreign Trading Corp. v. United States, 600 F.Supp. 226 (C.I.T.1984), *affirmed* 783 F.2d 1031 (Fed.Cir.1986) (exemption for watches includes solid-state digital watches).

[23] 19 U.S.C.A. § 2463(c).

[24] See Madison Galleries, Ltd. v. United States, 870 F.2d 627 (Fed.Cir.1989).

[25] 19 U.S.C.A. § 2463(b). Eligible articles qualifying for duty-free treatment:

(b)(1) The duty-free treatment provided under section 501 shall apply to any eligible article which is the growth, product, or manufacture of a beneficiary developing country if—

(A) that article is imported directly from a beneficiary developing country into the customs territory of the United States; and

(B) the sum of (i) the cost or value of the materials produced in the beneficiary developing country or any 2 or more countries which are members of the same association of countries which is treated as one country under section 502(a)(3), plus (ii) the direct costs of processing operations performed in such beneficiary developing country or such member countries is not less than 35 percent of the appraised value of such article at the time of its entry into the customs territory of the United States.

(2) The Secretary of the Treasury, after consulting with the United States Trade Representative, shall prescribe such regulations as may be necessary to carry out this subsection, including, but not limited to, regulations providing that, in order to be eligible for duty-free treatment under this title, an article must be wholly the growth, product, or manufacture of a beneficiary developing country, or must be a

that a "two-stage" substantial transformation process must also occur in order to qualify goods for GSP purposes.[26] Thus, the value of U.S.-grown corn did not count towards meeting the 35 percent requirement because the intermediate products into which it was turned did not qualify as Mexican in origin for lack of substantial transformation into a new and different article of commerce.[27] But the assembly of integrated circuits in Taiwan from slices containing many integrated circuit chips, gold wire, lead frame strips, molding compound and epoxy (all of which were U.S. in origin) did constitute a substantial transformation of such items into a new article of commerce. Thus the circuits could be deemed from Taiwan for purposes of the 35 percent value added GSP rule.[28]

One unusual feature of the rules of origin for the United States GSP program is that which favors selected regional economic groups. Goods made in the ANDEAN pact, ASEAN or CARICOM may be designated as "one country" for purposes of origin. So too may goods produced in the East African Community, the West African Economic and Monetary Union and the Southern African Development Community. This means that the value added requirement as applied in these regions is met if 35 percent of the value added has been created inside each group as opposed to inside any one nation of the group. It is notable that many other third world regional economic groups are not similarly treated, e.g. MERCOSUR, and the Gulf Council of the Middle East.

§ 10.11 U.S. Generalized System of Tariff Preferences—Graduation

As nations develop, U.S. law either bars their participation in the GSP program absolutely or vests discretion in the President to remove nations or products from its scope. Since 1984, developing nations with a per capita gross national product in excess of $8,500

new or different article of commerce which has been grown, produced, or manufactured in the beneficiary developing country; but no article or material of a beneficiary developing country shall be eligible for such treatment by virtue of having merely undergone—

(A) simple combining or packaging operations, or

(B) mere dilution with water or mere dilution with another substance that does not materially alter the characteristics of the article.

[26] See Torrington Company v. United States, 764 F.2d 1563 (Fed.Cir.1985). See generally Cutler, United States Generalized System of Preferences: the Problem of Substantial Transformation, 5 North Carolina Journal of International Law & Commercial Regulation, 393 (1980).

[27] Azteca Mill. Co. v. United States, 890 F.2d 1150 (Fed.Cir.1989).

[28] Texas Instruments Inc. v. United States, 681 F.2d 778 (C.C.P.A.1982). See Madison Galleries, Ltd. v. United States, 688 F.Supp. 1544 (C.I.T.1988) (blank porcelain from Taiwan substantially transformed when painted and fired in Hong Kong).

are totally ineligible for GSP duty free entry. The Bahamas, Bahrain, Brunei, Israel, Nauru and Bermuda have been disqualified under this rule. In addition, the President has a broad authority to "graduate" countries from the United States GSP program. The basic concept here is that certain nations are sufficiently developed so as to not need the benefits of duty free entry into the United States market. Discretionary graduation is based on an assessment of the economic development level of the beneficiary country, the competitive position of the imports and the overall national economic interests of the United States.[29]

In recent years, Presidents have been graduating more and more products from countries like India and Brazil. In January of 1989, President Reagan graduated all products from Hong Kong, Singapore, South Korea and Taiwan. At that time, these countries were the source of about 60 percent of all goods benefiting from the United States GSP program. Mexico then emerged as the chief beneficiary country under the program until late in 1993 when all of its products were removed from the GSP treatment in anticipation of the North American Free Trade Agreement. In 1997, President Clinton graduated Malaysia entirely from the GSP program. Other U.S. free trade partners, such as Jordan, Morocco and Peru, have also been eliminated as beneficiary countries.

§ 10.12 U.S. Generalized System of Tariff Preferences—Judicial and Administrative Remedies

Legal challenges to presidential revocations of duty free GSP treatment were originally filed with the U.S. Customs Court. This was the case despite contentions of inadequate legal remedies in that court and the fact that plaintiff could not pursue class action relief except in federal district court.[30] Litigation involving the GSP program is now commenced in the U.S. Court of International Trade.

The goods entering the United States duty free through the GSP program remain subject to the possibility of escape clause relief under Section 201 of the Trade Act of 1974.[31] Moreover, such goods may also be restrained pursuant to Section 232 of the Trade Expansion Act of 1962 in the name of the national security of the United States.[32]

---

29 See 47 Fed.Reg. 31,099, 31,000 (July 16, 1982).

30 Barclay Industries, Inc. v. Carter, 494 F.Supp. 912 (D.D.C.1980).

31 See 19 U.S.C.A. § 2251 and Chapter 15.

32 See 19 U.S.C.A. § 2463(c)(2).

§ 10.13 Caribbean Basin Initiative (CBI)

The European Union has had for many years a policy which grants substantial duty free entry into its market for goods originating in Mediterranean Basin countries. The United States has duplicated this approach for the Caribbean Basin. This is accomplished through the Caribbean Basin Economic Recovery Act of 1983.[33] For these purposes, the Caribbean Basin is broadly defined to include nearly all of the islands in that Sea, and a significant number of Central and South American nations bordering the Caribbean. So defined, there are 28 nations which could qualify for purposes of the United States Caribbean Basin Initiative. As with the GSP program, the Caribbean Basin Initiative (CBI) involves presidential determinations to confer beneficiary status upon any of these eligible countries. However, unlike the GSP, there are no presidential determinations as to which specific products of these countries shall be allowed into the United States on a duty free basis. All Caribbean products except those excluded by statute are eligible. Moreover, there are no "competitive need" or annual per capita income limits under the CBI. Lastly, unlike the GSP program which must be renewed periodically, the Caribbean Basin Initiative is a permanent part of the U.S. tariff system.

The United States has maintained a steady trade surplus with Caribbean Basin countries. Leading export items under the CBI are typically beef, raw cane sugar, medical instruments, cigars, fruits and rum. The leading source countries have often been the Dominican Republic, Costa Rica and Guatemala, now all U.S. free trade partners. The value of all CBI duty free imports now exceeds $1 billion annually, but the CBI countries fear a diversion of trade and investment to Mexico and Central America as the North American Free Trade Agreement (NAFTA) and the Central American Free Trade Agreement (CAFTA) mature.

§ 10.14 CBI Country Eligibility

The President is forbidden from designating Caribbean Basin Initiative beneficiaries if they are communist, have engaged in expropriation activities, nullified contracts or intellectual property rights of the U.S. citizens, failed to recognize and enforce arbitral awards, given preferential treatment to products of another developed nation, broadcast through a government-owned entity United States copyrighted material without consent, failed to sign a treaty or other agreement regarding extradition of United States citizens,

---

[33] Public Law 98–67, 97 Stat. 384 codified at 19 U.S.C.A. § 2701 et seq.

failed to cooperate on narcotics enforcement, or failed to afford internationally recognized workers rights. For these purposes, the definition of workers rights enacted in connection with the GSP program applies.[34] Since 2000, CBI countries must also show a commitment to implementing WTO pledges.

These prohibitions notwithstanding, the President can still designate a Caribbean Basin country as a beneficiary if he or she determines that this will be in the national economic or security interest of the United States. However, this can be done only in connection with countries that are disqualified as being communist, expropriators, contract or intellectual property nullifiers, nonenforcers of arbitral awards, unauthorized broadcasters, or those who fail to provide for internationally recognized workers rights. Thus, if a Caribbean nation is disqualified because it grants preferential trade treatment to products of another developed nation or refuses to sign an extradition treaty with the United States, there is no possibility of its designation as a beneficiary nation under the Caribbean Basin Initiative. As with the GSP statutory requirements, if the basis for the disqualification is expropriation or nullification of benefits, the President may override this disqualification if that nation is engaged in payment of prompt, adequate and effective compensation or good faith negotiations intended to lead to such compensation.

In addition, the President is required to take various factors into account in designating beneficiary countries under the Caribbean Basin Initiative. These include:

(1) the desire of that country to participate;

(2) the economic conditions and living standards of that nation;

(3) the extent to which the country has promised to provide equitable and reasonable access to its markets and basic commodity resources;

(4) the degree to which it follows accepted GATT rules on international trade;

(5) the degree to which it uses export subsidies or imposes export performance requirements or local content requirements which distort international trade;

---

[34] See § 10.9, supra.

(6) the degree to which its trade policies help revitalize the region;

(7) the degree to which it is undertaking self-help measures to promote its own economic development;

(8) whether it has taken steps to provide internationally recognized workers rights;

(9) the extent to which it provides adequate and effective means for foreigners to secure and enforce exclusive intellectual property rights;

(10) the extent to which the country prohibits unauthorized broadcasts of copyrighted material belonging to U.S. owners; and

(11) the extent to which it is prepared to cooperate with the United States in connection with the Caribbean Basin Initiative, particularly by signing a tax information exchange agreement.

Under these criteria, the President has designated a large number of the 28 eligible nations as beneficiary countries under the Caribbean Basin Initiative. These include Antigua and Barbuda, Aruba, the Bahamas, Barbados, Belize, the British Virgin Islands, Costa Rica, Dominica, the Dominican Republic, El Salvador, Grenada, Guatemala, Guinea, Haiti, Honduras, Jamaica, Monserrat, the Netherlands Antilles, Nicaragua, Panama, St. Christopher–Nevis, St. Lucia, St. Vincent and the Grenadines, and Trinidad and Tobago. Cuba is not even listed among the nations eligible for consideration in connection with the Caribbean Basin Initiative. Some of these countries are now U.S. free trade partners and therefore no longer CBI eligible.

U.S. Presidents have typically required of each potential beneficiary a concise written presentation of its policies and practices directly related to the issues raised by the country designation criteria listed in the Caribbean Basin Economic Recovery Act. Wherever measures were in effect which were inconsistent with the objectives of these criteria, U.S. presidents have sought assurances that such measures would be progressively eliminated or modified. For example, the Dominican Republic promised to take steps to reduce the degree of book piracy and the Jamaican and Bahamian governments promised to stop the unauthorized broadcast of U.S. films and television programs.[35]

§ 10.15 CBI Product Eligibility

Unless specifically excluded, all products of Caribbean Basin nations are eligible for duty free entry into the United States market. Certain goods are absolutely excluded from such treatment.[36] These include footwear, canned tuna, petroleum and petroleum derivatives, watches, and certain leather products. It should be noted that this listing of "import sensitive" products is different from but overlaps with that used in connection with the United States GSP program. Since 2000, products ineligible for CBI benefits enter at reduced tariff levels corresponding to Mexican goods under NAFTA . . . so-called "NAFTA parity".

One of the most critical of the products that may enter the United States on a duty free basis is sugar. But the President is given the authority to suspend duty free treatment for both sugar and beef products originating in the Caribbean Basin or to impose quotas in order to protect United States domestic price support programs for these products.[37] Sugar exports have traditionally been critical to many Caribbean Basin economies. Nevertheless, sugar import quotas into the United States from the Caribbean have been steadily reduced in recent years. For example, by 1988 the sugar quota allocations for some CBI countries reached a low of 25 percent of their 1983 pre-Caribbean Basin Initiative allocations.[38] Many consider the few duty free import benefits obtained under the Initiative to be more than counterbalanced by the loss in sugar exports to the United States market.

The rules of origin for determining product eligibility in connection with the Caribbean Basin Initiative are virtually the same as discussed previously under the GSP.[39] As a general rule, a substantial transformation must occur and a 35 percent value added requirement is imposed (but 15 percent may come from the United States). This percentage is calculated by adding the sum of the cost or value of the materials produced in the beneficiary country or two or more beneficiary countries plus the direct cost of processing op-

---

[35] 19 U.S.C.A. § 2702.

[36] See 19 U.S.C.A. § 2703(b).

[37] 19 U.S.C.A. § 2073(c) and (d).

[38] See Fox, Interaction of the Caribbean Basin Initiative and U.S. Domestic Sugar Price Support: A Political Contradiction, 8 Mississippi College Law Review 197 (1988).

[39] See HTS General Note 3(c)(v).

erations performed in those countries.[40] It should be noted that this approach effectively treats all of the CBI-eligible nations as a regional beneficiary since the 35 percent required value can be cumulated among them.

As under the GSP program, the President is given broad powers to suspend duty free treatment with reference to any eligible product or any designated beneficiary country.[41] Import injury relief under Section 201 of the Trade Act of 1974 can be invoked in connection with Caribbean Basin imports. And the equivalent of that relief is authorized specifically for agricultural imports upon similar determinations by the Secretary of Agriculture.[42] The effects of these protective proceedings may be diminished in the context of Caribbean Basin imports. Whenever the International Trade Commission is studying whether increased imports are a substantial cause of serious injury to a domestic industry under Section 201 or its agricultural equivalent, the ITC is required to break out the Caribbean Basin beneficiary countries. The President is given the discretion if he or she decides to impose escape clause relief to suspend that relief relative to Caribbean Basin imports. A similar discretion is granted to the President in connection with national security import restraints under Section 232 of the Trade Expansion Act of 1962. However, these discretionary provisions relate only to those goods that are eligible for duty free entry under the Caribbean Basin Initiative.[43]

In 1986, President Reagan initiated a special program for textiles produced in the Caribbean. Essentially, this program increases the opportunity to sell Caribbean textile products when the fabric involved has been previously formed and cut in the United States. If this is the case, there are minimum guaranteed access levels. This program is run in conjunction with Section 9802.00.80 of the Harmonized Tariff Schedule of the United States.[44]

The U.S.–Caribbean Basin Trade Partnership Act of 2000 grants duty-free and quota-free access to the U.S. market for apparel made from U.S. fabric and yarn. Apparel made from CBI fabric is capped for duty free into the United States. CBI textiles and apparel are subject to market surge safeguards comparable to those under NAFTA. Late in 2006, duty free treatment of Haitian apparel products was expanded under the HOPE Act. In certain cases, Haiti

40 19 U.S.C.A. § 2703(a).

41 19 U.S.C.A. § 2702(e).

42 19 U.S.C.A. § 2703(f).

43 See 29 U.S.C.A. § 2703(e).

44 See 51 Fed.Reg. 21,208 (June 11, 1986).

may utilize third country fabrics and still ship apparel duty free into the United States.

§ 10.16 Andean Trade Preferences

The Andean Trade Preference Act (ATPA) of 1991[45] authorizes the President to grant duty free treatment to imports of eligible articles from Colombia, Peru, Bolivia and Ecuador. Venezuela is not included as a beneficiary country under this Act. The Andean Trade Preference Act is patterned after the Caribbean Basin Economic Recovery Act of 1983. Goods that ordinarily enter duty free into the United States from Caribbean Basin nations will also enter duty free from these four Andean countries. The same exceptions and exclusions discussed above in connection with the Caribbean Basin Initiative generally apply. However, while the CBI is a permanent part of United States Customs law, the ATPA was only authorized initially for a period of ten years. Furthermore, the guaranteed access levels for Caribbean Basin textile products, separate cumulation for antidumping and countervailing duty investigations, and the waiver of the Buy American Act for procurement purposes are not authorized by the ATPA.

The Andean Trade Preference Act was renewed by the TPA–TAA through February 2006 retroactive to its expiry Dec. 4, 2001. Periodic renewals have followed. Textile and apparel products, and most other products previously excluded, are now included under the ATPA. Country eligibility for enhanced benefits includes consideration of steps taken to comply with WTO obligations, the protection of worker rights and combating corruption. Broadly speaking, the passage of the ATPA represents fulfillment of the elder President Bush's commitment to assist these nations economically in return for their help in containing narcotics. Peru and Colombia are now U.S. free partners, a status that removes ATPA benefits. Free trade negotiations with Ecuador and Bolivia have not succeeded, leaving their Andean benefits uncertain.

§ 10.17 African Trade Preferences

The Africa Growth and Opportunity Act of 2000[46] granted duty-free and quota-free access to the U.S. market for apparel made from U.S. fabric and yarn. Apparel made from African fabric is capped for duty free entry. The least developed sub-Saharan countries enjoy duty-free and quota-free apparel access regardless of the origin of the fabric. In 2008, the so-called "abundant supply" provision of

---

45 Public Law 102–82, 19 U.S.C.A. § 3201 et seq.

46 Public Law No. 106–200, 114 Stat. 252.

AGOA was repealed, thus assuring least-developed country textile exports to the United States. U.S. imports of AGOA textiles using third country fabrics have also been liberalized.

The Act also altered U.S. GSP rules to admit certain previously excluded African products on a duty-free basis, including petroleum, watches and flat goods. Sub–Saharan countries can export almost all products duty-free to the United States. These countries are encouraged to create a free trade area with U.S. support. African exports are subject to import surge (escape clause) protection and stringent rules against transshipments between countries for purposes of taking advantage of U.S. trade benefits.

§ 10.18 Section 9802.00.80 of the HTS

Section 9802.00.80 of the Harmonized Tariff Schedule of the United States (formerly Section 807.00 of the Tariff Schedule of the United States) is an unusual "duty free" provision. This section allows for the duty free importation of United States fabricated components that were exported ready for assembly abroad. If qualified, goods assembled abroad containing U.S. components are subject only to a duty upon the value added through foreign assembly operations regardless of where assembled. In order for this to be the case, Section 9802.00.80 requires that the components be fabricated and a product of the United States, that they be exported in a condition ready for assembly without further fabrication, that they not lose their physical identity by change in form, shape or otherwise, and that they not be advanced in value or improved in condition abroad except by being assembled and except by operations incidental to the assembly process such as cleaning, lubricating and painting.

The regulations issued in connection with Section 9802.00.80 indicate that there are other incidental operations which will not disqualify components from duty free re-entry into the United States. These include removing rust, grease, paint or other preservative coatings, the application of similar preservative coatings, the trimming or other removal of small amounts of excess material, adjustments in the shape or form of a component required by the assembly that is being undertaken, the cutting to length of wire, thread, tape, foil or similar products, the separation by cutting of finished components (such as integrated circuits exported in strips), and the calibration, testing, marking, sorting, pressing and folding and assembly of the final product.[47] In contrast, the regulations also

[47] 19 C.F.R. § 10.16(b).

provide examples of operations that are not considered incidental to assembly for these purposes. These examples include the melting of ingots to produce cast metal parts, the cutting of garments according to patterns, painting which is intended to enhance the appearance or impart distinctive features to the product, chemical treatment so as to realize new characteristics (such as moisture-proofing), and the machining, polishing or other treatment of metals which create significant new characteristics or qualities.[48]

If all of the Section 9802.00.80 criteria are met, the tariff that will be assessed upon the imported assembled product will be limited to a duty upon the full value of that product less the cost or value of U.S. made components that have been incorporated into it.[49] Those who seek to take advantage of Section 9802.00.80 must provide the United States Customs Service with a Foreign Assembler's Declaration and Certification. This is known as Form 3317. The assembly plant operator certifies that the requirements of Section 9802.00.80 are met, and the importer declares that this certification is correct. Billions of dollars of ordinarily tariffed value have been excluded as a result of this Customs law provision. Motor vehicles, semiconductors, office machines, textiles and apparel, and furniture are good examples of the kinds of products assembled abroad with fabricated U.S. components so as to meet the requirements of Section 9802.00.80. Historically, many of these products have been assembled in Japan, Germany or Canada. In more recent times, the assembly operations to which Section 9802.00.80 frequently applies have more commonly been found in the developing world.

§ 10.19 Maquiladoras

Section 9802.00.80 is applicable to goods imported into the United States from anywhere in the world. However, it is most frequently associated with Mexican maquiladoras. Maquiladoras are "in-bond" assembly plants that often take advantage of the duty free potential of Section 9802.00.80. Maquiladoras enjoyed a phenomenal popularity after 1982 when the Mexican peso was dramatically devalued. This had the practical effect of rendering Mexican labor costs lower than those of Taiwan, Hong Kong, Singapore and South Korea. These Asian nations were traditionally low-cost assembly plant centers. Since 1982, thousands of maquiladoras have been established in Tijuana, Ciudad Juarez, Neuvo Laredo and other border cities. They provide Mexico with hundreds of thousands of jobs and are a major source of foreign currency earnings. Electron-

---

48 19 C.F.R. § 10.16(c).

49 See generally 19 C.F.R. § 10.14 et seq.

ics, apparel, toys, medical supplies, transport equipment, furniture and sporting goods are examples of the types of industries that have been attracted south of the border. United States components, when assembled in maquiladoras and qualifying under Section 9802.00.80, are exported and then reimported on a duty free basis. Maquiladoras have been developed throughout the Caribbean Basin and Central America. Much to the frustration of organized labor, such offshore assembly operations exemplify the internalization of the United States manufacturing sector.

The maquiladora industry enjoyed explosive growth before and in the early years of NAFTA. Mexican law, like Section 9802.00.80, supports this growth. Various decrees permit goods to enter Mexico on a duty free basis *under bond* for purposes of assembly in maquiladoras. Mexican law permits duty free importation of equipment, technology and components for six months. At the end of that period the goods must be exported from Mexico, typically back to the United States. Except with special permission, which has been increasingly granted by the authorities, maquiladora-assembled goods may not enter the Mexican market. Investors may own maquiladoras, typically using 30–year land trusts (fideicomiso) and Mexican subsidiaries. Alternatively, they may lease assembly plant space from a Mexican company and operate a maquiladora from that space. The simplest way to enter into maquiladora assembly operations is to contract with a Mexican company to assemble the goods in question.

In 1998, Mexico's Ministry of Commerce and Industry Development (SECOFI) published an amended Maquiladora Decree. The revised Decree streamlines regulation of maquiladoras in Mexico, notably reducing SECOFI's discretion to deny, suspend or cancel maquila programs. A translation of the new Decree can be found at www.natlaw.com. Mexico was responding, in part, to increased assembly plant competition from Asia, especially China after its 2001 admission to the WTO.

The net result of the United States and Mexican law in this area is to create an interdependent legal framework mutually supportive of maquiladora operations. Many have characterized this legal framework as a "co-production" or "production sharing" arrangement between the two countries. However, utilization of maquiladoras is not limited to U.S. firms nor United States' components. Japanese and Korean companies have become major investors in maquiladora industries. To the extent that they utilize U.S. components, they may benefit from the duty free entry provisions of Section 9802.00.80. At this stage, however, some firms have moved their plants to Asia where lower labor costs prevail.

Until late in 1993, there was also a link between the United States System of Generalized Preferences (GSP) and Mexican maquiladoras. Under the rules of origin that govern the GSP program, if at least 35 percent of the value of a maquiladora product was of Mexican origin, it could qualify entirely for duty free entry into the United States. The possibility of this result caused many users of maquiladoras to seek out Mexican suppliers in order to try to meet the 35 percent rule of origin. This incentive was enhanced by the fact that South Korea, Singapore, Taiwan and Hong Kong were all graduated from the United States GSP program in 1989. Mexico was the largest source of GSP qualified goods entering the United States market prior to December, 1993 when all of its products were removed from the GSP program as a result of NAFTA.

The North American Free Trade Area incorporating Mexico, Canada and the United States creates an incentive to invest in Mexico. Nearly all Mexican-made goods are able to enter the United States market on a duty free basis. NAFTA phased out over seven years the duty free entry Section 9802.00.80 benefits applied to Mexican maquiladoras, but not as regards goods assembled with United States components from outside North America. NAFTA incentives, notwithstanding, there has been a decline in foreign investment in Mexico.

There is an evolutionary cycle in assembly plants-from cheap raw labor to more skill-oriented operations to capital-intensive manufacturing. One of the most interesting comparative questions is whether there is also an evolutionary process in the applicable laws of these countries. In other words, what legal regimes do developing nations have to adopt in order to first attract assembly operations and do they evolve from extremely accommodating to more demanding as the cycle reaches completion? Or, does the manufacturer's ability to go elsewhere to even cheaper labor markets (e.g., from Mexico to Guatemala to Haiti or from Hong Kong to the People's Republic of China to Vietnam) constantly temper the legal regimes regulating assembly plants? By 2009, assembly plants withdrawn from Mexico were based in China and Vietnam, with a few actually returning to North America due to rising costs.

§ 10.20 Section 9802.00.80 Case Law

There is a surprisingly large body of case law interpreting Section 9802.00.80. Much of it was developed when this provision was formally known as Section 807 of the Tariff Schedule of the United States. One issue is whether the United States components have been advanced in value or improved in condition abroad. If this is the case, duty free re-entry into the United States is prohibited. An early decision of the Court of Customs and Patent Appeals held that the export of U.S. fish hooks, which were assembled abroad into individually packaged assortments so as to meet the requirements of retail purchasers in the United States, were not advanced in value or improved in condition so as to be disqualified.[50] In another decision, U.S. revolvers were rechambered in Canada such that they no longer fired with accuracy .38 caliber bullets as originally designed. This change in condition caused the revolvers to be disqualified under Section 9802.00.80.[51] United States tomatoes shipped to Canada in bulk and sorted, graded as to color and size, and repackaged in smaller cartons were not changed, advanced in value or improved in condition so as to be disqualified from duty free re-entry.[52]

The buttonholing in Mexico of U.S. shirt components (cuffs and collar-bands) did not advance them in value nor improve their condition as a result of this incidental operation.[53] But polyester fabric exported from the United States to Canada where it was dyed and processed, and then exported back to the United States as finished fabric did involve an advancement in value and changing of the condition of the U.S. component so as to disqualify it from duty free entry.[54] Similarly, glass pieces produced in annealled form in the United States which were sent to Canada for heat treatment and returned for use as pieces of tempered glass were not capable of benefiting from duty free entry.[55] Terminal pins of U.S. origin were shipped to Mexico and incorporated into header assemblies and relays. This operation constituted an assembly which did not advance the value of the terminals nor improve their condition.[56]

Another requirement of Section 9802.00.80 is that the United States component be fabricated and ready for assembly without further fabrication. Circuit boards for computers made in the United States from foreign and U.S. parts qualify as fabricated components

---

50 United States v. John V. Carr & Son, Inc., 496 F.2d 1225 (C.C.P.A.1974).

51 A.D. Deringer, Inc. v. United States, 386 F.Supp. 518, 73 Cust.Ct 141 (1974).

52 Border Brokerage Co., Inc. v. United States, 314 F.Supp. 788, 65 Cust.Ct. 50 (1970).

53 United States v. Oxford Industries, Inc., 668 F.2d 507 (C.C.P.A.1981). See United States v. Mast Industries, Inc., 668 F.2d 501 (C.C.P.A.1981) (buttonholing and pocket slitting operations incidental to assembly process do not lead to duty free entry disqualification.)

54 Dolliff & Co., Inc. v. United States, 455 F.Supp. 618 (Cust.Ct.1978), *affirmed* 599 F.2d 1015 (C.C.P.A.1979).

55 Guardian Industries Corp. v. United States, 3 C.I.T. 9 (1982).

56 Sigma Instruments, Inc. v. United States, 565 F.Supp. 1036 (C.I.T.), *affirmed* 724 F.2d 930 (Fed.Cir.1983).

for these purposes.[57] In this case, the programmable read only memory (PROM) was programmed in the United States causing it to undergo a substantial transformation and become a United States product. Aluminum foil, tabs, tape, paper and mylar made in the United States and shipped to Taiwan in role form where they were used together with other articles of U.S. origin to produce aluminum electrolytic capacitors were not eligible for duty free entry because they were not "fabricated components" upon departure from the United States to Taiwan.[58] The fact that gold wire made in the United States was not cut until used for transistors assembled in Taiwan did not make it a U.S. component that was not ready for assembly abroad without further fabrication. The cutting of the gold wire was an incident of the assembly process.[59] But the assembly in Ecuador of flattened cylinders and ends into tunafish cans which were then packed with tuna and shipped back to the United States did not qualify under Section 9802.00.80.[60]

The failure to lock knitting loops to keep the knitting from unravelling in the United States meant that knitted glove shelves were not exported in a condition ready for assembly without further fabrication. The importer of those gloves was not entitled to duty free entry for the value of the shelves.[61] On the other hand, pantyhose tubes made in the United States were fully constructed and secured from unravelling by stitches. A closing operation did not create a new toe portion and the goods were permitted the benefits of Section 9802.00.80.[62] Likewise the joinder of molten plastic to the upper portion of a shoe abroad did not prevent the shoe vamp from duty free entry upon return to the United States. This operation did not constitute further fabrication of the vamp.[63]

The scoring and breaking of silicon slices along designated "streets" was an incidental operation to the assembly of transistors and therefore the slices were entitled to duty free entry into the United States.[64] Magnet and lead wire made in the U.S. and exported to Taiwan where it was wound into coils and cable harness put into television deflection yolks were entitled to duty free entry.[65] The two-step assembly process in this case did not defeat the appli-

---

57 Data General Corp. v. United States, 4 C.I.T. 182 (1982).

58 General Instrument Corp. v. United States, 67 Cust.Ct. 127 (1971).

59 General Instrument Corp. v. United States, 462 F.2d 1156 (C.C.P.A.1972).

60 Van Camp Sea Food Co. v. United States, 73 Cust.Ct. 35 (1974).

61 Zwicker Knitting Mills v. United States, 613 F.2d 295 (C.C.P.A.1980).

62 L'Eggs Products, Inc. v. United States, 704 F.Supp. 1127 (C.I.T.1989).

63 Carter Footwear, Inc. v. United States, 669 F.Supp. 439 (C.I.T.1987).

64 United States v. Texas Instruments, Inc., 545 F.2d 739 (C.C.P.A.1976).

65 General Instrument Corp. v. United States, 499 F.2d 1318 (C.C.P.A.1974).

cation of Section 9802.00.80. The burning of slots and holes in steel Z-beams in order to incorporate them into railroad cars was an operation incidental to the assembly process and therefore the beams were not dutiable.[66]

For Section 9802.00.80 to apply the components must be assembled abroad. It has been held that a needling operation causing fibers to be entwined with exported fabric in order to create papermaker's felts constituted an assembly abroad for these purposes.[67] Likewise the adhesion of Canadian chemicals to sheets of the United States polyester involved an assembly.[68] Another requirement of Section 9802.00.80 is that the components not lose their physical identity by change in form, shape or otherwise. Fabric components used to make papermaker's felts which were needled abroad and thus perforated with holes and changed in width did not lose their physical identity and therefore continued to qualify for duty free re-entry.[69] The absence of a loss of physical identity was apparently included as a requirement of Section 9802.00.80 in order to exclude U.S. components that are chemical products, food ingredients, liquids, gases, powders and the like. These products would presumably lose their physical identity when "assembled" abroad.[70]

---

66 Miles v. United States, 567 F.2d 979 (C.C.P.A.1978).

67 E. Dillingham, Inc. v. United States, 470 F.2d 629 (C.C.P.A.1972)

68 C.J. Tower & Sons of Buffalo, Inc. v. United States, 304 F.Supp. 1187 (Cust.Ct.1969).

69 E. Dillingham, Inc. v. United States, 470 F.2d 629 (C.C.P.A.1972)

70 See United States v. Baylis Bros., Co., 451 F.2d 643 (C.C.P.A.197_).

Chapter 11

CUSTOMS CLASSIFICATION, VALUATION AND ORIGIN

Table of Sections

§ 11.1 Purpose of Classification, Valuation and Origin

To calculate import duties, you must first determine the classification, country of origin and the customs valuation of goods. In other words, what is it, where is it from, and what is its customs value? Customs officials classify, value and identify the origin of imported merchandise. In some cases, the importer (and the exporter) may disagree with those conclusions reached by the official regarding the classification of the merchandise, its country of origin, and its valuation. This chapter concentrates on the customs process, those who play a role in the process, and some of the difficulties that may arise.

All foreign goods entering the United States must be identified in a process called classification. Classification takes two forms determining (1) the nature of the product, and (2) the product's country of origin. The first, looks to the nature of a product, such as whether an imported doll wig made from human hair should be classified as a wig of human hair, part of a doll, or as a toy.[1] The second, looks at what country or countries a product was made. For example, if the doll wig was made in Argentina from human hair from Cuba, is the doll wig a product of Argentina or Cuba? This form of classification by country may involve formal rules of origin.

Knowing the nature of the product allows Customs to determine the proper tariff that applies, because tariffs differ from nation to nation. In other words, knowing the country of origin informs Customs which tariff column to use. For example, different tariffs apply to countries granted most favored nation (MFN) status, countries denied such status, or countries with special or duty free tariff levels such as Canada and Mexico under the North American Free Trade Agreement (NAFTA), Caribbean Basin beneficiaries under the Caribbean Basin Economic Recovery Act, or other such agreements. Additionally, identification of the country of origin informs Customs of products that cannot be imported for reasons such as an embargo by the United States, like Cuba.

But even when the product and its source of origin have been identified, Customs must know the value of the product before the tariff can be determined. Assigning a value to an import is called valuation. Customs officials must be able to determine a value in order to calculate the appropriate import tariff, usually calculated as a percentage of the value. The task is easier if the product is entitled to duty free entry. In such case the valuation is not needed for purposes of collecting a tariff. But valuation remains useful for gathering information regarding the value of various classes of imports for statistical purposes.

---

[1] A hypothetical problem involving imported doll wigs and the process of classification and valuation was included in R. Folsom, M. Gordon & J. Spanogle, International Business Transactions: A Problem Oriented Coursebook 276 (2d ed. 1991). The hypothetical in the latest edition of this book involves classifying peanut butter-jelly swirl.

§ 11.2 The Actors Who Classify and Value—The Customs Service

The United States Customs Service, as part of the Department of the Treasury, administers the entry of goods into the Customs Territory of the United States, which includes the fifty states, the District of Columbia, and Puerto Rico.[2] This process allows Customs officials to detain and examine goods to determine compliance with all laws and regulations. Title 19 of the Code of Federal Regulations sets out extensive regulations governing such entry.[3]

An importable item must "pass customs". Usually, the passage through customs and physical entry into a country occur simultaneously. When goods arrive at the United States border, the consignee (or an agent, such as a customs broker) files both "entry" and "entry summary" forms which are used to determine the classification, valuation, origin and conformity to product standards of the imported goods. At the same time, a deposit of the amount of estimated customs duties is made with customs officials. A procedure for immediate release of imported goods is available, as is the use of consolidated periodic statements for all entries made during a billing period.

Because the entry process requires the importer to classify and value goods, a Customs Service official must determine the correctness of the documentation presented by the importer. If the Customs official rejects the importer's documentation, the decision may be appealed to the District Director (Regional Commissioner if for the port of New York), and to the Commissioner of Customs.[4]

Customs' decisions may be reviewed by the judiciary.[5] Specifically, the United States Court of International Trade (CIT),[6] which has exclusive jurisdiction.[7] Appeals from the CIT may be made to

---

[2] 19 U.S.C.A. § 1500, granting Customs authority to appraise, classify and liquidate merchandise entering the United States.

[3] Title 19 of the C.F.R. is divided into three chapters. Chapter I includes parts 1–199 entitles United States Customs Service, Department of the Treasury. Chapter II and Chapter III include parts 200 to the end and are entitled United States International Trade Commission, and International Trade Administration, Department of Commerce, respectively.

[4] 19 C.F.R. §§ 173–174. There is a process for omitting the review by the district director in certain instances, by application for "further review." See 19 C.F.R. § 174.23–174.27.

[5] See Dell Products v. U.S., 642 F.3d 1055 (Fed. Cir. 2011) (affirming an appeal from importer regarding Customs and Border Protection decision under Harmonized Tariff Schedule of the United States);

[6] 19 C.F.R. § 176.

[7] The CIT is the successor to the Customs Court.

the Court of Appeals for the Federal Circuit (CAFC).[8] From these specialized courts, appeals are ultimately made to the United States Supreme Court. In *United States v. Mead Corp.,* the U.S. Supreme Court held Customs Service classification rulings are not entitled to full administrative deference, but rather, such rulings are entitled to limited deference depending on their "thoroughness, logic and expertness, fit with prior interpretations, and any other sources of weight."[9]

As an additional precaution, on February 28, 2012, President Barack Obama, by way of an executive order, created the Interagency Trade Enforcement Center within the Office of the United States Trade Representative.[10] The primary purpose of the Center focuses on strengthening and coordinating the enforcement of U.S. trade rights under international law. The Order ensures compliance with domestic trade laws and international trade agreements through coordination between government agencies that have "trade related responsibilities."

On the international level, other actors involved in classification and valuation play an important role, including:

Secretariat of the Customs Cooperation Council (CCC). This Brussels-based organization formed under the Convention on the Commodity Description and Coding System (the Convention) as an administrative entity. Since 1970, the CCC has sought to develop an internationally accepted "Harmonized Commodity Coding and Description System." This system, called the Customs Cooperation Council Nomenclature (CCCN) gives nations a domestic law for classifying goods for all purposes, including the application of tariffs and gathering statistics. It was formerly known as the Brussels Tariff Nomenclature (BTN). The CCCN evolved into the Harmonized Tariff Schedule (HTS), which is the system in currently used by the United States.

The Customs Cooperation Council (CCC) is composed of four committees. These committees have worked closely with the HTS, however, only one remains active today, the Harmonized System Committee.

---

8 The CAFC is the successor to the Court of Customs and Patent Appeals.

9 533 U.S. 218, 121 S.Ct. 2164, 150 L.Ed.2d 292 (2001).

10 Exec. Order No. 13601, 77 Fed, Reg. 12981 (March 5, 2012).

§ 11.3 The Sources of Law for Classification, Valuation and Origin

The process of classification (of the item and the country of origin) and valuation requires us to turn to separate rules. Classification of products or materials requires use of the Harmonized Tariff Schedule, adopted by the enactment of the Omnibus Trade and Competitiveness Act of 1988. Classification of the country of origin tends to focus on theory developed in cases, whereas the process of valuation utilizes provisions in the Tariff Act of 1930, which generally follow the GATT Customs Valuation Code. The statutory development of classification of products and valuation follows.

Classification. Although most nations used the internationally accepted Brussels Tariff Nomenclature (BTN), the United States refused to participate in the system. Instead, the United States used its own system of classification, found within the Tariff Schedule of the United States (TSUS). These two systems created very different classifications for United States exports destined to a nation using the BTN, and those classifications of products entering the United States from other nations. What might be very narrowly defined in one system, might be very broadly defined in another. It made achieving fairness in lower tariffs for certain products quite difficult. What was called a widget in the foreign nation, might be a gadget in the United States.

As a result of using a separate system, the United States became increasingly isolated, and it became apparent that the United States TSUS would have to give way to the BTN. In 1982, after much urging from other major trading partners, the United States began converting to the HTS, the effective successor to the BTN. The HTS is administered by the World Customs Organization (WCO) in Brussels. This conversion was completed by adoption of the HTS for all imports in the Omnibus Trade and Competitiveness Act of 1988, effective January 1, 1989.[11] Most United States exports enter other nations under the HTS, and now the same is true for products of those other nations entering the United States.

The HTS "nomenclature" has twenty sections, the majority of which group articles from similar branches of industry or commerce. For example, Section I includes live animals and animal products, Section II includes vegetable products, Section III includes animal

---

[11] P.L. 100–418, title I, §§ 1202–1217, Aug. 23, 1988, 102 Stat. 1107. The HTS is not published in the U.S. Code. The United States International Trade Commission maintains the current version, which is available from the Superintendent of Documents, U.S. Government Printing Office, Washington, D.C., 20402.

or vegetable fats, Section IV includes prepared foodstuffs, and Section V mineral products. The twenty sections are subdivided into 99 chapters, which in total list approximately 5,000 article descriptions in the heading and sub-heading format. These provisions apply to all goods entering the customs territory of the United States. Most problems arise when it is possible to classify imported goods under more than one heading.

Valuation. For many years the United States used the American Selling Price (ASP) system to determine the value of an imported good. This system valued an imported good at the level of the usual wholesale price that the same product was offered for sale, if manufactured and sold in the United States. Thus, the valuation had no relation to the cost of production in the foreign nation, which caused the system to be much criticized abroad.[12] Many other nations, especially in Europe, used a system based on the 1950 convention that established the Brussels Definition of Value. To many, the Brussels Definition was too general, and was not adopted by either the United States or Canada.

Harmonization of customs valuation became one of the most important topics at the 1979 GATT Tokyo Round, which produced the GATT Customs Valuation Code.[13] The United States abandoned the ASP when it adopted the GATT Customs Valuation Code in the Trade Agreements Act of 1979.[14] The GATT's approach to valuation differs significantly from the ASP because it values goods based on "positive" rather than "normative" economic principles. In other words, the Code values goods based on the transaction price (price paid or payable) and not what the value of the good should be. If the transaction price cannot be determined, several fallback methods in a descending order of applicability may be used.

Because the United States replaced the TSUS with the HTS for the classification of imports, and the ASP with the GATT Customs Valuation Code for valuation of imports, its classification and valuation systems obtained greater harmony with its major trading partners.

The Uruguay Round of negotiations ushered in the next stage of development of customs valuation. The World Trade Organiza-

---

[12] Such criticism was quite expected since United States domestic producers could indirectly control the valuation applied to foreign competitors' imports

[13] Its importance is reflected by its adoption by the European Union, Canada and the United States, plus such major trading nations as Australia, Japan, Spain (prior to joining the EU) and Sweden, and even important developing nations such as Argentina, Brazil, and India.

[14] 19 U.S.C.A. § 1401a.

tion replaced the GATT, and incorporated customs valuation provisions rather than having them exist as a separate external code. The three principal amendments to the Customs Valuation Code are discussed below. The provisions, which allow pre-shipment inspection are of considerable importance to customs procedures.[15] These provisions attempt to balance the interests of some nations in contracting with outside companies to determine whether imports were fairly valued in the invoice, with the interest of exporting nations to reduce or remove impediments to trade, not to increase them.

§ 11.4 Classification—Sample Provisions of the Harmonized Tariff System

In any classification dispute, two issues must be resolved: (1) under what category or categories is it proper to classify the goods; and, (2) if there are several permissible classifications, which one takes priority over the others? Although the HTSUS updates every five years to account for new products, obsolete products, and provide more thorough classifications, multiple classifications can still result.[16]

As to the first question, no provisions in the HTSUS "General Rules of Interpretation" (GRI) purport to limit the categorization of a product to a single categorization. In other words, the General Rule of Interpretation 2 (GRI 2) is inclusive, not exclusory, and the GRI 3 assumes that multiple categorizations will occur.

To solve the issue of multiple classifications, the GRIs provide priorities among competing categories, and the GRI 3(c) provides a "last resort" provision for cases where all else fails. However, even within the GRI, interesting ambiguities exist. For example, even though an international treaty produced the HTS and attempts to avoid the now-repealed TSUS system, a U.S. court may consult prior U.S. cases under the TSUS to interpret GRI 3(a)'s preference for "the most specific description."[17]

---

[15] See Creskoff, Pre–Shipment Inspection Programs: The Myth of Inconsistency with GATT Customs Valuation Provisions, 35 Fed.Bar News & J. 83 (1988).

[16] For example, in 2012 Chapter 3, covering "Fish and crustaceans, mollusks, and other aquatic invertebrates," now has a new heading for aquatic invertebrates (i.e. sea urchin and jellyfish), which had previously been classified only under "Other" or "Not Elsewhere Included." See Harmonized Tariff Schedule of the U.S., Annotated for Statistical Reporting Purposes (USITC Publ. 4299).

[17] See Mitsui Petrochemicals v. U.S., 21 C.I.T. 882, 887 (1997) (citing United States v. Siemens America, Inc., 653 F.2d 471 (C.C.P.A. 1981) (applying the "relative specificity" test under the Tariff Schedules of the United States)).

In addition to the GRI, the U.S. has allowed "[a]dditional U.S. Rules of Interpretation" and "the General Notes" in the HTS. These allow any determined attorney to create additional interpretations, and have particular importance because it is unclear whether the General Notes prevail over the GRIs and the Additional U.S. Rules, or vice versa. The best example of these possible conflicts arises when one tries to determine the priority between competing classifications. Should one first attempt to use the provisions of GRI 3, including the "last resort" provision in GRI 3(c)? Or, should one first attempt to apply the General Notes, especially Note 3(f)? And, what is the role of the Additional U.S. Notes to the Chapter Headnotes?

Below is a small portion of the extensive classification schedule of the United States.[18] The provision illustrates two features of the HTS. First, the notes preceding the chart provide comments on what the chapter does or does not cover. And second, the illustration shows the schedule of tariffs in the various columns.

CHAPTER 67

PREPARED FEATHERS AND DOWN AND ARTICLES MADE OF FEATHERS OR OF DOWN; ARTIFICIAL FLOWERS; ARTICLES OF HUMAN HAIR

Notes

1. This chapter does not cover:

(a) Straining cloth of human hair (heading 5911);

(b) Floral motifs of lace, of embroidery or other textile fabric (section XI);

(c) Footwear (chapter 65);

(d) Headgear or hair-nets (chapter 65);

(e) Toys, sports equipment, or carnival articles (chapter 95); or

(f) Feather dusters, powder-puffs or hair sieves (chapter 96).

[18] See Harmonized Tariff Schedule of the U.S., Annotated for Statistical Reporting Purposes (USITC Publ. 4299).

Heading Subheading	Stat. Suf. & cd		Article Description	Units of Quantity	Rates of Duty		
					General	Special	
6703.00			Human hair, dressed, thinned, bleached or otherwise worked; wool or other animal hair or other textile materials, prepared for use in making wigs or the like:				
6703.00.30	00	1	Human hair.............	kg	Free		20%
6703.00.60	00	4	Other......................	kg	Free		35%
6704			Wigs, false beards, eyebrows and eyelashes, switches and the like, of human or animal hair or of textile materials; articles of human hair not elsewhere specified or included:				
			Of synthetic textile materials:				
6704.11.00	00	3	Complete wigs......	No.	Free		35%
6704.19.00	00	5	Other................	X	Free		35%
6704.20.00	00	2	Of human hair.........	X	Free		35%
6704.90.00	00	7	Of other materials.....	X	Free		35%

§ 11.5 Classification—The Meaning of the Headings in the HTS

The heading in the above excerpt is used under the General Rules of Interpretation to determine classification of products.[19] Customs must apply the rule of relative specificity in the classification process, which requires that goods be classified under the provision that most specifically describes it. Here, false eyelashes made of human hair, for human adult use appear to fall under Chapter 67 because it is an article of human hair. However, it seems that this commodity may fit under more than one heading. This potential problem will be discussed in the next section.

§ 11.6 Classification—The Meaning of the Notes in the HTS

The notes at the beginning of chapters in the HTS provide a useful tool in classification. They are to be used in addition to the terms of the headings, under the General Rules of Interpretation.[20] For example, Note 1 in Chapter 67 states footwear cannot be classified under Chapter 67, but is the subject of Chapter 64. These

---

[19] General Rules of Interpretation are reproduced in the Selected Documents section.

[20] Id.

"chapter notes" should not be confused with the Explanatory Notes to the Harmonized System,[21] nor the General Notes to the HTS.[22]

§ 11.7 Classification—The Meaning of the Columns in the HTS

After looking through the applicable chapter notes, the next step is to look at the columns. The United States HTS utilizes a combined number system, including the six digits used internationally, and adding further digits for more subdivisions and statistical use. As seen in the above excerpt the first column, titled "Heading/Subheading", has eight digits. The first six are the heart of the HTS, and must be adopted by all contracting nations. The first two (67 in the excerpt) repeat the chapter. The second two designate the heading (03 for Human hair, etc., 04 for Wigs, etc., in the excerpt). The next two are subheadings. The additional two numbers provide further sub-subheadings (.30 for Human hair and .60 for Other in the excerpt),[23] and the columns titled "Stat. Suf. & cd" help maintain records for statistical purposes.

The three-column section entitled "Rates of Duty" discloses the rate of duty for the particular article. The Column 1 rates apply to nations that receive most favored nation (MFN) status. MFN tariffs are set by GATT/WTO negotiations and are now referred to officially as "normal" tariffs. The "General" column applies to most MFN nations. The "Special" column applies to nations that have tariff preferences, making these nations even more favored than the most favored. The tariffs may be commodities, which enter duty free or with less than the general MFN rate. The capital letters denote different special preferential tariff programs. For example, A means nations qualifying under the Generalized System of Preferences (GSP),[24] B means commodities under the Automotive Products Trade Act, C means products under the Agreement on Trade in Civil Aircraft, CA means commodities under the Canada–United States Free Trade Agreement, E means commodities under the Caribbean

[21] The Explanatory Notes to the Harmonized System are part of the documents of the Customs Cooperation Council in Brussels which may have some influence on the classification. They are discussed in § 5.8, infra.

[22] These General Notes identify the customs territory of the United States, list nations to which Column 2 rates of duty apply, define symbols for special treatment such as the Caribbean Basin nations, give definitions, abbreviations, items exempted from coverage and rules on commingled goods. See ITC Pub. 2333 (1991).

[23] The use of an additional four digits is permitted by the Convention and other nations have adopted their own form of using these additional digits. Such use will lead to some lessening of the uniformity of the system.

[24] An A* appears if a country is specifically ineligible.

Basin Economic Recovery Act,[25] IL means commodities under the United States–Israel Free Trade Area, and NA means commodities under the North American Free Trade Agreement.

Column 2 applies to all nations, which are not entitled to Column 1 rates of duty. These countries are listed in General Note 3(b). They include principally nations under communist or socialist rule. Essentially these counties are "least" favored nations, although that term perhaps ought to be saved for those nations, which are excluded from trading with the United States altogether.

While it might seem the HTS offers a fairly easy resolution to classification, it does only when a commodity clearly fits into one chapter, one heading, and if present one sub-heading. Fortunately, that is often the case, but many commodities are not clearly allocated within the system, and multiple possibilities for their classification may exist. This is the subject of much of the remainder of this chapter.

§ 11.8 Classification—Applying the General Rules of Interpretation

While the Customs Service classifies goods, the importer (also the foreign exporter) has an obvious interest in the classification, because when the goods are classified at a high rate of duty applicable, the transaction may not go forward. Thus, the United States importer may consider the classification themselves. If the importer's conclusion is not the same as the Customs Service (meaning undoubtedly that the latter will be a classification at a higher rate of duty), the importer may (1) decide not to import the goods, (2) pay the higher duty, or (3) challenge the Customs' determination.

The process of determination, whether conducted by Customs or the importer, must use the rules of interpretation of the United States (e.g. the General Rules of Interpretation and the Additional U.S. Rules of Interpretation). A walk through those rules illustrates how difficult the classification process can be.

Headings and relevant section or chapter notes (Rule 1). The legal classification of a good is determined according to (1) the terms of the *headings*; (2) any relative *section*; and (3) *chapter notes*.[26] This means the section, chapter and sub-headings are subordinated to the headings in importance. If the headings and notes do not otherwise require, one turns to the additional provisions of the General

25 The symbol E* appears if a country is ineligible.

26 General Rules of Interpretation 1.

Rules,[27] and also to the Additional U.S. Rules of Interpretation.[28] The General Rules specifically note that the "table of contents, alphabetical index, and titles of sections, chapters and sub-chapters" are only for reference, not legal classification.[29]

Heading references to articles (Rule 2(a)). When any reference in a heading is to an *article,* as opposed to a material or substance, the reference is to be understood to include that article in an incomplete or unfinished state as long as it "has the essential character" of the complete or finished article.[30] The reference also includes that article unassembled or disassembled.[31] This emphasis on the *material* as well as on the *function* of the good replaces emphasis on how the goods are used under the TSUS.

Heading references to a material or substance. (Rule 2(b)). If the reference heading describes a *material* or *substance,* as opposed to an article, it should be understood to refer to mixtures or combinations of that material or substance with other materials or substances.[32] Also, any reference to goods of a given material or substance should include a reference to goods consisting wholly or partly of such material or substance. The obvious problem with this is that when the goods are only partly of a material or substance, the other party may have its own classification. This can also occur when there are mixtures or combinations. The Rules acknowledge this and require one to move on to Rule 3.

Classification under two or more headings—most specific description (Rule 3(a)). When goods may be classified under two or more headings,[33] the most specific description is preferred over the *more general description.*[34] This rule parallels the long used "rule of relative specificity," and decisions under that rule may continue to be of some use.[35] However, if each possible heading refers only to a *part* of the material or substances in mixed or composite goods, or of the

27 Id.

28 The Additional U.S. Rules of Interpretation are found immediately following the General Rules in the HTS, as adopted in the United States. These additional rules often include methods of interpretation used under the prior classification system in the United States.

29 General Rules of Interpretation 1.

30 General Rules 2(a).

31 Id. Rule 2 generally follows the previous position under the TSUS.

32 General Rules 2(b).

33 This applies to Rule 2(b) discussed above and to any other situation where two or more headings seem possibly applicable.

34 General Rules 3(a).

35 That includes the doctrine that an *eo nomine* description prevails over headings having only general or functional descriptions.

items in a set for retail sale,[36] the headings must be considered equally specific. This is so even if one heading provides a more complete or precise description of the goods.[37] If this occurs, one must move to Rule 3(b).

Classification under two or more headings—essential character (Rule 3(b)). If an item cannot be classified under the most specific description test in Rule 3(a), then it must be classified with regard the material or component that gives the items their *essential character.*[38] While no similar provision existed in the TSUS[39] and the HTS does not strictly define "essential character," it has some parallel under the TSUS definition of the term "almost wholly of." Even some United States cases hold "almost wholly of" may be used while defining "essential character." However, the determination is fact-intensive[40] and should still be made on a case-by-case basis.

Classification under two or more headings—last in numerical order (Rule 3(c)). If classification is not possible using either the most specific description or essential character tests, the rules move from a substantive classification method to one based simply on location. More specifically, the proper classification is the one heading, which occurs last in numerical order among those which might be applicable.[41]

Goods unclassifiable under Rules 1–3—most akin (Rule 4) When no headings appear directly applicable, the goods should be classified under the heading the goods are *most akin.* While this test has been used very infrequently, it is essentially a "do the best the headings allow" test, and may result in two or more headings being equally "most akin." In such case one should try to find which is "more" akin. However, if uncertainty still results, move on to Rule 5.

Specially shaped or fitted cases for goods—classed with their contents (Rule 5(a)). Containers, such as camera cases, musical instrument cases, gun cases, drawing instrument cases, and necklace cases, which are "specially shaped or fitted" are classified with the

---

[36] In April 2011, the Federal Circuit held that "goods put up in sets for retail sale" include goods that are packaged together in a certain manner at the time they enter the United States, and does not include secondary materials that the customer must purchase separately. Dell Prod. LP v. U.S., 642 F.3d 1055, 1060 (Fed. Cir. 2011).

[37] General Rules 3(a).

[38] General Rules 3(b).

[39] A "chief value" determination applied, no less capable of exact determination.

[40] CamelBak Prod. LLC v. United States, 649 F.3d 1361, 1369 (Fed. Cir. 2011).

[41] General Rules 3(c).

goods they serve, if they enter with those goods and are suitable for long term.[42]

However, the rule does not apply if the containers give the whole its essential character. For example, expensive carved tea caddies containing tea would not be classified as tea, because the container is not shaped to fit the tea (as is a musical instrument case) and the container gives the whole (tea plus caddy) the essential character.

Packing materials and containers—classed with their contents (Rule 5(b)). Subject to the provisions of Rule 5(a), packing materials and containers that enter with goods are classified as the goods if they are the normal kind used in packaging or containers.[43] However, this is not true when the materials or containers are suitable for repetitive use.

Rules 5(a) and (b) are specific and apply only in limited situations. In fact, in most cases when a clear classification cannot be determined after using Rule 4, it will be necessary to go on to the final General Rule 6 for additional guidance.

Subheadings and subheading notes (Rule 6). The subheadings, found in the first "Heading/Subheading" column of each chapter in the tariff schedules define goods more specifically than the heading. When subheadings or subheading notes are used, and two or more subheadings on the same level seem applicable, the process follows the outline in the rules discussed above.[44]

§ 11.9 Classification—The Additional U.S. Rules of Interpretation

The six General Rules of Interpretation make up the classification system provided by the HTS. However, when the United States adopted this system, it added its own rules, called the "Additional U.S. Rules of Interpretation." In addition to applying the General Rules, these rules must also be examined to determine whether a use is (1) consistent with the General Rules; (2) helpful where the General Rules do not lead to a satisfactory conclusion; or (3) conflict with the conclusion reached under the General Rules.

Classification controlled by use other than actual use (U.S. Rule 1(a)). If a classification is controlled by use other than actual use,

---

42 General Rules 5(a).

43 General Rule 5(b).

44 General Rules 6.

and there is no special language or context mandating otherwise, it must be the use in the United States. More specifically, the use in the United States at, or immediately prior to, the time of importation. Furthermore, the controlling use must be the *principal* use (which exceeds any other single use).[45] This requirement steps away from the Rule's past reference to chief use (which exceeds all other uses).

Classification controlled by actual use (U.S. Rule 1(b)). The rule is similar to the above. However, to satisfy this provision, the imported goods must, (1) be the use intended at the time of importation, (2) the goods are so used, and (3) proof thereof is furnished within three years after the date the goods are entered.[46]

Parts and accessories—general v. specific (U.S. Rule 1(c)). Where a provision specifically describes a part or accessory, it must be used over a general "parts and accessories" provision.[47] Thus, the import of bicycle chains would be classified as bicycle chains if described specifically, and not under a "catch-all" "other parts and accessories" category. This rule provides consistency with the General Rules' preference for specificity, even though the General Rules do not specifically contain a rule for parts.[48]

Textile materials (U.S. Rule 1(d)). The principles of section XI, which govern mixtures of two or more *textile* materials, apply to any goods in any provision where textile material are named.[49] Textiles have their own mystique, and are subject to special trading rules throughout the world. These provisions assure the special rules of classification for textile materials are applied throughout the tariff schedules wherever textile material is mentioned.

Conflicts between General Rules and Additional U.S. Rules. When a conflict arises between the application of the General Rules and the Additional U.S. Rules, no guidance exists within the rules to handle that situation. However, it seems likely that the Additional U.S. Rules would supplant as well as supplement the General Rules. But, the likelihood for such conflict is slim because the Additional U.S. Rules were not intended to set forth views where the United States differs with the HTS. Instead, the Rules provide a necessary supplement.

---

45 U.S. Rules 1(a).

46 U.S. Rules 1(b).

47 U.S. Rules 1(c).

48 However, individual chapter and section notes sometimes include parts rules.

49 U.S. Rules 1(d).

Fair and accurate application of the above rules is not an easy task, and certainly does not mean that all reasonable minds (including those found in the Customs Service) will reach the same conclusion. However, another important source should be considered while classifying products, the "United States Customs Service, Guidance for Interpretation of Harmonized System."

§ 11.10 Classification—United States Customs Service, Guidance for Interpretation of Harmonized System

When the HTS was adopted in 1989, some questions existed as to how Customs would classify some of the materials developed over the years. Of specific concern was the use of the Explanatory Notes to the Harmonized System, and reports of the Nomenclature Committee, which administered the Customs Cooperation Council (CCC) Nomenclature. Additionally, how letters from the Secretariat of the CCC would be used was unclear, and rulings and regulations from the customs administrations of other nations. The United States Customs Service soon issued the *Guidance for Interpretation of Harmonized System.*[50] The guide makes several points quite clear.

United States Customs Service does not seek uniformity of interpretation with other nations. While the Harmonized System Committee (HSC) under Article 7 of the Convention functions to provide uniformity, the United States Customs Service does not. To illustrate, the United States does not to alter "sections, chapters, headings or subheadings" of the HTS, and will consider background documents to avoid such alterations. However, the Customs Service will not purposely make its interpretations of the HTS consistent with the interpretations of other HTS member nations. If serious inconsistencies in interpretation result, the HTS will likely be modified to minimize the inconsistency, such as by further refining the classification.

Use of Explanatory Notes to the Harmonized System. These notes are the official interpretation of the Harmonized System created by the Customs Cooperation Council. According to the Custom Service, Customs should use the notes as a useful tool, providing guidance, but should not treat them as dispositive.[51] Further, because the Explanatory Notes are amended from time to time and reflect changes in interpretation, they should be consulted periodically as changes are adopted. The only other document given this status by Congress

---

[50] 54 Fed.Reg. 35127 (1989).

[51] See Conf.Rep. No. 100–576, 100th Cong., 2d Sess. 549 (1988).

are the "similar publications of the Council," which essentially refers to the Compendium of Classification Opinions because it is the only similar publication.

Use of the Compendium of Classification Opinions. The Harmonized System Committee (HSC) writes these opinions on the classification of different products. They are the result of requests presented to the HSC, and have the same weight as Explanatory Notes. Additionally, the Opinions are the official interpretation of the HSC on the particular issue decided.

Harmonized System Committee Reports. In addition to opinions, the HSC periodically issues reports on various subjects. While they do not have the same weight as the Explanatory Notes or Compendium of Classification Opinions, they may be helpful in determining the intention of the HSC. However, the reports of committees within the HSC, such as the Nomenclature Committee, carry virtually no weight, but may nevertheless be of some assistance in interpretation. Of even less use are the "working documents" of the Nomenclature and Classification Directorate of the CCC. They are the basis of discussions in HSC sessions, but they may not necessarily reflect the intent of the HSC.

Rulings of Other Countries. Because other nations that have adopted the HTS use the same General Rules of Interpretation, Section and Chapter Notes, and first six digits in the classification tables, their customs administration decisions are sometimes presented to the United States Customs Service. In general, U.S. Customs does not follow other nations' rulings because their decisions "may have been subject to political realities or domestic regulations which are different from our own." The meaning of this has not been further defined, but illustrates that there may be political pressure to classify goods so as to more readily admit them to, or more readily exclude them from, the United States. In any event, these foreign rulings are considered "merely instructive of how others" classify imports.

Position papers. Before a session of the HSC, U.S. Customs, the International Trade Commission, and the Bureau of Census prepare position papers for the session. These papers do not reflect Customs' position in the interpretation of the HTS and are considered to have no value, although they are occasionally circulated and obtained by importers or their counsel.

These notes, opinions, reports, rulings and papers all add to the process of interpretation, a layer which did not exist before the adoption of the HTS by the United States. Awareness of their use by the Customs Service may be helpful to United States counsel, but should not expect to be given weight beyond that announced by the Customs Service and as described above.

§ 11.11 Classification—Decisions of United States Courts

While it may seem strange to suggest that decisions of United States courts may not be applicable in interpreting the HTS, that may be correct for decisions interpreting the prior TSUS.[52] Interpretations of the United States HTS must follow the procedure outlined above. Certainly decisions rendered subsequent to the adoption of the HTS in 1988, which interpret the HTS, will be useful. But in many cases decisions have little usefulness because they apply to a narrow set of issues affecting specific goods where two or more classification possibilities exist. Although the HTS has a different process, the approach used in the past may find use in the future. Thus, some earlier decisions may be useful to understand the analytical process used by the courts.[53]

For example, prior United States decisions applying the rule of relative specificity may be used in interpreting General Rule of Interpretation Rule 3(a), which uses a kind of "rule of relative specificity" under the wording "most specific description."[54]

§ 11.12 Rules of Origin—Substantial Transformation, Proposed Uniform Approach

The second form of classification determines the country of origin of the items to be imported. Unlike, the determination of the proper classification discussed above, the country of origin determination discloses whether Column 1 or Column 2 rates of duty apply. If Column 1 rates of duty apply, the goods may qualify for preferential or duty free treatment, if from a country of origin that qualifies under "Special" in Column 1.[55]

---

[52] See JVC Company of America v. United States, 234 F.3d 1348 (Fed.Cir.2000).

[53] For example, the Mattel, Inc. v. United States decision, 287 F.Supp. 999 (Cust.Ct.1968), might be used when the issue involves priority of one classification over another.

[54] See, e.g., Great Western Sugar Co. v. United States, 452 F.2d 1394 (C.C.P.A.1972).

[55] The Court of International Trade requires importers seeking preferential tariff treatment to verify the country of origin of their goods. "Reasonable care" must be exercised, not just simple reliance on the exporter's assertions of origin. Failures in this regard can result in collection of lost duties and penalties. United States v.

Additionally, knowing the country of origin uncovers more general prohibitions of trade with that country, because the United States nearly always has several nations with which it does not trade by legislative or presidential declaration.[56] The United States may also put limits on products entering from a specific foreign nation. This limitation may be the result of a formal quota,[57] or an informal voluntary restraint agreement (VRA). VRAs have in the past covered a wide range of products (e.g., steel, vehicles, electronics), and have been a device adopted by the United States (and other areas such as the European Union) as executive policy in order to discourage legislative action to establish mandatory and involuntary quotas to reduce trade imbalances.[58] VRAs are now generally prohibited under the WTO Safeguards Agreement (1995).

Counsel representing an importer must know the framework for determining the country of origin of articles.[59] Eligibility of entry often depends on country of origin determination.[60] Country of origin law does not have as consolidated a framework as for classification of the goods discussed above. Although the classification is dealt with exclusively in the HTS, working within that system is not a simple matter. Determination of the country of origin requires using rules that may apply in a spectrum of different areas. While there are several references to various aspects of the rule of origin in different sources of law, the *substantial transformation* test (treated below) in its various costumes, has traditionally been *the* test.

In 2008, the Bureau of Customs and Border Protection proposed shifting to a single uniform approach to determine the origin of imported goods.[61] Although Customs and Border Protection withdrew the proposal, if adopted, it would have abandoned the historic test for the "substantial transformation" of foreign goods. The proposal elicited so many responses that the time for public comment on the proposal was extended twice. Most of the responses opposed

---

Golden Ship Trading Co., 2001 WL 65751 (C.I.T.2001) (T-shirts imported from Dominican Republic under Caribbean Basin Act were from China).

[56] These prohibitions may extend to both exports and imports, but may have certain exceptions, such as medical supplies.

[57] Quotas are regulated by the Customs Service. See 19 C.F.R. Part 132.

[58] See, e.g., Note, Voluntary Restraint Agreements: Effects and Implications of the Steel and Auto Cases, 11 N.C.J. Int'l L. & Com.Reg. 101 (1986).

[59] Counsel may wish to obtain a ruling from Customs in advance of importation. See 19 C.F.R. §§ 177.1–177.11.

[60] The United States must know whether the country of origin is one entitled to most favored nation treatment.

[61] *Uniform Rules of Origin for Imported merchandise, Notice of Proposed Rulemaking*, 73 FR 43,385 (2008).

the proposal because the rule could have substantially impacted the cost of entry into the United States, place undue burdens on those in the trading community, and cause the importation process to become more complex.[62] Eventually, in 2010 the Bureau of Customs and Border Protection abandoned the proposal.

Under the proposed WTO Agreement on Rules of Origin, there will be an effort to harmonize the rules of origin on a world-wide basis. A committee of experts is charged with creating rules which are "objective, understandable, and predictable." They are likely to differ from the core U.S. rule. Special rules of origin apply to the various U.S. duty free entry programs, most notably NAFTA which relies principally on changes in tariff classifications and regional value content to determine which goods may freely be traded. See Chapter 21. It is expected that any WTO agreement on rules of origin will adopt similar approaches.

§ 11.13 Rules of Origin—Sources of Law

Tariff Act of 1930. Section 304 of the Tariff Act requires every article of foreign origin, or its container imported into the United States to be marked in a conspicuous place with the English name of the country of origin.[63]

Trade Agreements Act of 1979. Section 308 of the Act provides various definitions, including the rule of origin for eligible products.[64] The definition focuses on the concept of substantial transformation,[65] leaving the courts to interpret the meaning of substantial transformation.

Code of Federal Regulations, Country of Origin Marking. Part 134 of 19 C.F.R. provides rules governing the country of origin *marking*. These regulations implement or reflect the provisions noted above

---

62 Vivian C. Jones and Michael F. Martin, INTERNATIONAL TRADE: RULES OF ORIGIN, Cong. Res. Serv., RL 34524 at 2 (January 5, 2012).

63 19 U.S.C.A. § 1304. For example the product has to say "Made in Spain" rather than "Made in Espana." The HTS governs treatment of containers and holders for imported merchandise. See 19 C.F.R. § 1202. The purpose of the rule is essentially to inform the public. Also, the Trademark Act of 1946, 15 U.S.C.A. §§ 1051–1127, does not allow admission of goods of foreign origin if they have a mark or name intended to lead the United States public to believe the product was made in the United States, or any country other than its true country of origin.

64 19 U.S.C.A. § 2518.

65 "An article is a product of a country or instrumentality only if (i) it is wholly the growth, product, or manufacture of that country or instrumentality, or (ii) in the case of an article which consists in whole or in part of materials from another country or instrumentality, it has been substantially transformed into a new and different article of commerce with a name, character, or use distinct from that of the article or articles from which it was so transformed." 19 U.S.C.A. § 2518(4)(B).

in both the Tariff Act of 1930 and the HTS. The regulations define articles subject to the marking, with special rules for articles repacked or manipulated, and ones usually combined with another article.[66] Rules also specify how containers or holders must be marked,[67] exceptions to the marking requirements,[68] method and location of marking,[69] and the consequences of finding articles not legally marked.[70] Essentially, the consequences for not properly marking a good are (1) properly mark the goods; (2) return the goods to the foreign nation; or (3) destroy the goods.[71]

Generally, a single country of origin must be determined for labeling purposes, even though the product may have been made in several countries. The country of origin, as determined by Customs, may not disclose other nations that may have participated in the process. While this may be important to the United States consumer, who may not wish to purchase products from a country substantially benefiting from the sale, but it is not important to the determination of the official country of origin. It may also be important to the United States government because it may not trade with the country that has substantially benefited from the importation, but was not the official country of origin.

Special Rules—The North American Free Trade Agreement (NAFTA). In drafting the NAFTA, as with drafting the earlier Canada–United States Free Trade Agreement, there was considerable concern that products entering the United States, as products of Canada or Mexico, actually had little fabrication or processing in those countries. To prevent this, special NAFTA rules of origin (discussed in Chapter 21) were adopted, which include articles governing customs procedures for the certification of origin.

The procedures create a North American "Certificate of Origin" and require extensive verification provisions. The exporter provides the Certificate of Origin when the importer tries to claim the duty free tariff treatment offered by the NAFTA.[72] However, a Certificate of Origin is not required for goods valuing $1,000 or less, or where a member state has waived their use.[73] A member state may conduct verification through written questionnaires, visits to the premises

---

[66] 19 C.F.R. §§ 134.13–134.14.

[67] 19 C.F.R. §§ 134.21–134.26.

[68] 19 C.F.R. §§ 134.31–134.36.

[69] 19 C.F.R. §§ 134.41–134.47.

[70] 19 C.F.R. §§ 134.51–134.55.

[71] 19 C.F.C. § 134.51(a).

[72] NAFTA Art. 501.

[73] NAFTA Art. 503.

exporter/producer, or other procedures the member states agree.[74] Verification is of considerable concern to the United States because it does not want Mexico to be used as a base for transshipping products from outside the NAFTA area, especially from Asia. The Court of International Trade requires importers seeking preferential tariff treatment to verify the country of origin of their goods. "Reasonable care" must be exercised, which requires more than simple reliance on the exporter's assertions of origin. Failure to do so can result in collection of lost duties and penalties.[75]

Decisions of United States Courts. There are several areas where Customs is required to determine the country of origin. However, the determinations sometimes lead to problems. For example, products from countries that the United States does not trade may be transshipped through a country that the United States does trade. Products from countries subject to high rates of duty in Column 2 may be transshipped through countries subject to lower rates of duty in Column 1. Products with most favored nation status, Column 1 rates of duty, may be transshipped through a country with special access, such as a Caribbean nation. Exporters from a nation that has agreed to a voluntary restraint agreement may try to exceed the agreed upon numbers by having the products transshipped through a nation without such a quota. As the United States enters into free trade agreements such as NAFTA, other nations may attempt to take advantage of that relationship by having goods transshipped through Canada or Mexico into the United States.

Fortunately, some case law has evolved, addressing the country of origin issue. Those cases, which involve one specific area, may be helpful in addressing another. For example, a case that has identified the country of origin, may be useful in determining whether the agreed amount under a voluntary restraint agreement has been exceeded.[76] Or may be helpful where products are allegedly violating the rules of the generalized system of preferences. Thus, when dealing with a country of origin issue, cases outside the scope of the form of entry (i.e., GSP, VRA, NAFTA, etc.) must be consulted. However, overall the cases utilize the same substantial transfor-

---

[74] NAFTA Art. 506.

[75] United States v. Golden Ship Trading Co., 2001 WL 65751 (Ct. Intl' Trade 2001) (T-shirts imported from Dominican Republic under Caribbean Basin Act were from China).

[76] See, e.g., Superior Wire, A Div. of Superior Products Co. v. United States, 669 F.Supp. 472 (C.I.T.1987), *affirmed* 867 F.2d 1409 (Fed.Cir.1989).

mation test, whether the matter involves quota restrictions or trade preferences.[77]

§ 11.14 Rules of Origin—Applicable Legal Theories

While some consistency in the identification of the country of origin exists, the process requires more than simply reading the label, which states the country of origin. Because a nation may do little more to an item than sew on the country of origin label, the product itself must be measured. The tests tend to be product specific, and because so many product variations exist, many variations in application may result.

Substantial transformation test. As stated above, the principal focus in a country of origin determination examines whether the product was substantially transformed in the country claiming the country of origin status.[78] One of the principal cases defining substantial transformation in the United States, an early United States Supreme Court decision, involves drawbacks.[79] The Court held substantial transformation occurs when a product is transformed into a new and different article "having a distinctive *name, character or use.*"[80] However, while this case provides a standard, it has been applied in many different ways.[81] For example, while a name change alone would not always be sufficient, such as from "wire" to "wire rod,"[82] a court held that changing heat-treated steel to galvanized steel was sufficient. More specifically, because the annealing process involved substantial manufacturing, which ultimate strengthened the steel and made it resistant to corrosion, it caused a substantial transformation to occur.[83]

---

[77] See Ferrostaal Metals Corp. v. United States, 664 F.Supp. 535, 538 (C.I.T.1987) (case law does not suggest that the court should depart from "policy-neutral rules governing substantial transformation in order to achieve wider import restrictions in particular cases.").

[78] This test is in the Trade Agreements Act of 1979. See 19 U.S.C.A. § 2518(4)(B).

[79] Anheuser–Busch Brewing Ass'n v. United States, 207 U.S. 556, 28 S.Ct. 204, 52 L.Ed. 336 (1908).

[80] Id. at 562, 28 S.Ct. at 206.

[81] But it is applied by the courts. See, e.g., Texas Instruments Inc. v. United States, 681 F.2d 778, 782 (C.C.P.A.1982).

[82] See Superior Wire, A Div. of Superior Products Co. v. United States, 669 F.Supp. 472 (C.I.T.1987) (the court noted that in recent years the focus was on a change in use or character).

[83] Ferrostaal Metals Corp. v. United States, 664 F.Supp. 535 (C.I.T.1987) (there was a "significant altering" of the "mechanical properties and chemical composition of the steel").

Courts tend to concentrate on changes in *character* or *use* rather than in the name of the product. Also, they often develop subtests appropriate for a particular kind of article. For example, whether a *significant value* was added, or *additional costs* were incurred. But each test leads to some subjective evaluation, which provides a sort of sense of whether the product is really from the state country. While the substantial transformation test has been criticized,[84] it remains the applicable law.

Value-added test. This test provides a more exacting process. It looks at how much value has been added as a percent of the value of the original product. There may be situations where no substantial transformation has occurred, but where significant value has been added to the original product.[85] What if a completed shirt with K–Mart logo buttons has those buttons removed and buttons are added with the logo of the most prestigious (currently) designer? If the result is the retail price may be trebled would that satisfy the value added test? There has certainly been minimal processing. Was the added value any more than the cost of the new buttons and their application? Isn't the high price really added in the United States by the consumers' willingness to pay more for apparent prestige? It seems that there must be some real value, such as labor or capital equipment, added in the country claiming to be the country of origin.

Considerations. However a court reaches a decision in a country of origin question, it is likely to have considered most of the following changes:

1. Change in name (and change in tariff classification);

2. Change in physical appearance;

3. Change in material substance (at each stage of manufacture);

4. Change in apparent use;

5. Change in value of item in the mind of the consumer;

6. Additional capital vested in article;

---

[84] Maxwell, Formulating Rules of Origin for Imported Merchandise: Transforming the Substantial Transformation Test, 23 J. Int'l L. & Econ. 669 (1990).

[85] One may nevertheless claim this to be a substantial transformation of value, if not of substance.

7. Additional labor vested in article;

8. Type of processing;

9. Affect of processing; and

10. Change in method of distribution.

There is no secret formula for determining which factor, if any, plays the most significant role. The end result may seem much like a test parallel to Justice Stewart's obscenity test—"I'll know it when I see it."

§ 11.15 Valuation—United States Law

The law applicable to classification of products is limited by the United States adoption of the HTS. The case law tends to evolve through variations of the substantial transformation test. The law applicable to valuation can be found in the United States Tariff Act of 1930, as amended. However, the United States' commitment to the GATT Customs Valuation Code, and the successor World Trade Organization must be considered.

For the most part, the United States Tariff Act of 1930 incorporates the GATT Customs Valuation Code of 1979.[86] However, because the United States adopted that GATT Code in 1979 amendments to the Tariff Act of 1930, some of the prior methods of interpretation of valuation may continue to be considered by courts.[87]

§ 11.16 Valuation—The Law of the GATT/WTO

Of the several codes adopted by the GATT in the Tokyo Round and renewed in the Uruguay WTO Round, the Agreement on the Implementation of Article VII of the General Agreement on Tariffs and Trade (GATT Customs Valuation Code) is of considerable importance to the United States.[88] While Article VII of the GATT, titled "Valuation for Customs Purposes," established a form of transaction value before, it was not until the Customs Valuation Code was adopted that the form of valuation by a descending order of tests was introduced. This form of valuation was incorporated into

---

[86] 19 U.S.C.A. § 1401a. See Sherman, Reflections on the New Customs Valuation Code, 12 Law & Pol'y Int'l Bus. 119 (1980).

[87] The same is true of other areas with pre-Code established procedures. See Snyder, Customs Valuation in the European Economic Community, 11 Georgia J. Int'l & Comp.L. 79 (1981).

[88] Geneve, 1979, GATT, 26th Supp. BISD 116 (1980). See Davey, Customs Valuation: Commentary on the GATT Customs Valuation Code (1989).

the United States law in 1979, and is the source of law one must turn for valuation of imports.

§ 11.17 Valuation—Appraisal of Imported Merchandise

Imports of merchandise are valued according to a series of alternative methods,[89] but not alternative methods in the sense that Customs may use any method it chooses. Nor may Customs reject information provided if based on the use of generally accepted accounting procedures.[90] The methods of valuation are set forth in the order of use. Most valuations never go beyond the first, the transaction value.

§ 11.18 Valuation—Transaction Value

All merchandise imported into the United States must be appraised. First, Customs considers the transaction value of the merchandise.[91] The transaction value is often referred to as the *invoice value* because in the absence of over or under invoicing, it would be the value of the transaction. The statute describes the transaction value as the *price actually paid or payable.*[92] In other words, it is the price when sold for exportation to the United States, also known as the wholesale price.[93] This may be confusing where there are several contracts, in addition to the actual contract between the buyer-seller. This situation can occur as between a party to the sale and the party's parent entity,[94] or between a foreign seller and United States company acquiring items purchased by the foreign seller from a foreign manufacturer.[95]

---

[89] Merchandise is defined as of the same class or kind as other merchandise if within a group or range which is produced by a particular industry or industrial sector. 19 U.S.C.A. § 1401a(e)(2).

[90] 19 U.S.C.A. § 1401a(g)(3).

[91] 19 U.S.C.A. § 1401a(a)(1)(A).

[92] 19 U.S.C.A. § 1401a(b)(1). Price actually paid or payable is defined in 19 U.S.C.A. § 1401a(b)(4). Disbursements by the buyer for the benefit of the seller are included, as when the buyer disburses some funds to the agent's seller who assists in bringing about the sale. Moss Mfg. Co., Inc. v. United States, 714 F.Supp. 1223 (C.I.T.1989), *affirmed* 896 F.2d 535 (Fed.Cir.1990).

[93] As of January 1, 2011, Customs and Border Protection

[94] Nissho Iwai American Corp. v. United States, 786 F.Supp. 1002 (C.I.T.1992), *aff'd in part, rev'd in part* 982 F.2d 505 (Fed.Cir.1992) (holding the master contract between the buyer and seller controls, rather than the contract price paid by the seller's Japanese company's parent to primary manufacturer).

[95] See Brosterhous, Coleman & Co. v. United States, 737 F.Supp. 1197 (C.I.T.1990)

Also, the transaction value may include some elements that create doubt as to application of duties. For example, quota charges clearly separated on the invoice are nevertheless includable.[96] Rebates to the price actually paid or payable made after the merchandise has entered the United States are disregarded in determining the transaction value.[97] However, dividing the assembly (service) price from the consumer (sale of goods) price for made-to measure clothing does not relieve the importer from duty on the former portion, the full cost is subject to duty.[98]

Five other categories of associated costs must be also added to the transaction value. Some are costs, which may be part of the price paid or payable, but some are costs, which, if not subject to tariffs, could be split off from the price of the goods and paid separately, thus avoiding or evading proper duty.[99] These additional costs subject to duty are:

1. Packing costs incurred by the buyer.[100] If incurred by the seller they would be part of the price paid for the merchandise, probably buried in the price of the goods.

2. All selling commission incurred by the buyer with respect to the imported merchandise.[101]

3. The value of any assist, apportioned as appropriate.[102] An assist includes a very broad range of benefits, and is the subject of an extensive definitional provision.[103]

4. Any royalty or license fee related to the goods, which the buyer pays directly or indirectly as a condition of the sale.[104] This

---

96 Generra Sportswear Co. v. United States, 905 F.2d 377 (Fed.Cir.1990).

97 19 U.S.C.A. § 1401a(b)(4)(B). See Allied Int'l v. United States, 795 F.Supp. 449 (C.I.T.1992) (importer has the burden of showing that the rebate occurred on or before date of entry).

98 E.C. McAfee Co. v. United States, 842 F.2d 314 (Fed.Cir.1988).

99 See All Channel Products v. United States, 787 F.Supp. 1457 (C.I.T.1992), *judgment affirmed* 982 F.2d 513 (Fed.Cir.1992) (inland freight charges separately invoiced properly included in transaction value); United States v. Arnold Pickle & Olive Co., 659 F.2d 1049, 68 C.C.P.A. 85 (1981) (inspection costs).

100 19 U.S.C.A. § 1401a(b)(1)(A).

101 19 U.S.C.A. § 1401a(b)(1)(B). See Jay–Arr Slimwear Inc. v. United States, 681 F.Supp. 875 (C.I.T.1988).

102 19 U.S.C.A. § 1401a(b)(1)(C).

103 19 U.S.C.A. § 1401a(h)(1). See, e.g., Texas Apparel Co. v. United States, 883 F.2d 66 (Fed.Cir.1989), *cert. denied* 493 U.S. 1024, 110 S.Ct. 728, 107 L.Ed.2d 747 (1990) (sewing machine costs constitute an assist in manufacturing jeans). See Collins, The Concept of Assist as Applied to Customs Valuation of Imported Merchandise, 1991 Detroit Col.L.R. 239.

104 19 U.S.C.A. § 1401a(b)(1)(D).

can be a difficult provision to interpret. However, if a buyer pays a flat fee per year directly to the designer of the goods, no matter how many are sold, the buyer may escape duty. But, any payment related to the number sold seems subject to duty.

5. Any direct or indirect accrual to the seller from the subsequent resale, disposal, or use of the goods.[105] This prevents the sale at a low base price, with the buyer required to pass on a percentage to the seller after the goods are resold.

The price paid or payable shall be increased by any of the above five additions, if it can be shown that they have not already been included in the price paid or payable by "sufficient" information.[106] The statute defines sufficient information as that which "establishes the accuracy of such amount, difference, or adjustment."[107] Where sufficient information is not available, and it seems like one or more of the five additional amounts exist, the transaction value is not determinable, and one must move to the next section in the chronology of applicable provisions.[108]

Where the transaction value is determinable, as discussed above, it will be considered the *appraised* value only if certain further conditions exist. The first of these conditions requires the buyer to dispose of or use the goods without restriction, except restrictions that (1) are required by law, (2) limit resale to a geographical area, or (3) do not substantially affect the value.[109]

The second condition requires that there may not be any condition or consideration affecting the sale of or the price paid or payable where the value of the condition or consideration cannot be determined.[110]

The third states that no part of the proceeds from the use or resale may accrue directly or indirectly to the seller, unless that amount is calculable under the provisions noted above.[111]

The fourth requires the buyer and seller to be either unrelated, or if related that the transaction is acceptable.[112] Because buyers

---

105 19 U.S.C.A. § 1401a(b)(1)(E).

106 19 U.S.C.A. § 1401a(b)(1).

107 19 U.S.C.A. § 1401a(b)(5).

108 Id.

109 19 U.S.C.A. § 1401a(b)(2)(A)(i).

110 19 U.S.C.A. § 1401a(b)(2)(A)(ii).

111 19 U.S.C.A. § 1401a(b)(2)(A)(iii). The above provision is 19 U.S.C.A. § 1401a(b)(1)(E).

112 19 U.S.C.A. § 1401a(b)(2)(A)(iv).

and sellers are often related through a parent and subsidiary relationship, the statute sets forth special rules. Often the prices reflected in transfers within an organization do not truly reflect arm's length prices because they want to avoid taxes, avoid tariff duties, or for other purposes.[113] The transaction value in such a transaction will be the appraised value, as long as (1) the circumstances of the sale do not suggest the relationship influenced the price, and (2) the transaction value approximates either the transaction value in an unrelated parties transaction, the deductive value, or computed value for identical or similar merchandise.[114]

This exception introduces the concepts of *deductive* value and *computed* value, both alternative valuations methods discussed below. The exception also requires defining both *identical* merchandise and *similar* merchandise.[115] The comparison values referred to above must be values for merchandise entering the United States on or around the same time as the merchandise in question.

The values used for comparison purposes usually consists of identical or similar goods,[116] however, varying method of sales may distort the comparison between the goods. Consequently, the values used must consider these differences, if based on sufficient information, in commercial levels, quantity levels and any costs, commissions, values, fees and proceeds in § 1401a(b)(1), discussed above.[117]

While the above identifies provisions designating the composition of the transaction value, specific items should not be included in the transaction value, including:

First, transaction value should not include any reasonable cost or charge for either (1) construction, erection, assembly, or maintenance of, or technical assistance to the merchandise after importation, or (2) transportation after importation.[118]

---

[113] Transfer pricing is discussed in chapter 24.

[114] 19 U.S.C.A. § 1401a(b)(2)(B).

[115] 19 U.S.C.A. § 1401a(h)(2) & (4).

[116] See Walter Holm & Co. v. United States, 3 C.I.T. 119 (1982) (use of value of exports of cantaloupes through Laredo, Texas, to determine value of same items through Nogales, Arizona).

[117] 19 U.S.C.A. § 1401a(b)(2)(C).

[118] 19 U.S.C.A. § 1401a(b)(3)(A). International transportation is separately excluded in 19 U.S.C.A. § 1401a(b)(4)(A).

Second, transaction value should not include the customs duties or other federal taxes imposed upon importation, nor federal excise tax.[119]

Transaction value of identical and similar merchandise. This separate section largely draws from the above section applicable to transaction value. The identical merchandise value method is used when the transaction value cannot be determined or used. When the identical merchandise value cannot be used, the similar merchandise value should be used.[120] Where the transaction value has been determined above for identical merchandise or for similar merchandise, as defined in the statute,[121] it must be adjusted. This adjustment requires consideration of all different commercial level or quantity level of sales for identical or similar merchandise.[122] It must also be based on sufficient information. Where two or more comparison transactions exist, the appraisal of the imported merchandise will be based on the lower or lowest of the comparison values.[123]

§ 11.19 Valuation—Deductive Value

The most important question is when will the deductive method of valuation be used? Deductive value should be used when the above transaction value does not lead to an acceptable determination to Customs.[124] However, the importer may request that the computed value discussed below be used in place of the deductive value.[125] If computed value does not prove possible, the deductive value must be used next.[126]

Deductive value may be applied to the merchandise being appraised, or to either identical or similar merchandise.[127] The deductive value focuses on unit value,[128] and constitutes the most appropriate value as determined in one of three ways.

---

119 19 U.S.C.A. § 1401a(b)(3)(B).

120 19 U.S.C.A. §§ 1401a(a)(1)(B) & (C).

121 19 U.S.C.A. § 1401a(h)(2) & (4).

122 19 U.S.C.A. § 1401a(c)(2).

123 Id.

124 19 U.S.C.A. § 1401a(a)(1)(D).

125 19 U.S.C.A. § 1401a(a)(2).

126 Id.

127 19 U.S.C.A. § 1401a(d)(1).

128 Unit value is the price the merchandise is sold (1) in the greatest aggregate quantity, (2) to unrelated persons, (3) at the first commercial level after importation (at level i and ii discussed below), or after further processing (at level iii discussed below), (4) in a total volume which is both greater than the total volume sold at any

The first method applies when the merchandise imported is sold (1) in the condition as imported, and (2) at or about the date of importation. The deductive value is the unit price at which the merchandise is sold in the greatest quantity.[129]

The second method applies when the merchandise imported is sold in the condition as imported, but not at or about the date of importation. The deductive value in this case is the unit price at which the merchandise is sold in the greatest quantity, but within 90 days after importation.[130]

The third method is where the merchandise is neither sold in the condition imported nor within 90 days after importation. The deductive value is the unit price at which the merchandise, after further processing, is sold in the greatest quantity within 180 days of importation.[131] This third method only applies at the election of the importer and upon notification to the customs officer.[132]

If the deductive method applies, some reductions from the unit price may result, including commissions, additions for profit and expenses, costs of domestic and international transportation, customs duties and other federal taxes on the merchandise. If the third method of deductive value is used, the costs of additional processing may reduce the unit price.[133] However, deductions for profits and expenses must be consistent with profits and expenses in the United States for similar merchandise, and any state or local taxes on the importer relating to the sale of the merchandise is considered an expense.[134]

There may also be an increase to the unit price, if such costs have not already been included, amounting to the packing costs incurred by the importer or buyer.[135]

A final provision requires one to disregard any sale to a person who supplies an assist for use in connection with the merchandise.[136]

---

other unit price, and sufficient to establish the unit price. 19 U.S.C.A. § 1401a(d)(2)(B).

[129] 19 U.S.C.A. § 1401a(d)(2)(A)(i).

[130] 19 U.S.C.A. § 1401a(d)(2)(A)(ii).

[131] 19 U.S.C.A. § 1401a(d)(2)(A)(iii).

[132] Id.

[133] 19 U.S.C.A. § 1401a(d)(3)(A).

[134] 19 U.S.C.A. § 1401a(d)(3)(B).

[135] 19 U.S.C.A. § 1401a(d)(3)(C).

[136] 19 U.S.C.A. § 1401a(d)(3)(D).

Where deductive value is inapplicable, or where the importer has chosen to pass over deductive value, the next method is computed value.

§ 11.20 Valuation—Computed Value

Computed value should be used when transaction and deductive value methods do not provide an appropriate result. However, the importer may skip over the deductive value tests and go straight to the computed value test.[137] The computed value determination consists of the sum of four parts.[138]

First, computed value considers the cost or value of materials and fabrication or processing,[139] but it does not include any internal tax by the exporting country if the tax is remitted upon exportation.[140]

Second, compute value considers the profit and expenses of the amount usually associated with the same kind of merchandise.[141] They are based on producer's profits and expenses, unless inconsistent with those for sales of the same class or kind of merchandise by producers in the country exporting to the United States, in which case there is a calculation of such profits and expenses using the "sufficient information" procedure.[142] For example, freight costs incurred through the shipment of tomato paste from Mexico to the United States should be included in the computed value.[143] Also, the costs of a warranty for aircraft should be included as profit, less expenditures the manufacturer-seller establishes as incurred by the warranty obligations in curing defects.[144]

Third, computed value includes any assist if not already included in the amount above.[145] Computing the value of jeans would

---

[137] 19 U.S.C.A. § 1401a(a).

[138] 19 U.S.C.A. § 1401a(e)(1). For cases which have used the constructed value approach, see Campbell Soup Co., Inc. v. United States, 107 F.3d 1556 (Fed. Cir. 1997) (calculating the computed value of transported tomato paste from Mexico to United States); New York Credit Men's Adjustment Bureau, Inc. v. United States, 314 F.Supp. 1246 (Cust.Ct.1970), *affirmed* 342 F.Supp. 745 (Cust.Ct.1972).

[139] 19 U.S.C.A. § 1401a(e)(1)(A). See Texas Apparel Co. v. United States, 698 F.Supp. 932 (C.I.T.1988), *affirmed* 883 F.2d 66 (Fed.Cir.1989), *cert. denied* 493 U.S. 1024, 110 S.Ct. 728, 107 L.Ed.2d 747 (1990).

[140] 19 U.S.C.A. § 1401a(e)(2)(A).

[141] 19 U.S.C.A. § 1401a(e)(1)(B). See Braniff Airways, Inc. v. United States, 2 C.I.T. 26 (1981).

[142] 19 U.S.C.A. § 1401a(e)(2)(B).

[143] Campbell Soup Co., Inc. v. United States, 107 F.3d 1556 (Fed. Cir. 1997)

[144] Braniff Airways, Inc. v. United States, 2 C.I.T. 26 (1981).

[145] 19 U.S.C.A. § 1401a(e)(1)(C).

allow the addition of the cost or value of the sewing machines used to produce the jeans.[146] Finally, packing costs are included in the computed value.[147]

§ 11.21 Valuation—Value When Other Methods Are Not Effective

If the value cannot be determined under the above-discussed methods, there is a final method for calculating value. It is to derive a value using the methods set forth above, and then adjusting them to the extent necessary to achieve a reasonable result.[148] But in making such an appraisal, the statute prohibits using any of seven items.[149]

(1) United States selling price of United States produced merchandise,

(2) any system using the higher of two alternatives,

(3) domestic market price in country of exportation,

(4) cost of production for identical or similar merchandise which differs from such cost of production determined under the computed value method,

(5) price for export to a country other than the United States,

(6) minimum values, or

(7) arbitrary or fictitious values.

As first noted, transaction value expressed in the invoice is used in the vast majority of cases. However, when challenges to transaction value appear, the procedure may become more complex. While any of the determinations of Customs may be challenged, the cost of such challenge for all but the largest importers will often result in paying the Customs determined value, or not importing the goods. Counsel should calculate the possible rates of duty under all the possible alternatives and should only import the products if the rate of duty is acceptable and does not cause the price for resale to

---

146 Texas Apparel Co. v. United States, 698 F.Supp. 932 (C.I.T.1988), *affirmed* 883 F.2d 66 (Fed.Cir.1989), *cert. denied* 493 U.S. 1024, 110 S.Ct. 728, 107 L.Ed.2d 747 (1990).

147 19 U.S.C.A. § 1401a(e)(1)(D).

148 19 U.S.C.A. § 1401a(f)(1).

149 19 U.S.C.A. § 1401a(f)(2).

be either excessive, or more than would result from using United States products which may cost more to produce, but do not have added duty.

Chapter 12

ANTIDUMPING DUTIES

Table of Sections

---

§ 12.1 Overview—Antidumping Duties (ADs) and Countervailing Duties (CVDs)

Chapters 9, 10, and 11 examined governmental regulation of international trade, and in particular the international and national rules for the imposition of tariffs. At the core of the international system defined by the various agreements in the World Trade Organization (WTO) system is a principle of binding tariffs applied equally to all WTO member states (the most-favored-nation principle). The WTO system allows, however, certain exceptions, the two most important of which are "antidumping duties" (ADs) and "countervailing duties" (CVDs). This Chapter will analyze antidumping duties; Chapter 13 will then examine the subject of governmental subsidies and the allowed response of countervailing duties.[1]

Under both antidumping duties and countervailing duties, a country may impose duties on an imported item above that otherwise allowed by the generally applicable tariff schedule. Antidumping duties are an allowed trade response where an enterprise prices its goods for sale in the country of importation at a level that is less than that charged for comparable sales in the home country (*i.e.*, at "less than fair value" (LTFV)). Countervailing duties are allowed as a trade response to direct or indirect "subsidies" granted by another country in order to position its exports more competitively in the international marketplace.

The WTO system recognizes and permits both antidumping duties and countervailing duties, providing of course the respective requirements are satisfied. Each "trade remedy" also is governed by a separate WTO Covered Agreement that provides more detail on the circumstances under which member states may impose the exceptional duties. Because each is mandatory in the WTO system, the special WTO agreements provide the foundation for a reasonably uniform body of legal rules for trade remedies among the more than 150 WTO member states.

The substantive grounds for the imposition of trade remedies are different for each of the two exceptions, but the injury standard is essentially the same. Under the WTO Antidumping Agreement and the WTO Subsidies and Countervailing Measures Agreement, generally a country may impose a special duty on products of another WTO member state only if two requirements are met. First, the country must find sufficient evidence of an unfair trade practice, either dumping (sales at less than fair value) or prohibited or actionable subsidies. Second, the practice must cause a sufficiently significant injury to a domestic industry. In the case of dumping or subsidies, this requires proof that the practice has caused or threatens to cause a "material injury" to a domestic industry or that it has "materially retarded" the establishment of such an industry.

---

[1] Chapter 15 will examine a third allowed response to import competition: temporary "safeguard" (or "escape clause") measures. This form of governmental protection against import competition is substantially less common.

Neither of the two trade remedies in favor of domestic producers is based, however, on any notion of reciprocity. That is, neither arises because another country has restricted the importation of U.S. goods into its markets. Antidumping and countervailing duties instead address only unfair selling prices for the dutiable imported goods themselves.

§ 12.2 Dumping—What Is It and Why Is It Done?

Dumping involves an exporter selling goods abroad at a lower price than it charges for the same goods in the home market (the "normal" or *"fair"* value). This alone is not sufficient however. Antidumping duties are allowed as a trade response only if the practice causes or threatens to cause a material injury to an industry in the export market. Dumping is recognized by most of the trading world as an unfair practice (akin to price discrimination as an antitrust offense). As noted, dumping is the subject of a special WTO Agreement that defines when dumping occurs, what constitutes a material injury, and the rules on the calculation of an allowed antidumping duty response by the offended country.

The economics of dumping arise from a producer's opportunity to compartmentalize the overall market for its product, thus permitting it to offer the product for sale at different prices in different geographic areas. Only if trade barriers or other factors insulate each market sector from others is there opportunity to vary substantially the product's price in different sectors of the global market. For example, a producer can securely "dump" products in an overseas market at cheap prices and at high volume only if it can be sure that the product market in its home country is immune from return penetration by these products. The objectives of dumping include increasing marginal revenues, ruining a competitor's market position, and developing a new market on an expeditious basis.

On the other hand, a sale at less than the home price may not necessarily represent an unfair trade practice; it may instead merely result from a short-term need to introduce new products, sell off excess inventory, or conduct a distress sale in difficult financial circumstances. Indeed, "dumping" products in order to establish a foothold in a new foreign market or to raise brand awareness in an existing market may make sense as a marketing technique. Because the motivations for selling a product at low prices are numerous and varied, it often is very difficult to determine whether "actionable" dumping is occurring in any particular case. In any event, the ultimate economic rationality of dumping remains the subject of vigorous debate among economists.

§ 12.3 The WTO Antidumping Agreement (1994)

The law regarding dumping has been the repeated subject of discussion in the various rounds of negotiations under the General Agreement on Tariffs and Trade (GATT) and (later) the WTO. A technical area, antidumping remedies were for many years principally used by developed nations to protect against competition from developing country imports. Then, in a remarkable transfer of legal technology, the principles endorsed by various GATT antidumping agreements took hold in newly developing countries. Today, antidumping duties are as likely to be imposed on U.S. exports by Mexico, India or China, as vice-versa. Antidumping proceedings remain the preferred trade remedy of domestic producers. The European Union and India are the top users of antidumping remedies, with products from China by far the top target of antidumping duties.

Late in 1993, the Uruguay Round of GATT negotiations came to a successful conclusion and President Clinton notified Congress of his intent to sign the many "covered agreements" that resulted from those negotiations. One of those agreements is yet another attempt at a codification of antidumping law. As a basic matter, Article VI of the longstanding GATT grants WTO member states the right to impose antidumping duties. But the more detailed standards for such duties are set forth in a separate WTO Agreement, "The Agreement on Implementation of Article VI of GATT 1994."

The WTO Antidumping Agreement, adopted from the earlier Tokyo Round GATT "Antidumping Code," focuses on dumping determinations (particularly criteria for allocating costs) and material injury determinations (particularly causation). The Antidumping Agreement provides that dumping occurs with respect to a product if its export price is less than the "normal value." It defines the "normal value" of a good as the comparable price, in the ordinary course of trade, for the same or a similar product "when destined for consumption in the exporting country." Thus, in evaluating whether an export price constitutes dumping, the best baseline for comparison is the domestic sales price of comparable goods in the exporting country (*i.e.*, the home country).

However, such comparable sales may not be available, either because comparable products are not sold domestically or because the usual retail transaction there is not comparable (*e.g.*, leasing rather than a sale). In that situation, the Antidumping Agreement provides a hierarchy of alternative computation methods to achieve an approximate evaluation. Among these alternatives, the preferred one uses the *price* for the same or a similar product in the ordinary course of trade for export to a third country. The next preferred alternative is to calculate the *cost* of production of the exported goods in the country of origin, plus a reasonable amount for profits and for administrative, selling and any other general costs. In either case, the value thus determined is then compared against the price charged on the export price to the target country.

The Agreement then has detailed rules that permit a member state to impose an antidumping duty only if a sale at less than fair value has caused a sufficient injury to a domestic industry. The Agreement defines the required level of injury as a "material injury" or "threat of material injury" to a domestic industry or a "material retardation of the establishment of such an industry." And such an injury determination is permitted only on "positive evidence" and an "objective determination" of the volume of dumped imports and the effect on domestic prices as well as the consequent impact on domestic producers of the dumped product.

Because the United States has agreed to abide by the Antidumping Agreement, each of these requirements is reflected in conforming provisions of the U.S. Tariff Act of 1930. The remaining Sections of this Chapter will examine in detail these rules of antidumping law.

The WTO Antidumping Agreement also has a few special rules that are worthy of emphasis. First, it forbids duties for *de minimis* dumping, defined as less than two percent of the product's export price; in such cases member states must terminate any antidumping investigations immediately. Second, the Agreement permits "cumulation" of imports—*i.e.*, imports of the same goods from more than one country—if the dumping from each is more than *de minimis* and this is otherwise appropriate under the circumstances. Third, it recognizes, but does not expressly allow or disallow, antidumping petitions by employees and their union representatives. Fourth, the Agreement obligates member states to notify the WTO of any changes to their domestic antidumping laws as well as any related administrative actions. More generally, a special WTO "Committee on Anti-Dumping Practices" oversees implementation of the Agreement by member states.

Finally, when another member state challenges the imposition of antidumping duties before the WTO, the Dispute Settlement Body (DSB) panel may rely on the facts developed in the domestic administrative proceedings and must accept those facts if the domestic evaluation "was unbiased and objective, even if the panel might have reached a different conclusion." Agreement also expressly allows for "competing, reasonable interpretations" of its obligations under the domestic law of its member states.

§ 12.4 The Evolution of U.S. Antidumping Law

The United States was an early advocate of the perspective that dumping constitutes an unfair trade practice. Indeed, complaints about dumping were recorded as the subject of a protest by Secretary of the Treasury Alexander Hamilton in 1791. In general, U.S. antidumping statutes compare the price at which articles are imported or sold within the United States with their price in the country of production at the time of their export to the United States. This approach was first established by the Antidumping Act of 1916, a rarely-invoked criminal statute prohibiting "predatorily low price levels."[2] This statute, which also created a private remedy for treble damages, required proof of an intent to seriously injure or destroy a U.S. industry. The European Union, Japan, and other states successfully challenged this 1916 Act in WTO dispute settlement proceedings as inconsistent with the Antidumping Agreement. The pressure of the adverse rulings by the WTO's DSB ultimately led the United States to repeal the Act in 2004.

The modern U.S. rules and procedures governing antidumping duties are set forth in a statute that is still known as the Tariff Act of 1930;[3] but Congress has enacted amendments to this statute numerous times. The most important of these for present purposes came through the Uruguay Round Agreements Act of 1994 (URAA),[4] by which (as the name suggests) Congress amended the Tariff Act to implement the numerous Uruguay Round WTO agreements, including the Antidumping Agreement. Finally, the Code of Federal Regulations contains more detailed rules on the requirements for, calculation of, and process for assessing antidumping duties.[5]

U.S. law places authority for administering antidumping law in two different governmental agencies.[6] Generally, the Secretary of Commerce (which in turn has delegated specific authority to its International Trade Administration (ITA)) is the "Administering Au-

---

[2] 15 U.S.C. §§ 71–77.

[3] Codified at 19 U.S.C. §§ 1671–1677g.

[4] Public Law No. 103–465, 108 Stat. 4809.

[5] The principal U.S. antidumping regulations are found in 19 C.F.R. Part 351.

[6] For more on the administrative processes governing antidumping duties see §§ 12.22 through 12.25 *infra*.

thority,"[7] which is responsible for all administration determinations except those relating to injury to a domestic industry. Injury determinations are the responsibility of the International Trade Commission (ITC).[8] To provide guidance on the application of the applicable statutory and regulatory rules, the International Trade Administration publishes an "Antidumping Manual," the most recent version of which is from 2009.[9]

Sections 12.5 through 12.19 below will examine in detail the substantive rules of U.S. law on antidumping determinations. In brief, and in conformity with the WTO Antidumping Agreement, the fundamental determination under U.S. law is whether a sale is at "less than fair value" (LTFV).[10] This requires a comparison of the U.S. price of imported goods with their "normal value." "Normal value" is usually determined by the price charged for the goods in the exporter's *domestic* market (the home market) in the ordinary course of business.[11] The ITA then compares this value with the price of the goods for export to the United States.[12] As noted, the ITC separately makes determinations on injury and causation in antidumping proceedings. In order to impose antidumping duties, the Tariff Act requires an affirmative determination by the ITC that a challenged practice presents an actual or threatened "material injury" to a domestic industry or that it has "materially retarded" the establishment of such an industry.[13]

If sales are both at LTFV and cause or threaten "material injury" to a domestic industry, then the Tariff Act declares that an antidumping duty "shall be imposed."[14] Thus, antidumping duties are a statutory remedy, one which the President cannot veto or affect (except by the extraordinary act of negotiating an international trade agreement).

---

7 19 U.S.C. § 1677(1). Prior to 1980, the Treasury Department was the "administering authority", but the Secretary of Commerce was so designated in 1980. *See President's Reorganization Plan No. 3 of 1979*, 44 Fed. Reg. 69,273 (1979), and Executive Order 12188, 45 Fed. Reg. 989 (1980).

8 19 U.S.C. §§ 1673(2) and 1677(2).

9 Import Administration Antidumping Manual (2009), available at http://ia.ita.doc.gov/admanual/index.html.

10 19 U.S.C. § 1673(1).

11 19 U.S.C. §§ 1673(1), 1677b. *See also* §§ 12.6–12.9 *infra.*

12 19 U.S.C. §§ 1673(1), 1677a. *See also* § 12.10 *infra.*

13 19 U.S.C. § 1673(2). *See also* §§ 12.12–12.18 *infra.*

14 19 U.S.C. § 1673.

§ 12.5 The Basic Dumping Determination

The Basic Measure. The ITA determines whether foreign merchandise[15] is, or is likely to be, sold in the United States at less than fair value (LTFV) by comparing the foreign market value (the "normal value") of the goods to the price charged for export to the United States (the "United States price"). If the former exceeds the latter, dumping has occurred. Much turns, therefore, on the definitions of these two central concepts. Sections 12.6 through 12.9 below will examine the calculation of the foreign market value. Section 12.10 below will then analyze the appropriate comparison price regarding the export of the goods to the United States.

The Dumping Margin. As noted, if a sale both (a) is at LTFV and (b) meets the statutory material injury requirement, then the Tariff Act provides that an antidumping duty "shall be imposed."[16] The amount of the duty will correspond to the "dumping margin." The ITA normally compares the "weighted-average" foreign market value with the "weighted-average" U.S. price for the dumped product.[17] The term "weighted average dumping margin" is a percentage that is determined with reference to the "aggregate dumping margins" of the exporter or producer for the type of products at issue.[18] For large capital goods, however, the ITA will typically use the actual normal value and the U.S. price on a transaction-to-transaction basis.[19] Whichever calculation method is used, the "dumping margin"—and thus the amount of the antidumping duty—corresponds to the amount by which the foreign market "normal value" of the goods exceeds the price charged in the export to the United States.[20] The dumping margin may be different for similar merchandise from different foreign states, and may also be different for different manufacturers from the same foreign state.

§ 12.6 Foreign Market Value—"Normal Value"

The first step in the analysis is to determine the appropriate value of the allegedly dumped goods in a relevant foreign market.

---

15 Antidumping law generally does not apply to services, but also is not limited to "cash-only sales." *See* U.S. v. Eurodif S. A., 555 U.S. 305 (2009).

16 19 U.S.C. § 1673.

17 19 U.S.C. § 1677(35)(B).

18 *Id.*

19 19 U.S.C. § 1677(35)(A).

20 *Id.*

The Tariff Act refers to this value as the "normal value."[21] It recognizes three different measures for this normal value:

Home Market Price. The standard measure of the "normal value" is the price at which the foreign merchandise is first sold for consumption—in usual quantities, in the ordinary course of trade, and preferably at the same level of trade—in the exporting country ("home market price").[22]

Third Country Price. If, however, sales in the home market are nonexistent or too small to form an adequate basis for comparison (usually, less than five percent of the total sales of the goods to the United States), then export sales to other countries may be used for the normal value ("third country price").[23] Sales intended to establish fictitious markets in the source country, however, cannot be considered.[24]

Constructed Value. If comparable merchandise is not offered for sale either in the home market or for export to third countries, the ITA is authorized to calculate a "constructed" value.[25] In such a case, the ITA will build a figure based on the sum of three elements: (1) First, it will calculate the actual costs of production and processsing of the goods. (2) To this basic cost figure it will add the exporter's actual "selling, general, and administrative expenses" as well as actual profits for the goods. If actual numbers are not available for this element, then the ITA will use one of three alternatives: (a) the specific exporter's costs and profits for goods of the "same general category," (b) the weighted average of costs and profits for like goods by other exporters subject to the investigation, or (c) the costs and profits determined by the ITA "based on any other reasonable method." (3) Finally, the ITA will add the costs of containers and other coverings for the goods as well as all other expenses incidental to shipping the goods to the United States.[26] If the foreign producer is in a non-market economy, then the ITA will construct an appropriate value based either on various "factors of production" or on "surrogate country prices" (see Section 12.8 below).[27]

The time and place for determining the normal value is often crucial. The Tariff Act requires that the relevant time for measuring

---

21 19 U.S.C. §1677b.

22 19 U.S.C. §1677b(a)(1)(B)(i).

23 19 U.S.C. § 1677b(a)(1)(B)(ii).

24 19 U.S.C. § 1677b(a)(2).

25 19 U.S.C. § 1677b(a)(4), (e).

26 19 U.S.C. § 1677b(e).

27 19 U.S.C. § 1677b(c). For more detail on this issue see § 12.9 *infra.*

the sales in the foreign country must "reasonably correspond[]" to the time used to calculate the comparison export price to the United States.[28] That is the time when the product is "first sold (or agreed to be sold) before the date of importation by the producer or exporter of the subject merchandise outside of the United States to an unaffiliated purchaser in the United States."[29] That is also the date for determining the appropriate exchange rate for converting prices in foreign currency into U.S. dollars.[30]

In determining foreign market value, the ITA may use averaging and generally recognized sampling techniques whenever there is a significant volume of sales or number of adjustments.[31] The authority to select averages and statistical sampling "rests exclusively" with the Secretary of Commerce (and thus the ITA).[32]

When the goods are manufactured in one country and then shipped to another, from which they are exported to the United States, a question arises as to which foreign country is the relevant one. The Act provides a partial answer. Generally, the price in country of transshipment (the "intermediate country") is the correct one *unless*:

(A) the producer knew at the time of the sale that the subject merchandise was destined for exportation;

(B) the goods are merely transshipped through the intermediate country;

(C) sales of the goods in the intermediate country are too small to form an adequate basis for comparison; or

(D) the goods are not produced in the intermediate country.[33]

Other issues relating to the determination of foreign market value are discussed below. These problems include issues arising out of sales at less than the costs of production; constructed values; imports from nonmarket economy countries; special rules for multinational corporations; and adjustments necessary to ensure a proper comparison of value with price.

---

28 19 U.S.C. § 1677b(a)(1)(A).

29 19 U.S.C. § 1677a(a).

30 *See* 19 U.S.C. § 1677b–1.

31 19 U.S.C. § 1677f–1.

32 19 U.S.C. § 1677f–1(b).

33 19 U.S.C. § 1677(a)(3).

§ 12.7 Sales Below Cost Disregarded

The central question in most antidumping proceedings is whether and to what degree the foreign producer or exporter is selling its goods in the home market below the cost of production. Sales are below cost if they do not recover total costs, both fixed and variable, over a commercially reasonable period. Thus, a significant volume of sales by a foreign producer at prices that cover only its variable costs can be disregarded by the ITA in its calculation of the foreign market value of the goods. The Tariff Act explicitly authorizes the ITA to disregard sales at less than the cost of production when it makes its "normal value" determinations.[34]

The ITA will investigate this issue whenever it "has reasonable grounds to believe or suspect" that sales of the goods under investigation "have been made at prices which represent less than the cost of production." If the ITA determines that such sales (a) have occurred "within an extended period of time in substantial quantities," and (b) "were not at prices which permit recovery of all costs within a reasonable period of time," then it "may" disregard the sales in determining the "normal value."[35] Thus, recovery of start-up costs may be prorated over commercially reasonable periods. A decision to disregard sales below cost from the normal value calculation naturally raises the average cost and thus increases the potential to find dumping. A decision to include such sales has the opposite effect.

If the ITA disregards sales as below the cost of production, it will make its "normal value" determination based on the remaining sales of the goods "in the ordinary course of trade."[36] And if no sales are made in the ordinary course of trade, the ITA must instead use the "constructed value" of the goods.[37]

§ 12.8 Nonmarket Economy Constructed Values

The ITA will always use the "constructed value" to determine the foreign market value of imports from nonmarket economy countries.[38] The actual prices used in the exporter's (home) foreign market are deemed irrelevant because they are assumed to be determined bureaucratically and not by market forces. That is, they are

---

[34] 19 U.S.C. § 1677b(b).

[35] *Id.*

[36] *Id.*

[37] *See* § 12.9 *infra.*

[38] 19 U.S.C. § 1677b(c).

not sufficiently subject to the forces of competition to form an accurate standard for comparison.

The Tariff Act delegates to the ITA the authority to determine when imports are from a "nonmarket economy country,"[39] and then insulates that administrative determination from judicial review.[40] The Act nonetheless gives the ITA a basic definition—whether the country's economy operates on "market principles" so that home market sales reflect "fair value." It then provides five factors to consider.[41] The factors include the convertability of the foreign country's currency, the extent to which wages and prices are determined by government action or free bargaining, the extent of government ownership of the means of production, the receptivity to private foreign investment, and "such other factors as the [Commerce Department] considers appropriate."[42] Although the Act speaks in terms of a country by country decision, the ITA has more often analyzed the particular industrial segment involved.

If the imports are from a nonmarket economy (NME) country, the Act directs the ITA to "construct" a foreign market value by determining the factors of production (labor, materials, energy, capital, etc.) actually used by the NME to produce the imported goods.[43] The ITA then determines a value for each of those "factors of production" according to the prices or costs in a market economy that is appropriate under the circumstances. Surrogate countries are appropriate if they are "at a level of economic development comparable to that of the nonmarket economy country" and also are "significant producers of comparable merchandise."[44]

The Act then directs the ITA to add to the cost of production—again, as constructed based on the factors of production—appropriate amounts for general expenses, profits, and the packaging of the goods for shipment to the United States. The amounts for general expenses and profits are to be derived from sales of the same class or kind of merchandise in the "country of exportation,"[45]

---

[39] 19 U.S.C. § 1677(18)(A), (C).

[40] 19 U.S.C. § 1677(18)(D).

[41] 19 U.S.C. § 1677(18)(B).

[42] *Id.*

[43] 19 U.S.C. § 1677b(c)(1).

[44] 19 U.S.C. § 1677b(c)(4). *See also, e.g.*, Ad Hoc Shrimp Trade Action Comm. v. United States, 618 F.3d. 1316 (Fed. Cir. 2010)(upholding the ITA's decisions in an antidumping order covering shrimp from Vietnam that calculated surrogate values based on survey data from comparable suppliers as "the best available information").

[45] 19 U.S.C. § 1677b(e)(1)(B).

but this term simply means an "appropriate" market economy country.

In recognition of some of the difficulties with a "cost of production" approach, the Act provides an exception to the constructed value method outlined above, by allowing the use of a method of constructing a foreign market value for imports from a NME based on actual sale *prices*. The ITA may use this alternative method if it finds that the best available information on the factors of production is not adequate. In such a case, the ITA will find a "surrogate" market economy country (a) that produces goods that are the same as or similar to the merchandise imported from the NME, and (b) that is "at a level of economic development comparable to that of the nonmarket economy country." Then, the ITA will construct a value based on the *price* at which such goods are "sold in other countries, including the United States."[46] Such a methodology does not require the ITA to construct a value based on the factors of production.

Several problems arise in the application of this scheme. First, "appropriate" market economy countries may be limited or unavailable. Second, the surrogate market economy countries selected may be obviously inappropriate, when compared to the level of economic development of the NME. Third, producers in such countries may not furnish the necessary information, even though the ITA is authorized to use the "best available information."[47] Fourth, there is no necessary relationship between the price so constructed by the ITA and any price that the NME producer may decide to charge. This leaves the NME producer or exporter always open to antidumping duties, and there is no pre-transaction analytical path for avoiding such duties.

§ 12.9 ____Market Economy Constructed Values

The ITA may use constructed values not only for imports from NME countries, but in other circumstances as well. It is directed to construct a foreign market value whenever merchandise comparable to the imported merchandise is not offered for sale either in the home market of the foreign producer or exporter or for export from that home market to other countries.[48] A constructed foreign market value is also to be used when so many sales in the home market are below the cost of production, and therefore are disregarded,

---

[46] 19 U.S.C. § 1677b(c)(2).

[47] 19 U.S.C. § 1677b(c)(1).

[48] 19 U.S.C. § 1677b(a)(4).

such that the remaining sales provide an inadequate basis for determining foreign market value.[49]

In such a case, the ITA will calculate the foreign market value based on one of three methodologies: (1) the producer's actual costs, plus sales, general, and administrative expenses, and plus a profit for the specific product under investigation; *or* (2) the producer's actual costs and profit for the products in the same category as those under investigation; *or* (3) a weighted average of other producers' actual costs and profit for the category of products under investigation.[50]

Special Rule for Multinational Corporations. The Act also has a special rule for determining the foreign market value of merchandise produced by a corporation with production facilities in two or more countries. This "special rule for certain multinational corporations" applies when there are insufficient sales by that producer in its home market on which to base a comparison of its export sales to the United States.[51] If the foreign market value of the goods produced in the country of exportation is less than the price of the goods produced in the corporation's facilities in another country, the ITA "shall" construct a foreign market value which reflects the price of the goods produced in the nonexporting country.

§ 12.10 United States Price

To determine whether dumping exists, the ITA will compare the foreign market value ("normal value") of the goods with the price charged for export to the United States. The Tariff Act recognizes two different methods for calculating this price:

Export Price. The ITA generally uses the "export price" for the price of the goods for exportation to the United States. This is the price at which the goods are first sold *outside* of the United States to an unaffiliated person before the goods are imported into the United States.[52] The standard example of this is when a foreign producer or exporter contacts an unaffiliated U.S. business in order to distribute a foreign product in the United States and the parties agree on the sale terms (price, quantity, delivery, etc.).

Constructed Export Price. If, however, the foreign exporter first sells the goods to an *affiliated* person outside the United States

---

[49] 19 U.S.C. § 1677b(b).

[50] 19 U.S.C. § 1677b(e).

[51] 19 U.S.C. § 1677b(d).

[52] 19 U.S.C. § 1677a(a).

(such that this "export" price is not a reliable one), then the ITA may use the "constructed export price."[53] This is the price at which the goods are first sold to an unaffiliated person *in* the United States irrespective of whether it occurs before or after importation. This typically occurs when a foreign exporter or producer first sells to a U.S. subsidiary, and in that case the relevant price is that charged by the subsidiary to the first unaffiliated U.S. buyer.

§ 12.11 "Foreign Like Product" Determinations and Required Adjustments

The entire analysis above depends upon a comparison of the United States price against the price of a "foreign like product,"[54] a concept also relevant in injury determinations by the ITC.[55] Because merchandise sold in foreign markets is often different, due to cultural, technical or legal constraints, the determination of comparability of merchandise sold in the foreign market to the imported merchandise is often a crucial one. The Act provides a definition, with a hierarchy of criteria.[56] Under the basic definition, merchandise that is identical in physical characteristics, and produced in the same country by the same person as the imported merchandise, is to be categorized as a "foreign like product."[57]

If such identical merchandise is not available, the ITA next looks for merchandise that is (a) produced in the same country by the same person, (b) has similar component materials, and (c) is approximately equal in value to the imported merchandise.[58]

If neither of these reference points is available, the ITA is to look at merchandise that (a) is produced in the same country by the same person and is of "the same general class or kind as the subject merchandise," (b) is like that merchandise "in the purposes for which used," and (c) in the judgment of the ITA "may reasonably be compared with" the imported merchandise.[59] In practice, the ITA considers similarities in the physical characteristics, use and expectations of ultimate purchasers, including advertising of the product, and distribution channels.

---

53 19 U.S.C. § 1677a(b).

54 19 U.S.C. § 1677b(a)(1)(A), (B).

55 *See* § 12.13 *infra*.

56 19 U.S.C. § 1677(16).

57 19 U.S.C. § 1677(16)(A).

58 19 U.S.C. § 1677(16)(B).

59 19 U.S.C. § 1677(16)(C).

A considerable number of adjustments are necessary to obtain comparable prices for goods sold in home markets and for export to the United States. To determine the United States price, packing costs and container costs are added to the purchase price or exporter's sales price, if they are not already included in that price.[60] If generally applicable taxes are either not collected or are rebated by the exporting government, these also may be included in the determining United States price.

Adjustments deducted from the purchase price or exporter's sales price include any expenses, such as freight or insurance costs, included in that price and attributable to the costs of bringing the goods from the country of export to the United States as well as most export taxes of the exporting country.[61] Deductions also are appropriate for any commissions and other expenses for making sales in the United States and for the costs of additional processing or assembly in the United States after importation and before sale.[62] However, the additional cost of U.S. product liability insurance is not a permitted adjustment.[63]

Adjustments and exchange rate conversions are also made to determine the foreign market value of the goods. Exchange rate conversions are required whenever the foreign market price or the United States price is not in U.S. dollars. The rates for the relevant sales period as determined quarterly by the Federal Reserve Bank of New York are ordinarily used except when those rates are fluctuating rapidly. In such cases, the ITA will test whether the dumping margin remains if the rates from the prior quarter are used. If the margin disappears, the dumping is attributed to exchange rate fluctuations and the ITA may determine that no dumping occurred.

To obtain an equivalent of the United States price, the ITA will add to the foreign market value an amount equal to the packing costs and container costs for shipment to the United States.[64] Allowances may be made for sales at different trade levels (wholesale versus retail), quantity or production cost discounts, differences in the circumstances of sale, and physical differences in the merchandise.[65] Differences in the circumstances of the sale include credit terms, warranties, servicing, technical assistance, and advertising

[60] 19 U.S.C. § 1677a(c)(1)(A).

[61] 19 U.S.C. § 1677a(c)(1)(B)-(C).

[62] 19 U.S.C. § 1677a(d).

[63] *See* Carlisle Tire & Rubber Co. v. United States, 622 F. Supp. 1071 (C.I.T. 1985).

[64] 19 U.S.C. § 1677b(a)(6).

[65] *See* 19 U.S.C. § 1677b(a), (b).

allowances. Adjustments for cost differences in the circumstances of sale are allowed even if they do not give rise to comparable price increases in the foreign market. This is true even if they involve rebates or discounts not made available to all purchasers.[66] These decisions reflect the substantial deference the courts give to the ITA on the important issue of adjustments to its price and value calculations.

§ 12.12 The Injury Determination

As noted in the Overview in Section 12.1, antidumping proceedings in the United States are conducted in two stages. In the second stage, the International Trade Commission (ITC) must determine whether the dumping has caused material injury to concerned domestic industries.[67] The following sections review the material injury determination under U.S. law, including market definition, injury factors, and causation.

Thus, the injury determination by the ITC involves three separate inquiries:

(1) First, the ITC must define the relevant "domestic like product" and relevant domestic industry;

(2) Second, the ITC must determine whether that industry is suffering or threatened with a sufficiently serious injury; and

(3) Third, the ITC must determine whether a causal link exists between the injury and the sale at LTFV (*i.e.*, the dumping).

The most important of these steps is the determination of whether a domestic industry is suffering a sufficient injury due to a dumping practice. The Tariff Act provides that an affirmative injury determination is required when an industry in the United States is materially injured or is threatened with material injury by reason of dumped imports, or the establishment of an industry in the United States is materially retarded.[68] Both the "material injury"[69] and the "threat of material injury"[70] standards apply to established industries, and substantial overlap exists between the two. Nonethe-

[66] *See* Zenith Radio Corp. v. United States, 783 F.2d 184 (Fed. Cir. 1986).

[67] 19 U.S.C. § 1673(2).

[68] *Id.*

[69] 19 U.S.C. § 1677(7).

[70] 19 U.S.C. § 1677(7)(F).

less, the Act makes clear that they are independent grounds for a sufficient injury to justify antidumping duties.[71]

§ 12.13 ____The "Like Product" and Relevant Domestic Industry Determinations

In order to assess "material injury," the ITC and the ITA must first identify the relevant products and relevant domestic industry affected by an alleged dumping practice. The ITA necessarily focuses on which foreign products are like those alleged to be dumped in the United States. For its part, the ITC also must define the relevant domestic industry that produces like products in order to make its injury determinations.

The term "domestic like product" is defined by the Tariff Act as one that is "like, or in the absence of like, most similar in characteristics and uses with" the foreign product under investigation.[72] The "like product" determination is a factual issue for which the ITC weighs six relevant factors: "(1) physical characteristics and uses; (2) common manufacturing facilities and production employees; (3) interchangeability; (4) customer perceptions; (5) channels of distribution; and, where appropriate, (6) price."[73]

Separately, the ITA and the ITC must define the relevant domestic industry potentially affected by dumped products. The Tariff Act defines the relevant domestic "industry" as those domestic producers, "as a whole," of a "domestic like product" or as those producers "whose collective output of a domestic like product constitutes a major proportion" of the total domestic production.[74] Although these definitions apply to both the ITA and the ITC, they do not always agree on the outcome. The ITA and ITC may assess injury on a geographically regional basis if local producers sell most of their production in the regional market, and the demand in the regional market is not supplied by other U.S. producers outside that region.[75]

The determination of domestic "like products" and the relevant domestic industry can be decisive for ITA dumping determinations,

---

[71] 19 U.S.C. § 1673(2).

[72] 19 U.S.C. § 1667(10).

[73] Cleo Inc. v. U.S., 501 F.3d 1291, 1295 (Fed. Cir. 2007). The ITA's identification of the category of goods sold at less than fair value is not binding on the ITC's "like product" determination for injury purposes. *See* Hosiden Corp. v. Advanced Display Mfrs. of Am., 85 F.3d 1561, 1568 (Fed. Cir. 1996).

[74] 19 U.S.C. § 1677(4)(A).

[75] 19 U.S.C. § 1677(4)(C).

but especially for ITC injury determinations. Some early cases on the subject, which have paved the way for later determinations, illustrate the point. In one early case, for example, the ITC excluded large screen TVs from the U.S. domestic industry definition. This had the effect of giving Japanese TV exports a much larger market share in the United States, thus supporting an affirmative injury determination.[76] In another early decision, the ITC narrowly defined the relevant U.S. industry as the canned mushrooms industry, noting that fresh and canned mushrooms were not always interchangeable. This narrow market definition again supported a preliminary injury determination.[77] Variations on the theme of defining "domestic like products" can occur if the ITC decides it is appropriate to exclude domestic companies that also import the allegedly dumped goods or are related to the importer or foreign producer.[78] The ITC may also define the domestic industry regionally in situations where this reflects market realities.[79] Thus, which U.S. firms the ITC chooses to include or exclude in its "domestic like product" definition is an important threshold issue in material injury analysis.

§ 12.14 ___Material Injury

There are two potential perspectives on the appropriate meaning of "material." The first is that the term means any economic harm that is more than trivial, inconsequential, or *de minimis*. The second is that it contemplates a higher threshold, something not quite as hurtful as the "serious injury" required for escape clause relief,[80] but yet still serious in the ordinary sense of that word. The consensus view is that the spirit of Article VI of the GATT embraces the higher standard.

The Tariff Act thus defines material injury as "harm which is not inconsequential, immaterial, or unimportant."[81] (The same standard applies in CVD proceedings[82] and much of the law in the area is therefore interchangeable.) In assessing this essential "material injury" standard, the Act *requires* the ITC to consider three factors:

---

[76] *See Television Sets from Japan*, U.S.I.T.C. Publ. No. 367 (March 1971).

[77] Canned Mushrooms from the People's Republic of China, U.S.I.T.C. Publ. No. 1324 (Dec. 1982).

[78] 19 U.S.C. § 1677(4)(B).

[79] 19 U.S.C. § 1677(4)(C).

[80] *See generally* Chapter 15.

[81] 19 U.S.C. § 1677(7)(A).

[82] *See* Chapter 13.

(1) The volume of imports of the merchandise subject to investigation;

(2) The effect of these imports on prices in the United States for like products; and

(3) The impact of these imports on domestic producers of like products, but only in the context of domestic U.S. production operations.[83]

The Act also *permits* the ITC to consider "such other economic factors as are relevant to the determination regarding whether there is material injury by reason of imports."[84]

The ITC is required to explain its analysis of each factor considered and the relevance of each to its determination.[85] The Tariff Act nonetheless provides that the "presence or absence" of any of the three mandatory factors should "not necessarily give decisive guidance" to the ITC in its material injury determination, and the ITC is not required to give any particular weight to any one factor.[86] The factors are examined through extensive statistical analyses. This analysis occurs on industry-wide basis and not on a company-by-company basis. The ITC may select whatever time period best represents the business cycle, best captures the competitive conditions in the industry, and most reasonably allows it to determine whether an injury exists.[87]

The Tariff Act also gives detailed guidance for the ITC's assessment of each of the three mandatory considerations for a material injury determination:

Volume of Imports. The Tariff Act requires the ITC to consider the absolute volume of imports or any increase in volume of imports in evaluating the volume of imports subject to investigation. This assessment may be made in relation to production or consumption in the United States. The standard in this evaluation is whether the volume of imports, viewed in any of the above ways, is significant.[88]

---

[83] 19 U.S.C. § 1677(7)(B)(i). *See also* Angus Chemical Co. v. United States, 140 F.3d 1478 (Fed. Cir. 1998)(holding that consideration of these three factors is mandatory).

[84] 19 U.S.C. § 1677(7)(B)(ii).

[85] 19 U.S.C. § 1677(7)(B).

[86] 19 U.S.C. § 1677(7)(E)(ii).

[87] 19 U.S.C. § 1677(7)(C).

[88] 19 U.S.C. § 1677(7)(C)(i).

Data relating to the volume of imports are an important factor in the ITC's injury determinations. In particular, the ITC is more concerned with the dynamics of the market share, such as a significant increase in market penetration, than it is with the size of market share. It is also primarily concerned with the effects that market share changes might have on profits and lost sales. The ITC may also find a sufficient injury even where a specific producer has a small market share, but imports from its home country as a whole are increasing rapidly, such that the U.S. domestic industry must reduce its prices in response. On the other hand, a large market share for the importer, coupled with increases in production, domestic shipments, exports, employment and profits of the domestic industry, may indicate that no material injury is occurring.

Price Effects. While price issues are obviously crucial to any determination of dumping margins, they have no strict correlation to injury determinations. However, under the Tariff Act, the ITC may consider the effect of the dumped imports upon prices for like products in the domestic market. This is done to the extent that such a consideration assists in evaluating whether (1) there is significant "price underselling" in the imported merchandise as compared with the price of like products of the United States;[89] and (2) the effect of the imported merchandise is otherwise to depress domestic prices to a significant degree or to prevent price increases that otherwise would occur.[90] If there is no price underselling, but instead the exporters cut their U.S. prices to effectively meet price competition from U.S. producers, this is traditionally considered only "technical dumping" and precludes a finding of material injury. The rationale for this approach focuses upon the purposes behind antidumping law, *i.e.*, to prevent unfair dumping not to protect against procompetitive trade practices. Thus, technical dumping constitutes a defense to U.S. material injury determinations.

Price underselling is not a *per se* basis for a finding of injury. For example, if the demand for the product is not price sensitive, price underselling will not be a central consideration. Price underselling in fact may be irrelevant, even if domestic producers are losing sales in the United States, if their inability to sell goods is not attributable to dumped imports. For example, the industry's decline may have been caused by its failure to develop, produce, and market a competitive product. (The next Section will analyze causation issues in more detail.)

---

[89] 19 U.S.C. § 1677(7)(C)(ii)(I).

[90] 19 U.S.C. § 1677(7)(C)(ii)(II).

Substantial underselling, on the other hand, will lead to an affirmative injury finding where the market is price sensitive. The ITC looks for a pervasive pattern of underselling. If the ITC finds that demand for a specific product is price sensitive and importers are engaging in price underselling, it will then examine whether domestic producers are being forced into price suppression[91] or actual price cutting.[92] Because price suppression can be as severe a burden to domestic producers as can an actual price cutting, the ITC will find an injury if it determines that, in order to respond to dumping practices, domestic producers have lowered or have been unable to raise their prices to accommodate rising costs.

Domestic Industry Impact. The impact on a domestic industry of an allegedly dumped product commonly is the most important consideration in the ITC's injury analysis. Because of this, the Tariff Act provides supplemental factors for the ITC to consider. These include (1) actual and potential decline in "output, sales, market share, profits, productivity, return on investments, and utilization of capacity," (2) impact on domestic prices, (3) actual and potential "negative effects on cash flow, inventories, employment, wages, growth, ability to raise capital, and investment," (4) actual and potential negative effects "on the existing development and production efforts of the domestic industry," and (5) in specific cases, the magnitude of the margin of dumping.[93]

The ITC must evaluate all these relevant economic factors within the context of the business cycle and conditions of competition in the affected industry.[94] But the ITC traditionally relies primarily on two of the factors in making this determination. First, the industry must be in a distressed or a stagnant condition. Second, the low domestic price levels must be a factor in the industry's difficulties (*e.g.*, high unemployment or low capacity utilization rate), and these low prices must be having a serious negative effect on profits.

The ITC will often base an affirmative determination of material injury on severe downward trends in profitability among domestic producers. In one early case, the ITC found that a drop in the

---

[91] Price suppression arises when the domestic industry can affect smaller price increases on those articles directly competitive with dumped imports than it can on those articles that directly compete with non-dumped imports.

[92] Price cutting arises when the domestic industry is compelled to lower its prices to meet the prices of dumped imports in an attempt to protect its market share.

[93] 19 U.S.C. § 1677(7)(C)(iii).

[94] 19 U.S.C. § 1677(7)(C), last paragraph.

ratio of net profit to sales from 5.55 percent to 1.05 percent over a three year period, coupled with a seventy-five percent decline in the aggregate profit in the relevant industry in the same period justified an affirmative determination of material injury.[95] Thus, it is not necessary that an industry suffer an actual loss as a prerequisite to a finding of material injury. On the other hand, simply because an industry is experiencing a decline in profitability does not require a finding of material injury due to dumping.[96] Other factors unrelated to dumping, such as general economic conditions and industry overexpansion, may be the cause.

The effect of dumped imports on employment in the relevant domestic industry often is a significant factor. Employment data are not dispositive, because decreases in the level or rate of employment may be due to a broad spectrum of economic factors unrelated to dumping. (The economic downturn since 2008 provides ample proof of this point.) Nonetheless, sudden changes in domestic employment during the period of dumping can be an important signal for the ITC that dumping is causing a material injury. For example, in one early case the ITC found that a thirty-five percent drop in employment during the period of dumping was a reasonable indication of material injury.[97] On the other hand, an increase in employment levels and hours worked can be a strong indication that dumping did not cause a material injury to the relevant industry.

Finally, the utilization of plant capacity can be a significant factor in material injury determinations. Again, however, such capacity utilization data commonly is affected by a variety of factors. For example, the ITC found a reasonable indication of material injury from the fact that capacity utilization in the affected industry fell from eighty-eight percent to seventy-seven percent in two years.[98] In contrast, the ITC found no material injury in a case where capacity utilization similarly dropped from eighty-five to seventy-seven percent, because in that instance frequent equipment breakdowns and quality control disruptions were the actual cause of the decline.[99]

---

[95] Sugars and Syrups from Canada, 46 Fed. Reg. 51,086-01 (1981).

[96] *See* GEO Specialty Chems. Inc. v United States, 2009 WL 424468 (CIT 2009) (upholding an ITC determination that imports of glycine did not cause a material injury because the declining profits were the fault of the domestic industry).

[97] Montan Wax from East Germany, 45 Fed. Reg. 73,821-02 (1980).

[98] Carbon Steel Wire Rod from Brazil, Belgium, France, and Venezuela, 47 Fed. Reg. 13,927-01 (1982).

[99] Crystal from Italy and Austria, 45 Fed. Reg. 31,830-03 (1980).

§ 12.15 ____Threat of Material Injury

The ITC may also make an affirmative determination of injury if it finds that dumped imports represent a "threat of material injury" to a domestic industry. The Tariff Act lists a variety of "economic factors" that the ITC "shall consider" in making such a determination in an antidumping proceeding:

(1) any "unused production capacity or imminent, substantial increase in production capacity in the exporting country . . . indicating the likelihood of substantially increased imports" into the United States;

(2) "a significant rate of increase of the volume or market penetration of imports . . . indicating the likelihood of substantially increased imports";

(3) whether imports are coming to the United States "at prices that are likely to have a significant depressing or suppressing effect on domestic prices, and are likely to increase demand for further imports";

(4) the existing inventories of the imported products;

(5) the potential that the low prices for the imports will cause other production facilities in the foreign country to switch to the products at issue; and

(6) "the actual and potential negative effects on the existing development and production efforts" of the industry in the United States.[100]

Beyond these, the Tariff Act requires the ITC to consider "any other demonstrable adverse trends that indicate the probability" of a material injury to a domestic industry.[101]

The Tariff Act obligates the ITC to consider these factors "as a whole" in making a determination of a threat of material injury. Therefore, the presence or absence of any one factor is not determinative. In any event, the determination "may not be made on the basis of mere conjecture or supposition."[102]

The case of *Rhone Poulenc, S.A. v. United States* represents a good example of the analysis of the *threat* of material injury stand-

---

[100] 19 U.S.C. § 1677(7)(F)(i).

[101] *Id.*

[102] 19 U.S.C. § 1677(7)(F)(ii).

ard.[103] That case involved the shipment of package anhydrous sodium metasilicate from France to the United States. The U.S. industry comprised four companies, only one of which was demonstrably injured. *Rhone Poulenc* was an appeal to the U.S. Court of International Trade (CIT) from an ITC decision concerning the "threat of material injury" standard. The court first rejected the importers' argument that the extent of market penetration by imports is the crucial factor in determining whether such a threat exists. Instead, the court found that it is proper for the ITC to consider, in determining the likelihood of future injury, the developing trends in the indicators used to determine whether an actual injury has occurred. These indicators of actual injury include the volume of imports, the effect of imports on prices, and the impact of the imports on the domestic industry. The court also held that the ITC also may look at likely future conduct of the producers or exporters of the dumped products.

§ 12.16 ___Material Retardation

The Tariff Act recognizes as an independent ground for an affirmative injury determination by the ITC that a dumped import product has "materially retarded" the establishment of an industry in the United States. The standard for "material retardation" is applied to new industries, *i.e.*, those that have made a substantial commitment to begin production, or have recently begun production.[104] As the ITA notes in its Antidumping Manual, however, this ground "has rarely been asserted by a petitioner in an antidumping duty investigation. Nearly all antidumping investigations have been initiated on the basis of petitions by established manufacturers of the domestic like product."[105]

§ 12.17 Causation

Causation of material injury by dumping is a required element in addition to, and independent of, the finding of material injury, threat of material injury or the material retardation of the establishment of a domestic industry. As a practical matter, however, the two separate inquiries (injury and causation) are closely linked. As a result, when it has found a material injury from a dumping practice the ITC has tended to make an affirmative injury determination without a lengthy analysis of the causal link between them. In

---

[103] 592 F. Supp. 1318 (C.I.T. 1984).

[104] For a rare analysis of this standard see BMT Commodity Corp. v. United States, 667 F. Supp. 880 (C.I.T. 1987), *affirmed* 852 F.2d 1285 (Fed. Cir. 1988), *cert. denied*, 489 U.S. 1012 (1989).

[105] Antidumping Manual, *supra* footnote 9, Ch. 18, I, § III.D.

a negative injury determination, on the other hand, the ITC may engage in a rather detailed analysis of causation.

The Tariff Act requires a simple causation element: that the material injury to a domestic industry is "by reason of" the dumped imports.[106] (Again, the same standard applies in CVD proceedings and the law in this area is largely interchangeable.[107]) The causation requirement is not a high one. Imports need only be *a* cause of material injury, and need not be the most substantial or primary cause of injury suffered by domestic industry.[108] The "by reason of" standard nonetheless "mandates a showing of causal—not merely temporal—connection between the LTFV goods and the material injury."[109] The Tariff Act does not require that the ITC use any particular methodology in making such a determination, and it "need not isolate the injury caused by other factors from injury caused by unfair imports."[110] Nonetheless, the Federal Circuit has made clear that "causation is not shown if the subject imports contributed only 'minimally or tangentially to the material harm.'"[111]

In short, the causation element of an affirmative injury determination can be satisfied if the dumped products contribute in any noteworthy way to the conditions of the domestic injury.[112] Under this "contributing cause" standard, causation of injuries may be found despite the absence of correlation between dumped imports and the alleged injuries if there is substantial evidence that the volume of dumped imports was a contributing factor to the price depression experienced by the domestic injury.

In examining the causal link between the dumped imports and the material injury, the ITC must consider other causal factors that might be responsible for the alleged injury. The Federal Circuit has observed that, for example, "the increase in volume of subject imports priced below domestic products and the decline in the domes-

---

[106] 19 U.S.C. § 1673(2).

[107] *See* Chapter 13, § 13.18.

[108] *See* Nippon Steel Corp. v. Int'l Trade Comm'n, 345 F.3d 1379, 1381 (Fed. Cir. 2003)(observing that "'dumping' need not be the sole or principal cause of injury").

[109] Gerald Metals, Inc. v. United States, 132 F.3d 716, 720 (Fed. Cir. 1997).

[110] Bratsk Aluminium Smelter v. U.S., 444 F.3d 1369, 1373 (Fed. Cir. 2006)(*quoting* Taiwan Semiconductors Industry Ass'n v. Int'l Trade Comm'n, 266 F.3d 1339, 1345 (Fed. Cir. 2001)).

[111] *Id.*, 444 F.3d at 1373 (*quoting* Gerald Metals, Inc. v. U.S., 132 F.3d 716, 722 (Fed. Cir. 1997)).

[112] Antidumping Manual, *supra* footnote 9, Ch. 18, I, § III.F (observing that: [t]he courts have held that this causation standard is satisfied if the dumped imports contribute, more than minimally or tangentially, to the injured condition of the domestic industry").

tic market share are not in and of themselves sufficient to establish causation."[113] On this reasoning, the Federal Circuit has held that the ITC must consider "fairly traded imports" of non-dumped products as a relevant "other economic factor" for causation inquiries.[114] Thus, the ITC may uncover other major causes for the problems of the domestic industry. These may include huge unnecessary expenses, chronic excess capacity, inefficiency, poor quality, price sensitivity or increased domestic competition. Nonetheless, the presence of such major alternative causes of injury does not foreclose the possibility that imports have been *a* contributing cause of the industry's problems.[115]

The ITC may, but is not required to, consider the margin of dumping when evaluating causation. In practice the margin of dumping is an important factor in the ITC's causation analysis. If the dumping margin is slight or substantially lower than the margin of underselling, this may indicate that the injury was not caused by the dumped imports. The imports will still be able to undersell domestic producers, even if the prices of the imports are raised to their fair values. If, on the other hand, the dumping margin is higher than the margin of underselling, thereby enabling the foreign exporters to undersell domestic producers, the dumping can be the cause of the material injury because the foreign exporters may be able to undersell only because of the higher dumping margin.

§ 12.18 Cumulative Causation

Can "material injury" be caused by imports from exporters from more than one country through the cumulative effect of many small injuries? There are arguments against cumulating the sources of dumping to determine whether they collectively are a cause of material injury. For example, cumulation could penalize small suppliers who would not have caused injury if their dumping had been examined in isolation. Nevertheless, the WTO Antidumping Agreement expressly permits cumulation.[116]

In turn, the Tariff Act requires that the ITC cumulatively assess the impact of reasonably coincident dumped imports from two or more countries if the imports compete with like U.S. products. In

---

[113] *See* Bratsk Aluminium Smelter v. U.S., 444 F.3d 1369, 1374 (Fed. Cir. 2006).

[114] *See, e.g.,* Gerald Metals, Inc. v. United States, 132 F.3d 716, 723 (Fed. Cir. 1997).

[115] *See, e.g.,* Iwatsu Electric Co., Ltd. v. United States, 758 F. Supp. 1506 (C.I.T. 1991) (regarding small telephone systems); United Engineering & Forging v. United States, 779 F. Supp. 1375 (C.I.T. 1991), *opinion after remand* 14 ITRD 1748 (C.I.T. 1992)(regarding crankshafts).

[116] *See* Antidumping Agreement, art. 3.3.

specific, the Act requires the ITC to "cumulatively assess the volume and price effects of imports of the subject merchandise from all countries" with respect to which antidumping petitions were initiated on the same day, "if such imports compete with each other and with domestic like products in the United States market."[117] (An exception exists, however, for imports from beneficiary countries of the Caribbean Basin Initiative.[118]) The injury to a domestic industry is measured by the cumulated results of dumping on the ground that an injury caused by the collective effect of "many nibbles" is just as harmful as one caused by "one large bite." Cumulation also provides administrative ease, since the ITC is not required to allocate the amount of injury caused by each individual exporter.

The CIT has observed that to support a cumulation decision, the ITC "must find a reasonable overlap of competition between imports from the subject countries and the domestic like product."[119] In applying this "reasonable overlap" test, the ITC traditionally has applied a "four factor" test: "(1) fungibility; (2) sales or offers in the same geographic markets; (3) common or similar channels of distribution; and (4) simultaneous presence."[120]

§ 12.19 Negligible Dumping

The Tariff Act requires that an investigation be terminated with a negative injury determination if imports of the subject merchandise are negligible. The Act defines imports as "negligible" if they "account for less than three percent of the volume of all such merchandise imported into the United States" during a defined twelve-month period."[121] In the case of cumulated imports from a number of countries,[122] however, the "negligible" threshold rises to seven percent.[123] In computing import volumes for these purposes, the ITC "may make reasonable estimates on the basis of available statistics."[124]

---

[117] 19 U.S.C. § 1677(7)(G)(i). *See also* Hosiden Corp. v. Advanced Display Mfrs. of America, 85 F.3d 1561 (Fed. Cir. 1996).

[118] 19 U.S.C. § 1677(7)(G)(ii)(III).

[119] Nucor Corp. v. U.S., 594 F. Supp. 2d 1320, 1347 (C.I.T. 2008)(*quoting* Noviant OY v. United States, 451 F. Supp. 2d 1367, 1379 (C.I.T. 2006), *aff'd*, Nucor Corp. v. U.S., 601 F.3d 1291 (Fed. Cir. 2010).

[120] Nucor Corp. v. U.S., 594 F. Supp. 2d 1320, 1347 (C.I.T. 2008).

[121] 19 U.S.C. § 1677(24)(A)(i).

[122] *See* § 12.18 *supra*.

[123] 19 U.S.C. § 1677(24)(A)(ii).

[124] 19 U.S.C. § 1677(24)(C).

§ 12.20 Specific Issues in the U.S. Implementation of the WTO Antidumping Agreement

As noted above, Congress ratified and implemented the Uruguay Round accords of 1994 under the Uruguay Round Agreements Act (URAA).[125] For present purposes, the most significant aspect of the URAA was the amendment of the Tariff Act to conform to the WTO Antidumping Agreement. In nearly all respects, therefore, the important rules on dumping determinations as described in the Sections above conform to the requirements of the Antidumping Agreement. Nonetheless, the URAA brought about a few more specific changes that are worthy of emphasis here.

De Minimis Dumping. First, the URAA amended the Tariff Act to address "*de minimis*" dumping.[126] In specific, the Tariff Act now requires that, in making its preliminary determination, the administrating authority (the Secretary of Commerce/ITA) disregard any weighted average dumping margin less than two percent ad valorem or the equivalent specific rate for the subject merchandise. Any weighted average dumping margin that is *de minimis* must also be disregarded by the administrating authority when making its final determinations.[127]

Statutory Time Limits. A significant new effect from the adoption of the URAA is the imposition of strict new statutory timelines for dumping determinations by the ITA. In the case of an antidumping petition, the ITA must make an initial determination within twenty days after the date on which a petition is filed. This time limit may be extended to forty days if the ITA is required to poll or otherwise determine support for the petition by the industry and exceptional circumstances exist.[128] Time limits are also imposed on the ITC in its determination of whether there is a reasonable indication of injury.[129] Separately, the ITC must conduct a review no later than five years after an antidumping duty order is issued to determine whether revoking the order would likely lead to continuation or recurrence of dumping and material injury. Known as the "sunset provision," this new requirement will result in periodic reviews of antidumping orders.[130]

---

125 Public Law No. 103–465, 108 Stat. 4809.

126 19 U.S.C. 1673b(b)(3).

127 19 U.S.C. 1673d(a)(4).

128 19 U.S.C. 1673a(c).

129 19 U.S.C. 1673b(a).

130 19 U.S.C. § 1675(c).

Notice and Comment. The URAA requires that the ITC provide all parties to a proceeding with an opportunity to comment, prior to a formal decision, on *all* information collected in the investigation.

Other Issues. The URAA requires the ITC to consider the magnitude of the dumping margin (although not the magnitude of the margin of subsidization) in making material injury determinations. It also authorizes an adjustment to sales-below-cost calculations to accommodate start-up costs,[131] a new rule thought to be particularly beneficial to high-tech products. It also adds a new "captive production" section intended to remove such internal sales from ITC injury determinations.[132]

§ 12.21 ___WTO Dispute Resolution and U.S. Antidumping Actions

The WTO Appellate Body (AB) has taken a restrictive view of what constitutes permissible antidumping duties and in fact has repeatedly ruled against the United States in disputes with other countries. In the *Thai-steel from Poland* dispute, for example, the WTO rejected a cursory material injury determination by the ITC, stressing that all relevant economic factors must be considered. Similarly, in the *United States–Hot–Rolled Steel from Japan* dispute, the AB found bias in the determination of normal value when low-priced sales from a respondent to an exporter were automatically excluded. The AB also indicated that injury determinations must include an analysis of captive production markets in addition to merchant markets. It thus observed that causation in such determinations must be rigorously scrutinized.

Separately, a WTO panel ruled that the Commerce Department's refusal to revoke an antidumping order against South Korean DRAMS was inconsistent with Article 11.2 of the Antidumping Agreement. Hence, U.S. regulations regarding the likelihood of continued dumping after a three-year hiatus are suspect under the Antidumping Agreement. The Court of International Trade, on the other hand, has found that the U.S. regulations in question are consistent with the WTO Antidumping Agreement. The Court took the position that the WTO panel ruling was not binding precedent, merely persuasive.

The Zeroing Controversy. In a series of decisions that ran through 2011, the WTO's Appellate Body also repeatedly ruled

---

[131] 19 U.S.C. § 1677b(f)(1)(c).

[132] 19 U.S.C. § 1677b(f)(1)(c)(iii).

against "zeroing," a methodology used in dumping margin calculations by the United States and other countries. To understand this practice, first note that a foreign producer likely will have numerous sales in its home country. As a result, in order to calculate the "home market price," the ITA must use the *average* price from all such sales.[133] This average price is then compared to the "export price" to yield the dumping margin. Under zeroing, however, the ITA in effect considered only those home market sales that were *above* the export price; for sales *below* the export price, it simply assigned a "zero" (*i.e.*, not a negative number). Because on average this meant a higher home country comparison price, it also resulted in a higher average dumping margin.

In a series of decisions, WTO panels declared that this practice violates the United States' obligations under the Article 2.4 of the Antidumping Agreement.[134] Notwithstanding these decisions, the Federal Circuit repeatedly upheld the methodology as a reasonable interpretation of the actual language in the Tariff Act.[135] In response to the repeated adverse rulings by the WTO, however, the ITA now has proposed to discontinue permanently the practice of zeroing.[136]

The "Byrd Amendment" Controversy. The WTO Appellate Body also ruled against the United States with respect to the Continued Dumping and Subsidy Offset Act of 2000 (CDSOA, also known as the "Byrd Amendment"). The controversial aspect of that Act was a mechanism under which the U.S. government funneled the antidumping duties it collected back to the members of the affected domestic industry. As a result, CDSOA in effect subsidized domestic industries through antidumping procedures, because it made those industries the financial beneficiaries of any duties ultimately assessed.

Nine other member states of the WTO promptly challenged CDSOA pursuant to the procedures set forth in the WTO's Dispute Settlement Understanding (DSU). Following unsuccessful negotiations, a WTO panel concluded that CDSOA was inconsistent with Articles 5.4, 18.1, and 18.4 of the antidumping Agreement (as well

---

[133] *See* 19 U.S.C. § 1677(35).

[134] *See, e.g.*, Appellate Body Report, *United States—Laws, Regulations and Methodology for Calculating Dumping Margins ("Zeroing")*, ¶ 222, WT/DS294/AB/R, adopted May 9, 2006.

[135] *See, e.g.*, *Corus Staal BV v. U.S. Dep't of Commerce*, 395 F.3d 1343 (Fed. Cir. 2005).

[136] *See* Antidumping Proceedings: Calculation of the Weighted Average Dumping Margin and Assessment Rate in Certain Antidumping Proceedings, 75 Fed. Reg. 81533 (Dep't Commerce Dec 28, 2010).

as various provisions of other WTO Agreements). The United States then appealed to the WTO's AB. In its report, the AB first observed that CDSOA was subject to the obligations in the Antidumping Agreement because it was a "specific action against" dumping. It also found that the only permitted responses to dumping under the Antidumping Agreement are "definitive antidumping duties, provisional measures and price undertakings." The AB ultimately concluded that, because CDSOA did not fall into any of these allowed responses to dumping, it was inconsistent with the United States' obligations under the Antidumping Agreement.[137]

When the United State failed to comply with this decision, the WTO authorized the claimant countries to retaliate in their domestic trade laws as permitted under Article 22 of the DSU.[138] Congress then bowed to the pressure created by the WTO decisions and repealed CDSOA effective October 1, 2007.

§ 12.22 Antidumping Procedures—Petition and Response

In an antidumping proceeding, the ITA determines whether the imports are being sold at less than fair value (LTFV), and the ITC makes a separate determination concerning injury to the domestic industry making like or similar products.

United States antidumping proceedings may be initiated by a petition of the Commerce Department itself or by a union or aggrieved business (or by a group association of aggrieved workers or businesses).[139] The petition requirements are set forth by regulation.[140] In general, antidumping proceedings involve the ITA first making a determination that a petition adequately alleges the relevant statutory requirements. But before initiating an investigation, the ITA must find that a sufficient percentage of the affected domestic industry supports the petition—for the Tariff Act requires that a petition be filed "by or on behalf of" the entire domestic industry.[141] Generally, this requires that the industry or workers who support the petition account for (a) at least twenty-five percent of

---

[137] *See* Appellate Body Report, *United States—Continued Dumping and Subsidy Offset Act of 2000*, WT/DS217/R, WT/DS234/R, Jan. 16, 2003.

[138] *See, e.g.,* United States—Continued Dumping and Subsidy Offset Act of 2000, Original Complaint by Canada—Recourse to Arbitration by the United States under Article 22.6 of the DSU, WT/DS234/ARB/CAN, 31 August 2004.

[139] 19 U.S.C. § 1673a.

[140] *See* 19 C.F.R. § 351.202.

[141] 19 U.S.C. § 1673a(b), (c)(4).

the total industry, and (b) more than fifty percent of those that have actually expressed an opinion for or against the petition.[142]

After an initial review, the ITA makes a determination—"on the basis of information readily available to it"—on whether the petition (a) alleges the elements necessary for the imposition of an antidumping duty and "contains information reasonably available to the petitioner supporting the allegations," and (b) has been filed "by or on behalf of the industry."[143] This inquiry cannot include any information furnished by respondents or a respondent's government. In other words, the ITA accepts or rejects the petition almost entirely on the basis of the information supplied by the petitioner.

Once the petition is accepted, the proceeding becomes genuinely adversarial if (as is commonly the case) the parties alleged to be dumping respond to the questionnaires on sales volumes and prices that the ITA creates and later verifies through on-site investigations. It is rare for the "defense" to have more than one month to respond. Any failure to respond or permit verification risks an ITA dumping decision on the "best information available" (see Section 12.23 immediately below), *i.e.* most likely the petitioner's or other respondent's submissions.[144] Because this obviously is an undesirable result, the best information available rule functions much like a subpoena. Most respondents answer the ITA's questionnaires. Protective orders preserve the confidentiality of the often strategically valuable information submitted to the ITA and ITC in dumping proceedings.[145] Such orders ordinarily preclude release to corporate counsel engaged in competitive decision-making, but permit release to outside counsel and outside experts.

§ 12.23 Administrative Determinations

Antidumping proceedings under U.S. law involve four stages. The ITC first makes a "preliminary determination," based on "the information available to it at that time," on whether there is "a reasonable indication" that the challenged practice presents a real or threatened material injury to the affected domestic industry.[146] If the ITC makes such a finding, the ITA then makes a preliminary determination, again based on the best "information available to it at that time," on whether there is "a reasonable basis to believe"

142 19 U.S.C. § 1673a(c)(4).

143 19 U.S.C. § 1673a(c).

144 *See* 19 U.S.C. § 1677e(b).

145 19 U.S.C. § 1677f.

146 19 U.S.C. § 1673b(a).

that goods are being sold at LTFV.[147] If the ITA makes such a preliminary determination, it proceeds to make a "final determination" concerning sales at LTFV.[148] If the ITA finds sales at LTFV as a final determination, the ITC then must make a final determination concerning injury.[149] Thus the chain of decision-making in antidumping proceedings runs as follows:

ITC Preliminary Injury Determination

ITA Preliminary Dumping Determination

ITA Final Dumping Determination

ITC Final Injury Determination

Congress has repeatedly amended U.S. antidumping law so as to accelerate the rate at which these determinations are made. At this point, it is common for the proceeding to be completed within one year. U.S. antidumping duties are then and in the future assessed retrospectively for each importation such that the amount payable varies for each importer and transaction.

Any goods imported after an ITA preliminary determination of sales at LTFV (Stage Two) will be subject to any antidumping duties imposed later, after final determinations are made.[150] In customs law parlance, liquidation of the goods is suspended. In "critical circumstances," the antidumping duties will also be imposed on goods entered ninety days *before* suspension of liquidation.[151] Critical circumstances exist when there is a prior history of dumping or the importer knew or should have known that the sales were below fair value, and there have been massive imports over a relatively short period of time.[152] Because the ITA has demonstrated a willingness to order retroactive antidumping duties and need not find injury as a result of the massive imports, the importer's risks in such a case may be substantial.

§ 12.24 ____The Importance of the ITA Preliminary Dumping Determination

As a practical matter, the ITA's *preliminary* determination that dumping has occurred will place significant, often overwhelming, pressure on the importers of the covered goods. This is so because at

---

[147] 19 U.S.C. § 1673b(b).

[148] 19 U.S.C. § 1673d(a).

[149] 19 U.S.C. § 1673d(b).

[150] 19 U.S.C. § 1673b(d).

[151] 19 U.S.C. 1673b(e).

[152] 19 U.S.C. 1673b(e)(1).

that point any covered goods become subject to antidumping duties that are ultimately determined once the ITA and ITC complete their investigations and make any affirmative final determinations. The preliminary determination, therefore, tends to discourage or even cut off the imports, because at that point importers generally must post cash or bonds to cover any duties as determined by the ITA in its preliminary determination. At a minimum, they likely will have to raise their import prices—unless and until either the ITA or the ITC makes a contrary final determination once the agencies have completed their respective administrative proceedings.

Thus, once a petition is filed, importers will not know what their liabilities for duties will be and must post an expensive bond in the meantime to gain entry. Foreign exporters frequently raise their "United States prices" to the level of home market prices soon after such a preliminary determination. If they do, antidumping law will have accomplished its essential purpose. However, the WTO GATT Antidumping Agreement and the U.S. Tariff Act disfavor termination of the proceeding on the basis of voluntary undertakings of compliance.[153]

United States antidumping proceedings may be settled by the ITA if the respondents formally agree to cease exporting to the United States within six months or agree to revise their prices so as to eliminate the margin of the dumping.[154] Because price revision agreements are hard to monitor, they are disfavored by the ITA. But an agreement to cease exports also cancels any outstanding suspension of liquidation. The total time secured in this manner may allow foreigners a window of opportunity to establish market presence prior to shifting production to the United States. If requested, the ITA and ITC may proceed to their final determinations after a settlement is agreed. If the respondents prevail, normal trading will resume; but if the petitioners prevail, the settlement agreement will remain in effect. The ITA monitors all settlement agreements and may assess civil penalties (in addition to antidumping duties) in the event of a breach.[155]

§ 12.25 Antidumping Duties and Reviews

The ITA's final determination of sales at LTFV establishes the amount of any antidumping duties. Because duties are not imposed to support any specific domestic price, they are set at the "margin of dumping" (the amount the "normal value" exceeds the United

[153] 19 U.S.C. § 1673c.

[154] 19 U.S.C. § 1673c(b).

[155] 19 U.S.C. § 1673c(i).

States price).[156] In the ordinary case, antidumping duties are retroactive to the date of the suspension of liquidation that occurred when the ITA made its preliminarily determination on dumping. However, if the ITC's final determination is one of threatened (not actual) domestic injury, the duties usually apply as from the ITC's final decision and not retroactively to the suspension date. The antidumping duty remains in force only as long as the dumping occurs. Upon request, annual ITA reviews are conducted.[157] The ITA also may review and revoke or modify any antidumping order if changed circumstances warrant such an action, but the burden of proof is on the proponent.[158] As noted above, in accordance with the WTO Antidumping Agreement the ITA must also conduct a review of final antidumping determinations every five years.[159]

Problems in assessing and collecting antidumping duties may arise because the antidumping duty order applies to goods that do not exactly correspond to normal U.S. Harmonized Tariff Schedule (HTS) classifications. While the ITA is given some leeway to modify an antidumping order to accommodate such problems, it may not use them as an excuse to exclude merchandise falling within the scope of the order. Where, on the other hand, merchandise is deliberately excluded from an original antidumping order, the ITA may not subsequently include that merchandise in an anticircumvention order (see Section 12.26 immediately below).[160]

§ 12.26 ____Anticircumvention

In 1988, Congress enacted important amendments to the Tariff Act to address the "circumvention" of antidumping duties. These "anticircumvention" rules entered into force while the subject was under discussion in the GATT Uruguay Round negotiations. Ultimately, the WTO Antidumping Agreement included no substantive rules on anticircumvention, but also did not forbid the practice.

The Tariff Act addresses circumvention in a variety of ways. First, it allows the ITA to ignore fictitious markets in the source country—a form of advance circumvention—when calculating the foreign market "normal value."[161] In addition, the ITA may include within the scope of an antidumping order merchandise "completed

---

[156] 19 U.S.C. § 1677(35).

[157] 19 U.S.C. § 1675(a).

[158] 19 U.S.C. § 1675(b).

[159] 19 U.S.C. § 1675(c).

[160] *See, e.g.*, Wheatland Tube Co. v. United States, 161 F.3d 1365 (Fed. Cir. 1998).

[161] 19 U.S.C. § 1677b(a)(2).

or assembled" in the United States if such merchandise includes "parts or components produced in the foreign country" that is the original subject of the order.[162] The principal requirements are that the process of completion or assembly in the United States is "minor or insignificant" and the value of the components themselves is a "significant portion of the total value of the merchandise."[163] Similarly, when the exporter ships the components to a third country for assembly and subsequent exportation to the United States, such circumvention efforts can be defeated by extending an antidumping order to those goods as well.[164] Again, such an action is appropriate if the assembly in the third country is "minor or insignificant" and the components themselves represent the principal value of the merchandise.[165]

§ 12.27 Appeals—United States Courts

The U.S. Court of International Trade. A party to an administrative antidumping proceeding may appeal an adverse final determination of the ITA or ITC to the U.S. Court of International Trade (CIT). The CIT was established in 1980 as the successor to the U.S. Court of Customs. The CIT is an Article III court, and its nine judges are appointed by the President with the Advice and Consent of the Senate. The CIT possesses all the powers in law and equity of a U.S. District Court, including the authority to enter money judgments against the United States, but with three general limitations. These limitations (a) prohibit its issuance of injunctions or writs of mandamus in challenges to trade adjustment rulings, (b) allow it to issue only declaratory relief in suits for accelerated review of pre-importation administrative actions, and (c) limit its power to order disclosure of confidential information to a narrowly defined class of cases.

The CIT has "exclusive" subject matter jurisdiction over suits against the United States, its agencies, or its officers arising from any law pertaining to revenue from imports, tariffs, duties or embargoes, or the enforcement of such laws and certain related regulations. The court's exclusive jurisdiction also includes any civil action commenced by the United States that arises out of an import transaction, the authority to review final agency decisions concerning antidumping duties and countervailing duties, and a review of eli-

162 19 U.S.C. § 1677j(a).

163 19 U.S.C. § 1677j(a)(2).

164 19 U.S.C. § 1677j(b).

165 *Id.*

gibility determinations for trade adjustment assistance (see Chapter 15).

Further Appeals. CIT decisions may be appealed first to the Court of Appeals for the Federal Circuit (formerly the Court of Customs and Patent Appeals), and ultimately to the U.S. Supreme Court.

§ 12.28 ____International Tribunals

International institutions also play an increasingly significant role in the resolution of trade disputes. The most important of these is the WTO's Dispute Settlement Body ("DSB"). Dissatisfied parties in domestic administrative proceedings may convince their government to challenge an adverse antidumping ruling before the DSB based on alleged violations of the WTO Antidumping Agreement. As Chapter 9 examines in detail, proceedings before the DSB are governed by a separate WTO Agreement, the Dispute Settlement Understanding (DSU). The DSU generally provides that the involved member states first must pursue consultations. If those consultations are not successful, either party may request that the DSB establish a panel to investigate the dispute and issue a written report. Panel decisions are appealable on issues of law to the WTO's Appellate Body.

Three points are worthy of emphasis concerning proceedings before the DSB. First, since the WTO came into being in 1994 dispute settlement before the DSB, once initiated, is compulsory and binding.[166] Second, this dispute settlement option is not open to private litigants, for only WTO member state governments may file an action before the DSB. Finally, although formally binding, the WTO has no direct power to compel compliance with its decisions. Nonetheless, it may order compensation for the aggrieved state(s) or authorize retaliatory trade sanctions, and these may provide a significant incentive for an offending state to bring its domestic law into compliance.

Separately, a special international institution exists for trade disputes involving the three member states of the North American Free Trade Agreement (NAFTA)—the United States, Canada, and Mexico. NAFTA uniquely provides for resolution of antidumping disputes through "binational panels." Such panels apply the domestic law of the importing country, and provide a substitute for judicial review of the decisions of administrative agencies of the importing country. Indeed, the initiation of a review under NAFTA divests

---

[166] For more detail, see Chapter 9.

the CIT of jurisdiction over the same dispute. Although the decisions of such binational panels are not formally binding in U.S. law, the ITA or ITC may decide to review any administrative action to conform to an adverse panel decision, including through a revocation or reduction of antidumping duties.

Chapter 13

SUBSIDIES AND COUNTERVAILING DUTIES

Table of Sections

§ 13.1 Subsidies and International Trade

A member state of the World Trade Organization (WTO) may impose an increased tariff on an imported item beyond the regular tariff schedule as a "countervailing duty." Such duties are based not on a foreign exporter selling goods at less than fair value, but rather on a foreign government providing "subsidies" that support production for exportation and thus permit the exporter to sell at lower prices in other countries. Subsidies come in many forms, including, among others, tax reductions or rebates; tax credits; loan guarantees; subsidized financing; equity infusions; and outright grants. Rapidly developing countries also routinely offer to give some form of subsidy for initial foreign investments designed to produce exports. But subsidies are not only a phenomenon for developing countries. In the United States, for example the Export-Import Bank (EXIMBANK)—the financing for which Congress extended and expanded in 2012—offers low cost loans to overseas buyers of products exported from the United States. Other developed countries have similar programs.

In theory, a countervailing duty offsets exactly the unfair subsidy. Proponents of countervailing duties argue that they are necessary to keep imports from being unfairly competitive based on foreign government support. Opponents of countervailing duties argue that there is no coherent standard of "fairness" to justify a rational assessment of such duties. They point out that, absent a predatory motive by a foreign government, there is no more reason to justify government action to protect a domestic producer disadvantaged by foreign competition than one disadvantaged by domestic competition. The result in each case is that the domestic resources used by the disadvantaged producer are shifted to their next highest value use and, viewing the world market as a unit, production efficiency worldwide is increased thereby. Opponents of countervailing duties also point out that it is often difficult to identify precisely when a subsidy exists as compared with general governmental actions to support beneficial commercial activity.

Countervailing duties (CVDs) complement the antidumping duties (ADs) examined in Chapter 12 above. These alternatives recognize that unfair international trade practices can arise either through practices of producers or exporters, or through unfair practices of foreign governments. The former are subject to AD law; the latter are subject to CVD law. The two can be equally harmful to domestic industries, and such domestic interests thus often simultaneously pursue both trade remedies.

§ 13.2 The WTO Agreement on Subsidies and Countervailing Measures (1994)

International concern with unfair subsidies and countervailing duties is reflected in Articles VI, XVI, and XXIII of the General Agreement on Tariffs and Trade (GATT) and in the more specific 1994 WTO "Agreement on Subsidies and Countervailing Measures" (SCM Agreement). Like the Antidumping Agreement, Congress approved and implemented the SCM Agreement through the Uruguay Round Agreements Act of 1994 (URAA).[1]

Under the SCM Agreement, government authorities in an importing member state may impose a CVD in the amount of the subsidy for as long as the subsidy continues. The SCM Agreement also provides substantive rules governing when, and under what circumstances, a member state may impose CVDs to offset a claimed subsidy. The CVD may only be imposed after an investigation, begun on the request of an affected industry, has "demonstrated" the existence of (1) a subsidy; (2) that has adverse trade effects, such as injury to a domestic industry; and (3) a causal link between the subsidy and the alleged injury.

The SCM Agreement attempts to shift the focus of subsidy rules from a national forum, as was the exclusive case under the GATT, to the multinational forum provided by the WTO. As a result, disputes over subsidies may occur either before national administrative authorities (according to prescribed procedures) or before the WTO's Dispute Settlement Body (or both).[2] In addition, a special WTO "Committee on Subsidies and Countervailing Measures" supervises the implementation of the SCM Agreement by the WTO member states.

The SCM Agreement generally defines a subsidy as a financial contribution provided by a government that confers a benefit on an exporter. The Agreement establishes three classes of subsidies: (1) prohibited subsidies (also known as "red light" subsidies); (2) actionable subsidies, *i.e.*, those that are permissible unless they cause adverse trade effects ("yellow light" subsidies); and (3) non-actionable and non-countervailable subsidies ("green light" subsidies). Under the terms of the SCM Agreement, however, the "green light" category expired in 2000. The SCM Agreement also granted special exemptions for developing countries that permitted them to phase out their export subsidies and local content rules on a gradual basis. These exemptions were to have expired by 2003, but as of 2013, eighteen countries—principally in the Caribbean and Central America—continue to operate under an extension of this deadline granted by the WTO's Committee on Subsidies and Countervailing Measures.

The SCM Agreement also prescribes procedural rules for the investigation and imposition of CVDs by domestic authorities. The-

---

1 Public Law No. 103–465, 108 Stat. 4809.

2 *See* §§ 13.20 and 13.25 *infra*.

se rules address, among other things, the initiation of CVD proceedings, the conduct of investigations, the calculation of the amount of the subsidy, and the right of all interested parties to present information. The Agreement also has special rules relating to subsidies that cause a "serious prejudice" to the interests of another member state (although most of these rules have lapsed). Finally, the SCM has rules on the gathering of evidence in CVD proceedings, on the imposition and collection of CVDs, on provisional measures, and on the permitted length of any allowed CVDs (typically five years).

§ 13.3 Historical Introduction to U.S. CVD Law

United States law has long considered the grant of a subsidy by a foreign government to aid its exporters to be an unfair trade practice. Laws granting a right to impose countervailing duties to counter unfair subsidies have existed since 1897, long before the creation of the GATT. The origin of U.S. laws against export "bounties" or "grants" can be traced to Section 5 of the Tariff Act of 1897.[3] For many years, this law vested almost complete discretion in the Treasury Department to levy CVDs as it saw fit. Several early CVD tariffs targeted tax subsidies on sugar exports.[4] And the U.S. Supreme Court essentially gave the Treasury Department *carte blanche* to impose CVDs whenever foreign governments favored exports reaching the United States.[5]

Prior to the Trade Act of 1974, U.S. law on CVDs was largely administered as a branch of U.S. foreign policy, not as a private international trade remedy.[6] Indeed, it was not until 1974 that negative bounty or grant determinations by the Treasury Department became subject to judicial review. The Trade Act of 1974 also gave private parties a number of procedural rights, notably time limits for Treasury decisions on their petitions for CVD relief and mandatory publication of Treasury rulings. It is from this point, therefore, that a systematic body of case law interpreting and applying U.S. bounty, grant, and CVD provisions began to develop.

The next major development in the U.S. statutes governing this field arrived in the Trade Agreements Act of 1979. This Act, *inter alia,* codified the rules on the use of CVDs to counteract unfair "ex-

---

[3] 30 Stat. 205.

[4] *See* Downs v. United States, 187 U.S. 496 (1903)(relating to Russia); United States v. Hills Bros., 107 Fed. 107 (2nd Cir. 1901)(relating to the Netherlands).

[5] *See* G.S. Nicholas & Co. v. United States, 249 U.S. 34 (1919).

[6] *See* Energetic Worsted Corp. v. United States, 53 C.C.P.A. 36 (1966)(relating to wool from Uruguay); United States v. Hammond Lead Products, 440 F.2d 1024 (C.C.P.A. 1971), *cert. denied* 404 U.S. 1005 (1971) (relating to Mexican lead).

port subsidies" as agreed in the Tokyo Round GATT Subsidies Code. In addition, the 1979 Act authorized limited use of CVDs against foreign *domestic* subsidies, a subject the GATT Subsidies Code did not address. The 1979 Act also adopted the GATT requirement of proof of an actual injury to a domestic industry.

The Uruguay Round Agreements Act of 1994 then implemented the numerous changes of the new WTO SCM Agreement into U.S. law. Most important, the URAA amended the Tariff Act of 1930 to reflect a rough arrangement similar to the "red light," "yellow light," and "green light" (now lapsed) categories of the SCM Agreement. The requirements of the earlier Tokyo Round Subsidies Code relating to material injury continued in substantially the same form.

§ 13.4 Two Statutory Tests

The United States currently has two statutory structures on countervailing duties. That is, Section 1671 of the Tariff Act of 1930 provides a different test for products imported from countries that participate in the WTO SCM Agreement (or its equivalent),[7] as compared to products imported from other countries.[8] The most important difference between the two is that for imports from a "Subsidies Agreement Country,"[9] CVDs may be imposed only upon an affirmative determination both that a countervailable subsidy exists *and* that a U.S. industry is "materially" injured, or threatened with such injury, or its development is materially retarded; for other countries, CVDs may be imposed *without* any finding of injury to a domestic industry. In most other significant respects, the two tests are the same.[10] Nonetheless, with the continuing growth in the membership of the WTO (over 150 member states as of 2013), the possibility of imposing CVDs without a showing of material injury is rapidly decreasing in significance.

§ 13.5 U.S. Implementation of the WTO SCM Agreement—In General

The U.S. statutory provisions on countervailing duties are set forth principally in Section 1671 of the Tariff Act of 1930.[11] As de-

---

[7] 19 U.S.C. § 1671(a)(2).

[8] 19 U.S.C. § 1671(a)(1).

[9] 19 U.S.C. § 1671(b)(defining a "Subsidies Agreement Country" as a WTO member state or a country the President has determined has laws that are 'substantially equivalent" to the SCM Agreement).

[10] *But see* § 1671(c)(identifying certain other general provisions that do not apply for countries that are not "Subsidies Agreement Countries").

[11] 19 U.S.C. § 1671 et seq.

rived from the SCM Agreement, Section 1671 imposes two general conditions on the imposition of countervailing duties. First, the International Trade Administration (ITA) in the Department of Commerce (the "administering authority") must determine that a foreign state is providing a countervailable subsidy to its exporters. Second, the International Trade Commission (ITC) must determine that imports benefiting from the subsidy injure, threaten to injure, or retard the establishment of a domestic industry in "material" way.[12] This second condition embraces proof of causation, a difficult CVD issue. If these conditions are met, a duty equal to the net subsidy "shall be imposed" upon the imports.

Like antidumping duties, countervailing duties are a statutory remedy, one which the President cannot veto or (in general) otherwise affect. If an injured U.S. industry believes that a countervailable subsidy exists, it generally may pursue CVD proceedings to their conclusion over the President's objection simply by refusing to withdraw a petition once filed.[13] The President nonetheless may have substantial influence in bringing a CVD proceeding to a positive end. Section 1671 allows the suspension of a proceeding if the subsidizing foreign government or exporters accounting for substantially all of the exports agree to cease exporting to the United States or to eliminate the subsidy within six months.[14] The subsidy may be eliminated by imposition of either an export tax or a price increase amounting to the net subsidy. In "extraordinary circumstances" benefiting the domestic industry, the ITA may also suspend a proceeding in the case of a settlement agreement reducing the subsidy by at least eighty-five percent and preventing price cutting in the United States.[15] These approaches, which are increasingly common, may effectively give exporters a brief window of opportunity to enter the U.S. market at subsidized price levels prior to shifting production to the United States.

Although an exporter may receive the subsidy through public or private sources, all U.S. determinations to date have involved foreign governmental subsidies. Thus, these cases are usually determined on a country-wide basis (for instance, steel from India[16]), and CVD orders usually apply to all imported goods of a particular tariff classification from a particular country—including indirect

---

[12] 19 U.S.C. § 1671(a).

[13] 19 U.S.C. § 1671(a)(providing that in the event of a countervailable subsidy that causes a sufficient injury, a CVD "shall be imposed").

[14] 19 U.S.C. § 1671c(b).

[15] 19 U.S.C. § 1671c(c).

[16] *See* United States Steel Corp. v. U.S., 2009 WL 5125921 (CIT 2009), *aff'd*, 425 Fed. Appx. 900 (Fed. Cir. 2011).

imports shipped via other countries. This is one of the few instances in which the GATT/WTO allows an importing country to engage in discriminatory conduct.

As noted, the United States amended its rules on countervailing duties in 1994 to conform to the SCM Agreement. The amendments changed many concepts under U.S. law and, although with a slightly different structure, the U.S. rules on CVDs in large measure are consistent with the substance of the SCM Agreement. In nearly all respects, therefore, the important rules on the imposition of CVDs under U.S. law as described in the Sections below conform to the substance of the WTO SCM Agreement.

In general, the U.S. rules state that "there shall be imposed . . . a countervailing duty" (CVD) if the ITA determines that an exporting country is providing, "directly or indirectly," a "countervailable subsidy," and the ITC makes an affirmative injury determination.[17] U.S. law defines three elements for the imposition of a CVD: (1) a "subsidy," (2) that is "specific," and (3) that causes or threatens to cause a material injury to a domestic industry.[18] If all three elements are satisfied, the ITA must impose a CVD "equal to the amount of the net countervailable subsidy."[19]

The following sections will analyze in detail each of the three required elements for the imposition of a CVD.

§ 13.6 The Subsidy Requirement

The first step in the analysis for the imposition of a CVD is a finding of a "subsidy." The Tariff Act defines this term as a "financial contribution" by a governmental entity that confers a "benefit" on the producer or exporter of the subsidized product.[20] It includes governmental grants, loans, equity infusions, and loan guarantees, as well as tax credits and the failure to collect taxes. It can also include a governmental purchase or sale of goods or services on advantageous terms.[21] Further, direct governmental action is not required: A subsidy may also arise if a government provides any of the above through a private body.

---

[17] 19 U.S.C. § 1671(a).

[18] *Id.*

[19] *Id.*

[20] 19 U.S.C. § 1677(5).

[21] 19 U.S.C. § 1677(5)(D). *See also* United States Steel Corp. v. U.S., 2009 WL 5125921 (CIT 2009)(upholding an imposition of CVDs on steel from India because the Indian government sold input goods to exporters "for less than adequate remuneration"), *aff'd,* 425 Fed. Appx. 900 (Fed. Cir. 2011).

A financial contribution provides a "benefit" if it grants an exporter a better deal than would be available through normal market mechanisms. The Tariff Act states that this "normally" occurs: (1) in the case of an equity infusion, "if the investment decision is inconsistent with the usual investment practice of private investors"; (2) in the case of a loan, if the recipient gains an advantage as against a "comparable commercial loan"; (3) in the case of a loan guarantee, if there is a difference between the fee the recipient paid as compared to the fee for "a comparable commercial loan"; (4) in the case of governmental goods or services, if they "are provided for less than adequate remuneration"; and (5) in the case of goods purchased from the exporter, if the goods are purchased "for more than adequate remuneration."[22]

§ 13.7 The Specificity Requirement

In addition to a financial contribution that confers a benefit, the Tariff Act requires that the resulting subsidy be "specific" to a particular industry or enterprise. This is where U.S. law uses a slightly different structure as compared to the SCM Agreement (although, again, the substance is largely the same). U.S. law thus refers to "export subsidies" (see § 13.8 below) to correspond to the "prohibited" (red light) subsidies under the SCM Agreement. These are deemed to be specific as a matter of law. Similarly, U.S. law refers to "domestic subsidies" (see § 13.9 below) to correspond to "actionable" (yellow light) subsidies under the SCM Agreement. These may be subject to CVDs if they cause adverse effects to a domestic industry based on a variety of further factual considerations.

Two other categories originally recognized under the SCM Agreement, and incorporated into U.S. law, have lapsed.[23] A so-called "dark amber" subsidy was one that exceeded five percent of the cost basis of the product, or provided debt forgiveness, or covered the operating losses of a specific enterprise industry more than once. The dark amber provisions lapsed in 2000. As noted above, the "green light" category of allowed subsidies—for industrial research and development, regional development, and adaptation of existing facilities to new environmental standards—also lapsed after five years and was not renewed.[24]

---

22 19 U.S.C. § 1677(5)(E).

23 *See* 19 U.S.C. § 1677(5B)(A)-(E).

24 *See* § 13.2, *supra*.

§ 13.8 Export Subsidies

The clearest example of a "specific" subsidy is a direct export incentive provided by a foreign government, such as an export credit on taxes or export loan guarantees at less than commercial rates. U.S. CVD law provides that a subsidy is an "export subsidy," and thus is specific as a matter of law, if "in law or in fact" it is "contingent upon export performance," even where the condition is only one of several.[25] The same applies for a subsidy that is "contingent upon the use of domestic goods over imported goods" ("import substitution subsidy").[26]

As noted, these rules correspond to the "prohibited" (red light) subsidies under the SCM Agreement. (Annex I to the SCM Agreement also provides an "Illustrative List of Export Subsidies.") A footnote to the SCM Agreement explains that a subsidy also is contingent on exports if it is "in fact tied to actual or anticipated exportation or export earnings."[27] A 2011 WTO Appellate Body decision in the long-running dispute between the European Union and the United States over aircraft subsidies explained that this concept applies, "[w]here the evidence shows, all other things being equal, that the granting of the subsidy provides an incentive to skew anticipated sales towards exports."[28] Although U.S. law does not expressly incorporate the language of the SCM Agreement footnote, a fair interpretation of the definition of an "export subsidy" would seem to capture it as well.

Other examples of an export subsidy might include governmental loans at below market interest rates or with uncompensated deferrals of payments of the principal. If these benefits are used to induce the building of a plant with a capacity too large for the local market, an export subsidy may exist. Outright cash payments to exporters, export tax credits, and accelerated depreciation benefits specifically for exporters provide additional examples of clearly countervailable export subsidies.

More difficulties arise in analyzing whether tax rebates confer the type of benefits that would equate with an export subsidy. Remission or deferral of, or exemption from, a direct tax on exports is a countervailable subsidy. But the remission of an indirect tax (sales tax, value added tax, etc.) is not a "specific" subsidy, as long

---

25 19 U.S.C. § 1677(5A)(B).

26 19 U.S.C. § 1677(5A)(C).

27 *See* SCM Agreement, art. 3.1(a), footnote 4.

28 *See* Report, *European Communities and Certain Member States—Measures Affecting Trade in Large Civil Aircraft*, ¶ 1047, WT/DS316/AB/ (May 18, 2011).

as it is not excessive. However, a foreign government that makes payments to exporters must show a clear link between the amount, eligibility, and purpose of the payments and the actual payment of indirect taxes, and then document the link.

At one time, the amount of a U.S. CVD would be reduced by the "nonexcessive" amount of the remission of an indirect tax. The Tariff Act now provides, however, a definition of "net subsidy" that allows certain subtractions. These include (1) application fees to qualify for the subsidy, (2) any reduction in the value of the subsidy due to a governmentally mandated deferral in payment, and (3) export taxes intended to offset the subsidy.[29]

§ 13.9 ___Domestic Subsidies

The Tariff Act as amended by the URAA in 1994 generally covers the SCM Agreement category of "actionable" (yellow light) subsidies under the concept of a "domestic subsidy." Under the SCM Agreement such subsidies are permissible (and thus may not be subject to CVDs), but only if they do not cause "adverse effects."[30]

Under the Tariff Act, a domestic subsidy exists if as a matter of law or fact it is provided to a specific enterprise or industry, even if not linked to export performance.[31] The Act lists four "guidelines" for determining whether a subsidy so qualifies as a domestic subsidy:

(1) If the subsidizing country "expressly limits access" to the subsidy to an enterprise or industry, then it is "specific as a matter of law."

(2) If the subsidy is in fact automatically granted to all enterprises or industries that meet written and objective criteria or conditions, it is "not specific as a matter of law."

(3) But a subsidy may be "specific as a matter of fact" where the actual recipients are limited in number; one enterprise or industry is the predominant user or receives a "disproportionately large amount" of the subsidy; or the manner in which the granting authority exercises its discretion indicates that one enterprise or industry is favored over others.

---

[29] 19 U.S.C. § 1677(6).

[30] SCM Agreement, art. 5.

[31] 19 U.S.C. § 1677(5A)(D).

(4) Finally, a subsidy is specific if it is limited to an enterprise or industry in a "designated geographic region" and is granted by the governmental authority of that region.[32]

For purposes of each of these guidelines, the Tariff Act makes clear that a reference to an enterprise or industry includes "a group of such enterprises or industries."[33]

§ 13.10 ___Upstream Subsidies

A foreign government may, as discussed in the preceding two Sections, subsidize the actual exportation of a product, whether in law or in fact. Alternatively, it may subsidize component parts or raw materials that are incorporated into the final exported product. The latter are called "upstream subsidies" and are subject to CVDs if they both bestow a competitive benefit on the product exported to the United States and have a significant effect on its cost of production.[34] A competitive benefit arises if the price of the subsidized "input product" (the component or raw material) to the producer of the final product is less than it would have been "in an arms-length transaction."[35] Upstream subsidies then become "countervailable subsidies" if this competitive benefit functions to create or support an import substitution subsidy or a domestic subsidy.[36]

The amount of the benefit from an upstream subsidy is determined by calculating the subsidy rate on the input and then determining what percentage of the cost of the final product is represented by the subsidized input. By regulation the ITA has stated that, if the subsidy so calculated represents more than five percent of the total cost, it will presume that there is a "significant effect;" if it is less than one percent, The ITA will presume no significant effect.[37] However, both presumptions are rebuttable, and the ITA also will consider whether "factors other than price, such as quality differences," are "important determinants" in the competitiveness of the final product.[38]

---

[32] 19 U.S.C. § 1677(5A)(D)(i)-(iv).

[33] 19 U.S.C. § 1677(5A)(D), last paragraph.

[34] 19 U.S.C. § 1677–1(a). *See also* 19 U.S.C. § 1671(e)(providing for the inclusion of upstream subsidies in CVDs).

[35] 19 U.S.C. § 1677–1(b).

[36] 19 U.S.C. § 1677–1(a)(stating that an upstream subsidy is one "other than an export subsidy"); 19 U.S.C. §§ 1677(5)(C)(referring to import substitution subsidies), and 1677(5)(D)(referring to domestic subsidies).

[37] 19 CFR § 351.523(d)(1) (2013).

[38] 19 CFR § 351.523(d)(2) (2013).

The Tariff Act has specialized rules for processed agricultural products. A subsidy provided to producers of a "raw agricultural product" is deemed to be provided to the producer of the processed agricultural product if (1) the demand for the "raw" product is substantially dependent upon the demand for the processed product, and (2) the processing adds only limited value to the raw product.[39]

§ 13.11 ___*De Minimis* Subsidies

De minimis subsidies, defined in Tariff Act as subsidies of "less than 0.5 percent *ad valorem,*" are disregarded, with the result that the Act does not permit the imposition of CVDs on the imported goods.[40] However, when the ITA calculates country-wide CVD rates, it uses a fair average of aggregate subsidy benefits to exports of all firms from that country. In making such calculations, the ITA must include not only sales by exporters who receive substantial subsidy benefits, but also sales by exporters who receive zero or *de minimis* subsidies, when calculating the weighted average benefit conferred.[41] Thus, in such circumstances, the CVD imposed may not exceed the weighted average benefit received by all exporters of the goods subject to the CVD proceeding. The *de minimis* 0.5 percent rule need not be utilized in sunset reviews of CVDs every five years.[42]

§ 13.12 CVDs and Nonmarket Economies

The subject of subsidies is particularly difficult with respect to non-market economies (NMEs). The longstanding view was that CVDs for products from NMEs are not appropriate because the NME government in effect is responsible for the entire economy. In accordance with this view, the Federal Circuit Court of Appeals ruled in 1986 that economic incentives given to encourage exportation by the government of an NME cannot create a countervailable "subsidy."[43] The court's rationale was that, even though an NME government provides export-oriented benefits, the NME can direct sales to be at any price, so the benefits themselves do not distort competition. The court also suggested that imports from NMEs with

---

[39] 19 U.S.C. § 1677–2.

[40] Although the Tariff Act generally refers to one percent, see 19 U.S.C. § 1671b(b)(4), the ITA has refined the standard to .05 percent. *See* 19 CFR § 351.106(c)(1) (2013).

[41] *See* Ipsco, Inc. v. United States, 899 F.2d 1192 (Fed. Cir. 1990).

[42] *See* Report of the Appellate Body, U.S. *CVD on Certain Corrosion—Resistant Steel Flat Products from Germany*, WT/DS213/AB/R (Dec. 19, 2002).

[43] Georgetown Steel Corp. v. United States, 801 F.2d 1308 (Fed. Cir. 1986).

unreasonably low prices should be analyzed under the rules for antidumping duties.

For some time, one strong view was that Congress implicitly approved of this reasoning when it enacted important amendments to the Tariff Act in 1988, and again in 1994. Those amendments addressed *dumping* from NMEs, but did not address *subsidies* for exports from NMEs.[44] Thus, for many years it was assumed that unfair trade practices by NMEs would only be subject to antidumping reviews and not CVD reviews. But in a major reversal, the Commerce Department in 2007 started pursuing CVD cases against China despite its NME status under U.S. trade law. In 2008, it then imposed substantial CVDs on steel pipe from China.[45] It did the same in 2010 for certain imports from Vietnam.[46]

In 2011, however, the Federal Circuit rejected this effort based on its reading of congressional intent in the substantial amendments of CVD law in 1994.[47] But in March, 2012, Congress then stepped in and annulled the Federal Circuit's decision by special legislation, with the result that countervailing duties also may be imposed on goods from non-market economies such as China and Vietnam.[48] Thus, the criteria used to determine whether a country has a nonmarket economy in antidumping proceedings[49] will apply for U.S. countervailing duty law as well. These criteria focus principally upon government involvement in setting prices or production levels, private versus collective ownership, and market pricing of inputs.[50]

§ 13.13 The Injury Determination

CVD proceedings in the United States for Subsidies Agreement Countries (and only such countries[51]), are conducted in two stages. The ITA is responsible for assessing the substantive grounds for the imposition of a CVD as discussed in Sections 13.5 through 13.11

---

44 *See, e.g.,* 19 U.S.C. §§ 1677b(c) and 1677(18).

45 *See* 73 Fed. Reg. 40,480 (July 15, 2008).

46 *See* 75 Fed. Reg. 23,670 (May 4, 2010).

47 *See* GPX Int'l Tire Corp. v. United States, 666 F.3d 732, 745 (Fed. Cir. 2011).

48 *See* PL 112–99 (March 12, 2012), codified at 19 U.S.C. § 1671(f). In 2013, the Court of International Trade, in a decision sure to be appealed, held that retroactive application of this statute to past CVDs on NMEs was not unconstitutional. Guangdong Wireking Housewares & Hardware Co., Ltd. v. United States, 2013 WL 951006 (C.I.T. 2013).

49 *See* Chapter 12, § 12.8.

50 *See id.*

51 *See* § 13.2 *supra* (noting that an injury determination is required only for "Subsidies Agreement Countries").

above.[52] In the second stage, the International Trade Commission (ITC) must determine whether the subsidization of the imported merchandise has caused or threatens material injury to a domestic industry.[53] The following sections review the material injury determination under U.S. law, including market definition, injury factors, and causation.

The injury determination by the ITC involves three separate inquiries:

(1) First, the ITC must define the relevant "domestic like product" and relevant domestic industry;

(2) Second, the ITC must determine whether that industry is suffering or threatened with a sufficiently serious injury; and

(3) Third, the ITC must determine whether a causal link exists between the injury and the "countervailable subsidy."

The most important of these steps is the determination of whether a countervailable subsidy causes a sufficient injury to a domestic industry. The Tariff Act provides that an affirmative injury determination is required when an industry in the United States is materially injured or is threatened with material injury by reason of dumped imports, or the establishment of an industry in the United States is materially retarded.[54] Both the "material injury"[55] and the "threat of material injury"[56] standards apply to established industries, and substantial overlap exists between the two. Nonetheless, the Act makes clear that they are independent grounds for a sufficient injury to justify a CVD.[57]

The law governing the injury determination for the imposition of CVDs in nearly all significant respects is the same as that for imposing antidumping duties. Indeed, the definitions of the relevant product market, the relevant industry, and the three alternatives for an affirmative injury determination are essentially identical for CVDs and ADs. Thus, the analysis of the injury determination for CVDs below will often be the same as, or will liberally refer to, the injury analysis for ADs in Chapter 12.

---

52 *See* generally 19 U.S.C. § 1671(a)(1).

53 19 U.S.C. § 1671(a)(2).

54 *Id.*

55 19 U.S.C. § 1677(7).

56 19 U.S.C. § 1677(7)(F).

57 19 U.S.C. § 1671(a)(2).

§ 13.14 ___The "Like Product" and Relevant Domestic Industry Determinations

In order to assess "material injury," the ITC must first identify the relevant products and relevant domestic industry affected by a countervailable subsidy.

With regard to the product market, the Tariff Act uses the term "domestic like product." This term is defined, for both CVDs and ADs, as one that is "like, or in the absence of like, most similar in characteristics and uses with" the foreign product under investigation.[58] The "like product" determination is a factual issue for which the ITC weighs six relevant factors: "(1) physical characteristics and uses; (2) common manufacturing facilities and production employees; (3) interchangeability; (4) customer perceptions; (5) channels of distribution; and, where appropriate, (6) price."[59] In a CVD proceeding, the ITC must define the relevant product and industry for an assessment of the harm caused by a subsidized product upon importation. The ITA undertakes a similar analysis in AD proceedings in order to determine the foreign market value ("normal value") for the imported merchandise.[60] Because the concept of "like product" is used for a different purpose, the ITA's definition and methodology in determining whether dumping has occurred is not binding on the ITC's analysis of "like product" for CVD cases.[61]

Separately, the ITC in a CVD proceeding must define the relevant domestic industry potentially affected by a proscribed subsidy practice. The Tariff Act defines the relevant domestic "industry" as those domestic producers, "as a whole," of a "domestic like product" or as those producers "whose collective output of a domestic like product constitutes a major proportion" of the total domestic production.[62] Again, although these definitions apply to both the ITA and the ITC, they do not always agree on the methodology or outcome.

In addition, the ITC may create regional geographic product markets if the local producers sell most of their production in the regional market, and the demand in the regional market is not supplied by other U.S. producers outside that region.[63] If the relevant

---

58 19 U.S.C. § 1667(10).

59 Cleo Inc. v. U.S., 501 F.3d 1291, 11294–1295 (Fed. Cir. 2007).

60 *See* Chapter 12, § 12.6.

61 Cleo Inc. v. U.S., 501 F.3d 1291, 1295 (Fed. Cir. 2007); Mitsubishi Elec. Corp. v. U.S., 898 F.2d 1577 (Fed. Cir. 1990).

62 19 U.S.C. § 1677(4)(A).

63 19 U.S.C. § 1677(4)(C).

domestic injury in such a region is harmed, then there is material injury to a domestic industry.

§ 13.15 ____Material Injury

The Tariff Act defines material injury as "harm which is not inconsequential, immaterial, or unimportant."[64] (The same standard applies in AD proceedings,[65] and again much of the law in the area is therefore interchangeable.) In assessing this essential "material injury" standard, the Act *requires* the ITC to consider three factors:

> (1) The volume of imports of the merchandise subject to investigation;
>
> (2) The effect of these imports on prices in the United States for like products; and
>
> (3) The impact of these imports on domestic producers of like products, but only in the context of domestic United States production operations.[66]

The Act also *permits* the ITC to consider "such other economic factors as are relevant to the determination regarding whether there is material injury by reason of imports."[67]

The ITC is required to explain its analysis of each factor it considers and the relevance of each to its determination.[68] The Tariff Act nonetheless provides that the "presence or absence" of any of the three mandatory factors should "not necessarily give decisive guidance" to the ITC in its material injury determination, and the ITC is not required to assign any particular weight to any one factor.[69] The factors are examined through extensive statistical analyses. This analysis occurs on industry-wide basis and not on a company-by-company basis. The ITC may select whatever time period best represents the business cycle and competitive conditions in the industry and most reasonably allows it to determine whether an injury exists.[70]

---

[64] 19 U.S.C. § 1677(7)(A).

[65] *See* Chapter 12, § 12.14.

[66] 19 U.S.C. § 1677(7)(B)(i). *See also* Angus Chemical Co. v. United States, 140 F.3d 1478 (Fed. Cir. 1998)(holding that consideration of these three factors is mandatory).

[67] 19 U.S.C. § 1677(7)(B)(ii).

[68] 19 U.S.C. § 1677(7)(B).

[69] 19 U.S.C. § 1677(7)(E)(ii).

[70] 19 U.S.C. § 1677(7)(C).

The Tariff Act also gives detailed guidance for the ITC's assessment of each of the three mandatory considerations for a material injury determination. This guidance applies to both CVD and AD proceedings.

Volume of Imports. The Tariff Act requires the ITC to consider the absolute volume of imports or any increases in volume in evaluating the volume of imports subject to investigation. This assessment may be made in relation to production or consumption in the United States. The standard in this evaluation is whether the volume of imports, viewed in any of the above ways, is significant.[71]

Price Effects. Under the Tariff Act, the ITC must consider the effect of the subsidized imports on prices for like products in the domestic market. This is done to the extent that such a consideration assists in evaluating whether (1) there is significant price underselling by the imported merchandise as compared with the price of like products of the United States,[72] and (2) whether the effect of the imported merchandise is otherwise to depress domestic prices to a significant degree or to prevent price increases that otherwise would have occurred to a significant degree.[73]

Domestic Industry Impact. Similar to AD proceedings, the impact on a domestic industry of an allegedly subsidized product commonly is the most important consideration in the ITC's injury analysis. Because of this, the Tariff Act provides supplemental factors for the ITC to consider. These include: (1) actual and potential decline in "output, sales, market share, profits, productivity, return on investments, and utilization of capacity"; (2) impact on domestic prices; (3) actual and potential "negative effects on cash flow, inventories, employment, wages, growth, ability to raise capital, and investment"; and (4) actual and potential negative effects "on the existing development and production efforts of the domestic industry."[74]

The ITC must evaluate all these relevant economic factors within the context of the business cycle and conditions of competition in the affected industry.[75] But traditionally the ITC has relied primarily on two of the factors in making this determination. First, the industry must be in a distressed or a stagnant condition. Se-

[71] 19 U.S.C. § 1677(7)(C)(i).

[72] 19 U.S.C. § 1677(7)(C)(ii)(I).

[73] 19 U.S.C. § 1677(7)(C)(ii)(II). For more detail on the role of "price underselling" in the ITC's determination of injury see Chapter 12, § 12.14.

[74] 19 U.S.C. § 1677(7)(C)(iii).

[75] 19 U.S.C. § 1677(7)(C), last paragraph.

cond, the low domestic price levels must be a factor in the industry's difficulties (*e.g.*, high unemployment or low capacity utilization rate), and these low prices must have a serious negative effect on profits.

The ITC will often base an affirmative determination of material injury on severe downward trends in profitability among domestic producers. But even in a case of declining profitability, increasing production, shipments, capacity, and market share may demonstrate to the ITC that the affected industry is in a healthy state.[76] Thus, the ITC may make a negative determination concerning material injury even if the industry is experiencing decreases in profitability.

Like AD proceedings, the effect of subsidized imports on employment in the relevant domestic industry may also be significant. Again, employment data are not dispositive due to the broad spectrum of economic factors that may affect such data, many of which may not be attributable to foreign subsidization. However, a change in domestic employment during the period under investigation is one factor to be considered. A decrease in employment during the period of investigation may be an indication of injury, whereas increasing employment commonly is a fact that supports a negative injury determination.

Finally, and again like AD proceedings, plant capacity utilization can be an important factor. Falling capacity utilization may indicate material injury if no other explanation exists, but the ITC can make negative injury determinations despite falling capacity utilization, if the decline is caused by other factors, such as frequent equipment breakdowns and quality control disruptions.

§ 13.16 ____Threat of Material Injury

The ITC may also make an affirmative determination of injury if it finds that a proscribed subsidy practice represents a "threat of material injury" to a domestic industry. The Tariff Act lists a variety of "economic factors" that the ITC "shall consider" in making such a determination in an antidumping proceeding. Again, these factors apply for AD proceedings as well, and Chapter 12 analyzes them in detail.[77]

---

[76] *See, e.g.*, Nucor Corp. v. U.S., 675 F. Supp. 2d 1340 (C.I.T. 2010)(relating to a revocation of CVDs after a review); American Spring Wire Corp. v. U.S., 590 F. Supp. 1273 (C.I.T. 1984), *affirmed sub nom.* Armco, Inc. v. U.S., 760 F.2d 249 (Fed. Cir. 1985).

[77] *See* Chapter 12, § 12.15.

The Tariff Act nonetheless adds one "economic factor" that is relevant only for CVD proceedings. For such proceedings, the ITC must also consider "the nature of the subsidy . . . and whether imports of the subject merchandise are likely to increase."[78]

§ 13.17 ___Material Retardation

For a CVD proceeding as well, the Tariff Act recognizes as an independent ground for an affirmative injury determination by the ITC that a countervailable subsidy has "materially retarded" the establishment of an industry in the United States. This standard of its nature is relevant to new or nascent domestic industries Like AD proceedings,[79] this ground for an affirmative injury determination has not been a significant one in CVD cases.

§ 13.18 ___Causation

In addition to a sufficient injury to a domestic industry as described in Sections 13.15 through 13.17 above, the ITC must also find causation. As with AD proceedings, however, when the subsidization and material injury already exist, there is a natural tendency to make an affirmative determination for a CVD without a lengthy analysis of the causal link between the two. In a negative injury determination, on the other hand, the ITC may engage in a rather detailed analysis of causation.

The Tariff Act sets out a simple causation standard: that material injury must occur "by reason of" the subsidization of the imports.[80] The same standard applies in AD proceedings, and once again the law in this area is largely interchangeable.[81] The Tariff Act does not require that the ITC use any particular methodology in making such a determination, and it "need not isolate the injury caused by other factors from injury caused by unfair imports."[82] Thus, the causation requirement is not a high one. Imports need only be a cause of material injury, and need not be the most substantial or even primary cause. Again, the causation standard may be satisfied if the subsidized imports simply contribute to the conditions of the domestic injury. Under this "contributing cause" standard, causation may exist despite the absence of a correlation be-

78 19 U.S.C. § 1677(7)(F)(i)(I).

79 *See* Chapter 12, § 12.16.

80 19 U.S.C. § 1671(a)(2)

81 *See* Chapter 12, § 12.17.

82 Bratsk Aluminium Smelter v. U.S., 444 F.3d 1369, 1373 (Fed. Cir. 2006)(*quoting*Taiwan Semiconductors Industry Ass'n v. Int'l Trade Comm'n, 266 F.3d 1339, 1345 (Fed. Cir. 2001)).

tween subsidized imports and the alleged injuries, if substantial evidence exists that the volume of subsidized imports was a contributing factor in the price depression experienced by the domestic injury. Nonetheless, as the Federal Circuit has made clear in an AD case, "causation is not shown if the subject imports contributed only 'minimally or tangentially to the material harm.'"[83]

Like AD proceedings, the ITC must consider causal factors other than subsidies in CVD cases.[84] An industry that is prospering during times of greater import penetration will find it difficult to persuade the ITC that subsidized imports are the cause of any material injury to it. The existence of extraneous injury factors will not, however, necessarily preclude an affirmative finding of material injury for purposes of the Tariff Act, as long as the subsidies are a contributing cause to the material injury of the domestic industry. The ITC is not required to weigh the effects from the subsidized imports against the effects associated with other factors, if the subsidization is a contributing cause of the injury. Nonetheless, the ITC may uncover other major causes for the problems of the domestic industry. These may include huge unnecessary expenses, chronic excess capacity, inefficiency, poor quality, price sensitivity or increased domestic competition.

§ 13.19 ____Cumulative Causation

Similar to an AD proceeding,[85] the Tariff Act requires that the ITC cumulatively assess the impact of reasonably coincident subsidized imports from two or more countries if the imports compete with "like products" in the United States. In specific, the Act requires the ITC to "cumulatively assess the volume and price effects of imports of the subject merchandise from all countries" with respect to which CVD proceedings were initiated on the same day, "if such imports compete with each other and with domestic like products in the United States market."[86] The reasoning for this approach, again, is that the injury caused by the cumulative effect of "many nibbles" is just as harmful as that caused by "one large bite."

The Court of International Trade has observed that to support a cumulation decision, the ITC "must find a reasonable overlap of

---

[83] *Id.*, 444 F.3d at 1373 (*quoting*Gerald Metals, Inc. v. U.S., 132 F.3d 716, 722 (Fed. Cir. 1997)).

[84] Taiwan Semiconductors Industry Ass'n v. International Taiwan Semiconductors Industry Ass'n v. International Trade Com'n, 266 F.3d 1339, 1345 (Fed. Cir. 2001)(so holding with respect to an AD proceeding).

[85] *See* Chapter 12, § 12.18.

[86] 19 U.S.C. § 1677(7)(G)(i).

competition between imports from the subject countries and the domestic like product."[87] In applying this "reasonable overlap" test, the ITC traditionally has applied a four factor test: (1) the degree of fungibility; (2) the presence of sales or offers in the same geographic markets; (3) the existence of common or similar channels of distribution; and (4) whether there is a simultaneous presence in the relevant market.[88] However, neither the "reasonable overlap' test nor the four factors test is "singularly dispositive or the sole factors the ITC may consider."[89]

When cumulating, it is not necessary to find, for each country, a separate causal link between imports and U.S. material injury. Such multiple country cumulation should be distinguished from the "cross cumulation," which is also allowed by the Tariff Act. Cross cumulation involves consideration by the ITC of both dumped and subsidized imports into the United States. The net effect of U.S. rules on cumulation of import injury is to encourage petitioners to name as many countries as possible as the source of their problems and combine these in a single proceeding.

§ 13.20 Countervailing Duty Procedures

As noted in Section 13.4 above, the Tariff Act applies different rules for the imposition of CVDs depending on whether the source country is or is not a "Subsidies Agreement Country."[90] The major difference between the two is that for a "Subsidies Agreement Country" a determination of both a countervailable subsidy and an injury is required; for other countries, only a finding of a countervailable subsidy is necessary.[91] Thus, the administrative procedure for deciding whether to impose CVDs for a Subsidies Agreement Country is the same as that for antidumping duties[92] and involves the ITA and ITC (see below) making both preliminary and final determinations. But for subsidized products from other countries, a decision by the ITA on the existence of a countervailable subsidy is alone sufficient to impose CVDs.

[87] Nucor Corp. v. U.S., 594 F. Supp. 2d 1320, 1347 (C.I.T. 2008)(*quoting* Noviant OY v. United States, 451 F. Supp. 2d 1367, 1379 (C.I.T. 2006), *aff'd*, Nucor Corp. v. U.S. 601 F.3d 1291 (Fed. Cir. 2010).

[88] *Id.*, at 1347.

[89] *Id.*

[90] *See* § 13.4 *supra*.

[91] 19 U.S.C. § 1671(a)(1), (2).

[92] *See* Chapter 12, § 12.22.

§ 13.21 Administrative Determinations

Two different governmental agencies are involved in administering U.S. CVD law: The International Trade Administration (ITA), which is part of the Commerce Department and thus the Executive Branch, and the International Trade Commission (ITC), which is an independent agency created by Congress.

The chain of decision-making in CVD proceedings depends, again, on whether a Subsidies Agreement Country is involved. If not, the proceeding is totally before the ITA. This will be a two-stage proceeding:

ITA Preliminary Countervailable Subsidy Determination.

ITA Final Countervailable Subsidy Determination.

If, in contrast, a Subsidies Agreement Country is the source of the challenged goods, then a four-stage proceeding will apply:

ITC Preliminary Injury Determination.

ITA Preliminary Countervailable Subsidy Determination.

ITA Final Countervailable Subsidy Determination.

ITC Final Injury Determination.

The CVD process may be initiated by either the Department of Commerce or by a union or business (or group or association of aggrieved workers or businesses).[93] The petition requirements are set forth by regulation.[94] Pre-filing contact with the ITA and (if necessary) the ITC can often resolve any problems regarding the contents of the petition. Petitioners may also access the ITA's library of information on foreign subsidy practices.

The ITA first examines, "on the basis of sources readily available" to it, the "accuracy and adequacy" of the evidence provided in the petition, and determines whether the petition (a) alleges the elements necessary for the imposition of a CVD and "contains information reasonably available to the petitioner supporting the allegations," and (b) has been filed "by or on behalf of the industry."[95] In other words, the ITA essentially accepts or rejects the petition based only on readily available information, which most often means only that provided by the petitioner.

---

[93] 19 U.S.C. § 1671a(a), (b). *See also* 19 U.S.C. § 1677(9)(C)-(G)(defining such entities as a relevant "interested party" that may initiate a CVD petition).

[94] *See* 19 C.F.R. § 351.202.

[95] 19 U.S.C. § 1671a(c).

Like AD proceedings, the ITA must find that a sufficient percentage of the affected domestic industry supports a CVD petition—for the Tariff Act requires that a petition be filed "by or on behalf of" the entire domestic industry.[96] Generally, this requires that the industry or workers who support the petition account for (a) at least twenty-five percent of the total industry, and (b) more than fifty percent of those that have actually expressed an opinion for or against the petition. [97]

Once the petition is accepted, the ITC makes a preliminary determination as to a real or threatened material injury within sixty-five days of the filing of the petition based on the best information available to it at that time.[98] If the ITC makes such a finding, the ITA must then make a preliminary determination on whether there is "a reasonable basis to believe or suspect" based on the best information available that there is a countervailable subsidy with respect to the covered merchandise.[99] The time for making this decision may be extended if the petitioner so requests, or if the ITA determines both that the parties are cooperating and that the case is extraordinarily complicated.[100] The time period may also be extended for "upstream subsidy" investigations.[101]

If the ITA makes a preliminary determination that a countervailable subsidy exists, it must, within seventy-five days, both make a "final determination" on the existence of a countervailable subsidy and calculate the amount of the proposed CVD.[102] If the ITA makes a positive finding on a countervailable subsidy, the ITC then must make a final determination on material injury within 120 days after the ITA's preliminary determination or forty-five days after the ITA's final determination.[103] If both the ITA and ITC make affirmative final determinations in their respective areas of responsibility, then the ITA must enter a CVD order and assess the CVD on the covered goods "equal to the amount of the net countervailable subsidy."[104] If the ITA makes a negative preliminary determination, but

[96] 19 U.S.C. § 1671a(c)(1)(A).
[97] 19 U.S.C. § 1671a(c)(4).
[98] 19 U.S.C. § 1671b(a).
[99] 19 U.S.C. § 1671b(b).
[100] 19 U.S.C. § 1671b(c).
[101] 19 U.S.C. § 1671b(g).
[102] 19 U.S.C. § 1671d(a).
[103] 19 U.S.C. § 1671d(b)(2).
[104] 19 U.S.C. §§ 1671(a), (c), 1671e.

then an affirmative final determination, the ITC must thereafter make its final determination within seventy-five days.[105]

In reaching their determinations, both the ITA and the ITC frequently circulate questionnaires to interested parties, including foreign governments and exporters. Since any failure to respond risks a determination on the "best information available," this results in the flow of significant and often strategically valuable business information to the government.

§ 13.22 The Importance of the ITA Preliminary Subsidy Determination

An ITA preliminary determination that a countervailable subsidy exists places great pressure on the importers of the foreign goods. Liquidation (entry of the goods subject to a determined rate of tariff) of all such merchandise is suspended by order of customs. Goods imported after an ITA preliminary determination of a countervailable subsidy will be subject to any CVD imposed later, after final determinations are made.[106] Such a preliminary determination, although subject to final determinations by the ITA and the ITC and appealable to the CIT, will effectively cut off further importation of the disputed goods unless an expensive bond is posted pending completion of the process. The respondent importer thus will want a speedy resolution, as its total costs for the imports will have become uncertain. It is for this reason that the Tariff Act is replete with time provisions designed to protect the importer by requiring decisions within specified time limits (see § 13.21 above). As with antidumping proceedings, most CVD proceedings are completed within one year.

At one level, then, a useful intermediate goal in representing a petitioner is to obtain an ITA preliminary determination concerning a "subsidy" that meets the statutory requirements. The respondent's "defense" to such efforts must be organized quickly, usually within thirty days of the filing of a CVD petition. The importer's ability to present a defense is handicapped by the nature of CVD proceedings—the actual target of the petition is the subsidy practices of foreign governments. Unlike most foreign exporters whose pricing decisions are the focus in AD proceedings, many foreign governments are loath to provide information necessary for an adequate response to a CVD complaint. Because the ITA and ITC are authorized to make decisions on the basis of the "information avail-

---

[105] 19 U.S.C. § 1671d(b)(3).

[106] 19 U.S.C. § 1671b(d).

able to it," any failure to adequately respond to a CVD complaint can contribute to adverse rulings. Moreover, responses by foreign governments and exporters to ITA questionnaires that cannot be verified by on-the-spot investigations are ignored and thus removed from the best information available for decision-making. This may leave only the petitioner's or other respondents' submissions for review—a one-sided proceeding almost sure to result in affirmative determinations.

The respondent-importer's uncertainties over the amount of duty owed after a preliminary ITA determination that a countervailable subsidy exists can increase for Subsidies Agreement Countries if the ITA decides that "critical circumstances" are present. In such cases, the suspension of liquidation of the goods applies not only prospectively from the date of such determination, but also retrospectively for ninety days.[107] For other countries, moreover, there is *no* time limit on retroactivity and no need for a "critical circumstances" determination.

§ 13.23 ___CVDs and Anticircumvention

The ITA final determination of the existence of a subsidy establishes the amount of any CVDs. Because duties are not imposed to support any specific domestic price, they are set only to equal the amount of the net subsidy.[108] The CVDs remain in force as long as the subsidization continues.

Like antidumping duties,[109] the Tariff Act also has rules that address the "circumvention" of CVDs. First, the ITA may include within the scope of a CVD order merchandise "completed or assembled" in the United States if such merchandise includes "parts or components produced in the foreign country" that are the original subject of the order.[110] The principal requirements are that the process of completion or assembly in the United States is "minor or insignificant" and the value of the components themselves is a "significant portion of the total value of the merchandise."[111] Second, when the exporter ships components to a third country for assembly and subsequent exportation to the United States, such circumvention efforts can be defeated by extending an antidumping order to those goods as well.[112] Again, such an action is appropriate if the assem-

107 19 U.S.C. § 1671b(e).

108 19 U.S.C. § 1671e.

109 *See* Chapter 12, § 12.26.

110 19 U.S.C. § 1677j(a).

111 19 U.S.C. § 1677j(a)(2).

112 19 U.S.C. § 1677j(b).

bly in the third country is "minor or insignificant" and the value of the components represents a "significant portion" of the total value.

Many petitioners in countervailing duty cases also seek antidumping duties[113] and other relief through "escape clause" or market disruption proceedings.[114] Thus, domestic producers seeking relief from import competition will often use a "shotgun" approach to obtain protective relief.

§ 13.24 Appeals

Judicial review "on the record" of final (not preliminary) decisions by the ITA and the ITC in both CVD and AD proceedings may be sought before the Court of International Trade (CIT). In turn, CIT decisions may be appealed first to the Court of Appeals for the Federal Circuit, and ultimately to the U.S. Supreme Court.

NAFTA. For proceedings arising out of exports from Canada and Mexico, however, NAFTA provides for resolution of antidumping and countervailing duty disputes through binational panels.[115] Such panels apply the domestic law of the importing country, and provide a substitute for judicial review of the decisions of administrative agencies of the importing country. Indeed, the initiation of a review under NAFTA divests the CIT of jurisdiction over the same dispute. Although the decisions of such binational panels are not formally binding in U.S. law, the ITA or ITC may decide to review any administrative action to conform to an adverse panel decision, including through a revocation or reduction of countervailing duties.

§ 13.25 ____WTO Proceedings

As noted in Chapter 12, international institutions also play an increasingly significant role in the resolution of trade disputes. The most important of these is the WTO's Dispute Settlement Body (DSB). Dissatisfied parties in domestic administrative proceedings may convince their government to challenge an adverse countervailing duty determination before the DSB based on alleged violations of the WTO SCM Agreement. As Chapter 9 examines in detail, proceedings before the DSB are governed by a separate WTO Agreement, the Dispute Settlement Understanding (DSU).

---

[113] *See* Chapter 12.

[114] *See* Chapter 15.

[115] Canada-United States Free Trade Agreement (1989), Chapter 19; NAFTA (1994), Chapter 19.

The SCM Agreement also has special rules regarding the resolution of subsidy disputes. The multilateral procedure under the WTO first provides for consultations between the complaining state and the subsidizing state. If these do not resolve the dispute within thirty days for a "red light" subsidy, or sixty days for a "yellow light" subsidy, either party is entitled to request that the DSB establish a panel to investigate the dispute and issue a written decision and report. The DSB panel will have ninety days (red light) or 120 days (yellow light) to investigate and prepare its report. The panel report is appealable on issues of law to the Appellate Body. The Appellate Body has thirty days (red light) or sixty days (yellow light) to decide the appeal. Panel and Appellate Body decisions are adopted without modification by the DSB unless rejected by an "inverted consensus" (again, see Chapter 9).

If a prohibited or actionable subsidy is found to exist, the subsidizing state is obligated under the WTO to withdraw the subsidy. If the subsidy is not withdrawn within a six-month period, the AB may authorize the complaining state to take countermeasures. Such countermeasures need not be in the form of countervailing duties, but may instead comprise increased tariffs by the complaining state on exports from the subsidizing state.

Chapter 14

UNITED STATES IMPORT CONTROLS AND NONTARIFF TRADE BARRIERS

Table of Sections

---

§ 14.1 Import Quotas and Licenses

Goods imported into the United States may have to qualify within numerical quota limitations imposed upon importation of that item or upon that kind of item. Import quotas may be "global" limitations (applying to items originating from anywhere in the world), "bilateral" limitations (applying to items originating from a particular country) and "discretionary" limitations. Bilateral limitations may be found in an applicable Treaty of Friendship, Commerce and Navigation or in a more narrow international agreement. Discretionary limitations, when coupled with a requirement that importation of items must be licensed in advance by local authorities, provide an effective vehicle for gathering statistical data and for raising local revenues. "Tariff-rate quotas" admit a specified quantity of goods at a preferential rate of duty. Once imports reach that quantity, tariffs are normally increased.

If a quota system is created, a fundamental subsidiary issue is: How will the quotas be allocated? The Customs Service generally administers quotas on a first-come, first-served basis. This approach creates a race to enter goods into the United States. One potential allocation method is through the use of licenses, which would be the documentation for administration of such quantitative restrictions. Licensing of imports can work a trade restrictive effect. International concern about delays which result from cumbersome licensing procedures was manifested in the 1979 Tokyo Round MTN

Import Licensing Code (which most developing countries refused to sign). The United States adhered to this Code, as did a reasonable number of other nations. The Uruguay Round made an Agreement on Import Licensing Procedures (1994) binding on all World Trade Organization members. The Agreement's objectives include facilitating the simplification and harmonization of import licensing and licensing renewal procedures, ensuring adequate publication of rules governing licensing procedures, and reducing the practice of refusing importation because of minor variations in quantity, value or weight of the import item under license.

The President is authorized to sell import licenses at public auctions.[1] One advantage of an auction system is its revenue raising potential. The U.S. Tariff Act of 1930 also provides that to the extent practicable and consistent with efficient and fair administration, the President is to insure against inequitable sharing of imports by a relatively small number of the larger importers.[2] In fact, allocating quotas among U.S. importers rarely happens. Rather, in the past, quotas have been part of a "voluntary restraint" or orderly market agreement between the U.S. and one or more foreign governments, and represent adherence by those governments to U.S. initiatives. The negotiations have typically concentrated on obtaining foreign government agreement to limitations on exportation of their products into the U.S. market, and have not pursued limitations on who might use the resulting allocations. Thus, instead of an auction system, the U.S. has usually used a Presidentially managed system of import allocations, especially in regard to agricultural import quotas.

§ 14.2 U.S. Import Restraints

The United States has employed import quotas for many years. Tariff-rate quotas have been applied to dairy products, olives, tuna fish, anchovies, brooms, and sugar, syrups and molasses. Quite a few absolute quotas originate under Section 22 of the Agricultural Adjustment Act.[3] These quotas are undertaken when necessary to United States farm price supports or similar agricultural programs. They have used on animals feeds, dairy products, chocolate, peanuts, and selected syrups and sugars. U.S. quotas and tariff-rate quotas on sugar and sugar-containing products, designed to reinforce U.S. price support and loan programs, have notably increased domestic costs well above world prices. These quotas are adminis-

1 19 U.S.C.A. § 2581.

2 Id.

3 7 U.S.C.A. § 624.

tered by the Department of Agriculture by allocating certificates to sugar exporting countries. Only Mexico, under NAFTA, is permitted unlimited sugar exports into the United States. Some U.S agricultural quotas are being "tariffied" under the WTO Agreement on Agriculture. Some quotas imposed by the U.S. are sanctions for unfair trade practices, as against tungsten from China. Other quotas originate in international commodity agreements, and important restraints on textile imports were achieved as a result of the international Multi–Fiber Arrangement (phased out under the WTO Textiles Agreement).

The Agricultural Act of 1949 requires the President to impose global import quotas on Upland Cotton unless the Secretary of Agriculture determines that its average price exceeds certain statutory limits.[4] This provision tends to be countercyclical to market forces for cotton in the United States, meaning the greater the U.S production of cotton, the more restrictive the quota. Brazil successfully challenged parts of this program in a WTO dispute proceeding. See Chapter 9. A similar countercyclical system applies under the Meat Import Act of 1979. To avoid meat import quotas, the president usually negotiates "voluntary restraint" agreements with major meat exporting countries such as Australia.

Generally speaking, the United States maintains an open market for competitive trade in services. One major exception is maritime transport. In this area, the U.S. protects its domestic industry from import competition under the Merchant Marine Act of 1920 ("Jones Act") and other statutes. For example, the shipment of Alaskan oil is reserved for U.S.-flag vessels as is the supply of offshore drill rigs. The Jones Act most notably prohibits foreign vessels from transporting goods or passengers between U.S. ports and on U.S. rivers, lakes and canals. The reservation of goods for U.S.-flag ships (such trade is known as cabotage) is very significant economically, amounting to some $6.4 billion annually with a heavy concentration in petroleum products.

Lastly, the United States sometimes imposes import restraints for national security or foreign policy reasons. Many of these restraints originate from Section 232 of the Trade Expansion Act of 1962. This provision authorizes the President to "adjust imports" whenever necessary to the national security of the country. Trade embargoes are sometimes imposed on all the goods from politically incorrect nations (e.g., Cuba). The Burmese Freedom and Democracy Act of 2003 (Public Law 108–61) banned the importation of Bur-

---

4 7 U.S.C.A. § 1444.

mese goods, in protest against repression of democracy in that country. Recognizing pro-democracy developments in Myanmar, this ban was lifted in 2012. Product-specific import bans also exist for selected goods, e.g., narcotic drugs and books urging insurrection against the United States.[5] The importation of "immoral" goods is generally prohibited[6], even for private use, and the obscenity of such items is decided by reviewing the community standards at the port of entry.[7] Generally, as well, goods produced with forced, convict, indentured or bonded child labor are excluded from the United States.[8] This ban has been applied to certain goods from the People's Republic of China.[9]

The materials that follow selectively present United States law governing import controls and nontariff trade barriers. "Voluntary" export restraints (VERs) and orderly marketing agreements (OMAs) limiting exports into the U.S. market have been applied to textiles, autos, steel, machine tools and semiconductors. Their use is now severely limited by the WTO Agreement on Safeguards.[10]

§ 14.3 Nontariff Trade Barriers

There are numerous nontariff trade barriers applicable to United States imports. Many of these barriers arise out of federal or state safety and health regulations. Others concern the environment, consumer protection, product standards and government procurement. Many of the relevant rules were created for legitimate consumer and public protection reasons. They were often created without extensive consideration of their international impact as potential nontariff trade barriers. Nevertheless, the practical impact of legislation of this type is to ban the importation of nonconforming products from the United States market. Thus, unlike tariffs which

---

5 21 U.S.C.A. § 171 and 19 U.S.C.A. § 1305.

6 19 U.S.C.A. § 1305.

7 United States v. Various Articles of Obscene Merchandise, 536 F.Supp. 50 (S.D.N.Y.1981).

8 19 U.S.C.A. § 1307. The 1997 Bonded Child Labor Elimination Act amended 19 U.S.C. § 1307 to prohibit the U.S. importation of goods produced by "bonded child labor." Such labor is defined as work or service exacted by confinement against his or her will from persons under age 15 in payment for debts of parents, relatives or guardians, or drawn under false pretexts. Section 307 bans products of convict, forced and indentured labor. See China Diesel Imports, Inc. v. United States, 870 F.Supp. 347 (C.I.T. 1994) (Chinese government documents referring to factory as "Reform through Labor Facility" probative of convict labor origin of goods; exclusion order affirmed; U.S. consumption demand exception applies only to forced and indentured labor). On standing to sue to block importation of prohibited labor goods, see McKinney v. United States Department of Treasury, 799 F.2d 1544 (Fed.Cir.1986) (causal link between imports and clear economic injury must be shown).

9 See, e.g., 57 Fed.Reg. 9469 (March 18, 1992).

10 See Chapter 15.

can always be paid and unlike quotas which permit a certain amount of goods to enter the United States market, nontariff trade barriers have the potential to totally exclude foreign exports.

The diversity of regulatory approaches to products and the environment makes it extremely difficult to generalize about nontariff trade barriers. The material in Section 14.5 concerns health restrictions relating to food, safety restrictions relating to consumer products, environmental auto emissions standards and selected other NTBs. These areas have been chosen merely as examples of the types of NTB barriers to the United States market, and are by no means exhaustive. Special NTB rules apply in the context of the Canada–U.S. Free Trade Agreement and the NAFTA.[11] Sanitary and phytosanitary (SPS) measures dealing with food safety and animal and plant health regulations are the subject of a Uruguay Round WTO accord.

The European Union and the United States, and (separately) Canada and the U.S., have agreed to Mutual Recognition Agreements on certain product standards. Each side will test their exports according to the other's standards. A second test in the country of importation will no longer be necessary. The Agreements should reduce the trade restraining potential of regulations applicable to telecommunications equipment, medical devices, pharmaceuticals, recreational craft, electrical safety and electromagnetic compatibility.

§ 14.4 Public Procurement

Where public procurement is involved, and the taxpayer's money is at issue, virtually every nation has some form of legislation or tradition that favors buying from domestic suppliers. In federal nations like the United States, these rules can extend to state and local purchasing requirements. The principal United States statute affecting imports in connection with government procurement is the Buy American Act of 1933.[12] This Act requires the government to buy American unless the acquisition is for use outside the U.S.,[13] there are insufficient quantities of satisfactory quality available in the U.S., or domestic purchases would be inconsistent with the public interest or result in unreasonable costs.

---

11 See Chapter 21.

12 41 U.S.C.A. §§ 10a–10d.

13 See the U.S. Balance of Payments Program, 48 C.F.R. § 225.302 et seq., creating procurement preferences for materials used outside the U.S. but suspended if the Code on Procurement applies.

As currently applied, the United States Buy American Act requires federal agencies to treat a domestic bid as unreasonable or inconsistent with the public interest only if it exceeds a foreign bid by more than six percent (customs duties included) or ten percent (customs duties and specific costs excluded). Exceptions to this general approach exist for reasons of national interest, certain designated small business purchases, domestic suppliers operating in areas of substantial unemployment and demonstrated national security needs. Bids by small businesses and companies located in labor surplus areas are generally protected by a 12 percent margin of preference. Bids from U.S. companies are considered foreign rather than domestic when the materials used in the products concerned are below 50 percent American in origin. These rules apply to civil purchasing by the United States government,[14] but are suspended for purchasing subject to the GATT/WTO Procurement Codes as implemented by the Trade Agreements Act of 1979 and the Uruguay Round Agreements Act of 1994.

The Department of Defense has its own Buy American rules. Generally speaking, a 50 percent price preference (customs duties excluded) or a 6 or 12 percent preference (customs duties included) whichever is more protective to domestic suppliers is applied. However, intergovernmental "Memoranda of Understanding" (MOU) on defense procurement provide important exceptions to the standard Department of Defense procurement rules.[15] Additional procurement preferences are established by the Small Business Act of 1953.[16] Under this Act, federal agencies may set-aside certain procurement exclusively for small U.S. businesses. In practice, the federal government normally sets aside about 30 percent of its procurement needs in this fashion. Special set-aside rules apply to benefit socially and economically disadvantaged minority-owned businesses. These preferences are excepted from U.S. adherence to the GATT/WTO Procurement Codes under a U.S. reservation.

A number of federal statutes also contain specific Buy American requirements. These include various GSA, NASA and TVA appropriations' bills, the AMTRAK Improvement Act of 1978,[17] the Public Works Employment Act of 1977,[18] various highway and

---

[14] See Executive Order No. 10582 (Dec. 17, 1954), 19 Fed.Reg. 8723 *as amended by* Exec. Order No. 11051 (Sept. 27, 1962), 27 Fed.Reg. 9683 and Exec. Order No. 12148, July 20, 1979, 44 Fed.Reg. 43239.

[15] See Self–Powered Lighting, Ltd. v. United States, 492 F.Supp. 1267 (S.D.N.Y.1980).

[16] 15 U.S.C.A. §§ 631–648. See 48 C.F.R. §§ 19.000–.902.

[17] Pub.L. 95–421.

[18] 42 U.S.C.A. § 6705.

transport acts,[19] the Clean Water Act of 1977,[20] and the Rural Electrification Acts of 1936 and 1938.[21] Many of these statutes involve federal funding of state and local procurement. Most are generally excepted from the GATT/WTO Procurement Codes as applied by the United States.

The Buy American Act generally conformed to the GATT Code on Government Procurement negotiated during the Tokyo Round. However, Congress expressed its displeasure with the degree to which that Code opened up sales opportunities for United States firms abroad. It therefore amended the Buy American Act in 1988 to deny the benefits of the Procurement Code when foreign governments are not in good standing under it. United States government procurement contracts are also denied to suppliers from countries whose governments "maintain . . . a significant and persistent pattern of practice or discrimination against U.S. products or services which results in identifiable harm to U.S. businesses."[22] Presidential waivers of these statutory denials may occur in the public interest, to avoid single supply situations or to assure sufficient bidders to provide supplies of requisite quality and competitive prices.

The European Union was one of the first to be identified as a persistent procurement discriminator by the USTR. This identification concerns longstanding heavy electrical and telecommunications disputes that were partly settled by negotiation in 1993 The remaining disputes led to U.S. trade sanctions and European retaliation. This did not occur with Greece, Spain and Portugal (where the EU procurement rules do not apply), and with Germany which broke ranks and negotiated a pathbreaking bilateral settlement with the U.S. In 1993, also, Japan was identified as a persistent procurement discriminator in the construction, architectural and engineering areas.

The Tokyo Round GATT Procurement Code was not particularly successful at opening up government purchasing. Only Austria, Canada, the twelve European Union states, Finland, Hong Kong, Israel, Japan, Norway, Singapore, Sweden, Switzerland and the United States adhered to the Procurement Code. This was also partly the result of the 1979 Code's many exceptions. For example, the Code did not apply to contracts below its threshold amount of

---

19 See, e.g., Highway Improvement Act of 1982, Pub.L. 97–424.

20 33 U.S.C.A. § 1295.

21 7 U.S.C.A. § 903.

22 41 U.S.C.A. § 10d.

$150,000 SDR (about $171,000 since 1988), service contracts, and procurement by entities on each country's reserve list (including most national defense items). Because procurement in the European Union and Japan is often decentralized, many contracts fall below the SDR threshold and were therefore exempt. By dividing up procurement into smaller contracts national preferences were retained. U.S. government procurement tends to be more centralized and thus more likely covered by the Code. This pattern helps explain why Congress restrictively amended the Buy American Act in 1988.

In addition to the Buy American Act, state and local purchasing requirements may inhibit import competition in the procurement field. For example, California once had a law which made it mandatory to purchase American products. This law was declared unconstitutional as an encroachment upon the federal power to conduct foreign affairs.[23] A Massachusetts ban on contracts with companies invested in Burma was preempted by federal sanctions adopted in 1997 against Burma.[24] State statutes which have copied the federal Buy American Act, on the other hand, and incorporated public interest and unreasonable cost exceptions to procurement preferences, have generally withstood constitutional challenge.[25] A Pennsylvania statute requiring state and local agencies to ensure that contractors do not provide products containing foreign steel was upheld by the Third Circuit Court of Appeals.[26] This case illustrates the inapplicability of the Tokyo Round Procurement Code to state and local purchasing requirements.[27]

A practice known as "unbalanced bidding" has arisen in connection with the Buy American Act. Unbalanced bidding involves the use of United States labor and parts by foreigners in sufficient degree so as to overcome the bidding preferences established by law for U.S. suppliers. This occurs because the United States value added is *not* included in the calculations of the margin of preference for the U.S. firms. Thus foreign bids minus the value of work done in

---

[23] Bethlehem Steel Corp. v. Board of Commissioners of the Department of Water and Power of the City of Los Angeles, 276 Cal.App.2d 221, 80 Cal.Rptr. 800 (1969).

[24] Crosby v. National Foreign Trade Council, 530 U.S. 363, 120 S.Ct. 2288, 147 L.Ed.2d 352 (2000).

[25] See K.S.B. Technical Sales Corp. v. North Jersey District Water Supply Commission of the State of New Jersey, 75 N.J. 272, 381 A.2d 774 (1977), *appeal dismissed* 435 U.S. 982, 98 S.Ct. 1635, 56 L.Ed.2d 76 (1978).

[26] Trojan Technologies, Inc. v. Pennsylvania, 916 F.2d 903 (3d Cir.1990), *cert. denied* 501 U.S. 1212, 111 S.Ct. 2814, 115 L.Ed.2d 986 (1991).

[27] See Southwick, Binding the States: A Survey of State Law Conformance with Standards of the GATT Procurement Code, 13 U.Pa.J.Int'l Bus.L. 57 (1992).

the U.S. are multiplied by the 6, 12 or 50 percent Buy American Act preference. If the U.S. bids are above the foreign bids but within the margin of preference, the U.S. company gets the contract. If the U.S. bids are higher than the foreign bids plus the margin of preference, the foreigners get the contract.[28]

Chapter 13 of the 1989 Canada–United States Free Trade Area Agreement opens government procurement to U.S. and Canadian suppliers on contracts as small as $25,000. However, the goods supplied must have at least 50 percent U.S. and Canadian content. The NAFTA also establishes distinct procurement regulations. The thresholds are $50,000 for goods and services provided to federal agencies and $250,000 for government-owned enterprises (notably PEMEX and CFE). These regulations are particularly important because Mexico, unlike Canada, has not traditionally joined in GATT/WTO procurement codes.[29]

The Uruguay Round Procurement Code replaced the Tokyo Round agreement. It is one of very few WTO agreements that is optional. The WTO Code expands coverage to include procurement of services, construction, government-owned utilities, and some state and local (subcentral) contracts. Various improvements to the procedural rules surrounding procurement practices and dispute settlement attempt to reduce tensions in this difficult area. For example, an elaborate system for bid protests is established. Bidders who believe the Code's procedural rules have been abused will be able to lodge, litigate and appeal their protests. The United States has agreed, with few exceptions, to bring all procurement by executive agencies subject to the Federal Acquisition Regulations under the Code's coverage (i.e., to suspend application of the normal Buy American preferences to such procurement).

That said, thirteen U.S. states have not ratified this WTO Procurement Agreement. The United States, amid considerable controversy, adopted "Buy American" steel rules in the Obama administration economic stimulus plan, exempting WTO Procurement Code participants and U.S. free trade agreements. Additional Buy American preferences were created by the Obama administration auto bail-out plans.

§ 14.5 Product Standards

Widespread use of "standards" requirements as NTB import restraints resulted in 1979 in the GATT Agreement on Technical

28 See Allis–Chalmers Corp. v. Friedkin, 635 F.2d 248 (3d Cir.1980)

29 See generally Chapter 15 on free trade agreements of the United States.

Barriers to Trade (called the "Standards Code").[30] This Code was made operative in the United States by the Trade Agreements Act of 1979,[31] and was followed by a reasonable number of other nations. Its successor is the Uruguay Round Agreement on Technical Barriers to Trade (1994). This agreement is binding on all WTO members. In general, this Code deals with the problem of countries' manipulation of product standards, product testing procedures, and product certifications in order to slow or stop imported goods. The Code provides, in part and subject to some exceptions, that imported products shall be accorded treatment (including testing treatment and certification) no less favorable than that accorded to like products of national origin or those originating in any other country. It also requires that participating nations establish a central office for standards inquiries, publish advance and reasonable notice of requirements that are applicable to imported goods, and provide an opportunity for commentary by those who may be affected adversely. The Code establishes an international committee to deal with alleged instances of noncompliance.

Under United States law,[32] state and federal agencies may create standards which specify the characteristics of a product, such as levels of quality, safety, performance or dimensions, or its packaging and labelling. However, these "standards-related activities" must not create "unnecessary obstacles to U.S. foreign trade," and must be demonstrably related to "a legitimate domestic objective" such as protection of health and safety, security, environmental or consumer interests. Sometimes there is a conflict between federal and state standards. For example, federal law licensing endangered species' articles preempted California's absolute ban on trade in such goods.[33] The Office of the USTR is charged with responsibility for implementation of the Standards Code within the United States.[34] The Secretary of Commerce maintains a "standards information center" (National Bureau of Standards, National Center for Standards and Certification Information), in part to "serve as the central national collection facility for information relating to standards, certification systems, and standards-related activities, whether such standards, systems or activities are public or private, domestic or foreign, or international, regional, national, or local [and

---

[30] See 18 Int'l Legal Mat. 1079.

[31] 19 U.S.C.A. § 1531 et seq.

[32] 19 U.S.C.A. § 2531.

[33] Man Hing Ivory and Imports, Inc. v. Deukmejian, 702 F.2d 760 (9th Cir.1983).

[34] 19 U.S.C.A. §§ 2541, 2552.

to] make available to the public at . . . reasonable fee . . . copies of information required to be collected."[35]

There are numerous nontariff trade barriers applicable to United States imports. Many of these barriers arise out of federal or state safety and health regulations. Others concern the environment, consumer protection, product standards and government procurement. Many of the relevant rules were created for legitimate consumer and public protection reasons. They were often created without extensive consideration of their international impact as potential nontariff barriers. Nevertheless, the practical impact of legislation of this type is to ban the importation of nonconforming products from the United States market. Thus, unlike tariffs which can always be paid and unlike quotas which permit a certain amount of goods to enter the United States market, nontariff barriers have the potential to totally exclude foreign exports.

The diversity of U.S. regulatory approaches to products and the environment makes it extremely difficult to generalize about nontariff trade barriers. In 2008, all imports of plants and wood products (even toothpicks) were subjected to new disclosure duties that may inhibit trade. All foods imported into the United States are subject to inspection for their wholesomeness, freedom from contamination, and compliance with labeling requirements (including the 1993 nutritional labeling rules). This examination is conducted by the Food and Drug Administration using samples submitted to it by the United States Customs Service. If these tests result in a finding that the food products cannot be imported into the United States, they must be exported or destroyed. The Bioterrorism Act of 2002 requires all U.S. and foreign food companies selling in the United States to register with the Food and Drug Administration. Importers must notify the FDA in advance and in detail of food shipments, and keep records of suppliers and customers. The FDA can detain any food deemed a risk, including late or missing notice items.

The Consumer Products Safety Act bars the importation of consumer products which do not comply with the standards of the Consumer Products Safety Commission. Exporters of consumer products must certify that their goods conform to applicable United States safety and labeling standards. Any product that has a defect which is determined to constitute a "substantial product hazard" or is imminently hazardous may be banned from the United States market. The Customs Service may seize any such nonconforming

---

[35] 19 U.S.C.A. § 2544.

goods. These goods may be modified in order to conform them to U.S. Consumer Products Safety Commission requirements. Otherwise, such goods must be exported or destroyed, an end result notably applied in 2007 to children's toys from China.

United States environmental or conservation laws notably affecting international trade include:

- The Endangered Species Act of 1973 prohibiting import/export of endangered species.
- The "Pelley Amendment" authorizing import restraints against fish products of nations undermining international fisheries or wildlife conservation agreements.
- The High Seas Driftnet Fisheries Enforcement Act of 1992 banning imports of fish, fish products and sport fishing gear from countries violating the United Nations driftnet moratorium.
- The Sea Turtle Conservation Act prohibiting shrimp imports harvested with adverse effects on sea turtles first used in 1993 against shrimp from several Caribbean nations and now applicable globally to Thailand, India, China and Bangladesh among others.
- The Wild Bird Conservation Act banning imports of tropical wild birds.
- The Antarctic Marine Living Resources Convention Act prohibiting import/export of living resources.
- The African Elephant Conservation Act restricting ivory imports.

GATT/WTO Product Standards Law

United States standards have been attacked in international tribunals as violating international obligations. Sometimes the standards have been upheld, sometimes not. For example, a binational arbitration panel established under Chapter 18 of the Canada–U.S. FTA issued a decision upholding a United States law setting a minimum size on lobsters sold in interstate commerce. The panel found that, since the law applied to both domestic and foreign lobsters, it was not a disguised trade restriction. On the other hand, in 1991, a GATT panel found that United States import restrictions designed to protect dolphin from tuna fishers did violate the GATT.

The panel ruled that GATT did not permit any import restrictions based on environmental concerns, whether they were considered disguised trade restrictions or not. This decision suggested repeal of a number of United States laws which concern health, safety and environmental conditions in exporting nations. A 1994 decision by a second GATT panel recognized the legitimacy of extraterritorial environmental regulations, but ruled against the tuna boycott of the U.S. because of its focus on production methods.

Nevertheless, in 2008, Mexico initiated WTO proceedings against U.S. "dolphin-safe" label rules and a Ninth Circuit decision (*Earth Island Institute v. Hogarth*, 494 F.3d 757 (2007)) requiring zero use of purse seine nets for such labels. In 2010, the U.S. commenced NAFTA proceedings seeking to force Mexico to withdraw its WTO complaint and re-file it under NAFTA. "Standards" disputes are supposed to be resolved exclusively under NAFTA Chapter 20 procedures and trade rules that strongly favor national laws. In 2011, a WTO panel held in favor of Mexico's complaint, which Mexico declined to re-file under NAFTA.

In 1998, the WTO Appellate Body ruled against a U.S. ban on shrimp imports from nations that fail to use turtle exclusion devises comparable to those required under U.S. law. The Appellate Body found the U.S. ban "arbitrary" and "unjustifiable". The standards of other nations have also been challenged as violations of GATT obligations. For example, the United States has criticized European Union bans of imports of meat from the United States, first for containing certain hormones, later for unsanitary conditions in U.S. meatpacking facilities. In 1997, and again in 2004, the WTO Appellate Body ruled against the EU hormone-treated beef ban, citing lack of an adequate scientific basis as required under the WTO SPS Code. See Chapter 9.

§ 14.6 Product Markings (Origin, Labels)

The United States requires clear markings of countries of origin on imports. This can be perceived, especially by those abroad, as a nontariff trade barrier intended to promote domestic purchases. Section 304 of the Tariff act of 1930 establishes the basic rules for origin markings.[36] Every imported article of foreign origin (or its container) must be marked conspicuously, legibly, indelibly and as permanently as practical in English so as to indicate to ultimate purchasers its country of origin.[37] In 2008, as part of the Farm Bill,

[36] 19 U.S.C.A. § 1304.

[37] See Precision Specialty Metals, Inc. v. United States, 116 F.Supp 2d 1350 (C.I.T.2000).

new import disclosure and country of origin requirements were broadly created for plants and wound products.

The principle sanction for failure to properly mark imports is the imposition of statutory tariffs of 10 percent ad valorem, which are imposed in addition to regular duties and even if the goods would ordinarily enter the U.S. duty free. Importers ordinarily receive notice from the Customs Service and an opportunity to comply with marking requirements. Any untimely failure to comply can result in liquidated damages proceedings by Customs against the importer. The amount of damages assessed will vary with the frequency and circumstances of the offense, and will be assessed as a percentage of the appraised value of the merchandise. In severe cases, Customs may seek civil penalties under Section 592 of the Tariff Act of 1930.[38] This provision generally sanctions imports under false documents. Furthermore, criminal sanctions are also possible, either for use of false documents[39] or altering a required marking with concealment intended.[40] The latter penalties can rise to $250,000 or one year imprisonment or both. The severity of these sanctions must be measured against the temptation of traders to alter country of origin markings so as to obtain duty free or quota free entry of goods into the United States.

Various exceptions apply to the U.S. country of origin marking requirements.[41] These include goods that are incapable of being marked, goods economically prohibitive to mark (unless the failure to do so was a deliberate attempt at avoiding the law), or goods that will be injured if marked. If the containers will reasonably indicate origin to the ultimate consumer, or the import circumstances or character of the goods necessarily convey knowledge of their source, no marking is required. Nor is it mandatory to mark goods not intended for resale, goods which when processed will obliterate the mark, goods over twenty years old and goods intended for export without entering U.S. commerce. Certain United States fishery products, products of U.S. possessions and products that originally came from the U.S. and are being imported are likewise exempt. Lastly, there is a "J-list" of specific goods that have been individually ruled exempt by the Secretary of the Treasury.[42] These include items like cordage, buttons, nails, etc., all of which must be marked by container.

---

38 19 U.S.C.A. § 1592.

39 18 U.S.C.A. § 1001.

40 19 U.S.C.A. § 1304.

41 See 19 C.F.R. § 134.32.

42 See 19 C.F.R. § 134.33.

Special regulations govern the marking requirements for imported textiles. These are created by the Textile Fiber Products Identification Act.[43] This Act is enforced by the U.S. Federal Trade Commission. It mandates disclosure of country of origin, generic fiber contents and the name or identification number of the manufacturer or marketer. Violation of the Textile Fiber Products Identification Act amounts to a violation of Section 5 of the Federal Trade Commission Act.[44] This means that F.T.C. cease and desist order proceedings, injunction actions, civil penalties and consumer redress relief can follow. Similar but not identical labelling requirements are established by the Wool Products Labelling Act[45] (country of origin required) and the Fur Products Labelling Act[46] (country of origin not required). These laws are also enforced by the Federal Trade Commission.

Significant litigation has ensued under the Tariff Act country of origin requirements regarding when a U.S. manufacturer is to be deemed the "ultimate purchaser" which may render the goods exempt from marking. In a major decision by the Court of Customs and Patent Appeals, wooden brush handles from Japan were processed in the U.S. by inserting bristles which obliterated the marking. The CCPA, adopting a common rationale in U.S. customs law, held that the handles had undergone a "substantial transformation" into a new product in the United States and were thus subject only to container marking obligations.[47] In contrast, when leather uppers for shoes were imported from Indonesia, the Court of International Trade required individual markings despite the attachment of soles in the U.S. and argument that a "substantial transformation" had taken place.[48] Gifts of products to ordinary consumers (umbrellas to racetrack patrons) may still require origin markings even if the donor would be exempt.[49]

Other litigation has focused on the duty to mark origin "conspicuously." The Court of International Trade initially reversed a "plainly erroneous" Customs Service position that frozen food markings at the rear of the package (Made in Mexico) were conspicu-

---

[43] 15 U.S.C.A. § 70–70K.

[44] 15 U.S.C.A. § 45.

[45] 15 U.S.C.A. § 68–68j.

[46] 15 U.S.C.A. § 69–69j.

[47] United States v. Gibson–Thomsen Co., 27 C.C.P.A. 267 (1940), *superseded by regulation as stated in* Cumins Engine Co. v. United States, 83 F.Supp.2d 1366 (C.I.T.1999).

[48] Uniroyal, Inc. v. United States, 542 F.Supp. 1026 (C.I.T.1982), *affirmed* 702 F.2d 1022 (Fed.Cir.1983).

[49] Pabrini, Inc. v. United States, 630 F.Supp. 360 (C.I.T.1986).

ous.[50] The Court took the position that such markings did not give U.S. consumers realistic choices when shopping and noted the health risks associated with such goods. Subsequently, the Court of International Trade vacated this opinion.

[50] Norcal/Crosetti Foods, Inc. v. United States Customs Service, 758 F.Supp. 729 (C.I.T.1991), *opinion vac'd* 790 F.Supp. 302 (C.I.T.1992).

Chapter 15

ESCAPE CLAUSE (SAFEGUARD) PROCEEDINGS; TRADE ADJUSTMENT ASSISTANCE

Table of Sections

§ 15.1 Prospects for Relief

One way that U.S. businesses may seek protection (safeguards) from import competition is by initiating what are known as "escape clause" or market disruption proceedings under the Trade Act of 1974. In contrast to most other statutory trade law remedies, these "safeguard" proceedings are not targeted at unfair practices. Rather, the goods are assumed to be fairly traded but the new imports are in such an unexpected volume that temporary protection is appropriate to allow the domestic industry to adjust to the new competitive environment. Escape clause proceedings can involve imports from anywhere in the world and are authorized by Section 201 of the Trade Act.[1] Escape clause proceedings are also often found in the bilateral trade agreements of the United States.

---

1 19 U.S.C. § 2251.

Market disruption proceedings concern imports from communist nations and are authorized by Section 406 of the 1974 Trade Act.[2] These proceedings are similar but not identical. Either may result in the imposition of U.S. import restraints or presidential negotiation of export restraints from the source country. Escape clause and market disruption proceedings are anticipated by Article XIX of the General Agreement on Tariffs and Trade (GATT). A more specific World Trade Organization (WTO) "Safeguards Agreement" also emerged from the 1994 Uruguay Round of negotiations.[3]

Import injury relief available under the Trade Act of 1974 is basically of two kinds: (1) Presidential relief designed to temporarily protect domestic producers of like or directly competitive products; and (2) governmental assistance to workers and firms economically displaced by import competition. This assistance is intended to enhance job opportunities and competitiveness. Protective relief tends to be awarded when the President believes that a U.S. industry needs some time to adjust to specific trade developments, while governmental assistance is seen as a means to accommodate the injury caused by import competition more generally. Adjustment to import competition is the longer term goal, resulting in more competitive U.S. industries and markets.

§ 15.2 The Impact of Limited Judicial Review

Judicial review of escape clause and market disruption proceedings and remedies is very limited. As the Federal Circuit observed in *Corus Group PLC. v. International Trade Commission*, "under the escape clause provision of the Trade Act of 1974, . . .'[f]or a court to interpose, there has to be a clear misconstruction of the governing statute, a significant procedural violation, or action outside delegated authority.'"[4] This flows from the President's broad constitutional powers over foreign affairs. Derivatively, the actions of the International Trade Commission (ITC, or Commission) in these proceedings are likewise sheltered from extensive judicial review.[5] This means that the decisions of the ITC are critical to obtaining escape clause relief.

Nonetheless, GATT compensation duties, U.S. free trade agreements, presidential prerogatives, and important amendments

---

2 19 U.S.C. § 2436.

3 *See* § 15.3 *infra*.

4 352 F.3d 1351, 1361 (Fed. Cir. 2003)(*quoting*Maple Leaf Fish Co. v. United States, 762 F.2d 86, 89 (Fed. Cir. 1985).

5 *Id. See also* Maple Leaf Fish Co. v. United States, 762 F.2d 86 (Fed. Cir. 1985).

to Section 201 in 1988 and 1994 have significantly reduced the potential for success under these proceedings. During the 1990s, there were very few Section 201 or Section 406 proceedings. Indeed, since 2003 the ITC has not instituted any Section 201 proceedings (although it has instituted six under a special rule for Chinese imports arising from China's accession to the WTO[6]). The main focus of U.S. escape clause relief has instead become trade adjustment assistance, as Sections 15.14 and 15.15 will discuss in detail.

§ 15.3 The WTO Safeguards Agreement

One of the important regulatory products of the Uruguay Round negotiations under the auspices of GATT was a "WTO Agreement on Safeguards" on the subject of escape clause and related "gray area" protective measures. Under the Safeguards Agreement, the imposition of temporary protective relief from imports does not require a showing of any unfair trade practice, such as dumping or governmental granting of subsidies. But as a result, the injury standard is higher: Such duties are permitted only where increased imports cause a "*serious* injury or threat thereof" (emphasis added) to a domestic industry. (For antidumping duties and countervailing duties, the standard is merely "material" injury.[7])

In addition, the Safeguards Agreement permits such escape clause measures "only to the extent necessary" to prevent or remedy such an injury and to "facilitate adjustment." Such measures are allowed for a maximum of four years, and on a progressively decreasing basis (although, upon a further investigation, a member state may extend the measures, but not beyond a total period of eight years).

Perhaps the most important provision of the Safeguards Agreement is that it expressly prohibits a member state from seeking, undertaking, or maintaining voluntary export or import restraint agreements (VERs or OMAs).[8] Such agreed arrangements to limit trade competition were quite common, especially by developed countries to protect against unwanted imports, prior to the adoption of the Safeguards Agreement in 1994.

Protective safeguard remedies are often in the form of tariff increases and tariff rate quotas (TRQs). In general, such remedies must be applied on an MFN-basis to imports regardless of their source. The right to retaliate, absent a compensation settlement,

---

6 *See* § 15.12 *infra*.

7 *See* Chapter 12, §12.12, Chapter 13, § 13.13.

8 *See* Safeguards Agreement, art. 11.

when another country invokes escape clause relief is suspended if the safeguard action is for less than three years. Special rules limit the use of safeguard measures against imports from developing countries and allow such countries to impose safeguard measures to protect domestic industries for up to ten years.

Congress ratified and implemented the Uruguay Round accords in December of 1994 through the Uruguay Round Agreements Act (URAA).[9] This Act changed a number of rules of U.S. law relating to escape clause relief. The most notable of these were: (1) clarifications of the meaning of the significant terms "domestic industry," "serious injury," and "threat of serious injury"; (2) changes to the allowed terms for relief to provide an initial period of up to four years and an overall limit of eight years; (3) a requirement that any relief actions exceeding one year be "phased down at regular intervals" during the relief period; (4) an allowance of ITC investigations at the request of the President or on petition by an industry with respect to continuing a relief measure; (5) certain new rules to protect confidential business information collected in connection with a proceeding; and (6) an allowance of expedited proceedings in "critical circumstances."[10]

The more general effect of URAA was to bring U.S. escape clause law into compliance with the Safeguards Agreement. Therefore, except as to certain doubts noted in Section 15.13, the standards and procedures for the granting of escape clause relief as described in the Sections below conform to the substance of the WTO's Safeguards Agreement.

§ 15.4 Escape Clause Proceedings—Petitions

Decisions about the granting of escape clause relief are made by the President upon the recommendation of the ITC. Any entity that is representative of an industry, including a "trade association, firm, certified or recognized union, or group of workers," may file a petition requesting such import relief.[11] The petition must state the "specific purposes" for any requested action "which may include facilitating the orderly transfer of resources to more productive pursuits, enhancing competitiveness, or other means of adjustment to new conditions of competition."[12] The ITC also must initiate an escape clause proceeding at the request of the President, the United

---

[9] Public Law No. 103–465, 108 Stat. 4809.

[10] A summary of these changes is available in the International Trade Commission's "Annual Report" of 1995.

[11] 19 U.S.C. § 2252(a)(1).

[12] 19 U.S.C. § 2252(a)(2).

States Trade Representative, and certain congressional committees, and may do so "on its own motion."[13]

The Trade Act makes clear that the purposes of the safeguards relief are to enhance competitiveness and otherwise assist an industry to adjust to unexpected competitive conditions.[14] The petition may request provisional relief pending the outcome of an escape clause proceeding. Petitions under Section 201 also must show that a substantial number of the companies or workers in the industry support the petition, as the Trade Act requires that the petitioning "entity" be "representative of an industry."[15] In this sense, the petitioner is like a class action representative. While it is not necessary for all companies or workers in the industry to support the petition, a substantial proportion must do so because Section 201 is focused upon industry-wide relief.

The petitioner industry or worker group may—and is well advised to—submit its own specific plan "to facilitate positive adjustment to import competition" during the term of any protective relief.[16] This is often done because the Commission is required in conducting its escape clause investigation to seek information on actions being taken or planned by the firms and workers in the industry to make a positive adjustment to import competition. Moreover, the Commission is authorized to accept "commitments" regarding such action if it affirmatively determines that the statutory criteria of Section 201 are met.[17]

§ 15.5 ITC Investigations

Upon the filing of a petition that meets the statutory requirements, the ITC must "promptly" begin an investigation to determine whether the import competition meets the statutory standard for temporary escape clause relief.[18] Separately, if the industry is unable to adequately document its case for escape clause relief, it may be able to convince the Commission to do this on its own under what is known as a general Section 332 investigation.[19] If successful, a Section 332 investigation will shift the burden and the cost of preparing a Section 201 proceeding from the industry or its representatives to the Commission.

---

13 19 U.S.C. § 2252(b)(1)(A).

14 19 U.S.C. § 2252(a)(2).

15 19 U.S.C. § 2252(a)(1).

16 19 U.S.C. § 2252(a)(4).

17 19 U.S.C. § 2252(a)(4)–(7).

18 19 U.S.C. § 2252(b)(1)(A).

19 19 U.S.C. § 1332.

As the Commission's investigation proceeds, it will develop an extensive questionnaire to send to domestic producers. This questionnaire focuses on the kinds of information the Commission needs in order to assess the statutory criteria for escape clause relief. Although industry members typically support escape clause relief, they may not wish to reveal all the information requested in the questionnaire. If this is the case, the ITC can obtain subpoena enforcement from the U.S. District Court for the District of Columbia.[20] The hearings held by the ITC in connection with escape clause proceedings involve testimony under oath and the right of cross examination by opposing parties. Thus, for example, importers that do not wish to see restrictive measures imposed may oppose the domestic industry and its witnesses. The various procedures governing escape clause investigations by the ITC are defined in 19 C.F.R. Parts 201 and 206. The entire ITC investigation normally takes about six months.

§ 15.6 The Statutory Criteria for Escape Clause Relief

Section 201 of the Trade Act of 1974 requires proof of an increase in imports that substantially causes or threatens to cause serious injury to domestic industries producing like or directly competitive articles.[21]The ITC traditionally has divided this statutory standard for escape clause relief into three separate criteria. In order to make an affirmative determination on an escape clause petition, the ITC must find, as it stated in the famous (or infamous) *Steel Safeguards* determination, that:

> (1) imports of the subject article are in *increased quantities* ...;
>
> (2) the domestic industry producing an article that is like or directly competitive with the imported article is *seriously injured or threatened with serious injury*; and
>
> (3) the article is being imported in such increased quantities as to be a *substantial cause* of serious injury or threat of serious injury to the domestic industry.[22]

---

[20] 19 U.S.C. § 1333(b).

[21] 19 U.S.C. § 2251(a).

[22] *See* U.S. International Trade Commission—*Steel*, Investigation No. TA–201–73, at 27 (Pub. No. 3479, Dec., 2001).

Of these three, the causation and injury criteria are the most consequential. They are the subject of separate analyses in Sections 15.8 and 15.9 below.

Increased Quantities. The increased quantities of imports test is comparatively uncontroversial. But for clarity, the Trade Act emphasizes that the required "increase" in imports may be (a) "either actual or relative to domestic production," and (b) based on a consideration of imports from all sources. Relative increases occur when domestic production declines when measured against imports. Imports could thus be declining in an absolute sense but nonetheless increasing in a relative sense if domestic production is declining at an even faster rate.[23]

§ 15.7 Relevant Domestic Industry

The focus of an escape clause proceeding is the harm caused to a domestic industry. Thus, the ITC must first identify the relevant domestic industry. But this in turn requires an identification of the relevant domestic products affected by the imports. The Trade Act focuses on the domestic industry that "produc[es] an article like or directly competitive with the imported article."[24] In determining what constitutes a "like product," the ITC has traditionally considered a wide variety of factors, including "the physical properties of the product, its customs treatment, its manufacturing process (*i.e.*, where and how it is made), its uses, and the marketing channels through which the product is sold."[25]

Escape clause proceedings nonetheless commonly involve disputes as to the definition of the "competitive" imported article. Typically, domestic producers will want to define the imported article broadly so as to enhance the possibility of proving domestic injury as well as of obtaining broader relief. Importers of the product in question will want to define the imported article narrowly or in terms of separate categories so as to minimize the potential for escape clause remedies.

One issue concerning the definition of the domestic industry is whether it can involve various stages of processing. In other words, the issue is whether the imports must be at the same level of processing as the domestic industry. Once a uncertain area, the Trade Act now specifically states that various stages of processing may be

---

23 *See* 19 U.S.C. § 2252(c)(1)(C).

24 19 U.S.C. § 2252(b)(1)(A).

25 *See* U.S. International Trade Commission—*Steel*, Investigation No. TA–201–73, at 30 (Pub. No. 3479, Dec., 2001).

considered in defining the relevant imported product. This has the practical effect of allowing the imported article to be at a different level of process from that which causes injury to the domestic industry.[26]

The next step is to identify the relevant domestic industry with respect to the relevant competitive products. The Trade Act defines the relevant "domestic industry" as either all of the producers of the articles at issue or "those producers whose collective production of the like or directly competitive article constitutes a major proportion of the total domestic production" of those articles.[27]

Having defined the industry, the Commission then must decide which particular companies belong to it. This is not always easy. In the ITC's automobile investigation during the serious economic downturn of the 1970s, for example, the Commission had to decide whether dealers and independent parts suppliers were part of the same domestic industry. It found that neither were part of the domestic industry because the dealers did not produce any article, and the independent suppliers of parts did not produce products that were like or directly competitive with the final product.[28]

To guide this difficult issue, the Trade Act provides specific instructions to the ITC: First, if a domestic company is also an importer, the ITC may only consider as part of the domestic industry that part of the business that relates to domestic production.[29] Second if a domestic company produces more than one article, the ITC may treat as part of such domestic industry "only that portion or subdivision of the producer which produces the like or directly competitive article."[30] Finally, if the domestic producers are concentrated in one geographic area of the country and the imports also are concentrated in that area, the ITC may treat as the relevant domestic industry "only that segment of the production located in such area."[31]

---

[26] *See* 19 U.S.C. § 2481(5).

[27] 19 U.S.C. § 2252(c)(6)(A).

[28] *See* U.S. International Trade Commission—*Certain Motor Vehicles and Certain Chassis and Bodies Thereof*, Investigation No. TA–201–44 (Publ. No. 1110, Dec., 1980).

[29] 19 U.S.C. § 2252(c)(4)(A).

[30] 19 U.S.C. § 2252(c)(4)(B).

[31] 19 U.S.C. § 2252(c)(4)(C).

§ 15.8 Substantial Causation

The issue of causation commonly is among the most controversial in escape clause proceedings. As a general matter, the Trade Act requires that the ITC "investigate any factor which in its judgment may be contributing to increased imports of the article under investigation."[32] But it also provides that the ITC "shall" consider the condition of the domestic industry not only at the specific time of the petition but over "the course of its relevant business cycle."[33]

The Trade Act defines "substantial cause" as "a cause which is important and not less than any other cause."[34] Thus, as the ITC has observed, "increased imports must be both an important cause of the serious injury or threat and a cause that is equal to or greater than any other cause."[35] The Act directs the ITC to consider all relevant economic factors, including "an increase in imports (either actual or relative to domestic production) and a decline in the proportion of the domestic market supplied by domestic producers."[36] As a more general matter, the Trade Act obligates the ITC to "examine factors other than imports" that may be the cause of an injury to a domestic industry.[37] However, the ITC may not aggregate the cause of declining demand associated with a recession or economic downturn into "a single cause" of serious injury or threat of injury.[38]

Of its nature, the adjective "substantial" leaves considerable latitude to the ITC in making its determinations of import injury under Section 201. The difficulty with the "substantial cause" element comes in determining whether increased imports are "equal to or greater than" the myriad of other competing factors that may cause harm to an industry. Management may be inept; labor may be underproductive or overly costly; general economic trends may be predominantly negative; and technological innovations may be causing obsolescence. Myriad causes may be at play. Whether one cause is more substantial than another is often very difficult to pinpoint with precision.

The issue of causation also may be affected by political currents at the ITC. For example, the controversial *Steel* decision of 2001

---

[32] 19 U.S.C. § 2252(c)(5).

[33] 19 U.S.C. § 2252(c)(2).

[34] 19 U.S.C. § 2252(b)(1)(B).

[35] *See* U.S. International Trade Commission—*Steel*, Investigation No. TA–201–73, at 34 (Pub. No. 3479, Dec., 2001).

[36] 19 U.S.C. § 2252(c)(1)(C).

[37] 19 U.S.C. § 2252(c)(2)(B).

[38] 19 U.S.C. § 2252(c)(2)(A).

was initiated by the U.S. Trade Representative and clearly unfolded in an atmosphere of political support for the steel industry at the highest levels of government.[39] In another controversial case, ITC refused to consider a general recession as a more substantial cause for a decline in the U.S. motorcycle industry.[40] On this point, Congress was forced to step in to clarify by express language that, as noted above, the ITC may not aggregate the causes of declining production associated with a general economic downturn into a single cause.[41] The point of this rule is that increasing imports may also be a "substantial cause" of a serious injury to a domestic industry even during a serious recession.

The Trade Act requires that the ITC not only "investigate" other contributing factors, but also that it then "take into account all economic factors which it considers relevant" in making its ultimate determination.[42] In carrying out this obligation, the ITC in fact has considered a wide array of causes in past decisions, including the following alternative causes of injury to domestic industries:

(1) Consumer cycles that affect product purchases;

(2) fundamental changes in consumption;

(3) governmental regulation;

(4) industry competition;

(5) management decision making;

(6) trends in imports, domestic consumption and production;

(7) price changes in the product market;

(8) business cycle changes;

(9) labor contract negotiations; and

(10) world price and competitive conditions.[43]

Finally, the legislative history of the Trade Act itself expressly identified other types of causes that may be more important than

---

39 *See* U.S. International Trade Commission—*Steel*, Investigation No. TA–201–73 (Pub. No. 3479, Dec., 2001).

40 U.S. International Trade Commission—*Heavy Weight Motorcycles, & Engines & Power Train Subassemblies Therefor*, Investigation No. TA–201–47 (1983).

41 *See* 19 U.S.C. § 2252(c).

42 19 U.S.C. § 2252(c)(1).

43 For a review of these alternative causation factors, see especially U.S. International Trade Commission—*Carbon & Certain Alloy Steel Products* (Publ. No. 1553, July, 1984).

increased imports, such as "changes in technology or in consumer tastes, domestic competition from substitute products, plant obsolescence, or poor management."[44]

§ 15.9 Serious Injury

A less developed, but nonetheless also potentially controversial, area of ITC determinations under Section 201 involves the question of what constitutes "serious injury" to the domestic industry. The statutory criteria indicate that loss of production should be the relevant inquiry, whereas loss of market share is relevant primarily to causation.

The Trade Act defines a "serious injury" as "a significant overall impairment in the position of the domestic industry."[45] In making its determinations with reference to a serious injury to a domestic industry, the Trade Act requires the ITC to take into account the following specific "economic factors":

(1) the significant idling of productive facilities;[46]

(2) the inability of a significant number of firms to carry out domestic production at a reasonable level of profit; and

(3) significant unemployment or underemployment within the domestic industry.[47]

Due to the decline in safeguards proceedings in recent years, most of the ITC authority on the serious injury test comes from some time ago. (An exception is the *Steel* safeguards case from 2001, which also is examined in Section 15.13 below.) From its earlier cases, the ITC has interpreted the term "serious injury" to mean damage of a grave or important proportion.[48] In a decision denying relief to U.S. cigar producers, the Commission determined that a marked decline in U.S. consumption of large cigars was a more important cause of injury than import competition.[49] Similarly, it found that a decline in housing construction was more important to the injury suffered by door manufacturers than was import competi-

---

44 *See* Sen. Rep. No. 93–1298, at 121 (1974).

45 19 U.S.C. § 2252(c)(6)(C).

46 The term "significant idling of productive facility" includes the closing of plants or underutilization of production capacity. *See* 19 U.S.C. § 2252(c)(6)(B).

47 19 U.S.C. § 2252(c)(1)(A).

48 U.S. International Trade Commission—*Bolts, Nuts & Screws of Iron or Steel* (Publ. No. 747, Nov., 1975).

49 U.S. International Trade Commission—Wrapper Tobacco (Publ. No. 746, Nov., 1975).

tion.[50] In most of its decisions concerning causation and serious injury, the Commission ordinarily reviews the economic trends over the past five years so as to screen out temporary problems.

The Trade Act also states that a mere "threat" of serious injury is sufficient. This means a "serious injury that is clearly imminent."[51] The Act provides further guidelines on this alternative injury standard as well. It directs the ITC to consider:

> (1) declines in sales or market share and higher and growing inventories as well as downward trends in production, profits, wages or employment in the domestic industry;
>
> (2) the extent to which the industry is unable to generate adequate capital to finance modernization or maintain existing levels of research and development; and
>
> (3) the extent to which the U.S. market is the focal point for the diversion of exports of the article in question by reason of trade restraints in other countries.[52]

In actual practice, however, there may be little difference between evaluating actual and threatened injury in escape clause proceedings.

Whether there is serious injury or threat of serious injury will of course depend upon the definition of the domestic industry. This is a bit like deciding what is the relevant market in U.S. antitrust litigation. Sub-markets, including sub-product markets and sub-geographic markets, can clearly contain a relevant domestic industry for purposes of Section 201. The ITC has in fact used tariff classifications of the United States in order to determine the domestic industry. Using such classifications has the practical feature of allowing identifiable tariff relief if that is ultimately granted.

Because the injury determination is closely tied to the definition of the affected domestic industry, the parties typically attempt to promote either a broader or narrower definition depending on whether they are the petitioner or respondent industry. Importers may contest the definition initially offered by the domestic industry so as to decrease the perception that like or directly competitive products are at risk or to reduce the measurement of increase in

---

[50] U.S. International Trade Commission—*Birch Plywood Door Skins* (Publ. No. 743, Oct., 1975).

[51] *See* 19 U.S.C. § 2252(c)(6)(D).

[52] *See* 19 U.S.C. § 2252(c)(1)(A).

imports. The definition of the industry will also impact on the question of causation. This was a principal issue in the *Heavy Weight Motorcycles* case. In that highly controversial decision, the Commission ruled that imported sub-assemblies were not directly competitive with domestic sub-assemblies because the imports were captively consumed.[53]

Similar issues were raised in the automobile investigation in the 1980s. The domestic industry argued that passenger cars should be defined as a single industry producing automobiles and light trucks. Importers who opposed the escape clause proceeding sought to subdivide the industry into large automobiles and small automobiles. The Commission ultimate determined that three different industries were involved: passenger automobiles, light trucks, and medium-heavy weight trucks.[54]

§ 15.10 ITC Escape Clause Relief Recommendations

The statute requires the ITC to report its findings on an escape clause petition to the President within 120 days after the petition is filed.[55] If the ITC determines that the case is "extraordinarily complicated," the deadline is extended to 150 days.[56] If the ITC decides that the statutory criteria of Section 201 are met, it "shall" make recommendations to address the serious injury or threat thereof to the domestic industry as well as consider the most effective means to allow that industry to make a positive adjustment to import competition.[57]

The Trade Act authorizes the Commission to choose from a menu of relief options. It may recommend an increase in or the imposition of a tariff or a tariff rate quota, a modification or imposition of an import quota, various trade adjustment measures including trade adjustment assistance, or any combination of these options.[58] No initial recommended relief may exceed four years and, if renewed, the total may not exceed eight years.[59] In addition, the

[53] *See* U.S. International Trade Commission—*Heavy Weight Motorcycles*, Investigation No. TA–201–47 (Publ. No. 1342, Feb., 1983).

[54] *See* U.S. International Trade Commission—*Certain Motor Vehicles and Certain Chassis and Bodies Thereof*, Investigation No. TA–201–44 (Publ. No. 1110, Dec., 1980).

[55] 19 U.S.C. § 2252(b)(2)(A).

[56] 19 U.S.C. § 2252(b)(2)(B).

[57] 19 U.S.C. § 2252(e).

[58] 19 U.S.C. § 2252(e)(2).

[59] *See* 19 U.S.C. § 2252(e)(2), § 2253(e).

Commission may recommend that the President initiate international negotiations to address the underlying cause of the increase in imports.[60] Interestingly, only those members of the ITC who vote affirmatively on the satisfaction of the Section 201 criteria in the first place are eligible to vote on the recommendations to the President. Dissenting members appear to have no input on relief recommendations.[61]

The ITC's report to the President will also include any adjustment plans submitted by the domestic industry in its petition and any commitments made by firms and workers in that industry in order to facilitate positive adjustment to import competition.[62] The Commission's report must also analyze the long- and short-term economic effects of the relief it recommends. The report to the President is advisory, but if the President decides not to follow any recommended import relief, Congress may pass a joint resolution by majority vote of both houses disapproving of the President's action. The President may veto this joint resolution, but of course Congress may override that veto. If this were to occur, then the Commission's original relief recommendations would be implemented.[63]

§ 15.11 ___Presidential Relief Decisions

The Trade Act authorizes the President to grant escape clause relief *only if* the ITC has made an affirmative finding that the increased imports have caused or threaten to cause serious injury to a domestic industry.[64] But if the ITC makes an affirmative finding, the Act requires the President to take "all appropriate and feasible action within his power" to facilitate efforts by the industry to make "a positive adjustment to import competition."[65]

Presidential Discretion. Notwithstanding the mandatory nature of this language, the President, as the Federal Circuit has observed, "has broad latitude to determine the type of action to take."[66] The President need not follow the ITC's relief recommendations. Thus, even though the word "shall" is used, the Act leaves substantial discretion to the President in defining the appropriate protective action. In other words, unlike antidumping and counter-

---

60 19 U.S.C. § 2252(e)(4)(A).

61 19 U.S.C. § 2252(e)(6).

62 19 U.S.C. § 2252(e)(5)(B).

63 *See* 19 U.S.C. § 2253(b), (c).

64 *See* 19 U.S.C. § 2253(a)(1)(A).

65 *Id.*

66 Corus Group PLC. v. International Trade Comm'n., 352 F.3d 1351, 1354 (Fed. Cir. 2003).

vailing duty proceedings, the President has effective control over both whether any relief will be given in a Section 201 proceeding, and what form that relief will take (providing, again, that the ITC makes an affirmative injury determination). Indeed, the President need not take any action at all.

If the President decides to provide escape clause relief, the Trade Act gives the President "an expansive, non-exclusive list"[67] of available relief measures. These include a tariff, a tariff rate quota, an import quota, adjustment assistance, orderly marketing agreements with foreign countries,[68] an allocation among importers by auction of import licenses, international negotiations, legislative proposals, or any combination thereof.[69] Duty free treatment under the Generalized System of Tariff Preferences of the United States is automatically suspended if the President decides to impose an escape clause tariff.

In deciding whether to grant escape clause relief, the President is directed to take into account the following: the ITC's report; the extent to which the workers and firms in the industry are benefiting from trade adjustment assistance;[70] the efforts being made by the industry to make a positive adjustment to import competition; the likelihood of effectiveness of relief in facilitating such adjustment; and the short- and long-term economic and social costs of the relief relative to their short- and long-term economic and social benefits.[71] The President must also consider other factors related to the national economic interest of the United States, including but not limited to, the economic and social costs if relief is not granted, the impact on consumers and on competition in domestic markets, and the impact on U.S. industries if other nations were to take retaliatory action.[72] Consumer interests have sometimes been critical of the President's decision to grant escape clause relief. Various presidents have noted that such relief can as a practical matter increase prices to consumers and that this would be adverse to the national economic interests of the United States. The argument that escape clause relief may cause inflation in the United States is a variation on this theme.

---

[67] *Id.*

[68] As noted in § 15.3 above, however, the WTO Safeguards Agreement expressly prohibits such agreements to limit import competition. *See also* Safeguards Agreement, art. 11.

[69] 19 U.S.C. § 2253(a)(3).

[70] *See* §§ 15.14 and 15.15 *infra.*

[71] 19 U.S.C. § 2253(a)(2)(A)-(E).

[72] 19 U.S.C. § 2253(a)(2)(F).

The Trade Act further directs the President to consider the extent to which there is a diversion of foreign exports to U.S. markets by reason of foreign restraints, the potential for circumvention of any relief taken, the national security interests of the United States, and those factors that the Commission is required to consider in reaching its recommendations.[73] These considerations have frequently caused Presidents to deny escape clause relief. This is consistent with the President's primary role in foreign affairs. Thus, for example, the President once decided not to grant escape clause relief regarding imports of copper when doing so might have influenced then-pending negotiations under the auspices of GATT and with the United Nations Conference on Trade and Development (UNCTAD) about the commodities trade.[74] A similar refusal to grant relief in connection with imports of copper was based on the need for the U.S. exporters of copper to obtain adequate export earnings.[75] In the latter case, the President expressly declared that "granting import relief is not consistent with our national economic interest."[76]

Limits on Escape Clause Relief. Although the President has almost unlimited discretion on the form of escape clause relief, the Trade Act places some outer limits: First, because escape clause relief is intended to be temporary, no relief ordered by the President may exceed four years initially, and eight years in total; second, no additional tariffs resulting from escape clause proceedings may exceed fifty percent *ad valorem* of the rate existing at the time of the escape clause proceeding; finally, if the ordered relief exceeds one year, it "shall be phased down at regular intervals during the period in which [it] is in effect."[77]

Petitioners in escape clause proceedings should consider in advance which form of relief they hope to receive. Tariffs may not provide effective relief because of floating currency values. For example, if the dollar increases in value relative to the currency of the principal exporters to United State, imports will become cheaper and the negative impact of tariffs might be offset. On the other hand, if the dollar declines in value, the relative production costs in the export countries will increase and the escape clause tariffs will provide even greater protection (unless of course adjusted upon review). Thus, tariff relief may or may not provide the type or level of

---

[73] 19 U.S.C. § 2253(a)(2)(G)-(J).

[74] Domestic Copper Industry, 43 Fed. Reg. 49523 (Oct. 24, 1978).

[75] *See* Copper Import Relief Determination, 49 Fed. Reg. 35609 (1984).

[76] *Id.*

[77] 19 U.S.C. § 2253(e).

protection the petitioners anticipate. For one thing, the importers may simply pay the increased tariffs if allowed by the economics of the market.

One reason why protective escape clause relief is difficult to obtain is that the WTO Safeguards Agreement entitles most trading partners to seek compensation for the adverse effects of any relief granted by another member state. Formal retaliation through a return suspension of concessions on exports generally is prohibited for three years. But because escape clause proceedings do not concern any unfair trade practice, protective relief measures typically are a source of substantial friction in world trade. This perspective helps explain why the President frequently decides that it is not in the economic interest of the United States to impose escape clause relief or, if granted, decides to terminate the relief earlier than originally ordered.

The President thus has provided escape clause relief in relatively few instances. Again, Congress can (but never has chosen to) override any presidential denial of escape clause or market disruption relief recommended by the ITC. Congress can do so by adopting a joint resolution of disapproval. Once this is enacted, the President is required to adopt the import relief previously recommended by the Commission. However, the President may veto this joint resolution, in which case an override of the President's veto is required to obtain relief.[78]

Reviews. If the President decides to impose protective escape clause relief, the ITC must monitor the granted relief during the period it is in effect.[79] The President also may later decide to reduce, modify, terminate, or extend the relief.[80] The level of the relief granted, however, cannot be increased. In the subsequent proceedings, the Commission's role is advisory, but if the period of relief exceeds three years, it must provide reports to the President and Congress on any continuing injury and on the progress of the domestic industry in adjusting to import competition.[81] The President may alter existing escape clause relief if he or she finds that the domestic industry has failed to make adequate efforts to adjust to import competition, the circumstances have sufficiently changed to

---

78 *See* 19 U.S.C. § 2253(b), (c).

79 19 U.S.C. § 2254(a).

80 19 U.S.C. § 2254(b).

81 19 U.S.C. § 2254(a)(2).

warrant a reduction or termination in relief, or upon the request of the domestic industry.[82]

Amendments to the Trade Act of 1974 adopted in 1988, and reaffirmed in the URAA in 1994, promote the goal of adjustment to import competition instead of trade protection relief. This is accomplished by strongly encouraging the submission of adjustment plans and commitments by petitioners for Section 201 relief, and by expanding the range of remedies the Commission may recommend to the President in escape clause proceedings to *any* action that will facilitate adjustment. Further, the standards for presidential relief mandate a determination that the relief will facilitate efforts by the domestic industry to make a positive adjustment to import competition. Finally, as noted immediately above, the Trade Act requires increased monitoring of Section 201 relief plans and imposes time limits on any relief granted by the President. Thus, as compared to the past, Section 201 of the Trade Act is now considerably less protectionist and more adjustment-oriented.

§ 15.12 Special Safeguards Rules for Chinese Imports

In addition to the general rule in Section 201, U.S. law has a special provision—which arose in connection with China's accession to the WTO in 2000—for safeguard measures relating to imports from China. Because of worries over a flood of inexpensive Chinese imports, these "Section 421" safeguard measures require only that increased imports be a "significant cause" of a "material" injury to a domestic industry.[83] These standards are significantly lower than for regular safeguard measures, which (as noted above) require a cause that is "equal to or greater than any other cause" and a real or threatened "serious" injury to a domestic industry.

In recent years, the special Section 421 safeguards rule has played a much more significant role than the traditional Section 201 rule. Between 2003 and 2012, the ITC initiated six investigations under Section 421, but none under Section 201. A prominent example is President Obama's imposition in June 2009 of protective tariffs of thirty-five percent on vehicle tires from China.[84] Pursuant to the special authorization for such actions in China's WTO Accession Protocol, however, the United States may not initiate such China-specific actions after the end of 2013.

---

[82] 19 U.S.C. § 2254(b)(1).

[83] 19 U.S.C. § 2451(a), (c).

[84] *See* Proclamation No. 8414, 74 Fed. Reg. 47,861 (Sept. 17, 2009).

§ 15.13 WTO Rulings on U.S. Escape Clause Cases

The rulings of the WTO's Appellate Body concerning the Safeguards Agreement have strictly limited the use of escape clause remedies. Indeed, the United States has lost a number of related disputes before the WTO, including in complaints brought by Australia and New Zealand on lamb; by the European Union on wheat gluten; by India and Pakistan on wool shirts and blouses; by South Korea on line pipe; and by Japan and numerous others on steel.

In 2001 alone, the Appellate Body (AB) ruled against the United States in three separate safeguard cases. In *U.S.–Wheat Gluten from the EC*, the AB emphasized the critical issue of causation. The AB found that the ITC's causation analysis lacked clarity and inadequately addressed factors other than imports that may have caused domestic industry injury. It also criticized the U.S. for a failure to give timely notice and to allow for a "meaningful exchange" in the required consultations. In *U.S.–Lamb Meat from New Zealand*, the AB reiterated that all causation factors must be isolated and examined. Further, it rejected the "domestic industry" definition adopted by the ITC because growers were included. Both of these decisions also emphasized the need for the ITC to find "unforeseen developments" in its injury determinations. The third 2001 AB ruling against U.S. safeguard measures concerned cotton yarn from India and Pakistan. In this decision, the AB rejected an exclusion of vertically integrated yarn producers from the definition of "domestic industry."

In its 2002 decision on U.S. safeguards on line pipe from Korea, the WTO similarly criticized the ITC for a "mere assertion" that challenged imports were "an important cause of serious injury and . . . not less than any other cause." More generally, the AB has repeatedly emphasized that the United States may not exclude consideration of imports from NAFTA countries (Canada and Mexico) in making safeguard determinations (the concept of parallelism).

The U.S. Steel Safeguards Case. Perhaps the most controversial recent escape clause action by the United States was the imposition of tariffs on steel by President Bush in 2002. The ITC found, following an extensive investigation and numerous hearings, that certain categories of steel imports caused, or threatened to cause, serious injury to the domestic steel industry. President Bush then imposed on the covered steel products annually decreasing tariffs of up to thirty percent, although only for a three-year period.[85] This

---

85 *See* Proclamation No. 7529, 67 Fed. Reg. 10553 (Mar. 5, 2002).

escape clause relief was tempered by exclusions for selected steel from selected countries. Most Australian and Japanese steel products, for example, were not subject to the extra U.S. tariffs. About half of all E.U. steel imports were exempt. Canada and Mexico, as members of NAFTA, were fully exempt.

Opponents promptly challenged the imposition of the safeguard measures in both U.S. courts and the WTO. The Federal Circuit upheld the action as a matter of domestic law.[86] But numerous WTO member states then challenged the imposition of this safeguard relief before the WTO's Dispute Settlement Body. In 2003, the Appellate Body ultimately ruled that the special U.S. tariffs on steel were illegal under the WTO Safeguards Agreement.[87] The AB held that the U.S. erred in utilizing the protective tariffs some four years after the surge of steel imports during the Asian economic meltdown of the late 1990s, and in excluding NAFTA partners Canada and Mexico. It also found that the ITC failed to address the requirement of "unforeseen developments." Although the AB acknowledged that the term does not appear in the Safeguards Agreement, it reiterated its earlier holdings that the Agreement must be understood against the backdrop of GATT Article XIX, which conspicuously includes such a requirement.

The European Union then threatened over $2 billion annually in retaliatory tariffs on U.S. exports of clothing, citrus, and boats, products thought to be politically damaging to the Bush Administration. But before the WTO could authorize such sanctions, President Bush—pursuant to corresponding authority in the Trade Act[88]—terminated the tariffs in December, 2003, reasoning that the effectiveness of the tariffs "ha[d] been impaired by changed economic circumstances."[89]

(Interestingly, in the meantime domestic interests separately petitioned the ITA and ITC to impose CVDs or Ads on many of the same products. Reasoning that the temporary safeguard measures effectively mitigated the damaging effects of imports, the ITC concluded that there was no material injury to justify responsive duties on either basis.[90])

---

86 *See* Corus Group PLC v. ITC, 352 F.3d 1351 (Fed. Cir. 2003).

87 *See* Appellate Body Report, *U.S.-Definitive Safeguard Measures on Imports of Certain Steel Products*, WT/DS248/AB/R, *et al.* (adopted Dec. 10, 2003).

88 19 U.S.C. § 2254(b)(1).

89 *See* Proclamation No. 7741, 68 Fed. Reg. 68,483, ¶ 6 (Dec. 4, 2003).

90 *See* Nucor Corp. v. U.S., 414 F.3d 1331 (Fed. Cir. 2005).

§ 15.14 Trade Adjustment Assistance—Individual and Company Assistance Criteria

The idea of trade adjustment assistance (TAA) has its origins in programs intended to assist people who were dislocated when the European Community (now Union) was established. Its adoption in the United States has had a checkered history, particularly as regards congressional willingness to fund trade adjustment assistance. The first authority for such assistance was provided in the Trade Expansion Act of 1962. However, no assistance was actually provided until 1969.

The Trade Act of 1974 made trade adjustment assistance a greater possibility. But dramatic increases in payments to workers under the program during the early 1980s caused the Reagan Administration to seek to repeal the Trade Adjustment Assistance Program. During the 1980s, tighter eligibility requirements and shrinking budgetary allocations reduced the scope of the program. It was not until the Omnibus Trade and Competitiveness Act of 1988 that significant funds were committed to trade adjustment assistance and the program was reauthorized through 1993. Nonetheless, actual payment of adjustment assistance to workers occurred slowly, and assistance to companies was extremely difficult to obtain. Trade adjustment assistance programs of the United States were consolidated and expanded in 2002, including for the first time worker assistance with health insurance, coverage of "secondary workers," a new pilot program on wage insurance for older workers, benefits for family farmers and ranchers, and expanded training and income support.

Trade adjustment assistance is designed to provide financial relief to workers (and, to a lesser extent, firms) for the effects of the increased imports—not to prevent, reduce, or restrict the imports. Escape clause relief is always considered temporary, but adversely affected workers may obtain "adjustment assistance" payments and other displacement benefits for a longer period.

Trade adjustment assistance decisions are made by the U.S. Department of Labor. U.S. law permits petitions for trade adjustment assistance by a "group of workers," unions, or "employers of such workers."[91] Generally, three groups of workers may be eligible for adjustment assistance: (1) those who have lost their jobs because increased imports caused significant harm to production by their former employer; (2) those who lost their jobs because increased im-

---

[91] 19 U.S.C. § 2271.

ports caused their former employer to shift production to a foreign country; and (3) "adversely affected secondary workers"—those who lost their jobs with a supplier of a primary firm harmed by increased imports.[92]

Distilled to its essence, the Trade Act requires for a grant of trade adjustment assistance that the Secretary make an affirmative finding on two elements:

First, there must be *negative employment effects* from trade in the form of the loss or threatened loss of jobs by "a significant number or proportion of the workers" in a firm.

Second, there must be evidence of *causation*. The Secretary may find such causation in one of two ways:

(a) Sales or production by the firm have decreased absolutely, imports of directly competitive goods (or their component parts) or services have increased, *and* the increase in imports "contributed importantly" to the loss or threatened loss of the workers' jobs;

or

(b) the workers' firm moved production or services to a foreign country or has begun importing its products or services from a foreign country, *and* either of these things "contributed importantly" to the loss or threatened loss of the workers' jobs.[93]

These criteria are related to but not identical with those considered by the ITC in connection with escape clause proceedings. For example, the term "contributed importantly" means a cause which is important but not necessarily more important than any other cause.[94] This is a lesser standard than the required "substantial causation" for Section 201 proceedings.[95] Whether imports are "like or directly competitive" with domestic products is a question of interchangeability or substitutability. The fact that imports are actually decreasing does not *per se* eliminate the possibility of trade

[92] 19 U.S.C. §§ 2271(a), 2272(b). For a case analyzing the special requirements for "adversely affected secondary workers" see Former Employees of Southeast Airlines v. U.S. Secretary of Labor, 774 F .Supp. 2d 1333 (C.I.T 2011).

[93] 19 U.S.C. § 2272(a).

[94] 19 U.S.C. § 2272(c)(1).

[95] *See* § 15.8 *supra.*

adjustment assistance. The critical issue is whether those imports have "contributed importantly" to unemployment.[96]

Congress expanded the trade adjustment assistance programs significantly 2009 and 2011. Such expansions and extensions of trade adjustment assistance often are closely connected with the granting of Trade Promotion Authority ("fast track") by Congress to the President for free trade agreements, as well as to actual congressional approval of such agreements once concluded by the President. An example is the extension of the enhanced TAA programs in 2011 in connection with the approval of the free trade agreements with South Korea, Colombia, and Panama.

Among the variety of benefits and services now available for eligible workers are the following: employment counseling and job referrals; job search allowances for travel and related costs; "relocation allowances" to cover moving expenses; retraining assistance; and, perhaps most important, simple income support after state unemployment benefits have run out. The recent expansions of the TAA programs also now allow financial assistance for health insurance as well as special wage subsidies for workers over fifty. Adjustment assistance also is available to workers whose plants relocate to U.S. free trade partners, or GSP, CBI, Andean or African trade preference countries.

Congress also has authorized a separate, but more limited, program of Trade Adjustment Assistance for Firms (TAAF) which is administered by the Department of Commerce.[97] Assistance to companies is primarily limited to technical aid.[98] Companies may receive adjustment assistance only if the Secretary of Commerce finds that a significant number of their workers have been separated or threatened with separation, that sales or production have decreased absolutely, and that increased importation of like or directly competitive articles contributed importantly to these results.[99] Agricultural firms may apply for adjustment assistance. Although once authorized by statute, Congress has not been willing to fund trade adjustment assistance for communities impacted by import competition.

---

[96] For an analysis of the importance of the "contributed importantly" standard in a long-running disagreement between the Secretary of Labor and the Court of International Trade see Chen v. Solis, 2009 WL 2058659 (C.I.T 2009).

[97] *See* 19 U.S.C. § 2341.

[98] *See* 19 U.S.C. § 2342(b).

[99] *See* 19 U.S.C. § 2341(c).

A grant of trade adjustment assistance does not require an affirmative determination by the ITC on import injuries (as is required for protective relief, *see* above). Such separate assistance flows from the separate determinations by the Secretaries of Labor and Commerce under the Trade Act of 1974. One important difference is the fact that in adjustment assistance proceedings the effect of imports on the industry as a whole is not at issue. The focus is instead on specific workers and specific companies. Whenever the ITC commences an investigation for purposes of Section 201 escape clause proceedings, the Secretary of Labor is required to begin a parallel investigation as to the likelihood and number of workers who may be certified as eligible for trade adjustment assistance. The Secretary of Labor then prepares a report which is forwarded to the President along with the report of the ITC concerning the escape clause petition.

§ 15.15 ____Secretary of Labor Determinations

The Trade Act gives considerable discretion to the Secretary of Labor in making trade adjustment assistance determinations. The Court of International Trade has thus held that it will uphold a grant of such assistance "if it is supported by substantial evidence on the record and is otherwise in accordance with law."[100] Substantial evidence merely means "such relevant evidence as a reasonable mind might accept as adequate to support a conclusion."[101]

In making determinations as to worker eligibility, the Secretary of Labor must obtain from the workers' firm whatever information he or she "determines to be necessary to make the certification."[102] This may be done "through questionnaires and in such other manner as the Secretary determines appropriate."[103] The Secretary may also seek additional information from officials or employees of the workers' firm, customers of the workers' firm, and officials of "certified or recognized unions" for the workers.[104] The Trade Act also expressly gives the Secretary subpoena powers.[105] But he or she must ensure confidentiality for any secret business information gathered in the process.[106]

---

[100] *See* Former Employees of Western Digital Technologies, Inc. v. U.S. Secretary of Labor, 2012 WL 7006347, at *3 (C.I.T 2012) and 19 U.S.C. § 2395(b).

[101] Former Emps. of Barry Callebaut v. Chao, 357 F.3d 1377, 1380–81 (Fed. Cir. 2004)(*quoting* Universal Camera Corp. v. NLRB, 340 U.S. 474, 477 (1951)).

[102] 19 U.S.C § 2272(d).

[103] *Id.*

[104] *Id.*

[105] 19 U.S.C. § 2272(d)(3)(B).

[106] 19 U.S.C. § 2272(d)(3)(C).

The Secretary of Labor may conduct investigations in any reasonable manner.[107] But he or she must publish in the Federal Register a notice of the fact that an eligible group of workers has filed a petition for certification for trade adjustment assistance benefits, and must publish a summary of the determinations on that petition.[108] Once an investigation is commenced, "the Labor Department is vested with considerable discretion in the conduct of its investigation of trade adjustment assistance claims."[109] Nonetheless, "there exists a threshold requirement of reasonable inquiry" by the Secretary.[110] This means, for example, that petitioners do not have a right to a trial-type hearing with cross examination of the witnesses of the Department of Labor as part of the process of determining eligibility for trade adjustment assistance. If, however, the CIT finds that the Department did not conduct a "reasonable inquiry," it may remand the case to require further investigation.[111]

Until recently, services were not covered by worker adjustment assistance programs. Thus, in the 1970s and 1980s courts held that workers engaged in airline services, automobile services, and shipyard maintenance services were not impacted by the importation of "articles" within the meaning of the Trade Act.[112] As amended, the Trade Act now expressly covers workers that have lost their jobs because, among other reasons, their employer either (a) has lost sales or production due to "imports of articles *or services* like or directly competitive with articles produced *or services* supplied by" the employer,[113] or (b) shifted work to a foreign country "in the production of articles or the supply of *services* like or directly competitive with articles which are produced or *services* which are supplied by" the employer.[114]

---

[107] Abbott v. Donovan, 570 F. Supp. 41 (C.I.T. 1983), *appeal after remand* 588 F. Supp. 1438 (1984).

[108] 19 U.S.C. § 2271(a)(3).

[109] Former Employees of Invista, S.A.R.L. v. U.S. Sec'y of Labor, 714 F. Supp. 2d 1320, 1329 (C.I.T 2010).

[110] *Id.* (*quoting* Former Employees of Hawkins Oil & Gas, Inc. v. U.S. Sec'y of Labor, 814 F. Supp. 1111, 1115 (1993)).

[111] *See* 19 U.S.C. § 2395(b) and Former Employees of Fairchild Semi-Conductor Corp. v. U.S. Sec'y of Labor, 2008 WL 1765519 (C.I.T 2008).

[112] *See, e.g.,* Woodrum v. United States, 737 F.2d 1575 (Fed. Cir. 1984); Miller v. Donovan, 568 F. Supp. 760 (C.I.T. 1983); Pemberton v. Marshall, 639 F.2d 798 (D.C. Cir. 1981); Fortin v. Marshall, 608 F.2d 525 (1st Cir.1979).

[113] 19 U.S.C. § 2272(a)(2)(A).

[114] 19 U.S.C. § 2272(a)(2)(B).

Chapter 16

UNITED STATES EXPORT CONTROLS

Table of Sections

§ 16.1 Governance of Exports

Unlike the control of imports, the laws regulating exports are briefer and rely on the issuance of extensive administrative regulations. For example, the *statutes* prohibiting U.S. persons from assisting boycotts against friendly nations fill only a few pages. But the *regulations* and examples of prohibited and permissible conduct fill dozens of pages in the Code of Federal Regulations. The control of exports, meaning their limitation, quite expectantly creates some conflict by way of the diminished economic benefit to the United

States that might otherwise be gained from export trade. Indeed, the statement of policy in the Export Administration Act indicates that it is only after consideration of the impact of restrictions on the economy that export restrictions are adopted, and only to the extent necessary.[1]

Exports are controlled for three reasons stated in the governing rules—(1) to protect against the drain of scarce materials and reduce inflation from foreign demand, (2) to further U.S. foreign policy, and (3) to assure national security.[2] These goals are expressed in the principal export enactment, the Export Administration Act (EAA), and are implemented by means of licensing requirements.[3] But the EAA does not contain many substantive provisions regulating exports. They are contained in the Export Administration Regulations (EAR). These regulations constitute an extensive set of provisions detailing the governance of exports.

Governance of exports is principally by The Department of Commerce's Bureau of Industry and Security (BIS). But other departments also have some regulatory authority, especially the Department of State where the goods are "dual-use" items, meaning that they have both commercial and military application. Application for a license may be done electronically under the Simplified Network Application Process Redesign (SNAP-R), but only if the exporter has a BIS granted Company Identification Number (CIN).

§ 16.2 The Meaning of a "License"

Prior to 1996 changes, exporters sent items abroad under either a "general" license or a "validated" license. The general license was used for most exports and did not require prior approval by the

---

1 50 U.S.C.A.App. § 2402.

2 15 C.F.R. § 730.6.

3 The EAA of 1979 has been amended several times. It expired in 1994 but has been kept in force ever since by the President declaring a state of emergency under the International Emergency Economic Powers Act (IEEPA). 50 U.S.C.A. §§ 1701–1706. The President is required to report to Congress every six months on the national emergency. The report is more an outline of changes in export rules and actions taken than a disclosure of any conditions which any "reasonable man" might conclude constitute a national emergency. The Congress and the President have allowed the EAA to expire because of the continuing conflict between the Congress and the President regarding control over export trade. Unhappy with what Congress presents as a new framework for regulating exports, usually granting little discretion to the President to curtail exports to countries for U.S. foreign policy reasons, the President threatens a veto, the act is not passed, and the provisions of the old act remain in force under the International Emergency Economic Powers Act. Waiting for a "better" new law from Congress which does not so severely limit discretionary power of the President, with legislators annually predicting that it will be passed "this year", the wait is about to reach twenty years without any reasonable expectation that a new law will be forthcoming "this year or next."

Department of Commerce. When most goods were shipped and a "Shipper's Export Declaration (SED)" was filled out, the SED constituted a general license. Validated licenses were issued only upon application to and approval by the Department of Commerce.

The current regulations eliminate the terms "general license" and "validated license". "License" refers to an authorization to export granted by the Department of Commerce. The change is to some degree a matter of semantics. General licenses, which were in a sense "self-granted", are abolished in favor of referring to such exports as exports permitted without any license. The new "license" replaces the old "validated license." But much more was accomplished in the rearrangement of the regulations. The myriad of "special" licenses has been redone. There are now ten general prohibitions making up Part 736 of the C.F.R., rather than the previous scattering of the prohibitions throughout the regulations. These prohibitions indicate the circumstances where a license must be obtained.

§ 16.3 Export Administration Regulations

The Export Administration Regulations[4] govern most export activity, including the issuance of licenses. The regulations are implemented and enforced by the Bureau of Industry and Security (BIS). The regulations include helpful provisions for the exporter that attempt to explain the regulations in simple terms. The regulations introduce the exporter to considerable new terminology.[5] The export of some commodities and technical data is absolutely prohibited, while other commodities are permitted to be exported under a range of lenient to severe restrictions. Special provisions of the EAA apply to further control the proliferation of missiles, and chemical and biological weapons.[6] The EAR has integrated the role of the former Coordinating Committee for Multilateral Export Controls (COCOM), a group of nations which sought to keep sensitive material from communist dominated nations. COCOM was abolished soon after the Soviet Union was dismantled.[7] The United States enacted the Enhanced Proliferation Control Initiative (EPCI), motivated by the Iraq conflict. This enactment seeks to establish greater control where commodities or technical data are destined for a prohibited nuclear, chemical or biological weapons or missile development use or end user. Considerable emphasis is placed on making

---

4 15 C.F.R. §§ 730–774.

5 Terms are defined in 50 U.S.C.A.App. § 2415, and in 15 C.F.R. § 772.

6 50 U.S.C.A.App. §§ 2410b and c.

7 COCOM expired in 1994. It has been replaced by the Wassenaar Arrangement, discussed below in § 16.17.

the exporter aware of the nature of the buyer and where the items are going.

The Department of Commerce has considerable discretion to allow or block exports where they are subject to licensing. In addition, certain *items* may be subject to mandatory controls, just as certain *destinations* may be subject to mandatory controls (e.g., a boycott that disallows most or all exports, such as with Cuba or North Korea). Actually, these mandatory controls allow some deviation, usually by the President rather than an agency exercising discretion. Some examples of mandatory controls include the Nuclear Non–Proliferation Act regulations governing exports that have nuclear explosive capability, unprocessed timber under the Forest Resources Conservation and Shortage Relief Act (FRCSRA 1990), oil for purposes of conservation or to establish reserves, and oil from certain locations such as the North Slope of Alaska. Exports are thus subject to a mix of regulations *by* different persons or agencies, *of* different products, *for* different purposes, and *to* different places.

§ 16.4 Steps for Using the Export Administration Regulations

Part 730 provides a general introduction to the EAR. It outlines the scope of the regulations, statutory authority, defines "dual use" exports (generally civil versus military), other agencies which participate in the regulation of exports, extraterritorial application of regulations, purposes of control, and limited situations requiring licenses. Part 732 includes the 29 steps for using the EAR. They include an overview, steps regarding the scope of the EAR, the ten general prohibitions, License Exceptions, Shipper's Export Declaration and other documents and records, and other requirements.

The overview notes some important questions to which the exporter must give thought, such as—What is the item? Where is it going? Who will actually receive and use it? What will it be used for?[8] This will help the exporter determine whether the EAR are applicable. The first six steps regarding the scope of the EAR cover (1) items subject to the exclusive jurisdiction of another federal agency; (2) publicly available technology and software; (3) reexport of U.S. origin items; (4) foreign made items incorporating less than a *de minimis* level of U.S. parts, components and materials; (5) foreign made items incorporating more than a *de minimis* level of U.S. parts, components and materials; and (6) foreign made items pro-

---

8 15 C.F.R. § 732.1.

duced with certain U.S. technology for export to specified destinations.

§ 16.5 General Prohibitions[9]

If an export is subject to the EAR, the general prohibitions, as well as the License Exceptions, must be reviewed to determine if a license is necessary. This part informs the exporter of both the facts that make the proposed transaction subject to the general prohibitions, and the nature of the general prohibitions.

§ 16.6 Determination of the Applicability of the General Prohibitions

Five factors help determine the obligations of the exporter under the ten general prohibitions.[10] They are:

1. Classification of the item using the Country Control List (CCL).

2. Destination of the item using the CCL and Country Chart.

3. End-user referring to a list of persons the exporter may not deal with.

4. End-use.

5. Conduct such as contracting, financing, and freight forwarding in support of a proliferation project.

The ten general prohibitions follow, with commentary under the following headings:

1. General Prohibition One—Export and reexport of controlled items to listed countries (Exports and Reexports).

2. General Prohibition Two—Reexport and export from abroad of foreign-made items incorporating more than a *de minimis* amount of controlled U.S. content (Parts and Components Reexports).

3. General Prohibition Three—Reexport and export from abroad of the foreign-produced direct product of U.S.

---

9 15 C.F.R. Part 736.

10 15 C.F.R. § 736.2.

technology and software (Foreign–Produced Direct Product Reexports).

4. General Prohibition Four—Engaging in actions prohibited by a denial order (Denial Orders).

5. General Prohibition Five—Export or reexport to prohibited end-uses or end-users (End–Use End–User).

6. General Prohibition Six—Export or reexport to embargoed destinations (Embargo).

7. General Prohibition Seven—Support of Proliferation Activities (U.S. Person Proliferation Activity).

8. General Prohibition Eight—In transit shipments and items to be unladen from vessels or aircraft (Intransit).

9. General Prohibition Nine—Violation of any order, terms, and conditions (Orders, Terms, and Conditions).

10. General Prohibition Ten—Proceeding with transactions with knowledge that a violation has occurred or is about to occur (Knowledge Violation to Occur).

In preparing these prohibitions, the Commerce Department rejected a number of suggestions to liberalize existing reexport controls, such as to create a separate part for reexports. Reexports create a problem with the nation from which the item may be reexported, which nation may object to any extraterritorial application of the U.S. rules. Some comments noted that although the new regulations were intended to be easier to use and less complex than the old, the new regulations created a system just as complex.

§ 16.7 Overview of Export Controls

The Commerce Control List (CCL—Part 774) is maintained by the BIS. The CCL includes all items (i.e., commodities, software, and technology) subject to BIS controls. The CCL does not include items exclusively governed by other agencies. But where there is shared governance, the CCL will note other agency participation. Knowing the Harmonized Code (customs classification for tariff purposes) Schedule B number does not help to determine whether or not an export license is required. That number is used by the Census Bureau for trade statistics. It is only the ECCN that will indicate whether or not an export license is required. If no license is required it is considered to be NLR.

§ 16.8 The Commerce Control List (CCL)

The CCL is contained in Supplement No. 1 to Part 774. Supplement No. 2 to Part 774 contains the General Technology and Software Notes relevant to entries in the CCL. The CCL basic structure includes the following ten general categories:

0. Nuclear Materials, Facilities, and Equipment (and Miscellaneous Items)

1. Materials, Chemicals, "Microorganisms," and Toxins

2. Materials Processing

3. Electronics

4. Computers

5. Telecommunications and Information Security

6. Sensors and Lasers

7. Navigation and Avionics

8. Marine

9. Propulsion Systems, Space Vehicles, and Related Equipment

Within each of the above ten categories are five different groups of items, identified by the letters A through E, as follows:

A. Systems, Equipment, and Components

B. Test, Inspection, and Production Equipment

C. Material

D. Software

E. Technology

To classify an item the exporter determines the general characteristics that will usually be expressed by one of the categories. Having the appropriate category, the next step is to match the characteristics and functions with one of the groups. For example, a common television would be in category 3 and group A. The first digit and letter of the ECCN would thus be 3A.

This is followed by another digit that differentiates individual entries by the types of controls associated with the second digit. The Reasons for Control are as follows:

0. National Security reasons (including Dual Use and International Munitions List) and Items on the NSG Dual Use Annex and Trigger List

1. Missile Technology reasons

2. Nuclear Nonproliferation reasons

3. Chemical & Biological Weapons reasons

9. Anti-terrorism, Crime Control, Regional Stability, Firearms Convention, etc.

There may be more than one reason for control of a particular item. If so the first digit in the above list would appear as the second digit in the ECCN. The third digit in the ECCN reflects the possible unilateral and multilateral controls.

§ 16.9 License Requirements, License Exceptions and List of Items Controlled Sections

Next to each ECCN is a brief description, followed by "License Requirements", "License Exceptions", and "List of Items Controlled" sections.

"License Requirements" identifies all possible Reasons for Control in order of precedence. Items within a particular ECCN number may be controlled for more than one reason. All the possible Reasons for Control are as follows:[11]

AT Anti–Terrorism

CB Chemical & Biological Weapons

CC Crime Control

EI Encryption Items

---

[11] 15 C.F.R. § 738.2(d)(2)(i).

MT Missile Technology

NS National Security

NP Nuclear Nonproliferation

RS Regional Stability

SS Short Supply

XP Computers

SI Significant Items

The applicable reasons appear in one of two columns in the License Requirements, entitled "Control(s)". The second column, entitled "Country Chart", identifies a column name and number for each applicable Reason for Control (e.g., CB Column 1). Once the exporter has determined that the item is controlled by a specific ECCN, information contained in the "License Requirements" section of the ECCN in combination with the Country Chart will allow a decision regarding the need for a license.

"License Exceptions" is used after it is determined that a license is required. It provides a brief eligibility statement for each ECCN-driven License Exception that may be applicable to the transaction. This is intended to help the exporter decide which ECCN-driven License Exception should be considered before submitting an application.[12] License Exceptions, the subject of Part 740, includes numerous categories. In the regulations, several exceptions were "bundled" under the grouping symbol LST (limited value shipments (LVS), shipments to group B countries (GBS), civil end-users (CIV), technology and software under restriction (TSR) and computers (APP)). But objections by exporters with automated processes, who complained that an additional step was created, resulted in 1996 changes which dropped the LST, "debundled" the process, putting each exception into its own section. This makes them similar to other separated exceptions (i.e., temporary imports and exports (TMP), servicing and parts replacement (RPL), governments and international organizations (GOV), gift parcels and humanitarian donations (GFT), some technology and software (TSU), baggage (BAG), aircraft and vessels (AVS) and additional permissive reexports (APR)). Part 740 is an extensive and important part of the EAR. It is followed by three supplements to Part

---

12 15 C.F.R. § 738.2(d)(2)(ii).

740, including (1) Country Groups, (2) meeting basic human needs, and (3) favorable treatment countries (ENC).

§ 16.10 The Commerce Country Chart

Consulting the Country Chart is an essential step in determining the need for a license. It is useful in all cases except where short-supply reasons apply, or where there are unique entries.[13] The Country Chart is Supplement No. 1 to Part 738, and over several pages lists countries alphabetically. Territories, possessions, and departments are not listed, but are subject to the same rules as the governing country. On the right of the listed countries are the numerous columns identifying the various Reasons for Control. There may be one, two or three columns under a particular Reason for Control. They correlate to references in the License Requirements section of the applicable ECCN. There may be an "x" in one or more of the cells. Where it appears in more than one cell, there will be multiple reviews.

§ 16.11 Determining the Need for a License[14]

Having determined that the item to be exported is controlled by a specific ECCN number, the exporter uses information in the "License Requirements" section of the ECCN entry in combination with the Country Chart. The need for a license is thus determined. Using the CCL "Controls" the exporter learns the reasons for control. Turning to the Country Chart and finding the appropriate country and the heading(s) for the reason(s), and with the column identifiers from the ECCN, the exporter looks for an "x". If found in the cell on the Country Chart, the exporter knows a license is required. A license application must be submitted unless a License Exception applies. Turning to the License Exceptions in the ECCN entry list, if a "yes" appears a further search of Part 740 will disclose whether an exception is available. Where there is no "x" in the cell on the Country Chart, a license is not required for control and destination, but one or more of General Prohibitions Four through Ten may prohibit the export. One can thus go to Parts 758 and 762 for information on export clearance procedures and record keeping.

§ 16.12 Advisory Opinions

A party who wishes to know whether a license is required may obtain an Advisory Opinion from the BIS.[15] Receipt of an opinion

---

13 15 C.F.R. § 738.3.

14 15 C.F.R. § 738.4.

15 15 C.F.R. § 748.3.

does not mean the subsequent application will be granted, opinions are not binding. But the BIS is likely to help the applicant in the preparation of an application which will meet the Advisory Opinion's requirements. An applicant may wish to avoid asking for an Advisory Opinion for fear that the opinion will be unfavorable. But if an export is made without an opinion and is in violation of the law, the sanctions may be severe.[16] Certainly, obtaining an unfavorable opinion and then exporting without a license creates a rather clear case of intent to disregard the law. But the Advisory Opinion is a good route to follow. If an unfavorable opinion is received, the BIS may explain what is required to obtain permission, unless the case is a clear one where no exports are permitted.

Support documents may be required along with an application.[17] Numerous countries are exempt from the need of support documents, mostly (1) any exports or reexports in the Western Hemisphere, (2) sales to government purchasers, and licenses submitted under special procedures, such as by A.I.D., or under the Special Comprehensive License procedure. When support documentation is required, the required data is to gain information about the disposition of the items, and to answer questions about national security controls and certain destinations. The transaction may require an End–User Certificate, or a Statement of Ultimate Consignee and Purchaser.[18]

§ 16.13 Issuance and/or Denial of Applications[19]

Part 750 describes the BIS's process for reviewing a license application, including processing times, denials, revocations, issuance, duplicates, transfers, and shipping tolerances on approved licenses. The part also includes information on processing Advisory Opinion requests.

The BIS undertakes a complete review of the application, including an analysis of the license and support documentation, plus a consideration of the reliability of each party to the transaction, including any intelligence information. The Departments of Defense, Energy, State, and the Arms Control and Disarmament Agency may also have review authority. Furthermore, the BIS may request review by other departments or agencies, which may agree to review, or waive review.

---

16 Persons convicted of a violation of any statute specified in § 11(h) of the EAA may not apply for any export license for ten years. 15 C.F.R. § 748.4(c).

17 15 C.F.R. § 748.9.

18 See also 15 C.F.R. § 748.10–13, and Supplements.

19 15 C.F.R. Part 750.

There has been a continuing dispute between Commerce and State over control of technology that seems to fall within the jurisdiction of each department. While the Arms Export Control Act gives State exclusive authority to issue jurisdiction determinations, Commerce has attempted to obtain concurrent authority to issue commodity jurisdiction determinations. Hearings were held in 1995 by the Senate Armed Services Committee after complaints that Commerce had issued export licenses for stealth technology that was under the jurisdiction of State. State intervened to stop the shipments, determined that they had jurisdiction, and denied the license. This kind of dispute has made it difficult to reach agreement on a new Export Administration Act. With proposals to abolish Commerce and transfer much of its export jurisdiction to State, the issue could become moot. There is little likelihood that State will agree to the transfer of any authority to Commerce.

Delay has been used by the government, especially by the Department of Defense, as a means of discouraging exports which might be permissible, but to which the Department objects. The *Daedalus Enterprises, Inc. v. Baldrige* case is an example.[20] Twenty-nine months after the filing of an application, the Department of Commerce had not reached a decision. The company had to seek a court order that the Secretary comply with the statutory timetable. There is little a company can do. It may not export the goods when the time period has expired if no response has been made by the government. It must go to court at each stage when the government fails to comply with the statute. Fortunately, the *Daedalus* case is an exception, and this kind of delay has been much diminished. The filing process is considerably improved. Furthermore, the President in 1996 made a major transfer of authority over encryption devices from the Department of State to the Department of Commerce.

§ 16.14 Timetable for Application Review

The BIS is required to resolve all applications, or refer them to the President, within 90 calendar days from the date of registration by the BIS. That is the date the BIS enters the application into the electronic license processing system.[21] Where there are deficiencies, the BIS tries to contact the applicant to obtain needed information. If no contact is made, the license is returned with notations of the deficiencies. This may cause a suspension in the processing time. If another department or agency is involved, or if government-to-government assurances or consultations are involved, there are ad-

[20] 563 F.Supp. 1345 (D.D.C.1983).

[21] 15 C.F.R. § 750.4.

ditional time requirements for making requests and analyzing their results. When certain countries are involved, such as Congressional designated terrorist supporting nations, Congress may have to be notified, delaying the application for another 60 days.

§ 16.15 Issuance of a License[22]

A license is issued for a transaction, or series of transactions. The application may be approved in whole or in part. A license number is issued along with and a validation date. The license number must be used when discussing the license with the Department of Commerce. Nonmaterial changes may be made without obtaining a "Replacement" license.

§ 16.16 Revocation or Suspension of a License[23]

All licenses may be revised, suspended, or revoked. This may occur without notice when the BIS learns that the EAR have been violated or are about to be violated. The exporter may have to stop a shipment about to be made, or if possible one that is already en route. When revocation or suspension occurs, the exporter is required to return the license to the BIS. Appeals from actions taken under the EAA or the EAR by the BIS are allowed for most actions.[24] There is an internal appeal process prior to appealing to the federal courts.

§ 16.17 Review of Export Applications by International Agencies

In December, 1995, 28 nations,[25] including the United States, agreed to establish a new export control regime that would assume some of the functions of the expired COCOM. The Wassenaar Arrangement on Export Controls for Conventional Arms and Dual–Use Goods and Technologies (the organizational meeting was in Wassenaar, the Netherlands; the secretariat was established in Vienna) fell short of U.S. expectations, not containing a requirement of prior notification of sales by one country to other countries in the group. A second concern is the lack of agreement on prohibiting dual-use goods and conventional weapons to civilian as well as mili-

---

22 15 C.F.R. § 750.7.

23 15 C.F.R. § 750.8.

24 15 C.F.R. § 756.1.

25 Australia, Austria, Belgium, Canada, the Czech Republic, Denmark, Finland, France, Germany, Greece, Hungary, Iceland, Italy, Japan, Luxembourg, the Netherlands, New Zealand, Norway, Poland, Portugal, the Russian Federation, the Slovak Republic, Spain, Sweden, Switzerland, Turkey, the United Kingdom, and the United States. Several other nations have since joined.

tary end-users in such nations as Iran, Iraq, Libya, and North Korea. An additional concern is the lack of transparency in exchanging information on exports of dual use goods and conventional arms.

There are other multilateral export regimes, including the Nuclear Suppliers group (NSG), the Australia Group (AG), the Missile Technology Control Regime (MTCR), and the Technical Advisory Committees (TACs). It is reasonably safe to assume that the goals of these groups govern products carefully controlled under U.S. law.

§ 16.18 Shipper's Export Declaration (SED) and Automated Export System (AES)

The exporter is responsible for following the regulations that govern carrying out the export.[26] This is so whether a license is issued or the exporter relies on a License Exception. The most important responsibility is the proper preparation of the Shipper's Export Declaration (SED), or Automated Export System (AES) record. They are primarily statements to the U.S. government used for gathering information to prepare trade statistics. There are numerous exemptions, such as gift parcels, aircraft and vessels, governments and international organizations, technology and software, and tools of trade.

As many as one-half the filings contain errors of omission or commission, according to the Bureau of Census and U.S. Customs Service. The two organizations have compared SEDs with outbound vessel manifests and discovered numerous inaccuracies in the vessel manifests as well as the SEDs. Cargo is often manifested not on the vessel actually carrying the goods, but on the manifest of a later departing vessel. The reason is the failure of exporters (and forwarders) to supply SEDs with complete and accurate information when the goods are shipped. This causes difficulties for Customs in detecting export law violations, and creates inaccurate trade statistics. Unless voluntary compliance improves, Customs may delay or detain an increasing number of shipments where filings are not presented with complete and accurate information.

§ 16.19 Fines, Suspensions and Revocation of Export Authority

Some means of enforcement is necessary to assure compliance with rules. The export laws and regulations are no exception. Violation of laws and regulations governing exports brings into play both

[26] 15 C.F.R. § 758.3.

the basic law and the regulations. The EAA contains provisions governing violations of both the EAA and EAR.[27] The Export Administrative Regulations contain supplementary provisions.[28] The general sanction for violations of the export laws, where the conduct was entered into *knowingly,* is a fine of the higher of $50,000 or five times the value of the exports.[29] This can obviously be *very* substantial.[30] *Willful* violations, with knowledge that the commodities or technology will be used to benefit, or are destined for, a controlled country, may result in a fine for business entities of the higher of $1 million or five times the value of the exports.[31] For individuals who engage in such willful violations the fine is $250,000 and/or 10 years imprisonment. This provision covers misuse of licenses. Cases involving violations of the licensing requirements tend to be quite complex.[32] If the party exported to a controlled country commodities or technology under a license with knowledge that the commodities or technology were being used for military or intelligence gathering purposes, and willfully fails to report this use, the business entity fine is the same as above, the higher of $1 million or five times the value of the exports, but for the individual the imprisonment drops to five years, with the fine remaining the same, $250,000.[33] Even possession of goods or technology either with the intent to export in violation of the law or knowing that the goods might be so exported, can result in a fine.

Perhaps the most severe statutory penalty in the EAA is in the civil penalty section. The Department of Commerce may impose a fine of $10,000 for violations (in certain cases up to $100,000), and they may *suspend or revoke the authority to export.*[34] This is a most severe sanction used only in extreme cases. It was used in the Toshiba dispute, where Toshiba (Japan) and Köngsberg (Norway) enterprises sold the Soviet Union technology allegedly useful for developing submarine propellers which would be sufficiently silent

27 50 U.S.C.A.App. § 2410. See www.bis.doc.gov, for considerable information concerning enforcement.

28 15 C.F.R. Part 764.

29 50 U.S.C.A. App. § 2410(a).

30 See United States v. Ortiz de Zevallos, 748 F.Supp. 1569, 1573 (S.D.Fla.1990), *judgment reversed* in United States v. Macko, 994 F.2d 1526 (11th Cir.1993). See also United States v. Brodie, 403 F.3d 123 (3d Cir. 2005).

31 50 U.S.C.A. App. § 2410(b)(1).

32 United States v. Pervez, 871 F.2d 310 (3d Cir.1989); *cert. denied* 492 U.S. 925, 109 S.Ct. 3258, 106 L.Ed.2d 603 (1989).

33 50 U.S.C.A. App. § 2410(b)(2).

34 50 U.S.C.A. § 2410(c).

to avoid detection.[35] The result was enactment of the Multilateral Export Control Enhancements Act in 1988,[36] amending the EAA and providing trade prohibition sanctions for two to five years.[37] These sanctions are applied whether or not the other nations take action against their companies. The EAR repeat and expand upon these statutory sanctions. They further add provisions dealing with actions including "causing, aiding, or abetting" a violation,[38] and "solicitation and attempt", and "conspiracy."[39] Further details are provided addressing misrepresentation and concealment of facts, or evasion,[40] failing to comply with reporting and record keeping requirements',[41] alterations of documents,[42] and acting contrary to the terms of a denial order.[43]

The political nature of export controls is emphasized by judicial refusal to agree to a settlement negotiated between a company accused of violations of the export laws and the Justice Department. In one instance a bargained for $1 million fine was rejected by the court, which imposed a $3 million fine.[44]

§ 16.20 Administrative Proceedings and Denial Orders

Administrative procedures which supplement the Administrative Procedures Act are the subject of a separate Part of the EAA and EAR.[45] They provide the framework for proceedings dealing largely with denial of export privileges and civil penalties. Appeals are the subject of several parts of the regulations.[46] The denial of export rights occurs principally either as an administrative sanction for violation of the EAR, or as a temporary measure when there is

---

35 See Robert van den Hoven van Genderen, Cooperation on Export Control Between the United States and Europe: A Cradle of Conflict in Technology Transfer? 14 N.C.J.Int'l L. & Com.Reg. 391 (1989).

36 It was part of the 1988 Omnibus Trade and Competitiveness Act. See 50 U.S.C.A.App. § 2410a.

37 50 U.S.C.A.App. § 2410a.

38 15 C.F.R. § 764(2)(b).

39 15 C.F.R. § 764(2)(c) & (d).

40 15 C.F.R. § 764.2(g) & (h).

41 15 C.F.R. § 764.2(i).

42 15 C.F.R. § 764.2(j).

43 15 C.F.R. § 764.2(k).

44 United States v. Datasaab Contracting A.B. (D.D.C.Criminal No. § 84–00130, 4–27–84).

45 50 U.S.C.A.App. § 2412; 15 C.F.R. Parts 756, 764, and 766. One court has held that attorneys' fees of a prevailing defendant are not allowable under § 2412, because Congress did not make the Equal Access to Justice Act part of the EAA. See Dart v. United States, 961 F.2d 284 (D.C.Cir.1992).

46 15 C.F.R. Part 764. See Iran Air v. Kugelman, 996 F.2d 1253 (D.C.Cir.1993).

evidence of an imminent violation of the EAR. A denial order prohibits the party from any exports, unless there are exceptions in the order. The denial order states the extent to which exports are restricted. Because all denial orders are not the same, it is important to read carefully any specific denial order to determine the extent of the denial.

The denial order also affects persons dealing with the denied party.[47] The denied party may not be part of a transaction nor receive any benefit from a transaction. What are subject to regulation are essentially items of U.S. origin, or foreign items which require reexport permission. A person who deals with a denied party is not innocent if there is no knowledge of the denial status; everyone is responsible for knowing that any person with whom they engage in transactions is *not* on the denial list.

Licensed items to be shipped to a denied party may place the exporter at risk. The denial order must be checked to determine the extent of the loss of export privileges *if* the sale to the denied party is a product to be reexported, or it releases controlled technical data to a denied foreign national. A person may buy products from a denied party in the United States, however, unless the intention is to subsequently export the product, which would give a "benefit" to the denied party. A transaction within a foreign country may be prohibited, as the foreign recipient of U.S. origin items may not sell them to a denied party even if the sale occurs within the foreign nation.[48] This purportedly applies whether or not the foreign firm is a U.S. subsidiary.

§ 16.21 Enhanced Proliferation Control Initiative (EPCI)

The EPIC consists of Sections 744.1–744.6 of the C.F.R. The initiative addresses how technology and goods are *used* rather than by their *description*. They include essentially the "design, development, production, stockpiling, or use" of nuclear explosive devices, missiles, or chemical or biological weapons. The end result is that a license is required where otherwise it might not be. Exporters are thus given the responsibility to know more about their dual-use goods. The use of the EPCI in the control of weapons of mass destruction, especially after September 11, 2001, is clear.

---

[47] It could even limit employment of a denied party, to the extent that the party could not engage in transactions subject to the EAR.

[48] This is not likely to be acceptable to the foreign country, which is apt to consider the prohibition an unreasonable extension of U.S. laws into its territory. A foreign court might order the transaction to take place.

§ 16.22 Designation as a Foreign National

Although it is part of sanctions, being designated a foreign national merits separate consideration because it is so potentially restrictive. The Office of Foreign Assets Control (OFAC) in the Department of the Treasury may designate individuals and companies owned or controlled by, or acting for or on behalf of, targeted companies. They become so-called "specially designated nationals" or "SDNs." Their assets are blocked and U.S. persons are for the most part prohibited in dealing with them. The list of such designated nationals exceeds 550 pages. It can be a devastating designation and effectively end trade with the United States.

Chapter 17

THE FOREIGN CORRUPT PRACTICES ACT AND ILLEGAL PAYMENTS ABROAD

Table of Sections

§ 17.1 Foreign Policy Based Laws—The Antiboycott Laws and the FCPA

Two special sets of laws that affect exports and foreign investments address specific foreign policy issues. First, the antiboycott laws and regulations (chapter 18) were enacted to reduce U.S. participation in the Arab nations' boycott of Israel. Second, the Foreign Corrupt Practices Act of 1977 (FCPA) was enacted to reduce U.S. participation in making certain payments or giving of items of value to foreign government officials in an attempt to influence government decisions.[1] These are two examples of laws enacted to achieve political, as opposed to international trade, goals. Anyone dealing with the FCPA should read the Department of Justice Resource Guide to the U.S. Foreign Corrupt Practices Act, published in November, 2012. See http://www.justice.gov/criminal/fraud/fcpa/guidance.

§ 17.2 History of the FCPA

The FCPA resulted from disclosures made to the Special Investigator of the Watergate investigations that many U.S. corporations had made payments to foreign officials to influence official government decisions affecting the companies. The FCPA is a response to real and perceived harm to U.S. foreign relations with important, developed friendly nations, and the interest of the United States to prevent U.S. persons from making payments which might embarrass the United States in conducting foreign policy. SEC investigations disclosed a large number of payments by U.S. corporations to foreign officials. Names of alleged recipients were disclosed, causing considerable embarrassment (Prince Bernard of the Netherlands), and even withdrawal or removal from office (Prime Minister Tanaka of Japan[2]), of national leaders. Ultimately, many consent agreements were concluded between the U.S. government and U.S. companies charged with making questionable payments. The agreements usually provided that names of foreign officials who received payments would be held confidential if the companies would disclose the payments. Considerable debate ensued in the press, generally attacking the U.S. companies and including little about the way business was conducted in many other nations,

---

[1] The law firm Sherman & Sterling produces a 400 page FCPA Digest of Cases and Review Releases Relating to Bribes to Foreign Officials under the Foreign Corrupt Practices Act of 1977 (March 4, 2010) that is an excellent assist in dealing with bribes to foreign officials. There is also an excellent annual FCPA conference by the American Conference Institute. See www.FPCAconference.com.

[2] Lockheed was alleged to have paid $1.4 million to Prime Minister Tanaka, which led to his removal and imprisonment. See 134 Cong. Rec. S9617–18 (July 14, 1988) (quoting statement of Senator Proxmire).

where bribes were not only commonplace but a precondition to doing business. There were legitimate concerns that several large U.S. corporations' payments had been extremely harmful to U.S. foreign relations. Some new legislation was inevitable. Morality was at stake. Many foreign observers, especially from other major exporting nations, did not object to the proposed legislation. Preventing U.S. persons from making such payments would give foreign businesses a competitive advantage. Some foreign observers wondered why Americans needed to make such public disclosure of their moments of transgression. The inevitable legislation occurred in 1977 with the enactment of the FCPA.[3] It has had two principal amendments: in 1988 and 1998.

§ 17.3 Amendments in 1988

The 1988 amendments removed some of the strictness of the initial act.[4] The level of conduct required to violate the Act was altered in favor of U.S. business by substantial elimination of the "reason to know" standard when payments made to agents might be passed on to foreign officials. The amendment requires that payments to agents must have been knowingly made, and includes a definition of such knowledge. One leading proponent of the original provision in the Senate was so incensed at the change that he suggested that the new loophole established by the amendment was "big enough to fly a Lockheed through."

§ 17.4 Amendments in 1998

The FCPA was again amended in 1998, to comply with U.S. obligations under the 1997 OECD Convention on Combating Bribery of Foreign Officials in International Business Transactions.[5] The Convention included language, added to the FCPA, making it unlawful to make payments to gain "any improper advantage" in order to obtain or renew business. The FCPA was further amended to expand its scope to cover prohibited acts by "any person." The 1998 amendments both significantly expanded who is covered and added an alternate jurisdiction provision. Domestic concerns other than issuers and "other" persons are now included, the latter making the FCPA cover all *foreign* natural and legal persons who commit acts while in the United States.[6] The amendments also reach payments

[3] Pub.L. 95–213, 91 Stat. 1494, Dec. 19, 1977 (amending the Securities Exchange Act of 1934, 15 U.S.C.A. §§ 78q(b), 78dd, 78ff(a)).

[4] 15 U.S.C.A. §§ 78q(b), 78dd, 78ff(a).

[5] Pub.L. 105–366, Nov. 10, 1998 (International Anti-bribery & Fair Competition Act).

[6] 15 U.S.C.A. §§ 78dd–2, 78dd–3.

by U.S. businesses and persons taking place wholly outside the United States, and payments to officials of international agencies. Finally, penalties for non-U.S. citizen employees and agents of U.S. employers and principals, previously limited to civil sanctions, now include the same criminal sanctions as for U.S. citizen employees and agents.

§ 17.5 Responses from Other Nations

Following the conclusion of the OECD Convention in 1997, several nations adopted domestic antibribery laws. But the number has been disappointing to the Convention's advocates. In the first year of the Convention, only 12 of 34 signatories enacted domestic laws to implement the Convention. But Japan's Ministry of International Trade and Industry (MITI) began immediately to adopt measures consistent with the OECD guidelines,[7] and Canada enacted an antibribery law that adopted the OECD recommendation to prohibit tax deductions for bribes.[8] Other major trading nations have adopted a variety of laws and policies addressing bribery of foreign officials, including China, Russia, and the United Kingdom. Nigeria's president sent its principal bribery enforcement official on a year long assignment. He had been an effective leader in combating bribery.[9] Adoption and enforcement of antibribery policies often differs, but some foreign enforcement actions have gained attention, in Brazil, Finland, France, Germany, India, Ireland, Japan, the Philippines, and the United Kingdom.[10]

The Inter-American Convention Against Corruption was adopted in 1996 by the OAS, and the Group of States Against Corruption (GRECO) was established in 1999 by the European Council. They had by late 2012, 31 and 46 participants, respectively. The United States participates in both.

There is an OECD Working Group on Bribery that has issued reviews of several nations' laws. Many nations have been criticized by the OECD, perhaps using the strongest language with the United Kingdom for its alleged failures to update its laws and urging the government to do so. In 2010, the UK Bribery Act was adopted with broad and strict coverage extending to payments to private parties

---

[7] Japan adopted an Unfair Competition Act which bans bribes to foreign officials.

[8] Canada adopted the Corruption of Foreign Public Officials Act, but is the only OECD nation to prohibit tax authorities to report suspicions of bribery to law enforcement officials.

[9] See 43 Int'l Lawyer 784 (2009).

[10] Id. at 784–789.

as well as officials. But the Act also contains an "adequate procedures" compliance defense.

The United Nations finally came into the game in 2004, after years of inability to agree and failure to acknowledge that perhaps some governments were responsible for their officials' actions in receiving bribes from foreign entities. Because the UN Convention went beyond the scope of the RFCPA and OECD enactments, including procedures for recouping bribes, it was thought to be the answer to the need for a more multinational approach to bribery. But many of the worst offending nations, including China and Russia, have acted to make the UN Convention just so many words. The UN Convention Against Corruption is welcome, and was ratified by the United States in 2006, and by 163 countries as of late 2012. Nevertheless, the OECD appears to have largely preempted the field with respect to serious attention.

§ 17.6 Definitional Challenges

One difficulty with the FCPA is defining what constitutes a wrongful payment. Because the payment is made to a foreign official, cultural standards of that official's nation may affect the payment. Conflicts of interest by government officials are governed by very different notions in each country. While apparently no foreign country has written laws permitting foreign officials to accept bribes to influence their conduct, the "operational code" or unwritten law of many countries makes that very conduct commonplace. The FCPA imposes a U.S. ethic on conduct in the United States and abroad by U.S. persons, and to conduct within the United States by foreign persons. But the FCPA does not prohibit bribes qua bribes: it prohibits only actions that violate the express language of the Act.

§ 17.7 Exempting Minor Payments

In defining conduct that violates the FCPA it was understood that certain minor payments to minor foreign officials for minor activities should not be condemned. The original act defined "foreign official" to exclude foreign employees "whose duties are essentially ministerial or clerical."[11] But the 1988 amendments altered this to specifically exclude acts that were "routine government action."[12] Only a few court decisions interpret the language of the FCPA, making the often uncertain meaning of the definitions in the amended law very important.

---

11 15 U.S.C.A. § 78dd–1(b) (1977).

12 15 U.S.C.A. § 78dd–1(b).

§ 17.8 Who Is Covered?

In addition to limiting prohibited payments to certain kinds of payments, the drafters of the Act also had to consider the scope of coverage regarding who would fall within the prohibitions of the Act. That meant both which persons would be subject to an action for making prohibited payments, and which persons abroad had to be the recipients of the payments for the transaction to be unlawful. The amendments in 1998 expanded the scope of coverage of payors, extending to "any person", natural or legal, United States or foreign, acting within United States territory. Omitted are foreign persons acting outside the United States. But as to payees, the Convention mandates are quite narrow, and required no amendments to the FCPA. The Convention, for example, does not cover payments to political parties, party officials, or candidates (except in some one-party states). Such payments, however, are covered under the FCPA.

§ 17.9 Prohibited Payments

The FCPA made it unlawful for an issuer of registered securities under § 12 of the SEA, or an issuer required to file reports under § 15(d) of the SEA, to make certain payments to foreign officials or other persons. The FCPA also requires those issuers to maintain accurate financial records which would disclose such payments. The Act additionally extends the scope of prohibited payments to any issuer *or domestic concern* making use of the mails or any means or instrumentality of interstate commerce,[13] thus effectively extending the liability to all corporations, in a manner not unlike the insider trading provisions of § 10 of the SEA. These rules allegedly were based on a shareholder's right to know if its corporation books were inaccurate, if management used corporate money to violate U.S. or foreign laws, if bribes were paid with corporate funds, or if payments were made to consultants with no accountability as to the disbursements by the consultants.

The 1988 amendments retained much of the 1977 act's structure, but made very important changes and additions. The most significant and controversial change was removing the "reason to know" language from the provision regulating payments to third persons that might be passed on to government officials.[14] This language was replaced with a "knowing" standard for liability, and a

---

[13] 15 U.S.C.A. §§ 78dd–1(a), 78dd–2(a). The latter part also defines both "domestic concern" and "interstate commerce." See § 78dd–2(h)(1) and (5).

[14] 15 U.S.C.A. §§ 78dd–1(a)(3), 78dd–2(a)(3) (1977).

complex definition of "knowing" violations.[15] The amendments in 1998 expanded the scope of prohibited payments by including payments made to secure "any improper advantage."

The current FCPA remains relatively concise. After establishing accounting standards,[16] it prohibits payments to certain foreign officials directly, or by way of third persons, when such payments are for the purpose of influencing any act or decision of the foreign official,[17] inducing the foreign official to act or refrain from acting in violation of the official's duty,[18] inducing the foreign official to use influence with a foreign government or instrumentality to influence that government's or instrumentality's act or decision,[19] or to secure any improper advantage.[20] There follows an important exception for routine government action,[21] which is further defined in a separate section.[22] The Act then establishes as an affirmative defense, cases where the payment was lawful under the *written* laws of the foreign country, or was a "reasonable and bona fide expenditure."[23] The Act also defines of "foreign official", "public international organization", "knowing", and "routine governmental action."[24] Added in 1998 is a provision for alternative jurisdiction.[25] This provision extends jurisdiction to issuers and U.S. persons who are officers, directors, employees, or agents (and shareholders acting on behalf) of issuers acting corruptly *outside* the United States, regardless of whether the act involved the use of the mails or any means or instrumentality of interstate commerce. "U.S. person" is defined. Concluding provisions of the Act consist of a penalty section with some exceptionally severe sanctions, including fines up to $1 million and ten years' imprisonment for individuals, and fines to $2.5 million for enterprises.[26]

---

[15] 15 U.S.C.A. § 78dd–1(f)2.

[16] 15 U.S.C.A. § 78m(b).

[17] 15 U.S.C.A. § 78dd–1(a)(1)(A)(i).

[18] 15 U.S.C.A. § 78dd–1(a)(1)(A)(ii).

[19] 15 U.S.C.A. § 78dd–1(a)(1)(B).

[20] 15 U.S.C.A.§§ 78dd–1(a)(1)(A)(iii), 78dd–1(a)(2)(A)(iii), 78dd–1(a)(3)(A)(iii). The content of these provisions is essentially repeated in sections 78dd–2 and 78dd–3.

[21] 15 U.S.C.A. § 78dd–1(b).

[22] 15 U.S.C.A. § 78dd–1(f)(2).

[23] 15 U.S.C.A. § 78dd–1(c).

[24] 15 U.S.C.A. §§ 78dd–1(f), 78dd–2(h). Section 78dd–2(h) also defines "domestic concern" and "interstate commerce."

[25] 15 U.S.C.A. § 78dd–1(g).

[26] 15 U.S.C.A. § 78ff.

§ 17.10 Accounting Standards

One approach used in the FCPA to discourage illegal payments is to require issuers subject to the SEA to maintain certain accounting records that assist in disclosing payments that might violate the other substantive sections of the FCPA. The original law generated considerable criticism about standards that threatened harsh penalties for even slight, incorrect accounting entries. The standards further required considerable documentation of foreign transactions. The 1988 amendments addressed what was a concern for "reasonable detail" and "reasonable assurances" in internal accounting controls, and indicate that the Act does not cover technical or insignificant errors in record keeping. Liability is to be imposed on persons who "knowingly circumvent or knowingly fail to implement a system of internal controls or knowingly falsify any book, record or account."[27]

§ 17.11 What Is Given?

The persons described above who are subject to the Act may not "make use of the mails or any means or instrumentality of interstate commerce *corruptly*" where the act is "in furtherance of" any one of several actions, including an:

1. offer,
2. payment,
3. promise to pay, or
4. authorization of the payment

"of any money", or an:

1. offer,
2. gift,
3. promise to give, or
4. authorization of the giving

"of anything of value."[28]

---

[27] 15 U.S.C.A. § 78m(b)5.

[28] 15 U.S.C.A. §§ 78dd–1(a), 78dd–2(a).

Thus, the Act divides numerous "giving" actions between giving either money or anything of value. The fact that something offered, promised or given has a very small value does not remove it from the Act. There is no *de minimis* exemption. The exemptions exist in *to whom* the item is offered, promised, or given, or *for what purpose* the item is offered, promised, or given.

§ 17.12 Acting "Corruptly"

The act of offering, promising or giving must be done *corruptly*. "Corruptly" is not defined in the Act. If all of the provisions are met, i.e., a payment is made to a defined foreign official and there is no statutory affirmative defense, does the government nevertheless have to prove that the act was done corruptly? Or does the giving to a foreign official where there is no statutory defense constitute a corrupt act? The word "corruptly" seems unnecessary; the FCPA prohibits certain conduct, about which persons might debate endlessly regarding whether it is corrupt conduct. One decision suggests that the word "corruptly" means that the court or jury determines whether the conduct violates the provisions of the Act, rather than meeting some external definition of "corrupt".[29] The party charged must be the one who acts corruptly; carrying out an employer's instructions might not be acting corruptly.[30] Thus, an employee of a U.S. aircraft-maintenance contractor who made a "gesture" to the chief of maintenance for Nigerian Air Force cargo planes, in the form of purchasing airline tickets for the official's honeymoon, after the contract was awarded to the U.S. company, was entitled to a new trial to determine whether the employee met the "corrupt" standard.[31]

An unusual comment in the Senate Committee Report on the 1977 Act stated:

> That the payment may have been first proposed by the recipient rather than the U.S. company does not alter the corrupt purpose on the part of the person paying the bribe. On the other hand true extortion situations would not be covered by this provision since a payment to an official to keep an oil rig from being dynamited should not be held to be made with the requisite corrupt purpose.[32]

---

[29] See United States v. Liebo, 923 F.2d 1308 (8th Cir.1991).

[30] Id.

[31] Id.

[32] Senate Report No. 114, 95th Cong. 10 (1977).

This would be a useful defense where there is clearly an attempt to extort money from the company or individual. But it may be very difficult to prove, and may require the kind of dramatic case noted in the Senate Report.

§ 17.13 Foreign Official

The definition of a foreign official has long been debated between the government and critics. Defendants have argued that employees of state-owned companies are not foreign officials under the FCPA. Justice and the SEC disagree. The issue is before the federal Eleventh Circuit

The offer, promise, or gift may not be made to any person in any one of three classes. One class is a payment to any *foreign official* if the offer, promise, or gift is either (1) to influence an official act or decision, induce an act or omission in violation of lawful duty, or secure any advantage, or (2) to induce the use of the official's influence with a foreign government or instrumentality in order to "affect or influence" any act thereof, and where the ultimate purpose is assisting the issuer in either obtaining or retaining business, or directing business to any person.[33] The "obtaining or retaining" business language was discussed in *United States v. Liebo,* where the court held the standard had been met.[34] It later came before the court in *United States v. Kay*, where the Fifth Circuit found the "obtaining or retaining" business to mean more than bribes beyond payments sufficient only to "obtain or retain government contracts."[35] But it also held that bribes did not have to rise to the level of influencing awarding contracts to violate the Act.

In addition to defining "knowing", the Act offers some help in defining the term "foreign official."[36] A foreign official is any "officer or employee" of any foreign government, or department, agency, or instrumentality thereof. "Official" is thus very broadly defined to include the lowest-level employee.[37] Also included are persons acting in an *official capacity* for or on behalf of a government or international organization. Added in 1998 were officers or employees of international organizations. The addition of international organizations substantially expands the scope of the FCPA. When payments to only foreign *government* officials were covered, it was necessary

[33] 15 U.S.C.A. §§ 78dd–1(a)(1), 78dd–2(a)(1).

[34] 923 F.2d 1308 (8th Cir.1991).

[35] 359 F.3d 738 (5th Cir.2004).

[36] 15 U.S.C.A. §§ 78dd–1(f)(1), 78dd–2(h)(2).

[37] But the exceptions for routine government actions are most likely to apply to payments to relatively low-level employees.

to define "government." That is not always easy. Some entities, such as the Vatican, the PLO, or a territory over which there is some government control, may or may not be considered governments.

§ 17.14 Foreign Political Party, Official, or Candidate

An offer, promise, or gift may not be made to any *foreign political party* or *official of that party* or *candidate for political office,* if it is (1) to influence such party in an official act or decision, induce an act or omission in violation of lawful duty, or secure any improper advantage, or (2) to induce the use of that party's influence with a foreign government or instrumentality to "affect or influence" any act thereof. The ultimate purpose must be to assist the issuer in either obtaining or retaining business, or directing business to any person.[38] "Candidate" may be difficult to define, since it may not be clear that a person is a candidate at the time of making a payment. The act does not specifically cover a person intending to become a candidate.

§ 17.15 Any Person "While Knowing"

An offer, promise, or gift may not be made to *any person,* while *knowing* it will be offered, promised, or given to (1) a foreign official, (2) a foreign political party, (3) an official of a foreign political party, or (4) a candidate for foreign political office, where the purpose is the same as in the first two sections above.[39] This third category of persons to whom payments are prohibited governs payments to persons hired as agents or consultants, but adds the very important requirement that a payment to such third party be made "while knowing" that the money or item of value will be passed on to a prohibited person. In the original Act the language was "knowing or having reason to know."[40] The "having reason to know" language was the subject of continual criticism by business persons, who believed it created an unfair and ambiguous standard that placed the burden on the business to prove that its conduct was proper. Although proponents of the original language lost the fight to retain it in the 1988 amendments, added to the Act was a broad definition of "knowing". The definition seems to be so broad to possibly include within the definition of the word "knowing" some actual "reason to know" criteria. The definition of "knowing" states that knowing conduct is where either (1) the person is *aware* of the conduct, that

[38] 15 U.S.C.A. §§ 78dd–1(a)(3), 78dd–2(a)(3).

[39] 15 U.S.C.A. §§ 78dd–1(a)(3), 78dd–2(a)(3).

[40] 15 U.S.C.A. §§ 78dd–1(a)(3), 78dd–2(a)(3) (1977).

"such circumstance" exists, or the result is "substantially certain" to occur, or (2) the person has a "firm belief" that such circumstance exists or the result is substantially certain to occur.[41] The provision then adds that the knowing standard is met if the person is "aware of a high probability" of the existence of such circumstance, *unless* the person "actually believes" that such circumstance does not exist.[42] Does the "high probability" language carry the knowing standard into the territory of a reason to know standard? The definition certainly modifies what might normally be considered a knowing standard, and will be the subject of considerable debate when it comes to an argument before the courts.

§ 17.16 *De Minimis* or "Grease" Payments

The FCPA might leave one with the sense that the Act extended far beyond what Congress initially wished to label as corrupt, into the area of the myriad of minor "grease" payments made to government officials (usually too nominal in amount to have a third party involved) to do what they are supposed to do, but to do it in a shorter period of time. Probably few persons who have crossed a border into Mexico or further South driving a car filled with personal belongings (but no illegal items) have not paid the customs officials a few dollars to avoid having to unload every item, and to speed the car on its way without a lengthy inspection. Probably many business persons have paid a small amount to a customs official to expedite the processing of goods needed for an impatient customer. The FCPA needed some exception for "minor" payments, without compromising its premise that "corrupt" payments ought not be allowed. The result is that corruption has a *de minimis* element, but it is not defined by dollar amount. Payments made to obtain or retain business are not minor payments. Furthermore, even *de minimis* payments may be subject to the accounting requirements.

§ 17.17 "Facilitating or Expediting Routine Governmental Action"

The original Act exempted payments to minor government officials for acts that were ministerial, using language to exempt payments to foreign government employees "whose duties are essentially ministerial or clerical."[43] The 1988 amendments changed that to create an exception for "facilitating or expediting" payments when

---

41 15 U.S.C.A. §§ 78dd–1(f)(2)(A), 78dd–2(h)(3)(A).

42 15 U.S.C.A. §§ 78dd–1(f)(2)(B), 78dd–2(h)(3)(B).

43 15 U.S.C.A. § 77dd–1(b) (1977).

the purpose is to "expedite or to secure the performance of a routine governmental action."[44] A "routine governmental action" is defined in the Act,[45] in four specific sections and one general subsection. Specifically allowed are payments made when:

1. obtaining permits, licenses, or other official documents which are part of the process of qualifying to do business in the country,

2. processing such papers as visas and work orders,

3. providing police protection, mail pick-up and delivery, or scheduling inspections which are associated with the performance of a contract or related to transit of goods across country, and

4. providing telephone service, power and water supply, loading and unloading cargo, or protecting perishables from deterioration.

A final, fifth class encompasses "actions of a similar nature."

Specifically exempted from being considered a "routine governmental action" is any decision by a foreign official about the terms of a new contract, the awarding of such contract, continuing business, or any action by any official involved in the process of new or renewal business.[46]

There is a very large gap between what is specifically allowed and what is specifically disallowed. One of the least clear areas involves the extent to which foreign officials may be entertained. Entertaining is not always motivated solely by courtesy. Foreign officials are usually entertained as part of the process of receiving the award of a contract, or establishing or continuing a business. The line of legitimacy must fall somewhere between reasonable expenses associated with normal business, and unreasonable expenses associated with unreasonable influence. Finding that line is helped by the special provisions providing affirmative defenses.[47]

---

[44] 15 U.S.C.A. §§ 78dd–1(b), 78dd–2(b).

[45] 15 U.S.C.A. §§ 78dd–1(f)(3), 78dd–2(h)(4).

[46] 15 U.S.C.A. §§ 78dd–1(f)(3)(B), 78dd–2(h)(4)(B).

[47] 15 U.S.C.A. §§ 78dd–1(c), 78dd–2(c).

§ 17.18 Lawful under "Written" Laws

The FCPA establishes two basic classes of affirmative defenses. The first is when the payment, gift, offer, or promise is lawful under the *written* laws and regulations of the foreign country.[48] Since nations uncommonly enact laws giving legitimacy to what may be common but corrupt practices of its officials, this section is likely to be of little use. Were it to allow payments where the *unwritten* laws, i.e., the expected and common practice, mandate payments, the loophole would be considerably wider than merely enough to fly a Lockheed through. To be safe, counsel should obtain an opinion in writing from foreign local counsel that identifies the written law or regulation that allows a payment. It is of course possible that payments may be allowed to political campaigns under local written law, but not personally to serving officials to influence their official decisions.

§ 17.19 "Reasonable and Bona Fide Expenditures"

The second specific affirmative defense is when the payment, gift, offer or promise is a "reasonable and bona fide expenditure, such as travel and lodging expenses" that a foreign official incurs, and which is related to either (1) the promotion, demonstration, or explanation of products or services, or (2) the execution or performance of a contract.[49] While the first part of this section broadens the permissible payments, the second part narrows it. Noticeably excluded are such payments when the contract is being considered, either initially or for renewal. But a carefully crafted corporate policy might provide that even in the advance of obtaining a contract or having it renewed, payments to foreign officials are exclusively based on promotions, demonstrations, and/or explanations relating to the performance of the contract if granted or renewed.

The Department of Justice issued an Opinion approving some planned paid travel for Chinese journalists to a Trace International event in China[50]. This DOJ procedure may be the best process to follow for travel expenses about which a corporation has some doubt.

---

[48] 15 U.S.C.A. § 77dd–1(c)(1).

[49] 15 U.S.C.A. § 77dd–1(c)(2).

[50] See 43 Int'l Lawyer 783 (2009). U.S. Dep't of Justice, Foreign Corrupt Practices Act Review, Opinion Procedure Release No. 08–03 (July 11, 2008).

§ 17.20 Enforcement Authority

The severity of penalties for violations of the FCPA mandates close consideration of its provisions by all persons doing business abroad. Violations of the FCPA are dealt with principally by the SEC (which monitors the record keeping) and the Department of Justice (which enforces the antibribery provisions). Comparatively few actions have been brought by the Department of Justice and reached the appellate courts. One example, involving the International Harvester Company, alleged participation in a series of charges relating to dealings with officials of Petroleos Mexicanos (PEMEX), the national oil company.[51] But it is not only the largest U.S. corporations which have been the subject of actions. Another action involved an individual who owned a postage stamp concession for a Caribbean island and who paid for flights for citizens to return to the island to vote for the reelection of the president, allegedly to influence the government to renew the concession.[52]

Investigations are often reported in the news, suggesting that U.S. persons and companies have not ceased making payments to foreign officials.[53] Some of the most controversial allegations in the past few years involved IBM and Mexico in 1993, during the sensitive negotiations for the North American Free Trade Agreement.[54] An Iranian-born British businessman was retained by IBM to be its agent in a tender bid for a new air-control system in Mexico City. The agent alleged that soon after a meeting with several Mexican officials at which they tried to obtain a $1 million bribe, IBM's bid was rejected and the contract given to the French Thomson Company. The agents' subsequent public disclosure and numerous newspaper articles led nowhere, but caused a sensation in Mexico early in 1993. The Minister of Communications was ousted in a cabinet reorganization. The agent alleged that the Mexican government later tried to buy him off. IBM did not support the agent in his claims, and settled with the agent out-of-court. The whole episode illustrates many problems. The U.S. government showed no inclination to become involved or investigate the matter. There were foreign

---

[51] The company pleaded guilty to conspiracy to violate the FCPA. See McLean v. International Harvester Co., 902 F.2d 372 (5th Cir.1990); McLean v. International Harvester Co., 817 F.2d 1214 (5th Cir.1987); Executive Legal Summary No. 5, Business Laws, Inc. 100.03 (Hancock ed., Oct. 1988).

[52] Executive Legal Summary No. 5, Business Laws, Inc., 100.03, 100.04 (Hancock ed., Oct. 1988).

[53] See, e.g., Some Weapons Makers Are Said To Continue Illicit Foreign Outlays, Wall St.J., Nov. 5, 1993, at 1, discussing GE, Teledyne Inc., Litton Industries, Inc., Loral Corp., and United Technologies Corp. problems.

[54] See The Independent, August 29, 1993, Sunday Review at 2; The Financial Post, Oct. 27, 1993, at 13.

policy problems, NAFTA priorities, perhaps a sense that the whole story was not implausible, but a realization that this is how things work. Aliases or no names, secret meetings, finger pointing, and leaks to the press are all part of the game. No one seems to have asked how the French Thomson Company got the bid so quickly after IBM was rejected.

Later, IBM was again in the news regarding an investigation of bribes in Argentina to obtain a $250 million contract to modernize the computer system for the Banco de la Nación.[55] IBM allegedly paid bribes to CCR, a computer systems company, in connection with obtaining a contract with Nación, money which soon found its way into Swiss accounts.[56]

Major prosecutions occurred in 2008 and 2009 of Siemens and Halliburton/KBR. Early in 2010 it was reported that investigations of Daimler resulted in a settlement where Daimler agreed to pay $185 million in fines. A New York Times article in December 2012 covered more than three full pages describing bribes allegedly made by Walmart in Mexico, The payments seem certain to lead to a Department of Justice investigation. The focus on these high profile companies does not mean that smaller companies that have no compliance plans have escaped attention.

The Department of Justice Resource Guide to the U.S. Foreign Corrupt Practices Act of November 2012 includes examples of how companies avoid prosecution. It is a highly recommended guide to anyone dealing with the FCPA. It is available as a *pdf* document from the GPO.

§ 17.21 Consent Decrees

Few of the cases investigated ever come to court.[57] Most cases are resolved by consent decrees. Corporations prefer to accept a negotiated fine rather than litigate in the federal courts.[58] Furthermore, corporations usually prefer to avoid the publicity accompanying charges of making foreign payments corruptly. There is also the problem that the payment usually occurs in a foreign country and

---

[55] National Law Journal, Mar. 3, 1997, at B16.

[56] Financial Times, Oct. 19, 1995, at 5.

[57] See United States v. McLean, 738 F.2d 655 (5th Cir.1984), *cert. denied* 470 U.S. 1050, 105 S.Ct. 1748, 84 L.Ed.2d 813 (1985).

[58] The FCPA Reporter includes information regarding consent decrees and guilty pleas. The names of corporations charged are well known, including such companies as Ashland Oil, General Electric, Goodyear International, International Harvester, and Lockheed Martin.

proof of the payment is difficult to establish. The foreign country is not likely to assist in allowing discovery or taking depositions.

§ 17.22 Charges of Accounting and Illegal Payment Violations

More actions have been brought charging violations of the accounting provisions as opposed to making illegal payments. The proof of accounting violations is mostly available in the United States, where the corporate books are located. But the books often disclose little to auditors, since payments may be made to persons who appear to be legitimate foreign consultants, and thus are listed only as payments made to consultants, not to foreign officials.

§ 17.23 Additional Charges

Persons charged by the government with violations of either the accounting requirements or the payments provisions may face other charges. Competitors may bring claims under RICO, antitrust, or direct FCPA theories. Employees who are dismissed for refusing to comply with orders to make foreign payments may bring unlawful discharge suits, usually in the form of a breach of contract action, or become whistle-blowers and tell all to the government.[59] Shareholders may initiate derivative suits. Finally, a foreign government whose officials are offered bribes may take action.

§ 17.24 Penalties: Record Keeping and Accounting Violations

Section 78m(b) violations, the record-keeping and internal accounting-control standards section, may lead to penalties of $100 per day during the period in which the company fails to comply with the requirements. These are civil rather than criminal penalties. But where there is (1) a willful violation of the provisions, or (2) a willful and knowing making of a false or misleading statement in filed applications, statements or reports, a criminal penalty may be imposed of not more than $1,000,000, or not more than ten years imprisonment, or both.[60]

---

[59] A whistle-blower's experience at GE is described in Some Weapons Makers Are Said To Continue Illicit Foreign Outlays, Wall St.J., Nov. 5, 1993, at 1.

[60] 15 U.S.C.A. § 78ff(a). An exchange may be fined up to $2,500,000 Proof of no knowledge of the rule or regulation will avoid imprisonment. Id.

§ 17.25 Penalties: Illegal Payment Violations

Section 78dd–1 and § 78dd–2 violations for making illegal payments are governed in these two different provisions, for issuers and domestic concerns, respectively, and their officers, directors, agents, and shareholders acting on behalf of the entity. Each section leads to the same levels of penalties.[61] The entities are subject to fines of not more than $2 million, and civil penalties of not more than $10,000. The officers, directors, employees, agents, and shareholders acting on behalf of the concerns are subject to fines up to $100,000, or five years' imprisonment, or both, if the violation was willful.[62] They are also subject to civil penalties up to $10,000, without the willful requirement. Any fine imposed on a person under the above provisions, criminal or civil, may not be paid by the company, directly or indirectly. These penalties illustrate that the government is serious about violations of the FCPA.[63]

Some significant recent prosecutions and settlements include (1) Lucent Technologies, Inc., involving payments to Chinese officials and resulting in Lucent agreeing to pay criminal and civil penalties of $2.5 million, (2) AGA Medical Corporation involving China again with a $2 million fine, (3) Aibel Group Limited involving Nigeria and an agreed to $4.2 million fine, and (4) Siemens AG involving bribes paid in numerous countries and an agreed to fine of $1.6 billion which also involved German government enforcement cooperation. Siemens alone settled for $800 million. The Siemens cases involved the Oil-for-Food program, which itself resulted in four other settlements, against Akzo Nobel of the Netherlands—$3 million in penalties, against Flowserve Corporation—$10.55 million of criminal and civil penalties, against AB Volvo—$12.6 million in penalties, and against Fiat—$17.8 million civil and criminal penalties. An early 2010 report indicated that Daimler settled with the SEC, agreeing to pay $185 million in fines ($96.3 million criminal and $91.4 million civil). The 2008 Siemens' settlement remains the largest to date.

There have also been individual prosecutions, including some high profile persons. Albert Stanley, CEO of KBR, a subsidiary of Halliburton, agreed to serve seven years in prison and pay $10.8

[61] 15 U.S.C.A. §§ 78ff(c) and 78dd–2(g).

[62] Only willful violations are subject to criminal penalties. See Trane Co. v. O'Connor Securities, 718 F.2d 26 (2d Cir.1983).

[63] Two units of Litton Industries pleaded guilty in 1999 to fraud and conspiracy in making payments to obtain defense business in Greece and Taiwan. Litton agreed to pay $18.5 million to settle the matter (including an amount to reimburse the Department of Justice for the costs of the investigation).

million in restitution. Halliburton was run by later-to-be Vice-president Richard Cheney.

§ 17.26 Review Process

The FCPA requires the Department of Justice to establish a procedure allowing persons to request an opinion about proposed activity that might create some FCPA concern.[64] The first step is for the person or company to present to the Department of Justice details of the proposed transaction. The person or company may only rely upon a review letter signed by the Assistant Attorney General (or delegate) in charge of the criminal division. The procedure has not been used very often, possibly because of concern about identifying foreign officials and the consequences if the review request information is not held confidential.[65] The 1988 amendments provide more definitional information of what may be allowed, and may lead to even less use of the review procedure. The DOJ has rejuvenated the opinion procedure, issuing several opinions in 2008. Several questions were addressed, about disclosures, takeovers, acquisitions by auction and payment of some travel expenses.[66]

§ 17.27 When to Use Review Process?

The review process should be used when a company is clearly uncertain about the lawfulness of the proposed payments, and believes that the information it will provide to the Department will not be disclosed, or will not cause injury if disclosed, and that the protection afforded by the request outweighs the potential harm to the company if it does not disclose and is later challenged.

§ 17.28 Actions by the Government

The FCPA was drafted with the intent that the Department of Justice and the SEC would enforce the law. The former would challenge illegal payments and the latter would challenge record keeping and accounting procedures. That is the way the Act has functioned. But, as in the case of many federal laws, questions have been raised regarding the extent to which the FCPA creates private rights of action and other suits.

---

[64] 15 U.S.C.A. §§ 78dd–1(e), 78dd–2(f). The review procedure is contained in 28 C.F.R. § 50.18.

[65] Furthermore, information provided in a review request might be used against the person in a criminal prosecution. See John W. Bagby, Enforcement of the Accounting Standards in the Foreign Corrupt Practices Act, 21 Am.Bus.L.J. 213 (1983).

[66] See 43 Int'l Lawyer 782–784 (2009).

§ 17.29 Private Right of Action

There have not been many suits charging violations of the FCPA initiated by private individuals or companies against other private parties. One federal circuit court has held that there is no private right of action under the FCPA.[67] The case involved donations Philip Morris allegedly promised a Venezuelan Children's Foundation (the wife of the President of Venezuela was the president of the Foundation) for benefits to Philip Morris in obtaining Venezuelan tobacco. Two U.S. tobacco producers sued Philip Morris for harm caused by the alleged violation of the FCPA (and antitrust law). The *Lamb* decision is influential and law in the Sixth Circuit, but may not be the last word on the issue. With the recent substantial increase in enforcement by several governments there may be a significant increase in bribery-related private civil litigation.

§ 17.30 Employee Suits

If a company intends to make payments to foreign officials that appear likely to be in violation of the FCPA, the payments will obviously require acts by company employees. Very large payments are likely to be authorized and possibly made directly by senior officers. Other payments may be authorized by senior officials but be made by lower level employees who are in more frequent contact with the foreign officials. In some cases, the lower level employees, such as sales or purchasing agents, decide upon and make the payments on their own. If executives decide to make payments and delegate making those payments to another employee, the decision-makers are in jeopardy of the employee refusing to participate and, if dismissed for the refusal, bringing a lawsuit. The FCPA itself does not provide any basis for a corporate employee to bring a claim against the corporation where the corporation appears to have made the employee the scapegoat for allegedly unlawful payments.[68] The original 1977 Act included what was known as the Eckhardt provision, which did not allow actions to be brought against employees without first going against the employer. The amendments in 1988 reversed this and allow such actions. An employer may now urge the government to bring suit directly against the employee who made the payment,

---

[67] Lamb v. Phillip Morris, Inc., 915 F.2d 1024 (6th Cir.1990), *cert. denied* 498 U.S. 1086, 111 S.Ct. 961, 112 L.Ed.2d 1048 (1991). See also Citicorp Int'l Trading Co., Inc. v. Western Oil & Refining Co., 771 F.Supp. 600 (S.D.N.Y.1991) (applying the well established four-part Cort v. Ash test to determine that there is no private cause of action); Shields on Behalf of Sundstrand Corp. v. Erickson, 710 F.Supp. 686 (N.D.Ill.1989) (violations of financial and accounting controls do not give rise to private right); Lewis v. Sporck, 612 F.Supp. 1316 (N.D.Cal.1985) (same conclusion).

[68] McLean v. International Harvester Co., 817 F.2d 1214 (5th Cir.1987), *appeal after remand* 902 F.2d 372 (5th Cir.1990).

even if the payment was authorized by other higher level officers. The possibility of a scapegoat is back. But the scapegoat employee may not be without a remedy. That employee is likely to be or soon become a *former* employee, and may have an action against the company.

Ashland Oil Inc., learned that firing an employee for refusing to make an illegal payment abroad is costly.[69] Ashland's vice-president William McKay was instructed but refused to make an illegal payment to an official in Oman. McKay later cooperated with SEC and IRS investigations of the payment. Another executive, Harry Williams, was sympathetic to McKay's attempt to change the corporate policy at Ashland. Both were soon no longer employed. They sued Ashland for wrongful discharge and received a verdict of nearly $70 million, later settled for $25 million. A key to the settlement was a provision in McKay's employment contract that he would not be compelled to make unlawful payments. It is an appropriate employment contract provision for an officer, because many states do not allow suits for termination in the absence of a contractual provision. Any suit commenced under such a contract provision would be based on the contract and not the FCPA. It would therefore not face the uncertain issue noted above of bringing private suits under the Act. Because it is a suit based on breach of the employment contract, it requires inquiry only regarding the company's act of demanding a payment that, if made, would be a violation.[70]

Teledyne Systems faced another possible use of the FCPA: whistle-blower suits. A significant military contractor, Teledyne became involved in several whistle-blower suits in the early 1990s. One filed by a former program manager for Teledyne in the Middle East alleged a payment to an Egyptian general to help obtain Air Force contracts.[71]

§ 17.31 Suits Charging Competitor with Violation of FCPA

A person or company believing that a competitor violated the FCPA and obtained business at the company's expense has several choices. First, a direct suit charging a violation of the FCPA may

---

69 See Marshall Sella, More Big Bucks in Jury Verdicts, 75 A.B.A. Journal 69 (July 1989). See also Williams v. Hall, 683 F.Supp. 639 (E.D.Ky.1988).

70 See also Pratt v. Caterpillar Tractor Co., 149 Ill.App.3d 588, 102 Ill.Dec. 900, 500 N.E.2d 1001 (1986), *appeal denied* 114 Ill.2d 556, 107 Ill.Dec. 68, 506 N.E.2d 959 (1987), holding that the FCPA did not create a basis for a state claim of retaliatory discharge.

71 See At Teledyne, A Chorus of Whistle–Blowers, Business Week, Dec. 14, 1992, at 40.

fail as in the case of the Philip Morris experience discussed above, because it is an attempt to bring a private cause of action.[72] Second, a suit might be based on violations of antitrust laws. A third choice is a violation of the Racketeer Influenced and Corrupt Organizations Act (RICO).[73] In each of the latter two actions, the corrupt payment would be *evidence* of the wrong alleged, but not used as the basis of the suit, and thus the suit would not fail as a disallowed private right of action. A fourth possible cause of action would be for tortious interference with a current or prospective business relationship.[74]

A RICO action was brought in *W.S. Kirkpatrick & Co., Inc. v. Environmental Tectonics Corp., Int'l.*[75] Environmental Tectonics was an unsuccessful bidder for a contract with the Nigerian Air Force. The company complained that Kirkpatrick had paid unlawful bribes to Nigerian officials. The company sued under the federal RICO statute. The court ruled that the act of state doctrine did not apply because the lawfulness of acts of a foreign government in its own territory were not at issue, but only the motives of foreign officials in accepting payments. The case was remanded. RICO thus may be an effective method for private suits involving violations of the FCPA, unless RICO is amended to diminish its scope.

As the incidents of such cases as Ashland and Environmental Tectonics become more common, companies may be more inclined to develop serious internal policies which are intended both to prevent company officials from making such payments abroad and to assure that they are in fact not made. Facing litigation by dismissed employees who refused to make illegal payments, and by competitors injured by such payments, companies may find it better to stop such payments rather than attempting to hide them.

---

[72] Lamb v. Phillip Morris, Inc., 915 F.2d 1024 (6th Cir.1990), *cert. denied* 498 U.S. 1086, 111 S.Ct. 961, 112 L.Ed.2d 1048 (1991).

[73] 18 U.S.C.A. §§ 1961–1968.

[74] See discussion in Citicorp Int'l Trading Co., Inc. v. Western Oil & Refining Co., Inc., 771 F.Supp. 600 (S.D.N.Y.1991).

[75] 493 U.S. 400, 110 S.Ct. 701, 107 L.Ed.2d 816 (1990).

Chapter 18

UNITED STATES BOYCOTT AND ANTI–BOYCOTT LAW

Table of Sections

§ 18.1 Boycott and Antiboycott Laws

The United States engages in both boycott and antiboycott practices. In the past few decades the United States has boycotted or embargoed goods from or to such countries as Cuba, Iran, Iraq, Libya, Nicaragua, North Korea, South Africa, Rhodesia and Vietnam. The effectiveness of these boycotts in achieving political goals has been widely debated.[1] The U.S. boycotts have not all been unilateral. It has engaged in collective sanctions when many others have joined, such as the U.N. trade boycott against Iraq after the invasion of Kuwait,[2] against Serbia and Montenegro after the Serbian-promoted invasion of Bosnia,[3] and against Libya after killings

1 See Gary C. Hufbauer, Jeffrey J. Schott & Kimberly Ann Elliot, Economic Sanctions Reconsidered (1990).

2 See United Nations Security Council Resolution 661 (1990).

3 See United Nations Security Council Resolution 757 (1992).

of protesters. Less "collective" were the trade sanctions imposed on Argentina by the United States and the European Economic Community after the Argentine invasion of the Falklands/Malvinas Islands.[4]

The United States has engaged in boycotts when many have participated, such as the U.N. collective sanctions, and it has sometimes stood nearly alone among major nations in implementing boycotts, such as that directed against Cuba. Additionally, the United States has engaged in long term boycotts, notably against Cuba, and very brief boycotts, such as limits on exports to Europe which might be used in the construction of a gas pipeline from the USSR after the Soviet invasion of Poland. There is little doubt that in the future unilateral or collective boycotts will continue to be part of U.S. foreign policy.

The United States has only one significant experience with the use of the U.S. antiboycott law. That is the Arab boycott of Israel. The U.S. law was adopted exclusively because of the Arab boycott of Israel. But nowhere does the law specifically mention either Arabs or Israel. Furthermore, the law is likely to remain on the books long after the Arab boycott ends. The law is directed to prohibiting U.S. persons from participating in or supporting boycotts by foreign nations against other foreign nations friendly to the United States.

§ 18.2 Boycott Laws and International Law

International law scholars have long debated whether boycotts violate international law.[5] But boycotts have been used frequently as an instrument of international law to achieve political goals,[6] such as actions by the United Nations. A primary boycott, which involves a curtailment of trade with another nation, generally is regarded as not constituting a violation of international law. But that view may differ when the boycotted nation is little more than an economic dependent of the boycotting nation. Even when the boycott assumes secondary or tertiary characteristics, international law may not be violated. It is when the boycotting nation carries the

[4] See Domingo E. Acevedo, The U.S. Measures Against Argentina Resulting from the Malvinas Conflict, 78 Am.J.Int'l L. 323 (1984).

[5] See, e.g., Margaret P. Doxey, Economic Sanctions and International Enforcement (1980); Christopher C. Joyner, The Transnational Boycott as Economic Coercion in International Law: Policy, Place and Practice, 17 Vand.J.Transnat'l L. 205 (1984).

[6] They may be referred to as "self-help" or unilateral measures. The Restatement (Third) of Foreign Relations Law addresses unilateral measures in § 905, as does the International Law Commission's Draft Articles on State Responsibility (Part Two), in Articles 12–14. Both assume similar approaches. Neither constitute law; they reflect the perceptions (and sometimes goals) of their drafters.

boycott to a stage of economic warfare, such as a blockade, that it more readily conflicts with international law, especially when human rights issues arise. Further obscuring the issue is whether there must be some act by the nation boycotted which justifies the boycotting action of the other.[7]

A *blockade* of another nation may constitute a violation of international law, but some may be reluctant in labeling a blockade such a violation when it appears to be the only likely alternative to armed conflict. Few disagree as to which is the less harmful alternative, but that does not reject the idea that both may be violations of acceptable international conduct.

However elevated the argument over the norms of international law may soar to academic heights, nations will continue to use boycotts as instruments of foreign policy. The use of boycotts by the United States illustrates that it is quite an extensive, although perhaps not always effective, instrument of that policy.

§ 18.3 The Structure of United States Boycott Law

With whom the United States does *not* trade tends to be the decision of the President, although the Congress may act in special situations to deny trade benefits. Trade embargoes or other sanctions are often imposed quickly, following some act which the U.S. President finds politically unacceptable. The Department of Commerce participates in the process of enforcing trade sanctions by controls on exports to various nations. Although the Congress governs foreign commerce and specifically *exports* by means of the Export Administration Act, Congress tends to leave to presidential discretion the imposition of sanctions against specific countries. This is not always the case, however. Congress may enact specific laws targeting particular nations. An example is the Cuban Democracy Act of 1992, which placed severe limitations on trade with Cuba, including trade by U.S. controlled subsidiaries abroad.[8] When Congress does act, it usually provides that its law will be carried out with additional regulations. The Export Administration Act has substantial regulations that are enforced largely by the Department of Commerce.

---

7 A critical point is whether the boycotted state must have committed an illegal act. The majority view seems to be that the act need not be illegal, it may simply be "unfriendly."

8 Pub.L. No. 102–484, §§ 1706–12, 106 Stat. 2315, 2578–81 (1992).

When the United States wishes to go further than to simply deny most favored nation status to a foreign nation, it may totally prohibit trade. Congressional action is likely to target a specific nation. When Congress prohibits trade, or delegates such authority to the President, there is a shift of much of the enforcement (and enactment of regulations) responsibility from the Department of Commerce to the Department of the Treasury. Part of the reason is that Treasury has an extensive framework of regulations governing the control of foreign assets.[9] The Office of Foreign Assets Control (OFAC) of Treasury has jurisdiction over a broad range of controls on transactions between U.S. persons and persons in foreign countries.[10] When those latter persons are in certain foreign countries, the controls may prohibit nearly any form of "transaction" or "transfer". A transaction or transfer may involve money or goods or services. Certain transactions or transfers may be absolutely prohibited, others may be subject to special licensing.[11]

The general regulations governing foreign assets control are followed by a series of mostly country-specific regulations.[12] These regulations vary in intensity of restrictiveness, but follow a general format including (1) the relation of the regulations to other laws and regulations, (2) what transactions are prohibited, (3) definitions, (4) interpretations, (5) licensing process, (6) reports, (7) penalties and (8) procedures. Some of the provisions are brief, others extensive. To give an idea of how these restrictions function, the experience of Cuba is outlined in the following section.

The Office of Foreign Assets Control has two forms of sanctions. One is financial sanctions and asset freezes. The second is trade and commercial embargoes. They may be used selectively or quite comprehensively. Selective sanctions may include blocking assets held in the United States, limitations on engaging in contracts, travel, transportation, or even exporting any goods or services. Selective sanctions have been used against various countries, including former "communist bloc" nations, South Africa, Iran and Angola. Comprehensive sanctions usually involve all the available options, and have been used against Cuba, Iran, Iraq, Libya, North Korea and parts of the former Yugoslavia.

---

9 31 C.F.R. Parts 500–585.

10 For a clash of OFAC and the Constitution see Looper v. Morgan, 1995 WL 499816 (S.D.Tex.1995) (regarding the search of an attorney's briefcase upon entry to the United States in search of documents supporting violations of the Libyan sanctions).

11 Licensing is in 31 C.F.R. Part 500, subpart E.

12 OFAC's list of sanction programs in effect as of April, 2013, includes Balkans, Belarus, Burma, Cote d'Ivoire, Cuba, Congo, Iran, Iraq, Lebanon, Liberia, Libya, North Korea, Somalia, Sudan, Syria, and Zimbabwe.

The Cuban sanctions discussed immediately below represent the most severe sanctions yet adopted. They were partly used as a model for the 1996 Iran and Libya Sanctions Act, often referred to as the D'Amato Act.[13] This Act, following the Libertad Act, requires the President to impose sanctions against *foreign* companies that invest more than $20 million a year in the development of petroleum resource production in Iran, or more than $40 million in Libya. The proposed $2 billion investment in Iran by the French Total company in the late 1990s generated a conflict between France and the United States over possible sanctions, which the U.S. President did not impose although he was under pressure to do so. If sanctions had been imposed, this matter quickly would have been taken to the WTO by the European Union on behalf of France.

Although the focus of this chapter is on federal law, in the past few years a number of state and local governments have adopted boycott provisions. The provisions for the most part limit government procurement for reasons of perceived violations of human rights (a principal target has been Burma (Myanmar)), religious freedom (many countries), and the failure to deal with the return of Holocaust assets (Switzerland). These laws have created a separate (from federal sanctions) opposition among some foreign nations. The EU initiated a challenge under the WTO government procurement rules against a 1996 Massachusetts law addressed to Burma. Federal sanctions were authorized against Burma in 1997,[14] but the law did not discuss preemption. In a case against the Massachusetts law brought by the National Foreign Trade Council, the federal district court, the federal circuit court and the U.S. Supreme Court all held for the NFTC.[15] The federal ruling caused the EU to withdraw its action under the WTO dispute resolution procedures.

§ 18.4 Trade Restrictions: The Case of Cuba

The trade boycott of Cuba illustrates how the United States carries out a unilateral boycott. The Cuban boycott has endured longer than current sanctions against other nations. Furthermore, Cuba has received attention by Congress and the U.S. President of varying levels of forcefulness over the past three decades, often in direct relation to U.S. political campaigns.

---

[13] Pub.L. No. 104–172, 110 Stat. 1541 (1996).

[14] Omnibus Consolidated Appropriations Act, Pub.L. No. 104–208, § 570, 110 Stat. 3009, 3009–166–167, on September 30, 1996.

[15] National Foreign Trade Council v. Baker, 26 F.Supp.2d 287 (D Mass.1998), *aff'd*, National Foreign Trade Council v. Natsios, 181 F.3d 38 (1st Cir.1999), *aff'd sub nom.*, Crosby v. National Foreign Trade Council, 530 U.S. 363, 120 S.Ct. 2288, 147 L.Ed.2d 352 (2000) (holding Massachusetts' Burma law invalid under the Supremacy Clause because it threatens to frustrate federal statutory objectives).

The boycott of Cuba began as a response to the Cuban nationalization of all U.S. citizens' properties in 1959 and 1960,[16] and to the trade agreement concluded by Cuba with the USSR in February, 1960. The U.S. Congress amended the Sugar Act of 1948 giving the President authority to alter the Cuban sugar quota. The President used this authority during the height of the July, 1960, bitterness to nearly totally remove the extensive quotas, leaving Cuba with no access to the U.S. sugar market. In October, 1960, the President imposed an extensive embargo on shipments of goods to Cuba, except for nonsubsidized food, medicines, and medical supplies. With the cessation of diplomatic relations, the United States has continued the boycott without a break, but the intensity of the boycott has varied. The boycott provisions were amended in 1975 to allow foreign subsidiaries of U.S. companies to trade with Cuba. These amendments followed U.S. threats to tighten controls on foreign subsidiaries that caused several foreign governments to angrily denounce the policy, and even threaten nationalization of the companies. After 1975, U.S. subsidiaries abroad developed significant trade with Cuba. This trade angered anti-Castro groups in the United States, and led to the enactment of the Cuban Democracy Act in 1992. The Cuban Assets Control Regulations were amended to reflect the Act's strict provisions. However extensive and restrictive the laws appear, the United States is one of Cuba's major trading partners.

Proponents of the Cuban Democracy Act were also urging adoption of a much harsher act, which would allow litigation by current U.S. citizens who were Cuban nationals at the time of the Castro expropriations, seeking compensation from persons currently using expropriated properties. This became the Cuban Liberty and Democratic Solidarity (Libertad) Act (more commonly known as Helms–Burton), enacted in March, 1996,[17] only because of the emotions aroused due to the shooting down of two U.S. civilian aircraft by Cuba near Cuban territory. The Act included two very controversial sections. The first, Title III, created a right of action in U.S. courts for a U.S. national with a claim that Cuba expropriated property after January 1, 1959, against any person who is "trafficking" in such property. Trafficking is quite broadly defined, including not only such actions as selling, buying, leasing, or transferring, but also engaging in a "commercial activity using or otherwise benefit-

[16] The expropriations effectively commenced under the Agrarian Reform Law on June 1, 1959, but did not reach their zenith until the resolutions issued under the authority of the major nationalization law of July, 1960. See Michael Wallace Gordon, The Cuban Nationalizations: The Demise of Foreign Private Property (1976).

[17] Pub.L. No. 104–114, 110 Stat. 785 (Mar. 12, 1996).

ting from confiscated property."[18] The Act authorizes the President to suspend the effectiveness of Title III actions for successive periods of six months. President Clinton issued such suspension every six months beginning in August, 1996, throughout his term, and each president elected since has continued that practice. These suspensions were the only reason the European Union deferred its request for a panel under the WTO to challenge the extraterritorial effects of the Libertad Act. The United States has stated that it would use the national security defense under the WTO, and also in response to any similar challenge brought by Canada or Mexico under the NAFTA.[19]

The second important part of the Act, Title IV, requires that the Secretary of State deny visas for entry into the United States to corporate officers, principals, shareholders and even the spouse, minor children or agents of such persons, if they are trafficking in or have confiscated property.[20] This authority has been used against officials of Canadian, Israeli, and Mexican companies.

Other nations and organizations have responded in very strong terms against the Libertad Act by adopting blocking laws and enacting resolutions.[21] Cuba enacted its own response to the Libertad Act, which, *inter alia*, denies any possible compensation in a future settlement with the government of Cuba to anyone attempting to take advantage of the Libertad Act by using the U.S. courts under Title III.[22] Finally, the Florida legislature largely deferred to the Miami Cuban-American groups and passed a state version of Helms–Burton, essentially a "feel good" action since the federal government had pre-empted governance of trade with Cuba. Florida later passed first one law attempting to ban any Florida university researchers from traveling to Cuba using private funds, even if licensed by the federal government, and then a second, the 2008 Sellers of Travel Act, setting huge fees on federally authorized trav-

---

[18] Libertad Act § 4(13).

[19] The use of the national security defense was strongly criticized in such a case, where there was no foreseeable security threat.

[20] Id. at § 401.

[21] See, e.g., Peter Glossop, Canada's Foreign Extraterritorial Measures Act and U.S. Restrictions on Trade with Cuba, 32 Int'l Lawyer 93 (1998); Mexico: Act to Protect Trade and Investment from Foreign Statutes which Contravene International Law, with Introductory note by Jorge Vargas, 36 Int'l Legal Materials 133 (1997); Douglas H. Forsythe, Introductory Note, Canada: Foreign Extraterritorial Measures Act Incorporating the Amendments Countering the U.S. Helms–Burton Act, 36 Int'l Legal Materials 111 (1997); Protecting Against the Effects of the Extraterritorial Application of Legislation Adopted by the Third Country, E.U. Council Regulation 2271/96, 1996 O.J. (L 309), reprinted in 36 Int'l Legal Materials 127 (1997).

[22] Ley de Reafirmacion de la Dignidad y Soberania Cubana (Ley No. 80), Dec. 24, 1996.

el agencies in Florida that booked flights to Cuba. Both were quickly overturned by the federal district court. The more recent thinking from the Miami legislator who promoted those laws is to punish exiles who visit Cuba by taking away their food stamps and Medicaid.

The Cuban Assets Control Regulations, approximately four dozen pages and nearly 150 separate provisions, are the principal regulations which govern trade with Cuba.[23] The application of the Regulations is limited by the Cuban Democracy Act, which removed administrative discretion in allowing some trade with Cuba from foreign subsidiaries. Furthermore, the Regulations may not conflict with the Trading with the Enemy Act,[24] or the Foreign Assistance Act of 1961, both as amended.[25] The administration of the Regulations is delegated to the Office of Foreign Assets Control (OFAC) of the Department of the Treasury.

The Regulations prohibit certain transactions and transfers, where Cuba or a Cuban national is involved. The scope is very wide, including various transfers involving (1) currency, securities, and gold or silver coin or bullion; (2) property or indebtedness; and (3) any form where the transfer is one which attempts to evade or avoid the first two prohibitions.[26] But the Secretary of the Treasury is given authority to authorize such transfers. Imports are prohibited if (1) Cuban in origin,[27] (2) the goods have been in Cuba (including transported through), or (3) if made from any Cuban parts.[28] There are a few exceptions to the trade restrictions. One is a limited exception allowing trade in informational materials, such as some books.[29] More recently cash sales of certain agricultural products have been allowed. The trade prohibitions conclude with a restriction that disallows (1) any vessel which has entered a Cuban port for trade purposes from entering a U.S. port for 180 days after the departure from Cuba, or (2) any vessel carrying goods or passengers to or from Cuba (or goods in which a Cuban has any inter-

---

[23] 31 C.F.R Part 515. OFAC publishes a useful overview of the regulations. See 2013 Guide to OFAC Compliance Regulations at www.OFAC-Guide.com.

[24] The original powers of the President were in the Trading With the Enemy Act (TWEA) of 1917. The President delegated authority to Treasury in accordance with the TWEA. The International Emergency Economic Powers Act (IEEPA) was enacted in 1988 and substantially replaced the TWEA. The authority of the President continues under the IEEPA.

[25] 31 C.F.R. § 515.101.

[26] 31 C.F.R. § 515.201.

[27] See, e.g., United States v. Plummer, 221 F.3d 1298 (11th Cir.2000).

[28] 31 C.F.R. § 515.204.

[29] 31 C.F.R. § 515.206. But no cigars or rum. The regulations even prohibit a U.S. citizen or legal resident alien from smoking a Cuban cigar or drinking Cuban rum while in a third country. One might think that OFAC has more important things to do than produce and publish Cuban Cigar Updates.

est) from entering any U.S. port with such goods or passengers on board.[30]

The Regulations were modified in September, 2009, to increase allowed family visits and remittances, and increase permitted telecommunications. Additionally legislation in 2009 created a new *general* license to allow travel related transactions linked to commercial marketing of agricultural commodities, medicine, or medical devices. The new U.S. administration under President Obama seemed less inclined to source U.S. foreign policy towards Cuba in Miami, but even as 2010 unfolded there was no major step toward removing the trade embargo. What has become important is an apparent relaxation by OFAC of the zealous control demanded by a decreasing number of Cuban exiles.

While general tourist travel is permitted, almost any U.S. national can find a group to travel with, especially church groups. The addition of the general license covering considerable travel has opened travel to many U.S. nationals without Cuban relatives.

The prohibitions are followed by quite extensive definitions.[31] While nearly all of the definitions create little problem, one is of considerable importance to U.S. businesses with subsidiaries. A "person subject to the jurisdiction of the United States," upon whom the Regulations impose trade restrictions, includes, "any corporation, partnership, or association, wherever organized or doing business, that is owned or controlled by persons" citizen or resident of the United States or where an entity is organized under the laws of the United States.[32] The meaning of "owned" or "controlled" is not included in the Regulations. The focus of the Cuban Democracy Act is to limit trade with Cuba from foreign subsidiaries of U.S. corporations. It has brought negative responses from the European Union (and separately from member states of the EU), Canada, Argentina, Mexico, and the U.N. General Assembly. It is one more example of the extraterritorial application of U.S. laws, and one more example of foreign rejection of such application.

Until this point, the Regulations are mostly prohibitory. But the next section contains important provisions covering "licenses, authorizations, and statements of licensing policy."[33] These provisions authorize the Secretary of the Treasury to issue licenses in a

---

[30] 31 C.F.R. § 515.207. These vessel restrictions were added to comply with § 1706(b) of the Cuban Democracy Act.

[31] 31 C.F.R. Subpart C.

[32] 31 C.F.R. § 515.329(d).

[33] 31 C.F.R. Subpart E.

wide variety of circumstances, including (1) for certain judicial proceedings to take place, (2) to determine persons to be unblocked nationals, (3) and to allow transfers by operations of law. The provisions of most importance for U.S. business interests allow some limited trade with Cuba by U.S. owned or controlled firms.[34] But it was this provision which was the principal focus of the Cuban Democracy Act, which reversed a decade old policy allowing Treasury to license foreign subsidiaries to trade with Cuba.[35] The current law prohibits the issuance of any such licenses to contracts entered into after the enactment of the Cuban Democracy Act. The governments of the foreign nations in which many U.S. subsidiaries are located, however, have enacted laws which mandate that the subsidiaries disregard the U.S. restrictions. It must be assumed that some trade continues without any attempt to obtain a license.

The subsequent subpart governs reports, and requires reports by any person engaging in any transaction subject to the Regulations.[36] Thus, a U.S. company trading through a subsidiary may twice violate the law, first by trading and second by failing to report the trade. Penalties are contained in the next provisions,[37] and are severe. Fines may reach $1 million for willful violations, with a maximum of $500,000 as civil penalties.[38] If experience with the antiboycott Regulations discussed below offers any parallel, consent decrees are likely to be the method used to respond to investigated violations. Just as the antiboycott provisions have not eliminated violations, these boycott provisions are unlikely to eliminate violations. That becomes even more clear when it is realized that with antiboycott violations there is no violation of foreign law when the violation of the U.S. law occurs. But in the case of these boycott Regulations, a U.S. firm in violation of some of the provisions may have a mitigating argument not present in the antiboycott situation—to comply with the U.S. law means violation of the law of the nation in which the U.S. subsidiary is incorporated and operating.

---

34 31 C.F.R. § 515.559.

35 Cuban Democracy Act § 1706(a).

36 31 C.F.R. § 515.601.

37 31 C.F.R. Subpart F.

38 See United States v. Brodie, 403 F.3d 123 (3d Cir. 2005); United States v. Plummer, 221 F.3d 1298 (11th Cir. 2000); United States v. Macko, 994 F.2d 1526 (11th Cir. 1993); and United States v. Ortiz de Zevallos, 748 F.Supp. 1569 (S.D.Fla. 1990), all dealing with violations of the Cuban boycott rules.

§ 18.5 United States Reaction to the Arab Boycott of Israel: The Antiboycott Laws

Two important historic events surrounding the conflict between businesses' freedom to export and the government's political goals led to special rules governing exports. The first was the Arab nations' extensive international primary, secondary and tertiary boycott of Israel.[39] The boycott is inconsistently applied by the Arab nations. Where the product or project is of high priority, the Arab nations either ignore their own boycott or grant a waiver.[40]

The Arab boycott of Israel led to the adoption of U.S. laws and regulations prohibiting U.S. persons from complying with or supporting any boycott by a foreign nation against a nation friendly to the United States.[41] Nowhere in the law is there any direct reference to either Israel or any specific Arab nation, but of 376 boycott requests notified to the Office of Antiboycott Compliance in 2011, 369 involved Arab League members. The antiboycott laws owe their existence to a long and bitter struggle within Congress, and between Congress and the administration, over the creation of rules that would prohibit U.S. companies from assisting the Arab nations in their attempts to harm Israel.[42] Prior to the enactment of federal export laws dealing with the Arab boycott of Israel, several states enacted similar laws, and the federal tax and antitrust laws were used to deter U.S. companies from compliance with boycott requests. Although the boycott of Israel by the Arab nations is the reason the federal law exists, there has been some question raised about the applicability of the law to foreign boycotts against South Africa. The Department of Commerce interpreted the law as not applicable to the (since terminated) boycotts against South Africa. The law does affect many commercial relationships between U.S. persons and Middle-Eastern governments, private individuals, and banks.

---

39 A primary boycott is where one nation, for example, Oman, refuses to deal with another, for example, Israel. The boycott is secondary when the boycotting nation (Oman) refuses to deal with any third party nation, such as the United States, if that nation deals with the boycotted nation, Israel. The tertiary boycott arises when the boycotting nation (Oman) refuses to deal with the third party nation (the United States), if any of the elements of its products are from a fourth party nation company (e.g., The Netherlands) which trades with the boycotted nation (e.g., Israel).

40 See Abrams v. Baylor College of Medicine, 581 F.Supp. 1570, 1576 n. 3 (S.D.Tex.1984) for an example of a waiver of the boycott regarding medical equipment from a blacklisted company.

41 Export Administration Act of 1979, 50 App.U.S.C.A. § 2407; Export Administrative Regulations, 15 C.F.R. Part 760.

42 The history of the boycott provisions is contained in Trane Co. v. Baldrige, 552 F.Supp. 1378 (W.D.Wis.1983).

The second event leading to special rules governing exports evolved from the discovery during the Watergate investigations that many U.S. companies had made payments to foreign officials to encourage those officials to purchase the goods of the company making the payments, or extend other favors such as allowing a foreign investment. Congressional reaction was much swifter than in the case of the Arab boycott. Congress adopted amendments to the securities laws to prohibit certain payments and regulate reporting of payments, in legislation called the Foreign Corrupt Practices Act.[43] Congress instead might have further amended the Export Administration Act to prohibit such payments, but the securities laws already addressed reporting and accounting requirements and that was one method used to regulate payments abroad. The FCPA added new reporting and accounting requirements which would help identify payments abroad. Prohibiting certain payments abroad, the second part of the FCPA, could be monitored by a company's records of payments. Use of the securities laws additionally meant that the Department of Justice would be the agency to pursue violations. The antiboycott provisions were under the jurisdiction of the Department of Commerce, thought to be somewhat more lenient than Justice.[44]

§ 18.6 Export Administration Act

Enforcement of the antiboycott laws lies largely within the Department of Commerce Bureau of Industry and Security. The Export Administration Act (EAA) governs the export of goods from the United States, including the antiboycott provisions. These antiboycott provisions, and the regulations, prohibit U.S. persons from participating in boycotts by a foreign nation against third nations that are friendly toward the United States. The statutory language is very broad, not unlike the concept of the U.S. antitrust laws. The EAA structure requires the President to issue regulations that prohibit any U.S. person from engaging principally in two different areas of activity, *refusals to deal* and *furnishing information*, if such actions further or support a boycott by one foreign nation against another foreign nation that is friendly to the United States.[45] There is a further provision that applies particularly to banks, that prohibits certain actions with regard to letters of credit which also may further or support a boycott. These prohibitions are included in six

---

[43] Foreign Corrupt Practices Act of 1977 (as amended in 1988 and 1998), 15 U.S.C.A. §§ 78q(b), 78dd, 78ff(a). The FCPA is the subject of the previous chapter.

[44] There have been attempts by businesses to shift the jurisdiction of the FCPA from Justice to Commerce.

[45] 50 App.U.S.C.A. § 2407(a)(1).

sections of the law.[46] The law subsequently states that the regulations should provide exceptions governing some six classes of activity.[47] Further mandated is reporting to the Secretary of Commerce any request to furnish information.[48] Violations of these provisions are subject to the same statutes that govern other violations of the export laws.

§ 18.7 Export Administration Regulations

Supplementing the EAA are Export Administration Regulations (EAR).[49] They include very extensive examples of conduct which provide guidance in determining whether specific conduct may constitute a violation of the EAA and EAR. Many of the examples are of common occurrences where companies are in jeopardy of refusing to deal or furnishing prohibited information. Use of these examples is essential to determining both the sense of the administration in interpreting the law, and the likelihood that the conduct in question may be challenged. The examples in the regulations follow the pattern of the principal statute. Thus, the regulations begin (after a section with definitions[50]) with examples of the classes of prohibited conduct,[51] and are followed by examples of the classes of exceptions.[52] Following the regulations are a series of sixteen Supplements that include Department of Commerce interpretations of various provisions, with some suggested contractual provisions that may avoid challenges by the Department.

§ 18.8 Prohibited Actions Must Be Done Intentionally

The purpose of the antiboycott provisions is to prohibit any U.S. person "from taking or knowingly agreeing to take [certain actions] with intent to comply with, further, or support any boycott" against a country friendly to the United States.[53] It specifically exempts boycotts pursuant to U.S. law. The requirement of intent is essential, but what constitutes intent may seem marginal. In *United States v. Meyer,*[54] the defendant Meyer was held to have knowledge that a form required by Saudi Arabia to have a trade-

---

46 50 App.U.S.C.A. § 2407(a)(1)(A)–(F).

47 50 App.U.S.C.A. § 2407(a)(2)(A)–(F).

48 50 App.U.S.C.A. § 2407(b)(2).

49 15 C.F.R. Part 760.

50 15 C.F.R. § 760.1.

51 15 C.F.R. § 760.2.

52 15 C.F.R. § 760.3.

53 50 App.U.S.C.A. § 2407(a)(1).

54 864 F.2d 214 (1st Cir.1988).

mark registered in that country was not used to obtain information needed for the registration, but to further the boycott of Israel. Meyer claimed that his actions were inadvertent and not intentional, but Meyer's knowledge and intention were rather clearly illustrated by his receipt of information from the Department of State that it could not notarize the form because of the boycott, and his subsequent acquisition of a notarization through the U.S.–Arab Chamber of Commerce.[55] The *Meyer* decision involves a clear attempt to find a way past the law. *Meyer* thus is not very helpful for a case where the intent is based on less apparent criteria. But it does emphasize that *inadvertent* compliance is not a violation.

§ 18.9 Refusals to Deal

The first prohibition in the EAA is against directly refusing to do business with or in the boycotted country, or with a national or resident of that country. Also prohibited is any refusal to do business with the boycotted country by agreement with or response to requests from any other person.[56] This means a U.S. company may not refuse to do business with Israel at the request of the central boycott office of the Arab nations in Damascus. Intent to refuse to do business is not established by the absence of any business relationship with the boycotted country.

The Export Administration Regulations, which include subsections further defining the meaning of refusing to do business, expand upon this prohibition.[57] The regulations make it clear that a refusal to do business may be established by a course of conduct as well as a specific refusal, or by a use of any "blacklist" or "whitelist". They emphasize, nevertheless, that intent to comply with or support a boycott is required. The regulations also suggest what does *not* constitute a refusal to do business, such as an agreement to comply generally with the laws of the boycotting country. There does not have to be an agreement not to do business. Compliance with a request, or a unilateral decision, if for boycott reasons, will suffice. These regulations raise one especially difficult issue—the use of a list of suppliers. The regulations give a specific example, although specific examples are usually left for the "examples" section.[58] A U.S. person under contract to provide management services for a construction contract may provide a list of qualified bidders for the

---

55 A strong dissent inappropriately relied on an inapplicable case to argue that the required level of intent was not met.

56 50 App.U.S.C.A. § 2407(a)(1)(A).

57 15 C.F.R. § 760.2(a). See also Supplements to Part 760.

58 15 C.F.R. § 760.2(a)(6).

client if the service is customary, and if qualified persons are not excluded because they are blacklisted.

The regulations and especially the examples disclose the nearly unlimited possible configurations of fact situations that may give rise to problems. Consider only a few possible variations, from which numerous additional variations may be easily considered:

1. A U.S. company is doing business in Israel, but wants to do business in Arab nations while retaining the Israel business. This creates a problem if the Arab nations have alternative sources for the goods, especially from companies in nations which do not have antiboycott laws, meaning essentially all other nations in the world.

2. Same as above but the company would like to terminate the business in Israel because:

a. it believes in or doesn't really care about the boycott. The company is in danger of challenge by the Department of Commerce. But is a business likely to state that it believes in or doesn't care about the boycott?

b. the Israel business is not as large as the potential Arab nations business and the company does not have the capacity to do business in both. As long as the decision is not boycott based, it is proper to drop the Israel business. But it may have to prove that its motives were business and not boycott based.

c. the company had planned to close the Israel business because it has been losing money. It had best be able to prove that loss.

3. The company trades with Arab nations and would also like to do business with Israel. It knows if it does do business with Israel it may lose the business with the Arab nations.

4. The same but the company is willing to drop the business with the Arab nations. It may do so without violating the boycott rules because Israel is not boycotting the Arab nations.

5. The company is doing business in both Israel and Arab nations. The Arabs do not know this. The company wants to drop the Israel business because it fears that the Arabs will learn of that business and terminate very profitable Arab business.

Prior to 1985–86, the focus of the Department of Commerce was on reporting violations. But in 1986 the Department, concerned about its limited resources, began to concentrate on the blacklist, religious discrimination, and refusals to deal. These are viewed by the Department as the most serious violations.

The regulations attempt to cover many variations, but obviously cannot offer an example for each possible situation. Refusals to deal arise for reasons both directly related and totally unrelated to the boycott. When normally justified business reasons for refusing to deal begin to show a pattern of not dealing for reasons consistent with a boycott, however, the party is in some danger of a challenge from Commerce. But the law does include language of intent, which is most difficult to show from a pattern of conduct that indicates good business reasons for refusing to deal.

§ 18.10 Discriminatory Actions

The second statutorily prohibited conduct is refusing to employ or otherwise discriminating against any U.S. person on the basis of race, religion, sex, or national origin, where such conduct is intentional and in furtherance of an unlawful boycott.[59] This section addresses the Arab nations' attempts to cause harm to Jewish people wherever they may live, rather than to harm Israel as a nation. Thus, a company may not refuse to employ Jewish persons so that it may gain favor with Arab clients. In one of the few court decisions involving the antiboycott provisions, Baylor College of Medicine was found to have persistently appointed non-Jewish persons for a project with Saudi Arabia.[60]

The antidiscrimination section of the EAA includes both refusals to employ and *other discrimination*. For example, a requirement that a U.S. company not use a six-pointed star on its packaging of products to be sent to the Arab nation would be a violation because it is part of the enforcement effort of the boycott. But it is not a violation if the demand is that no symbol of Israel be included on the packaging. The former is a religious symbol generally, the latter an acceptable request which does not include reference to any person's

---

[59] 50 App.U.S.C.A. § 2407(a)(B). Even if employment discrimination is not boycott based, and thus not a violation of the EAA, it may violate other laws, such as civil rights legislation.

[60] Abrams v. Baylor College of Medicine, 581 F.Supp. 1570 (S.D.Tex.1984), *aff'd*, 805 F.2d 528 (5th Cir.1986). The case also deals with the issue of the right to bring a private action. Using the Cort v. Ash factors test the court held that there is an implied right under the EAA.

religion.[61] This illustrates a general attempt to acknowledge that the boycotting nations are entitled to have *some* control over what comes into their nation. They are entitled to say no imports may be stamped "Products of Israel", but they may not attack the Jewish religion more broadly by requiring certification that no religious symbols appear on any packages. The United States is attempting to say by the law and regulations that the Arab nations may have a right to engage in a primary boycott against Israel, but they may not draw U.S. persons into supporting that boycott.

The regulations governing discriminatory actions make it clear that such actions must involve "intent to comply with, further or support an unsanctioned foreign boycott."[62] The regulations further state that the boycott provisions do not supersede or limit U.S. civil rights laws.[63]

§ 18.11 Furnishing Information Regarding Race, Religion, Sex, or National Origin

The third specific prohibition relates to the refusal to hire for reasons that would violate U.S. civil rights laws. This provision effectively means furnishing information with respect to race, religion, sex or national origin.[64] It is a brief provision is supplemented by regulations which state that it shall apply whether the information is specifically requested or offered voluntarily and whether stated in the affirmative or negative.[65] Furthermore, prohibited information includes place of birth or nationality of the parents, and information in code words or symbols that would identify a person's race, religion, sex, or national origin.[66] The regulations also reaffirm the element of intent.[67]

The examples in the regulations illustrate the difficulty of clearly defining "prohibited information". If the boycotting nation requests a U.S. company to give all employees who will work in the boycotting nation visa forms, and these visa forms request otherwise prohibited information, the company is not in violation for giving the forms to its employees or for sending the forms back to the boycotting country party. This is considered a ministerial function

---

[61] These are examples included in 15 C.F.R. § 760.2(b), examples (viii) and (ix). See Supplements to Part 760.

[62] 15 C.F.R. § 760.2(b)(2).

[63] 15 C.F.R. § 760.2(b)(3).

[64] 50 App.U.S.C.A. § 2407(a)(C).

[65] 15 C.F.R. § 760.2(c)(2).

[66] 15 C.F.R. § 760.2(c)(3).

[67] 15 C.F.R. § 760.2(c)(4).

and not support of the boycott. But the company may not itself provide the information on race, religion, sex, or nationality of its employees, if it meets the intent requirement. The company might certify that none of its employees to be sent to the boycotting nation are women, where the laws of the boycotting country prohibit women from working. The reason for such submission has nothing to do with the boycott.

§ 18.12 Furnishing Information Regarding Business Relationships—The Use of "Blacklists"

The fourth prohibition is one that is often at issue. It involves the use of blacklists. Some Arab nations maintain a blacklist of persons and companies with whom they will not do business. Arab nations often ask a prospective commercial agreement party to certify that none of the goods will include components obtained from any companies on the blacklist.

Persons are prohibited from furnishing information about an extensive list of business activities ("including a relationship by way of sale, purchase, legal, or commercial representation, shipping or other transport, insurance, investment, or supply"[68]), with an equally extensive list of business relationships ("with or in the boycotted country, with any business concern organized under the laws of the boycotted country, with any national or resident of the boycotted country, or with any other person which is known or believed to be restricted from having any business relationship with or in the boycotting country"[69]). At the end is a statement that the section does not prohibit furnishing "normal business information in a commercial context as defined by the Secretary." Thus, entities are very extensively governed with regard to the flow of information between the company and the boycotting country.

The regulations develop this already expansive section.[70] The prohibited information may not be given whether directly or indirectly requested or furnished on the initiative of the U.S. person.[71] The Secretary's definition of normal business in a commercial context is that related "to factors such as financial fitness, technical competence, or professional experience" as might be normally found in documents available to the public, such as "annual reports, disclosure statements concerning securities, catalogues, promotional

---

68 50 App.U.S.C.A. § 2407(a)(D).

69 Id.

70 15 C.F.R. § 760.2(d).

71 15 C.F.R. § 760.2(d)(2)(ii).

brochures, and trade and business handbooks."[72] Such public information may not be supplied if in response to a boycott request.[73] But it may be supplied if it could be used by the boycotting country to further the boycott—knowledge and intent on the part of the U.S. person is the key to making the furnishing of the information unlawful. There are numerous examples of this prohibition, many referring to use of blacklists. For example, a person may not certify that its suppliers are not on a furnished blacklist.[74] If a company is on the blacklist, or if it wishes to know whether it is on the blacklist, it may request such information.[75] That is not furnishing information. But if it furnishes information in order to be removed, it may be in violation. If a company believes it is on the blacklist but no longer would be listed were the Arab nations to know the true facts, supplying those facts may constitute a violation.[76] The same may occur when a company believes it is mistakenly listed, and wishes to make this known to the Arab nations. Companies have removed their names, but it must be done with great care.

The most publicized blacklist case involved Baxter International Inc., a large U.S. medical supply company.[77] As a result of an informant's disclosure, Baxter was investigated and charged with violating the EAA because of the way in which it attempted to have its name removed from the Arab blacklist.[78] Commerce was prepared to charge Baxter and a senior officer with providing over 300 items of prohibited information to Syrian authorities and a Saudi Arabian firm. The company and the officer admitted civil and criminal violations and were assessed total civil penalties of $6,060,600—the highest at the time. The case would not have succeeded without the informant providing substantial documentation of the violations.

§ 18.13 Prohibition of Intentional Evasion

The EAA and the regulations each include a section that states that no U.S. person may take any action with intent to evade the

[72] 15 C.F.R. § 760.2(d)(3).

[73] 15 C.F.R. § 760.2(d)(4).

[74] 15 C.F.R. § 760.2(d) example (x).

[75] 15 C.F.R. § 760.2(d) example (xv).

[76] A U.S. subsidiary of the French cosmetics company L'Oreal provided the parent information to assist in removal from the blacklist. Providing this information and failing to report to the Commerce department led to L'Oreal agreeing to pay $1.4 million in civil penalties. See, e.g, Los Angeles Times, August 30, 1995, at Part D.

[77] See, e.g., The Case Against Baxter International, Business Week, Oct. 7, 1991, pg. 106.

[78] See 5 OEL Insider 7 (Dec. 1993).

law.[79] Permitted activities are not to be considered an evasion of the law. An example of an evasion is placing a person at a commercial disadvantage or imposing on that person special burdens because that person is blacklisted or otherwise restricted from business relations for boycott reasons.[80] Another evasion may be use of risk-of-loss provisions that expressly impose a financial risk on another because of the import laws of a boycotting country, unless customarily used.[81] Two final suggested evasions are the use of dummy corporations or other devices to mask prohibited activities, or diverting boycotting country orders to a foreign subsidiary.[82]

§ 18.14 Reporting Requirements

Under the title "Foreign policy controls," the EAA includes very important provisions that require the reporting of the receipt of any request for the "furnishing of information, the entering into or implementing of agreements, or the taking of any other action" outlined in the policy section[83] of the EAA.[84] The receipt of any such request must be reported to the Secretary of Commerce. Failure to report boycott associated requests is perhaps the most frequent violation of the EAA. The report must include any information the Secretary deems appropriate and must state whether the person intends to comply or has complied with the request. These reports are public records, except to the extent that certain confidential information is included that would cause a competitive disadvantage to the reporting person.

The regulations include quite extensive provisions, covering (a) the scope of reporting requirements, (b) the manner of reporting, and (c) the disclosure of information.

Scope of reporting requirements. Whenever a person receives a written or oral request to take any action in furtherance or support of a boycott against a friendly foreign country it must be reported. The request may be to enter into or implement an agreement. It may involve a solicitation, directive, legend, or instruction asking for information or action (or inaction). The request must be reported whether or not the action requested is prohibited, except as the regulations provide.[85] That essentially means reporting is required if

---

[79] 50 App. U.S.C.A. § 2407(a)(5); 15 C.F.R. § 760.4.

[80] 15 C.F.R. § 70.4(c).

[81] 15 C.F.R. § 760.4(d).

[82] 15 C.F.R. § 760.4(e).

[83] 50 App. U.S.C.A. § 2402(5).

[84] 50 App. U.S.C.A. § 2407(b).

[85] 15 C.F.R. § 760.5(a)(1).

the person knows or has reason to know that the purpose of the request is to enforce, implement, or otherwise support, further or secure compliance with the boycott.[86]

When a request is received by a U.S. person located outside the United States (subsidiary, branch, partnership, affiliate, office, or other controlled permanent foreign establishment), it is reportable if received in connection with a transaction in interstate or foreign commerce.[87] A general boycott questionnaire, unrelated to any specific transaction, must be reported when that person has or anticipates a business relationship with or in the boycotting country, also in interstate or foreign commerce.

The reporting requirements apply whether the U.S. person is an exporter, bank, or other financial institution, insurer, freight forwarder, manufacturer, or other person.[88] If the information about a country's boycotting requirements is learned by means of the receipt or review of books, pamphlets, legal texts, exporter's guidebooks, and other similar publications, it is not considered a reportable request. The same is true of receipt of an unsolicited bid where there is no intention to respond.[89]

The regulations include ten specific requests that are not reportable. They were added because of the customary use of certain terms for boycott and non-boycott purposes, Congressional mandates for clear guidelines in uncertain areas, and the Department of Commerce's desire to reduce paperwork and costs. They are:[90]

> (i) request to refrain from shipping goods on a carrier flying the flag of a particular country, or that is owned, chartered, leased or operated by a particular country or its nationals or residents; or a request for certification to such effect;
>
> (ii) request to ship goods, or refrain from shipping goods, on a prescribed route, or a certification request of either;

[86] 15 C.F.R. § 760.5(a)(2).

[87] Id., citing 15 C.F.R. §§ 760.1(c) and (d). The definition of "interstate or foreign commerce" is the subject of a Department of Commerce interpretation in Supplement No. 8 to Part 760.

[88] 15 C.F.R. § 760.5(a)(3).

[89] 15 C.F.R. § 760.5(a)(4). A definition of "unsolicited invitation to bid" is included in Supplement No. 11 to Part 769.

[90] 15 C.F.R. § 760.5(a)(5); see also Supplement No. 10(b) to Part 760.

(iii) request for an affirmative statement or certification regarding the country of origin of goods;

(iv) request for an affirmative statement or certification of supplier's or manufacturer's or service provider's name;

(v) request to comply with laws of another country except where it requires compliance with that country's boycott laws;

(vi) request to individual for personal information about himself or family for immigration, passport, visa, or employment requirements;

(vii) request for an affirmative statement or certification stating the destination of exports or confirming or indicating the cargo will be unloaded or discharged at a particular destination;

(viii) request to supply a certificate by the owner, master, charterer, or any employee thereof, that a vessel, aircraft, truck, or other transport is eligible, permitted, nor restricted from or allowed to enter, a particular port, country or group of countries under the laws, rules, or regulations of that port, country or countries;

(ix) request for a certificate from an insurance company stating the issuing company has an agent or representative (plus name and address) in a boycotting country; or

(x) request to comply with term or condition that vendor bears the risk of loss and indemnify the purchaser if goods are denied entry for any reason if this clause was in use by the purchaser prior to January 18, 1978.

The Department of Commerce periodically is to survey domestic concerns to determine the worldwide scope of boycott requests received by U.S. subsidiaries and controlled affiliates regarding activities outside U.S. commerce.[91] This is to cover requests that would be required to be reported but for the fact that they involve commerce outside the United States. Information collected from U.S. persons will include the number and nature of non-reportable

---

[91] 15 C.F.R. § 760.5(a)(7).

requests received, action requested, action taken, and countries making such requests.

Manner of reporting requests. Every request must be reported; however, only the first need be reported when the same request is received in several forms.[92] But each different request regarding the same transaction must be reported. Each U.S. person receiving a request must report the request, but one person may designate another to make the report, such as a parent reporting on behalf of a subsidiary.[93]

Disclosure of information. The third part of the regulations applying to reporting states that the reports shall become public records, except for "certain proprietary information."[94] The reporting party may certify that the disclosure of information relating to the (1) quantity, (2) description, or (3) value of any articles, materials or supplies (including technical data and other information), may place the company at a competitive disadvantage. In such case the information will not be made public. But the reporting party must edit the public inspection copy of the accompanying documents as noted below, and the Secretary may reject the request for confidentiality for reasons either of disagreement regarding the competitive disadvantage, or of national interest in not withholding the information.[95] If such decision is made, the party must be given an opportunity to comment.

Because the report is made public, one copy must be submitted intact and the other may be edited in accordance with the above limitations. Any additional material considered confidential may also be deleted, as may be any material not required to be reported.[96] The copy is to be marked "Public Inspection Copy."

§ 18.15 Violations and Enforcement

Violations and enforcement of the antiboycott laws are subject to the same provisions as violations and enforcement of the export laws.[97] The enforcement of the antiboycott laws has generated few court decisions. Most have involved issues of constitutionality, crea-

92 15 C.F.R. § 760.5(b)(1).

93 15 C.F.R. § 760.5(b)(2).

94 15 C.F.R. § 760.5(c)(1).

95 Id.

96 15 C.F.R. § 760.5(c)(2).

97 50 App.U.S.C.A. §§ 2410, 2411 and 2412. See supra, chapter 17. Considerable information on the boycotts is at www.bis.doc.gov, including major cases

tion of private rights of action, or the statute of limitations.[98] Several persons have had licenses suspended and fines exceeding $5 million have been levied. Most of these cases involved the receipt of requests for information from Arab countries. In instances where the companies had complied with the request, the Department of Commerce and the company usually agreed on a fine as part of a consent decree. The procedures were dealt with administratively, and the decisions are found only in some private reporters.[99] One of the largest civil penalties was imposed in a settlement with Baxter International Inc., in 1993. Baxter, a Swiss subsidiary, and an officer paid a penalty totaling $6,060,600. For all of 2011 eight companies paid penalties totaling $129,300.

The Department of Commerce began in 1986 to emphasize what it considered the most serious violations, involving the blacklist, religious discrimination and refusals to deal. The number of reported court decisions remains very small. Although in the early 1990s the number of reported Arab requests for information had diminished, cases such as Baxter illustrate that violations continue to occur.

U.S. subsidiaries that carry out boycott activities of foreign parents are within the reach of the provisions. The French L'Oreal, S.A. cosmetics company requested information from two U.S. subsidiaries, Parbel of Florida, Inc. (formerly Helena Rubenstein, Inc.) and Cosmair, Inc., about their business relationships in or with Israel. More than 100 items of information were provided, and no report of the request was made to Commerce. The two subsidiaries (and individual corporate counsel for Cosmair) agreed to fines exceeding $1.4 million in 1995.

§ 18.16 Private Right of Action

As is the case with so many laws, there is no clear indication whether the EAA includes a private right of action. A federal district court in Texas, in *Abrams v. Baylor College of Medicine,*[100] addressing a claim by two Jewish medical students that Baylor University denied them opportunities when it excluded Jews from medical teams it sent to Saudi Arabia, found an implied right of action

---

[98] United States v. Core Laboratories, Inc., 759 F.2d 480 (5th Cir.1985) (EAA and the statute of limitations); Abrams v. Baylor College of Medicine, 581 F.Supp. 1570 (S.D.Tex.1984), *aff'd* 805 F.2d 528 (5th Cir.1986) (EAA and affirming private right of action); Bulk Oil (ZUG) A.G. v. Sun Co., Inc., 583 F.Supp. 1134 (S.D.N.Y.1983), *aff'd* 742 F.2d 1431 (2d Cir.1984), *cert. denied* 469 U.S. 835, 105 S.Ct. 129, 83 L.Ed.2d 70 (1984) (EAA and rejecting private right).

[99] See Int'l Boycotts (Business Law Inc.); Boycott L. Bull.

[100] 581 F.Supp. 1570 (S.D.Tex.1984), *aff'd* 805 F.2d 528 (5th Cir.1986).

by applying the factors in the *Cort v. Ash* decision of the U.S. Supreme Court.[101] The Fifth Circuit upheld the decision. But in *Bulk Oil (ZUG) A.G. v. Sun Co.,* the Second Circuit rejected the existence of a private right of action, affirming a New York federal district court decision involving an accusation of violation of the antiboycott provisions by failing to deliver oil to Israel.[102]

[101] 422 U.S. 66, 95 S.Ct. 2080, 45 L.Ed.2d 26 (1975).

[102] 583 F.Supp. 1134 (S.D.N.Y.1983), *aff'd* 742 F.2d 1431 (2d Cir.1984), *cert. denied* 469 U.S. 835, 105 S.Ct. 129, 83 L.Ed.2d 70 (1984).

Chapter 19

UNITED STATES SECTION 301 PROCEEDINGS—SPECIAL 301 PROCEDURES

Table of Sections

---

§ 19.1 Foreign Country Practices and Market Access

Section 301 of the Trade Act of 1974 is one of the most highly political remedies concerning United States trade relations. Basically, this section applies when United States rights or benefits under international trade agreements are at risk or when foreign nations engage in unjustifiable, unreasonable or discriminatory conduct. Thus Section 301 is primarily focused on the activities of foreign governments. Although it has been used to protect United States markets from foreign imports, Section 301 has been most notably applied to open up foreign markets to United States exports, investments and intellectual property rights. The focus has been on foreign market access for U.S. goods and services.

Most Section 301 proceedings have been resolved through negotiations leading to alteration of foreign country practices. Ultimately, if the President or United States Trade Representative (USTR) is not satisfied with any negotiated result in connection with a Section 301 complaint, the United States may undertake unilateral retaliatory trade measures. Unlike subsidy, dumping, escape clause and market disruption proceedings, Section 301 of the Trade Act of 1974 has no origins in or other imprimatur of legitimacy from the GATT/WTO. Indeed, the unilateral nature of Section 301 is thought by many to run counter to the multilateral approach to trade relations. Brazil lodged but did not actively pursue a complaint about Section 301 during the Uruguay Round negotiations.

Although the U.S. has been a strong supporter of the GATT over the years, Section 301 reflects U.S. frustration with multilateral methods and procedures. It has received hostile responses from United States trade partners, especially after the amendments to Section 301 implemented in 1988 through the Omnibus Trade and Competitiveness Act. These amendments include the so-called "Super 301 Procedures" and the "Special 301 Procedures" discussed below. The offenses under Section 301 are now primarily subject to the authority of the United States Trade Representative as opposed to the President. The 1988 Act also introduces the concept of mandatory versus discretionary retaliation. Offenses for which retaliation is mandatory involve the breach of international agreements to which the United States is a party and unjustifiable trade practices. The USTR has discretionary authority to retaliate under Section 301 regarding unreasonable or discriminatory practices of foreign countries.

Late in 1999, a panel of the World Trade Commission concluded that Section 301 was not inconsistent with U.S. obligations under the WTO (WTO/DS 152/1). The panel relied heavily on President Clinton's Congressionally approved statement that the U.S. would refrain from Section 301 retaliation until the WTO has ruled on disputes falling within its domain. Should some future U.S. administration fail to adhere to this policy, the WTO panel indicated that Section 301 would violate the WTO Dispute Settlement Understanding.

§ 19.2 The Evolution of Section 301

The origins of Section 301 can be traced to a trade dispute between the United States and the European Community (now Union) during the 1960s. This dispute became known as "the Chicken War." Basically, United States chicken producers had mechanized and developed a large export market in the European Union. The Union sought to protect its smaller chicken producers and did so by establishing a minimum price for imported chicken. This had the effect of drastically curtailing United States exports into the European market. At that time, there was no vehicle through which the United States growers could express their complaints over this practice. Nevertheless, the United States government sought to resolve the dispute through the nullification and impairment provisions of Article XXIII of the GATT. These attempts failed and ultimately the United States imposed unilateral trade restraints upon European Union exports as a matter of compensation for the minimum import price program. In the Chicken War, the retaliatory tariffs concerned brandy, trucks and potato starch. These trade restraints, while arguably compensating the United States as a nation, did little to satisfy the chicken exporters. In other words, the remedy was not linked to the source of the complaint, a reality that remains in Section 301 law.

As the Chicken War was in progress, the Trade Expansion Act of 1962 was adopted. Section 252 of that Act specifically authorized the President to retaliate against foreign import restrictions imposed in breach of GATT obligations. Furthermore, the President was authorized to impose higher tariffs or other import restraints on the products of countries that established burdensome restraints upon U.S. exports of agricultural goods. The latter could be imposed regardless of whether the import restraints of the foreign country constituted a breach of the GATT. Section 252 of the Trade Expansion Act of 1962 thus preceded and anticipated Section 301 of the Trade Act of 1974.

The President exercised retaliatory authority under Section 252 only twice. Both cases involved the imposition of import restraints because of agricultural disputes. Between 1974 and 1979, the first of the private petitions for Section 301 action were considered. However the typical result was to refer the dispute to the GATT organization which deliberated at length and effectively turned the disputes into issues for review during the Tokyo Round of GATT negotiations concluded in 1979. Congress was not happy with these results, and in the Trade Agreements Act of 1979 imposed a variety of time limitations in connection with Section 301 complaints. Congress also expanded the range of complaints that could be filed and on balance sought to rejuvenate Section 301.

From 1979 through the 1980s, the number of Section 301 investigations initiated by private complaints increased considerably. Through the Trade and Tariff Act of 1984, Congress continued to seek to make Section 301 an effective trade remedy. Its availability for complaints in the field of intellectual property rights and trade involving services was made clear. Nevertheless, a significant number of these complaints were still being referred to the GATT and its remarkably slow dispute settlement procedures. Through the Omnibus Trade and Competitiveness Act of 1988, Congress expressed its displeasure with GATT as a dispute settlement forum by indicating that under appropriate circumstances Section 301 investigations and remedies can proceed notwithstanding the fact that GATT dispute settlement has not run its full course. At the same time, Congress switched the ultimate authority for determining Section 301 offenses and Section 301 remedies from the President to the United States Trade Representative.

The bottom line after all of these legislative efforts on the part of Congress to invigorate Section 301 is that it became a significant forum for opening up foreign markets to United States exports. This forum can be accessed by private initiative as well as governmental action.

§ 19.3 The Impact of the WTO Dispute Settlement Understanding

United States membership in the World Trade Organization since 1995 has committed it to multilateral dispute settlement of disputes arising out of the numerous WTO agreements. If the dispute is covered by a WTO agreement, the United States is obliged to pursue remedies under the WTO Dispute Settlement Understanding.[1] Section 301 petitions falling within the scope of the WTO routinely trigger USTR complaints with the multilateral Dispute Settlement Body. The United States has been involved in more WTO disputes (as a complaining and responding party) than any other member country. The DSU creates procedures under which unilateral retaliation is restrained until the offending nation has failed to conform to a WTO panel or Appellate Body ruling. Unilateral retaliation is then authorized by the WTO in an amount equal to the damages incurred.

However, when a petition concerns subject matter not covered by a WTO agreement (media goods) or a country that is not a WTO member (Iran), Section 301 and its unilateral remedies remain in full force and effect.

§ 19.4 Mandatory versus Discretionary Offenses and Remedies

Section 301 of the Trade Act of 1974 vests in the United States Trade Representative the power to determine when the *rights* of the United States under any trade agreement are being denied, when foreign country practices are inconsistent with or otherwise denying the *benefits* to the United States of trade agreements, or foreign countries are engaged in unjustifiable practices that burden or re-

---

1 See Chapter 9.

strict United States commerce. An affirmative finding by the USTR in connection with any of the above now requires mandatory retaliation on the part of the United States "subject to Presidential direction."[2]

The USTR is not required to take action whenever the dispute has been adjudicated within the GATT/WTO and there has been a finding that United States rights under a trade agreement are not being denied or that the foreign country practices under dispute are not in violation of nor impair the benefits of the United States under any trade agreement. In addition, the USTR does not have to take retaliatory action if he or she determines that the foreign country in question is taking satisfactory measures to grant the rights of the United States under a trade agreement or has agreed to eliminate or phase out the practices that are in dispute. If this is not possible, but the foreign country agrees to provide the United States with compensatory trade benefits satisfactory to the USTR, no mandatory retaliation will take place. In extraordinary cases, the USTR need not undertake retaliatory action if that would have an adverse impact on the United States economy substantially out of proportion to the benefits of that action or would cause serious harm to the national security of the United States.[3]

Section 301 also authorizes the USTR to determine when foreign countries are engaged in unreasonable or discriminatory practices that burden or restrict United States commerce. If such findings are reached, the Trade Representative (subject to directives from the President) may decide to undertake retaliatory action.[4] Hence, these offenses do not require mandatory retaliation; they are discretionary.

With reference to both mandatory and discretionary actions under Section 301, the USTR is authorized to withdraw the benefits of trade agreements enjoyed by the foreign country engaging in the offending activities, impose tariffs or other import restrictions upon the goods of those nations, and enter into binding international agreements to eliminate or phase out the unfair practices or to provide the United States with compensatory trade benefits. If the dispute concerns services, and many recent Section 301 disputes have been focused upon services, the USTR may restrict any "service sector access authorization" under United States law. Presumably, for example, the USTR subject to presidential directives could deny

[2] 19 U.S.C.A. § 2411.

[3] 19 U.S.C.A. § 2411(a)(2).

[4] 19 U.S.C.A. § 2411(b).

access to foreign banks by withholding licenses from federal authorities. It is less clear, but appears possible, that the USTR could order state authorities to deny similar access to the services sector.[5]

One problem with Section 301 remedies is that they need not necessarily benefit those who have been injured by foreign country practices. Thus, for example, if the complaint concerns European Union export subsidies on sugar, the ultimate retaliatory action taken by the United States may involve the imposition of tariffs upon European wine. Similarly, if the dispute concerns the intellectual property rights afforded pharmaceuticals in Brazil, the ultimate Section 301 remedy may impose quotas or other trade restraints upon Brazilian hardwoods.

§ 19.5 Statutory Definitions

The provisions of Section 301 are remarkably broad and open-ended in language. The statute therefore seeks to define with greater specificity some of the important terms involved. These definitions are found in Section 301(d) of the Trade Act of 1974.[6] One important definition provides an expansive interpretation of the appropriate international commerce to which Section 301 applies. For these purposes, commerce includes trade in goods and services, and foreign direct investment by United States persons with implications for trade in goods or services.

Foreign country practices are "unreasonable" if they are unfair and inequitable, regardless of whether they are in violation of or inconsistent with the international legal rights of the United States. Unreasonable practices include those which deny fair and equitable opportunities for the establishment of a business abroad, those which provide inadequate or ineffective protection of intellectual property rights, those which deny market opportunities as a result of systematic anticompetitive activities of private firms, and those which constitute export targeting (defined to mean any government scheme designed to assist its exporters in becoming more competitive). Unreasonable practices include those which constitute a persistent pattern of conduct that denies workers the right to associate, organize or bargain collectively. They also include practices which tolerate forced or compulsory labor, fail to provide a minimum working age for children, or fail to provide general standards on minimum wages, hours of work and occupational safety and health requirements. However, Section 301(d) indicates that foreign coun-

5 19 U.S.C.A. § 2411(c)(2).

6 19 U.S.C.A. § 2411(d).

try practices are not to be treated as unreasonable if the USTR determines that nation is taking action which demonstrates a significant and tangible advancement towards providing the rights and standards discussed above or that the practices in question are not inconsistent with the level of economic development of the foreign country. Where appropriate, the absence or presence of reciprocal opportunities in the United States for foreign nationals shall be taken into account in determining whether any particular practice is unreasonable.

It is important to bear in mind that this lengthy definition of unreasonable foreign country practices coincides with discretionary USTR action if such practices are found. The other discretionary category under Section 301 includes foreign country practices which are "discriminatory." Section 301(d) defines discriminatory as any practice which denies national or most favored nation treatment to United States goods, services or investment. The prohibition against "unjustifiable" foreign country practices is expanded by a definition which indicates that such practices must violate or be inconsistent with the international legal rights of the United States. These include those which deny national or most favored nation treatment, the right of establishment or the protection of intellectual property rights. Unjustifiable practices, if determined to exist by the USTR, mandate retaliatory action by the United States.

Perhaps the most critical difference in the Section 301(d) definitions of Section 301 offenses concerns international legal rights. This is part of the definition of unjustifiable practices, but not found in connection with unreasonable or discriminatory practices. There is no requirement that unreasonable, discriminatory or unjustifiable practices violate or contradict any international agreement to which the United States is a party. Thus the international legal rights which must be breached in order to find an unjustifiable practice may turn upon customary international law of trade. The statutory definitions of unreasonableness reviewed above were greatly expanded in 1988. This suggests that the most likely avenue of success under Section 301 is in pleading unreasonable practices.

§ 19.6 Petitioning and Consultation Procedures

Section 302 of the Trade Act of 1974 permits any interested person to file a petition with the United States Trade Representative requesting action under Section 301. Complaints from U.S. industries have in fact driven most Section 301 proceedings, and they can be screened by the USTR before filing. The USTR is given 45 days within which to determine whether to initiate an investigation. Interested parties may include but are not limited to domestic companies and workers, representatives of consumer interests, U.S. exporters, and any industrial users of goods or services potentially affected by Section 301 actions.[7] The Trade Representative's powers to initiate investigations under Section 301 appear to be completely discretionary. That is to say, if the USTR is not persuaded by the petition and supporting documents, no Section 301 procedures will be commenced. This is true for both mandatory and discretionary action under Section 301. However, if the USTR decides not to initiate an investigation, he or she must inform the petitioner of the reasons why and publish notice of that determination together with its reasons in the Federal Register.[8]

If the USTR decides to initiate an investigation under Section 301, he or she then publishes a summary of the petition and is required to provide an opportunity for the presentation of views including a public hearing. The USTR may self-initiate Section 301 investigations.[9] The USTR is not required to initiate any investigation if he or she determines that to do so would be detrimental to United States economic interests.[10] Once an investigation under Section 301 is launched, either by petition or self-initiation, the USTR must consult with the foreign country alleged to have engaged in unfair trade practices. If a mutually acceptable solution is not reached, and the complaint concerns a breach of an international agreement to which the United States is a party, the USTR is obliged to commence dispute settlement procedures as provided for in that agreement.[11]

The regulations which detail the procedures and conduct of investigations in connection with Section 301 are found at 15 C.F.R. 2006 et seq. An interagency committee composed of staff from the Departments of State, Treasury, Commerce, Justice, Agriculture, Labor and the Council of Economic Advisors is involved in the decisionmaking under Section 301. This Committee is sometimes called the "Section 301 Committee" and its report and advice will be considered by the USTR in making Section 301 determinations. The input of this Committee does not diminish the discretion of the USTR in deciding whether to commence a Section 301 investigation. When a petition is received from the private sector alleging a Section 301 offense, the USTR typically notifies the country that is the

---

[7] 19 U.S.C.A. § 2411(d)(9).

[8] 19 U.S.C.A. § 2412(a).

[9] 19 U.S.C.A. § 2412(b).

[10] 19 U.S.C.A. § 2412(b).

[11] 19 U.S.C.A. § 2413(a).

object of the complaint. That country may supply any relevant information it chooses. In the absence of such a response, the USTR is entitled to proceed on the basis of the "best information available."[12] This will often as a practical matter be the information submitted by the petitioner or otherwise derived from the Section 301 Committee or other independent sources. Thus the procedures utilized in Section 301 make it imperative that private petitioners properly document the nature of their complaint.

The rules require that a private petition for Section 301 action describe the petitioner's interest that is allegedly impacted by the foreign country practice about which the petitioner is complaining. If the complaint is based upon international agreements to which the United States is a party and the denial of rights thereunder, this must be clearly cited and documented. The petition must specifically identify the foreign country alleged to be engaging in a Section 301 offense. It must identify the specific product or service which is the subject of the complaint. Most importantly, the petition must show exactly how the practice in question is inconsistent with a trade agreement or is otherwise unjustifiable, unreasonable or discriminatory and that it burdens or restricts United States commerce. Lastly, the petitioner must indicate whether any other requests for relief under the Trade Act of 1974 or other United States law have been filed.

Once the USTR determines to initiate an investigation under Section 301, the petitioner has 30 days to submit a written request for a public hearing.[13] Any other interested person can also submit an application for such a hearing. Section 305 of the Trade Act of 1974 allows U.S. companies and other interested persons to essentially request of the USTR information necessary to substantiate a Section 301 complaint. Such requests have the practical effect of obliging the USTR to provide any such available information, and perhaps even to require the USTR to contact foreign governments in order to satisfy this request for information. Such requests can amount to a kind of preliminary Section 301 investigation before formal investigations are initiated.[14]

§ 19.7 USTR Determinations

Since the amendments of 1988, the USTR is required to make a determination of whether foreign country practices are actionable under Section 301 regardless of whether any retaliatory action is

---

[12] 15 C.F.R. § 2006.4.

[13] 19 U.S.C.A. § 2414(b).

[14] See 19 U.S.C.A. § 2411(d)(2).

taken. For many years disputes concerning export subsidies, particularly export subsidies of the European Union, dominated Section 301 proceedings.[15] Whenever Section 301 complaints involve an alleged breach of United States benefits under an existing international agreement, such as the package of WTO agreements, the USTR must initiate the dispute settlement procedures of that agreement.

Since 1988, the USTR is required to determine whether unfair practices have occurred under Section 301 within certain time limits. These are 12 months in cases involving export subsidies and practices not covered by trade agreements, 18 months in trade agreement cases other than subsidies unless the dispute settlement procedures of the relevant agreement are concluded earlier. Generally speaking, the USTR must determine whether a Section 301 offense has occurred in all instances where an investigation has been commenced within a 12–month deadline. These time limits could pressure the USTR into making a determination before the international dispute settlement procedures of the WTO or other trade agreements are concluded.[16]

§ 19.8 Section 301 in Action

There have been a large number of complaints and investigations under Section 301 of the Trade Act of 1974. In some instances, complaints under Section 301 have been dismissed by the President or USTR as without merit. In other instances, the complaints led to a GATT/WTO dispute settlement panel which decided against the position of the United States. This has the effect of terminating the Section 301 proceeding. Many Section 301 complaints have been resolved to the satisfaction of those concerned through international negotiations. For example, in the early 1970s, a shipping company complained about the discriminatory practices of the government of Guatemala. The United States undertook negotiations with that government and reached an agreement satisfactory to the complainant.[17] In the same year, Canada had been imposing a quota on the importation of eggs from the United States. A trade association complaint to the USTR led to negotiations and an increase in this quota.[18] An exporter of thrown silk to Japan complained about the

---

15 See Bishop, The Multilateral Trade Negotiations, Subsidies and the Great Plains Wheat Case, 16 International Lawyer 339 (1982).

16 See generally Bliss, The Amendments to Section 301: An Overview and Suggested Strategies for Foreign Response, 20 Law & Policy of International Business 501 (1989).

17 See 41 Fed.Reg. 26758 (1976).

18 41 Fed.Reg. 9430 (1976).

difficulties in obtaining import licenses for such silk. This complaint led to the threat of retaliatory action against Japanese-made silk products. However, subsequent negotiations resulted in an agreement which caused the Japanese to remove their import licensing restraints.[19]

A lengthy Section 301 complaint concerned European Union tariff restraints in connection with the export of Florida citrus products. In this case, the GATT (pre-WTO) did not provide an adequate dispute resolution forum, and the United States decided to retaliate by imposing substantial tariffs on European pasta products. Europe in turn retaliated with tariff increases on U.S. walnuts and lemons. Ultimately the United States and the European Union agreed to mutual elimination of the tariffs in question. This result did not really resolve the underlying dispute concerning the export of citrus products from the United States to Europe.[20] One Section 301 complaint involved the Cigar Association of America. This complaint was against Japanese practices which had the effect of raising the price on U.S. cigars and making them difficult to market in Japan. International negotiations led to the formation of a GATT dispute settlement panel. However, this panel did not need to complete its task because the Japanese government agreed to substantial reductions in the relevant tariffs and retail requirements.[21]

While many Section 301 complaints have concerned export opportunities for United States firms, some have involved import competition. For example, a complaint was filed against Taiwanese subsidies of rice exports. International negotiations led to an agreement limiting these subsidized exports such that the Section 301 complaint was withdrawn.[22]

The United States Trade Representative has occasionally commenced Section 301 proceedings on its own initiative. For example, the Brazilian "informatics policy" was challenged in this manner. This policy discriminated against foreign computer and high technology imports principally through local content requirements and the grant of exclusive monopolies. International negotiations, backed up by a threat by the United States to suspend the benefits for Brazil under the U.S. Generalized System of Tariff Preferences, eventually resulted in an opening of the Brazilian in-

---

19 43 Fed.Reg. 8876 (1978).

20 See 50 Fed.Reg. 26143 (1985).

21 See 44 Fed.Reg. 19083 (1979), 44 Fed.Reg. 64938 (1979) and 46 Fed.Reg. 1388, 1389 (1981).

22 See 48 Fed.Reg. 56289 (1983), 49 Fed.Reg. 10761 (1984).

formatics market.[23] Another example of a self-initiated Section 301 proceeding concerned Korea's restraints on foreign insurance companies. Korean law was discriminatory and failed to give foreign companies the same benefits that domestic firms obtained. An international settlement was reached between the United States and Korea which gave access to that market for life and non-life insurance.[24] Korea was also the object of another Section 301 investigation concerning its intellectual property rights. These were thought to be inadequate, particularly in the copyright area. International negotiations led to the creation of a comprehensive copyright system for Korea, including coverage of computer software. Amendments were also made to the Korean patent laws and the country joined the Universal Copyright Convention.[25]

Several Section 301 disputes have been resolved with Thailand. Following Section 301 success at opening the Japanese, Taiwanese and South Korean markets to United States cigarettes, the first dispute concerned Thai tariffs on U.S. cigarettes. United States producers petitioned under Section 301, and a lengthy investigation resulted in the formation of a GATT dispute settlement panel. This panel ruled against the tariffs and Thailand removed them.[26] A second Section 301 complaint by the International Intellectual Property Alliance and others led to an investigation focused on Thai piracy of audio and video cassettes. A substantial Thai industry had developed around such activities. The USTR threatened removal of Thailand's GSP duty free tariff entry benefits and the imposition of a total U.S. barrier to Thai imports. Thailand capitulated and announced copyright reforms targeted at cassette piracy.[27]

A longstanding dispute between the United States and Japan concerning semiconductor products resulted in a Section 301 complaint in the late 1980s. The essence of the complaint was that a prior agreement concerning trade in such products between the two nations had been breached and therefore the United States intended to impose tariffs on certain imports from Japan.[28] The United States argued that Japan had not opened up its market sufficiently to foreign semiconductor manufacturers and had not avoided dumping of Japanese-made semiconductors in various markets around the world. Thus the heart of this complaint was that the benefits of

---

23 See 51 Fed.Reg. 35993.

24 See 51 Fed.Reg. 29443.

25 See 51 Fed.Reg. 29445.

26 55 Fed.Reg. 49724 (USTR 1990).

27 56 Fed.Reg. 67114 (USTR 1991).

28 See 52 Fed.Reg. 13412 (1987).

an international agreement previously made were being denied to the United States and that this constituted a burden or restraint on U.S. commerce. The United States did impose additional duties on Japanese data processing machines, rotary drills and color television sets. However, these duties were suspended when the USTR found improved compliance by the Japanese with the semiconductor agreement.[29]

Section 307 of the Trade and Tariff Act of 1984 focuses specifically on export performance requirements created by foreign countries. Such requirements are thought by many United States investors to be unreasonable. Section 307 requires the USTR to enter into consultations with any foreign country imposing export performance requirements in an effort to seek to alleviate them when they adversely the economic interests of the United States. If such consultations do not result in a settlement, the USTR is authorized to impose import restraints on the products or services of the country in question.[30] In one instance, for example, the USTR was able to successfully negotiate away export performance requirements maintained by the Taiwanese relative to automobiles.[31]

The Telecommunications Trade Act of 1988[32] focuses upon foreign market opportunities in the telecommunication field. It is integrated into Section 301 procedures and administrative determinations. In undertaking retaliation, however, the USTR is directed to target telecommunications industry exports to the U.S. unless other action would be more effective in opening up foreign export markets. Section 1374 of the 1988 Act requires the USTR to identify priority countries whose practices cause the greatest telecommunications trade barriers. South Korea and the European Union were so identified in 1989. Ensuing negotiations resulted in a market-opening telecommunications agreement with South Korea and the European Union.

In the fall of 1991, the USTR initiated a prominent investigation of restrictive trade practices of the People's Republic of China. This investigation was undertaken in part to mitigate Congressional frustration over President Bush's continued willingness to grant most-favored-nation tariff status to Chinese goods despite record U.S. trade deficits with the PRC (second only to Japan). The Section 301 investigation focused upon PRC import quotas, prohibitions and

---

29 See 52 Fed.Reg. 22693 (1987).

30 See 19 U.S.C.A. § 2112(g)(3).

31 See 51 Fed.Reg. 41558.

32 Pub.L. 100–418.

licensing procedures, and PRC technical barriers to trade (e.g., standards, testing and certification requirements). It also challenged the failure to publish PRC laws, regulations, judicial decisions and administrative rulings relating to import restraints. Additional discussions regarding PRC tariffs (ranging up to 200 percent) and import taxes were held. The main thrust of the proceeding was to open up China's markets to U.S. exports.

Since China was not a member of the GATT, and in spite of U.S. bilateral trade agreements with the PRC, the USTR proceeded with this investigation on an unfair practices' basis. This meant that no trade agreement dispute settlement procedures were triggered. The Section 301 investigation was in addition to the Special 301 priority country investigation of PRC practices in the intellectual property field.

In October of 1992 the United States and China signed a memorandum of understanding that narrowly avoided massive, unilateral Section 301 trade sanctions. The People's Republic agreed to phase out by the end of 1977 numerous nontariff trade barriers, including import licenses, quotas and bans as well as regulatory restraints. The removal of these barriers will improve U.S. export possibilities for telecommunications equipment, airplanes, machinery, agricultural goods, electrical appliances, computers, auto parts and pharmaceuticals. Furthermore, China promised to undertake a series of significant tariff cuts no later than the end of 1993. All of China's import-substitution regulations and policies are to be eliminated. In particular, the PRC will not condition entry into its market upon technology transfers. All laws, regulations, policies and decrees dealing with China's import and export system will be published on a regular basis and no such rules can be enforced unless they have been made readily available to foreign traders and governments. The goal is complete "transparency" of PRC trade law and an end to the use of secret internal directives. For its part, the United States committed itself to full GATT/WTO membership for the PRC, which was finally realized in 2001.

§ 19.9 Special 301—Prioritization of U.S. Intellectual Property Rights Disputes with Foreign Countries

Unlike the Super 301 procedures, which expired in 1991, the Special 301 procedures established by the 1988 Omnibus Trade and Competitiveness Act are permanent features of United States trade legislation. These procedures are located in Section 182 of the Trade

Act of 1974.[33] Under these procedures the United States Trade Representative is required to identify foreign countries that deny adequate and effective protection of intellectual property rights, or deny fair and equitable access to United States persons that rely upon intellectual property protection. As with the Super 301 procedures, the USTR is given discretion to determine whether to designate certain of these countries to be "priority countries." If so designated, a mandatory Section 301 investigation must follow in the absence of a determination that this would be detrimental to U.S. economic interests or a negotiated settlement of the intellectual property dispute. Once designated, Special 301 investigations and retaliations against priority countries must ordinarily be decided within 6 months by the USTR. This is a fast track when compared with Super 301 procedures. Whether to retaliate or not is discretionary with the USTR, but retaliation is not authorized if the country in question enters into good faith negotiations or makes "significant progress" in bilateral or multilateral negotiations towards increased protection for intellectual property rights.

In identifying priority foreign countries in the intellectual property field, Section 182 indicates that the USTR is to prioritize only those countries that have the most "onerous or egregious" practices, whose practices have the greatest adverse impact on United States products, and are not entering into good faith negotiations bilaterally or multilaterally to provide adequate and effective protection of intellectual property rights.[34] For these purposes, the term "persons that rely on intellectual protection" covers those involved in copyrighted works of authorship or those involved in the manufacture of products that are patented or subject to process patents.[35] Interestingly, this definition does not include those who rely on United States trademarks. However, the relevant definitions include trademarks in connection with the denial by foreign countries of adequate and effective protection of intellectual property rights. The definition of practices that deny fair and equitable market access in connection with intellectual property rights appear to be limited to copyrights and patents. This denial must constitute a violation of provisions of international law or international agreements to which both the United States and that country are parties or otherwise constitute a discriminatory nontariff trade barrier.[36]

---

[33] 19 U.S.C.A. § 2242.

[34] 19 U.S.C.A. § 2422(b).

[35] 19 U.S.C.A. § 2242(d).

[36] Id.

Regular reports to Congress are required of the USTR by Section 182. As with the Super 301 procedures, the USTR has chiefly placed foreign country intellectual property practices on watch lists rather than formally designating priority countries. These watch lists are divided as between "priority watch lists" and "secondary watch lists." Many nations have been listed by the USTR since 1989 in this fashion. This has the practical effect of placing pressure on those nations to enter negotiations with the United States that will improve their protection of intellectual property rights. The use of these lists gives the USTR more room to negotiate settlements with the countries concerned. In April of 1991, the USTR formally named China, India and Thailand as the first "priority countries" for Special 301 purposes. Thus the formal process of negotiation backed up by a mandatory Section 301 investigation and potential sanctions was begun. Thailand was cited for its failure to enforce copyrights and for the absence of patent protection for pharmaceuticals. India was named because its patent laws are deficient from the U.S. perspective, particularly on compulsory licensing and the absence of pharmaceutical protection. Extensive book, video, sound recording and computer software piracy in India was also cited.

The United States Trade Representative has long been skeptical of the PRC commitment to intellectual property rights. In 1991 she commenced a Special 301 investigation into the adequacy of China's computer software and other intellectual property regulations. Absent satisfaction through negotiations, the U.S. threatened massive retaliatory trade sanctions blocking Chinese exports to America. Early in 1992, a last minute agreement was reached on significant reform of China's copyright, patent and trade secret laws. In the copyright area, China agreed to join the Berne Convention and the Geneva Convention on Phonograms, to extend protection to existing as well as new works, and to treat computer programs as literary works protected for 50 years. Accession to the Berne Convention will remove the barrier to Chinese copyright protection of works by most foreigners, including U.S. citizens, first published outside the PRC.

Regarding patents, China promised full protection for pharmaceuticals and agricultural chemicals with a 20–year patent term. It also promised a substantial waiver of the risk of compulsory licensing for all U.S. holders of Chinese patents, including a ban on such licensing if the U.S. holder does not manufacture the product in the PRC. This promise does not appear to apply to European or Japanese owners of Chinese patents. Trade secrets will be protected by legislation against unauthorized use or disclosure, including that by third parties. China and the United States reached another crisis-ridden agreement on intellectual property early in 1995. This agreement emphasizes enforcement issues in the PRC, particularly regarding pirate CD plants. It does not preclude Section 301 action by the United States. In 1996, China was identified as a priority foreign country under Special 301. Shortly thereafter yet another crisis-ridden agreement on intellectual property was reached by the United States and the PRC. This agreement, once again, avoided massive mutual trade sanctions.

United States Special 301 investigations and watch lists, now including "Out-of-Cycle Reviews of Notorious Markets", have continued relentlessly in spite of the TRIPs agreement. The USTR has filed numerous TRIPs complaints with the WTO. Filings have been made, for example, against Denmark, Sweden, Ireland, Ecuador, Greece, Portugal, India, Russia, Pakistan, Turkey and, not surprisingly, China.

Chapter 20

ANTITRUST LAWS (U.S. AND EUROPE)

Table of Sections

§ 20.1 Sherman Act Prohibitions and Remedies

The first federal antitrust statute was the Sherman Act of 1890. The early state statutes and the Sherman Act reflected a "populist" movement in United States society in the late 19th Century. This movement opposed the formation of large and economically powerful "trusts" by the captains of the American industrial revolution. Perhaps the most famous of all trusts was that put together by the Rockefellers to control the oil industry.

The Sherman Act contains two basic prohibitions. Section 1 prohibits every contract, combination or conspiracy in restraint of trade. Section 2 prohibits monopolization, attempts to monopolize, and combinations or conspiracies to monopolize. Both of these prohibitions extend to interstate commerce within the United States and, under Section 7 of the Sherman Act, to United States foreign commerce. Section 7 concerns the "extraterritorial" application of the Sherman Act to foreign enterprises and restraints of trade undertaken outside the limits of the United States which have "direct, substantial and reasonably foreseeable" effects on U.S. commerce. Extraterritorial U.S. antitrust jurisdiction has always been controversial and is discussed separately in this chapter.

Originally enacted as misdemeanors, the Sherman Act prohibitions have now become felony criminal offenses. Among the family of nations with antitrust-type laws, the United States is almost unique in criminally sanctioning anticompetitive behavior. Persons violating either Section 1 or Section 2 of the Sherman Act may be imprisoned up to three years or fined up to $350,000. Corporations held to violate those sections may be fined up to $10,000,000. In fact, criminal prosecutions under the Sherman Act are rare. Perhaps the most common kind of activity which is criminally prosecuted is bidrigging on government contracts.

The Sherman Act also created a powerful private remedy, treble the actual damages suffered as a result of an antitrust violation. This remedy has been carried forward and is now found in Section 4 of the Clayton Act. When combined with class action and parens patriae procedures before federal and state courts, and the constitutional right to a jury trial in civil litigation, treble damages is transformed into an incredibly powerful remedy. Private treble damages actions account for approximately 85 percent of all antitrust litigation. No other nation permits the bulk of its antitrust law enforcement to be accomplished by private parties. In the United States, this result is rationalized as promoting the enforcement of extremely important, almost quasi-constitutional law. The Supreme Court has repeatedly referred to the Sherman Act as "the economic constitution of the United States" or the "Magna Carta of free enterprise." Private antitrust litigants are often said to function as "attorneys general" when seeking to obtain treble damages relief.

§ 20.2 Reasonable and Unreasonable (Per Se) Restraints of Trade

After a period of "trust busting" led by President Theodore Roosevelt at the turn of the century, the Supreme Court of the United States rendered its famous decision in *Standard Oil Company of New Jersey v. United States.*[1] In this decision, the Supreme Court

---

1 221 U.S. 1, 31 S.Ct. 502, 55 L.Ed. 619 (1911).

held that Sections 1 and 2 of the Sherman Act apply only to *unreasonable* restraints of trade and monopolization activities. The *Standard Oil* case thus stands for the well-known proposition that the "rule of reason" governs Sherman Act law. In applying this approach to the Rockefellers and the Standard Oil Company of New Jersey, the Supreme Court ordered dissolution of this "trust" into approximately 30 oil companies. Whether a comparable remedy will be applied to Microsoft remains to be seen.

The courts have created categories of restraint of trade offenses which are treated as *per se* unreasonable, that is to say presumptively illegal. These categories historically have included: (1) horizontal price fixing;[2] (2) vertical price fixing or minimum resale price maintenance;[3] (3) horizontal market division or customer allocation;[4] (4) certain tying arrangements;[5] and (5) certain commercial group boycotts.[6] The term "horizontal" applies to the activities of persons who operate at the same economic level, e.g., manufacturers, wholesalers, etc. Thus a horizontal price fixing, market division or customer allocation conspiracy would be among manufacturers, wholesalers or retailers, but not as between them. Such conspiracies are often referred to as cartels. The term "vertical" applies to relationships between actors who function at different economic levels, e.g., wholesalers and retailers. Thus a vertical price fixing conspiracy could be reflected in contracts between manufacturers and wholesalers or as between wholesalers and retailers.

---

[2] United States v. Trenton Potteries Co., 273 U.S. 392, 47 S.Ct. 377, 71 L.Ed. 700 (1927); Catalano, Inc. v. Target Sales, Inc., 446 U.S. 643, 100 S.Ct. 1925, 64 L.Ed.2d 580 (1980). Compare Broadcast Music, Inc. v. Columbia Broadcasting System, Inc., 441 U.S. 1, 99 S.Ct. 1551, 60 L.Ed.2d 1 (1979); Arizona v. Maricopa County Medical Society, 457 U.S. 332, 102 S.Ct. 2466, 73 L.Ed.2d 48 (1982); N.C.A.A. v. Board of Regents of University of Oklahoma, 468 U.S. 85, 104 S.Ct. 2948, 82 L.Ed.2d 70 (1984) (Rule of Reason cases).

[3] Dr. Miles Medical Co. v. John D. Park & Sons Co., 220 U.S. 373, 31 S.Ct. 376, 55 L.Ed. 502 (1911); California Retail Liquor Dealers Ass'n v. Midcal Aluminum, Inc., 445 U.S. 97, 100 S.Ct. 937, 63 L.Ed.2d 233 (1980) *reversed by* Leegin Creative Products, Inc. v. PSKS, Inc., 551 U.S. 877, 127 S.Ct. 2705, 168 L.Ed.2d 623 (2007).

[4] United States v. Topco Associates, 405 U.S. 596, 92 S.Ct. 1126, 31 L.Ed.2d 515 (1972); Palmer v. BRG of Georgia, Inc., 498 U.S. 46, 111 S.Ct. 401, 112 L.Ed.2d 349 (1990).

[5] Jefferson Parish Hospital District No. 2 v. Hyde, 466 U.S. 2, 104 S.Ct. 1551, 80 L.Ed.2d 2 (1984); Eastman Kodak Co. v. Image Technical Services, Inc., 504 U.S. 451, 112 S.Ct. 2072, 119 L.Ed.2d 265 (1992).

[6] Klor's, Inc. v. Broadway–Hale Stores, 359 U.S. 207, 79 S.Ct. 705, 3 L.Ed.2d 741 (1959); FTC v. Superior Court Trial Lawyers Association, 493 U.S. 411, 110 S.Ct. 768, 107 L.Ed.2d 851 (1990). Compare NCAA v. Board of Regents of the University of Oklahoma, 468 U.S. 85, 104 S.Ct. 2948, 82 L.Ed.2d 70 (1984); Northwest Wholesale Stationers, Inc. v. Pacific Stationery and Printing Co., 472 U.S. 284, 105 S.Ct. 2613, 86 L.Ed.2d 202 (1985); FTC v. Indiana Federation of Dentists, 476 U.S. 447, 106 S.Ct. 2009, 90 L.Ed.2d 445 (1986) (Rule of Reason cases).

The Supreme Court in recent years has indicated that none of these *per se* rules is absolute, and that in special circumstances the rule of reason will prevail. For example, the traditional (now rejected) *per se* rule against resale price maintenance (RPM) was tempered by an exception for most consignment sales,[7] by removing maximum RPM from *per se* treatment,[8] and by allowing manufacturers to suggest resale prices and unilaterally refuse to deal with distributors who do not comply (the "*Colgate* doctrine").[9]

These trends have revived interest in just exactly what the rule of reason is all about. The classic statement of the rule appears in *Board of Trade of Chicago v. United States*[10] where Justice Brandeis stressed analysis of the competitive significance or competitive impact of the restraints at issue. Recent cases sometimes also allow economic efficiency and noncompetitive business justifications to be weighed in the rule of reason calculus, and it is clear that nonprice vertical restraints are to be judged under such an approach.[11] Thus, most territorial and customer allocations by manufacturers among their distributors are evaluated in terms of their intrabrand versus interbrand competitive effects and marketing efficiency. These decisions, and others, suggest that the traditional distinction in U.S. antitrust law between rule of reason analysis and *per se* treatment of restraints of trade is breaking down and that a new synthesis, the contours of which are not yet clear, is emerging.

§ 20.3 Monopolization

Section 2 of the Sherman Act is primarily concerned with single firm market power. Attempts to monopolize have never been easily proved because the Supreme Court has required a "dangerous probability of success" in addition to proof of specific intent and acts undertaken to monopolize.[12] The typical analysis in monopolization cases first involves a definition of the market in which the defendant is alleged to have monopoly power and engaged in monopoliza-

---

7 But see Simpson v. Union Oil Co., 377 U.S. 13, 84 S.Ct. 1051, 12 L.Ed.2d 98 (1964).

8 Atlantic Richfield Co. v. USA Petroleum Co., 495 U.S. 328, 110 S.Ct. 1884, 109 L.Ed.2d 333 (1990); State Oil Co. v. Kahn, 522 U.S. 3, 118 S.Ct. 275, 139 L.Ed.2d 199 (1997).

9 Monsanto Co. v. Spray–Rite Service Corp., 465 U.S. 752, 104 S.Ct. 1464, 79 L.Ed.2d 775 (1984); Business Electronics Corp. v. Sharp Electronics Corp., 485 U.S. 717, 108 S.Ct. 1515, 99 L.Ed.2d 808 (1988).

10 246 U.S. 231, 38 S.Ct. 242, 62 L.Ed. 683 (1918). See National Society of Professional Engineers v. United States, 435 U.S. 679, 98 S.Ct. 1355, 55 L.Ed.2d 637 (1978).

11 Continental T.V., Inc. v. GTE Sylvania Inc., 433 U.S. 36, 97 S.Ct. 2549, 53 L.Ed.2d 568 (1977).

12 Swift & Co. v. United States, 196 U.S. 375, 25 S.Ct. 276, 49 L.Ed. 518 (1905).

tion. This is known in antitrust parlance as "defining the relevant market." Each market for purposes of Section 2 will be defined in terms of product and geographic scope. In *United States v. E.I. du Pont de Nemours & Co.,*[13] the Court emphasized that all "reasonably interchangeable" products should be included in defining the relevant product market. Geographically, markets are defined for purposes of Section 2 in terms of the area of effective competition faced by the alleged monopolist. Typically, this is the whole or part of the United States, but may exclude Hawaii or Alaska. Market shares are the beginning of an analysis of market power necessary to the monopolization offense under Section 2.

Assuming that the defendant in a Section 2 case has monopoly power in the relevant market, the next step is to examine whether exclusionary practices were used in obtaining this power or maintaining it. Such practices are referred to as "acts of monopolization." Common allegations of acts of monopolization have involved predatory pricing, price discrimination, tying practices, refusals to deal and mergers and acquisitions. In the famous *Alcoa* decision, Judge Learned Hand emphasized that the creation of new plants designed to meet market needs constituted an act by Alcoa of monopolization of the U.S. virgin aluminum ingot market.[14]

In recent years, other language in Judge Hand's opinion has been used to defeat allegations of monopolization when monopoly power has been achieved as a result of superior foresight, skill and industry. Thus, for example, Eastman Kodak Co. was held not to have monopolized under Section 2 as a result of its product market innovations which were not disclosed in advance to competing companies.[15] In 1982, partly because of the internationalization of the computer market, the government dropped its longstanding monopolization case against IBM. Shortly thereafter, it also settled another large monopolization case against American Telephone & Telegraph. This settlement, somewhat like the famous dissolutions under *Standard Oil of New Jersey,* resulted in the creation of a number of regional telecommunications companies and the breakup of the world's largest corporation.

§ 20.4 Clayton Act Prohibitions

Critics of the Sherman Act and the *Standard Oil* decision mounted a legislative campaign which resulted in two major federal antitrust statutes in 1914. The first of these statutes was the Clay-

---

13 351 U.S. 377, 76 S.Ct. 994, 100 L.Ed. 1264 (1956).

14 United States v. Aluminum Co. of America, 148 F.2d 416 (2d Cir.1945).

15 Berkey Photo, Inc. v. Eastman Kodak Co., 603 F.2d 263 (2d Cir.1979).

ton Act of 1914, and the second was the Federal Trade Commission Act, also of 1914. The Clayton Act prohibits four kinds of activities if they involve commodities (not services) and may tend to substantially lessen competition in any line of commerce:

(1) price discrimination, subject to "cost justification" and "meeting competition" defenses (Section 2);

(2) exclusive dealing and tying arrangements (Section 3);

(3) mergers and acquisitions (Section 7); and

(4) interlocking company boards of directors (Section 8) (rarely invoked).

§ 20.5 Mergers and Acquisitions

The statutory prohibitions found in the Clayton Act are drafted in detailed language that has often led to narrow interpretations following the literal language of the statute. For example, initial interpretation of Section 7 did not permit coverage of assets acquisitions as distinct from stock mergers. It took, instead, an amendment in 1951 for asset acquisitions to fall under the jurisdictional scope of Section 7 of the Clayton Act. Section 7 is, since 1975, subject to "premerger notification." These requirements (sometimes known as "Hart–Scott–Rodino" notifications) stipulate that parties to large mergers and acquisitions must give the Justice Department and the Federal Trade Commission advance notice of their intentions. This advance notice allows the government antitrust authorities to review proposed mergers and acquisitions from the perspective of their potential to violate Section 7 of the Clayton Act and the desirability of challenging them in court. Of all the mergers that take place in the United States annually, including those involving takeovers by foreign firms, probably less than 1 percent are required to be notified to the federal antitrust authorities.

Under the Reagan and Bush administrations, vertical mergers were almost never challenged and very few horizontal mergers were subject to court proceedings under Section 7. Some mergers approved by the federal authorities have been subsequently challenged by a state Attorney General.[16] The states have, in general, become quite active in the mergers area and have adopted their own set of Horizontal Mergers Guidelines through the National Associa-

---

[16] See California v. American Stores Co., 495 U.S. 271, 110 S.Ct. 1853, 109 L.Ed.2d 240 (1990).

tion of Attorneys General (NAAG).[17] Private challenges to mergers can also occur, and did so notably in the hostile takeover of British Consolidated Gold Fields by Minorco (a Luxembourg company controlled by the two leading South African gold producers). Gold Fields sought to block the takeover on antitrust grounds in the United States, Britain, South Africa, Australia and the European Union. These efforts failed everywhere except before a U.S. federal district court judge who issued an injunction against the takeover which was upheld by the Second Circuit Court of Appeals.[18]

§ 20.6 Price Discrimination, Exclusive Dealing and Tying Offenses

The price discrimination prohibition found in Section 2 of the Clayton Act was once the source of considerable public prosecution by the Federal Trade Commission. It was amended in the 1930s in an attempt to protect small retailers from the growing competitive pressures of chain stores. These amendments were undertaken in the Robinson–Patman Act of 1936. In this effort, Section 2 has largely proved unsuccessful. Chain stores are now a prominent form of merchandising in the United States. However, the prohibition against price discrimination remains law, despite considerable efforts at repeal. Its primary significance today is to permit private parties to sue for treble damages as victims of price discrimination practices. Thus, for example, small retailers of liquor may join together in a lawsuit which charges manufacturers with discriminating in price in favor of chain stores to their detriment. These small retailers often succeed in settling for or recovering at judgment substantial sums.

Section 3 of the Clayton Act concerns sales and distribution agreements. In general, exclusive dealing contracts have not been frequently challenged by the government or private parties. This is because the government now takes the position that exclusive dealing contracts are a variation on vertical integration, which may permit desirable economic efficiencies. Exclusive dealing arrangements are generally treated under the "rule of reason."

Section 3 also prohibits what are known as "tying arrangements." A tying arrangement must involve two separate products: the tying product and the tied product. The essence of the arrange-

---

17 The NAAG guidelines are reproduced in R. Folsom, State Antitrust Laws (Matthew Bender).

18 Consolidated Gold Fields v. Anglo American Corp., 698 F.Supp. 487 (S.D.N.Y.1988), *affirmed* 871 F.2d 252 (2d Cir.1989), *cert. dismissed* 492 U.S. 939, 110 S.Ct. 29, 106 L.Ed.2d 639 (1989).

ment is coercion. The seller forces the buyer to take the tied product in order to get the tying product. If such activities may substantially lessen competition in any line of commerce, there is a violation of Section 3. Tying practices are also extensively litigated under Section 1 of the Sherman Act as restraints of trade. Under Section 1, the Supreme Court has traditionally viewed tying arrangements as a "per se offense." Per se offenses are those activities which the courts have treated as without redeeming virtues and therefore presumptively unreasonable. The case law on tying arrangements under Section 1 of the Sherman Act and Section 3 of the Clayton Act is extensive, complex, and not entirely consistent. Although the Supreme Court has recently affirmed the appropriateness of *per se* treatment for tying arrangements,[19] a number of lower court decisions indicate that it is a rather soft *per se* rule.

§ 20.7 The Federal Trade Commission Act

The second statute enacted in 1914 was the Federal Trade Commission Act. Under Section 5 of that Act, "unfair methods of competition" are prohibited. A number of leading cases of the United States Supreme Court indicate that Section 5 covers all of the types of activities prohibited by the Sherman and Clayton Acts. The FTC Act can also be construed to reach anticompetitive methods that are not clearly prohibited by those statutes, but which the Commission in its administrative wisdom determines unfair. Thus the Federal Trade Commission Act is said to "fill in the gaps" of federal antitrust law.

While Section 5 is arguably the most vague of all federal antitrust statutes, it is enforced exclusively by an administrative agency, the Federal Trade Commission. Over the years, the Commission has had a sporadic record in accomplishing its mission. The Commission is composed of five persons nominated by the President and confirmed by the Senate, no more than three of whom can be from the same political party. Despite the political nature of the appointment process to the Federal Trade Commission, the Commission is "an independent agency." It is supposed to exercise its statutory authority to act against unfair methods of competition without influence from the President or the Congress. In recent years, this supposition has been called into question as Congress, through its budget powers, has increasingly involved itself in policy and enforcement decisions of the Federal Trade Commission. A favorite

---

[19] See Jefferson Parish Hospital District No. 2 v. Hyde, 466 U.S. 2, 104 S.Ct. 1551, 80 L.Ed.2d 2 (1984); Eastman Kodak Co. v. Image Technical Services, Inc., 504 U.S. 451, 112 S.Ct. 2072, 119 L.Ed.2d 265 (1992).

method of control is to deny the Commission the power to spend money on specified law enforcement proceedings.

The antitrust remedies available to the Commission are limited to issuance of "cease and desist orders" against parties found to violate Section 5. Additional remedies can follow, including civil penalties and restitution, only if there is noncompliance with such orders. There is no private right of action to enforce Section 5 of the Federal Trade Commission Act. Because the only remedies available are public remedies, and the Commission inevitably has scarce resources, the ability to monitor and regulate unfair methods of competition under the FTC Act is limited.

The Federal Trade Commission can also enforce all of the prohibitions found in the Clayton Act. However, it cannot enforce Sections 1 or 2 of the Sherman Act. Today, the Commission's primary activity is evaluating mergers under the premerger notification rules of Section 7 of the Clayton Act. It is hard to see that the Commission's efforts since 1914 have lent much precision to the field of antitrust law. It has instead become a variable agency often swinging from periods of inaction to dramatic enforcement proceedings along with the tides of United States politics and the prevailing winds of antitrust.

§ 20.8 Extraterritorial U.S. Antitrust in Perspective—Blocking Statutes

After some initial hesitation,[20] United States courts have long asserted the right to apply the Sherman Antitrust Act to foreign commerce intended to or affecting the United States market. Perhaps the most famous application of this approach was by Judge Learned Hand in the *Alcoa* case.[21] This decision is the origin of the "effects test" governing extraterritorial U.S. antitrust jurisdiction. It was affirmatively applied in *Alcoa* to a foreign cartel acting almost entirely outside the United States but with clear restraint upon U.S. imports. In some cases, this approach has been tempered to allow consideration and balancing of the interests of comity and foreign countries in the outcome.[22] This results in a kind of jurisdic-

---

[20] See especially, American Banana Co. v. United Fruit Co., 213 U.S. 347, 29 S.Ct. 511, 53 L.Ed. 826 (1909).

[21] United States v. Aluminum Co. of America, 148 F.2d 416 (2d Cir.1945).

[22] See especially Timberlane Lumber Co. v. Bank of America, 549 F.2d 597 (9th Cir.1976); Mannington Mills, Inc. v. Congoleum Corp., 595 F.2d 1287 (3d Cir.1979); Compare Laker Airways Ltd. v. Sabena, Belgian World Airlines, 731 F.2d 909 (D.C.Cir.1984) and Uranium Antitrust Litigation, 617 F.2d 1248 (7th Cir.1980) (jurisdictional rule of reason rejected).

tional "rule of reason" and is supported by the American Law Institute's Third Restatement of Foreign Relations Law.[23]

In 1982, Congress amended the Sherman Act and the Federal Trade Commission Act by enacting the Foreign Trade Antitrust Improvements Act.[24] Section 402 of the Act added a new Section 6a to the Sherman Act, which states:

> This Act shall not apply to conduct involving trade or commerce (other than import trade or import commerce) with foreign nations unless—
>
> (1) such conduct has direct, substantial, and reasonably foreseeable effect—
>
> (A) on trade or commerce which is not trade or commerce with foreign nations, or on import trade or import commerce with foreign nations; or
>
> (B) on export trade or export commerce with foreign nations, of a person engaged in such trade or commerce in the United States; and
>
> (2) such effect gives rise to a claim under the provisions of this Act, other than this section.

If this Act applies to such conduct only because of the operation of paragraph (1)(B), then this Act shall apply to such conduct only for injury to export business in the United States.[25]

The FTAIA makes it clear that the Sherman Act no longer applies to transactions the principal effects of which are felt in markets wholly outside the United States.[26] The Act accomplishes this

---

23 Section 403 (1987).

24 Pub. L. No. 97–290, 96 Stat. 1233 (1982) (codified in scattered sections of 12 and 15 U.S.C.). The Foreign Trade Antitrust Improvements Act [hereinafter FTAIA] was part of the Export Trading Company Act. The Export Trading Company Act consists of four separate titles, each of which applies to a different type of activity. Title IV, the Foreign Trade Antitrust Improvements Act of 1982, deals with the extraterritorial reach of the antitrust laws.

25 15 U.S.C. § 6a.

26 See F. Hoffmann–La Roche Ltd. v. Empagran S.A., 542 U.S. 155, 161, 124 S.Ct. 2359, 159 L.Ed.2d 226 (2004) ("The FTAIA seeks to make clear to American exporters (and to firms doing business abroad) that the Sherman Act does not prevent them from entering into business arrangements (say, joint-selling arrangements), however anticompetitive, as long as those arrangements adversely affect only foreign markets.") *See also* United States v. Anderson, 326 F.3d 1319, 1329, *reh'g, en banc, denied,* (11th Cir.), *cert. denied*, 540 U.S. 825, 124 S.Ct. 178, 157 L.Ed.2d 46 (2003) ("In 1982, Congress enacted the Foreign Trade Antitrust Im-

by first laying down a "general rule placing *all* (non-import) activity involving foreign commerce outside the Sherman Act's reach."[27] Then, the FTAIA creates an exception to the general rule: that exception brings such conduct back within the Sherman Act's reach *provided that* the conduct *both* (i) sufficiently affects American commerce, *i.e.*, it has a "direct, substantial, and reasonable foreseeable effect" on American domestic, import or (certain) export commerce, *and* (2) has an effect of a kind that antitrust law considers harmful, *i.e.*, the "effect" must "give ris[e] to a [Sherman Act] claim.[28]

The extraterritorial reach of the antitrust laws was addressed by the U.S. Supreme Court in a divided decision in *Hartford Fire Insurance Co. v. California*.[29] The majority opted for an extraterritorial application unless there was a "true conflict." What a true conflict means was left to future debate, but it appeared to mean that the Sherman Act would be applied unless the foreign law required the American party to act in a manner which is in violation of U.S. law, or compliance with the laws of both nations is impossible. The case raises doubt about the status of interest balancing in any situation where U.S. laws are applied extraterritorially and create a conflict.[30] The Circuit Courts have been divided on the impact of *Hartford Fire* on comity analysis. Predictably, the Ninth Circuit has resisted abandonment of its *Timberlane* approach.[31] The Second Circuit, on the other hand, has fully embraced the true conflict doctrine.[32] Most courts and commentators see comity as "more an aspiration than a fixed rule" after *Hartford Fire*.[33]

---

provements Act . . . to limit American courts' jurisdiction over international commerce to transactions that affect the American economy.").

[27] F. Hoffmann–La Roche Ltd. v. Empagran S.A., 542 U.S. 155, 162, 124 S.Ct. 2359, 159 L.Ed.2d 226 (2004) (emphasis in original).

[28] 542 U.S. at 162 (emphasis in original). Whether the FTAIA imposes substantive or merely jurisdictional bars has been much debated. See Animal Science Products v. China Minerals Corp., 654 F.3d 462 (3d Cir. 2011).

[29] 509 U.S. 764, 113 S.Ct. 2891, 125 L.Ed.2d 612 (1993).

[30] For a debate regarding the meaning of the decision, see Andreas F. Lowenfeld, Conflict, Balancing of Interests, and the Exercise of Jurisdiction to Prescribe: Reflections on the Insurance Antitrust Case, 89 Am.J. Int'l L. 42 (1995); Phillip R. Trimble, The Supreme Court and International Law: The Demise of Restatement Section 403, 89 Am.J.Int'l L. 53 (1995); Larry Kramer, Extraterritorial Application of American Law after the Insurance Antitrust Case: a Reply to Professors Lowenfeld and Trimble, 89 Am.J.Int'l L. 750 (1995).

[31] Metro Industries, Inc. v. Sammi Corp., 82 F.3d 839 (9th Cir.1996), *cert. denied* 519 U.S. 868, 117 S.Ct. 181, 136 L.Ed.2d 120 (1996).

[32] In re Maxwell Communication Corp., 93 F.3d 1036 (2d Cir.1996).

[33] United States v. Nippon Paper Indus. Co., Ltd., 109 F.3d 1 (1st Cir.1997), *cert. denied* 522 U.S. 1044, 118 S.Ct. 685, 139 L.Ed.2d 632 (1998) (*criminal* extraterritorial antitrust jurisdiction affirmed).

Principles of comity significantly influenced the Supreme Court's decision in the *Empagran* decision[34] which held that the FTAIA did not permit a plaintiff injured by independent foreign effects of conduct occurring in foreign commerce to sue under the Sherman Act. One basis for its decision was that in construing the FTAIA, deemed ambiguous, the Court said it must "avoid unreasonable interference with the sovereign authority of other nations" and consider international disagreements with U.S. antitrust policies and remedies.[35]

Some limits on the extraterritorial reach of the Sherman Act are created by the act of state doctrine and the Foreign Sovereign Immunities Act.[36] But in the main, United States antitrust law has been applied to foreigners and overseas activities with a zeal sometimes approaching religious fervor. Amendments to the Sherman Act in 1984 stress the "direct, substantial and reasonably foreseeable" nature of effects on United States foreign commerce as a prerequisite to antitrust jurisdiction. Nevertheless, the potential for conflict in this field is enormous. For example, a multinational enterprise (MNE) headquartered in the U.S. but doing business in England could be constrained by United States antitrust law from fixing prices, yet permitted by EU competition law to do exactly that. Assuming that the price fixing in question has effects in both markets, what course of action is to be followed? There is no easy answer. When the MNE is located within a country other than one of the Member States of the EU or the United States, but engages in activity having effects within those markets, the problem potential of extraterritoriality may be even more acute. Reconciling a conflict of antitrust laws applied extraterritorially by these two jurisdictions could become a flashpoint in international business transactions.

Blocking Statutes

Extraterritoriality is a matter of balance. The executive, legislative, and judicial branches of government in the United States have reached out extraterritorially in the law of admiralty, antitrust, crime, labor, securities regulation, taxation, torts, trademarks

---

[34] F. Hoffman–La Roche Ltd. v. Empagran S.A., 542 U.S. 155, 124 S.Ct. 2359, 159 L.Ed.2d 226 (2004).

[35] 542 U.S. at 164.

[36] Even when there are effects in the U.S.A., extraterritorial antitrust conspiracies are not actionable unless those effects "give rise" to the plaintiff's antitrust claim. No subject matter jurisdiction exists. See Den Norske Stats Oljeselskap As v. HeereMac Vof, 241 F.3d 420 (5th Cir.2001), *cert. denied* 534 U.S. 1127, 122 S.Ct. 1059, 151 L.Ed.2d 967 (2002), *rehearing denied* 535 U.S. 1012, 122 S.Ct. 1597, 152 L.Ed.2d 512 (2002) (Norwegian oil company claims fail).

and wildlife management. A balance drawn wrongly by one nation invites retaliatory action by others. In the case of antitrust judgments emanating from courts in the United States, most notably the "Uranium Cartel" treble damages litigation of the late 1970s,[37] many nations consider that the balance has been wrongly drawn. At least nine nations (Australia, Canada, France, Germany, Netherlands, New Zealand, Philippines, South Africa and the United Kingdom) have taken retaliatory action by enacting "blocking statutes." In addition, the 41 Commonwealth nations have resolved general support for a position similar to that of the United Kingdom.

The United Kingdom blocking statute is the Protection of Trading Interests Act of 1980. This Act (without specifying United States antitrust law) makes it difficult to depose witnesses, obtain documents or enforce multiple liability judgments extraterritorially in the U.K. Violation of the 1980 Act may result in criminal penalties. Furthermore, under the "clawback" provision of the Act, parties with outstanding multiple liabilities in foreign jurisdictions (e.g., U.S. treble damages defendants) may recoup the punitive element of such awards in Britain against assets of the successful plaintiff. The British Act invites other nations to adopt clawback provisions by offering clawback reciprocity. United States attorneys confronted with a blocking statute need to understand that multiple liability judgments combined with contingency fee arrangements are virtually unknown elsewhere.

The extensive array of pre-trial discovery mechanisms allowed in U.S. civil litigation rarely, if ever, have a counterpart in foreign law. Discovery subpoenas originating in United States litigation are often "shocking" to many foreign defendants. And the U.S. Supreme Court has ruled that use of letters rogatory under the Hague Convention is not obligatory.[38] It is the blocking of discovery that potentially most threatens the extraterritorial application of United States laws, especially antitrust. Since U.S. courts may sanction parties who in bad faith fail to respond to discovery requests, foreign defendants requesting help from their home governments under blocking statutes are especially at risk. On the other hand, good faith efforts to modify or work around discovery blockades may favor foreign defendants. Such defendants are often caught in a "no win" situation. Either way they will be penalized.

---

[37] See Uranium Antitrust Litigation (Westinghouse Electric Corp. v. Rio Algom Limited), 617 F.2d 1248 (7th Cir.1980).

[38] Société National Industrielle Aérospatiale v. U.S. District Court, 482 U.S. 522, 107 S.Ct. 2542, 96 L.Ed.2d 461 (1987).

The reasons advanced to support an extraterritorial application of United States antitrust laws are founded on the idea that some extraterritorial extension is necessary to prevent their circumvention by multinational corporations which have the business sagacity to ensure that anticompetitive transactions are consummated beyond the territorial borders of the United States. An extraterritorial extension of antitrust laws can also help to ensure that the U.S. consumer receives the benefit of competing imports, which in turn may spur complacent domestic industries. The effect of foreign auto imports on the car manufacturers in the United States may be cited as an example. In an increasingly internationalized world, extraterritorial antitrust may merely reflect economic reality.

On the other hand, the British argue that extraterritoriality permits the United States to unjustifiably "mold the international economic and trading world to its own image." In particular, the "effects test" doctrine creates legal uncertainty for international traders, and U.S. courts pay little attention to the competing policies (interests) of other concerned governments. As the House of Lords has stated: "It is axiomatic that in anti-trust matters the policy of one state may be to defend what it is the policy of another state to attack."[39] The British also argue, not without some support, that customary international law does not permit extraterritorial application of national laws. In making this argument, the British have a convenient way of forgetting about the extraterritorial scope of Articles 101 and 102,[40] which are now part of their law. Moreover, in a curious reversal of roles illustrating the extremes of the debate, the British government applied the Protection of Trading Interests Act to block the pursuit of treble damages in U.S. courts by the liquidator of Laker Airway against British Airways and other defendants. A House of Lords decision reversed this ban but retained government restrictions on discovery related to the case.[41]

§ 20.9 The Goals of European Union Competition Policy

In Europe, the field of law that Americans call "antitrust" is generally referred to as "competition law." Although some nations in Europe have active competition law policies (notably Britain and Germany), none surpass the embracement of competition as a public good by the European Community.

---

39 Rio Tinto Zinc Corp. v. Westinghouse Electric Corp., 2 W.L.R. 81 (1978).

40 See Section 32.27.

41 British Airways Board v. Laker Airways, 3 W.L.R. 413 (1984).

The primary purpose of competition policy in Europe is preservation of the trade and other benefits of economic integration. The removal of governmental trade barriers unaccompanied by measures to ensure that businesses do not recreate those barriers would be an incomplete effort. Competing enterprises might agree to geographically allocate markets to each other, making the elimination of national tariffs and quotas by Treaty irrelevant. Similarly, a dominant enterprise in one state might tie up all important distributors or purchasers of its goods through long-term exclusive dealing contracts. The result could make entry into that market by another business exceedingly difficult. By assisting in the formation and maintenance of an economic community, business competition law is an important component in competition policy. It prevents enterprise behavior from becoming a substantial nontariff trade barrier to economic integration.

The secondary purpose of European competition policy is not unique to regional integration. This purpose is the attainment of the economic benefits generally thought to accrue in any economy organized on a competitive basis. These benefits are many Perhaps most important of all, an economy characterized by competitive enterprise answers the questions of economic organization by maximizing the market desires of its human constituents. A genuinely competitive market is responsive to individual choice in a way that acknowledges and promotes diversity. Competition among businesses protects the public interest in having its cumulative demand for goods and services provided at the lowest possible prices and with the greatest possible degree of responsivity to public tastes. It is in this sense that a competitive economy is said to be guided by the principle of "consumer welfare" or "consumer sovereignty." When, for example, European law prevents competing enterprises from fixing prices for their goods or prevents a dominant enterprise from charging monopoly prices at the consumers' expense, such law helps to realize the economic benefits of competition within the Euro-economy.

§ 20.10 Article 101—Restraints of Trade

Article 101(1) of the Treaty on the Functioning of the European Union (TFEU) deals with concerted business practices, business agreements and trade association decisions. When they have the potential to affect trade between member states *and* have the object or effect of preventing, restricting or distorting competition *within* Europe, such business activities are deemed incompatible with the Common Market and are prohibited. The focus of Article 101(1) is thus on cartels. By way of example, Article 101(1) lists certain prohibited activities:

(1) the fixing of prices or trading conditions;

(2) the limitation of production, markets, technical development or investment;

(3) the sharing of markets or sources of supply;

(4) the application of unequal terms to equivalent transactions, creating competitive disadvantages; and

(5) the conditioning of a contract on the acceptance of commercially unrelated additional supplies.

Article 101(2) voids agreements and decisions (or severable parts thereof) prohibited by Article 101(1). Thus the prohibitions of Article 101(1) against anticompetitive activity are absolute and immediately effective under 101(2) without prior judicial or administrative action. The open-ended text of 101(1) gives considerable leeway for interpretation and enforcement purposes. It has, for example, been interpreted to cover nonbinding "gentlemen's agreements."[42] Trade association "recommendations" influencing competition are caught.[43] It also generates considerable uncertainty as to the validity of many business agreements, since full market analyses of their competitive and trade impact are often required. However, Article 101(3) permits Article 101(1) to be declared inapplicable when agreements, decisions, concerted practices or classes thereof:

(1) contribute to the improvement of the production or distribution of goods, or to the promotion of technical or economic progress; while

(2) reserving to consumers an equitable share of the resulting benefits; and neither

(3) impose any restrictions not indispensable to objectives 1 and 2 (i.e., least restrictive means must be used); nor

(4) make it possible for the businesses concerned to substantially eliminate competition.

---

[42] ACF Chemiefarma v. Commission (1970) Eur.Comm.Rep. 661.

[43] Re ANSEAU–NAVEWA (1983) Eur.Comm.Rep. 3369.

The prohibitions of Article 101(1) may be tempered by "declarations of inapplicability" (exemptions) only when the circumstances of Article 101(3) are present. As befits exemptions from broad prohibitions, the terms of 101(3) are more narrow and specific. Such legal issues are often considered simultaneously in the process of analyzing the market impact of restrictive agreements, decisions and concerted practices. The net result is not unlike the "rule of reason" approach found in United States antitrust law.

§ 20.11 Commission Investigations, Attorney–Client Privilege, Shared Prosecutorial Powers

In March of 1962 the Council of Ministers adopted Regulation 17 on the basis of proposals from the Commission. Regulation 17 has been the major piece of secondary law under Articles 101 and 102. Effective May 1, 2004, Regulation 17 was replaced by Regulation 1/ 2003. These regulations establish the scheme of enforcement for competition law. The Commission, for the most part its Competition Directorate–General or department, has a wide range of powers.

The regulations confer investigatory powers in the Commission to conduct general studies into economic sectors and to review the affairs of individual businesses and trade associations. The Commission may investigate in response to a complaint or upon its own initiative. These powers are particularly significant because (except in the case of mergers) notification of restrictive agreements, decisions and practices to the Commission, although at times beneficial, is not mandatory. The Commission may request all information *it* considers necessary, and examine and make copies of record books and business documents.

Written communications with external EU-licensed lawyers undertaken for defense purposes are confidential and need not be disclosed.[44] Written communications with in-house lawyers are *not* exempt from disclosure, nor are communications with external *non-*EU counsel.[45] Thus communications with North American attorneys (who are not also EU-licensed attorneys) are generally discoverable. For example, the Commission obtained in-house counsel documents from John Deere, Inc., a Belgian subsidiary of the United States multinational. These documents were drafted as advice to management on how to avoid competition law liability for export prohibition restraints. They were used by the Commission to justify the finding

[44] AM & S Europe Ltd. v. Commission (1982) Eur.Comm.Rep. 1575.

[45] *Id.*

of an intentional Article 101 violation and a fine of 2 million EUROs.[46] United States attorneys have followed these developments with amazement and trepidation. Disclaimers of possible nonconfidentiality are one option to consider in dealing with clients. At a minimum, U.S. attorneys ought to advise their clients that the usual rules on attorney-client privilege may not apply.

In conducting its investigations, the Commission may ask for verbal explanations on the spot and have access to premises. One author refers to these powers as "dawn raids and other nightmares." Nevertheless, the Court of Justice has affirmed this right of hostile access.[47] Effective May 1, 2004, subject to the issuance of a local court warrant, this right of access extends to private homes and motor vehicles of corporate directors, managers and other staff. In these matters the Commission acts on its own authority provided there are reasonable grounds to believe that relevant books or records are kept in these locations. It must, however, inform member states prior to taking such steps and may request their assistance. The member states must render assistance when businesses fail to comply with competition law investigations of the Commission.

Businesses involved in the Commission's investigatory process have limited rights to notice and hearing.[48] They do not have access to the Commission's files. Any failure on the part of an enterprise to provide information requested by the Commission or to submit to its investigation can result in the imposition of considerable fines and penalties. For example, the Belgian and French subsidiaries of the Japanese electrical and electronic group, Matsushita, were fined by the Commission for supplying it with false information about whether Matsushita recommended retail prices for its products. These sanctions are civil in nature and run against the corporation, not its directors or management.

The Commission has increased the use of its investigatory powers. Several procedural requirements for Commission investigations and hearings have been discussed by the Court of Justice. One notable Court decision upheld the authority of the Commission to conduct searches of corporate offices without notice or warrant when it has reason to believe that pertinent evidence may be lost.[49]

---

[46] John Deere v. Commission (1985) 28 Off.J.Eur.Comm. L/35, 58.

[47] Hoechst v. Commission (1987) Eur.Comm.Rep. 1549; Dow Chemical Nederland BV v. Commission (1987) Eur.Comm.Rep. 4367; NV Samenwerkende Elektriciteits-produktiebedrijven (SEP) v. Commission (1991) Eur.Comm.Rep. II–1497 (Case T–39/90).

[48] Commission Regulation 99/63. See generally Hoffmann–La Roche v. Commission (1979) Eur.Comm.Rep. 461.

[49] Re National Panasonic (1980) Eur.Comm.Rep. 2033.

Another notable decision permitted a Swiss "whistle blower" who once worked for Hoffmann–La Roche (a defendant in competition law proceedings) to sue the Community in tort for disclosure of his identity as an informant.[50]

Regulation 17 and Regulation 1 envision significant cooperation and information sharing between European and national authorities in the field of competition law. Effective May 1, 2004, enforcement of Articles 101 and 102 has been shared with the competition agencies and national courts of the member states. A new European Competition Network was established to facilitate cooperative law enforcement and minimize divergent application of competition law principles, with the Commission to act as final arbiter on substantive matters. The principal reason for this sharing of enforcement duties is to allow the Commission to focus its energies on price fixing, cartel arrangements and other serious violations.

The Court of First Instance (now the General Court) has ruled that the Commission can refuse to pursue a competition law complaint if an adequate remedy is available from a national court.[51] This decision supports the Commission's customary practice of decentralized "subsidiarity" in the competition law field. Since May 1, 2004, national courts may ask the Commission for support regarding Article 101 or 102, with the Commission and national authorities empowered to file opinions with the national courts. Moreover, in all cases affecting member state trade, Regulation 1/ 2003 permits the Commission to issue ex ante binding decisions determining that a particular agreement or practice does not infringe European competition law. Such decisions would preclude different results at the national level.

§ 20.12 Commission Prosecutions and Sanctions

In addition to its investigatory powers, the Commission is authorized to determine when violations of the competition law provisions occur. This is the source of the Commission's power to render enforcement decisions. A regulation limits the time period in which the Commission may render a decision in competition law cases to five years. All Commission decisions, including enforcement decisions and decisions to investigate, fine or penalize must be published and are subject to judicial review. These appeals are heard by the General Court.

---

[50] Adams v. Commission (1985) Eur.Comm.Rep. 3539.

[51] Automec SRL v. Commission (1992) Eur.Comm.Rep. 2223 (Case T–24/90).

During interim periods, the Commission has the power to order measures indispensable to its functions.[52] Interim relief should be granted when there is prima facie evidence of a violation and an urgent need to prevent serious and irreparable private damage or intolerable damage to the public interest. La Cinq, a private television service twice denied membership in the European Broadcasting Union, successfully met these criteria. The Court of First Instance rebuked the Commission's refusal to grant provisional Article 102 protection.[53]

Before deciding that a competition law breach has occurred, the Commission issues a statement of "objections." This statement must reveal which facts the Commission intends to rely upon in reaching a decision that a violation has occurred.[54] A hearing can then be requested by the alleged violator(s) or any interested person. These hearings are conducted in private, with separate reviews of complainants and witnesses. The Commission must disclose only those non-confidential documents in its file upon which it intends to rely and are necessary to prepare an adequate defense.[55] After the hearing, the Commission consults with the Advisory Committee on Restrictive Practices and Monopolies, which is composed of one civil servant expert from each member state. The results of this consultation are not made public. Having consulted the Committee, the Commission is then free to render an enforcement decision.

In its enforcement decision, the Commission may require businesses to "cease and desist" their infringing activities. In practice, this power has sufficed to permit the Commission to order infringing enterprises to come up with their own remedial solutions. However, the Commission may not, at least in an Article 101 proceeding, require a violator to contract with the complainant.[56] Daily penalties may be imposed to compel adherence to the order to cease and desist. Commission decisions on violations are also accompanied by a capacity to substantially fine any intentionally or negligently infringing enterprise. When appeals are lodged against Commission decisions imposing fines and penalties, payment is suspended but interest is charged and a bank guarantee for the amounts concerned must be provided.[57]

---

[52] Camera Care v. Commission (1980) Eur.Comm.Rep. 119.

[53] La Cinq v. Commission (1992) Eur.Comm.Rep. 1 (Case T–44/90).

[54] AEG v. Commission (1983) Eur.Comm.Rep. 3151.

[55] VBVB and VBBB v. Commission (1984) Eur.Comm.Rep. 19.

[56] Automec SRL v. Commission (1992) Eur.Comm.Rep. 2223 (Case T–24/90). Compare Article 82 case law on refusals to deal by dominant firms.

[57] Hasselblad v. Commission (1982) Eur.Comm.Rep. 1555.

In the early years, fines and penalties actually levied by the Commission were few, relatively small in amount and frequently reduced on appeal to the Court of Justice. As competition law doctrine has become clearer, these trends have all been reversed. In its more recent decisions, the Court has upheld substantial fines and penalties imposed by the Commission in competition law proceedings and recognized their deterrent value.[58] In 2001, for example, the Commission imposed competition law fines of more than $850 million on European companies for conspiring to fix prices and divide up the vitamins market. Fines against other cartels have ratcheted up since Regulation 1 took effect in 2004, hitting *inter alia* producers of industrial bags, copper fittings, fasteners, hydrogen peroxide, acrylic glass, car glass, synthetic rubber, gas insulated switches, and lifts and escalators. By 2007, Microsoft had paid over 2 billion Euros in fines and penalties. In 2013, Microsoft was hit with a $732 million fine for failure to honor its commitment under a settlement agreement to offer Windows users a choice of rival web browsers.

Any complete picture of the development of Article 101 must account for the Commission's informal negotiations as well as its decisions to prosecute infringing activities. Business compliance with Articles 101 and 102 is often achieved short of a formal Commission decision. Word of informal file-closings is occasionally revealed. In *Re Eurofima*,[59] for example, the Commission terminated proceedings without issuing a decision. In the process of responding to complaints from suppliers, the Commission was able to secure termination of infringing conduct from Eurofima, the most important buyer of railway rolling stock in the Common Market. Eurofima also undertook to continue to comply with competition law. The Commission announced these results in a press release.

§ 20.13 Article 101—Group Exemptions

The Commission received an onslaught of Article 101(3) notifications in 1962 when Regulation 17 took effect. The vast majority of the business activities involved in this deluge were in the distribution and licensing areas. As a result, the Commission sought and obtained authorization in 1965 from the Council to formulate, for limited time periods, group "declarations of inapplicability" under Article 101(3). These are commonly known as "group or block exemptions." The Council granted this authorization, noting that Article 101(3) allows "classes" of exempt agreements.

---

[58] See Musique Diffusion Francaise SA v. Commission (1983) Eur.Comm.Rep. 1825.

[59] (1973) Common Mkt.L.Rep. D217.

Group exemptions, guidelines and policy announcements by the Commission in areas where group exemptions have not yet been promulgated, invite businesses to conform their agreements and behavior to their terms and conditions. In other words, group exemptions rely upon confidential business self-regulation.

After a number of test enforcement decisions and definitive rulings by the Court of Justice, the Commission issued Regulation 67 in 1967. It became the first of a series of group exemptions. Regulation 67/67 was replaced in 1983 by Regulation 1983/83. These regulations concerned exclusive dealing methods of distribution. Exclusive dealing agreements ordinarily involve restrictions on manufacturers and independent distributors of goods. These restraints concern who the manufacturer may supply, to whom the manufacturer or distributor may sell, and from whom the distributor may acquire the goods or similar goods. Exclusive dealing agreements should be distinguished from agency or consignment agreements where title and most risk remain with the manufacturer until the goods are sold by their retail agents to consumers. The announced policy position is that competition law will not require a manufacturer to compete with its agents. Exclusivity in genuine retail agency agreements is therefore legal.

The group exemptions for exclusive dealing, exclusive purchasing and franchise agreements were replaced in 2000 by Regulation 2790/99, known as the "vertical restraints regulation." In 2010, a new vertical restraints regulation was issued: Regulation 330/10. These Regulations are discussed in Chapter 22.

A series of Commission regulations have followed the pattern established by Regulation 67. Test cases are initiated by the Commission before the European Court prior to creating a group exemption. Group exemptions now exist for motor vehicle distribution and servicing agreements (Regulation 461/2010), production specialization agreements among small firms (Regulation 1218/2010), and research and development agreements among small firms (Regulation 1217/2010). The formerly separate group exemptions for patent licensing and know-how licensing have been merged under the technology transfers Regulation 240/96, superceded by Regulation 772/2004. See Chapter 23.

§ 20.14 Article 102

Article 102 of the Treaty on the Functioning of the European Union (TFEU) prohibits abuses by one or more undertakings of a dominant position within a substantial part of the Common Market insofar as the abuses may affect trade between member states. The existence of a dominant position is not prohibited by European law. Only its abuse is proscribed.

Article 102 proceeds to list certain examples of what constitute abuses by dominant enterprises:

(1) the imposition of unfair prices or other trading conditions;

(2) the limitation of production, markets or technical development which prejudices consumers;

(3) the application of dissimilar conditions to equivalent transactions, thereby engendering competitive disadvantages; and

(4) the subjection of contracts to commercially unrelated supplementary obligations.

These examples are remarkably, although not exactly, similar to the examples of anticompetitive agreements, decisions and concerted practices provided in Article 101. Indeed, insofar as two or more enterprises are abusing their dominant market position under Article 102 they may well be simultaneously engaging in an Article 101(1) infringement. However, fines for the same conduct under both Articles will not be permitted by the Court of Justice.[60]

Article 102 differs fundamentally from Article 101. There are no provisions to declare abuses by dominant enterprise(s) automatically void, nor to permit any exemptions from its prohibitions. Article 102 might be viewed as a *per se* rule of law. Thus, under the administrative framework of EU competition law, no individual or group exemptions can be granted by the Commission for Article 102. The absence of exemptions from Article 102 means that there is little incentive for dominant firms to notify their abuses to the Commission. Negative clearances are obtainable, however, indicating that the Commission sees no grounds for intervention on the facts and law before it. Quite understandably, few requests for Article 102 clearances have been made. Regulation 1 grants the Commission the same powers with reference to Article 102 as it possesses under Article 101 to obtain information, investigate corporate affairs, render infringement decisions, and fine or penalize offenders.

---

60 ACF Chemiefarma v. Commission (1970) Eur.Comm.Rep. 661.

A few Commission decisions concerning Article 102 have their origins in complaints to the Commission from competitors or those abused. Generally, however, the Commission has acted on its own initiative in Article 102 proceedings. Some of the Commission's decisions have been the subject of appeal to the Court of Justice, which occasionally has received Article 102 issues on reference from national courts under the preliminary ruling procedure. A limited number of cases have been resolved informally through Commission negotiations. To highlight the more important developments in the interpretation of the language and scope of Article 102, a selection of cases and issues follows.

§ 20.15 Article 102—Dominant Positions

Unless an enterprise or group of enterprises possesses a dominant position within a substantial part of the Common Market, no questions of abuse can arise. A dominant position may exist on either the supply or demand side of the market.[61]

In establishing the existence of dominant positions, the Commission has tended to look at commercial realities, not technical legal distinctions. For example, the only two producers of sugar in Holland were legally and financially independent of each other. In practice they systematically cooperated in the joint purchase of raw materials, the adoption of production quotas, the use of by-products, the pooling of research, advertising and sales promotion, and the unification of prices and terms of sales. To other enterprises they appeared as if a single firm. They were involved in over 85 percent of the sales of sugar in Holland. The Commission and the Court of Justice held them to be a single enterprise for the purpose of assessing the existence of a dominant position under Article 102.[62] The Commission has recently found support for its "collective dominance" theory of liability under Article 102.[63] This theory may bear upon oligopolies within the Common Market.

A celebrated merger case involved Continental Can, a large U.S. corporation.[64] It is a leading case on the existence of a domi-

---

[61] Re Eurofima (1973) Common Mkt.L.Rep. D217 (dominant buyer). In 1997, the commission issued a "Notice on the Definition of Relevant Market For Purposes of Community Competition Law" (O.J. 1997 C372/5). This Notice covers Article 81 and 82 cases, as well as mergers and acquisitions.

[62] Re European Sugar Cartel (1973) Common Mkt.L.Rep. D65 (Commission); (1975) Eur.Comm.Rep. 1663 (Court of Justice).

[63] See Societa Italiano Vetro SpA v. Commission (1992) Eur.Comm.Rep. 1403 (Cases T–68/89, 77/89, 78/89).

[64] Europemballage Corporation and Continental Can Co., Inc. v. Commission (1972) Common Mkt.L.Rep. D11 (Commission); (1973) Eur.Comm.Rep. 215 (Court of Justice).

nant position under Article 102 law. Evidence of Continental Can's worldwide and German national market strength in the supply of certain metal containers and tops, a concentrated market characterized by ineffective consumers and competitors, and strong technical and financial barriers to entry were sufficient for the Commission to find the existence of a dominant position in certain areas of Germany. In so doing, the Commission stressed that enterprises are in a dominant position:

> when they have the power to behave independently, which puts them in a position to act without taking into account their competitors, purchasers or suppliers . . . This power does not necessarily have to derive from an absolute domination . . . it is enough that they be strong enough as a whole to ensure to those enterprises an overall independence of behavior, even if there are differences in intensity in their influence on different partial markets.[65]

Power to behave independently of competitors, purchasers or suppliers amounting to a dominant position must be exercisable with reference to the supply or acquisition of particular goods or services, i.e., a market. In *Continental Can* the Commission distinguished between that enterprise's powerful position around the world and in Europe with reference to the generic market for light metal containers, and its dominant position in Germany with reference to the particular markets for preserved meat and shellfish tins and metal caps for glass jars. Thus, initial Commission selection of the appropriate geographic and product market is the key to its analysis of whether a dominant position exists or not. It is also the key to the utility of its dominant position formula as set out in the *Continental Can* opinion. On such selection hinges the determination of the market power of the enterprise concerned. The broader the market for goods or services is defined (light metal cans versus cans for preserved meat, etc.), the less likely there will be overall independence of behavior from competitors, purchasers or suppliers. The same is true for broader geographic markets selected by the Commission (e.g., Europe versus Germany or parts thereof).

On appeal to the Court of Justice, the Commission's guiding principles for determining the existence of a dominant position under Article 102 were not seriously questioned. The Court did challenge the Commission's delineation of the relevant *product* market and its failure to explain in full how Continental Can had the power to behave independently in the preserved meat, shellfish, and metal

---

65 Id.

top markets. Its German market shares were, by the Commission's calculation, 75, 85, and 55 percent respectively. Regarding the first criticism the Court said:

> The products in question have a special market only if they can be individualized not only by the mere fact that they are used for packaging certain products but also by special production characteristics which give them a specific suitability for this purpose.[66]

In other words the Commission failed to make clear, for the purpose of assessing the existence of a dominant position, why the markets for preserved meat tins, preserved fish tins, and metal tops for glass jars should be treated separately and independently of the general market for light metal containers.

The Commission's failure here overlapped with the Court's second point:

> A dominant position in the market for light metal containers for canned meat and fish cannot be decisive insofar as it is not proved that competitors in other fields but not in the market for light metal containers cannot, by mere adaptation, enter this market with sufficient strength to form a serious counterweight.[67]

The Court felt that the existence or lack of competition from substitute materials such as plastic or glass as well as potential competition from new entrants to the metal container industry or purchasers who might produce their own tins were also aspects of market power insufficiently explored by the Commission. Under the Commission's own formula for establishing a dominant position, the Court annulled the decision because it did not "sufficiently explain the facts and appraisals of which it [was] based."

The Court's emphasis in *Continental Can* on "special production characteristics," entry barriers and potential competition amounted to instructions to the Commission to do its homework a little better in future market power analyses under Article 102. Evaluating potential competition, of course, involves hypothetical calculations with which even an expert Commission would have difficulty. Yet these factors, as well as those considered by the Commission, made up the commercial realities of the German marketplace for canned meat and fish tins and metal tops for glass jars.

---

[66] Id.

[67] Id.

What is clear from the Court's *Continental Can* opinion is that dominance can be found under Article 102 in sub-product markets such as these, provided the Commission is exhaustive in its research and analysis.

Subsequent opinions of the Court have elaborated upon the product market analysis presented in *Continental Can.* The "interchangeability" of products for specific uses is a critical factor in determining the relevant product market under Article 102.[68] Thus, bananas were a proper product market since their interchangeability with other fresh fruits was limited.[69] And the replacement market for tires (as distinct from original equipment) is another submarket capable of sustaining a dominant position.[70] In exceptional circumstances, even a brand name product may be the relevant submarket.[71]

The Court has held that a market share of 40 percent may constitute dominance under Article 102.[72] Such a percentage is well below the threshold market share associated with monopolization cases under Section 2 of the Sherman Antitrust Act. While the Court has said that a market share of 5 or 10 percent would ordinarily rule out the existence of a dominance, exceptional circumstances could show such a position. Moreover, a large market share (say 50 percent or more) is presumptive proof of a dominant position.[73]

Partial *geographic* markets can also be relevant to Article 102 market power analyses. A dominant position must exist within a "substantial" part of the Common Market. The Commission discussed geographic markets amounting to the whole of Germany in its opinion concerning tins and metal tops. Yet each of these products has different transport costs. The geographic commercial realities of competition in metal tops, given their relatively low level of transport costs, are likely to be much broader than that for tins. The same comparison can be made as between small and large tins. The Court held that the Commission's geographic delineation of the markets for large and small tins in *Continental Can* was at odds

---

[68] Hoffmann–La Roche v. Commission (1979) Eur.Comm.Rep. 461.

[69] United Brands Co. v. Commission (1978) Eur.Comm.Rep. 207.

[70] Michelin NV v. Commission (1983) Eur.Comm.Rep. 3461.

[71] General Motors Continental NV v. Commission (1975) Eur.Comm.Rep. 1367 (legal monopoly over import certificates for which excessive prices were charged); Hugin Cash Registers Ltd. v Commission (1979) Eur.Comm.Rep. 1869 (spare parts for brand name product must be supplied to service competitor.)

[72] See United Brands v. Commission (1978) Eur.Comm.Rep. 207.

[73] See Hoffmann–La Roche v. Commission (1979) Eur.Comm.Rep. 461.

with some of its own evidence on their relative transport costs. The commercial realities of potential competition in small tins appeared to go beyond the national boundaries of Germany. Thus the Commission's delineation of the particular geographic markets in *Continental Can* was insufficiently explained and appraised. Later decisions have deferred to the Commission's expertise and discretion in selecting relevant geographic markets. Belgium, Holland, and Southern Germany, for example, have been held substantial parts of the Common Market for Article 102 purposes.[74]

When exclusive intellectual property rights are conferred by national states, the question of the existence of a dominant position remains vital. A patent, copyright or trademark for an individual product does not necessarily give an enterprise independent market power.[75] Other patented or nonpatented products of a similar nature may provide effective market competition and thereby protect suppliers and purchasers from abuse. The full market power analysis required in *Continental Can* must be undertaken. Similarly, the absence of patent rights is no barrier to finding a dominant position where know-how and costly and complex technology give former patent holders complete market power.[76]

§ 20.16 Article 102—Abuse

If the existence of a dominant position in the supply or acquisition of certain goods or services within a substantial part of the Common Market has been established, the next issue under Article 102 is whether an abuse or exploitation of that position has occurred. In *Commercial Solvents,* the Commission and the Court of Justice found abuse in the activities of the only producer in the world of aminobutanol, a chemical used in the making of the drug ethambutol. Commercial Solvents, a U.S. corporation, sold the chemical in Italy to its subsidiary, Istituto Chemioterapico, which in turn sold it to Zoja, an Italian firm making the drug. After merger negotiations between Istituto and Zoja broke off, Zoja sought but failed to get supplies of the chemical from Istituto.

Upon receiving a complaint from Zoja, the Commission commenced Article 102 infringement proceedings. It eventually held that the refusal to deal of Commercial Solvents and Istituto (viewed

---

[74] Re European Sugar Cartel (1975) Eur.Comm.Rep. 1663.

[75] Parke, Davis v. Probel and Centrafarm (1968) Eur.Comm.Rep. 55; Sirena v. Eda GMBH (1971) Eur.Comm.Rep. 69. But see Radio Telefis Eireann v. Commission (Magill TV Guide), 4 Common Mkt.L.Rep. 586 (1991).

[76] Commercial Solvents Corp. v. Commission (1973) 12 Common Mkt.L.Rev. D50 (Commission); (1974) Eur.Comm.Rep. 223 (Court of Justice).

as one enterprise) amounted to an abuse. Commercial Solvents, through its Italian subsidiary, was ordered to promptly make supplies of aminobutanol available to Zoja at a price no higher than the maximum which it normally charged.[77]

In *Re GEMA*, the only German authors' and composers' rights licensing society was in possession of a dominant position within a substantial part of the Common Market. This dominant position was reinforced by agreements with other societies in Europe granting exclusive rights to the various national markets. The societies were extremely advantageous and profitable to recording artists who otherwise faced formidable, if not impossible, tasks of distributing rights to their copyrighted goods on an individual basis to record manufacturers and other users. These commercial realities reinforced the Commission's conclusion that GEMA's market position was a dominant one.

The Commission instituted Article 102 infringement proceedings *sua sponte*.[78] It decided that the imposition of higher license fees on importers of records and tape recorders, compared with fees imposed on German manufacturers, was restrictive of competition between them and therefore an abuse of GEMA's dominant position relative to its purchasers. GEMA similarly abused its dominant position by extending its members' copyrights to noncopyrighted works through a system of package license fees that failed to distinguish between copyrighted and noncopyrighted works. By discriminating through loyalty rebates between German users and users from different member states, GEMA abusively helped to prevent the establishment of a single common market for the supply of recording services. In other words, it also abused its market power concerning potential competitors.

GEMA's discrimination against foreign members regarding management positions and a supplementary benefits scheme also constituted abuses of its dominant position. Requirements imposed on members to assign their rights to GEMA for the whole world and all marketing categories were deemed unnecessary to its operation and fell into the same category. GEMA members were also abusively excluded, by their contract terms, from recourse to the courts in the event of disputes as to distribution of GEMA funds. By requiring a six-year term, by obliging assignment of all future works during that six-year period, and by establishing a lengthy period of waiting to be eligible for certain payments, GEMA abused its domi-

---

77 Id.

78 (1971) Common Mkt.L.Rep. D35; (1972) Common Mkt.L.Rep. 694

nant position through agreements with its supplier-members. By generally curtailing their mobility to join other societies in the Common Market, GEMA inhibited the process of economic integration and the creation of a single market for music publishers.

Many of the abuses found in *GEMA* do not fall under the examples provided by the Treaty terms of Article 102. From this survey of some of the abuses found, it should be apparent that once a dominant position is established the Commission feels free to roam the whole of the behavior of the dominant enterprise. Anticompetitive aspects of contractual and noncontractual relations between GEMA and its members, GEMA's constitution, its general commercial practices, and its relations with record manufacturers and users of rights were reviewed and subjected to the Commission's regulation. Another decision involves a French society of musical composers' rights.[79]

Hoffmann–La Roche, the large multinational Swiss firm, was fined for abusing its dominant position in seven vitamin markets in Europe. It used a network of exclusive or preferential supply contracts, along with loyalty rebates, to reinforce its dominance by cornering retail markets.[80] United Brands, a U.S. multinational, abused its dominant position in bananas through discriminatory, predatory and excessive pricing in various countries. Its abuses also extended to refusals to deal with important past customers and prohibiting the resale of bananas. Excessive pricing occurred when its banana prices bore little relation to the economic value of the bananas supplied.[81] This particular finding of the Commission however, was quashed on appeal by the Court of Justice. Taking into account the "high profits" involved, the Commission fined United Brands 1,000,000 EUROs. In the Commission's opinion, this was a "moderate" fine under the circumstances.

The Court of Justice has held that predatory pricing can constitute an abuse of a dominant position in violation of Article 102. Predatory pricing below average total cost (as well as below average variable cost) may be abusive if undertaken to eliminate a competitor. Regarding the former, pricing below average total cost could drive out competitors as efficient as the dominant firm but lacking

---

[79] See Greenwich Film Production, Paris v. SACEM (1979) Eur.Comm.Rep. 3275. See generally regarding copyright abuses, Radio Telefis Eireann v. Commission (Magill TV Guide), 4 Common Mkt.L.Rep. 586 (1991).

[80] Hoffmann–La Roche v. Commission (1979) Eur.Comm.Rep. 461.

[81] United Brands v. Commission (1976) Eur. Comm. Rep. 425 (1978) Eur.Comm.Rep. 207.

its extensive financial resources.[82] Abuses by Microsoft and Intel have recently led to staggering fines and penalties. These cases are discussed in Section 20.19.

§ 20.17 The Extraterritorial Reach of Articles 101 and 102

There is a question about the extent to which the competition rules of Europe extend to activity anywhere in the world, including activity occurring entirely or partly within the territorial limits of the United States, Mexico or Canada. Decisions by the Commission and the Court of Justice suggest that the territorial reach of Articles 101 and 102 is expanding and may extend to almost any international business transaction.

For an agreement to be incompatible with the Common Market and prohibited under Article 101(1), it must be "likely to affect trade between Member States" and have the object or effect of impairing "competition within the Common Market." Taken together, these requirements amount to an "effects test" for extraterritorial application of Article 101. This test is similar to that which operates under the Sherman Act of the United States.

The Court has repeatedly held that the fact that one of the parties to an agreement is domiciled in a third country does not preclude the applicability of Article 101(1). Swiss and British chemical companies, for example, argued that the Commission was not competent to impose competition law fines for acts committed in Switzerland and Britain (before joining the EU) by enterprises domiciled outside its scope even if the acts had effects within the Common Market.[83] Nevertheless, the Court held those companies in violation of Article 101 because they owned subsidiary companies within the Union and controlled their behavior. The foreign parent and its subsidiaries were treated as a "single enterprise" for purposes of service of process, judgment, and collection of fines and penalties. In doing so, the Court observed that the fact that a subsidiary company has its own legal personality does not rule out the possibility that its conduct is attributable to the parent company.

The Court has extended its reasoning to the extraterritorial application of Article 102. A United States parent company, for example, was held potentially liable for acquisitions by its subsidiary

82 Akzo Chemie BV v. Commission (1991) Eur.Comm.Rep. 3359 (Case C–62/86).

83 See ICI v. Commission (1972) Eur.Comm.Rep. 619.

which affected market conditions within the Common Market.[84] In another decision, the Court held that a Maryland company's refusal to sell its product to a competitor of its affiliate company was a result of united "single enterprise" action.[85] It proceeded to state that extraterritorial conduct merely having "repercussions on competitive structures" in the Common Market fell within the parameters of Article 102. The Court ordered Commercial Solvents, through its Italian affiliate, to supply the competitor at reasonable prices.

In 1988, the Court of Justice widened the extraterritorial reach of Article 101 in a case where wood pulp producers from the U.S., Canada, Sweden and Finland were fined for price fixing activities affecting Union trade and competition. These firms did not have substantial operations within Common Market; they were primarily exporters to it. This decision's utilization of a place of implementation "effects test" is quite similar to that used under the Sherman Act.[86] And the reliance by the U.S. exporters upon a traditional Webb–Pomerene export cartel exemption from United States antitrust law carried no weight in European law. The Court has also affirmed the extraterritorial reach of Articles 101 and 102 to airfares in and out of Europe.[87]

§ 20.18 United States Antitrust Cooperation Agreements

Some evidence of international antitrust cooperation is contained in a 1976 recommendation of the OECD which provides for notification of antitrust actions, exchanges of information to the extent that the disclosure is domestically permissible, and where practical, coordination of antitrust enforcement. The OECD resolution served as a model for the 1972 "Antitrust Notification and Consultation Procedure" between Canada and the United States, and the 1976 antitrust cooperation agreement with the Federal Republic of Germany. Following the "Uranium Cartel" litigation, Australia and the United States reached an Agreement on Cooperation in Antitrust Matters (1982) to minimize jurisdictional conflicts. Australia has taken the position that United States courts are not proper institutions to balance interests of concerned countries within the context of private antitrust litigation. The Agreement on Cooperation provides that when the Government of Australia is concerned

---

[84] See Europemballage Corp. and Continental Can Co., Inc. v. Commission (1973) Eur.Comm.Rep. 215.

[85] See Commercial Solvents Corp. v. Commission (1974) Eur.Comm.Rep. 223.

[86] Woodpulp Producers v. Commission (1988) Eur.Comm.Rep. 5193.

[87] Ahmed Saeed Flugreisen v. Zentrale zur Bekämpfung unlauteren Wettbewerbs (1989) Eur.Comm.Rep. 838.

with private antitrust proceedings pending in a United States court, the Government of Australia may request the Government of the United States to participate in the litigation. The United States must report to the court on the substance and outcome of consultations with Australia on the matter concerned. In this way Australia's views and interests in the litigation and its potential outcome are made known to the court. The court is not required to defer to those views, or even to openly consider them. It merely receives the "report." Australia, in turn, has indicated a willingness to be more receptive to discovery requests in United States antitrust litigation and to consult before invoking its blocking statute.

Similar arrangements have been made in the Memorandum of Understanding Between the U.S. and Canada With Respect to the Application of National Antitrust Laws (1984) and more generally in the context of NAFTA. No such agreement has been reached with the United Kingdom, with whom the extraterritoriality issue remains contentious, a fact which has led some to wonder whether the United States ought to have its own blocking statute against extraterritorial European competition law.

The International Antitrust Enforcement Assistance Act of 1994 (P.L. 103–438) authorizes mutual assistance agreements between the DOJ and FTC and their foreign counterparts. Such assistance includes the disclosure and sharing of evidence. The first International Antitrust Enforcement Assistance Agreement was completed between Australia and the United States in 1997. Its focus is on mutual assistance for criminal investigations. The agreement is especially notable in light of a 1997 decision of the First Circuit Court of Appeals that the Sherman Act applies criminally to foreign companies (in this case, Nippon Paper Industries). Additional antitrust cooperation agreements were negotiated with Israel, Japan and Brazil in 1999, and Mexico in 2000.

In August of 1995, the United States and Canada signed an antitrust and deceptive practices cooperation agreement, followed by a "comity" agreement in 2004 not unlike that between the EU and the United States (see below).

§ 20.19 United States–European Antitrust Cooperation

In 1991 the European Community (of which Britain is still a member) and the United States reached an antitrust cooperation agreement. This accord commits the parties to notify each other of imminent enforcement action, to share relevant information and consult on potential policy changes. It was prominently used in 1994 to jointly settle charges of restrictive trade practices with the Microsoft Corporation. An innovative feature is the inclusion of "comity" principles, each side promising to take the other's interests into account when considering antitrust prosecutions. Since the Commission has traditionally permitted U.S. lawyers to appear before it on competition law matters, the FTC announced on the same day as the signing of the antitrust cooperation agreement that European lawyers would be permitted to appear before it on a reciprocal basis.

The agreement has had a significant effect on mergers of firms doing business in North America and Europe. Each side has agreed to notify and consult with the other regarding antitrust matters, including mergers and acquisitions, that "may affect important interests." In its first six months of operation, about 45 notifications were exchanged between the Commission, the U.S. Federal Trade Commission, and the Antitrust Division of the U.S. Justice Department. A large portion of these notifications concerned international mergers and acquisitions. Since both Europe and the U.S. have premerger notification systems, the exchange of such information has increased rapidly. In the first year after the cooperation agreement, U.S. antitrust enforcers sent 37 such notifications to the European Commission and received 15 in return. About 20 percent of all the mergers reviewed by the Commission under its competition law were simultaneously being reviewed by U.S. antitrust authorities. See Chapter 26 for a more extensive treatment of EU mergers regulation and its impact on U.S. firms.

In April of 1997 the Justice Department made its first "positive comity" request to the European Commission under the U.S.–E.U. Antitrust Cooperation Agreement. The Justice Department has asked the Commission to investigate alleged anticompetitive conduct by European airlines regarding U.S.-based airline computer reservation systems (CRS). In 1998, the European Union and the United States signed a "Positive Comity Agreement." This agreement reinforces the 1991 Cooperation Agreement by establishing procedures for positive comity requests and responses, including parallel investigations such as against Microsoft. The Agreement can be found at *www.usdoj.gov*.

In the more recent round of public prosecutions of Microsoft focused on Windows as a monopoly, the United States settlement reached in 2001 is less demanding than the Commission abuse of a dominant position judgment of 2004, which requires an unbundling of media playback capabilities. This example reaffirms that transatlantic antitrust "cooperation" need not necessarily result in similar outcomes. In 2007, the Court of First Instance (now the General Court) broadly confirmed the Commission's 2004 decision. Shortly thereafter, Microsoft settled the prosecution by altering its operating systems' licensing arrangements to favor "open source" software developers (e.g., Linux). Prior to settlement, Microsoft had been fined, including daily noncompliance penalties, in excess of 2 billion EUROs. By 2008, the Commission was investigating Microsoft's bundling of its web browser with Windows, and the compatibility of its Office software with rival programs. Other U.S. technology firms are also under the EU competition law microscope: Qualcomm, Intel, Google and Apple included. In 2009, the Commission fined Intel a massive 1.06 billion EUROs for abusing its dominant position in microprocessors for PCs. Intel's price discounts and loyalty rebates were the center of this judgment.

Chapter 21

FREE TRADE AGREEMENTS AND CUSTOMS UNIONS, NAFTA IN OUTLINE

Table of Sections

---

§ 21.1 Introduction

There is a massive movement towards free trade agreements and customs unions throughout the world, though not often of the consequence of that occurring in Europe and North America. Some of these developments are a competitive by-product of European and North American integration. Others simply reflect the desire (but not always the political will) to capture the economic gains and international negotiating strength that such economic relations can bring. This is particularly true of attempts at free trade and customs unions in the developing world. The explosion of such agreements creates systemic risks for the World Trade Organization. It reports that nearly all of its members are partners in one or more regional or bilateral trade agreements. Here is a sampling of such agreements: Hong Kong–China, Japan–Singapore, Russia–CIS states, New Zealand–China, Mexico–Israel, Canada–Peru, EU–South Africa, Chile–South Korea, the South Asian Free Trade Area (India, Pakistan, Bangladesh, Nepal, Bhutan, Sri Lanka) . . . and the list goes on. One reason for this proliferation of free trade and customs union agreements may be doubts about the prospects of success for the Doha Round of WTO negotiations. Over half of all world trade now occurs under free trade agreements.

There is a continuum of sorts, a range of options to be considered when nations contemplate economic integration. In "free trade areas," tariffs, quotas, and other barriers to trade among participating states are reduced or removed while individual national trade barriers vis-à-vis third party states are retained. "Customs unions" not only remove trade barriers among participating states, but they also create common trade barriers for all participating states as regards third-party states. "Common markets" go further than customs unions by providing for the free movement of factors of production (capital, labor, enterprise, technology) among participating states.

"Economic communities" build on common markets by introducing some harmonization of basic national policies related to the economy of the community, e.g. transport, taxation, corporate behavior and structure, monetary matters and regional growth. Finally, "economic unions" embrace a more or less complete harmonization of national policies related to the economy of the union, e.g. company laws, commercial treaties, social welfare, currencies, and government subsidies. The difference between an economic community and an economic union relates only to the number and importance of harmonized national policies.

All such agreements are inherently discriminatory in their trade impact. As nonuniversalized trade preferences, they tend to simultaneously *create trade* among participating states and *divert trade* between those states and the rest of the world. Thus, while trade creation may represent an improvement in the allocation of scarce world resources, trade diversion may generate an opposite result.

With free trade agreements, diversionary trade effects are usually not distinct because of the absence of a common trade wall against outsiders. Trade diversion nonetheless occurs. "Rules of origin" in free trade area agreements keep third-party imports from seeking the lowest tariff or highest quota state and then exploiting the trade advantages within a free trade area. Under rules of origin, free trade areas are "free" only for goods substantially originating therein. This causes member state goods to be preferred over goods from other states. Rules of origin under a free trade agreement can be as trade diversionary as common external tariffs in customs unions.

§ 21.2 GATT Article 24

Article 24 of the GATT (1947 and 1994) attempts to manage these internal trade-creating and external trade-diverting effects. Free trade area and custom union proposals must run the gauntlet of a formal GATT/WTO review procedure during which "binding" recommendations are possible to bring the proposals into conformity. Such recommendations might deal with Article 24 requirements for the elimination of internal tariffs and other restrictive regulations of commerce on "substantially all" products originating in a customs union or free trade area. Or they might deal with Article 24 requirements that common external tariffs not be "on the whole higher or more restrictive" in effect than the general incidence of prior existing national tariffs. The broad purpose of Article 24, acknowledged therein, is to facilitate trade among the GATT contracting parties and not to raise trade barriers.

It is through this review mechanism that most free trade and customs union agreements have passed *without* substantial modification. The GATT, not economic agreements, most often has given way. For example, during GATT review of the 1957 Treaty of Rome creating what we now call the European Union, many "violations" of the letter and spirit of Article 24 were cited. The derivation of the common external tariff by arithmetically averaging existing national tariffs was challenged as more restrictive of trade than previous arrangements. Such averaging on a given product fails to take account of differing national import volumes. If a product was faced originally with a lower than average national tariff and a larger than average national demand, the new average tariff is clearly more "restrictive" of imports than before. Averaging in high tariffs of countries of low demand quite plausibly created more restrictions on third-party trade. If so, the letter and spirit of Article 24 were breached.

Despite these and other arguments, the Treaty of Rome passed through GATT study and review committees without final resolution of its legal status under Article 24. Postponement of these issues became permanent. GATT attempts—through the lawyer-like conditions of Article 24 to maximize trade creation and minimize trade diversion—must be seen as generally inadequate. Treaty terms became negotiable demands that were not accepted. Decades later, the ineffectiveness of GATT/WTO supervision of free trade and customs union agreements continues. At best Article 24 exerts a marginal influence over their contents. Whether the extraordinary proliferation of preferential agreements undermines or supports WTO trade policies is hotly debated.

§ 21.3 GATS Integrated Services Agreements

Since 1995 "economic integration agreements" (EIAs) covering services are permitted under Article 5 of the General Agreement on Trade in Services (GATS). Such agreements, which can be staged, must have "substantial sectoral coverage," eliminate "substantially" all discrimination in sectors subject to multilateral commitments, and not raise the "overall" level of barriers to trade in GATS services compared to before the EIA. EIAs involving developing nations are to be accorded "flexibility." Like GATT Article 24 customs unions, there is an Article 5 duty to compensate EIA nonparticipants.

Review of GATS Article 5 notifications is undertaken, when requested by the WTO Council for Trade in Services, by the Committee on Regional Trade Agreements. Thus, whereas CRTA examinations of GATT Article 24 agreements are required, such examinations are optional under GATS. Nevertheless, numerous Article 5 examinations have been conducted, including notably the services components of NAFTA, the EEC Treaty (1957) and EU Enlargement (2004), Japan's FTAs with Singapore, Mexico and Malaysia, China's FTAs with Hong Kong and Macau, and various U.S. bilaterals. None of these examinations have resulted in a final report on consistency with GATS Article 5. This pattern continues the GATT/WTO record of regulatory failure regarding economic integration agreements.

§ 21.4 Developing World Integration

Developing nations in Africa, the Caribbean, Central America, South America and Southeast Asia (among others) had free trade and customs union agreements in place as early as the 1960s. In 1979, under what is commonly called the Enabling Clause, the GATT parties decided to permit developing nations to enter into differential and more favorable bilateral, regional or global arrangements among themselves to reduce or eliminate tariffs and nontariff barriers applicable to trade in goods. Like Article 24, the Enabling Clause constitutes an exception to MFN trade principles. It has generally been construed to authorize third world free trade area and customs union agreements. Whether the Enabling Clause was intended to take such agreements out of Article 24 and its requirements, or be construed in conjunction therewith, is unclear. However, the creation of alternative notification and review procedures for Enabling Clause arrangements suggests Article 24 is inapplicable.

Notification to GATT of Enabling Clause arrangements is mandatory. Since 1995, the WTO Committee on Trade and Development (CTD) is the forum where such notifications are reviewed, but in practice not examined in depth. Enabling Clause arrangements should be designed to promote the trade of developing countries and not raise external trade barriers or undue trade difficulties. Consultations with individual GATT members experiencing such difficulties must be undertaken, and these consultations may be expanded to all GATT members if requested. Unlike GATT Article 24 and GATS Article 5, neither compensation to nonparticipants nor formal reporting on the consistency with the Enabling Clause of developing nation arrangements is anticipated. The ASEAN–China (2004), India–Sri Lanka (2002), and "revived" Economic Community of West African States (ECOWAS 2005) agreements illustrate notified but unexamined preferential arrangements sheltered by the Enabling Clause.

Africa

Several groups have been formed in Africa. In 1966 the central African countries of Cameroon, Central African Republic, Chad, Congo (Brazzaville) and Gabon formed the Economic and Customs Union of Central Africa (Union Douaniere et Économique de l'Afrique Centrale: UDEAC) to establish a common customs and tariff approach toward the rest of the world and to formulate a common foreign investment code. Implementation has proceeded very slowly. In 1967 Kenya, Tanzania and Uganda created the East African Community (EAC) in an attempt to harmonize customs and tariff practices among themselves and in relation to other countries. The practical effect of that Community has frequently been negated by political strife. In 1974 six French speaking West African nations formed the West African Economic Community (known by its French initials CEAO). This Community is a sub-group within and pacesetter for ECOWAS, the Economic Community of West African States.

ECOWAS was created in 1975 by Dahomey, Gambia, Ghana, Guinea, Guinea–Bissau, Ivory Coast, Liberia, Mali, Mauritania, Niger, Nigeria, Senegal, Sierra Leone, Togo and Upper Volta to coordinate economic development and cooperation. Some progress on liberalized industrial trade has been made and a Cooperation, Compensation and Development Fund established. During the 1980s the pace of regionalization quickened. ECOWAS countries agreed upon formulative policies for the Community, especially regarding air transport, communications, agriculture, freedom of movement between Member States, currency convertibility, and a common currency. ECOWAS (now the West African Economic and Monetary Union, WAEMU)and CARICOM have agreed upon policies and programs for mutual promotion of inter-Community trade. In June of 1991, the Organization of African Unity (OAU) member states agreed to a Treaty Establishing the African Economic Community. This wide-ranging Treaty embraces 51 African nations, and includes a regional Court of Justice. In September of 1995, 12 southern African countries, with South Africa under Mandela participating for the first time, targeted free trade under the Southern African Development Community. A 20–member Common Market for Eastern and Southern Africa (COMESA) has also been announced.

Islamic World

Bahrain, Kuwait, Oman, Qatar, Saudi Arabia, and United Arab Emirates have formed the Gulf Cooperation Council (GCC) with objectives to establish freedom of movement, a regional armaments industry, common banking and financial systems, a unified currency policy, a customs union, a common foreign aid program, and a joint, international investment company, the Gulf Investment Corporation (capitalized in 1984 at two and one-half billion dollars). The Council has already implemented trade and investment rules concerning tariffs on regional and imported goods, government contracts, communications, transportation, real estate investment, and freedom of movement of professionals. Progress has been made on a Uniform Commercial Code and a Commission for Commercial Arbitration of the Gulf states. In 1987, the GCC entered into negotiations with the EU which resulted in a major 1990 trade and cooperation agreement. In 2003, the non-Arab states of Iran, Pakistan, Turkey, Afghanistan and five Central Asian nations joined together in an Economic Cooperation Organization Trade Agreement (ECOTA). In 2004, Jordan, Egypt, Tunisia and Morocco concluded their Agadir free trade agreement.

Latin America and Caribbean

Other regional groups have been established in Latin America and the Caribbean. Since 1973, the Caribbean countries of Barbados, Belize, Dominica, Jamaica, Trinidad–Tobago, Grenada, St. Kitts–Nevis–Anguilla, St. Lucia, and St. Vincent have participated in the Caribbean Community (CARICOM), an outgrowth of the earlier Caribbean Free Trade Association. In 1958 Costa Rica, El Salvador, Guatemala, Honduras and Nicaragua formed the Central American Common Market (CACM), another victim of political strife, but still functioning in a limited way. Numerous countries in Latin America were members of the Latin American Free Trade Association (LAFTA) (1961) which had small success in reducing tariffs and developing the region through cooperative industrial sector programs. These programs allocated industrial production among the participating states.

The Grand Anse Declaration commits CARICOM to establishment of its own common market. The Latin American Integration Association (LAIA) (1981), the eleven member successor to LAFTA, is continuing arrangements for intra-community tariff concessions. They agreed to a 50 percent tariff cut on LAIA goods. Antigua, Dominica, Grenada, Montserrat, St. Kitts–Nevis, St. Lucia, St. Vincent and the Grenadines have formed the Organization of Eastern Caribbean States (OECS) in part "to establish common institutions which could serve to increase their bargaining power as regards third countries or groupings of countries". Some 37 nations signed the Association of Caribbean States agreement in 1994 with long-term economic integration goals.

Latin America became a central focus in the 1990s of economic integration. Mexico not only has a free trade agreement with the United States and Canada, it has also agreed to free trade with Colombia, Venezuela, Chile, Bolivia, Costa Rica, Nicaragua, Guatemala, Honduras, El Salvador, Peru and Uruguay. It has even negotiated free trade agreements with the European Union and EFTA (European Free Trade Assn). Argentina, Brazil, Paraguay and Uruguay signed a treaty establishing the MERCOSUR (Southern Cone) common market in March of 1991 and Chile and Bolivia joined them as Associates in 1996. Venezuela under Chavez finally obtained membership in 2012. All of this activity occurs against the background of the Free Trade Area of the Americas (FTAA) initiative of Presidents Clinton and George W. Bush.

ANCOM ("The Cartegena Agreement") was founded by Bolivia, Chile, Colombia, Ecuador, and Peru in 1969 primarily to counter the economic power of Argentina, Brazil and Mexico and to reduce dependency upon foreign capital and technology. Its Decision No. 24 regulating foreign investment and technology transfers was widely copied during the 1970s. A major boost came in 1973 with the addition of Venezuela, but some of the fragile dynamics of the regional grouping are illustrated by Chile's withdrawal in 1977, Bolivia's withdrawal in 1981 and resumption of membership barely four months later, and Peru's economic (but not political) withdrawal in 1991 and return in 1996. In 2003 the ANCOM and MERCOSUR groups nominally agreed upon free trade, at least partly to counterbalance United States power in the FTAA negotiations. The United States, pursuing in turn a divide and conquer strategy, has been negotiating bilateral free trade agreements with all ANCOM members save Venezuela.

§ 21.5 The Association of Southeast Asian Nations (ASEAN)

Some interesting moves toward third world free trade and rulemaking have been taken by the Association of Southeast Asian Nations (ASEAN). Its problems, failures and successes are representative of third world attempts at legal and economic integration. ASEAN has its genesis in the 1967 Bangkok Declaration, with common trade rules in various states of growth, implementation and retrenchment. ASEAN has internal tariff preferences, industrial development projects, "complementation schemes," and regional joint ventures, all discussed below.

An important juncture in the integration process is the point in time at which member countries of a regional group accept a supranational mechanism for enforcing the regime's law irrespective of national feelings and domestic law within a member country. The 1957 Treaty of Rome provided for a supranational European Court of Justice, which decided quickly upon a mandatory enforcement stance regarding national (Member State) compliance with regional law. ASEAN does not have a comparable enforcement mechanism. A vigorous administrator can also make regional law a reality. In Europe, the Commission frequently issues regulations and decisions which are binding within the territories of Member States. These rules are enforced through fines and penalties, and ultimately by the Court of Justice and European Court of First Instance. Violations are investigated and, if necessary, prosecuted by the Commission. In contrast, the ASEAN Secretary–General once remarked that ASEAN's Secretariat was "a postman collecting and distributing letters." The surrender of national sovereignty to ASEAN institutions has been a painfully slow process. That said, NAFTA provides an alternative example of achieving free trade without significantly surrendering national sovereignty to regional institutions.

ASEAN was formed in 1967 by Indonesia, Malaysia, the Philippines, Singapore and Thailand. Brunei joined in 1984, Vietnam in 1995. Laos and Myanmar(Burma) joined in 1997, and more recently Kampuchea (Cambodia) became a member. Rarely have such culturally, linguistically and geographically diverse nations attempted integration. The Bangkok Declaration establishing ASEAN as a co-operative association is a broadly worded document. Later proposals were made for a formal ASEAN treaty or convention, but were rejected as unnecessary. The Bangkok Declaration sets forth numerous regional, economic, cultural and social goals, including acceleration of economic growth, trade expansion and industrial collaboration.

The Bangkok Declaration establishes several mechanisms, but little supranational legal machinery, to implement its stated goals. An annual ASEAN Meeting of Foreign Ministers is scheduled on a rotational basis among the Member States. Special meetings are held "as required". The Declaration provides for a Standing Committee composed of the Foreign Minister of the State in which the next annual Ministerial Meeting is to be held, and includes the ambassadors of other ASEAN States accredited to that State. The Declaration also provides for "Ad Hoc Committees and Permanent Committees of specialists and officials on specific subjects". Each Member State is charged to set up a National Secretariat to administer ASEAN affairs within that Member State and to work with the Ministerial Meeting and the Standing Committee.

There have been relatively infrequent meetings of the ASEAN heads of government. This contrasts with the semiannual European "summits" that have kept that group moving forward along the path of integration. The third ASEAN summit was held in Manila in 1987. This summit produced an agreement for the promotion and protection of investments by ASEAN investors (national and most-favored-nation treatment rights are created), made revisions to the basic ASEAN joint venture agreement, and continued the gradual extension of regional tariff and nontariff trade preferences. Goods already covered by the ASEAN tariff scheme were given a 50 percent margin of preference. New items received a 25 percent preferential margin. The nontariff preferences generally co-opt GATT rules, e.g. regarding technical standards and customs valuation.

The fourth ASEAN summit in 1992 committed the parties to the creation of a free trade area within 15 years. Five years were cut from this schedule by agreement in 1994, but operational reality has eluded ASEAN free trade. In 2003, a "watershed" date for complete integration in an ASEAN Economic Community targeted

2020. In 2007, this target date was changed to 2015, a reflection of the fear that ASEAN risks being overwhelmed by the powerhouse economies of China, India and Japan.

§ 21.6 East Asian Integration

East Asia, ranging from Japan in the North to Indonesia in the South, enjoyed truly remarkable economic growth during the 1980s and 1990s. When the Asian financial crisis hit in 1997–98, the region took it on the chin economically, but bounced back quickly. United States and other foreign investors participated in this growth largely on a country-by-country basis. All signs are that rapid growth, especially in China, will continue.

East Asia, unlike Europe or NAFTA, has not developed a formal agreement with uniform trade, licensing and investment rules. Only recently has the APEC (Asia–Pacific Economic Cooperation) group even begun to address this idea. The APEC group is comprised of Asia–Pacific nations including the United States. Late in 1994 the APEC nations targeted free trade and investment for industrial countries by 2010 and developing countries by 2020. Nine industries have been selected for initial trade liberalization efforts.

With the European Union and the North American Free Trade Area maturing rapidly, one provocative question is the future of Japan. It is not in the interests of any nation that Japan should feel economically isolated or threatened. Yet it is hard to imagine incorporating Japan into the NAFTA, though some have suggested this. To some degree, what appears to be happening is that regional integration in East Asia is growing along lines that follow Japanese investment and economic aid decisions. Japan now has "economic cooperation" agreements with ASEAN, Thailand, Malaysia, the Philippines, Indonesia, Vietnam, Switzerland, India and Brunei.

The role of China in all of this is critical. China and Japan are clearly rivals for economic leadership of the region. China is pushing for influence in the East Asian economic sphere. Hong Kong's return in 1997 and Macau in 1999 moved in this direction. China is cultivating trade and investment relations with Singapore, South Korea, Taiwan and, to a lesser extent, Japan. China also has free trade deals with Hong Kong, Chile, Costa Rica, Peru, Singapore, Pakistan, New Zealand and others. ASEAN and China have a free trade agreement, achieved before that of Japan. Some commentators foresee, as a practical matter, the emergence of a powerful Southern China coastal economic zone embracing Hong Kong, Taiwan, Guangdong and Fujian.

§ 21.7 Getting to NAFTA

The United States has entered into a growing number of major free trade agreements. The first was with Israel, enacted through the United States–Israel Free Trade Area Implementation Act of 1985.[1] The Israeli–U.S. Agreement (IFTA) was fully implemented by January 1, 1995. The second was with Canada, and this agreement was adopted through the United States–Canada Free Trade Area Agreement Implementation Act of 1988.[2] The Canada–U.S. Agreement (CUFTA) was fully implemented by January 1, 1998. The United States negotiated along with Canada and Mexico a three-way North American Free Trade Area Agreement (NAFTA). The NAFTA took effect January 1, 1994 with full implementation in nearly all areas by the year 2003. NAFTA was incorporated into United States law by the North American Free Trade Agreement Implementation Act of 1993.[3]

Late in 2001, Jordan and the United States agreed on free trade. In 2003, the United States reached free trade agreements with Chile and Singapore, notably incorporating coverage of E–Commerce and digital products. Early in 2004, free trade between the United States and five Central American states (CAFTA) plus the Dominican Republic, and with Australia and Morocco, was agreed. More bilateral free trade deals have been struck with Bahrain, Oman and Peru, and additional agreements with Panama, Colombia and South Korea took effect in 2012. These trade agreements provide new duty free import opportunities into the U.S. market. Unlike the Generalized System of Preferences (GSP) program and the Caribbean Basin Initiative,[4] these agreements are reciprocal. That is to say they open up foreign markets to United States exports on a duty free basis. In addition, they establish detailed rules targeting nontariff trade barriers (NTBs) among the parties.

The evolutionary character of the free trade agreements of the United States is readily apparent. The first agreement in 1985 with Israel is noticeably narrower in scope and level of legal detail that in 1994 with Canada and Mexico on NAFTA. And the second with Canada in 1989 was nothing less than path breaking; the most sophisticated free trade agreement in the world. Yet, for full understanding, each agreement must be viewed in its own geopolitical

---

1 Public Law 99–47, 98 Stat. 3013, June 11, 1985.

2 Public Law 100–449, 102 Stat. 1851, 19 U.S.C.A. § 2112 Note.

3 Public Law 103–182, 107 Stat. 2057.

4 See Chapter 10.

and economic context. The economic integration of Canada and the United States was a certainty. The blueprint was already there. For most Canadians and Americans, revising the design to include Mexico required considerably more effort and discomfort. The discomfort came from years of observing protectionist Mexican trade policies, uncontrolled national debt, corruption, and the sense, somehow, that Mexico just did not "fit." In the end, these perspectives were overcome.

Mexico under Presidents de la Madrid, Salinas, Zedillo, and Fox had been unobtrusively breaking down its trade barriers and reducing the role of government in its economy. More than half of the enterprises owned by the Mexican government a decade ago have been sold to private investors, and more are on the auction block. Tariffs have been slashed to a maximum of 20 percent and import licensing requirements widely removed. Export promotion, not import substitution, became the highest priority. Like the U.S. and Canada, Mexico (since 1986) participates in the General Agreement on Tariffs and Trade (GATT) and World Trade Organization (WTO). This brings it into the mainstream of the world trading community on a wide range of fronts, including participation in nearly the full range of the Uruguay Round agreements.

Mexican debt, hopefully, promises to become a manageable problem, although the collapse of the peso in 1994 and its slide in 2008/09 cast doubt on this. One party rule has ended nationally and in several states, with signs of an ever more pluralistic democracy on the horizon. Admittedly, political and economic corruption still runs deep within Mexico, but the winds of change are blowing. Major prosecutions of leading police, union and business leaders are underway. Perhaps most significantly, the rapid privatization of the state-owned sector of the economy combined with increasing tolerance of international competition has reduced not only the need for government subsidies but also the opportunity for personal enrichment by public officials.

Presidents Bush and Salinas, and Prime Minister Mulroney, pushed hard in 1991 to open "fast track" negotiations for a free trade agreement. In 1992, these efforts reached fruition when a NAFTA agreement was signed by Canada, the United States and Mexico with a scheduled effective date of Jan. 1, 1994. President Bush submitted the agreement to Congress in December 1992. President Clinton supported NAFTA generally, but initiated negotiations upon taking office for supplemental agreements on the environment and labor. This delayed consideration of the NAFTA agreement in Congress until the Fall of 1993. Ratification was considered under fast track procedures which essentially gave Congress 90 session days to either ratify or reject NAFTA without amendments. After a bruising national debate that fractured both Democrats and Republicans with each party doing its best to avoid Ross Perot's strident anti-NAFTA attacks, ratification was achieved in mid-November, just weeks before NAFTA's effective date. During this same period, Canada's Conservative Party suffered a devastating defeat at the polls. This defeat was partly a rejection by the Canadian people of the earlier ratification of NAFTA under Prime Minister Mulroney.

The United States is Mexico's largest trading partner, accounting for nearly 70 percent of all Mexican trade and more than 60 percent of its foreign direct investment. In contrast, trade with Mexico in 1994 totaled only 7 percent of all U.S. international trade. Those facts help explain why Mexico has been the major beneficiary of the NAFTA accord.

§ 21.8 The NAFTA Agreement in Outline—Goods

Although each partner affirmed its rights and obligations under the General Agreement on Tariffs and Trade (GATT), the NAFTA generally takes priority over other international agreements in the event of conflict. The NAFTA, for example, prevailed over the former Multi–Fiber Arrangement on trade in textiles. Certain exceptions to this general rule of supremacy apply; the trade provisions of the international agreements on endangered species, ozone-depletion and hazardous wastes notably take precedence over the NAFTA (subject to a duty to minimize conflicts). Unlike the GATT, the NAFTA makes a general duty of national treatment binding on all states, provinces and local governments of the three countries.

Prior to NAFTA, Mexican tariffs on U.S. goods averaged about 10 percent; U.S. tariffs on Mexican imports averaged about 5 percent. Under NAFTA, Mexican tariffs will be eliminated on all U.S. exports within ten years except for corn and beans which are subject to a fifteen-year transition. United States tariffs on peanuts, sugar and orange juice from Mexico will also last 15 years. Immediate Mexican tariff removals under the "A" list covered about half the industrial products exported from the United States. Further tariff eliminations were made for the "B" list after 5 years, and will occur for the "C" list when the treaty matures in ten years. Accelerated tariff reduction may occur by bilateral accord. The existing Canada–U.S. tariff reduction schedule remained in place.

NAFTA trade is subject to "rules of origin" that determine which goods qualify for its tariff preferences. These include goods wholly originating in the free trade area. A general waiver of the NAFTA rules of origin requirements is granted if their non-regional value consists of no more than 7 percent of the price or total cost of the goods. Goods containing non-regional materials are considered North American if those materials are sufficiently transformed so as to undergo a specific change in tariff classification. Some goods, like autos and light trucks, must also have a specified North American content. Ultimately, 62.50 percent of the value of such vehicles must be North American in origin. A 60 percent regional content rule will apply to other vehicles and auto parts. After 10 years, U.S. auto producers will no longer need to manufacture in Mexico in order to sell there.

Regional value may be calculated in most cases either by a "transaction value" or a "net cost" method. The former avoids costly accountings. The latter is based upon the total cost of the goods less royalties, sales promotion, packing and shipping, and allowable interest. Either requires manufacturers to trace the source of non-NAFTA components and maintain source records. The net cost method must be used for regional value calculations concerning automotive goods. Uniformity of tariff classification and origin decisions is promoted by NAFTA regulations, a common Certificate of Origin, and a trilateral working group.

Special rules of origin apply to free trade in textiles and apparel under NAFTA. For most products, a "yarn forward" rule applies. This means that the goods must be produced from yarn made in a NAFTA country. A similar "fiber forward" rule applies to cotton and man-made fiber yarns. Silk, linen and certain other fabrics in short supply within NAFTA are treated preferentially, as are yarns, fabrics and apparel covered by special tariff rate quotas. Safeguard import quotas and tariffs may be imposed during the transition period if a rise in textile and apparel trade causes serious damage. Other special rules of origin have been created for electronics. For example, if the circuit board (motherboard) is made in North America and transformed in the region so as to change a tariff classification, the resulting computer may be freely traded.

Import and export quotas, licenses and other restrictions are gradually being eliminated under NAFTA subject to limited rights to restrain trade, e.g. to protect human, animal or plant health, or to protect the environment. Customs user fees on internal NAFTA trade were eliminated in 1999 and existing tariff drawback refunds or waivers were removed by January 1, 2001. These changes, it is thought, will discourage the creation of "export platforms" in one NAFTA country to serve markets in the other member states by insuring that non-NAFTA components and materials are tariffed. NAFTA essentially phased out maquiladora tariff preferences over 7 years, notably disadvantaging producers who source heavily outside North America.

Export taxes and new waivers of customs duties are banned with few exceptions. Once goods are freely traded under NAFTA, they are subject to nondiscriminatory national treatment, including at the provincial and state levels of government. Goods sent to another NAFTA country for repair or alteration may return duty free.

Distinct rules govern energy and petrochemical products. Perhaps most notably, Mexico reserved to its state (as its Constitution provides) the oil, gas, refining, basic petrochemical, nuclear and electricity sectors. A limited range of new investment opportunities were created for non-basic petrochemicals, proprietary electricity facilities, co-generation and independent power production. As under the GATT, minimum or maximum import or export price controls are prohibited on energy products, but licensing systems may be used. Trade quotas or other restraints are permissible only in limited circumstances, e.g. short supply conditions, and a general duty of national treatment applies. Mexico, unlike Canada, has not committed itself to energy sharing during times of shortage.

A second set of distinct rules apply to agricultural trade. These are undertaken principally through separate bilateral agreements between the U.S. and Mexico and Canada and Mexico. The United States–Mexico agreement converts all nontariff trade barriers to tariffs or tariff rate quotas. These will be phased out over a maximum of 15 years. Roughly half of the bilateral trade in agriculture was made duty-free immediately. Under special rules, trade in sugar will be gradually liberalized with all restraints removed over 15 years. Safeguard tariff action may be undertaken during the first 10 years when designated "trigger" levels of agriculture imports are reached. All three countries have agreed to combat agricultural export subsidies, including consultation and what amounts to joint action against third-country subsidies affecting any one of their markets. Special rules of origin apply in the agricultural sector and standards on pesticide residues and inspections are being harmonized.

Another food-related issue is sanitary and phytosanitary measures against health, diseases, contaminants or additives (collectively known as SPS protection). Each country retains the right to establish its own SPS levels of protection provided they are based upon scientific principles and a risk assessment, apply only as needed and do not result in unfair discrimination or disguised restrictions on trade. Each NAFTA nation is committed to accepting the SPS measures of the others as equivalent to its own provided the exporting country demonstrates that its measures achieve the importing country's chosen level of protection. This is facilitated by procedural transparency rules requiring public notice of any SPS measure that may affect NAFTA trade. A committee on SPS measures strives to facilitate all of these principles and to resolve disputes.

Technical standards and certification procedures for products are classic nontariff trade barriers. The NAFTA reaffirmed each country's commitment to the GATT Agreement on Technical Barriers to Trade (1979). In addition, each must provide national treatment and most favored nation treatment. As in the food products area, international standards are used whenever possible, but each country may have more stringent requirements. Procedural transparency rules and a committee on standards are also created. One innovation of note allows companies and other interested parties to participate directly in the development of new standards anywhere within NAFTA. All three countries have agreed not to lower existing environmental, health and safety standards and to attempt to "upwardly harmonize" them. States, provinces and localities can adopt more stringent requirements in these fields provided they are scientifically justifiable, transparent and applied equally to local and imported goods. All health, safety and environmental regulations must be necessary, represent the least trade restrictive way of achieving these goals, and based on scientific principles and risk assessment. Loans from the newly created North American Development Bank help finance the border cleanup by Mexico and the U.S.

Escape clause rules and procedures are generally applicable to United States–Mexico trade under the NAFTA. These permit temporary trade relief against import surges subject to a right of compensation in the exporting nation. During the 10–year transition period, escape clause relief may be undertaken as a result of NAFTA tariff reductions only once per product for a maximum in most cases of 3 years. The relief is the "snap-back" to pre-NAFTA tariffs. After the transition period, escape clause measures may only be undertaken by mutual consent. If a global escape clause proceeding is pursued by one NAFTA partner, the others must be excluded unless their exports account for a substantial share of the imports in question (top five suppliers) and contribute importantly to the serious injury or threat thereof (rate of growth of NAFTA imports must not be appreciably lower than total imports).

There are a variety of other areas of law impacted by the NAFTA accord. Government procurement, apart from defense and national security needs, generally follows nondiscriminatory principles on the supply of goods and services (including construction services) to federal governments. The threshold for the application of the NAFTA to such procurement is $50,000 U.S. for goods and services, and $6.5 million U.S. for construction services. When state enterprises (e.g. PEMEX and CFE), not agencies, are the buyers, thresholds of $250,000 U.S. and $8 million U.S. respectively apply. The use of offsets or other requirements for local purchases or suppliers are prohibited. Independent bid challenge mechanisms must be created by each member state and transparency in the bidding process promoted by timely release of information. These provisions are particularly important because Mexico, unlike Canada, is not a signatory to the GATT/WTO Procurement Code. They do not apply to state and local procurement.

§ 21.9 The NAFTA Agreement in Outline—Services

Cross-border trade in services is subject to national treatment, including no less favorable treatment than that most favorably given at federal, state or local levels. No member state may require that a service provider establish or maintain a residence, local office or branch in its country as a condition to cross-border provision of services. However, a general standstill on existing discriminatory or limiting laws affecting cross-border services has been adopted. Mutual recognition of professional licenses is encouraged (notably for legal consultants and engineers), but not made automatic. All citizenship or permanent residency requirements for professional licensing have been eliminated.

Additionally, a NAFTA country may deny the benefits of the rules on cross-border provision of services if their source is in reality a third country without substantial business activities within the free trade area. For transport services, these benefits may be denied if the services are provided with equipment that is not registered within a NAFTA nation. Most air, maritime, basic telecommunications and social services are not covered by these rules, nor are those that are subject to special treatment elsewhere in the NAFTA (e.g. procurement, financing and energy). Even so, the NAFTA considerably broadens the types of services covered by free trade principles: accounting, advertising, architecture, broadcasting, commercial education, construction, consulting, enhanced telecommunications, engineering, environmental science, health care, land transport, legal, publishing and tourism. Whereas the CUFTA allowed free trade in services only for those sectors that were positively listed in the agreement, the NAFTA adopts a broader "negative listing" approach. All services sectors are subject to free trade principles unless the NAFTA specifies otherwise.

Unlike CUSFTA, the NAFTA creates a timetable for the removal of barriers to cross-border land transport services and the establishment of compatible technical, environmental and safety standards. This extends to bus, trucking, port and rail services. It should eliminate the historic need to switch trailers to Mexican transporters at the border. Cross-border truck deliveries in the border states were supposed to come on line late in 1995, but U.S. concerns about the standards of Mexican carriers and (one suspects) Teamsters Union influence have delayed this result. After 6 years, truckers were supposed to be able to move freely anywhere within NAFTA. In 2001, Mexico prevailed in a NAFTA arbitration panel on truck access to the United States. President George W. Bush has indicated that the U.S. will comply. Bus services should have been totally free within 3 years, and 100 percent investment in Mexican truck and bus companies will be possible after 10 years. The bus services dispute may go to arbitration. Investment in port services was immediately opened. However, national restraints upon domestic cargo carriage (cabotage) are retained and the commitment to harmonize technical and safety laws was made subject to a 6–year "endeavor."

Public telecommunications networks and services must be opened on reasonable and nondiscriminatory terms for firms and individuals who need the networks to conduct business, such as intracorporate communications or so-called enhanced telecommunications and information services. This means that cellular phone, data transmission, earth stations, fax, electronic mail, overlay networks and paging systems are open to Canadian and American investors, many of whom have entered the Mexican market. Each NAFTA country must ensure reasonable access and use of leased private lines, terminal equipment attachments, private circuit interconnects, switching, signaling and processing functions and user-choice of operating protocols. Conditions on access and use may only be imposed to safeguard the public responsibilities of network operators or to protect technical network integrity. Rates for public telecommunications transport services should reflect economic costs and flat-rate pricing is required for leased circuits. However, cross-subsidization between public transport services is not prohibited, nor are monopoly providers of public networks or services. Such monopolies may not engage in anticompetitive conduct outside their monopoly areas with adverse affects on NAFTA nationals. Various rights of access to information on public networks and services are established, and the NAFTA limits the types of technical standards that can be imposed on the attachment of equipment to public networks.

§ 21.10 The NAFTA Agreement in Outline—Investment and Financial Services

Investment in the industrial and services sectors of the NAFTA nations is promoted through rules against nondiscriminatory and minimum standards of treatment that even benefit non-NAFTA investors with substantial business operations in a NAFTA nation. For example, an Asian or European subsidiary incorporated with substantial business operations in Canada will be treated as a Canadian investor for purposes of NAFTA. Investment, for these purposes, is broadly defined to cover virtually all forms of ownership and activity, including real estate, stocks, bonds, contracts and technologies. National and most favored treatment rights apply at the federal, state and local levels of government, and to state-owned enterprises (e.g. PEMEX, Canadian National Railway Corporation). Furthermore, each country is to treat NAFTA investors in accordance with "international law," including fair and equitable treatment and full protection and security. Performance requirements, e.g. specific export levels, minimum domestic content, domestic source preferences, trade balancing, technology transfer and product mandates are disallowed in all areas except government procurement, export promotion and foreign aid. Senior management positions may not be reserved by nationality, but NAFTA states may require that a majority of the board of directors or committees thereof be of a designated nationality or residence provided this does not impair the foreign investor's ability to exercise control.

A general right to convert and transfer local currency at prevailing market rates for earnings, sale proceeds, loan repayments and other investment transactions has been established. But this right does not prevent good faith and nondiscriminatory restraints upon monetary transfers arising out of bankruptcy, insolvency, securities dealings, crimes, satisfaction of judgments and currency reporting duties. Direct and indirect expropriations of investments by NAFTA investors are precluded except for public purposes and if done on a nondiscriminatory basis following due process of law. A right of compensation without delay at fair market value plus interest is created.

In the event of a dispute, a NAFTA investor may (and quite a few have)[5] elect as between monetary (but not punitive) damages through binding arbitration in the home state of the investor under the ICSID Convention if both nations are parties, the Additional Facility Rules of the ICSID if only one nation is a party to the Convention or the UNCITRAL arbitration rules. An arbitration tribunal for investment disputes will be established by the Secretary–General of ICSID if the parties are unable to select a panel by choosing one arbitrator each and having those arbitrators choose a third. However, there are no time limits for the arbitration and either side may appeal the award to the courts. Alternatively, the investor may pursue judicial remedies in courts of the host state.

The NAFTA investment code does not apply to Mexican constitutionally-reserved sectors (e.g. energy, railroads and boundary and coastal real estate) nor Canada's cultural industries. It does, however, remove Mexican foreign investment controls for U.S. and Canadian investors below an initial $25 million U.S. threshold phased-up to $150 million U.S. in ten years and opened new Mexican mining ventures to NAFTA investors after 5 years. Canadian review of direct U.S. investments in excess of $150 million U.S. and indirect investments in excess of $450 million (indexed for inflation from Jan. 1, 1993) continue. Maritime, airline, broadcasting, fishing, nuclear, basic telecommunications, and government-sponsored technology consortia are exempt from the NAFTA investment rules. All of the NAFTA countries have agreed not to lower environmental standards to attract investment and permit (as Mexico requires) environmental impact statements for foreign investments. However, apart from consultations, there was no retaliatory remedy in this area prior to the environmental side agreement discussed below.

Financial services provided by banking, insurance, securities and other firms are separately covered under the NAFTA. Trade in such services is generally subject to specific liberalization commitments and transition periods. Financial service providers, including non-NAFTA providers operating through subsidiaries in a NAFTA country, are entitled to establish themselves anywhere within NAFTA and service customers there (the right of "commercial presence"). Existing cross-border restraints on the provision of financial services were frozen and no new restraints may be imposed (subject to designated exceptions). Providers of financial services in each NAFTA nation receive both national and most favored nation treatment. This includes equality of competitive opportunity, which is defined as avoidance of measures that disadvantage foreign pro-

---

[5] See Chapter 27.

viders relative to domestic providers. Various procedural transparency rules are established to facilitate the entry and equal opportunity of NAFTA providers of financial services. The host nation may legislate reasonable prudential requirements for such companies and, under limited circumstances, protect their balance of payments in ways which restrain financial providers.

The following are some of the more notable country-specific commitments on financial service made in the NAFTA:

United States—A grace period allowed Mexican banks already operating a securities firm in the U.S. to continue to do so until July of 1997.

Canada—The exemption granted U.S. companies under the Canada–U.S. FTA to hold more than 25 percent of the shares of a federally regulated Canadian financial institution was extended to Mexican firms, as was the suspension of Canada's 12 percent asset ceiling rules. Multiple branches may be opened in Canada without Ministry of Finance approval.

Mexico—Banking, securities and insurance companies from the U.S. and Canada are able to enter the Mexican market through subsidiaries and joint ventures (but not branches) subject to market share limits during a transition period that ended in the year 2000 (insurance) or 2004 (banking and securities). Finance companies are able to establish separate subsidiaries in Mexico to provide consumer, commercial, mortgage lending or credit card services, subject to a 3 percent aggregate asset limitation (which does not apply to lending by affiliates of automotive companies). Existing U.S. and Canadian insurers could expand their ownership rights to 100 percent in 1996. No equity or market share requirements apply for warehousing and bonding, foreign exchange and mutual fund management enterprises.

§ 21.11 The NAFTA Agreement in Outline—Intellectual Property

The NAFTA mandates adequate and effective intellectual property rights in all countries, including national treatment and effective internal and external enforcement rights. Specific commitments are made for virtually all types of intellectual property, including patents, copyrights, trademarks, plant breeds, industrial designs, trade secrets, semiconductor chips (directly and in goods incorporating them) and geographical indicators.

For copyright, the NAFTA obligates protection for computer programs, databases, computer program and sound recording rentals, and a 50 year term of protection for sound recordings. For patents, the NAFTA mandates a minimum 20 years of coverage (from date of filing) of nearly all products and processes including pharmaceuticals and agricultural chemicals. It also requires removal of any special or discriminatory patent regimes or availability of rights. Compulsory licensing is limited. Service marks are treated equally with trademarks. Satellite signal poaching is illegal and trade secrets are generally protected (including from disclosure by governments). The NAFTA details member states' duties to provide damages, injunctive, antipiracy and general due process remedies in the intellectual property field. This has, for example, reinforced major changes in Mexican law.

§ 21.12 The NAFTA Agreement in Outline—Other Provisions

The provisions on temporary entry visas for business persons found in the CUSFTA are extended under the NAFTA. These entry rights cover business persons, traders, investors, intra-company transferees and 63 designated professionals. Installers, after-sales repair and maintenance staff and managers performing services under a warranty or other service contract incidental to the sale of equipment or machinery are included, as are sales representatives, buyers, market researchers and financial service providers. White collar business persons only need proof of citizenship and documentation of business purpose to work in another NAFTA country for up to 5 years. However, an annual limit of 5,500 additional Mexican professionals may temporarily enter the United States during the first 10 years of the NAFTA. Apart from these provisions, no common market for the free movement of labor is undertaken.

The NAFTA embraces a competition policy principally aimed at state enterprises and governmentally sanctioned monopolies, mostly found in Mexico. State owned or controlled businesses, at all levels of government, are required to act consistently with the NAFTA when exercising regulatory, administrative or governmental authority (e.g. when granting licenses). Governmentally-owned and privately-owned state-designated monopolies are obliged to follow commercial considerations in their transactions and avoid discrimination against goods or services of other NAFTA nations. Furthermore, each country must ensure that such monopolies do not use their positions to engage in anticompetitive practices in non-monopoly markets. Since each NAFTA nation must adopt laws against anticompetitive business practices and cooperate in their enforcement, Mexico has revived its historically weak "antitrust" laws. A consultative Trade and Competition Committee reviews competition policy issues under the NAFTA.

Other notable provisions in the NAFTA include a general duty of legal transparency, fairness and due process regarding all laws affecting traders and investors with independent administrative or judicial review of government action. Generalized exceptions to the agreement cover action to protect national security and national interests such as public morals, health, national treasures, natural resources, or to enforce laws against deceptive or anticompetitive practices, short of arbitrary discriminations or disguised restraints on trade. Balance of payments trade restraints are governed by the rules of the International Monetary Fund. Taxation issues are subject to bilateral double taxation treaties, including a new one between Mexico and the United States. The "cultural industry" reservations secured by the CUSFTA now cover Canada and Mexico, but are not extended to Mexican–U.S. trade. A right of compensatory retaliation through measures of equivalent commercial effect is granted when invocation of these reservations would have violated the Canada–U.S. FTA but for the cultural industries proviso.

The NAFTA is not forever. Any country may withdraw on 6 months notice. Other countries or groups of countries may be admitted to the NAFTA if Canada, Mexico and the United States agree and domestic ratification follows. In December of 1994, Chile was invited to become the next member of the NAFTA. Negotiations have stalled for want of U.S. Congressional fast track negotiating authority.

§ 21.13 Dispute Settlement under NAFTA

The institutional dispute settlement arrangements accompanying the NAFTA are minimal. A trilateral Trade Commission (with Secretariat) comprised of ministerial or cabinet-level officials meets at least annually to ensure effective joint management of the NAFTA is established. The various intergovernmental committees established for specific areas of coverage of the NAFTA (e.g. competition policy) to oversee much of the work of making the free trade area function. These committees operate on the basis of consensus, referring contentious issues to the Trade Commission.

Investment, dumping and subsidy, financial services environmental, labor and standards disputes are subject to special dispute resolution procedures. A general NAFTA dispute settlement procedure is also established (Chapter 20). A right of consultation exists when one country's rights are thought to be affected. If consultations do not resolve the issue within 45 days, the complainant may convene a meeting of the Trade Commission. The Commission must seek to promptly settle the dispute and may use its good offices, mediation, conciliation or any other alternative means. Absent resolution, the complaining country or countries ordinarily commence proceedings under the GATT/WTO or the NAFTA. Once selected, the chosen forum becomes exclusive. However, if the dispute concerns environmental, safety, health or conservation standards, or arises under specific environmental agreements, the responding nation may elect to have the dispute heard by a NAFTA panel.

Dispute settlement procedures under Chapter 20 involve nonbinding arbitration by five persons chosen in most cases from a trilaterally agreed roster of experts (not limited to NAFTA citizens), with a special roster established for disputes about financial services. A "reverse selection" process is used. The chair of the panel is first chosen by agreement or, failing agreement, by designation of one side selected by lot. The chair cannot be a citizen of the selecting side but must be a NAFTA national. Each side then selects two additional arbitrators who are citizens of the country or countries on the *other* side. The Commission has approved rules of procedure including the opportunity for written submissions, rebuttals and at least one oral hearing. Expert advice on environmental and scientific matters may be given by special procedures accessing science boards. Strict time limits are created so as to keep the panel on track to a prompt resolution. Within 90 days an initial confidential report must be circulated, followed by 14 days for comment by the parties and 16 days for the final panel report to the Commission.

Early NAFTA Chapter 20 arbitrations have concerned Canadian tariffication of agricultural quotas (upheld), U.S. escape clause relief from Mexican corn broom exports (rejected) and a successful Mexican challenge of the U.S. failure to implement cross-border trucking. Once the Trade Commission receives a final arbitration panel report, the NAFTA requires the disputing nations to agree within 30 days on a resolution (normally by conforming to the panel's recommendations). If a mutually agreed resolution does not occur at this stage, the complaining country may retaliate by suspending the application of equivalent benefits under the NAFTA. Any NAFTA country may invoke the arbitration panel process if it perceives that this retaliation is excessive.

When NAFTA interpretational issues are disputed before domestic tribunals or courts, the Trade Commission (if it can agree) can submit an interpretation to that body. In the absence of agreement within the Commission, any NAFTA country may intervene and submit its views as to the proper interpretation or application of the NAFTA to the national court or tribunal.

The independent binational review panel mechanism established in the CUSFTA for dumping and subsidy duties is carried over into NAFTA, along with the extraordinary challenge procedure to deal with allegations about the integrity of the panel review process. Chapter 19 panels are substituted for traditional judicial review at the national level of administrative dumping and countervailing duty orders. Mexico has undertaken major improvements to its law in this area. The procedures and rules for such panels generally follow those found in the CUSFTA. They are limited to issues of the consistency of the national decisions with domestic law, and once again have been numerous.

In addition, a special committee may be requested by any country believing that another's domestic law has prevented the establishment, final decision or implementation of the decision by such a panel. A special committee may also be invoked if the opportunity for independent judicial review on a dumping or subsidy determination has been denied (a concern focused especially on Mexico). This committee's findings, if affirmative, will result in member state consultations. Absent resolution, the complainant may suspend the panel system or benefits under the NAFTA agreement.

§ 21.14 The Side Agreements on Labor and the Environment

The NAFTA side agreements on labor (NAALC) and the environment (NAAEC) do not create additional substantive regional rules. Rather the side agreements basically create law enforcement mechanisms. The side agreements commit each country to creation of environmental and labor bodies that monitor compliance with the adequacy and the enforcement of *domestic* law. The Commission for Environmental Cooperation (CEC) (Montreal) and three National Administrative Offices (NAO) concerning labor matters are empowered to receive complaints. Negotiations to resolve complaints first ensue.

In the absence of a negotiated solution, the NAAEC establishes five environmental dispute settlement mechanisms. *First*, the CEC Secretariat may report on almost any environmental matter. *Second*, the Secretariat may develop a factual record in trade-related law enforcement disputes. *Third*, the CEC Council can release that record to the public. *Fourth*, if there is a persistent pattern of failure to enforce environmental law, the Council will mediate and conciliate. *Fifth*, if such efforts fail, the Council can send the matter to arbitration and awards can be enforced by monetary penalties.

The NAALC labor law enforcement system is a calibrated four-tier series of dispute resolution mechanisms. *First*, the NAOs may review and report on eleven designated labor law enforcement matters that correspond to the NAALC Labor Principles. *Second*, ministerial consultations may follow when recommended by the NAO. *Third*, an Evaluation Committee of Experts can report on trade-related mutually recognized labor law enforcement patterns of practice concerning eight of the NAALC Labor Principles (excluding strikes, union organizing and collective bargaining). *Fourth*, persistent patterns of failure to enforce occupational health and safety, child labor or minimum wage laws can be arbitrated and awards enforced by monetary penalties.

The NAAEC and NAALC law enforcement mechanisms have been used more frequently than many expected. Quite a few labor law enforcement complaints have focused on the organization of "independent" unions in Mexico. United States plant closings and treatment of immigrant workers have also been reviewed. Regarding the environment, a wide range of complaints have been filed asserting inadequate Canadian, Mexican and U.S. law enforcement. None of these environmental disputes have proceeded beyond development of a factual record.

§ 21.15 Expanding NAFTA

When Canada and the United States agreed to free trade in 1989, there was no expectation of extension of that agreement to Mexico or any other country. The NAFTA agreement, on the other hand, specifically anticipates growth by accession. Article 2204 invites applications to join NAFTA by countries or groups of countries without regard to their geographic location or cultural background. This is unlike the European Union which only allows "European" nations to join. Australia, South Korea, New Zealand and Singapore have, for example, all expressed interest in NAFTA. Canada would also like to see European nations actively considered for membership.

The NAFTA Free Trade Commission is authorized to negotiate the terms and conditions of any new memberships. The resulting accession agreement must be approved and ratified by each NAFTA nation. Practically speaking, as in the European Union, this means that current members can veto NAFTA applicants.

In December of 1994, at the "Summit of the Americas" in Miami, Canada and Mexico joined the United States in formally inviting Chile to apply for NAFTA membership. This invitation went nowhere because Congress repeatedly refused to authorize "fast track" negotiations by President Clinton. Fast track negotiations provide assurance to all concerned that Congress would not be able to alter the terms and conditions of Chile's accession. Under fast track, Congress would have to approve or disapprove the agreement by majority vote. Apart from partisan politics, one thorny issue was whether there would be side agreements with Chile on labor and the environment.

Absent fast track authority, Chile, Canada and Mexico all steered different courses. Mexico and Chile renegotiated and expanded their pre-NAFTA free trade agreement. Canada and Chile reached agreement in 1997 on free trade along with side agreements that are similar to NAAEC and NAALC. Chile in 1996 became a free trade associate of MERCOSUR, the Southern Cone common market of Brazil, Argentina, Paraguay and Uruguay. All these free trade commitments flowed partly from want of U.S. fast track authority. They had an impact on trade and investment patterns. Some U.S. companies with Canadian subsidiaries, for example, shifted production and exports to Canada in order to take advantage of Canada–Chile free trade.

§ 21.16 The USTR, Fast Track and Bilateral Trade Agreements

Removing trade barriers is usually done on a reciprocal basis, and requires lengthy bargaining and negotiations between sovereign states. Congress is not adapted to carry on such negotiations, so it routinely delegates limited authority to the President to negotiate agreements reducing import restrictions when the President finds that such restrictions, either of the United States or of a foreign country, are unduly burdensome. Some recent efforts to reduce trade restrictions have been multilateral efforts (e.g., the WTO and the North American Free Trade Agreement). Others have been bilateral, such as the U.S. free trade agreements. In these situations, Congress intermittently since 1974 has given quite broad authority to the President, or his representative, to reduce or eliminate United States tariffs on a reciprocal "fast track" basis. Fast track originated as a compromise after Congress refused to ratify two major components of the Kennedy Round of GATT negotiations.

Since the 1980s, a United States Trade Representative (USTR) is appointed by the President, with the advice and consent of the

Senate. The Office of the USTR has been the principal vehicle through which trade negotiations have been conducted in recent years on behalf of the United States. For example, the international setting in which the USTR frequently functions is that provided by the WTO and NAFTA, and to a lesser extent by the International Monetary Fund (IMF). The USTR is the contact point for persons who desire an investigation of instances of noncompliance with any trade agreement.

The Trade Act of 2002 (P.L. 107–210) authorized President Bush to negotiate international trade agreements on a fast track basis, a procedure that requires Congress to vote within 90 legislative days up or down, without amendments, on U.S. trade agreements. In return, Congress receives substantial notice and opportunity to influence U.S. trade negotiations conducted by the USTR. See 19 U.S.C. § 3801 et seq. The President and the USTR quickly completed and Congress approved free trade agreements with Chile and Singapore, and thereafter with Morocco, Australia, Central America/Dominican Republic, Peru, Jordan, Oman, and Bahrain. The President's fast track authority expired in July of 2007 with agreements for Colombia, Panama and Korea signed but approval by Congress was delayed several years into the Obama administration. For U.S. free trade partners, fast track suggests that once they reach a deal Congress cannot alter it, though in recent years Congress has effectively tacked on additional requirements, notably regarding labor and the environment.

Hundreds of bilateral free trade agreements lattice the world, including for example the European Union and South Africa, Canada and Costa Rica, China and Chile, Japan and Singapore. Mexico has dozens of bilateral free trade agreements. At this point the only nation without a bilateral free trade deal is Mongolia. A variety of factors help explain why bilaterals have become the leading edge of international trade law and policy. Difficulties encountered in the Uruguay, "Seattle" and Doha Rounds of multilateral trade negotiations are certainly crucial. GATT/WTO regulatory failures regarding bilaterals have also fueled this reality. Yet these "negatives" do not fully explain the feeding frenzy of bilaterals. A range of attractions are also at work. For example, bilaterals often extend to subject matters beyond WTO competence. Foreign investment law is a prime example, and many bilaterals serve as investment magnets. Government procurement, optional at the WTO level, is often included in bilaterals. Competition policy and labor and environmental matters absent from the WTO are sometimes covered in bilaterals. In addition, bilaterals can reach beyond the scope of existing WTO agreements. Services is one "WTO-plus" area where this is clearly true. Intellectual property rights are also being "WTO-plussed" in bilateral free trade agreements. Whether this amounts to competitive trade liberalization or competitive trade imperialism is a provocative question.

§ 21.17 Free Trade in the Americas

The United States "Enterprise for the Americas Initiative" (EAI) under elder President Bush raised hopes of economic integration throughout the Americas against a background of competitive regionalism in trade relations, especially between the European Union and North America. At the Americas Summit in Miami, President Clinton and 33 Latin American heads of state (only Fidel Castro was absent) renewed this hope by agreeing to commence negotiations on a Free Trade Area of the Americas (FTAA). The year 2005 was targeted at the Summit for creation of the FTAA. Preparatory working groups have regularly met since 1995 to discuss the following topics: (1) Market Access; (2) Customs Procedures and Rules of Origin; (3) Investment; (4) Standards and Technical Barriers to Trade; (5) Sanitary and Phytosanitary Measures; (6) Subsidies, Antidumping and Countervailing Duties; (7) Smaller Economies; (8) Government Procurement; (9) Intellectual Property Rights; (10) Services; (11) Competition Policy; and (12) Dispute Settlement. It is expected that each of these areas would be covered in any FTAA agreement. Formal FTAA negotiations were delayed several times, particularly because of differences between Brazil-led MERCOSUR and U.S.-led NAFTA.

The absence of fast track authority and the general perception that political support for free trade in the United States is weak has clearly slowed FTAA developments. MERCOSUR and Brazil in particular seized the opportunity to move towards a South American Free Trade Area (SAFTA). Presumably, SAFTA would be in a much better position to negotiate terms and conditions with NAFTA than individual countries or sub-groups within South America. To that end, Bolivia, Peru, Chile and Venezuela are already MERCOSUR free trade associates and negotiations with virtually all South American nations are in progress. Venezuela has a socialist-style Trade Treaty for the Peoples with Cuba, Bolivia Ecuador, Nicaragua and Honduras. Late in 2003, MERCOSUR and the Andean Community (ANCOM) signed a free trade deal. Indeed, MERCOSUR is even negotiating along the same lines with Canada, Mexico, the Central American states, and the European Union.

In 2002, a bipartisan Congress authorized President George W. Bush to negotiate free trade agreements on a fast track basis. This authorization is valid until June 1, 2005 subject to possible extension. President Bush, following the pattern established by Canada and Mexico, rapidly concluded a bilateral U.S. free trade agreement with Chile, including coverage of the environment and labor.

The 2002 Congressional authorization of fast track free trade negotiations covers the FTAA. President George W. Bush sought such an agreement, while simultaneously negotiating U.S. free trade deals with five Central American states (CAFTA, finalized early in 2004), the Dominican Republic (2004), Peru (2007), Colombia (2012) and Panama (2012). Such a "divide and conquer" strategy undermines Brazil's hopes for a united South/Central American negotiating front for the FTAA. It also reflects the reality of the United States playing catch up with Canada (which has free trade agreements with Chile and Costa Rica) and Mexico (which has numerous Latin American free trade agreements).

Divisions were particularly evident during the November 2003 FTAA ministerial meeting in Miami. Lowered expectations, known as FTAA–Lite, reflect U.S. refusal to budge on agricultural protection and trade remedies, and Brazilian refusal to fully embrace investment, intellectual property, services and procurement "free trade." Absent successful resolution of these issues in the WTO Doha Round negotiations, an unlikely prospect at this writing, FTAA–Lite, even with different levels of country commitments, seems unlikely.

§ 21.18 U.S. Free Trade Agreements—NAFTA Plus and Minus

United States free trade agreements since NAFTA have evolved substantively under a policy known as "competitive liberalization." For example, coverage of labor law has been narrowed to core ILO principles: The rights of association, organization and collective bargaining; acceptable work conditions regarding minimum wages, hours and occupational health and safety; minimum ages for employment of children and elimination of the worst forms of child labor; and a ban on forced or compulsory labor. Coverage of labor and environmental law enforcement is folded into the trade agreement (compare NAFTA's side agreements) and all remedies are intergovernmental (compare private and NGO "remedies" in the side agreements).

Other NAFTA-plus provisions have emerged. These are most evident regarding foreign investment and intellectual property. Regarding investor-state claims, for example, post–NAFTA U.S. free trade agreements insert the word "customary" before international law in defining the minimum standard of treatment to which foreign investors are entitled. This insertion tracks the official Interpretation issued in that regard under NAFTA. In addition, the contested terms "fair and equitable treatment" and "full protection and security" are defined for the first time:

> "fair and equitable treatment" includes the obligation not to deny justice in criminal, civil, or administrative adjudicatory proceedings in accordance with the principle of due process embodied in the principal legal systems of the world; and 'full protection and security" requires each Party to provide the level of police protection required under customary international law.

More significantly perhaps, starting with the U.S.—Chile FTA, these agreements contain an Annex restricting the scope of "indirect expropriation" claims:

> "Except in rare circumstances, nondiscriminatory regulatory actions by a Party that are designed and applied to protect legitimate public welfare objectives, such as public health, safety, and the environment, do not constitute indirect expropriations."

Hence the potential for succeeding with "regulatory takings" investor-state claims has been reduced. Moreover, the CAFTA–DR agreement anticipates creating an appellate body of some sort for investor-state arbitration decisions.

Regarding intellectual property, NAFTA—plus has moved into the Internet age. Protection of domain names, and adherence to the WIPO Internet treaties, are stipulated. E-commerce and free trade in digital products are embraced, copyrights extended to rights-management (encryption) and anti-circumvention (hacking) technology, protection against web music file sharing enhanced, and potential liability of Internet Service Providers detailed.

Less visibly, pharmaceutical patent owners obtain extensions of their patents to compensate for delays in the approval process, and greater control over their test data, making it harder for generic competition to emerge. They also gain "linkage," meaning local drug regulators must make sure generics are not patent-infringing before their release. In addition, adherence to the Patent Law Treaty (2000) and the Trademark Law Treaty (1994) is agreed. Anti-counterfeiting laws are tightened, particularly regarding destruction of counterfeit goods.

Other NAFTA-plus changes push further along the path of free trade in services and comprehensive customs law administration rules. Antidumping and countervailing duty laws remain applicable, but appeals from administrative determinations are taken in national courts, not binational panels. Except for limited provisions in the Chile—U.S. agreement, business visas drop completely out of U.S. free trade agreements, a NAFTA—minus development.

In sum, the United States has generally used its leverage with smaller trade partners in the Americas to obtain more preferential treatment and expanded protection for its goods, services, technology and investors. It has given up relatively little in return, for example a modest increase in agricultural market openings. The net results substantively suggest that the NAFTA/MERCOSUR divide is deepening.

§ 21.19 Quebec and NAFTA

The Canadian Constitution of 1982 was adopted by an Act of the British Parliament. As such, the Act and Constitution of 1982 are thought to bind all Canadian provinces including Quebec. That province, however, has never formally ratified the Constitution of Canada. Since 1982 a series of negotiations have attempted to secure Quebec's ratification, and all have failed miserably.

In 1987, for example, the "Meech Lake Accord" was reached. This agreement recognized Quebec as a "distinct society" in Canada. What the practical consequences of this recognition would have been will never be known. Quebec's adherence to the Meech Lake Accord was nullified when Manitoba, New Brunswick and ultimately Newfoundland failed to ratify the Accord. A second set of negotiations led in 1992 to the Charlottetown Accord which also acknowledged Quebec as a distinct society with its French language, unique culture and Civil Law tradition. This time a national referendum was held and its defeat was overwhelming. Quebec, five English-speaking Canadian provinces, and the Yukon territory voted against the Charlottetown Accord.

The failure of these Accords moved Quebec towards separation from Canada. In 1994 and again in 2012, the Parti Quebecois came to power. It held a provincial referendum on separation in 1995. By the narrowest of margins, the people of Quebec rejected separation from Canada. Just exactly what "separation" would have meant was never entirely clear during the debate, perhaps deliberately so.

In 1998, Canada's Supreme Court ruled that Quebec could not "under the Constitution" withdraw unilaterally. To secede Quebec would need to negotiate a constitutional amendment with the rest of Canada. The rest of Canada would, likewise, be obliged to enter into such negotiations if a "clear majority" of Quebec's voters approved a "clear question" on secession in a referendum. Subsequently, the Canadian Parliament legislated rules which will make it difficult for Quebec to separate, should it ever wish to do so. That prospect now seems more remote, particularly because the Parti Quebecois lost power in 2003.

If Quebec ever separates from Canada this will raise fundamental issues about Quebec and NAFTA. Would Quebec be forced to negotiate for membership in NAFTA? If so, would English-speaking Canada veto its application? Might Quebec's relationship to Canada continue in some limited manner (such as for defense and international trade purposes) such that NAFTA is not an issue at all? Might Quebec automatically "succeed" to the NAFTA treaty, thus becoming a member without application? Customary international practice maintains existing treaties when nations sub-divide. This practice was applied to the Czech Republic, Slovakia, and various states of the former Yugoslavia. Thus custom suggests that fears in Quebec about losing NAFTA benefits are exaggerated.

§ 21.20 A NAFTA/Free Trade in the Americas Timeline

1986	Canada–U.S. free trade negotiations commence. Mexico joins the GATT. Uruguay Round of GATT negotiations launched.
1989	CUSFTA enters into effect.
1991	Congress extends fast track authority to NAFTA and Uruguay Round, MERCOSUR created by Brazil, Argentina, Paraguay and Uruguay.
1992	NAFTA signed by Presidents Bush and Salinas, Prime Minister Mulroney.
1993 (August)	Side agreements on North American Labor and Environmental Cooperation concluded under President Clinton.
1993 (October)	Vice President Gore "defeats" Ross Perot in nationally televised NAFTA debate.
1993 (November)	U.S. Congress ratifies NAFTA and sides agreements.
1993 (December)	Uruguay Round agreements concluded.
1994	NAFTA enters into effect.
1994 (December)	Miami Summit supports creation by 2005 of a

	Free Trade Area of the Americas (FTAA).
1994–95	Mexican peso crashes, U.S. organizes rescue package.
1995	Uruguay Round agreements enter into effect. WTO created. Negotiations commence for Chile to join NAFTA. Quebec voters barely reject separation from Canada.
1997	Canada and Chile agree on free trade with side agreements. Mexico revises its free trade agreement with Chile.
1995–2002	Congress refuses to authorize fast track negotiations. Mexico agrees to free trade with Colombia, Venezuela, Costa Rica, Bolivia, Nicaragua, Guatemala, Honduras, El Salvador, Peru and Uruguay. Canada agrees to free trade with Costa Rica.
2002	Congress authorizes bilateral and FTAA fast track negotiations.
2003	U.S.–Chile agree on free trade.
2004	U.S.–CAFTA plus Dominican Republic agree on free trade.
2005	FTAA deadline is not met, CAFTA–DR agreement passes House of Representative by two votes.
2006/2007	Panama, Peru and Colombia agree on free trade with the U.S. Venezuela applies for MERCOSUR membership, creates Peoples' Trade Treaty (ALBA) with Cuba, Bolivia, Nicaragua, and Ecuador.
2007 (July)	U.S. fast track authority expires.
2007 (October)	Costa Rican people barely approve CAFTA.
2008 (Jan)	U.S.–Peru and Canada–Peru FTAs take effect
2009–2012	U.S.—Panama and U.S.—Colombia FTAs stalled then ratified. Venezuela joins MERCOSUR. Canada free trades with Colombia and Panama.

Chapter 22

FRANCHISING AND TRADEMARK LICENSING

Table of Sections

§ 22.1 Franchising Abroad

Franchising constitutes a rapidly expanding form of doing business abroad. Most franchisors have established fairly standard contracts and business formulae which are utilized in their home markets, and receive counsel on the myriad of laws relevant to their domestic business operations. Approaches to developing, defining and managing franchise relationships that have worked domestically may not work abroad. For example, agreements authorizing development of multiple locations within a given territory and, possibly, subfranchising by a master franchisee are often used overseas while infrequent in the United States.

International franchising confronts the attorney with the need to research and evaluate a broad range of foreign laws which may apply in any particular jurisdiction. Such laws tend to focus on placing equity and control in the hands of local individuals and on regulating the franchise agreement to benefit the franchisees. In addition, counsel should be sensitive to the cultural impact of foreign franchising. For example, the appearance of a franchise building or trademark symbol may conflict in a foreign setting with traditional architectural forms (such as in European cities) or nationalist feelings hostile to the appearance of foreign trademarks on franchised products (such as in India or Mexico). Cultural conflicts can diminish the value of international franchises. To anticipate and solve legal and cultural problems, foreign counsel is often chosen to assist in the task of franchising abroad.

This chapter explores some of the concerns a franchisor or prospective franchisee may encounter in opting for, negotiating, drafting or enforcing an international franchise agreement. Although patents, copyrights and trademarks may all be involved in international franchising, trademark licensing is at the core of most international franchise agreements. Many rightly consider franchising to be a U.S. invention, but foreigners have rapidly been developing international franchising systems. Thus, while the primary focus in this chapter is on the problems of United States franchisors who intend to go abroad, additional coverage is given to United States law relevant to franchising.

§ 22.2 Trademark Protection

Virtually all countries offer some legal protection to trademarks, even when they do not have trademark registration systems. Trademark rights derived from the use of marks on goods in commerce have long been recognized at common law and remain so today in countries as diverse as the United States and the United Arab Emirates. The latter nation, for example, had no trademark registration law in 1986, but this did not prevent McDonald's from obtaining an injunction against a local business using its famous name and golden arches without authorization.[1] However, obtaining international trademark protection normally involves separate registration under the law of each nation. Over three million trademarks are registered around the globe each year. In the United States, trademarks are protected at common law and by state and federal registrations. Federal registration is permitted by the U.S. Trademark Office for all marks capable of distinguishing the goods on which they appear from other goods.[2] Unless the mark falls within a category of forbidden registrations (e.g., those that offend socialist morality in the People's Republic of China), a mark becomes valid for a term of years following registration.

In some countries (like the U.S. prior to 1989), marks must be used on goods before registration. In others, use is not required and speculative registration of marks can occur. It is said that ESSO was obliged to purchase trademark rights from such a speculator

---

1 Case No. 823/85. See 76 Trademark Reports 356 (1986).

2 15 U.S.C.A. § 1052.

when it switched to EXXON in its search for the perfect global trademark. Since 1989, United States law has allowed applications when there is a bona fide intent to use a trademark within 12 months and, if there is good cause for the delay in actual usage, up to 24 additional months.[3] Such filings in effect reserve the mark for the applicant. The emphasis on bona fide intent and good cause represent an attempt to control any speculative use of U.S. trademark registrations.

The scope of trademark protection may differ substantially from country to country. Under U.S. federal trademark law, injunctions, damages and seizures of goods by customs officials may follow infringement. Other jurisdictions may provide similar remedies on their law books, but offer little practical enforcement. Thus, trademark registration is no guarantee against trademark piracy. A pair of blue jeans labeled "Levi Strauss made in San Francisco" may have been counterfeited in Israel or Paraguay without the knowledge or consent of Levi Strauss and in spite of its trademark registrations in those countries. Trademark counterfeiting is not just a third world problem, as any visitor to a United States "flea market" can tell. Congress created criminal offenses and private treble damages remedies for the first time in the Trademark Counterfeiting Act of 1984.

In many countries trademarks (appearing on goods) may be distinguished from "service marks" used by providers of services (e.g., the Law Store), "trade names" (business names), "collective marks" (marks used by a group or organization), and "certificate marks" (marks which certify a certain quality, origin, or other fact). Although national trademark schemes differ, it can be said generally that a valid trademark (e.g., a mark not "canceled," "renounced," "abandoned," "waived" or "generic") will be protected against infringing use. A trademark can be valid in one country (ASPIRIN brand tablets in Canada), but invalid because generic in another (BAYER brand aspirin in the United States).

Unlike patents and copyrights, trademarks may be renewed in perpetuity. A valid mark may be licensed, perhaps to a "registered user" or it may be assigned, in some cases only with the sale of the goodwill of a business. A growing example of international licensing of trademarks can be found in franchise agreements taken abroad. And national trademark law sometimes accompanies international licensing. The principal U.S. trademark law, the Lanham Act of 1946, has been construed to apply extraterritorially (much like the

[3] 15 U.S.C.A. § 1051(b).

Sherman Antitrust Act) to foreign licensees engaging in deceptive practices.[4] Foreigners who seek a registration may be required to prove a prior and valid "home registration," and a new registration in another country may not have an existence "independent" of the continuing validity of the home country registration. Foreigners are often assisted in their registration efforts by international and regional trademark treaties, discussed below.

§ 22.3 Quality Controls

Because franchising links trademarks with business attributes, there is a broad duty in the law for the franchisor to maintain quality controls over the franchisee, particularly in the business format franchise system. Any failure of the franchisor to maintain such quality controls could cause the trademark in question to be abandoned and lost to the franchisor.[5] In order to maintain adequate quality controls, the franchisor must typically police the operations of the franchisee.[6]

Broadly speaking, the duty to maintain quality controls arises because a trademark is a source symbol. The public is entitled to rely upon that source symbol in making its purchasing decisions so as to obtain consistent product quality and attributes. International franchisors operating at a distance from their franchisees must be especially concerned with quality controls. On the other hand, excessive control or the public appearance of such control may give rise to an agency relationship between the franchisor and the franchisee. Such a relationship could be used to establish franchisor liability for franchisee conduct, including international product and other tort liabilities.[7] It may be possible to minimize these risks through disclaimer or indemnification clauses in the franchise agreement.

§ 22.4 Copyright Protection in Franchising

Although franchising primarily focuses upon trademarks and trademark licensing, the use of copyrights frequently parallels such activity. For example, the designs and logos of the franchisor may be copyrighted, and certainly its instruction manual and other such written communications to franchisees should be copyrighted. These

---

[4] See especially Scotch Whiskey Association v. Barton Distilling Co., 489 F.2d 809 (7th Cir.1973).

[5] See, e.g., Yamamoto & Co. v. Victor United, Inc., 219 U.S.P.Q. 968 (C.D.Cal.1982).

[6] See Dawn Donut Co. v. Hart's Food Stores, Inc., 267 F.2d 358 (2d Cir.1959).

[7] See Hanson, The Franchising Dilemma: Franchisor Liability for Actions of a Local Franchisee, 19 N.C.Central L.J. 190 (1991).

copyrights benefit in many countries from the Universal Copyright Convention (UCC) of 1952 and the Berne Convention of 1886. The United States now adheres to both of these conventions. Under the UCC, copyright holders receive national treatment, translation rights and other benefits. This convention will excuse any national registration requirement provided a notice of a claim of copyright is adequately given. However, in the United States, a reservation was made such that registration of foreign copyrights is required if the only convention under which foreigners are seeking such protection is the Universal Copyright Convention of 1952.

On the other hand, if the foreigner comes from a nation which also adheres to the Berne Convention, national treatment and a release from registration formalities is obtained. The Berne Convention permits local copyright protection independent of protection granted in the country of origin and does not require copyright notice. Prior to 1987, most United States copyright holders acquired Berne Convention benefits by simultaneously publishing their works in Canada, a member country. Since 1987 the United States has ratified the Berne Convention. This has the practical effect of eliminating registration requirements for foreign copyright holders. It also extends United States copyright relations to approximately 25 new nations.

§ 22.5 Protection of Franchise Trade Secrets

Franchise formulae often involve utilization of trade secrets. This may range from recipes and cooking techniques to customer lists, pricing formulas, market data or bookkeeping procedures. It is extremely difficult to protect such trade secrets under United States law. The first problem arises from the concept of what is a trade secret. Generally speaking, abstract ideas or business practices which do not involve an element of novelty are not considered trade secrets.[8] Even if franchise trade secrets are involved, maintaining such secrets can be difficult given the wide number of persons who may have access to the confidential information. Even though the franchisees may warrant to maintain such secrets, once released into the business public there may not be an effective way to recapture the secret or remedy the harm.[9]

The duty not to disclose trade secrets should be extended to employees of the franchisee. This can be done by permitting dissemination only on a need-to-know basis. However, it may be impossible

---

[8] See Kewanee Oil Co. v. Bicron Corp., 416 U.S. 470, 94 S.Ct. 1879, 40 L.Ed.2d 315 (1974).

[9] See Smith v. Dravo Corp., 203 F.2d 369 (7th Cir.1953).

not to permit certain employees from the knowledge of cooking procedures or recipes, for example. Once again the remedies and efforts to recapture the secret are likely to be inadequate.[10] Terminated employees and terminated franchisees are another fertile source of the loss of trade secrets. Tort remedies employing misappropriation theories may prevent the utilization or disclosure by such persons of trade secrets where there is a possibility of competition with the franchisor.[11] Damages are generally viewed as an inadequate remedy in the trade secret field because the harm of the loss of the secret is irreparable.

§ 22.6 The Franchise Agreement, U.S. Franchising

International franchising raises a host of legal issues under intellectual property, antitrust, tax, licensing and other laws. The significance of these issues is magnified by the rapid growth of international franchising. Hundreds of U.S. companies have, in total, tens of thousands of foreign franchises. Nearly 70 percent of these franchisors started in Canada, with Japan and Britain following. Some United States investors have found franchising the least risky and most popular way to enter Eastern Europe. But franchising is not just a United States export. Many foreign franchisors have entered the U.S. market.

Most franchisors have standard contracts which are used in their home markets and receive counsel on the myriad of laws relevant to their business operations. Such contracts need to be revised and adapted to international franchising without significantly altering the franchisor's successful business formula. Franchise fees and royalties must be specified, the provision of services, training, and control by the franchisor detailed, the term and area of the franchise negotiated ("master franchises" conveying rights in an entire country or region are common in international franchise agreements), accounting procedures agreed upon, business standards and advertising selected, insurance obtained, taxes and other liabilities allocated, default and dispute settlement procedures decided. At the heart of all franchise agreements lies a trademark licensing clause conveying local trademark rights of the franchisor to the franchisee in return for royalty payments.

Franchising is an important sector in the United States economy. Thousands of franchisors have created and administer fran-

---

[10] See Shatterproof Glass Corp. v. Guardian Glass Co., 322 F.Supp. 854 (E.D.Mich.1970) *affirmed* 462 F.2d 1115 (6th Cir.1972).

[11] See FMC Corp. v. Taiwan Tainan Giant Industrial Co., 730 F.2d 61 (2d Cir.1984).

chise systems throughout the nation. U.S. franchisees number in the hundreds of thousands. These franchisees are typically independent business persons, and their local franchise outlets employ millions of people. It has been estimated that approximately one-third of all retail sales in the United States take place through franchised outlets. Just as U.S. franchisors have found franchising particularly effective for market penetration abroad, Canadian, European and Japanese companies are increasingly penetrating the U.S. market through franchising.

Franchising is a business technique that permits rapid and flexible penetration of markets, growth and capital development. In the United States, there are traditional distinctions between product franchises and business format franchises. Product franchises involve manufacturers who actually produce the goods that are distributed through franchise agreements. For example, ice cream stores, soft drink bottling companies and gasoline retailers are often the subject of product franchises. Business format franchises are more common. These do not involve the manufacture by the franchisor of the product being sold by the franchisee. More typically, the franchisor licenses intellectual property rights in conjunction with a particular "formula for success" of the business. Fast food establishments, hotels, and a variety of service franchises are examples of business format franchising.

U.S. regulation of franchise relationships occurs at both the federal and state levels of government. Such regulation can be as specific as the Federal Trade Commission Franchising Rule and state franchise disclosure duties or as amorphous as the ever present dangers of state and federal antitrust law.

§ 22.7 Regulation of International Franchising

Were franchising unaffected by regulation, the attorney's role would be limited to negotiation and drafting of the agreement. But international franchising is increasingly regulated by home and host jurisdictions, including regional groups like the European Union (EU). In third world countries, especially Latin America, technology transfer laws aimed principally at international patent and know-how licensing also regulate franchise agreements. These laws benefit franchisees and further development policies, e.g., the conservation of hard currencies by control of royalty levels. In 1986, the European Court of Justice issued a major opinion on the legality of franchise agreements under EU competition law.[12] This decision

[12] Pronuptia de Paris GmbH v. Pronuptia de Paris Irmgard Schillgallis (1986) Eur.Comm.Rep. 353. See Section 18.11.

indicates that Union law can depart significantly from leading United States antitrust law on market division arrangements for distributors.[13] The EU first implemented a comprehensive regulation on franchise agreements in 1988.[14]

There is often a perception of being invaded culturally that follows franchising. Local laws sometimes respond to the cultural impact of foreign franchises, but this did not stop McDonald's from opening in Moscow with great success. In India and Mexico, nationalist feelings hostile to the appearance of foreign trademarks on franchised products have produced laws intended to remove such usage. For example, the Mexican Law of Inventions and Trademarks (1976) (repealed 1987) anticipated requiring use of culturally Mexican marks in addition to marks of foreign origin. Dual marks are now voluntary in Mexico and prohibited by NAFTA. Other nations require local materials (olive oil in the Mediterranean) to be substituted. This could, for example, alter the formula for success (and value) of fast food franchises. Still others (e.g., Alberta, Canada) mandate extensive disclosures by franchisors in a registered prospectus before agreements may be completed. Disclosure violations can trigger a range of franchisee remedies: recision, injunctions and damages. Such laws are also found in many of the states of the United States.

Franchise advertising must conform to local law. For example, regulations in the People's Republic of China prohibit ads which "have reactionary . . . content." Antitrust and tax law are important in international franchising. Double taxation treaties, for example, will affect the level of taxation of royalties. Antitrust law will temper purchasing requirements of the franchisor, lest unlawful "tying arrangements" be undertaken. Tying arrangements involve coercion of franchisees to take supplies from the franchisor or designated sources as part of the franchise.

Such arrangements must, by definition, involve two products: the tying and tied products. They are subject to a complex and not entirely consistent body of case law under the U.S. Sherman Antitrust Act, Articles 101 and 102 of the TFEU and other laws. For example, one leading United States antitrust case treats the trademark licenses as a separate tying product and the requirement of

---

[13] Compare Continental T.V., Inc. v. GTE Sylvania Inc., 433 U.S. 36, 97 S.Ct. 2549, 53 L.Ed.2d 568 (1977) (location clauses not per se illegal); American Motor Inns, Inc. v. Holiday Inns, Inc., 521 F.2d 1230 (3d Cir.1975) (allocation of franchisor/franchisee towns and territories *per se* illegal).

[14] Commission Regulation No. 4087/88, replaced by Regulation 2790/99, and replaced again by Regulation 330/10, discussed in Section 18.12.

the purchase by franchisees of non-essential cooking equipment and paper products unlawful.[15] Another case permits franchisors to require franchisees to purchase "core products" (e.g., chicken) subject to detailed specifications, or from a designated list of approved sources.[16] Sometimes the "core product" and the trademark license are treated as a single product incapable of being tied in violation of the law.[17] Still another leading case suggests that anything comprising the franchisor's "formula for success" may possibly be tied in the franchise contract.[18] This may be notably lawful if there was full pre-contract disclosure by the franchisor.

§ 22.8 The Paris Convention as Applied to Trademarks

The premium placed on priority of use of a trademark is reflected in several international trademark treaties. These include the 1883 Paris Convention for the Protection of Industrial Property, the 1957 Arrangement of Nice Concerning the International Classification of Goods and Services, and the 1973 Trademark Registration Treaty. The treaties of widest international application are the Paris Convention and the Arrangement of Nice, to which the United States is a signatory. The International Bureau of the World Intellectual Property Organization (WIPO) in Geneva plays a central role in the administration of arrangements contemplated by these agreements.

The Paris Convention reflects an effort to internationalize some trademark rules. In addition to extending the nondiscriminatory principal of national treatment and providing for a right of priority of six months for trademarks, the Convention mitigates the frequent national requirement that foreigners seeking trademark registration prove a pre-existing, valid and continuing home registration. This makes it easier to obtain foreign trademark registration, avoids the possibility that a lapse in registration at home will cause all foreign registrations to become invalid, and allows registration abroad of entirely different (and perhaps culturally adapted) marks. The Paris Convention right of priority eliminates the need to simultaneously file for trademark protection around the globe. Filings

15 Siegel v. Chicken Delight, Inc., 448 F.2d 43 (9th Cir.1971), *cert. denied* 405 U.S. 955, 92 S.Ct. 1172, 31 L.Ed.2d 232 (1972).

16 Kentucky Fried Chicken Corp. v. Diversified Packaging Corp., 549 F.2d 368 (5th Cir.1977).

17 Krehl v. Baskin–Robbins Ice Cream Co., 664 F.2d 1348 (9th Cir.1982) (franchisees must buy Baskin–Robbins ice cream).

18 Principe v. McDonald's Corp., 631 F.2d 303 (4th Cir.1980), *cert. denied* 451 U.S. 970, 101 S.Ct. 2047, 68 L.Ed.2d 349 (1981) (franchisees required to lease land and buildings from McDonald's).

abroad that are undertaken within six months of the home country filing for trademark registration will take priority.

The Paris Convention has in excess of 170 member nations. Since the Convention provides that any domestic trademark registration filing gives rise to priority in all Paris Convention countries, this means that foreign marks registered in countries that do not require use of the mark on an actual product can be obtained in the United States. In other words, foreign trademarks that are not used are entitled under the Paris Convention to U.S. trademark registration. Since 1988, the foreign applicant must state a bona fide intention to use the mark in commerce, but actual use is not required prior to registration.[19]

The Paris Convention also deals with unregistered trademarks. Article 6bis requires the member nations to refuse to register, to cancel an existing registration or to prohibit the use of a trademark which is considered by the trademark registration authorities of that country to be "well known" and owned by a person entitled to the benefits of the Paris Convention. This provision concerns what are called "famous marks" and prevents their infringement even if there has been no local registration of the mark. This is a remarkable development because it effectively creates trademark rights without registration. It has, for example, been successfully invoked in the People's Republic of China in order to protect against infringing use of Walt Disney and other well-known trademarks. In protecting such marks, China sided with the interpretation of the Paris Convention that marks that are well-known internationally deserve protection, even if not well known locally.

§ 22.9 The Nice Agreement on Trademark Classification

The Nice Agreement addresses the question of registration by "class" or "classification" of goods. In order to simplify internal administrative procedures relating to marks, many countries classify and thereby identify goods (and sometimes services) which have the same or similar attributes. An applicant seeking registration of a mark often is required to specify the class or classes to which the product mark belongs. However, not all countries have the same classification system and some lack any such system. Article 1 of the Nice Agreement adopts, for the purposes of the registration of marks, a single classification system for goods and services. This has brought order out of chaos in the field.

---

[19] 15 U.S.C.A. § 1126(e).

§ 22.10 International Trademark Registration Treaties

The 1973 Vienna Trademark Registration Treaty (to which the United States is a signatory) contemplates an international filing and examination scheme like that in force for patents under the Patent Cooperation Treaty of 1970.[20] This treaty has not yet been fully implemented, but holds out the promise of reduced costs and greater uniformity when obtaining international trademark protection. The 1994 Trademark Law Treaty substantially harmonized trademark registration procedures. Numerous European and Mediterranean countries are parties to the 1891 Madrid Agreement for International Registration of Marks. Since 2002, the United States has joined in the Madrid Protocol of 1989. This agreement permits international filings to obtain national trademark rights in about 90 countries and is administered by WIPO. A Common Market trademark can now be obtained in the European Union, an alternative to national trademark registrations and the "principle of territoriality" underlying IP laws.

§ 22.11 The *Pronuptia* Case

The European Union (EU) has become an active regulator of franchise agreements. Prior to *Pronuptia*,[21] the Commission had never sought to apply Article 101 of the Treaty on the Functioning of the European Union (TFEU) to franchise agreements. *Pronuptia* arose from the refusal of a franchisee to pay license fees to the franchisor. The distribution of the Pronuptia brand wedding attire in the Federal Republic of Germany was handled by shops operated by the German franchisor and by independent retailers through franchise agreements with that franchisor. The franchisee had obtained franchises for three areas (Hamburg, Oldenburg and Hannover). The franchisor granted the franchisee exclusive rights to market and advertise under the name of "Pronuptia de Paris" in these specific territories. The franchisor promised not to open any shops or provide any goods or services to another person in those territories. The franchisor also agreed to assist the franchisee with business strategies and profitability.

The franchisee agreed to assume all the risk of opening a franchise as an independent retailer. The franchisee also agreed to the following: (1) To sell Pronuptia goods only in the store specified in the contract and to decorate and design the shop according to the

---

20 See Chapter 23.

21 Pronuptia de Paris GmbH v. Pronuptia de Paris Irmgard Schillgallis (1986) Eur.Comm.Rep. 353.

franchisor's instructions; (2) to purchase 80 percent of wedding related attire and a proportion of evening dresses from the franchisor, and to purchase the rest of such merchandise only from sellers approved by the franchisor; (3) to pay a one time entrance fee for exclusive rights to the specified territory and a yearly royalty fee of 10 percent of the total sales of Pronuptia and all other products; (4) to advertise only with the franchisor's approval in a method which would enhance the international reputation of the franchise; (5) to make the sale of bridal fashions the franchisee's main business purpose; (6) to consider the retail price recommendations of the franchisor; (7) to refrain from competing directly or indirectly during the contract period or for one year afterward with any Pronuptia store; and (8) to obtain the franchisor's prior approval before assigning the rights and obligations arising under the contract to a third party.

In due course, the case was referred to the European Court of Justice. The Court's judgment concentrates on the crucial issue of whether franchise agreements come within Article 101. The Court draws a preliminary distinction between "distribution" franchises such as Pronuptia as opposed to "service" and "production" franchises. The Court concludes that a franchising system as such does not interfere with competition. Consequently, clauses essential to enable franchising to function are not prohibited. Thus, the franchisor can communicate know-how or assistance and help franchisees apply its methods. The franchisor can take reasonable steps to keep its know-how or assistance from becoming available to competitors. Location clauses forbidding the franchisee during the contract, or for a reasonable time thereafter, from opening a store with a similar or identical object in an area where it might compete with another member of the franchise network were necessary for distribution franchises and therefore permissible. The obligation of the franchisee not to sell a licensed store without prior consent of the franchisor was similarly allowable.

Clauses necessary to preserve the identity and reputation of the franchise network, such as decorations and trademark usage, were upheld. The reputation and identity of the network may also justify a clause requiring the franchisee to sell only products supplied by the franchisor or by approved sources, at least if it would be too expensive to monitor the quality of the stock otherwise. Nevertheless, each franchisee must be allowed to buy from other franchisees. The requirement of uniformity may also justify advertisement approvals by the franchisor, but the franchisee must be allowed to set and advertise resale prices. The Court rejected the view that clauses tending to divide the Common Market between franchisor and franchisee or between franchisees are always necessary to protect the knowhow or the identity and the reputation of the network.

The location clause in *Pronuptia* was seen as potentially supporting exclusive territories. In combination, location clauses and exclusive territories may divide markets and so restrict competition within the network. Even if a potential franchisee would not take the risk of joining the network by making its own investment because it could not expect a profitable business due to the absence of protection from competition from other franchisees, that consideration (in the Court's view) could be taken into account only under an Article 101(3) individual exemption review by the Commission. The Commission, in fact, ultimately granted such an exemption to Pronuptia.[22]

§ 22.12 EU Regulations 4087/88, 2790/1999 and 330/10

The Commission, following the European Court of Justice decision in *Pronuptia,*[23] adopted a group exemption regulation (No. 4087/88) for franchise agreements under Article 101(3).[24] This regulation detailed permissible franchise restraints (the "white list") and impermissible obligations (the "black list"). Its terms were widely followed in drafting European franchise agreements. Any failure to adhere to the regulation could result in serious competition law (antitrust) sanctions.[25]

Regulation 4087/88 was superceded by Regulation 2790/1999, the vertical agreements regulation. This regulation was more economic and less formalistic than Regulation 4087/88. Supply and distribution agreements of firms with less than 30 percent market shares are generally exempt; this is known as a "safe harbor." Companies whose market shares exceed 30 percent may or may not be exempt, depending upon the results of individual competition law reviews by the Commission under Article 101(3). In either case, no vertical agreements containing so-called "hard core restraints" are exempt. These restraints concern primarily resale price maintenance, territorial and customer protection leading to market allocation, and in most instances exclusive dealing covenants that last more than five years.

22 Re Pronuptia, 30 O.J.Eur.Comm. 39 (L13/1987).

23 Pronuptia de Paris GmbH v. Pronuptia de Paris Irmgard Schillgallis (1986) Eur.Comm.Rep. 353.

24 O.J. 1988 L539/46.

25 See Chapter 20.

In 2010, a new vertical restraints Regulation 330/10 (with accompanying Guidelines) was issued. Its content is similar to that of 1999. Restrictions on the use of the Internet by distributors with at least one "brick-and-mortar" store are treated as a hardcore restraints. For example, distributors cannot be required to reroute Internet customers outside their territories to local dealers. Nor can they be forced to pay higher prices for online sales ("dual pricing"), or be limited in the amount sales made via the Internet, although a minimum amount of offline sales can be stipulated. Generally speaking, distributors may sell anywhere in the EU in response to customer demand ("passive sales"). Restraints on "actively" soliciting sales outside designated distributor territories, including by email or banner web advertising, are permissible. *Both* supplier and distributor must have less than 30% market shares to qualify for the 2010 "safe harbor."

Chapter 23

PATENT AND KNOWHOW LICENSING

Table of Sections

§ 23.1 Protecting Patents and Knowhow

This chapter concerns the most common form of lawful international technology transfer—patent and knowhow licensing. Before any patent licensing can take place, patents must be acquired in all countries in which the owner hopes there will be persons interested in purchasing the technology. Even in countries where the owner has no such hope, patent rights may still be obtained so as to foreclose future unlicensed competitors. Licensing is a middle ground alternative to exporting from the owner's home country and direct investment in host markets. It can often produce, with relatively little cost, immediate positive cash flows. After a brief introduction to patents and knowhow, the main themes of this chapter are standard licensing contract terms and the regulation of international licensing agreements.

§ 23.2 The Nature of Patents

For the most part, patents are granted to inventors according to national law. Thus, patents represent *territorial* grants of exclusive rights. The inventor receives Canadian patents, United States patents, Mexican patents, and so on. There are relatively few jurisdictions without some form of patent protection. However, legally protected intellectual property in one country may not be protected similarly in another country. For example, many third world nations *refuse* to grant patents on pharmaceuticals. These countries often assert that their public health needs require such a policy. Thailand has been one such country and unlicensed "generics" have been a growth industry there. Similarly, most European countries do not grant patents on medical and surgical therapeutic techniques for reasons of public policy.

Nominal patent protection in some developing nations may lack effective forms of relief—giving the appearance but not the reality of legal rights. Since international patent protection is expensive to obtain, some holders take a chance and limit their applications to those markets where they foresee demand or competition for their product. Nevertheless, U.S. nationals continue to receive tens of thousands of patents in other countries. But the reverse is also increasingly true. Residents of foreign countries now receive over 50 percent of the patents issued under United States law. In many countries, persons who deal with the issuance and protection of patents are called patent agents. In the United States, patent practice is a specialized branch of the legal profession. Obtaining international patent protection often involves retaining the services of specialists in each country.

What constitutes a "patent" and how it is protected in any country depends upon domestic law. In the United States, a patent issued by the U.S. Patent Office grants the right for 20 years to exclude everyone from making, using or selling the patented invention without the permission of the patentee.[1] The United States traditionally granted patents to the "first to invent," not (as in many other countries) the "first to file." In 2013, the U.S. switched to first to file rules. Patent infringement can result in injunctive and damages relief in the U.S. courts. "Exclusion orders" against foreign-made patent infringing goods are also available. Such orders are frequently issued by the International Trade Commission under Section 337 of the Tariff Act of 1930,[2] and are enforced by the U.S. Customs Service. A U.S. patent thus provides a short-term legal, but not necessarily economic, monopoly. For example, the exclusive legal rights conveyed by the patents held by Xerox on its photocopying machines have not given it a monopoly in the marketplace. There are many

---

1 35 U.S.C.A. § 154.

2 See Chapter 24.

other producers of non-infringing photocopy machines with whom Xerox competes.

There are basically two types of patent systems in the world community, registration and examination. Some countries (e.g., France) grant a patent upon "registration" accompanied by appropriate documents and fees, without making an inquiry about the patentability of the invention. The validity of such a patent grant is most difficult to gauge until a time comes to defend the patent against alleged infringement in an appropriate tribunal. In other countries, the patent grant is made following a careful "examination" of the prior art and statutory criteria on patentability or a "deferred examination" is made following public notice given to permit an "opposition." The odds are increased that the validity of such a patent will be sustained in the face of an alleged infringement. The United States and Germany have examination systems. To obtain U.S. patents, applicants must demonstrate to the satisfaction of the Patent and Trademark Office that their inventions are novel, useful and nonobvious. Nevertheless, a significant number of U.S. patents have been subsequently held invalid in the courts and the Patent Office has frequently been criticized for a lax approach to issuance of patents. Much of this growth is centered in high-tech industries, including computer software and business methods patents, for example Amazon's "Buy Now with 1-Click" software patent. The U.S. has also been criticized for sometimes allowing patents on "traditional knowledge" (e.g., Mexican Enola Beans) found primarily in the developing world.

The terms of a patent grant vary from country to country. For example, local law may provide for "confirmation," "importation," "introduction" or "revalidation" patents (which serve to extend limited protection to patents already existing in another country). "Inventor's certificates" and rewards are granted in some socialist countries where private ownership of the means of production is discouraged. The state owns the invention. This was the case in China, for example, but inventors now may obtain patents and exclusive private rights under the 1984 Patent Law. India requires pharmaceutical patents to be "more efficacious" than existing drugs, an "anti-evergreening" requirement the Indian Supreme Court aplied to deny Novartis a patent for its cancer drug Gleevac. Some countries, such as Britain, require that a patent be "worked" (commercially applied) within a designated period of time. This requirement is so important that the British mandate a "compulsory license" to local persons if a patent is deemed unworked. Many developing nations have similar provisions in their patent laws . . the owner must use it or lose it.

§ 23.3 The Nature of Knowhow and Trade Secrets

Knowhow is commercially valuable knowledge. It may or may not be a trade secret, and may or may not be patentable. Though often technical or scientific, e.g., engineering services, knowhow can also be more general in character. Marketing and management skills as well as simply business advice can constitute knowhow. If someone is willing to pay for the information, it can be sold or licensed internationally.

Legal protection for knowhow varies from country to country and is, at best, limited. Unlike patents, copyrights and trademarks, you cannot by registration obtain exclusive legal rights to knowhow. Knowledge, like the air we breathe, is a public good. Once released in the community, knowhow can generally be used by anyone and is almost impossible to retrieve. In the absence of exclusive legal rights, preserving the confidentiality of knowhow becomes an important business strategy. If everyone knows it, who will pay for it? If your competitors have access to the knowledge, your market position is at risk. It is for these reasons that only a few people on earth ever know the Coca Cola formula, which is perhaps the world's best kept knowhow.

In the United States, the Economic Espionage Act of 1996 creates *criminal* penalties for misappropriation of trade secrets for the benefit of foreign governments or anyone. For these purposes, a "trade secret" is defined as "financial, business, scientific, technical, economic or engineering information" that the owner has taken reasonable measures to keep secret and whose "independent economic value derives from being closely held." In addition to criminal fines, forfeitures and jail terms, the Act authorizes seizure of all proceeds from the theft of trade secrets as well as property used or intended for use in the misappropriation (e.g., buildings and capital equipment).

Protecting knowhow is mostly a function of contract, tort and trade secrets law. Employers will surround their critical knowhow with employees bound by contract to confidentiality. But some valuable knowledge leaks from or moves with these employees, e.g., when a disgruntled retired or ex-employee sells or goes public with the knowhow. The remedies at law or in equity for breach of contract are unlikely to render the employer whole. Neither is tort relief likely to be sufficient since most employees are essentially judgment proof, although they may be of more use if a competitor induced the breach of contract. Likewise, even though genuine trade secrets are protected by criminal statutes in a few jurisdictions, persuading the prosecutor to take up your business problem is not easy and criminal penalties will not recoup the trade secrets (though they may make the revelation of others less likely in the future).

Despite all of these legal hazards, even when certain knowhow is patentable, a desire to prolong the commercial exploitation of that knowledge may result in no patent registrations. The international chemicals industry, for example, is said to prefer trade secrets to public disclosure and patent rights with time limitations. Licensing or selling such knowhow around the globe is risky, but lucrative.

§ 23.4 International Patent and Knowhow Licensing

This section concerns the most common form of lawful international technology transfer-patent and knowhow licensing. Before any patent licensing can take place, patents must be acquired in all countries in which the owner hopes there will be persons interested in purchasing the technology. Even in countries where the owner has no such hope, patent rights may still be obtained so as to foreclose future unlicensed competitors. Licensing is a middle ground alternative to exporting from the owner's home country and direct investment in host markets. It can often produce, with relatively little cost, immediate positive cash flows.

International patent and knowhow licensing is the most critical form of technology transfer to third world development. From the owner's standpoint, it presents an alternative to and sometimes a first step towards foreign investment. Such licensing involves a transfer of patent rights or knowhow (commercially valuable knowledge, often falling short of a patentable invention) in return for payments, usually termed royalties. Unlike foreign investment, licensing does not have to involve a capital investment in a host jurisdiction and may be tax-advantaged. However, licensing of patents and knowhow is not without legal risks.

From the licensee's standpoint, and the perspective of its government, there is the risk that the licensed technology may be old or obsolete, not "state of the art." Goods produced under old technology will be hard to export and convey a certain "second class" status. On the other hand, older more labor intensive technologies may actually be sought (as sometimes done by the PRC) in the early stages of development. Excessive royalties may threaten the economic viability of the licensee and drain hard currencies from the country. The licensee typically is not in a sufficiently powerful position to bargain away restrictive features of standard international licenses. For all these reasons, and more, third world countries frequently regulate patent and knowhow licensing agreements. Such law is found in the Brazilian Normative Act No. 17 (1976) and the Mexican Technology Transfer Law (1982) (repealed 1991), among others. Royalty levels will be limited, certain clauses prohibited (e.g., export restraints, resale price maintenance, mandatory grantbacks to the licensor of improvements), and the desirability of the technology evaluated.

Regulation of licensing is not limited to the developing world. The European Union extensively regulates patent and knowhow licensing.[3] In the United States, there is a less direct form of licensing regulation via antitrust law.[4]

The licensor also faces legal risks. The flow of royalty payments may be stopped, suspended or reduced by currency exchange regulations. The taxation of the royalties, if not governed by double taxation treaties, may be confiscatory. The licensee may abscond with the technology or facilitate "gray market" goods[5] which eventually compete for sales in markets exclusively intended for the licensor. In the end, patents expire and become part of the world domain. At that point, unless the technology is somehow tied to a protected trade secret, the licensee has effectively purchased the technology and becomes an independent competitor (though not necessarily an effective competitor if the licensor has made new technological advances).

Licensing is a kind of partnership. If the licensee succeeds, the licensor's royalties (often based on sales volumes) will increase and a continuing partnership through succeeding generations of technology may evolve. If not, the dispute settlement provisions of the agreement may be called upon as either party withdraws from the partnership. Licensing of patents and knowhow often is combined with, indeed essential to, foreign investments. A foreign subsidiary or joint venture will need technical assistance and knowhow to commence operations. When this occurs, the licensing terms are usually a part of the basic joint venture or investment agreement. Licensing may also be combined with a trade agreement, as where the licensor ships necessary supplies to the licensee, joint venturer,

---

[3] See Section 23.8.

[4] See generally the *Antitrust Guidelines for the Licensing for Intellectual Property* issued by the U.S. Dept. of Justice and the Federal Trade Commission on April 6, 1995. BNA–ATRR, Vol. 68, No. 1708 (April 13, 1995), Special Supplement. These Guidelines are primarily domestic in orientation, but also apply to international licensing.

[5] See Chapter 24.

or subsidiary. Such supply agreements have sometimes been used to overcome royalty limitations through a form of "transfer pricing," the practice of marking up or down the price of goods so as to allocate revenues to preferred parties and jurisdictions (e.g. tax havens).

§ 23.5 International Acquisition of Patents

The principal treaties regarding patents are the 1970 Patent Cooperation Treaty and the 1883 Paris Convention for the Protection of Industrial Property, frequently revised and amended. To some extent, the Paris Convention also deals with trademarks, servicemarks, trade names, industrial designs, and unfair competition. Other recent treaties dealing with patents are the European Patent Convention (designed to permit offices at Munich and The Hague to issue patents of all countries party to the treaty), the European Community Patent Convention (designed to create a single patent valid throughout the EU) and the 1994 Eurasian Patent Convention (which does the same for Russia and the Central Asian states).

Paris Convention

The Paris Convention,[6] to which over 170 countries including the U.S. are parties, remains the basic international agreement dealing with treatment of foreigners under national patent laws. It is administered by the International Bureau of the World Intellectual Property Organization (WIPO) at Geneva. The "right of national treatment" (Article 2) prohibits discrimination against foreign holders of local patents and trademarks. Thus, for example, an American granted a Canadian patent must receive the same legal rights and remedies accorded Canadian nationals. Furthermore, important "rights of priority" are granted to patent holders provided they file in foreign jurisdictions within twelve months of their home country patent applications. But such rights conceivably may not overcome prior filings in "first to file" jurisdiction.

Patent applications in foreign jurisdictions are not dependent upon success in the home country: Patentability criteria vary from country to country. Nevertheless, the Paris Convention obviates the need to file simultaneously in every country where intellectual property protection is sought. If an inventor elects not to obtain patent protection in other countries, anyone may make, use or sell the invention in that territory. The Paris Convention does not attempt to reduce the need for individual patent applications in all jurisdic-

---

6 21 U.S.T. 1583, T.I.A.S. No. 6295, 828 U.N.T.S. 305 (Stockholm revision).

tions where patent protection is sought. Nor does it alter the various domestic criteria on patentability.

Patent Cooperation Treaty

The Patent Cooperation Treaty (PCT),[7] to which about 140 countries including the U.S. are parties, is designed to achieve greater uniformity and less cost in the international patent filing process, and in the examination of prior art. Instead of filing patent applications individually in each nation, filings under the PCT are done in selected countries. The national patent offices of Japan, Sweden, Russia and the United States have been designated International Searching Authorities (ISA), as have the European Patent Offices at Munich and The Hague. The international application, together with the international search report, is communicated by an ISA to each national patent office where protection is sought. Nothing in this Treaty limits the freedom of each nation to establish substantive conditions of patentability and determine infringement remedies.

However, the Patent Cooperation Treaty also provides that the applicant may arrange for an international preliminary examination in order to formulate a nonbinding opinion on whether the claimed invention is novel, involves an inventive step (non-obvious) and is industrially applicable. In a country without sophisticated search facilities, the report of the international preliminary examination may largely determine whether a patent will be granted. For this reason alone, the Patent Cooperation Treaty may generate considerable uniformity in world patent law. In 1986 the United States ratified the PCT provisions on preliminary examination reports, thereby supporting such uniformity.

§ 23.6 European Patents

The 1973 European Patent Convention (EPC)[8] established the European Patent Offices (EPO) in Munich and The Hague. It allows applicants to simultaneously apply for national patent rights in any of the contracting countries. These include all of the EU nations save Spain, plus a number of other European states. The applicant must meet the requirements for patentability established by the EPC. Challenges to patentability decisions by the EPO may be made within 9 months after granting of the patent. Thereafter, challenges must be made in national courts subject to national patent laws. Thus, the EPC basically presents a one-stop opportunity

---

7 28 U.S.T. 7645, T.I.A.S. No. 8733.

8 13 Int'l Legal Mats. 268 (1974).

to obtain a basket of national patents in Europe. It does not foreclose the option of individual national patent applications.

A European Union Patent Convention (CPC) will finally come into force in 2014. The Convention originally provided that it had to be ratified by all members before becoming effective. However, a conference was held in December 1985. It produced a "Community Patent Agreement," a "Protocol" on the settlement of disputes regarding infringement and validity of Community patents, a "Protocol" amending the Community Patent Convention, and two "Protocols" on a Community Court of [Patent] Appeals. It was agreed in 1985 that if unanimous CPC ratification was not achieved by December 31, 1991, a lesser number of required ratifications would suffice. The Convention was therefore expected to come into force before the end of 1992, but realization of this goal remained elusive until 2012 when 25 of the EU member states agreed to move forward on "enhanced cooperation" to create a "unitary" patent. The abstainers were Italy and Spain, miffed because their languages are not used, only French, English and German.

The Unitary Patent regime will allow applications for a Common Market patent valid in 25 contracting states. Applications will be handled by the EPO in Munich. A Unitary patent may be granted, revoked or transferred. Licenses for part of the Union will be possible. The Unitary Patent will be an alternative to (but not a replacement for) national or EPO patent rights. Its signatories are required to harmonize national patent laws to conform to Unitary Patent rules on infringement, litigation procedures, exhaustion of rights and other issues. A new Unified Patent Court primarily based in Paris will become the final arbiter on unified patent disputes, though references to the European Court of Justice on questions of interpretation of Unitary Patent regulations and the EU directive in biotech inventions are mandatory. By 2021, patent disputes concerning nationally issued or EPO patents will also be exclusively resolved by the Unified Patent Court. A special Court of Appeals for patent matters will be created in Luxembourg.

§ 23.7 European Patent and Knowhow Licensing

In its 1982 *Maize Seed* judgment, the European Court of Justice addressed patent license restrictions under the Community's competition rules.[9] The Commission waited for this judgment before publishing the 1984 group exemption under Article 101(3) TFEU for patent licensing agreements. In this case, a research institute fi-

---

[9] Nungesser v. Commission (1982) Eur.Comm.Rep. 2015. For an overview of the European competition law, see Chapter 20.

nanced by the French government (INRA) bred varieties of basic seeds. In 1960, INRA assigned to Kurt Eisele plant breeder's rights for maize seed in the Federal Republic of Germany. Eisele agreed to apply for registration of these rights in accordance with German law. In 1965, a formal agreement was executed by the parties. This agreement consisted of five relevant clauses.

Clause 1 gave Eisele the exclusive rights to "organize" sales of six identified varieties of maize seed propagated from basic seeds provided by INRA. This enabled Eisele to exercise control over distribution outlets. Eisele undertook not to deal in maize varieties other than those provided by INRA. Clause 2 required Eisele to place no restriction on the supply of seed to technically suitable distributors except for rationing in conditions of shortage. The prices charged to the distributors by Eisele were fixed in consultation with INRA, according to a specified formula. Clause 3 obligated Eisele to import from France for sale in Germany at least two-thirds of that territory's requirements for the registered varieties. This restricted Eisele's own production and sale to only one-third of the German market. Clause 4 concerned the protection by Eisele of INRA's proprietary rights, including its trademark, from infringement and granted Eisele the power to take any action to that end. Clause 5 contained a promise by INRA that no experts to Germany of the relevant varieties would take place otherwise than through the agency of Eisele. This meant that INRA would ensure that its French marketing organization would prevent the relevant varieties from being exported to Germany to parallel importers.

In September 1972, it became apparent that dealers in France were selling the licensed varieties of maize seed directly to German traders who were marketing the products in breach of the breeder's rights claimed by Eisele. This resulted in an action by Eisele in the German courts against one of the traders. The parties reached a court approved settlement under which the French trader promised to refrain from offering for sale without permission any variety of maize seed within the rights held by Eisele, and to pay a fine. In February 1974, another breach took place, this time advertising in the German press by a French dealer. In response to threats of legal proceedings, this dealer lodged a complaint with the Commission alleging breach of the Treaty of Rome competition rules.

The Commission considered both the agreement and the settlement to violate Article 101(1) because they granted an exclusive license and provided absolute territorial protection. The Court of Justice reversed the Commission with respect to exclusivity, but upheld the Commission with respect to absolute territorial protection. The Court drew a distinction between "open" licenses which do not necessarily fall under Article 101(1), and "closed" licenses which do so.

Open license agreements are those which do not involve third parties. In *Maize Seed,* the obligation upon INRA or those deriving rights through INRA to refrain from producing or selling the relevant seeds in Germany was treated as an open license term. The Court held such clauses necessary to the dissemination of new technology inasmuch as potential licensees might otherwise be deterred from accepting the risk of cultivating and marketing new products. The Court defined closed licenses as those involving third parties. Thus, the obligation upon INRA or those deriving rights through INRA to prevent third parties from exporting the seeds into Germany without authorization, Eisele's concurrent use of his exclusive contractual rights, and his breeder's rights, to prevent all imports into Germany or exports to other member states were invalid under Article 101(1).

The Commission of the European Community adopted in 1984 a patent licensing group exemption regulation under Article 101(3).[10] It acknowledged that patent licensing improves the production of goods and promotes technical progress by allowing licensees to operate with the latest technology. The Commission also believes that patent licensing increases both the number of production facilities and the quantity and quality of goods in the Common Market. Commission Regulation 2349/84 covered patent licensing agreements and licensing agreements for both patents and knowhow. Commission Regulation 556/89 covered pure knowhow licensing agreements, also exempting them under the terms of Article 101(3). Knowhow was broadly conceived in this regulation. Nonpatented technical information (*e.g.,* descriptions of manufacturing processes, recipes, formulae, designs or drawings) was the focus of Regulation 556/89.

§ 23.8 European Transfer of Technology Regulation

In 1996 the Commission enacted Regulation 240/96 on the application of Article 101(3) TFEU to transfer technology agreements. The intention of this Regulation was to combine the existing patent and knowhow block exemptions into a single regulation covering technology transfer agreements, and to simplify and harmonize the rules for patent and knowhow licensing. It was also intended to en-

---

[10] Commission Regulation 2349/84.

courage dissemination of technological knowledge and promote the manufacture of more technologically advanced goods.

Transfer of Technology Regulation 772/2004

The detailed regulation of technology transfer agreement clauses contained in Regulation 240/96 was replaced by Regulation 772/2004, which applies to patent, know-how and software copyright licensing. The new Regulation distinguishes agreements between those of "competing" and "noncompeting" parties, the latter being treated less strictly than the former. Parties are deemed "competing" if they compete (without infringing each other's IP rights) in either the relevant technology or product market, determined in each instance by what buyers regard as substitutes.[11] If the competing parties have a *combined* market share of 20 percent or less, their licensing agreements are covered by group exemption under Regulation 772/2004.[12] Noncompeting parties, on the other hand, benefit from the group exemption so long as their *individual* market shares do not exceed 30 percent.[13] Agreements initially covered by Regulation 772/2004 that subsequently exceed the "safe harbor" thresholds noted above lose their exemption subject to a two-year grace period.[14] Outside these exemptions, a "rule of reason" approach applies.

Inclusion of certain "hardcore restraints" causes license agreement to lose their group exemption. For competing parties, such restraints include price fixing,[15] output limitations on both parties,[16] limits on the licensee's ability to exploit its own technology,[17] and allocation of markets or competitors (subject to exceptions).[18] Specifically, restraints on active and passive selling by the licensee in a territory reserved for the licensor are allowed, as are active (but not passive) selling restraints by licensees in territories of other licensees.[19] Licensing agreements between noncompeting parties may not contain the "hardcore" restraint of maximum price fixing.[20] Active selling restrictions on licensees can be utilized, along with passive selling restraints in territories reserved to the licensor or (for

11 Regulation 772/2004, Article 1(1)j.

12 *Id.*, Article 3(1).

13 *Id.*, Article 3(2).

14 *Id.*, Article 8(2).

15 *Id.*, Article 4(1)(a).

16 *Id.*, Article 4(1)(b).

17 *Id.*, Article 4(1)(d).

18 *Id.*, Article 4(1)(c).

19 *Id.*, Article 4(1)(c)(iv) and (v).

20 *Id.*, Article 4(2)(a).

two years) another licensee.[21] For these purposes, the competitive status of the parties is decided at the outset of the agreement.[22]

Other license terms deemed "excluded restrictions" also cause a loss of exemption.[23] Such clauses include: (1) mandatory grant-backs or assignments of severable improvements by licensees, excepting nonexclusive license-backs;[24] (2) no-challenges by the licensee of the licensor's intellectual property rights, subject to the licensor's right to terminate upon challenge;[25] and (3) for noncompeting parties, restraints on the licensee's ability to exploit its own technology or either party's ability to carry out research and development (unless indispensable to prevent disclosure of the licensed Know-how).[26]

In all cases, exemption under Regulation 772/2004 may be withdrawn where in any particular case an agreement has effects that are incompatible with Article 101(3) TFEU.[27]

§ 23.9 Technology Transfers

The process of transferring technology involves an agreement which outlines the relationship between the transferor and the transferee. The extent to which the agreement is detailed may depend upon the character of the transferee.

Subsidiary or affiliate as transferee. Even when the technology is transferred to a wholly owned subsidiary in a foreign nation, there is almost always some agreement, at the very least for tax purposes. The corporate structure using a parent and subsidiary (the latter being an entity incorporated under the laws of the foreign host nation) demands that the separate nature of the two entities be maintained. If not, the parent may be held responsible for the debts of the subsidiary under veil piercing theory. Consequently, the transfer of technology from a parent to a subsidiary should be at arms length and represented by a written agreement.[28] But if the parent is convinced that there is little likelihood that the subsidiary's management will adversely affect the value of the technology, or pro-

---

21 *Id.*, Article 4(2)(b).

22 *Id.*, Article 4(3).

23 *Id.*, Article 5.

24 *Id.*, Article 5(1)(a).

25 *Id.*, Article 5(1)(b) and (c).

26 *Id.*, Article 5(2).

27 *Id.*, Article 6.

28 If it is not an arms length transaction, there may be accusations that transfer pricing is involved.

duce poor quality goods using the technology, there are likely to be fewer provisions in the agreement than where the transferee is an independent entity, unrelated to the transferor.

Independent transferee. When the agreement is to transfer technology to an entity which is not part of the transferor's corporate structure, such as a subsidiary or affiliate, there will be a sense that more detail ought to appear in the technology agreement. For example, disputes will not be settled "within" the company, as they may when the transfer of technology is to a subsidiary, but by judicial or arbitral tribunals. A transfer within a corporate structure is usually easily worked out, but a transfer to an independent transferee may involve considerable negotiation of many details.

§ 23.10 Regulations in the Country of the Transferee

When there are no transfer of technology rules in the country of the transferee, the technology transfer agreement is the conclusion of the bargaining of the two parties, the transferor and the transferee. The agreement will not be public; it will not be registered. But when the transfer of technology is to some nations, especially developing nations and nonmarket economy nations, there may be a third party, i.e., the government, involved both in the determination and regulation of what may and may not be included in the technology transfer agreement, and in approving the agreement. During the 1970s a number of developing nations enacted transfer of technology laws.[29] The laws were adopted both as part of the general attempt to control foreign investment and technology transfers, but also to preserve scarce hard currency at a time of severe balance of payment problems. The developing nations viewed technology transfers as an area of investment where there were serious abuses, and believed that their laws would adequately address these issues.[30] The principal abuses were thought to include the following:

1. Transfer of obsolete technology;

2. Excessive price paid for the technology;

---

[29] For example, Mexico adopted a transfer of technology law in 1972. It was amended in 1982 but remained restrictive. In 1991 it was replaced by a law which removed the focus on restrictions and replaced this focus with more investment encouraging and protecting provisions.

[30] See Radway, Antitrust, Technology Transfers and Joint Ventures in Latin American Development, 15 Lawyer Am. 47 (1983).

3. Limitations on use of new developments by the transferee by grantback provisions;

4. Little research performed by the transferee;

5. Too much intervention by the transferor in transferee activities;

6. Limitations on where the transferee may market the product;

7. Requirements that components be purchased from the transferor which are available locally or could be obtained from other foreign sources more cheaply;

8. Inadequate training of transferee's personnel to do jobs performed by personnel of the transferor;

9. Transfer of technology which has adequate domestic substitutes and is therefore not needed;

10. Too long a duration of the agreement; and

11. Application of foreign law and use of foreign tribunals for dispute resolution.

These do not establish an exclusive list. Some nations had different reasons for wishing to more closely govern technology transfers. But these reasons provide an outline of what areas transfer of technology laws in the 1970s attempted to govern.

The result of these restrictive laws was the transfer of less technology, and of technology less valuable to the parent. It was often older technology over which the company was willing to relinquish some control. The bureaucracies established to register and approve or disapprove the agreements were often staffed with persons who knew little about technology, less about international business, but who possessed all of the inefficiency and incompetence of many developing nation government agencies. The laws did not bring in more technology, but less. The consequence was that they did not serve the purpose of helping the balance of payments. Furthermore, the nations which adopted strict rules regulating the transfer of technology often did not have laws which protected intellectual property.

In the 1980s, these restrictive laws were dismantled in many countries, whether by formal repeal or replacement by more transfer encouraging and intellectual property protecting laws, or by a relaxed interpretation of the laws and a general automatic approval of what the transferor and transferee agreed upon. In the 1990s transferring technology increased.[31] Ironically, some technology agreements which were used in the 1960s before the enactment of the strict laws, and which became unusable after such enactments, are now once again be used in the developing world but regulated in the European Union (above). Much of the remainder of this chapter will focus on the nature of modern transfer of technology agreements.

§ 23.11 Different Kinds of Agreements

There are many variations of technology transfer agreements. But they all in some way address the transfer of intellectual property. The agreement may be exclusively for that purpose, or the transfer may be part of a larger agreement, such as the creation of a joint venture. What is included within the definition of intellectual property or technology transfers tends to be quite broad. The transfer may involve property which is granted protection under such laws as those protecting and regulating patents, copyrights and trademarks, or the transfer may involve property which is not granted such protection, but where some protection is maintained by controlling who obtains the knowledge. The previous chapter discussed the licensing of two forms of property, franchises and trademarks. This chapter considers licensing patents, trade secrets and knowhow.

A comparatively new form of transferring technology is by way of a strategic alliance. It is a kind of joint venture where two firms (or more) from different nations agree to jointly exploit technology. The participants often make different contributions to the alliance—one may contribute technology, another capital, or a distribution network, or service facilities, etc. Perhaps the most important part of a strategic alliance is the technology license agreement. It is not always clear whether the alliance structure also transfers enforcement rights to the licensee of the technology.[32]

---

[31] But it has only increased when the nations not only dismantled their restrictive transfer of technology laws, but also adopted laws protecting intellectual property, including knowhow.

[32] See J. Atik, Technology and Distribution as Organizational Elements Within International Strategic Alliances, 14 U. Pa. J. Int'l Bus. L. 273 (1993).

§ 23.12 Agreement to License a Patent

The agreement to license a patent is a common form of agreement. The transferor presumably owns a valid patent and wishes to transfer its exploitation. Exploiting the patent widely may gain the most return from the limited period the property is granted patent protection. The transferor will likely have sought patent protection in the transferee's nation, just as it has registered the patent in its home nation. Both prevent others from using the patent. Transferring the patent does not create this protection from the use by others; it may well place the patent at risk. The protection is gained by national or multinational permission or agreement included in treaties and laws. The patent is not transferred by the registration abroad, but by the transfer agreement. There are thus two stages which are important for counsel. The first is gaining protection of the patent under the laws of every nation where the patent might be transferred, or where one fears that local parties may try to exploit the property. The second is transferring its use to a firm abroad. It is the licensee which will exploit the patent, and may be required by the agreement, or by virtue of the agreement, to undertake considerable expenditure in such exploitation.

§ 23.13 Agreement to License Knowhow or Trade Secrets

This information, or intellectual property, is often not available to the public. It is safe in some nations only as long as it can be kept from others. But many nations, both developed and an increasing number of developing, protect knowhow. Knowhow and trade secrets may be related to patents, in that it may deal with how the products are used, the cost of production, where they can best be marketed, etc. For example, a product which is expensive to produce may be difficult to market without knowledge of those who may be able to afford its purchase. A list of names of persons with the money and inclination to make such purchase may be a precondition to successful production and sales. The value of knowhow will vary considerably from one form to another. Knowhow can be very tenuous in its capacity to be protected, making the agreement an important device to establish the rules for its use by a licensee. Much of the agreement will focus on the protection and limits of permitted use of the knowhow.

All WTO member-nations are obliged under the TRIPs agreement to protect trade secrets. Because some nations do not protect knowhow or other proprietary information, it must be protected in the transfer agreement. What becomes important is for the transferee to agree to the contractually stated conditions of its use, and to assume responsibility for its improper dissemination to the public or other persons, particularly competitors. In a country where no protection is granted by law, dissemination may cause a severe financial loss to the transferor. Protecting the knowhow from such loss is thus central to an agreement to license knowhow.

§ 23.14 Agreement as Part of a Foreign Direct Investment

Any foreign direct investment which includes the transfer of some technology may include the transfer in an agreement which also includes the direct investment, quite possibly in a joint venture contract. Whether there is such an agreement will depend on the laws of the host nation. Sometimes foreign direct investment requires nothing more than entering the host nation with a branch operation or establishing a local wholly owned subsidiary. The articles of incorporation of the subsidiary will not include anything relating to the transfer of technology to the subsidiary. There will be a separate transfer of technology agreement. But in many nations which restrict foreign investment, there may be an agreement which expresses the total relationship, including the transfer of technology.[33] Investment in nations which mandate joint ventures are the most likely situations where the investment agreement will also include the technology transfer provisions. There is nothing wrong with combining transfer of technology provisions in a larger scope agreement, but the agreement ought to be just as detailed regarding technology provisions as it would standing alone as a separate agreement.

Where technology is transferred within the context of a joint venture or other form of investment agreement, the agreement ought to be clear as to the access of the host nation joint venture partner to any sensitive technology. Particularly where there is knowhow transferred, the foreign investor may wish to control the local party's access to the technology.[34] India demanded in the 1970s that the Coca–Cola company alter its structure from a wholly foreign owned investment to a joint venture. While the Indian gov-

---

[33] For example, the few foreign investments established in Cuba must comply with the broad and often vague provisions of the out-of-date 1982 joint venture law. That law notes the need for foreign technology and that a formal agreement with the government for an investment must also outline the nature of any technology transfers. Little technology is being transferred because there is little protection to technology under Cuban law.

[34] While the local party may be one trusted by the foreign investor, unless there are restrictions on the transfer of ownership interests, that party may change and bring into the ownership and management persons less trusted.

ernment did not expressly state that the foreign parent would have to share the secret formula, the government did say that such sharing would be the natural consequence of the partnership sense of the joint venture. Coca–Cola would not disclose the technology, and withdrew from India, not to return until the 1990s, when India had relaxed its previously strict foreign investment rules.

§ 23.15 Other Forms of Agreement

Transfers may assume other functions or address other matters than noted above. They sometimes apply to a particular area because of the frequent use of licensing for that area.

Franchises. An example of a special form of licensing is the licensing of a franchise abroad.[35] While some franchises own their outlets, many are franchised to local investors. The licensing may involve transfers of trade secrets, knowhow, trademarks, patents and copyrights. All will be included in the same franchise agreement.

Computer software. The laws of some nations do not recognize computer software as protectable property by copyright or as a trade secret, thus making a transfer particularly risky.[36] Even when there is legal recognition of computer software as protectable property, however, it may be best not to transfer it if the risk of loss is high. Where the computer technology is contained in the end product, such as the bar coding process for retail products, the software technology may be protected by retaining it in the home country and only transferring the end use product.

Management contracts. Many enterprises, especially in the hotel industry, function by means of management contracts. The transfer usually involves knowhow, the knowledge of how to operate a facility. Often the most important aspect of the transfer is the experience of the manager of the management company. That experience is reflected in the manager's day to day decisions. It is an experience which has proven that it has value. For example, many Cuban government organizations attempted to manage hotels to develop tourism beginning in the mid–1980s. But the hotels were inefficiently managed until foreign management was obtained.

Training contracts. Knowledge of how to undertake a particular function or functions has value. That knowledge may be transferred

---

35 Franchises are discussed in chapter 18 which addresses trademarks.

36 It may be recognized as property protected by copyright.

as any other knowhow. The management contract noted above may include training of host nation persons in hotel management.[37]

[37] Even if the management contract is not also a training contract, there will be a certain amount of transfer of training involved, simply by the other employees viewing how a well managed unit functions.

Chapter 24

COUNTERFEIT, INFRINGING AND GRAY MARKET IMPORTS—UNITED STATES SECTION 337 PROCEEDINGS

Table of Sections

---

§ 24.1 Technology Transfers

The predominant vehicle for controlling technology transfers across national borders is the "license" or "franchise" contract. The holder of a patent, copyright or trademark in one country first acquires the legally protected right to the same in another country. This is a time consuming and expensive process. Convincing new franchising operations or other holders of patents, trademarks and copyrights of the value of securing international protection is often a role which falls to counsel. The holder then licenses foreign rights, usually for a fee known as royalty, to a persons in those countries. Thus, the licensor typically conveys to the licensee rights to make, use or sell the technology. The very sharing of intellectual property rights across borders raises a risk that proprietary control of the technology may be lost, or at a minimum, that a competitor will be created. For these reasons, international licensing agreements are complex legal documents that need to be carefully negotiated and drafted. Absent licensed transfers, piracy of intellectual property is increasingly commonplace. Indeed, in some countries such theft has risen to the height of development strategy.

Issues surrounding the transfer of knowledge across national borders have provoked intense discussions during the last decade. The discussions promise to continue unabated. At the core is the desire of third world countries (often advanced developing countries like China, Brazil, and India) to obtain protected information quickly and affordably irrespective of the proprietary rights and profit motives of current holders (usually persons from the most developed countries). Developing countries want production processes which maximize inexpensive labor but which result in products that are competitive in the international marketplace. Capital intensive production processes (e.g., robot production of automobiles) may be of less interest. MNEs may be willing to share (by way of license or sale) a good deal of proprietary information, but are reluctant to part with their "core technology."

The developing nations (as a "Group of 77"), the industrialized nations, and the nonmarket economy nations have tried to agree in UNCTAD upon an international "Code of Conduct" for the transfer of technology. Wide disparities in attitudes toward such a Code, which has now gone through many drafts, have been reflected by the developing nations' insistence that it be "internationally legally binding," and the industrialized nations' position that it consist of "guidelines" for the international transfer of technology. Some economics of the debate are illustrated by the fact that persons in the United States pay millions of dollars in royalties for the use of imported technology, but received billions in royalty payments from technology sent abroad. Many considered development of an international technology transfer Code the most important feature of the North–South dialogue between developed and developing nations. But it was not to be. Instead to some degree the TRIPs Agreement from the Uruguay Round of GATT negotiations functions as such a code.

Among the industrialized countries, efforts often occur to acquire (even by way of stealing) "leading edge" technology. One example in the 1980s involved attempted theft of IBM computer technology by Japanese companies ultimately caught by the F.B.I. In the United States, the Office of Export Administration uses the export license procedure to control strategic technological "diversions." But falsification of licensing documents by prominent Norwegian and Japanese companies allowed the Soviets to obtain the technology for making vastly quieter submarine propellers. In the ensuing scandal, "anti-Toshiba" trade sanctions were adopted in the United States. Leading Japanese executives resigned their positions, which is considered the highest form of apology in Japanese business circles. In 2009, U.S. officials seized about $260 million in counterfeit goods. Chinese gangs accounted for the bulk of these goods, which were most often footwear, consumer electronics, luxury goods and pharmaceuticals. U.S. military and civilian procurement agencies have begun actively targeting counterfeit suppliers. An Anti-Counterfeiting Trade Agreement (ACTA) is in the works, though China is not expected to participate.

Theft of intellectual property and use of counterfeit goods are rapidly increasing in developing and developed countries. Such theft is not limited to consumer goods (Pierre Cardin clothing, Rolex watches). Industrial products and parts (e.g., automotive brake pads) are now being counterfeited. Some countries see illegal technology transfers as part of their strategy for economic development. They encourage piracy or choose not to oppose it. Since unlicensed producers pay no royalties, they often have lower production costs than the original source. This practice fuels the fires of intellectual property piracy. Unlicensed low-cost reproduction of entire copyrighted books (may it not happen to this book) is said to be rampant in such diverse areas as Nigeria, Saudi Arabia, and South Korea. Apple computers have been inexpensively counterfeited in Hong Kong. General Motors estimates that about 40 percent of its auto parts are counterfeited in the Middle East. Recordings are duplicated almost everywhere without license or fee. And the list goes on.

§ 24.2 Counterfeit Goods, U.S. Remedies

Legal protection against intellectual property theft and counterfeit goods is not very effective. The four principal U.S. remedies are: (1) seizure of goods by Customs; (2) infringement actions in federal courts; (3) criminal prosecutions or treble damages actions under the Trademark Counterfeiting Act of 1984; and (4) Section 337 proceedings. Each of these is discussed below.

The Anticounterfeiting Consumer Protection Act of 1996, Public Law 104–153 (110 Stat. 1386), made a number of statutory changes intended to combat counterfeiting. Trafficking in counterfeit goods is now an offense under the RICO Act (Racketeer Influenced and Corrupt Organizations Act). Importers must disclose the identity of any trademark on imported merchandise, ex parte seizures by law enforcement officers of counterfeit goods and vehicles used to transport them are widely authorized, damages and civil penalties that can be recovered from counterfeiters and importers were increased, and the Customs Service's authority to return counterfeit merchandise to its source (and potential re-entry into commerce) has been repealed. Customs must now destroy all counterfeit merchandise that it seizes unless the trademark owner otherwise consents and the goods are not a health or safety threat.

In the United States, the Copyright Felony Act of 1992 criminalized all copyright infringements. The No Electronic Theft Act of 1997 (NET) removed the need to prove financial gain as element of copyright infringement law, thus ensuring coverage of copying done with intent to harm copyright owners or copying simply for personal use. The Digital Millennium Copyright Act of 1998 (DMCA) brought the United States into compliance with WIPO treaties and created two new copyright offenses; one for circumventing technological measures used by copyright owners to protect their works ("hacking") and a second for tampering with copyright management information (encryption). The DMCA also made it clear that "webmasters" digitally broadcasting music on the internet must pay performance royalties. Criminal and civil sanctions apply.[1]

§ 24.3 Customs Service Seizures

United States trademark and copyright holders may register with the Customs Service and seek the blockade of pirated items made abroad. Such exclusions are authorized in the Tariff Act of 1930 and the Copyright Act of 1976.[2] The thrust of these provisions is that unauthorized imports bearing U.S. registered trademarks or copyrights may be seized by the Customs Service. Trade names that have been used for at least six months can also be recorded with the Customs Service. Such recordation permits those names to receive the same relief accorded registered trademark and copyright holders when imports that counterfeit or simulate those trade names are found.[3] Since these trademark, copyright and trade name remedies are only available to United States citizens, distributors of foreign goods must ordinarily be assigned United States trademark rights held by foreigners. Such assignments would permit the dis-

---

1 See, e.g., Universal City Studios, Inc. v. Shawn C. Reimerdes, 111 F.Supp.2d 294 (2000) (injunction against anti-encryption software).

2 See 19 U.S.C.A. § 1526(a) (trademarks) and 17 U.S.C.A. § 602(b) (copyrights). See also 19 C.F.R. § 133, Parts A, D.

3 See 19 C.F.R. § 133, Parts B, C.

tributor to seek a new registration from the Patent and Trademark Office so as to be able to invoke these trade remedies.

The importation of semiconductor chip products or equipment that contains a semiconductor chip design or "mask work" registered with the U.S. Copyright Office is prohibited.[4] As with trademarks, copyrights and trade names, the owner of such a mask work may register it with the U.S. Customs Service or the U.S. International Trade Commission so as to invoke trade remedies which will preclude infringing products and equipment from entering into the United States. The Customs Service also administers a high-tech copyright protection program specially targeted at pirated computer programs.[5] Generally, the Customs Service will seize infringing programs if there is proof of access by the infringer and a "substantial similarity" between the imports and the registered program.[6]

There are some differences in Customs Service seizure proceedings depending upon whether the product seized is alleged to be a trademark counterfeit or a copyright counterfeit. The Customs Service rules indicate that in administrative hearings the burden is on the importer to demonstrate why allegedly counterfeit trademarked goods should be released, whereas the burden is on the copyright owner to prove that copyrighted goods are being pirated. These burdens are different because of the greater difficulties in proving copyright infringements. The Second Circuit has ruled that the Customs Service must employ the "average purchaser test" in determining whether imports are counterfeits subject to seizure and forfeiture.[7] In this case, the Service had used experts to determine differences in the trademark such that it was deemed not a counterfeit (merely infringing) and therefore admissible if the confusing mark was obliterated. The consumer test mandated by the Second Circuit should give greater protection from counterfeits.

Attorneys invoking the Customs Service process frequently sense the inadequacy of relief against counterfeit goods. The first problem is simply knowing when counterfeit goods are likely to enter the United States market. The Customs Service has enormous duties and can only pay limited attention to the possibility that certain goods are pirated. This is understandable. How is the Customs Service officer to know that the goods are pirated? Can the Customs

---

[4] See 17 U.S.C.A. § 601(a).

[5] See 19 C.F.R. § 133.31 et seq.

[6] See Webster and Pryor, Customs Administration of the High-tech Copyright Protection Program, 73 J. Pat. & Trademark Off. Society 538 (1991).

[7] Montres Rolex, S.A. v. Snyder, 718 F.2d 524 (2d Cir.1983), *cert. denied* 465 U.S. 1100, 104 S.Ct. 1594, 80 L.Ed.2d 126 (1984).

Service do anything more than look at the invoice in a cursory way? Pirates often take great pains to imitate the logo and trademarks they are copying. This makes such piracy non-obvious.

Copyright piracy of sound recordings is even more difficult to ascertain. It cannot reasonably be expected of the Customs Service that they will play records and tapes in order to determine that they are counterfeit goods. To make customs relief effective it is necessary for private interests to notify the Customs Service that a suspected shipment of counterfeit goods is about to or has arrived in the United States. Companies are increasingly hiring private detectives in order to assist with this task. Private detectives might also be used to try to locate pirated copies and counterfeiting operations inside the United States.

A second frustration with Customs Service relief concerns narrow Customs Service interpretations, such as in the *ROMless Computers* case.[8] In that decision, the Customs Service refused to seize ROMless computers alleged to be in violation of Apple Computer Company copyrights. The practical effect of this decision was to permit ROMless computers to enter the U.S. market, and thereafter be altered in rather simple fashion so as to become effective competitors and arguably infringers of copyrights held by the Apple Computer Company. By removing the ROM (Read Only Memory operating system computer program) unit from the computers, the importers eliminated the only copyrighted element in the computer and thereby nullified attempts at blocking importation of these goods:

> Assuming without deciding that the making of the "ROMless" computers constitutes a contributory infringement against the copyright holder's copyrights, the importation of such merchandise is not prohibited by 17 U.S.C. 602(b). While the phrase "an infringement of copyright" arguably includes contributory copyright infringement, preventing the importation of "ROMless" computers would be inconsistent with other language in the statute. The objects against which the provisions of 17 U.S.C. 602(b) are directed are copies or phonorecords of a work that have been acquired outside the United States.
>
> With regard to the very computer programs in issue, the statutory copyright requirement of fixation has been held to be satisfied through the embodiment of these programs in ROM

8 See 9 BNA U.S. Import Wkly 1062 (May 30, 1984).

devices. . . . Furthermore, computer programs contained in ROMs can be perceived, reproduced, or otherwise communicated therefrom with the aid of other computer equipment. Accordingly, the provisions of 17 U.S.C. 602(b) are operative against ROMs (or diskettes, tapes, or other devices for fixed storage of software) that contain unlawful reproductions of copyrighted computer software, for these items are copies within the meaning of that section. . . . Therefore, inasmuch as "ROMless" computers do not include such copies upon arrival in the United States, they may enter the country without violation of 17 U.S.C. 602(b).

§ 24.4 Section 337 Proceedings (Intellectual Property)

This section focuses on the application of Section 337 of the Tariff Act of 1930 to imports that infringe U.S. intellectual property rights. A later section in this chapter focuses upon non-intellectual property rights' cases, and there are two additional sections discussing Section 337 procedures and remedies generally.

Patent piracy is most often challenged in proceedings against unfair import practices under Section 337 of the Tariff Act of 1930.[9] Section 337 proceedings traditionally have involved some relatively complicated statutory provisions. Prior to 1988, the basic prohibition was against: (1) unfair methods of competition and unfair acts in the importation of goods (2) the effect or tendency of which is to destroy or substantially injure (3) an industry efficiently and economically operated in the U.S. Such importation was also prohibited when it prevented the establishment of an industry, or restrained or monopolized trade and commerce in the U.S. Section 337 proceedings are *in rem* which explains why they are preferable to a series of *in personam* actions for infringement in the federal courts.

The Omnibus Trade and Competitiveness Act of 1988 revised Section 337. The requirement that the U.S. industry be efficiently and economically operated was dropped. Proof of injury to a domestic industry is *not* required in intellectual property infringement cases. The importation of articles infringing U.S. patents, copyrights, trademarks or semiconductor chip mask works[10] is specifical-

---

[9] 19 U.S.C.A. § 1337.

[10] The Semiconductor Chip Protection Act of 1984 (17 U.S.C.A. §§ 901–914) provides a national system for the registration of original mask works. Only a mask work that was first commercially exploited in the United States, or which was owned by a national or domiciliary of the United States or a national, domiciliary, or sover-

ly prohibited provided a U.S. industry relating to such articles exists or is in the process of being established. Such an industry exists if there is significant plant and equipment investment, significant employment of labor or capital, or substantial investment in exploitation of the intellectual property rights (including research and development or licensing). This test has origins in prior ITC case law.[11] There is also prior case law on the question of whether an American industry is "in the process of being established."[12]

Determination of violations and the recommendation of remedies to the President under Section 337 are the exclusive province of the International Trade Commission (ITC). Most of the case law under Section 337 concerns the infringement of patents. Trademark, copyright and mask work infringements may also be pursued under Section 337.[13] In copyright cases, the petitioner must prove ownership of the copyright and the fact of copying.[14] While not quite a per se rule, it is nearly axiomatic that any infringement of United States patent rights amounts to an unfair import practice for purposes of Section 337.[15] Both product and process patents are entitled to protection under Section 337. But in a major decision affecting biotechnology firms, the Federal Circuit Court of Appeals refused relief when the U.S. patent owner had no claim either to the final product or the process used to create it even though the foreign party had to use the patented product to create the product being imported into the United States.[16] Had the same activity been undertaken in the U.S., an infringement would most probably have been found. Section 337 can be used to obtain exclusionary orders based upon misappropriation abroad of trade secrets of U.S. compa-

eign authority of a foreign nation that is a party to a treaty affording protection to mask works to which the United States is also a party or a stateless person at the time of its first commercial exploitation outside the United States, is entitled to registration. The owner of a registered mask work has exclusive rights to reproduce the work by optical, electronic, or any other means and to import or distribute a semiconductor chip product in which the mask work is embodied. The violation of any of these exclusive rights would amount to infringement. However, the owner of a particular semiconductor chip product made by the owner of the mask work, or by any person authorized by the owner of the mask work, may import, distribute, or otherwise dispose of or use, but not reproduce, that particular semiconductor chip product without the authority of the owner of the mask work. Reverse engineering of the mask work is permitted for the purpose of teaching, analysis or evaluation or for the purpose of making another original mask work.

[11] See Airtight Cast–Iron Stoves, 3 ITRD 1158, U.S.I.T.C. Pub. No. 1126 (1980).

[12] See Caulking Guns, 6 ITRD 1432, U.S.I.T.C. Pub. No. 1507 (1984).

[13] 19 U.S.C.A. § 1337(a).

[14] See Coin–Operated Audio–Visual Games and Components, 1981 WL 50518, U.S.I.T.C. Pub. No. 1160 (June 1981).

[15] See Synthetic Star Sapphires, § 316, No. 13 (Sept. 1954), *aff'd sub nom.* In re Von Clemm, 229 F.2d 441 (C.C.P.A.1955).

[16] Amgen, Inc. v. U.S. Int'l Trade Comm., 902 F.2d 1532 (Fed.Cir.1990).

nies. Such complaints are governed by federal common law (not state law).[17]

All legal and equitable defenses (but not counterclaims) may be presented, including attacks upon the validity or enforceability of the patent.[18] A patent license term requiring all "litigation" to take place in California barred pursuit of Section 337 relief.[19] The ITC's refusal to entertain a Section 337 proceeding because the complainant's patent was unenforceable due to prior inequitable conduct was upheld by the Federal Circuit Court of Appeals.[20] This decision illustrates the power of the ITC, as a practical matter, to rule on patent validity. International Trade Commission decisions on patent validity, and Federal Circuit Court of Appeals opinions on appeal from the ITC, can be treated as preclusive fact findings under collateral estoppel principles in ordinary federal court proceedings.[21] Res judicata effect is ordinarily denied given the fundamental differences between ITC administrative and federal judicial proceedings concerning patent validity.[22]

Patent-based Section 337 proceedings are multiplying. ITC decisions take about 12 to 15 months, versus three to five years for federal court lawsuits. General exclusion orders are typically sought. Hearings are held before one of four administrative law judges specializing in patent law, with final decisions taken by the ITC. Infringing products are excluded from importation during the appeals process. About one-fourth of all 337 proceedings find infringements. In 2007, in a major decision, the ITC excluded the importation of cell phones containing Qualcomm microchips found to infringe Broadcom parents. Invocation of Section 337 in patent disputes will be influenced by the U.S. Supreme Court's ruling in *KSR International Co. v. Teleflex, Inc.* (April 30, 2007) where it unanimously held that a patent combining pre-existing elements is invalid if the combination is no "more than the predictable use of prior art elements according to their established functions" (obvious). Likewise, the Supreme Court's cautious consideration of business method patents in *Bilski v. Kappos* (June 28, 2010) will influence Section 337 disputes.

---

17 See Tian Rui Group v. Int'l Trade Commission, _Fed. Cir._(2011) (misappropriation in China from licensees of wheel production trade secrets of U.S manufacturer).

18 19 U.S.C.A. § 1337(c).

19 Texas Instruments Inc. v. Tessera, Inc., 231 F.3d 1325 (Fed.Cir.2000).

20 LaBounty Manufacturing, Inc. v. U.S. ITC, 958 F.2d 1066 (Fed.Cir.1992).

21 In re Convertible Rowing Exerciser Patent Litigation, 814 F.Supp. 1197 (D.Del.1993).

22 Id.

An increasing number of foreign owners of U.S. patents are invoking 337 procedures. About half of all such complaints are settled, often using cross-licensing among the parties. Section 337 proceedings can result in general exclusion orders permitting seizure of patent counterfeits at any U.S. point of entry. Apple Computer, for example, was able to get such an order against computers sold under the label "Orange" that contained infringing programs and color display circuits.[23] However, as previously noted, the Customs Service finds it extremely difficult when inspecting invoices and occasionally opening boxes to ascertain which goods are counterfeit or infringing. Many counterfeits do look like "the real thing." For most seizure remedies to work, the holder must notify the Customs Service of an incoming shipment of patent offending goods. Such advance notice is hard to obtain.

Section 337 exclusion orders can be used against gray market imports (see Part C below). In one decision, the Federal Circuit Court of Appeals upheld the ITC's order against used Kubota-brand tractors.[24] This decision relies heavily on the existence of material differences between the gray market tractors and those distributed by authorized Kubota dealers in the U.S. These differences included parts and the absence of English-language labels and instructions.

A 1989 decision by a General Agreement on Tariffs and Trade (GATT) panel ruled that Section 337 violates the national treatment provisions of Article III:4 of the GATT. The panel was persuaded that imported goods are treated less favorably (i.e., more severely) under Section 337 in terms of patent infringement remedies than domestic goods which are remedied in the federal courts. The panel's decision was ultimately adopted by the GATT Council and the U.S. indicated that it would consider ways to reach compliance after the TRIPs accord was finalized. The Uruguay Round Agreements Act of 1994 did not alter the substance of Section 337 law. It did make procedural changes (such as allowance of counterclaims in Section 337 proceedings) intended to address the issue of an imbalance in patent infringement remedies. The federal district courts must stay infringement proceedings at the request of the respondent to Section 337 actions.

§ 24.5 Infringement Actions

Another alternative available to counsel attempting to assist U.S. firms combating foreign counterfeiting of their products is in-

---

[23] In Re Certain Personal Computers and Components Thereof, 6 ITRD 1140, 1984 Copr.L.Dec. p 25651, U.S.I.T.C. Pub. No. 1504.

[24] Gamut Trading Co. v. U.S. I.T.C., 200 F.3d 775 (Fed.Cir.1999).

fringement relief, including temporary restraining orders, injunctions, damages and an award of the defendant's profits. The major problem with infringement relief is the inability of United States trademark, patent and copyright owners to get effective jurisdiction over and relief from foreign counterfeiters. Infringement and contributory infringement actions can be used more effectively against the importers, distributors or retailers of counterfeit goods. But relief against one such party may merely shift counterfeit sales to another who must then be brought to court, and then another, and another, etc. While such proceedings can result in *ex parte* seizure orders of counterfeit goods already in the United States, they do not represent a long term solution to production of counterfeit goods in foreign jurisdictions.

Most injunctive and damages relief remains illusory, but it can sometimes be useful. For example, it has been held that counterfeit goods seized *ex parte* under the Lanham Trademark Act can be destroyed upon court order.[25] Civil remedies are *not* limited to simply removing the offending trademark.[26]

Infringement and treble damages actions may be commenced in United States courts against importers and distributors of counterfeit goods, but service of process and jurisdictional barriers often preclude effective relief against foreign pirates. Even if such relief is obtained, counterfeiters and the sellers of counterfeit goods have proven adept at the "shell game," moving across the road or to another country to resume operations. Moreover, the mobility and economic incentives of counterfeiters have rendered the criminal sanctions of the Trademark Counterfeiting Act of 1984 (below) largely a Pyrrhic victory. Ex parte seizure orders are also available under the 1984 Act and the Lanham Trademark Act when counterfeit goods can be located in the United States. Goods so seized can be destroyed upon court order.

§ 24.6 Criminal Prosecutions

Many states have enacted criminal statutes to combat increased counterfeiting of goods and services in the United States. After much debate, Congress enacted the Trademark Counterfeiting Act of 1984.[27] Criminal penalties are established for anyone who "intentionally traffics or attempts to traffic in goods or services and knowingly uses a counterfeit mark on or in connection with such

---

[25] Fendi S.a.s. Di Paola Fendi E Sorelle v. Cosmetic World, 642 F.Supp. 1143 (S.D.N.Y.1986).

[26] Id.

[27] 18 U.S.C.A. § 2320 et seq.

goods or services." Treble damages or profits (whichever is greater) and attorney fees may be recovered in civil actions unless there are "extenuating circumstances." Ex parte seizure orders for counterfeit goods may be issued by the federal courts. Parallel imports of genuine or "gray market goods" (goods legitimately produced overseas but imported into the United States via unauthorized distribution channels, infra) and "overruns" (goods produced without authorization by a licensee) are expressly *excluded* from the Act's coverage. The real problem with criminal sanctions as a remedy for counterfeiting is to persuade public prosecutors to take these crimes seriously and to allocate law enforcement resources to them.

§ 24.7 International Solutions

International solutions to the problem of intellectual property piracy have been no less elusive. A draft "Anti–Counterfeiting Code" received close scrutiny in the Uruguay Round of negotiations. Although the TRIPs accord incorporates some coverage of counterfeiting, it is not the encompassing anti-counterfeiting code that the developed world sought. The TRIPs agreement does mandate border measures to block the release of counterfeit goods into domestic circulation. It also requires criminal penalties for willful trademark counterfeiting or copyright piracy undertaken on a commercial scale. However, the TRIPs agreement does not reject the practice of re-exportation of counterfeit merchandise. Re-exportation has the practical effect of pushing the problem on some other jurisdiction and does not represent a final solution from the point of view of the infringed party.

France and Italy have made it illegal to knowingly purchase counterfeit goods. For example, if a student buys a "Louis Vuitton" bag for $15 in a Paris or Florence flea market, he or she may be arrested, fined and imprisoned. France has gone a step further. A new agency monitors Internet piracy. French offenders are subject to a "three strikes" rule: Two warnings are issued before Net accesses can be terminated and fines imposed by court order. South Korea and Taiwan also employ warnings and penalties against illegal downloading.

Various United States statutes authorize the President to withhold trade benefits from or apply trade sanctions to nations inadequately protecting the intellectual property rights of U.S. citizens. This is true of the Caribbean Basin Economic Recovery Act of 1983,[28] the Generalized System of Preferences Renewal Act of

---

[28] See Chapter 10.

1984,[29] the Trade and Tariff Act of 1984 (amending Section 301 of the 1974 Trade Act),[30] and Title IV of the 1974 Trade Act as it applies to most-favored-nation tariffs.[31] Slowly this carrot and stick approach has borne fruit. Under these pressures for example, Singapore drafted a new copyright law, Korea new patent and copyright laws, and Taiwan a new copyright, patent, fair trade and an amended trademark law. Brazil introduced legislation intended to allow copyrights on computer programs. Though these changes have been made, there is some doubt as to the rigor with which the new laws will be enforced when local jobs and national revenues are lost.

§ 24.8 Gray Market Goods

One of the most controversial areas of customs law concerns "gray market goods," goods produced abroad with authorization and payment but which are imported into unauthorized markets. Trade in gray market goods has dramatically increased in recent years, in part because fluctuating currency exchange rates create opportunities to import and sell such goods at a discount from local price levels. Licensors and their distributors suddenly find themselves competing in their home or other "reserved" markets with products made abroad by their own licensees. Or, in the reverse, startled licensees find their licensor's products intruding on their local market shares. In either case, third party importers and exporters are often the immediate source of the gray market goods, and they have little respect for who agreed to what in the licensing agreement. When pressed, such third parties will undoubtedly argue that any attempt through licensing at allocating markets or customers is an antitrust or competition law violation.

In times of floating exchange rates, importers have found that by shopping around the world for gray market goods they can undercut local prices with "parallel imports." This explains in large part the dramatic growth in trade in gray market goods in recent years. Gray market goods have become an important source of price competition in the United States marketplace, particularly in years when the U.S. dollar is strong. Some retail firms, like K–Mart, are major traders of gray market goods.

A decline of the dollar against the Japanese yen or EURO would reduce the flow of gray market *imports* from those sources, but perhaps increased the flow of gray market *exports* from the U.S. to those countries. For example, assume a Cadillac sells in the U.S.

---

[29] See Chapter 10.

[30] See Chapter 19.

[31] See Chapter 10.

for $30,000 and a Mercedes in Germany for 30,000 EUROs. At exchange rate of .75 EUROs to the dollar, the dollar is very strong. Mercedes sells in Germany for $22,500, Cadillac sells in the U.S. for 40,000 EUROs. This encourages importing cars bought in Germany to the U.S. The cars are converted to U.S. specifications for $2,000 and sold for $24,500 by nonauthorized companies, often independent Mercedes repair shops. Then the dollar drops in value to 1.50 EUROs. Now you must pay $45,000 in Germany to buy a Mercedes, but need only 20,000 EUROs to buy a Cadillac. This encourages exporting cars bought in the U.S. to Germany.

In most cases, the manufacturer is not unhappy at selling the product, whether it is sold in the regular market or gray market. But the manufacturer may do better when its product is sold through the regular distributor. First, this lessens the need to face angry authorized distributors as in the above Mercedes situation. Furthermore, when the dollar is strong there is a very substantial price differential. This profit is effectively divided between the manufacturer and the U.S. distributor.

§ 24.9 The U.S. Customs Service Position

In the early part of the century, gray market litigation provoked a Supreme Court decision blocking French cosmetics from entering the United States.[32] A United States firm was assigned the U.S. trademark rights for French cosmetics as part of the sale of the United States business interests of the French producer. The assignee successfully obtained infringement relief in federal district court against Katzel, an importer of the French product benefiting from exchange rate fluctuations. On appeal, the Second Circuit vacated this relief in a holding which followed a line of cases allowing "genuine goods" to enter the U.S. market in competition with established sources. The Supreme Court ultimately reversed the Second Circuit emphasizing the trademark ownership (not license) and independent public good will of the assignee as reasons for its reversal.

Genuine Goods Exclusion Act

Congress, before the Supreme Court reversal, passed the Genuine Goods Exclusion Act, now appearing as Section 526 of the Tariff Act of 1930.[33] This Act bars *unauthorized importation* of goods bearing trademarks of U.S. citizens. Registration of such marks with the Customs Service can result in the seizure of unauthorized imports.

---

[32] A. Bourjois & Co. v. Katzel, 260 U.S. 689, 43 S.Ct. 244, 67 L.Ed. 464 (1923).

[33] 19 U.S.C.A. § 1526.

Persons dealing in such imports may be enjoined, required to export the goods, destroy them or obliterate the offending mark, as well as pay damages. The Act has had a checkered history in the courts and Customs Service. The Customs Service view (influenced by antitrust policy) was that genuine (gray market) goods may be excluded only when the foreign and U.S. trademark rights are not under common ownership or control, or those rights have been used without authorization. The practical effect of this position was to admit most gray market goods into the U.S., thereby providing substantial price competition, but uncertain coverage under manufacturers' warranty, service and rebate programs. Some firms, like K–Mart, excel at gray market importing and may provide independent warranty and repair service contracts. Since 1986, New York and California require disclosure that manufacturers' programs may not apply to sellers of gray market goods.

An attempt in 1985 by Duracell to exclude gray market batteries alternatively under Section 337 of the Tariff Act of 1930 as an unfair import practice was upheld by the U.S. International Trade Commission, but denied relief by President Reagan in deference to the Customs Service position.[34] Despite that position, injunctive relief under trademark or copyright law is sometimes available against gray market importers and distributors.[35] Injunctive relief, however, applies only to the parties and does not prohibit gray market imports or sales by others. This remedy is thus useful, but normally insufficient.

A split in the federal Courts of Appeal as to the legitimacy in light of the Genuine Goods Exclusion Act of the Customs Service position on gray market imports resulted in a U.S. Supreme Court ruling.[36] In an extremely technical, not very policy-oriented decision, the Supreme Court arrived at a compromise. The Customs Service can continue to permit entry of genuine goods when there is common ownership or control of the trademarks. The Service must seize such goods only when they were authorized (licensed), but the marks are not subject to common ownership or control. For these

[34] See Duracell, Inc. v. U.S. International Trade Commission, 778 F.2d 1578 (Fed.Cir.1985). Compare Bourdeau Bros. Inc. v. Int'l Trade Comm., 444 F.3d 1317 (2006) (goods produced in U.S., exported to Europe, importation can be blocked if materially different from goods sold in USA).

[35] See especially, CBS, Inc. v. Scorpio Music Distributors, Inc., 569 F.Supp. 47 (E.D.Pa.1983), *affirmed* 738 F.2d 424 (3d Cir.1984) (copyright infringement relief granted); NEC Electronics, Inc. v. CAL Circuit Abco, Inc., 810 F.2d 1506 (9th Cir.1987), *cert. denied* 484 U.S. 851, 108 S.Ct. 152, 98 L.Ed.2d 108 (1987) (trademark infringement relief denied).

[36] K Mart Corp. v. Cartier, Inc., 486 U.S. 281, 108 S.Ct. 1811, 100 L.Ed.2d 313 (1988).

purposes, "common ownership or control" is defined as a 50 percent shareholding or the effective control of policy and operations. Gray market goods originating from such "affiliated companies" will still be allowed to enter the United States.[37] However, a Fifth Circuit decision indicates that close and profitable business ties between a foreign trademark owner and the foreign owner of U.S. trademark rights do not amount to "common control." Rolex was thus able to obtain a Customs Service forfeiture ruling against gray market imports of its watches by Wal–Mart. The court applied a strict common ownership test to Section 526.[38] The Tenth Circuit affirmed summary judgment in favor of an Oklahoma company owning U.S. trademark rights to "Vittoria" for bicycle tires. The rights were transferred by an Italian company, the maker of the tires. The "common control" exception to gray market trademark protection did not apply because there was at most "a close business relationship" between the two companies.[39]

Many believe that the bulk of U.S. imports of gray market goods have continued under the Supreme Court's *K Mart* ruling. However, this perspective is somewhat undermined by treatment of gray market imports under other statutory regimes.

§ 24.10 Trademark and Copyright Remedies

Section 42 of the Lanham Trademark Act prohibits the importation of goods that copy or simulate a registered U.S. trademark.[40] In *K Mart,* the U.S. Supreme Court specifically declined to review the legality of barring gray market goods under this provision. Some courts have denied relief under Section 42 against gray market imports. These cases stress the absence of consumer confusion when genuine goods are involved.[41] Other courts have reached conclusions that in the absence of adequate disclosure Section 42 is actionable against gray market goods that materially differ in physical content from those sold in the U.S.A.[42] However, when there are

---

[37] See 19 C.F.R. §§ 133.21(c), 133.2(d).

[38] United States v. Eighty–Three Rolex Watches, 992 F.2d 508 (5th Cir.1993)., *cert. denied* 510 U.S. 991, 114 S.Ct. 547, 126 L.Ed.2d 449 (1993).

[39] Vittoria North America, LLC v. Euro–Asia Imports, Inc., 278 F.3d 1076 (10th Cir.2001).

[40] 15 U.S.C.A. § 1124.

[41] See, e.g., Monte Carlo Shirt v. Daewoo International (America) Corp., 707 F.2d 1054 (9th Cir.1983); Bell & Howell: Mamiya Co. v. Masel Supply Co., Corp., 719 F.2d 42 (2d Cir.1983).

[42] See Lever Bros. Co. v. United States, 877 F.2d 101 (D.C.Cir.1989); Ferrero U.S.A., Inc. v. Ozak Trading, Inc., 753 F.Supp. 1240 (D.N.J.1991), *affirmed* 935 F.2d 1281 (3d Cir.1991); Société Des Produits Nestle, S.A. v. Casa Helvetia, Inc., 982 F.2d 633 (1st Cir.1992); Lever Bros. Co. v. United States, 981 F.2d 1330 (D.C.Cir.1993).

material differences, labeling suffices to avoid Section 42.[43] A Second Circuit decision relying upon Section 32 of the Lanham Act also supports blocking imports of materially different gray market goods.[44] In this case, Cabbage Patch dolls produced in Spain under license came with birth certificates, adoption papers and instructions in Spanish, but were otherwise the same product. The U.S. manufacturer refused to register these dolls, leading to numerous complaints by parents and children. These complaints supported the court's injunction against importation of the dolls from Spain under Section 32. Section 32 provides trademark owners with remedies against persons who, without consent by the owner, use a "reproduction, counterfeit, copy or colorable imitation" of a mark so as to cause confusion, mistake or deception.[45] However, a Ninth Circuit decision relying of Sections 32 and 43(a) (country of origin markings) of the Lanham Act leads to the opposite conclusion, finding no support for the argument that gray market imports can be remedied under those provisions.[46]

Sections 103 and 602 of the Copyright Act provide that importing goods into the U.S. without the consent of copyright owners is an infringement.[47] But Section 109 limits the distribution rights of copyright owners under what is known as the "first sale doctrine."[48] This doctrine limits the owner's control over copies to their first sale or transfer. Two Third Circuit decisions split on the use of copyright law against gray market imports in spite of the first sale doctrine.[49] In *Sebastian,* the Third Circuit held that a U.S. manufacturer who sells goods with copyrighted labels to foreign distributors is barred by the first sale doctrine from obtaining import infringement relief. In *Scorpio,* where the goods were manufactured abroad under license by the U.S. copyright holder, such relief was granted. The Supreme Court subsequently held that the first sale doctrine bars injunctive relief under the Copyright Act[50] against goods previously exported from the USA. Reversing the Ninth Circuit, the Supreme

---

[43] See the U.S. Customs Service Regulation at 19 C.F.R. § 133.23.

[44] Original Appalachian Artworks v. Granada Electronics, Inc., 816 F.2d 68 (2d Cir.1987), *cert. denied* 484 U.S. 847, 108 S.Ct. 143, 98 L.Ed.2d 99 (1987). Accord, Société Des Produits Nestle, S.A. v. Casa Helvetia, Inc., 982 F.2d 633 (1st Cir.1992).

[45] 15 U.S.C.A. § 1114.

[46] NEC Electronics v. CAL Circuit Abco, Inc., 810 F.2d 1506 (9th Cir.1987), *cert. denied* 484 U.S. 851, 108 S.Ct. 152, 98 L.Ed.2d 108 (1987).

[47] 17 U.S.C.A. § 106.

[48] 17 U.S.C.A. § 109.

[49] Columbia Broadcasting System v. Scorpio Music Distributors, 569 F.Supp. 47 (E.D.Pa.1983), *affirmed* 738 F.2d 424 (3d Cir.1984) (relief granted); Sebastian Int'l, Inc. v. Consumer Contacts (PTY), Ltd., 847 F.2d 1093 (3d Cir.1988) (relief denied).

[50] Quality King Distributors, Inc. v. L'ANZA Research International, Inc., 523 U.S. 135, 118 S.Ct. 1125, 140 L.Ed.2d 254 (1998).

Court has also barred injunctive relief under the Copyright Act even if the goods are foreign made.[51]

§ 24.11 Gray Market Goods in Other Jurisdictions

An excellent review of the treatment of gray market goods in other jurisdictions is presented in an article by Takamatsu.[52] This review is of particular interest to U.S. *exporters* of gray market goods. For the most part, his review indicates that other jurisdictions permit gray market goods to enter. This is true of the *Parker Pen* cases under Japanese law,[53] the *Maja* case under German law[54] and the *Agfa–Gevaert* case in Austria,[55] all of which are reviewed by Takamatsu. Canadian Superior Court law strongly supports free trade in gray market goods.[56]

The legal analysis contained in these opinions has been very influential in European Union licensing law.[57] EU law basically posits that once goods subject to intellectual property rights of common origin have been sold on the market with authorization, the holders can no longer block importation of those goods ("parallel imports") through the use of national property rights. Such use is not thought to have been intended as part of the original grant of rights and is said to have been "exhausted" upon sale. An extensive body of law permits parallel imports (even of qualitatively different goods) as part of the promotion of the Common Market and rejects attempts to divide the market territorially along the lines of national property rights. Product labeling as to source and contents is thought sufficient notice to consumers that qualitatively different goods are involved.

---

[51] See Kirtsaeng v. John Wiley & Sons, ___U.S.___ (March 19, 2013) *reversing* Parfums Givenchy, Inc v. Drug Emporium, 38 F.3d 477 (9th Cir.1994)., *cert. denied* 514 U.S. 1004, 115 S.Ct. 1315, 131 L.Ed.2d 197 (1995) and Costco Wholesale Corp. v. Omega SA, ___ U.S. ___(2010) *affirming by a tie vote* 541 F 3d 982 (9th Cir. 2008).

[52] Takamatsu, Parallel Importation of Trademarked Goods: A Comparative Analysis, 57 Wash.L.Rev. 433 (1982).

[53] NMC Co. v. Schulyro Trading Co., Feb. 20, 1970 (Osaka Dist. Ct., 234 Hanrei Taimuzu 57) reprinted in English at 16 Japanese Annual of Int'l Law 113 (1972) affirmed by Osaka High Court. See Nestle Nihon K.K. v. Sanhi Shoten (unreported Tokyo Dist.Ct. May 29, 1965) summarized in T. Doi, Digest of Japanese Court Decisions in Trademarks and Unfair Competition Cases (1971).

[54] Fed.Sup.Ct. (W.Ger.) Jan. 22, 1964, 41 Bundesgerichtshof 84 summarized in 54 Trademark Rep. 452 (1964).

[55] Agfa–Gevaert GmbH v. Schark, Sup.Ct. (Aus.), Nov. 30, 1970.

[56] Consumers Distributing Co., Ltd. v. Seiko Time Canada Ltd., 1 Sup.Ct. 583 (1984). But see Mattel Canada Inc. v. GTS Acquisitions, 27 C.P.R.(3d) 358 (1989) (preliminary injunction against identical gray market goods).

[57] See Chapter 23.

In a major decision, the European Court of Justice has ruled that trademark rights can be used to block gray market imports into the Common Market. These rights are not exhausted once the goods are voluntarily put into the stream of international commerce. An Austrian maker of high-quality sunglasses was therefore entitled to bar imports from Bulgaria.[58] In *Zino Davidoff, SA*, and *Levi Strauss* the European Court of Justice affirmed the right of trademark owners to block gray market sales of their goods sold at prices below those they utilize in the EU. No "implied consent" to gray market imports was found via the sale of goods outside the EU.[59]

§ 24.12 Section 337—Complaint and Response

Section 337 complaints may be filed by domestic producers with the International Trade Commission in Washington, D.C., provided the complainants have not agreed by contract to litigate all disputes elsewhere.[60] The complainant must be a representative of the industry. The complaint itself must contain a statement of the facts alleged to constitute unfair import methods or acts. The complaint must also specify instances when unlawful importations occurred, the names and addresses of respondents, and if they exist, a description of any related court proceeding. The complaint must describe the domestic industry that is affected by the import practices and the petitioner's interest in that industry. If the case involves intellectual property rights, detailed information regarding the patent, copyright, trademark or mask work must be provided. Lastly, the complaint must indicate what relief is sought.[61] Section 337 complainants are subject to the "duty of candor" recognized in *Convertible Rowing Exercisers*.[62] This duty is violated by (1) a failure to disclose material information or a submission of false material information and (2) an intent to mislead.

Once a complaint is filed, or the Commission decides to start a Section 337 proceeding on its own initiative, an investigation is normally commenced. The Commission takes the position that it is not obliged to commence an investigation after the filing of a private complaint. Its Office of Unfair Imports (OUI) takes 30 days to exam-

---

58 Silhouette International v. Hartlauer, 1998 WL 1043033 (July 16, 1998).

59 Cases C–414–99, 415/99 and 416/99, 2001 WL 1347061 (Levi jeans sold by supermarket in Britain) (Nov. 20, 2001).

60 See Texas Instruments Inc. v. Tessera, Inc., 231 F.3d 1325 (Fed.Cir.2000) (agreement that all litigation must take place in California precludes Section 337 complaint).

61 C.F.R. § 210.20 (1990).

62 Inv. No. 337–TA–212, U.S.I.T.C. Pub. No. 2111 (1988).

ine the sufficiency of the complaint. This Office is an independent party in Section 337 proceedings charged with representing the public interest. Pre-filing review of draft complaints by the OUI is possible, and counsel for the respondents may also seek to have the OUI recommend against proceeding with a Section 337 complaint. Although it is a rare event, the Commission occasionally has declined to pursue a Section 337 investigation. If this happens, the complaint is dismissed.[63] The Commission has maintained its discretionary authority to review Section 337 complaints despite statutory language which would appear to be mandatory.[64] Thus, it has dismissed complaints where there is insufficient data to support the allegations, or the allegations themselves are insufficient to prove a Section 337 violation.[65] The complainant may of course amend and refile its complaint. Furthermore, a rejection of Section 337 complaints by the Commission can be appealed to the Federal Circuit Court of Appeals.[66] The Commission serves the complaint on foreign parties, thus avoiding the delay of international service of process. Parties who fail to appear can default, and have exclusion orders automatically entered against them.

The respondents in Section 337 proceedings are given an opportunity to submit written briefs regarding the complaint. Such briefs should respond to each allegation in the complaint and set forth any defenses. Section 337 complaint and response requirements are reproduced in Section 20.27 of this chapter. Failure to provide a response to the complaint can result in a determination that the facts alleged in the complaint are deemed admitted.[67] For example, if the complaint is based upon patent infringement, the respondent would typically allege non-infringement by suggesting that the product is not covered by the patent and/or the invalidity of the patent. An unusual aspect of Section 337 proceedings is the appointment of an investigative attorney by the ITC to represent the public interest. This attorney is a party to the investigation and may participate in discovery and hearings to the full extent of the complainant and respondent.[68]

---

[63] See 19 C.F.R. § 210.12.

[64] See 19 U.S.C.A. § 1337(b)(1).

[65] See Certain Fruit Preserves in Containers Having Lids With Gingham Cloth Design, Docket 1056 (May 21, 1984); Certain Architectural Panels, Docket 1122 (November 30, 1984).

[66] See Syntex Agribusiness, Inc. v. U.S. International Trade Commission, 617 F.2d 290 (C.C.P.A.1980) and 659 F.2d 1038 (C.C.P.A.1981).

[67] 19 C.F.R. § 210.21.

[68] 19 C.F.R. § 210.4.

§ 24.13 Section 337—Temporary Relief

If the Commission decides, in the process of its investigation, that there is reason to believe that a violation of Section 337 has occurred, it may order the goods to be excluded from entry into the United States or permit entry only under a bond as a temporary remedy.[69] Such remedies require proof not only of the reasons to believe in the violation, but also of an immediate and substantial injury to the domestic industry in the absence of a temporary remedy.[70] The statute now requires that the Commission consider the public interest in making temporary remedial decisions in connection with Section 337. Thus, the Commission ends up balancing the probability of the complainant's success on the merits, the prospect for immediate and substantial harm to the domestic industry if no relief is granted, the harm to the respondent if such relief is granted, and the effect that temporary remedies would have on the public interest.[71] If the Commission is concerned that the complainant may possibly have filed a frivolous claim or that the harm to the respondent is particularly large, it can require the complainant to post a bond in order to get temporary relief. Decisions about temporary relief are made by the administrative law judge in the case, although they may be modified or vacated by the Commission upon review.[72]

§ 24.14 Section 337—Administrative Process

Section 337 investigations normally last one year but may be extended to eighteen months in complicated cases. This relatively short period has been described as "due process with dispatch." Section 337 investigations are the only investigations conducted by the International Trade Commission that are governed by the Administrative Procedure Act. Thus, the investigation will follow the established procedures for discovery under the Federal Rules of Civil Procedure, pre-hearing conferences, an initial determination of the issues by an administrative judge, and final review by the Commission.[73] One problem is the frequent need for extraterritorial discovery in Section 337 cases. Another issue is sanctions for abuse of discovery,[74] although findings of default can be made. Section 337 discovery responses are typically due in 10 days, much more rapidly

69 19 U.S.C.A. § 1337(e).

70 See Certain Apparatus, 12 ITRD 1841, U.S.I.T.C. Pub. No. 1132 (April 1981).

71 19 U.S.C.A. § 1337(e).

72 19 C.F.R. § 210.24(17).

73 See 19 C.F.R. §§ 2210.1–2210.71.

74 See Certain Concealed Cabinet Hinges and Mounting Plates, 12 ITRD 1841 (Jan. 8, 1990).

than in civil litigation. Although the Commission is authorized to promulgate rules allowing costs and attorneys' fees as sanctions, it has not yet done so. In contrast, the Commission has aggressively enforced its protective orders against disclosure of confidential and business information of a proprietary character.[75] At any point during its investigation, the Commission may decide to settle the proceedings by consent order or by agreement of the parties. This happens reasonably often, especially when the parties to an intellectual property case agree to a licensing arrangement. In either case, the Commission will review the motion to terminate or a proposed consent order from the standpoint of the public interest in the proceeding. An arbitration agreement between parties who are contesting a Section 337 proceeding is no grounds for terminating the ITC investigation.[76]

When the International Trade Commission reviews the advisory decision of the administrative law judge in Section 337 proceedings, it need not undertake a review of that entire determination. It is sufficient for purposes of appeal that the Commission decides the case on the basis of a single dispositive issue. For example, in patent infringement litigation, if the Commission decides that there was no infringement, it need not render decisions concerning any other issues in the Section 337 proceeding.[77] Thus it was only this issue that could be appealed to the Federal Circuit Court of Appeals. Put another way, the only issues that can be appealed are those upon which the Commission has decided, and this is true even in cases concerning temporary relief under Section 337.[78]

§ 24.15 Section 337—Sanctions

If the Commission ultimately decides that an unfair import method or act has been committed, it is authorized to issue a cease and desist order or an exclusion order barring the goods from entering the United States. Any violation of those orders is punishable by civil penalties up to $100,000 per day or twice the value of the merchandise in question. Final ITC determinations under Section 337 are appealed directly to the Federal Circuit Court of Appeals.

---

75 See Certain Electrically Resistive Monocomponent Toner, 10 ITRD 1672 (1988).

76 Farrel Corp. v. U.S. ITC, 949 F.2d 1147 (Fed.Cir.1991), *cert. denied* 504 U.S. 913, 112 S.Ct. 1947, 118 L.Ed.2d 551 (1992).

77 Beloit Corp. v. Valmet Oy, 742 F.2d 1421 (Fed.Cir.1984), *cert. denied* 472 U.S. 1009, 105 S.Ct. 2706, 86 L.Ed.2d 721 (1985).

78 See Warner Bros., Inc. v. U.S. International Trade Commission, 787 F.2d 562 (Fed.Cir.1986).

The Federal Circuit Court of Appeals has ruled that the ITC may impose civil penalties for violation of consent orders (as well as cease and desist orders) that terminate patent infringement investigations under Section 337.[79]

§ 24.16 Section 337—Settlements

As the Section 337 investigation proceeds, the complainant may move for a summary determination by the ITC. This is analogous to summary judgment under the Federal Rules of Civil Procedure.[80] If the complaint concerns patent infringement, one solution is for the parties to enter into a licensing agreement. However, the parties must give the Commission a copy of their complete agreement. The Commission's investigative attorney then comments on the settlement and the administrative law judge makes an initial decision as to whether to terminate the investigation on the basis of the settlement. This determination is sent to the Commission for final approval.[81] The purpose of these procedures is to insure that the public interest is preserved as part of the patent infringement dispute settlement.

In non-patent cases, the typical route for settlement is by consent order. To do this, a joint motion is filed by all of the complainants, the Commission's investigative attorney, and one or more of the respondents.[82] This typically occurs before the commencement of the hearing before the administrative law judge. Consent settlements of this type must contain admissions of all jurisdictional facts, waivers of rights to seek judicial review or other means of challenging the consent order, and an agreement that the enforcement, modification and revocation of the order will be undertaken pursuant to ITC rules. The consent order typically is not deemed to constitute an admission of a violation of Section 337 and usually states that it is undertaken solely for settlement purposes.[83] There is a ten-day notice period which allows any interested party to comment on the proposed termination of a Section 337 proceeding on the basis of a consent order.[84]

---

[79] San Huan New Materials High Tech, Inc. v. ITC, 161 F.3d 1347 (Fed.Cir.1998).

[80] 19 C.F.R. § 210.50.

[81] 19 C.F.R. § 210.51.

[82] 19 C.F.R. § 211.20.

[83] 19 C.F.R. § 211.22.

[84] 19 C.F.R. § 211.20.

§ 24.17 Section 337—ITC Public Interest Review

The International Trade Commission is not required to impose a Section 337 remedy if it finds a violation. Its remedial powers are discretionary. In deciding whether to accept proposed consent orders or to impose any remedy, the Commission is required to consider all of the public comments that have been received, the effect upon the public health and welfare of the United States, the effect upon competitive conditions in the U.S. economy, the effect on production of like or directly competitive articles in the United States, and its effect upon U.S. consumers.[85] The Commission has rarely invoked the public interest exception to Section 337 relief. When it has, the domestic industry typically was unable to supply critically needed items[86] or the public's strong interest in the research overrode patent rights.[87]

§ 24.18 Section 337—ITC General Exclusion and Cease and Desist Orders

The International Trade Commission may issue three different kinds of remedies under Section 337. The first is an exclusion order of a limited or general nature, and this type of relief predominates in intellectual property cases. The second is a cease and desist order, and this type of relief is often issued if there are significant inventories of the offending product already imported into the United States. The effect of such a cease and desist order is to prevent further distribution within the country. The Commission is expressly authorized to issue exclusion orders and cease and desist orders together.[88] In either case, the Commission may authorize entry of the goods under bond pending the President's final determination in the proceeding. The amount of the bond varies from case to case, but is generally intended to offset the competitive advantages that are perceived to exist. Such bonds have ranged upwards to 600 percent of the value of the imports.[89] Many Section 337 bonds have been determined by measuring the difference between the complainant's prices in the U.S. and the customs value of the imports. Forfeiture orders are relatively uncommon and typically follow notice by the Secretary of the Treasury that forfeiture would result from further importation of goods that offend Section 337.

---

85 19 U.S.C.A. § 1337(d), (e), (f).

86 See Automatic Crankpin Grinders, 2 ITRD 5121, U.S.I.T.C. Pub. No. 1022 (1979) (engine parts needed to meet fuel efficiency standards); Certain Fluidized Supporting Apparatus reported at 7 I.T.R.D. 1089 (1984).

87 Certain Inclined–Field Acceleration Tubes, 2 ITRD 5572 (1980).

88 19 U.S.C.A. § 1337(f).

89 See Certain Cube Puzzles, supra.

Plaintiffs usually wish to obtain general exclusion orders in intellectual property cases. Such orders will keep out all infringing products. The problem with this approach is that it may unfairly bar the importation of goods that resemble but do not infringe the patented product. This is a generally undesirable result that the Commission will try to avoid.[90] Consequently, the Commission requires those seeking general exclusion orders to prove a widespread pattern of unauthorized use of the patented invention and reasonable inferences that foreign manufacturers other than the respondents may attempt to enter the United States market with infringing goods.[91] A widespread pattern of unauthorized use can be demonstrated by the importation of the infringing goods by numerous companies, by pending foreign infringement suits based upon foreign patents which correspond to the United States patent at issue, or by other evidence which demonstrates a history of unauthorized foreign use of the invention.[92] In providing evidence that it is reasonable to infer that other foreign manufacturers may attempt to enter the U.S. market, plaintiffs may offer proof of the established demand for the product, the existence of a distribution system in the United States for its marketing, the cost to foreigners of manufacturing or creating a facility capable of manufacturing the goods, the ease and number of foreign manufacturers who could retool so as to produce the offending article, and the cost of such retooling.[93] As these criteria suggest, obtaining a general exclusion order is not always easy, and certainly not automatic.

§ 24.19 Section 337—Presidential Veto

Any order issued by the International Trade Commission under Section 337 goes into effect immediately. However, the President may veto that order for public policy reasons.[94] Vetoes by the President of Commission orders in Section 337 proceedings are rare and not generally reviewable by the courts.[95] The President has sixty days within which to make a decision concerning ITC orders under Section 337. If the President does not take action within this period, then the order becomes final.[96] Final ITC orders under Section 337

---

[90] See Certain Cloisonne Jewelry, 8 ITRD 2028, U.S.I.T.C. Pub. No. 1822 (March 1986).

[91] See Certain Airless Spray Pumps and Components Thereof, 3 ITRD 2041, U.S.I.T.C. Pub. No. 1199 (1981).

[92] Id.

[93] Id.

[94] 19 U.S.C.A. § 1337(j).

[95] Duracell, Inc. v. U.S. International Trade Commission, 778 F.2d 1578 (Fed.Cir.1985).

[96] Id.

remain in effect until the Commission decides that there is no longer reason to continue the order.[97] Any violation of an outstanding ITC order under Section 337 can incur a civil penalty of up to $10,000 per day or twice the domestic value of the goods sold, whichever is greater.[98]

§ 24.20 Section 337—ITC Opinion Letters

The ITC follows the practice of issuing informal or formal opinion letters in connection with Section 337 matters. Requests for informal opinions from the ITC staff should be addressed to the Assistant General Counsel of the Commission. Formal opinions actually issued by the Commission itself may be obtained if the staff opinion letter is adverse or a formal opinion is just simply necessary. Requests for such opinions are filed with the Secretary of the Commission.[99]

---

[97] 19 U.S.C.A. § 1337(k).

[98] 19 U.S.C.A. § 1337(j).

[99] 19 C.F.R. § 211.54.

Chapter 25

INTRODUCTION TO FOREIGN DIRECT INVESTMENT

Table of Sections

---

§ 25.1 Why Invest Abroad?

Foreign direct investment (FDI) abroad often occurs subsequent to less extensive contact with the foreign country in the form of trading finished goods or transferring technology to have goods produced under license in a foreign nation. Individuals and multinationals have many reasons to invest abroad. It may be part of an initial overall plan to produce goods or provide services worldwide. It may be the next progression considered after the home market is saturated. A further step, increasingly undertaken in the United States and the European Union, is to move the state of incorporation to another country where the corporation organizational and regulatory laws are more favorable. It is not an action without critics, especially in the country the corporation is departing. But the reality is that bad hosts cause guests to depart. For example, what if Bank of America moved its place of incorporation and management center to Zurich, Switzerland, in reality to benefit from more favorable executive compensation laws, but for the publicly stated reason that the company's business was increasingly centered in Europe? The generally accepted rule that the law of the state of incorporation applies to internal affairs may encourage such moves.

A foreign investment may be less than fully voluntary in some instances. For example, a corporation of one country may remain even when some significant characteristics suggest incorporation in another country. The corporation may not wish to risk disturbing the corporation's domestic market share at home, even though its sales are increasingly abroad in countries where labor costs are lower. Avoiding high tariffs may be a factor in deciding whether to stay or move. So may be a perception that the country is moving less toward remaining a market economy. A move might be considered when a licensee abroad is creating problems, and the company believes it can make a better product or provide a better service on its own. Poor-quality products or services produced by licensees is often the reason for assuming control of production abroad. Whatever the motivation, foreign investment will almost always encounter laws in the host nation that differ from the laws regulating investment in the home nation.[1] Movement of the place of incorporation will not be favorable until balancing all corporate interests are considered and deemed to favor the foreign country.

Investment abroad involving the creation of new businesses, and the capital transfers to underwrite them, is often referred to as foreign direct investment (FDI).[2] It means ownership and control of the enterprise abroad, whether branch or subsidiary in form. Enterprises which undertake foreign investment are referred to by

---

1 Host-nation is used to identify the nation in which the investment is made. Home-nation is used to designate the nation from which the investment capital and technology comes, meaning usually the nation in which the multinational parent is incorporated and has its management center.

2 In contrast to indirect investment such as by purchases of shares of an existing company.

several names, multinational corporations (MNCs) or enterprises (MNEs), or transnational corporations (TNCs) or enterprises (TNEs). More important than what they are called are their percentages of ownership and control by the home-nation individual or entity. Share ownership discloses whether or not the enterprise is a joint venture involving two countries, and which country is likely to assert authority over the enterprise. Both the governments of the home nation (place of incorporation) and the foreign host nation (place of the productive part of the business) may attempt to assert such authority, leading to intergovernmental conflicts.

Foreign investment is a major part of the business of many companies chartered in developed nations. Especially since the early 1980s, multinational enterprises have moved toward global production and division of labor. As a result, global foreign direct investment rose to over $2 trillion by the opening of this century. Intraregional foreign investment is another aspect of this development. The creation of the European Community (now European Union) in 1958, and the adoption of the North American Free Trade Agreement in 1994, stimulated increased foreign investment within these trading areas.[3] The completion of the Uruguay GATT Round in late 1993 added new WTO investment rules (TRIMs). These new rules have encouraged even more foreign investment.

The composition of the rules which should govern foreign investment has been a subject of frequent debate among developed and developing countries. The North–South dialogue[4] led in the 1970s to both restrictive United Nations General Assembly Resolutions,[5] and restrictive foreign investment laws in many developing

---

[3] There are many other regional trade groups which have promoted increased investment as well as trade.

[4] The North–South dialogue split developed countries in the northern hemisphere from less developed countries generally in the southern hemisphere. The less developed countries argued that they were poor because the developed countries were rich, and that the development gap was increasing. The less developed countries made demands that were largely aspirational, and invariably unrealistic. They wanted transfers of the most advanced technology at little or no cost, increased investment capital in companies with majority local control and ownership and both forgiveness of old debt and assurances of new borrowing with few restrictions as to use. The dialogue was most active in the late 1960s and through the 1970s. It became unraveled with the debt defaults in the early 1980s, and the election of more market oriented leaders in many developing nations who realized that development lay more in local effort than foreign largesse.

[5] The two most significant were the Charter of Economic Rights and Duties of States, Dec. 12, 1974, U.N.G.A.Res. 3281 (XXIX), 29 U.N. GAOR, Supp. (No. 31) 50, U.N.Doc. A/9631 (1975), reprinted in 14 Int'l Legal Mat. 251 (1975), and the Declaration on the Establishment of a New International Economic Order, May 1, 1974, U.N.G.A.Res. 3201 (SBVI), 6 (Special) U.N. GAOR, Supp. (No. 1) 3, U.N.Doc. A/9559 (1974), reprinted in 13 Int'l Legal Mat. 715 (1974). A proposed U.N. Code of Conduct on Transnational Corporations was never enacted. These "aspirational" declarations

nations.[6] But after the debt crisis in the early 1980s, and the subsequent election of governments more determined to join the developed world than to lead the third world, impediments to foreign investment began to be dismantled. Nationalizations in the 1960s and 1970s gave way to privatizations in the 1980s and 1990s. Investment restrictions gave way to investment incentives, as nations that had rejected foreign investment now welcomed it. Involuntary joint ventures gave way to voluntary joint ventures. But even though this recent liberalization has provided investors with significant opportunities in many foreign nations, obstacles to foreign investment remain, and old ones may be exhumed as governments change. This chapter focuses upon some of the typical regulations that investors may confront in attempting to *establish* or *acquire* and to *operate* enterprises in foreign countries. Later chapters discuss more specifically investment issues in developing and in nonmarket or transitional economy nations, and in regional areas in Latin America and Europe. This chapter also examines efforts to reduce or limit foreign investment barriers by means of bilateral or multilateral agreements, especially within the GATT/WTO and the NAFTA.

§ 25.2 The Language of Investment Barriers—TRIMs

Foreign investment barriers that individual nations impose have come to be described in the past few years as "trade related investment measures" or TRIMs, language incorporated in the WTO. Although many countries impose TRIMs, the developed and developing countries have different views regarding their economic effects. Developed nations argue that TRIMs cause investors to base their decisions on considerations other than market forces. The principle of national treatment that mandates that foreign-controlled enterprises receive no less favorable treatment from governments than their domestic counterparts, embodies this idea. Led by the United States, the developed nations have tried to limit TRIMs through the General Agreement on Tariffs and Trade (GATT)/ World Trade Organization (WTO) process.

---

of the developing nations and the UN General Assembly were never very effective, and with the focus shifting to incentives for investment since the early 1980s, UN control is very much on the back burner.

[6] See, e.g., Mexican Law to Promote Investment and Regulate Foreign Investment of 1973, translated in 1 Michael Wallace Gordon, Multinational Corporations Law (1982); Indian Foreign Investment Regulation Act of 1973, in 1982 Bus. Int'l 92 (Mar. 19); Nigerian Enterprises Promotion Decree of 1977, in 6 Investment Laws of the World (ICSID1982). Each of these restrictive laws of the 1970s has been repealed, amended, or emasculated by regulation or policy.

Developing nations take a less negative view of TRIMs. They believe TRIMs provide a means of host nation control over various aspects of foreign multinational enterprise activity. Specifically, they believe that TRIMs serve as useful policy tools to promote government objectives in furthering economic development and ensuring balanced trade. Additionally, developing nations have quite vigorously defended the use of TRIMs as an aspect of national sovereignty, historically to maintain control over natural resources and more recently to preserve domestic culture.

The overall data as to whether TRIMs successfully meet policy objectives or always cause inefficiency appears mixed. Also unclear is exactly what form of practice the term TRIMs encompasses. The Uruguay Round of GATT, leading to the creation of the WTO, defined fourteen practices as TRIMs. U.N. commentators have broken these into four categories: local content, trade-balancing, export requirements, and the broad area of investment incentives.[7] The first three serve as restrictions or barriers, while the fourth encourages investment. Some viewers divide foreign investment laws into different groups.[8] Rather than discuss the broad area of incentives, which typically involves tax benefits, this chapter focuses more on barriers to investment.

The term "performance requirements" often refers to barriers that governments use to condition entry, often through a screening mechanism. In order to distinguish between the incentives and barriers, barrier TRIMs are often called trade related performance requirements (TRPRs).[9]

---

[7] Sometimes, however, a foreign investment law that is actually restrictive is introduced by a government as an investment encouraging law, and therefore an "incentive" law. This may be the first law adopted that allows foreign investment after a long period of little or no foreign investment, such as the 1982 Cuban joint venture foreign investment law. The Cuban government viewed it as an incentive law, a view nearly unanimously rejected by potential foreign investors. The law was replaced in 1995 by a better law, but not a law that has been successful in drawing any significant foreign investment. Furthermore, other Cuban government policies remain discouraging to foreign investors.

[8] Foreign investment laws are divided into four categories as well: export requirements, local content requirements, investment incentives, and transfer of technology requirements. See also Cynthia Day Wallace, Legal Control of the Multinational Enterprise 37 (1983).

[9] The term "trade related investment measure" is sometimes considered synonymous with performance requirements, but it may more accurately encompass all measures, including incentives. The U.S. government does not clearly distinguish these measures.

§ 25.3 Governance by Home Nations

Governance of multinational enterprises may be divided into three spheres. They are governance by the home nation, by the host nation, or by multi-nation organizations. One might also wish to add a fourth, governance by international law. Although the latter might constitute an ideal method in an ideal world, international legal norms that govern multinational enterprises are few in number and contested in status.

The regulation of a U.S. multinational abroad by the home nation is essentially a matter of U.S. federal law. These laws tend to fall into one of two classes. First are those laws enacted to deal with domestic issues, and without serious consideration of their impact on foreign activities of U.S. enterprises. Examples are the federal securities and antitrust laws. Both have extraterritorial effect, although the potential impact abroad was not seriously debated when they were enacted. Second are laws that address specific foreign policy issues and are intended to achieve what are largely political goals. Examples are the Foreign Corrupt Practices Act (FCPA) and the antiboycott laws. There are other laws that affect multinationals' actions abroad, such as tax laws that may encourage investment in friendly nations, customs provisions allowing assembly abroad of U.S. made parts with duties applied only to the value added abroad when the products re-enter the United States, and the generalized system of preferences (GSP) that is intended to assist development. But what is missing are laws of home nations enacted to address special interests of the developing nations when they host foreign investment. Foreign nations should nevertheless understand that home nations in which multinationals are registered and usually "seated" tend only to enact laws that are in the best interests of the home nations, usually without serious regard for any special interests of the various possible host nations. Thus it is only the host nations' laws that may effectively regulate multinational activity in the host nation.

One form of governance by home nations, in a kind of collective sense, is the work of the Organisation for Economic Cooperation and Development (OECD). The OECD was for many years composed of developed Western European nations plus such other nations as the United States, Japan, Australia, New Zealand, Canada, Finland and Turkey. But it began to expand in the 1990s with the transition of non-market economies to market economies. The OECD recommends only a modest form of "governance", and its efforts have not been enacted into national laws. What the OECD has accomplished is the creation of Guidelines for the conduct of multinational enterprises. The Guidelines consist of recommendations regarding how multinationals ought to act in foreign nations. In the late 1990s the OECD engaged in extensive discussions to develop a Multilateral Agreement on Investment (MAI). But it stalled over several issues, as discussed below. The discussions are certain to continue, especially in view of the success of the OECD in completing the Convention on Combating Bribery of Foreign Officials in International Business Transactions.

§ 25.4 Governance by Host Nations

The laws enacted in the 1970s by host nations to govern foreign investment tended to be very restrictive. Some of their characteristics are discussed below.[10] Mandatory joint ventures was a key element.[11] But foreign investors in developing nations with restrictive laws often were able to avoid joint ventures. An "operational code" or unwritten law existed that allowed much needed foreign investment to avoid the harsh rules of the host nation that were generally believed to be mandatory rules affecting foreign investment.[12]

Host nation laws of the 1970s that governed foreign investment tended to evolve from two quite different perspectives. One group which enacted restrictive laws mandating joint ventures included nations which already had considerable foreign investment, such as India, Mexico, and Nigeria. These nations viewed the new laws as a way to gain greater control over foreign multinationals and to allow their nationals to participate in the equity and management of the means of production in the nation. At the same time nonmarket

---

[10] In addition to restrictions based on the desire to have host nation nationals participate in equity and management, restrictions may be imposed when investment is believed to infringe upon national sovereignty, is contrary to a development plan, is unbalanced in favor of the foreign party, creates environmental damage, or violates host nation law.

[11] See, e.g., Wolfgang G. Friedmann & J.P. Beguin, Joint International Business Ventures in Developing Countries (1971); Andrzej Burzynski & Julian Jurgensmeyer, Poland's New Foreign Investment Regulations: An Added Dimension to East–West Industrial Cooperation, 14 Vand.J.Transnat'l L. 17 (1981); Thomas M. Franck & K. Scott Gudgeon, Canada's Foreign Investment Control Experiment: The Law, the Context and the Practice, 50 N.Y.U.L.Rev. 76 (1975); Michael Wallace Gordon, The Joint Venture as an Institution for Mexican Development: A Legislative History, 1978 Ariz.St.Univ.L.J. 173; Martin F. Klingenberg & Joseph E. Pattison, Joint Ventures in the People's Republic of China: The New Legal Environment, 19 Va.J.Int'l L. & Econ. 807 (1979); Covey Oliver, The Andean Foreign Investment Code: A New Phase in the Quest for Normative Order as to Direct Foreign Investment, 66 Am.J.Int'l L. 763 (1972); James F. Pederson, Joint Ventures in the Soviet Union: A Legal and Economic Perspective, 16 Harv.Int'l L.J. 390 (1975); Niki Tobi, Legal Aspects of Foreign Investment in Nigeria, 18 Indian J.Int'l L. (1978).

[12] See Michael Wallace Gordon, Of Aspirations and Operations: The Governance of Multinational Enterprises by Third World Nations, 16 Inter–American L.Rev. 301 (1984).

economy nations were beginning to adopt joint venture laws that were used to admit for the first time in decades some limited foreign equity. The reason was usually that the nation needed technology that would not be transferred unless it accompanied an equity investment. Nations adopting such laws included several Eastern European nations, plus China and Cuba.[13] Nearly all of the world's nations that experimented with a nonmarket economy have more recently adopted investment laws that have eliminated many of the more restrictive features of investment laws of the 1970s.[14] Foreign investors often preferred to establish an investment in these nations rather than in the developing, market economy nations. That decision was perplexing to the latter nations. Those latter nations failed to realize that they were becoming more restrictive than they had been before, while the nonmarket economy nations were becoming less restrictive than before. Overall, whether nonmarket or developing (or both), new investment entered these nations in the 1970s far more cautiously than it has since the late 1980s, when the restrictive laws began to be dismantled, in application if not in existence.

Governance by host nations has been a dynamic process. By the early 1990s the restrictiveness of the earlier laws had largely been replaced by laws encouraging foreign investment. The changes were both internally induced after the financial crises of the early 1980s when foreign debts could not be paid in many nations, and externally induced in order to participate in regional pacts and the GATT. The decade of the 1990s was clearly one of marketization and privatization, rather than nationalization. That remained true through the first decade of the new century. Written incentives to invest were replacing unwritten policy-based disincentives.

In addition to legislation governing foreign investment, there may be constitutional provisions that affect investment. These may

---

13 The development of investment laws in China and Cuba are discussed in Jian Zhou, National Treatment in Foreign Investment Law: A Comparative Study From a Chinese Perspective, 10 Touro Int'l L. Rev. 39 (2000); Zhang Lixing, The Statutory Framework for Direct Foreign Investment in China, 4 Fla.Int'l L.J. 289 (1989); Lynn McGilvray–Saltzman, Joint Venture Associations: Cuba Reopens its Doors to Foreign Investment, 1 Fla.Int'l L.J. 45 (1984).

14 See, e.g., Foreign Investment Law of Mongolia of 1990, translated in 30 Int'l Leg.Mat. 263 (1991); National Investment (Promotion and Protection) Act of 1990 (applicable on the mainland only, the 1986 act remains effective in Zanzibar), 30 Int'l Leg.Mat. 890 (1991); Foreign Investment Law of Vietnam of 1987, amended several times; O.Plotnikov, Ukraine: Capacity for Growth, 9 Dec. 2012. www.iflr.com/IssueArticle/3129630.

reserve areas for national ownership,[15] allocate regulation to or among specific government agencies,[16] and generally outline the form of economy the nation has adopted.[17] When China initially welcomed foreign investment with the adoption of a law on joint ventures in 1979, it first amended the Constitution of 1978 to sanction foreign investment. If a foreign investment law is inconsistent with the nation's constitution, but is not questioned by the current government, problems may arise for the foreign investor with a later government not inclined to view the investment law as liberally as the prior government. In many civil law nations the weight given to the constitution is less than in the United States, often because there may be no process of judicial review to test legislation against the constitution.

Host nations often strongly promote foreign investment and offer diverse incentives to foreign investors. Even states or provinces within nations offer incentives, creating some issues with federal policy.[18]

§ 25.5 Governance by Multi–Nation Organizations and International Law

The principal multi-nation organization that has attempted to regulate multinationals is the United Nations. The United Nations and its subsidiary organizations, however, have had little success in developing an effective, widely accepted regulatory scheme for multinationals. This should not be surprising because the United Nations is a large organization with diverse cultural, economic, and political norms. However laudable have been the efforts to develop a code of conduct for multinationals, the record to date has not been impressive. The role of the United Nations, especially the Centre on Transnational Corporations, has become somewhat obscure as developing nations and nonmarket economies increasingly adopt less restrictive investment laws. The aspirations of developing nations of the 1970s, to achieve development through transfers (reparations for alleged abuses of colonialism, transfers of technology based on ideas being the patrimony of mankind rather than subject to private

---

15 The Mexican Constitution reserves basic petroleum production to the nation by vesting ownership of the land in the nation. The nation retains all subsurface rights when surface ownership is sold. Mex. Const., art. 27.

16 The Indian Constitution outlines government involvement in investment, including the ability to exclude private participation. Indian Const., arts. 19 and 301.

17 The constitutions of nonmarket economies often reserve the means of production and distribution to the state.

18 A. Vila, The Role of States in Attracting Foreign Direct Investment, 16 Law & Bus. Rev. Am. 259 (2010).

ownership, etc.), have been largely subordinated to a desire to achieve development through self-help.

Part of the efforts of the developing nations in the 1970s involved the creation of international norms that would control multinationals, such as the UN initiated code of conduct. Not only did these efforts fail, but the development of international law in general has been disappointing in its failure to establish legal norms for both multinationals and host nations. For example, the most contentious issue, compensation rights subsequent to expropriation, was before the International Court of Justice in the *Barcelona Traction* decision, but the court focused on a narrow issue of ownership and did not address compensation.[19]

The OECD has also participated in developing rules governing foreign investment. It has conducted work on a Multilateral Agreement on Investment (MAI). The United States urged that this Agreement further liberalize investment, and address such issues as national treatment, standstill, roll-back, non-discriminatory most favored nation treatment, and transparency. The OECD is considering such issues as free movement of executives, foreign investor rights to participate in privatization, monopolies, intellectual property rights, portfolio investment, restrictions on investment in sensitive areas, relations with regional organizations, authority over investment by sub-federal government (i.e., states and provinces), protection of culture by limitations on investment, and dispute settlement. Developing nations have expressed concern that the MAI may be an attempt by the OECD to monopolize market share by industrialized nations' corporations in the developing world. There were expectations that the MAI would be completed by April, 1998, for the annual OECD ministerial meeting. But the United States would not agree to EU insistence that an exception would be created for the EU, so that it could deny non-EU investment benefits granted exclusively within the market. The United States further rejected the "cultural exception" and the "public order" clauses. The cultural exception would allow nations to limit investment when it had an adverse impact on the host nation's culture (promoted by France and Canada). The public order clause would permit withholding national treatment in industries considered essential to national security, law enforcement, and public order. The United States tabled many exceptions to the applicability of the proposed Agreement's provisions, and insisted that the MAI would not extend to the United States. April came and went and the MAI remained in the negotiation stage. France, in frustration, withdrew from the

---

[19] Barcelona Traction, [1970] I.C.J. Rep. 3.

talks in October. The year (1998) ended without completion of the Agreement, and without any expectation that it would soon conclude. At the end of the first decade of the new century it remained dormant.

The earlier focus on investment rules by the United Nations has been renewed, but this time as a joint effort with the International Chamber of Commerce (ICC) in Paris. Rather than the restrictive approach taken by the United Nations in the 1960s and 1970s, the UN–ICC effort may produce investment guidelines for the private sector to promote better private sector involvement in the UN's decision-making processes, and more private sector participation in the economic development of the poorest countries. This joint effort has not been successful; the principal focus of the ICC with regards to investment rules by the UN has involved the latter's attempts to control climate, and the former's concern that any such UN controls may harm investment.

The World Bank, home of the successful International Centre for the Settlement of Investment Disputes (ICSID), is another organization that has drafted guidelines on foreign investment. They are important to investors seeking World Bank assistance.

A study in Canada (Industry Canada) suggests that the MAI will not eliminate some important barriers because it does not lead to the "deeper integration" that may be the only way to eliminate some barriers.[20] The report illustrates how as some barriers are eliminated, such as mandatory joint ventures or local content requirements, other barriers arise. It notes some of the following barriers:

1. Antitrust policies such as merger laws that prohibit takeovers for economic or social reasons.

2. Administrative procedures such as using required takeover reviews to demand performance requirements.

3. Structuring corporations with voting schemes that permit effective control by a small group representing a small proportion of the shares but with ability to block a takeover.

4. Anti-takeover laws that restrict voting rights of individuals or groups, such as in some American states.

---

[20] "Foreign Investment Research: Messages and Policy Implications," Industry Canada.

5. Restrictions on privatized government companies such as the U.K. and Italian use of "golden shares" to prevent changes of control.

6. Structures such as the Japanese *keiretsu* that essentially precludes a hostile takeover, or large bank holdings that block takeovers.

7. Limited role of stock markets with few listings, and high local concentrations of ownership that are hard to dislodge.

The report noted how such trade agreements as the NAFTA (Chapter 11) may dismantle some barriers, but also emphasized the limited range of issues that the NAFTA addressed in opening foreign investment. Some of the barriers are deeply rooted and long-established practices, that were never adopted as barriers, but have come to function as such.

Despite the efforts of the UN and OECD, the most effective control of the multinational remains by the laws of the host nation, and by the WTO. It is thus the form of those laws that is of most concern to an investor planning a foreign investment, and is the subject of the some of the comments below. The form of these laws within the WTO are called TRIMs. For the smaller NAFTA, Chapter 11 has reasonably successful rules on investment.

§ 25.6 Restrictions upon Entry

At what point in the investment process the government regulation or law takes effect presents another key distinction. Some nations make *entry* very difficult, by mandatory review of proposed investment, requirements of joint ventures or exemptions gained only after long negotiation and concessions, restrictions on acquisitions, and numerous levels of permission from various ministries and agencies. Mexico, until the late 1980s, possessed in its legal structure an example of each such restriction. But by 1994 it had repealed nearly all of these restrictions, a necessary change for Mexico to participate in the NAFTA.

Restrictions upon entry tend to assume one of two forms. Nations which recognize the corporate form sometimes restrict the maximum foreign equity allowed. Additional rules may also limit the foreign management or control to a minority interest. The enterprises resulting from these restrictions are referred to as equity joint ventures. But where host nations do not recognize the corporate entity, foreign equity cannot be governed by way of limiting share ownership. These nations are the nonmarket economies. Those which remain do not usually allow private ownership of the means of production and distribution, and usually do not have corporation laws. The manner of control over permitted foreign investment is by means of contract. The foreign investor's rights are detailed in what is referred to as a contractual joint venture.[21] The foreign party receives a percentage of the profits and is granted certain management rights. As nonmarket nations have converted to market economies, they have adopted corporation laws and shifted from the use of contractual to equity joint ventures. Many have also shifted from mandatory to voluntary joint ventures. In some cases the shift has involved a change from contractual joint ventures directly to permitting wholly foreign owned corporate entities, without an intermediate stage of mandating equity joint ventures.

§ 25.7 Restrictions During Operations

Some nations allow entry with comparative ease. Once established, however, the *operation* of the enterprise may be subject to various restrictions that divert time and resources from the main purpose of the investment. Government oversight may be extensive, with frequent visits from different officials to the degree that it becomes more harassment than regulation. Restrictions are often imposed on repatriating capital or sending profits or royalties abroad, or receiving hard currency to pay for needed imports. Currency restrictions have long been associated with foreign investment in developing nations such as Brazil, although less so with Mexico.

Another form of restriction on operations is performance requirements that mandate minimum local content, specify use of local labor, and mandate levels of technology used in production. The elimination of performance requirements has been a focus of multinational negotiations, especially in the GATT, where the adoption of the WTO TRIMs Agreement has resulted in a diminished use of such restrictions.

The worldwide economic declines in 2008 brought more demands for corporate regulation, especially in the financial sector. Most of the discussion was focused on such financial issues as lending practices, hedges, and especially executive compensation that is not linked to performance. How this will evolve, both with regard to the form of new rules and the impact on the movement of capital, remains unknown.

---

[21] See, e.g., Van Uu Nguyen, Foreign Investment in Vietnam Through Business Cooperation Contracts, 28 Int'l Lawyer 133 (1994). Vietnam does allow the creation of a limited liability company, but it is not required for foreign investment

§ 25.8 Restrictions upon Withdrawal

The withdrawal of foreign investment may be subject to restrictions. These restrictions may affect the ability to repatriate capital, the liability of the foreign parent or other subsidiaries in the country for debts of the withdrawing entity, and the removal of physical assets from the country. Potential investors should evaluate the restrictiveness at each level in determining whether or not to invest. Termination of an investment by bankruptcy may introduce the foreign investor to different theories of bankruptcy, including liability of the parent for debts of the foreign subsidiary.

§ 25.9 Prohibitions and Limitations on Ownership

Although restrictions may assume a seemingly infinite number of alternatives, there are several forms that continue to appear in the laws of various nations. They may be laws that generally govern foreign investment, or laws that limit foreign investment by means of anti-monopoly or restrictive trade practice rules.[22] Or they may be more general laws restricting the flow of foreign capital, with a consequent ability of a nation to govern the purpose of capital inflows for investment.

Total prohibition in certain sectors. Almost every nation prohibits foreign investment in certain sectors. Both developed and developing nations limit investment where national security is threatened. But the developing nations sometimes increase the scope of prohibited investment to a degree that may suggest the nation is really a nonmarket economy—it mandates state ownership of most of the means of production and distribution. Foreign investment is most often prohibited in the exploitation of the nation's most important natural resources.[23] Mexico, for example, has long prohibited nearly all foreign investment in the petroleum industry. Canada's early foreign investment regulations discouraged foreign investment in railroads by limiting ownership of Canadian railroads receiving government aid to British subjects. Canada also restricted natural resources, limiting oil and gas leases, mining, and exploration assis-

---

[22] See, e.g., the Indian Monopoly and Restrictive Trade Practices Act of 1969, which applied to investments exceeding a certain size or which were "dominant undertakings;" A.Lee, Myanmar's Long-Awaited Foreign Investment Law Analysed, 9 Nop. 2012. www.iflr.com/Article/3115717.

[23] Cynthia D. Wallace, Legal Control of Multinational Enterprise 45 (1983) (giving examples of broad bans in Sweden, Norway, Switzerland, and particularly Japan, which had indicated as many as 22 protected industries, some going beyond those that might reasonably be attributed to national sovereignty, such as drugs and data processing). Aeronautics, high-tech, petroleum, and iron and steel industries, also rank high among the key sectors protected by European nations, even those with generally open investment policies, such as Germany.

tance grants to Canadian companies, or foreign companies having at least 50 percent Canadian ownership or being listed on the Canadian stock exchange.

Outside this hemisphere, similar restrictions on foreign investment have been imposed by many nations. For example, India reserved some industries to its public sector in its Industrial Policy Resolution of 1948.[24] In the 1970s India took such a strong position about limiting foreign investment that it attempted to force foreign owned corporations in India to reduce ownership to less than 50 percent. IBM and Coca-Cola withdrew.

Additionally, some sectoral barriers through legislation and national monopolies remain impediments to FDI and intraregional direct investment in the European Union.[25] Other areas often restricted in various nations relate to the nation's infrastructure, such as transportation (in addition to railroads), communications, and electricity. The prohibitions may further reach some basic petrochemical production.

Reservation of investment to domestic private investors. A second group of industries may be permitted as private rather than national ownership, but the private owners must be host-nation nationals. These are industries where the nation believes that public national ownership is not necessary, but the nation prefers to reserve the areas for their own nationals. The reasons may be no greater than protectionism and the power of lobbying efforts of domestic industry which does not wish to compete with foreign owned investment. If the nation admits private ownership in a specific industry, it may have difficulty reserving that industry for its own nationals if the nation is a member of the GATT/WTO. The current trend is to require that the nation offer the same investment opportunities to foreigners that it offers to its own nationals, under the concept of national treatment. This could cause nations to move these industries not to ownership by nationals or foreigners, but exclusively to state ownership.

Foreign investment allowed. Industries not included in the protected classes mentioned above may have foreign ownership participation.

---

[24] Note, Foreign Investment in India, 26 Colum.J. Transnat'l L. 609, 640 (1988). See also, What to watch under India's new companies law, 9 Aug. 2012, www.iflr.com/Article/3073414.

[25] S. Thomsen & S. Woolcock, Direct Investment and European Integration Competition Among Firms and Governments 89 (1993) (citing transportation, telecommunications, and utilities as typical protected industries; also noting that intra-EU investors have much less trouble than non-EU investors as the EU removes many barriers within the region).

But that foreign private ownership may be limited to joint ventures, and possibly only minority interests. In some joint venture laws, it appears at first that all areas are open to foreign investment, because the law does not reserve any spheres of activity for the state or its nationals. This was true of the Cuban joint venture law of 1982,[26] but it was clear that foreign investment was to be directed to restoring Cuba's tourist industry, which would help obtain foreign currency. The Tanzanian law specifically prohibited foreign participation only in petroleum and minerals, but the Investment Promotion Centre could refuse investments in other areas, particularly if they were not joint ventures.[27] The Namibian law referred only to "eligible investment", without defining what areas were open or closed to foreign investment.[28]

Outright bans on foreign investment appear less frequent than equity limitations, but such laws present the first question a foreigner looking to invest abroad must consider—is the industry in which I am interested open to me? If the industry is one which is historically sensitive, such as natural resources and transportation, the answer may remain—no, it is not open to foreign investment. Where foreign investment is limited to minority participation in joint ventures in all industries not subject to even greater restrictions, the country is not a very receptive location for foreign investment. It is also unlikely to be a member of the GATT/WTO.

Equity percentage limitations. The equity percentages allowed to be owned by foreign investors have varied with the type of industry and the host nation's goal in applying the restriction. The reason for equity percentage limitations may be to allow the amount to depend on (1) what the investment is perceived to offer the nation, such as needed technology, or (2) an economic/social philosophy that foreign investment is inherently evil and to be prohibited. The former may be overcome by the foreign investor, the latter often may not. For years the nonmarket economy nations adopted the latter view, but

---

[26] Economic Associations Between Cuban and Foreign Entities, No. 50 (Feb. 15, 1982), translated in Possibility of Joint Ventures in Cuba, Cámara de Comercio de la República de Cuba 8 (Feb. 1982). Regulations were issued in September, 1982. See Regulations complimentary to decree Law No. 50 of 15 Feb. 1982, Cámara de Comercio de la República de Cuba (Sept. 1982). Cuba adopted a new investment law in 1995.

[27] The law does not address joint ventures, but it appears that the Centre has the authority to demand them for approval.

[28] Namibia Foreign Investments Act of 1990, 31 Int'l Leg.Mat. 205 (1992). But the Act allowed the Ministry to issue notices regarding areas reserved for Namibians, which was broadly defined as areas of "services or the production of goods which can be provided or produced adequately by Namibians."

moved to the former when it was apparent that those nations' development levels had remained at best static.

When nations adopt mandatory joint venture rules, they often limit foreign ownership to a minority share, usually 49 percent.[29] The reason is stated to be a preference to keep a majority of the ownership and control in the hands of nationals. If the nation decides to allow majority control to be owned by foreign investors, it often takes the additional step and allows the investment to be *wholly* foreign owned. If there is one certain characteristic of equity percentage limitations, it is that they are neither likely to remain static over a number of years, nor likely to be enforced absolutely. An unwritten code usually allows selective, needed investment to enter with total foreign ownership. The host nation often will waive restrictive equity limitations. Several reasons are commonly found in exception provisions in written investment laws, or in the unwritten "operational code", the unwritten policy of the government. They include the following:

1. *Technology*. Some companies with high technology, such as IBM, have been able to avoid joint venture mandates and retain total ownership.[30] What form of technology will gain such a waiver is likely to vary from one nation to another. Where there is a transfer of technology law, it is likely to state several reasons for registering a technology agreement which discloses the nation's interests. They include technology that assists import substitution, the most up-to-date technology, technology in high priority areas such as computers, technology intended to enhance job opportunities, and technology viewed as reasonable in cost.

2. *Plant location*. The willingness to locate a production facility away from already saturated areas, such as the most populated cities, will increase chances of gaining a waiver. Some countries specify areas that the nation feels

[29] The arrangement is called differently in different nations. For example, in India it is "foreign collaboration." See Kurk, Foreign Collaboration Agreements: Policy as Law, 9 J. Indian L. Inst. 66 (1967); Note, Foreign Investment in India, 26 Colum. J. Transnat'l L. 609 (1988).

[30] The experience of IBM in Mexico is an example. Contrastingly, IBM withdrew from India in the late 1970s when India demanded that IBM convert its wholly foreign parent owned investment in India to a joint venture. Minority shares would be owned by the parent with the majority owned by Indian nationals. See generally, Gucharan Das, India Unbound (2001); Foreign Investment in India—A Valuable Proposition, www.articlesbase.com (2006).

are already sufficiently industrialized,[31] other specify areas that they have designated for industrial development, or simply mention "less developed" areas.[32]

3. *Education.* The willingness to establish training centers in the host nation, especially centers that will teach jobs to function with new technology, is a method of gaining a waiver.[33]

4. *Research and development.* A major criticism of many nations is that multinationals only export their technology while undertaking all the research to develop that technology in their home nation. Being willing to undertake some research and development in a host nation may gain a waiver of maximum equity participation requirements.

5. *Balance imports with exports.* Because of chronic shortages of hard currencies, many host nations grant waivers of investment restrictions where the investment will require little demand on the host nation's scarce hard currency reserves. Thus, exporting part of the production to earn sufficient hard currency to pay for imports and cover profit and royalty payments may be decisive. The host nation's appreciation will increase as the export earnings continue to exceed the import demand. China placed great emphasis on exports, it was the key to obtaining permission to establish a wholly owned foreign investment under the 1986 joint venture law.[34]

6. *Sourcing capital from abroad.* In addition to shortages of foreign currency, some nations have shortages of domestic currency to lend to companies. They often wish to reserve that lending capacity for locally owned business. Thus, commencing an investment with capital from outside the host nation is another possible key to gaining a waiver.

---

[31] Mexico has preferred to keep new investment out of Mexico City, Guadalajara and Monterrey.

[32] Namibia Foreign Investment Law of 1990, art. 6(3)(b)(iv).

[33] The Namibian Investment Law of 1990, for example, gave special regard to the training of Namibians. Art. 6(3)(b)(ii).

[34] Law of the People's Republic of China on Wholly Foreign–Owned Enterprises of 1986, art. 3. See also V. Bath, Foreign Investment, the National Interest and National Security—Foreign Direct Investment in Australia and China, 34 Sydney L. Rev. 5 (2012); Foreign Investment in China Falls, Business Spectator, 18 Dec. 2012, www.businessspectator.com.au.bs.nsf; China: New Review Procedures for Foreign Investment in China, www.mondaq.com/x/123290 (2011).

Not only developing nations have experimented with limitations on foreign ownership of domestic business. During the 1970s, Canada enacted a restrictive investment law, although the provisions were never as restrictive as the foreign investment laws of India, Mexico, and Nigeria. The Foreign Investment Review Act of 1973 placed Canada in a unique position. It rendered Canada a legitimate contender to the title "developing nation." There were complex rules governing foreign investment, especially acquisitions. There was a Foreign Investment Review Agency with powers not greatly different than the powers of the Mexican Foreign Investment Commission. But this restrictive Canadian law was replaced in 1985 with the more investment-encouraging law—the Investment Canada Act. Parts of that Act have remained in place and were integrated into the framework of investment rules both under the Canada–United States Free Trade Agreement and the subsequent North American Free Trade Agreement.

Reasons for accepting equity restrictions. Foreign investors generally prefer to have total ownership of their foreign investments. Why would a foreign investor agree to limit participation to a minority interest?

An investment in place at the time of enactment of a government demand to either convert to a joint venture or withdraw from the nation may be less costly to continue as a joint venture with a minority position than to withdraw from the country. A local partner may be an asset if market penetration is difficult or political contacts are critical. But it is unlikely that the parent company will increase its investment or transfer the latest technology to the joint venture enterprise. The foreign entity will thus become quite unlike other wholly owned foreign investments of the multinational. It will remain relatively static while other foreign wholly owned company investments receive any needed additional capital and the latest technology.

If the market in the host nation has good long term prospects, and the restrictive joint venture laws are viewed as being transitory and likely to be modified in the future, it may be appropriate to accept a joint venture and invest. In Mexico in the 1970s, the willingness of Japanese investors to enter joint ventures with minority participation placed pressure on U.S. firms to accept the same limits on ownership, and even to offer better deals because of the growing Mexican desire to lessen reliance on U.S. investment. But new investment was never as extensive as it would have been without the restrictive laws of the 1970s, illustrated by the rapid increase in new foreign investment since those laws were repealed in the 1990s and Mexico entered both GATT and NAFTA.

If the host nation offers attractive investment incentives, accepting limitations on equity and management participation may be a fair trade, especially if the incentives are available immediately and the joint venture rules are likely to fade in time.

Retroactive effect of equity limitations. To force foreign investment already in existence to convert to joint ventures may give rise to claims of expropriation. Consequently, countries usually applied the laws to new investment, but often added provisions that made it very difficult for current investment to continue without conversion. For example, the Mexican 1973 Investment Law was not retroactive on its face,[35] but regulations denied permission to enter new lines of products or establish new locations without conversion to a joint venture.[36] India's Foreign Exchange Regulation Act of 1975 separately classified existing and new investment, granting the latter favorable treatment because it complied with joint venture mandates.[37] But the Indian government began to place pressure on all foreign investment to convert to joint ventures, leading to conflicts with many companies, and the withdrawal of Coca Cola and IBM. Conversion to a joint venture for Coca Cola would have meant disclosing the "secret formula";[38] conversion for IBM would have been contrary to a long-held policy to not participate in joint ventures.[39]

§ 25.10 Limitations on Acquisitions

A frequently used method to invest abroad is to acquire a locally owned company in the foreign nation. Such foreign acquisition has all the characteristics of an acquisition in the United States. That includes both the loss of an opportunity to increase the number of competitors in the business were the investing company to commence a new company ("greenfields investment") rather than acquire an existing company, and the consequences of vertical inte-

---

[35] One Mexican author, however, considered the law to constitute "creeping" expropriation. See Luis Creel, "Mexicanization": A Case of Creeping Expropriation, 22 Sw.L.J. 281 (1968).

[36] See Ignacio Gomez–Palacio, Defining "New Lines of Products" Under Mexico's Foreign Investment Law, 8 Calif.West.Int'l L.J. 74 (1978).

[37] See A. Jayagovinda, Regulation of Foreign Enterprises in India: An Enquiry into Foreign Exchange Regulation Act, 1973, 17 Indian J.Int'l L. 325 (1977).

[38] See Dennis J. Encarnation & Sushil Vachani, Foreign Ownership When Hosts Change the Rules, 63 Harv.Bus.Rev. 152 (1985).

[39] See McLellan, Why IBM Must Withdraw from India in June, 24 Datamation 181 (1978). IBM's experience with Mexico, contrastingly, was successful. It was granted waivers from the mandatory joint ventures. See IBM to Bid Again to Build Computers in Mexico, Miami Herald, Feb. 4, 1985, Bus. Monday, at 23.

gration if the company acquired is the distribution channel while the company acquiring is the producer, or vice versa. But these antitrust issues have not been the reason foreign nations have often prohibited foreign investment by means of acquisition of a host nation company. The reason has been the replacement of a locally owned business by a foreign owned business. The nation may be particularly concerned where the proposed acquisition is of a large domestic industry that is thought to *be* a domestic industry. For example, a proposed foreign acquisition of General Motors would create far more objection than proposed foreign acquisitions of 1,000 companies, each one–1,000th the size of GM, but not thought of *as American*. Even more sensitive may be proposed acquisitions of enterprises bearing the name of the nation, such as Mexicana airlines or Canadian Pacific railway. American incorporated airlines, wishing to merge or have some close linkage with large foreign airlines, have often been rejected in their attempts. The objection is thus often more cultural and emotional than economic. Foreign acquisition may provide an infusion of needed capital not available at home, and bring new management ideas where old management has lacked creativity and been stagnant. Restrictions on acquisitions are thus often based more on the feared *loss* of a domestic company, than the feared *addition* of a new foreign company. This means foreign investors and their lawyers have a different obstacle to overcome to obtain approval of an acquisition as opposed to a new investment.

Prohibiting *any* foreign investment in a particular sector is protective of domestic industry. Prohibiting foreign investment by means of *acquisitions* does not assure protection for domestic industry, since it allows competition to exist by the establishment of a new industry that is foreign owned. Thus protectionist arguments urge restrictions on all investment, not only acquisitions. The decision often is given to a foreign investment review agency.

§ 25.11 Limitations on Management

A limitation on the permitted foreign equity may not mean an inability to control the investment. Host nation majority owners may elect foreign management. Some host nation laws, however, stipulate that the percentage of foreign management may be no greater than the permitted equity participation.[40] But even this lim-

---

[40] The 1973 Mexican Investment Law stated, "The participation of foreign investment in the administration of the business enterprise may not exceed its participation in the capital." Law to Promote Mexican Investment and to Regulate Foreign Investment, art. 5 (1973). The provision does not appear in the current Mexican investment law.

itation may be unimportant if the local board is dominated by host nation nationals who are all profit motivated entrepreneurs whose goals are far more aligned with the foreign affiliate than with host nation government officials who believe that local management should be committed to pursuing national social goals.

§ 25.12 Performance Requirements

Restrictive investment laws often include performance requirements. These may mandate that manufactured products contain a certain minimum percentage of local content, thus protecting many smaller local suppliers. Other requirements may address the use of local labor. Labor requirements may cover both the employment of local persons, and establishing facilities for training new employees, including management level positions. The performance requirements may also mandate that a certain percentage of the production be exported, often in order to balance import needs against exports to avoid drawing on scarce foreign exchange.[41] Finally, there may be mandates regarding the level of technology used in the production, often requiring that the technology be as current as technology of the company used in the home nation. Transfer of technology requirements may also include mandated licenses to locals, or stipulations as to what technologies the investor may introduce. Performance requirements have been limited by the adoption of the WTO TRIMs Agreement.

§ 25.13 Limitations on Transfer of Capital and Earnings

One aspect of the import/export performance requirement is to alleviate trade imbalances, reflected in part by the flow of capital in or out of a country. Some countries have no systematic restrictions on movements of capital such as foreign exchange controls, limits on borrowing, transfer pricing, as well as repatriation of earnings. Ironically, restricting remittance of earnings does not always solve balance-of-payments problems; it may rather cause companies to maintain a static position with respect to their capital, and freeze the flow of currency, both inbound and outbound, to the nation.

Repatriation of assets, profits, or royalties may have to be reviewed by a national bank. This is often the case even where the

---

[41] The Mexican 1989 investment regulations required that a company established under the regulations (which exempted the company from joint venture mandates) maintain "during the first three years of its operations, a position of equilibrium in its balance of foreign currency." Regulations of the Law to Promote Mexican Investment and to Regulate Foreign Investment, Diario Oficial, art. 5, IV, 16 May 1989.

general policy is to allow relatively free transfer of currencies. Similar approval may be needed to pay for necessary imports. Some countries have been notorious for demanding that all receipts in foreign currencies be converted to the host nation (usually soft) currency. Any foreign currency thereafter needed to pay for imports or to remit home as profits must be approved. This restrictive policy often leads to double billing for exports, with part of the price going directly to the home nation. Such transfers are as commonly practiced as they are as commonly deemed unlawful.

Brazil and Argentina are examples of nations that have relied heavily on currency restrictions. The restrictions have been government responses to a frustrating inability to control inflation and indexation. Argentina even partly linked the Argentine currency with the U.S. dollar, which constituted a form of official dual currency in Argentina. Such currency linkages rarely last. Brazil has reduced restrictions on capital and profit repatriations, but it has a history of currency restrictions and investors are always concerned that restrictions will be restored. Mexico, contrastingly, imposed currency restrictions only during a brief four-month period in 1982.[42] As a result of considerable inflation, capital flight from Mexico increased dramatically in the early 1980s. To conserve remaining hard currency, the government nationalized banks and imposed exchange controls in August, 1982. The elected but not yet inducted president terminated the controls a few months later. The banking industry was partially opened to foreign investment several years later. Mexico's entry into NAFTA a decade later accelerated Mexico's return to private ownership of and foreign participation in banking.

India seems to have stood somewhere between Mexico and Brazil. While repatriations were generally freely allowable, they were controlled by the Reserve Bank of India and subject to numerous restrictions. Yet the Indian practice was generally thought to be accommodating to foreign investment.[43] If a repatriation or divestment was particularly large, the Indian government might stagger it over several years to cushion its impact on India's persistent foreign exchange difficulties.

China, as part of obtaining export oriented or technologically advanced status, encourages investors to reinvest profits in China

---

[42] See Stephen Zamora, Peso–Dollar Economics and the Imposition of Foreign Exchange Controls in Mexico, 32 Am.J.Comp.L. 99 (1984).

[43] See Khanna, Licensing Technology and Joint Ventures in India, Indo–Am. Bus. Times, May, 1987, at 24.

rather than remitting them abroad.[44] Such encouragement is generally present in most nations, both because it reduces demand on foreign currency reserves and adds to the industrial base of the nation. Reinvestment is often the only real choice for a foreign investment, since idle funds may be taxed or diminished in value if there is indexation in the nation which does not apply to such funds.

§ 25.14 Current Trends in Enacting and Enforcing Restrictions

The enactment of restrictive investment laws was most prominent in the 1970s. Two important occurrences in the 1980s tended to stop the enactment of restrictive investment laws. The first was the debt crisis in the early 1980s, which caused nations to realize that restrictive investment laws did not contribute to economic growth and exports. The second was the dismantling of the USSR and the commencement of the transition of many nonmarket economies to market economies. Even nonmarket economies outside the Eastern Europe and USSR group were making such changes. Vietnam, for example, first adopted a foreign investment law in 1987, and has since amended it several times.[45] Tanzania and Mongolia both enacted investment laws in 1990, neither of which has any reference to mandatory joint ventures.[46] The former USSR first adopted joint venture legislation in 1987, with modifications in 1988 and 1989, and a new law in 1990.[47] The law was quite liberal, which is the direction taken by the new nations that were formerly part of the USSR. Poland enacted a series of investment laws, each more liberal than the previous. The 1991 law eliminated the previously required approval process for many investments.[48]

By the late 1980s nearly all developing and nonmarket economies had begun to open their economies to more foreign direct investment, even though their earlier announced reservations about

---

44 Zhang Lixing, The Statutory Framework for Direct Foreign Investment in China, 4 Fla.J.Int'l L. 289, 305, 310–11 (1989).

45 See Van Uu Nguyen, Foreign Investment in Vietnam Through Business Cooperation Contracts, 28 Int'l Lawyer 133 (1994). The Vietnamese laws become important to United States investors because of the restoration of trading relations in early 1994.

46 Foreign Investment Law of Mongolia of 1990, translated in 30 Int'l Leg.Mat. 263 (1991); National Investment (Promotion and Protection) Act of 1990 (Tanzania), in 30 Int'l Leg.Mat. 890 (1991).

47 A brief description of the USSR laws is included in William G. Frenkel, Introductory Note to the 1990 Decree, 30 Int'l Leg.Mat. 913 (1991). See also 30 Int'l Leg.Mat. 266 (1991).

48 Polish Law on Companies with Foreign Participation, June 14, 1991, translated in 30 Int'l Leg.Mat. 871 (1991), including a useful Introductory Note by Ania M. Frankowska & Radoslon Gronet.

extensive participation in the means of production and distribution by foreign enterprises remained in many existing written laws. There was a reluctance at first to repeal these laws, which were often popular with the liberal media and academics. The nations instead began to relax their enforcement of the restrictive laws. While foreign nations, both developing and nonmarket, previously had brought many, and sometimes all, industries within the ambit of foreign equity limitations or prohibitions, these governments began in the mid–1980s to administer those laws with increasing flexibility. At times, the way the laws read and the way they were applied seemed quite opposite.[49] In the 1990s, the laws began to be modified to reflect the reality of practice, and to reflect obligations under bilateral investment agreements and multilateral agreements such as the GATT/WTO.

§ 25.15 TRIMs

The GATT Uruguay Round produced important new investment rules. Prior to this Round, the GATT had not directly governed foreign investment.[50] The new rules were thus quite a significant development. But as must be expected with any large organization with members possessing divergent views, the investment provisions of the GATT are not as comprehensive as those in the much smaller NAFTA.

The GATT/WTO investment rules are included in the "Agreement on Trade–Related Investment Measures." These measures, commonly called TRIMs, first set forth a national treatment principal. TRIMs which are considered inconsistent with GATT/WTO obligations are listed in an annex, and include such performance requirements as minimum domestic content, imports limited or linked to exports, and restrictions on access to foreign exchange to limit imports for use in the investment. Developing countries are allowed to "deviate temporarily" from the national treatment concept, thus diminishing in value the effectiveness of the GATT/WTO investment provisions, and obviously discouraging investment in nations which have a history of imposing investment restrictions, thus making such agreements as the NAFTA all the more useful and likely to spread.

---

[49] There was in effect an operational code, an unwritten law which stated "how things really worked". See Michael Wallace Gordon, Of Aspirations and Operations: The Governance of Multinational Enterprises by Third World Nations, 16 Inter–American L.R. 301 (1984).

[50] Foreign investment was originally to have been governed by a proposed World Trade Organization, discussed at the Bretton Woods conference near the end of World War II. The U.S. Senate was hostile to the idea, and the ensuing GATT did not regulate foreign investment.

The essence of the GATT/WTO TRIMs is to establish the same principle of national treatment for investments as has been in effect for trade. TRIMs are incorporated in the overall structure of the GATT/WTO, alongside trade measures, rather than being treated as a distinct area. Because all the deficiencies of the GATT/WTO with regard to trade measures may apply to TRIMs, it remains to be seen how effective these measure will be in governing foreign investment. Because the measures are much less certain than those included in bilateral investment treaties and small-area free trade agreements, it is likely that much of the regulation of foreign investment will develop in their context rather than within the GATT/WTO.

The WTO has a working party on trade and investment which has been discussing new investment rules. To some degree the collapse of the OECD discussions regarding the proposed Multilateral Agreement on Investment in late 1998 shifted the discussion to the WTO. The EU wanted investment policy to be a major issue in a comprehensive millennium round of trade talks it had hoped to commence in 1999. The unsettled nature of the Seattle WTO meeting in early 2000 delayed further development. By early 2013 there was no immediate prospect of new WTO investment rules.

§ 25.16 Foreign Investment Treaties

The decade of the 1990s was an active period for the signing of bilateral investment treaties (BITs). The principal focus was the protection and promotion of foreign investment.[51] The focus of a BIT is on the protection of existing foreign investment, not providing guarantees for market access in the pre-investment stage. A benefit of such an agreement is that its provisions prevail over domestic law, although the agreements usually allow for exceptions to investment protection when in the interests of national security.

It is not only the United States which has emphasized these treaties; they are common features of most developed nations in their relations with host nations for foreign investment. For example, China has investment protection agreements with an impressive list of nations, including Australia, Austria, Belgium, Luxembourg, Denmark, France, Germany, Japan, the Netherlands, and the United Kingdom. The European Union as a group, and the United States, have been at various stages of developing a BIT with China.

---

[51] Another form of treaty important to foreign investment has been for the avoidance of double taxation and prevention of tax evasion.

The investment treaties of interest to U.S. investors are those which have been concluded by the United States with other nations. Because the process of enactment of these agreements is a continuing one, the number in existence is certain to increase in the coming years. The existence of the WTO TRIMs provisions may reduce the number of bilateral treaties, but they will be used because they are able to tailor the provisions to meet the unique needs of the two nations. The parties must be careful, however, that concessions granted may be demanded by other WTO members under MFN concepts.

§ 25.17 United States Investment Treaties

The United States has entered into numerous bilateral investment treaties (BITs) in the past two decades. The reason is twofold. The earlier Friendship, Commerce and Navigation treaties (FCNs) were not effective investment protection treaties. Furthermore, other multinational forums, especially the United Nations, failed to enact investment protection and promotion rules, leaving the gap to be filled by bilateral agreements, especially between developed and developing nations respectively. The WTO TRIM rules are a step in the right direction, but remain less specific than agreements among smaller groups of nations (such as the NAFTA) or bilateral agreements.

The United States may participate in bilateral arrangements which are not treaties, but rather constitute cooperative statements of policies regarding direct investment. Japan and the United States signed such a statement by means of letter exchanges on a diplomatic level. One of the objectives of the letter exchange was to increase foreign investment in each nation by the other nation's investors.[52] But the exchange seems more a U.S. attempt to further remove obstacles to U.S. investment in Japan than the reverse.

§ 25.18 The Unwritten Law: Operational Codes[53]

Nations currently allowing foreign investment often strive to create regulations that narrowly fall short of the degree of restrictiveness that would cause a large scale withdrawal of foreign direct investment. Multinationals react adversely to any form of regulation and often attempt to convince host nation authorities that the nation either has achieved the nadir of restrictiveness, or, more

[52] Japan–United States: Policies and Measures Regarding Inward Direct Investment and Buyer–Supplier Relationships, reprinted in 34 Int'l Legal Materials 1341 (1995).

[53] This material is extracted from Michael Wallace Gordon, Of Aspirations and Operations: The Governance of Multinational Enterprises by Third World Nations, 16 Inter–American L.Rev. 301 (1984).

likely, that the nation is retarding development. They argue that the restrictiveness has increased above the "Edge of Discouragement", that level of restrictiveness beyond which foreign investors will withhold investment. Each host nation has such a level which the combination of its written and unwritten laws must not exceed if the nation truly wants to receive foreign investment.

The Edge of Discouragement slopes upwards in the degree of acceptable restrictiveness over time. Foreign investors learn to function in an atmosphere of increasing restrictiveness, as long as the point of investment impossibility is not reached. It is difficult for host nations to determine the optimum level for the regulation without discouraging foreign direct investment. No two developing or nonmarket nations possess such similar domestic, political, economic, and social characteristics that a uniform code of regulation of foreign direct investment could be produced. The framework of any one nation for the governance of foreign direct investment consequently may consist of a sophisticated and finely tuned set of norms, or it may include elements of regulatory absurdity, based on misconceptions either of the impact of the foreign investment, or the ability of the host nation to regulate without causing the withdrawal of needed foreign investment.

A tier of multinational governance consists of regulations by multi-nation organizations, although the adequacy of this type of regulation is questionable when directed at conduct in developing host nations. The principal multi-nation organization which has attempted to regulate multinationals is the United Nations. The United Nations and its subsidiary associations have had little success, however, in developing an effective, widely accepted regulatory scheme for multinational enterprises. This should not be surprising because it is a large organization with a wide diversity of cultural, economic and political characteristics and goals. That is as it should be. However ideally conceived to govern multinationals objectively the United Nations may have been, the record to date is not impressive.

Whether several of the United Nations pronouncements affecting multinationals constitute international law is an important issue that has become largely academic. Of greater importance is their disclosure of the aspirations of the large majority of the developing and nonmarket members, and a few developed nations. Because they reflect the aspirations of these nations, they may be called "Aspirational Declarations". They are written, but not law.

Aspirational Declarations assume particular importance not because they may constitute international law but because they disclose current sentiments and the direction of possible future law. They create a norm of expected conduct, a moral code promoted by developing and nonmarket nations as proper and reasonable conduct for multinationals. But they are more than a moral code. They may be a precursor of customary international law or they may become part of the written or unwritten laws of specific host nations governing foreign investment. The laws and policies of several host nations share a close identity with Aspirational Declarations of multi-nation organizations.

Apart from being indicators of future action, Aspirational Declarations serve another important function. They offer developing nations strong words to use that may temper adverse public reaction to governments plagued by economic and political troubles. They may serve, in a sense, as doctrines of collective insecurity.

On a graph, the Aspirational Declarations belong above the Edge of Discouragement. If these declarations were the norm of regulation, most foreign direct investment would withdraw. The reluctance of host nations to incorporate these declarations into their domestic law, and the Operational Code's extreme variance with the concepts of the declarations, also reinforces that they are more restrictive than is acceptable.

If one is asked how multinationals are governed, the common response is to concentrate exclusively on those written laws of the host nations that directly or indirectly regulate foreign direct investment. This is the second level of governance, referred to as the "Public Code". This code is written and it is law, in contrast to the Aspirational Declarations, which are written but are not law. A nation's Public Code includes constitutional provisions affecting foreign direct investment (such as labor and social security rules), statutes, published administrative regulations and widely distributed regulations or decisions of foreign investment agencies.

Although a nation's Public Code governing foreign direct investment may be extensive, it serves as the basis—the mental framework—of regulation of foreign direct investment for that developing nation. But even in those nations that have an extensive Public Code, multinational advisors should not rely on that written law as constituting the total framework of investment regulation. Awareness of the Operational Code is necessary, as is awareness of any impact that the nation's participation in the formulation of Aspirational Declarations would have on the functioning of both the Operational and Public Codes.

Properly locating the Public Code on a graph creates some difficulty because the graph generally applies to foreign direct investment in all developing and nonmarket nations. But a graph may be done for individual nations. Conclusions drawn as to the plotting of the restrictiveness over time are limited to an increasing degree of restrictiveness, or an upward sloping line, because Public Codes differ from nation-to-nation. It is preferable to show this line not as a constantly increasing line but one which increases in abrupt increments. Elements of the Public Code are enacted periodically, usually when the Operational Code has become so cumbersome and confusing that it is necessary to transfer some elements to the Public Code. This reduces investor confusion and increases predictability for those investors only familiar with the Public Code.

The Operational Code, the third control level, is the pivotal concept for multinational enterprises to understand. It is important largely because it is not written, or, where written, is not publicly disclosed. Indeed, by definition it may not be publicly disclosed. When elements of the Operational Code become so well-known to the investing community and are no longer considered secret, these elements tend to assume the status of the Public Code, yet remain unwritten. There is consequently a small part of the Public Code which is not formally written. But it is likely to become part of the written Public Code in its next revision. Nevertheless, the government may continue to deny its existence, even in the face of overwhelming public acknowledgment of its existence.

The definition of the Operational Code suggests that it is limited to formal unwritten regulations and decisions, but it may also include formal written regulations and decisions that either are not publicly available or discoverable. Two examples of written elements of the Operational Code illustrate this point. The National Commission on Foreign Investment in Mexico reviewed petitions from foreign investors requesting exceptions from the now-repealed 1973 Mexican Investment Law. A company could request a waiver from the requirement of Mexicanization to allow it to expand its current production at a new location or begin production of new products. Either, in the absence of being granted an exception, required Mexicanization of the entire company.

The Commission's written decisions were not released to the public, but they disclosed a great deal about the Operational Code and the criteria the government applied in reaching decisions on these petitions. Over time, these decisions were obtained by some Mexican lawyers representing multinationals. Their release eventually would become so extensive they would be common knowledge. They were then no longer part of the Operational Code but transformed by the extent of the public knowledge to the Public Code. These decisions were already written and constituted pronouncements of an entity with decision-making authority, therefore, there was no need to pass through the formal legislative process to become part of the Public Code. When the Public Code was next revised, these concepts would very probably integrated into the investment regulation laws. That happened with the enactment of the 1993 Mexican Investment Law.

In contrast to formerly non-disclosed pronouncements, there are regulations issued by various ministries which have not been kept secret. Although technically part of the Public Code, they exist in such large numbers and are so difficult to locate that they must be considered part of the Operational Code. Brazilian lawyers deal with such rules in the form of what are known as "drawer" regulations. These are regulations that have been issued by various ministries that, even though not labeled secret, have not been publicly disseminated. They are kept in a ministry official's drawer, removed on one occasion when considering a proposed foreign investment, and left in the drawer on another. Even when a drawer regulation is noted by the official it may be applied with an inconsistency permitted by the lack of public disclosure. Both the Mexican Commission decisions and these Brazilian regulations may be considered part of the Operational Code, although they are in fact *written* decisions and regulations.

The Operational Code is always somewhat at variance with the Public Code, but it must not deviate from the Public Code so extensively that it generates uncertainty that reduces foreign investor confidence in the regulatory structure. The Operational Code directly conflicts with the Public Code when, although positive law provisions of the Public Code do not contain exceptions, the law is waived according to the Operational Code. Any such waiver would be an Operational Code provision directly contrary to written law which would constitute a serious source of misunderstanding for potential foreign investors. This would be a far more serious problem than where a sizable variance exists between the Codes only in an indirect form. A direct conflict with the Public Code may lead to litigation against a host country over the Operational Code.

An indirect variance exists when positive statements of the Public Code are conditioned by exception provisions, but the government so routinely grants exceptions that the positive law effectively becomes a nullity. It is a potential source of conflict because unknowing foreign investors may believe the Public Code to be routinely applied. If the variance between the Operational Code and Public Code becomes extreme, it is mandatory, and in the best interest of a nation, to enact a new investment law. The new law should add to the Public Code those elements of the Operational Code the government wishes to acknowledge as now being appropriately part of the Public Code, and those which it believes create unacceptable conflicts by remaining within the Operational Code. The government will still not acknowledge Operational Code provisions it does not want admitted to the public. For example, Operational Code requirements mandating payments to government officials to expedite services, to grant exceptions, or even to refuse to enforce the Public Code, are not appropriate subjects to publicly acknowledge, and thus remain perpetually hidden in the Operational Code.

To place the Operational Code in the graph it must be emphasized that Operational Codes by their nature are not well defined. But for a general representation the line should relate to the Public Code and move upwards (or downwards) without the abrupt steps of the Public Code since the Operational Code is constantly undergoing modification.

It is as important for a host nation government to be aware of the divergence of its Operational Code from the Public Code, as it is for multinationals to be aware of that divergence and the progressively changing content of the Operational Code. A company failing to appreciate these movements is not in a secure position to predict future movements if it is ignorant of the existence of the Operational Code and the degree to which it varies from the Public Code. In some cases, particularly in the small dependent nations, the government tries to maintain a narrow gap between the Public Code and the Operational Code. If a dominant multinational enterprise in that nation is able to influence the Operational Code, it may function according to a lenient Operational Code but defend its actions on the basis of the more restrictive Public Code. The graph of such a nation would show a more restrictive Public Code than the Operational Code (at least for the dominant investor). There may be a benefit to the nation because it limits the single, dominant multinational to benefitting from the lenient Operational Code and enforces the more restrictive Public Code for other new investments.

The Operational Code has numerous facets. It has different rules applicable to multinationals with different levels of power to demand a lenient Operational Code. It reflects the nation's need to be flexible so as to obtain investment, particularly in crucial areas. The Operational Code under which IBM functions in many nations, where its computer technology has a monopoly position and where such technology is of critical need to development, is in stark contrast to the Operational Code applicable to a multinational entering an industry saturated by domestic-owned enterprises. The Operational Code applicable to IBM may be less restrictive than the Public Code, while that applicable to the latter multinational may be so severely restrictive that it works to eliminate foreign direct investment that might compete with inefficient local industry.

The Operational Code occupies an important position in a host nation's governance of foreign direct investment because it allows the government to treat different multinational enterprises in specific ways thought to be best for the nation. It may even treat different nations' multinational enterprises differently, hidden from obligations of MFN treatment. An investor with leverage may be able to enter without accepting a joint venture with majority host nation equity, but other enterprises, even those manufacturing similar products, may be required to comply with a Public Code mandating the joint ventures. More important than permitting unequal treatment, however, is that a potentially unpopular, flexible, Operational Code is hidden from public criticism. Nationalistic pressures may have caused the enactment of a restrictive Public Code for foreign investment that is unrealistic and certain to discourage all investment. By use of a liberal Operational Code, however, the government is able to function pragmatically while public opinion remains nationalist.

The most successful multinational enterprises are those that are aware of the various sources of law affecting foreign investment. This awareness, however, should not be misinterpreted as constituting control by the multinational enterprise. A multinational that appears to have a foreign investment with attributes that differ from provisions of the Public Code may simply understand the Operational Code better than others. The Operational Code cloaks much activity of foreign direct investment. It may lead to increased criticism from the public sector, particularly the press and academia, that may identify practices of multinationals which appear to the public to be at variance with the Public Code. The multinationals, however, have not necessarily violated the law; they have rather followed the Operational Code completely in accordance with the practices of the host nation government.

§ 25.19 Other Forms of Foreign Investment

There are some unique forms of foreign investment that have gathered their own rules as an overlay to the rules discussed above.

Countertrade. Investment may assume the form of a countertrade agreement, where production is established in the host nation and the profit is received exclusively as a share of the production.[54] This is usually called "compensation" or "buy-back". In such case the foreign investor may agree to build a production plant in the foreign nation and take as compensation or profit a part of the production of the plant. It is a form used mainly when the foreign nation is very short of hard currency. Compensation agreements are usually of fairly long duration, since it may take years to pay for the plant by the share of the plants production. The foreign investor must be able to market the production, and often negotiates a low price for the goods (in the form of a higher percentage of the production than might otherwise be called for).

Border industries and economic zones. A unique form of foreign investment has taken place for several decades along the borders of the United States and Mexico, called the border industries or *maquiladoras.* A foreign, primarily United States, company establishes an assembly plant across the border in Mexico to take advantage of low labor costs. Mexico in turn would not apply its former, restrictive foreign investment rules to the maquiladoras. With the adoption of the NAFTA, and Mexico's dismantling of its restrictive rules, the advantages of the maquiladora are considerably reduced.[55] The maquiladora concept is related to the use of free trade or economic zones, common in many countries.

Free trade or economic zones. Free trade or economic zones are geographic areas, often at a port, where foreign investors are allowed to exist with few domestic restrictions.[56] The foreign investor provides raw materials and goods are manufactured or assembled in the economic zone for subsequent export. One common rule is that the products may not be distributed in the domestic market.[57] The bene-

---

[54] Countertrade is discussed in chapter 5.

[55] See, e.g., Panel Discussion, The Mexican Maquiladora: Rumors of its Death Are Premature, 7 U.S.–Mexico L.J. 203 (1999); Cheryl Schechter & David Brill, Jr., Maquiladoras: Will the Program Continue? 23 St. Mary's L.J. 697 (1992); Note, Mexico's Maquiladora Industry & Other Manufacturing Facilities in Mexico, 15 Loyola L.A. Int'l & Comp.L.J. 965 (1993).

[56] See, e.g., Samuels, Freeports, Free Trade Zones, 9 Bus.L.Rev. 109 (1988); D.L.U. Jayawardena, Free Trade Zones, 17 J.World Trade L. 427 (1983).

[57] There may be exceptions, but in such case import duties will almost certainly be applied.

fits of the zone are (1) lower labor costs and conditions, and (2) the country in which the zone is located does not impose tariffs on either the parts entering the zone or the products leaving the zone, provided that they are exported. The benefit of the zone to the host nation is principally the jobs produced in the zone.

Lease financing. Lease financing involves financial (or operational) leasing of equipment to manufacture products. It is often a part of an investment arrangement, and may help reduce demands on foreign exchange (lease versus purchase). It also may allow the nation to obtain high technology equipment under lease.

§ 25.20 Taxation of Foreign Investment

As noted above, many developed nations have concluded tax treaties with nations in which their multinationals invest, essentially to avoid double taxation. Even though a nation may have a liberal foreign investment law, unless there is a reasonably clear expression of the form of taxation facing the investment, investment will be slow to enter. Some nations offer tax incentives to foreign investment, such as tax holidays that defer tax for a certain number of years, or rebates when profits are reinvested rather than repatriated. The tax benefits are often linked to investment in high priority areas, such as those that generate foreign exchange for the host country. Tax benefits may extend beyond a tax on profits to taxation of royalties, taxes on imports and exports, sales and consumption taxes, and taxes on personal income of expatriates. One problem for foreign investors is the dynamics of taxation in foreign nations. Tax burdens change frequently and incentives received one year may be far less valuable in another.

Tax units, whether nations or states, are always concerned when reporting methods tend to diminish income expectations. Two issues relate to transfer pricing and the unitary tax. If a foreign company reduces its taxable income in a host nation by intra-company transfers at prices which do not reflect arms-length transactions, the host nation may respond with methods to restructure the transfers, and possibly impose sanctions. Secondly, when the subsidiary reports an income that as a percentage of the world wide corporate entity's income is considerably lower than the percent of assets, employees, and sales within the host nation, the host nation may adopt a unitary tax that replaces a tax based on reported income by adjusting that income to parallel the percent of assets, employees, and sales in the jurisdiction.

§ 25.21 Currency Issues

Currencies of developing nations are almost uniformly considered to be "soft" currencies, although they are rarely as controlled as the *soft* currencies of nonmarket economies. It may be that merely being a developing nation means that the currency is soft But within the developing nation world there are *soft* currencies and there are *softer* currencies. The softest of these currencies may be as nearly controlled as the currencies of a nonmarket economy. But few developing nations have the kind of controls formerly used in nonmarket economies, where entering persons were required to convert so much hard currency for the soft local currency, and where no currency could be taken out of the nation. Every transaction by foreigners has to be accounted for upon exiting the country, and what local currency had not been spent had to be left within the country, often used to purchase tourist items in a shop at the point of departure. Common as such practices were three to four decades ago, they were largely dismantled as part of the transitional process to market economies.

The currency controls in developing nations often amount to attempts to fix the rate of exchange rather than allow it to freely float, or to link the currency to a hard currency. When the currency is formally linked to a hard currency, such as to the dollar for some Latin American nations, the currency has two problems. First, the country's monetary policy effectively is transferred to the linked nation.[58] Second, the linking may prove to be artificial and cause a parallel free market rate to arise.[59] The country may use the parallel free market rate as a guide against which to devalue the fixed official rate. Mexico for many years linked the Mexican peso to the dollar, and sometimes adjusted the peso daily, often with a slight daily slippage or decline in the peso against the dollar.

Many developing nations compound currency problems with high inflation. High inflation tends not to be a characteristic of nonmarket economies, at least until they become nations in transition. A nation with high inflation cannot long keep its currency pegged to that of a low inflation developed nation. There must be periodic devaluations or the developing nation currency will be highly overvalued. This will cause a parallel market at market rates to develop, will encourage nationals to move currency abroad, and may cause the economy to "dollarize." The latter occurs when there

---

[58] If the dollar falls against other hard currencies, such as the yen or Euro or Pound Sterling, the developing nation's currency also falls.

[59] The parallel market may be allowed to exist, or be suppressed to the extent possible, and become a black market currency.

is little faith in the local currency and nationals begin to deal with a hard foreign currency. As inflation reaches four figures or more, business persons often become more concerned with currency issues than with the primary purpose of the business.

Western traders normally require that goods or services be paid for in hard currency, the rate of which generally reflects market conditions and is convertible to other currencies. But a few developing nations' currencies are relatively hard, and generally convertible to other hard currencies. Some developing nations have laws that mandate that any international contract performed in the nation, or any debt due, must be paid in the official national currency. Such laws do not succeed where the currency is soft and unacceptable as a commercial form of payment. Thus an international agreement may stipulate that the contract is to be considered performed outside the developing nation and payment is to be made in a hard currency outside the developing nation. It may even be helpful to have the contract executed in the United States (or another hard currency nation), and stipulate that title to exports from the United States passes before shipment, so as to have as many links as possible outside the developing nation, even though that is where the much of the performance actually occurs.

Currency issues complicate trade and investment, but they not to halt trade and investment unless they become so extreme that they overwhelm the principal trade or investment project. Since currency problems are usually an incident of being a developing nation, traders and investors have learned how to deal with them.

> Currencies in nonmarket economies are also usually "soft" currencies. Nonmarket economy currency "official" exchange rates are established and rigidly protected by the government. These rates do not reflect market factors. Nonmarket economies frequently have multiple exchange rates. There is an "official" rate, and such other rates as a tourist rate, and perhaps a commercial rate. All are artificial and set by the government. There is additionally likely to be a black market rate that the government may attempt to suppress. Any artificial exchange rate tends to cause the currency to be rejected in international currency markets, although the nonmarket economy may attempt to keep the currency completely out of any international trading. But most transitional nations have attempted to stabilize their currencies. The transitional process has brought some "hardness" to these currencies. One intermediate measure for Eastern European nations in transition from nonmarket to market economies was to peg the domestic currency at a float-

ing rate to a Western hard currency, initially the German Deutschmark, and subsequently the Euro. With later entry into the European Union, the Euro became in most instances the nation's official currency. That may not guarantee long term economic development, as reflected in the experience of Cyprus.

Loans to purchase products usually must be repaid in hard currency. Such demands have a restrictive effect on trade. Hard currency reserves must be earned to be spent. Many nonmarket economies are reluctant to spend their hard currency reserves unless the product is of high priority.

Several of the new nations created by the changes in the former Soviet Union have an even more basic currency problem. These newly independent nations have only recently introduced a national currency. They are attempting the very difficult task of simultaneously establishing an independent nation, introducing major structural reforms, and modernizing their infrastructure and industry. Several new nations that were formerly part of the Soviet Union continued to use the ruble until their own currency was established, or having established their own, used both. The ruble's problems thus extended beyond Russia's borders. The new currencies often had few assets backing them. The nations' leaders may have little experience in developing an economy or dealing with financial markets. But these new linked currencies have become independent from the ruble, and many have been gaining reputations as reasonably stable currencies.

§ 25.22 Goals of Privatization

Developing nations. The reasons countries privatize is not always made clear. Many developing nations have struggled with a mix of private and state ownership which they call a "mixed" economy. But the proportion of the mix is never very clear. Furthermore, it is also uncertain how the government will allocate the private sector between host nation nationals and foreign investors. While privatization has important economic consequences for the nation, it is always the result of political decisions.

Developing nations have turned to privatization to reduce the financial burden on the state from operating many businesses at a loss. But privatization is also thought to make profitable state-owned businesses operate even more profitably. A company might operate in the domestic market with a profit, where its products are necessaries and there is no foreign competition. But as the nation reduces tariffs on imports, these businesses must change to survive. Privatization is sometimes the first change.

Privatization was much discussed in developing nations in the mid–1980s, but in practice the idea was mostly mythical. Privatization plans were announced, but the obstacles to a successful privatization were often considerable. Brazil once announced a sale of "one company per month" but added little detail to assure success. It never materialized. To some extent actual and effective privatization in many developing nations did not commence until the nonmarket nations in Eastern Europe began serious privatizations at the beginning of the 1990s. Privatization in developing nations is obviously less extensive than privatization in nonmarket economies. In the latter, often all the means of production and distribution was state owned, even small stores. Furthermore, all housing was often state owned. Developing nations' privatization usually affects medium to large businesses.

There is no common plan of privatization. Nations have developed many different plans, often carefully watching how privatization functions in other nations and making small adjustments. There are common characteristics to privatization plans, such as dealing with retention of employees, granting employees or nationals priority in purchasing businesses, and listing enterprises to be privatized. Because privatization is a relatively new phenomenon, there has been much trial and error in developing a plan appropriate to the particular state and appropriate to the goals of privatization.

The goals of privatization in developing economies are more associated with the need to reduce state expenditures than with a philosophical change of economic theory from socialism to capitalism. Most nonmarket economies have pursued privatization to assist the change to a nonmarket economy. Certainly, some philosophical change has occurred in developing nations. Many governments in the 1970s thought greater state ownership of the means of production and distribution was an appropriate social goal. Having established that in a usually quite nominal dimension, changes in attitudes reversed based on more fundamental theories than the need to reduce state subsidization of business. Many transitional and developing nation administrations are theoretically committed to the idea of a market economy. But it is often difficult to gain public acceptance of the idea when populist remnants endure, and even assume control. In nonmarket economies privatization is one element of the commitment to change. In developing nations there is usually no such pronounced change in process.

Once the concept of privatization has been accepted by a nation, rules must be developed to carry out the privatization. If the rules are unrealistic state owned businesses will remain unsold. The concept will remain a myth. The nation will either abandon the process or make adjustments to make the plan successful. Those adjustments must be made in many areas where there are obstacles to privatization.

Nonmarket economy nations. State ownership of the means of production and distribution has not been successful. It has caused inefficiency and the production of poor quality goods that have not found markets abroad. The cost of maintaining so many state enterprises has placed an unbearable economic burden on the state. Nearly all of the nonmarket economies have chosen as a principal method of transition greater private ownership of commercial enterprises. Privatization of state owned firms has been a major method of foreign investment in these nations. The process has gone beyond factories to stores and apartment buildings, and selected services. Not all industries and services are on national schedules for privatization, many associated with national security and some "essential" services remain state owned.

The pace of privatization and the methods used vary country-to-country. Few of these nations have had much experience, even prior to communist rule, with modern Western style capitalism and private ownership of property and business enterprises. Some Eastern European nations have a history of capitalism and industrialization, with small shops and farms. But the history of the region consists primarily of agrarian peasant societies with a landed aristocracy. Entrepreneurs and shopkeepers were not at the center of government or society, and there are few persons left who had actual experience with markets where they existed during the first half of the last century.

Most of the nonmarket economies have learned that privatization increases productivity and removes a very costly burden from government financial support. Success in one privatized industry leads to more privatization. But there seems to be an inconsistency in the motivations behind privatization in different countries.

Some nations are using privatization to achieve what they refer to as a "mixed" economy, allowing private enterprise in certain sectors but retaining substantial state ownership in others. What the proper mix is to be is never very clearly identified, and the concept seems subject to continual alteration as industries retained under state ownership become a financial burden. Some nations have used privatization to lower the foreign debt, using the proceeds to pay down outstanding obligations. Others have used the process to broaden the base of private ownership in the middle class. The plans of some countries often seem based only on political publicity, such as Brazil's idea of "one company per month." There is some dislike of the idea of privatization, not only in the nonmarket economies but developing nations as well. To avoid public anger, Mexico has referred to the process as "disincorporation" rather than privatization. There is yet no clear plan in many countries that informs potential foreign investors of the nation's real commitment to the privatization process.

Once the process is made part of the nation's economic transitional plan, it must be realized that it is a long process to change a nation with no private ownership of the means of production and distribution to one where private ownership is the dominant mode. Full conversion must be measured in several decades rather than several years, even where the goal is made clear and principal obstacles are removed. Those obstacles are many.

§ 25.23 Obstacles to Privatization

Developing nations. The once largely myth of privatization in developing nations has turned to reality. But the process has proven difficult. There are many obstacles, which if not corrected or surmounted, tend to return the plan to mythology.

Absence of an adequate legal infrastructure. Developing nations usually have in place a legal infrastructure with market economy characteristics, unlike the situation facing nonmarket economies in transition. But there are often inadequate structures to help raise capital, such as a viable stock market and securities regulation law. Also, few developing nations have effective rules governing monopolies and restrictive trade practices. Mexico, for example, only a few decades ago created a commission to deal with restrictive trade practices.[60] Nevertheless, most developing nations have effective company laws, commercial codes, laws governing property transfers, and bankruptcy or insolvency laws. Even when the laws and institutions are created there may be an absence of the educated human resources required to function effectively. The result may be no enforcement or a very harsh and arbitrary enforcement.

---

[60] The absence of laws often also means an absence of regulatory institutions. In some cases the rules are in place but there are no enforcement institutions, such as in the area of protecting the environment.

One concern special to privatization is dealing with claims against the property being privatized by former owners. This is a serious issue in privatization in former nonmarket economy nations. In most developing nations the state owned enterprises were not formerly privately owned entities that were expropriated, and the issue is not often present.

There is another infrastructure that is often lacking in developing nations and in nonmarket economics. It is the infrastructure of airports, roads, ports, waterways, telecommunications, water treatment, and power plants, all needed to allow business to function and grow. Often these are all state-owned and operated inefficiently and without adequate capital. They are areas where privatization is often most needed to diminish such a serious obstacle to encouraging foreign investment. In recent years there has been a major emphasis in some developing nations, especially in Latin America, in developing this infrastructure with foreign private assistance.

Government approval process. Because the essence of privatization is the sale of state-owned properties, the government is obviously involved. Often, the state creates a privatization commission to carry out the process. But, where a specific case becomes a public issue, there may be pressure on the central administration to influence decisions of the special commission. Privatization can become a very volatile issue, especially when the workers feel threatened by the process and seek public support for stopping the process.

The government must decide what to privatize. In nonmarket economies the question becomes: "is everything to be sold?" But in developing nations the state does not own everything, and the question is more limited to: "is everything the state does own on the list?" The state is likely to control the process by controlling what will be sold at a given time. There may be a list of state enterprises to be sold, or the state may be open to offers to purchase almost any state-owned enterprise.[61]

Government approval creates opportunities for requests for bribes. Many developing nations governments have institutionalized corruption. The privatization process creates new opportunities and new forms of corruption. Management (i.e., government employees) of the state owned enterprises may oppose the privatization unless they are paid-off, or hired-on, by the purchasers. Many government employees see the proceeds of the sale as a one-time wind-

[61] There are likely to be some state enterprises not on the list, such as petroleum and some natural resource related industries.

fall, which they have an opportunity to share in personally. It is difficult to participate in privatization in many countries without confronting demands for payments that will likely create issues under the U.S. Foreign Corrupt Practices Act.[62]

Participation of workers in the approval process. Workers often view privatization as a threat to their jobs. They have good reason. Usually the state enterprise has more employees than are needed to perform the business function. Privatization means a reduction of the workforce in most cases. As a consequence of this, workers are sometimes given some voice in the sale of an enterprise. But they are rarely given the final say, since they are likely to vote against the sale to preserve their jobs. What they may receive are rights to participate in the equity of the new privately owned enterprise. They may be similar to rights sometimes granted generally to nationals.

Rights of nationals to preferences. While employees may participate in the approval process, all nationals may have preference rights to purchase shares in the entity being sold. The reason is to allow nationals to share in the sale of assets. But there is less such motivation in developing nations than in nonmarket economies. In the latter, nationals have not been able to own the means of production and distribution, and privatization is a method of allowing them to begin to become owners. In developing nations, ownership of private business has almost always been a possibility, if not of the particular industry or plant being privatized. Furthermore, nationals of developing nations are more likely to have had the means to become owners, since unlike in the nonmarket economies, there were no limits on their earnings.

When governments set aside so much of the enterprise to be privatized for possible purchase by nationals or employees, they may issue coupons or vouchers to the nationals or employees. The vouchers may be used for any privatization, or for a specific industry being privatized. A danger is to allow too much of the enterprise to be acquired by nationals at a nominal price paid for the coupons or vouchers. The principal purchaser of the majority interest will not be willing to subsidize the acquisition of shares by nationals. If the per share price paid by nationals is far less than that paid by the foreign investor, the latter may reject the acquisition unless the price is low, notwithstanding the sale of some shares to nationals. The value of a privatized enterprise is one of the most difficult calculations for the government to make.

---

[62] The Foreign Corrupt Practices Act is the subject of chapter 17.

Method of valuation. There is probably no more difficult aspect of privatization than establishing a value for an enterprise to be privatized. The book value of a developing nation state owned company is not likely to be any more reflective of the value than in the case of a privately owned business in the United States.

Where it is difficult to determine a fair value, the government may wish to have an auction.[63] Foreign investors may not wish to engage in a bidding process, and the auction process clearly drives away some prospective buyers. Most purchasers wish to be the only negotiating company, so as to avoid losing the expense of competitive bidding.

Valuation difficulty is not limited to developing nation privatizations. It is even more difficult in nonmarket economies. Furthermore, there have been experiences in developed nations that have privatized state owned companies at either too high prices (bringing no interest), or too low prices (bringing many buyers and the creation of a second market after the sale at a considerably higher price).

Treatment of *foreign investment.* The privatization process in developing nations assumes the participation of foreign investment. There is usually thought to be insufficient capital in the private sector to purchase the enterprises. However, some enterprises which are to be privatized may be limited to private ownership by host nation nationals. Or there may be limitations on the foreign share acquired, bringing into the privatization mandatory joint ventures. Sometimes there are attempts to first sell the business to nationals, with a subsequent opening of the remaining shares to foreign investment. This is not likely to attract many foreign investors when it means acquisition of a minority share. The reality is that the capital needed to privatize is usually mostly located abroad, and sooner or later the nation must adapt the privatization plan to including foreign investors. If there are limits on foreign investment, the largest industries will go unsold.

Miscellaneous. Privatization contains many unknowns for both the government and potential foreign investors. The government views the process as relieving it of a financial burden and acquiring a substantial payoff. The foreign investor often views the process as a

---

[63] They may wish to use an auction method even where there is a reasonably certain calculation of value. The auction may bring a buyer who is willing to pay more than the enterprise would be worth to most buyers. But a purchase at too high a price could lead to disappointment with the business by the purchaser, and an early insolvency.

means of entering the nation and possibly obtaining a good investment at a favorable price. Neither the nation nor the foreign investor may be fully satisfied, and may discover that the time and expense necessary to complete the privatization is far in excess of what was expected.

Additional problems that face foreign investors acquiring an enterprise through privatization include the possibility that there may be demands that the company continue to produce the same products, or export so much production. The company must know what the demands will be that will interfere with its making choices.

State owned companies may not have shares. There may have to be a creation of a new enterprise with shares by the government so that there are shares to sell. Alternatively, the state may sell the assets to an entity which creates a local business to accept such assets. This latter may be more favorable if there are hidden liabilities that must be addressed if shares are bought. Buying specific assets may avoid assuming non-disclosed liabilities. In any event, even when shares are bought, there may be an agreement by the selling government to assume all liabilities not stipulated in the sales agreement.

Privatization has been especially successful in nonmarket economies with small to medium businesses. But in developing nations, there are usually few small to medium sized business that are state owned. Where there are they have sold reasonably well. Selling the largest businesses in any form of economy has more complex problems than selling smaller businesses. The workforce is likely to be more vocal and more powerful in the largest businesses. Valuation is usually more difficult, and there are fewer buyers who can afford such businesses. In many cases, the largest business have been acquired by consortia, often comprising investors from several foreign nations.

The complexities of the privatization process, and especially the problems associated with being unable to fire workers, replacing obsolete technology, assuming responsibility for environmental damage claims, valuing the business, understanding and correcting poor (or different) accounting procedures, and having little previous quality control, have led many foreign investors to follow the "greenfields" method of investing. That method suggests forming an entirely new company rather than acquiring an existing state-owned one.

Nonmarket economy nations. Until a very few years ago, privatization was much discussed but little activated. It was one of the myths of foreign investment. As the myth became reality, mainly with the political changes in Eastern Europe and the former USSR, it became apparent that the process of privatization would be difficult, even with a new positive government backing.

Absence of an adequate legal infrastructure. Nonmarket economies long functioned without the legal framework necessary in a market economy. Constitutional amendments have been required to change the fundamental philosophy, and alter fundamental notions of ownership of property. New laws have been enacted to address the formation and operation of business enterprises, transfers of property, bankruptcy, banking, and securities regulation.[64] Many new laws have been viewed by foreign investors as being too broad and allowing too much discretion to government officials. In addition to the laws, new institutions have to be established, such as a stock market and securities regulation agency.[65] There have been disputes regarding whether federal or local (state or provincial) laws ought to govern, with federal law predominating. As the nations began to acknowledge private ownership, many citizens and emigres presented claims for the return of properties expropriated decades ago. Such claims affect foreign investors, who may be pursuing an acquisition of a small business claimed by a host nation citizen. Of major concern has been the obligation of new owners to clean up past environmental damage. Foreign investors need to learn if there are any claims of environmental damage against the state and whether there are laws allocating the responsibility for their correction. An agreement to acquire a state owned business ought to have an indemnification provision obligating the state to pay any former claims.

As nonmarket economies in transition enact new market oriented laws, the risk to foreign investors will be much reduced. The manner of development of the new legal infrastructure discloses much about the commitment of the host nation to a serious process of allowing foreign investment and achieving a market economy.

Government approval process. Many nonmarket economies have added a special agency to deal with privatization. That is helpful if it does not merely add one additional layer of bureaucracy to the

---

[64] Principal models have been the laws of Germany and the United States.

[65] Part of the problem with the earlier structures was that so much was done by a kind of unwritten law or administrative policy that was often elusive in source. See, e.g., Bernard Black, Reinier Kraakman & Anna Tarassova, Russian Privatization and Corporate Governance: What Went Wrong? 52 Stan. L. Rev. 1731 (2000).

approval process. In some cases the specialized agency shares authority with another agency. The specialized agency may develop a list of approved companies for privatization. But "spontaneous" privatization, where foreign investors identify a company and propose privatization, has been accepted and successful in some cases.

Government approval creates the possibility of requests for bribes. Unfortunately, the nonmarket economies in transition have been a major source of such requests, matching some of the developing nations in demanding payments for official action.

Participation of workers in the approval process. Workers may have to participate in the approval of the sale of enterprises. Before the disintegration of Yugoslavia, workers owned the plants in which they worked and there was thus a constitutional obstacle to the sale. In other nations, enterprise workers' councils may have the right to approve a sale. Even where there does not seem to be any formal process for workers' approval, the concern for the workers sometimes leads to a kind of informal approval, a sensing of the workers' attitudes before official government approval is granted. The likely primary concern of workers is loss of employment. One reason privatization is adopted is to reverse the overemployment consequence of state ownership with no accountability for costs of production. If workers are given approval rights, privatization may prove impossible, and essentially be a mythical characteristic of the transition.

Rights of nationals to preferences. While workers in the factory may participate in the approval process, both workers and nationals in general may have preference rights to purchase shares. The national motivation is to allow nationals to share in ownership. But since nationals would probably not have very much savings, they cannot afford to pay the per share price offered by a foreign investor. Governments have thus sometimes set aside so much percentage of a company to be privatized for local ownership. It is often accomplished by a coupon or voucher scheme, where the government issues coupons or vouchers of a set value to all nationals. The state privatization agency first determines the approximate value of an enterprise to be privatized. The agency then issues an appropriate number of stock shares. The coupons or vouchers may be redeemed for shares of an enterprise or traded with others, or sold. Shares may then be redeemed through the state privatization agency or on the stock exchange.

In some countries, employees are granted the first opportunity to purchase shares of the factory or establishment where they work.

The initial issue of coupons or shares are to employees or specific buyers only, and may not be freely transferred. This method is consistent with the nonmarket economy tradition of common or collective ownership, only under this system the workers truly own the factory instead of the state owning it for them. This program has run into resistance, particularly in Russia, from factory managers who fear losing their jobs to the workers, or worse yet to strangers when the workers later trade or sell their shares. The nationals are allowed to sell the vouchers to other nationals, or use them to acquire shares in companies. Because nothing is paid for such shares, a foreign investor is likely to calculate the per share value considering the dilution effect by the percentage of shares acquired by nationals. While the process is fair to nationals, it overlooks the fact that the nations need capital, and for every share of stock given to nationals, the foreign investor is going to reduce its offer to offset the "free" shares to nationals.

Treatment of foreign investment. The privatization framework may include limitations on foreign participation. That may be by absolute prohibition in some privatizations, leaving the enterprises for exclusively local private ownership, or by limitations allowing joint ventures. The joint venture law thus becomes interrelated with the privatization process. Sometimes foreign investors are given last priority, to allow as many enterprises as possible to be owned by nationals, with foreign investors allowed to invest in what remains. But while this might suggest that foreign investors are given only the scraps, the fact is that nationals do not have the resources to purchase anything but a small fraction of their nation's industries.

Some of the rules are based on incorrect assumptions regarding what foreign investors want. They are interested in direct investment, not a scattered portfolio investment. And they are interested in control. If the host nations expect to obtain foreign technology, capital and distribution outlets, they have to give up more than many governments have been willing to acknowledge.

Method of valuation. Establishing a value for an enterprise to be privatized is as difficult in a nonmarket economy nation as in a developing nation. Book value possesses all the problems of book value in the United States, plus even greater distortions due to accounting practices that do not adhere to market policies. But book value may be used, especially to set the value (at a low amount) for purchases by workers. The government may use one valuation method for purchases by nationals, another (higher value) for purchases by foreign investors.

One prevalent form of valuation is really not a valuation method at all. It is by auction, perhaps with a minimum base. But many foreign investors prefer to negotiate a price and not be one of several players in bidding for a company. Former losers at auctions may be discouraged from committing the time and expense to be a participant in the future.

Setting the value of a company to be privatized is not only a problem for nonmarket economy nations. The experience of the United Kingdom in privatizing several state owned companies illustrates setting prices too low or too high. When too low, the market quickly raises the price to a market level and the government is quickly aware of what they have lost by undervaluation. When too high, there may be no buyers and the process has to be repeated. It may become a costly procedure.

Miscellaneous. Privatization is a rather traumatic experience for the government, and also for the foreign investor. There are many uncertainties, as noted above. The government sees a benefit in both raising a great deal of hard currency, and ending a constant drain on the economy in subsidizing an unprofitable enterprise.[66] The most difficult obstacle is concern for workers. Mythical privatization procedures stipulated that no workers could be fired. That meant the foreign private investor would be expected to subsidize overemployment in the same way as the state had in the past. That could hardly be called a market economy system.

Some additional problems facing the foreign investor involve demands that the company continue to produce the traditional products, export demands, and limitations on salary disparities of foreign managers and domestic employees. Another problem is whether to sell the assets and then have a new company formed, or form a new state owned company and then sell the company with all its assets. The practice seems to be to create a company that is then sold.

Privatization has thus far been very successful with small to medium sized enterprises. This applies whether the enterprise is sold to domestic or foreign investors. Many foreign investors have preferred to acquire smaller companies in the service sector, thus avoiding some of the many problems associated with large manufacturing state controlled industries. It is more complex to establish valuation for the larger factories, and it is much more difficult to

---

[66] Not all enterprises privatized were unprofitable. The government may be privatizing to get out of ownership altogether, or to sell an enterprise that is profitable but could be even more so under private ownership.

locate willing buyers, especially if the operation is inefficient, uses outdated technology, or requires environmental repair.

Ironically, privatization may be more successful where a single agency has the primary responsibility for devising and executing the plan. Where decentralization has occurred, bureaucracy has been replaced by chaos and unpredictability. For example, in Russia, the government issued vouchers for individual stock purchase, but delegated the implementation and schedule of privatization to municipal authorities. Consequently, in several cities, the authorities and factory managers conspired to either block privatization or to appropriate the enterprises for themselves. The legal system proved inadequate to cope with such corruption and misappropriation.

Rather than proceed with immediate privatization, some nations are taking an intermediate step of reforming the structure of state enterprises. These governments are introducing market factors of production and commercial accountability, while retaining state ownership. This requires a separation of the functions of management of state owned property and the management activity of the enterprise. Companies are restructured as either joint stock or limited liability companies, while remaining under the control of the appropriate ministries.

A variation of the above transforms the state owned enterprises into single owner corporations, with the state as the initial owner. Management is then contracted out. A majority percentage of the shares is turned over to investment groups, and the companies become joint stock corporations upon termination of the management contract. To encourage local purchase, some will offer a lease-to-own option or credit at preferential loan rates.

The complexities of the privatization process in nonmarket as well as developing nations have led many foreign investors to reject the privatization route and follow the "greenfields" method of investing.

§ 25.24 Human Rights and Environmental Challenges to Foreign Investors

Foreign investors have always faced possible litigation in the host nation. Jurisdiction in the host nation is rarely a problem because the company is clearly there and doing business. But a foreign owned subsidiary in the host nation often has few assets in that nation. While they may be sufficient to satisfy judgments dealing with such common issues as a job related injury to an employee, or a contract breach, they are insufficient when multiple plaintiff actions are brought for alleged large scale injury such as environmental damage or labor abuses. In such actions the defendants include both the foreign parent and the host nation subsidiary, leading to jurisdiction issues if the suit is brought in the host nation. But such suits more often are brought in the United States, often in state courts where juries are perceived as hostile to multinational corporations, such as South Texas or Mississippi.[67] Initiated by attorneys with contingent fee contracts and who demand punitive damages, human rights abuses, environmental damages, and even cultural genocide have been the charges in an increasing number of suits against some of the largest corporations in the United States, including Del Monte, Dupont, Exxon Mobil Corp., Ford Motor Company, Freeport–McMoran, Texaco, Union Carbide, and United Technologies. The principal basis for these suits has been alleged violations of international law and specifically of the U.S. Alien Tort Claims Act. Much of this litigation has evolved since the 1980 *Filártiga v. Peña–Irala* decision.[68]

Filártiga did not involve a corporate defendant. It was brought by a Paraguayan citizen, Filártiga, residing in the United States, against one Peña, another Paraguayan citizen in the United States on a tourist visa. Peña had been the Inspector General of the Police in Asunción, Paraguay, and allegedly tortured and killed the son of Filártiga. The case was based principally on violations of the Alien Tort Claims Act, a 1789 enactment of Congress to address quite different concerns, such as acts of piracy. It was rarely used until *Filártiga*. But its brevity and breadth provided the court a foundation to find Peña in violation as the court had little trouble in holding that death by torture constituted a violation of international law. When the court rendered its opinion in 1980 the floodgates opened for many suits that tried to enlarge the scope of violations of international law. And for another challenge important to international business—could the defendants be foreign corporations?

How expansive an interpretation should be given the ATCA's "violation of the law of nations" language is yet undetermined. Certainly torture and extra-judicial killing are such violations. So perhaps are hostage taking and aircraft sabotage, and acts of terrorism. But the cases have tested the ATCA's language in two ways.

---

[67] The U.S. parent will usually argue lack of jurisdiction over the parent because it operates in the foreign host nation solely through a host nation corporation. This usually leads to veil piercing charges and defenses based on *forum non conveniuens*.

[68] 630 F.2d 876 (2d Cir. 1980).

One is the scope of acts within a category that appear at first glance to constitute international law violations, but may encompass less clear violations, such as torture (e.g., cutting off hands versus sleep deprivation) and human rights (extra-judicial killing of political dissidents versus relocating indigenous people to build a dam). The second debate is whether to bring within violations of international law areas where there is uncertainty about whether acts violate treaties or customary international law. The most frequently litigated may be violations of environmental laws. While there are many domestic environmental laws, there is considerable debate as to whether there is any international environmental law, especially customary law. A more recent basis for litigation is alleged "cultural genocide,"[69] charging displacement and relocation of indigenous peoples.

While the above issues could be debated and litigated in cases against officials of the foreign nations, subject to jurisdiction in U.S. courts, the far deeper pockets are those of multinational corporations. It was inevitable that suits would be brought against corporate defendants. The first to establish corporate liability was *Doe v. Unocal*, brought by Burmese nationals charging human rights violations by the defendant for complicity with the government in using forced labor in the construction of an oil pipeline.[70]

Sosa v. Alvarez–Machain, a U.S. Supreme Court decision limited the ATCA, but left it unclear how it would affect corporate liability.[71] The issue of corporate liability under the ATCA, was subsequently raised in *Kiobel v. Royal Dutch Petroleum Co. Kiobel* involved human rights claims by Nigerian refugees arising but taking place outside the United States. As this hornbook went to press the Supreme Court ruled unanimously that the ATCA could not be used because there is a presumption against extraterritoriality of a U.S. law. That presumption is not easily displaced, and mere presence of a corporation in a foreign country is not a sufficient reason for displacement. While the decision was unanimous, four justices believed that corporations may be "today's pirates." Immediate reaction was that the decision will substantially eliminate the currently popular litigation for foreign plaintiff's based on nothing more than

---

[69] Beanal v. Freeport–McMoran, Inc., 197 F.3d 161 (5th Cir. 1999) (brought on grounds of human rights violations, environmental torts and abuses, and genocide and cultural genocide).

[70] 110 F.Supp.2d 1294 (C.D.Cal.2000). The chronology of corporate liability under the ATCA is in Presbyterian Church of Sudan v. Talisman Energy, Inc., 244 F.Supp.2d 289, 308 (S.D.N.Y. 2003). See also Courtney Shaw, Uncertain Justice: Liability of Multinationals Under the Alien Tort Claims Act, 54 Stan.L.Rev. 1359 (2002).

[71] 542 U.S. 692, 124 S.Ct. 2739, 159 L.Ed.2d 718 (2004).

a U.S. corporation's presence in a foreign nation. The question now becomes: what more is needed?

Sosa did not involve a corporate defendant, but an individual claiming that his abduction constituted a violation of international law under the ATCA. The case brought the U.S. Supreme Court into the debate over the limits of the ATCA. The Court rejected the defendant's argument that the ATCA does not provide a cause of action, but found that the abduction of Alvarez–Machain in Mexico and transportation to the United States for trial did not violate the law of nations. The Court gave several reasons for judicial caution in applying too broad an interpretation of the ATCA.

Sosa v. Alvarez–Machain may have diminished the availability of reliance upon the ATCA for suits against foreign corporations, not because the defendants are corporations but because the scope of the ATCA is more limited than prior to the decision. *Sosa* has not ended suits against foreign investors, since other grounds remain, such as the Racketeer Influenced and Corrupt Organizations Act, the federal question statute, and such traditional actions as wrongful death, false imprisonment, assault, intentional infliction of emotional distress and negligence.[72]

§ 25.25 The Applicable Law and Dispute Resolution

Investment disputes often involve claims by the foreign investor that the host nation interfered with the investment to the degree that it constitutes a taking of property. A taking may violate international law, but that area is poorly defined in international law and disputed by different nations.[73] Investors prefer to rely on other means for dispute settlement where the procedural rules and applicable law are agreed upon.

Host nation law may include how investment disputes are to be resolved. Often the law provides for stages beginning with a form of mediation, then arbitration, and if not satisfied through use of the courts. This may be unsatisfactory to the foreign investor if the membership of the mediation and arbitration panels, and the rules under which they operate, favor the host nation. A more neutral settlement process is usually preferred.

---

[72] The ATCA and each of these examples of causes of action were grounds in Doe v. Unocal Corp., 110 F.Supp.2d 1294 (C.D.Cal.2000). The case was appealed, 395 F.3d 932 (9th Cir.2002). After a majority of the 9th Circuit voted to have an *en banc* rehearing, and a few months after the Sosa decision, a settlement was reached.

[73] The expropriation of property is the subject of chapter 29.

In host nations which are federations of states or provinces, there may be concern regarding the applicability of local law. Where there are differences in national and local laws, the general rule is that the national law will prevail. But where the local law supplements or fills gaps in the national law, foreign investors will have two sets of laws with which to comply. There is an added cost to functioning in such a system. U.S. investors should have no difficulty in understanding such a system, there is none more complex than the federation of states which constitutes the United States.

§ 25.26 Bilateral Investment Treaties (BITs)

International law has been slow to establish standards regarding how nations should treat foreign investment. The United Nations' efforts to draft a code of conduct for multinational enterprises did not include provisions for the conduct of host nations. Such process was thus quite unsatisfactory to foreign investors, who sought assistance from their home nations when their property was taken by the host nation. Bilateral investment treaties have provided some help. To promote national treatment and protect U.S. investors abroad, the United States embarked on the BIT program in the early 1980s.[74] The BIT program followed earlier extensive use of Friendship, Commerce, and Navigation (FCNs) treaties.

Unlike the FCNs, the model BIT distinguishes treatment for foreign owned, domestically incorporated subsidiaries and branches of foreign firms for some provisions, particularly employment. As a result of the *Sumitomo Shoji America v. Avagliano* decision,[75] the FCN treaty afforded no protection to a foreign company using its nationals in hiring. Under the typical BIT, explicit freedom to hire nationals exists in a narrow range of management provisions, helping roll back the traditional TRIM of local management provisions. But investment screening mechanisms and key sectors often remain exempt from BIT protections, typically listed in an Annex to a BIT. While elimination of foreign direct investment screening and imposition of performance requirements has been an object of the BIT program, these provisions of the model BIT have been weakened in the treaties currently in force.[76]

---

[74] See K. Scott Gudgeon, United States Bilateral Investment Treaties, 4 Int'l Tax & Bus.Law. 105 (1986); Pamela Gann, The United States Bilateral Investment Treaty Program, 21 Stanford J.Int'l L. 373 (1985). See, *supra* at §25.17.

[75] 457 U.S. 176, 102 S.Ct. 2374, 72 L.Ed.2d 765 (1982).

[76] See Gudgeon, supra note 1, at 126–7 (observing that BITs with Egypt, Haiti, and Zaire have the weakest language ["shall seek to endeavor/avoid" trade related performance requirements], while BITs with Senegal and Panama include qualifications, such as exemption for Panama's investment incentive program).

The United States has entered into a number of bilateral investment treaties (BITs), as well as a number of less formal bilateral trade agreements. The trade agreement may refer to investment as an area for further discussion.[77] The bilateral *investment* treaties, however, do address investment issues. They tend to replace earlier Friendship, Commerce & Navigation treaties because they apply to investments. While many of the first BITs were negotiated with small developing countries,[78] more recently the United States has signed BITs with such important trading nations as Argentina.[79] The Argentina–United States BIT follows the U.S. BIT prototype of addressing both *investment protection* and *investor access* to each other's markets.

The BITs do not prohibit nations from enacting investment laws, but provide that any such laws should not interfere with any rights in the treaty. The free access aspect of some BITs may not be perceived as a right. Thus investment laws might be enacted that limit access to certain areas, but would not create a right of the other party to challenge the law under the BIT.

One important provision the United States seeks to include in its BITs is the "prompt, adequate and effective" concept (if not always the language) of compensation subsequent to expropriation. Many of the nations that have recently agreed to this language disputed its appropriateness during the nationalistic North–South dialogue years of the 1960s and 1970s. But as the developing nations began to promote rather than restrict investment, they began to accept the idea that expropriated investment had to be compensated reasonably soon after the taking ("prompt"), be based on a fair valuation ("adequate"), and be paid in a realistic form ("effective"). The Argentina–United States BIT uses language referring to the "fair market value . . . immediately before the expropriatory action".[80]

Most BITs do not include provisions for consultations when differences arise in the interpretation of the treaty. The Argentina–United States and Sri Lanka–United States BITs are exceptions.

---

[77] The Mongolia–United States Agreement on Trade Relations, Jan. 23, 1991, 30 Int'l Leg.Mat. 515 (1991), provides for further cooperation in the form of reaching agreement on investment issues, including the repatriation of profits and transfer of capital. See art. X(1). The United States often refers to these agreements as Trade and Investment Framework Agreements, and has them with such nations as South Africa, Nigeria, Uruguay, Georgia, Iceland, Turkey, and New Zealand.

[78] For example, Haiti, Mongolia, Panama, Senegal, Sri Lanka and Zaire. And more recently in Rwanda.

[79] Argentina–United States Treaty Concerning the Reciprocal Encouragement and Protection of Investment, Nov. 14, 1991.

[80] Argentina–United States BIT, art. IV(1).

BITs do often provide for arbitration, sometimes with no necessary recourse to prior exhaustion of local remedies.

The BIT process is quite dynamic. Each successive agreement with a new country may include some new provisions. The United States has a prototype agreement, but it has been modified as host nations have sought new foreign investment and have been willing to sign a BIT to establish the most attractive conditions for that investment. It is certain that the BITs in existence today will not be identical to BITs executed in years ahead. BITs are an important contribution of the developed home nation to their multinationals investing abroad. They establish some ground rules for investment on a bilateral treaty basis that should not be unilaterally altered by the host nation to impose restrictions on the investments that are inconsistent with the BIT. Certainly, revolutionary governments have ignored similar agreements in the past and may in the future. But the BITs do provide some investment security, at least as long as the host governments remain relatively stable, and receptive to foreign investment.

Similar to the United States in attempting to protect its investors, the European Union has addressed the problems with some 1,200 bilateral investment agreements between member states and non-EU countries. The EU brought foreign investment under exclusive EU competence in the Lisbon Treaty, which became effective in 2009. In late 2012 the EU adopted a new Regulation on bilateral investment agreements. It affects both existing agreements, which the EU will attempt to replace over time, and new EU-wide agreements, such as ones being discussed with significant trading partners including as China, Canada and Singapore.

§ 25.27 International Centre for the Settlement of Investment Disputes (ICSID)

More than 140 nations have become parties to the 1966 Convention on the Settlement of Investment Disputes Between States and Nationals of Other States.[81] The Convention provided for the creation of the International Centre for the Settlement of Investment Disputes as part of the World Bank.[82] The Convention and Centre provide for a form of arbitration of investment disputes, of-

---

[81] TIAS 6090, implemented in the United States in 22 U.S.C.A. §§ 1650 and 1650a.

[82] The Centre publishes the useful semiannual journal, the ICSID Review–Foreign Investment Law Journal. See, e.g., A. Ekpombang, The Legal Framework of Foreign Investment in Rwanda, 26 ICSID For. Inv. L.J. (2011); O. Sandrock, Right of Foreign Investors to Access German Markets, 25 ICSID For.Inv.L.J. (2010).

fering an institutional framework for the proceedings. Jurisdiction under the Convention extends to "any legal dispute arising directly out of an investment, between a Contracting State or . . . any subdivision . . . and a national of another Contracting State." But the parties must consent in writing to the submission of the dispute to the Centre. Once given, the consent may not be withdrawn.

Disputes regarding jurisdiction may be decided by the arbitration panel and appealed to a committee (ad hoc) created from the Panel of Arbitrators by the Administrative Council of the ICSID. The jurisdiction of the tribunal, challenged in a United States court, may well lead to a refusal to uphold the decision.[83] Concern regarding the jurisdictional limitations led to the creation of the Additional Facility, which may conduct conciliations and arbitrations for what are rather special disputes.[84] It was not created to deal with the ordinary investment dispute, but with disputes between parties with long-term special economic relationships involving substantial resource commitments. The Additional Facility may be used only with the blessing of the ICSID Secretary General.

Chapter 11 of the North American Free Trade Agreement governs foreign investment and provides for the resolution of investment disputes between the government of a member state and a private investor of another member state. These disputes may be submitted to arbitration under the ICSID Convention where the government and investors are both from member countries. But Canada and Mexico are not yet ICSID members, leaving the arbitration to be done under either the ICSID Additional Facility Rules or the UNCITRAL Rules.[85] Only UNCITRAL Rules are available for disputes between Mexico and Canada since neither is an ICSID member.

The World Bank has another organization important to foreign investment, the Multilateral Investment Guarantee Agency (MIGA). MIGA provides investment insurance not unlike the United States Overseas Private Investment Corporation's (OPIC) insurance program.[86]

---

83 The ICSID is discussed in W. Michael Reisman, Systems of Control in International Adjudication & Arbitration (1992).

84 The Additional Facility has its own arbitration rules.

85 The first two NAFTA investment disputes, each involving a U.S. investor and the Mexican government, chose to use the ICSID Additional Facility Rules, the first investment disputes anywhere to do so. See Metalclad Corp. v. United Mexican States (Case ARB(AF)/97/1); Azinian et al and the United Mexican States (Case ARB(AF)/97/2) (reported in 14 ICSID Review—Foreign Investment L.J. 538 (1999)).

86 Both MIGA and OPIC are discussed in chapter 28.

Chapter 26

INVESTING IN EUROPE

Table of Sections

This chapter focuses upon investing in Europe. It is written primarily for an audience located outside Europe, and its emphasis is on investing in the European Union. The underlying assumption is that foreign investors are seeking to and will increasingly treat Europe as a regional market, not a series of individual national markets nor as a group of regional markets. Thus, although the relevant laws of the European country where the investment will be made always need to be consulted and can vary greatly, this chapter primarily covers regional investment and trade law in Europe. It is this body of law that governs the operational realities of the market called Europe. And it is this market potential that so attracts foreign investors. For much more extensive coverage, see Folsom's *Principles of European Union Law.*

§ 26.1 Introduction

Investors in the European Union have a great interest in how well its common market works. Their basic goal is to sell in a regional (not a national) market. This chapter highlights the law governing free movement of goods, money and services. It also very selectively focuses upon the development of common policies of particular concern to foreign investors (with emphasis on U.S. interests). Space does not permit treatment of European law governing medical and food products, free movement of people, worker and professional rights, banking, insurance, investment advisors, transportation, value-added and excise taxation, broadcasting and media products, computer software, commercial agents, corporate taxation, subsidies, industrial and intellectual property, procurement, products liability, consumer protection, advertising, companies, the environment, energy, telecommunications, agricultural and fisheries policy, customs, trade,[1] franchising,[2] patent and know-how licensing,[3] distribution and antitrust.[4] All of these subjects are treated in Folsom's *Principles of European Union Law*.

§ 26.2 A Single Market

A TIMELINE OF EUROPEAN INTEGRATION

A timeline presenting major developments in European integration follows:

1948—Benelux Customs Union Treaty

1949—COMECON Treaty (Eastern Europe, Soviet Union)

1951—European Coal and Steel Community ("Treaty of Paris")

1957—European Economic Community (EEC) ("Treaty of Rome")
European Atomic Energy Community Treaty (EURATOM)

1959—European Free Trade Area Treaty (EFTA)

1968—EEC Customs Union fully operative

1973—Britain and Denmark switch from EFTA to EEC; Ireland joins EEC; Remaining EFTA states sign industrial free trade treaties with EEC

1979—Direct elections to European Parliament

1981—Greece joins EEC

---

1 See Chapters 12 and 13.

2 See Chapter 22.

3 See Chapter 23.

4 See Chapter 20.

1983—Greenland "withdraws" from EEC

1986—Spain and Portugal join EEC, Portugal leaves EFTA

1987—Single European Act amends Treaty of Rome to initiate campaign for a Community without internal frontiers, qualified majority legislative voting commences in earnest

1990—East Germany merged into Community via reunification process

1991—COMECON defunct; trade relations with Central Europe develop rapidly

1993—Maastricht Treaty on European Union (EU) ratified and operational, EEC officially becomes EC

1994—European Monetary Institute established

1995—Austria, Finland, and Sweden join EU, Norway votes no again

1999—Amsterdam Treaty ratified and operational

1999—Common currency (EURO) managed by European Central Bank commences with 11 members

2003—Treaty of Nice ratified and operational, draft Constitution for Europe released

2004—Cyprus, Estonia, Slovenia, Poland, Hungary, the Czech Republic, Slovakia, Latvia, Lithuania, Malta join EU

2005—Constitution for Europe overwhelmingly defeated in France, Netherlands

2007—Accession of Bulgaria and, Romania, Reform Treaty proposed

2008—Irish voters reject Reform Treaty

2009—Irish voters approve Reform Treaty, which takes effect Dec. 1, 2009, EU Charter of Fundamental Rights becomes binding law, EU accedes to European Convention on Human Rights, Treaty of Rome becomes Convention on the Functioning of the European Union (TFEU)

2010—Greece and Ireland bailed out, 1 trillion temporary EURO safety net created for financial crises

2011—Portugal bailed out, EURO in crisis

2012—Spanish and Italian banks bailed out, Greece bailed out again, EURO in extreme crisis, Treaty on Stability, Coordination and Governance (TSCG) adopted by 25 member states creating permanent European Stability Mechanism crisis loan fund and a Fiscal Compact with balanced budget rules, ECB agrees to buy unlimited short-term national bonds

2013—Croatia joins EU, Cyprus bailed out

****

The campaign for a European Community without internal frontiers was the product of Commission studies in the mid–1980s which concluded that a hardening of the trade arteries of Europe had occurred. The Community was perceived to be stagnating relative to the advancing economies of North America and East Asia. Various projections of the wealth that could be generated from a truly common market for Western Europe suggested the need for revitalization. A "white paper" drafted under the leadership of Lord Cockfield of Britain and issued by the Commission in 1985 became the blueprint for the campaign.

The Commission's white paper identified three types of barriers to a Europe without internal frontiers—physical, technical and fiscal. Physical barriers occur at the borders. For goods, they include national trade quotas, health checks, agricultural monetary compensation amount (MCA) charges, statistical collections and transport controls. For people, physical barriers involve clearing immigrations, security checks and customs. Technical barriers mostly involve national standards and rules for goods, services, capital and labor which operate to inhibit trade among the member states. Boilers, railway, medical and surgical equipment, and pharmaceuticals provide traditional examples of markets restrained by technical trade barriers. Fiscal barriers centered on different value-added and excise taxation levels and the corresponding need for tax collections at the border. There were, for example, wide value-added tax (VAT) differences on auto sales within the Common Market.

The Commission (Cecchini Report) estimated that removal of all of these barriers could save the Community upwards of 100 billion ECUs (European Currency Units) in direct costs. In addition, another roughly 100 billion ECUs may be gained as price reductions and increased efficiency and competition take hold. Overall, the

Commission projected an increase in the Common Market's gross domestic product (GDP) of between 4.5 to 7 percent, a reduction in consumer prices of between 6 to 4.5 percent, 1.75 to 5 million new jobs, and enhanced public sector and external trade balances. These figures were thus said to represent "the costs of non-Europe."

Single European Act

Major amendments to the Treaty of Rome (now TFEU) were undertaken in the Single European Act (SEA) which became effective in 1987. Amendments to the Treaty can occur by Commission or member state proposal to the Council which calls an intergovernmental conference to unanimously determine their content. The amendments are not effective until ratified by all the member states in accordance with their respective constitutional requirements. Proposals originating in the Commission's 1985 white paper on a Europe without internal frontiers were embodied in the Single European Act. The SEA amendments not only expanded the competence of the European institutions, but also sought to accelerate the speed of integration by relying more heavily on qualified majority (not unanimous) voting principles in Council decision-making.

The Single European Act envisioned the adoption of hundreds of new legislative measures designed to fully integrate the Common Market by the end of 1992. Nearly all of these measures and more were adopted by the Council. Implementation at the national level proceeded more slowly and even now remains a concern. By 1996, the Commission reported that the single market program had increased internal trade by 20–30%, added 1% in GDP growth annually, and generated over 900,000 jobs.

§ 26.3 The EURO

Preparing for the EURO: The European Monetary System

Capital movements legislation of the 1990s, combined with the various banking and investment services reforms and Maastricht amendments, promised to bring forth a remarkable new financial sector in the European Union. It also supported the EURO replacing national currencies. For Germany, with the strongest currency in the Union and memories of hyper-inflation between the two World Wars, supporting the EURO had to result in money "as good as the Deutschmark." A EURO Zone without Germany was a non-sequitur. In moving step-by-step toward monetary union, the member states created the European Monetary System (EMS). When the EMS was established in 1979, member states deposited 20 percent of their gold and dollar assets with the European Monetary Cooperation Fund in exchange for an equivalent amount of European Currency Units (ECUs). This fund was used as a non-cash means of settlement between central banks undertaking exchange rate support.

The legal basis for the European Monetary System and European Currency Units was substantially advanced by the Single European Act of 1987. This article committed the member states to further development of the EMS and ECU, recognized the cooperation of the central banks in management of the system, but specifically required further amendment of the Treaty if "institutional changes" were required. In other words, a common currency managed by a central bank system was *not* part of the campaign for a Europe without internal frontiers. Draft plans for such developments surfaced in the Commission using the U.S. Federal Reserve Board as a model. Britain, always concerned about losses of economic sovereignty, proposed an alternative known as the "hard ECU." This proposal would have retained the national currencies but added the hard ECU as competitor of each, letting the marketplace in most instances decide which currency it preferred.

In December of 1989, the European Council (outvoting Britain) approved a three stage approach to economic and monetary union (EMU). Stage One began July 1, 1990. Its focus was on expanding the power and influence of the Committee of Central Bank Governors over monetary affairs. This Committee was a kind of EuroFed in embryo. It was primarily engaged in "multilateral surveillance." Stage One also sought greater economic policy coordination and convergence among the member states.

Stage Two anticipated the creation of a European Union central banking system, but functioned with the existing national currencies in the context of the EMS and ERM. Stage Two was a learning and transition period. In October of 1990, it was agreed (save Britain) that Stage Two would commence January 1, 1994. This deadline was actually met, and the European Monetary Institute was installed in Frankfurt. It was the precursor to the European Central Bank. Stage Three involved the replacement of the national currencies with a single currency, the EURO, managed by a European Central Bank. In December of 1991, agreement was reached at Maastricht to implement Stage Three no later than Jan. 1, 1999 with a minimum of seven states. Britain and Denmark reserved a right to opt out of Stage Three.

Admission to the EURO Zone

All member states wishing to join the EURO Zone in 1999 had to meet strict economic convergence criteria on inflation rates, government deficits, long-term interest rates and currency fluctuations. To join the third stage, a country was supposed to have an inflation rate not greater than 1.5 percent of the average of the three lowest member state rates, long-term interest rates no higher than 2 percent above the average of the three lowest, a budget deficit less than 3 percent of gross domestic product (GDP), a total public indebtedness of less than 60 percent of GDP, and no devaluation within the ERM during the prior two years. These criteria continue to govern admission of other member states into the EURO zone. One could argue they have been honored more in the breach than conformity

The economic performance of member states in 1997 became the test for admission to the economic and monetary union. Since both France and Germany had trouble meeting the admissions criteria, this opened a window for much more marginal states such as Belgium, Italy and Spain to join immediately in 1999. Eleven of the then fifteen EU members commenced the EURO Zone. Greece subsequently in 2001 was deemed "qualified" for the EURO Zone based upon (as we now know) dubious financial data. As expected, Denmark, Britain and Sweden opted out of initial participation in the common currency. The Danes did so by voting No in a year 2000 national referendum. The Swedes voted similarly in 2003. By 2013, Slovenia, Malta, Estonia, Cyprus and Slovakia had joined the EURO zone, for a total of 17 out of 27 member-states of the Union, with Latvia in the wings. The world financial crisis of 2008–09 initially increased the interest of some outside the EURO zone, notably Iceland, to partake of its relative stability. Denmark, Latvia, Lithuania and Bulgaria pegged their national currencies to the EURO.

On January 1, 1999, the participating states fixed the exchange rates between the EURO and their national currencies. National notes and coins were removed from the market by July 2002 as the EURO was installed. The EURO has been used for most commercial banking, foreign exchange and public debt purposes since 1999. It has also been adopted (voluntarily) by the world's securities markets, and by Monaco, San Marino, the Vatican, Andorra, Montenegro and Kosovo.

The arrival of the EURO had important implications for the United States and the dollar. For decades, the dollar had been the world's leading currency, although its dominance has been declining since the early 1980s. Use of the Deutsche Mark and Yen in commercial and financial transactions, and in savings and reserves, had been steadily rising. The EURO was expected to continue the dollar's decline in all of these markets. It was certainly the hope of many Europeans that they have successfully created a rival to the dollar.

European Central Bank

It was also agreed at Maastricht that in the third stage the European Central Bank (ECB) and the European System of Central Banks (ECSB) would start operations. The ECB and ECSB are governed by an executive board of six persons appointed by the member states and the governors of the national central banks. The ECB and the ECSB are independent of any other European institution and in theory free from member state influence. Their primary responsibility is to maintain price stability, specifically keeping price inflation below two percent per year. In contrast, the U.S. Federal Reserve has three primary responsibilities: maximum employment, stable prices and moderate long-term interest rates.

The main functions of the ECB and ECSB are: (1) define and implement regional monetary policy; (2) conduct foreign exchange operations; (3) hold and manage the official foreign reserves of the member states; and (4) supervise the payments systems. The ECB has the exclusive right to authorize the issue of bank notes within the Common Market and must set interest rates to principally achieve price stability. The Court of Justice may review the legality of ECB decisions.

Under the EURO's founding rules, the ECB worked closely with the Ecofin Council's broad guidelines for economic policy, such as keeping national budget deficits below 3 percent of GDP in all but exceptional circumstances (2 percent decline in annual GDP). If the Ecofin considered a national government's policy to be inconsistent with that of the region, it could recommend changes including budget cuts. If appropriate national action did not follow such a warning, the Ecofin could have required a government to disclose the relevant information with its bond issues, blocked European Investment Bank credits, mandated punitive interest-free deposits, or levied fines and penalties.

Regrettably, the fiscal enforcement system established when the EURO was created did not work. Sanctions for failure to comply with the 3 percent budget deficit rule were held unenforceable by the Court of Justice. See *Commission v. Council* (2004) Eur.Comm.Rep. I–6649 (Case C–27/04). Since 1999, many EURO states have been under threat of sanctions for failure to comply with the 3 percent budget deficit rule, most notably Greece, Portugal, Spain, Italy and Ireland after the global financial meltdown of 2008–09. Yet no EURO Zone member state was ever sanctioned, suggesting this system for controlling national deficits is toothless. It has essentially been replaced by the 2012 Treaty on Stability, Coordination and Governance (TSCG, below).

Financial Bailouts

The global meltdown also caused financial markets to finally realize that national debt issued in EUROs by different Zone members came with different levels of risk. Interest rates rose on Greek, Portuguese, Irish and other bonds, while German and to a lesser extent French EURO bonds held firm. Despite a specific TFEU Article 125 prohibition against Union bailouts of member state governments, as the market-driven European financial crisis of 2010/11 demonstrated, bailouts of debt-ridden EURO zone members may occur. Joining with the IMF, a 110 billion EURO rescue package for Greece was organized over German laments. Fearing a cascade of financial crises in Spain, Portugal, Italy and Ireland, a 1 trillion EURO liquidity safety net (EFSF) was devised using EU-backed bonds, special purpose EU-guaranteed investment loans, and more IMF funds. In addition, the ECB for the first time began buying EURO zone national government bonds in the open market.

All this caused Germany to publicly re-think its traditional role as paymaster and proponent of the European Union and EURO. Clearly the EURO was not as good as the fondly remembered Deutschmark. Sure enough, Ireland tapped into this safety net for over 100 billion EUROs late in 2010 followed by Portugal in 2011. In 2012, massive loans to Spanish and Italian banks and their governments staved off bailouts and moderated interest rates, and Greece was bailed out a second time. Cyprus was bailed out in 2013 under conditions that "bailed in" bank bondholders and uninsured bank depositors. These actions ran down the safety net and ECB resources. Most private holders of Greek debt have been pushed into a renegotiated deal with roughly a 50% "haircut" in the value of their holdings. Since 2013, EU bailouts require sovereign bond holders to take losses under "collective action clauses" designed to keep individual investors from blocking restructured debt deals. Mandatory losses can be imposed when Euro-zone nations are deemed insolvent by the European Central Bank, the European Commission and the IMF, the "Troika", and the Euro-zone finance ministers unanimously are in accord.

Treaty on Stability, Coordination and Governance (TSCG), ECB Bond Buying

In March of 2012, with market pressures and threats of a Greek default or exit from the EURO Zone escalating, 25 of the 27 EU members (minus Britain and the Czech Republic) adopted a Treaty on Stability, Coordination and Governance (TCSG) intended to provide a "permanent" solution to the EURO crisis. Only Ireland allowed its voters a referendum on this Treaty, which was negotiated outside the regular TFEU framework. The Irish, their bailout in progress, voted in favor of ratification by approximately a 60% margin. Importantly, ratification by the German Parliament was upheld by Germany's Constitutional Court under that country's "eternal democracy" clause. The TCSG has two principal components: The European Stability mechanism (ESM) and a "Fiscal Compact."

Effective in 2013, the ESM created a permanent 900 billion EURO loan fund, 27% of which is financed by Germany. Any increase in the ESM fund must be approved by the German Parliament. EURO Zone countries may apply for bailout loans conditioned upon fiscal and economic reforms. As a general rule, all EURO Zone national parliaments must approve of any ESM rescue package. Finland has indicated its approval may require loan collateral. The "Fiscal Compact" incorporates a "balanced budget" rule. "Automatic corrective measures" apply if excessive budgets are reached. The EU Commission monitors national budget deficits and breach of the Compact can result in enforcement actions before the European Court of Justice with penalties payable to the ESM.

In addition, in 2012, the European Central Bank announced its willingness to buy unlimited, short-term national government bonds if an ESM rescue is secured by a EURO Zone member. Germany's revered Bundesbank openly opposed this announcement, which had the support of the Merkel government. Like ESM loans, such purchases will be conditioned upon fiscal and economic austerity commitments with the ECB serving as the regulator of Zone banks. The extent of the ECB's regulatory powers was much debated, though ECB licensing and penalty powers over banks represented a regulatory base line.

Thus there is a three-part attempt at "permanently" solving the EURO crisis: The ESM, Fiscal Compact and ECB bond buying. This attempt once again seeks to come to grips with systemic flaws that have haunted the EURO since its creation....can national spending policies be stabilized, coordinated and governed in support of a common currency? Since all EURO Zone countries are jointly liable for

ESM and ECB monies, this amounts to a partial mutualization of national debt risk. It is not, however, as some have suggested is needed, EURO bonds backed by the EURO Zone. That said, the TGSG is certainly a step in that direction.

§ 26.4 Free Movement of Goods

North American traders and investors should understand that the free movement of goods within Europe is based upon the creation of a customs union. Under this union, the member states have eliminated customs duties among themselves.[5] They have established a common customs tariff for their trade with the rest of the world. Quantitative restrictions (quotas) on trade between member states are also prohibited, except in emergency and other limited situations.[6] The right of free movement applies to goods that originate in the Common Market *and* to those that have lawfully entered it and are said to be in "free circulation."[7]

Measures of Equivalent Effect

The establishment of the customs union has been a major accomplishment, though not without difficulties. The member states not only committed themselves to the elimination of tariffs and quotas on internal trade, but also to the elimination of "measures of equivalent effect."[8] The elastic legal concept of measures of equivalent effect has been interpreted broadly by the European Court of Justice and the Commission to prohibit a wide range of trade restraints, such as administrative fees charged at borders which are the equivalent of import or export tariffs.[9] Charges of equivalent effect to a tariff must be distinguished from internal taxes that are applicable to imported and domestic goods. The latter must be levied in a nondiscriminatory and nonprotective manner (Article 110, TFEU), while the former are prohibited entirely (Articles 28, 30). There has been a considerable amount of litigation over this distinction.[10]

The elasticity of the concept of measures of an equivalent effect is even more pronounced in the Court's judgment relating to quotas.

5 Article 30, Treaty on the Functioning of the European Union (TFEU).

6 Articles 34–37, TFEU.

7 Articles 28–29, TFEU.

8 See especially Articles 30, 34 and 35, TFEU.

9 Rewe Zentralfinanz v. Landwirtschaftskammer Westfalen–Lippe (1973) Eur.Comm.Rep. 1039; Commission v. Italy (1969) Eur.Comm.Rep. 193. But see Commission v. Germany (1988) Eur.Comm.Rep. 5427.

10 See e.g. Industria Gomma, Articoli Vari v. Ente Nazionale ENCC (1975) Eur.Comm.Rep. 699.

This jurisprudence draws upon an early Commission directive (no longer applicable) of extraordinary scope.[11] In this directive, the Commission undertook a lengthy listing of practices that it considered illegal measures of effect equivalent to quotas. It is still occasionally referenced in Commission and Court of Justice decisions. Its focus is on national rules that discriminate against imports or simply restrain internal trade.

Cassis Formula

In a famous case, the Court of Justice ruled that Belgium could not block the importation of Scotch whiskey via France because of the absence of a British certificate of origin as required by Belgian customs law.[12] The Court of Justice held that any national rule directly or indirectly, actually or potentially capable of hindering internal trade is generally forbidden as a measure of equivalent effect to a quota. However, *if* European law has not developed appropriate rules in the area concerned (here designations of origin), the member states may enact "reasonable" and "proportional" (no broader than necessary) regulations to ensure that the public is not harmed.[13] This is often referred to as the "*Cassis* formula". Products meeting reasonable national criteria, the *Cassis* opinion continues, may be freely traded. This is the origin of the innovative "mutual reciprocity" principle used in significant parts of the legislative campaign for a Europe without frontiers.

The *Cassis* decision suggests use of a Rule of Reason analysis for national fiscal regulations, public health measures, laws governing the fairness of commercial transactions and consumer protection. Environmental protection and occupational safety laws of the member states have been similarly treated. Under this approach, for example, a Danish "bottle bill" requiring use of approved containers was therefore unreasonable.[14] However, the Danes' argument that a deposit and return system was environmentally necessary prevailed. This was a reasonable restraint on internal trade recognized by the Court under the *Cassis* formula for analyzing compelling state interests. Likewise, a Belgian law prohibiting the

---

[11] Procureur du Roi v. Dassonville (1974) Eur.Comm.Rep. 837.

[12] Commission Directive 70/50 on the Abolition of Measures which have an Effect Equivalent to Quantitative Restrictions, 1970 O.J. L13/29 (Special Edition) (I), p. 17.

[13] See the "Cassis de Dijon" case, Rewe Zentral AG v. Bundesmonopolverwaltung für Branntwein (1979) Eur.Comm.Rep. 649 (German *minimum* alcoholic beverage rule not reasonable).

[14] Commission v. Denmark (1988) Eur.Comm.Rep. 4607.

importation of general wastes from neighboring countries was found reasonable and not in breach of Community free trade principles.[15]

Under *Cassis*, national rules requiring country of origin or "foreign origin" labels have fallen as measures of effect equivalent to quotas.[16] So have various restrictive national procurement laws, including a "voluntary" campaign to "Buy Irish."[17] Minimum and maximum retail pricing controls can also run afoul of the Court's expansive interpretations.[18] Compulsory patent licensing can amount to a measure of equivalent effect nullified by operation of regional law. The U.K. could not compulsorily require manufacturing within its jurisdiction.[19] Member states may not impose linguistic labelling requirements so as to block trade and competition in foodstuffs. In this instance, a Belgian law requiring Dutch labels in Flemish areas was nullified as in conflict with the Treaty.[20] These cases vividly illustrate the extent to which litigants are invoking the TFEU and the *Cassis* formula in attempts at overcoming commercially restrictive national laws.

There are cases which suggest that "cultural interests" may justify national restrictions on European trade. For example, British, French and Belgian bans on Sunday retail trading have survived initial scrutiny under the *Cassis* formula.[21] French legislation prohibiting the sale or rental of cassettes within one year of a film's debut also survived such scrutiny.[22] And British prohibitions of sales of sex articles except by licensed sex shops are compatible.[23] National laws prohibiting sales below cost, when applied without discrimination as between imports and domestic products, are not considered to affect trade between the member states. In this re-

---

[15] Commission v. Belgium (1992) Eur.Comm.Rep. I–4431 (Case C–2/90).

[16] Commission v. Ireland (1981) Eur.Comm.Rep. 1625; Commission v. United Kingdom (1985) Eur.Comm.Rep. 1202.

[17] Commission v. Ireland (1988) Eur.Comm.Rep. 4929 (product standards); Commission v. Ireland (1982) Eur.Comm.Rep. 4005 (Buy Irish). But see Apple and Pear Development Council (1983) Eur.Comm.Rep. 4083 (permissible promotion of local agricultural products).

[18] Re Ricardo Tasca (1976) Eur.Comm.Rep. 291; Openbaar Ministerie v. Van Tiggele (1978) Eur.Comm.Rep. 25.

[19] Commission v. United Kingdom (1992) Eur.Comm.Rep. I–0829 (Case C–30/90).

[20] Piageme ASBL v. Peeters BVBA (1991) Eur.Comm.Rep. I–2971 (Case C–369/89).

[21] Torfaen Borough Council v. B+Q PLC Ltd (1989) Eur.Comm.Rep 3851; UDS v. Sidef Conforma & Ors (1991) Eur.Comm.Rep. 997 (Case C–312/89); Le Marchandise & Ors (1991) Eur.Comm.Rep. 1027 (Case C–332/89).

[22] Cinéthèque SA v. Federation Nationale des Cinémas Francais (1985) Eur.Comm.Rep. 2605.

[23] Quietlynn Ltd. v. Southend Borough Council (1990) 1 Eur.Comm.Rep. 3051.

markable decision signaling a jurisprudential retreat, the ECJ ruled that such laws may not be challenged under the traditional *Cassis* formula.[24] Deceptive trade practices laws ordinarily do not amount to "selling arrangements,"[25] but national laws regulating sales outlets[26] and advertising[27] may.

In recent years, member state regulations capable of being characterized as governing "marketing modalities" or "selling arrangements" have sought shelter under *Keck*. For example, the French prohibition of televised advertising (intended to favor printed media) of the distribution of goods escaped the rule of reason analysis of *Cassis* in this manner. Some commentators see in *Keck* and its progeny an unarticulated attempt by the Court to take subsidiarity seriously. Others are just baffled by its newly found tolerance for trade distorting national marketing laws. But the Court of Justice has poignantly refused to extend *Keck* to the marketing of services, and some commentators suggest *Keck* may be fading into obscurity.

The Court has made it clear that all of the Rule of Reason justifications for national regulatory laws are temporary. Adoption of Common Market legislation in any of these areas would eliminate national authority to regulate trading conditions under *Dassonville, Cassis* and (presumably) *Keck*.[28] These judicial mandates, none of which are specified in the TFEU, vividly illustrate the powers of the Court of Justice to expansively interpret the Treaty and rule on the validity under European law of national legislation affecting internal trade in goods.

§ 26.5 Article 36 and the Problem of Nontariff Trade Barriers

As in the world community, the major trade barrier within Europe has become NTBs. To some extent, in the absence of a harmonizing directive completely occupying the field,[29] this is authorized.

---

[24] See Re Keck & Mithouard (1993) Eur.Comm.Rep. 6097 (Cases C–267/91, C–268/91).

[25] Verband Sozialer Wettbewerb v. Clinique Laboratories (1994) Eur.Comm.Rep. I–317.

[26] Commission v. Greece (1995) Eur.Comm.Rep. I–1621

[27] Societe d'Importation Edouard Leclerc–Siplec v. TF1 Publicite (1995) Eur.Comm. I–179. *Compare* Konsumertombusmannen (KO) v. Gourmet International Products ABS, (GIP) (2001) Eur.Comm.Rep. I–6493.

[28] Oberkreisdirektor des Kreises Borken v. Moorman B.V. (1988) Eur.Comm.Rep. 4689.

[29] See Firma Eau de Cologne v. Provide (1989) Eur.Comm.Rep. 3891 and Publico Ministero v. Ratti (1979) Eur.Comm.Rep. 1629 (Article 36 preempted by directives). But see Article 114 TFEU regarding internal market directives where member

Article 36 TFEU permits national restraints on imports and exports justified on the grounds of:

(1) public morality, public policy ("ordre public") or public security;

(2) the protection of health and life of humans, animals or plants;

(3) the protection of national treasures possessing artistic, historical or archeological value[30]; and

(4) the protection of industrial or commercial property

Article 36 amounts, within certain limits, to an authorization of nontariff trade barriers among the member nations. This "public interest" authorization exists in addition to, but somewhat overlaps with, the Rule of Reason exception formulated in *Dassonville* and *Cassis* above. However, in a sentence much construed by the European Court of Justice, Article 36 continues with the following language: "Such prohibitions or restrictions shall not, however, constitute a means of arbitrary discrimination or a disguised restriction on trade between member states."

Case Law

In a wide range of decisions, the Court of Justice has interpreted Article 36 in a manner which generally limits the ability of member states to impose NTB barriers to internal trade. Britain, for example, may use its criminal law under the public morality exception to seize pornographic goods made in Holland that it outlaws,[31] but not inflatable sex dolls from Germany which could be lawfully produced in the United Kingdom.[32] Germany cannot stop the importation of beer (e.g., Heineken's from Holland) which fails to meet its purity standards.[33] This case makes wonderful reading

states retain certain Article 36 prerogatives and cases allowing member states to "supplement" directives on the basis of genuine need, including Ministère Public v. Grunert (1980) Eur.Comm.Rep. 1827; In re Motte (1985) Eur.Comm.Rep. 3887; Ministére Public v. Muller (1986) Eur.Comm.Rep. 1511; Ministére Public v. Bellon (1990) Eur.Comm.Rep. 4683.

[30] See Council Directive 93/7 securing the right of return of national cultural treasures removed unlawfully after Dec. 31, 1992.

[31] Regina v. Henn and Darby (1979) Eur.Comm.Rep. 3795.

[32] Conegate Ltd. v. H.M. Customs and Excise (1986) Eur.Comm.Rep. 1007.

[33] Commission v. Germany (1987) Eur.Comm.Rep. 1227. But see Aragonesa de Publicidad Exterior SA (APESA) + Anor v. Departamento de Sanidad y Seguridad Social (1991) Eur.Comm.Rep. 4151 (Cases C–1/90 and C–176/90) (advertising ban applied to strong alcoholic beverages can be justified on public health grounds).

as the Germans, seeking to invoke the public health exception of Article 36, argue all manner of ills that may befall their populace if free trade in beer is allowed. Equally interesting are the unsuccessful Italian health protection arguments against free trade in pasta made from common (not durum) wheat.[34]

But a state may obtain whatever information it requires from importers to evaluate public health risks associated with food products containing additives that are freely traded elsewhere in the Common Market. This does not mean that an importer of muesli bars to which vitamins have been added must prove the product healthful, rather that the member state seeking to bar the imports must have an objective reason for keeping them out of its market.[35] Assuming such a reason exists, the trade restraint may not be disproportionate to the public health goal.[36] A notable 2002 ECJ opinion invalidated a French public health ban on U.K. beef imports maintained after a Commission decision to return to free trade following the "mad cow" outbreak.[37]

Public security measures adopted under Article 36 can include external as well as internal security. An unusual case under the public security exception contained in Article 36 involved Irish petroleum products' restraints.[38] The Irish argued that oil is an exceptional product always triggering national security interests. Less expansively, the Court acknowledged that maintaining minimum oil supplies did fall within the ambit of Article 36. The public policy exception under Article 36 has been construed along French lines (ordre public). Only genuine threats to fundamental societal interests are covered.[39] Consumer protection (though a legitimate rationale for trade restraints under *Dassonville* and *Cassis*), does not fall within the public policy exception.[40] Permitting environmental protesters to block the Brenner Pass for 30 hours is acceptable public policy in support of fundamental assembly and expression rights.[41]

---

[34] Re Drei Glocken GmbH and Criminal Proceedings against Zoni (1988) Eur.Comm.Rep. 4233, 4285.

[35] Officer van Justitie v. Sandoz BV (1983) Eur.Comm.Rep. 2445.

[36] Commission v. United Kingdom (UHT Milk) (1983) Eur.Comm.Rep. 203.

[37] National Farmers' Union v. Secrétariat Général (2002) Eur.Comm.Rep. I–9079.

[38] Campus Oil Ltd. v. Minister for Industry and Energy (1984) Eur.Comm.Rep. 2727.

[39] See Regina v. Thompson (1978) Eur.Comm.Rep. 2247 (coinage).

[40] Kohl KG v. Ringelhan and Rennett SA (1984) Eur.Comm.Rep. 3651.

[41] Schmidberger v. Austria (2003) Eur.Comm.Rep. I–5659 (Case C–112/00).

§ 26.6 Intellectual Property Rights as European Trade Barriers

A truly remarkable body of case law has developed around the authority granted national governments in Article 36 to protect industrial or commercial property by restraining imports and exports. These cases run the full gamut from protection of trademarks and copyrights to protection of patents and knowhow. There is a close link between this body of case law and that developed under Article 101 concerning restraints on competition.[42]

Trade restraints involving intellectual property arise out of the fact that such rights are nationally granted. Owners of intellectual property rights within the Union are free under most traditional law to block the unauthorized importation of goods into national markets. There is a strong tendency for national infringement lawsuits to serve as vehicles for the division of the Common Market. Although considerable energy has been spent by the Commission on developing Common Market patents that would provide an alternative to national intellectual property rights, these proposals have yet to be fully implemented. In 1993, the Council reached agreement on a Common Market trademark regime. And the Council adopted Directive 89/104, which seeks to harmonize member state laws governing trademarks. In the copyright field, several directives have harmonized European law, perhaps most importantly on copyrights for computer software (No. 91/250).

Exhaustion Doctrine

The European Court of Justice has addressed the problems under Article 36 and generally resolved against the exercise of national intellectual property rights in ways which inhibit free internal trade. In many of these decisions, the Court acknowledges the existence of the right to block trade in infringing goods, but holds that the *exercise* of that right is subordinate to the TFEU. The Court has also fashioned a doctrine which treats national intellectual property rights as having been *exhausted* once the goods to which they apply are freely sold on the market. One of the few exceptions to this doctrine is broadcast performing rights which the Court treats as incapable of exhaustion.[43] Records and CDs embodying such rights are, however, subject to the exhaustion doctrine once released into the

---

[42] See Chapter 20.

[43] See Coditel v. Ciné Vog Films SA (1980) Eur.Comm.Rep. 881; (1982) Eur.Comm.Rep. 3381.

market.[44] Such goods often end up in the hands of third parties who then ship them into another member state.

The practical effect of many of the rulings of the Court of Justice is to remove the ability of the owners of the relevant intellectual property rights from successfully pursuing infringement actions in national courts. When intellectual property rights share a common origin and have been placed on goods by consent, as when a licensor authorizes their use in other countries, then infringement actions to protect against trade in the goods to which the rights apply are usually denied. It is only when intellectual property rights do not share a common origin or the requisite consent is absent that they stand a chance of being upheld so as to stop trade in infringing products.[45] Compulsory licensing of patents, for example, does not involve consensual marketing of products. Patent rights may therefore be used to block trade in goods produced under such a license.[46] But careful repackaging and resale of goods subject to a common trademark may occur against the objections of the owner of the mark.[47]

Centrafarm Case

An excellent example of the application of the judicial doctrine developed by the Court of Justice in the intellectual property field under Article 36 can be found in the *Centrafarm* case.[48] The United States pharmaceutical company, Sterling Drug, owned the British and Dutch patents and trademarks relating to "Negram." Subsidiaries of Sterling Drug in Britain and Holland had been respectively assigned the British and Dutch trademark rights to Negram. Owing in part to price controls in the UK, a substantial difference in cost for Negram emerged as between the two countries. Centrafarm was an independent Dutch importer of Negram from the UK and Germany. Sterling Drug and its subsidiaries brought infringement actions in the Dutch courts under their national patent and trademark rights seeking an injunction against Centrafarm's importation of Negram into The Netherlands.

---

[44] Musik–Vertrieb membran Gmbh v. GEMA (1981) Eur.Comm.Rep. 147.

[45] See CNL–Sucal v. HAG (1990) Eur.Comm.Rep. 3711 (Case C–10/89) (wartime expropriation of trademark removes common origin).

[46] Pharmon BV v. Hoechst AG (1985) Eur.Comm.Rep. 2281.

[47] Hoffman–LaRoche & Co. AG v. Centrafarm Vertriebsgesellschaft Pharmazeutischer Erzeugnisse mgH (1978) Eur.Comm.Rep. 1132; Pfizer, Inc. v. Eurim–Pharm GmbH (1981) Eur.Comm.Rep. 2913.

[48] Centrafarm BV and Adriaan de Peipjper v. Sterling Drug Inc. (1974) Eur.Comm.Rep. 1147.

The Court of Justice held that the intellectual property rights of Sterling Drug and its subsidiaries could not be exercised in a way which blocked trade in "parallel goods." In the Court's view, the exception established in Article 36 for the protection of industrial and commercial property covers only those rights that were specifically intended to be conveyed by the grant of national patents and trademarks. Blocking trade in parallel goods after they have been put on the market with the consent of a common owner, thus exhausting the rights in question, was not intended to be part of the package of benefits conveyed. If Sterling Drug succeeded, an arbitrary discrimination or disguised restriction on Union trade would be achieved in breach of the language which qualifies Article 36. Thus the European Court of Justice ruled in favor of the free movement of goods within the Common Market even when that negates clearly existing national legal remedies.

Only in the unusual situation where the intellectual property rights in question have been acquired by independent proprietors under different national laws may such rights inhibit internal trade.[49] While the goal of creation of the Common Market can override national intellectual property rights when internal trade is concerned, these rights apply fully to the importation of goods from outside the European Union.[50] North American exporters of goods allegedly subject to rights owned by Europeans may therefore find entry into the EU challenged by infringement actions in national courts. This is notably true regarding trade in gray market goods.[51] Levi Strauss successfully cited *Silhouette* to keep low-price (made in the USA) Levi's out of the EU.

§ 26.7 NTBs and the Single Market

Nontariff trade barrier problems were the principal focus of the campaign for a fully integrated Common Market. Many legislative acts have been adopted, or are in progress, which target NTB trade problems. When possible, a common European standard is adopted. For example, legislation on auto pollution requirements adopts this methodology. Products meeting these standards may be freely traded in the Common Market. Traditionally, this approach (called

---

[49] See Terrapin (Overseas) Ltd. v. Terranova Industrie CA Kapferer & Co. (1976) Eur.Comm.Rep. 1039; CNL–Sucal v. HAG (1990) Eur.Comm.Rep. 3711 (Case C–10/89).

[50] See E.M.I. Records Ltd. v. CBS United Kingdom Ltd. (1976) Eur.Comm.Rep. 811 and Silhouette International v. Hartlauer, No. C–355/96 (July 16, 1998) (gray-market goods).

[51] Silhouette International v. Hartlauer (1998) Eur.Comm.Rep. I–4799 (Case C–355/96); Zino Davidoff SA v. A + G Imports Ltd. (2001) Eur.Comm.Rep. I–8691 (Cases C–414/99 to 416/99).

"harmonization") has required the formation of a consensus as to the appropriate level of protection.

Once adopted, harmonized standards must be followed. This approach can be deceptive, however. Some harmonization directives contain a list of options from which member states may choose when implementing those directives. In practice, this leads to differentiated national laws on the same so-called harmonized subject. Furthermore, in certain areas (notably the environment and occupational health and safety), the TFEU expressly indicates that member states may adopt laws that are more demanding. The result is, again, less than complete harmonization.

Harmonization Principles

Many efforts at the harmonization of European environmental, health and safety, standards and certification, and related law have been undertaken. Nearly all of these are supposed to be based upon "high levels of protection."[52] Many have criticized what they see as the "least common denominator" results of harmonization of national laws under the campaign for a Europe without internal frontiers. One example involves the safety of toys. Directive 88/378 permits toys to be sold throughout the Common Market if they satisfy "essential requirements." These requirements are broadly worded in terms of flammability, toxicity, etc. There are two ways to meet these requirements: (1) produce a toy in accordance with CEN standards (drawn up by experts); or (2) produce a toy that otherwise meets the essential safety requirements. Local language labeling requirements necessary for purchaser comprehension have generally, though not always, been upheld.[53]

The least common denominator criticism may be even more appropriate to the second legislative methodology utilized in the internal market campaign. The second approach is based on the *Cassis* principle of mutual reciprocity. Under this "new" minimalist approach, European legislation requires member states to recognize the standards laws of other member states and deem them acceptable for purposes of the operation of the Common Market.[54] However, major legislation has been adopted in the area of professional services.[55] By mutual recognition of higher education diplomas based

---

[52] Article 114, TFEU.

[53] *See* Piageme & Orrs v. Peeters (1995) Eur.Comm.Rep. I–2955; Colim v. Bigg's Continent Noord (1999) Eur.Comm.Rep. I–3175.

[54] See, e.g., Council Resolution on a New Approach to Technical Harmonization and Standards, 1985 O.J. C136/1.

[55] See Council Directives, 89/48, 92/51, 2005/36.

upon at least three years of courses, virtually all professionals have now obtained legal rights to move freely in pursuit of their careers. This is a remarkable achievement.

§ 26.8 Product Standards and Testing

An important part of the single market campaign against non-tariff trade barriers (NTBs) of great interest to international business involves product testing and standards. More than half of the legislation involved in the single market campaign concerned such issues. Since 1969, there has been a standstill agreement among the member states to avoid the introduction of new technical barriers to trade. A 1983 directive requires member states to notify the Commission of proposed new technical regulations and product standards. The Commission can enjoin the introduction of such national rules for up to one year if it believes that a regional standard should be developed.[56] The goal was to move from national regulatory approvals to one unified system embodying essential requirements on health, safety, the environment and consumer protection. Goods that meet these essential requirements bear a "CE mark" and can be freely traded. Manufacturers self-certify their compliance with relevant European standards. Design and production process standards generally follow the ISO 9000 series on quality management and assurance. Firms must maintain a technical file documenting compliance and produce the file upon request by national authorities.

Standards Bodies

Private regional standards bodies have been playing a critical role in the development of this system. These include the European Committee for Standardization (CEN), the European Committee for Electrotechnical Standardization (CENELEC), and the European Telecommunications Standards Institute (ETSI). Groups like these have been officially delegated the responsibility for creating thousands of technical product standards. They have been turning out some 150 common standards each year. For example, directives on the safety of toys, construction products and electromagnetic compatibility have been issued.[57] These directives adopt the so-called "new approach" of setting broad standards at the regional level which if met guarantee access to every member state market. Under the "old approach", which still applies to most standards for processed foods, motor vehicles, chemicals and pharmaceuticals,

---

[56] Council Directive 83/169.

[57] See Council Directives 88/378, 89/106 and 89/336.

European legislation on standards is binding law. The technical specifications and testing protocols of these directives must be followed and (unlike the new approach) the member states may add requirements to them. Under either approach, goods meeting these standards will bear a CE mark. North American producers have frequently complained that their ability to be heard by European standards' bodies is limited. They have had little influence on product standards to which they must conform in order to sell freely in the Common Market.

Testing and Certification

Testing and certification of products has been another part of the single market campaign. The main concern of North American companies is that recognition be granted of U.S., Canadian and Mexican tests. In the past, many North American exporters have had to have their goods retested for European purposes. The EU is generally committed to a resolution of such issues under what it calls a "global approach" to product standards and testing. This involves creation of a regional system for authorizing certification and testing under common rules and procedures.[58] In negotiations undertaken as part of the Uruguay Round on revising the Standards Code of the GATT, the EU indicated its commitment to giving recognition to "equivalent technical regulations" of other nations, and to avoidance of unnecessary obstacles to trade. The Transatlantic Partnership dialogue between Europe and the United States has successfully achieved mutual recognition on a range of product standards and testing.

§ 26.9 Freedom to Provide and Receive Services across European Borders

The freedom of nonresidents to provide services within other parts of the Common Market is another part of the foundations of the TFEU[59] The freedom to provide services (including tourism) implies a right to receive and pay for them by going to the country of their source.[60] Industrial, commercial, craft and professional services are included within this right, which is usually not dependent upon establishment in the country where the service is rendered.[61]

---

[58] Council Resolution Dec. 21, 1989, O.J. C10 (Jan. 16, 1990).

[59] Articles 56 and 57, TFEU.

[60] Luisi and Carbone v. Ministero del Tesoro (1984) Eur.Comm.Rep. 377; Cowan v. Le Tresor Public (1989) Eur.Comm.Rep. 195 (British tourist entitled to French criminal injury compensation).

[61] Commission v. Germany (1986) Eur.Comm.Rep. 3755; Ministère Public v. van Wesemael (1979) Eur.Comm.Rep. 35 (employment agencies).

In other words, the freedom to provide or receive services across borders entails a limited right of temporary entry into another member state.

The Council has adopted a general program for the abolition of national restrictions on the freedom to provide services across borders. This freedom is subject to the same public policy, public security and public health exceptions applied to workers and the self-employed.[62] The Council's program has slowly been implemented by a series of legislative acts applicable to professional and nonprofessional services. As with the right of self-establishment, discrimination based upon the nationality or nonresidence of the service provider is generally prohibited even if no implementing law has been adopted.[63] However, in parallel with law developed in connection with the free movement of goods, the Court of Justice in *van Binsbergen* indicated that member governments may require providers of services from other states to adhere to professional public interest rules. These rules must be applied equally to all professionals operating in the nation, and only if necessary to ensure that the out-of-state professional does not escape them by reason of establishment elsewhere.

In other words, if the professional rules (e.g., ethics) of the country in which the service provider is established are equivalent, then application of the rules of the country where the service is provided does not follow. Following *Cassis,* and notably not *Keck,* the Court of Justice has affirmed member state marketing controls over the sale of lottery tickets (social policy and fraud interests) and over "cold calling" solicitations for commodities futures. Telemarketing in most other areas is forbidden, except with prior consumer consent, under a 1977 directive.

Financial Services

Bankers, investment advisors and insurance companies long awaited the arrival of a truly common market. Their right of establishment in other member states has existed for some time. The right to provide services across borders without establishing local subsidiaries was forcefully reaffirmed by the Court of Justice in

62 Article 74, TFEU.

63 Van Binsbergen v. Bestuur van de Bedrijfsvereniging voor de Metaalnijverheid (1974) Eur.Comm.Rep. 1299 (legal representation); Coenen v. Sociaal Economische Raad (1975) Eur.Comm.Rep. 1547 (insurance intermediary).

1986.[64] This decision largely rejected a requirement that all insurers servicing the German market be located and established there.

Legislative initiatives undertaken in connection with the single market campaign created genuinely competitive cross-border European markets for banking, investment and insurance services. Licensing of insurance and investment service companies and banks meeting minimum capital, solvency ratio and other requirements as implemented in member state law is done on a "one-stop" home country basis. Banks, for example, cannot maintain individual equity positions in non-financial entities in excess of 15 percent of their capital funds, and the total value of such holdings cannot exceed 50 percent of those funds.[65] They can participate and service securities transactions and issues, financial leasing and trade for their own accounts. The proposed investment services directive requires home country supervision of the "good repute" and "suitability" of managers and controlling shareholders.

Member states must ordinarily recognize home country licenses and the principle of home country control. For example, Council Directive 89/646 ("the Second Banking Directive") employs the home country single license procedure to liberalize banking services throughout the region. However, host states retain the right to regulate a bank's liquidity and supervise it through monetary policy and in the name of the "general good." Similarly, no additional insurance permits or requirements may be imposed by host countries when large industrial risks (sophisticated purchasers) are involved. However, when the public at large is concerned (general risk), host country rules still apply.[66] Major auto and life insurance directives employing one-stop licensing principles were adopted in 1990.[67] The auto insurance directive reproduces the large versus general risk distinctions found in the Second Non–Life Insurance Directive. Host country controls over general risk auto insurance policies were retained until 1995. Host country permits are also required when life insurers from other member states actively solicit business.

Reciprocity and the United States

There was a rush by non-member state bankers, investment advisors and insurers to get established in the EU before January 1, 1993 in order to qualify for home country licenses. North Americans and others have been particularly concerned about certain features

---

64 Commission v. Germany (1986) Eur.Comm.Rep. 3755.

65 Council Directive 89/646.

66 Council Directive 88/357 ("the Second Non–Life Insurance Directive").

67 Council Directives 90/619 (life insurance) and 90/618 (auto insurance).

of the legislation mandating effective access in foreign markets for European companies before outsiders may benefit from the liberalization of financial services within the Common Market. This problem is generally referred to as the "reciprocity requirement." It is this kind of requirement that gave the campaign for a Europe without internal frontiers the stigma of increasing the degree of external trade barriers. Many outsiders, in rhetoric which sometimes seems excessive, refer to the development of a "Fortress Europe" mentality and threat to world trading relations.

Since state and federal laws governing banking, investment services and insurance are restrictive, and in no sense can it be said that one license permits a financial company to operate throughout the United States, one result of European integration has arguably been reform of United States regulatory legislation. Since 1994, the U.S. has noticeably relaxed its rules on interstate banking and largely repealed the Depression-era Glass–Steagall Act limitations on universal banking.

§ 26.10 Equal Pay and Equal Treatment (Comparable Worth)

Article 157 is probably the most prominent element in European social policy. It is derived from International Labor Organization Convention No. 100 which three states, including France, had adopted by 1957. The French were rightfully proud of this tradition of nondiscrimination between the sexes on pay. They also appreciated that gender-based inequality in pay in other member states could harm the ability of their companies to compete. Article 157 thus enshrines the principle that men and women shall receive equal pay for equal work, a rough equivalent to what is termed "comparable worth" in the United States and a brave new world for investors in Europe.

Equal Pay, Comparable Worth

Article 157 has been the subject of voluminous legislation and litigation. It applies, quite appropriately, to the European Community as an employer.[68] Early on, the Court of Justice decided that the Article 157 on equal pay for equal work is directly effective law.[69] This decision allows individuals to challenge pay discrimination in public and private sector jobs. The ruling was applied pro-

---

[68] Sabbatini, née Bertoni v. European Parliament (1972) Eur.Comm.Rep. 345; Razzouk v. Commission (1984) Eur.Comm.Rep. 1509 (working conditions)

[69] Defrenne v. Sabena (1976) Eur.Comm.Rep. 455.

spectively by the Court of Justice so as to avoid large numbers of lawsuits for back pay.

In *Defrenne,* a flight attendant for Sabena Airlines was able to allege illegal discrimination in pay and pension benefits (as a form of deferred pay) to stewards and stewardesses on the basis of Article 157 law before a Belgian work tribunal. European law in this area enshrines the principle of "comparable worth," a most controversial issue in United States employment law. Furthermore, women who are paid less than men performing work of less worth may claim relief.[70] The hard questions are how to determine what constitutes "equal work" requiring equal pay under Article 157 or what "women's work" is worth more than that being done by men (again requiring pay adjustments). For example, does secretarial work equal custodial work? Is the work of an airline attendant worth more than that of an airline mechanic? What about speech therapists (mostly women) and pharmacists (mostly men).[71]

Council Directive 75/117 complements Article 157. It makes the principle of equal pay apply to work of *equal value* (to the employer). This mandates establishment of nondiscriminatory job classifications to measure the comparable worth of one job with another. The Commission successfully enforced Directive 75/117 in a prosecution before the European Court of Justice against the United Kingdom. The Sex Discrimination Act of 1975, adopted expressly to fulfill Article 157 obligations, did not meet European standards because employers could block the introduction of job classification systems.[72] Danish law's failure to cover nonunionized workers also breached the equal pay directive.[73] But its implementation under German law, notably by constitutional provisions, sufficed to meet regional standards.[74]

In determining equal or greater values, most states favor a job content approach. Content is determined through job evaluation systems which use factor analysis. For example, in Great Britain a job is broken down into various components such as skill, responsibility, physical requirements, mental requirements, and working conditions. Points or grades are awarded in each of these categories and totaled to determine the value of the job. Different factors may be balanced against each other. In Ireland, the demand of physical work can be balanced against the concentration required in particu-

---

70 Murphy v. An Bord Telecom Eireann (1988) Eur.Comm.Rep. 673.

71 *See* Enderby v. Frenchay Health Authority (1993) Eur.Comm.Rep. I–5535.

72 Commission v. United Kingdom (1982) Eur.Comm.Rep. 2601.

73 Commission v. Denmark (1986) 1 Common Mkt.L.Rep. 44.

74 Commission v. Germany (1986) 2 Common Mkt.L.Rep. 588.

lar skills. This is known as the "total package" approach. The equal job content approach relies on comparisons. This raises the question of which jobs should be deemed to be suitable for comparison. The member states have taken different approaches to this question. In Britain the comparison must be drawn from the same business establishment. In contrast, the Irish Anti–Discrimination Pay Act provides for "comparisons in the same place," and "place" includes a city, town or locality. This approach is designed to ensure that legitimate regional differences in pay are not disturbed.

Defenses

Employer defenses also vary from member state to member state. In Ireland, employers may justify a variation if they can show "grounds other than sex" for a disputed variation in pay. In Britain, employers will succeed if they can prove a "genuine material factor which is not the difference of sex." In Germany, the employer can prove that "material reasons unrelated to a particular sex" justify the differential. A further consideration in the implementation of equal pay laws has been the existence of pre-existing wage schedules set by collective agreement. In Britain and Italy, courts have held that collective agreements relating to pay cannot be changed or altered except where direct discrimination can be shown.

The burden of proving "objectively justified economic grounds" to warrant pay differentials is on the employer.[75] When a woman succeeds a man in a particular position within a company (here a warehouse manager), she is entitled to equal pay absent a satisfactory explanation not based upon gender.[76] The same is true of part-time (female) workers doing the same job as full-time (male) workers.[77] Free travel to railway employees upon retirement cannot go only to men.[78] And "pay" includes retirement benefits paid upon involuntary dismissal, which cannot be discriminatory.[79] But a protocol adopted at the 1991 Maastricht Summit makes this ruling prospective only. Pay also includes employer-paid pension benefits which cannot be for men only.[80] In this decision the Court refused to remove the retroactive effect of its judgment suggesting that *Defrenne* was adequate notice of the direct effect of Article 157 upon

[75] Council Directive 97/80.

[76] Macarthys Ltd. v. Smith (1980) Eur.Comm.Rep. 1275.

[77] Jenkins v. Kingsgate (Clothing Productions) Ltd. (1981) Eur.Comm.Rep. 911.

[78] Garland v. British Rail Engineering, Ltd. (1982) Eur.Comm.Rep. 359.

[79] Barber v. The Guardian Royal Exchange Assurance Group (1990) 1 Eur.Comm.Rep. 1889.

[80] Worringham and Humphreys v. Lloyds Bank Ltd. (1981) Eur.Comm.Rep. 767.

employers. Mobility, special training and seniority may be objectively justifiable grounds for pay discrimination.[81]

Equal Treatment

The principle of equal pay for equal work has been extended by Council Directive to *equal treatment* regarding access to employment, vocational training, promotions, and working conditions (e.g. retirement deadlines).[82] This directive prohibits discrimination based upon sex, family or marital status. The Equal Treatment Directive is limited by three exceptions. Member states may distinguish between men and women if: (1) sex is a determining factor in ability to perform the work; (2) the provision protects women; or (3) the provision promotes equal opportunity for men and women. Equal treatment must be extended to small and household businesses.[83] Dutch Law compulsorily retiring women at age 60 and men at age 65 violated the directive.[84] Women cannot be refused employment because they are pregnant even if the employer will suffer financial losses during maternity leave.[85] Maternity and adoption leave benefits for women, however, need not be extended to men.[86] The dismissal of a woman because of repeated absences owing to sickness is lawful provided the same absences would lead to the dismissal of men.[87] General prohibitions against night work by women but not men violate equal treatment Directive 76/207. The French government failed to justify this criminal law on any special grounds.[88]

Equality also governs social security entitlements[89] such as disability or caring for the disabled pay.[90] Social security benefits

---

[81] Union of Commercial and Clerical Employees v. Danish Employers Assn *ex parte* Danfoss, 1989 Eur.Comm.Rep. 3199.

[82] Council Directive 76/207 (issued under Article 235).

[83] Commission v. United Kingdom (1983) Eur.Comm.Rep. 3431.

[84] Beets–Proper v. Van Lanschot Bankiers NV (1986) Eur.Comm.Rep. 773. See Council Directive 86/378 (equal treatment regarding pensions).

[85] Dekker v. Stichting Vormingscentrum voor Jong Volwassenen Plus (1990) Eur.Comm.Rep. 3941 (Case C–177–88).

[86] Hofmann v. Barmer Ersatzkasse (1984) Eur.Comm.Rep. 3047; Commission v. Italy (1983) Eur.Comm.Rep. 3273 (adoption leave benefits).

[87] Hertz and Aldi Marked (1990) Eur.Comm.Rep. 3979 (Case C–179/88).

[88] Ministère Public v. Stoeckel (1991) Eur.Comm.Rep. 4047 (Case C–345–89).

[89] Council Directive 79/7. An important exception allows state pension schemes to retain different retirement ages for men and women. See Regina v. Secretary of State for Social Security (1992) Eur.Comm.Rep. 4297 (Case C–9/91) and Article 7(1)(a) of Directive 79/7. But severe disablement allowances (SDA) and invalid care cannot be provided on the basis of different ages. Secretary of State for Social Security v. Thomas (1993) Eur.Comm.Rep. 1247 (Case C–328/91).

[90] Drake v. Chief Adjudication Officer (1986) Eur.Comm.Rep. 1995.

cannot be based upon marital status.[91] Women police officers cannot be denied arms when men are not, even in the interest of "public safety" and "national security."[92] Equal treatment requires the elimination of preferences based upon gender in laws governing collectively bargained employment agreements.[93] The Council adopted a declaration in December 1991 endorsing the Commission's recommended Code of Practice on sexual harassment. This Code rejects sexual harassment as contrary to equal treatment law, specifically Council Directive 76/207. But the equal pay and equal treatment directives fail to cover significant categories of women workers; part-time, temporary and home workers.[94] Additional legislation in these areas can be expected.

Although Article 157 on equal pay is directly effective law binding upon public and private employers, it is not yet clear to what degree the equal treatment directives discussed above have that effect. Clearly these directives are binding on the member states and public corporations as employers.[95] The private sector must comply after national implementing legislation is adopted, but if that legislation is deficient the only remedy is a prosecution of the member state by the Commission.[96] There is a trend within the jurisprudence of the Court of Justice towards recognition of a broad human right of equality before the law. This is evidenced in a number of Article 157 cases, which suggests that the private sector will eventually be bound by all European legislation on equal pay and equal treatment even in the absence of or in spite of national implementing law.

Affirmative Action

Predictably, questions of "affirmative action" have arisen in the context of Article 157 law. A controversial decision of the Court of Justice invalidated a Bremen regulation giving women of equal qualifications priority over men where women made up less than

---

91 Id.

92 Johnston v. Chief Constable (1986) Eur.Comm.Rep. 1651. See generally Articles 223–225, Treaty of Rome.

93 Commission v. France (1988) Eur.Comm.Rep. 6315 (Case 312/86) (preferences for women must be removed).

94 See Jenkins v. Kingsgate Ltd. (1981) Eur.Comm.Rep. 911 (part-time workers paid less, and though largely female, no EC law violation). Compare Bilka–Kaufhaus v. Weber 1986–2 Common Mkt.L.Rep. 701.

95 See especially Marshall v. Southampton and South–West Hampshire Area Health Authority (Teaching) (1986) Eur.Comm.Rep. 723 (discriminatory retirement ages unlawful); Foster v. British Gas (1990) Eur.Comm.Rep. 3313 (Case 188/89).

96 See Duke v. GEC Reliance Ltd. (1988) 1 All Eng.Rep. 626 (discriminatory retirement ages lawful).

half the relevant civil service staff. While not strictly a quota, the Court found that Bremen had exceeded the limits of the equal treatment directive in promoting equality of opportunity.[97] Article 157(4) TFEU, as amended by the Amsterdam Treaty in 1999, attempts to address such issues. It allows member states to maintain or adopt "measures for specific advantages" in order to make it "easier" for the "under represented sex" to pursue vocational activity or to prevent or compensate for "disadvantages" in professional careers. Specific reservation of University professorships for women in Sweden likewise fell upon ECJ review.[98] Sweden now uses increasing targets for women in full professorships.

Gender and Other Discrimination

Although Article 157 on equal pay is directly effective law binding upon public and private employers throughout the Union (*Defrenne*), it is not yet clear to what degree the equal treatment directives cited above have that effect. Clearly these directives are binding on the member states and public corporations as employers.[99] The private sector must comply after national implementing legislation is adopted, but if that legislation is deficient the only remedy may be prosecution of the member state by the Commission.[100] There is a trend within the jurisprudence of the Court of Justice towards recognition of a broad human right of equality before the law. This is evidenced in a number of Article 157 cases, reliance upon the European Human Rights Convention in developing general principles of EU law, and in revised Articles 8–10 TFEU, which suggests that the private sector will eventually be bound by all European Union legislation on equal pay and equal treatment even in the absence of or in spite of national implementing law.[101] Combatting discrimination based on sex, racial or ethnic origin, religion or belief, disability age or sexual orientation was made a central EU policy principle by the Reform Treaty of 2009.

---

[97] Kalanke v. Freie Hansestadt Bremen (1995) Eur.Comm.Rep. I–3051.

[98] Abrahamsson and Anderson v. Fogelqvist (2000) Eur.Comm.Rep. I–5539.

[99] *See especially* Marshall v. Southampton and South–West Hampshire Area Health Authority (Teaching) (1986) Eur.Comm.Rep. 723 (discriminatory retirement ages unlawful); Foster v. British Gas (1990) 1 Eur.Comm.Rep. 3313.

[100] *See* Duke v. GEC Reliance Ltd. (1988) 1 All Eng.Rep. 626 (discriminatory retirement ages lawful).

[101] National courts have a duty to interpret national law in furtherance of EU directives.

§ 26.11 Social Policy—Occupational Safety, the Social Fund and Social Charter

Investors in the European Union encounter a host of "social policy" regulations. The Treaty on the Functioning of the European Union (TFEU) is dominated by economic affairs. Nevertheless, Europe has always sought to provide for some of the concerns of the human beings who are impacted by the winds of economic change. Articles 151–164 TFEU seek to improve working conditions and standards of living on a harmonized basis. The right of nationals to move freely to take up employment has been solidified. Europe's social policy builds upon this basic right. Article 160, for example, led to the enactment of social security legislation to insure coverage for those who exercise their right to move freely to work.

A major impetus came in 1987 with the addition of Article 154 by the Single European Act. This article focuses on health and safety in the working environment. Acting by a qualified majority vote, the Council in cooperation with the Parliament is empowered to issue directives establishing minimum requirements in this field. It has done so, for example, on visual display units, heavy load handling and exposure to biological agents and carcinogens. More generally, Council directives now establish minimum safety and health requirements for most workplaces, equipment used by workers, and protective devices. Article 154 specifically requires such directives to avoid imposing administrative, financial and legal constraints that would hold back the creation and development of small and medium-sized enterprises. Like the 1987 amendments creating the Environmental Policy, Article 154 allows member states to maintain or introduce more stringent legal rules on working conditions, provided these are compatible with the Treaty.

The European Social Fund comes out of the regional budget. It is used to pay up to 50 percent of the costs of the member states under their vocational retraining and worker resettlement programs. European rules have substantially harmonized these programs. Unemployment compensation is also funded when plants are converted to other production for workers who are temporarily suspended or suffer a reduction in working hours. They retain the same wage levels pending full re-employment. Commission Decision 83/516 extended the operation of the European Social Fund to promoting employment among those under age 25, women who wish to return to work, the handicapped, migrants and their families, and the long-term unemployed.

Social Charter

The single market campaign has a social dimension that sometimes surprises U.S. investors. Labor unions have been especially concerned about the prospect of "social dumping," the relocation of companies to states with weaker unions and lower wages. There is no regional legislation on minimum wages and none is expected in the near future. One response to these concerns led to the Charter of Fundamental Social Rights For Workers, adopted in 1989 by 11 member states less Britain through the European Council. The Charter proclaims the following fundamental social rights for workers:

(1) freedom of movement and choice of occupations;

(2) fair remuneration (sufficient to have a decent standard of living);

(3) improved living and working conditions (e.g., paid leave);

(4) adequate social security benefits;

(5) free association in unions, including the right *not* to join, and the right to strike;

(6) nondiscriminatory access to vocational training;

(7) equal treatment for women and men;

(8) development of rights to access to information, and rights of consultation and participation;

(9) satisfactory health and safety conditions at work;

(10) for the young, a minimum employment age of 15, substantial limitations on night work for those under 18, and start-up vocational training rights;

(11) for retirees, the right to assistance "as needed" and a decent standard of living; and

(12) for the disabled, assistance to integrate socially and professionally.

The Charter was to be implemented immediately by the member states in "accordance with national practices." In addition, for each item listed above, regional legislation was anticipated.

Adoption of this legislation was slow chiefly because Britain held a veto power in the Council over employment matters under the Single European Act. The Commission, however, drafted a number of Social Action Program legislative measures. One such measure guaranteeing minimum maternity leave benefits of 14 weeks at statutory sick pay rates was adopted by the Council in 1992. A woman's employment cannot be terminated because she is pregnant. In addition, pregnant women are entitled to switch from night work, exempted from work detrimental to their health, and entitled to take paid leave for pre-natal check-ups. This directive required substantial improvements to existing legislation in Ireland, Portugal and the United Kingdom. Unpaid parental leave rights are detailed in Directive 96/34.

Social Protocol and Policy

In December 1991 at the Maastricht Summit agreement was reached, save Britain, on a "social policy protocol" facilitating adoption by the other eleven member states of laws by qualified majority vote governing many areas which bridge workers' interests and company operations. Some suggested that the "social protocol" would have been more accurately labeled a "workers' rights protocol". It focused on working environment issues including conditions of labor, health and safety, disclosure of information, sex discrimination, and worker consultation. The "social protocol" thus overlapped considerably with the Social Charter.

Despite its repeated opposition to development of a "social dimension," the United Kingdom under Conservative rule adopted or implemented over half of the measures noted in the Social Charter. What the Conservatives consistently objected to were rules relating directly to the employee-employer relationship, not worker benefits such as pregnancy leave or health or safety measures. Nevertheless, the Court of Justice repeatedly ruled against Britain in litigation challenging the adequacy of its implementation of worker-related directives (e.g., on collective redundancies and transfers of enterprises). And, in a major decision, the Court ruled over vehement objection that the "working time" directive (No. 93/104) was properly adopted by qualified majority vote on the basis of Article 153's authorization of worker health and safety law.[102] This ruling had the practical effect of avoiding Britains's Social Protocol opt out rights. The directive creates, inter alia, a minimum right to four weeks of paid vacation. The United Kingdom under the Labour Par-

[102] United Kingdom v. Council (1996) Eur.Comm.Rep. I–5755.

ty administration of Prime Minister Blair opted into the EU's Social Policy.

As amended, Articles 151–161 of the TFEU (the "social chapter") embrace social goals reflecting the Social Charter. There is express authority for EU legislation on worker health and safety, work conditions, information and consultation of workers, and gender equality, mostly using qualified majority voting and co-decision Parliamentary powers. However, there is no authorization for EU action on matters of pay, and rights of association, strike and lockout. EU legislation can occur by unanimous vote on social security, co-determination, worker protection upon termination, and employment of third country nationals.

§ 26.12 Company Law, European Companies

Article 49 on the right of establishment entitles companies based in one member state to set up agencies, branches or subsidiaries in other member states, even when this avoids paid-in capital requirements.[103] Thousands of U.K. companies have been set up to avoid Continental paid-in capital requirements. In the absence of an EU convention on legal personalities, nothing in the right of establishment permits a company to freely transfer its place of incorporation (seat) and administrative center to another member state without home state permission where that is required. In this case, the British Daily Mail newspaper sought to change to Dutch citizenship to take advantage of lower taxes.[104]

However, two decisions of the European Court of Justice, *Überseering*[105] and *Centros,*[106] hold that a company formed under the laws of one member state of the European Union may move or establish its entire operations to or in any other member state. The Court explicitly clarified that it does not constitute an abuse of the principle of freedom of establishment if the purpose is to circumvent the application of the stricter company or tax laws of the member state in which the company is operating by forming a company or branch in another member state with more liberal laws. It further stated that all questions relating to the company's status (liability of limited partners and managing directors, capital requirements, etc.) must be governed by the law of incorporation of the company. It is widely thought that these decisions will avoid restrictive Ger-

---

[103] Centros v. Erhvervs–OG Selskabsstyrelsen (1999) Eur.Comm.Rep. II–1459.

[104] Re Daily Mail (1988) Eur.Comm.Rep. 5483.

[105] Uberseering BV v. NCC Nordie Construction Co. (2002) Eur.Comm.Rep. I–9919.

[106] (1999) Eur. Comm. Rep. II–1459.

many company law rules by, for example as in *Uberseering*, incorporation in the Netherlands.

Company Law Directives

The Council has adopted a number of non-controversial coordination directives advancing Union company law. These in theory seek to avoid the race to the bottom problems associated with Delaware corporate law in the United States. The first directive sets out requirements for disclosure, validity and nullity of share capital companies. The ECJ has ruled that the listing of grounds for nullifying the formation of a company found in the First Company Law Directive 68/151 exhausts all such possibilities. Grounds for nullification based upon the Spanish Civil Code requirement of "causa" could not be utilized since that Code must be construed in conformity with Directive 68/151.[107] The second deals with the classification, subscription and maintenance of capital of public and large companies.[108] Increases in share capital must be approved by company shareholders with preemptive rights preserved. This obligation is derived from Article 25 of the Second Company Law Directive, which has direct effect in Union law.[109] Companies are generally forbidden from acquiring their own shares. Governmental acts authorizing increases in company capital to ensure survival which prejudice the preemptive rights of shareholders are impermissible under Directive 77/91.[110] The Second Company Law Directive was amended in late 1992 to close a loophole by prohibiting parent companies from buying through subsidiaries more than 10 percent of their own shares when faced with hostile takeovers.[111]

The Third Company Law Directive concerns the internal merger of public companies. Modern procedures for mergers with related and unrelated companies are established. Asset and liability acquisitions and new company formations are allowed. Shareholder rights are specified. The Sixth directive governs sales of assets of public companies, including certain shareholder, creditor and work-

---

[107] Marleasing SA v. La Comercial Internacional de Alimentación SA. (1990) 1 Eur.Comm.Rep. 4135. Regarding the first directive, *see also* Daihatsu Handler v. Daihatsu Deutschland (1997) Eur.Comm.Rep. I–6843; Commission v. Germany (1998) Eur.Comm.Rep. I–5449.

[108] Karella & Anor v. Greek Minister for Industry, Energy and Technology (1991) Eur.Comm.Rep. I–2691 (Cases C–19 and C–20/90).

[109] *Id.* Regarding the second directive, *see also* Siemens v. Nold (1996) Eur.Comm.Rep. I–6017; Pafitis v. Trapeza Kentrikis Ellados (1996) Eur.Comm.Rep. I–1347.

[110] Kerafina–Keramische und Finanz Holding AG & Anor v. Hellenic Republic (1992) Eur.Comm.Rep.I–5699 (Cases C–134/91, C–135/91).

[111] *See* Council Directive 92/101.

ers' rights. The Fourth standardizes the treatment of annual accounts (*e.g.,* in their presentation, content, valuation and publication). It requires public presentation of a "true and fair view" of company assets, liabilities, finances, profits and losses. Small and medium-sized firms can publish abridged accounts. All companies must present comparable figures for the preceding year. Valuation of assets and liabilities must be prudent, consistent and reflect the company as a going concern. The Fourth directive even details the notes that must accompany annual accounts. In addition, shareholders must be given a report by management annually on the development of the business, future plans, research activities and company purchases of its own shares. There is a permissive provision relating to inflation or current cost accounting. There is some doubt about the degree of relation to similar requirements of the United Kingdom accounting bodies or "generally accepted accounting practices" in the United States. Directive 2001/65 spells out "fair value" accounting rules, notably for derivatives. Regulation 1606/2002 mandated use of International Accounting Standards by publicly traded companies. In 2006, new rules on the auditing of company accounts were adopted, as well as substantial amendments to EU accounting Directives 2006/46 and 2006/43.

The Sixth Company Law Directive adopted in 1982 complements the third directive and addresses the division or "scission" of public limited companies, where they wind up without liquidation. The Seventh concerns requirements for consolidated accounts of groups of companies. Consolidated accounts must follow the rules of the fourth directive as supplemented by the seventh. Consolidated accounts are required if an EU firm has legal or *de facto* control over other companies through majority shareholdings, appointment or removal power over management in a subsidiary, the right to exercise dominant influence, or the possibility of shareholder agreements conveying majority voting rights. Consolidated accounts must treat the group as a single enterprise regarding transactions among the companies. The Eighth Company Law Directive provides certain minimum standards and qualifications for auditors of company accounts. The Ninth Directive facilitates electronic shareholder voting, proxy voting and shareholder questioning rights.

Works Councils

Several controversial proposals for company law directives are in varying stages of evolution. These include a fifth directive on company structure and administration which has been long delayed due to differing views about the functions of single and two-tier boards of directors and officers, and worker representation at these levels. Another controversial topic (the "Vredeling proposal") would have required substantial information sharing between companies and their employees. The 1994 "works council" Directive 94/45 requires councils in companies with more than 1000 employees operating with 150 employees in at least two member states. Workers must be given information on and an opportunity to respond to a broad range of topics including the firm's economic and financial situation, employment, work methods and mergers and layoffs. But the information can be withheld when disclosure might "seriously harm" the functioning of the company or be "prejudicial" to it. Thousands of works councils now operate with little controversy. The European Court of Justice has held Directive 94/45 applies to parent companies located outside the EU.[112] It was revised and codified in Directive 2009/38.

Other less controversial directives have also been pursued. The Ninth directive concerns liability on the part of parent companies for the debts of subsidiaries they effectively control. The Tenth directive deals with cross-border company mergers. The Eleventh (adopted in 1989) involves disclosure by branches operating in other EU states, and the Twelfth (also adopted in 1989) affects single member private limited liability companies. Hostile takeovers, a sensitive area, are the subject of the Thirteenth company law directive (No. 2004/25). This directive requires equal treatment of shareholders, and specifies permissible defensive measures.

European Companies

An amended proposal for a European Company was submitted by the Commission to the Council in August 1989. Nineteen years had passed since the submission of the first proposal in 1970, and 14 years since the last amended proposal in 1975. In that period, considerable harmonization had been accomplished by way of directives. Finally, late in 2001, a European Company Statute was finalized, taking effect in 2004. Forming a European Company ("Societas Europeae" or SE) is optional. An SE operates on a European-wide basis governed by EU law. A regulation establishes its company law rules, while a directive covers worker involvement in SE. Under the Statute, an SE registered in one member state can freely move its registered office to another. SEs may be privately or publicly traded companies. SE, at least in theory, will remove the need for costly networks of subsidiaries throughout the European Union. Large legal and administrative cost savings are expected to be realized.

---

[112] Gesamtbetriebsrat der Kühne + Nagel AG – Co. KG v. Kühne + Nagel AG + Co. KG (2004) Eur.Comm.Rep. I–00000 (Case 440/00).

SE must be registered in the member state where it has its administrative head office, and the Statute does not significantly alter applicable taxation.

Regarding worker participation, the issue that held up the SE proposal for over 30 years, the first duty is to try negotiate agreement on employee involvement. Failing that, Standard Principles attached to the directive require regular reports, consultation and information exchange between management and worker representatives. Such reports must detail business plans, production and sales, management changes, mergers, divestments, potential closures and layoffs, and the implications of all this to workers. In the case of a European Company created by merger, the Standard Principles apply when at least 25 percent of the employees had the right to participate before the merger. However, member states need *not* implement the directive on participation for SEs created by mergers, but if so the SE can be registered only if an agreement with the employees is reached, or when no employees were covered by participation rules before the SE was created.

§ 26.13 Early Law on Mergers and Acquisitions

One alternative to direct investment in Europe is to purchase an existing business. Traditionally, the law governing such acquisitions was almost exclusively national. Since 1990, the EU actively regulates sizeable mergers and acquisitions as part of its competition policy. European law in this area is summarized below. Special attention should also be paid to the United States–European Community Antitrust Cooperation Agreement (1991) under which coordinated exchanges of information and review of transnational mergers occur. This Agreement is reviewed in Chapter 20.

In 1965 the Commission announced in a memorandum to the member states that concentration ought to be encouraged to achieve efficiency and economies of scale, and to combat competition from large United States and Japanese multinational firms. These rationales had supported a long line of merger approvals by the Commission under its coal and steel concentration controls. It was not until a European merger boom was in progress and extensive studies revealed increasing trends toward industrial concentration that the Commission took action against a merger in *Continental Can*.[113]

The Commission decided Continental Can abused its dominant positions in the manufacture of meat and fish tins and metal caps in Germany in only one fashion, by announcing an 80 percent control

---

113 (1972) Common Mkt.L.Rep. D11.

bid for the only Dutch meat and fish tin company. The Commission reasoned that Continental Can would strengthen its dominant German market position through this Dutch acquisition, to the detriment of consumers, and that this amounted to an abuse. The Commission emphasized that potential competition between companies located within Europe was to be eliminated. Acting quickly before the merger was a *fait accompli,* the Commission underscored its inability to block proposed mergers. Continental Can was given six months to submit proposals for remedying its infringement.

On appeal to the Court of Justice, Continental Can argued that the Commission was acting beyond its powers in attempting to control mergers under Article 102.[114] The Advocate General to the Court concurred. Nevertheless, the Court chose to go beyond the limits of the language of Articles 101 and 102 and interpret them in light of basic EU tasks and activities. The Court reasoned teleologically that both Articles were intended to assist in the maintenance of nondistorted competition. If businesses could freely merge and eliminate competition, a "breach in the whole system of competition law that could jeopardize the proper functioning of the common market" would be opened.

> There may therefore be abusive behavior if an enterprise in a dominant position strengthens that position so that the degree of control achieved substantially obstructs competition, i.e. so that the only enterprises left in the market are those which are dependent on the dominant enterprise with regard to their market behavior.[115]

One problem with relying on Article 102 for control of mergers and acquisitions was the absence of any pre-merger notification system. Once a merger is completed, it is always difficult to persuade a court or tribunal that dissolution is desirable or even possible. The key to effective mergers regulation, as the United States has learned under its Hart–Scott–Rodino pre-merger notification rules,[116] is advance warning and sufficient time to block anticompetitive mergers before they are implemented.

After the ruling of the Court of Justice in *Continental Can,* the Commission submitted a comprehensive mergers' control regulation to the Council for its approval. Nearly twenty years later, a regulation on mergers was finally implemented.

---

114 (1973) Eur.Comm.Rep. 215.

115 Id.

116 15 U.S.C.A. § 18A.

§ 26.14 Commission Regulation of Mergers and Acquisitions, Case Examples

In December of 1989, the Council of Ministers unanimously adopted Regulation 4064/89 on the Control of Concentrations Between Undertakings ("Mergers Regulation"). This regulation became effective Sept. 21, 1990 and was expanded in scope by amendment in 1997 (Regulation 1310/97) and significantly revised in 2004. It vests in the Commission the *exclusive* power to oppose large-scale mergers and acquisitions of competitive consequence to the Common Market and the European Economic Area.

Applicability, Advance Notice

For EU regulatory purposes, a "concentration" includes almost any means by which control over another firm is acquired. This could be by a merger agreement, stock or asset purchases, contractual relationships or other actions. Most full function joint ventures creating autonomous economic entities are caught by this test. Thus "control" triggering review can be achieved by minority shareholders, such as when they exercise decisive influence over strategic planning and investment decisions.[117] "Cooperative joint ventures" between independent competitors may also be subject to from the Mergers Regulation.[118]

The control process established by the Mergers Regulation commences when a concentration must be notified to the Commission on Form CO in one of the official languages. This language becomes the language of the proceeding. Form CO is somewhat similar to second request Hart–Scott–Rodino pre-merger notification filings under U.S. antitrust law. However, the extensive need for detailed product and geographic market descriptions, competitive analyses, and information about the parties in Form CO suggests a more demanding submission. Form CO defines a product market as follows:

> A relevant product market comprises all those products and/or services which are regarded as interchangeable or substitutable by the consumer, by reason of the products' characteristics, their prices and their intended use.

Meeting in advance of notification with members of the Commission on an informal basis in order to ascertain whether the "con-

[117] See Conagra/IDEA, 1991 O.J. C175/18; EIF/BC/CEPSA, 1991 O.J. C172/8; Usinor/ASD 1991 O.J. C193/34.

[118] See Article 4(2).

centration" has a regional dimension and is compatible with the Common Market has become widely accepted. Such meetings provide an opportunity to seek waivers from the various requests for information contained in Form CO. Since the Commission is bound by rules of professional secrecy, the substance of the discussions is confidential.

The duty to notify applies within one week of the signing of a merger agreement, the acquisition of a controlling interest or the announcement of a takeover bid.[119] The Commission can fine any company failing to notify it as required.[120] The duty to notify is triggered only when the concentration involves enterprises with a combined worldwide sales turnover of at least 5 billion EUROs,[121] *and* two of them have an aggregate regional turnover of 250 million EUROs, and each of the undertakings involved does not achieve more than two-thirds of its aggregate Union-wide turnover within one and the same state.[122] Additionally, since 1997, mergers with a combined aggregate worldwide turnover of more than 2.5 billion EUROs and significant member state and regional turnovers must be notified.[123]

As a general rule, concentrations meeting these criteria cannot be put into effect and fall exclusively within the Commission's domain. The effort here is to create a "one-stop" regulatory system. However, certain exceptions apply so as to allow national authorities to challenge some mergers. For example, this may occur under national law when two-thirds of the activities of each of the companies involved take place in the *same* member state.[124] The member states can also oppose mergers by appealing Commission decisions when their public security is at stake, to preserve plurality in media ownership, when financial institutions are involved or other legitimate interests are at risk.[125] If the threshold criteria of the Mergers Regulation are not met, member states can ask the Commission to investigate mergers that create or strengthen a dominant position in that state.[126] This is known as the "Dutch clause." States that lack national mergers' controls seem likely to do this. Similarly, if the merger only affects a particular market sector or region in one

---

[119] Article 4(1).

[120] Article 14(1).

[121] For banks and insurance companies, an amount equal to one-tenth of assets will be used as a proxy for sales turnover.

[122] Article 1(2).

[123] Article 1(3).

[124] Article 1(2).

[125] Article 21(3).

[126] Article 22(3).

member state, that state may request referral of the merger to it. This is known as the "German clause" reflecting Germany's insistence upon it. It has been sparingly used by the Commission.

Once a concentration is notified to the Commission, it has one month to decide to investigate the merger. If a formal investigation is commenced, the Commission ordinarily then has four months to challenge or approve the merger.[127] During these months, in most cases, the concentration cannot be put into effect. It is on hold.

The Commission evaluates mergers in terms of their "compatibility" with the Common market. The 1990 Mergers Regulation stated that if the concentration created or strengthened a dominant position such that competition was "significantly impeded," it was incompatible. Effective May 1, 2004, this test was replaced by a prohibition against merges that "significantly impede effective competition" by creating or strengthening dominant positions. Thus the new test focuses on effects not dominance. A set of Guidelines on Horizontal Mergers issued by the Commission in 2004 elaborate upon this approach. It is thought that this change will bring EU and U.S. mergers law closer together (the U.S. test is "substantial lessening of competition").

During a mergers investigation, the Commission can obtain information and records from the parties, and request member states to help with the investigation. Fines and penalties back up the Commission's powers to obtain records and information from the parties.[128] If the concentration has already taken effect, the Commission can issue a "hold-separate" order.[129] This requires the corporations or assets acquired to be separated and not, operationally speaking, merged. Approval of the merger may involve modifications of its terms or promises by the parties aimed at diminishing its anticompetitive potential. If the Commission ultimately decides to oppose the merger in a timely manner, it can order its termination by whatever means are appropriate to restore conditions of effective competition (including divestiture, fines or penalties). Such decisions can be appealed to the General Court under "fast track" procedures intended to promote judicial review within a year. As a practical matter, most merger proposals do not last that long. Hence, a negative Commission decision usually kills a merger.[130]

---

[127] Article 10.

[128] Articles 11–15.

[129] Articles 7 and 10.

[130] See Gencor Ltd. v. EC Commission, 1999 CEC 395. *See* also France v. EC Commission, 1998 Eur.Comm.Rep. I–1375.

The Commission may be found liable in damages for intervening unlawfully against mergers, notably when making manifest procedural errors. Commission decisions to clear joint ventures or mergers can, in rare cases, be annulled.

Case Examples

The first merger actually blocked by the Commission on competition law grounds was the attempted acquisition of a Canadian aircraft manufacturer (DeHaviland-owned by Boeing) by two European companies (Aerospatiale SNI of France and Alenia e Selenia Spa of Italy).[131] Prior to this rejection in late 1991, the Commission had approved over 50 mergers, obtaining modifications in a few instances. The Commission, in the DeHaviland case, took the position that the merger would have created an unassailable dominant position in the world and the European market for turbo prop or commuter aircraft. If completed, the merged entity would have had 50 percent of the world and 67 percent of the European market for such aircraft. In contrast, the Commission approved (subject to certain sell-off requirements) the acquisition of Perrier by Nestlé.[132] Prior to the merger, Nestlé, Perrier and BSN controlled about 82 percent of the French bottled water market. Afterwards, Nestlé and BSN each had about 41 percent of the market. The sell-off requirements were thought sufficient by the Commission to maintain effective competition. The case also presents interesting arguments that the Commission, in granting approval, disregarded fundamental workers' social rights. This issue was unsuccessfully taken up on appeal by Perrier's trade union representative.

In 1997, the Commission dramatically demonstrated its extraterritorial jurisdiction over the Boeing–McDonnell Douglas merger. This merger had already been cleared by the U.S. Federal Trade commission. The European Commission, however, demanded and (at the risk of a trade war) got important concessions from Boeing. These included abandonment of exclusive supply contracts with three U.S. airlines and licensing of technology derived from McDonnell Douglas' military programs at reasonable royalty rates. The Commission's success in this case was widely perceived in the United States as pro-Airbus.

The Commission blocked the MC Worldcom/Spring merger in 2001, as did the U.S. Dept. of Justice. Both authorities were worried about the merger's adverse effects on Internet access. For the

[131] 1991 O.J. L334/42.

[132] O.J. L356/1 (Dec. 5. 1992).

Commission, this was the first block of a merger taking place outside the EU between two firms established outside the EU. Much more controversy arose when in 2001 the Commission blocked the GE/Honeywell merger after it had been approved by U.S. authorities. The Commission was particularly concerned about the potential for bundling engines with avionics and non-avionics to the disadvantage of rivals. This reasoning was rejected on appeal, by the ECJ, but the merger was never completed. The United States and the EU, in the wake of GE/Honeywell, have agreed to follow a set of "Best Practices" on coordinated timing, evidence gathering, communication and consistency of remedies.

The General Court overturned a 1999 decision of the European Commission blocking the $1.2 billion merger of Airtours and First Choice Holidays. This was the first reversal of a merger prohibition since the 1990 inception of the review process. The GC judgment confirmed that transactions can be blocked on collective dominance grounds, but found that the Commission had failed to meet the three conditions for proving collective dominance: (1) each member of the dominant group is able to determine readily how the others are behaving, (2) there is an effective mechanism to prevent group members from departing from the agreed-upon policy, and (3) smaller competitors are unable to undercut that policy.

In June of 2002 the European Court of Justice issued three decisions on the use by member states of so-called "golden shares." Such shares allow governments to retain veto rights with respect to acquisitions of or other significant accumulations in privatized businesses. The court outlawed a golden share decree allowing France to block a foreign takeover of a privatized oil company. The golden share decree created a barrier to the free movement of capital. The court also outlawed a law giving Portugal the ability to block the acquisition of controlling stakes in privatized state companies, but determined as a matter of public interest that Belgium could retain its golden share in recently privatized canal and gas distribution companies.

In October of 2002, acting under its new fast track review procedures, the General Court overturned two additional mergers decisions of the Commission. In both the Court found serious errors, omissions and inconsistencies. Credible evidence, not assumptions or "abstract and detached analysis," must be tendered to prove both the strengthening or creation of a dominant position, and the likelihood that the merger will significantly impede competition.

Chapter 27

INVESTING IN NAFTA

Table of Sections

§ 27.1 Investment Laws of Canada

Although U.S. persons often view Canada in a mirror and see themselves, thus assuming that Canadians and the Canadian government will be very receptive to foreign investment, the policies of Canada over the years reflect an ambivalence toward such investment. Canada has long regulated foreign investment by both federal and provincial laws. Soon after its creation as a federation in 1867, Canada established high tariffs to protect infant industries from imports from the United States. This caused U.S. manufacturers to invest in Canada to surmount the tariff wall. Soon the United States was the principal source of foreign investment, and for many U.S. companies Canada was a natural location for their first foreign investment.

Most restrictive Canadian investment laws have focused on specific sectors, such as financial institutions, transportation, natural resources[1] and, quite importantly, publishing.[2] Canada was al-

[1] Oil and gas acquisitions were prohibited until the *Masse Policy*, adopted in 1992, was rescinded, leaving such regulation to the Investment Canada Act, which

ways a natural target for investment from the United States, especially since so much of the industrial development of the United States occurred relatively near the Canadian border. Canada's attitude toward foreign investment remained quite receptive until nationalistic forces in the 1960s began to challenge an open investment policy. The first measure of significance was the creation of the Foreign Investment Review Agency (FIRA) in 1974, which allowed the federal government to review proposed foreign investment, especially acquisitions of Canadian companies, and in some cases deny their development. The National Energy Program in 1980 was intended to *reduce* foreign ownership in the oil and gas industry. Most of that foreign ownership was by U.S. companies.

A Conservative government elected in 1984 replaced the FIRA with the Investment Canada Act (ICA) (1985),[3] that continues to govern foreign investment in Canada—especially acquisitions. When the CFTA was adopted, it incorporated part of the ICA, providing that a review of an acquisition under the ICA would not be subject to the CFTA dispute settlement provisions.[4] The ICA was to be amended to comply with the CFTA, but considerable definitional language in the ICA was retained by reference. When NAFTA was adopted, excluded from its dispute settlement provisions were decisions by Canada following a review under the ICA. This, plus Canada's exclusion of "cultural industries" by incorporation of the CFTA provisions, indicates that Canada has insisted on retaining considerable domestic control over certain foreign investment, especially the acquisition of Canadian owned industries, and most especially "cultural" industries. It has not, however, stopped significant foreign investment in Canada. While overall it diminished in 2010 with the appreciation of the Canadian dollar, investment increased from the United States. Over the past ten years, however, U.S. investment in Canada has declined. At the same time, investment from Asia/Oceania increased. That continued when Malaysian state owned Petronas (oil) acquired Progress Energy for $6 billion. A month later China's state-owned CNOOC (oil) acquired Nexen of Canada for $15 billion.

---

allowed such investment but required approval of some acquisitions. However, the threshold before approval was required was quite high, making the law less restrictive than it otherwise appeared.

[2] Canada considers publishing to be a cultural industry. Until restrictions in the Canadian *Baie Comeau Policy* on ownership of publishing were relaxed, foreign investment in publishing was very difficult.

[3] R.S. 1985, ch. 28 (1st Suppl.), *as amended* by 1988 ch. 65 and Investment Canada Regulations SOR/85–611, *as amended* by SOR/89–69.

[4] CFTA Art. 1608(1).

§ 27.2 Investment Laws of Mexico

The United States has never viewed Mexico with the same mirror as it does Canada, seeing itself in the reflection. Despite all the differences between Canada and the United States, Canada usually has been viewed an equal by the United States. Not so with Mexico. The United States has viewed Mexico as something less than a partner. The United States views Mexico as needing the United States, but the United States has not viewed itself as needing Mexico. Mexico has responded accordingly, with suspicion and deliberation. NAFTA has to some degree come to help. There is better mutual respect.

Canada never really flirted with socialism, as Mexico did in the 1970s by substantially increasing national ownership of the means of production and distribution. The Mexican investment law, the transfer of technology law, and the trade names and inventions law, all enacted in the 1970s, were models of restrictive laws of developing nations adopted during the tense and often bitter North–South dialogue, when developing nations argued that they were poor because the developed nations were rich, and that there had to be a transfer of wealth from the latter to the former.

Several Mexican government actions reducing foreign ownership of specific foreign investment brought considerable industrial production and distribution into government ownership long before the 1973 law. Mexico opened to foreign investment with few restrictions during the *Porfiriato*, the 1876–1911 reign of Porfirio Díaz. But the state assumed a more restrictive role with the new 1917 Constitution, which followed the revolutionary turmoil begun in 1910. It soon became apparent that the state would begin to intervene in many areas of established foreign investment. After an unsuccessful attempt by Mexico to participate in the foreign owned petroleum industry in 1925, a labor dispute led to the total nationalization of the industry in 1938, reducing in the minds of many Mexicans the apparent conflict with Article 27 of the Mexican Constitution. The 1938 change decreed that all natural resources were owned by the nation. Two years later, the government severely limited foreign participation in the communications sector.

A 1944 Emergency Decree was the first broad attempt to regulate foreign investment, and limited certain investments to joint ventures. The joint venture concept was extended by a Mixed Ministerial Commission established in 1947, although it was of limited effectiveness. The 1950s saw the introduction of further limited control of specific industries, and electric power was nationalized in

1960. Mining became subject to a 1961 Act, but the next dozen years were relatively free of significant changes.

A strict 1972 Law for the Registration of the Transfer of Technology and the Use and Exploitation of Patents and Marks,[5] forewarned the coming restrictiveness toward foreign investment. The 1973 Law to Promote Mexican Investment and Regulate Foreign Investment,[6] to some degree pulled together the policies of encouraging but limiting foreign investment that had been introduced during the previous several decades, and were clearly part of the Echeverrían administration policy that began in 1970. The 1973 law classified investments, limiting some to state ownership, some to private ownership exclusively by Mexican nations, and some where minority foreign participation would be allowed. The law did not apply retroactively, but if a company expanded into new lines of products or new locations, it was expected to Mexicanize, meaning to sell majority ownership to Mexicans. But escape provisions and the operational code in Mexico (the way things really work), resulted in few existing companies converting to Mexican majority ownership. What the laws did accomplish was to significantly curtail new foreign investment. A new institution, the National Commission on Foreign Investment, assumed substantial discretionary power to carry out the new rules.

What President Echeverría started, his successor, José López Portillo, continued when he entered office in 1976. His final year in office, 1982, saw first, the amendment of the 1972 Transfer of Technology Law, retaining its restrictiveness and extending its scope, and second, the nationalization of the banking industry. His successor, Miguel de la Madrid, assumed control of a nation with a defaulted national debt, a plunging currency, and diminished interest of foreign investors. Realizing that Mexico must change its policies, de la Madrid issued investment regulations in 1984 that partly relaxed the restrictiveness of the 1970s. Further regulations were issued in the following years, and in 1989, the first year of Carlos Salinas de Gortari's presidency, new regulations were issued that were so inconsistent with the clear philosophy of the restrictive 1973 law that their constitutionality was questioned. The direction was turned: Mexico's ascension into the stratosphere of developing-nation restrictiveness toward foreign investment had reached its apogee in 1982, and was coming back to earth. Foreign investment was returning. It was further encouraged by Mexico's admission into the GATT in 1984, after years of internal debate. The 1993 re-

[5] See Diario Oficial, Dec. 30, 1972.

[6] Diario Oficial, Mar. 9, 1973.

placement of the 1973 Investment Law, twenty years after its introduction, ended an unsettling era of Mexican foreign-investment policy.

This 1993 Investment Act[7] was a highlight of the Salinas administration, an encouragement to the many investors who had made commitments to Mexico during his administration, and a stepping stone to participation in the NAFTA the following year. The 1993 law improved access to investment in Mexico, containing investment attracting provisions absent from the earlier law. Formally abandoned was the mandatory joint venture focus, although it was never successful. But some significant restrictions remained, including control over natural resources, reservation of some areas of investment for Mexican nationals, and retention of remnants of the Calvo doctrine that attempted to limit a foreign investor's use of its own nation to pursue diplomatic efforts in the event of an investment conflict with Mexico. But the law nevertheless was a huge reversal of the policies of the 1970s, and it both established a more efficient National Registry of Foreign Investment and allowed proposals to be assumed to have been approved if they were not acted upon within the established time-frame. Regulations adopted in 1999 were consistent with both the 1993 law and its investment-encouraging philosophy. As the new century began, Mexico was not yet as open to foreign investment as were Canada and the United States, but it had established a sufficiently respectful base from which to participate in the NAFTA foreign investment framework. It was quite a remarkable transformation and a credit to several of Mexico's leaders.[8]

Not much has changed in Mexico in this new century with regard to its legal framework for foreign investment. However, in 2012 Mexico enacted a resolution that makes it even easier to establish agencies and subsidiaries of foreign businesses.[9]

---

7 See Diario Oficial, Dec. 27, 1993.

8 See generally Matt Roland, Overview of Foreign Direct Investment in Mexico, www.ventanaonlinemagazin.com, at 26, Jan. 17, 2013, Alejandro Hazera, The Changing Philosophy of Mexican Foreign Investment Laws. www.mattrinmexico.blogspot.com; Jorge A. Vargas, Mexico's Foreign Investment Act of 1993, Mexican Law (J. Vargas ed. 1998); Ewell E. Murphy Jr., Access and Protection for Foreign Investment in Mexico under Mexico's New Foreign Investment Law and the North American Free Trade Agreement, 10 ICSID Rev. Foreign Investment L.J. 54 (1998).

9 The Resolution establishes criteria for the application of Article 17 of the 1993 foreign investment law.

§ 27.3 Mexican and Canadian Foreign Investment Review Procedures

If foreign investment is allowed under certain conditions, there must be some entity assigned the decisional role in accepting or rejecting proposals. Quite obviously where foreign investment is totally prohibited, no such review entity is necessary. Consequently, as nations which prohibited investment began to open to limited foreign investment, an entity was created to review proposed foreign investment. Investment screening agencies were granted, or over time assumed, very substantial power in molding the nation's foreign investment sector. This was especially true where the agency had discretion to admit otherwise prohibited foreign investment under exception clauses, whether those exceptions were contained in written law or unwritten administrative policy. Sometimes review power was given to a ministry, other times to a specialized agency.

A screening process allows a government to control foreign entry on a case-by-case basis. The written law may be quite restrictive, but the screening process may allow the entry of foreign investment deemed necessary for development. That may mean admission of investment which brings to the country advanced technology. Proposals granted permission and proposals denied permission often illustrated what the nation was willing to grant exceptions for, which could help a prospective foreign investor. But decisions of foreign investment review agencies which might disclose the reasoning process were usually not available to the public. Some of the reasons a nation might give approval to a proposed investment are discussed above as reasons a nation might grant a waiver from restrictive maximum equity percentages.

The individual analysis of proposed foreign investment by a review agency makes evaluation of potential foreign investments very flexible. This in turn makes government action more difficult to predict, but allows governments the ability to place conditions on foreign investment without a total ban.

Screening agencies are often thought to be the exclusive patrimony of developing and nonmarket economy nations. That is not the case. Essentially all nations limit foreign investment, including the most developed nations. The reasons may appear to be different, but may mask the most common reason—the protection of domestic industries. The United States has a process to review foreign investment. The European Union also has restrictions on foreign investment.

The examples of Canada and Mexico. The investment screening processes introduced by Canada and Mexico in the early 1970s departed from their earlier unrestrictive foreign investment policies. Their 1970s screening mechanisms have survived, notwithstanding the dismantling of most investment restrictions in the 1980s and the creation of the North American Free Trade Agreement.

The Foreign Investment Review Agency (FIRA), the first Canadian foreign investment screening process, arose in part from political pressures, with the ruling Liberal party looking to maintain its legislative coalition.[10] The FIRA was formed in 1973 and provided the cornerstone of an expanded effort to control foreign investment in Canada, while maintaining some of the traditional open investment attitude of previous years. A grandfather clause exempted from review existing investments as well as profits reinvested in similar businesses. The FIRA appeared to target the expansion of foreign control of Canada's economy, rather than foreign investment as a whole.[11] The overall goal remained simple: to ensure that new foreign investment would benefit Canada.

The Investment Canada Act of 1985 replaced the Foreign Investment Review Agency with Investment Canada, a new agency "to advise and assist" the Minister in reviewing investment and more generally in administering the Act. What was to be reviewed was considerable less encompassing than under the earlier FIRA.

The Canada–United States Free Trade Agreement of 1989 included a full chapter on investment,[12] which further opened Canada for U.S. investment under the principal of national treatment. The Agreement allowed Canada to continue to review the acquisition of control of Canadian businesses, but included within the scope of such review far fewer businesses. Canada's participation in the NAFTA brings additional investment rules into force. It incorporates the national treatment principal. The review process established under the Investment Canada Act remains in place, with specific reference in the NAFTA that decisions of Canada in reviewing acquisitions are not subject to Chapter 11 or Chapter 20 dispute

---

10 Thomas M. Franck & K. Scott Gudgeon, Canada's Foreign Investment Control Experiment: the Law, the Context and the Practice, 50 N.Y.U.L.Rev. 76, 111 (1975).

11 FIRA § 2(1) (describing the purpose of the Act, to ensure that acquisition of Canadian enterprises by those not already carrying on business in Canada, or those whose new businesses in Canada would be unrelated to the businesses they already have, would continue only if the investment would be likely to significantly benefit Canada).

12 CFTA, chapter 15.

resolution panels or procedures.[13] The Canadian policy thus has been to retain a modest measure of reviewing authority of only the largest acquisitions.

The since-repealed Mexican 1973 Investment Law also created a screening agency, the National Commission on Foreign Investment.[14] The Commission was granted considerable review power over approving new foreign investment, including exemptions from joint venture mandates, acquisitions, and expansion of existing investment. The Investment Law allowed quite flexible administration, but it was unclear at the outset whether that flexibility would serve the government's or foreign investor's goals. The law imposed fines and prison terms for using Mexican nominees to subvert the requirements. The Mexican law included an investment limitation not present in the Canadian regime—existing enterprises could not expand in similar businesses without agency review, because *foreign controlled* Mexican firms were considered foreign investors. The result of both the Canadian FIRA and Mexican FIL acts was similar: the imposition of entry conditions upon foreign investors.

The 1989 Regulations to the 1973 Mexican Investment Law changed the screening process in some key respects, but not the screening entity. The Regulations, designed to increase foreign investment, waived Commission approval for investments that met certain conditions. While the screening process did become more streamlined, performance requirements did not vanish. The 1993 Investment Law, that replaced both the 1973 law and the 1989 regulations, retained the Commission as a review agency, but with review authority closer to review procedures in the Regulations than to procedures in the earlier restrictive law.

Mexico's participation in the NAFTA means the applicability of the same Chapter 11 investment rules as for Canada. The difference is that while Canada has retained the review process developed under the Investment Canada Act, Mexico specifically is allowed to retain review by the Mexican National Commission on Foreign Investment, with such review of acquisitions not subject to the Chapter 11 or Chapter 20 dispute resolution panels and procedures.[15] For comparison, the United States reserved no process of review of acquisitions in the NAFTA, but it is certain that review under the amended U.S. Exon–Florio law will continue.

[13] NAFTA chapter 11, Annex 1138.2.

[14] Mexican 1973 Investment Law, chapter III, art. 11.

[15] NAFTA chapter 11, Annex 1138.2.

The trend to reduce the restrictiveness of foreign investment laws has led to a reduction of the role of a review agency or commission, if not an abolition of the agency itself. That is true not only of Canada and Mexico. India, for example, also streamlined its foreign investment approval scheme during the mid–1980s.[16] But even the much more liberal written laws of India in the 1990s continue to retain the use of review agencies, even though they may not have as much authority to restrict foreign investment as in previous decades.[17]

The process of review by foreign investment review agencies usually includes the application of specific guidelines, but nevertheless allowing considerable discretion in the evaluation of the investment. Since foreign investment has to benefit the host nation for approval, the review process necessarily requires an evaluation of what constitutes a benefit. The process usually requires an application filed with the review agency with approval in the form of permission or a kind of license. While the agency granting permission or issuing licenses may have considerable discretion, some nations have formal development plans (usually a five- or ten-year plan) with which the reviewing agency must comply in granting permission.[18] The review process usually includes scrutiny regarding the proposed investment's benefits to the nation. It is likely to consider some of the following:

1. Effect on the economic development of the nation;

2. Degree of participation of host-nation citizens in the business;

3. Location of the new business;

4. Effect on competition in the industry;

5. Effect on productivity, efficiency, technological development, and product innovation;

6. Effect on balance of payments, which may mean amount of exports generated by the new business;

---

16 Note, Foreign Investment in India, 26 Colum.J.Transnat'l L. 609, 630 (1988).

17 See Indian Foreign Exchange Regulation Act of 1973. See also 1992 Bus. Int'l 92 (Mar. 92). Another example in Africa is the 1990 Namibia Foreign Investment Act, which established an Investment Centre in the Ministry of Trade and Industry to administer the Act. 31 Int'l Leg.Mat. 205 (1992).

18 While nonmarket economies are often most associated with such plans, such market economy nations as Mexico and India have used plans. Knowledge of these plans is important; they may disclose sectors in which a nation is especially interested in developing, and which may be the beneficiary of incentives.

7. Ability of the nation to increase its role in the world market;

8. Creation of new training and job opportunities;

9. Establishment of research and development facilities;

10. Impact on culture; and

11. Use of external capital sources for borrowing.

Many of these points may have to be addressed in seeking approval of a new investment or acquisition. It means a lengthy process in many cases, and an expensive one. It is never clear how much weight will be given any one of the different factors. The weight may change according to circumstances within the nation. For example, if the nation has a favorable trade balance and substantial hard currency, little weight is likely to be given to whether exports exceed imports and raise hard currency. How the process proceeds in two nations, Canada and Mexico, is discussed immediately below as an example.

The decision of the review agency may be final, or it may be appealable to another agency within the government or to the courts. But the process of review is largely a factual determination, and the foreign investor is advised to place great emphasis on establishing the benefit of the proposed investment to the host nation.

Canadian review process. The factors that the Canadian Foreign Investment Review Agency uses in evaluating whether new investment will "significantly benefit" Canada are included in the Investment Canada Act and reflect the TRIMs described above, and some of the various separate criteria noted immediately above. These factors include the effects on economic activity, participation by Canadians, productivity, efficiency, innovation, technological development, competition, culture, and role in world markets.[19] A "net benefit" test is usually applied. The review of cultural investments was shifted to Canadian Heritage in the late 1990s.

Most new foreign investment in Canada is not reviewed,[20] review being limited to *acquisitions*.[21] The Investment Canada Act

[19] Investment Canada Act of 1985, art. 20.

[20] Canada has reserved the right to review investment in certain stipulated cultural industries. See ICA arts. 14.1(9), 15. This right is retained in the NAFTA.

[21] The earlier Canadian Foreign Investment Review Act did provide for a review of new investment, with complex provisions regarding investor eligibility and control. Under the Investment Canada Act, new investment is subject only to notification procedures. Part III, Arts. 11–13.

raised the minimum threshold level of dollars for a reviewable acquisition, shortened the time for government review, and streamlined the process and standards for review. The ICA also included a series of stages where acquisitions by Americans (principally U.S. nationals) would not require review if they exceeded certain levels.[22]

Mexican review process. The factors that the Mexican National Commission of Foreign Investment (Commission) will consider in allowing exceptions to the 49 percent maximum for foreign equity, reflect, as in Canada, the four trade related investment measures (TRIMs) and trade related performance requirements (TRPRs). The Commission also issues general resolutions of interpretation and application. The procedure requires the Commission to act within 45 business days, or the application is automatically approved.

§ 27.4 U.S. Regulation of Foreign Investment

The Exon–Florio amendment to the Defense Production Act of 1950, passed as part of the Omnibus Trade and Competitiveness Act of 1988,[23] granted the President the authority to investigate and suspend or prohibit transactions leading to the control of American firms by foreign persons, based on national-security concerns.[24] Exon–Florio is the only U.S. law that broadly regulates foreign investment. Furthermore, its application may arise throughout the investment process.

Although a trade regulation provision based upon national security such as Exon–Florio may pose a potential for mischief against foreign investors by the government, foreign acquisitions of U.S. companies were thought at the inception of Exon–Florio not likely to be obstructed. History has verified this prediction, with perhaps one or two notable exceptions.

There are two basic problems that Exon–Florio presents to foreign investors. The first is that Exon–Florio issues may arise

---

[22] The stages progressed from review for any acquisition above $25 million at the time of enactment, to only those above $150 million after 1992. Art. 14.1. In 2008 the threshold for investments from WTO countries had been increased to Can$295 million. For non-WTO and certain industries, such as culture, transportation, and financial services, there is a low Can$5million threshold.

[23] 50 U.S.C.A.App. § 2170; See also 31 C.F.R. § 800.101.

[24] See generally Jose Alvarez, Political Protectionism and United States International Investment Obligations in Conflict: The Hazards of Exon–Florio, 30 Va.J.Int'l. 1 (1989).

The main point of contact in the United States for inquires about the Exon–Florio law is the Committee on Foreign Investment in the United States (CFIUS), in the Office of International Investment, Department of the Treasury. See generally <www.treas.gov/>.

throughout the life of the investment. Foreign acquisitions that could affect national security must be reported to CFIUS at the outset to allow the government to make a determination; otherwise, the government may be prompted to investigate on its own and possibly order divestment. The result could be that foreign investors have acquired property without very clear title.[25]

The second problem is the uncertainty about the definition of national security under Exon–Florio. The Exon–Florio Regulations offer few bright-line tests. That confirms CFIUS, the President's designated center of investigation, as the omnipotent reviewer of foreign acquisitions. Exon–Florio initially earned the nickname "Lawyers Full Employment Act" because of the potentially broad scope of national security.[26] CFIUS has interpreted national security on a case-by-case basis, leaving other companies, even in similar industries, somewhat baffled about the criteria used to evaluate the transaction. But Exon–Florio does include a list of factors to be considered in the evaluation of a transaction's national security implications.[27] There nevertheless remains concern about the potential abuse of the broad language and consequent wide scope of Exon–Florio's national security language.

§ 27.5 History of CFIUS and Evolution of Exon–Florio to the Foreign Investment and National Security Act (FINSA)

Before the enactment of Exon–Florio, when the concern for widespread Arab buyouts of American businesses in the 1970s was perceived as a threat to national security, the U.S. executive, seeking a compromise with the Congress, agreed to create the Committee on Foreign Investment in the United States (CFIUS) as an interagency, interdepartmental group to investigate inward foreign direct investment and recommend policy. CFIUS, which would have no real screening or review power, would serve at the President's discretion; for example, President Carter's administration investigated only one transaction.

During President Reagan's second term, the concern turned more toward the increasing trade deficit and the "Japanese threat." There were large inflows of foreign investment in the 1980s, alt-

[25] See Group Sees Problems with Treasury's Draft Foreign Acquisition Regulations, 57 Antitrust & Trade Reg.Rep. (BNA) No. 1425, at 95 (July 20, 1989).

[26] Soon after the law was passed, CFIUS reportedly received notice of a planned acquisition of swimming pool companies. See Martin Tolchin & Susan J. Tolchin, Selling Our Security: The Erosion of America's Assets 51 (1992).

[27] See 50 U.S.C.A.App. § 2170(f)(4).

hough they were not limited to Japanese investors. The administration began to intervene in these inflows more frequently, especially when they constituted planned acquisitions of U.S. companies. The policy of open versus controlled investment seemed most confused when the Japanese electronics conglomerate Fujitsu sought to acquire an 80 percent share in Fairchild Semiconductor.[28] Fairchild had openly solicited the bid. Even though the French concern Schlumberger already owned Fairchild, the Commerce, Defense, and Justice departments all joined to oppose the proposed acquisition. The Department of Justice was concerned with antitrust implications,[29] while the departments of Commerce and Defense appeared to object primarily in order to force Japanese markets to open more. Because of the extensive concern Fujitsu withdrew its proposed acquisition, even though CFIUS at the time lacked the power to block the sale.

By 1988, Congress seemed intent on creating some mechanism to review proposed foreign investment in the United States. The determination was increased when the proposed foreign purchase of Phoenix Steel was announced. Phoenix Steel was a producer of many items procured by the Department of Defense. The purchaser, represented by a Hong Kong agent, was to obtain financing for the acquisition from the People's Republic of China.[30] CFIUS had no authority to block the sale, but it nevertheless began an investigation because many of Phoenix's products were subject to export controls. Representative Florio of New Jersey proposed foreign-investment control legislation that would allow the President to block the sale of a U.S. owned company to any entity with financing by a potential enemy, to ensure that the U.S. firm's controlled technology would not be acquired by the foreign nation. The administration accepted the Exon–Florio proposal as a compromise because competing bills would have imposed even greater reporting and disclosure requirements on foreign investors, which the administration opposed. One competing proposal required any foreign investor acquiring a five percent or greater interest to report to the Department of Commerce certain information which would become available to the public.

---

[28] The policy issues of foreign investment, such as whether it benefits or harms the United States, should controls be extended beyond national security, etc., have never been addressed thoroughly. Exon–Florio's vague language does not help resolve these questions.

[29] See Division is Probing Effects of Merger of California, Japanese Computer Firms, 51 Antitrust & Trade Reg.Rep. (BNA) No. 1282, 803 (Nov. 27, 1986).

[30] See Bid for U.S. Steel Mill by Company Backed by P.R.C. Raises Export Control Questions, 5 Int'l Trade Rep. (BNA) 239 (Feb. 24, 1988).

After the enactment of Exon–Florio in 1988, several amendments were proposed that would have increased the regulation of foreign investment. These proposals were partly due to the belief that Treasury was attempting to weaken the law through the adoption of lenient regulations.[31] Consequently, some of the proposed amendments would have replaced Treasury as the chair of CFIUS with either the department of Commerce or Defense.[32] Nevertheless, the amendments that were passed in 1992 did not alter CFIUS's structure but did modify when and how CFIUS must investigate.[33]

Significant changes to Exon–Florio were made in 2007, with the adoption of the Foreign Investment and National Security Act (FINSA), amending the Defense Production Act within which Exon–Florio is buried. The Dubai World Ports 2006 bid to operate several U.S. ports received CFIUS approval. It also received front-page news coverage. Congress immediately addressed the issue and FINSA was the result. The Dubai Ports proposal was dropped.

FINSA was principally intended to amend Exon-Florio to reform the process by which CFIUS undertakes national security reviews of proposed foreign acquisitions of U.S. businesses, with special scrutiny of acquisitions by foreign state-owned corporations. FINSA made other important changes, including identifying critical infrastructure that is to be reviewed, codifiying modifications to CFIUS, emphasizing the importance of national security, and expanding the number of risk factors taken into consideration in CFIUS reviews.

§ 27.6 When and How CFIUS Reviews Proposed Foreign Investment under Exon–Florio

Exon–Florio authorizes the President or President's designee to investigate the national security impact of "mergers, acquisitions, and takeovers" by or with foreign persons that could result in con-

---

[31] See Treasury Official Concedes Aim to Weaken Rules for Exon–Florio Takeover Amendment, 55 Antitrust & Trade Reg. Rep. (BNA) No. 1395, at 1013 (Dec. 15, 1988).

[32] See Bill Offered to Strengthen Law Governing Foreign Acquisitions, 8 Int'l Trade Rep. (BNA) 947 (June 19, 1991).

[33] The 1992 Byrd Amendment included a non-binding resolution that to CFIUS membership should be added the Director of the Office of Science and Technology Policy and the Assistant to the President for National Security. Congress wanted more representation which would be likely to be concerned with foreign acquisitions and take a harder line on CFIUS than would other departmental heads. In response to this resolution, Executive Order 12860 was issued expanding CFIUS' membership to add the two aforementioned persons and also the Assistant to the President for Economic Policy, bringing the membership to eleven.

trol by foreign persons.[34] Most investigations are at the discretion of CFIUS after receipt of written notification as prescribed by the regulations.[35] CFIUS has 30 days after notification to decide whether or not to investigate,[36] and 45 days after that to investigate and make a recommendation to the President. The President next has 15 days to either (1) suspend or prohibit the acquisition, merger, or takeover, or (2) seek divestiture for an already completed transaction.[37] He may direct the Attorney General to seek appropriate relief in U.S. district courts to enforce his decision.

The President must make two findings in order to exercise his authority. First, he must believe that there is "credible evidence" that the foreign interest would exercise "control" which might threaten "national security." Second, he must believe that other provisions of law, aside from the International Emergency Economic Powers Act, provide inadequate authority to safeguard national security. Although these two findings remain prerequisites to presidential action, they are not subject to judicial review under the statute.

Although considerable debate occurred, "national security" remains undefined in either the law or regulations. But the Exon–Florio provisions suggest that the President consider several factors

[34] See 50 U.S.C.A. App. § 2170(a); 53 Fed.Reg. 43,999 (1988) (President naming Secretary of Treasury as lead investigator and head of CFIUS); 31 C.F.R. § 800.203 (1992) (defining "Committee" and "Chairman of the Committee" as CFIUS and the Secretary of the Treasury); Executive Order No. 11858, 40 Fed.Reg. 20,263, 3 C.F.R. 1971–1975 Comp., 990 as amended, reprinted in 15 U.S.C.A. § 78b note (establishing CFIUS, which includes Treasury, State, Defense, Commerce and Justice Departments, the U.S. Trade Representative, and other executive chairs); 31 C.F.R. §§ 800.202—800.221 (definitions unique to Exon–Florio).

[35] See 31 C.F.R. § 800.401 (establishing procedures for notice to CFIUS; providing for notification by individual members of the Committee, where the member has reason to believe national security to be adversely affected; and setting a three-year time limit for such self-starting notice); 31 C.F.R. § 800.402 (describing the information that CFIUS requires for voluntary notices). But see 50 U.S.C.A. App. § 2170(b) (requiring mandatory investigations when an entity seeking control in a merger, takeover, or acquisition is itself controlled or acting on behalf of a foreign government).

[36] The investigation is mandatory where a foreign government controlled entity or agent is involved. This was part of the 1992 Byrd Amendment resulting from the Thomson/LTV case discussed below.

[37] Notice may be submitted and CFIUS review commenced at any time while the transaction is pending or after it is completed. But there is a three-year limitation after the transaction is completed, unless the CFIUS chairman, consulting with other members, requests an investigation. To avoid the possibility of having a completed transaction questioned, companies sometimes submit a voluntary notice to commence review before completing the transaction. Any transaction which has been the subject of CFIUS review or investigation is not subject to later Presidential action. Thus, even when there seems to be little apparent impact on national security, a review request might be useful.

in evaluating national security concerns. These are mainly directed to the capacity of domestic industry to meet national defense requirements in view of the proposed takeover. Amendments to Exon–Florio have added as factors for presidential consideration both the potential for proliferation of missiles and nuclear and biological weapons, as well as the potential effect of the transaction on U.S. leadership in technology that affects national security.

Any information filed with CFIUS is largely confidential, although some releases of information may be made to authorized members of Congress. Critics have charged that CFIUS has abused the confidentiality provisions in some cases, and also has left important players out of the investigation process until after CFIUS has made its decisions.[38] The confidentiality provision has made official reports of cases impossible but has protected both the interests of foreign investors and national security. The manner in which CFIUS and the President have applied the law, and the criticism generated from such application, have focused on the proper meaning of three terms—"mergers, acquisitions, and takeovers," "control", and "national security." The statute and regulations confine the application of the Exon–Florio law to "mergers, acquisitions, and takeovers" of U.S. businesses leading to foreign control. Any such transaction concluded on or after the 1988 effective date of Exon–Florio is subject to review.

The regulations take into account devices created to avoid Exon–Florio review, such as foreign controlled corporations seeking to purchase U.S. businesses using American agents supposedly acting independently. As Treasury drafted the regulations, Rep. Florio and other commentators wondered about the applicability of the law toward other types of transactions, such as proxy solicitations which might lead to foreign control, foreign bank financing which might lead to control by default, joint ventures, and "greenfield" investments.[39] The regulations address most of those issues, although they include few "bright-line" tests.

Exon–Florio does not apply to portfolio investments, such as investments where the foreigner obtains ten percent or less of voting securities solely for investment purposes; investments where the foreign buyer has the same parent as the target; or other investments where the foreign investor does not acquire managerial control of a U.S. business. Joint ventures, originally thought to be

---

38 See Martin Tolchin & Susan J. Tolchin, Selling Our Security: The Erosion of America's Assets 61 (1992).

39 See Treasury Proposes Rules on Foreign Mergers, Acquisitions, and Takeovers, 57 Antitrust & Trade Reg. Rep. (BNA) No. 1424, at 46 (July 13, 1989).

exempt from Exon–Florio review, are included. Foreign persons soliciting proxies in order to obtain control are also covered. The regulations do not subject lending transactions by foreign persons to Exon–Florio review, unless the lender assumes some degree of control, at either the time that the loan is made or when default appears imminent.

As the above comments suggest, what *control* would be exercised by the foreign person is the key to determining whether a transaction is within the scope of Exon–Florio. The regulations define "control" without limitation on voting percentages or majority ownership, but as "the power, direct or indirect, whether or not exercised . . . to determine, direct, take, reach or cause decisions" in a series of key areas. These areas include the transfer (sale, lease, mortgage or pledge) of assets, the dissolution of the business, the closing or relocation of research and development facilities, terminating or not fulfilling the business contracts, and amending the Articles of Incorporation of the business with regard to any of the aforementioned matters.[40] In addition, when examining control, if more than one foreign person is involved, CFIUS may consider the possibility of their acting in concert. However, an *unrelated* group of foreign investors holding a majority of shares in a U.S. company will not be assumed to control that company.

In contrast with the attempt to define "control," Exon–Florio and its associated regulations do not define "national security." Many of the public comments during Treasury's drafting of the regulations urged a specific definition, but the statute and regulations consciously leave the determination of a national security concern to the President's discretion.[41] Few involved in regulating foreign investment outside the administration were satisfied with that result. Some in Congress thought that the White House interpreted "national security" under Exon–Florio too narrowly, equating it only with military security.[42] The General Accounting Office (GAO) criticized CFIUS for not determining if anti-competitive behavior by foreign firms might jeopardize national security. A former Attorney General and Secretary of Defense, speaking for a segment of the foreign investment regulatory community, criticized the rules lack

---

[40] The Industrial Security Regulations, allowing the DOD to block an acquisition where there will be access to classified information, include a much more extensive definition of "foreign ownership, control or influence."

[41] See H.R. Conf. Rep. No. 576, 100th Cong. (1988). See also Set of Principles on S & T Cooperation Would Be Valuable. NEC Official Says, 10 Int'l Trade Rep. (BNA) 663 (Apr. 21, 1993) (a White House official hinting that a definition of "national security" may be forthcoming).

[42] See Narrow Interpretation of Statute Hobbles Exon–Florio Reviews, Lawyers Told, 9 Int'l Trade Rep. (BNA) 325 (Feb. 19, 1992).

of national -security criteria because more mergers and acquisitions may fall under review than Congress intended.[43] Nevertheless, administration officials stressed the need for "national security" to have a broad scope and not be confined to particular industries, and be particularly applicable should the target company provide products or technologies essential to the U.S. defense industrial base.[44]

§ 27.7 Application of Exon–Florio: Cases

The application of Exon–Florio in real situations resolves some of the apparent ambiguity with regard to the meaning of "national security" and the other important statutory and regulatory terms. By 1992, fifteen years before the FINSA amendments and well before China became the major focus of the law, CFIUS had reviewed 650 proposed acquisitions. Twelve detailed investigations led to two withdrawals, but only one presidential order of divestment. Because of CFIUS' confidentiality requirements, no official reports or summaries of its investigations under Exon–Florio exist for lawyers or investors to consult. Instead, secondary sources must be used to draw meanings given to the statute and regulations. The cases when the President chose not to act when the parties themselves withdrew and the one case when the President actually ordered divestment present some general patterns of what foreign investors may expect from a CFIUS investigation under Exon–Florio.

Huels AG of Germany/Monsanto. The Department of Defense prompted one of the first investigations under Exon–Florio, because the U.S. semiconductor research consortium that the DOD sponsors, SEMATECH, wanted guaranteed access to silicon wafers manufactured by Monsanto Electronic Materials Co., which was about to be sold to Huels AG, a German company. Although CFIUS recommended that the President allow the transaction to go forward, notwithstanding the objections of 29 congressmen, CFIUS obtained as part of its approval written assurances that SEMATECH would retain access and no technology would transfer for five years.[45] There appeared to be a quid pro quo that CFIUS would not disapprove the takeover in return for Huels' assurances, creating a per-

---

[43] See Seminar Probes Impact of Investment by Japanese Firms in the U.S. Economy (Elliot Richardson quoted), 57 Antitrust & Trade Reg. Rep. (BNA) No. 1426, at 137 (July 27, 1989).

[44] See Foreign Acquisitions and National Security: Hearing Before House Subcom. on Commerce, Consumer Protection, and Competitiveness of the Comm. on Energy and Commerce, 101st Cong. (1990) (statements of assistant secretaries in Treasury and Commerce).

[45] See Bush Clears Sale of U.S. Manufacturer of Silicon Wafers to German Corporation, 56 Antitrust & Trade Reg.Rep. (BNA) No. 1402 at 232 (Feb. 9, 1989) (Rep. Florio observing that Huel's parent's owners could not be identified).

formance requirement for foreign investment. CFIUS apparently imposed a similar requirement on Matra SA of France when it sought to purchase Fairchild industries, requiring a restructured export control system as a condition for CFIUS approval. Foreign investors therefore may have to agree to government-imposed conditions on their transactions, with CFIUS approval received only after an Exon–Florio investigation is conducted as a bargaining tool.

British Tire & Rubber (UK)/Norton. The administration is not alone in using Exon–Florio as a bargaining tool. U.S. companies which are targets of hostile takeovers by foreign investors have used Exon–Florio as one method to oppose proposed takeovers.[46] Within two months of passage of the law, companies began to invoke Exon–Florio to delay or discourage takeovers.[47] This led many to conclude that the Exon–Florio process was easily abused. Critics argued that existing DOD regulations could handle true national-security concerns, and that Exon–Florio only added a political element to the ability of foreign investors to acquire U.S. companies.

A good example of an American firm using political pressure on a foreign buyer through Exon–Florio and other mechanisms is the attempted purchase of the Norton Company of Worcester, Mass., by British Tire and Rubber, PLC (BTR). Norton manufactured ceramic ball bearings used in the space shuttle. More than 200 congressmen urged an investigation, including Senator Kerry of Massachusetts, who noted Norton's role in the Massachusetts economy as justification for an investigation in addition to national security reasons. The Massachusetts state legislature soon enacted a law depriving BTR of control should the purchase succeed, leading BTR to pull out, and a French buyer to make a friendly offer at a much higher price. No security concerns were raised when the friendly French buyer appeared offering a better price, even though Norton had earlier argued that BTR planned to dismember Norton and reduce its research and development budgets to the detriment of national security.[48] This led many to conclude that the Exon–Florio process was easily abused. Critics argued that existing DOD regulations could handle true national security concerns, and that Exon–Florio only added a political element to the ability of foreign investors to acquire U.S. companies.

---

[46] See Jonathan A. Knee, Limiting Abuse of Exon–Florio by Takeover Targets, 23 Geo.Wash.J.Int'l L. & Econ. 475 (1989).

[47] See New Omnibus Trade Law May Provide Weapon Against Foreign Takeover Bids, 55 Antitrust & Trade Reg.Rep. (BNA) No. 1390, at 853 (Nov. 10, 1988).

[48] See John Burgess, Norton's Defense: The British Are Bad

China Nat'l Aero Tech./NAMCO. While some firms use a CFIUS investigation to scare away hostile foreign investors, the one transaction that the President decided to reject had already been finalized at the time of the order.[49] The order forced the foreign entity to divest. The target was MAMCO Manufacturing, Inc., a U.S. company in Seattle that manufactured metal parts for commercial aircraft made by Boeing. MAMCO mainly supplied Boeing, and although some of its products were subject to export controls, MAMCO had no contracts involving classified information. The buyer was China National Aero–Technology Import and Export Corp. (CATIC), owned by the People's Republic of China. During the investigation, it appeared that CATIC had previously violated export control laws concerning aircraft engines purchased from General Electric. But concerns about CATIC went beyond export control problems with China. Administration sources revealed that CATIC had been trying to obtain technology to build jet fighters capable of refueling during flight. In addition, there were concerns by the administration and Congress that the Chinese government used CATIC as a base for covert operations in the United States.

The Executive Order directing CATIC to divest itself of MAMCO contained none of the above concerns or information, but simply stated that the two requirements of Exon–Florio had been satisfied: There existed credible evidence of a threat to national security, and no other provision of law could protect the national security interest. Considering the relatively low level of technology involved, however, the President's action on CFIUS' unanimous recommendation to terminate the investment surprised many observers, leading some to believe that the national security concern was a pretext for other political motives. Foreign investor lobbying organizations agreed with this perception, fearing that Exon–Florio would become a foreign policy tool. But the administration stressed that the order did not constitute a change in America's general policy of openness toward investment from foreigners or reflect upon the PRC in particular. But the order seemed to be some indication that investment owned or supported by foreign governments would receive particular scrutiny under Exon–Florio.

Nakamichi/Applied Magnetics. MOST, a U.S. incorporated subsidiary of Nakamichi Corp. of Japan, agreed to purchase the Optical Products Division of U.S. Applied Magnetics Corporation. Although

[49] See President Invokes Exon–Florio, Blocks Acquisition of Aircraft Components Maker, 58 Antitrust & Trade Reg.Rep. (BNA) No. 1452, at 225 (Feb. 8, 1990); Bush Cancels China Purchase of U.S. Firm, San Francisco Chronicle, Feb. 3, 1990, at A1; Stuart Auerbach, President Tells China to Sell Seattle Firm, Wash. Post, Feb. 3, 1990, at A1

about 98 percent of OPD's sales were optical heads for computers, the products have application in some weapons systems. CFIUS reviewed the application and approved the sale one day before the inauguration of President Clinton. Congress was unaware of the ongoing review until the announced approval. But some members quickly intervened and produced evidence allegedly showing that the CFIUS review was based on misleading and incomplete information. That would allow reopening of the review process. Although much publicity followed there was no further review, but a clear warning sounded that a clearance by CFIUS may lead to public outcry if the process had remained silent until the CFIUS decision.

Thomson/LTV. By 1992, Congressional dissatisfaction with how the President and CFIUS had interpreted Exon–Florio led to proposals for new and stricter controls. The circumstances that led to the first substantive amendments to the Exon–Florio law involved foreign-government participation in a proposed acquisition, the attempted purchase of the missile division of LTV Corp. by Thomson–CSF, a conglomerate partially owned (58 percent) and financed by the French government.[50]

LTV, a defense contractor, had been operating under bankruptcy protection since 1986. Thomson made a bid for $450 million in association with an American investment bank and Northrop, the U.S. aircraft company, to buy LTV's aircraft and missile business.[51] Thomson outbid the U.S. defense contractor Martin Marietta by nearly $100 million. Martin Marietta was the buyer LTV favored because of the prospective problems Thomson would have with CFIUS.[52] To diminish concerns regarding national security, Thomson initially proposed to the DOD to structure its purchase of LTV through an agreement that would allow some control over LTV. As pressure increased, Thomson withdrew that proposal and stated that a proxy agreement would suffice, with the proxies being U.S. citizens who had no prior connection to the parties. But Thomson was unable to satisfy DOD demands to protect classified information.[53]

There was immediate adverse Congressional reaction, acknowledging that the United States and France were allies, but not-

---

50 See Foreign Investment: Thomson–CSF Bid for LTV "Watershed Event," Leading to New Controls, ABA Seminar Told, 9 Int'l Trade Rep. (BNA) 1781 (Oct. 14, 1992).

51 The bankruptcy court approved the sale.

52 Thomson filed the notice for review under Exon–Florio.

53 The DOD has separate authority under the Industrial Security Regulations to protect classified information, including the ability to block an acquisition.

ing that French interests have not always been the same as America's.[54] Administration officials were reluctant to discuss even the general policy of allowing a foreign government-owned or-controlled company to purchase a U.S. defense contractor while the investigation was in process. Because the DOD apparently did not at first intend to object to the sale, it was criticized for failing to consider the questionable record of Thomson and the French government in exporting weapons to countries with which the United States did not have good relations, such as Iran, Libya, and Iraq, and also for ignoring a Defense Intelligence Agency warning of extensive technology leakage. The lesson is that even "friendly" nations may have skeletons in the closet which the DOD and other critics of a proposed investment will quickly make public. France's military policy, which is made independently of NATO's, did not help.

Other commentators remained equally critical of Thomson's proposal suggesting that although an open-door policy makes sense for *private* foreign investors, that policy should be reexamined where foreign *governments* are involved, especially in this case, where LTV's products could not be replaced by another domestic firm. Exon–Florio (as it then existed) did not seem an appropriate vehicle to carry out a policy intended to prevent foreign government ownership of defense contractors.

It became apparent during the controversy over LTV that the CFIUS was almost certain to recommend that the President block the transaction. Consequently, Thomson first withdraw its bid to restructure the deal and ultimately withdrew completely, leading to a suit by LTV for breach of contract.[55] Martin Marietta soon submitted a higher bid, justified because it would not have to compete with the inexhaustible resources of a government-assisted competitor.

During and following the Thomson–LTV attempted merger, Congress, not the President and CFIUS, assumed the lead role. Congress led the effort to gain more information on Thomson, and as a result of its hearings to reconsider the policy of open direct investment involving foreign governments, Thomson's bid was withdrawn. Because of the perception that the administration took up the case only with prompting by Congress, amendments to Exon–Florio soon appeared on Capitol Hill.

---

[54] See French Government Ownership of Thomson Should Bar LTV Acquisition, Panel Told, 9 Int'l Trade Rep. (BNA) 1017 (June 10, 1992). The Senate even passed a non-binding resolution (vote of 93–4) finding the proposed acquisition to be harmful to national security.

[55] See LTV Sues Thomson–CSF for Failure To Pay $20 million After Bid Withdrawal, 9 Int'l Trade Rep. (BNA) 1395 (Aug. 12, 1992).

The committee working on what would become the Byrd Amendment to Exon–Florio identified three factors of greatest concern in the attempted merger. First, LTV was a substantial contractor with the DOD and NASA, and was the largest contractor ever for sale to a foreign firm. Second, as much as 75 percent of the work LTV did for the DOD required access to highly classified information that is generally prohibited for foreign nationals or representatives of foreign interests. Third, the French government owned 58 percent of Thomson's stock.[56] Of considerable concern to the committee was that government ownership would introduce into the company's decision-making process the foreign government's political and diplomatic interests, which may contrast with those of the United States.

Two major amendments to Exon–Florio are directly attributable to the experience of the failed Thomson purchase of LTV. When Congress assumed the lead in that investigation, the President appeared to be slow to react to the attempted takeover involving a foreign government. The first change sought by Congress was to remove any presidential and CFIUS reticence in carrying out their responsibilities under Exon–Florio. The Byrd Amendment *requires* the President or his designee to investigate if the purchasing foreigner is "controlled by or acting on behalf of a foreign government." The "acting on behalf" language is not without some ambiguity. It remains unclear whether this would include a lesser form of control as defined in the regulations (issued before the Byrd Amendment), consequently increasing Exon–Florio's coverage when a foreign government is involved. But the Byrd Amendment does add a new concept of "effective control" by a foreign government, which may increase the ambiguity of the meaning of "control by a foreign government."

The second important amendment forbids the sale of some U.S. companies to certain foreign investors, principally those involved with foreign governments. In a separate section of Exon–Florio, entities controlled by a foreign government are prohibited from acquiring certain department of Energy or Defense contractors. Such contractors may not be acquired by entities controlled by or acting on behalf of foreign governments if they work under a national security program that cannot be done without access to a "proscribed category of information." Furthermore, any firm awarded at least $500 million in prime DOD contracts or at least $500 million in prime Department of Energy contracts under national security programs

[56] See S.Rep. No. 352, 102d Cong. (1992); see also H.R. Conf. Rep. No. 966, 102d Cong. (1992).

may not be acquired. There may be an escape clause, however. Section 2170a(b) suggests that if foreign investors are patient and go through an investigation that ends without suspension or prohibition, the acquisition restraints may not apply.[57]

There is an additional amendment which requires the President to report to Congress his Exon–Florio decision, including a detailed explanation of how the decision was reached. These reports are not disclosed to the public under an exemption to the Freedom of Information Act.

The Thomson–CSF experience nearly established a process that Congress decided that it did not want followed. The earlier described proposed acquisition by CATIC, owned by the Chinese government, also resulted in a failed acquisition attempt, although due to action rather than a somewhat coerced withdrawal. Although the cases involve different national security concerns, the pattern exists that if a foreign government plays a role in a foreign investment, CFIUS, or perhaps its apparent watchdog, the Congress, will examine the proposal very carefully. Exon–Florio has proven to be a law the operation of which Congress views very carefully, ready to enter into the review of a proposed acquisition with the threat of amendments that would undo any CFIUS or presidential approval.

Subsequent to the Thomson–CSF attempted merger, other sensitive cases have been heard by CFIUS. When China or mid-East countries are involved there seems to be immediate suspicion of the intention of the proposed acquisition. Thus the Dubai Ports case, eventually ended without the proposed acquisition, but with the adoption of FINSA, and various proposals associated with the economic downturn in 2008. That included GM's proposed sale of Hummer to a Chinese firm.

More recently challenged was a proposal by one of China's richest men, Wu Jialiang, CEO of Ralls Corp., to build a wind farm in Oregon near a naval weapons training facility. CFIUS blocked the proposal and Ralls challenged the decision, leading to President Obama becoming the first president to issue an order in 22 years supporting a CFIUS ruling. Only a month earlier two other Chinese companies had investment proposals blocked. It seems likely that China, with its aggressive policy to increase foreign investment

---

[57] This section may mean either that such acquisitions are permitted only if an Exon–Florio review has been completed. And a decision made not to block, or that such acquisitions are permitted unless they are actually blocked by an Exon–Florio proceeding. As a practical matter, an Exon–Florio notice filing is most likely in such a case, and, consequently, there will be an examination by CFIUS.

throughout the world, will be the most frequent nation before CFIUS for decades to come.

§ 27.8 Defenses to Exon–Florio

If a foreign investor's proposed transaction is blocked, or if a completed transaction is ordered divested, the foreign investor may have some recourse despite a finding that the investment adversely affects national security. As noted above, the Exon–Florio law states that the President's findings with regard to national security are not subject to judicial review. But courts may find that statutes designed to protect nationals security do not preclude all judicial review on the merits.[58] The requirement in § 2170(g) that the President report his findings in detail to Congress indicates that Congress intended to oversee the President's discretion. Additionally, the Fifth Amendment, as interpreted in *Goldberg v. Kelly*,[59] recognizes due process rights in an administrative proceeding based upon a balancing test of the party's and the government's interests. If the President orders divestment, the foreign investor might claim that the consequence of such summary action is a "grievous loss" because of the President's action, not justified by an inadequate government interest cloaked in a nebulous concept of national security. Depending on the sensitivity of the national security interest, a divestment order, because of the substantial property loss, may justify more formal procedural protections than CFIUS standard procedures of investigation. There is nevertheless a mystique about national security that may lead courts to avoid opening the door to a proceeding in which the injured investor attempts to mandate that the government prove what the government will insist cannot be made the subject of inquiry for national-security reasons.

Additionally, foreign investors could challenge a divestment order issued pursuant to Exon–Florio as a taking for public use requiring just compensation, provided investors could prove a property loss. But such an argument must overcome the government's substantial public purpose in protecting national security.

Application of Exon–Florio might also produce conflicts with bilateral investment treaties (BITs) and friendship, commerce, and navigation treaties (FCNs) that the United States has concluded with other nations to promote open investment and guarantee national treatment in the United States and abroad. Foreign investment proponents have argued that the government should interpret

---

58 See Note, Proposals for Limiting Foreign Investment Risk Under the Exon–Florio Amendment, 42 Hastings L.J. 1175, 1229 (1991).

59 397 U.S. 254, 90 S.Ct. 1011, 25 L.Ed.2d 287 (1970).

national security under Exon–Florio as defined in these treaties, rather than a broader version including economic issues.[60] Under FCN treaties, however, national security usually constitutes an exception to the principal of national treatment. Foreign investors may attempt to have presidential orders under Exon–Florio reviewed by means of an interpretation of the exception that requires resolution by the International Court of Justice (ICJ). The principal obstacle, however, is that standing before the ICJ is provided only to governments, thus requiring the foreign investor's home nation to commence the proceeding.[61] By contrast, bilateral investment treaties provide procedures for resolving investment disputes through binding arbitration. But it is unclear whether their security exceptions are wholly discretionary or subject to judicial review.[62]

One further option, considering the political sensitivity of foreign investment in the United States, is to advance policy arguments to Congressional members interested in the investment. More than 100 members of Congress prompted the investigation into the proposed purchase of the Massachusetts based Norton Company by British Tire and Rubber. The case demonstrated the politicization of the review process. In addition to the usual justifications for following a generally open investment policy, as described above, foreign investors might argue that a broad interpretation of Exon–Florio would cause defense production companies needing capital to survive would be forced to dissolve in the absence of a foreign infusion through an acquisition, thus causing a loss of production.[63] But in most cases the foreign interest in the U.S. target company is matched by domestic interest, although by means of an offer for less than that offered by the foreign investor.

§ 27.9 Exon–Florio Viewed from Abroad

Foreign nations have not viewed the Exon–Florio law very favorably. The C.D. Howe Institute of Canada has noted that Canadian investors are concerned with the vague definition of "national security" and likely variations in interpretations by successive ad-

---

60 See Martin Tolchin & Susan J. Tolchin, Selling Our Security: The Erosion of America's Assets 67 (1992).

61 It is further likely that under present attitudes toward the ICJ in the United States, jurisdiction of the ICJ would not be recognized by the United States.

62 See Jose Alvarez, Political Protectionism and United States International Investment Obligations in Conflict: the Hazards of Exon–Florio, 30 Va.J.Int'l L. 1, 37 (1989). Bilateral investment treaties are discussed in chapter 25 on investment control laws.

63 See Tolchin & Tolchin, supra note 6, at 67.

ministrations.[64] The 1992 amendments were viewed in Canada as a further barrier to investment because they failed to define "defense critical technology."[65] The European Union also objects to Exon–Florio's vagueness in the definition of national security.[66]

If national security is to mean something more than national security, the law ought to be modified to express an intention to use foreign investment review as a review based on economic and/or political concerns. Most of the trading partners of the United States view Exon–Florio in its current clothes as a law used differently by successive administrations to achieve political goals in permitting foreign investment, with little real analysis of the national security implications that are purportedly the foundation of the review process.

It is fair to comment that Exon–Florio is not well regarded abroad. It has allegedly led to diminished foreign investment in U.S. defense contractors.[67] But that is, of course, intended if such investment would threaten national security. Exon–Florio seems unlikely to go away. Exon–Florio is part of the government's "discretionary" power to deal with foreign trade and investment. Once given, it is hard to retrieve. But, in focus, some 98 percent of proposed acquisitions since 1988 that have been notified under the law have been approved without a full investigation.

§ 27.10 The Development of NAFTA Investment Rules

Unsuccessful attempts to develop an International Trade Organization under the failed Havana Charter after (WWII) (when the successes included the creation of the IMF, World Bank and GATT), left an investment rule abyss until bilateral investment treaties began to be used by European nations in the late 1950s.[68] While rules for investment were not successfully developed on a multilateral

[64] See NAFTA's Investment Provisions Improve Over FTA's, But Problems Remain Report Says, 10 Int'l Trade Rep. (BNA) 498 (Mar. 24, 1993).

[65] See Canadian List of U.S. Trade Barriers Wide–Ranging but Small, Wilson Says, 10 Int'l Trade Rep. (BNA) 582 (Apr. 7, 1993), (discussing Canada's 1993 register of U.S. barriers to trade).

[66] See EC Report on U.S. Barriers Issued on Eve of Talks Between Officials, 10 Int'l Trade Rep. (BNA) 659 (Apr. 21, 1993); EC's Van Agt Expresses Concern with U.S. Protectionist Tendencies, 10 Int'l Trade Rep. (BNA) 994 (June 16, 1993).

[67] See Changes Since Thomson/LTV Controversy Have Shrunk Defense Investment, Bar Told, 10 Int'l Trade Rep. (BNA) 1859 (Nov. 3, 1993).

[68] See A.J. Pappas, References on Bilateral Investment Treaties, 4 ICSID Rev. 189 (1989). The United States joined in their use in the 1970's. See K. Scott Gudgeon, United States Bilateral Investment Treaties: Comments of Their Origin, Purposes, and General Treatment Standards, 4 Int'l Tax & Bus. L. 105 (1986).

basis by the UN's Code of Conduct attempts during the 1970s, the issue of the settlement of investment disputes took a major step with the 1965 conclusion of the Convention on the Settlement of Investment Disputes Between States and Nationals of Other States.[69] The Convention established within the World Bank an affiliated institution called the International Center for the Settlement of Investment Disputes (ICSID).

The GATT was never intended to include investment rules, they were to be in the failed ITO agreement. Although one of the later GATT rounds might have addressed the issue, there were many obstacles, not the least being the problem of potential U.S. Congressional opposition to such a major change or addition to the GATT, that had not been approved by the Congress in the first place. When the Uruguay Round of negotiations to develop the World Trade Organization began, intending to lead to an expansion of the GATT, it was clear that it would have to face a vote in Congress. Investment rules were a major focus of the negotiations. By the time the WTO was adopted, with its Trade Related Investment Measures (TRIMs), the NAFTA, with its Chapter 11 on investment, was already in place. The Canada–U.S. Free Trade Agreement had covered investment in a modest manner, but with little attention to investment dispute settlement.

The NAFTA provisions carry further the investment provisions of the CFTA. Adding Mexico to form the NAFTA meant addressing several investment law problems that had not been at issue in relations between Canada and the United States. One was Mexico's adherence to the Calvo doctrine.[70] Furthermore, Mexico was reluctant to accept international law as the law applicable in determining compensation subsequent to an expropriation. Mexico has long rejected the U.S. view that international law requires prompt, adequate and effective compensation. Mexico believed the applicable law was domestic law, and the standard to be closer to "appropriate" or "just" than to the U.S. view.[71]

---

[69] Mar. 18 1965, 17 U.S.T. 1270, T.I.A.S. 6090, 575 U.N.T.S. 159.

[70] See generally Donald R. Shea, The Calvo Clause: A Problem of Inter–American and International Law and Diplomacy (1955).

[71] See generally Gloria L. Sandrino, The NAFTA Investment Chapter and Foreign Direct Investment in Mexico: A Third World Perspective, 27 Vand. J. Transnat'l L. 259 (1994); Stephen Zamora, NAFTA and the Harmonization of Domestic Legal Systems: The Side Effects of Free Trade, 12 Ariz. J. Int'l & Comp. L. 401 (1995); Note, NAFTA's Provision for Compensation in the Event of Expropriation: A Reassessment of the "Prompt, Adequate and Effective" Standard, 31 Stan. J. Int'l L. 423 (1995).

§ 27.11 The Scope of Coverage of the NAFTA

The NAFTA investment provisions in Chapter 11 are divided into two major sections. Section A covers investment rules, and Section B the settlement of investment disputes. Chapter 11 applies to all investments, as defined in Article 1139; exempted are financial services contained in Annex III, and where special social services (police, public health, etc.) are performed. But if a provision of Chapter 11 conflicts with a provision in another chapter, the latter prevails.

The investment provisions of Chapter 11 are a major step in the multilateral agreement process. They are far more developed than those contained in the earlier CFTA, and even than those in the more recent WTO. They are a model for the development of a Free Trade Agreement of the Americas (FTAA). But, however rational the progress in the development of the NAFTA investment rules may appear, these rules are not without their critics. The absence of serious attention to the environment and labor issues led to the adoption of NAFTA based environmental and labor side agreements. The negotiations for the FTAA must address both of these issues. But that is not enough to satisfy some critics. The rhetoric of the North–South dialogue of the 1960s and 1970s has never really gone away. It appears in the legal academy within the larger framework of "critical legal studies." Turning their attention to the NAFTA, some scholars suggest that the NAFTA is little more than a way for the United States to further dominate investment in Mexico, by establishing rules which for the most part govern the conduct of Mexico in admitting investment, but omitting any consideration of the responsibilities of the foreign investor. Often spoken in the broad language of the UN of the 1970s, if they are to be understood their criticisms need to be expressed in more specific and less rhetorical language that may allow fair consideration during the process of negotiation of future multinational trade agreements. The process of the development of the FTAA will tell us whether critical legal studies has any role to play.

While we often have stereotyped Mexico as a difficult nation in which to invest, and Canada as welcoming, we are to learn that stereotypes are often mythical. The NAFTA does not require each Party to repeal all laws governing foreign investment. What it does require is that each Party treat investors of other Parties in certain ways. But there are also exceptions that allow the perpetuation of some vestiges of earlier restrictionist policies. Whether or not justified, they are part of the NAFTA, and they are effective. Our interest is principally in the way in which the NAFTA affects our investment, rather than in whether or not national or local laws of the Parties are violated by the acts of the Canadian and Mexican governments. But we have learned that national laws remain applicable; what NAFTA tries to accomplish is to control those laws.

§ 27.12 NAFTA Chapter 11—General Rules

Section A of NAFTA Chapter 11 includes several general rules which require each Party to offer specific treatment to investors of each other Party. The most important is *national treatment*, requiring treatment to investors of another Party "no less favorable than that it accords" to the Party's own investors. This is similar to the provision that follows, *most-favored nation treatment,* that a Party accord investors of another Party treatment no less favorable than that it accords to any other Party or non-Party. There is also a requirement that the treatment of investors of another Party meet a minimum standard, incorporating a rule of "international law, including fair and equitable treatment and full protection and security." These provisions are a kind of boiler-plate framework, and they have roots in the GATT treatment obligations applicable to international trade in goods. The concept in the NAFTA applies equally to goods, services, technology, and investment. But foreign investment has some special requirements, and several NAFTA provisions attempt to deal with them.

One ongoing concern of foreign investors has been *performance requirements,* local mandates that a certain percentage of the goods or services be exported, or be of domestic content, or meet a balance between import needs and exports, or link local sales to the volume of exports, or contain certain technology transferred from abroad, or mandate meeting certain exclusive sales targets. Each of these is addressed in the NAFTA, with certain exceptions. Perhaps the second most disliked domestic restriction on foreign investment are mandated levels of local equity, the *involuntary joint venture*. A prohibition against a minimum level of domestic equity is included in the national treatment provision. There is also a prohibition against a minimum number of local persons being appointed to senior management. But there may be a local requirement that a majority of the board of directors (or a board committee) be nationals or residents, as long as the investor is not therefore impaired in controlling the investment. A fourth investor concern is free transferability of profits, royalty payments, etc., both during the operation and upon liquidation of the investment. The agreement attempts to assure this right, with some exceptions dealing with such issues as bankruptcy, securities trading, and criminal offenses (money laundering).

The above areas of concern deal mostly with the ability to commence and operate an investment free from certain restrictions. There is another time in the life of a business that has perhaps long been the most significant risk for foreign investors: when the business is nationalized or expropriated. The NAFTA includes an eight-part article outlining rules for both the taking and the compensation. Nowhere do the words "prompt, adequate, and effective" appear, although that has long been the standard the U.S. government has argued to be the mandate of international law. It is a standard specifically rejected by Mexico subsequent to the nationalization of petroleum in 1938. The language of the NAFTA addresses each of these areas, however. Compensation shall be "equivalent to the fair market value of the expropriated investment immediately before the expropriation took place . . . ," which certainly meets a prompt standard. But there may be disputes over whether an expropriation has occurred. In such instance prior compensation will not have been made. The adequacy issue is covered by the NAFTA requirement of "fair market value," and the effectiveness by the requirement of payment in a "G7 currency," or by implication one convertible to such currency. The expropriation article is likely to be the subject of considerable debate. Indeed, it has already been used to challenge actions that are not traditional nationalizations, but are more common regulatory standards that act as impediments to the effective operation of an investment.[72]

§ 27.13 NAFTA Chapter 11—Investment Dispute Resolution

Section B of NAFTA Chapter 11 governs the settlement of investment disputes between a Party and an investor of another Party.[73] This part of Chapter 11 establishes a procedure for claims against states. It proceeds first by consultation or negotiation, and then moves directly to arbitration under the ICSID Convention, the latter's Additional Facility Rules, or UNCITRAL Arbitration Rules. Arbitration is to be under the ICSID Convention where both the disputing Party *and* the Party of the investor are parties to the Convention (only the United States is an ICSID party), or under the ICSID Additional Facility Rules if either the disputing Party or the

[72] See, e.g., Anthony DePalma, Mexico is Ordered to Pay a U.S. Company $16.7 Million, N.Y.Times, Aug. 31, 2000, at C4 (state government's enforcement of environmental laws amounted to an expropriation); Timothy Pritchard, Law Suits are Prompting Calls for Changes to Clause in NAFTA, N.Y.Times, June 19, 1999, at C2 (Canadian claiming California environmental law violated Ch. 11); William Glaberson, NAFTA Invoked to Challenge Court Award, N.Y. Times, Jan. 28, 1999, at C6 (Canadian company claiming Mississippi jury award violated Ch. 11).

[73] See, e.g., Donald S. Macdonald, Chapter 11 of NAFTA: What Are the Implications for Sovereignty?, 24 Can.-U.S. L.J. 281 (1998).

Party of the investor is not a party to the Convention(applicable for disputes between United States and Mexico, or United States and Canada), or under the UNCITRAL arbitration rules (applicable for disputes between Canada and Mexico). But the matter is not fully shifted to these forms of arbitration: such issues as the selection of arbitrators, the place of arbitration, and enforcement are covered in the NAFTA. There have been numerous investor–state claims' proceedings under Section B.[74]

[74] See R. Folsom, *NAFTA and Free Trade in the Americas* Nutshell (2012), Chapter 6.

Chapter 28

OPIC AND MIGA INVESTMENT INSURANCE

Table of Sections

§ 28.1 OPIC—Role and Structure

The Overseas Private Investment Corporation's (OPIC's) mandate is to "mobilize and facilitate the participation of U.S. private capital and skills in the economic and social development of less developed friendly countries and areas, thereby complementing the development assistance objectives of the United States."[1] Guided by the expected economic and social development impact of a project, and its compatibility with other U.S. projects,[2] preferential consideration is given to investment projects in countries having low per-capita income. But, the President may designate other countries as beneficiaries under separate authority.[3] Countries may be denied OPIC insurance if they do not extend internationally recognized workers' rights to workers in that country, but the President may waive this prohibition on national economic interest grounds.[4]

---

1 22 U.S.C.A. § 2191.

2 22 U.S.C.A. § 2191(1).

3 19 U.S.C.A. § 2702.

4 22 U.S.C.A. § 2191a. A subsection makes China ineligible for insurance unless the President grants authorization.

OPIC began as a government entity to insure U.S. investment abroad against (1) inconvertibility of local currency, (2) expropriation or confiscation of U.S. owned property, or (3) war, revolution, insurrection, or civil strife. All are subject to definition, generally left to principles of U.S. or international law. Claims would be paid by OPIC, which would then be subrogated to the investor's claims against the government. The U.S. government had far more leverage in exacting compensation than single investors.

As is the case of so many organizations formed for a specific purpose, OPIC began to assume roles related and sometimes unrelated to its original mandate. As has been the case of the IMF and the World Bank, OPIC has become a broader "development" agency. Building upon its guarantees and political risk insurance OPIC has assumed a lending role (with loan guarantees) for such projects as the Kenya Women's Finance Trust, a water desalination plant in Algeria, and constructing four solar power plants in Peru. The role of risk insurance which was OPIC's initial function has continued, and has become at least partially shared with the successful Multilateral Investment Guarantee Agency (MIGA), discussed below.

OPIC has broad power to engage in such insurance activities as to insure, reinsure,[5] cooperate in insuring,[6] enter into pooling or risk-sharing agreements, and hold ownership in investment insurance entities.[7] But its role is not limited to insurance. In addition to insuring investment risks, OPIC has some financing authority.[8] It provides loans which are sponsored by or significantly involve U.S. small businesses. OPIC may also guarantee loans, regardless of the size of the company.[9] Although OPIC currently provides financing worldwide, much of its initial focus was for investments in Latin America. But it does not offer financing in nations which do not have bilateral agreements with OPIC. There has been a dramatic increase in financing in Eastern Europe. More recently, OPIC created new private equity investment funds—the Modern Africa Growth and Investment Company Fund, and the New Africa Opportunity Fund. These two funds address nations long thought overlooked. The Arab Spring events have led OPIC to shift some focus to the Middle-East and North Africa.

OPIC operates with a fifteen member board of directors that includes eight appointed by the President from outside the govern-

---

5 22 U.S.C.A. § 2194(f).

6 22 U.S.C.A. § 2194(a)(2).

7 22 U.S.C.A. § 2194(f).

8 22 U.S.C.A. § 2194(c).

9

ment.[10] At least two of the eight must be experienced in small business, one each in organized labor and cooperatives. Other board of director members include the Administrator of the U.S. Agency for International Development, the U.S. Trade Representative or the Deputy, the President of OPIC, and four members who are senior officials of such entities as the Department of Labor. The OPIC President and CEO is appointed by the President, taking into account private business experience.[11] It is this composition that causes it to be referred to as a "quasi private/quasi public" organization.

§ 28.2 OPIC—Investor Eligibility

OPIC is a U.S. program for U.S. business. Eligibility is limited to U.S. citizens, U.S. corporations, partnerships, or other associations "substantially beneficially owned" by U.S. citizens. "Substantial beneficial ownership" ordinarily means that more than 50 percent of each class of issued and outstanding stock must be directly or beneficially owned by U.S. citizens. Foreign corporations, partnerships and other associations are also eligible if they are 95 percent owned by U.S. citizens.[12] If it appears from all the circumstances that foreign creditors can exercise effective control over an otherwise eligible corporation, no insurance will be written.

§ 28.3 OPIC—Insurance Programs

The three principal investment risks noted above ((1) inconvertibility of currency, (2) expropriation or confiscation of property, and (3) property loss caused by war, revolution, insurrection, or civil strife) were the initial reason for the existence of OPIC. A fourth class has been added called "business interruption" due to any of the principal three risks.

Inconvertibility. Before insurance against inconvertibility of currency is approved, the investor must obtain assurance from the host country that investor earnings will be convertible into dollars and that repatriation of capital is permitted. If the currency thereafter becomes inconvertible by act of the government, OPIC will accept the foreign currency, or a draft for the amount, and will provide the investor with U.S. dollars.

Expropriation. Expropriation is broadly defined and "includes, but is not limited to, any abrogation, repudiation, or impairment by a

---

[10] 22 U.S.C.A. § 2193(b).

[11] 22 U.S.C.A. § 2193(c).

[12] 22 U.S.C.A. § 2198(c).

foreign government of its own contract with an investor with respect to a project, where such abrogation, repudiation, or impairment is not caused by the investor's own fault or misconduct, and materially adversely affects the continued operation of the project."[13] OPIC contracts have followed a more specific and enumerative approach, because the law does not define specifically what actions constitute expropriation. OPIC's standard insurance contract contains a lengthy description of what is considered to be expropriatory action sufficient to require OPIC payment. That definition may help an investor in drafting a contract with the foreign host government, because that government will have to deal with OPIC once OPIC has paid the investor's claim.

The OPIC insured U.S. investor must exhaust local remedies before OPIC is obligated to pay any claim. All reasonable action must be taken by the investor, including pursuing administrative and judicial claims, to prevent or contest the challenged action by the host government. Upon payment of the claim, OPIC is subrogated to all rights to the investor's claim against the host government. Because the United States (OPIC) must deal with the foreign government, OPIC will not write any insurance in a foreign country until that country agrees to accept OPIC insurance and thus to negotiate with OPIC after claims have been paid.[14]

War, Revolution, Insurrection or Civil Strife. The third form of coverage, "war, revolution, insurrection, or civil strife," (political violence) is not defined by the statute. The usual OPIC contract provides protection against:

> injury to the physical condition, destruction, disappearance or seizure and retention of Covered Property directly caused by war (whether or not under formal declaration) or by revolution or insurrection and includes injury to the physical condition, destruction, disappearance or seizure and retention of Covered Property as a direct result of actions taken in hindering, combating or defending against a pending or expected hostile act whether in war, revolution, or insurrection.[15]

Civil strife is politically motivated violence (e.g., civil disturbances, riots, acts of sabotage, terrorism). Added to the OPIC statute in 1985 was a provision providing that:

---

[13] 22 U.S.C.A. § 2198(b).

[14] 22 U.S.C.A. § 2197(a).

[15] OPIC Contract Art. 1.07.

> Before issuing insurance for the first time for loss due to business interruption, and in each subsequent instance in which a significant expansion is proposed in the type of risk to be insured under the definition of "civil strife" or "business interruption", the Corporation shall . . . submit to [Senate and House Committees] . . . a report with respect to such insurance, including a thorough analysis of the risks to be covered, anticipated losses, and proposed rates and reserves and, in the case of insurance for loss due to business interruption, an explanation of the underwriting basis upon which the insurance is to be offered.[16]

§ 28.4 OPIC—Investment Insurance Terms

Since its inception, OPIC has funded, guaranteed, or insured more than $180 billion worth of investments. While OPIC may not apply more than ten percent of the maximum to any one investor,[17] it would seem unjustified according to risk management principles to allocate anywhere near that to a single investor, especially if most of the investment was located in a single foreign nation. OPIC in 1990 insured General Electric Company's Hungarian investment for $141 million, which might be questioned were risk management principles to govern investment decisions.[18] Foreign policy often appears to influence the decision. That policy has increasingly benefitted Africa, which has become a major focus of OPIC programs. In 2008, OPIC announced over $200 million in investment support in Africa, plus almost $150 million in the Middle-East. That creates some concern, because OPIC's increasing attention to socially and environmentally responsible investments may conflict with the use of risk management principles that are essential to insurance.

§ 28.5 OPIC—Eligible Investments

The creating legislation authorizes OPIC to carry out its functions "utilizing broad criteria".[19] OPIC must consider investment eligibility in accordance with extensive guidelines that provide that OPIC conduct operations on a self-sustaining basis. It must consider the economic and financial soundness of the project; use private credit and investment institutions along with OPIC's guarantee authority; broaden private participation and revolve its funds through selling its direct investments to private investors; apply principles

---

16 22 U.S.C.A. § 2194(a)(4).

17 22 U.S.C.A. § 2194(a)(3).

18 The World Bank's MIGA reinsured $50 million of this project, thus lessening the full exposure of OPIC.

19 22 U.S.C.A. § 2191.

of risk management; give preferential consideration to projects involving small business (at least 30 percent of all projects); consider less developed nation receptiveness to private enterprise; foster private initiative and competition and discourage monopolistic practices; further balance of payment objectives of the United States; support projects with positive trade benefits to the United States; advise and assist agencies of the United States and other public and private organizations interested in projects in less developed nations; avoid projects which diminish employment in the United States; refuse projects which do not have positive trade benefits to the United States; and refuse projects which pose an unreasonable or major environmental, health, or safety hazard, or result in significant degradation of national parks and similar protected areas. OPIC must also operate consistently with the goals of U.S. law relating to protection of environment and endangered species in less developed nations. Additionally, it must limit operations to nations which provide or are in the process of providing internationally recognized rights for workers. That includes right of association, right to organize and bargain collectively, prohibition of forced or compulsory labor, minimum age for employment, and acceptable conditions of work. Such requirement is often observed more on paper than in practice in many of the countries listed as acceptable for OPIC assistance. Finally, OPIC must consider the host nation's observance of and respect for human rights. The political and economic changes in Eastern European countries since the late 1980s have resulted in considerable OPIC activity in that area.

OPIC participates only in *new* investments (loans or insurance) because its role is to encourage new investment, not facilitate existing investment. Each proposed investment is evaluated by OPIC to consider, in addition to the above eligibility requirements, the extent to which the U.S. participant has long-term management arrangements with the new enterprise, the extent of private participation and whether the project is likely to assist further development of the host nation's private sector. Loans or the contribution of goods or services to foreign governments will not be insured unless they are part of a construction contract. Nor will OPIC insure the credit or solvency of the foreign government. OPIC insures or provides a guarantee only for projects in countries that have signed an agreement with the United States for OPIC programs.

§ 28.6 OPIC—Claims and Dispute Settlement

Claims presented by insured investors are "settled, and disputes arising as a result thereof may be arbitrated with the consent of the parties, on such terms and conditions as OPIC may determine."[20] OPIC insurance contracts have stated that "any controversy arising out of or relating to this Contract or the breach thereof shall be settled by arbitration in accordance with the then prevailing Commercial Arbitration Rules of the American Arbitration Association." The arbitration process is important: OPIC has challenged a number of claims presented to it by U.S. companies claiming to have lost property through expropriations.

Under AID, from 1966 to 1970, $3.5 million was paid to settle eight claims. From 1971 through most of 2012, OPIC agreed to 292 insurance claim settlements which totaled $970.8 million, constituting either cash settlements to investors or OPIC guaranties of host nation obligations. OPIC had denied twenty-eight claims, fourteen of which had been submitted to arbitration by the investors. Only two claims were pending at the end of 2012.

Since 1978, OPIC has had the authority to deny loss claims if the investor, a controlling shareholder, or any agent of the investor has engaged in any act which resulted in a conviction under the 1977 Foreign Corrupt Practices Act, and such act has been the "preponderant" cause of the loss.[21] There have been few convictions under the FCPA, however, since most charges lead at most to a consent decree involving a fine.

§ 28.7 OPIC—Private Insurers

OPIC continues to investigate methods of transferring its insurance coverage to private insurers. Even though some members of Congress view insurance of private investment abroad as best allocated exclusively to the private sector, it seems likely that OPIC will survive because its programs provide insurance for risks not broadly acceptable to the private insurance industry, and there are foreign policy considerations which may conflict with traditional risk management principles in establishing insurance premium rates. Further assuring its existence is its broadening scope of lending.

§ 28.8 Investment Insurance on an International Level

The concept of offering insurance for various investment risks which led to the creation of OPIC in the United States, and to similar programs in several other nations, has been built upon on an international level by the World Bank's 1988 creation of the Multi-

---

[20] 22 U.S.C.A. § 2197(i).

[21] 22 U.S.C.A. § 2197(*l*).

lateral Investment Guarantee Agency (MIGA). This organization, part of the World Bank, was intended to encourage increased investment to the developing nations by offering investment insurance and advisory services.[22] Voting power is equally divided between the industrial and developing nation groups. Shares are proportional to member nations' shares of World Bank capital. Unlike OPI, MIGA is not a lending agency, but its parent organization—the World Bank—serves principally as a lender.

Creating MIGA within the World Bank structure offers benefits a separate international organization lacks. MIGA has access to World Bank data on nations' economic and social status. This gives considerable credibility to MIGA, and encourages broad participation. It is not certain how MIGA has affected national programs, such as OPIC.[23] A U.S. based company, for example, may prefer dealing with OPIC because of greater confidence of claims being paid (until MIGA actually develops a record of claims payments), of maintaining information confidentiality, and benefiting from legal processes established in bilateral investment treaties. But U.S. companies may find MIGA insurance available where OPIC is not. Rather than being an alternative to OPIC, MIGA should be viewed as compatible with OPIC. For example, International Paper Investments of the United States obtained MIGA insurance for risks of currency transfer, expropriation, and war and civil disturbance, plus additional political risk insurance from OPIC.

Banks have found MIGA attractive because bank regulators in some countries have exempted commercial banks from special requirements for provisioning against loss where loans or investments are insured by MIGA. Furthermore, investors in nations without adequate national insurance programs have very much welcomed MIGA's creation. But even some of the newly industrializing nations, such as India and Korea, have adopted national programs. MIGA is not intended to replace national programs, but to extend the availability of investment insurance to many areas where it was not previously available, which in turn is expected to assist economic development in those areas. MIGA's success will likely be where it fills gaps rather than where it competes with established and suc-

[22] MIGA publishes a newsletter "MIGA NEWS", available at MIGA, World Bank, 1818 H Street, N.W., Washington, D.C. 20433. The advisory service is provided by MIGA's Foreign Investment Advisory Service, a joint venture with the IFC and World Bank. MIGA has a homepage at www.miga.org, and it's Investment Promotion Agency Electronic Network is at www.ipanet.net.

[23] Several U.S. foreign investment projects have turned to MIGA for insurance, including McDonald's in Chile, Citibank in Argentina, Turkey and Pakistan, Bank of America in Pakistan, Bank of Boston in Argentina, Mobil Corporation in Saudi Arabia, and Coca Cola in Poland.

cessful national insurance programs. Those gaps are substantial and MIGA has a very major role to play in the world.

Unlike national programs, such as OPIC, MIGA has the leverage of a large group of nations behind it when it presses a claim. Only experience will disclose the extent to which politics will enter MIGA's claims procedures. The clear intention of MIGA is to avoid political interference and consider the process solely as creating legal issues. The last three decades have been quiet times for foreign investment with regard to the occurance of the risks insured against by OPIC and MIGA. But the risks are perceived as sufficiently likely that OPIC and MIGA have been quite busy writing new insurance.

§ 28.9 MIGA—Insurance Programs

Risks covered by MIGA are noncommercial and include risks of currency transfer; expropriation; war, terrorism, and civil disturbance; breach of contract; and failure to honor sovereign financial obligations, all actions by the host government. Only developing nations are eligible locations for insured investments.

Currency Transfer. This insurance is similar to that offered by OPIC. It covers losses incurred when an investor is unable to convert host nation currency into foreign exchange and transfer that exchange abroad. Host nation currency may be that obtained from profits, principal, interest, royalties, capital, etc. The insurance covers refusals and excessive delays where the host government has failed to act, where there have been adverse changes in exchange control laws or regulations, or where conditions in the host nation that govern currency transfer have deteriorated. Currency devaluations are *not* covered. Such devaluations are often the cause of substantial losses, but these are commercial losses attributed to changes that are to some extent predictable, and are not carried out by host nations to harm investment. Indeed, currency devaluations are usually extreme measures to address changing demand for the nation's currency.

Expropriation. This is insurance for partial or total loss from acts that reduce ownership of, control over, or rights to the insured investment. Included is "creeping" expropriation, where a series of acts has the same effect as an outright taking. Not covered are nondiscriminatory actions of the host government in exercising its regulatory authority.

Valuation for compensation is net book value; that may mean inadequate compensation where book value reflects historic costs. Loans and loan guarantees are compensated to the extent of the outstanding principal and interest. Compensation is paid at the same time as the insured assigns its rights in the investment to MIGA, which then may take action against the expropriating government.

War, Terrorism, and Civil Disturbance. Losses for damage, disappearance, or destruction to tangible assets by politically motivated acts of war or civil disturbance, such as revolution, insurrection, *coups d'etat*, sabotage, and terrorism. Compensation is for the book value or replacement cost of assets lost, and for the repair of damaged assets. This insurance also covers losses attributable to an interruption in a project for a period of one year. This is business interruption coverage, and becomes effective when the investment is considered a total loss. Book value is the measure of compensation.

Breach of Contract. This special insurance covers losses caused by the host government's breach or repudiation of a contract. When there is an alleged breach or repudiation, the foreign investor must be able to invoke an arbitration clause in the contract and obtain an award for damages. If that award is not paid by the host government, MIGA provides compensation.

Failure to Honor Sovereign Financial Obligations. More recently added, this insurance is for losses from the failure of a government to make payments when due where there is an unconditional (not subject to defenses) obligation or guarantee related to an eligible investment. The investor does not need to obtain an arbitral award.

§ 28.10 MIGA—Eligible Investments

MIGA insurance may cover, to a maximum of U.S. $220 million per project and usually for a maximum of fifteen years, new equity investments, shareholder loans or guaranties, and non-shareholder loans. Also covered are technical assistance and management contracts, asset securitization, capital market bond issues, leasing, services, and franchise and licensing agreements. MIGA will insure acquisitions under a state privatization program, an important program in view of the rapid pace of privatization in developing nations, Eastern European nations, and parts of the former Soviet Union.

Two member countries are involved. First, investors must be from a member country, and only foreign investors qualify. With Agency approval, however, domestic investors may receive coverage for projects where they bring assets back to their nation. This special allowance is intended to promote the return of capital transferred to safe havens during times of political or economic uncertainty. Second, the location of approved investments must be in developing member nations which approve the insurance. There was considerable discussion regarding insuring only in developing nations which adopted standards for protecting foreign investment, but the final Convention did not include any such standards. Member nation standards for protecting foreign investment may nevertheless be a factor in writing insurance, if any measure of risk management principles is to be followed. Since the viability of MIGA is dependent both on its care in selecting risks to insure, and its ability to negotiate settlements after paying claims, the right of subrogation is extremely important.

§ 28.11 MIGA—Eligible Investors

An investor seeking MIGA insurance must be a national or member country *other than* the country in which the investment is to be made. The test of nationality for corporations is incorporation and having its principal place of business in the member nation, *or* being majority owned by nationals of the member nation. Commercially operated state owned corporations are eligible if it operates on a commercial basis. Even non-profit organizations are eligible if they operate on a commercial basis.

§ 28.12 MIGA—Scope of Coverage

MIGA covers investments under a standard term of fifteen years, which may be increased to twenty years if MIGA determines that the longer term is justified by the nature of the project. If the insurance is for a loan, the term follows the duration of the loan agreement. Once written, MIGA is not able to terminate the coverage except for default by the investor. The insured investor, however, is entitled to cancel the insurance on any anniversary date after the third.

Premiums are based on a risk assessment which includes consideration of the political and economic conditions in the host nation. They average about one percent of the insured amount per year. Rates vary, however, depending on the industry and type of coverage. MIGA can insure equity investments to ninety percent of the initial contribution, plus 180 percent to cover earnings. Contracts such as for technical assistance are covered to ninety percent of the value of the payments due under the agreement. Loans and loan guarantees are also insured to ninety percent of the principal and interest that will accrue over the term of the loan. These figures are maximum available guarantees. The *current* amount is that in force for the given year. The difference between the maximum and current amount is referred to as the *standby* amount of guarantee, and constitutes a reserve coverage that the investor may place in effect each year to cover changes in the value or amount of investment at risk.

§ 28.13 MIGA—Claims

In all but two cases, MIGA has resolved disputes that would have led to claims. It has paid four additional claims related to damage from war and civil disturbance. The first was for an equity investment in a power corporation in Indonesia, which was suspended by a presidential decree due to an economic crisis. The second was for war and civil disturbance, a guerilla attack in Nepal had damaged a hydroelectric plant, and also dealt with a power project. The third claim involved a toll road project in Argentina when the nation faced yet another financial crisis.

With a history of only four paid claims, and MIGA's success in finding a resolution without the investor resorting to the claims process, on any basis of measurement MIGA appears to be a successful entity and a welcome addition to OPIC for U.S. investors. Choosing MIGA or OPIC for a U.S. investor planning an investment abroad is not a coin toss. In one case MIGA may be the better or only choice. In another OPIC may be better. In still other cases, either OPIC or MIGA may be appropriate. Finally, there may be instances when a project has several aspects which call for use of both MIGA and OPIC.

Chapter 29

EXPROPRIATION OF AN INVESTMENT

Table of Sections

---

§ 29.1 Avoiding the Risk of Expropriation

Avoiding the risk may depend upon the form of expropriation. While most attention focuses on direct expropriation—when part or all of the investment is taken by the host nation government, and indirect expropriation—various actions that make continuation of the investment impossible, such as excessively high tax rates, forced joint ventures, excessive government control, mandatory use of domestic inputs, and mandatory export levels.

The risk of expropriation cannot be fully avoided, and insurance should be considered, especially that provided either by the U.S. Overseas Private Investment Corporation (OPIC) or the World Bank's Multilateral Investment Guarantee Agency (MIGA).[1] Taking measures to avoid the risk of expropriation cannot assure a foreign investor that expropriation will not occur. Many of the expropriations of the last century resulted from revolutions (USSR, Cuba, Mexico, Nicaragua) or very significant alterations in the government through elections (Chile), or in post-independence nationalism (Indonesia). A significant development has been the increasing use of bilateral investment agreements or treaties, which include requirements of prompt, adequate, and effective compensation (or equivalent language)

§ 29.2 Legal Choices Following Expropriation

If a taking occurs, there are several issues that will face the expropriated foreign investor. What law will apply: the law of the place of the taking, international law, or the law of the forum? Was the taking for a public purpose, or was it retaliatory or discriminatory? Was proper compensation forthcoming? Must remedies be exhausted in the taking nation? If the investor whose property has been taken attempts to sue the taking government in courts in the United States, or in third nations, what are the likely defenses?

§ 29.3 What Law Applies and What Is that Law?

There has been continuing debate about both the choice of law issue with respect to expropriation law and, assuming international law applies or is to be considered, what does that law state? The Mexican expropriation of foreign petroleum interests in 1938 commenced a dialogue between Mexico and the United States regarding

---

[1] See, *supra*, Chapter 28.

the applicable law.[2] Mexico insisted that Mexican domestic law applied, which required compensation. The United States insisted that international law applied, which also required compensation. The United States argued that compensation had to be made in accordance with an alleged "prompt, adequate, and effective" international law standard. The U.S. government position has continued to be that the standard is "prompt, adequate, and effective," even though this view receives inconsistent support abroad and even within the United States by many jurists. The U.S. business community, nevertheless, tends to support the U.S. government position.

The use of bilateral investment agreements or treaties (BITs) adds a set of rules which diminishes the choice of law issue, such as rules governing what compensation is required, when it must be paid, and in what form.

§ 29.4 Applying Domestic Law of the Taking Nation

While there does seem to be agreement that international law is applicable to takings of foreign property, that has been challenged in two ways. First, the U.N. Charter of Economic Rights and Duties of States affirms the right of nations to expropriate property, and states that compensation issues are to be settled by "domestic law of the nationalization State," unless otherwise agreed.[3] Second, when a nation expropriates foreign property, it tends to find greater comfort in arguing the applicability of its own law, which invariably is less demanding in requiring compensation than whatever standard the international community has approved.

§ 29.5 Applying International Law

Even if the parties agree that international law is applicable, it may be difficult to determine what international law requires. It may be "prompt, adequate and effective" compensation, as the United States argues, or "just" compensation, as the Restatement of Foreign Relations suggests, or "appropriate" compensation, as U.N.

---

[2] The views expressed in letters exchanged by the governments are included in 3 Green H. Hackworth, Digest of International Law 655–65 (1942).

[3] Dec. 12, 1974, U.N.G.A. Res. 3281 (XXIX), 29 U.N. GAOR, Supp. (No. 31) 50, U.N. Doc. A/9631 (1975), reprinted in 14 Int'l Legal Mat. 251 (1975). This Charter, which does not constitute international law, was passed over the objection to this provision by 16 nations, mostly the largest industrialized nations, including the United States. The Charter illustrates the diversity of opinion regarding expropriation arising with the achievement of independence by many former colonies of the industrialized nations.

Resolution 1803 proposed in 1962, and which seems to have been adopted by tribunals and courts more than any other standard.

§ 29.6 Investment Treaties

The possibility of having to address these issues suggests that investment agreements should include a provision providing for compensation under a standard of prompt, adequate, and effective. The United States continues to try to include in bilateral investment treaties (BITs) a provision for compensation based on such standard. That is helpful to U.S. investors abroad. But governments change, and the most contentious compensation issues have arisen when there is an expropriation following a revolution or radical realignment of a government, such as in Cuba. In such case, even contractual provisions for payment according to prompt, adequate, and effective criteria may be ignored by the new government in the taking nation.

§ 29.7 Public Purpose under International Law

A sovereign nation has full and permanent sovereignty over its natural resources and economic activities.[4] That sovereignty gives the nation the right to take privately-owned property, whether that property is owned by the country's nationals or foreigners. These are long held concepts that exist on both an international and domestic level. Most national (and state or provincial) constitutions express this right. But the theory of taking does not allow the taking for any reason or upon any whim of the prevailing government. There must be a public purpose. There are two problems with the public purpose, however. First is its definition, and second is determining who is to measure public purpose in an international expropriation.

§ 29.8 Defining Public Purpose

There has never been a very clear definition of public purpose. It is often expressed in such broad words as "improvement of the social welfare or economic betterment of the nation." Does this mean such specific goals as improved infrastructure, better medical care, lower rates for basic services such as electricity, more adequate housing, or a lower infant-mortality rate? Or does it mean something more general, such as a shift to a different fundamental economic theory, by increasing or making exclusive the state owner-

---

[4] That is clearly stated in the U.N. Resolution on Permanent Sovereignty Over Natural Resources, Dec. 14, 1962, U.N.G.A.Res. 1803 (XVII), 17 U.N. GAOR, Supp. (No. 17) 15, U.N.Doc. A/5217 (1963), reprinted in 2 Int'l Legal Mat. 223 (1963).

ship of the means of production and distribution.[5] The proper definition may be what the taking nation says it is, but at least there seems to be agreement that some legitimate public purpose is a necessary component of a lawful expropriation, and the taking nation must offer some rational purpose for the taking.

§ 29.9 Who Measures Public Purpose?

Defining public purpose does not end the problem. When one state has taken the property of nationals of another, what court should sit in judgment of the public purpose issue, both to define it and to determine whether it is likely to be or already has been met? A court in the taking nation is not likely to overrule the taking for lack of public purpose justifications. The ideal setting for establishing these rules is the International Court of Justice. But that court has not yet proven to be an effective body to develop an international law of expropriation. Such development is thus left to national courts and various tribunals. These have tended to shy away from addressing the public purpose issue.[6] That has been because of both the conceptual difficulty with the issue and the fact that foreign investors whose properties have been expropriated usually are not interested in restitution of their property as long as the taking government is in office. The foreign investors are interested in receiving compensation. Consequently, while the public purpose element of expropriation is present and should be considered, there are other elements of expropriation more likely to be the subject of investor concern.

§ 29.10 Retaliation and Discrimination Defined

In addition to lacking a public purpose, an expropriation may be unlawful if it were in retaliation for acts of the government of the person who owned the property,[7] or if it discriminated against a particular person or government.[8] The Cuban expropriations were examples of both. The first expropriations were exclusively of U.S. property (i.e., discrimination), and were in response to the United

[5] Public purpose, with respect to the Cuban expropriations, is explored in Michael Wallace Gordon, The Cuban Nationalizations: The Demise of Foreign Private Property (1976).

[6] See Martin Domke, Foreign Nationalizations, 55 Am.J.Int'l L. 585 (1961).

[7] Proof of a retaliatory purpose may actually constitute proof of the *absence* of a public purpose. If the reason for an expropriation is retaliation, it can hardly be considered a public purpose.

[8] If an expropriation is undertaken solely to discriminate against a foreign nation, it may constitute proof of both a lack of a public purpose and retaliation. The three elements, public purpose, retaliation, and discrimination, are thus often quite interrelated.

States eliminating the Cuban sugar quota (i.e., retaliation). Both were reasons for U.S. courts holding the expropriations to have been unlawful.[9]

The taking of some property of only one nation's nationals is not necessarily discriminatory. A country may decide to nationalize one sector, such as mining. That sector might be owned exclusively by nationals of one foreign nation. It could be difficult in such case to conclude whether the taking was based on the desire to have the state own all mining interests, because it was believed more sound economically or preferable for national security reasons, or was based on an intention to discriminate against one nation and take its property, whether it consisted of mining properties or hotels or anything else.

§ 29.11 Retaliation and Discrimination Subordinated to Compensation

However important it may be to understand the issues of public purpose, retaliation and discrimination, the real issue is likely to be the payment of compensation. If a foreign investor is compensated satisfactorily, there is likely to be little concern with the technicalities of lawfulness or unlawfulness of the taking under international law because of the public purpose, retaliation, or discrimination characteristics of the taking. The investor may be concerned with the loss of future business, however, and may wish to consider the prospects of a return of the property after the new, hostile government is either replaced or adopts a different attitude toward foreign investment or the foreign investor.

§ 29.12 The Uncertainty of International Law

As noted above, if the expropriated foreign property owner is satisfactorily compensated, that is likely to end the matter. A ruling by any dispute settling entity, court, or tribunal, domestic or international, that the expropriation was unlawful, is a purely pyrrhic victory if there is no satisfactory compensation. What, therefore, is the proper measure of compensation?

The U.S. government's repeatedly stated position regarding compensation is that it is (1) required under international law, and it (2) must be prompt, adequate, and effective.[10] The first view, that

[9] See Banco Nacional de Cuba v. Sabbatino, 376 U.S. 398, 84 S.Ct. 923, 11 L.Ed.2d 804 (1964), and especially the decisions of the district court, 193 F.Supp. 375 (S.D.N.Y.1961), and the circuit court of appeals, 307 F.2d 845 (2d Cir.1962).

[10] See Oscar Schachter, Editorial Comment, Compensation for Expropriation, 78 Am.J.Int'l L. 121 (1984).

international law requires compensation, is generally shared by jurists within the United States and abroad. But the second view, the prompt, adequate, and effective standard, is the subject of vigorous debate and is rejected by many U.S. and foreign jurists. The two parts are often discussed as one issue.

The first international court case usually referred to that discussed expropriation is the 1928 *Chorzów Factory* decision of the Permanent Court of International Justice (PCIJ).[11] That case referred only to a duty of the "payment of fair compensation." That seems less stringent than the "prompt, adequate, and effective" standard alleged to be the prevailing international law by U.S. Secretary of State Hull in 1938 in his notes to the Mexican government.[12] There has been little further guidance from the PCIJ or its successor—the International Court of Justice. The narrow focus in the latter's *Barcelona Traction* decision[13] added very little, if anything, to the international law of expropriation compensation.

A subsequent dispute involving an intervention which allegedly caused the company to file for bankruptcy was decided by a chamber of the International Court of Justice.[14] It involved the interpretation of the Treaty of Friendship, Commerce, and Navigation between the United States and Italy, most specifically issues regarding interference with the U.S. company's right to "control and manage" its operation in Italy. The measure of damages became an issue, and was not dealt with very clearly, partly because of the uncertainty of the company's ability to function during the period of intervention and the appropriateness of damages after filing bankruptcy. But the ruling was that Italy had not violated international law in its requisition or intervention. Furthermore, since the damages were conditioned upon liability, there was no final decision as to their measure.

---

[11] P.C.I.J., Ser.A, No. 17 (1928). The earlier 1922 Norwegian Shipowners' Claims arbitration referred to "just compensation" as determined by the "fair actual value at the time and place". Norwegian Shipowners' Claims (Norway v. U.S.), 1922 1 U.N.Rep.Int'l Arb.Awards 307.

[12] 3 Green H. Hackworth, Digest of International Law 655 (1942).

[13] Barcelona Traction, Light & Power Co. (Second phase) (Belg. v. Spain), 1970 ICJ Rep. 3. The case is discussed in Herbert W. Briggs, Barcelona Traction: The *Jus Standi* of Belgium, 65 Am.J.Int'l L. 327 (1971); F.A. Mann, The Protection of Shareholders' Interests in the Light of the *Barcelona Traction* Case, 67 Am.J.Int'l L. 259 (1973).

[14] Elettronica Sicula S.p.A. (ELSI), Judgment (U.S. v. Italy), 1989 ICJ Rep. 15. The case is discussed in Ignaz Seidl–Hohenveldren, ELSI and Badger: The Two Raytheon Cases, 26 Rivista de Diritto Internazionale Privato e Processuale 261 (1990); F.A. Mann, Foreign Investment in the International Court of Justice: The *ELSI* Case, 86 Am.J.Int'l L. 92 (1992).

Debate over the proper level of compensation continues without anything resembling a consensus. But some standards have developed that might be applied by a court or tribunal. The alternatives seem to use elastic words or terms, but when further defined, there may be less difference than is at first thought to exist.

§ 29.13 Prompt, Adequate, and Effective Compensation

The "prompt, adequate and effective" standard is likely to be applied by (1) U.S. courts or tribunals applying a U.S norm of compensation theory, or searching for an international standard, or (2) U.S. courts or tribunals applying an agreement between the parties or nations that calls for the application of the prompt, adequate, and effective standard, such as a bilateral investment treaty. There is no assurance, however, that a U.S. court or tribunal searching for "the" international law will arrive at a prompt, adequate, and effective standard. The 1981 *Banco Nacional v. Chase Manhattan Bank* decision suggested that the consensus of nations was to apply an "appropriate" standard, and quoted one highly regarded American author who rejected the prompt, adequate, and effective standard as a norm of international law.[15]

Because of the very limited number of judicial decisions discussing the compensation issue, decisions of arbitration panels are often useful to compare with cases. In the *LIAMCO* arbitration, the arbitrator suggested that the prompt, adequate, and effective standard was not the only standard, and interpreted the contract to conclude that under general principles of law only "equitable" compensation was required.[16] But the arbitrator included in the award a substantial amount for lost profits, a conclusion suggesting the adoption of a *full* compensation standard.

§ 29.14 Appropriate Compensation

The "appropriate" compensation norm is the standard in U.N. Resolution 1803 of 1962, which in the view of many jurists,[17] remains the most likely norm to be applied. It has been suggested as the standard in the *Banco Nacional* decision noted above, and in at

---

[15] Banco Nacional de Cuba v. Chase Manhattan Bank, 658 F.2d 875 (2d Cir.1981). The court quoted Professor Wolfgang G. Friedmann.

[16] Libyan American Oil Co. v. Libyan Arab Republic, 20 Int'l Legal Mat. 1 (1981).

[17] See, e.g., Richard B. Lillich, The Valuation of Nationalized Property in International Law: Toward a Consensus or More "Rich Chaos"?, in Richard B. Lillich (ed. & contrib.), 3 The Valuation of Nationalized Property in International Law 183 (1975).

least two important international arbitrations, the *TOPCO/CALASIATIC* and *AMINOIL* cases.[18]

§ 29.15 Fair Compensation

The "fair" compensation standard was used in the much-discussed but little followed *Chorzów Factory* PCIJ decision, noted above. However, fair compensation has not generally been accepted as the proper standard, and has not become an accepted norm of international law. That is at least partly due to the broad sense of what fair might include. A legal norm deserves greater definition.

§ 29.16 Just Compensation

The Restatement (Third) of the Foreign Relations Law of the United States adopted "just" in place of "appropriate", largely to avoid a possible inclusion of host nation demanded deductions under an "appropriate" standard. Several expropriating nations had calculated compensation by taking the company's value of the property and deducting what were called "excess profits" or "improper pricing" of resources to arrive at a conclusion that either no compensation was due, or that the company actually owed the expropriating nation. But it is hard to envision a taking nation agreeing that while such deductions could be allowed under an "appropriate" standard, they could not under a "just" standard.

§ 29.17 Restitution as a Substitute for Compensation

The expropriated foreign investor may prefer to have the property returned rather than receive compensation. This is not likely to be the case where there has been a revolution with an investment-hostile government, such as Cuba, but may be appropriate where a counter-revolution has soon restored an investment welcoming government. There is some precedent for restitution. In the *TOPCO/CALASIATIC* arbitration, following expropriations of Texas Overseas Petroleum Corporation and California Asiatic Oil Company by Libya, the sole arbitrator, Professor Dupuy (Secretary General of the Hague Academy of International Law), noted that the *Chorzów Factory* decision suggested that *restitutio in integrum* remains international law, and ordered Libya to resume performance of the agreement.[19] But in the *BP Arbitration* the arbitrator, Swe-

18 Texas Overseas Petroleum Co/California Asiatic Oil Co. v. Government of the Libyan Arab Republic, 17 Int'l Legal Mat. 3, 29 (1978), 53 ILR 389 (1979) (English trans.); Arbitration between Kuwait and the American Independent Oil Co. (AMINOIL), 21 Int'l Legal Mat. 976 (1982).

19 17 Int'l Legal Mat. 1, 32 (1978).

dish Judge Lagergren, stated that the *Chorzów Factory* rule of *restitutio in integrum* was meant only to be used to calculate compensation, suggesting adherence to a full compensation theory.[20]

§ 29.18 Mandatory Questions under Any Standard

Whatever standard is chosen, three questions must be asked. First, *how much* is to be paid? Second, in *what form* is it to be paid? And third, *when* must it be paid? If the answers to these questions are the full value of the property, in convertible currency, and immediately or very soon, then the standard that is being applied seems to be the "prompt, adequate, and effective" standard argued by the United States to constitute international law. The Iran–United States Claims Tribunal, meeting in the Hague for over three decades, never formally applied a "prompt, adequate, and effective" standard.[21] But claims approved by the tribunal have been paid *promptly* from the funds established for the purpose, they have been paid in dollars (that surely constitutes *effective* payment), and the methods of valuation used seem to satisfy any reasonable *adequacy* standard.[22]

If the consensus is an "appropriate" standard, tribunals that have gained the respect of the majority of the international community, including the main industrialized nations, seem to be applying a standard that is "fair, just, and appropriate" as well as "prompt, adequate, and effective". For now, and perhaps until or unless the investment restrictiveness of the 1970s returns, the demand for a norm allowing only partial compensation has little backing.[23]

§ 29.19 Exhaustion of Local Remedies

Seeking compensation from the expropriating government is not only appropriate, but may be a precondition for initiating an

---

[20] British Petroleum Exploration Co. v. Libyan Arab Republic, 53 ILR 297 (1973).

[21] The Tribunal has used a "just" standard, which is stated in the U.S.–Iran Treaty of Amity, Economic Relations and Consular Rights. Aug. 15, 1955, 8 UST 899, ITAS No. 3853, 284 UNTS 93. The standard is stated as "prompt payment of just compensation." But it goes on to state that it must be paid in "an effectively realizable form" and must be for the "full equivalent of the property taken", thus becoming nearly a prompt, adequate, and effective standard. See David Caron, The Nature of the Iran–United States Claims Tribunal and the Evolving Structure of International Dispute Resolution, 84 Am.J. Int'l L. 104 (1990).

[22] The Iran–United States Tribunal is quite unique, however, because of the initial agreement to deposit considerable funds to meet approved claims.

[23] See Patrick M. Norton, A Law of the Future or a Law of the Past? Modern Tribunals and the International Law of Expropriation, 85 Am.J. Int'l L. 474 (1991).

insurance claim.[24] It is reasonable to first seek compensation from the one who has committed the wrong.[25] That idea makes sense when the expropriation is not part of a total change in economic theory following a revolution that includes the expropriation of all private property. The taking nation may be prepared to compensate properties taken in a selective nationalization, such as a taking of all telecommunications or air transportation enterprises. But when a nationalization occurs of the dimensions of those in the former Soviet Union, China, Eastern Europe, and Cuba, there is little reason either for the expropriated property owner to attempt to exhaust local remedies, or for that party to be forced to do so before the presentation of insurance claims. Nevertheless, it is probably appropriate for the expropriated party to make some attempt against the taking government, if nothing more than a formal written protest of the taking and a demand for compensation. The problem arises when the nation expresses a willingness to hear such claims, but the circumstances and unfolding facts seem clearly to suggest that the willingness to discuss compensation is illusory.[26] The expropriated property owner may have to be prepared to establish that local remedies are inadequate before seeking remedies at home or in third party nations. Adequate proof justifying the futility of pursuing local remedies may take time to accumulate. The proof should illustrate deficiencies with the court or tribunal system of the taking nation, the method of valuation, the ability of the country to pay settled claims, and the appropriateness of the form of any payment the taking nation can afford. The experience with taking nations where the taking is part of a major economic, political, and social revolution clearly suggests that local remedies are likely to very unsatisfactory to the expropriated property owners, and that they will have to seek assistance outside the taking nation.

§ 29.20 Assistance of the Government—The "Calvo Clause"

Expropriated U.S. investors usually report the expropriation to the U.S. Department of State. Diplomatic pressure may be essential to success in dealing with the taking nation. The U.S. executive has frequently intervened subsequent to foreign nationalizations of U.S. property. While diplomatic intervention may be helpful and may lead to government sanctions against the taking nation, there is one concern that frequently faces the U.S. investor abroad—the applica-

24 See G. Law, The Local Remedies Rule in International Law (1961).

25 See Mummery, Increasing the Use of Local Remedies, 58 Proceed.Am. Soc'y Int'l L. 107 (1964), tracing the idea to the Bible.

26 Cuba offered compensation in the form of bonds that deserved the term "junk bonds" long before Wall Street popularized them decades later.

tion by the taking nation of the "Calvo Clause", or something comparable.[27]

The Calvo Clause espouses a theory, sometimes expressed in an agreement signed by the foreign investor, that a foreign investor is entitled to treatment no different than that given domestic investors,[28] and recourse to one's diplomatic channels may result in a *forfeiture* of the property. The Calvo Clause was included in Article 3 of the restrictive 1973 Mexican Investment Law, but there is no instance of any property forfeiture in Mexico, or in other nations which have either adopted the Calvo Clause concept formally in investment legislation, or made it a part of investment rhetoric.[29] The concept of the Calvo Clause improperly frustrates the right of a nation to diplomatic intervention to protect property of its citizens. If a government does intervene, it may not be clear whether it does so at the request of the expropriated foreign investor, or on its own initiative. If the latter, it is unfair to conclude that the property is therefore forfeited because of any act of the investor. While the idea that foreign investors ought to be entitled to no better treatment than nations may seem sensible, the real world does give foreign investors alternatives not available to nationals. One is diplomatic negotiations. When the Calvo Clause goes beyond being a statement of exhaustion of local remedies to being an exclusionary rule precluding any other subsequent remedies, it loses much of its respect and viability.

§ 29.21 Lump–Sum Agreements and Claims Commissions

Where there has been an extensive nationalization of foreign property, such as by the Soviet Union, China, Eastern European nations, and Cuba, the most likely conclusion is by a lump-sum settlement under the terms of a later binational agreement. Lump-sum settlements are common, but they remain questionable as a part of the jurisprudence of the international law of compensation.[30] Any

---

[27] Donald R. Shea, The Calvo Clause (1955).

[28] This part of the concept means that the foreign investor is entitled to no better treatment than a national, and thus is left exclusively to local remedies. It is consequently interrelated with the exhaustion of local remedies concept.

[29] The concept was not included in the 1993 Mexican Investment Law, which is more investor friendly than the 1973 law. The NAFTA foreign investment provisions eliminate the Calvo Clause as a threat to a Canadian or U.S. investor, a major concession by Mexico.

[30] Dictum in Barcelona Traction suggests that lump-sum settlements are not sources of law for compensation. Barcelona Traction, Light & Power Co., Ltd. (Belgium v. Spain), 1970 I.C.J. 3, 40. See also Brice Clagett, Just Compensation in International Law: The Issues Before the Iran–United States Claims Tribunal, in Richard

agreed upon lump sum is subsequently divided among claimants who have quite likely filed claims years earlier, soon after the expropriations occurred.[31] For example, the Cuban nationalizations occurred between 1959 and the early 1960s. The Cuban Claims Act was passed in 1964, providing for claims to be filed between 1965 and 1967, extended later to 1972. At the end claims allowed amounted to U.S. $1.76 billion.[32] The valuation method ranged from strict reliance on book value to a usually much higher going concern value.[33]

The Iran–United States Claims Tribunal was created in 1981 as part of the settlement of the crisis between Iran and the United States arising from the 1979 hostage taking at the U.S. Embassy in Tehran. The only reason Iran agreed to the tribunal was because the United States had frozen Iranian assets. Claims had to be filed by January 19, 1982, and approximately 1,000 were so filed for amounts of $250,000 or more, and 2,800 were filed for smaller claims. Most claims have been satisfied but a few large and complex claims remain.

The Hague Tribunal has tended to interpret its obligation to provide full compensation to mean something closer to going concern value than book value.[34] Arguing for acceptance of a claim under a going concern value does not assure that one will receive that higher amount, but it may mean a claim accepted for an amount higher relative to other U.S. claimants, and thus ultimate receipt of a higher amount in the pro rata apportioning of any agreed settlement.

Cuba will not be able to pay the full amount of the claims. A Cuban government willing to negotiate the claims will not likely agree that the amount as determined by the United States is cor-

---

B. Lillich (ed. & contrib.) 4 The Valuation of Nationalized Property in International Law 31 (1987). Other scholars dispute this narrow view of international law sources.

[31] See generally Richard B. Lillich, International Claims: Their Adjudication by National Commissions (1962).

[32] See Michael Wallace Gordon, The Cuban Claims Act: Progress in the Development of a Viable Valuation Process in the FCSC, 13 Santa Clara Law. 625 (1973).

[33] The statute authorizes the use of several methods of valuation. See 22 U.S.C.A. § 1623(a). The valuation is to use "applicable principles of international law, justice, and equity." Id. See 22 U.S.C.A. § 1623(k).

[34] The experience with Iran differs markedly from the case of Cuba. Iran agreed to the payment of claims only because it had very substantial sums on deposit in the West, which were blocked. It agreed to the claims process as a means to gain access to those funds. But Cuba had no such large sums in foreign banks. Sums that remain frozen in U.S. banks will probably be part of a future settlement agreement, with additional sums to be paid from renewed trade with the United States, possibly with restoration of some sugar quota.

rect, partly because there was never any Cuban representation at the claims hearings. Cuba will not be able to afford to pay some $2 billion (and counting) in claims, and the experience of U.S. claims commissions is the ultimate payment of a substantially lower negotiated amount than the full value of previously documented claims.

The Cuban Claims Act process is part of the larger U.S. Foreign Claims Settlement Commission. A *mixed* commission to settle claims was created following the U.S. revolutionary war.[35] But it was not effective and was followed by a *national* commission to determine claims after a lump-sum settlement agreement was concluded in 1803. Over the next century the United States established national commissions to distribute funds received in settlements with Great Britain, Brazil, China, Denmark, France, Mexico, Peru, the Two Sicilies, and Spain. Between World Wars I and II both national and mixed claims commissions were used, but the national commission prevailed.

Foreign countries often prefer the use of a national claims commission to distribute an agreed upon total sum as the country prefers. The Iran–United States Claims Tribunal is quite unique in this respect, it varies from the norm at least partly because the U.S. hostages were involved, and there was no time to conduct a lengthy process to determine how much money to demand from Iran. But the use of a national commission, in the manner of the Cuban Claims Commission, is likely to be the way future claims are settled that lack the unique characteristics of the Iranian case.

The Foreign Claims Settlement Commission was established in 1954 as a separate entity when the earlier International Claims Commission was abolished. Its function is essentially judicial, and the benefit of its existence (as opposed to using the district courts, for example) is its ability to acquire expertise in the narrow area of adjudication of foreign claims. Evidence of valuation of property lost abroad is difficult to obtain, and that form of evidence demanded in the courts is rarely available. In 1980, after a number of years of relative inactivity, the FCSC was transformed into a separate and independent agency within the Department of Justice. Any sums obtained by the United States are distributed according to the statute.

Special funds have been created in the Treasury for specific claims, relating to claims and agreements with Yugoslavia and the People's Republic of China. Each real or expected settlement with

[35] The Jay Treaty of 1794 established the first claims commission for the new United States.

an expropriating nation must necessarily be kept separate from another, thus the statutes have titles covering special procedures for various specific takings. These include claims against (1) Bulgaria, Hungary, Romania, Italy, and the Soviet Union; (2) Czechoslovakia; Cuba and China; (3) German Democratic Republic; and (4) Vietnam. Each is related to takings following significant disturbances, principally war and revolution. The statute illustrates a pattern of procedural provisions which will likely be adopted for any future losses by U.S. citizens abroad where the takings are of all the property of U.S. citizens.

Some claimants might prefer bringing their own suits against the foreign government if they are able to locate property owned by that foreign government situated in the United States. That has not proven very successful in most cases, however. When a nation undertakes a massive expropriation of the property of a foreign nation it usually removes as much property as possible from that nation. The inability of Iran to do so motivated Iran to agree to the Iran–United States Claims Tribunal. Cuba successfully transferred large sums out of the United States before remaining assets were frozen by the Congress. Thus, there may be little sense in seeking a judgment in a U.S. court if there is no property to attach and it is evident that the hostile taking nation will reject any attempt to enforce the judgment in the taking nation. Furthermore, the United States may make filing claims before a national commission the only available procedure. Many investors who were in the process of suing Iran at the time of the resolution of the hostage dispute and the establishment of the claims tribunal were angered that the agreement included removal of their claims from courts to the tribunal. Requiring all U.S. claimants to use this same process may benefit relations between the nations, but may not satisfy some claimants who were able to attach specific property of the foreign government, and who believe they might receive a greater share of their claim by separate litigation.

Separate litigation will often be attempted by frustrated expropriated investors, perhaps more successfully when the expropriations have not been massive takings as discussed above, but more selective takings of only certain property. Thus, some thought should be given to these individual suits against foreign governments for expropriations.

§ 29.22 Suing in United States Courts

When a U.S. investor sues a foreign government for taking property, two special defenses are likely to be made by the foreign government. The first is that the defendant is a sovereign which is immune from suit. The second is that the act of taking was a sovereign act occurring within the territory of the nation and thus constituted an "act of state" that should not be adjudicated in the courts of a foreign nation. There is much written about these two subjects. There are some principal features of these two theories, particularly as they apply to expropriation.

§ 29.23 Foreign Sovereign Immunity

When the circumstances for state immunity are present, the court relinquishes jurisdiction to adjudicate or enforce over the foreign state. Because state immunity is influenced by the state's concepts of separation of powers and notions of comity, state immunity theory assumes different forms in different nations. Somewhat paradoxically, state immunity is contained in statutes in several common law tradition nations, but is found only in the case law of many civil law tradition nations. State immunity theory in the United States developed in case law exclusively, until the enactment of the Foreign Sovereign Immunities Act (FSIA) of 1976.[36] The experience in the United Kingdom is similar; case law prevailed until the enactment of the State Immunity Act 1978.[37] On the continent, the theory long remained in case law, but is at least partly now under the 1972 European Convention on State Immunity and Additional Protocol.

§ 29.24 History and Rationale

The roots of U.S. state immunity precedent go back to *The Schooner Exchange v. McFaddon.*[38] Chief Justice Marshall stated in this Supreme Court decision that the courts of the United States lacked jurisdiction over an armed ship of a foreign state (France) located in a U.S. port. When engaged in official acts *(jure imperii)* the sovereign (whether ancient prince or modern state):

> [b]eing in no respect amenable to another; and being bound by obligations of the highest character not to degrade the dignity of his nation, by placing himself or its sovereign rights within the jurisdiction of another, can be supposed to enter a foreign territory only under an express license, or in the confidence that the [absolute] immunities belonging to his independent

---

36 28 U.S.C.A. §§ 1330, 1602–1611.

37 See Michael Wallace Gordon, Foreign State Immunity in Commercial Transactions § 17 (Butterworths 1991).

38 11 U.S. (7 Cranch) 116, 3 L.Ed. 287 (1812).

> sovereign station, though not expressly stipulated, are reserved by implication, and will be extended to him.[39]

But Chief Justice Marshall was also aware of the logic of limits on immunity, acknowledging a distinction between the private property of a person who happens to be a prince, and the military force of a sovereign power. Had he been confronted with a case of commercial activity by a sovereign, the long struggle with state immunity theory in the United States might have been prevented.

Immunity of a sovereign nevertheless was consistently found to be absolute, regardless of the nature of the activity. Although it may have appeared from *The Schooner Exchange* that state immunity is domestic law, it is as well an accepted principle of customary international law.[40] Customary international law offered some support in the mid-part of the 20th century to nations (i.e., United Kingdom) confronting the absolute/restrictive debate, but the evolution from absolute to restrictive theory was less influenced by international law than developing state concepts of the role of the state in modern society.

The doctrine of state immunity would have caused little difficulty had sovereigns engaged only in "sovereign" acts. But modern states engage in many private transactions (*jure gestionis*). The doctrine of absolute and unqualified immunity gave way to a restrictive theory which denied immunity when the sovereign descended into the market place.

Many states became private traders, engaging in the operation of transportation, telegraph and telephone services, radio and television communications, and the production of goods (extraction of natural resources, tobacco and matches, etc.). Commercial transactions gave rise to disputes and brought into the courts of one nation the trading sovereigns of another. National courts were slow to alter the absolute immunity doctrine. Rather surprisingly, in civil law tradition nations on the Continent case law was where the evolution from absolute theory to restrictive theory occurred, while in common law tradition nations, courts struggled with such evolution and the restrictive theory only took root clearly with the enactment of legislation. As early as 1857 in Belgium, in *Etat du Perou v. Krelinger,*[41] the restrictive theory began to be accepted on the Con-

---

39 11 U.S. (7 Cranch) at 137.

40 See Berizzi Brothers Co. v. The Pesaro, 271 U.S. 562, 46 S.Ct. 311, 70 L.Ed. 1088 (1926).

41 P.B. 1857–II–348.

tinent. An Italian decision in 1882, *Morellet C. Goveruo Danese,*[42] continued the movement, as have Austrian and German courts in the 20th century.

The Department of State regularly requested immunity when friendly nations were sued in U.S. courts. But in 1952, the Department of State sent what became known as the "Tate Letter" to the Department of Justice, announcing that Department of State policy was "to follow the restrictive theory of sovereign immunity in the consideration of requests of foreign governments for a grant of sovereign immunity."[43] The letter stated:

> It is realized that a shift in policy by the executive cannot control the courts but it is felt that the courts are less likely to allow a plea of sovereign immunity where the executive has declined to do so. There have been indications that at least some Justices of the Supreme Court feel that in this matter courts should follow the branch of the Government charged with responsibility for the conduct of foreign relations.

Although the Tate Letter announced an acceptance of the restrictive theory of sovereign immunity, it offered no guidelines or criteria to distinguish a state's public acts from its private acts. Until the passage of the Foreign Sovereign Immunities Act twenty-four years later, the application of the restrictive theory proved troublesome. The courts generally complied with "suggestions" of immunity from the Department of State, and foreign sovereigns were often successful in urging the Department to support immunity for the kind of private acts the restrictive theory was intended to address. But even when state immunity was codified in the 1976 FSIA, it was uncertain to what degree separation of powers principles would induce a judicial caution about embarrassing the executive branch in its role as the primary organ of international policy. Moreover, and "(p)erhaps more importantly, in the chess game that is diplomacy only the executive has a view of the entire board and an understanding of the relationship between isolated moves."

§ 29.25 The Foreign Sovereign Immunities Act of 1976

The enactment of the Foreign Sovereign Immunities Act was intended to relieve the government of diplomatic pressures, "thereby eliminating the role of the State Department in such questions

---

[42] (1882) Guir. It. 1883–I–25.

[43] 24 Dept. State Bull. 984 (1952).

and bringing the United States into conformity with the immunity practice of virtually every other country."[44] The FSIA additionally illustrated to litigants that sovereign immunity decisions would be made on legal rather than political grounds. The old suggestion of immunity made by the executive was abrogated by the FSIA.[45] In adopting the restrictive theory, the FSIA established legal standards applicable to claims of immunity made by foreign sovereigns, whether the litigation was in a state or federal court in the United States. But the FSIA also guarantees foreign states the right to remove civil actions from a state court to a federal court, thus allying fears of "local" treatment and contemplating the development of a fairly uniform body of law in the federal courts. That body has proven to be less than uniform; one court has described it as a "statutory labyrinth that, owing to the numerous interpretive questions engendered by its bizarre structure . . . has . . . been a financial boon for the private bar but a constant bane of the federal judiciary".[46]

A further goal of the FSIA was to provide a procedure for service of process and obtaining *in personam* jurisdiction, thus avoiding the past practices of plaintiffs seizing property of foreign states to force an appearance. And finally, the FSIA allows execution upon commercial assets, although the requirements for execution are stricter than those for jurisdiction to adjudicate.

§ 29.26 Who Is a Sovereign?

State immunity is a defense that is the patrimony of foreign states. A "foreign state" includes "a political subdivision of a foreign state or an agency or instrumentality of a foreign state."[47] An "agency or instrumentality of a foreign state" is any entity:

> (1) which is a separate legal person, corporate or otherwise, and
>
> (2) which is an organ of a foreign state or political subdivision thereof, or a majority of whose shares or other ownership interest is owned by a foreign state or political subdivision thereof, and

[44] Martropico Compania Naviera S.A. v. Perusahaan Pertambangan Minyak Dan Gas Bumi Negara (Pertamina), 428 F.Supp. 1035, 1037 (S.D.N.Y.1977).

[45] Republic of Philippines v. Marcos, 665 F.Supp. 793 (N.D.Cal.1987).

[46] Gibbons v. Udaras na Gaeltachta, 549 F.Supp. 1094, 1105 (S.D.N.Y.1982).

[47] 28 U.S.C.A. § 1603(a).

(3) which is neither a citizen of a State of the United States [as defined in the Act], . . . nor created under the laws of any third country.[48]

The distinction between a foreign state and agency or instrumentality is important: a foreign state is not liable for the acts of its agencies or instrumentalities in the absence of piercing the corporate veil. There is a presumption that the foreign state is separate from its instrumentalities that may only be overcome by showing (1) that the corporate entity was so controlled that there was a principal/agent relationship, or (2) that allowing the distinction would work fraud or injustice.[49] The Vatican has been held to be a foreign state.[50] The PLO has been denied such status.[51] Foreign trade organizations of nonmarket nations have usually been held to be instrumentalities, as have state owned corporations engaged in a wide variety of activities, such as airlines, mining, shipping, banking, and production such as steel.

The FSIA does not address the status of international organizations as foreign states. Courts have denied such status to OPEC,[52] granted it to the British West Indies Central Labour Organization,[53] and in other cases suggested that it did not have to reach a decision because immunity would exist (or not exist) whether absolute or restrictive theory applied. In 2010, the Supreme Court held that the FSIA does not apply to government officials, leaving that issue to federal common law.[54]

§ 29.27 Jurisdictional Issues

The FSIA is federal law. The law is based on the theory that a foreign state is "presumptively immune" from the jurisdiction of a U.S. court. The court lacks subject matter jurisdiction unless a specific exception applies.[55] Subject matter jurisdiction is conferred by

---

[48] 28 U.S.C.A. § 1603(b).

[49] First Nat'l City Bank v. Banco Para El Comercio Exterior de Cuba (Bancec), 462 U.S. 611, 103 S.Ct. 2591, 77 L.Ed.2d 46 (1983).

[50] English v. Thorne, 676 F.Supp. 761 (S.D.Miss.1987).

[51] National Petrochemical Co. of Iran v. M/T Stolt Sheaf, 860 F.2d 551 (2d Cir.1988).

[52] International Ass'n of Machinists and Aerospace Workers v. OPEC, 477 F.Supp. 553, 560 (C.D.Cal.1979), *aff'd*, 649 F.2d 1354 (9th Cir.1981), *cert. denied*, 454 U.S. 1163, 102 S.Ct. 1036, 71 L.Ed.2d 319 (1982).

[53] Rios v. Marshall, 530 F.Supp. 351 (S.D.N.Y.1981).

[54] Yousuf v. Samantar, 130 S.Ct. 2278, 176 L.Ed.2d 1047 (2010).

[55] See Saudi Arabia v. Nelson, 507 U.S. 349, 113 S.Ct. 1471, 123 L.Ed.2d 47 (1993); Argentine Republic v. Amerada Hess Shipping Corp., 488 U.S. 428, 109 S.Ct. 683, 102 L.Ed.2d 818 (1989); Verlinden B.V. v. Central Bank of Nigeria, 461 U.S. 480, 103 S.Ct. 1962, 76 L.Ed.2d 81 (1983).

§ 1330(a) to permit a nonjury civil action against a foreign state not entitled to immunity. If the court has subject matter jurisdiction under § 1330(a), and if service of process is made in accordance with § 1608, and if constitutional due process requirements are met, then the court has personal jurisdiction over the foreign state under § 1330(b). But, as noted, this jurisdiction is effective only when the foreign state is not entitled to immunity.

The principal function of the FSIA is to confer immunity upon a defendant foreign state. A court clearly lacks jurisdiction unless one of the exceptions applies. It should thus be apparent that "(u)nder the analytic structure of the Act, the existence of subject matter and personal jurisdiction, the requisites for service of process, and the availability of sovereign immunity as a defense are intricately coordinated inquiries."[56] Understanding the Congressional pattern of subject matter and personal jurisdiction under the FSIA requires one additional essential comment, that the "Act cannot create personal jurisdiction where the Constitution forbids it. Accordingly, each finding of personal jurisdiction under the FSIA requires, in addition, a due process scrutiny of the court's power to exercise its authority over a particular defendant."[57] The FSIA "is designed to embody the 'requirements of minimum jurisdictional contacts and adequate notice.'"[58]

§ 29.28 Exceptions to Sovereign Immunity—Waiver

A foreign state is not immune in any case "in which [it] has waived its immunity either explicitly or by implication, notwithstanding any withdrawal of the waiver . . . except in accordance with the terms of waiver."[59]

Implied waivers are not easily established. A foreign state does not waive its state immunity by entering into a contract with another nation. That contract may give rise to a commercial exception issue, but a waiver must be intentional and knowing.[60] How a foreign state responds to a complaint is important to determining the existence of an implicit waiver. Entering a general appearance may

---

56 Velidor v. L/P/G Benghazi, 653 F.2d 812, 817 (3d Cir.1981).

57 Texas Trading & Milling Corp. v. Federal Republic of Nigeria, 647 F.2d 300, 308 (2d Cir.1981), *cert. denied* 454 U.S. 1148, 102 S.Ct. 1012, 71 L.Ed.2d 301 (1982).

58 East Europe Domestic Int'l Sales Corp. v. Terra, 467 F.Supp. 383, 387 (S.D.N.Y.1979).

59 28 U.S.C.A. § 1605(a)(1).

60 Transamerican Steamship Corp. v. Somali Democratic Republic, 767 F.2d 998 (D.C.Cir.1985).

constitute a waiver, as might failure to appear altogether.[61] But failing to timely answer or file motions, such as a motion to dismiss, will not automatically waive immunity.

Explicit waivers are more readily identifiable, such as those found in treaties. For example, the United States has waived immunity with respect to commercial and other activities in some of its treaties of Friendship, Commerce, and Navigation (FCN). The language used in the waiver is important—a commonly used provision in FCN treaties that immunity shall not be claimed from "suit, execution or judgment, or other liability" is not an explicit waiver from prejudgment attachment.[62]

A second source of explicit waivers is in private agreements. For example, a loan document providing that "The Borrower can sue and be sued in its own name and does not have any right of immunity from suit with respect to the Borrower's obligations under this Letter or the Notes," has been held to be an explicit waiver of a right to raise the defense of state immunity for a prejudgment attachment.

§ 29.29 Exceptions to Sovereign Immunity—Commercial Activity

The commercial activity exception is the reason the FSIA was enacted. Law prior to the passage of the Act was unclear about whether a restrictive theory of sovereign immunity excluded acts which were commercial in *nature* or commercial in *purpose*. The FSIA chooses those commercial in *nature*, by defining "commercial activity" as:

> either a regular course of commercial conduct or a particular commercial transaction or act. The commercial character of an activity shall be determined by reference to the nature of the course of conduct or particular transaction or act, rather than by reference to its purpose.[63]

Determining what activity of the foreign state is alleged to be commercial is obviously a precondition to determine whether that activity is commercial and whether it fits into one of the three clas-

---

[61] Von Dardel v. USSR, 623 F.Supp. 246 (D.D.C.1985, vacated 736 F.Supp. 1 (D.D.C. 1990)). See also Frolova v. USSR, 761 F.2d 370 (7th Cir.1985).

[62] Libra Bank Ltd. v. Banco Nacional de Costa Rica, S.A., 676 F.2d 47 (2d Cir.1982).

[63] 28 U.S.C.A. § 1603(d).

ses of commercial activity which deny immunity to the foreign state. The FSIA defines those three classes as:

> A foreign state shall not be immune from the jurisdiction of courts of the United States or of the States in any case . . . in which the action is based upon a commercial activity carried on in the United States by the foreign state; or upon an act performed in the United States in connection with a commercial activity of the foreign state elsewhere; or upon an act outside the territory of the United States in connection with a comercial activity of the foreign state elsewhere and that act causes a direct effect in the United States.[64]

The legislative history of the FSIA suggests that a commercial activity is one which an individual might customarily carry on for profit. If the activity is one which normally could be engaged in by a private party, it is commercial and a foreign state is not immune, but if the activity is one in which only a state can engage, it is noncommercial under the FSIA. The focus is not on whether the defendant generally engages in commercial activities, but on the particular conduct giving rise to the action.[65]

The proper focus is on the *nature* of the activity rather than its *purpose*. Cases have found commercial activity to include purchasing grain from a U.S. company under a U.S. government program, a Republic of Ireland joint venture with two U.S. citizens to manufacture plastic cosmetic containers, a Turkish government owned gun manufacturer selling in the United States, contracts for tours of USSR artists to the United States and Great Britain, and a Polish government owned company selling golf carts in the United States. Noncommercial activities have included nationalizing plaintiff's corporation, establishing terms and conditions for removal of natural resources from its territory, and granting and revoking a license to export a natural resource.

In 1992 the U.S. Supreme Court addressed the definition of commercial activity and came down strongly against any interpretation based on the *purpose* of the activity.[66] The court said the issue is whether the actions that the foreign state "performs (whatever the motive behind them) are the type of actions by which a private party engages in 'trade and traffic or commerce'".

---

[64] 28 U.S.C.A. § 1605(a)(2).

[65] Brazosport Towing Co., Inc. v. 3,838 Tons of Sorghum Laden on Board, 607 F.Supp. 11 (S.D.Tex.1984).

[66] Republic of Argentina v. Weltover, Inc., 504 U.S. 607, 112 S.Ct. 2160, 119 L.Ed.2d 394 (1992).

The FSIA and pleas of sovereign immunity after expropriations are important. Since considerable U.S. litigation against foreign sovereigns follows noncompensated nationalizations, the view that a "nationalization is the quintessentially sovereign act, never viewed as having a commercial character," obviously is a disappointment to many subjects of nationalization.[67] The exception contained in § 1605(a)(3), discussed in the next section below—rights taken in violation of international law—may apply to some nationalizations, depending on the relation of the property located in the United States to the property nationalized.

The three part commercial activity test of § 1605(a)(2) requires the commercial activity to bear some relationship to the United States. The first part is "action based upon a commercial activity carried on in the United States by the foreign state." This is the easiest part of the test and essentially involves how much commercial activity was done in the United States, and what is the link between the cause of action and the commercial activity. "Substantial contact" with the United States is sufficient. The second part of the test deals with an "act performed in the United States in connection with a commercial activity of the foreign state performed elsewhere." It is the least used of the three parts since many of the acts complained of occur outside the United States; when they do occur in the United States the matter is often considered under or in combination with part one of the test. It is the third part of the test, an "act outside . . . the United States in connection with a commercial activity of the foreign state and that act causes a direct effect in the United States," that has been the most difficult to define. Since many acts do occur abroad, the "direct effect" language is often the focus of attention. The federal circuit courts have been split on what constitutes a direct effect. Some followed the view that it must be "substantial and foreseeable", drawing upon the Restatement of Foreign Relations section on jurisdiction to prescribe.[68] Others have rejected this and believe direct effect to be satisfied where there is some financial loss.[69] This division was answered by the Supreme Court in 1992, when the Court rejected the House Report and Restatement views that direct effect meant both "substantial" and "foreseeable" and ruled that an effect is direct if it "follows 'as an

[67] Alberti v. Empresa Nicaraguense de la Carne, 705 F.2d 250 (7th Cir.1983).

[68] Maritime Int'l Nominees Establishment v. Republic of Guinea, 693 F.2d 1094 (D.C.Cir.1982).

[69] Texas Trading & Milling Corp. v. Federal Republic of Nigeria, 647 F.2d 300 (2d Cir.1981).

immediate consequence of the defendant's . . . activity,"[70] accepting the *Texas Trading* position.

§ 29.30 Exceptions to Sovereign Immunity—Violations of International Law

Rights in property taken in violation of international law may preclude the defense of sovereign immunity if:

> that property or any property exchanged for such property is present in the United States in connection with a commercial activity carried on in the United States by the foreign state; or that property or any property exchanged for such property is owned or operated by an agency or instrumentality of the foreign state and that agency or instrumentality is engaged in a commercial activity in the United States.[71]

This section may be used to respond to noncompensated expropriations of property, but the decisions have interpreted the provisions more restrictively than what many scholars thought the FSIA intended to reach. The "property tracing" feature of the FSIA severely limits the use of this alternative violation of international law provision of the FSIA. The FSIA is not a helpful statute to persons whose property has been expropriated by a foreign state.

§ 29.31 Act of State Doctrine

The defense of sovereignty immunity often is accompanied by the separate defense of "act of state". Acceptance of either defense generates judicial abstention. The sovereign immunity doctrine mandates that a foreign sovereign may not be sued in the courts of other nations, thus focusing on who should or should not be sued. It is concerned with the *status* of the defendant. Contrastingly, the act of state doctrine suggests that courts of one nation will not sit in judgment of the acts of a foreign sovereign that occurred in the foreign state, thus focusing on what is or is not a proper subject matter. It is concerned with the *acts* of the defendant. The act of state "operates as an issue preclusion device."[72] Sovereign immunity is jurisdictional in nature. If immunity exists, the court lacks jurisdiction. But the act of state doctrine does not deprive a court of juris-

---

[70] Republic of Argentina v. Weltover, Inc., 504 U.S. 607, 112 S.Ct. 2160, 2168, 119 L.Ed.2d 394 (1992), citing Texas Trading & Milling Corp. v. Federal Republic of Nigeria, 647 F.2d 300, 311 (2d Cir.1981), *cert. denied* 454 U.S. 1148, 102 S.Ct. 1012, 71 L.Ed.2d 301 (1982).

[71] 28 U.S.C.A. § 1605(a)(3).

[72] National American Corp. v. Federal Republic of Nigeria, 448 F.Supp. 622, 640 (S.D.N.Y.1978), *aff'd*, 597 F.2d 314 (2d Cir.1979).

diction. Where the act of state doctrine is at issue, the court has jurisdiction but decides, for act of state reasons, not to decide the issue.

Sovereign immunity in the United States is governed by the FSIA, which has exemption provisions for certain commercial activity, and for certain violations of international law. Those two issues have not escaped the act of state doctrine, which has not been the subject of legislation parallel to the FSIA. The act of state doctrine in the United States is not governed by statute but rather by case law. That case law includes debate regarding its application to violations of international law. Congressional anger over *Banco Nacional de Cuba v. Sabbatino*,[73] led to legislation mandating that courts not accept the defense in some instances where there are alleged violations of international law, whether the doctrine applies to bar a counterclaim, whether it applies to an act in violation of a treaty, uncertainty over the situs of an act of state, and most recently, whether it applies to motives rather than acts of foreign state officials. But of most concern to those engaged in international business transactions is the debate regarding the existence of a commercial exception to the doctrine.

§ 29.32 History of Act of State Doctrine

The doctrine can be traced to the 1674 English case of *Blad v. Bamfield*.[74] It also exists in the jurisprudence of France, Germany, Greece, Italy, The Netherlands, Switzerland, and other countries. The initial important U.S. decision is *Underhill v. Hernandez*.[75] There the Supreme Court stated that:

> Every sovereign state is bound to respect the independence of every other state, and the courts of one country will not sit in judgment on the acts of the government of another, done within its own territory. Redress of grievances by reason of such acts must be obtained through the means open to be availed of by sovereign powers as between themselves.[76]

The *Underhill* litigation arose from claimed damages suffered by the plaintiff (Underhill) at the hands of a Venezuelan revolutionary army commander (Hernandez) during an alleged false arrest in Venezuela. The United States had subsequently recognized

[73] 376 U.S. 398, 84 S.Ct. 923, 11 L.Ed.2d 804 (1964).

[74] 36 All E.Eng.Rep. 992, applied in 1981 in Buttes Gas and Oil Co. v. Hammer (No. 3), [1981] 3 All E.R. 616.

[75] 168 U.S. 250, 18 S.Ct. 83, 42 L.Ed. 456 (1897).

[76] Id. at 252, 18 S.Ct. at 84.

the revolutionary government. The doctrine as expressed in *Underhill* was reaffirmed in the modern classic, *Sabbatino.*

§ 29.33 Act of State and the Expropriation of Property

Banco Nacional de Cuba v. Sabbatino began the contemporary history of the act of state doctrine and its applicability to expropriations.[77] The case involved rights to property affected by the Cuban nationalization of property in 1960. Justice Harlan stated:

> [T]he Judicial Branch will not examine the validity of a taking of property within its own territory by a foreign sovereign, extant and recognized by this country at the time of suit, in the absence of a treaty or other unambiguous agreement regarding controlling legal principles, even if the complaint alleges that the taking violates customary international law.[78]

Justice White dissented, stating:

> I do not believe that the act of state doctrine, as judicially fashioned in the Court, and the reasons underlying it, require American courts to decide cases in disregard of international law and of the rights of litigants to a full determination on the merits.[79]

The Supreme Court decision was not well received by many members of Congress. The Sabbatino Amendment to the Foreign Assistance Act was quickly passed, and stated:

> Notwithstanding any other provisions of law, no court in the United States shall decline on the ground of the federal act of state doctrine to make a determination on the merits giving effect to the principles of international law in a case in which a claim of title or other right [to property] is asserted by any party including a foreign state . . . based upon . . . a confiscation or other taking . . . by an act of that state in violation of the principles of international law, including the principles of compensation and the other standards set out in this subsection: *Provided,* That this subparagraph shall not be applicable . . . (2) in any case with respect to which the President determines that application of the act of state doctrine is required in that particular case by the foreign policy interests of the Unit-

77 376 U.S. 398, 84 S.Ct. 923, 11 L.Ed.2d 804 (1964).

78 Id. at 428, 84 S.Ct. at 940.

79 Id. at 441, 84 S.Ct. at 946.

ed States and a suggestion to this effect is filed on his behalf in that case with the court.[80]

This Sabbatino Amendment (also called the Second Hickenlooper Amendment) led to a reversal of the *Sabbatino* decision on remand.[81] But in the years that followed, the courts have not applied very enthusiastically this hurriedly adopted reversal of a doctrine adopted and long approved by the judicial branch.

§ 29.34 Act of State Encounters Some Limits

The act of state doctrine, subsequent to the formation of much of its characteristics in expropriation cases, was for several years expanded in scope, but in 1990 encountered a Supreme Court contraction in *W.S. Kirkpatrick & Co. v. Environmental Tectonics Corp., Int'l.*[82] In the *Kirkpatrick* case Environmental Tectonics learned that the reason it had lost a contract with Nigeria was that Kirkpatrick had bribed Nigerian government officials. Environmental Tectonics sought damages against Kirkpatrick, which raised the act of state doctrine in that proof of the bribe might require the court to consider an act of the foreign state. The Circuit Court declined to apply the act of state doctrine because the Department of State said that such inquiry would not cause embarrassment to U.S. foreign relations. But the Supreme Court rejected that reasoning, refusing to apply the doctrine because it did not involve an inquiry into the lawfulness of an act of the foreign government, but merely the consideration of the motivations of foreign officials. This test will need some refining. One can think of situations where judicial consideration of an act of a foreign state would cause little embarrassment, but inquiry into the motives of another act would cause great embarrassment to U.S. foreign relations. *Kirkpatrick* is an important decision, suggesting to lower courts a method by which the act of state may be considerably diminished in application in future cases.

§ 29.35 Act of State and the Separation of Powers

The act of state doctrine is punctuated by unclear contours, debatable exceptions and an unsympathetic Congressional response. The cases illustrate that the doctrine is deliberate but flexible.

---

[80] 22 U.S.C.A. § 2370(e)(2). The bracketed words were added in 1965 to clarify that the doctrine continued to apply to acts not involving the taking of property.

[81] Banco Nacional de Cuba v. Farr, 243 F.Supp. 957 (S.D.N.Y.1965), *aff'd*, 383 F.2d 166 (2d Cir.1967), *cert. denied*, 390 U.S. 956, 88 S.Ct. 1038, 19 L.Ed.2d 1151 (1968).

[82] 493 U.S. 400, 110 S.Ct. 701, 107 L.Ed.2d 816 (1990).

There is general agreement that the doctrine is grounded in self-imposed judicial restraint. The doctrine rests upon considerations of international comity and separation of powers between the executive and judicial branches of the government. It is intended to avoid embarrassment in the conduct of the nation's foreign relations. One has only to envision a justice of peace court in the United States, proclaiming the illegality of actions taken in a foreign country by the highest officers of that government, to sense the international prudence of such a doctrine.[83]

The act of state doctrine's interface with the separation of powers, between the executive and judicial branches of the U.S. government, has been discussed by courts for over twenty years in large part because of *Bernstein v. N.V. Nederlandsche–Amerikaansche Stoomvaart–Maatschappij*.[84] In *Bernstein* the court was inclined to apply the act of state doctrine, but the Department of State urged the court to refrain and to proceed with an examination of the legal issues. The court concluded:

> [I]n the prior appeal in this case . . . because of the lack of a definitive expression of Executive Policy, we felt constrained to follow . . . [the act of state doctrine] . . . Following our decision, however, the State Department issued . . . [a policy statement intended] . . . to relieve American courts from any [such] restraint upon the exercise of their jurisdiction. . . . In view of this supervening expression of Executive Policy, we amend our mandate . . . [that the act of state doctrine precludes judicial inquiry].[85]

The validity of this "*Bernstein* exception" to the act of state doctrine was before the Supreme Court in *First National City Bank v. Banco Nacional de Cuba*.[86] Reversing the lower court, three justices, as a plurality, wrote:

> [W]here the Executive Branch, charged as it is with primary responsibility for the conduct of foreign affairs, expressly represents to the Court that application of the act of state doctrine would not advance the interests of American foreign policy, that doctrine should not be applied by the courts. In so doing, we of course adopt and approve the so-called *Bernstein* exception to the act of state doctrine.

---

[83] See DeRoburt v. Gannett Co., Inc., 548 F.Supp. 1370, 1380 (D.Haw.1982).

[84] 210 F.2d 375 (2d Cir.1954).

[85] Id. at 375–376.

[86] 406 U.S. 759, 92 S.Ct. 1808, 32 L.Ed.2d 466 (1972), *reh'g denied*, 409 U.S. 897, 93 S.Ct. 92, 34 L.Ed.2d 155 (1972).

> We believe this to be no more than an application of the classical common law maxim that "[t]he reason of the law ceasing, the law itself also ceases". . . . Our holding is in no sense an abdication of the judicial function to the Executive Branch.[87]

Two concurring Justices and four dissenting Justices disagreed, however, the latter writing:

> As six members of this Court recognize today, . . . [it] is clear that the representations of the Department of State are entitled to weight for the light they shed on the permutation and combination of factors underlying the act of state doctrine. But they cannot be determinative. . . .
>
> The task of defining the contours of a political question such as the act of state doctrine is exclusively the function of this Court. . . . The "*Bernstein*" exception relinquishes the function to the Executive by requiring blind adherence to its requests that foreign acts of state be reviewed. Conversely, it politicizes the judiciary.[88]

Four years later, in *Alfred Dunhill of London, Inc. v. Republic of Cuba*,[89] four dissenting justices wrote:

> [S]ix members of the Court in *First National* . . . disapproved finally the so-called *Bernstein* exception to the act of state doctrine, thus minimizing the significance of any letter from the Department of State . . . the task of defining the role of the judiciary is for this court, not the Executive Branch.

Constitutional effect aside, a *Bernstein* letter from the Department of State to a court may be quite persuasive in providing the court a reason to avoid application of the doctrine. Lack of such a letter may not result in a reverse conclusion; in 1982, the Department of State advised the Solicitor General that "courts should not infer from the silence of the Department of State that adjudication in . . . (a pending) case would be harmful to the foreign policy of the United States."[90]

---

87 Id. at 768, 92 S.Ct. at 1813.

88 Id. at 790, 92 S.Ct. at 1824.

89 425 U.S. 682, 725, 96 S.Ct. 1854, 48 L.Ed.2d 301 (1976).

90 See 22 Int'l Legal Mat. 207 (1983).

The *Kirkpatrick* decision supports the view of *Dunhill* that it is the function of the judiciary rather than the executive to define the role of the judiciary in addressing acts of foreign states. The Supreme Court in *Kirkpatrick* did not reject any role for the executive, but clearly rejected the Circuit Court's giving "full faith and credit" to the letter from the Department of State.

§ 29.36 Act of State and Some Exceptions

As in the case of the application of sovereign immunity, there are exceptions to the act of state doctrine. One exception, where the act violates international law, has been discussed above. Two other actions that are debated as constituting exceptions are waiver and commercial activity.

Waiver. A sovereign sometimes appears to expressly waive its right to raise the act of state defense. But it is not clear whether the sovereign might retract the waiver. If revocable, it would seem that the doctrine actually cannot be waived. A further question is whether the imposition of a counterclaim by a defendant sovereign constitutes a waiver. A majority of the Court in the *First National* decision suggested no, but it was not part of the opinion. If the sovereign brings an action in a U.S. court, it is not stripped of its right to invoke the act of state as a defense to a counterclaim just because it thereby waives its right to avoid a counterclaim on grounds of sovereign immunity. A clear and unambiguous statement by a foreign state that it does not object to judicial scrutiny of a state act may influence a court, but other factors may also be considered.[91]

Commercial activity. Uncertainty also clouds the issue of the existence of a commercial activity exception to the act of state doctrine. The Supreme Court in the *Dunhill* case has stated that:

> [T]he concept of an act of state should not be extended to include the repudiation of a purely commercial obligation owed by a foreign sovereign or by one of its commercial instrumentalities. . . . In their commercial capacities, foreign governments do not exercise powers peculiar to sovereigns. . . . Subjecting them in connection with such acts to the same rules of law that apply to private citizens is unlikely to touch very sharply on "national nerves."[92]

---

[91] Compania de Gas de Nuevo Laredo, S.A. v. Entex, Inc., 686 F.2d 322 (5th Cir.1982).

[92] Alfred Dunhill of London, Inc. v. Republic of Cuba, 425 U.S. 682 695, 704, 96 S.Ct. 1854, 48 L.Ed.2d 301 (1976).

The *Dunhill* case has become known as the "commercial exception" to the act of state doctrine, notwithstanding that only four justices joined in that part of the opinion, and that four other justices wrote:

> [I]t does not follow that there should be a commercial act exception to the act of state doctrine. . . .
>
> The carving out of broad exceptions to the doctrine is fundamentally at odds with the careful case-by-case approach adopted in *Sabbatino*.[93]

The ambiguity of the court has led to different views expressed in lower federal courts. One court stated:

> consideration of the commercial nature of a given act is compelled if the doctrine is to be applied correctly. In this connection, attention is owed not to the purpose of the act but to its nature. The goal of the inquiry is to determine if denial of the act of state defense in the case under consideration will thwart the policy concerns in which the doctrine is rooted.[94]

But another court observed:

> While purely commercial activity may not rise to the level of an act of state, certain seemingly commercial activities will trigger act of state considerations. . . . When the state *qua* state acts in the public interest, its sovereignty is asserted. The Courts must proceed cautiously to avoid an affront to that sovereignty. . . . [W]e find that the act of state doctrine remains available when such caution is appropriate regardless of any commercial component of the activity involved.[95]

If a commercial exception is not to be granted, determining that the situs of the activity (commercial or not) is not in the foreign state may cause judicial rejection of the doctrine. This has proven important to the international debt issue. If nonpayment is held to have occurred at the office of the lending bank in the United States, the doctrine may be rejected as a defense.[96]

---

93 Id. at 725, 96 S.Ct. at 1876.

94 Sage Int'l, Ltd. v. Cadillac Gage Co., 534 F.Supp. 896, 905 (E.D.Mich.1981).

95 IAM v. OPEC, 649 F.2d 1354, 1360 (9th Cir.1981).

96 Allied Bank Int'l v. Banco Credito Agricola de Cartago, 757 F.2d 516 (2d Cir.1985), *cert. denied*, 473 U.S. 934, 106 S.Ct. 30, 87 L.Ed.2d 706 (1985).

§ 29.37 Act of State and Congress

Congress does not like to enact legislation that will be annulled by the courts on the basis of the act of state doctrine. A recent example is the 1996 Cuban Liberty and Democratic Solidarity (LIBERTAD) Act [a.k.a. Helms Burton Act]. The act stated that: "No court of the United States shall decline, based upon the act of state doctrine, to make a determination on the merits in an action brought under paragraph (1)"[97]

[97] 22 USCS § 6082(6).

Chapter 30

INTERNATIONAL BUSINESS LITIGATION

Table of Sections

---

§ 30.1 Introduction

If the plaintiff is "foreign" and the defendant is domestic, or the plaintiff is domestic and the defendant is foreign, we must know the meaning of "foreign." If one assumes that foreign means another state, as many states interpret the word, what should we call people from other nations? Not foreigners. Outlanders? Others? It may be equally confusing when a state's laws refer to an action within the state as opposed to an action outside the state, as many states do in reference to the rules for service of process It is one thing to serve process in a neighboring state, and quite another to serve process in another nation, yet some states do not make any distinction.

Each of the topics which are covered in this chapter, such as personal jurisdiction, service of process, and *forum non conveniens,* should be familiar to any law student who has completed a year or two of law school. But that familiarity is based upon transactions between persons from different states rather than different nations. When one studies *international* litigation, each of these areas will be revisited, and each will raise very different issues than were discussed in the basic course in Civil Procedure. Consider only one example, service of process. The law that governs service of process in the various states may be different, but all have some similar characteristics. It is usually agreed the process is effective when actually given to the defendant, but when that person is not available the rules for service vary greatly. U.S. state law tends to focus on substituted service by such means as a registered letter. Some foreign nations allow service by posting a notice on the courthouse door, or by service on a willing neighbor. Service is considered so fundamentally different in different nations that nations have adopted what is known as the Hague Service Convention, which attempts to include rules acceptable to the agreeing parties.

An inevitable consequence of increased trade and investment is increased conflict requiring some method of dispute resolution. That means addressing the differences between the applicable nations in each of the subject areas discussed in this chapter.

Litigation may not be the method selected or preferred to resolve an international dispute arising from trade or investment. There are numerous methods to resolve cross border business disputes. Arbitration is commonly used for commercial contracts. Trade agreements have developed unique processes for dispute resolution, notably the dispute panel process, often combining elements of litigation and arbitration. But many international business disputes remain handled by traditional litigation.

§ 30.2 Personal Jurisdiction

There is interplay between minimum contacts and due process. We might list minimum contacts to include having an office or employees in the state, amount of business and its frequency, and use of services within the state such as banking.

Where a suit is initiated in the United States and the defendant believes a *forum non conveniens* motion will prevail, possible defects in jurisdiction are overlooked for the moment, or deferred pending the resolution of the *forum non conveniens* motion. The reason may be that predicting answers to questions of jurisdiction is less certain than predicting answers to *forum non conveniens*.[1]

Both state and federal courts are bound by federal Constitutional limitations. State courts may be further limited by state constitutional limitations, but many states have long-arm statutes

---

[1] A parallel situation arises when a foreign state is sued in a U.S. court. The court may first turn to the Foreign Sovereign Immunities Act and address the questions (1) whether the party is a state, and (2) whether there is a commercial activity, or waiver or other immunity exception. If the defendant is not a state, or an exception is not present, there is no need to address the jurisdiction issue.

which extend to, if not beyond, the federal limits.[2] A necessary return to *International Shoe* may cause nightmares to the reader but there is no other way to present personal jurisdiction in international litigation then to start with the classic test of minimum contacts discussed in that venerable decision.[3] Minimum contacts were held necessary to meet constitutional due process requirements under the Fourteenth Amendment. Perhaps in no other area of constitutional law have the courts been able to adopt various and varying approaches to the meaning of due process than in the progeny of *International Shoe*.

Although *International Shoe* did not involve a foreign defendant, that extension would later occur.[4] But before the venture into personal jurisdiction over foreign defendants, the Supreme Court issued *Worldwide Volkswagen*.[5] The Court held that a defendant must have "purposefully directed" its activities toward the forum state. The defendant would have to have anticipated being subjected to the forum state's courts, and there should be some link between the injuries and the defendant's activities in the state. The Court listed several factors, emphasizing the number, nature, and quality of contacts, as well as the source and connection of the action with the above three contacts. The often mentioned "stream of commerce" test uses the quantity and quality contacts.

The first significant Supreme Court decision with foreign defendants was the *Asahi* decision.[6] A motorcycle tire failed and the driver and passenger were injured and killed, respectively. The valve stem was allegedly the defective part of the tire, and had been made by Asahi, a company in Japan. It was purchased by the Taiwan tire manufacturer. The tire manufacturer was sued in Califor-

---

2 If they extend beyond they are in violation of the federal Constitution. But not all assertions of jurisdiction are tested in the courts at all, and not all decisions which may be in violation are appealed.

3 International Shoe Co. v. Washington, 326 U.S. 310, 66 S.Ct. 154, 90 L.Ed. 95 (1945).

4 Foreign defendants benefit under the Fifth Amendment due process requirements. See, e.g., Mathews v. Diaz, 426 U.S. 67, 96 S.Ct. 1883, 48 L.Ed.2d 478 (1976), Wong Wing v. United States, 163 U.S. 228, 16 S.Ct. 977, 41 L.Ed. 140 (1896).

5 World–Wide Volkswagen Corp. v. Woodson., 444 U.S. 286, 100 S.Ct. 559, 62 L.Ed.2d 490 (1980). It is essentially a domestic case, the German parent was not a defendant.

6 Asahi Metal Indus. Co., Ltd. v. Superior Court, 480 U.S. 102, 107 S.Ct. 1026, 94 L.Ed.2d 92 (1987). Perhaps the Helicopteros Nacionales de Colombia v. Hall, 466 U.S. 408, 104 S.Ct. 1868, 80 L.Ed.2d 404 (1984), decision should be acknowledged as the first, but the Asahi case is the first where the court seems truly aware that the defendants are foreign and that such fact might mean some different analysis.

nia state court, and cross-complained against Asahi.[7] The California Supreme Court upheld jurisdiction over Asahi, but the U.S. Supreme Court reversed. The Court was unanimous in its ruling that jurisdiction was improper. But the reasoning was not unanimous. There was general agreement that the *International Shoe* decision applied, and that there must be *both* minimum contacts and constitutional due process. But there was disagreement regarding the standard to determine minimum contacts. Four justices found the "stream of commerce" theory insufficient, rejecting meeting this step by finding the product was brought into the forum by the consumer. Some action by the defendant was needed to satisfy a substantial connection theory. The defendant would have to take some action "*purposefully directed toward the state*."[8] Four other justices preferred the stream of commerce theory without additional conduct. The split of opinion regarding minimum contacts has not helped subsequent cases; federal circuits and state courts have also split on which side they favored.[9]

If the minimum contacts test is satisfied, the court next considers reasonableness—whether exercising jurisdiction meets the *International Shoe* "notions of fair play and substantial justice." It is not easy to establish unreasonableness.

Simply listing minimum contacts and assuming that they are somehow weighed is incorrect. The minimum contacts must be sufficient to conclude that the defendant "purposely availed itself of the benefits and burdens of doing business" in the subject state. Purposely availed" itself has become a new term of art to be debated seemingly without end, in the same manner as "stream of commerce."[10]

The finding of minimum contacts seems to imply that reasonableness exists. *Asahi* suggests consideration of the burden on the defendant of litigating in the forum state, the interests of the for-

---

[7] The result might have been different had the action been initiated directly by the California parties against the valve manufacturer. See Restatement (Third) of Foreign Relations Law, § 421, reporters' note 2, at 310.

[8] 480 U.S. at 112 (emphasis in original).

[9] See, e.g., Gould v. P.T. Krakatau Steel, 957 F.2d 573 (8th Cir.1992), *cert. denied*, 506 U.S. 908, 113 S.Ct. 304, 121 L.Ed.2d 227 (1992) (Sale of Indonesian company's product to N.Y. corporation with subsequent sending of product to Arkansas does not meet test), Mason v. F. LLI Luigi & Franco Dal Maschio, 832 F.2d 383 (7th Cir.1987) (Sale of Italian goods to Maryland with subsequent sending of product to Illinois does meet test), Microsoft Corp. v. Very Competitive Computer Prod. Corp., 671 F.Supp. 1250 (N.D.Cal.1987) (Sale of Taiwanese product to California through another Taiwanese company does meet test).

[10] See, e.g., Frederick Juenger, A Shoe Unfit for Globetrotting, 28 Univ. Calif. Davis L.J. 1027 (1995).

eign state, the interests of the plaintiff in obtaining relief, the interests of the interstate judicial system in efficient resolution of cases, and the shared interests of the states in furthering substantive social policies.[11] The Court in *Asahi* was concerned with the burden placed on the Asahi company in defending the action in a foreign (U.S.) forum. It additionally noted that "great care and reserve should be exercised when extending our notions of personal jurisdiction in the international field."[12] With these principal cases providing guidelines, however conflicting, the state and federal courts are now left to work out the details when the defendant is foreign. There are certain to be new cases that ultimately reach the Supreme Court.

General and Specific Jurisdiction. An additional jurisdictional issue that had developed in domestic cases but is clearly also confronted in international cases is general versus specific jurisdiction. Specific jurisdiction is generally thought to be where the court may only adjudicate claims related to the defendant's contacts with the forum, while general jurisdiction envisions adjudication of any claims against the defendant because of the aggregate of contacts with the forum.[13] The U.S. Supreme Court views general jurisdiction when the defendant's activities constitute "continuous and systematic general business contacts."[14] Debate reigns whether the standard should be the same for foreign defendants, partly based on concern for reciprocal treatment of U.S. companies abroad.[15]

Veil Piercing to Obtain Jurisdiction. When the defendant is the parent of a subsidiary corporation located in the United States and subject to jurisdiction, a court may extend jurisdiction to the parent in what is often a poorly analyzed piercing of the corporate veil. Veil piercing usually involves linking the two enterprises, but in jurisdiction cases, the analysis often appears less demanding, using agency concepts more freely and replacing "formal relationships" with "economic realities."[16] A conclusion that pierces the veil of the U.S. entity means that jurisdictional factors of minimum contacts and due process are less complex. Additionally, because the parent

---

11 See also Burger King Corp. v. Rudzewicz, 471 U.S. 462, 105 S.Ct. 2174, 85 L.Ed.2d 528 (1985).

12 480 U.S. at 114.

13 Restatement (Third) of Foreign Relations § 421, reporters' note 3.

14 Helicopteros Nacionales de Colombia, S.A. v. Hall, 466 U.S. 408, 416, 104 S.Ct. 1868, 80 L.Ed.2d 404 (1984).

15 See, e.g., Note, Jurisdiction: Personal Jurisdiction Over an Alien Corporation, 26 Harv. Int'l L.J. 630, 634 (1985).

16 Andrulonis v. United States, 526 F.Supp. 183, 188 (N.D.N.Y.1981). See also Meyers v. ASICS Corp., 711 F.Supp. 1001, 1004 (C.D.Cal.1989).

and subsidiary are one, service of process on the U.S. entity will constitute service on the whole entity, including the foreign parent.

International Law and Jurisdiction. International law limitations on extraterritorial extensions of jurisdiction may conflict with U.S. personal jurisdiction rules. U.S. courts considering personal jurisdiction in international cases generally have been disappointing in failing to consider international law rules, instead focusing on the traditional minimum contacts and due process issues.[17] U.S. administrative agencies have similarly attempted to assert jurisdiction abroad beyond what appear to be acceptable international limits. When *foreign* courts or tribunals have considered the U.S. extraterritorial assertions of jurisdiction, the U.S. rules have not been well received.[18] The Restatement of Foreign relations in its *jurisdiction to adjudicate* provisions suggests "reasonableness" as the standard in assert jurisdiction, but this Restatement provision has received at best limited acceptance by U.S. courts.[19]

In one of its more recent decisions on personal jurisdiction, the U.S. Supreme Court has addressed the issue whether one must first challenge jurisdiction before *forum non conveniens*, ruling that there is no mandate to first establish jurisdiction.[20]

Jurisdiction in Foreign Nations. Jurisdiction in other nations, in particular civil law based nations, is fundamentally different in contrast to U.S. personal and subject matter jurisdiction. For example, the nations within the European Union have harmonized jurisdiction under the EU Regulation on Jurisdiction and the Recognition and Enforcement of Judgments in Civil and Commercial Matters (the Brussels Regulation). There is no distinction between personal and subject matter jurisdiction in the Brussels Regulation, but there is a distinction between jurisdiction and special jurisdiction. Special jurisdiction involves exceptions to the general principal

---

[17] See, e.g., Dieter Lange & Gary B. Born, The Extraterritorial Application of National Laws (1989); Harold G. Maier, Resolving Extraterritorial Conflicts, or "There and Back Again," 25 Va. J. Int'l L. 7 (1984); Harold G. Maier, Extraterritorial Jurisdiction at a Crossroads: An Intersection Between Public and Private International Law, 76 A. J. Int'l L. 280 (1982).

[18] See Compagnie Euro des Petroles SA v. Sensor Nederland BV reprinted in 22 I.L.M. 66 (1983), Fruehauf Corp. v. Massardy, Court of Appeals Paris, 14th Chamber. Decision of May 22, 1965, La Gazette du Palais, Paris, 1965, reprinted in 5 I.L.M. 476 (1966).

[19] The Restatement on Foreign Relations Law is often more aspirational than a reflection of the current status of the law. It is as essential to know its limitations as it is important to be familiar with its substance. It reflects a great deal of effort by some exceptionally capable scholars and practitioners.

[20] Sinochem Int'l Co., Ltd. v. Malaysia Int'l Shipping Corp., 549 U.S. 422, 127 S.Ct. 1184, 167 L.Ed.2d 15 (2007).

that jurisdiction is vested in courts of a particular state where the defendant is domiciled and that jurisdiction must be interpreted restrictively.

There is no concept within the EU that allows a court to first determine whether it has jurisdiction, and then separately determine whether it should go forward with those principles. Jurisdiction in the EU is often said to be a relationship between the court and the claim, whereas in the United States it is between the court and the defendant. This has ramifications in such areas as *forum non conveniens* as it exists in common law nations. *Forum non conveniens* allows a court to dismiss a case because it is allegedly better heard in an alternative and adequate forum. In Europe the rule is essentially that if jurisdiction is present the court must go forward and address the claim.

Because jurisdiction in Europe is related more to the nature of the claim than to the various claims that may be brought against the defendant, one does not find a claim in contract that grants jurisdiction as well to a claim in tort, which must have its own separate jurisdictional basis.

Another comparison is Japan, which after WWII adopted a code of civil procedure influenced by the then existing German code. But Japan has developed in case law a concept called *jōri* which introduces a fairness discussion that is closer to the U.S. due process theory.[21]

§ 30.3 Subject Matter Jurisdiction

Statutes often express an intention to apply only to domestic actions, or to additionally apply to foreign actions. More difficult is when no clear intention is stated. Subject matter jurisdiction extending beyond the borders becomes limited only by other obstacles such as personal jurisdiction, ability to serve process, and sometimes notions of comity which cause a court to avoid going forward. A court may also avoid the issue by of subject matter jurisdiction by refusing to hear the matter for *forum non conveniens* reasons.

The general rule is that a federal statute is to be applied only within the territory unless there is clear Congressional intent to apply the statute to conduct abroad.[22] But there are statutes with

---

21 Goto v. Malaysia Airline, 35 Minshū (No. 7) 1224 (Supreme Court, Oct. 16, 1981), *translated in* 26 Japanese Annual of International Law 122 (1983).

22 See EEOC v. Arabian Am. Oil Co., 499 U.S. 244, 111 S.Ct. 1227, 113 L.Ed.2d 274 (1991).

very little expression of such legislative intent with a substantial history of extraterritorial application. The best example may be the Sherman Act which refers only to trade "involving" foreign commerce.[23] There was little foreign commerce when the act was passed in 1890 and foreign commerce was not an issue in its debate. Another example is the Securities Exchange Act of 1934, which was directed to certain securities schemes in the United States, but also has been widely applied to international transactions.

Although specific laws may permit extraterritorial application, some courts have adopted an interest balancing analysis to determine whether the court will go ahead notwithstanding statutory intent. In the extensively debated *Timberlane* decision,[24] the often ambitious federal Ninth Circuit introduced a balancing of interests test. Followed by some courts,[25] and consistent with the Restatement,[26] the test was challenged in the Supreme Court *Hartford Fire Insurance* decision.[27] These decisions at least send a signal to Congress that if it intends to have a law applied extraterritorially, it should make that clear in the legislation. If the intent is clear, the laws application extraterritorially is more certain and the use of a balancing test in most cases is diminished, if not precluded. It may seem strange that Congress has not more frequently provided its position on the extraterritoriality of a law that it enacts. But few have ever charged the U.S. Congress with clarity or consistency.

Foreign nations have reacted strongly to the extraterritorial application of U.S. laws, especially the antitrust laws. The reaction has come in two forms. Most reaction has focused on "blocking" laws, which prohibit their courts from providing any assistance in suits which assert what the foreign nation believes to be excessive extraterritoriality, such as allowing the taking of any evidence in the nation.[28] A few countries have gone further and adopted "claw-

---

[23] 15 U.S.C.A. § 1.

[24] Timberlane Lumber v. Bank of America, 549 F.2d 597 (9th Cir.1976).

[25] See, e.g., Mannington Mills, Inc. v. Congoleum Corp., 595 F.2d 1287 (3d Cir.1979).

[26] Restatement (Third) of Foreign Relations Law of the United States § 415 (1987).

[27] Hartford Fire Ins. Co. v. California, 509 U.S. 764, 113 S.Ct. 2891, 125 L.Ed.2d 612 (1993). See also Laker Airways v. Sabena Belgian World Airlines, 731 F.2d 909 (D.C.Cir.1984).

[28] See, e.g., Art. 1A French Penal Code Law (C.Pen) No. 80–538, Protection of Trading Interests Act of 1980 (U.K.), Ontario Business Protection Act, R.S.O. Chap. 56 (1980). See also, Bate C. Toms, The French Response to Extraterritorial Application of United States Antitrust Laws, 15 Int'l Law. 585 (1981); Brigette Ecolivet Herzog, The 1980 French Law on Documents and Information, 75 Am. J. Int'l L. 382 (1981), Note, The Protection of Trading Interests Act of 1980: Britain's Response to U.S. Extraterritorial Antitrust Enforcement, 2 Nw J. Int'l Law & Bus. 476 (1980).

back" provisions, allowing a defendant who has been subjected to a judgment to take at least part of the damages back from any assets the plaintiff has in the country.[29] A further but as of yet little adopted alternative is for the foreign country to adopt its own laws which are a mirror image to the challenged U.S. law, a kind of "what's good for the goose is good for the gander" approach, especially when it comes to punitive damages.

§ 30.4 Service of Process

Service of process will be ineffective if it is not in conformance with the law of the forum. There may be options, but whichever method is used must conform. U.S. plaintiffs pursuing litigation in the United States against foreign defendants too often attempt to use shortcuts that prove to be the plaintiff's downfall. For example the U.S. plaintiff may not adequately provide translations of the papers required abroad for a recognized claim. The U.S. concept of "tag" jurisdiction obtained by the U.S. party, perhaps by serving the foreign party while in a New York City airport awaiting the final leg on a flight to Europe from Brazil. The fortuities perceived to be gained by the U.S. party in tracking down the defendant during a layover in the airport may not seem so clever when a later judgment is rejected when an attempt is made to enforce it abroad.

Service of Process abroad is effectively regulated by two conventions. The larger in scope is the Hague Convention on the Service Abroad of Judicial and Extrajudicial Documents (Hague Service Convention).[30] The second is the Inter–American Convention.[31] Rule 4(f) of the Federal Rules of Civil Procedure provides for the service of process abroad, requiring use of the treaties. If service is not available under treaty agreements, the Rule provides for alternative means of service. Use of the treaty process should result in service acceptable to the foreign country, but use of the alternative means may not. When using alternative means consideration must be given to the rules in the country where service is to be made. Ineffective service will make enforcement of a judgment very unlikely in the foreign nation.

---

[29] See, e.g., Protection of Trading Interests Act of 1980 (U.K.), Art. 6 (recovery of awards of multiple damages).

[30] Hague Convention on the Service Abroad of Judicial and Extrajudicial Documents in Civil or Commercial Matters, done Nov. 15, 1965, 20 U.S.T. 362.

[31] Inter–American Convention on Letters Rogatory, *done* Jan 30, 1975, *entered into force for the U.S.*, Aug. 27, 1988, S. Treaty Doc. 98–27, 98th Cong., 2d Sess. (1984); Additional Protocol to the Inter–American Convention on Letters Rogatory, *done* May 8, 1979, *entered into force for the U.S.*, Aug. 27, 1988, S. Treaty Doc. 98–27, 98th Cong., 2d Sess (1984).

Service under the Hague Convention is available in some forty participating countries, including such major nations as Belgium, Canada, China, France, Germany, Italy, Japan, Netherlands, Poland, Spain, Switzerland, the United Kingdom, and the United States. Some participating countries have made special reservations which affect the method of service. The service is exclusive, stating in Art. 1 that the Convention "shall apply in all cases, in civil or commercial matters, where there is occasion to transmit a judicial or extrajudicial document for service abroad."[32] Service is made upon a "central authority" in the foreign nation, which subsequently transmits the documents to the proper location. There is some limited authority to send documents by mail,[33] but whether such method of sending constitutes service is debated.[34]

Although the Convention is generally considered to be exclusive, it is not applicable if service may be made on a U.S. subsidiary of a foreign corporation. In *Volkswagenwerk, A.G. v. Schlunk*,[35] service made on Volkswagen of America (VWOA—a U.S. corporation) was held proper to reach Volkswagenwerk (VWAG—the German parent corporation). The Convention was held not to be applicable in a decision applying veil piercing alter ego theory, but without the usual substantive analysis that accompanies veil piercing cases. Cases subsequent to *Schlunk* have been inconsistent in the applicability of the Convention to state law substituted service provisions. But fears that *Schlunk* would cause retaliation abroad have proven unfounded.

The Inter–American Convention and its Additional Protocol have been ratified by most Latin American nations and the United States. The Convention is limited to letters rogatory, essentially requests from one country through its courts to another country through its courts to assist the administration of justice. Its purpose is similar but less encompassing than the Hague Service Convention. If both are applicable, the Inter–American Convention applies. But the Inter–American Convention is not exclusive, as is the Hague Service Convention. A party thus might use state methods of

---

[32] See Société Nationale Industrielle Aerospatiale v. United States Dist. Court, 482 U.S. 522, 107 S.Ct. 2542, 96 L.Ed.2d 461 (1987) (comparing Hague Service Convention with Hague Evidence Convention).

[33] Hague Service Convention, art. 10.

[34] See, e.g., Ackermann v. Levine, 788 F.2d 830 (2d Cir.1986); Bankston v. Toyota Motor Corp., 889 F.2d 172 (8th Cir.1989); Honda Motor Co., Ltd. v. Superior Court, 10 Cal.App.4th 1043, 12 Cal.Rptr.2d 861 (1992); Suzuki Motor Co., Ltd. v. Superior Court, 200 Cal.App.3d 1476, 249 Cal.Rptr. 376 (1988); Shoei Kako Co. v. Superior Court, 33 Cal.App.3d 808, 109 Cal.Rptr. 402 (1973). The cases are commented on in David Epstein, International Litigation §4.03 (1998).

[35] 486 U.S. 694, 108 S.Ct. 2104, 100 L.Ed.2d 722 (1988).

service that if transmitted to an Inter–American Convention nation would be effective, but that if transmitted to a Hague Service Convention nation not a party to the Inter–American Convention would fail because the Hague Service Convention would be applicable and exclusive.

Service which does not comply with an applicable convention will almost certainly cause any judgment to be rejected if there is an attempt to enforce it abroad. The German government made it very clear in the *Schlunk* case that unless service was made on VWAG under the Convention that German courts would not enforce a judgment.[36] There is thus a certain coercive effect to these service conventions, whether or not they are viewed as exclusive. If they are not followed, enforcement of a judgment will likely be denied.

As with so many conventions, certain provisions become a major problem in applying the Convention. So it has been with Article 10 of the Hague Service Convention, which allows service by mail. Many Convention states have made reservations or declarations prohibiting service by mail to be made within their nation. Some courts interpret the word "send" in Article 10 to mean proper service, but other courts have rejected that view.[37] Mail service is thus a form that should be used very carefully, with knowledge of the interpretation of Article 10 in the foreign forum.

§ 30.5 Choice of Forum

Choice of forum is associated with several questions. It principally involves conscious choices made by the parties to an agreement to decide in advance the proper forum. But any agreement thus entered into may not override rules of jurisdiction of the chosen forum. It is a very old principle that parties may not force upon a forum the hearing of their dispute.

Selecting a forum may be useful for commercial agreements, but is less useful for torts. However, some torts are covered by choice of law agreements, even when they are contained in an agreement not bargained at arm's length, but rather the consequence of purchasing a ticket for an event, or shares of stock, or an automobile.

Choice of forum is also associated with subject matter jurisdiction, in the sense that a choice of forum agreement by parties does

---

36 Brief for Volkswagenwerk, A.G. at 16, Volkswagenwerk, A.G. v. Schlunk, 486 U.S. 694, 108 S.Ct. 2104, 100 L.Ed.2d 722 (1988).

37 Bankston v. Toyota Motor Corp., 889 F.2d 172 (8th Cir. 1989).

not establish subject matter jurisdiction. The choice of forum agreement may meet a court hostile to any thought that it will be ousted of jurisdiction.[38] It may, however, assist courts where there is subject matter jurisdiction in two or more locations. Finally, choice of forum by a plaintiff in initiating litigation has some influence on a defendant's motion to dismiss for *forum non conveniens* reasons.

Most jurisdictions accept the parties' forum selection. When parties choose a third nation as the forum, there should be some assurance that the courts of that chosen nation will assume jurisdiction. Within the European Union, under the Brussels Convention, parties from two EU nations may select another nation within the EU.[39] Choosing a nation with a civil law tradition legal system introduces a very different form of litigation, where there will be a process of gathering evidence until the case is ready for a decision by the assigned judge. There is no trial as known in common law systems. For parties in civil law nations, the idea of a trial may be as much of a concern as the absence of one to a party from a common law system.

If there is any doubt as to the acceptability of forum selection clauses in the United States, the *Carnival Cruise Lines, Inc. v. Shute* decision is mandatory reading.[40] In *Carnival,* a plaintiff from the state of Washington purchased a cruise ticket for a cruise out of Los Angeles. The ticket contained a forum selection clause designating Florida courts, the home state of the cruise line. The plaintiff fell and was injured in international waters. The Supreme Court upheld the forum selection provision, which was never negotiated, unconvinced that it would be an unreasonable burden on the plaintiff to bring suit in Florida. The Court did not believe that Florida was a "remote alien forum", language taken from the earlier *Bremen* decision.[41] The Florida court was not "seriously inconvenient" and it was not unreasonable for Carnival Cruise Lines to want to consolidate cases brought against it in Florida. But if a "remote al-

---

[38] Albemarle Corp. v. AstraZeneca UK Ltd., 2009 WL 902348 (D.C.C. Mar. 31, 2009)(Fed. Dist. Ct.of South Carolina).

[39] Convention on Jurisdiction and Enforcement of Foreign Judgments in Civil and Commercial Matters at Brussels, Sept. 27, 1968, Art. 17–1. 8 I.L.M. 229 (1969). See Art. 23. The Brussels Regulation does not address adhesion contracts, perhaps because an adhesion contract may be considered no contract at all under the Brussels Regulation definition of "agreement."

[40] 499 U.S. 585, 111 S.Ct. 1522, 113 L.Ed.2d 622 (1991). Compare with Sun Trust Bank v. Sun Int'l Hotels, Ltd., 184 F.Supp.2d 1246 (S.D. Fla. 2001).

[41] M/S Bremen v. Zapata Off–Shore Co., 407 U.S. 1, 92 S.Ct. 1907, 32 L.Ed.2d 513 (1972) (provision choosing London courts upheld).

ien forum" is stipulated rather than bargained, a court may reject the clause.[42]

Forum selection clauses are also used to designate arbitration in lieu of judicial resolution. These provisions may conflict with provisions in the legislation generating the conflict that are alleged to give exclusive jurisdiction to courts in the United States. Two U.S. Supreme Court 5–4 decisions involving arbitration selection clauses in antitrust and securities cases upheld such clauses.[43] The reasons were partly because they were international agreements, and international agreements are commonly resolved by international arbitration. The need for predictability in international commerce may be persuasive in overriding notions that the U.S. Congress meant to restrict application of the law to U.S. courts.

There is interplay among (1) choice of forum agreements, (2) the concept of mandatory law, and (3) arbitration. Mandatory law means law that may not be derogated from. A frequent example is the Carriage of Goods at Sea Act (COGSA). If COGSA is the governing law, can it be ousted by a choice of forum that designates arbitration? The Supreme Court, in *Vimar Seguros v Reaseguros, S.A. v. M/V Sky Reefer*,[44] held that that there was no longer a mandatory law exception to the parties ability to choose an arbitration forum.

In addition to the Hague Service Convention and the Hague Convention on the Taking of Evidence Abroad in Civil or Commercial Matters (Hague Evidence Convention), both of which having been well received by many nations, there is now a Hague Convention on Choice of Courts Agreements. It is a parallel to the New York Arbitration Convention in establishing rules applicable to litigation as opposed to arbitration. The Convention is intended to enforce private party agreements specifying the proper *court* and including some rules for recognizing and enforcing decisions of the forum so selected. But it has not been a successful agreement, a very few nations have adopted this long negotiated convention.

---

42 See Lauro Lines SRL v. Chasser, 490 U.S. 495, 497, 109 S.Ct 1976, 104 L.Ed.2d 548 (1989). But see Spradlin v. Lear Siegler Management Services Co., 926 F.2d 865 (9th Cir.1991) (Saudi Arabia standard contract forum selection upheld in contract for services to be performed in Saudi Arabia).

43 Scherk v. Alberto–Culver Co., 417 U.S. 506, 94 S.Ct. 2449, 41 L.Ed.2d 270 (1974) (securities law issues). Mitsubishi Motors Corp. v. Soler Chrysler–Plymouth, 473 U.S. 614, 105 S.Ct. 3346, 87 L.Ed.2d 444 (1985) (antitrust issues).

44 515 U.S. 528, 115 S. Ct. 2322, 132 L.Ed. 2d 462 (1995) (reasoning that its previous decision in Scherk had so decided).

§ 30.6 *Forum Non Conveniens*

The *forum non conveniens* doctrine is a creature of equity. It allows a court to dismiss a case that it believes is better brought in another forum. Many cases are brought in the United States for no reason other than that appears to be where the rainbow ends in a pot of gold—called punitive damages. U.S. lawyers are notorious for going abroad to sign-up foreign plaintiffs for a suit in the United States. Shopping in the United States is a major pastime. It has more recently included foreigners shopping not for goods but for a favorite forum.

Not all nations recognize the doctrine, but some reach a similar conclusion under other titles.[45] It is generally a doctrine of the common law commenced and developed in cases rather than legislation. The U.S. doctrine has origins in *Gulf Oil Corp. v. Gilbert*,[46] a case involving two U.S. forum choices even though it has had immense impact on the use of the theory in international litigation—when the alternate forums are from two different countries. In *Gilbert*, the Supreme Court allowed courts to decline to exercise jurisdiction where public and private factors favored another forum. This theory was adopted in two important international cases. First, in *Piper Aircraft Co. v. Reyno*,[47] a court granted a *forum non conveniens* motion to dismiss a suit in the United States in favor of Scotland, where the plaintiffs represented Scottish decedents for a crash of a U.S. made aircraft flown by a Scottish pilot that crashed in Scotland. Scots law was clearly less favorable, but the Court significantly negated the consideration of relative favorableness of the law. Second, in *In re Union Carbide Corp. Gas Plant Disaster,*[48] the court dismissed a case on behalf of numerous Indian nationals injured in an explosion in the Union Carbide subsidiary plant in Bhopal, India. The court accepted as conditions for the dismissal Union Carbide's agreement to submit to jurisdiction in India, a condition that has become common in *forum non conveniens* dismissals.

The test has evolved to include several considerations. There must be an available and adequate alternative forum. The plaintiff's choice is weighed against all private interests. When private

---

[45] See, e.g., Republic of Bolivia v. Philip Morris Cos, 39 F. Supp. 2d 1008 (S.D. Tex. 1999). There appear to be some Scottish origins to the Forum Non Conveniens doctrine. See generally Paxton Blair, The Doctrine of Forum Non Conveniens in Anglo–American Law, 29 Colum. L. Rev. 1 (1929).

[46] 330 U.S. 501, 67 S.Ct. 839, 91 L.Ed. 1055 (1947).

[47] 454 U.S. 235, 102 S.Ct. 252, 70 L.Ed.2d 419 (1981).

[48] 809 F.2d 195 (2d Cir.1987), *cert. denied*, 484 U.S. 871, 108 S.Ct. 199, 98 L.Ed.2d 150 (1987).

interests are generally equal public interests are considered.[49] The defendant should submit to the jurisdiction of the foreign forum. Each of these has been subject to development in the case law.

Available and adequate alternative forum. The law of any alternate forum, whether common or civil law based, will be different from that where the suit was filed. That is not sufficient in itself to find the alternative forum inadequate. *Gilbert* held that the test must be to allow dismissal only where holding the trial in the forum poses a heavy burden on the defendant or the court, and the plaintiff is unable to note sufficiently convincing reasons for his choice. Often the choice is made to obtain punitive damages and obtain representation on a contingent fee basis. Neither is sufficient justification for retaining the suit in the forum chosen by the plaintiff.

Many nations have suspect legal systems that only by stretching the definition provide due process. But courts are hesitant to dismiss an action when the defendant's argument is based on the theory that the foreign forum is inefficient, corrupt, and/or has a judiciary subject to intimidation. A very few cases in U.S. courts have dismissed a case for these reasons, even though every lawyer engaged in international litigation can list nations where they do not believe fairness is understood to be part of the procedure, or a principal goal of the judges.

An important aspect of *forum non conveniens* is that the court is not forcing the case upon the foreign courts. Whether or not the plaintiff re-files in the foreign forum is his choice. Opponents of *forum non conveniens* have consistently, and unsuccessfully, argued that the dismissal *requires* that the plaintiff file the suit in the foreign forum. The truth is usually that the first forum was chosen solely because of the availability of legal representation on a contingent fee basis, and the possibility of receiving a very large award because of punitive damages. Few courts outside the United States offer such large returns on such small investments.

Private and public interest factors. U.S. courts consider both private and public interest factors. Such factors may overcome the strong presumption favoring the plaintiff's initial choice of forum. Private interest factors might include location of the witnesses, ability to depose persons, access to sources of proof such as important records, ability to implead possible third-party defendants, need to

---

[49] In Lubbe et al v. Cape Plc [2000] 4 All E.R. 268, 1 W.L.R. 1545 [2000], the House of Lords rejected the use of public interest factors in a *forum non conveniens* decision.

translate documents, language of the chosen forum, and other matters going to the general convenience of the parties.

Public interest factors, on the other hand, usually involve matters of public policy or legal certainty. Such consideration, in the view of many civil law jurists, interferes with the notion that jurisdiction should not be declined if it is present. The English legal system, which has always been thought to favor *forum non conveniens*, has rejected the use of public interest factors.[50] But that may be doubtful since many public interest factors may be rephrased as private interest factors.

Forum non conveniens motions are presented by defendants as part of litigation strategy. If they are successful, the case is sometimes moved to a forum far distant where the case dies. The death is because the U.S. attorneys no longer have visions of large punitive damage awards. Indeed, they may have little involvement as attorneys in the foreign forum. The defendants in both the *Piper* and *Bhopal* cases were obviously pleased with the outcome. The *Piper* case has never gone to trial in Scotland. The *Bhopal* case resulted in a settlement far less than what might have been a jury's award in the United States, and there is doubt that the settlement funds have ever reached the injured plaintiffs. Courts have thus increasingly asked about the nature of the proceeding in the foreign forum, especially about the nature of the process. If there is a viable legal system that provides for the resolution of disputes of the form presented, the *forum non conveniens* motion may be granted. But if the system is inefficient and corrupt, a *forum non conveniens* motion is unlikely to be granted.

One problem for defendants and their attorneys in obtaining a successful *forum non conveniens* ruling is that control over the case may be diminished or lost. If the case is moved abroad, the attorneys likely will not be able to appear before the foreign court, and foreign counsel must be hired. The U.S. defendant will have to learn about the foreign law and legal system. The better choice for a defendant may be to keep the matter in the U.S. court but to seek application of foreign law. Many such cases merit the application of foreign law, and when a court so rules the difficulty of proving foreign law may be an impossible burden for the plaintiff. It is a difficult choice for lawyers because the law of *forum non conveniens* seems sufficiently elastic that it is hard to predict the outcome, and additionally hard to predict possible conditions that the court may

---

[50] Lubbe and Others v. Cape PLC,[2000} 2 Lloyd's Rep. 383 (H.L.); See also, Owusu v. Jackson, C-281/02 [2005] E.C.R. 0.

impose upon the defendant in return for granting the *forum non conveniens* motion. The law is a product of equity, and like equity it is somewhat amorphous and difficult to foresee.

There is a movement, largely in Latin America, called Parlatino which tried to block dismissals in a U.S. court after a *forum non conveniens* based dismissal occurred in a major case involving plaintiffs from twelve nations.[51] Parlatino has not been successful, largely because its supporters misconstrue the theory. Because it has had no impact on dismissals based on *forum non conveniens*, some of the nations have tried another tactic—they have changed their domestic law to allow the damage law of the dismissing country to be used in the case when refiled in their nation. That has led to some very large judgments. But when attempts to enforce such judgments have been made in U.S. courts, grounds for nonrecognition have blocked such attempts.

§ 30.7 Choice of Law

Choice of law has two sides. First is as part of a conflicts of law determination when a court is using conflicts rules to determine what law applies. Second is when parties wish to argue that a foreign law is applicable and are faced with convincing the court of its merits and, if accepted, proving the foreign law. A generally accepted principle is that the court determining the proper law will use its own choice of law rules.

For the conflicts determination, parties to commercial contracts are allowed under most jurisdictions to choose the applicable law in the contract. When they do not, the court will turn to its own conflicts rules in seeking to apply what may be the law that has the "most significant relationship to the transaction",[52] or that "bears an appropriate relation",[53] or of the country "with which it is most closely connected."[54]

Torts raise different issues. Because they are not usually expected, they are less often provided for. But there are many attempts to designate the applicable law (and forum) for torts arising from contracts selling vacations, cruises, etc. They are often upheld. When there is no such "choice" of the applicable law, a court will either apply the law of the place of the injury under the *lex loci de-*

---

51 Delgado v. Shell Oil Co., 890 F.Supp. 1324 (S.D.Tex 1995).

52 Restatement, Conflicts of Law (Second) (1971) § 188.

53 U.C.C. § 1–105.

54 Convention on the Law Applicable to Contractual Obligations (EEC) (1980) art. 4.

licti rule, or consider a wide variety of facts to determine the appropriate law.

Cross-border litigation inherently provides for the possible applicability of the law of at least two nations. Because of the international character of a transaction, the parties frequently choose the applicable law, often in conjunction with a choice of forum provision. The parties should be fully aware of the substance of each possibly applicable law before stipulating the chosen law. For example, a U.S. party selling goods to a German party might discover that the German law favors the seller in such a transaction. The U.S. party in such case would want to specify that German law applies, and might even gain concessions from the German party on other issues if the German party prefers German law not because it has been researched but because it is German and "probably" better than U.S. law.

Just as a choice of forum agreement may not thrust subject matter jurisdiction upon a court, a choice of law provision may not thrust that decision upon the court. With subject matter jurisdiction and choice of forum, it is usually a matter of whether the court has the capacity to hear the case. Contrastingly, with choice of law, it is usually a question of whether the court is willing to hear the case applying the law of a foreign nation. Courts usually respect a choice of law provision, especially in a commercial contract where the choice is between the laws of the parties' nations. At the other end is where the choice has no relevance to the contract, such as where German and U.S. parties choose the law of Outer Mongolia. A court is likely to reject such choice, perhaps because the chosen law has no linkage to the case, but also because the court may feel uncomfortable in applying the law of a nation without a highly developed contract law that may be difficult to prove.

A court asked to accept the application of a foreign law is likely to inquire about whether that law will cover the dispute. If a foreign law is chosen that provides no cause of action or inadequate remedies, the court may reject the application of such foreign law. There thus may be some process, possibly a hearing, where the court conducts an analysis of the substance of the foreign law and even whether it is likely that translations of the law can be obtained and experts can be found to explain the law to the court. Because the court does not "know" foreign law, it must be proved.[55] That means

[55] Rule 44.1 of the Federal Rules of Civil Procedure states that the court's determination of foreign law is treated the same as a ruling on a question of law.

the judge has little if any knowledge of the substance of the foreign law and is entirely at the mercy of the experts used by the parties.

A party intending to use foreign law must give notice of such intent. Any form is adequate that does not create an "unfair surprise."[56] What is presented in proving foreign law is limited only in that it must be relevant.

There is a relationship between choice of law and *forum non conveniens*. When a court considers a motion to dismiss for *forum non conveniens* reasons, the court may believe a foreign forum is more appropriate because the law of that foreign nation is the proper choice of law.

What if the court believes a case should be decided under foreign law but neither of the parties raises that issue? Should the court decide that such a choice is present and request that the parties brief the issue, or fall back on the law presumed by the parties to apply—likely the law of the forum, or perhaps the court will undertake proving the foreign law without assistance from the attorneys. The court may be left to determining the foreign law, or it may reject such task regardless of any due process question.

§ 30.8 Antisuit Injunctions

Complex international litigation may create a situation where a suit is initiated in one nation by a foreign plaintiff against several defendants, including one or more from the foreign plaintiff's nation. Such was the case when Laker Airways initiated litigation in the United States against several U.S. and foreign airlines, including two from the United Kingdom. England was the home of Laker Airways.[57] The British defendants asked an English court to enjoin Laker Airways from pursuing the suit in the United States against the two British airlines because such litigation had only one proper forum—England. The injunction is called an "antisuit injunction." The U.S. court rejected the injunction granted by the English court, and a serious conflict was avoided only after the House of Lords overturned the injunction, although preserving the concept.

Although the U.S. court in *Laker* rejected the English antisuit injunction, the concept had been accepted in some U.S. courts. Some federal circuits have granted antisuit injunctions, generally apply-

[56] See Laminoirs–Trefileries–Cableries de Lens, S.A. v. Southwire Co., 484 F.Supp. 1063, 1067 (N.D.Ga.1980).

[57] See Laker Airways, Ltd. v. Sabena, Belgian World Airlines, 731 F.2d 909 (D.C.Cir.1984).

ing a multi-part test which considers such issues as: Would the foreign litigation frustrate a policy of the U.S. forum, be vexatious or oppressive, threaten the court's jurisdiction, or prejudice other considerations.[58] *Laker*, however, narrowed the concept, allowing it to protect the jurisdiction of the court or prevent the litigant from evading public policies of the forum.[59]

Antisuit injunctions are unusual because courts often allow parallel proceedings to continue in two jurisdictions. A judgment of a U.S. court will be considered *res judicata.* So may the foreign judgment. Thus, which party receives the first judgment may have the advantage, encouraging a race to judgment. But, however undesirable it is to encourage such a race, courts have not granted antisuit injunctions just to stop a race.

The impact of parallel proceedings will occur when the judgment is enforced. If the winner of the race's victory is accepted abroad and the judgment is enforced, the judgment was given *res judicata* effect. But it is not clear that it will be so recognized. The foreign court may reject the U.S. decision for traditional reasons justifying nonrecognition and enforcement of foreign judgments, which may incorporate some of the justifications for granting antisuit injunctions. A U.S. judgment entered after an antisuit judgment is granted abroad, will not be enforced in the foreign court. But the intention of an antisuit injunction in a case such as *Laker* is not to allow a judgment in the United States which will be enforced from U.S. assets of the foreign defendant.

The *Laker* decision and subsequent developments in the use of antisuit injunctions is only one part of the larger issue of the extraterritorial application of a nation's laws. Perhaps the first question to be asked is: Should any nation's laws have any effect abroad? The answer of necessity must be yes, or borders would gain a more certain rigidity, and many benefits of globalization would be lost. The United States has approached extraterritorality partly by assuming it has the authority to control the conduct of any person or entity

---

[58] In re Unterweser Reederei, GMBH, 428 F.2d 888 (5th Cir.1970), *affirmed en banc*, 446 F.2d 907 (5th Cir.1971), *vacated on other grounds sub nom.*, M/S Bremen v. Zapata Off–Shore Co., 407 U.S. 1, 92 S.Ct. 1907, 32 L.Ed.2d 513 (1972). See also Seattle Totems Hockey Club, Inc. v. National Hockey League, 652 F.2d 852 (9th Cir.1981), *cert. denied*, 457 U.S. 1105, 102 S.Ct. 2902, 73 L.Ed.2d 1313 (1982).

[59] For decisions subsequent to *Laker*, see China Trade & Dev. Corp. v. M.V. Choong Yong, 837 F.2d 33 (2d Cir.1987) (reversing an injunction); Gau Shan Co. v. Bankers Trust Co., 956 F.2d 1349 (6th Cir.1992), *appeal after remand,* 966 F.2d 1452 (6th Cir.1992) (reversing an injunction); Allendale Mut. Ins. Co. v. Bull Data Sys., Inc., 10 F.3d 425 (7th Cir.1993); Mutual Serv. Casualty Ins. Co. v. Frit Indus., Inc., 805 F.Supp. 919 (M.D.Ala.1992), *affirmed without opinion*, 3 F.3d 442 (11th Cir.1993).

abroad as long as the U.S. court has jurisdiction. That in itself raises objections from abroad, as does any law that impacts its territory adversely.

Considering two laws that were passed in the United States years ago, the Sherman Antitrust Act in 1890 and the Securities & Exchange Act in 1934, neither law in debate received much comment about its impact or application abroad. Those laws did not express any suggestion that they were to be applied abroad, where they might have been expected to generate adverse reaction from the foreign governments. Regardless, both laws have been extensively applied extraterritorially. These two laws by their language *were not* intended to correct cross border issues, but they have been so applied for decades.

Another two laws are specifically and intentionally directed to cross-border conduct: The antiboycott provisions of the Export Administration Act and the Foreign Corrupt Practices Act. The former provisions were enacted exclusively to address the Arab boycott of Israel; the latter to address what are referred to as "corrupt" payments made by U.S. persons and businesses to foreign officials. These two laws by their language *were* intended to correct cross border issues, and they have been so applied for decades.

Whether or not a law suggests any intention of extraterritorial application, a U.S. Supreme Court decision that has been largely ignored, *EEOC v. Arabian American Oil Co.,*[60] expressed the premise that laws are presumed to *lack* extraterritorial reach.

The conflicts that have arisen over the general concept of extraterritoriality are numerous, including the above discussion of antisuit injunctions. The debate has led to the adoption by many nations of laws that attempt to nullify or minimize the impact of U.S. laws affecting the foreign nation's presumed sovereignty. That includes the adoption of such laws as the U.K.'s Protection of Trading Interests Act of 1980, the theory of which has been copied in many nations in what are called "blocking statutes." It includes such areas as discovery abroad, taking evidence abroad, and enforcing judgments abroad, especially when U.S. courts award damages which are for the most part unheard of outside the United States. Some nations have gone further, allowing a "clawback" of certain damages.

---

60 499 U.S. 244, 111 S.Ct. 1227, 113 L.Ed 3d 274 (1991).

One should not leave this subject by suggesting that only the United States imposes its laws upon foreign parties. The European Union, despite its denial, also applies laws extraterritorially.[61]

§ 30.9 Proving Foreign Law

Unfortunately, many cases are filed in U.S. courts with a complaint drafted without any thought that foreign law might be applicable. For example the complaint may include several counts that may correctly make reference to U.S. law, but have no relevance if foreign law applies. For example, most civil law nations do not provide causes based on an alleged civil conspiracy or unjust enrichment. Additionally, most foreign courts do not grant punitive damages. Sometimes the plaintiff will attempt to equate a foreign concept as being the same as a U.S. concept. Thus, when a plaintiff has asked for punitive damages, and the law of Mexico is to apply, Mexico's "moral damage" law may be misconstrued to be the same as punitive damages.

Proving foreign law in a U.S. court very likely will include various forms of written and oral testimony. Often affidavits of experts are submitted,[62] with the experts appearing at trial to support and respond to questions about their opinions.[63] Usually when foreign law must be proved, experts will be practitioners or academics from the foreign country. But often those persons, unless they have received some of their legal education in the United States, may not be effective in explaining a very different legal system to an American judge. In such case U.S. comparative law experts may be helpful in explaining to the judge the nature of the perceived differences between the laws of the two nations.

If the opposing lawyers do not recognize that the case involves the application of foreign law, and proceed on the assumption that U.S. law applies, they may be asked by the court to present opinions on the foreign law. If the lawyers fail to do so, there is a split of authority regarding whether the U.S. judge may or must undertake the proof of foreign law. A court may conduct its own research, which also may be helpful when the experts are divided on the meaning of the foreign law. That is usually the case.

---

[61] See Ralph Folsom, Practitioner Treatise on International Business Transactions (2012), Chapter 20 on EU Business Competition Law.

[62] See Bing v. Halstead, 495 F.Supp. 517 (S.D.N.Y.1980) (affidavits resulting in granting summary judgment).

[63] See John R. Brown, 44.1 Ways to Prove Foreign Law, 9 Marq. Law. 179 (1984).

Proof of foreign law often requires obtaining translations. Some foreign laws are available in English, especially constitutions and important codes such as civil and commercial codes. If there is a published version of the foreign statutes, it is likely to have been translated objectively and thus will be accepted by the court. Where the parties have to translate foreign statutes or cases, they may do so with a choice of words favoring their case. The court may have to choose between two versions. Translations of foreign cases are not often undertaken, sometimes because of their length and thus expense, and sometimes because they are written very abstractly and are difficult to understand by a U.S. judge who lacks experience with foreign materials. When they do exist, they may be very helpful because a U.S. judge may not wish to interpret a foreign statute in a manner that is not clear from the language unless the foreign court has already given a similar or consistent interpretation. The Internet has made it possible to locate many translations of foreign laws into English, or at least disclose sources for purchasing translations.

§ 30.10 Depositions and Document Discovery Abroad

For a trial in the United States gathering evidence is far easier when both the defendant and the evidence are in the United States. But when the evidence is located abroad, and especially when the defendant resides abroad, obtaining evidence may become very difficult.[64]

The rules for obtaining evidence are the rules of procedure of the forum and any applicable international conventions or treaties such as the Hague Evidence Convention. When personal jurisdiction has been obtained by use of disputed extraterritorial application of U.S. law, gathering evidence abroad because of the court's authority resulting from personal jurisdiction may conflict with foreign laws blocking the production of evidence. Numerous suits are filed by U.S. lawyers who proceed under the forum's rules of evidence only to discover they need a short course in obtaining evidence abroad to save their suit. Part of that short course must be learning that some practices of obtaining evidence permitted in the United States constitute *criminal* conduct in foreign nations.[65]

---

[64] If the defendant is a U.S. citizen or resident, however, a U.S. court may subpoena the defendant to appear in the United States, and produce specified documents. 28 U.S.C.A. § 1783(a).

[65] Especially in France and Switzerland. See David Epstein et al, International Litigation § 10.03 n. 5.

If U.S. notions of proper evidence paralleled those in foreign nations there would be far less trouble. The problem in gathering evidence abroad is not that all foreign nations prevent other nations from obtaining evidence in their nations. The problem is that the U.S. concept of evidence extends beyond nearly all other nations' rules regarding what may be obtained. In most civil law tradition nations, judges with substantial discretion closely regulate gathering evidence. Attorneys are for the most part not left on their own to collect what they think would be useful, with occasional forays into court for new orders of production.

Civil law nation judges determine who may be witnesses. The judges ask questions they originate or those referred to them by the lawyers which they have approved. Requests for documents must be specific, disallowing requests, for example, for any documents that might have affected the design and manufacture of a product involved in an injury. If we sometimes think of our own process as condoning "fishing expeditions" for evidence, other nations are likely to interpret our method of fishing as using drift nets miles long that catch everything that the net surrounds. Other nations have effectively banned our nets.

As a civil process unfolds in the United States, the search for evidence begins at an early stage, well before the trial. Much that the lawyers are seeking will help in the further development of the case. There may have been very little, if any, evidence present when a brief and general complaint was filed. Much of what *is* subsequently obtained will never be used. This pretrial discovery is neither fully understood nor accepted by many civil law tradition nations. They sometimes think that "pretrial" means before the suit is filed.[66] Obviously, evidence needs to be gathered before the day of the trial, just as it is gathered over a period of time in a civil law nation and not all presented at one time for the judge's consideration. The dislike for pretrial evidence is made apparent in the Hague Evidence Convention,[67] allowing a convention participant to make a declaration that disallows letters of request seeking "pretrial discovery of documents."[68]

Obtaining evidence abroad comes in two general areas, deposing witnesses and obtaining physical evidence, principally written documents. If depositions are permitted by the foreign nation, they

---

[66] Their misunderstanding is perhaps because they view the stage like a grand jury proceeding, where evidence is gathered and presented before an indictment.

[67] Hague Convention on the Taking of Evidence Abroad in Civil or Commercial Matters, Mar. 18, 1970, 8 I.L.M. 37 (1965).

[68] Id., Art 23. Most signatories have issued such a declaration.

are sometimes taken before a person commissioned by the U.S. court.[69] U.S. consular officers are ordinarily used as the designated commissioners to take the testimony, but a foreign official or private person may be appointed. In some countries the testimony may only be taken under rules of the country that disallow the use of a commissioner appointed by the U.S. court. The foreign rules may even prohibit taking any testimony by deposition. In such case the U.S. court may be able to issue a letter of request to a court in the foreign nation asking that it issue an order to take the testimony.[70] The letter may be accepted under notions of comity.

When the court in the United States approves discovery of documents abroad, the laws of the foreign nation may admit or block such discovery. The process of discovery may be similar to taking depositions when letters of request are used as opposed to appointment of a commissioner.

The above discussion involves use of procedural rules of the separate nations, and the application of comity. But another route is present. Many countries, including the United States, are parties to the Hague Evidence Convention. This Convention provides for three methods of obtaining evidence abroad. First is use of a letter of request to the "Central Authority" in the foreign nation. That authority sends the request to the appropriate court. Second is by means of a request to take evidence before a diplomatic or consular officer in the foreign country. Third, a request may be made to have a commissioner appointed to take evidence. These three parallel the methods outlined above under the Federal Rules of Civil Procedure, but there are variations. One most important question for nations adhering to the Convention is whether it is the *exclusive* method of taking evidence abroad.

For the United States, the Supreme Court answered that it is not the exclusive method in *Societe Nationale Industrielle Aerospatiale v. United States.*[71] The Court did not even impose a rule that the Convention must be used first, with subsequent resort to the rules of the forum. Use of the Convention would seem to mean use of a form approved by the foreign nation, and more likely to be respected. The majority of decisions since *Aerospatiale,* however, have not required use of the Convention as a necessary first option. But the fact remains that the view of the United States is the view of

---

69 Fed. R. Civ. P. 28(b)(4).

70 Some nations require the letters of request to be submitted through diplomatic channels rather than court-to-court.

71 482 U.S. 522, 107 S.Ct. 2542, 96 L.Ed.2d 461 (1987).

only one side, the requirements of the foreign nation in which discovery is sought have to be considered.

§ 30.11 Recognition and Enforcement of Foreign Judgments

Judgments in one state of the United States are recognized in other states under the "full faith and credit" clause of the U.S. Constitution. But there is no application of this doctrine to foreign judgments. Foreign judgments are recognized and enforced in many nations, but only under often strict rules that allow careful scrutiny of many aspects of the original judgment. No rule exists in the United States prohibiting enforcement. Enforcement is currently a matter for separate state decision. Negotiations at The Hague for an international convention on jurisdiction and the enforcement of foreign judgments have been underway for years. They are yet to conclude with a final document. When that is accomplished, there is no certainty that it will be adopted in the United States.[72] It is unlikely, for example, that judgments from nations with corrupt or poorly developed nations will be enforced by U.S. courts. For example, several judgments in Nicaraguan courts against U.S. corporations for alleged injuries to Nicaraguan workers resulted in awards of many millions of dollars. The decisions were riddled with inequities and failure to include the most fundamental due process. They have been uniformly rejected by U.S. courts.

The rule adopted from English law is that a foreign money judgment is only *prima facie* evidence of the matter decided. But the U.S. Supreme Court rejected this position in *Hilton v. Guyot,*[73] and adopted a rule based on comity. This federal law decision presented an analysis of certain elements of the foreign decision, such as whether there was an opportunity for a fair trial before a court of competent jurisdiction, and whether the system of justice was impartial. Additionally discussed was whether the foreign nation would enforce a U.S. judgment, meaning the consideration of reciprocity. But this was not a judgment which established a rule effective in the states, although the evolving state law has drawn heavily from the *Hilton* decision.

States courts have differed on the issue of reciprocity. Similarly state legislatures adopting judgment statutes have differed on in-

[72] See generally Russell Weintraub, How Substantial is Our Need for a Judgments–Recognition Convention and What Should We Bargain Away to Get It?, 24 Brook. L. Rev. 167 (1998); Cromie, A Choice Between Evils, New Law Journal, at 1244 (Aug. 16, 1996).

[73] 159 U.S. 113, 16 S.Ct. 139, 40 L.Ed. 95 (1895).

cluding reciprocity as a requirement for enforcement. Although the law developed in the courts of the states after *Hilton*, in the last half of the last century states began to adopt the Uniform Foreign Money–Judgments Recognition Act.[74] Those states that have not adopted the UFMJRA either reject judgments and require a de novo trial, or they recognize and enforce judgments after applying tests not usually at great variance with the *Hilton* decision theory.[75] Conditions imposed may include reciprocity, acceptable personal and subject matter jurisdiction by the foreign court, adequate notice to the defendant, absence of fraud, and absence of any conflict with public policy of the United States.[76] Those states that have adopted the UFMJRA follow a procedure that includes considerations of some of these very same factors,[77] but the Act does not include reciprocity.[78]

A related issue to the enforcement of the judgment is what the enforcing state should do when the original judgment is in a foreign currency. Judgments are usually given in the currency of the forum, and in some cases this is a mandatory rule.[79] The principal issue for courts has been establishing the time of conversion of the currency of the judgment to the currency of the enforcing forum.[80] Some jurisdictions use the time of the act establishing the cause of action, others use the date of the judgment and others use the date of payment. The Uniform Foreign Money Claims Act has adopted the date of payment.[81] The Restatement of Foreign Relations suggests use of the date which would best "serve the ends of justice in the circumstances."[82]

---

74 About 30 states have adopted a form of this 1962 uniform law, including its updated version the 2005 Uniform Foreign-Country Money Judgments Recognition Act.

75 See, e.g., Koster v. Automark Ind., Inc., 640 F.2d 77 (7th Cir.1981).

76 See. E.g., Hunt v. BP Exploration Co. (Libya) Ltd., 492 F.Supp. 885 (N.D.Tex.1980).

77 See, e.g., Bank of Nova Scotia v. Tschabold Equipment Ltd., 51 Wash.App. 749, 754 P.2d 1290 (1988).

78 Reciprocity has nevertheless been added by several states when adopting the UFMJRA.

79 Judgments in U.S. courts may be in foreign currencies. See, e.g., In re Oil Spill by the Amoco Cadiz Off the Coast of France on March 16, 1978, 954 F.2d 1279, 1328 (7th Cir.1992).

80 See Freeman, Judgments in Foreign Currency—A Little Known Change in New York Law, 23 Int'l Law. 73 (1989) (adopting the date of the judgment).

81 About twenty states have adopted this uniform law. See Prefatory Note to Uniform Foreign Money Claims Act, 13 Uniform Laws Annotated 23 (1990 Supp.).

82 Restatement (Third) of the Foreign Relations Law of the United States § 823.

Chapter 31

INTERNATIONAL COMMERCIAL ARBITRATION

Table of Sections

Dispute resolution in international business transactions ranges from friendly consultations to litigation everywhere. In between, nonbinding conciliation and mediation do their best at facilitating a compromise, an approach common to Asia. In between also lies international commercial arbitration, a binding alternative to days in court. The volume of international commercial arbitration has grown enormously in recent decades, particularly in the Americas, Europe, and the Middle-East.

One variation of a *forum* selection clause is one that chooses no court at all, but selects an alternate dispute resolution mechanism such as an arbitration tribunal. For a long time the courts of many nations resisted validating such clauses, holding that they deprived the parties of due process of law (a reaction one might expect toward a competitor). For example, England was slow to adopt arbitration anywhere near to its current use, largely due to the belief that adversaries were entitled to their day in court. Legislatures were far more sympathetic to allowing arbitration, and around the early years of the last century began to enact statutes validating arbitration clauses. The issue now is firmly settled.

In addition to arbitration, there are many even less formal alternate dispute resolution mechanisms. The mini-trial, for example, comes in a variety of packages, each with a different impact on resolution of the dispute. It can be nonbinding if used with a "neutral advisor", it can be semi-binding if its results are admissible in later judicial proceedings, or it can be binding before a court appointed master.[1]

§ 31.1 Why Arbitrate?

The growth of international commercial arbitration is in part a retreat from the vicissitudes and uncertainties of international business litigation.[2] More positively, international commercial arbitration offers predictability and neutrality as a forum (who knows which court you otherwise may end up in) and the potential for specialized expertise (most judges have relatively little experience in applying international or foreign law). International commercial arbitration also allows the parties to select and shape the procedures and costs of dispute resolution. That said, international commercial arbitration procedures are often informal and not laden with legal rights. To quote Judge Learned Hand:

> Arbitration may or may not be a desirable substitute for trials in courts; as to that the parties must decide in each instance. But when they have adopted it, they must be content with its informalities; they may not hedge it about with those procedural limitations which it is precisely its purpose to avoid. They must content themselves with looser approximations to the enforcement of their rights than those that the law accords them, when they resort to its machinery.[3]

One of the most attractive attributes of international commercial arbitration is the enforceability in national courts of arbitral awards under the 1958 U.N. Convention on Recognition and Enforcement of Arbitral Awards, commonly called the New York Convention.[4] Roughly 150 nations participate in the New York Convention. There is no comparable convention for the enforcement of court judgments, although lengthy negotiations took place around the end of the last century for the adoption of a Hague Convention on Jurisdiction and Enforcement of Judgments. It was not concluded. Only a less encompassing 2005 Convention on Choice of Court Agreements

---

[1] For a review of the variety of such alternative dispute resolution mechanisms, see Nelson, "Alternatives to Litigation of International Disputes," 23 *Int'l Lawyer* 187 (1989).

[2] See Chapter 30.

[3] American Almond Products Co. v. Consolidated Pecan Sales Co., Inc., 144 F.2d 448, 451 (2d Cir.1944).

[4] U.N. Convention on Recognition and Enforcement of Arbitral Awards (1958), 21 U.S.T. 2517, 330 U.N.T.S. 38.

was concluded, but it has not been successful in attracting signatories.

Other less encompassing agreements governing aspects of arbitration exist, one of the more important to the United States being the Inter-American Convention on International Commercial Arbitration, commonly called the Panama Convention.[5] That 1975 Convention renders arbitral awards enforceable in Latin America. It has attracted nineteen members, nearly all the nations of Latin America with the exception of Cuba.

Another major advantage of international commercial arbitration is the support of legal regimes that give arbitration agreements dispositive effects. In the United States, for example, the Federal Arbitration Act provides a level of legal security unknown to international business litigation. Many countries have similar statutes, thus avoiding issues of subject matter and personal jurisdiction, *forum non conveniens,* and the like.[6] Professor Park has noted that, excepting New York, there are no statutory frameworks supporting court selection clauses at the state or federal level.[7] In worst case scenarios, parties selecting a court to resolve their disputes may end up with a court that refuses to hear the case.

One of the least attractive attributes of international commercial arbitration is the minimal availability of pre-trial provisional remedies.[8] In addition, many arbitrators focus on splitting the differences between the parties, not the vindication of legal rights which in courts might result in "winner takes all." But such extreme results could permanently disrupt otherwise longstanding and mutually beneficial business relationships. Perhaps, therefore, "splitting the baby" through arbitration really is the optimal outcome, even when the split is not equal.

Clearly international commercial arbitration has its pros and cons. Regardless of which way you would like to see the balance tipped, the use of arbitral dispute resolution methods is. One distinguished set of authors believes that this trend is hardly surprising. Here is their analysis of why:

---

5 Inter–American Convention on International Commercial Arbitration of 1975, 14 I.L.M. 336 (1975).

6 See Park, "When and Why Arbitration Matters" in Hartwell (ed.), The Commercial Way of Justice (1997); Richards v. Lloyd's of London, 107 F.3d 1422 (9th Cir.1997) *reversed* 135 F.3d 1289 (9th Cir.1998).

7 Park, "Bridging the Gap in Forum Selection: Harmonizing Arbitration and Court Selection," 8 Transnat'l Law & Contemp. Probs. 19 (Spring 1998).

8 See Borden, Inc. v. Meiji Milk Products Co., 919 F.2d 822 (2d Cir.1990), *cert. denied*, 500 U.S. 953, 111 S.Ct. 2259, 114 L.Ed.2d 712 (1991).

Trade and investment across state lines is on the rise, and parties from different jurisdictions who engage in such activity frequently seek the comparative neutrality of a non-state tribunal to resolve their differences. Parties to a transaction from different states may be reluctant to submit to the jurisdiction of the courts of the other. This reluctance may arise from lack of enthusiasm about operating in another language, or according to the procedures and, insofar as it infiltrates procedure, the substantive law of another state. In some circumstances, one party may fear that the courts of the other may have a preference for their own nationals, may share a dislike of a particular foreign nationality or may, in cases involving very large amounts of money, lean toward finding in favor of their national because of the consequences for their national economy and political system. Where one of the parties is a state or state agency, a non-state party may prefer arbitration to submitting a dispute to the courts of the other contracting party. Arbitration may thus serve to "equalize" the non-state entity by transferring the dispute to a setting which may be designed to minimize or ignore the sovereign character of one of the parties rather more than would a national court.

Arbitration may also be utilized because the various national laws which might be relevant have not developed enough to treat problems raised in a pioneer industry. Thus issues regarding intellectual property rights in computer software of companies from different states may be submitted to arbitration as a way of resolving a dispute by shaping new law on the matter. In some circumstances potential litigants may also seek out arbitration because it is touted as more rapid, private and cheaper than domestic adjudication, though many of these characteristics of international commercial arbitration may be relative and sometimes overstated.

International commercial arbitration is also on the increase because many national court systems not only help international arbitration but appear anxious to externalize a larger amount of the disputes that are formally within their jurisdiction. The willingness of national courts to compel parties who have made prior commitments to engage in private arbitration and then to enforce the awards that ensue, subject only to limited judicial review, increases the likelihood that parties will resort to that mode of dispute resolution.[9]

§ 31.2 Types of International Commercial Arbitrations

There are two distinct types of international commercial arbitrations: ad hoc and institutional. Ad hoc arbitrations involve selection by the parties of the arbitrators and rules governing the arbitration. The classic formula involves each side choosing one arbitrator who in turn together agree upon a third arbitrator. The ad hoc arbitration panel selects its procedural rules (such as the UNCITRAL Arbitration Rules). Ad hoc arbitration can be agreed upon in advance or, quite literally, selected ad hoc as disputes arise.

Institutional arbitration involves selection of a specific arbitration center or "court," often accompanied by its own rules of arbitration. Institutional arbitration is in a sense pre-packaged and the parties need only "plug in" to the arbitration system of their choice. There are numerous competing centers of arbitration, each busy marketing its desirability to the world business community. Some centers are longstanding and busy, such as the International Chamber of Commerce "Court of Arbitration" in Paris, which has its own Rules of Arbitration. Other centers are more recent in time and still struggling for clientele, such as the Commercial Arbitration and Mediation Center for the Americas, the Kuala Lumpur Regional Arbitration Center, and the Cairo Regional Center for International Arbitration.

Ad hoc arbitration presupposes a certain amount of goodwill and flexibility between the parties. It can be speedy and less costly than institutional arbitration. The latter, on the other hand, offers ease of incorporation in an international business agreement, supervisory services, a stable of experienced arbitrators and a fixed fee schedule. The institutional environment is professional, a quality that sometimes can get lost in ad hoc arbitrations. Awards from well-established arbitration centers (including default awards) are more likely to be favorably recognized in the courts if enforcement is needed. Many institutional arbitration centers now also offer "fast track" or "mini" services to the international business community.

Uncertainty about identity of the country and the court in which a dispute may be heard, about procedural and substantive rules to be applied, about the degree of publicity to be given the pro-

---

9 W. Michael Reisman, W. Laurence Craig, William W. Park & Jan Paulsson, International Commercial Arbitration (Foundation Press 1997).

ceedings and the judgment, about the time needed to settle a dispute, and about the efficacy which may be given to a resulting judgment, all have combined to make arbitration the preferred mechanism for solving international commercial disputes. Some Western European countries long have been accustomed to arbitration (e.g., see English Arbitration Act of 1889 and English Arbitration Act of 1950, as amended by Arbitration Act of 1979); the London Court of Arbitration, a private arbitration institution, has existed since 1892. The United States has had a Federal Arbitration Act since 1947.[10] Arbitration in international commercial contracts is favored by the People's Republic of China, if mediation and conciliation fails, either through the Chinese International Economic and Trade Arbitration Commission (CIETAC) or the Chinese Maritime Arbitration Commission (MAC). Most of the nations of the former Soviet Union also favor arbitration, and have organizations similar to the Chinese CIETAC and MAC. In terms of volume, CIETAC is now the world's largest arbitration center.

The Japan Commercial Arbitration Association has been active since 1953. Virtually all countries in Africa have arbitration statutes. Latin America, historically disadvantaged in many arbitral awards, increasingly is accepting arbitration. For example, the 1975 Inter–American Convention on International Commercial Arbitration[11] provides, in part, that "The Governments of the Member States of the Organization of American States . . . have agreed that . . . an agreement in which parties undertake to submit to arbitral decision any differences . . . with respect to a commercial transaction is valid." The 1979 Inter–American Convention on Extraterritorial Validity of Foreign Judgments and Arbitral Awards expands upon the scope of the 1975 Convention.

§ 31.3 Mandatory Law

Almost all jurisdictions have enacted law they consider "mandatory," *i.e.* public law that private parties cannot avoid by contract. Exactly where the line is drawn between mandatory and non-mandatory law is crucial to international commercial arbitration.

Many lower U.S. federal courts had held that "mandatory laws" could not be the subject matter of arbitration because of the public interest indicated by the legislative intent underlying the enactment of mandatory law and the public policy favoring judicial enforcement of such law. However, the Supreme Court has rejected

---

[10] 9 U.S.C.A. § 1 et seq.

[11] See 14 Int'l Legal Mat. 336.

that doctrine. In *Scherk v. Alberto–Culver Co.*[12], the Court held that Securities and Exchange Commission law issues arising out of an international contract are subject to arbitration under the Federal Arbitration Act *(9 U.S.C.A.* § 1 et seq.) despite the public interest in protecting the U.S. investment climate. In *Mitsubishi Motors Corp. v. Soler Chrysler–Plymouth, Inc.*[13], the Court held that antitrust claims arising out of an international transaction were arbitrable, despite the public interest in a competitive national economy, and the legislative pronouncements favoring enforcement by private parties. In *Vimar Seguros y Reaseguros, S.A. v. M/V Sky Reefer*,[14] claims that the foreign arbitrators would not apply the U.S. mandatory COGSA bill of lading law were rejected on the ground that the United States could "review" the arbitral award at the award-enforcement stage. That power may, however, be very narrow under the 1958 United Nation's Convention on the Recognition and Enforcement of Foreign Arbitral Awards (the New York Convention), discussed below.

In both *Mitsubishi Motors* and *M/V Sky Reefer*, the Court determined that issues arising out of international transactions involving U.S. mandatory law were arbitrable. However, in *dictum* at the end of the *Mitsubishi* opinion, the Court stated that U.S. courts would have a second chance at the enforcement stage to examine whether the arbitral tribunal "took cognizance of the antitrust claims and actually decided them." Similar language can be found in *M/V Sky Reefer* regarding COGSA claims. It would seem to be difficult to fit any such examination by the U.S. courts properly into the structure of the New York Convention. It is not clear whether *Mitsubishi* invites the U.S. courts merely to examine whether the arbitrators state that they considered the antitrust issues, or further invites them to examine whether the arbitrators considered these issues *correctly* (review on the merits). The former can be evaded by a mechanical phrase; the latter can harm the arbitral process, especially if the parties have chosen non–U.S. law to govern their agreement.

In either case, arbitrators' enforcement of U.S. antitrust laws may not be to the standards of U.S. courts, and the status of recognition and enforcement of arbitral awards involving antitrust issues

---

12 417 U.S. 506, 94 S.Ct. 2449, 41 L.Ed.2d 270 (1974).

13 473 U.S. 614, 105 S.Ct. 3346, 87 L.Ed.2d 444 (1985). The Ninth, Eleventh, and First Circuits have held that because of *Mitsubishi* private antitrust claims are arbitrable. See Seacoast Motors of Salisbury, Inc. v. DaimlerChrysler Motors Corp., 271 F.3d 6 (1st Cir. 2001), *cert. denied* 535 U.S. 1054, 122 S.Ct. 1911, 152 L.Ed.2d 821 (2002).

14 515 U.S. 528, 115 S.Ct. 2322, 132 L.Ed.2d 462 (1995).

is not yet clear. Under the New York Convention, a mere "misunderstanding," or error in interpretation, of a mandatory law by an arbitral tribunal has generally not been held to "contravene public policy." The cases are split as to whether even a "manifest disregard" of U.S. law constitutes such a violation of public policy. Awards have been upheld which violate the U.S. Vessel Owner's Limitation of Liability Act, previously considered mandatory law. Thus, it is not certain, under the New York Convention, that U.S. courts retain the review powers assumed by the *Mitsubishi* and *M/V Sky Reefer* Courts to be available at the "award-enforcement stage" of the proceedings.

§ 31.4 International Arbitration Rules: UNICITRAL

The factors considered above are incorporated in Model International Commercial Arbitration Rules[15] issued in 1976 by the United Nations Commission on International Trade Law (UNCITRAL) following ten years of study. They were revised in 2010. The UNCITRAL Rules are intended to be acceptable in all legal systems and in all parts of the world. Rapidly developing countries favor the Rules because of the care with which they have been drafted, and because UNCITRAL was one forum for developing arbitration rules in which their concerns would be heard. The Arbitral Institute of the Stockholm Chamber of Commerce has been willing to work with the UNCITRAL Rules, as has the London Court of Arbitration. The Iran–United States Claims Tribunal has used the UNCITRAL Rules in dealing with claims arising out of the confrontation between the two countries in 1980. Unlike the Stockholm Chamber of Commerce Rules, the UNCITRAL Rules are not identified with any national or international arbitration organization.

Among other things, UNCITRAL rules provide that an "appointing authority" shall be chosen by the parties or, if they fail to agree upon that point, shall be chosen by the Secretary–General of the Permanent Court of Arbitration at the Hague (comprised of a body of persons prepared to act as arbitrators when requested). The UNCITRAL rules also cover notice requirements, representation of the parties, challenges of arbitrators, evidence, hearings, the place of arbitration, language, statements of claims and defenses, pleas to the arbitrator's jurisdiction, provisional remedies, experts, default, rule waivers, the form and effect of the award, applicable law, settlement, interpretation of the award, and costs. In 2012, UNCITRAL issued a pre-release of its "Recommendations to assist ar-

[15] See 15 Int'l Legal Mat. 701 (1978).

bitral institutions and other interested bodies with regard to arbitration under the UNCITRAL Arbitration Rules as revised in 2010." They will replace recommendations issued in 1982.

In addition to its 1976 Model Arbitration Rules, UNCITRAL also promulgated a 1985 Model Law on International Commercial Arbitration, amended in 2006.[16] While the Model Rules are directed to potential or actual disputing parties, the Model Law is directed to states. The Model Law, or legislation based on the Model Law, has been enacted in more than sixty nations. It has also been enacted as state law by several states, including California, Connecticut, Florida, Illinois, Louisiana, Oregon, and Texas. There seems to be no competing federal law which would pre-empt the application of these enactments. Additionally, China has not adopted the law, but both Hong Kong and Macao have. Similarly, the United Kingdom has not adopted the law, but both Bermuda and Scotland have.

Under the UNCITRAL Model Law, submission to arbitration may be *ad hoc* for a particular dispute, but is accomplished most often in advance of the dispute by a general submission clause within a contract. Under Article 8 of the Model Law, an agreement to arbitrate is specifically enforceable.

Although no specific language will guarantee the success of an arbitral submission, UNCITRAL recommends the following model submission clause:

> Any dispute, controversy or claim arising out of or relating to this contract, or the breach, termination or invalidity thereof, shall be settled by arbitration in accordance with the UNCITRAL Arbitration Rules as at present in force.

§ 31.5 International Arbitration Rules: ICSID

Some of the same issues discussed immediately above are also incorporated in the text of the Arbitration Rules adopted under the 1966 Convention on the Settlement of Investment Disputes Between States and Nationals of Other States (TIAS 6090), to which over 140 countries are parties. The Convention was implemented in the United States by 22 U.S.C. § 1650 and § 1650a. An arbitral money award, rendered pursuant to the Convention, is entitled to the same full faith and credit in the United States as a final judg-

---

16 www.uncitral.org. See Lowry, Critical Documents Sourcebook Ann. 345 (1991).

ment of a court of general jurisdiction in a state of the United States.[17]

The 1966 Convention provided for the establishment of an International Center for the Settlement of Investment Disputes (ICSID), as a non-financial organ of the World Bank (the International Bank for Reconstruction and Development). ICSID is designed to serve as a forum for both conciliation and arbitration of disputes between private investors and host governments. It provides an institutional framework within which arbitrators, selected by the disputing parties from an ICSID Panel of Arbitrators or from elsewhere, conduct arbitration in accordance with ICSID Rules of Procedure for Arbitration Proceedings. Arbitrations are held in Washington D.C. unless agreed otherwise.

Under the 1966 Convention (Article 25), ICSID's jurisdiction extends only "to any legal dispute arising directly out of an investment, between a Contracting State or . . . any subdivision . . . and a national of another Contracting State, which the parties to the dispute consent in writing to submit to the Centre. Where the parties have given their consent, either in respect of future disputes or in respect of existing disputes, no party may withdraw its consent unilaterally." Thus, ICSID is an attempt to institutionalize dispute resolution between States and non-State investors. It therefore always presents a "mixed" arbitration.

If one party questions such jurisdiction (predicated upon disputes arising "directly out of" an investment, between a Contracting State and the national of another, and written consent to submission), the issue may be decided by the arbitration tribunal (Rule 41). A party may seek annulment of any award by an appeal to an ad hoc committee of persons drawn by the Administrative Council of ICSID from the Panel of Arbitrators under the Convention (Article 52). Annulment is available only if the Tribunal was not properly constituted, exceeded its powers, seriously departed from a fundamental procedural rule, failed to state the reasons for its award, or included a member who practiced corruption.

The Convention's 1966 jurisdictional limitations have prompted the ICSID Administrative Counsel to establish an Additional Facility for conducting conciliations and arbitrations for disputes which do not arise directly out of an investment and for investment disputes in which one party is not a Contracting State to the Convention or the national of a Contracting State. The Additional Facil-

---

[17] 22 U.S.C.A. § 1650a.

ity is intended for use by parties having long-term relationships of special economic importance to the State party to the dispute and which involve the commitment of substantial resources on the part of either party. The Facility is not designed to service disputes which fall within the 1966 Convention or which are "ordinary commercial transaction" disputes. ICSID's Secretary General must give advance approval of an agreement contemplating use of the Additional Facility. Because the Additional Facility operates outside the scope of the 1966 Convention, the Facility has its own arbitration Rules.

The ICSID Arbitration Rules have become adopted for use in trade disputes between States and investors. Under NAFTA Chapter 11 and DR-CAFTA Chapter 10.

§ 31.6 ICC and LCIA Arbitral Rules and Clauses

Many parties use the Rules of the Court of Arbitration of the International Chamber of Commerce (ICC) at Paris or of one of its national committees, such as the international commercial panel of the American Arbitration Association. The ICC Rules are modern, most recently updated in 2012, and often used in international arbitration. Some 11,000 arbitrations have been administered by the ICC.[18]

Although the ICC International Court of Arbitration is not a court in the judicial meaning of that label, its primary role is to administer arbitrations. The Court does not itself resolve disputes, such function being that of independent arbitral tribunals appointed under the ICC Rules, a major goal of the Court is to see that arbitral awards are enforceable at law.

The London Court of International Arbitration (LCIA), with roots to 1883, is generally conceded to be the leading global forum for dispute resolution using arbitration, although it also is active in mediation. The London Court has its own rules and procedures.

The Court of Arbitration of the ICC in Paris recommends use of the following model clause for the adoption of its rules:

> All disputes arising in connection with the present contract shall be finally settled under the Rules of Conciliation and Arbitration of the International Chamber of

[18] See W. Laurence Craig, William W. Park, and Jan Paulsson, International Chamber of Commerce Arbitration (3rd Edition, 2000). www.iccwbo.org. www.lcia-arbitration.com.

> Commerce by one or more arbitrators appointed in accordance with the said Rules.

Parties who wish to refer any dispute to the equally active London Court of International Arbitration may use the following model clause:

> The validity, construction and performance of this contract (agreement) shall be governed by the laws of England and any dispute that may arise out of or in connection with this contract (agreement), including its validity, construction and performance, shall be determined by arbitration under the Rules of the London Court of International Arbitration at the date hereof, which Rules with respect to matters not regulated by them, incorporate the UNCITRAL Arbitration Rules. The parties agree that service of any notices in reference to such arbitration at their addresses as given in this contract (agreement) (or as subsequently varied in writing by them) shall be valid and sufficient.

§ 31.7 Enforcement of Arbitral Awards: The New York Convention

Arbitration is only as useful as its decisions are recognized and enforced. Perhaps no other instrument has been more important to the success of international arbitration than the New York Convention.

In approximately 150 countries, the enforcement of arbitral awards is facilitated by the 1958 United Nations Convention on the Recognition and Enforcement of Foreign Arbitral Awards (the "New York Convention").[19] "[T]he principal purpose underlying American . . . implementation . . . was to encourage the recognition and enforcement of commercial arbitration agreements in international contracts and to unify the standards by which agreements to arbitrate are observed and arbitral awards are enforced in the signatory countries."[20] In an abbreviated procedure, under 9 U.S.C.A. §§ 203, 208, federal district courts entertain motions to confirm or to challenge a foreign award.

---

[19] 21 U.S.T. 2518, T.I.A.S. No. 6997, 330 U.N.T.S. 38, implemented in the United States by 9 U.S.C.A. §§ 201–208. www.newyorkconvention1958.org.

[20] Scherk v. Alberto–Culver Co., 417 U.S. 506, 520 n. 15, 94 S.Ct. 2449, 41 L.Ed.2d 270 (1974).

The New York Convention commits the courts in each Contracting State to recognize and enforce arbitration clauses and written arbitration agreements for the resolution of international commercial disputes. Where the court finds an arbitral clause or agreement, it "*shall* . . . refer the parties to arbitration, unless it finds that the said agreement is null and void, inoperative, or incapable of being performed" (emphasis added).[21] The New York Convention also commits the courts in each Contracting State to recognize and enforce (under local procedural rules) the awards of arbitral tribunals under such clauses or agreements, and also sets forth the limited grounds under which recognition and enforcement may be refused. Under the New York Convention, grounds for refusal to enforce include:

(1) incapacity or invalidity of the agreement containing the arbitration clause "under the law applicable to" a party to the agreement,

(2) lack of proper notice of the arbitration proceedings, the appointment of the arbitrator or other reasons denying an adequate opportunity to present a defense,

(3) failure of the arbitral award to restrict itself to the terms of the submission to arbitration, or decision of matters not within the scope of that submission,

(4) composition of the arbitral tribunal not according to the arbitration agreement or applicable law, and

(5) non-finality of the arbitral award under applicable law.[22]

In addition to these grounds for refusal, recognition or enforcement may also be refused if it would be contrary to the public policy of the country in which enforcement is sought, or if the subject matter of the dispute cannot be settled by arbitration under the law of that country.[23] Courts in the United States have taken the position that the "public policy limitation on the New York Convention is to be construed narrowly [and] to be applied only where enforcement would violate the forum state's most basic notions of morality and justice."[24] Recourse to other limitations of the Convention, in order to defeat its applicability, has been greeted with judi-

---

21 Article II(3).

22 Article V.

23 *Id.*

24 Fotochrome, Inc. v. Copal Co., Ltd., 517 F.2d 512 (2d Cir.1975).

cial caution in the absence of violation of basic U.S. notions of morality and justice.[25] However, the Second Circuit has held that the doctrine of *forum non conveniens* applies in arbitral award confirmation proceedings under the New York Convention.[26]

Whether the N.Y. Convention applies generally turns upon where the award was or will be made, not the citizenship of the parties.[27] A growing number of courts in developing nations are issuing injunctions against arbitration proceedings before they commence. Many of these injunctions seem deliberately intended to protect local companies. Parties who proceed to arbitrate after such an injunction has been issued do so at their peril. Subsequent enforcement of the award under the New York Convention in the enjoining nation will almost certainly be voided on grounds of public policy. Hence enforcement can only proceed in non-enjoining jurisdictions, assuming that their public policy permits this.

§ 31.8 Arbitration Agreements, Arbitrators and Awards under U.S. Law

Arbitration agreements, traditionally called *compromis,* come in a variety of forms. Many arbitration centers sponsor model clauses that can be incorporated into business agreements. The New York Convention obliges courts of participating nations, upon request, to refer disputes to arbitration unless the agreement is "null and void, inoperative or incapable of being performed."[28] The existence and validity of an arbitration agreement must be proved, and can be litigated before the arbitration takes place.

Article II(2) of the New York Convention requires states to recognize written arbitration agreements *signed* by the parties "or contained in an exchange of letters or telegrams." In most jurisdictions exchanges of fax, email, and the like embracing arbitration will also be recognized. However, arbitration clauses in unsigned purchase orders do not amount to a written agreement to arbitrate.[29] Pre-arbitration litigation often revolves around motions to compel arbi-

---

[25] Parsons & Whittemore Overseas Co., Inc. v. Societe Generale De L'Industrie Du Papier (RAKTA), 508 F.2d 969 (2d Cir.1974).

[26] In re Monegasque de Reassurances S.A.M. v. Nak Naftogaz of Ukraine, 311 F.3d 488 (2d Cir.2002).

[27] See Ministry of Defense of the Islamic Republic of Iran v. Gould Inc., 887 F.2d 1357 (9th Cir.1989), *cert. denied*, 494 U.S. 1016, 110 S.Ct. 1319, 108 L.Ed.2d 494 (1990).

[28] Article II(3).

[29] Kahn Lucas Lancaster, Inc. v. Lark Int'l Ltd., 186 F.3d 210 (2d Cir.1999).

tration.[30] If no such motion is made, and a court judgment is rendered (even by default), the right to arbitrate may be waived.[31] Delays in triggering arbitration or invocation of litigation rights may constitute a waiver of arbitration rights.[32]

Whether a valid agreement to arbitrate exists depends on the specifics of the arbitration clause, not the entire business agreement. The arbitration clause is severable, and issues of validity (such as fraud in the inducement of the arbitration clause and unconscionability) directed to it.[33] Many courts will stretch the limits of the New York Convention in order to uphold an arbitration clause.[34] When there is a battle of forms, the same judicial bias towards arbitration is often found.[35] But, in most cases, the disputes must "arise under" the business transaction to be arbitrable,[36] and legal claims falling outside the transaction remain in court.[37]

The closure or misdescription of an arbitration center designated in the agreement (e.g., the New York Chamber of Commerce) is no barrier to arbitration. A substitute arbitrator will be appointed by the court if the parties cannot agree.[38] The U.S. Supreme Court has held that arbitrators are subject to "requirements of impartiality" and must "disclose to the parties any dealings that might create an impression of possible bias."[39] That said, most U.S. courts are loathed to intrude or vacate an arbitration award on disclosure grounds.[40]

---

[30] See, e.g., Tennessee Imports, Inc. v. P.P. Filippi & Prix Italia, S.R.L., 745 F.Supp. 1314 (M.D.Tenn.1990).

[31] See Menorah Insurance Co. v. INX Reinsurance Corp., 72 F.3d 218 (1st Cir.1995).

[32] See O.J. Distributing, Inc. v. Hornell Brewing Co., 340 F.3d 345 (6th Cir.2003); Colón v. R. K. Grace & Co., 358 F.3d 1 (1st Cir.2003).

[33] Prima Paint Corp. v. Flood & Conklin Mfg. Co., 388 U.S. 395, 87 S.Ct. 1801, 18 L.Ed.2d 1270 (1967). See Republic of Nicaragua v. Standard Fruit Co., 937 F.2d 469 (9th Cir.1991). See also Hunt v. Up North Plastics, Inc., 980 F.Supp. 1046 (D.Minn.1997), *cert. denied*, 503 U.S. 919, 112 S.Ct. 1294, 117 L.Ed.2d 516 (1992).

[34] See Sphere Drake Insurance PLC v. Marine Towing, Inc., 16 F.3d 666 (5th Cir.1994), *cert. denied* 513 U.S. 871, 115 S.Ct. 195, 130 L.Ed.2d 127 (1994) (absence of signature to standard insurance policy contract no barrier to arbitration).

[35] See I.T.A.D. Associates, Inc. v. Podar Bros., 636 F.2d 75 (4th Cir.1981).

[36] See Mediterranean Enterprises, Inc. v. Ssangyong Corp., 708 F.2d 1458 (9th Cir.1983).

[37] Id. See Coors Brewing Co. v. Molson Breweries, 51 F.3d 1511 (10th Cir.1995).

[38] See Astra Footwear Industry v. Harwyn International, Inc., 442 F.Supp. 907 (S.D.N.Y.1978).

[39] Commonwealth Coatings Corp. v. Continental Casualty Co., 393 U.S. 145, 89 S.Ct. 337, 21 L.Ed.2d 301 (1968).

[40] See Andros Compania Maritima v. Marc Rich & Co., 579 F.2d 691 (2d Cir. 1978).

There is a split of opinion as to whether the implied ground of "manifest disregard of the law" bars enforcement of an arbitral award in U.S. courts under the New York Convention. The Second Circuit, and most other circuits, believe so,[41] while the Eleventh Circuit says no.[42] Article V of the New York Convention does not recognize manifest disregard of the law as a basis for denial of enforcement.

Another issue concerning the New York Convention is whether to adjourn U.S. enforcement proceedings if parallel proceedings to vacate the award have been commenced in the country of arbitration. Despite the risks of forum shopping and delay, the Second Circuit indicated that adjournment can be appropriate, depending upon the circumstances.[43] The Second Circuit has also denied use of 28 U.S.C. § 1782 to obtain compulsory non-party discovery in private commercial arbitrations. The issue was whether the I.C.C. in Paris constituted a "tribunal" within the scope of that statute.[44]

Cases in the United States have pointed out that parties cannot refer a dispute to a court while an arbitration is in progress,[45] or block enforcement of an award in the United States in reliance upon the fact that the award, although binding in the country where rendered, is under appeal there.[46] Interim orders of arbitrators, such as records disclosures, may be enforceable "awards" under the N.Y. Convention.[47] After the arbitration is concluded, a party may not be able to block enforcement of the award in reliance upon the United

---

[41] Yusuf Ahmed Alghanim & Sons v. Toys 'R' Us, Inc., 126 F.3d 15 (2d Cir.1997), *cert. denied* 522 U.S. 1111, 118 S.Ct. 1042, 140 L.Ed.2d 107 (1998); Westerbeke Corp. v. Daihatsu Motor Co., Ltd., 304 F.3d 200 (2d Cir.2000); Duferco International Steel Trading v. T. Klaveness Shipping, 333 F.3d 383 (2d Cir.2003); Hardy v. Walsh Manning Securities, LLC, 341 F.3d 126 (2d Cir.2003). In view of Hall Street Associates, LLC v. Mattel, Inc., 552 U.S. 576, 128 S.Ct. 1396 (2008), doubt exists as to the current view in the Second Circuit. The Hall decision has been criticized in subsequent lower federal court decisions. See, e.g., Robert Lewis Rosen Assoc., Ltd. v. Webb, 566 F.Supp2d 228 (S.D.N.Y. 2008); F.Hoffman-LaRoche Ltd. V. Qiagen Gaithersburg, Inc., 2010 WL 3184228 (S.D.,N.Y. 2010).

[42] Industrial Risk Insurers v. M.A.N. Gutehoffnungshutte GmbH, 141 F.3d 1434 (11th Cir.1998), *cert.denied* 525 U.S. 1068, 119 S.Ct. 797, 142 L.Ed.2d 659 (1999).

[43] Europcar Italia, S.p.A. v. Maiellano Tours, Inc., 156 F.3d 310 (2d Cir.1998).

[44] National Broadcasting Co. v. Bear Stearns & Co., 165 F.3d 184 (2d Cir.1999).

[45] Siderius, Inc. v. Compania de Acero del Pacifico, S.A., 453 F.Supp. 22 (S.D.N.Y.1978).

[46] Fertilizer Corp. of India v. IDI Management, Inc., 517 F.Supp. 948 (S.D.Ohio 1981).

[47] See Publicis Communication v. True North Communications, Inc. 206 F.3d 725 (7th Cir.2000).

States Foreign Sovereign Immunities Act[48], but a court may decline to enforce in reliance upon the Act of State Doctrine.[49] One court has granted enforcement, under the Convention, of a New York award rendered in favor of a non-citizen claimant against a non-citizen defendant.[50] Awards entirely between U.S. citizens are not subject to the New York Convention unless they concern property located abroad, envisage performance or enforcement abroad, or have some other reasonable relation with foreign state(s).[51]

When arbitral awards are annulled at their situs, courts in enforcing jurisdictions have taken different positions on the enforceability of the award. French courts enforced an improperly vacated award to the detriment of the claimant who had prevailed in a second arbitration.[52] A U.S. federal district court refused to honor the clearly legitimate annulment of an arbitral award by an Egyptian court because the parties had agreed not to appeal the award.[53] The Second Circuit, on the other hand, recognized the annulment of two arbitral awards vacated by a Nigerian court and refused enforcement.[54] The New York Convention does not address the treatment of annulled arbitral awards.

The U.S. Supreme Court has repeatedly affirmed that arbitrators have jurisdiction to decide their own jurisdiction (competence).[55] The Court has indicated that questions of the arbitrability of disputes may be arbitrated, but only if the parties have manifested a *clear* willingness to be bound by arbitration on such issues.[56] Silence or ambiguity should favor judicial review of arbitrability issues.[57] Arbitration clauses that adopt the UNITRAL Rules meet

---

[48] See Ipitrade International, S.A. v. Federal Republic of Nigeria, 465 F.Supp. 824 (D.D.C.1978) and Creighton Ltd. v. Government of Qatar, 181 F.3d 118 (D.C.Cir.1999).

[49] Libyan American Oil Co. v. Socialist People's, etc., 482 F.Supp. 1175 (D.D.C.1980).

[50] Bergesen v. Joseph Muller Corp., 548 F.Supp. 650 (S.D.N.Y.1982).

[51] 9 U.S.C. § 202 (1994).

[52] Hilmarton v. OTV, 1997 Rev. Arb. 376, note Ph. Fouchard discussed in Park, "Duty and Discretion in International Arbitration," 93 Am. J. Int'l Law 805 (1999).

[53] Chromalloy Aeroservices v. Egypt, 939 F.Supp. 907 (D.D.C.1996). See Park, *supra.*

[54] Baker Marine (Nig.) Ltd. v. Chevron (Nig.) Ltd., 191 F.3d 194 (2d Cir.1999).

[55] See, e.g., Howsam v. Dean Witter Reynolds, Inc., 537 U.S. 79, 123 S.Ct. 588, 154 L.Ed.2d 491 (2002); Pacificare Health Systems, Inc. v. Book, 538 U.S. 401, 123 S.Ct. 1531, 155 L.Ed.2d 578 (2003).

[56] First Options of Chicago, Inc. v. Kaplan, 514 U.S. 938, 115 S.Ct. 1920, 131 L.Ed.2d 985 (1995).

[57] *Id.*

the requirement of clarity to arbitrate arbitrability because Article 21 conveys jurisdictional issues to the tribunal.[58]

U.S. courts are split on whether contract parties may alter the scope of judicial review of arbitration awards. Three Circuits reject expansion of statutory or common law review standards.[59] The Ninth and Tenth Circuits permit contractual expansion of judicial review standards.[60] Attempts at *narrowing* statutory standards are likely to be rejected.[61]

§ 31.9 Arbitration Awards Rejected: A Case Study

A case that may consume years until it is resolved evidences the fragility of arbitration awards regardless of the New York Convention.

Spanish owned Repsol, S.A., is an oil and gas company operating in more than two-dozen nations and is the 15th largest petroleum refining company. It does not have especially good relations with the U.S. government ever since it contracted in 2009 with Cuba to drill and extract oil, and in 2010 agreed to invest US$10 billion in Iran. But the investment that has challenged the effectiveness of arbitration involving developing nations is with Argentina, not Cuba or Iran. In 1999, Repsol acquired control (57 percent) of YPF, Argentina's major oil company, worth somewhere between U.S. $15 and 20 billion. In April, 2012, Argentina expropriated 51 percent of YPF. Repsol commenced proceedings at ICSID. ICSID previously has fined Argentina for failure to comply with arbitral awards, and few believe Repsol will be any more successful in the event it wins an award from ICSID. Among other actions, Repsol attached Argentina's sail training ship while at an African port. It was two months before the ship was released. The Repsol case has huge political issues, and comes at a time when Argentina, financially unstable, has again made moves to take over the Falklands/Malvinas islands.

[58] Wal–Mart Stores, Inc. v. PT Multipolar Corp., 202 F.3d 280 (9th Cir.1999) (unpublished).

[59] See Roadway Package System, Inc. v. Kayser, 257 F.3d 287 (3d Cir.2001); Syncor Int'l Corp. v. McLeland, 120 F.3d 262 (4th Cir.1997), *cert. denied*, 522 U.S. 1110, 118 S.Ct. 1039, 140 L.Ed.2d 105 (1998); Gateway Techn., Inc. v. MCI Telecomm. Corp., 64 F.3d 993 (5th Cir.1995).

[60] See Kyocera Corp. v. Prudential–Bache Trade Services, Inc., 341 F.3d 987 (9th Cir.2003), *cert. dismissed*, 540 U.S. 1098, 124 S.Ct. 980, 157 L.Ed.2d 810 (2004); Bowen v. Amoco Pipeline Co., 254 F.3d 925 (10th Cir.2001).

[61] See Hoeft v. MVL Group, Inc., 343 F.3d 57 (2d Cir.2003).

Spain and Argentina have a bilateral investment treaty (BIT) that provides for arbitration of investments at the World Bank's ICSID. If Argentina's previous experience continues, Argentina will lose the arbitration and then denounce the award. But Spain and Argentina have long standing positive relationships. Nevertheless, that has not stopped Spain from announcing commercial restrictions. Argentina's main objection is with Repsol's practice of distributing most of its profits to its shareholders, Argentina would prefer them to be invested in new oil and gas production.

The Repsol case is unusual in that Argentina is not as poor as it would suggest. It has huge natural resources and despite debt defaults in 2001, has seen some economic growth. The dispute continues with what has occurred over the last half-century when successive Argentine governments shifted from policies of nationalization to privatization and back to nationalization again. While the arbitration under ICSID will presumably proceed, the satisfaction of any award to Repsol is doubtful and raises significant questions about the usefulness of BITs and the New York Convention when dealing with parts of the developing world. Many developing nations have applauded the Argentine actions over the years.

Table of Cases

Index

References are to Sections